THE ROUGH GUIDE TO

Ireland

There are more than two hundred Rough Guide titles covering destinations from Alaska to Zimbabwe and subjects from Acoustic Guitar to Travel Health

Forthcoming travel guides include

Devon & Cornwall • Ibiza • Iceland • Malta
Tenerife • Vancouver

Forthcoming reference guides include

Cuban Music • Hip-Hop • Personal Computers
Pregnancy & Birth • Trumpet & Trombone

Rough Guides Online

www.roughguides.com

ROUGH GUIDE CREDITS

Text editor: Judith Bamber, Paul Gray, Lisa Nellis and Matthew Teller

Series editor: Mark Ellingham

Editorial: Martin Dunford, Jonathan Buckley, Jo Mead, Kate Berens, Amanda Tomlin, Ann-Marie Shaw, Helena Smith, Orla Duane, Olivia Eccleshall, Ruth Blackmore, Geoff Howard, Claire Saunders, Gavin Thomas, Alexander Mark Rogers, Polly Thomas, Joe Staines, Andrew Tomičić, Richard Lim, Duncan Clark, Peter Buckley, Sam Thorne, Lucy Ratcliffe, Clifton Wilkinson, David Glen (UK); Andrew Rosenberg, Mary Beth Maioli, Stephen Timblin, Yuki Takagaki (US)

Production: Susanne Hillen, Andy Hilliard, Link Hall, Helen Ostick, Julia Bovis, Michelle Draycott, Katie Pringle, Robert Evers, Mike Hancock, Zoë Nobes

Cartography: Melissa Baker, Maxine Repath, Ed Wright, Katie Lloyd-Jones

Picture research: Louise Boulton, Sharon Martins

Online: Kelly Cross, Anja Mutić-Blessing, Jennifer Gold, Audra Epstein, Suzanne Welles (US)

Finance: John Fisher, Gary Singh, Edward Downey, Mark Hall, Tim Bill

Marketing & Publicity: Richard Trillo, Niki Smith, David Wearn, Chloë Roberts, Birgit Hartmann, Claire Southern (UK); Simon Carloss, David Wechsler, Kathleen Rushforth (US)

Administration: Tania Hummel, Demelza Dallow, Julie Sanderson

ACKNOWLEDGEMENTS

Margaret Greenwood would like to thank John Lahiffe at Bord Fáilte, Anne and Frank Greenwood; Cath Greenwood, Lily, Flo and Bruce; Claire Rooney; Mary White and John Bolger; Marleena dry Koningen; Con, Rosie and Siobhan Lynch; Niall, Ger and Luke Shanahan; Cath Hampshire and family; Bill Ward and the many people around the country who have made this book such a pleasure to research.

Geoff Wallis wishes to thank the following for their support, advice and assistance: staff at Bord Fáilte (especially John Lahiffe in London), North West Tourism staff in Letterkenny, the Northern Ireland Tourist Board (especially Orla Farren in Belfast), Eamonn Jordan, Seán MacLoskey, Mary Reynolds, Majella Mackin and Nick Newton, Joan Pyne, Hostelling International Northern Ireland and Stena Line.

Mark Connolly would like to thank the Connolly, Alexander and Killough families, Heather and Oceana Munro, Gregory Woulahan, Justin Rami, Michael McCullough, Brian McAllister, Anne Guilhot, Luciara Vicente, Dimitris Stamou, Wendy Williamson, Susan Daly and the staff at the Dublin and Galway tourist boards.

PUBLISHING INFORMATION

This sixth edition published April 2001 by Rough Guides Ltd, 62–70 Shorts Gardens, London WC2H 9AH.

Distributed by the Penguin Group:

Penguin Books Ltd, 27 Wrights Lane, London W8 5TZ

Penguin Putnam, Inc. 375 Hudson Street, NY 10014, USA

Penguin Books Australia Ltd, 487 Maroondah Highway, PO Box 257, Ringwood, Victoria 3134, Australia

Penguin Books Canada Ltd, 10 Alcorn Avenue, Toronto, Ontario, Canada M4V 1E4

Penguin Books (NZ) Ltd, 182–190 Wairau Road, Auckland 10, New Zealand

Typeset in Linotron Univers and Century Old Style to an original design by Andrew Oliver.

Printed in England by Clays Ltd, St Ives plc.

Illustrations in Part One and Part Three by Edward Briant.

Illustrations on p.1 & p.663 by Katie Pringle

Euro banknotes draft design on p.1 © EWI.

784pp – Includes index

A catalogue record for this book is available from the British Library

ISBN 1-85828-690-5

THE ROUGH GUIDE TO
Ireland

written and researched by

Mark Connolly, Margaret Greenwood, Hilda Hawkins and Geoff Wallis

THE ROUGH GUIDES

TRAVEL GUIDES • PHRASEBOOKS • MUSIC AND REFERENCE GUIDES

We set out to do something different when the first Rough Guide was published in 1982. Mark Ellingham, just out of university, was travelling in Greece. He brought along the popular guides of the day, but found they were all lacking in some way. They were either strong on ruins and museums but went on for pages without mentioning a beach or taverna. Or they were so conscious of the need to save money that they lost sight of Greece's cultural and historical significance. Also, none of the books told him anything about Greece's contemporary life – its politics, its culture, its people, and how they lived.

So with no job in prospect, Mark decided to write his own guidebook, one which aimed to provide practical information that was second to none, detailing the best beaches and the hottest clubs and restaurants, while also giving hard-hitting accounts of every sight, both famous and obscure, and providing up-to-the-minute information on contemporary culture. It was a guide that encouraged independent travellers to find the best of Greece, and was a great success, getting shortlisted for the Thomas Cook travel guide award, and encouraging Mark, along with three friends, to expand the series.

The Rough Guide list grew rapidly and the letters flooded in, indicating a much broader readership than had been anticipated, but one which uniformly appreciated the Rough Guide mix of practical detail and humour, irreverence and enthusiasm. Things haven't changed. The same four friends who began the series are still the caretakers of the Rough Guide mission today: to provide the most reliable, up-to-date and entertaining information to independent-minded travellers of all ages, on all budgets.

We now publish more than 150 titles and have offices in London and New York. The travel guides are written and researched by a dedicated team of more than 100 authors, based in Britain, Europe, the USA and Australia. We have also created a unique series of phrasebooks to accompany the travel series, along with an acclaimed series of music guides, and a best-selling pocket guide to the Internet and World Wide Web. We also publish comprehensive travel information on our Web site:

www.roughguides.com

HELP US UPDATE

We've gone to a lot of effort to ensure that the sixth edition of *The Rough Guide to Ireland* is accurate and up-to-date. However, things change – places get "discovered", opening hours are notoriously fickle, restaurants and rooms raise prices or lower standards. If you feel we've got it wrong or left something out, we'd like to know, and if you can remember the address, the price, the time, the phone number, so much the better.

We'll credit all contributions, and send a copy of the next edition (or any other Rough Guide if you prefer) for the best letters. Please mark letters: "Rough Guide Ireland Update" and send to:

Rough Guides, 62–70 Shorts Gardens, London WC2H 9AH, or Rough Guides, 4th Floor, 345 Hudson St, New York, NY 10014.

Or send email to: mail@roughguides.co.uk

Online updates about this book can be found on Rough Guides' Web site at www.roughguides.com

THE AUTHORS

Margaret Greenwood graduated from the University of Kent at Canterbury in 1981. Since then she has worked as a welfare rights campaigner and an English teacher. She has written extensively on Spain and has also worked on childrens' comics. She is a keen hill walker and has been a regular visitor to Ireland since the early 1980s.

After graduating from Queen's University Belfast, **Mark Connolly** taught English in Poland, Israel and Japan. He has worked as a radio journalist for BBC Radio Ulster and BBC Radio 5 and is currently based in Dublin.

Geoff Wallis is a freelance writer who has been contributing to Rough Guides since the early 1980s and has recently co-authored *The Rough Guide to Irish Music*. In his spare moments he hunts for rare records, plays the mandolin and is still seeking a cure for his addiction to Nottingham Forest.

READERS' LETTERS

Thanks to all the readers who have taken the time and trouble to write in with comments and suggestions:

Richard Terry, Caroline Robson, Anne Kristina McGlynn, Bernadette Fallon, Ki Robdon-Hunt, P O'Conner, Dick Bain, Graham Breeze, E. M. Parkes, Clara Jane Fanning, Shona Dodsworth, John Leahy, Shannon Redmond, Patricia Monaghan, Damian Patrick Sullivan, Richard Gaston, Sophie Latham, Marije Nijhof, Lennart Huizing, S. Stacey, Dr Charles Forsyth, Sandra Cruickshank, Graham Dunn, G. Thomas, Will Wheeler, Ralph Currlin, Nellie Cassin, Audrey Percy, Simon Ratsey, Sue O'Kane, Steve Warner, Mary Rothwell, Paul Anderson, Andrew Davidson, Myrtle Levis, Jennifer Hunter, Paul Donovan, Stephanie Grantham, Jack Susskind, Rachel Levinson, Aaron Campbell, Fiona MacCallum, David Ingleby, Geoffrey Pedley, Tara Manning, David and Margaret Battye, Krist Debruyn, Geraldine Exton, Lisa-Jane Bradbury, Alyson Dean, Sinead Nally, M. Guidolin, Rosalind J John, Jeff Probst, S. Livingston, Gail Burns, Louise Yourt, P. W. Spencer, Yvonne Sterling, Gary Stewart, P. M. Goodman, Christine Bell, Miriam Leham, Nereida Gonzalez, Joseph Lo, Gabby Musk and Anne Shardlow.

CONTENTS

• CHAPTER 3: LAOIS AND OFFALY 148–162

• CHAPTER 4: MEATH, LOUTH, WESTMEATH AND LONGFORD 163–213

• CHAPTER 5: WEXFORD, CARLOW AND KILKENNY 214–235

• CHAPTER 6: WATERFORD, TIPPERARY AND LIMERICK 236–277

• CHAPTER 7: CORK 278–316

• CHAPTER 8: KERRY 317–345

• CHAPTER 9: CLARE 346–368

• CHAPTER 10: GALWAY, MAYO AND ROSCOMMON 369–435

• CHAPTER 11: SLIGO AND LEITRIM 436–463

• CHAPTER 12: CAVAN AND MONAGHAN 464–473

• CHAPTER 13: DONEGAL 474–519

THE NORTH 521

• CHAPTER 14: BELFAST 524–554

• CHAPTER 15: ANTRIM AND DERRY 555–597

• CHAPTER 16: DOWN AND ARMAGH 598–637

• CHAPTER 17: TYRONE AND FERMANAGH 638–662

PART THREE CONTEXTS 663

LIST OF MAPS

MAP SYMBOLS

Motorway
Main road
Minor road
Pedestrianized street (town maps)
Footpath
Railway
Ferry route
Waterway
National border
County border
Chapter division boundary
Wall
Places to eat and drink
Accommodation
Point of interest
Airport
Museum
Country house
Castle
Abbey
Church (regional maps)
Ruins
Tower
Statue
Cave
Mountain range
Mountain peak
View
Parking
Hospital
Tourist office
Post office
Stadium
Building
Church
Park
National Park
Beach

INTRODUCTION

Landscape and people are what bring most visitors to Ireland – the Republic and the North. And once there, few are disappointed by the reality of the stock Irish images: the green, rain-hazed loughs and wild, bluff coastlines, the inspired talent for talk and conversation, the easy pace and rhythms of life. What is perhaps more of a surprise is how much variety this very small land packs into its countryside. The limestone terraces of the stark, eerie Burren seem separated from the fertile farmlands of Tipperary by hundreds rather than tens of miles, and the primitive beauty of the west coast, with its cliffs, coves and strands, seems to belong in another country altogether from the rolling plains of the central cattle-rearing counties.

It's a place to explore slowly, roaming through agricultural landscapes scattered with farmhouses, or along the endlessly indented coastline. Spectacular seascapes unfold from rocky headlands, and the crash of the sea against the cliffs and myriad islands is often the only sound. It is perfect if you want space to walk, bike or (with a bit of bravado) swim; if you want to fish, sail, or spend a week on inland waterways. In town, too, the pleasures are unhurried: evenings over a Guinness or two in the snug of a pub, listening to the chat around a blood-orange turf fire.

But there is another Ireland growing at a phenomenal pace alongside all of this. The extraordinary economic boom enjoyed by the Republic since the early 1990s has brought growth on an unprecedented scale. A country notoriously blighted by emigration is, at last, drawing people home with the lure of work. The conspicuous new wealth of many makes itself felt in every quarter of Irish life, but most especially in cities like Dublin and Galway where a proliferation of new bars, cafés and restaurants reveals a generation determined to enjoy life to the full. The cosmopolitan flavour of these cities is informed, in part, by the complex array of experiences brought home by returning ex-pats, more familiar with the ways of Melbourne and San Francisco, London and New York, than with those of the Aran Islands. The boom has its downsides – notably, spiralling property prices and the tensions brought about by increased immigration – but as a visitor you'll probably be most struck by the tremendous energy and palpable sense of confidence in the future, most especially in the young.

To act as a backdrop, there's a wealth of history. In every part of the island are traces of a culture established long before the coming of Christianity: sites such as Newgrange in County Meath or the clifftop fortress of Dún Aengus on Inishmore (the biggest of the Aran Islands) are among the most stupendous Neolithic remains in Europe, while in some areas of Sligo almost every hill is capped by an ancient cairn. In the depths of the so-called Dark Ages the Christian communities of Ireland were great centres of learning, and the ruins of Clonmacnois in County Offaly, the Rock of Cashel in Tipperary and a score of other monasteries are evocative of a time when Ireland won its reputation as a land of saints and scholars. Fortifications raised by the chieftains of the Celtic clans and the Anglo-Norman barons bear witness to a period of later turbulence, while the Ascendancy of the Protestant settlers has left its mark in the form of vast mansions and estates.

But the richness of Irish culture is not a matter of monuments. Especially in the Irish-speaking *Gaeltacht* areas, you'll be aware of the strength and continuity of the island's oral and musical traditions. Myth-making is for the Irish people their most ancient and fascinating entertainment. The ancient classics are full of extraordinary stories – Cúchulainn the unbeatable hero in war, Medb the insatiable heroine in bed, or Fionn Mac Cumhaill (Finn Mac Cool) chasing Diarmuid and Gráinne up and down the coun-

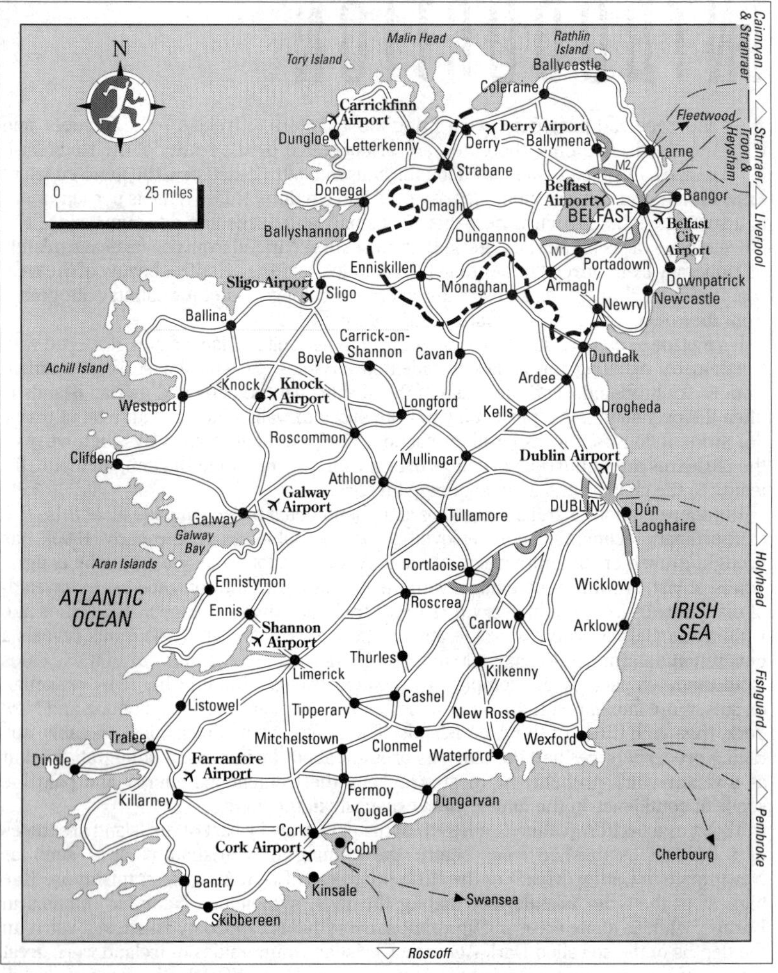

try – and tall tales, superstition-stirring and "mouthing off" (boasting) play as large a part in day-to-day life as they did in the era of the Táin Bó Cuailngè, Europe's oldest vernacular epic. As a guileless foreigner enquiring about anything from a beautiful lake to a pound of butter, you're ideally placed to trigger the most colourful responses. And the speech of the country – moulded by the rhythms of the ancient tongue – has fired such twentieth-century greats as Yeats, Joyce and Beckett.

Music has always been at the centre of Irish community life. You'll find traditional music sessions all around the touristed coasts and in the cities, too – some of it might be of dubious pedigree, but the *Gaeltacht* areas, and others, can be counted on to provide authentic renditions. Side by side with the traditional circuit is a strong rock scene, that has spawned Van Morrison, U2, Sinéad O'Connor and more recently The Divine Comedy and Jack Lukeman. And ever-present are the balladeers, fathoming and feeding the old Irish dreams of courting, emigrating and striking it lucky; there's hardly a dry eye in the house when the guitars are packed away.

The lakes and rivers of Ireland make it an angler's dream, but the sports that raise the greatest enthusiasm amongst the Irish themselves are speedier and more dangerous. Horse racing in Ireland has none of the socially divisive connotations present on the other side of the Irish Sea, and the country has bred some of the world's finest thoroughbreds. While association football is as popular as in most parts of the world now, Gaelic football, sharing elements of soccer and rugby (which itself has its hotbeds, notably in Limerick), still commands a large following. Hurling, the oldest team game played in Ireland, requires the most delicate of ball skills and the sturdiest of bones.

No introduction can cope fully with the complexities of Ireland's politics, especially the dramatic changes in Northern Ireland in recent years. However, throughout the guide we have addressed the issues wherever they arise, and in the introduction to the North on p.521 and at the end of the book, in the "Contexts" section, we have included pieces that give a general overview of the current situation. Suffice it to say that, just about everywhere hospitality is as warm as the brochures say, on both sides of the border.

Where to go

It's arguably the west coast that has the most appeal, where the demonically daunting peninsulas of the northern reaches are immediately contrasted a little inland by the mystical lakes of the Donegal highlands. The midwest coastline is just as strangely attractive, combining vertiginous cliffs, boulder-strewn wastes, and violent mountains of granite and quartz. In the south, the melodramatic peaks of the Ring of Kerry fall to lake-pools and seductive seascapes. Less talked about, but no less rewarding in their way, are the gentle sandy coves that Cork and Kerry share.

In the north of the island, the principal draw is the weird basalt geometry of the Giant's Causeway, not far from the lush Glens of Antrim. To the south of Belfast lies the beautiful walking territory of the softly contoured Mountains of Mourne, divided by Carlingford Lough from the myth-drenched Cooley Mountains.

The interior is nowhere as spectacular as the fringes of the island, but the southern heartlands of pastures and low wooded hills, and the wide peat bogs of the very centre are the classic landscapes of Ireland. Of the inland waterways, the most alluring are the island-studded Lough Erne complex of Fermanagh, and the River Shannon, with its string of huge lakes.

Some of the country's wildest scenery lies just offshore: the west-coast Aran Islands are the best known of the islands, but equally compelling are storm-battered Tory Island, to the far northwest and the savage Skelligs, off the southwest coast.

For anyone with strictly limited time, one of the best options must be to combine a visit to Dublin with the mountains and monastic ruins of County Wicklow. Dublin is an extraordinary combination of youthfulness and tradition, a modern European capital on a human scale with elegant Georgian squares and a vibrant cultural life. Belfast vies with Dublin in the vitality of its nightlife, while the cities of Cork and Galway have an energy and bustle that makes them a pleasure to visit.

When to go

Ireland's climate, determined by the pressure-systems of the Atlantic, is notoriously variable, and cannot be relied upon at any time of the year. Each year produces weeks of beautiful weather – the problem lies in predicting when they are likely to arrive. In recent years late spring and early autumn have seen some of the best of the weather, with May and September as the most pleasant months.

Geographically, the southeast is the driest and sunniest part of the country, and the northwest is the wettest. But regional variations are not particularly pronounced, the overall climate being characterized by its mildness – the country benefiting from the warming effects of the Gulf Stream. Even in the wetter zones, mornings of rain are frequently followed by afternoons of blue sky and sun – and besides, a downpour on a windswept headland can be exhilarating, and provides as good a pretext as any for repairing to the local pub, the hub of Irish social activity.

IRELAND'S CLIMATE

Average maximum and minimum daily temperatures (°C) and monthly rainfall (mm)

	Jan	Feb	Mar	Apr	May	Jun	Jul	Aug	Sep	Oct	Nov	Dec
Cork												
Max	9	9	11	13	16	19	20	20	18	14	11	9
Min	2	3	4	5	7	10	12	12	10	7	4	3
Rainfall	119	79	94	57	71	57	70	71	94	99	116	122
Dublin												
Max	8	8	10	13	15	18	20	19	17	14	10	8
Min	1	2	3	4	6	9	11	11	9	6	4	3
Rainfall	67	55	51	45	60	57	70	74	72	70	67	74
Valentia												
Max	9	9	11	13	15	17	18	18	17	14	12	10
Min	5	4	5	6	8	11	12	13	11	9	7	6
Rainfall	165	107	103	75	86	81	107	95	122	140	151	168

PART ONE

THE BASICS

GETTING THERE FROM BRITAIN

Choosing how to travel to Ireland depends heavily on the amounts of time and money available for your trip. Unless you live near a ferry port the cheaper options of train or coach travel can involve a lengthy and sometimes arduous journey. Flying is the quicker alternative and there are usually cheap tickets available to most of the Republic's airports and, increasingly, to Northern Ireland. However, at the peak times, such as the days preceding St. Patrick's Day and Easter, throughout July and August and in the week before Christmas, many of the low-cost fares may not apply or the few cheap seats may have been booked long in advance. It's worth looking out for deals advertised in one of the weekly newspapers catering for the Irish in Britain, such as the *Irish Post* or *Irish World*.

FLIGHTS

Flight time from London to the **Republic** is between an hour (to Dublin) and ninety minutes

TRAVEL AGENTS

Usit Campus, 32 Store St, London WC1 (☎020/7580 5522); other branches in Birmingham, Brighton, Bristol, Cambridge, Edinburgh, Manchester, Oxford and in YHA shops and on university campuses all over Britain (national telesales/bookings ☎0870/240 1010); *www.usitcampus.com*. Also USIT offices in Ireland. Student/ youth travel specialists.

STA Travel, 86 Old Brompton Rd, London SW7 3LH (☎020/7361 6161 for all European telesales); other offices in Birmingham, Bristol, Cambridge, Canterbury, Cardiff, Coventry, Durham, Glasgow, Leeds, Loughborough, Manchester, Nottingham, Oxford, Sheffield and Warwick; *www.statravel.com*. Specialists in low-cost flights and tours for students and under-26s.

IRELAND SPECIALISTS

Birmingham and West Midlands: Claddagh Travel, 199 High St, Erdington B23 6SY (☎0121/382 4803) and Fountain Court, Streethouse Lane B4 6DR (☎0121/200 3320); Ireland Direct, 115 Radford Rd, Coventry CV6 3BQ (☎0870/444 9090).

Bristol: Thorntons Travel Service, 48/54 Baldwin St BS1 1QP (☎01179/293211).

Edinburgh: Sibbald Travel, 86 South Clerk St EH8 9PT (☎0131/667 9172) and five other branches.

Glasgow: Going Places, 66 Gordon St G1 3TG (☎0141/221 5715); William Martin Travel, 184 Ingram St, G1 1ND (☎0141/552 5871).

Greater London: Abbey Travel, 89a High St, Wealdstone, Middx HA3 5DL (☎020/8861 5353) and 7, The Broadway, Greenford, Middx UB6 9PH (☎020/8570 1414); Pat Carroll Travel, 260 Kilburn High Rd, NW6 2BY (☎020/7625 9669); Tara Travel, 240–242 High Rd, Kilburn NW6 2BS (☎020/7625 8601, *www.taratravel.com*) and several other branches, including 758 Holloway Rd, N19 (☎020/7281 4171) and 75 High St, Lewisham SE13 (☎020/8318 7633).

Liverpool: Towns Travel, 114 County Rd L4 3QW (☎0151/733 1476); Wise Travel, 66 Allerton Rd L18 1NA (☎0151/733 1476).

Manchester: Curry Travel, 139 Wilbraham Rd, Fallowfield M14 7DS (☎0161/225 1133); Irish Travel Bureau, 1 Marsland Rd, Sale Moor M33 3HP (☎0161/976 3887).

(to Cork, Kerry, Knock, Shannon and Waterford). The main carriers are Aer Lingus, which flies from nine UK airports, and its main Irish competitor, Ryanair, which flies from eleven, while British Airways departs from seven. **Northern Ireland** is similarly well served: British Airways and British Midland run frequent daily flights from Heathrow to Belfast (1hr 15min), while easyJet has introduced a highly competitive service from Luton, and there are other flights to Belfast from fifteen

BRITAIN TO IRELAND FLIGHTS: ROUTES AND AIRLINES

Aberdeen to: Belfast International (British Airways).

Birmingham to: Belfast City (Jersey European); Belfast International (British Airways); Cork (Aer Lingus & Jersey European); Dublin (Aer Lingus & Ryanair); Knock (Aer Lingus); Shannon (Aer Lingus & Jersey European).

Blackpool to: Belfast City (Comed & Jersey European); Dublin (Comed).

Bournemouth to: Dublin (Ryanair).

Bristol to: Belfast City (Jersey European); Cork (British Airways); Dublin (Aer Lingus & Ryanair).

Cardiff to: Belfast City and Belfast International (British Airways); Dublin (Manx Airlines & Ryanair).

East Midlands to: Belfast International and Dublin (British Midland).

Edinburgh to: Belfast City and Belfast International (British Airways); Dublin (Aer Lingus).

Exeter to: Belfast City, Cork, Dublin and Shannon (Jersey European).

Glasgow to: Belfast City, Belfast International and Derry (British Airways); Cork (Aer Lingus); Dublin (Jersey European).

Leeds Bradford to: Belfast City (Jersey European); Dublin (Aer Lingus & Ryanair).

Liverpool to: Belfast City (British Airways); Belfast International (easyJet); Cork (Keenair); Dublin (Ryanair).

London City to: Dublin (City Jet & Jersey European).

London Gatwick to: Belfast City (Jersey European); Cork (British Airways); Dublin (British Airways & Ryanair); Shannon (British Airways).

London Heathrow to: Belfast International (British Airways & British Midland); Cork (Aer Lingus & British Airways); Dublin (Aer Lingus & British Midland); Shannon (Aer Lingus).

London Stansted to: Belfast City (Jersey European); Belfast International (Go); Cork, Derry, Kerry and Knock (Ryanair); Dublin (Aer Lingus & Ryanair); Shannon (Virgin Express); Waterford (British Airways).

Luton to: Belfast (easyJet); Dublin (Ryanair).

Manchester to: Belfast City, Belfast International, Cork, Derry, Knock, Shannon and Waterford (British Airways); Dublin (Aer Lingus & Ryanair).

Newcastle-upon-Tyne to: Belfast City (Gill Airways); Dublin (Aer Lingus).

Prestwick to: Dublin (Ryanair).

Sheffield to: Belfast City and Dublin (British Airways).

Southampton to: Belfast City and Dublin (British Airways).

Teesside to: Dublin (Ryanair).

AIRLINES

Aer Lingus ☎020/8899 4747 or 0845/973 7747, *www.aerlingus.ie.*

British Airways ☎0845/773 3377 or 722 2111, *www.britishairways.com* – travel shops in London at 115 Baker St, 101/2 Cheapside, 156 Regent St, also in Harrods and Selfridges stores and Victoria Station (all ☎0845/606 0747).

British European Airways ☎0870/567 6676, *www.jersey-eurpoean.co.uk.*

British Midland Airways ☎0870/607 0555, *www.britishmidland.com.*

City Jet ☎0845/744 5588.

Comed ☎01253/402661, *www.blackpool.airport.co.uk.*

easyJet ☎0870/600 0000, *www.easyjet.com.*

Gill Airways International ☎0191/214 6666, *www.gill-airways.com.*

Go ☎0870/607 6543, *www.go-fly.com.*

Keenair ☎0151/448 0606, *www.keenair.com.*

Manx Airlines ☎0845/7256256, *www.manx-airlines.com.*

Ryanair ☎0870/156 9569, *www.ryanair.com.*

Virgin Express ☎0800/891199, *www.virgin-express.com.*

regional airports. You can also fly to Derry from Stansted, Manchester and Glasgow.

There are usually reductions for mid-week travel, though the astonishingly complex **fare** structures are constantly changing, so it's always a good idea to check the latest special deals direct with the airlines or with your local travel agent. After these, the cheapest fares are usually called **APEX** (Advanced Purchase Excursion), available year round from most airlines. The conditions governing these tickets vary from airline to airline; however, most require that you stay one Saturday night, allow no changes and offer no refunds if you cancel your flight. In general, it's a good idea to book as far in advance as possible, and especially so if you intend to travel during peak times and/or to one of Ireland's regional airports.

Return fares from **London to Dublin** generally start at around £80, no matter the carrier nor point of departure, though it is possible to find some cheaper deals, particularly on Ryanair flights from Stansted or Gatwick. Flights from **London to Irish regional airports** tend to cost somewhat more. Return tickets for Aer Lingus's Heathrow to Cork flights start at around £90, while the best deal to Shannon is with Virgin Express whose flights from Gatwick cost around £110 return. Ryanair's flights from Stansted to Cork or Knock are priced from £80 return.

Fares **from UK regional airports** to Dublin can cost as little as £70 return for off-peak flights or APEX tickets, though regular tickets may cost substantially more. If you want to fly from a UK regional airport to Cork, Knock, Shannon or Waterford, you will probably find yourself paying around £120 for a return trip. You should expect to pay from £80 return for the cheapest tickets from UK regional airports to Belfast or Derry.

Flights from **London to Belfast** are also competitively priced. You can expect to pay around £70 for a midweek return flight from Heathrow to Belfast International with both British Midland and British Airways. Additionally, Jersey European Airways runs services from Stansted to Belfast International and from Gatwick to Belfast City with prices starting at £58 return, and Go operates from Stansted to Belfast International with return flights from £68. The same starting price applies to easyJet flights from Luton to Belfast International. The only carrier now flying from **London to Derry** is Ryanair, leaving from Stansted, whose tickets begin at £60 return.

If you want to bring a **bike** with you, most airlines will allow you to do so and don't charge (except Ryanair: £15 extra each way), as long as you don't exceed your baggage allowance. It makes sense to ask if the airline carries bikes before buying your ticket. It's also worth informing them in advance and to check in early – particularly if you are travelling to a small regional airport or during peak times, since carrying bikes is subject to available space.

YOUTH AND STUDENT FARES

Although there are few reductions on offer and the definition of "youth" varies between airlines (anything from under 20 to under 25), it is always worth asking, especially if you want a return period of longer than a month or a one-way ticket only. Students with an International Student Identity Card (ISIC; see p.14 for more on special passes) may be able to obtain reductions on some airlines when travelling off-peak.

If you are a student or **under 26** it's also worth checking fares through a specialist agency like STA or Usit Campus (see box on p.3 for addresses).

FERRIES

Nowadays, most **ferry services** are more like floating shopping precincts with restaurants, fast-food outlets, bars and stores. Journeys are relatively quick and comfortable. There are also catamaran or high-speed services on each of the main routes: Holyhead to Dún Laoghaire, Fishguard to Rosslare, Liverpool to Dublin, Cairnryan to Larne, Stranraer to Belfast, Troon to Belfast and Heysham to Belfast which cut sailing times almost in half (see box on p.6 for companies, routes and times). If you need a car when you get to Ireland, bringing your own is the best option – car rental in Ireland is among the most expensive in Europe (see "Getting Around" on p.32).

Ferry prices vary enormously depending on the time of year, and even the day and hour you travel, and some companies no longer advertise their full range of prices, but simply quote the starting point of the scale. Most ferry companies have **peak seasons** of July, August and Christmas and some also operate higher fares on bank holidays. In summer, in particular, car and foot passengers should always book in advance or risk turning up and not getting on the boat. Generally, midweek crossings are cheaper throughout the year, and many companies offer special **off-peak deals**,

FERRY COMPANIES, ROUTES AND TIMES

Irish Ferries, Reliance House, Water St, Liverpool L2 8TP (☎08705/171717, *www.irishferries.ie*); 150 New Bond St, London W1Y 0AQ (personal callers only).
Holyhead to Dublin Port (6 daily; Swift service 1hr 50min; ferry 3hr 15min); Pembroke to Rosslare (2 daily; 4hr).

Merchant Ferries, Canada Dock, No.3, Regent Rd, Kirkdale, Liverpool L20 8DF (☎0870/600 4321).
Liverpool to Dublin Port (1–2 daily; 7hr 30min).

Norse Irish Ferries, North Brocklebank Dock, Bootle, Merseyside L20 1BY (☎0151/944 1010).
Liverpool to Belfast (1 nightly, plus 1 Tues, Thurs & Sat daytime; 8hr 30min).

P&O European Ferries, Cairnryan, Stranraer, Wigtownshire DG9 8RF (☎0870/242 4777, *www.poirishsea.com*).
Cairnryan to Larne (2–8 daily; March–Dec fast ferry 1hr; Jan & Feb standard service 2hr 15min) Fleetwood to Larne (1 daily; 8hr); Liverpool to Dublin (1 daily; 8hr).

Seacat, Donegall Quay, Belfast (☎08705/523523, *www.seacat.co.uk*).
Heysham to Belfast (1–2 daily; 3hr 45min); Liverpool to Dublin (1 daily; 3hr 45min); Troon to Belfast (2 daily; 2hr 30min).

Stena Line, Charter House, Park St, Ashford, Kent TN24 8EX (☎08705/707070, *www.stenaline.co.uk*).
Fishguard to Rosslare (3–6 daily; catamaran 1hr 45min; ferry 3hr 30min); Holyhead to Dún Laoghaire (3–4 daily; 1hr 45min); Holyhead to Dublin Port (1–2 daily; 3hr 45min); Stranraer to Belfast (4–8 daily; HSS fast ferries 1hr 45min; ferry 3hr 15min); Stranraer to Larne (4–5 daily; 2hr 10min).

Swansea Cork Ferries, Harbour Office, King's Dock, Swansea, West Glamorgan SA1 1SF (☎01792/456116, *scferries@aol.com*).
Swansea to Cork (1 daily; 10hr).

three- or five-day return tickets, **APEX tickets** and various fares related to the number of passengers in a vehicle, including some **family fares**. Also bear in mind that prices are higher for the night-time crossings on some routes. In virtually all cases, bicycles are conveyed free of charge. Generally, combined bus/ferry or train/ferry tickets (see p.28) are good value.

The main crossing points to the **Republic** are from Holyhead on the Isle of Anglesey in North Wales and from Fishguard and Pembroke in southwest Wales. A standard return ticket for a car, its driver and one passenger on Stena Line's HSS service from **Holyhead to Dún Laoghaire** ranges upwards from £198 off-peak and from £338 in peak season and similarly from £40 return (off-peak) and from £50 (peak) for foot passengers. Bikes travel free on all Stena services carrying foot passengers. The same tickets on Stena's slower Superferry service from **Holyhead to Dublin Port** start at around £10 to £20 cheaper for a car, driver and one passenger, but note that foot passengers are not carried on this service. Irish Ferries also run from Holyhead to Dublin Port, charging return fares from £258 to £398 for a car, driver and one passenger on its Dublin Swift service and from £198 to £338 on the slower Cruise Ferry; fares for foot passengers are the same as Stena Line's for the high speed crossing and from £32 to £40 for the slower service. Again, Stena Line also has two services plying the longer **Fishguard to Rosslare** route: the high-speed Lynx service (from £218 off-peak and from £338 peak) and the Superferry (from £128 off-peak and from £278 peak); prices are for a car and two adults. Foot passenger return tickets cost from £50 (off-peak) to £59 (peak) and from £32 (off-peak) to £40 (peak). The range for the Irish Ferries four-hour crossing from **Pembroke to Rosslare** runs from £128 to £278 for a car and two adults while foot passengers are charged from £32 to £40.

Seacat operates the fastest crossing from **Liverpool to Dublin**, charging from £200 to £374 for a car, driver and one passenger. Foot passengers' return tickets cost from £38 to £60. Merchant Ferries' service regularly plies the route between **Liverpool and Dublin Port**. Standard return fares for a car and two passengers range from £158 to £258 on the daytime sailing and £188 to £358 for an overnight crossing (including a cabin). A special motorist return fare on the daytime sailing can cost as little as £120. Foot passengers are charged from £40 to £70 and may pay an additional £10 to £15 for an overnight cabin berth. P&O also operate a crossing from Liverpool to Dublin with a return trip costing from £150 to £280 for a car and two adults. Lastly, there's a sailing between **Swansea and Cork** operated by Swansea–Cork Ferries. Return fares for a car, driver and up to four adults cost from £139 (off-peak) to £378 (peak) and for foot passengers from £48 to £68; the fare for bicycles is £16 return. All crossings from Swansea are overnight and, though Pullman seats are provided, you might want to consider a cabin. These range in price from £34 per crossing for a standard 2-berth to £80 for a family suite (with a double bed and two berths). The return sailing from Cork takes place during the daytime except in off-peak periods. Note that there are no crossings from the second week in November to mid-March.

Most of the departure points for **Northern Ireland** are in southwest Scotland. The quickest option is the Stena Line service from **Stranraer to Belfast** and return fares cost £208 to £328 for a car including the driver and one passenger, with prices varying according to season and whether you choose the HSS or slower Superferry service. Foot passengers are charged from £40 to £50 for a return ticket. Stena Line has also reopened its **Stranraer to Larne** service and fares for this crossing are identical to its Belfast service. A little further north, P&O runs a fast ferry service from **Cairnryan to Larne**, costing from £184 to £324 for a car, driver and one passenger. Foot passenger rates for both of these services to Larne range between £36 and £50 return. Handy for those who live further north in Scotland or anyone first touring the Highlands, Seacat now operates a fast catamaran service from **Troon to Belfast**, costing from £200 to £374 for a car, driver and one passenger. Foot passengers are charged from £38 to £60. Exactly the same fares apply to its service from **Heysham** (on the Lancashire coast) **to Belfast**. P&O also runs a service from **Fleetwood to Larne** from a little further south, costing £120 to £220 return for a car, driver and one passenger; foot passengers' fares range from £40 to £60 return. Finally, Norse Irish Ferries operates a service from **Liverpool to Belfast**; fares for a car and two adults cost from £170 to £290 for daytime crossings with a return from £130 to £270. Overnight sailings range from £250 to a hefty £440 in high season, though for this you get a cabin, four-course dinner and breakfast. Foot passengers are charged from £50 to £60 (daytime return) or £70 to £90 (overnight return) with supplementary charges for cabins, if required. Advance booking is usually essential for this route.

Student reductions for foot passenger fares on ferries can be considerable: P&O charge only £22 to £40 for the Cairnryan to Larne crossing, and for Stranraer to Belfast routes, Stena Line charge £30 to £40, and Seacat £28 to £31. Savings on fares from Holyhead, Liverpool, Pembroke and Fishguard are generally between £5 to £15 on the standard fare. Reductions are also available for **senior citizens**.

COMBINATION TICKETS

If you want to enter Ireland through one port and leave by another, some ferry companies offer special **combination tickets**. Together P&O and Irish Ferries offer a seven-day **Circuit of Britain** ticket (mainly geared towards Irish travellers) which allows you one crossing on the Stranraer to Larne route and another on either the Holyhead to Dublin or Fishguard to Rosslare lines. The price for a car, driver and one passenger ranges from £169 to £219 and there are additional supplements of £15 per crossing for taking a high-speed sailing. Another deal is operated by Norse Irish Ferries and Merchant Ferries who have combined to offer a special Liverpool to Belfast, Dublin to Liverpool deal with return fares for a car and four adults priced from £165 to £385. For other trips, ferry companies usually add together the cost of two single passages.

TRAINS

Prices of combined train/sea tickets vary according to departure time and season and whether your journey qualifies for one of the several special offers available or can be booked some time in advance. It's usually more expensive to travel on high-speed ferries, in the daytime and during peak periods of Easter, July, August, Christmas and bank holidays. Journey times are considerably quicker than coaches: London, or Birmingham, to Dublin takes around seven hours; Manchester to Dublin takes around six hours; and add on an extra four hours to reach Belfast via these routes. Glasgow to Belfast via Stranraer is roughly four to five hours; plus an extra two hours from Edinburgh.

The return fare from London **to Dublin** ranges from £41 up to £76; from Birmingham tickets cost from £36 to £66; from Manchester £31 to £61; and from Glasgow £63 to £70. London **to**

TRAIN AND BUS COMPANIES

Eurolines, 52 Grosvenor Gardens, London SW1 0AU (☎020/7730 8235 or 0870/514 3219, *www.eurolines.com*).

National Rail Enquiry Service ☎0845/748 4950, *www.rail.co.uk*.

Ulsterbus Travel Centre, Europa Buscentre, Belfast BT12 5AH (☎028/9033 7003, *www.ulsterbus.co.uk*).

Rosslare costs from £40 to £62, and from Bristol £20 to £35 return. The standard fare from London **to Belfast** via Dublin is £78 return and Birmingham to Belfast is £73; both can be substantially reduced by taking the 4am sailing from Holyhead. Edinburgh to Belfast via Stranraer costs from £42 to £49, and from Glasgow £39 to £49. Simply book at a mainline station or travel agent.

Anyone **under 26** can get one-third off standard train fares by buying a Young Person's Railcard (£18) from any train station or at branches of Usit Campus (see p.3).

An **InterRail** pass is unlikely to be worth buying when travelling to Ireland unless you intend to travel extensively around the whole of Britain too or elsewhere in Europe. For ticketing purposes, Europe is divided into zones and a one-zone card, covering just Britain and Ireland, valid for 22 days, costs £159 for under-26s or £229 for over-26s. Passes are also available for two, three and all eight zones and these are valid for one month; prices range from £209 to £259 for under-26s and from £279 to £349 for over-26s. Note that InterRail passes are only available to people who have resided in one of the participating European countries for at least six months. However, non-residents may obtain a Eurail pass, see p.14. For train passes valid for travel in Ireland only, see "Getting Around", p.28.

BUSES

Getting to Ireland by bus is a slog, but very cheap. The main service is provided by Eurolines which operates a daily and nightly service from London **to Dublin** via Birmingham and Holyhead throughout the year with extra departures from May to October and over the Christmas period. The trip takes between eleven and thirteen hours, depending on the speed of the ferry, and costs from £37 return rising to £47 at peak times for the daytime service and from £47 increasing to a maximum of £55 for the night trip. A host of **connecting services** is available from Dublin, or there are daily direct services from London via Birmingham to Galway, Westport, Ballina and Sligo (all £45 to £58 return). Other Eurolines services to Dublin run daily from: Leicester via Nottingham; Leeds via Manchester and Liverpool; Bristol via Wolverhampton. There are also daily runs from London and Bristol to Waterford (£45 to £54), Cork, Killarney, Limerick and Tralee (all £45 to £58) using the Pembroke crossing, and connections are available at Rosslare (to Dublin), Waterford (to Kilkenny and Carlow), Cork (to Kinsale) and Limerick (to Roscrea and Ennis).

Getting to the North by bus is a little more expensive and prices are higher during July and August and in the week before Christmas. Eurolines runs a daily service from **London to Belfast** via Birmingham (12 hr), Manchester and Stranraer, charging from £39 to £60 return no matter where you board. Ulsterbus operates the following routes via Stranraer: from London to Belfast via Birmingham (£49 off-peak/£59 peak); from **Birmingham** via Manchester (£49/£59; 11hr); from **Edinburgh** via Glasgow (£39/£45; 9hr 30min).

There are reductions on Eurolines services of between twenty to thirty percent off standard fares for holders of National Express **Student**, **Young Person** (aged 16 to 25) and **Advantage** (aged over 50) cards all of which cost £9 (one year) or £19 (three years). Possession of a **Family Saver** card (£15 one year) allows children aged between 5 and 15 to travel free, if two adults pay the full return fare. All these cards and tickets for Eurolines services can be bought from the head office (see box), National Express Coach Stations in Birmingham, Leeds, Liverpool, London and Manchester, or from any travel agent acting as a National Express/Eurolines agent. Ulsterbus offers reductions of £4–6 on return tickets for 13–25 year olds and the over-60s. Tickets for its services are available by telephone from its Belfast office (see box), or from Eurolines or travel agents acting as National Express or Scottish Citylink agents.

PACKAGE HOLIDAYS

If you are looking for a specific holiday activity (such as angling, cycling, walking or golfing), heading for a busy festival or simply want to avoid

SPECIALIST TOUR OPERATORS IN BRITAIN AND IRELAND

Aer Lingus Holidays ☎0845/973 7747, *www.aerlingus.ie*. Dublin, Cork and Galway city holidays, coastal and country weekend breaks with accommodation, ranging from B&Bs to four-star hotels. Good fly-drive deals.

Conservation Volunteers Northern Ireland, 28 Glenstall Rd, Ballymoney, Co. Antrim BT53 7NB (☎028/2766 2273, *www.btcv.org*). Spend a week or weekend learning conservation skills, such as dry-stone walling, woodland management and wildflower planting.

Cresta Holidays, Tabley Court, Victoria St, Altrincham, Cheshire WA14 1EZ (☎0870/161 0909). Vast range of hotel and cottage holidays, river cruising, horse-drawn caravans, walking and golfing packages.

Drive Ireland, 311 Tower Building, Water St, Liverpool L3 1AS (☎0151/231 1480). Combined flight/accommodation/car rental deals, city breaks and coach tours.

Emerald Star, The Marina, Carrick-on-Shannon, Co. Leitrim (☎0782/0234, *www.emeraldstar.ie*). Specialist boat-holiday operator offering cruising packages on the Shannon and Erne waterways.

Flanagan & Sons World Travel, 115 Radford Rd, Coventry CV6 3BQ (☎0500/026385). Specialists in angling holidays at competitive rates. They also arrange combined ferry/flight and accommodation deals.

Gerry Feeney Travel Ltd, 8 Centre Way, High Rd, Ilford, Essex IG1 1ND (☎20/8514 5141, *www.travel-ireland.co.uk/contact.htm*). Fly- and ferry-drive packages, self-catering and coach tours.

Go Ireland, Killorglin, Co. Kerry (☎066/976 2094, *www.goireland.fexco.ie*). Guided walking holidays in Connemara, Donegal, Kerry and other counties; semi-guided cycling tours; specialist golfing holidays.

Irish Cycling Safaris, Belfield House, UCD, Dublin 4 (☎01/260 0749, *www.kerna.ie/ics*). Well-organized one-week guided tours for cyclists of all abilities in prime areas along the west coast from Cork to Donegal, with luggage van and hotel/guesthouse accommodation.

Irish Ferries Holidays, Reliance House, Water St, Liverpool L2 8TP (☎0870/5170 000, *www.irishferries.ie*). Competitively priced car rental available in its sail-drive and fly-drive packages, with a broad range of accommodation options. Also golfing, fishing and cruising holidays. Under-16s travel free.

Leisure Breaks & Golf, 33 Dovedale Rd, Liverpool L18 5EP (☎0151/734 5200). Very good range of activity holidays including riding, cycling, golf and horse-drawn caravanning. Also accommodation and ferry deals, and fly-drive packages.

Rural Cottage Holidays, St Anne's Court, 59 North St, Belfast BT1 1NB (☎028/9024 1110). Northern Ireland Tourist Board subsidiary offering reasonably priced, high standard, self-catering accommodation – often traditional cottages – in the Glens of Antrim, the Mournes, the Sperrins and Fermanagh Lakelands.

Slattery's Travel, 162 Kentish Town Rd, London NW5 2AG (☎020/7485 1438). Full range of transport (flight, ferries and bus travel, plus motoring holidays) and accommodation deals (hotels, country houses and self-catering). There's also horse-drawn caravans.

Stena Line Holidays, Stena Line Ltd, Charter House, Park St, Ashford, Kent TN24 8EX (☎0870/5747474, *www.stenaline.co.uk*). Full range of ferry, fly-drive, accommodation and self-catering packages. Under-16s travelling with a family in a car go free.

Swansea Cork Ferries, King's Dock, Swansea, West Glamorgan (☎01792/456116, *scferries@aol.com*). Activity holidays, self-catering packages in Cork and Kerry, and go-as-you-please-tours (you tell them where you want to go and they book hotels on your itinerary).

the hassle of making your own arrangements, there are numerous package deals available from tour operators. If you intend to rent a car, it's worth considering the various fly-drive and sail-drive offers available and the ferry companies often offer good packages including accommodation (see box).

GETTING THERE FROM THE USA AND CANADA

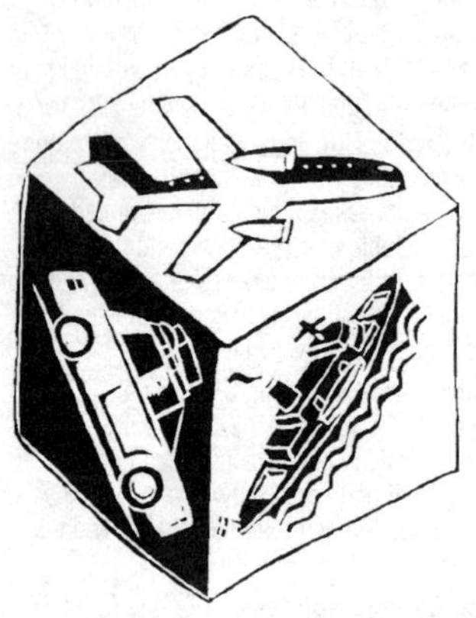

Ireland is easily accessible from the USA by a number of airlines that offer direct flights to the major gateways of Dublin, Shannon and Belfast. From Canada only indirect flights are available. Ferries and cheap flights also make Ireland easily accessible as part of a wider European travel itinerary.

SHOPPING FOR TICKETS

Leaving aside discounted tickets, the cheapest way to go is with an **APEX** (Advance Purchase Excursion) ticket, although these carry certain restrictions: you will probably have to book – and pay – 21 days before departure (though to get the very cheapest fares on certain routes, you may need to book ninety days in advance, spend at least seven days abroad (maximum stay three months), and you tend to get penalized if you change your schedule. There are also winter **Super-APEX** tickets, sometimes known as Eurosavers – slightly cheaper than an ordinary APEX, but limiting your stay to between seven and 21 days. Some airlines also issue **Special APEX** tickets to those under 24, often extending the maximum stay to a year. Many airlines offer youth or **student fares** to under-25s; a passport or driving licence is sufficient proof of age, though these tickets are subject to availability and can have eccentric booking conditions. It's worth remembering that most cheap return fares involve spending at least one Saturday night away and that many will only give a percentage refund if you need to cancel or alter your journey, so make sure you check the restrictions carefully before buying a ticket. Any local travel agent should be able to access up-to-the-minute fares, although in practice they may not have time to research all the possibilities – you might want to call the airlines directly or check online.

Discount outlets, however, can usually do better than any APEX and most student fares. They come in several forms. **Consolidators** buy up large blocks of tickets that airlines don't think they'll be able to sell at their published prices, and sell them at a discount. Besides being cheap, consolidators normally don't impose advance purchase requirements (although in busy times you'll want to book ahead just to be sure of getting a ticket), but they do often charge very stiff fees for date changes. Also, these companies' margins are pretty tiny, so they make their money by dealing in volume – don't expect them to entertain lots of questions. **Discount agents** – such as STA, Council Travel, Nouvelles Frontières, or oth-

AIRLINES IN NORTH AMERICA

Aer Lingus ☎1-800/IRISHAIR, *www.aerlingus.com.*

Air Canada ☎1-800/776-3000, *www.aircanada.ca.*

American Airlines ☎1-800/433-7300, *www.americanairlines.com.*

British Airways US ☎1-800/247-9297, Canada ☎1-800/668-1059, *www.britishairways.com.*

Delta Airlines US ☎1-800/241-4141, Canada ☎l-800/221-1212, *www.delta.com.*

United Airlines ☎1-800/241-6522, *www.united.com.*

Virgin Atlantic Airways ☎1-800/862-8621, *www.virgin.com.*

DISCOUNT AGENTS, CONSOLIDATORS AND TRAVEL CLUBS

Air Brokers International, 150 Post St, Suite 620, San Francisco, CA 94108 (☎1-800/883-3273 or 415/397-1383, *www.airbrokers.com*). Consolidator and specialist in RTW tickets.

Air Courier Association, 15000 W, 6th Ave, Suite 23, Golden, CO 80401 (☎1-800/282-1202, *www.aircourier.org*). Courier-flight broker.

Airtech, 588 Broadway, Suite 204, New York, NY 10017 (☎1-800/575-8324 or 212/219-7000, *www.airtech.com*). Standby seat broker; also deals in consolidator fares and courier flights.

Council Travel, Head Office, 205 E 42nd St, New York, NY 10017 (☎1-800/226-8624, or 212/822-2700, *www.counciltravel.com*). Other offices in Boston, Los Angeles, San Francisco and Washington. Nationwide US organization. Mostly, but by no means exclusively, specializes in student travel.

Educational Travel Center, 438 N Frances St, Madison, WI 53703 (☎1-800/747-5551, *www.edtrav.com*). Student/youth discount agent.

International Association of Air Travel Couriers, 220 South Dixie Highway, Lake Worth, FL 33460 (☎561/582-8320, *www.courier.org*). Courier-flight broker.

High Adventure Travel, 442 Post St, Suite 400, San Francisco, CA 94012 (☎1-800/350-0612 or 415/912-5600, *www.highadv.com*). RTW tickets. Web site features interactive database that lets you build and price your own RTW itinerary.

New Frontiers/Nouvelles Frontières, 12 E 33rd St, New York, NY 10016 (☎1-800/366-6387 or 212/779-0600, *www. newfrontiers.com*); 1001 Sherbrook East, Suite 720, Montréal, PQ H2L 1L3 (☎514/526-8444). French discount travel firm, mostly to Europe. Other branches in Los Angeles, San Francisco and Quebec City.

Now Voyager, 74 Varick St, Suite 307, New York, NY 10013 (☎212/431-1616, *www.nowvoyagertravel.com*). Courier-flight broker and consolidator.

STA Travel, 10 Downing St, New York, NY 10014 (☎1-800/777-0112 or 212/627-3111, *www.statravel.com*). Other offices including Boston, Chicago, Los Angeles, Minneapolis, Philadelphia and San Francisco. Specialists in independent travel.

TFI Tours International, 34 W 32nd St, New York, NY 10001 (☎1-800/745-8000 or 212/736-1160, *www.tfitoursinternational.com*). Consolidator.

Travac, 989 6th Ave, New York, NY 10018 (☎1-800/872-8800, *www.travac.com*). Consolidator and charter broker mostly to Europe; has another office in Orlando.

Travel Avenue, 10 S Riverside, Suite 1404, Chicago, IL 60606 (☎1-800/333-3335, *www.travelavenue.com*). Discount travel company.

Travel Cuts, 187 College St, Toronto, ON M5T 1P7 (☎1-800/667-2887 or 416/979-2406, *www.travelcuts.com*). Other offices include Calgary, Montréal, Vancouver, Winnipeg. Canadian student travel organization.

Uni Travel, 11737 Administration Drive, St Louis, MO 63146 (☎1-800/325-2222, *www.unitravel.com*). Consolidator.

ers listed above – also wheel and deal in blocks of tickets off-loaded by the airlines, but they typically offer a range of other travel-related services such as travel insurance, train passes, youth and student ID cards, car rentals and tours. These agencies tend to be most worthwhile to students and under-26s, who can often benefit from special fares and deals.

Travel clubs are another option for those who travel a lot – most charge you an annual membership fee, which may be worth it for discounts on air tickets, car rental and the like. You should also check the travel section in the Sunday *New York Times*; your own major local newspaper; browse the Internet on sites such as *www.travelocity.com* for current bargains; and consult a good travel agent.

Be advised also that the pool of travel companies is swimming with sharks – exercise caution with any outfit that sounds shifty or impermanent, and *never* deal with a company that demands cash up front or refuses to accept payment by credit card.

Regardless of where you buy your ticket, the **fare** will depend on **season**. Although these may vary from airline to airline, as a general rule, fares to Ireland are highest from the beginning of June through September and from December 12 to 31; they drop during the "shoulder" seasons, the beginning of October to around December 12; and you'll get the best deals during the low season,

SPECIALIST TOUR OPERATORS

All prices quoted exclude taxes and are subject to change. Accommodation is based on single person/double occupancy. Unless stated otherwise, round-trip flights are from New York.

Adventures Abroad ☎1-800/665-3998 or 604/303-1099, *www.adventures-abroad.com*. Specialists in small group tours. One week in Northern Ireland or the Republic from US$1136; two week combo from US$2277 (both land only).

Aer Lingus Vacations ☎1-800/474-7424, *www.aerlingus.com*. Airline tour department.

Art Horizons International ☎212/969-9410. Customized art and architecture tours.

Backroads ☎1-800/GO-ACTIVE,462-2848 or 510/527-1555, *www.backroads.com*. Eight days cycling in Co. Cork and Co. Kerry from US$2998 plus US$150 bike rental; six days walking from US$2698 (both land only).

Brian Moore International Tours ☎1-800/982-2299, *www.bmit.com*. Wide range of products including fly-drives, escorted tours plus customized chauffeur-driven tours, weddings, honeymoons, St Patrick's Day parades, gourmet, walking, horseback-riding.

Castles, Cottages and Flats ☎1-800/742-6030 or 617/646-6552, *www.castlescottages-flats.com*. Realize your fantasies of living in a medieval castle for roughly US$750–1000 per person, per night (land only). Plus other less exotic options.

Celtic International Tours ☎1-800/833-4373, *www.celtictours.com*. Customized packages, coach tours, fly-drives.

CIE Tours International ☎1-800/CIE-TOUR or 973/292-3438, *www.cietours.com*. Fly-drives, city breaks, coach tours available. Nine day"Irish Pub Tour" from US$1053 (airfare included).

Classic Adventures ☎1-800/777-8090, *www.classicadventures.com*. Fully escorted biking tours in the southwest from US$1829 for one week plus US$100 bike rental (land only).

Contiki Holidays ☎1-800/CONTIKI or 466-0610, *www.contiki.com*. Group tours for 18–35 year-olds. Nine days in the Republic of Ireland with optional two-night London add-on from US$759 (land only).

Destinations Ireland & Great Britain ☎1-800/832-1848; *www.01destinations.com*. Flexible range of travel products including walking, cycling, and car hire.

Distinctive Journeys ☎1-800/922-2060, *www.distinctivejourneys.com*. Customized deluxe packages to Ireland.

Fishing International ☎1-800/950-4242 or 707/542-4242, *www.fishinginternational.com*. A week of salmon fishing in the Shannon River with refurbished farmhouse accommodation, all meals, licence, instruction and fishing gear for US$1350 (land only).

Golf International ☎1-800/833-1389, *www.golfinternational.com*. Several packages, including seven days golfing in Ballybunion and Lahinch from US$1500 (land only).

International Gay Travel Association ☎954/776-3303. Trade group with lists of gay-owned or gay-friendly travel agents, accommodation and other travel businesses.

Irish American International Tours ☎1-800/633-0505. Group and individual customized packages, car rental, hotels, B&B, airline tickets, family reunions, winter pub tours, etc.

Irish Festival Tours ☎1-800/441-4277, *www.irishtours.com*. Among the tours offered are those hosted by entertainers and winter pub crawls.

Isle Inn Tours ☎1-800/237-9376, *www.isleinntours.com*. Irish travel specialists, trips include: cycling, walking, cruising, B&B.

Owenoak International ☎1-800/426-4498, *www.owenoak.com*. Customized tours and golf trips.

Saga Holidays ☎1-800/343-0273, *www.sagaholidays.com*. Specialists in group travel for seniors. "Round the Emerald Isle" fifteen-night escorted coach tour from US$1999 (airfare included).

January through May. If you want to travel during the Christmas–New Year period, book at least two or three months ahead.

A further possibility is to see if you can arrange a **courier flight**, although the hit-or-miss nature of these makes them most suitable for the single traveller who travels light and has a very flexible schedule. In return for shepherding a parcel through customs and possibly giving up your baggage allowance, you can expect to get a heavily discounted ticket. The duration of your stay is also likely to be restricted. A couple of courier "associations" (courier-flight brokers) are listed in the box on p.11.

Prices quoted are round-trip, assume midweek travel (add on US$50–75/CAN$75–112.50 for weekends), exclude taxes (around US$50–100/CAN$75–150) and are subject to availability and change.

FLIGHTS FROM THE USA

Aer Lingus, the national airline of Ireland, flies direct out of **Boston** and **New York** to both **Dublin** and **Shannon**. The APEX fares out of the East Coast to both these cities are roughly the same: starting at approximately US$320 (low season) or US$530 (high season). **From Chicago** the fares start at around US$430 (low season) or US$650 (high season). Also be on the lookout for Aer Lingus' special limited promotional fares, such as their two seats for the price of one offer, which crop up from time to time, most likely in the off-season, and are advertised in national newspapers. As always, a reputable discount agent, such as Council Travel or STA, should be able to sift through all the available fares and find one that best suits your particular travel requirements.

Of the **US airlines** that operate services direct to the Republic, Delta flies from **Atlanta** to both Shannon and Dublin. Their cheapest APEX fares range from approximately US$525 (low season) to US$860 (high). A number of carriers also fly **direct to Belfast**. Aer Lingus flies several days a week from New York. Fares start at approximately US$350 in low season, US$650 in high season.

The big airlines fly if not daily then at least three times a week, from Los Angeles, San Francisco and Seattle on the **West Coast** with transfers in New York, Atlanta and Dallas. Delta's Los Angeles to Dublin or Shannon service starts at US$580 (low season) and US$960 (high season), while British Airways has plenty of flights, and is competitive, with fares starting at around US$750 (low season) or US$1050 (high season) to London, where you can get a connecting flight. Prices quoted are round-trip, assume midweek travel (add on US$50–75 for weekends), exclude taxes (around US$50–100) and are subject to availability and change.

Flying time from New York is approximately five hours thirty minutes direct to Dublin and seven hours, with a necessary stopover, to Belfast. Flying time from Los Angeles is approximately ten hours and thirty minutes to Dublin, and twelve hours to Belfast, with a stopover somewhere en route.

FLIGHTS FROM CANADA

Aer Lingus does not fly out of Canada, but **Air Canada** flies indirect (with a change of plane in London) out of Toronto, Montréal and Vancouver to Dublin, Shannon and Belfast. APEX-type tickets from Toronto and Montréal to Dublin and Shannon are around Can$900 (low season)/Can$1200 (high season) and Can$1015/Can$1345 to Belfast. From Vancouver, expect to pay around Can$1170/Can$1460 to Dublin or Shannon and Can$1245/Can$1615 to Belfast.

For more options and potential for bargain fares, it may be worth considering flying to London first. British Airways flies from Toronto to London for around Can$725 (low season) or Can$975 (high season) and from Vancouver to London for roughly Can$960 (low season) or Can$1200 (high season). The add-on to the Republic or the North is around Can$150. But be warned that the fares for this last leg of the journey may come with more restrictions than the transatlantic tickets, especially with regard to changing your travel plans.

The actual **flying time** to Dublin from Toronto is approximately eight hours and from Vancouver between ten and eleven hours.

PACKAGES

Package tours may not sound like your kind of travel, but don't dismiss the idea out of hand. It's true that tours arranged in North America tend to be of the everybody-on-the-bus group variety, but many agents can put together very flexible deals, sometimes amounting to no more than a flight plus car or train pass and accommodation. If you're planning to travel in moderate or luxury style, and especially if your trip is geared around special interests, a package can work out cheaper than the same arrangements made on arrival. A package can also ensure a worry-free first week while you're finding your feet on a longer tour (of course, you can jump off the itinerary any time you like). Most companies will expect you to book through a local travel agent, and, since it costs the same, you might as well do that.

A variety of short excursions and specialized tours to Ireland are available from a number of organizations, including Aer Lingus, which offers a range of **fly-drive packages**. CIE Tours International is a good general operator to Ireland and also sells train passes. Other special-interest operators are listed on p.12.

EUROPEAN RAIL PASSES FOR NORTH AMERICAN AND AUSTRALASIAN TRAVELLERS

There are a number of European rail passes that can only be purchased before leaving home, though consider carefully how much travelling you are going to be doing: these all-encompassing passes only really begin to pay for themselves if you intend to see a fair bit of Ireland and the rest of Europe.

The best-known and most flexible is the **Eurail Youthpass** (for under-26s) which costs US$388/A$726 for fifteen consecutive days, and there are also one- and two-month versions; over-26's can buy a first-class version for US$554/A$1036 for the fifteen-day option. You stand a better chance of getting your money's worth out of a **Eurail Flexipass**, which is good for a certain number of travel days in a two-month period. This, too, comes in under-26/first-class versions: ten days cost US$458/A$856 for under-26s, US$654/A$1223 for over-26s, though it also comes in fifteen-day formats. These passes can be bought from the agents listed below and also from many regular travel agents, especially youth and student specialists (see listings on p.11 and p.15).

North Americans and Australasians are also eligible to purchase **more specific passes** valid for travel in Ireland only – see "Getting Around", p.28, for details.

RAIL CONTACTS IN NORTH AMERICA

CIE – Irish Rail and Bus Line ☎1-800/CIE-TOUR or 973/292-3438, *www.cie.ie.*

CIT Tours ☎1-800/CIT-RAIL, *www.cit-tours.com.*

Euro Vacations ☎1-888/281-EURO, *www.eurovacations.com.*

Rail Europe ☎1-800/4EURAIL in US, ☎1-800/361-RAIL in Canada, *www.raileurope.com.*

RAIL CONTACTS IN AUSTRALASIA

CIT, 263 Clarence St, Sydney (☎02/9267 1255 or 9299 4754); offices in Adelaide, Brisbane, Melbourne and Perth. Comprehensive range of rail passes. No NZ office – enquiries and reservations via Australian offices.

For students, programmes combining work and study with travel to Ireland are available from: The Irish American Cultural Institute, 1 Lackawanna Place, Morristown, NJ 07960 (☎973/605-1991, *www.irishaci.org*); The Council on International Education Exchange, 632 Third Ave, 20th Floor, New York, NY 10017 (☎1-800/40STUDY, *www.ciee.org*); Humanities Abroad, 11 Gloucester St, Boston, MA 02115 (☎1-800/754-9991, *www.humanitiesabroad.com*); and The American Institute for Foreign Study, College Division, 102 Greenwich Ave, Greenwich, CT 06830 (☎1-800/727-2437 or 203/869-9090, *www.aifs.org*). For general information and publications about studying abroad, try contacting the Institute of International Education, 809 UN Plaza, New York, NY 10017 (☎212/883-8200, *www.iie.org*).

GETTING THERE FROM AUSTRALIA & NEW ZEALAND

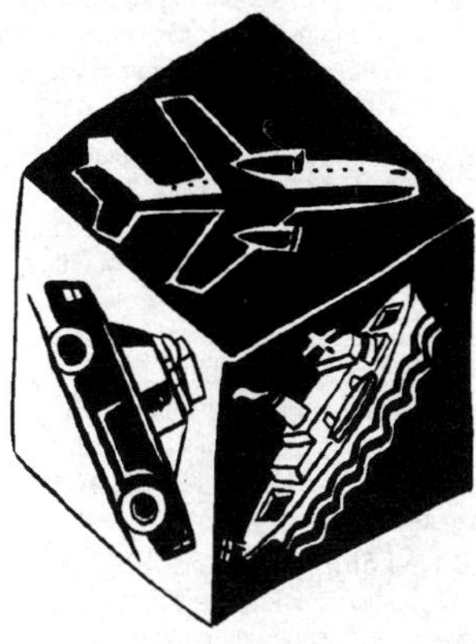

No direct scheduled flights are operated to Ireland from Australia or New Zealand; all require a transfer in London. British Airways, Aer Lingus and British Midland team up with a number of carriers to offer add-on fares to Dublin, Belfast, Cork, Shannon and Sligo. If you're on a budget it can work out cheaper to buy a low cost fare to London via Asia and either an add-on fare to Ireland with Aer Lingus or British Midland before you leave or pickup a bargain airfare to Ireland in London. Some flights via Asia involve a night's free overnight stop – often a needed break on long-haul flights – in the carrier's home city, with accommodation, meals and transfers included in the ticket price.

For most major airlines, regular return fares are seasonally adjusted – low season is from mid-January to the end of February and October to November; high season is mid-May to August and December to January, with the remainder of the year classed as "shoulder" season. Tickets purchased direct from the airlines tend to be expensive; **travel agents** generally offer much better

DISCOUNT AGENTS

All of the agents listed below will sell you discount flights, as well as acting as retail agents for tour companies such as Creative, Insight and Contiki, which offer accommodation packages, tours and car rental.

Anywhere Travel, 345 Anzac Parade, Kingsford, Sydney (☎02/9663 0411, *anywhere@ozemail.com.au*).

Budget Travel, 16 Fort St, Auckland, plus branches around the city (☎09/366 0061, and toll-free 0800/808 040, *www.budgettravel.co.nz*).

Destinations Unlimited, 220 Queen St, Auckland (☎09/373 4033).

Flight Centres, Australia: 82 Elizabeth St, Sydney (☎02/9235 3522); plus branches nationwide; for the nearest branch call ☎13 1600. New Zealand: 350 Queen St, Auckland (☎09/358 4310, toll-free ☎0200/354 448); plus branches nationwide; *www.flightcentre.com.au*.

Northern Gateway, 22 Cavenagh St, Darwin (☎08/8941 1394, *oztravel@norgate.com.au*).

STA Travel, Australia: 855 George St, Sydney; 256 Flinders St, Melbourne; other offices in state capitals and major universities; for nearest branch call ☎13 1776; fastfare telesales ☎1300/360 960. New Zealand: 10 High St, Auckland (☎09/309 0458); for nearest branch call ☎0800/874 773; fastfare telesales ☎09/366 6673; plus branches in major cities and university campuses; *www.statravel.com.au*.

Student Uni Travel, 92 Pitt St, Sydney (☎02/9232 8444); plus branches in Brisbane, Cairns, Darwin, Melbourne and Perth; *sydney@backpackers.net*.

Thomas Cook, Australia: 175 Pitt St, Sydney (☎02/9231 2877); 257 Collins St, Melbourne (☎03/9282 0222); plus branches in other state capitals; for the nearest branch call ☎13 1771; for telesales call ☎1800/801 002. New Zealand: 191 Queen St, Auckland (☎09/379 3920); *www.thomascook.com.au*.

Trailfinders, 8 Spring St, Sydney (☎02/9247 7666); 91 Elizabeth St, Brisbane (☎07/3229 0887); Hides Corner, Shield St, Cairns (☎07/4041 1199).

USIT Beyond, cnr Shortland St and Jean Batten Place, Auckland (☎09/379 4224 or toll-free on ☎0800/788 336); plus branches in Christchurch, Dunedin, Hamilton, Palmerston North and Wellington; *www.usitbeyond.co.nz*.

AIRLINES

Aer Lingus Australia ☎02/9244 2123, New Zealand ☎09/379 4455, *www.aerlingus.ie*. Daily direct flights to Cork, Dublin and Shannon from London.

Air New Zealand Australia ☎13/2476, New Zealand toll-free ☎0800/737 000, or ☎09/357 3000, *www.airnz.com*. Daily flights to London Heathrow from Brisbane, Melbourne, Sydney and Auckland, with a transfer in LA.

British Airways Australia ☎02/8904 8800, New Zealand ☎09/356 8690; *www.british-airways.com*. Daily flights to London Heathrow from Sydney either direct, or with a transfer in LA; twice weekly via Perth with either a transfer or overnight stop in Harare or Johannesburg; and daily from Auckland with a transfer in LA.

British Midland Australia ☎02/9959 3922, New Zealand ☎09/6234294, *www.iflybritishmidland.com*. Daily flights to Belfast and Dublin from London Heathrow.

Cathay Pacific Australia ☎13/1747 or ☎02/9931 5500, New Zealand ☎09/379 0861, *www.cathaypacific.com*. Several flights weekly to London Heathrow from Brisbane, Cairns, Melbourne, Perth, Sydney and Auckland, all with a transfer in Hong Kong.

Garuda Australia ☎1300/365 330, New Zealand ☎09/366 1855 or ☎1800/128 510. Several flights weekly from major cities in Australia and New Zealand to London Gatwick, with either a transfer or an overnight stop in Denpasar or Jakarta.

Japan Airlines Australia ☎02/9272 1111, New Zealand ☎09/379 9906, *www.japanair.com*. Daily flights to London Heathrow from Brisbane and Sydney, and several flights a week from Cairns and Auckland, all with either a transfer or overnight stop in Tokyo or Osaka. Code-share with Air New Zealand.

Malaysian Airlines Australia ☎13/2627, New Zealand ☎09/373 2741 or ☎0800/777 747, *www.malaysiaair.com*. Several flights weekly to London Heathrow from Sydney, Melbourne, Perth and Auckland with either a transfer or overnight stop in Kuala Lumpur.

Qantas Australia ☎13/1313, New Zealand ☎09/357 8900 or ☎0800/808 767, *www.qantas.com.au*. Daily flights to London Heathrow from major cities in Australia, either direct (with a short refuelling stop) or with a transfer in Singapore or Bangkok, plus twice weekly via Perth with either a transfer or overnight stopover in Harare or Johannesburg; daily flights from major cities in New Zealand to London Heathrow via Sydney, and with a transfer in Singapore, Bangkok or LA.

Royal Brunei Airlines Australia ☎07/3221 7757, no NZ office, *www.bruneiair.com*. Three flights weekly to London Heathrow from Brisbane, and two weekly from Darwin and Perth, all via Abu Dhabi and with a transfer or overnight stop in Brunei.

Singapore Airlines Australia ☎13/1011, New Zealand ☎09/303 2129 or ☎0800/808 909, *www.singaporeair.com*. Daily flights to London Heathrow from Brisbane, Melbourne, Perth, Sydney and Auckland, either direct or with a transfer in Singapore.

Sri Lankan Airlines Australia ☎02/9244 2234, New Zealand ☎09/308 3353. Three flights a week to London Heathrow from Sydney, with a transfer or overnight stop in Colombo.

Thai Airways Australia ☎1300/651 960, New Zealand ☎09/377 3886, *www.thaiair.com*. Several flights a week to London Heathrow from Brisbane, Melbourne, Perth, Sydney and Auckland, with either a transfer or overnight stop in Bangkok.

United Airlines Australia ☎13/1777, New Zealand ☎09/379 3800, *www.ual.com*. Daily flights to London Heathrow from Melbourne, Sydney and Auckland, with a transfer in LA.

deals, and have the latest information on limited special offers and stopovers. The best discounts are offered by companies such as Flight Centres, STA and Trailfinders (see box on p.15); these can also help with visas, travel insurance and tours. You might also want to have a look on the **Internet**; *www.travel.com.au* offers discounted fares online, as does *www.sydneytravel.com*.

Buying a flight to London is a worthwhile option, if you pick up one of the cheap deals offered by some carriers in low season, for example, A$1400 from Australia with Garuda, Royal Brunei and Sri Lankan Airlines. The add-on fare to destinations in Ireland is around A$180/NZ$210. See p.3 for details of discount agents who supply low-cost tickets.

If you're planning to visit Ireland as part of a wider world trip, then **Round-the-World tickets** offer greater flexibility and are better value than a straightforward return flight. For example, prices for a RTW ticket from Sydney or Auckland to Singapore or Bangkok, London, side trip to Dublin or Belfast, New York, Los Angeles, Auckland and back to Sydney start at around A$2399/NZ$2899; a ticket from Sydney to Auckland, Santiago, Rio, London, side trip to Dublin or Belfast, Paris, Bangkok, Singapore and back to Sydney starts at A$2499/NZ$2999.

FLIGHTS FROM AUSTRALIA

Airfares from **Australian east-coast gateways** are all pretty much the same: common rated (meaning there's no difference whether you're flying from Melbourne, Sydney or any other eastern gateway), with Ansett and Qantas providing a shuttle service to the point of international departure. Depending on the route and transfer time, flights between Australia and Britain take between 24 and 30 hours via Asia and 27 and 30 hours via the US. From Australia there are numerous indirect flights to Ireland via London with British Airways, Aer Lingus or British Midland providing the services from Heathrow to Belfast, Dublin, Cork, Shannon and Sligo. The cheapest fares are **via Asia** with the best value through-fare offered by Japan Airlines (which includes a stopover in either Tokyo or Osaka en route) from A$1350 low season to A$2400 high season. Thai Airways, Singapore Airlines, Cathay Pacific, Qantas, British Airways and Malaysia Airlines have through-fares to Ireland via their respective home cities for around A$1899–2600. Air New Zealand's fares **via the US** to Dublin via Los Angeles and Heathrow range from A$1999 to 2800

Fares from **Perth** and **Darwin** cost around A$100–200 less than from eastern gateways and A$400 more via the US.

FLIGHTS FROM NEW ZEALAND

Most airlines fly out of **Auckland**; add between NZ$150 and NZ$300 to the following fares for flights from **Christchurch** and **Wellington**. Fewer carriers fly from New Zealand than from Australia; however, routes are just as varied. British Airways, Aer Lingus and British Midland team up with several airlines to offer through services to Ireland via London from Auckland. **Via**

SPECIALIST TOUR OPERATORS

Adventure World (wholesaler), 73 Walker St, North Sydney (☎02/9956 7766 or 1800 221 931, *www.adventureworld.com.au*); 101 Great South Rd, Remuera, Auckland (☎09/524 5118). Agents for CIE bus tours, motoring holidays, Dublin city breaks and a range of car-accommodation packages.

Best of Britain, 352a Military Rd, Cremorne, Sydney (☎02/9909 1055). Flights, accommodation (B&Bs and apartments as well as hotels), car rental and city tours.

Blue Sky Travel, 6 Walls Rd, Penrose, Auckland (☎09/525 2363). Specializes in all Irish travel arrangements.

Contiki, 35 Spring St, Bondi Junction, Sydney (☎02/9511 2200 or ☎1300/301 835, *www.contiki.com*). Specializes in extended tours for 18 to 35-year-old party animals including their seven-day tour visiting Eire's most popular sights.

Eblana Travel, Level 4, 67 Castlereagh St, Sydney (☎02/9232 8144). A wide choice of accommodation, packages and tours.

Explore Holidays, Second Floor, 55 Blaxland Rd, Ryde, NSW (☎02/9857 6200, *www.exploreholidays.com.au*). A good selection of accommodation and tours throughout Ireland.

European Travel Office (wholesaler), 122 Rosslyn St, West Melbourne (☎03/9329 8844); Suite 410, 368 Sussex St, Sydney (☎02/9267 7714); 407 Great South Rd, Auckland (☎09/525 3074). Tours, car rental and accommodation for the independent traveller.

Qantas Holidays (bookings through travel agents only). Offer a range of accommodation, four- to seven-day sightseeing tours from Dublin and car rental.

Silke's Travel, 263 Oxford St, Darlinghurst, Sydney (☎02/9380 6244 or ☎1800/807 860, *www.silkes.com.au*). Specially tailored packages for gay and lesbian travellers.

Wiltrans Australia, 10/189 Kent St, Sydney (☎02/9255 0899). Agents for Maupintour's luxury all-inclusive fifteen-day bus tours of Ireland, staying in premier hotels and medieval castles.

Asia the lowest fares are with Japan Airlines from NZ$1800 low season to NZ$2400 high season (including an overnight stop in either Tokyo or Osaka), while Thai Airways, Singapore Airlines, Cathay Pacific, Qantas, and Malaysia Airlines also offer through-fares to Ireland via a transfer or overnight stop in their carrier's home city, for between NZ$2000 and NZ$2600. Air New Zealand and British Airways fares to Dublin and Belfast **via Los Angeles** and Heathrow are around NZ$2000 low season, N$2800 high season.

PACKAGE HOLIDAYS

If you are considering a **package holiday**, many agents can put together very flexible deals (amounting to no more than a flight plus car or train pass and accommodation) and special-interests **tours** (such as walking, cycling or staying in historic country houses). See p.17 for details of tour operators. For information on European train passes that you buy before you leave, see the box on p.14.

VISAS, CUSTOMS REGULATIONS AND TAX

British nationals born in the UK do not need a passport to enter the Republic or the North, but it is useful to carry one in case you use the medical services, and for cashing travellers' cheques. If you don't take a passport, be sure to have some other form of convincing ID. British passport holders *not* born in Great Britain or Northern Ireland must have a valid passport or national identity document. If you are a British national of Indian, Pakistani, Bangladeshi, Far Eastern or African descent, it is advisable to take along your passport (or your birth certificate), in spite of the fact that, technically speaking, you don't need one.

If you are an EU national, you can enter the **Republic** with either a national ID card or, even better, a passport, and you are entitled to stay for as long as you like. Travellers from the US, Canada, Australia and New Zealand are simply required to show a passport and can stay for up to ninety days, after which you'll need to apply to the nearest superintendent's office in the Garda Siochana (police) in the district in which you intend to stay – in Dublin apply to the Aliens Registration Office, Harcourt St (☎01/475 5555). All other visitors to the Republic should contact the Irish Embassy, in their home country, in advance as regulations vary. A comprehensive list of Irish consulates and embassies, along with visa information, is available on the Department of Foreign Affairs Web site: *www.irlgov.ie/iveagh*.

In the **North**, British regulations apply. This means that under the European Economic Area agreement of 1994 citizens of the European Union, Liechtenstein, Norway and Iceland can visit Northern Ireland with just a passport or national ID card. UK and Irish citizens need no ID or passport.

US, Canadian, Australian and New Zealand citizens can enter the country for up to six months with just a passport, provided they have an onward or return ticket and evidence of sufficient funds to support themselves for the duration of their stay. To extend a visit you need to apply for an extension of leave, before the six months period expires, to the Home Office Public Enquiry Office, Immigration and Nationality Directorate, Block C, Whitgift Centre, Croydon CR9 1AT (☎0870/606 7766). To arrange a visit of more than

EMBASSIES AND CONSULATES

IRISH

Australia: 20 Arkana St, Yarralumla, Canberra, ACT 2600 (☎02/6273 3022).

Britain: 17 Grosvenor Place, London SW1X 7HR (☎020/7235 2171).

Canada: 130 Albert St, Suite 1105, Ottawa, ON K1P 5G4 (☎613/223-6281).

New Zealand: 2nd Floor, Dingwall Building, Queen St, Auckland (☎09/302-2867).

United States: 535 Boylston St, Boston, MA 02116 (☎617/267-9330); 400 N Michigan Ave, Suite 911, Chicago, IL 60611 (☎312/337-1868); 345 Park Ave, 17th Floor, New York, NY 10154 (☎212/319-2555); 44 Montgomery St, Suite 3830, San Francisco, CA 94104 (☎415/392-4214); 2234 Massachusetts Ave NW, Washington, DC 20008 (☎202/462-3939). Information available online at *www.irelandemb.org*.

BRITISH

Australia: (High Commission), Commonwealth Ave, Yarralumla, Canberra, ACT 2600 (☎02/627 06666, *www.uk.emb.gov.au/*).

Canada: (High Commission), 80 Elgin St, Ottawa, ON K1P 5K7 (☎613/237-1530, *www.britain-in-canada.org*).

Ireland: 29 Merrion Rd, Dublin 4 (☎01/205-3700, *www.britishembassy.ie*).

New Zealand: (High Commission), 44 Hill St, PO Box 1812, Wellington (☎04/472-6049, *www.britain.org.nz*).

United States: 3100 Massachusetts Ave NW, Washington, DC 20008 (☎202/588-6500, *www.britainusa.com/*).

six months prior to your arrival, contact the British embassy or High Commission in your home country.

Citizens of most other nationalities require a visa, obtainable from the British consular office in the country of application. To find out if you need a visa, either contact your nearest British embassy or High Commission, or visit the British Foreign Office Web site: *www.fco.gov.uk*.

Travellers coming into the Republic or the North directly from another EU country do not have to make a declaration to **customs** at their place of entry and can effectively bring in almost as much wine or beer as they like – although the general rule for imports of alcohol and cigarettes is that goods should be for personal use only. However, there are still strict restrictions – details of which are prominently displayed in all duty-free outlets – on tax- or duty-free goods. There are import restrictions on a variety of articles and substances, from firearms to furs derived from endangered species, none of which should bother the average tourist. Visitors from mainland Britain can bring pets into the North and the Republic, although animals brought from elsewhere overseas are subject to tight quarantine restrictions. These restrictions can be addressed through the new **pet passport** scheme, which takes around seven months to prepare for and is only eligible for pets entering Britain via Dover, Portsmouth or the Euroshuttle. Once in England, pets with passports can be freely taken to Northern Ireland and the Republic. Detailed information is available from the Pets Travel Scheme helpline (☎0870 241 1710) and the website of the Ministry of Agriculture, Food and Fisheries: *www.maff.gov.uk*.

Throughout Ireland most goods are subject to **Value Added Tax** (VAT) at 17.36 percent in the Republic and 17.5 percent in the North. Visitors from non-EU countries can save a lot of money through the **Retail Export Scheme**, which allows a refund of VAT on goods to be taken out of the country. Note that not all shops participate in this scheme – enquire before you make your purchase – and you cannot reclaim VAT charged on hotel bills or other services. In order to make a **claim** you have to leave the country within three months of purchase. Some shops offer the lower price directly to the customer, and all you are required to do is hand in a receipt to customs as you leave the country, but this procedure does vary, so check at the time of purchase. Information online can be found at *www.revenue.ie*.

COSTS, MONEY AND BANKS

The currency in circulation in the Republic will remain the Irish pound, also known as the punt, up until 2002 when conversion to the euro will be complete (see the box below). The punt is divided into 100 pence as in Britain. Exchange rates vary, but currently one pound sterling is worth £1.31 punts and €1.66 euros; one US dollar is worth £0.93 punts, and €1.18 euros; and the Irish punt itself converts to €1.27 euros. For the best rates you should change money either in banks or bureaux de change; depending on who they bank with, visitors from Britain may find withdrawing money directly from their account via an ATM the best option of all. The currency in the North is pounds sterling, as in Britain, though the notes are different and are not readily accepted in mainland Britain. Prices quoted in this guide are in punts and euros for the Republic, and pounds sterling for Northern Ireland.

It may be a surprise to find that the **Republic** is not a cheap place to travel. The least expensive **accommodation** in a hostel bed will rarely cost less than £6/€7.62 a night, while bed and breakfast generally works out at £16–20/€20.36–25.70 per person sharing, £25–30/€31.74–38.09 in Dublin (and single travellers can expect to pay a supplement ranging from 25 to 50 percent extra in many instances – hostels aside). Reckon on about £5/€6.35 for a basic, filling **meal**, and on spending more than you expect on drink, partly because it's expensive and partly because so much social life and entertainment revolves around the pubs. In short, you're likely to spend an absolute minimum of £20/€25.70 a day, even if you're being very careful, and it's easy to find yourself getting through £30/€38.09 or more if you plan to live it up in the slightest. As always, if you're travelling in a group you may be able to save some money by sharing rooms and food. Prices in the **North** tend to be less expensive; in particular B&B accommodation, basic groceries and consumer goods which are all cheaper.

If you are planning on visiting a lot of **historic monuments** in the **Republic**, it may be worth buying a **Heritage Card** (£15/€19.05; children/students £10/€12.82), valid for one year from the date of purchase. This gives you unlimited admittance to sites cared for by **Dúchas**, the Heritage Service, which runs many parks, monuments and gardens. Cards can be bought from the

THE EURO

The Republic of Ireland is one of twelve European Union countries who have changed over to a single currency, the **euro** (€). The transition period, which began on January 1, 1999, is however lengthy: euro notes and coins are not scheduled to be issued until January 1, 2002, with the **Irish pound**, also known as the **punt**, remaining in place for cash transactions, at a fixed rate of £0.787564 to 1 euro, until it is scrapped entirely on February 28, 2002.

Euro notes will be issued in **denominations** of 5, 10, 20, 50, 100, 200 and 500 euros, and coins in denominations of 1, 2, 5, 10, 20 and 50 cents and 1 and 2 euros. Even before euro cash appears in 2002, you can opt to pay in euros by credit card and you can get travellers' cheques in euros – you should not be charged commission for changing them in any of the eleven countries in the euro zone (also known as "Euroland"), nor for changing from any of the old Euroland currencies to any other (French francs to Irish pounds, for example).

All prices in this book for costs in the Republic are given in both Irish pounds and the euro equivalent.

first Dúchas site you visit, or in advance from their main office at 6 Ely Place, Dublin 2 (☎01/647 2461 or within the Republic ☎1850 600601, *www.heritageireland.ie*). Monuments for which the card is valid are indicated throughout this book; membership of An Óige also includes discounts on access to certain sites (see **hostels** on p.36). In the **North**, the **National Trust** offers a similar deal, but there are a lot fewer sights. If, however, you are also visiting Britain, membership (£30; under-25s £15; family £57) may be worthwhile. Write to them at Rowallane House, Saintfield, Co Down BT24 7LH (or telephone for an application ☎028/9751 0721); alternatively, contact the National Trust Membership Department, PO Box 39, Bromley, Kent BR1 3XL (☎0208 3151111, *www.nationaltrust.org.uk*).

Throughout this guide, the full entry price for museums, art galleries and other sights has been given. Many places will also offer a **concessionary** price for children, students and those over 60, which is usually at least a third off the full amount.

CARRYING MONEY

The easiest way to draw cash is with a **debit or credit card**. If you are from the UK, some cashpoint cards allow you to withdraw money directly from your account. NatWest and HSBC customers can use any Ulster Bank ATM free of charge. Most sizeable towns throughout Ireland have at least one bank with a cash dispenser that will accept Visa and/or Mastercard and most also accept Plus and Cirrus. The majority of large department stores, petrol stations, hotels and upmarket restaurants in both the Republic and Northern Ireland accept the major credit cards – MasterCard, Visa and all cards carrying the Eurocard symbol, though Diners' Club and American Express are not widely accepted. However, credit cards are less useful in rural areas: smaller establishments all over the country, such as B&Bs, will often accept cash only.

Another easy and safe way to carry your money is in **travellers' cheques**, available for a small commission from any major bank. The most commonly accepted travellers' cheques are American Express, followed by Visa and Thomas Cook – most cheques issued by banks will be one of these brands. You'll usually pay commission again when you cash each cheque, or a flat rate – though no commission is payable on Amex cheques exchanged at Amex branches and the same goes for Thomas Cook cheques exchanged at Thomas Cook branches. Make sure you keep a record of the cheques as you cash them, so you'll be able to get the value of all uncashed cheques refunded immediately if you lose them.

BANKS AND BUREAUX DE CHANGE

Almost everywhere banks are the best places to change money and cheques; outside banking hours you'll have to use a bureau de change, widely found in most city centres and at international airports. Avoid changing money or cheques in hotels, where the rates are normally very poor.

The main high-street **banks** in the **Republic** are Allied Irish Bank, Bank of Ireland and Ulster Bank. All are open Monday to Friday 10am to 12.30pm and 1.30 to 4pm; banks in larger cities stay open all day and are open until 5pm one day a week, usually Thursday. It makes sense to change your money while in the cities since many small country towns are served by sub-offices open only on certain days of the week. **Foreign exchange counters** are open at Dún Laoghaire, Dublin Port and Rosslare **ferry terminals** and at all main **airports**: Dublin (daily 6am–8pm year round, staying open later during the summer); Shannon (daily except Christmas day, 6am–5.30pm); Cork (Mon–Fri 9am–5pm, Sat & Sun 11am–5pm, closed Christmas day); Knock International (summer daily 10.30am–5pm; winter Mon, Thurs, Fri & Sun opens 1hr before incoming and outgoing flights). In Dublin city, there are several **bureaux de change** and outlets where you can change money: these include Thomas Cook at 51 & 118 Grafton St, and 4 North Earl St, American Express at 41 Nassau St, and Dublin Tourism's main office on Suffolk Street.

In the **North**, the main high-street **banks** are linked with British ones: National Irish Bank (associated with HSBC in Britain); Ulster Bank (associated with NatWest) and Bank of Ireland. Main banks in large towns are open Monday to Friday 9.30am to 4.30pm, with some opening for longer hours and on Saturdays; outside the cities some may close between 12.30pm and 1.30pm. In very small villages the bank may only open on two or three days a week – so, as in the Republic, aim to get your cash in the bigger centres. Belfast International **airport** has a branch of Thomas Cook, there's a **bureau de change** at City of Derry Airport, but no foreign exchange facilities at

Belfast City airport. In Belfast itself, you can **change money** at the Post Office, 7 Shaftesbury Square, or at Thomas Cook, 11 Donegall Place (☎028/9088 3900). Thomas Cook also have a branch in Derry at Unit 7, Quayside Strand Rd (☎028/7185 2500).

EMERGENCIES

If, as a foreign visitor, you run out of money or there is some kind of emergency, the quickest way to get **money sent out** is to contact your bank at home and have them wire the cash to the nearest bank.

For **Americans and Canadians** – or any Amex cardholder – one of the quickest ways to get money from home is through American Express. The company allows cardholders to draw cash from their checking accounts, up to US$1000 every 21 days (over the counter) or seven days (from an ATM), as well as offering its own Moneygram Service (☎1-800/543-4080; *www.moneygram.com*), through which money can be sent to Europe. Another option is to have cash sent out through Western Union (☎1-800/325-6000; *www.westernunion.com*) to a nearby bank or post office (this service is available to any traveller, not just North Americans). Make sure you know when it's likely to arrive, since you won't be notified by the receiving office. Remember, too, that you'll need some form of identification when you pick up the money. Moneygram fees start at US$24, and Western Union US$29 for a wire of US$300; the fees do rise quite steadily and this is an expensive – albeit necessary at times – way to get money.

Finally, Americans in dire straits can arrange to have money sent to them via the State Departments' Citizen's Emergency Center (Mon–Fri 8am–10pm, Sat 9am–3pm ☎202/647-5225, at all other times 202/647-7000; *www.travel.state.gov*).

For **Australians and New Zealanders**, your best bet is to take a Visa or Mastercard, or a key (debit) card with Cirrus or Plus transaction facilities, with you. Otherwise you have to make arrangements for a possible international money transfer before you leave by nominating a bank and account number in Ireland, entrusting your bank account number with someone at home and paying a fee of A$25/NZ$30.

YOUTH AND STUDENT DISCOUNTS

There are various official and quasi-official youth/student ID cards available that soon pay for themselves in savings.

Full-time students are eligible for the **International Student ID Card** (ISIC). This entitles the bearer to discounts at some museums, theatres and visitor centres, but is perhaps most useful with an additional Travelsave Stamp (£8/€10.16), available at any USIT office in Ireland, offering reductions of up to fifty percent on Irish Rail services, along with discounts on Bus Éireann, B&I ferries and Northern Ireland Railways. The card, which costs £6 in Britain, £7/€8.89 in the Republic, US$20 in the US and A/NZ$16.50 in Australia and New Zealand, is available from branches of USIT in Ireland and Council Travel, STA and Travel Cuts around the world or online at *www.ciee.org*, *www.statravel.com* and *www.travelcuts.com* respectively.

The **International Youth Card** is available to anyone under 26 and can be obtained at any USIT office (£7 UK, £8/€10.16 Republic); take along valid ID and a passport photo. The card gives discounts on flights, and in the Republic, for an additional £7/€8.89, entitles you to up to fifty percent off train fares, though generally very little reduction on short journeys.

You have to be 25 or younger to qualify for a **GO-25 Card**, which buys discounts on air fares; the card costs $15 in the US, $16.50 in Australia and New Zealand, and £7 in the UK. It can be purchased through Council Travel in the US, Hostelling International in Canada (see p.11), STA in Australia and New Zealand (see p.15), and USIT in the UK, or online at the addresses listed above.

STA also sells its own ID card that's good for some discounts, as do various other travel organizations. A university photo ID might open some doors, too.

Also see p.20 for Heritage and National Trust cards.

INSURANCE AND HEALTH

As an EU country, Ireland has free reciprocal health agreements with other member states. To take advantage, British and other EU citizens will need form E111, available over the counter from main post offices. There are no inoculations required for travellers to Ireland, nor any particular health hazards to beware of beyond those of taking care when travelling in an unknown place. Still, you're as likely to fall ill or have an accident here as anywhere else, so it's as well to make sure you're covered by adequate travel insurance.

A typical **travel insurance** policy usually provides cover for the loss of baggage, tickets and – up to a certain limit – cash or cheques, as well as cancellation or curtailment of your journey. Most of them exclude so-called dangerous sports unless an extra premium is paid: in Ireland this can mean horse riding, windsurfing, trekking and mountaineering. Read the small print and benefits tables of prospective policies carefully; coverage can vary wildly for roughly similar premiums. Many policies can be chopped and changed to exclude coverage you don't need – for example, sickness and accident benefits can often be excluded or included at will. If you do take medical coverage, ascertain whether benefits will be paid as treatment proceeds or only after return home, and whether there is a 24-hour medical emergency number. When securing baggage cover, make sure that the per-article limit – typically under £500 equivalent – will cover your most valuable possession. If you need to make a claim, you should keep receipts for medicines and medical treatment, and in the event of having anything stolen, you must obtain an official statement from the police. Bank and credit cards often have certain levels of medical or other insurance included and you may automatically get travel insurance if you use a major credit card to pay for your trip.

Even with an E111, **UK citizens** would do well to take out an insurance policy before travelling to cover against theft, loss and illness or injury. Travel agents and tour operators are likely to require some sort of insurance when you book a package holiday, though according to UK law they can't make you buy their own (other than a £1 premium for "schedule airline failure"). If you have a good all-risks home insurance policy it *may* cover your possessions against loss or theft even when overseas. Many private medical schemes such as BUPA or PPP also offer coverage plans for abroad, including baggage loss, cancellation or curtailment and cash replacement as well as sickness or accident.

Americans and **Canadians** should also check that they're not already covered. Canadian provincial health plans usually provide partial cover for medical mishaps overseas. Holders of official student/teacher/youth cards are entitled to meagre accident coverage and hospital in-patient benefits. Students will often find that their student health coverage extends during the vacations and for one term beyond the date of last enrolment. Homeowners' or renters' insurance often covers theft or loss of documents, money and valuables while overseas, though conditions and maximum amounts vary from company to company.

HEALTH CARE

Visitors from **EU countries** are entitled to medical treatment in the **Republic** under the EU Reciprocal Medical Treatment arrangement. EU visitors should collect a form E111 from their Social Security office (or in Britain from any Post Office). Although an E111 is technically not a requirement for people from the UK, in reality it's essential to get the entitlement to free treatment and prescribed medicines (though this does not cover dental examinations, X-rays and so on). Even then, you can run into problems, and it makes sense to take your NHS card, too. Armed with these documents, check that the doctor you use is registered with the Health Board Panel, and make it clear you want to be treated under the European Union's social security arrangements. Similarly if you are admitted to hospital, make it clear you want to be treated within the EU Reciprocal Treatment scheme. The only other real problem is that in rural areas you may find yourself miles from the nearest doctor or hospital, and possibly even further from one prepared to treat you under the reciprocal arrangements.

British citizens need no documentation to be treated in the **North**; for non-British EU travellers, the requirements are the same as for the Republic.

Citizens of **non-EU countries** will be charged for all medical services except those administered by accident and emergency units at health service hospitals. Thus a US citizen who has been hit by a car would not be charged if the injuries simply required stitching and setting in the emergency unit, but would if admission to a hospital ward were necessary. Health insurance is therefore extremely advisable for all non-EU nationals.

Citizens of some countries may also enjoy a reciprocal agreement; in Australia, Medicare has such an arrangement with Ireland and Britain. Check before you leave. And remember that whatever your legal rights, the local doctor may not necessarily know anything about them.

INFORMATION, MAPS AND WEB SITES

There's no shortage of information published on Ireland, much of it free; it's well worth contacting the local office of the Irish Tourist Board (Bord Fáilte) and/or the Northern Ireland Tourist Board before you leave. Alternatively, the Internet has a wealth of sites, giving information not only on Ireland's history, culture and politics but also a range of practical advice on visiting the country.

Bord Fáilte and NITB offices outside Ireland are listed below. Once **in Ireland**, you'll find some kind of tourist office in nearly every town which has a reasonable number of tourists passing through: either a branch of Bord Fáilte or the NITB, or a locally run information centre, many of which open only for the summer. Most of these are listed in the relevant sections of the *Guide* and are usually extremely helpful, providing local maps and leaflets as well as information on where to stay (booking charge £1–2/€1.27–2.54). It has to be said, though, that they only give details on services which they have approved, thereby excluding some excellent hostels, campsites and private bus services, and they tend to be reluctant to show favouritism among hotels and restaurants, so always go to them for information, not advice. A Bord Fáilte or NITB recommendation implies a certain standard of service, however, so if you don't think your approved B&B comes up to scratch, they are the people you should complain to.

MAPS

A variety of large-scale **road maps** covering the whole of Ireland are available for general touring, such as the Michelin 1:400,000 (no. 405) or the AA 1:350,000. The four Ordnance Survey Ireland Holiday Maps, covering the North, West, East and South at a scale of 1:250,000, give more contour details and are probably the best all-purpose

BORD FÁILTE OFFICES ABROAD

Australia: Level 5, 36 Carrington St, Sydney NSW 2000 (☎02/9299 6177).

Britain: 150 New Bond St, London W1Y 0AQ (☎020/7493 3201). See also All Ireland Desk addresses given below.

New Zealand: Level 6, 18 Shortland St, Auckland 1 (☎09/379 8720).

US and Canada: 345 Park Ave, New York, NY 10154 (☎1-800/223-6400 or 212/418-0800, *www.io.ie*).

NORTHERN IRELAND TOURIST OFFICES ABROAD

Australia: at the same address as the Bord Fáilte office above.

Britain: All Ireland Desk, British Travel Centre, 1 Lower Regent St, London SW1 4PQ (drop-in only); 3rd Floor, 24 Haymarket, London SW1Y 4DG (☎08701/555250); 98 West George St, Glasgow G21 PJA (☎0141/572 4030).

Canada: 2 Bloor St, Suite 1501, Toronto, ON M4W 3E2 (☎1-800/576-8174 or 416/925-6368, *www.discovernorthernireland.com*).

New Zealand: at the same address as the Bord Fáilte office above.

US: 551 5th Ave, Suite 701, New York, NY 10176 (☎1-800/326-0036 or 212/922-0101, *www.interknowledge.com/northern-ireland*).

MAP OUTLETS

BRITAIN

Cardiff: Blackwell's, 13–17 Royal Arcade, Cardiff CF1 2PR (☎029/2039 5036).

Edinburgh: The Stationery Office Ltd, 71 Lothian Rd, Edinburgh EH3 9AZ (☎0131/228 4181, *www.thestationeryoffice.com*).

Glasgow: John Smith and Sons, 57–61 St Vincent St, Glasgow G2 5TB (☎0141/221 7472).

London: Daunt Books, 83 Marylebone High St, London W1 (☎020/8224 2295); National Map Centre, 22–24 Caxton St, London SW1 (☎020/7222 2486); Stanfords, 12–14 Long Acre, London WC2 (☎020/7836 1321, *sales @stanfords.co.uk*); The Travellers Bookshop, 13 Blenheim Crescent, London W11 (☎020/7229 5260, *www.thetravellersbookshop.co.uk*).

Maps by mail, phone, or email order are available from Stanfords.

US

Boston: The Globe Corner Bookstore, 28 Church St, Cambridge, MA 02138 (☎1-800/358-6013 or 617/497-6277, *www.globecorner.com*)

Chicago: Rand McNally, 444 N Michigan Ave, Chicago, IL 60611 (☎312/321-1751, *www.randmcnally.com*).

Los Angeles: Map Link Inc, 30 S La Patera Lane, Unit 5, Santa Barbara, CA 93117 (☎805/692-6777, *www.maplink.com*).

New York: The Complete Traveller Bookstore, 199 Madison Ave, New York, NY 10016 (☎212/685-9007); Rand McNally, 150 E 52nd St, New York, NY 10022 (☎212/758-7488, *www.randmcnally.com*).

San Francisco: The Complete Traveller Bookstore, 3207 Fillmore St, San Francisco, CA 92123 (☎415/923-1511); Rand McNally, 595 Market St, San Francisco, CA 94105 (☎415/777-3131, *www.randmcnally.com*); Phileas Fogg's Books & Maps, #87 Stanford Shopping Center, Palo Alto, CA 94304 (☎1-800/533-FOGG).

Seattle: Elliott Bay Book Company, 101 S Main St, Seattle, WA 98104 (☎1-800/962-5311 or 206/624-6600, *www.elliottbaybooks.com*); World Wide Books and Maps, 4411A Wallingford Ave N, Seattle, WA 98103 (☎1-888/534-3453 or 206/634-3453, *www.travelbooksandmaps.com*).

Washington DC: The Map Store Inc, 1636 Eye St NW, Washington, DC 20006 (☎1-800/544-2659 or 202/628-2608); Travel Books & Language Center, 4437 Wisconsin Ave, Washington, DC 20016 (☎1-800/220-2665).

Note: Rand McNally now has more than twenty stores across the US; call or visit their Web site (☎1-800/333-0136 ext 2111, *www.randmcnally.com*) for the address of your nearest store, or for direct mail maps.

CANADA

Montréal: Ulysses Travel Bookshop, 4176 St Denis, Montréal, PQ H2W 2M5 (☎514/843-9447, *www.ulyssesguides.com*).

Toronto: Open Air Books and Maps, 25 Toronto St, Toronto, ON M5C 2R1 (☎416/363-0719).

Vancouver: World Wide Books and Maps, 1247 Granville St, Vancouver, BC V6Z 1G3 (☎604/687-3320).

AUSTRALIA

Adelaide: The Map Shop, 6 Peel St, SA 5000 (☎08/8231 2033)

Brisbane: Worldwide Maps and Guides, 187 George St, Brisbane, QLD 4000 (☎07/3221 4330).

Cairns: Walkers Bookshop, 96 Lake St, QLD 4870 (☎07/4051 2410).

Melbourne: Mapland, 372 Little Bourke St, VIC 3000 (☎03/9670 4383).

Perth: Perth Map Centre, 1/884 Hay St WA 6000 (☎08/9322 5733).

Sydney: Travel Bookshop, Shop 3, 175 Liverpool St, NSW (☎02/9261 8200, or 02/9241 3554).

NEW ZEALAND

Auckland: Specialty Maps, 46 Albert St, Auckland 1 (☎09/307 2217).

Christchurch: Mapworld, 173 Gloucester St, Christchurch (☎03/374 5399, *www.mapworld.co.nz*).

maps on offer. These and others are widely available in Ireland.

For more detail, and for **walking**, the **Ordnance Survey** Discovery Series (1:50,000; a little over 1 mile: 1 inch) is generally the best option and now covers the whole island. Additionally, there are 1:25,000 maps on offer for certain tourist areas such as the Fermanagh Lakeland and Mourne Country. The old OS half-inch maps were surveyed in the nineteenth century and can be inaccurate over 1000 feet, so a certain amount of caution is advisable if using them.

For specialist interest maps it makes sense to check locally, as tourist boards or bookshops will often have something better than the above. For walking maps see "Sports and Activities" p.47.

USEFUL WEB SITES

The Internet is an excellent point of reference before travelling to and when you are in Ireland, not only for accessing general information about the country, but also for researching and booking accommodation and activities. In Ireland itself (even in the supposedly remote west) an Internet point is never far away, though the further west you go the more expensive it tends to be.

GENERAL INFORMATION

www.blather.net
An idiosyncratic site dealing with a range of Irish-related subjects, with a lively discussion forum.

www.indigo.ie
A huge site that lists everything from online recipes to cars with excellent reviews and a myriad of well-chosen links.

www.iol.ie, www.browseireland.com, www.searc.ie, www.touchtel.ie
These four excellent online resources collate and review sites relating to Ireland and offer good links, which makes them a good starting point for any online search or enquiry; *www.searc.ie* also offers an efficient, free service, answering any query you have about Ireland.

www.ireland.travel.ie
The official tourist-board site offering plenty of facts and information, though little practical advice.

www.ni-tourism.com
A site posted by the Northern Ireland Tourist Board outlining all officially approved tourist information.

www.visitdublin.com
An exceptional site on Dublin run by the local tourist authority.

HISTORY

www.bess.tcd.ie/ireland.ht
This is one of the best private sites relating to Ireland and is a good place to start an historical or academic-related search.

IRISH CUISINE

www.irishfood.com
This site speaks for itself, covering in delicious detail traditional Irish recipes and the best places to eat in the country.

MUSIC AND ENTERTAINMENT

www.entertainmentireland.ie
An up-to-date site listing concerts, festivals and special events throughout the country.

www.ohyeah.net
A well-produced site on music north of the border with updated listings, gig reviews and excellent links.

www.phantomfm.com
Established by a group of music enthusiasts to provide an alternative rock service for the Dublin area. It's an amateur site with lots of information not available in the conventional music press.

NEWS

www.irishnews.com
A must for anyone with an interest in the politics of Northern Ireland, this site also has links to travel information on the North, especially the Glens of Antrim.

www.irishtimes.com
The best news site relating to Ireland and posted much earlier than the print version of the paper is available. It offers an efficient free email service, and features information on the live entertainment scene in Dublin with excellent up-to-the-minute listings.

SPORT

www.setanta.com
A site offering comprehensive sports coverage including the Irish sports of Gaelic football and hurling, with quirky features and up-to-date results.

GETTING AROUND

Travel between major centres in the Republic is generally straightforward, with reliable – albeit infrequent and slow – public transport operated by the state-supported train and bus companies Iarnród Éireann (Irish Rail) and Bus Éireann. There are, however, glaring anomalies, and you should never assume that two major, local towns are necessarily going to be connected. It pays to think and plan ahead. Once off the main routes this becomes particularly important since it's quite usual for small towns and villages to be served by a couple of buses a week and no more. Transport in the North is similarly infrequent in rural areas. Ulsterbus is generally regular and dependable, as is the (limited) train network. Ireland's relatively quiet rural roads make car rental an attractive and increasingly popular option, allowing you to visit the more remote areas of the country; most towns throughout Ireland will have rental outlets, though the best value is usually found in Dublin. Parts of the country, especially in the west, are ideal for cycling and bikes are available for rent in even the smallest villages.

TRAINS

In the **Republic**, Irish Rail (Iarnród Éireann ☎01/836 6222) operates **trains** to many major cities and towns en route; on direct lines it's by far the fastest way of covering long distances, but the network is by no means comprehensive – Donegal, for instance, has no service at all. In general, train lines fan out from Dublin, with few routes running north–south across the country. So although you can get to the west easily by train, you can't sensibly use the train network to explore the west coast.

Train travel is not particularly cheap, either. If possible avoid travelling on Friday or Sunday when the prices are steepest and buy a return ticket as singles cost nearly as much. As a general example, an off-peak Dublin to Galway single ticket costs £16/€20.32, rising to £22/€27.94 on either a Friday or Sunday, a monthly return, excluding Friday and Sunday costs £22/€27.94. It's always worth asking about any special fares that may be on offer; or if you're doing a fair amount of travelling, it may be worth buying a **train pass**. Irish Rail's Irish Rover ticket, valid in the Republic and the North, costs £83.50/€106.04 for five days out of fifteen. A further option open to 16–26 year olds is the Faircard which gives a fifty percent discount on tickets. Available from any Iarnród Éireann office, it costs £8/€10.16 and is valid for a year.

Given the limited reach of the rail system, one of the most useful options is the Irish Explorer Ticket, a **combined rail and bus pass**, covering all intercity state and private rail and bus lines in the Republic (but no city transportation except DART, see p.64) and costing £67/€85.09 for any five days' travel out of fifteen consecutive days, and £90/€114.30 for eight out of fifteen days. For **unlimited train and bus travel** in the Republic and the North, an Emerald Card costs £115/€146.05 for eight days out of fifteen, £200/€254 for fifteen days out of thirty (same prices in Northern Ireland). Bear in mind, though, that the nature of travel in Ireland is such that you very rarely stick to your carefully drawn itinerary, and you may not get the value from your pass that you hope for. A Freedom of Northern Ireland Ticket, for daily (£10) or weekly (£37) unlimited travel on trains and all scheduled Ulsterbus services, is available at main bus and railway stations. The only service **between the Republic and the North** is the Dublin to Belfast express (6 each way daily, 2hr; £19/€24.13 single, £29/€36.83 return); this is quite an expensive option but is by far the most comfortable train in the country. Once **in the North**, you'll find only three short train routes, but these are efficient and reasonably cheap: a Belfast to Derry ticket will cost you £7.10 single, £12.60 return. If you are looking for a **train pass** a Runaround ticket is

valid on all Northern Irish trains for one week and costs around £37.

Students in possession of an ISIC card can buy a Travelsave stamp (£8/€10.16 from any USIT office in the Republic – Dublin, Cork, Galway, Limerick, Maynooth and Waterford), while in the North it's a Translink stamp (£7 from offices in Belfast, Coleraine, Derry and Jordanstown), which entitles you to discounts of fifty percent off standard train fares and thirty percent off bus fares.

The cost of taking **bikes** on trains varies between £4/€5.08 and £6/€7.62 per single journey in the Republic. In Northern Ireland it costs a quarter of the single fare.

North American travellers also taking in Great Britain might benefit from the **BritRail and Ireland Pass**, which entitles the holder to five days' unlimited travel within a month (US$528 first class, US$396 standard) or ten days within a month (US$752 first class, US$566 standard). The pass, which must be purchased before departure from North America, is available from Rail Europe (*www.raileurope.com*) and some travel agents (see p.14 for details of agents selling Irish and British passes).

For information on **Eurail** passes see p.14.

BUSES

Bus Éireann (☎836 6111) operates throughout the **Republic**, and its services are reliable, if infrequent. It's possible to travel by bus between all major towns, but routings can be complex, involving several connections, and hence very slow. Having said that buses are generally twenty to fifty percent cheaper than trains, with the best value given by **private local companies** which operate in most Irish counties (the names, telephone numbers and routes of these companies are listed at the end of each chapter).

Bus Éireann offers a number of passes ideal if you want to explore the country at your own pace. Rambler tickets (around £30/€38.10 for any three days out of eight; £70/€88.90 for any eight days out of fifteen; £100/€127 for fifteen days out of thirty) all give unlimited bus travel throughout the Republic; **students** can get reductions on standard fares if they have a Travelsave stamp (see p.29). It makes sense to pick up the relevant information for the area you intend to explore before you leave; remote villages may only have a couple of buses a week, so knowing when they are is essential.

Carrying a **bike** on a bus will cost you £5/€6.35 single regardless of length of journey, though be warned that the driver is under no obligation to take them and in any case usually only has room for one bike.

Private buses, which operate on many major routes, are often cheaper than Bus Éireann, and sometimes faster. They're very busy at weekends, so it makes sense to book ahead if you can; during the week you can usually pay on the bus. Prices for parts of the journeys are often negotiable, and bikes can be carried if booked with your seat.

You might want to consider one of the **hop-on-hop-off** bus services which allow you to travel around the country getting off at any given stop for as long as you like and then jumping back onto the bus again for a further section of the route. The more established firms offering this are Tír na nóg (☎01/836 4684, *www.tirnanog.com*), the well-run and informed Shamrocker (☎01/672 7651, *www.radicaltravel.com*) and the new – slightly rowdy – kid on the block, PaddyWagon Tours (☎01/672 6007, *www.paddywagon.iol.ie*). Each company offers either a full trip which lasts one week or a hop-on-hop-off service which must be completed within a year and costs from £150/€190.50. All of these companies run northern trips which take from four days to one week and cost from £70/€88.90 to £100/€127.

In the **North**, Ulsterbus runs regular and reliable services throughout the six counties, particularly to those towns not served by the train network. Students can get a fifteen percent discount on certain services with an ISIC card.

Details of bus services connecting principal towns and cities are given in "Travel Details" at the end of each chapter in this guide.

For details of **joint train and bus passes** see "Trains", p.28.

DRIVING

In order to **drive** in Ireland you must have a current driving licence; a licence from any EU country is equivalent to an Irish one. Licences from non-EU countries are valid for one year after entry into the country, providing it has been held for at least two years previous (it is also advisable to obtain an international driving permit from your home automobile association before leaving as some car rental companies require both). If you're bringing your own car into the country you should also carry your vehicle registration or ownership document at all times. Furthermore, you must be adequately **insured**, so be sure to check your existing policy.

Out of the main cities the **Republic's** roads remain relatively uncongested, making driving a very relaxing option. It also remains (along with Britain) one of the few countries in the world where you drive on the left, a situation that can lead to a few tense days of acclimatization for many overseas drivers. Unleaded petrol is about 75p/€0.95 per litre; the national **speed limit** is 55mph/88kph, except where posted otherwise. All passengers must wear **seat belts**, and motorbikers and their passengers must wear helmets. In remote areas, wandering cattle, unmarked junctions, and appallingly potholed minor roads are all potential dangers, particularly for motorbikes. Other hazards to watch out for include drunk drivers late at night, a continuing problem in spite of high accident rates and a concerted

MOTORING ORGANIZATIONS

American Automobile Association, 4100 E Arkanas Ave, Denver, CO 80222 (☎1-800/222-4357, *www.aaa.com*). Most member services apply only in the US and Canada, but the AAA can refer members to the AA and also provide international drivers' licences.

Australian Automobile Association, 216 Northbourne Ave, Canberra, ACT 2601 (☎02/6247 7311; www.aaa.asn.au/).

Automobile Association, Fanum House, Basingstoke, Hants RG21 2EA (☎0870/5448866); 36 Wellington Place, Belfast (☎028/9023 2131). Emergency number: ☎0800/887766.

Canadian Automobile Association: Each region has its own club – check the phone book for local address and phone number. Benefits are comparable to the AAA's.

Irish Automobile Association, 23 Suffolk Rd, Dublin (☎01/667 9481); Cork (☎021/4276922). Emergency number: ☎1-800/667788; *www.aaireland.ie*.

New Zealand Automobile Association, Floor 17, 99 Albert St, Auckland (☎09/377 4660, *www.aanz.co.nz/*).

Royal Automobile Club, PO Box 100, RAC House, 7 Brighton Rd, South Croydon CR2 6XW (☎020/8686 0088); 79 Chichester St, Belfast (☎028/9023 2640). Emergency number: ☎0800/828282.

CAR RENTAL FIRMS

IRELAND

Avis Dublin ☎01/874 5844, N.Ireland ☎0870/5900 500, Belfast ☎028/9024 0404, *www.avis.com*.

Budget Dublin ☎01/837 9611, N.Ireland ☎0800/181181, Belfast International Airport ☎028/9042 3332, 96–102 Great Victoria St, Belfast (☎028/9023 0700), Belfast City Airport ☎028/9045 1111, *www.budgetdrive.com*.

Europcar Dublin ☎01/614 2800, Dublin Airport ☎01/812 0410, Northern Ireland ☎0870/5607 5000, Belfast ☎028/9045 0904, *www.europcar.ie*.

Hertz Dublin ☎01/676 7476, Dublin Airport ☎01/844 5466, Northern Ireland ☎0870/599 6699, *www.hertz.com*.

Holiday Autos Dublin ☎01/872 9366, *www.holidayautos.co.uk/*.

BRITAIN

Autos Abroad ☎08700/667788, *www.autosabroad.co.uk*.

Avis ☎0870/5900 500, *www.avis.com*.

Budget☎0800/181181, *www.budgetdrive.com*.

Europcar/InterRent☎0870/6075000, *www.europcar.co.uk*.

Hertz ☎0845/755 5888, *www.hertz.com*.

Holiday Autos ☎0870/400 0099, *www.holidayautos.co.uk*.

NORTH AMERICA

Alamo domestic ☎1-800/327-9633, international ☎1-800/522-9696, *www.alamo.com*.

Avis domestic ☎1-800/831-2847, international ☎1-800/331-1084, *www.avis.com*.

Budget ☎1-800/527-0700, *www.budget.com*.

Europe By Car ☎1-800/223-1516, *www.europebycar.com*.

Hertz domestic ☎1-800/654-3131, international ☎1-800/654-3001, in Canada ☎1-800/263-0600, *www.hertz.com*.

Holiday Autos ☎1-800/422-7737, *www.holidayautos.com*.

National Car Rental ☎1-800/CAR-RENT, *www.nationalcar.com*.

AUSTRALIA

Avis ☎13 6333, *www.avis.com/au*.

Budget ☎1300/362 848, *www.budget.com.au*.

Hertz ☎1800/550 067, *www.hertz.com/au*.

Eurodrive ☎02/97259900.

NEW ZEALAND

Avis ☎09/526 2847 or 0800 655 111, *www.avis.com/nz*.

Budget ☎0800/ 652 227 or 09/375 2270, *www.budget.com/nz*.

Hertz ☎09/309 0989 or 0800 655 955, *www.hertz.com/nz*.

police crackdown. A cause of some confusion are "passing lanes" or "slow lanes", indicated by a broken yellow line, where you can pull over to the left for the car behind to overtake. However, they should be used with care as many have poor surfaces and can suddenly end with little or no warning. Be careful if you take a car to Dublin – congestion is chronic, theft and vandalism rates are high, and you're best advised to leave your car in a supervised car park.

Although nominally converted to metric measures, with kilometres indicated by green signs on all the main roads, Irish people still tend to think and talk in miles, while rural areas still retain the old black-and-white fingerpost signs in miles. There is also such a thing as an "Irish mile" – longer than the standard imperial measure – though this is rare and found only on very old signposts. **Unleaded petrol** is available almost everywhere. In all large towns a **disc parking** system is in operation: discs can be bought in newsagents and have to be displayed on the vehicle when parked in a designated area; failure to display a disc will result in clamping or towing, especially in Dublin and Galway.

Roads in the **North** are, in general, notably superior to those in the Republic. Driving is on the left and the rules of the road are as in Britain: speed limits are 30–40mph/50–60kph in built-up areas, 70mph/110kph on motorways (freeways) and dual carriageways and 60mph/100kph on most other roads. Car seat-belt and motorbike-helmet rules are the same as in the Republic (see p.30). Cars bearing large red "R" (Restricted) plates identify drivers who have passed their driving test within the past twelve months and are meant to keep to low speeds. Although security is not as rigorous as it was during the IRA's campaign, controlled parking is still in effect in some towns; a parked car in a control zone is considered a security risk and may result in a security alert. **Petrol prices** in the North are about 87p a litre.

In the Republic, the **Irish Automobile Association** (IAA) operates 24-hour emergency breakdown services. They also provide many other motoring services, including a reciprocal arrangement for free assistance through many overseas motoring organizations – check the situation with yours before setting out. You can ring the emergency numbers (see box on p.31) even if you are not a member of the respective organization, although a substantial fee will be charged. In the North, the **Automobile Association** (AA) and the **Royal Automobile Club** (RAC) both offer the same services as the IAA.

CAR RENTAL

Large international **car rental companies**, such as Hertz, have outlets in all major cities, airports and ferry terminals in the **Republic**: they're expensive at around £250–400/€317.50–508 a week, and, especially if you're travelling from North America, you'll probably find it cheaper to arrange things in advance. Booking a fly-drive or a train-sail-drive package is one of the cheapest ways to arrange car rental or, if you don't want to be so tied down, try an **agency** or **broker**, such as Holiday Autos, Global Leisure or Autos Abroad, who will arrange advance booking through a local agent and can usually undercut the big companies considerably.

If you haven't booked, then the smaller local firms can almost always offer better deals than the well-known names. You must produce a full valid driving licence (which you must have held without endorsement for at least two years); most companies will only rent cars to people over 23 years of age, though you might find some that will rent to drivers over 21; it will generally be more expensive if they do. It's advisable to take out a collision damage waiver with your car rental – otherwise expect to be liable for around £1000/€1270 damages in the event of an accident. If you intend to drive **across the border**, you should inform your rental company beforehand to check that you are fully insured.

Renting a car in the **North** involves much the same cost and age restrictions as in the Republic. There are fewer outlets, but rental is available in all major cities and at Belfast airport. Again, the cheapest deals are booked ahead, and here too you must inform the car rental company if you plan to cross the border.

HITCHING

In the **Republic** hitching is commonplace; for locals it's almost as much a normal part of getting around as using the bus and train networks, and for the visitor the human contact makes it one of the best ways to get to know the country. Knowing the shortcomings of public transport, many drivers readily give lifts, and it's not unusual to see single women with babies and the shopping or whole families waiting for a ride. It has to be borne in mind, however, that local people experience no real problems in getting lifts since they usually know just about everybody on the road; visitors can have a less easy time of it.

The chief problem if you plan to hitch extensively is lack of traffic, especially off the main roads, and if you are travelling around one of the tourist-swamped areas of the west, you may find there's a reluctance to pick up foreigners. That said, without transport of your own you are probably going to *have* to hitch if you want to see the best of Ireland's wild, remote places. Just be sure to leave yourself plenty of time.

Although it's probably safer than just about anywhere else in Europe, it goes without saying that hitching is never entirely risk-free, and on the whole it's best for women to avoid hitching alone.

Hitching a lift in the **North** is rather less straightforward and probably easiest for pairs of women who are obviously tourists. Men travelling alone or in pairs can still be viewed with suspicion and may find it impossible to get a lift. Men and women travelling together are at least in with a chance.

CYCLING

If you are lucky enough to get decent weather, cycling is one of the most enjoyable ways to see Ireland, ensuring you're continually in touch with the landscape. Roads are generally empty, though very poor surfaces may well slow you down.

Most airlines carry **bicycles** for free as long as you don't exceed your weight allowance; but be sure to check the regulations in advance (charters may be less obliging) and let them know when you book your ticket that you plan to carry a bike. Always deflate the tyres to avoid explosions in the unpressurized hold.

If you don't want to cycle long distances, it's easy and relatively cheap to **rent a bike** in most towns in the **Republic** and at a limited number of places in the **North** (most outlets are listed in the text); you can't take a rented bike across the border. Raleigh, who operate a national rental scheme and a choice of drop-off options, are the biggest distributors (£8–10/€10.16–12.70 per day, £35–40/€44.45–50.80 per week plus around £50/€63.50 deposit; collection and delivery service £10–15/€12.70–19.05). You can call their main office at Raleigh House, Kylemore Rd, Dublin 10 (☎01/626 1333, *raleigh@iol.ie*) to find out details of their agents throughout Ireland. Local dealers (including some hostels) are often less expensive. Wherever you rent your bike, it makes sense to check the tyres and brakes immediately and demand a pump and repair kit before you set off. You should also consider the terrain: if you plan on mountain biking, make sure your machine has enough gears to cope. **Cycle helmets** are available for rent at some shops, but if you want to be certain of wearing one, bring your own along.

In tourist spots at high season it's best to collect a bike early in the day (or book it the day before) as supplies frequently run out. If you arrive with your own bike, it's easy enough to carry it across long distances by train, less so by bus (see p.30). Local tourist offices will supply information on organized cycling tours, or contact ICS (see p.9).

Finally, a problem you may encounter – for some reason particularly in the west – is that of farmers' dogs chasing and snarling at your wheels. Should you be fortunate enough to be heading downhill at the time, freewheeling silently past cottages and farm entrances is perhaps the only humane way of minimizing the risk of savaged wheels and ankles.

ACCOMMODATION

Ireland offers a wide range of accommodation, from the spartan (camping for free in a farmer's field is usually possible if you ask permission first) to the luxurious (many of Ireland's elegant old country houses take bed-and-breakfast guests). There's also a huge number of hostels, which vary enormously, but all have at least the essentials of a bed and somewhere to cook, and some offer a great deal more. A notch up in price, in more or less the following order, come: bed and breakfasts (B&Bs), guesthouses, country houses and hotels. The majority of these are officially graded by the tourist boards on a set formula which, most of the time, gives a fair idea of what to expect. Prices quoted throughout this book indicate the price you can expect to pay for a double room in high season. The cost of a dormitory bed in a hostel in high season is generally around £8/€10.16. Where it exceeds £10/€12.70, this is indicated in the text. In B&Bs and hotels, rates for single rooms are generally considerably higher and can range from twenty-five to fifty percent more.

Whatever your budget, remember that accommodation can be difficult to find in **Dublin** at any time of year; in **July and August** accommodation in the cities and big tourist centres gets booked up well in advance, and during **festivals** things get even more hectic. For the really big festivals – like the Fleadh Cheoil and the Cork Jazz Festival (see p.46 for a full list of events) – there's often an extra accommodation office trying to cope with the overload, but you may still end up sleeping in a different town, or perhaps just revelling your way through to morning. The less famous festivals can be equally difficult for the spontaneous traveller. Since festivals take place all over Ireland throughout the summer, it's worth checking out where and when they are before you head off: check out Bord Fáilte's Web site (*www.ireland.travel.ie*), or call ☎020/7493 3201 in the UK to purchase a calendar of events for £1.50/€1.90.

B&BS, GUESTHOUSES AND HOTELS

B&Bs in the **Republic** vary enormously, but most are welcoming, warm and clean, with huge breakfasts including cereal, massive fry-ups of bacon, egg, sausage and tomato, toast and tea. Afternoon tea can usually be arranged and can be delicious, with homemade scones and soda bread – it will cost you around £3/€3.81 or £4/€5.08. Evening meals in guesthouses tend to be expensive – around £15/€19.05 – and generally need

ACCOMMODATION PRICE CODES

Throughout this book, prices of hotels, guesthouses and B&Bs have been graded with the codes below, according to what you can expect to pay for a double room in high season.

① Under £26 (or under £26/€33.01 in the Republic)

② £26–33 (or £26–33/€33.01–41.90 in the Republic)

③ £33–40 (or £33–40/€41.90–50.79 in the Republic)

④ £40–55 (or £40–55/€50.79–69.84 in the Republic)

⑤ £55–70 (or £55–70/€69.84–88.88 in the Republic)

⑥ £70–90 (or £70–90/€88.88–114.28 in the Republic)

⑦ £90–110 (or £90–110/€114.28–139.67 in the Republic)

⑧ £110–130 (or £110–130/€139.67–165.07 in the Republic)

⑨ Over £130 (or £130/€165.07 in the Republic)

ACCOMMODATION BOOKINGS

GULLIVER INFORES

Accommodation in the Republic and Northern Ireland can be booked in advance through the Tourist Board-approved agency, Gulliver InfoRes. The cost of booking a room in a hotel, B&B or guesthouse using the service is £3/€3.81 in the first instance and there is a non-refundable ten percent deposit taken on your credit card; subsequent bookings incur a fee of £1/€1.27 and again the ten percent deposit applies. There's a flat fee of £5/€6.35 to book self-catering accommodation. All calls to these numbers are free:

from within the **Republic of Ireland** ☎1800/668668

from the **UK** ☎0800/668 668 66

from the **US** ☎1800/3984376

A worldwide number is available subject to carriers accepting certain freephone numbers ☎00 800 668 668 66.

You can use Gulliver InfoRes to book online through the Web sites of the Irish tourist boards: *www.ireland.travel.ie* and *www.discovernorthernireland.com*, where the same charges apply as for telephone booking.

BORD FÁILTE WEB SITES

Online booking is also available via one of a growing number of accommodation Web sites. Bord Fáilte is the official tourist board of the Irish Republic and their Web sites only feature accommodation registered either with them or with the Northern Irish Tourist Board.

www.beourguest.ie
A comprehensive site detailing hotels, luxurious castles, country houses and homely guesthouses throughout the country. You can search by region, type and facilities.

www.camping-ireland.ie
Bord Fáilte camping and caravan sites around the country.

www.irelands-blue-book.ie
A small site detailing high-quality accommodation; produced by an association of country houses and restaurants in the Republic and Northern Ireland.

www.visitdublin.com
The official Web site of Dublin Tourism, detailing accommodation in the capital.

OTHER WEB SITES

www.hidden-ireland.com
Over thirty private country homes, chiefly in the Republic and generally chosen for their architectural merit and country house atmosphere. All Irish Tourist Board approved.

www.tourismresources.ie
A wide-ranging site including The Friendly Homes of Ireland Web pages that give the option of searching via categories such as child-friendly, less agile, self-catering cottages and working farms.

to be pre-booked. Bord Fáilte is the Republic's official tourist board and their registered B&Bs are generally pretty good, though it's not an absolute guarantee.

Don't assume that non-registered places will be of a lower standard – inclusion in the Bord Fáilte guide is voluntary, and a fair few simply choose not to bother. Many historic buildings are run as B&Bs, and they too can be surprisingly cheap. Many are managed by extremely good cooks, with some of the best and most inventive examples of new Irish cuisine on the menu.

You can expect to pay from around £16–20/€20.36–25.70 per person sharing, £25/€31.74 in Dublin (from £14/€17.78 for non-registered houses). **Bookings** for registered B&Bs can be made through tourist offices (with a booking fee of £1–2/€1.27–2.54) – well worth considering at busy periods, or you can do it yourself. Many phone numbers and addresses are given in the text of this guide. The most useful of a number of accommodation only guides available from Bord Fáilte is the *Town & Country Homes B&B Guide* (£3.50/€4.44), which also includes Web site addresses offering online booking facilities. It's available in tourist offices in Ireland or can be purchased by credit card over the phone in the UK (☎020/7493 3201). The Family Homes of Ireland is a smaller organization, their B&Bs tend to be slightly cheaper, and are particularly worth considering if you require single rooms; their brochure (£3/€3.75) is available from The Family Homes of Ireland, Oughterard, Co. Galway (☎091/552000, *www.family-homes.ie*). Alternatively, finding accommodation is simple enough in just about any town or touristy village – simply go into a pub and ask.

In the **North**, B&B accommodation costs much the same as in the Republic, perhaps a pound or two cheaper in country areas. It's worth ringing ahead if you're planning to stay in Belfast, Derry or one of the main resorts during festivals or high season. Addresses and phone numbers for B&Bs in all of the main centres are given in this guide; in addition the Northern Ireland Tourist Board's *Where to stay in Northern Ireland*, £4.99, gives extensive, highly detailed lists and is available from British bookshops and tourist offices in Ireland.

Accommodation in a **farmhouse** or in a cottage in the Republic can be arranged through Bord Fáilte; for all their simple rooms and turf fires, many "Rent-an-Irish-Cottage" cottages cluster in tiny tourist villages, so it's worth checking out exactly what the set-up is if you're after real solitude. That said, some are very good value; the Family Homes of Ireland (see above) also offers a good range. If you are travelling from the UK it is well worth checking out combined cottage and ferry deals from the major ferry companies.

Inns and **Travel Lodges** are a recent innovation providing good quality, if often rather characterless, accommodation, and for families and small groups are often less expensive than B&Bs: a typical room sleeping from two to three adults with two children costs around £52/€66.03 per night.

Hotels are generally more expensive, particularly in the cities; however, many of the swanky hotels slash their tariffs at weekends when the business types have gone home, or offer competitively priced low season deals. In smaller towns and villages, hotels are not always so pricey and may well be a lively social focus. Virtually all hotels have bars and provide meals to residents and non-residents alike.

HOSTELS

Hostel accommodation in Ireland has continued to grow hugely in breadth and quality recently, and staying in a hostel certainly doesn't mean subjecting yourself to the rigours of old-fashioned hostelling – although An Óige, the official Irish Youth Hostel Association in the Republic, and Hostelling International Northern Ireland (HINI), its counterpart in the North, still manage to satisfy more spartan tastes in some of their more remote hostels. That said, they also have some excellent newly refurbished hostels in prime locations. Hostels in the more popular areas tend to fill up very quickly in July and August, so booking in advance is strongly advised.

Independent hostels in both the Republic and the North are generally run along more relaxed lines, and as well as having traditional dormitory accommodation, a growing number have many private, double and family rooms. Some new city hostels compare favourably in terms of comfort with B&Bs. The majority are classed as **Independent Holiday Hostels** (IHH) and are recommended by Bord Fáilte, but you will also find some excellent (usually small) hostels that don't belong to An Óige, HINI or IHH; many of these are part of the Independent Hostel Owners organization (IHO). All independent hostels are privately owned, and they're all different, each reflecting the character and interests of its owner. Some are tucked away in such beautiful countryside that they're worth staying in for the setting alone. Very often the atmosphere is cosy and informal: you can stay in all day if you want, and there are no curfews or chores. On the downside, such is their popularity that some hostels cram people in to the point of discomfort. July and August are particularly bad, especially in the major cities and on the west coast, as are festival times. If you're relying on them it's worth ringing ahead to check what the situation is; or use the **book-a-bed-ahead** scheme or online booking facilities where available, to ensure a bed is kept for you. The IHH book-a-bed-ahead scheme allows you to book from one IHH hostel to another, usually for a charge of 50p/€0.66 per booking; the hostel owner will phone through your booking and on payment of £6.50/€8.25 will issue you with a ticket that guarantees your bed at the next hostel. Some hostels offer bike rental, some food: details are given in the text. Expect to pay around £7/€8.89 for a dormitory bed; £9–12/€11.43–

YOUTH HOSTEL ASSOCIATIONS

Hostelling International (*www.iyhf.org*) is an umbrella organization serving around five thousand youth hostels worldwide. Their comprehensive Web site gives access to information on all of their national offices and provides online booking and membership facilities. Membership prices shown below are for one year. Many youth hostel associations offer members discounts on some air and land travel, car rental, entrance fees to museums and historical sights, so it's worth checking out the details before you book your trip.

Australia: Australian Youth Hostels Association, 422 Kent Rd, Sydney (☎02/9261 1111, *www.yha.com.au*). Adult membership costs A$47 for a year (annual renewal is A$30); under-18s costs A$15.

Canada: Hostelling International – Canadian Hostelling Association, Room 400, 205 Catherine St, Ottawa ON K2P 1C3 (☎1-800/663-5777 or 1-613/237-7884, *www.hostellingintl.ca*). Adults CAN$25, under-18s CAN$12; two-year adult membership costs CAN$35.

England and Wales: Youth Hostel Association (YHA), Trevelyan House, 8 St Stephen's Hill, St Albans, Herts AL1 2DY (☎01727/855215, *www.yha.org.uk*). Adults £12, under-18s £6.

New Zealand: Youth Hostels Association of New Zealand, PO Box 436, 193 Cashel St, 3rd floor, Union House, Christchurch (☎03/379 9970, *www.yha.org.nz*). Adult membership costs NZ$40; under-18s NZ$15.

Northern Ireland: Hostelling International Northern Ireland, 22 Donegall Rd, Belfast BT12 5JN (☎028/9031 5435, *www.hini.org.uk*). Adults £10/€12.70, under-18s £6/€7.62.

Republic Of Ireland: An Óige, 61 Mountjoy St, Dublin 7 (☎01/830 4555, *www.irelandyha.org*). Adults/single-parent family £10/€12.70, under-18s £4/€5.08.

Scotland: Scottish Youth Hostel Association, 7 Glebe Crescent, Stirling FK8 2JA (☎01786/891400, *www.syha.org.uk*). Adults £6, under-18s £2.50.

US: Hostelling International–American Youth Hostels (HI–AYH), 773 15th St NW, Suite 840, Washington, DC 20005 (☎1-202/783-6161, *www.hiayh.org*). Adults US$25, under-18s free.

15.24 per person for private rooms where available (more in Dublin). Many hostels are open all year round. Where this is not the case, we have specified which months they are closed in the text. If you are planning on using hostels extensively, it's worth calling for their detailed lists in advance: for the IHH call ☎01/836 4700 (*www.hostels-ireland.com*), for the IHO call ☎073/30130 (*epcmedia.net/ihi/*). In recent years a number of independent hostels have turned to providing accommodation for refugees, so it's worth phoning ahead to check that they still cater for backpackers.

An Óige and HINI hostels are run more traditionally: many are closed during the daytime and enforce evening curfews, at least officially. Thanks to competition from other hostels though, you'll find many far more flexible than the rule book would suggest, and the quality of accommodation in newly refurbished hostels can be exceptionally good. Smaller dorms and private rooms are available in certain hostels; some are worth visiting for the location (which can often make up for the lack of facilities) and others, especially in the mountains, may be the only place to stay. In the Republic, An Óige membership – which includes membership of the umbrella organization, **Hostelling International** (HI), and therefore also membership of HINI – costs £10/€12.7 for adults and £4/€5.08 for under-18s, and can be obtained by visiting or writing to An Óige's main office in Dublin (see box above for details). In Northern Ireland, HINI membership (including membership of HI and therefore An Óige) costs £7 for adults and £3 for under-18s. Visitors from elsewhere in the UK, and foreign nationals, who wish to join HI once in the Republic or the North can do so. It is worth remembering that if you buy membership before leaving home some transport companies offer discounts; from Britain, Irish Ferries offer reductions on foot passenger fares, and certain car rental companies also offer reduced rates too. The members' handbook also lists discounts available at a range of historic sites, and in shops and visitor centres. If you turn up at an An Óige hostel as a non-member, you will be charged a nightly supplement of £1/€1.27, which accumulates so that after paying six you become a temporary member, though you are not eligible for the discounts that full membership entitles you to.

An Óige and HINI Hostels are graded according to the quality of facilities, and **prices** in the **Republic** vary accordingly, ranging between £7/€8.89 to £13/€16.51 for a dorm in high season; city hostels are generally the most expensive. It's worth getting a copy of the *An Óige Handbook*, which clarifies the intricacies of the system, lists every hostel in the association and gives details of HINI hostels; it's available from the address on p.37. An Óige also offers special accommodation-and-travel deals, which you should check out in advance – for instance, its combined transport to Ireland, hostel and train ticket is often very good value. In the **North**, charges for an overnight stay range from £7.50 to £10 for a dorm bed including linen.

CAMPING

The cheapest way to sleep in Ireland is to **camp** rough, although the distinct possibility of rain, without the facilities of a campsite, may put you off. You'll also find that some of the terrain is very tricky, especially in the areas of bog and rock in Clare, Donegal, Galway and Mayo. There's usually no problem if you ask to camp in a field, and in out-of-the-way places nobody minds where you pitch a tent (the only place you definitely can't camp in the Republic is in a state forest – but these are usually dark pine woods anyhow). You may find that the farmer will ask you for a pound or two if the field happens to be in a heavily touristed region such as Kerry, and if there's an organized site nearby you'll probably be directed to it, but other than this you can often camp for free. The cost of staying in **organized campsites** varies depending on the facilities offered, the number of people sharing, etc; expect to pay £5–8/€6.35–10.16 for two people in a small tent. Sites are listed throughout the *Guide*. It's also worth bearing in mind that many of the **hostels** will let you camp on their land for £3–4/€3.81–5.08 a night, with the use of kitchen facilities and showers.

FOOD AND DRINK

Ireland has no real tradition of eating out, but the range and quality of food has increased enormously in recent years, especially at the top end of the market, and this edition of the *Guide* includes the most luxurious and expensive of eating places, along with more everyday establishments. Outside smart restaurants the best of Irish food is to be found in seafood bars on the west coast and in the all-too-rare vegetarian cafés dotted around the country. These aside, the fresh, though rather plain, selection of vegetables, meat and breads available in the shops make self-catering a reasonable option; in some areas these can often be enlivened by a fine selection of Irish cheeses. If your budget is restricted, the best bet is to fill up with a hearty breakfast and/or a good lunch from a pub or coffee shop in the middle of the day, and then concentrate on drinking in the evening – few pubs serve food at night.

FOOD

Irish food is generally highly meat-oriented, and you don't have to be a vegetarian to find this wearing after a while. Having said that, meat in Ireland is generally of a good standard – lamb and steaks, in particular, are excellent – it's just that, after a while you begin to long for some variety in your diet and for something which hasn't been grilled or fried.

If you're staying in B&Bs, you'll most likely be served the hearty "traditional" Irish **breakfast** of sausages, bacon and eggs, which usually comes accompanied by generous quantities of delicious soda bread. Country pub **lunch** staples are usually meat and two veg, with plenty of potatoes and gravy, although you can usually get sandwiches (sometimes excellent, but often sliced white bread and processed cheese), and homemade soups can be very good too. Most larger towns have good, simple **coffee shops** (open daytime only) where you can get soup, sandwiches, cakes and scones, and a choice of one or two hot lunches. In the North expect enormous platters of meat, vegetables – most usually cabbage – and plenty of potatoes. It's worth remembering that many **hotels** in the Republic will offer food to non-residents so you can usually find a sandwich and a cup of coffee at any reasonable hour, which can be especially worth remembering on Sundays. You can generally order a plate of sandwiches and a pot of tea in pubs too – as long as it's before 6pm. This said, huge areas of the countryside offer no places to eat or drink at all – and many cafés and restaurants outside the cities close from September through to May. If you are going to explore the best of the landscape, you'll probably need to take your own provisions.

Many traditional Irish dishes, served up in abundance in many areas of rural Ireland, are based on the **potato** and you certainly do get an awful lot of them – often served up in several different forms in the same meal. Potato cakes can be magnificent – a flour and potato dough fried in butter – as can potato soup. **Irish stew** of varying qualities will be available almost everywhere. **Colcannon** – known as **champ** in the North – made up of cooked potatoes fried in butter with onions and cabbage, or leeks, is delicious. **Barm brack**, a sweet yeast bread with spices and dried fruits, is thoroughly traditional; **carrot cake** is perhaps a more recent introduction and is seen in coffee shops and tea rooms throughout the Republic.

Throughout Ireland's major **cities** it's a different story: in the Republic the economic boom of recent years coupled with the return of a large number of Irish people who have been living overseas, means that increasingly inexpensive lunch and dinner menus may just as easily see

Mediterranean influences as those of the traditional Irish farmhouse – and vegetarians can expect far more variety too.

RESTAURANTS AND SELF-CATERING

Once away from the pubs and coffee shops, food in Ireland is far more cosmopolitan than you might imagine – both in the cities and in some unexpected out-of-the-way places. Ireland's **gastronomic revolution**, that began around 1996 and has continued unabated ever since, has seen the development of a new Irish cuisine, consisting of elegant meals using local produce that are often adaptations of traditional recipes. Some **guesthouses**, particularly if they're historic buildings, serve very good food, in what can be very grand surroundings, and a growing number of excellent vegetarian and wholefood cafés offer a good budget alternative with a growing interest in the delights of organic food. Some impressive **seafood restaurants**, particularly along the west coast, serve freshly caught fish and seafood along with homegrown vegetables. Bars on the west coast are also a good bet for excellent salmon and crab salads and sandwiches, and there are numerous seafood festivals held around the coast. Irish **oysters** are famous: the season opens with an oyster festival at Clarinbridge on Galway Bay. **Salmon** and trout can also be fabulous, although away from the coast fish-farming is the norm. Outside the large cities there's a great deal of variation in opening times, especially in low season, and it's advisable to phone ahead if you have a particular restaurant in mind.

Catering for yourself, at least some of the time, may be a good option. Produce available in Ireland is usually fresh and excellent, but – aside from in the cities and some tourist towns on the west coast – it is limited in range (you won't find exotic fruits and vegetables, for instance). Irish potatoes, cabbages and carrots are delicious, though they can be surprisingly hard to buy in remote rural areas where the population may be too small to support even a grocer's shop. Meat is very good; bread and scones are wonderful, with a particularly wide variety on offer in the North. If you're travelling around the coast, you can sometimes buy seafood cheaply direct from the fishermen; this can throw up more unusual things – spider crabs and monkfish, for example – that you would be less likely to find in local fish shops. In many places you can gather your own mussels from the rocks – but be sure to check locally in case there's a sewage outlet nearby.

Dairy products, especially cheese, are excellent. The Irish cheese business has seen a definite upturn since the late 1980s, and now produces many delicious, often unpasteurized, cheeses. Look out for the creamy Cashel Blue, St Killian brie, and Gubbeen Farmhouse in West Cork as well as countless more idiosyncratic cheeses from smaller makers, many of whom like to experiment. There's no need to go to a smart restaurant to taste these – you can often find them in grocer's shops and markets.

DRINK

To travel through Ireland without visiting a **pub** would be to miss out on a huge chunk of Irish life, some would say the most important. Especially in rural areas, the pub is far more than just a place to drink. It's the communal and conversational heart of any Irish village, and often the cultural centre too. If you're after food, advice or company, the pub is almost always the place to head for; and very often they'll also be the venues for local entertainment, especially traditional and not so traditional music (see "Festivals and Entertainment", p.45).

Along with Mass and market day, the pub is the centre of Irish social activity: a cultural cliché, perhaps, but one that wears very well. Talking is an important business here, and drink is the great lubricant of social discourse. That said, it doesn't pay to arrive with too romantic a notion of what this actually means. Away from the cities and the touristed west coast, there are plenty of miserable, dingy bars where the only spark of conviviality is the dull glow of the TV. But in most big towns and cities you'll find bars heaving with life, and out in remote country villages it can be great fun drinking among the shelves of the ancient grocery shops-cum-bars you'll find dotted around.

While women will always be treated with genuine (unreconstructed) civility, it's true to say that the majority of bars in country areas are a predominantly male preserve. In the evening, especially, women travellers can expect occasional unwanted attention, though this rarely amounts to anything too unpleasant. Should your first encounters be bad ones, persist – the good nights will come, and will probably rank amongst the most memorable experiences of your trip. In the major cities and large towns things are a lot more balanced and women drinking in bars is totally the norm.

In the Republic, **opening hours** are Monday to Wednesday 10.30am to 11.30pm; Thursday, Friday and Saturday 10.30am to 12.30am; Sunday 12.30 to 11pm. In the **North** pubs are open Monday to Saturday 11am to 11pm, on Sunday 12.30 to 10pm.

WHAT TO DRINK

The classic Irish drink is, of course, **Guinness** ("a Guinness" is a pint; if you want a half of any beer, ask for "a glass") which, as anybody will tell you, is simply not the same as the drink marketed as Guinness outside Ireland. For one thing, good Guinness has to be kept properly, something non-Irish pubs abroad tend not to do; it has to be poured gradually (the ultimate gaffe in a pub is to ask them to hurry this process); and even across Ireland you'll taste differences. A proper pint of Irish Guinness is a dream, far less heavy than you may be used to, though still a considerably, filling drink. Other local stouts, like Beamish and Murphy's (a Cork stout, far sweeter and creamier), make for interesting comparison: they all have their faithful adherents.

If you want a pint of English-style **bitter**, then Smithwicks is the most commonly available option, though it has none of the flavour of a decent real ale. As everywhere, of course, **lager** is also increasingly popular: mostly Harp (made by Guinness) or Heineken. In recent years a number of **micro breweries** have popped up offering a range of beers – usually themed in some medieval fashion – made on the premises: generally there's a blond (lager), a red (ale) and a stout, with perhaps the addition of a wheat beer. Still really something of a novelty, these often have the advantage of being additive-free. Whatever your tipple, you're likely to find drinking in Ireland an expensive business at around £2.00 in the North and anything from £2–2.60/€2.54–3.30 in the Republic a pint.

Irish **whiskeys** – try Paddy's, Powers, Jameson's or, from the North, Bushmills – also seem expensive, but in fact the measures are far larger than those you'll get in mainland Britain. If you've come in from the cold you might like to try whiskey served warm with cloves and lemon – just ask for a hot whiskey. Asking for Scotch in an Irish pub is frowned on, and in any case anyone here will tell you that the Irish version is infinitely superior.

Wine is expensive in the Republic – expect prices in supermarkets to start at around £5/€6.35 a bottle (and in small villages in the west you can expect to pay £7/€8.89 at the very least), so if you are planning a self-catering holiday and travelling from Britain, it's worth bringing your own; in the North prices are similar to those in the rest of Britain.

Non-alcoholic drinks are limited to an uninspiring array of the usual soft drinks and bottled fruit juices. Among the most pleasant are Cidona (apple juice), plus a range of Irish mineral waters, some of which are available in a number of pleasantly unsweet, fruity flavours. Unless the bar is extremely busy, you can always get **coffee** (generally served with a dollop of full cream) or **tea**. You can usually get **Irish coffee** too (with whiskey and cream), which is delicious if not very traditional – it was invented at Shannon airport.

POST AND PHONES

In towns throughout Ireland you'll find fully automatic payphones in kiosks; instructions for use are on display, and internal and international calls can easily be made. A local call generally costs 30p minimum in the Republic, 20p in the North but, as you might imagine, long-distance daytime calls are very expensive. International calls are cheapest if dialled direct after 6pm. Cardphones, found in towns all over the country, are by far the most convenient way of making long-distance calls, avoiding the chugging of coins interrupting your call; they're also cheaper than coin-operated phones. Phonecards can be bought at newsagents and post offices – it's worth carrying one with you since cash-operated phones are rare in remote areas. If you make calls from a hotel or the like, expect a hefty premium charged on top of the normal price.

International dialling codes in the United Kingdom (including Northern Ireland) and Ireland follow the European standard – to call Ireland the code is 353, and for Northern Ireland, as part of the UK, it's 44. If you're calling the North from the Republic, however, the code is 048 followed by an eight digit number. Almost all telephone codes in Northern Ireland changed in 2000 and you may well come across out-of-date ones on leaflets, brochures and stationery. For details of all number changes in the North see the box on p.523.

There are few **fax offices** outside Dublin or Belfast. If you need to use a fax, ask at one of the swankier hotels – they're usually pleased to help and are unlikely to charge you an unreasonable rate. The other option is to enquire at the nearest Internet café as these sometimes have fax facilities. Internet access is available in most reasonably sized towns and in many hostels (see p.36).

Post to or from the **Republic** is generally reasonably fast and efficient. If it's something important, it's worth spending the extra for registered mail. An Post (the postal service) has three different charges for the Republic: letters and postcards to Ireland or Britain cost 30p; those going to any other European country cost 32p; cards or letters outside Europe cost 45p. Main post offices are open Monday to Friday 9am to 5.30pm, Saturday 9am to 1pm, and in cities and large towns until 5.30pm on Saturday. From the **North**, letters and postcards travel anywhere in the EU for 36p, for the rest of the world postcards are 40p and letters cost a minimum of 45p. Post office hours in the North are Monday, Tuesday, Thursday and Friday 9am to 5.30pm and Wednesday and Saturday 9am to 12.30pm – later on Saturday in some Belfast offices.

OPERATOR SERVICES

In the Republic:

Operator ☎10
Directory Enquiries within Ireland including Northern Ireland ☎11811
International Directory Enquiries ☎11818
International Operator Services ☎114
Telegrams ☎196

In the North:

Operator ☎100
Directory Enquiries ☎192
International Directory Enquiries ☎153
International Operator Services ☎155
Telegrams ☎0800 190190

THE MEDIA

NEWSPAPERS AND MAGAZINES

The most widely read **papers** in the **Republic** are the heavyweight *Irish Times* and the lighter *Irish Independent*. High-quality but remarkably slim papers, they really bring home just how small the population is. The *Times* is the more upmarket, a liberal newspaper with comparatively good foreign-news coverage and plenty of feature material on home news and sport. A newcomer on the national scene, *The Irish Examiner* (formerly *The Cork Examiner*), is, in its former provincial incarnation, the oldest daily published newspaper in the country; it has a softer focus with excellent local sports coverage. The *Star* is Ireland's tabloid, though the *Sun* and the *Mirror* both have an Irish edition. Sunday newspapers include the *Times* and *Independent* equivalents, the liberal *Sunday Tribune* and the more sensational *Sunday World*. British newspapers are generally available the same day in Dublin and other cities. Mostly conservative and varying widely in quality, there's a local daily paper in every county; some of the best are *The Kerryman*, *The Donegal Democrat* and *The Kilkenny People*.

In the **North**, all the main British papers are sold. Of the newspapers produced in Northern Ireland, the biggest seller is the evening paper, the *Belfast Telegraph*, which has a soft unionist stance while the morning papers are the *Irish News*, read by the Nationalist community, and the Unionist tabloid *News Letter*.

TELEVISION AND RADIO

In the **Republic**, RTE (Radio Telefís Éireann) runs two state-sponsored **television** channels: RTE 1 and Network 2. RTE 1 reflects the state broadcasting policy with an emphasis on public information and a commitment to Irish-language and bilingual programmes. Network 2 is more upbeat, with plenty of chat shows and youth-oriented programmes. There are two relatively new independent channels: TV3 which features mostly British and American soaps, films and sport, and the excellent Irish-language channel Telefís na Ghaeilge (TG4 as it is commonly referred to). TG4 has succeeded in its attempt to use the contemporary medium of television to reinvigorate the language, reflected in much of its programming which is youth-oriented, upbeat and visually progressive.

In the **North** you get the BBC whose strongest programming is related to politics: look out for the current affairs programme *Spotlight* on BBC1 on Tuesday evenings, while *Talkback* with David Dunseith, daily 11am to 1pm on BBC Radio Ulster, gives an insight into the complex sectarian politics of the North. The independent Ulster Television, the BBC's main rival, focuses on softer news issues. Many northerners also tune into RTE which can also be picked up north of the border. Throughout Ireland the four major English terrestrial TV channels are available on cable, as are satellite channels such as Sky One and Skysport.

RTE also runs three **radio** stations – Radio 1, 2 and FM3. **RTE1** is devoted to middle/highbrow music, and cultural and political programmes. **RTE 2** is a popular music channel with a more light-hearted feel; in the mornings for a flavour of everyday Irish life tune into RTE 2's *Gerry Ryan Show* from 9am to noon where the host has the ability to turn the most mundane subjects into highly entertaining radio. **FM3** is the national Irish-language station, Radio na Gaeltachta, which shares the frequency with classical music programming. **Today FM** was launched as an ambitious attempt to rival the state-owned media, and although its daytime output is rather uninspiring, its evening broadcasting, a mix of politics, satire and informed musical opinion is by far the best in the country: *The Last Word*, weekdays from 5 till 7pm, a current affairs programme hosted by the outspoken Eamonn Dunphy, is followed from 7 to 9pm by *Pet Sounds* where Tom Dunne trawls through his eclectic and, at times, idiosyncratic music collection, while the evening winds down to the dulcet tones of Kerryman Donal Dineen, an authority on contemporary electronic music. Deregulation of the radio has resulted in the growth of local radio on the FM airwaves. The quality varies, but you'll find some interesting fare, including all-Irish stations in Connemara and Ring, Co. Waterford, that are worth listening to for traditional music, country and western and insights into local issues.

OPENING HOURS AND HOLIDAYS

Business and shop opening hours in both Northern Ireland and the Republic are very similar to Britain's: approximately 9am to 5.30pm, Monday to Saturday. Many places in the towns stay open until 8pm or later on Thursdays and Fridays and most now open on Sundays from around noon until 6pm. The midweek half-day closing tradition survives in some of the smaller towns though even then you're likely to find somewhere open.

In the Republic, however, particularly away from the bigger towns, hours are more approximate, with later opening and closing times. In rural areas you can generally find someone to sell you groceries at any reasonable hour, even if they have to open their shop to do it – and very often the village shop doubles as the local pub. For banking hours see "Costs, Money and Banks" on p.21. On the main **public holidays** (see below), outside the cities virtually everything will be closed except the garages and pubs. Should St Patrick's Day or Orange Day happen to fall on a Saturday or Sunday, the holiday is carried over to the Monday.

There's no pattern to the opening and closing of **museums**, **archeological sites** and the like, though many close altogether for at least one day a week. Wherever possible, hours and prices are listed in the *Guide*. The bigger attractions will normally be open throughout the day, while smaller places may open only in the afternoon. Many sites away from the main tourist trails – especially houses or castles which are also private homes – are open only during the peak summer months.

Churches, at least if they're still in use, are almost always open, and if they're locked there's usually someone living nearby (often the priest) who will have the keys; otherwise, opening times will follow religious activity fairly closely.

PUBLIC HOLIDAYS

In the Republic:

New Year's Day
St Patrick's Day, March 17
Good Friday
Easter Monday
First Monday in May
First Monday in June
First Monday in August
Last Monday in October
Christmas Day
December 26

In the North:

New Year's Day
St Patrick's Day, March 17
Good Friday
Easter Monday
First Monday in May
Last Monday in May
Orange Day, July 12
Last Monday in August
Christmas Day
December 26

FESTIVALS AND ENTERTAINMENT

Virtually every village and town in Ireland seems to have a festival of some kind or other each year. Whatever the pretext for the celebration, it's usually also an excuse for serious partying. Well-established ones like the Cork Jazz Festival and the Wexford Opera Festival are major international events, and getting tickets for top performances can be well nigh impossible without advance planning. The very word "festival" seems to act as a magnet for all sorts of musicians, and many events are wonderfully overwhelming. No matter the size of the town, there's rarely enough room for all that's happening, with music and dancing bursting out of the official venues into surrounding streets and bars. The biggest of the annual events are listed here, but pick up a calendar of events at any major tourist office and you'll soon get a picture of the huge range of celebrations.

MUSIC

Apart from their sheer exuberance, the most enjoyable aspect of Irish festivals is, without doubt, the traditional music. Many festivals (the Irish for festival is *Fleadh* – pronounced fla) are devoted almost exclusively to this: the biggest of them is the **Fleadh Cheoil na hÉireann** (see box on p.46), which includes the finals of the All Ireland music and dance contests.

However, if you can't make it to a festival, there's usually plenty going on in the pubs and bars, especially in high season in the popular tourist spots. Music in Irish pubs is legendary, and there's lots on offer, though only a relatively small proportion of it is "traditional". The national hybrid form of country and western, country and Irish, is extremely popular with a host of regular gigs around the island. You'll still find that Irish staple, the showband, too, and there's a myriad of middle-of-the-road pop bands lurking in country areas. Ballads are another well-developed Irish music form though the term "ballad" is a bit of a catch-all and open to countless interpretations – it's generally some form of dull crooning, often accompanied by just a guitar and monotonous beatbox. Brace yourself for the worst, and from time to time you'll be very pleasantly surprised.

The cream of pub music, however, has to be the **traditional sessions** of fiddles, flutes, accordions, bodhrán (a drum) and, occasionally, singing. Interest from abroad and the tourist industry has much to do with the resurgence of this musical culture – but this hardly matters, since the music can be phenomenal. The west coast (especially around Clare, Donegal and Galway) has the best of the traditional scene. There's plenty in all the major cities, and pointers to the best sessions are given in the text. However, venues may change for all manner of reasons and it's wise to ask around and keep your ears open for local tips.

Traditionally Sunday evening was the night for sessions, and in rural areas this is often still the case (a throwback to restrictions on holy days that meant partying on Saturdays had to stop at midnight), but increasingly Friday and Saturday have become just as important, and, in summer, you may find something happening any night of the week. Things generally don't get going till late, and a bar that's still empty at 10pm may be a riot of music by half-past. While it's all extremely convivial and relaxed, if you're a musician yourself and want to join in, then do so tactfully. The first thing to do is sit and listen for a while – to make sure you can play to a high enough standard and are familiar with the repertoire – and then work out who the leader is and ask. If you're not playing, don't crowd the musicians; the empty seats around them are reserved for others who may arrive later.

MAJOR ANNUAL FESTIVALS AND EVENTS

Saint Patrick's Day (March 17; *www.stpatricksday.ie*): celebrations all over Ireland, including a national festival in Dublin and major events in all the larger towns and cities.

Irish Grand National (April): horse racing at Fairyhouse (Meath).

Cork International Choral Festival (April/May; *www.musweb.com/corkchoral.htm*): one of the big ones.

Foyle Film Festival (April/May): the best of new Irish and international film, Derry.

North-West 200 (May): the island's biggest motorcycle road racing event takes place on a circuit at Portstewart, Co. Derry.

Music Festival in Great Irish Houses (June): just what it says, classical music at venues around the country.

Irish Derby (June): and other important races at the Curragh (Kildare).

Willie Clancy Summer School (July): one of the biggest traditional music events of the year, based in Miltown Malbay, Co. Clare.

James Joyce Summer School (July; *www.artsworld.ie/joyce–school*): strictly for Joyce buffs, Dublin.

Galway International Arts Festival (July; *www.galwayartsfestival.ie*): festival of music, theatre and general partying – one of the best.

Galway Races (July/Aug): another important race meeting which is very popular.

Yeats International Summer School (Aug): this Sligo event has often courted controversy through its exploration of nationalistic themes.

Kilkenny International Arts Week (Aug): includes recitals, poetry readings, art exhibitions.

Rose of Tralee International Festival (Aug; *www.roseoftralee.ie*): a massive event, centred round a beauty contest.

Fleadh Cheoil na hÉireann (Aug; *www.comhaltas com*): the most important of all the traditional music festivals, held in a different town every year.

Oul' Lammas Fair (Aug): four hundred years old and still going strong, Ballycastle's traditional market fair is a major crowd-puller with music, dancing, sports and entertainment.

All Ireland Hurling and Football Finals (Sept): the biggest sporting events of the year, separated by a fortnight, in Dublin.

Lisdoonvarna Matchmaking Festival (Sept/Oct): plenty of traditional entertainment accompanies the lonely hearts side of the festivities.

Cork Film and Jazz Festivals (Oct; *www.corkfilmfest.org*): Ireland's major film event and an enormously popular jazz festival.

Wexford Opera Festival (Oct/Nov; *www.wexfordopera.com*): a large gathering of international renown.

Derry Halloween Carnival (Oct/Nov): street theatre, music and mayhem, especially during the fireworks display on October 31.

Belfast Festival at Queen's (Oct/Nov): major arts festival, Ireland's equivalent to Edinburgh, nowadays complete with its very own Fringe.

Comhaltas Ceoltóiri Éireann is an organization that exists purely to promote traditional music and culture, and evenings organized by them (not always in bars), though by their nature not spontaneous, are well worth looking out for. They are run by real enthusiasts, and the standard of playing is usually pretty high.

SPORTS AND ACTIVITIES

Ireland has two hugely popular indigenous amateur sports, hurling and gaelic football, with important matches attracting big crowds and passionate support. Hurling is a fifteen-a-side stick game, a precursor of hockey and lacrosse, but much faster and more competitive than either. Like rugby, there's an H-shaped set of goalposts and each team aims to score as many points as possible by either hitting the leather, baseball-sized ball (*sliotar*) over the crossbar for one point or into the net below for three points. The game's skill lies in control of the broad, wooden hurley stick (*camán)* and players can knock the ball along the ground, hit it through the air or run while balancing the ball on their stick. The ball can be caught by hand or with the hurley. The hurling season begins with local inter-county games in the early summer, progressing through provincial championships to reach its climax in the All Ireland Hurling Final on the first Sunday in September at Croke Park in Dublin. Cork, Kilkenny, Offaly and Tipperary are the most successful counties. Camogie, the women's version of hurling, is becoming increasingly popular, and well worth watching, if there's a match in the area.

Gaelic football is played on the same pitches as hurling and shares the same scoring system and team size. It has similarities with both rugby and association football, as the round, soccer-sized ball can be kicked, caught and passed by either boot or hand. However, running with the ball is only allowed if a player keeps control by tapping the ball from foot to hand every five steps. The season, which runs from early summer, is organized like hurling's, culminating in an All Ireland final at Croke Park on the third Sunday in September, a flavour of which can be gained from the excellent film shown as part of the Croke GAA Museum tour (see p.100). Details of fixtures for hurling and gaelic football can be obtained from the Gaelic Athletic Association (☎01/836 3222).

Rugby union and soccer are also extremely popular and tickets for international matches are very much in demand, especially in the Republic. The international **rugby** team is a joint Republic/Northern Ireland side, with home matches played at Dublin's Lansdowne Road Stadium (see p.123). The main event of the year is the Six Nations Championship, a series of international games against France, England, Scotland, Wales and, latterly, Italy played in Spring. **Soccer** is organized on a professional basis in both the North and the Republic, though the majority of players are semi-professional, with teams competing in the Irish League and League of Ireland respectively. Standards are not especially high and Irish teams rarely progress beyond the preliminary rounds of the European competitions. Northern Ireland's international matches are played at Windsor Park, Belfast (see p.551), and the Republic's at Lansdowne Road. Both international teams draw the overwhelming majority of their players from the English and Scottish leagues. The Northern Ireland side had its heyday in the 1980s, culminating in their famous 1–0 victory over hosts Spain in the 1982 World Cup, while the Republic gained a high profile and creditable international reputation in the early 1990s under the managership of the Englishman "Big Jack" Charlton – it's undoubted high point was the 1–0 defeat of Italy during the 1994 World Cup Finals. There's hope for the future too, as the Republic's youth team gained a remarkable third place in the 1997 World Finals and, uniquely, won both the under-16 and under-18 1998 European Championships. However, the most popular clubs here (and in the North) are Manchester United and Liverpool. Glasgow Celtic and Rangers are also popular in the North with support following sectarian Catholic and Protestant divisions.

Horse racing unites two Irish passions, horses and betting, and is carried out with a relaxed good humour that you shouldn't miss. Racing is concentrated around the Curragh, a grassy plain in Co. Kildare (see p.141), where the classic flat-race course of the same name is located, along with Punchestown race course and many of Ireland's famous stud farms. The Irish Grand National is run at Fairyhouse in Co. Meath in April, the Irish Derby at the Curragh in June. The flat-racing season runs from mid-March to early November while National Hunt racing over jumps takes place throughout the year. For details of the fixtures at Dublin's race course, Leopardstown, see p.123. Just as much fun and more easily accessible is **greyhound racing**. Shelbourne Park (☎668 3502) in Dublin is the country's most prestigious venue, although there are sixteen tracks across the country. Information on meetings is available from Bord na gCon, the Irish Greyhound Racing Board (☎061/316788).

Cycling is a hugely popular sport in Ireland, exemplified by the large crowds lining the route of the Irish sections of the 1998 Tour de France, a race won in 1987 by one of the country's sporting heroes, Stephen Roche. Another, Sean Kelly, was world number one from 1984 to 1988. There's an enormous number of **golf** courses here too, with major championships like the Irish Open in July. Both tourist boards produce information on where you can play and have details of holiday packages and accommodation.

Naturally, as this is an island, there are innumerable opportunities for sea **angling** and hundreds of lakes and rivers for fishing of the fly and game varieties. In general, the best of the sea angling takes place on the south and west coasts and Bord Fáilte can help with information. The high spot of the fly-fishing season is the emergence of the mayfly around mid-May when anglers flock to the best brown trout spots such as: Lower Lough Erne, Co. Fermanagh; Lough Derg, Co. Clare and the Corrib system, Co. Galway. There are plenty of other possibilities, however, and, again the tourist boards can assist.

The relatively sheltered waters of the east coast see most of the **sailing** activity, especially in Dublin Bay and further south around Arklow and Wexford, though there are excellent opportunities, too, in West Cork and on Lough Derg, Co. Clare. The south and southwest are most popular for cruising, though the Cork coast offers many possibilities for yachting. The rougher waters of the west coast restrict the options to the areas more protected from the elements, such as Galway Bay or Killybegs, Co. Donegal. On the north coast, Lough Swilly is increasingly popular, while on the other side of the border, there are numerous boating possibilities on Strangford Lough. For further information contact the Irish Sailing Association (☎01/280 0239). Inland waterways also offer **canoeing**, ranging from touring to rough- and white-water racing.

Wind-surfing and **water-skiing** are usually possible wherever there are good sailing waters and there are some fabulous beaches for **board-surfing**. Some of the best are: Barleycove beach, Co. Cork; Inch Strand and Castlegregory beach on, respectively, the south and north sides of the Dingle Peninsula. Further north, Easky, Co. Sligo offers perhaps the best of the lot, though Bundoran and Rossnowlagh beaches, Co. Donegal are close contenders. The Northern Ireland coast between Castlerock, Co. Derry and Portrush, Co. Antrim attracts hordes of board fanatics.

Situated in the path of the Gulf Stream, there are stupendous opportunities for **diving** off the Irish coast, from protected harbours for beginners to rocky cliff faces for the more experienced. There are plenty of places where you can learn to dive too. The Irish Underwater Council can provide details of clubs and courses (☎01/284 4601).

The Ulster Way was the first waymarked **walking** trail in Ireland and it's still the longest, running a 560-mile circuit of Northern Ireland and linked to trails from Donegal and Cavan. If you don't fancy the complete trek, the Northern Ireland Tourist Board publishes information on specific shorter walks, and the route guides published by the Sports Council for Northern Ireland at House of Sport, Upper Malone Road, Belfast BT9 5LA (☎028/9038 1222) are also useful. A variety of similar trails now exist in the Republic, ranging from walks through glens and mountains, such as the Wicklow Way, or around entire peninsulas, like the Beara and Dingle Ways. Although the walks are waymarked, you'll always need a good map as a standby. Local tourist offices and councils have produced map guides for some of the ways, as has East West Mapping, Ballyredmond, Clonegal, Enniscorthy, Co. Wexford (☎054/77835), which also sells trail guidebooks. These walks are maintained in the south by the National Waymarked Ways Committee (☎662 1444, *walsha@entemp.irlgov.ie*) who can give advice on which routes to take, while Bord Fáilte's publication *Walking Ireland* is a handy introduction to easier walks in the country. Particularly useful walking guides are listed in "Contexts", p.739.

Though Ireland's mountain ranges are not especially high, there are numerous opportunities for **rock-climbing**, expecially in Counties Cork and Kerry – the latter's Macgillycuddy's Reeks make up for their lack of height by spectacular settings. To the east, the Wicklow Mountains are hugely popular, while the craggy splendour and coastal setting of the Mourne Mountains in Co. Down are hard to beat. The Mountaineering Council of Ireland (☎01/450

WALKING SAFETY

Though one of the joys of hill- and mountain-walking in Ireland is the sheer solitude of the experience, bear in mind that the lack of other people in your vicinity can be a significant drawback if a mishap occurs. The Irish climate can seem pretty mild, but the temperature drops two to three degrees Celsius for every thousand feet climbed and a strong wind can make it seem even colder. Mist can suddenly transform your surroundings too, so a pleasant day at sea-level can rapidly become perilous higher up. If you're planning any walk, especially on high ground, consider the following:

1. Always plan your route carefully beforehand and ensure, especially, that it can be finished before nightfall. Average walking speed is around two and a half miles an hour. A map is essential and, if you're unfamiliar with your route, carry a compass too. A torch, small first aid kit and whistle are useful and the mountain distress signal is six blasts of a whistle per minute, followed by a pause.

2. Check weather forecasts in advance and, no matter the weather when you set out, ensure you have clothing suitable for changes – warm, wind- and water-proof. Walking boots are essential for all but the shortest and easiest of walks.

3. Always carry a reserve supply of high-energy food, such as chocolate or trail mix and also a hot drink.

4. Walking alone is inadvisable, except in populated areas or where there are plenty of other walkers. Even when walking in a group, it's advisable to let someone (your hostel or B&B for example) know where you're going and when you're likely to return. If you drive to your starting point, a note left visible in your car is another alternative.

5. Exercise caution when walking along cliff tops – some 'safe' walks can become perilous in high winds. Streams in flood are particularly dangerous too and bear in mind that most accidents occur on the way back when you're fatigued, especially on descents.

6. If an accident does happen and urgent assistance is needed, telephone ☎999 and ask for the Mountain Rescue, if you're on high ground, or the local Garda station.

7. Follow the Farmland Code of Conduct – remember that more often than not you'll be crossing someone's land, so respect the environment and leave everything as you found it, closing gates behind you.

7376, *www.mountaineering.ie*) publishes a Web site, a magazine, *Irish Mountain Log*, plus a number of guides and offers advice on a variety of peaks.

The number of rare species visiting Ireland makes the country a **birdwatching** paradise. Again, the tourist boards can provide details, as can the National Parks and Wildlife Service (☎01/661 3111), and the Irish Wildbird Conservancy (☎01/280 4322). In the North a good contact is the Royal Society for the Protection of Birds (☎028/9049 1547) while Birdwatch Northern Ireland has been established specifically to assist north-bound ornithologists (☎028/9069 3232). Useful Web sites relating to birdwatching in Ireland include *www.indigo.ie/~hutch/birdmap.html* and *www.geocities.com/rainforest/2801*.

SECURITY AND THE POLICE

The Republic is one of the safest countries in Europe in which to travel. That said, don't let the friendliness of people as a whole lull you into a general carelessness; like anywhere else visitors are seen as easy targets for petty thieves (particularly in the bigger cities) and women especially should always take note of our advice on choosing accommodation. Theft is very common in Dublin and some areas of the city can be unsafe: it's a good idea to take local advice about safety on the streets from your hostel or B&B. Although the North has opened up a lot in the last few years, there is still a security presence, and you should be careful in certain city areas. Personal security, and crimes against the individual are not a major worry except in certain areas of Dublin.

In the Republic, people generally have a healthy indifference to law and red tape, perhaps in part a vestige of pre-Independence days, when any dealings with the police smacked of collusion with the British. The **police** – known as **Garda** or Gardai – accordingly have a low profile. In rural areas the low level of crime is such that policing is minimal and, should you need them, you might spend an entire afternoon waiting for the Garda to arrive. If you have any dealings with the Garda at all, the chances are that you'll find them affable enough.

> The emergency numbers in both the North and the Republic are ☎999 and 112.

In the **North** the **Royal Ulster Constabulary** (RUC), which is in the process of being reorganized and may bear a new title, deal with all general civic policing and are the people you should go to if in difficulty. Police stations are heavily fortified and security inside is tight, but whatever their reputation, you'll find that the RUC are helpful in matters of everyday police activity.

Security measures have been considerably relaxed during the last few years. Permanent border controls are no longer operative and you will rarely see either a police road block or army foot patrol unless travelling through South Armagh and parts of Fermanagh. In the unlikely event that you do find yourself being quizzed about your movements and plans, simply be polite and co-operative and you should experience no problems.

Obviously, politics remains a sensitive subject in the North, and you should use your common sense about what you say to whom.

SEXUAL HARASSMENT, PREJUDICE AND RACISM

For women Ireland is wonderfully relaxing: the outlandish sexism of Irish society manifests itself in a male courtesy that can range from the genuine and delightful to the downright insufferable, but you are unlikely to experience any really threatening behaviour. Most uncomfortable situations can be defused by a straightforward, firm response. That said, don't believe the general view that *nothing* can happen to you. It is worth remembering that outside the cities, communities are very small, and local women you see hitching alone do so in safety because they know and are known by just about everybody on the road. Foreign travellers don't have that added security, and, though it is very unlikely, you could be unlucky. In particular, if you are travelling alone use only the budget accommodation that is listed in this guide or recommended by the tourist office, don't go with touts at stations, and exercise the kind of care in cities at night that you would in any other European country. In the case of serious assault, if possible contact a Rape Crisis Centre before going to the police (telephone numbers are given in chapter listings). Attacks are rare and the Garda, though well-meaning, have little experience of handling distressed women.

Black travellers to Ireland should not encounter any major problems while travelling around the country. That said, one of the most surprising aspects for many visitors is how homogeneous and socially conservative Irish society actually is: the main type of racism that may be encountered is a fairly innocuous type of naive ignorance that you might find in rural Ireland where locals are simply not used to seeing black people.

Although they should have little impact on a visitor to the city, it is worth being aware of racial tensions in some areas of inner-city Dublin. A more malicious type of racial intolerance is currently being directed toward increasing numbers of refugees living in inner-city areas. Due to governmental mismanagement, most migrants are obliged to wait for up to two years for a decision on residency, and during this period they are not permitted to work. The resulting development of small, impoverished ghettos of the socially dependent in these areas has led to some resentment, and unfortunately increased verbal, and, in some cases, physical racial abuse.

The **gay** community is both the biggest and least visible minority in Ireland. Although part of the UK, Northern Ireland was excluded from the 1967 Act that legalized homosexuality for consenting adults in Britain. This led one individual to take his case to the European Court of Human Rights in 1982, which brought the legal status of gays in Northern Ireland into line with the rest of the UK. In the Republic, homosexuality has only been legal since 1990, and a nominally wide-ranging Incitement Against Hatred Act was passed in 1994 specifically prohibiting discrimination against people on the grounds of sexual orientation as well as race. However, public indecency charges are still pursued – such as surveillance and arrest of gays cruising Dublin's Phoenix Park, and censorship laws are used to exclude gay material. Outside the big cities homosexuality is not at all socially accepted, and public displays of affection are out of the question.

TRAVELLERS WITH DISABILITIES

The disabled traveller in Ireland is not well served, and wheelchair users in particular are likely to find the lack of ramps, lifts and wide doors inconvenient. With this in mind, it is well worth contacting Comhairle in the Republic and the Northern Irish Tourist Board (NITB) for information before you travel. Comhairle publishes very useful and comprehensive survey guides of accommodation, tourist amenities and restaurants/pubs in the Republic. They also have listings of accessible toilets and provide the keys to

CONTACTS FOR TRAVELLERS WITH DISABILITIES

IN THE IRISH REPUBLIC

Comhairle, 44 North Great George's St, Dublin 1 (☎01/874 7503).

Irish Wheelchair Association, Blackheath Drive, Clontarf, Dublin 3 (☎01/833 8241, *info@iwa.ie*).

Mental Health Association of Ireland, Mensana House, 6 Adelaide St, Dún Laoghaire, Co. Dublin (☎01/284 1166).

Northern Irish Tourist Board, St Anne's Court, 59 North St, Belfast BT1 1NB (☎028/9024 6609).

IN BRITAIN

Disability Action, Portside Business Park, 189 Airport Rd West, Belfast BT3 9EP (☎028/9029 7880, *www.disabilityaction.org*).

Disabled Drivers Association, National Headquarters, Ashwellthorpe, Norwich NR16 1EX (☎01508/489449, *www.justmobility.co.uk/dda*). Membership organization offering concessions on ferries.

Disabled Drivers Motor Club, Cottingham Way, Thrapston, Northamptonshire NN14 4PL (☎01832/734724). Membership organization offering similar concessions on ferries to the Disabled Drivers Association.

Holiday Care Service, 2nd Floor, Imperial Building, Victoria Rd, Horley, Surrey RH6 7PZ (☎01293/ 774535). Information on all aspects of travel including restaurant access, accommodation, equipment, transport and useful contacts (50p per information sheet).

Royal Association for Disability and Rehabilitation (RADAR), 12, City Forum, 250 City Rd, London EC1V 8AF (☎020/7250 3222). All kinds of information and advice.

IN NORTH AMERICA

Directions Unlimited, 720 N Bedford Rd, Bedford Hills, NY 10507 (☎1-800/533-5343). Tour operator specializing in custom tours for people with disabilities.

Mobility International USA, PO Box 10767, Eugene, OR 97440 (Voice and TDD: ☎541/343-1284, *www.miusa.org*). Information and referral services, access guides, tours and exchange programmes. Annual membership US$35 (includes quarterly newsletter).

Society for the Advancement of Travel for the Handicapped (SATH), Suite 610, 347 5th Ave, New York, NY 10016 (☎212/447-7284, *www.sath.org*). Non-profit-making travel industry referral service that passes queries on to its members as appropriate.

Travel Information Service, Moss Rehabilitation Hospital, 1200 Tabor Rd, Philadelphia, PA 19141 (*www.mossresourcenet.org*). Excellent online resource for disabled travellers.

IN AUSTRALIA AND NEW ZEALAND

ACROD, PO Box 60, Curtin, ACT 2605 (☎02/6282 4333); 24 Cabarita Rd, Cabarita (☎02/9743 2699). Compiles lists of organizations, accommodation, travel agencies and tour operators.

Disabled Persons Assembly, 173 Victoria St, Wellington (☎04/801 9100). Resource centre with lists of travel agencies and tour operators for people with disabilities

them. Another useful publication is their *Dublin: A Guide for People with Disabilities,* with has detailed information on access to transport, toilets, public buildings, accommodation, shops and nightlife in the capital (all of the above publications are free). Wheelchair rental can be arranged in advance through the Irish Wheelchair Association.

Most of the major **ferry companies** offer good reductions to disabled drivers coming from mainland Britain: generally you need to be a member of the Disabled Drivers Association (DDA) or the Disabled Drivers Motor Club (DDMC); it's well worth enquiring about these in advance as they tend to vary considerably according to season.

In **Northern Ireland**, the very helpful NITB publish a guide to accessible accommodation, and their general guide to restaurants throughout the North highlights those with wheelchair ramps and facilities for disabled people (a nominal fee is charged for both publications). It is also worth contacting Disability Action for their holiday fact sheets which cover access to restaurants, accommodation, equipment and useful contacts.

DIRECTORY

CHILDREN Children are generally liked and indulged in Ireland, even if there are few places actually designed to cater for them. Baby supplies are easily obtained, and children are generally welcome at B&Bs (though few have cots or special facilities), in pubs during the daytime, and almost anywhere else.

CONTRACEPTIVES Throughout Ireland anyone over 18 can buy condoms at pharmacies (though in the Republic, where legal contraception was only introduced in 1992, you may still find places that don't sell them – or don't approve). The pill is available on prescription only.

ELECTRICITY In the Republic, electricity is 230V AC, in the North 240V AC. Plugs everywhere are British-style three square pins (just occasionally you may still find old round ones). In other words British appliances will work everywhere; North American ones will need both a transformer and a plug adapter; Australian and New Zealand appliances only an adapter.

LAUNDRY You'll find laundries only in the bigger towns and on large caravan/campsites. Hostels, though, will often have a washing machine for residents' use, and at many B&Bs they'll do your washing for you. Elsewhere it's worth taking along a tube of Travel Wash – designed to be used in hotel washbasins – which makes a lot less mess than powder.

TIPPING AND SERVICE CHARGE Tipping in restaurants in both the Republic and the North is at your discretion; if you are happy with the level of service and the meal, it is customary to leave an additional fifteen percent of the total bill.

TOILETS Public toilets are reasonably common in all the big towns, and generally acceptably clean, if no more. Or you can pop into the local pub, and stop for a drink while there. The Irish labels to look out for are *Fír* (Men) and *Mna* (Women).

WORK EU citizens are legally allowed to live and work in Ireland and most towns of any size will have a job centre advertising vacancies. Plenty of jobs are available in Dublin for waiters/waitresses, especially in the Temple Bar area. Another option for travellers is seasonal work in resorts or perhaps helping out in a hostel in return for board and pocket money. You'll need to search locally.

PART TWO

THE GUIDE

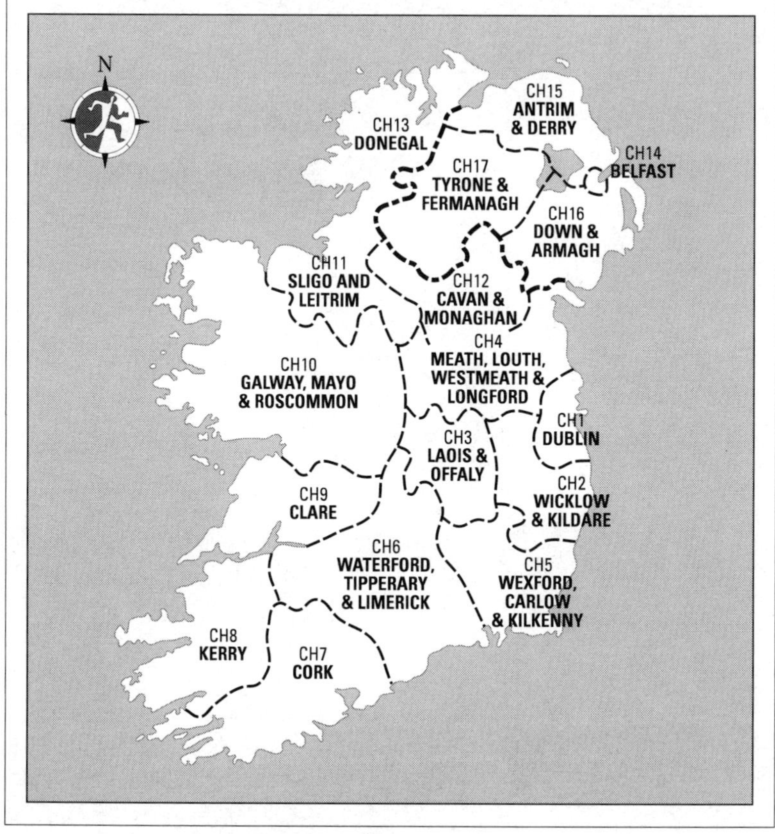

CHAPTER ONE

DUBLIN

Dubliners are fiercely proud of their city, and while **DUBLIN** is the Republic of Ireland's capital it is quite apart from, and can be dismissive of, the rest of the country – one Dublin wag once remarked with characteristic caustic humour that "the only culture outside Dublin is agriculture". Over the past decade, as young people from rural Ireland and all over Europe, gravitate toward the city to share in the wealth, not experienced since Dublin's much celebrated Georgian heyday, this urban/rural divide has started to wane. As a result Dublin exudes the style and confidence of any cosmopolitan European capital – most apparent at night when Dubliners party with a panache verging on the reckless. Dublin's economic upturn is impacting on the city's rapidly changing urban landscape too, with restaurants, cafés, bars and clubs opening in abundance, and Dublin's famous pub scene is now matched by an equally celebrated club scene. On the downside, however, its reputation as one of the party capitals of Europe has attracted droves of "alco-tourists" who arrive in the city for booze-fuelled weekends; they have become such a problem that some areas of the city, such as Temple Bar, have actually banned stag and hen parties.

The continual drift of population from the land to the capital has brought its fair share of problems too as Dublin is now bulging at the seams. Spend just a couple of days here and you'll come upon traffic congestion and inner-city deprivation as bad as any in Europe. The spirit of Dublin is undergoing massive upheavals too, with youthful enterprise set against a leaden traditionalism that harks back nostalgically, as in the words of one popular folk song, to "Dublin city in the rare old times". However, the collision of the old order and the forward-looking younger generations is an essential part of the appeal of this extrovert and dynamic city.

If you approach Dublin by sea, you'll have an opportunity to appreciate its magnificent physical setting, with the fine sweep of **Dublin Bay** and the weird, conical silhouettes of the Wicklow Mountains to the south providing an exhilarating backdrop. Central Dublin is not big, and it's easy to find your way around. One obvious axis is formed by the river, the **Liffey**, which runs from west to east and acts not only as a physical, but also a social and, at times, psychological dividing line. The **northside**, distinctly working class, with some areas blighted by unemployment and drugs, stands in stark contrast to the affluent neighbourhoods of the **southside**.

The transformation to top of Europe's economic class has cast the city economically and culturally into the heart of the continent. This new-found cosmopolitan chic has its

ACCOMMODATION PRICE CODES

Throughout this book, prices of hotels, guesthouses and B&Bs have been graded with the codes below, according to what you can expect to pay for a double room in high season. For more details on accommodation, see p.34.

① Under £26/€33.01	④ £40–55/€50.79–69.84	⑦ £90–110/€114.28–139.67
② £26–33/€33.01–41.90	⑤ £55–70/€69.84–88.88	⑧ £110–130/€139.67–165.07
③ £33–40/€41.90–50.79	⑥ £70–90/€88.88–114.28	⑨ Over £130/€165.07

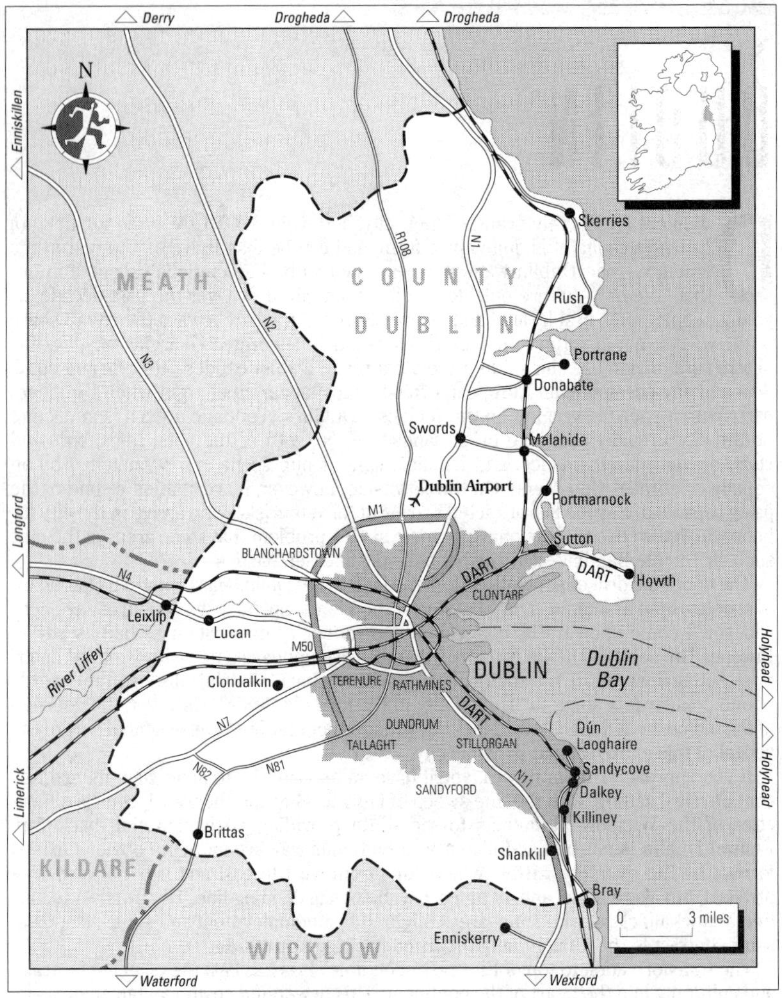

home in the vibrant **Temple Bar** area, "Dublin's Left Bank", with its numerous pubs, clubs, galleries and restaurants. However, for many visitors, the city's heart lies around the best of what is left of Georgian Dublin – the grand set pieces of **Fitzwilliam** and **Merrion** squares, and their graceful red-brick houses with ornate, fan-lighted doors and immaculately kept central gardens, and the wide but strangely decorous open space of St Stephen's Green. The elegant southside is also the setting for Dublin's august seat of learning, Trinity College and its famous library where you can see the exquisitely ornate *Book of Kells*; **Grafton Street**, the city's upmarket shopping area; and most of the city's museums and art galleries.

North of the Liffey, the main thoroughfare is **O'Connell Street**, on which stands the **General Post Office**, the scene of violent fighting in the Easter Rising of 1916.

Further north, among Georgian squares older and seedier than the ones you'll see on the southside, are the **Dublin Writers' Museum** and the **Hugh Lane Gallery**. West again, and you come to Dublin's biggest open space – indeed, one of the world's largest city parks – **Phoenix Park**, home of both the President's Residence and the zoo.

The urban sprawl quickly gives way to the genteel villages which punctuate the curve of Dublin Bay, from the fishing port of **Howth** in the north, to the southern suburbs of **Sandycove** with its James Joyce connections, **Dalkey**, made famous by the comic writer Flann O'Brien, and salubrious **Killiney**, now colonized by the rich and famous. Added to this is the fact that Dublin must be one of the easiest capitals to escape from, making it a good base for exploring the hills and coastline of Wicklow to the south and the gentler scenery to the north that leads up to the megalithic monuments of the verdant **Boyne Valley**.

Some history

Fort of the Dane
Garrison of the Saxon
Augustan capital
Of a Gaelic nation

Louis MacNeice
from *The Closing Album*, 1939.

Although the earliest evidence of a settlement beside the Liffey is on Ptolemy's celebrated map of 140 AD, which shows a place called Eblana on the site of modern Dublin, it is as a Viking settlement that Dublin's history really begins. The Norse raiders sailed up the Liffey and, destroying a small Celtic township, set up a trading post on the south bank of the river at the ford where the royal road from the Hill of Tara in the north crossed the Liffey on its way to Wicklow. The Vikings adopted the Irish name, Dubh Linn ("Dark Pool"), for their settlement, which soon amalgamated with another Celtic settlement, Baile Átha Cliath ("town of the hurdles", pronounced *Ballya-aw-kleea*, and still the Irish name for Dublin), on the north bank.

The next wave of invaders were the **Anglo-Normans**. In the twelfth century, the opportunistic Strongbow and a band of Welsh knights were sent over by Henry II in response to the beleaguered King of Leinster, Dermot McMurrough's request for help to regain his throne from the High King Rory O'Connor; in return he gave an oath of fealty. The invasion was successful, and the English king, concerned that Strongbow and his Welsh adventurers were becoming too powerful, fixed a court at Dublin. The city was thereby established as the centre of British influence in Ireland and set the precedent for the annual social and political gathering, known as the Seasons, which were to shape Dublin's role and character for the next seven centuries.

Because most of the early city was built of wood, only the two cathedrals, part of the Castle, and one or two churches have survived from before the seventeenth century. What you see today, in both plan and buildings, dates essentially from the **Georgian period**. By this time, soldiers in the service of the English monarchs, who had been rewarded with confiscated land, had begun to derive income from their new estates. As they began to replace their original fortified houses with something more fashionable, they wished also to participate in the country's burgeoning economic and political life, which was centred on Dublin. Their town houses (along with those of the growing business and professional classes), and the grandeur of the public buildings erected during this period, embodied the new confidence of the **British ruling class**. However, this was a group that was starting to regard itself not as British, but as Irish.

In the second half of the eighteenth century the wealth of this Anglo-Irish class was reflected in a **rich cultural life**; Handel's *Messiah*, for instance, was first performed in Ireland, while much of the architecture, furniture and silverware associated with the city dates from this period. Growing political freedom was to culminate in the parliament of 1782 in which Henry Grattan made a famous **Declaration of Rights**, modelled on the recent American example, which came very close to declaring Irish (by which he meant Protestant Anglo-Irish) independence. A severely limited and precarious enterprise, the Irish bid for self-government was soon to collapse, with the abortive **1798 Rebellion** and the **Act of Union** which followed in 1801.

The Act of Union may have shorn Dublin of its independent political power, but the city remained the centre of British administration, in the shape of the Vice Regent, and the Seasons continued to revolve around the Viceroy's Lodge (now the President's Residence) in Phoenix Park. Along with the rest of Ireland, Dublin entered a long **economic decline** and became the stage for much of the agitation that eventually led to Independence. The first step towards self-government came in 1829, when the Catholic lawyer (and Kerryman) Daniel O'Connell achieved limited Catholic emancipation, allowing Catholics to play some part in the administration and politics of their capital city and, in a signal victory, was elected Lord Mayor of Dublin. The city was also the centre of the **Gaelic League**, which, founded by Douglas Hyde in 1893, encouraged the formation of an Irish national consciousness through efforts to restore the native language and culture. This paved the way for the **Celtic literary revival** under W.B. Yeats and Lady Gregory and the establishment, in 1904, of the Abbey Theatre.

While political violence in nineteenth-century Dublin revolved around the independence issue, it was social politics, most especially the fight for the establishment of trade unionism, that resulted, at the turn of the century, in Dubliners taking to the streets in protest. In 1913, this came to a head in the **Great Lock-Out**, when forcibly unemployed workers and their families died of hunger and cold. Open violence hit the streets during Easter Week of **1916** in the uprising that was the main event in the long struggle for Irish independence. The prominent battles were fought in and around the centre of Dublin, and the insurgents made the General Post Office their headquarters (see p.96). The city's streets were once again the scene of violence during the brief **Civil War** that broke out after the creation of the Irish Free State in 1921, when supporters and opponents of the **partition** of Ireland fought it out across the Liffey, and the Four Courts, one of Dublin's great Georgian buildings, went up in flames after being seized by opponents of the Anglo-Irish Treaty.

The history of Dublin since Independence has been that of the capital of an old country yet a young nation endeavouring to leave behind its colonial past. It's to this, as well as the appalling condition of many of the old tenements, that the destruction of much of the Georgian city can be attributed. A corollary of the demolition of the city's Georgian buildings in the 1960s was the decanting of Dubliners to inadequately planned suburban estates, which today are blighted by some of the worst social conditions in Europe. Since the mid 1980s city planners have been aimed to reverse this trend of inner-city depopulation, with new apartment blocks being built in previously run-down areas to cater for the city's burgeoning and increasingly affluent middle classes.

One of the outstanding architectural successes of recent years has been the **new development** at **Temple Bar** (see p.87), which has done much to enhance the image and atmosphere of the city. Indeed, Dublin now has a new feel to it, a sense that the legacy of its colonial relationship with Britain has finally been put to one side, as the capital, along with the rest of the Republic, looks increasingly to Europe and America, rather than across the Irish Sea.

Arrival, information and transport

Buses from out of town, the airport included, will drop you at or close by the **Central Bus Station**, or Busáras (☎836 6111), in Store Street, behind the Custom House. Right by the river, this is dead central for almost anywhere in the city and is one of the few places you can leave luggage during the day (£2–3/€2.54–3.81). The city is served by two main **train stations**: Connolly and Heuston (☎836 6222). The former is on Amiens Street, behind the bus depot, while Heuston Station is in the west of the city just south of the river from Phoenix Park.

Coming in from the **airport**, six miles north of the centre, you can take the official airport bus for £3.50/€4.44 or a scheduled city bus (#41A or #41C) will do the same job for £1.15/€1.46. Either takes around half an hour to reach the bus station. Alternatively, a taxi will cost you not more than £12/€15.24. If you arrive by **ferry**, you'll come in at one of two harbours: Dún Laoghaire (pronounced *Learey*; for Stena Line services), six miles south, is on the efficient DART (Dublin Area Rapid Transport) city train network, which will whisk you into town in about twenty minutes; Dublin Port (Irish Ferries/B&I), one mile east of the centre itself, is served by local buses #53 and #53A, though it is common for coaches from the UK to continue to Busáras in Store Street. For information on leaving the city see "Listings", p.122.

The telephone code for Dublin is ☎01.

Information

Dublin Tourism's main office is housed in a converted church on Suffolk Street (July & Aug Mon–Sat 8.30am–6.30pm, Sun 10.30am–3pm; rest of year Mon–Sat 9am–5.30pm; ☎1850 230330, *www.visitdublin.com*). The office is always incredibly busy, but it has much of the most frequently needed information posted on the walls, and a vast collection of literature and maps (not all of it is free), as well as a bookshop and café. A room-booking service for accommodation in Dublin is also available and costs £3/€3.81, although if you have a credit card you can avoid the queues by using the private booking service recommended by Bord Fáilte (☎1800 668 668) instead for the same price. Other branches of Dublin Tourism's offices are at Dublin Airport (daily 8am–10pm; ☎844 5977), the port at Dún Laoghaire (opening times vary according to ferry times, minimum hours daily 9am–8pm; ☎284 6361) and at Dublin Port (June–Aug for ferry arrivals). Bord Fáilte has a much smaller office at Baggot St Bridge (9am–5.15pm; ☎1850 230330, *www.ireland.travel.ie*). An excellent branch of the Northern Ireland Tourist Board at 16 Nassau St (☎1850 230 230, *www.ni-tourism.com*), provides a high standard of service.

The **USIT office** is situated on Aston Quay just opposite O'Connell Bridge (Mon–Fri 9am–5.30pm, Sat 10am–1pm; ☎602 1600, *www.usitnow.ie*). USIT not only books bed and breakfasts during the summer but also has its own hostel, budget hotel and a travel agency offering student discounts on ferries and flights. Call in here for Travelsave stamps (see p.22), ISIC cards and information on everything that's going on in Dublin.

For **listings** of Dublin events, the best sources are the fortnightly magazine *In Dublin*, which you can pick up from any newsagent, and the *Dublin Event Guide*, free from the tourist office and most cafés around the city. *The Irish Times* and *Evening Herald* have theatre and cinema listings daily; the former also does a good weekly overview in its Saturday edition.

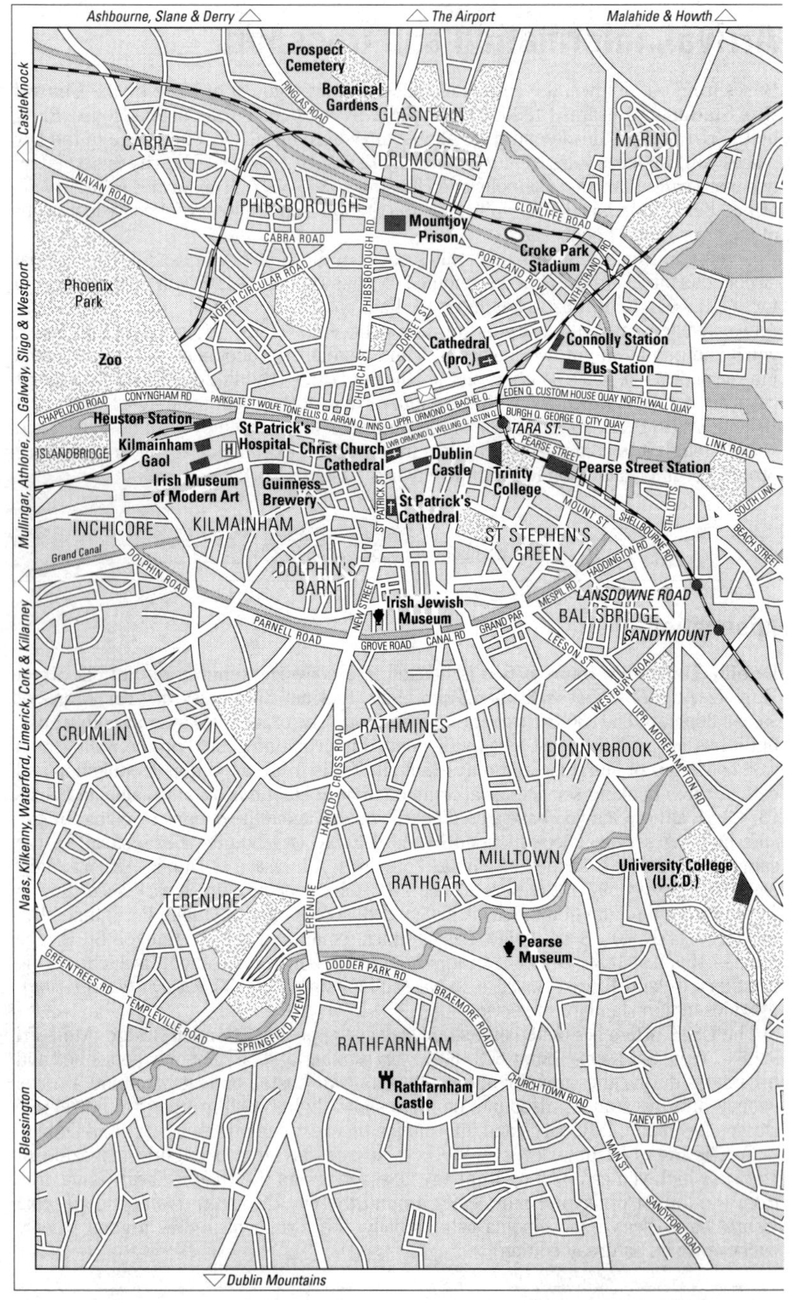

Ashbourne, Slane & Derry
The Airport
Malahide & Howth
CastleKnock
Mullingar, Athlone, Galway, Sligo & Westport
Naas, Kilkenny, Waterford, Limerick, Cork & Killarney
Blessington
Dublin Mountains
Prospect Cemetery
Botanical Gardens
GLASNEVIN
FINGLAS ROAD
CABRA
DRUMCONDRA
MARINO
NAVAN ROAD
PHIBSBOROUGH
Mountjoy Prison
CLONLIFFE ROAD
CABRA ROAD
Croke Park Stadium
PORTLAND ROW
NTH STRAND RD
NORTH CIRCULAR ROAD
PHIBSBOROUGH RD
DORSET ST
Phoenix Park
Zoo
CHURCH ST
Cathedral (pro.)
Connolly Station
Bus Station
CHAPELIZOD ROAD
CONYNGHAM RD
PARKGATE ST WOLFE TONE ELLIS Q. ARRAN Q. INNS Q. UPPR. ORMOND Q. BACHEL Q.
EDEN Q. CUSTOM HOUSE QUAY NORTH WALL QUAY
LWR ORMOND Q. WELLING Q. ASTON Q.
BURGH Q. GEORGE Q. CITY QUAY
Heuston Station
TARA ST.
St Patrick's Hospital
ISLANDBRIDGE
Kilmainham Gaol
Christ Church Cathedral
Dublin Castle
Trinity College
PEARSE STREET
Pearse Street Station
LINK ROAD
Irish Museum of Modern Art
Guinness Brewery
ST PATRICK ST
St Patrick's Cathedral
MOUNT ST
SHELLBOURNE RD
STH. LOTTS
SOUTH LINK
INCHICORE
KILMAINHAM
ST STEPHEN'S GREEN
BEACH STREET
Grand Canal
DOLPHIN ROAD
DOLPHIN'S BARN
HADDINGTON RD
MESPIL RD
LANSDOWNE ROAD
NEW STREET
Irish Jewish Museum
BALLSBRIDGE
PARNELL ROAD
GRAND PAR
SANDYMOUNT
GROVE ROAD
CANAL RD
LEESON ST
WESTBURY ROAD
UPR. MOREHAMPTON RD
CRUMLIN
HAROLDS CROSS ROAD
RATHMINES
DONNYBROOK
MILLTOWN
University College (U.C.D.)
RATHGAR
TERENURE
TERENURE
Pearse Museum
GREENTREES RD
DODDER PARK RD
BRAEMORE ROAD
TEMPLEVILLE ROAD
SPRINGFIELD AVENUE
RATHFARNHAM
CHURCH TOWN ROAD
Rathfarnham Castle
TANEY ROAD
MAIN ST
SANDYFORD ROAD

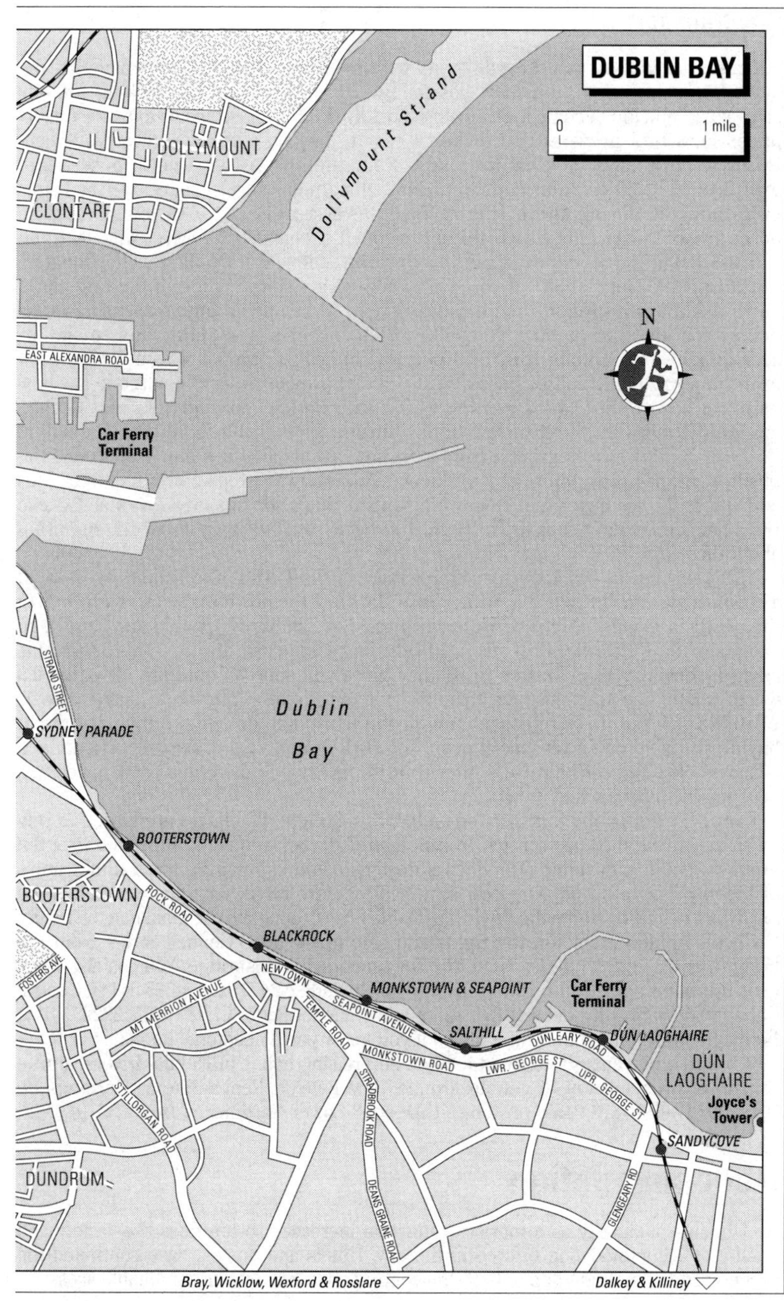
DUBLIN BAY
0
1 mile
N
Dollymount Strand
DOLLYMOUNT
CLONTARF
EAST ALEXANDRA ROAD
Car Ferry Terminal
Dublin Bay
STRAND STREET
SYDNEY PARADE
BOOTERSTOWN
BOOTERSTOWN
ROCK ROAD
BLACKROCK
FOSTERS AVE
NEWTOWN
MONKSTOWN & SEAPOINT
Car Ferry Terminal
SEAPOINT AVENUE
TEMPLE ROAD
MT MERRION AVENUE
SALTHILL
DUNLEARY ROAD
DÚN LAOGHAIRE
MONKSTOWN ROAD
LWR. GEORGE ST
UPR. GEORGE ST
DÚN LAOGHAIRE
Joyce's Tower
STILLORGAN ROAD
STRADBROOK ROAD
SANDYCOVE
GLENGEARY RD
DUNDRUM
DEANSGRAINE ROAD
Bray, Wicklow, Wexford & Rosslare
Dalkey & Killiney

City transport

It's customary to say that the way to get to know Dublin is to walk. It's true that the city's size makes this a practical possibility, but equally true that walking the city streets can quickly become a tiring slog. Luckily there's an extensive and reasonably priced local **bus network** that makes it easy to hop on a bus whenever you want. Buses start running between 6am and 6.30am, and the last city-centre buses leave town around 11.30pm. After midnight a limited night-bus service takes over and runs every hour. Maximum fare on the daytime bus system is £1.15/€1.46 and since all buses are exact fare only it's worth carrying a lot of change (the driver will issue you with a ticket in lieu of change, which can only be redeemed at Dublin Bus headquaters on 59 Upper O'Connell St.). If you don't know which stop to go to in the first place, either ask a bus inspector – there usually seems to be one around, dispensing directions – or invest in a bus timetable, which includes a **Dublin bus map**, for £1.50/€1.90 from Dublin Bus, 59 Upper O'Connell St (Mon–Fri 9am–5.15pm, Sat 9am–1pm; ☎873 4222 for city buses, ☎836 6111 for provincial services). A one-day bus-only pass costs £3.50/€4.44; an Explorer Ticket, a one-day bus-and-train pass (including DART) costs £5.20/€6.60; a four-day version of the latter is better value still at £10/€12.70. Passes are available from most newsagents. Finding your way around the bus system may prove more of a problem, although most stops now have timetables and routes for the buses that stop there. Dublin Bus also runs **city tours** and cheap **trips** outside Dublin to places the regular services don't visit, so it's worth enquiring about these.

The other useful city transportation service is the **DART**, the Dublin Area Rapid Transport system (☎836 6222), which links Howth to the north of the city with Bray to the south in County Wicklow, via such places as Sandycove, Monkstown and Dún Laoghaire. DART services are quick, efficient and easy to use, and the stretch that runs along Dublin Bay from Dalkey to Killiney gives you such an amazing view that it's worth taking the train just for that. It's not expensive – maximum single fare is £1.70/€2.15 – but if you're considering taking more than one or two trips, it's worth buying an Explorer Ticket (see above). The DART runs from 6.55am to 11.30pm and is accessible to wheelchair users, though in some stations there is a pronounced gap between the platform and the coach.

Because most public transport stops before midnight, Dubliners are forced to rely on an oversubscribed taxi service. Recent limited deregulation has helped alleviate the problem, but long post-midnight lines at designated ranks remain a frustrating feature of the city's night scene. The best served city-centre ranks are situated outside the *Shelbourne Hotel* on St Stephen's Green, Dame Street (opposite the main gate of Trinity College), Abbey Street (on the right-hand side going up O'Connell Street from the bridge), or close to *Jurys Hotel* and *The Towers* hotel in Ballsbridge. You can also book taxis by phone; some of the more reliable firms include ABC Taxis (☎285 5444), Central Cabs (☎365 555), City Cabs (☎872 7272) and National Radio Cabs (☎677 2222; 24hr). Finding a taxi after 11pm is difficult, so if you know you'll need one, book it.

If you're brave enough to face the often hair-raising habits of Dublin drivers, a **bike** can prove a useful way of getting around. Try Raleigh Rent-a-Bike at Hardings on Bachelor Walk (☎873 2455) or Rent-A-Bike at 58 Lower Gardiner St (☎872 5399).

Accommodation

As Dublin's popularity as a tourist destination increases so too does the variety and quality of accommodation offered in the city. Hotels and hostels have continued the recent trend of springing up in both the centre and previously unfashionable areas.

Generally, prices are cheaper on the northside and anywhere out of the centre. **Hotels** in Dublin are mostly expensive and sometimes no more comfortable than good guesthouses, but if you're travelling out of season, it's worth checking reductions, which can be considerable. Also, many swanky hotels drop their tariffs at the weekends when the business types have gone home. **B&Bs** are plentiful and of a high standard in the suburbs, but central B&Bs can be overpriced. If you're determined to be right at the heart of the action, and you are on a fairly limited budget, various well-organized official and private **youth hostels** are the cheapest option; most have some private rooms. Dublin Tourism's main office in Suffolk Street (see p.61) has lists of most places that are available, though there are many good options that, for various reasons, neither have nor want tourist-board recommendation. In summer it is highly advisable to book ahead, and imperative to do so on weekends.

Hotels

Dublin's hotels are on the whole rather pricey, but if you are looking for luxury, Georgian elegance and good food, there are a number to choose from.

North of the Liffey

Chief O'Neills, Smithfield, Smithfield Village (☎817 3838, fax 817 3839, *www.chiefoneills.ie*). This hotel is dedicated to a New York police commissioner (the eponymous Police Chief O'Neill) who collected traditional Irish music. With this as its theme it would have been easy for the designers to rely on the ubiquitous twee folksy aesthetic; things could not be further from the truth. This is an ultra-stylish, progressively designed hotel with bedrooms that are all simple lines with plenty of light and lots of high-tech gadgetry. The downside is that they are a little cramped and you get the feeling (most especially in the bathroom) that style takes priority over function. ⑨.

Gresham Hotel, 20–22 Upper O'Connell St (☎874 6881, fax 878 7175, *www.ryan-hotels.com*). First opened in 1817, the *Gresham* has since competed with the *Shelbourne* for the title of Dublin's most luxurious hotel. The rooms are spacious, colourful and well furnished, though one of the great strengths of the *Gresham* is the courteousness of its staff, a legacy of catering for Ireland's elite over a number of decades. If you are feeling a little romantic follow the example of Elizabeth Taylor and Richard Burton and take the penthouse for two months. ⑨.

Hotel Isaacs, Store St (☎855 0067, *www.isaacs.ie*). This hotel is aimed at those seeking affordable hotel accommodation. The building itself is spacious and light, the rooms comfortable and clean, and the price includes the standard fried breakfast. It's conveniently located directly opposite the bus depot and around the corner from Connolly train station. ⑥.

Jurys Custom House Inn, Custom House Quay (☎607 5000, *www.jurysdoyle.com*). Jurys' hotels have gained a reputation for high standards at affordable prices; this addition on the north east quay is no exception. Formerly a run-down dock area, the north quays are now flourishing with the Financial Services Centre at its hub, and, not surprisingly, *Jurys Custom House* is more business focused with fax and modem lines in the larger rooms. It also offers rooms that can accommodate up to four people, which make it a good family option. ⑥.

Morrison Hotel, Lower Ormond Quay (☎878 2999, fax 878 3185, *www.morrisonhotel.ie*). Dublin's trendiest residents are now tentatively tiptoeing across the new Millennium footbridge, into the unchartered waters of the city's northside, to frequent the city's most fashionable hangout with its very mellow bar, the *Morrison*. The creation of international designer John Rocha, it's an intoxicating mix of styles, with the understated bedrooms – all equipped with CD players and ISDN lines – contrasting with the extravagantly flamboyant public areas, and the equally flamboyant patrons who people them. ⑨.

Ormond Quay Hotel, Upper Ormond Quay (☎872 1811, fax 872 1362, *www.ormondqh.chamberwire.com*). An old hotel, formerly inhabitated by priests, barristers and, on the odd occasion, their clients (the Courthouse is next door). Joyce makes mention of the hotel in *Ulysses*, comparing the staff to Sirens, a theme used in the hotel's bar/restaurant. The hotel was recently refurbished to a high standard, and the bright, comfortable rooms, many overlooking the river, are adequately insulated from the constant stream of traffic along the busy quays. ⑥.

St Stephen's Green area

Buswell's, 23–27 Molesworth St (☎614 6500, fax 676 2090, *www.quinn-group.com*). A comfortable, well-run hotel in a Georgian terrace. Although recently renovated, the hotel retains its charm and style with ornamental fireplaces, antique furnishings and cosy bedrooms. ⑨.

Longfield's Hotel, 9–10 Fitzwilliam St East Lower (☎676 1367, fax 676 1542, *lfields@indigo.ie*). A small, friendly hotel, right in the heart of Georgian Dublin. *Longfield's* has the feel of a country guesthouse with period furnishings in both the rooms and public areas, welcoming open fires, and an excellent restaurant serving a mix of hearty French and Irish dishes. ⑧.

Merrion Hotel, Upper Merrion St (☎603 0600, fax 603 0700, *www.merrionhotel.com*) Situated opposite the government buildings is the latest jewel in Dublin's increasingly extravagant hotel crown. Centred on a Grade 1 Georgian town house, the *Merrion* has recently seen the addition of a beautifully executed garden wing, which houses one of the most important collections of contemporary Irish art in the country. The elegant bedrooms not only retain the style of the Georgian period, from crisp linen bedsheets to Italian marble bathrooms, but also cater for the needs of the modern traveller, with fax and Internet access as well as a minibar and a safe. ⑨.

Mont Clare, Merrion Square (☎607 3800, fax 661 5663, *montclares@ocallaghanhotels.ie*). Close to the National Gallery is the recently refurbished *Mont Clare*. The contemporary interior has generously-proportioned, well-furnished rooms with cool marble bathrooms. It's worth checking out the excellent weekend discounts offered here. ⑦.

The Old Schoolhouse, 2–8 Northumberland Rd, Ballsbridge (☎667 5014, *www.schoolhousehotel.com*). Set in a former derelict schoolhouse that was traditionally a landmark near the city's Grand Canal, this tastefully refurbished hotel offers modern, well-furnished rooms. The restaurant here is first rate, and a busy bar (especially on Sunday afternoons) sees patrons spilling out into the gardens. ⑥.

Shelbourne Méridien Hotel, St Stephen's Green North (☎676 6471, fax 661 6006, *www.shelbourne.ie*). Despite all the new kids on the block, it is the *Shelbourne* that retains the title as "the" hotel in Dublin. From the magnificent faux-marble entrance to the exquisite Waterford crystal chandeliers and Irish Chippendale furniture, the *Shelbourne* exudes style and history – it was here, in room 112, that the Irish constitution was drafted in 1921. The rooms are incredibly chic, with many of the older ones displaying pieces from the hotel's impressive antique collection. Those to the front of the hotel offer fine views over St Stephens Green, but can be a little noisy. ⑨.

Temple Bar and around

Adams Trinity, 28 Dame Lane (☎670 7100, fax 670 7101). A small hotel near Dublin Castle, with a generous welcome and comfortable rooms. Double-glazed windows manage to cut out most of the noise from the busy street below, and fine breakfasts are served in a gallery overlooking the bar. The hotel offers good weekend reductions, especially on its triple rooms, which may prove ideal for families. ⑦.

Bewley's, 19–20 Fleet St (☎670 8122, fax 670 8103, *bewleyshotel@eircom.net*). Small, friendly hotel next to the excellent *Palace Bar* on the edges of Temple Bar. The staff are exceptionally friendly and the old-style decor matches that of the famous *Bewley's* café below. The rooms are comfortable, though in summer the hotel can be a little airless. ⑦.

Central Hotel, 1–5 Exchequer St (☎679 7302, fax 679 7303, *reservations@centralhotel.ie*). This popular hotel, located amongst the red-bricked buildings of Victorian Exchequer Street, makes a perfect base for exploring the city. Bright colours throughout give the hotel a cheery feel. A pleasant lounge features contemporary Irish paintings. Of the two fine bars, *The Library* is popular with locals seeking a sanctuary from the increasingly hectic streets outside. ⑧.

The Clarence Hotel, 6–8 Wellington Quay (☎670 9000, fax 670 7800, *clarence@indigo.ie*). Originally opened in 1852, and now owned by U2, the *Clarence* was renowned as a popular clerical hangout, though these days the only cleric one might meet here is Mother Bernadette Mary (aka Sinead O'Connor). Further to extensive refurbishment, it's now a temple to ultra-modern design. A leather-lined lift leads to the smallish, though comfortable rooms all of which come with Egyptian linen. The hotel is home to the *Kitchen* nightclub, and the award-winning *Tea Rooms* restaurant. ⑨.

Harding Hotel, Copper Alley, Fishamble St (☎679 6500, fax 679 6504, *harding.hotel@usitworld.com*). On the fringes of Temple Bar, this bright, modern hotel is owned and run by the student travel company USIT, and thus aims to provide decent hotel accommodation to those travelling on a budget. The en-suite rooms are very comfortable, and since many accommodate up to three people they can prove excellent value for money; all are wheelchair accessible. ⑤.

Jurys Hotel, Christchurch Place (☎454 0000, fax 454 0012, *www.jurys.com*). A rather ugly building opposite Christchurch Cathedral. On the plus side, it's close to St Patrick's Cathedral, the Guinness factory and the Irish Museum of Modern Art. While not as comfortable as other branches in the city, the standards here are quite high, and, as with all Jurys' hotels, the flat rate for rooms makes it a good option for anyone travelling with small children. ⑥.

Temple Bar Hotel, 13–17 Fleet St (☎677 3333, fax 677 3088, *www.towerhotelgroup.ie*). A modern hotel, ideally placed for exploring the Temple Bar area. Rooms are larger than average with single and double beds, and excellent bathrooms with marble basins. Breakfast is served in a pleasant glass-roofed dining room. Triples are available, with under-12s staying for free, and there are reductions offered on weekend breaks. ⑧.

Ballsbridge

Berkeley Court, Lansdowne Rd (☎660 1711, fax 661 7238, *berkeleycourt@doylehotels.com*). The glass and concrete exterior disguise the inner elegance of this five-star hotel, set in its own grounds, in the heart of fashionable Dublin 4. Huge chandeliers light the elegant foyer, while the rooms are large and brightly painted with marble-tiled bathrooms. ⑨.

Jurys Hotel and The Towers, Pembroke Rd (☎660 5000, or 667 0033, *www.jurys.com*) Formerly two hotels *Jurys* and the *Towers* have been amalgamated, though both retain a distinct identity. *Jurys* is a huge, modern complex whose comfortable, spacious, though somewhat bland rooms, have become popular with the business community. The *Towers* has a warmer ambience, more suited to holidaymakers; rooms here are larger, and the wood finish, warm colours and comfy furniture give it a homely feel. ⑦.

Mount Herbert Guest House (☎668 4321, *www.mountherberthotel.ie*). A large hotel made up of several Victorian houses, and one of the less expensive options in this upmarket southside neighbourhood. The rooms are basic, though brightly painted, and all have TV and en-suite bathrooms. The house offers a play area for children. The restaurant serves hearty, if a little uninspiring, food. ⑦.

Dalkey and Killiney

The Court Hotel, Killiney Bay, Killiney (☎285 1622, fax 285 2085, *www.killineycourt.ie*). Large Victorian-style hotel set in pleasant grounds close to the DART station. The rooms are basic but comfortable with en-suite bathrooms and TVs, though try to secure one with a view of the sea. Check for weekend or family reductions. The hotel boasts two restaurants, one of which specializes in fish dishes. ⑥.

Fitzpatrick Castle Hotel, Killiney (☎284 0700, fax 285 0207, *www.fitzpatrickhotels.com*). A former stately home, with its own battlements, perched on the edge of Killiney Hill. Not surprisingly, many of the rooms offer fine, bay views, but for a real panorama head up the hill behind the hotel. The spacious rooms exude elegance, many with four-poster beds and antique furnishings, and the hotel has an excellent family-friendly policy with good child reductions and crèche facilities. Breakfast is not included in the price. ⑨.

Dún Laoghaire

Kingston Hotel, Adelaide St (☎280 1810, fax 280 1237, *www.kingstonhotel.com*). Don't be put off by the dreary facade of this large Victorian hotel as the inside is both welcoming and comfortable. The pale green rooms, while not luxurious, are adequate, with many overlooking the sea. This is a family friendly hotel that can prove a bargain if you book one of the rooms that sleep five people. ⑥.

Royal Marine Hotel, Royal Marine Rd (☎280 1911, fax 280 1089, *ryan@indigo.ie*). Built in 1870, the *Royal* Marine is a definite throwback to the nineteenth century, when Dún Laoghaire was a chic holiday resort. Although recently modernized, the hotel retains much of its former elegance: from the marble-floored foyer to the splendid bay-window suites with four-poster beds and antique furniture. The other rooms are a little more mundane, though many have magnificent bay views. ⑨.

Guesthouses and Bed and Breakfast

Bed and Breakfast places abound in Dublin, with the cheapest clustered around Connolly Station, especially on Gardiner Street, on the northside. In the south there are more salubrious, and more expensive, guesthouses in the Ballsbridge area, still within easy walking distance of the centre. The best balance between price and quality, though, generally involves staying further out in the suburbs; given the relatively small scale of the city, these places are definitely the better option.

Gardiner Street and around

Gardiner Street has the advantage of being close to both the bus (Busáras) and train (Connolly) stations, with bus #41 from the airport stopping on the street. However, it is prone to car theft and anyone with a car should consider whether or not secure car parking is available. Formerly, Lower Gardiner Street had a poor reputation and, although some pretty dingy places still remain, there is also a lot of excellent accommodation at reasonable prices.

Anchor Guest House, 49 Lower Gardiner St (☎878 6913, fax 878 8038, *www.anchorguesthouse.com*). Tastefully refurbished Georgian house offering comfortable rooms with TV and phone. A limited amount of parking is available, but be sure to book this in advance as street parking is not recommended. Discounts for children; infants free. ⑤.

Celtic Lodge Guesthouse, 82 Talbot St (☎677 9955, fax 878 8698). New guesthouse on a busy and slightly dowdy street, though only two minutes by foot to O'Connell Street. The en-suite rooms are clean and insulated from street noise. Breakfast is served in a bright canteen. No residents' lounge, but there is a bar. ⑤.

Charleville Lodge, 268–272 North Circular Rd, Phibsborough (☎838 6633, fax 838 5854, *www.charlevillelodge.ie*). One of the northside's best-regarded guesthouses. The en-suite bedrooms are tastefully decorated and the Stenson family serve a fine breakfast to their guests. Parking is available to the rear, and the owners can arrange baby-sitting. ⑥.

Clifden House, 32 Gardiner Place (☎874 6364, fax 874 6122, *www.clifdenhouse.com*). The quality of accommodation and warm hospitality of the owners, ensure this place is held in high regard by its many repeat guests. Don't be put off by the slightly run-down street (just off Mountjoy Square) as the Georgian house itself, with nine pleasant en-suite rooms, has been caringly refurbished. Children are welcome, and a baby-sitting service is available. ⑤.

Marian Guesthouse, 21 Upper Gardiner St (☎874 4129). A clean and friendly place with good breakfasts and no exploitive price hikes or single supplements at peak times. The rooms are basic and bathrooms shared, though this is reflected in the price. Highly recommended to those on a budget, especially lone travellers who want a basic, clean private room, as the rooms here cost little more than a dorm bed nearby. ③.

The Town House, 47–48 Lower Gardiner St (☎878 8808, fax 878 8787, *www.gtrotter@indigo.ie*). A refurbished Georgian house, once the home of playwrights Dion Boucicault and Lafcadio Hearn, which is more like a hotel in terms of ambience and service. There is secure parking, great breakfasts and all rooms are en suite with TV, fridge and tea maker. Beware of a considerable jump in price at the weekend. ⑤.

St Stephen's Green area

Fitzwilliam, 41 Upper Fitzwilliam St (☎660 0448, *info@fitzpark.ie*). Although recently restored, many of the original features of this splendid Georgian house have been preserved. The bedrooms are well equipped, though some, near to the top of the house, are on the small side. The breakfasts are of a high standard, and are all the more enjoyable when served in the opulent Grand Salon on the first floor. ⑥.

Number 31, Leeson Close, off Lower Leeson St (☎676 5011, fax 676 2929, *www.number31.ie*) A little difficult to find, tucked down a small lane off Leeson Street, but well worth the effort. A stylishly converted stable block forms the sitting and breakfast areas of this fine, secluded Georgian guesthouse. The owners' aim was to create the air of a country retreat in the city, and they have succeeded, most especially in the sunken lounge heated by a turf fire. Comfortable rooms and excellent breakfasts. ⑧.

Staunton's on the Green, 83 St Stephen's Green (☎478 2300, fax 478 2263, *hotels@indigo.ie*). An elegant Georgian house fronting onto St Stephen's Green, with private garden to the rear, offering stylish accommodation at a relatively reasonable price. The reception rooms are fine Georgian period pieces, and, while the bedrooms do not reflect the house's former elegance, they are very comfortable. A child-friendly policy with excellent reductions. ⑦.

Ballsbridge and Sandymount

Directly south of the centre, about two miles out, the upmarket inner suburbs of Ballsbridge (on bus routes #5, #6, #6A and #7) and Sandymount (buses #1, #2, #3 and #6) have a high standard of accommodation to offer. Both areas are well served by the DART train (take either the Sandymount, Landsdowne Road or Sydney Parade stops).

Aberdeen Lodge, 53–55 Park Ave, off Ailesbury Rd, Ballsbridge (☎283 8155, fax 283 7877, *aberdeen@iol.ie*). Close to the Sydney Parade DART station near Merrion Road, this large Edwardian house offers all the comforts expected from a stylish hotel. All the rooms are well equipped, but those with a private Jacuzzi offer the ultimate in comfort. Gardens, secure parking and baby-sitting services too. ⑦.

Anglesea Town House, 63 Anglesea Rd, Ballsbridge (☎668 3877). More like a country manor than a city town house, this is a congenial place with a warm welcome from the irrepressible proprietor, Helen Kirrane. The house is Edwardian, and the bedrooms, which retain a period feel (most have the original fireplaces intact), are comfy and spacious. The breakfast, made from home produce, is rightly regarded by many to be the best in the city. Reductions for seniors and children. Closed from December 15 to January 8. ⑦.

Mrs M. Bermingham, 8 Dromard Terrace, Sandymount (☎668 3861). This is a fine, traditional family run guesthouse in an ivy-covered period house near the beach in Sandymount, which has no aspirations beyond offering comfortable, clean rooms, good breakfasts and a warm welcome. A good choice for either a single traveller, or a family on a budget as there are child reductions; the owners also arrange baby-sitting. Closed Oct–April. ③.

Merrion Hall, 56 Merrion Rd, Ballsbridge (☎668 1426, *merrionhall@iol.ie*). This place was recently taken over, and renovated to an equally high standard, by the owners of *Aberdeen Lodge*. Bedrooms are spacious, and there is a comfy sitting-room area. Parking is limited, so it's a good idea to call ahead and reserve a space. Children are welcome, and there is a pleasant garden. ⑥.

Number Eighty-Eight, 88 Pembroke Rd, Ballsbridge (☎660 0277). Situated on stylish Pembroke Road, this makes an excellent base for exploring Dublin. The guesthouse has all the amenities of a good hotel (pool, Jacuzzi, gym, tennis and golf), while retaining personal service. It's advisable to book early as it can fill up with business groups. ⑦.

Glasnevin and Castlenock

The tree-lined Victorian suburbs of Glasnevin, to the north and west of the centre, and Castlenock, to the west of Phoenix Park, are both reasonable places to stay and are not too far from the centre.

Egan's Guesthouse, 7–9 Iona Park, Glasnevin (☎830 3611, fax 830 3312, *www.holiday/ireland.com*). *Egan's* has long been regarded as one of the best northside guesthouse options. The guesthouse is family run, and is situated on a very quiet road in a maze of red-bricked houses. There is car parking to the front of the house, and children are welcome here. Unusually breakfast is extra. ⑤.

Iona House, 5 Iona Park, Glasnevin (☎830 6217, fax 830 6743). Next door to *Egan's*, and signposted from the main Lower Drumcondra Road, is this fine guesthouse with well-furnished rooms (though avoid those to the back of the house on the first floor as they are somewhat cramped). The friendly owner does not apply a supplement for single occupancy. ⑤.

Mrs Mary McKay, *Deerpark House*, Castlenock Rd, near Phoenix Park gates (☎820 7466). The best way to locate this excellent guesthouse is to drive through Phoenix Park to its most westerly gate, Castlenock Gate, and you'll find it just to the right as you exit the park. A large, bright modern house, with conservatories to the front and side, that offers comfortable en-suite rooms, and is family friendly. ③.

Drumcondra and Clontarf

Drumcondra is a popular area, being close to the airport, well served by a number of bus routes (#11, #13 and #16, as well as airport buses), and just a short distance north of both the southside and the suburbs, which are easily reached via the new Drumcondra train link. East from Drumcondra, in Clontarf, you're into suburbia again, but close to the sea. Rates here are generally reasonable, with lots of places to choose from, particularly along the Clontarf Road, which runs right by the seafront. The only drawback is that buses from Clontarf terminate around Talbot Street in the north of the city, so getting to the southside can be time-consuming.

Mrs Maureen Black, 35 Ormond Rd, Drumcondra (☎837 0299). On a very quiet road just off the busy Drumcondra Road – if coming from the airport take the second left after the *Cat and Cage* pub – stands the home of the friendly Maureen Black. The area is as pleasant as the welcome, the rooms are en suite, and the couple who run it are extremely affable. ③.

Drumcondra House, 27 Lower Drumcondra Rd (☎855 0918). Coming from the airport, take the turning left at the railway bridge (emblazoned with the Guinness logo), to reach the new train station, and the house is just opposite. The house has been recently renovated to a very high standard, and has bright en-suite rooms. ③.

Eileen Kelly, *Torc House*, 17 Seacourt, off St Gabriels Rd, Clontarf (☎833 2547). An elegant, detached Georgian house off Seafield Road, which offers two en-suite and one standard room. the house is pleasant, and the Kelly's make fine hosts. Plenty of car parking available. Closed from November to April. ④.

Kathleen Hurney, 69 Hollybank Rd, Drumcondra (☎837 7907). If you are coming from the airport turn right at the popular *Fagan's* pub, onto the quiet red-bricked terrace to reach *Kathleen Hurney's*. The house is cheery and rooms are bright; only two rooms are en suite. Reductions for children. Non-smoking. ③.

The White House, 125 Clontarf Rd (☎833 3196). Very friendly house, with comfortable rooms, near Dublin Bay, that offers excellent value for money, and is on the city centre bus route. Booking early is advisable in the summer months. The breakfast served here is particularly substantial. ④.

Willowbrook, 14 Strandville Ave East, Clontarf (☎833 3115, *willowbrook@ireland.com*). A very comfortable, tastefully decorated house, which has three pleasant en-suite rooms. There is plenty of secure parking space to the front of the house. ④.

Hostels

Dublin's newer hostels tend to market themselves as budget accommodation rather than hostels (they feel there is something slightly pejorative about the term "hostel") and it is fair to say that there is a difference between these and old-fashioned hostels,

GAY-FRIENDLY ACCOMMODATION

Inn on the Liffey, 21 Ormond Quay Upper (☎677 0828, *www.homepage.eircom.net/nthedock/inn*). As the name suggests this guesthouse is found on the northern banks of the river Liffey. The rooms, while small, offer fine views of the river itself and all are en suite. Male customers receive free admission to the Dock, one of the city's most popular saunas. ③.

Frankies, 8 Camden Place (☎478 3087, *www.frankiesguesthouse.com*). Near both Grafton Street and Temple Bar this is a friendly place, though the rooms are on the small side. ⑤.

The Horse and Carriage Hotel, 15 Aungier St (☎478 3537 or 3087). Largest pink hotel in the city, but expect no frills or value for money, though the price does include admission to the Incognito sauna. ⑤.

Tig na mBan – *The Women's House* (☎473 1781). Offers self-catering or B&B near the city centre. ③.

not only in the price and generally higher standard of accommodation, but also in their emphasis on the individual rather than the communal; many have private and double rooms but often no sitting room. The hostels in the centre, especially around Temple Bar, tend to be very lively, so if you need a good night's rest it would be advisable to take one further out.

North of the Liffey

Abbey Hostel, O'Connell Bridge, 29 Bachelors Walk (☎878 0700, fax 878 0719, *www.abbey-court.com*). You can't get more central than this place, just off O'Connell Bridge. Rooms are fitted with a swipe-card security system and have storage cages under every bed. All rooms are en suite, and have excellent showers. There is no curfew, laundry and Internet facilities are available, and there's a large dining room and barbeque area. Dorms range from four- to twelve-bed and begin at £15/€19.05. Breakfast is included in the rates.

Abraham House, 82–83 Lower Gardiner St (IHH; ☎855 0600, fax 855 0598, *www.abraham-house.ie*). Like all hostels in Lower Gardiner Street, this one is handy for Busáras, and in addition, bus #41 from the airport stops outside. It's friendly and clean, with a self-catering kitchen, laundry, bureau de change, free hot showers and no curfew. There's also a secure car park. Four-bed and private rooms available. Dorms begin at £11/€13.97.

Cardijn House (or **Goin' My Way**), 15 Talbot St (IHH; ☎878 8484, *goinmyway@esatclear.ie*). The family run hostel above a newsagents is basic, clean, friendly and affordable, and a five-minute-walk from O'Connell Street. It's certainly not as plush as the new breed of hostel popping up on every street corner, but still maintains its following amongst the "old school" hostelling brigade who enjoy the communal aspect of shared accommodation. The hostel does not have a daytime lockout but is one of the few remaining hostels that does enforce a midnight curfew, suitable for those who want a quiet night's sleep. Closed Dec 20 to end Jan. Dorm bed prices begin at £9/€11.43.

Celts House, 32–33 Blessington St, just off Dorset St (☎ or fax 830 0657). The bright yellow, Georgian door sets the mood for this friendly hostel in the north of the city. Not a custom-made hostel, the converted house is adequate, if a little cramped, though it is a good place for making friends among the small number of guests. Dorm beds from £10/€12.70.

Dublin International Youth Hostel, 61 Mountjoy St (☎830 1766, fax 830 1600, *www.irelandyha.org*). Way up near the Black Church and Upper Dorset Street (bus #41 from the airport), is the northside headquarters of An Óige. This hostel was previously a convent, and it still retains some of the austere feel of its former incarnation. However, it is very well equipped and efficiently run, and attracts members of YHI and An Óige. The neighbourhood around the hostel, while once considered dangerous, has improved in recent years; nevertheless, it still pays to be vigilant at night. There are 460 beds and it is one of the few hostels in the city that offers parking facilities. Dorms from £11/€13.97.

Globetrotters Tourist Hostel, 46 Lower Gardiner St (IHH; ☎874 0592, fax 878 8787, *gtrotter@indigo.ie*). Superlative hostel with security-coded doors, first-rate showers and a breakfast that really sets you up for the day. The dining area is light and spacious and there's a small garden – great in summer. Be careful when booking to specify that it is in the hostel and not the guesthouse that you wish to stay. Dorms from £13/€16.51.

Isaac's Hostel, 2–5 Frenchman's Lane, just round the corner from Busáras (IHH; ☎836 3877, fax 874 1574, *www.isaacs.ie*). Otherwise known as the *Dublin Tourist Hostel*, this hostel is housed in an eighteenth-century wine warehouse, and offers a mix of accommodation, from dormitory bunks to single and double rooms. Breakfast isn't included in the price, but there's a good restaurant. Room lockout is from 11am to 2.30pm. No curfew. Dorms £9.50/€12.06.

Jacob's Inn, 21–28 Talbot Place (☎855 5660, fax 855 5664, *www.isaacs.ie*). Opposite the bus station this is impressive, flashy budget accommodation with lots of the extras, such as a swipe-card security system. All rooms are en suite with good lockers, and there's a decent kitchen. Dorms from £12/€15.24.

Litton Lane, 2–4 Litton Lane (☎872 8389, *www.irish-hostel.com*). This hostel is the younger sister of the excellent *Brewery Hostel* (see p.72), and is of an equally high standard. It's situated off Bachelor's Walk on the northside of the Liffey, and housed in a converted warehouse that was once one of the city's foremost recording studios. The showers are excellent, the hostel is open 24 hours, and there are no problems with security. Dorms £14/€17.78.

MEC Hostel, 44 North Great George's St (☎878 0071, fax 874 6472, *meccles@iol.ie*). A recently renovated hostel on possibly the finest Georgian street on the northside. The friendly staff and impressive Georgian building make this a great place to stay. In addition to dorm beds, self-catering apartments sleeping up to four people are available for around £300/€381.00 a week. Dorms start at £11/€13.97.

Temple Bar area

Barnacles Temple Bar House, Temple Lane (☎671 6277, fax 671 6591, *www.barnacles.ie*). Modern, well-equipped hostel in the centre of Temple Bar. There is no curfew and no lockout, and breakfast is included in the price. It is very popular, so be sure to book in advance. Dorms from £11/€13.97.

Kinlay House, 2–12 Lord Edward St (IHH; ☎679 6644, *www.kinlay.dub.in@usitworld.com*). This relaxed, friendly USIT hostel is well run and has good laundry and kitchen facilities. There's no curfew and it can be noisy at night. Breakfast is included in the price. Dorms from £10.50/€13.33.

Oliver St John Gogarty's, 18–21 Anglesea St (☎671 1822, fax 671 7637, *olivergogartys@hotmail.com*). Stylish though expensive communal accommodation, including rooftop apartments for up to four people at £150/€190.50 a week. *Gogarty's* shares its name and building with a pub, hugely popular with tourists, thus is more suited to partying than quiet contemplation. Dorms start at £17/€21.55.

St Stephen's Green and The Liberties area

Ashfield House, 19–20 D'Olier St (☎679 7734, fax 679 0852, *www.ashfieldhouse.ie*). A friendly, well-run and well-equipped hostel in a converted church close to Trinity. The rooms are spacious and most are en suite. Family rooms are available and under-10s stay free, though there is a weekend supplement of £2/€2.54. Dorms from £13/€16.51.

Avalon House, 55 Aungier St (IHH; ☎475 0001, fax 475 0303, *www.avalon-house.ie*). Impressive hostel in a red-brick Victorian ex-medical school close to St Stephen's Green and a stroll from Temple Bar. There's a fine if not substantial breakfast, excellent kitchen, good common room and restaurant, and the prices are comparatively reasonable, though, of late the standard of service is poor. No curfew. Dorms from £9/€11.43.

Brewery Hostel, 22–23 Thomas St West (☎453 8600, fax 453 8616, *www.irish-hostel.com*). Set in a converted library near the Guinness brewery, this hostel offers clean rooms with sturdy wooden bunks (regarded as the most comfortable in the city). Breakfast is included, and there's secure car parking. Dorms from £12.50/€15.87.

South of the city

Belgrave Hall, 34 Belgrave Square, Monkstown (☎284 2106, fax 280 5838, *www.dublinhostel.com*). This is an exceptional hostel in Dublin's salubrious Monkstown suburb, ten miles out of the city. The early Victorian house exudes character and warmth and has all its original features intact. The rooms are spacious and many boast period furniture. The proud owner, Dan Casey, is extremely helpful, as are the many Irish guests who come to study at the traditional music academy next door. With the closure of the hostel in Dún Laoghaire this is a good option for those arriving on the ferry. Dorms from £15/€19.05.

STUDENT ACCOMMODATION (SUMMER ONLY)

Trinity Hall, Dartry Rd, Rathmines (☎497 1772; buses #4 and #14A). Located three miles out of town, this place offers some family rooms where children under 10 can stay for £3/€3.81. Sports facilities are available. The single-room rate is £30/€38.10, and doubles cost £50/€63.50.

UCD Village, Belfield (☎269 7111; bus #10). UCD is a soulless modern campus about five miles south of the centre. A complex of modern single rooms with shared kitchens, dining area and shower room. It's a bit pricey at £26/€33.02, but a family or group might be interested in the four-room apartment, which costs £80/€101.60 per night, and £560/€711.20 per week.

Camping

There's no central campsite in Dublin, but there are several on the outskirts, including one south of Dún Laoghaire.

Comac Valley Caravan & Camping Park, Corkegh Regional Park, off the Naas Rd, Clondalkin (☎464 0644; buses #68, #68A, #69). Pleasant site set in landscaped grounds with views of Dublin Mountains.

Donabate, on the northside, a few miles beyond Swords (☎843 6008; bus #33B from Eden Quay). Fairly basic site with only limited space for tents, so phone in advance.

Shankill, close to the DART stop at Shankill (☎282 0011; buses #45, #45A, #46, #84). South of Dún Laoghaire and by the sea, within reach of secluded beaches.

The City

Dublin is divided into north and south with the river Liffey acting as a physical, social and at times psychological dividing line. Traditionally the southside has been regarded as the wealthier end of town, and certainly from a visitor's perspective it does possess the majority of the city's historic sites as well as being the home of the newer, more upmarket centres for shopping and socializing. The busy traffic intersection, **College Green**, which is framed by the elegant exteriors of Dublin's premier university **Trinity College** and the old eighteenth-century parliament building, now housing the **Bank of Ireland**, was once the central point of the old Viking city. Stretching south of here is the pedestrianized Grafton Street, the city's commercial and social hub, leading to the stylish Georgian streets that surround **St. Stephen's Green**. Heading directly west of Trinity College, however, will bring you to the narrow, cobbled lanes of the **Temple Bar** area, the centre for the city's nightlife, overlooked by the imposing facade of **Dublin Castle**, the seat of British rule until 1921. Further west still are Dublin's most important cathedrals, **Christchurch** and **St Patrick's**, it's near here that the rich smell of malting grain from the nearby **Guinness brewery** begins to fill the air.

On the northside of the river from the brewery is the historic **Smithfield** area, scene of the famous horse sales and home to the Jameson Whiskey distillery, east of which is the city's main thoroughfare, **O'Connell Street** from which the rebellion was launched that resulted in Irish independence.

College Green and Trinity College

In some ways the topography of Dublin has stayed remarkably constant since the city was founded, when the Vikings sited their Haugen or Thengmote, the central meeting place and burial ground, on what is now **College Green**. Formerly known as Hoggen Green, it remained the centre of administrative power in Ireland until the Act of Union. Today there is little green to be seen, except the small patch of coiffured lawn to the front of the gates of Ireland's most prestigious university, Trinity College. Opposite the college stands the classical facade of the Bank of Ireland which, for 71 years in the 18th century, acted as the country's parliament.

Trinity College

In comparison to the mighty facade of the Bank of Ireland opposite, the modest portico of **Trinity College** seems almost domestic in scale. Founded in 1591 by Queen Elizabeth I, it played a major role in the development of an **Anglo-Irish tradition**, with leading families often sending their sons to be educated here rather than in England. The statues outside represent Edmund Burke and Oliver Goldsmith, two of Trinity's most famous graduates. The philosopher and statesman Burke (1729–97) adopted an interesting political

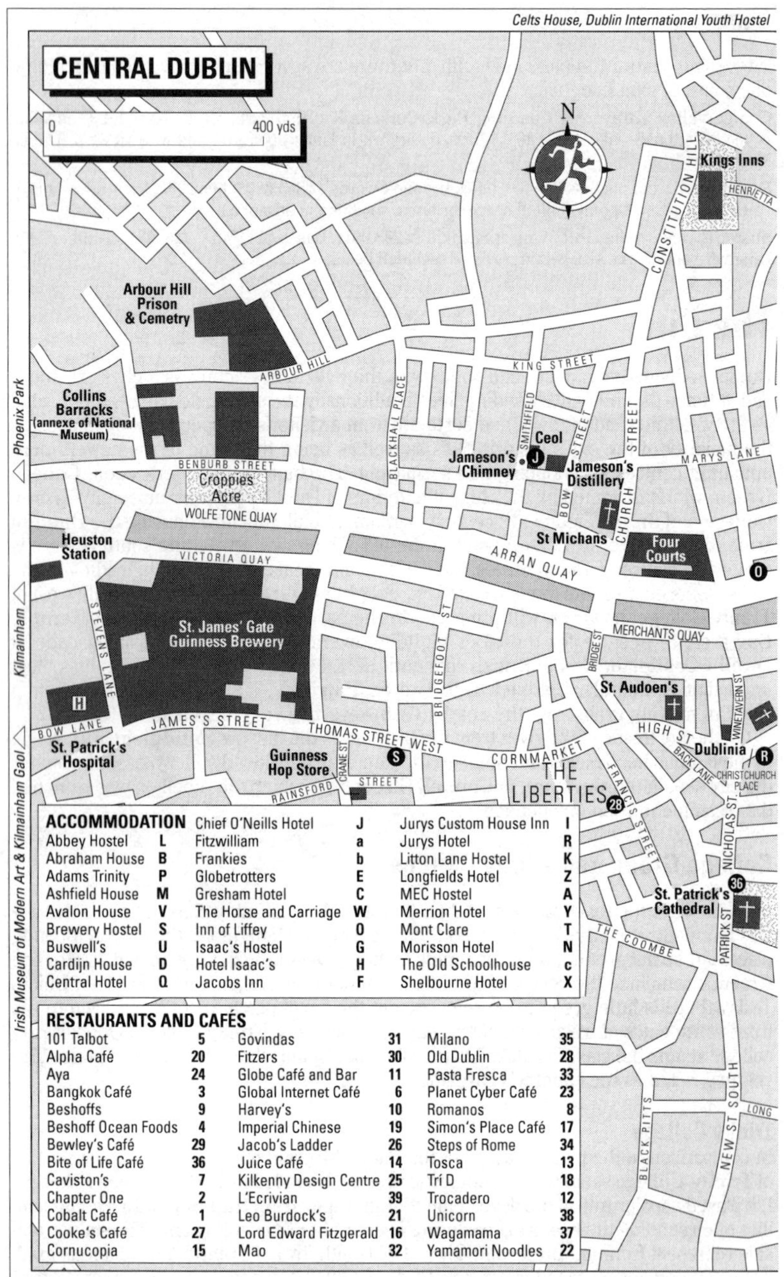

ACCOMMODATION

Abbey Hostel	L	Chief O'Neills Hotel	J	Jurys Custom House Inn	I
Abraham House	B	Fitzwilliam	a	Jurys Hotel	R
Adams Trinity	P	Frankies	b	Litton Lane Hostel	K
Ashfield House	M	Globetrotters	E	Longfields Hotel	Z
Avalon House	V	Gresham Hotel	C	MEC Hostel	A
Brewery Hostel	S	The Horse and Carriage	W	Merrion Hotel	Y
Buswell's	U	Inn of Liffey	O	Mont Clare	T
Cardijn House	D	Isaac's Hostel	G	Morisson Hotel	N
Central Hotel	Q	Hotel Isaac's	H	The Old Schoolhouse	c
		Jacobs Inn	F	Shelbourne Hotel	X

RESTAURANTS AND CAFÉS

101 Talbot	5	Govindas	31	Milano	35
Alpha Café	20	Fitzers	30	Old Dublin	28
Aya	24	Globe Café and Bar	11	Pasta Fresca	33
Bangkok Café	3	Global Internet Café	6	Planet Cyber Café	23
Beshoffs	9	Harvey's	10	Romanos	8
Beshoff Ocean Foods	4	Imperial Chinese	19	Simon's Place Café	17
Bewley's Café	29	Jacob's Ladder	26	Steps of Rome	34
Bite of Life Café	36	Juice Café	14	Tosca	13
Caviston's	7	Kilkenny Design Centre	25	Trí D	18
Chapter One	2	L'Ecrivian	39	Trocadero	12
Cobalt Café	1	Leo Burdock's	21	Unicorn	38
Cooke's Café	27	Lord Edward Fitzgerald	16	Wagamama	37
Cornucopia	15	Mao	32	Yamamori Noodles	22

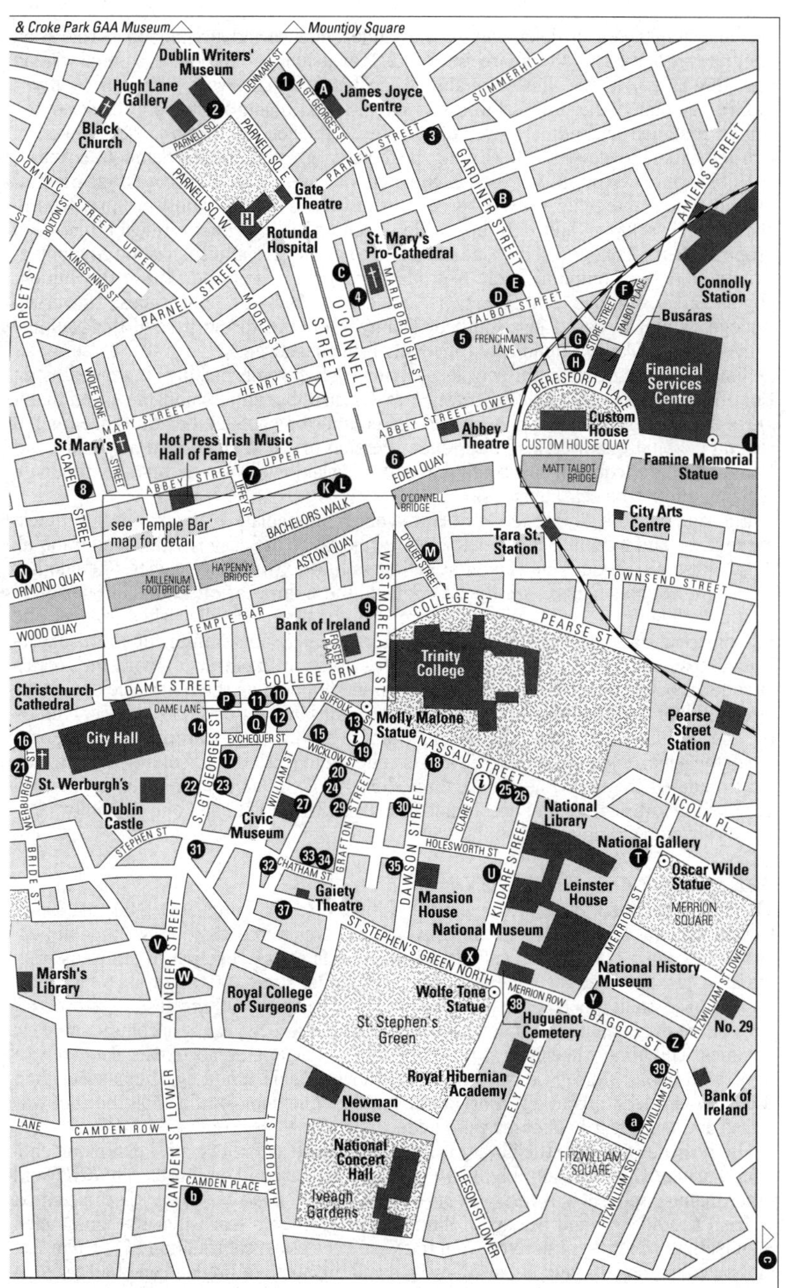

& Croke Park GAA Museum
Mountjoy Square
Dublin Writers' Museum
Hugh Lane Gallery
Black Church
James Joyce Centre
Gate Theatre
Rotunda Hospital
St. Mary's Pro-Cathedral
Connolly Station
Busáras
Financial Services Centre
Custom House
Abbey Theatre
Famine Memorial Statue
St Mary's
Hot Press Irish Music Hall of Fame
see 'Temple Bar' map for detail
City Arts Centre
Tara St. Station
Bank of Ireland
Trinity College
Christchurch Cathedral
City Hall
Molly Malone Statue
Pearse Street Station
St. Werburgh's
Dublin Castle
Civic Museum
National Library
National Gallery
Oscar Wilde Statue
Leinster House
Gaiety Theatre
Mansion House
National Museum
Marsh's Library
Royal College of Surgeons
Wolfe Tone Statue
National History Museum
Huguenot Cemetery
No. 29
St. Stephen's Green
Royal Hibernian Academy
Bank of Ireland
Newman House
National Concert Hall
Iveagh Gardens
Fitzwilliam Square
Merrion Square

position, simultaneously defending Ireland's independence and insisting on its role as an integral part of the British Empire (see p.719); Goldsmith (1728–94) was a noted wit and poet (see p.210). Other illustrious alumni include Jonathan Swift, author of *Gulliver's Travels* and many other satirical works (see pp.92 & 719), and Wolfe Tone, leader of the United Irishmen and prime mover of the 1798 Rebellion, as well as Bram Stoker, of *Dracula* fame, the playwright J.M. Synge and playwright and novelist Samuel Beckett.

Until recently, Trinity's Anglo-Irish connections gave it a strong **Protestant bias**. At its foundation, the college offered free education to Catholics who were prepared to change their religion, and right up to 1966 – long after the rule on religion had been dropped by the college itself – Catholics had to get a special dispensation to study at Trinity or risk excommunication. Nowadays, roughly seventy percent of the student population is Catholic, and Trinity is just one of Dublin's universities; University College Dublin is based just south of Donnybrook and forms part of the National University of Ireland; Dublin City University is in Glasnevin.

Simply as an architectural set piece, Trinity takes some beating. It served as an English university in the film *Educating Rita* – bizarre but understandable, given that it looks the way a great university should. Its cream-stone college buildings are ranged around cobbled quadrangles in a grander version of the arrangement at Oxford and Cambridge (the cobbles apparently have to be relaid every seven years as the land, reclaimed from the sea, subsides).

Entering the college via the **Front Gate** you are immediately struck with how quickly the noise and frenetic activity of the city gives way to the easy rhythms and tranquility of cloistered student life. The first buildings to catch your eye, facing one another across the cobbled square, are the **Chapel** and the **Examination Hall**, both designed by the Scottish architect Sir William Chambers who never actually visited Ireland. The Examination Hall's elegant, stuccoed interior makes a fine setting for the concerts sometimes held here (check the notice boards in the main entrance) while the room's chandelier once adorned the old Irish Parliament building on the other side of College Green. Beyond the chapel on the left is the **Dining Hall**, also used for exams, built by the German architect Richard Castle in 1743. The bell tower, or **Campanile**, in the middle of the square, was put up in 1853 and is believed to mark the site of the priory which long predated the university. A startling element of colour is introduced by the red brick of the Rubrics, student accommodation dating from 1712 and one of Trinity's oldest surviving buildings.

THE LIBRARY AND THE BOOK OF KELLS

The other early survivor is the famous **Library** (daily: June–Sept 9.30am-4.30pm; Oct–May noon–4.30pm; £4.50/€5.71), which receives a free copy of every book published in Britain and Ireland and also contains a famous collection of priceless Irish manuscripts, above all the celebrated **Book of Kells**. Some 200,000 of the total collection of three million books are held here in the old library and the rest are stored off site, where over half a mile of new shelving is needed every year to accommodate new volumes. The library itself is a long – 209ft in all – tall, aristocratic room, flooded with light, with books housed on two storeys of shelves. As designed by Thomas Burgh in the early eighteenth century, it originally had just one floor, but in 1859 the roof was raised and the upper bookcases were added.

On the ground floor of the library is a well-conceived and informative exhibition entitled "Turning Darkness into Light" which offers background on the *Book of Kells* (and other manuscripts such as the *Book of Armagh* and the *Book of Durrow*) in the context of Irish Christianity and the art of illumination. Here you learn that the illuminated manuscripts which were derived from the Celtic ecclesiastical tradition of St Columba, embraced not only Ireland but also Scotland and the north of England and had a strong influence on monastic institutions in mainland Europe. There's still some debate over whether the eighth-century *Book of Kells* was really copied and illuminated in Ireland at all; the location may have been Scotland – maybe Iona, St Columba's first Scottish port of call – or even Lindisfarne in northern England. At all events, the book was taken to the monastery of Kells in County Meath for safekeeping during the Viking raids of the ninth century, and, after a chequered history – during which it spent some time buried underground and some thirty of its pages disappeared, it was brought to Dublin in the seventeenth century. Totalling 680 pages, the *Book of Kells* consists of the four gospels of the New Testament, written in Latin. The book was re-bound in the 1950s into four separate volumes, of which two are on show at any one time: one open at a completely illuminated page, the other at a text page, itself not exactly unadorned, with patterns and fantastic animals intertwined with the capitals.

As famous as the *Book of Kells*, the **Book of Durrow** is in many ways equally interesting. It is the first of the great Irish illuminated manuscripts, dating from between 650 and 680 AD, and has, unusually, a whole page (known as the carpet page, for obvious reasons) given over to ornament. It's noticeable in all these early manuscripts that the depictions of the human form make no attempt at realism – St Matthew in the *Book of Durrow*, for instance, is apparently wrapped in a poncho, with no hands. The important thing is the pattern, which is derived from metalwork (as in the amazing Ardagh Chalice and Tara Brooch, which you can see in the National Museum close by). The characteristic spirals are always slightly asymmetrical – apparently another trick to ensure that the eye doesn't tire – and it's believed that the ornamentation in general had a symbolic meaning, although its full significance is not known.

After examining the books, you climb the stairs to the magnificent Long Room, at the far end of which are two early Irish **harps**, one of them traditionally known as Brian Boru's harp, although it's been dated to the fifteenth century, some four centuries after Boru defeated the Vikings at Clontarf in 1014. Also on display is an original copy of the 1916 **Proclamation of the Irish Republic**.

THE DUBLIN EXPERIENCE AND THE DOUGLAS HYDE GALLERY

In summer, visitors to the college tend to be steered towards the **Dublin Experience**, a forty-minute audiovisual display, which uses a combination of archive and new material to trace Dublin's and, to a lesser extent, Ireland's history. It's unlikely that it will give, as it claims, a "complete orientation to the city", but if you're footsore and still have money in your pocket, it may warrant a visit (June–Sept daily 10am–5pm on the hour ; £3/€3.81).

If you have time to explore, it's worth having a look at the carvings of animals, birds and foliage around the exterior and much of the interior of the museum on the right-hand side of New Square. They were executed by the O'Shea brothers who were hired and given free licence by the famous firm of architects, the Deanes. The brothers certainly didn't shrink from their task and produced a riot of eccentric ornamentation that earned them the displeasure of their employers and subsequent dismissal. Set just behind this is what is seen as the finest example of modern architecture in the city. Certainly not to everyone's taste, the Berkely Library wears its 1960s brutalist style firmly on its sleeve, though curiously it tends to complement, rather than jar, with its more antiquated neighbours. Behind the library stands the arts and science block, which is the centre for student life on campus. The **Douglas Hyde Gallery of Modern Art** (Mon–Wed & Fri 11–6pm, Thurs 11am–7pm, Sat 11am–4.45pm; free), in the same complex, is one of the city's few experimental art venues and always worth checking out; it also has a good bookshop.

The Bank of Ireland

Across the busy traffic interchange from the college, the massive **Bank of Ireland** has played an even more central role in the history of Anglo-Irish Ascendancy. When originally begun in 1729 by Sir Edward Lovett Pearce, it was envisaged as a suitably grand setting for the parliament of a nation, as the Anglo-Irish were coming to regard themselves, although Jonathan Swift, for one, had some typically tart opinions as to its worth:

As I stroll the city, oft I
Spy a building large and lofty
Not a bow-shot from the college
Half the globe from sense and knowledge.

The Ascendancy's efforts to achieve self-government culminated in the famous Grattan parliament of 1782, in which **Henry Grattan** – whose gesturing statue stands outside on College Green – uttered the celebrated phrase "Ireland is now a nation". The Protestant, Anglo-Irish parliament endorsed the country's Independence unanimously.

This period of nominal self-government was, however, short-lived; with the passing of the Act of Union in 1801, Ireland lost both its independence as a nation and its parliament (which acquiesced by voting itself obediently out of existence). With its original function gone, the building was sold to the Bank of Ireland for £40,000 two years later. Though not exactly geared up for coach parties, the bank does admit sightseers during normal banking hours (Mon–Wed & Fri 10am–12.30pm & 1.30–3pm, Thurs closes 5pm, guided tours Tues 10.30am, 11.30am, 1.45pm). Its interior is magnificently old-fashioned – you are shown around by ushers wearing costumes seemingly unchanged since the nineteenth century – and in winter, coal fires glow in the entrance hall's massive grates. In a room to the back of the bank is the atmospheric former **House of Lords**, with its coffered ceiling, oak surrounds and eighteenth-century Waterford glass chandelier, where you can see the mace from the old House of Commons and two 1733 Thomas Baille tapestries celebrating Protestant victories of the previous century: the Siege of Derry in 1689 and the Battle of the Boyne in 1690. Nearby on Foster Place, stands an armoury added during the Napoleonic Wars which now acts as an arts centre. It is also the venue for an exhibition on the "Story of Banking" which explains the role of the Bank of Ireland in the economic development of the country (Tues–Fri 10am–4pm; £1.50/€1.90).

Grafton Street to the National Museum

South of College Green stands the statue of Molly Malone, whose famous cry "alive, alive, o" could well describe **Grafton Street**, the vibrant stretch of pedestrianized road that runs from here to St Stephen's Green. The streets that surround Grafton Street frame Dublin's quality shopping area, where, in designer clothing stores and chic cafés, affluent Dubliners flaunt and dispose of their new-found prosperity. East of here is elegant Kildare Street, the most impressive legacy of the city's eighteenth-century wealth on which stands **Leinster House**, a magnificent Georgian town house which is now home to the Irish Parliament.

Grafton Street

Grafton Street is unabashedly commercial, but it's a pleasant enough place to while away some time – here, as in most cities, shopping is a way of life, and people come here as much to see and be seen as to buy. Dublin's leading department store, Brown Thomas, is a classy location for some retail therapy, while Powerscourt Town House is similarly upmarket and set back a little on Clarendon Street. As well as simply wandering in and out of its retail palaces, you can also take in the street life. Since it's pedestrianization, Grafton Street has become the centre of Dublin's burgeoning street theatre, and this is one of the few places where you'll find buskers. This vibrant street life is celebrated by the bawdy, musical hall representation of the city's most famous fishmonger, Molly Malone, by Jeanne Rynhart. Initially much maligned, not least because of Molly's striking décolletage, the statue has, in recent years, become very much part of Dublin life and is referred to affectionately as "The Tart with the Cart".

Unmissable in Grafton Street, even if you have no other business in the area, is **Bewley's coffee house** (daily 7.30am–7pm). While the café has moved somewhat upmarket in recent years and lost much of its former character it is still worth visiting to appreciate its dark wood and marble-tabled interior, lit by the magnificent stained-glass windows of Dublin artist Harry Clarke. *Bewley's* was once a Dublin institution where a cross-section of the city's population could be found in animated discussion over a cup of Dublin's other famous brew: *Bewley's* coffee. The coffee, sticky buns and world famous potato soup that made *Bewley's* a favourite with generations of Dubliners continue to be served here, and on the top floor, a small museum traces the history of this establishment. Additionally, plans are afoot to develop the small theatre space, which is currently used for lunchtime productions. Founded in the 1840s by the Quaker Bewley family, it became a workers' co-operative in 1971 and subsequently almost folded in 1986 provoking a national crisis until the government stepped in and offered to help before a buyer was secured. There are many branches of the chain popping up around the city but the two other traditional branches, each with a slightly different character, are in Westmoreland Street, which has wonderful Art Nouveau fireplaces (daily 7.30am–7pm), and on South Great George's Street, a smaller and more subdued incarnation (Mon–Sat 6.45am–6pm).

Close to Grafton Street is the **Dublin Civic Museum** at 58 South William St (Tues–Sat 10am–6pm, Sun 11am–2pm; free), a tiny establishment that is probably strictly for museum and history buffs. The display consists of a garbled but oddly intriguing collection of artefacts relating to the history of the city from Viking times to the present. You can see, among other things, the head of the statue of Lord Nelson that used to stand outside the General Post Office in O'Connell Street and was blown up by the IRA in 1966; one of the original 1916 proclamations of the Republic of Ireland; and fascinating minutiae such as timetables detailing the excruciatingly slow progress of that state-of-the-art mode of transport, the canal-boat, across Ireland in the late eighteenth and early nineteenth centuries.

Dawson Street

Dawson Street, just east of Grafton Street, is altogether quieter than its neighbour, and is home to some of Dublin's better **bookshops** (see p.121) as well as a number of august institutions. Chief among these is the **Mansion House**, a delicate building of 1710 weighed down by heavy Victorian wrought iron. This has been the official residence of the Lord Mayor since 1715 and was also where the *Dáil Éireann*, the Irish parliament, met in 1919 to ratify the Independence proclamation of 1916. The Mansion House isn't generally open to the public, but in any case there's not a great deal to be seen inside.

Next door, the decorous red-brick house containing the **Royal Irish Academy** is also closed to the public. One of the great learned institutions of Europe, it publishes books of Irish interest and has a weighty collection of Irish manuscripts. Next door again, **St Anne's** (Church of Ireland) church has an amazingly ornate Italianate facade which is a real surprise when you catch sight of it along Anne Street. Inside, behind the altar, are wooden shelves that were originally designed to take loaves of bread for distribution among the poor of the parish under the provisions of a 1720s bequest. On Thursday lunchtimes, St Anne's hosts a series of recitals and other cultural activities – check *In Dublin* for details.

Kildare Street: Leinster House

Moving east again, and marking the point where what's left of the Georgian city begins, Kildare Street is the really monumental part of the Grafton, Dawson, Kildare trio. The most imposing building is undoubtedly **Leinster House**, built in 1745 as the Duke of Leinster's town house. At that time, the fashionable area of Dublin was north of the river, and there were those who mocked him for building a town house in the south on what was then a greenfield site. The Kildare Street facade, facing the town, is built to look like a town house; the other side, looking out on to what is now Merrion Square, resembles a country house.

Today, this is one of the most important buildings in Dublin, housing the **Irish parliament** – the *Dáil Éireann*, or House of Representatives, and the *Seanad Éireann*, or Senate – as well as the **National Museum** and **National Library**. The Dáil (pronounced *Doil*) has 166 representatives – *Teachtaí Dála*, usually shortened to TDs – elected by direct proportional vote, representing 41 constituencies. The Senate is proposed on a vocational basis, with six members elected by the universities and eleven nominated by the Taoiseach (pronounced *Tee-shuck*), or Prime Minister. General elections take place at least every five years; presidential elections, which are also direct, are held every seven years. Mary Robinson, elected in 1990 as Ireland's first woman president, breathed welcome new life into this formerly symbolic role, testing its constitutional limitations by speaking out for women and the disadvantaged in society, while her successor, Mary McAleese, also broke new ground by becoming the first northener to hold the post.

There are **tours** of the Government Buildings on Saturdays from 10.30am to 3.30pm. Although admission is free, you'll need to get a ticket, available from the ticket office in the National Gallery, at the back of Leinster House; the tour lasts forty minutes and takes in the Taoiseach's office, the ceremonial stairs and the cabinet room. As the tour is popular, the best thing to do is get there early and put your name down for later in the day. If you go to the Kildare Street entrance to Leinster House and present your passport or prove you are a tourist – and the guard is in a good mood – you should be able to gain entry to the Dáil. The Parliament sits for ninety days a year, most of them between November and May on Tuesday from 2.30 to 8.30pm and Thursday from 10.30am to 5.30pm.

The National Library and National Museum

Whether or not the massive twin rotundas, added in 1890, housing the entrances of the National Library on the left and the National Museum on the right, do anything to complement the Georgian elegance of Leinster House is debatable. The **National Library** (Mon 10am–9pm, Tues & Wed 2–9pm, Thurs & Fri 10am–5pm, Sat 10am–1pm; free) is, however, worth visiting for its associations alone: it seems that every major Irish writer from Joyce onwards used it at some time, and the **Reading Room** is also the scene of Stephen Dedalus' great literary debate in *Ulysses*. The Library has a good collection of first editions and works of Irish writers, including Swift, Goldsmith, Yeats, Shaw, Joyce and Beckett. It's also often used for temporary exhibitions on Irish books and authors.

The **National Museum** (Tues–Sat 10am–5pm, Sun 2–5pm; free) is the place to go to see the treasures of ancient Ireland, as well as a small collection of artefacts – mainly silver, glass and ceramics – from Dublin's eighteenth-century heyday. It is national policy to gather treasures found all around the country in this one museum, so the place is a real treasure trove of wonderful objects. The really venerable exhibits, dating from the Irish **Bronze and Iron ages**, bear eloquent testimony to the ancient high culture of Ireland: there's **jewellery** ranging from the eighth to the first centuries BC, mainly the twisted gold bars known as torcs, cloak-fasteners and collars, and the beaten gold lunulae that are characteristic of the period.

The **medieval antiquities** are more spectacular still and include the **Tara Brooch** and the Ardagh Chalice, found in County Limerick in 1868, both of which date from the eighth century. The twelfth-century Cross of Cong, an ornate reliquary of wood, bronze and silver, is said to contain a fragment of the True Cross; and there's also an eleventh-century shrine, made of gold wire, that houses a bell said to have belonged to St Patrick. But perhaps the most impressive piece of Irish metalwork is the Tara Brooch, and it's thought that the patterns of manuscript illuminations such as the *Book of Kells*, which you can see in Trinity College Library, may be derived from this rich craft tradition. Remarkably, the Tara Brooch is decorated both on the front and the back, where the intricate filigree work could be seen only by the wearer – the brooch is displayed above a mirror so that you can see both sides.

One of the more recent finds is the **Derrynaflan Hoard**, a legacy of the metal-detecting fad which gripped Ireland in the 1980s. This collection of eighth- and ninth-century silver objects, including a chalice and a paten, was discovered in February 1980 in County Tipperary by amateur treasure hunters using a metal detector.

Right at the top of Kildare Street, at the point where it intersects with Nassau Street, the fussy, Venetian-inspired red-brick building on the corner used to house one of the major institutions of Anglo-Irish Dublin, the **Kildare Street Club** – the carved billiard-playing monkeys on the pillars hint toward the past use of the building as a gentlemen's playground. The place now houses the **Genealogical Office**, where you can trace the history of Irish names (call ☎661 4877 for details), the Heraldry Museum and the Alliance Française. The **Heraldry Museum** gives a general account of the development of its subject in Ireland and Europe (Mon–Fri 10am–12.30pm & 2–4.30pm).

St Stephen's Green

Walk to the bottom of Kildare Street and you'll emerge on the northeast side of **St Stephen's Green**, the focus of central Dublin's city planning. It's an oddly decorous expanse, neat and tidy with little bandstands and pergolas, laid out as a public park in 1880 by Lord Ardilaun (Sir Arthur Edward Guinness). It was an open common until 1663, and the final buildings ringing it went up in the eighteenth century; unfortunately, very few of these have survived, and their replacements speak eloquently of the failure of 1960s planning regulations. The **gardens**, with their ornamental pond, can be a pleasant place to while away some time on a sunny day, but in terms of architecture, or even city life, there's not a lot to see. The statue in memory of Wolfe Tone, backed by slabs of granite, is nicknamed "Tone-henge".

The northside of the square, known in the eighteenth century as the "Beaux Walk" for the dandies and glitterati who used to promenade there, is dominated by the **Shelbourne Hotel**. Fittingly, the *Shelbourne*, which boasts that it has "the best address in Dublin", continues to be a focus for the upper echelons of the city's social life. It's worth bearing in mind that, as with all Irish hotels, you can wander in for a drink and something to eat in the lobby at any time of day, even if you're not staying. The hotel's afternoon teas (from 3pm) are wonderful; but the airy, chandeliered lobby and the *Horseshoe* bar come into their own in the early evening, when the hotel is a great place for both celebrity-spotting and watching the parade of young Dubliners who are there to be seen. The *Shelbourne* is too well bred to pass comment on jeans and trainers in the lobby, but you'll feel out of place if you penetrate to the excellent (but expensive) restaurant (see p.66) unless you dress up a bit.

Just past the hotel, to the left of a shuttered garden, lies the **Huguenot Graveyard**, which dates from 1693. The Huguenots – French Protestants who fled persecution under Louis XIV, after the repeal of the Edict of Nantes in 1685 took away the religious privileges they had previously enjoyed – enriched cultural life all over Europe with their craftsmanship (their silverwork was particularly valued). Ireland was no exception, and this quiet burial place, with its understated French headstones, seems a particularly fitting tribute to their quietly industrious way of life; for more on the Huguenots in Dublin see p.94.

Linked to the east side of the Green by Hume Street is **Ely Place**, where you can see some of the best-preserved Georgian domestic buildings in Dublin.

The Catholic University of Ireland: Newman House

University College, Dublin's second-oldest university (after Trinity), is now at Belfield in the suburb of Donnybrook, but the first premises of its predecessor, the **Catholic University of Ireland**, are at nos. 85–86 on the southside of the Green and are now restored to something approaching their original appearance. The aim of the foundation was to provide a Catholic answer to the great academic traditions of Oxford and Cambridge, but, despite the appointment of John Henry Newman (who had famously converted from High-Church Anglicanism) as its rector, the new university was initially denied official recognition in Britain. Eventually, in 1853, it was successfully established as a University College. The poet and Jesuit priest Gerard Manley Hopkins (1844–89) had a chair here; the 1916 Republican leader Pádraig Pearse, prime minister Éamon de Valera, and James Joyce are among its more famous graduates.

The original, newly restored university buildings, collectively known as **Newman House** (June–Sept Mon–Fri noon–4pm, Sat 2–4pm, Sun 11am–1pm, guided tours only, on the hour; £3/€3.81), provide an unparalleled opportunity to get a taste of what the Georgian town houses of St Stephen's Green must have originally been like. No. 85 is a small, early Georgian villa built about 1738 for Hugh Montgomery, a wealthy Ulster landowner and member of parliament for County Fermanagh. This was one of the first town houses built by Richard Castle, or Cassels, the fashionable German country-house architect (who also designed Leinster House and, later, the Dining Hall at Trinity College), and shows his mastery of the more intimate scale of urban building.

The remarkable interior is worth visiting just to see the **Apollo Room**, with its stucco reliefs of the nine muses made by the brilliant Swiss stuccadores Paolo and Filippo Lanfranchini. Upstairs on the first floor, the restoration of a fine double-cube room with ceiling reliefs celebrating the subjects of good government and prudent economy has been recently completed with the ghastly colour schemes added in the 1940s stripped away so that the Lanfranchinis' work can be truly appreciated. Notice also the extraordinarily ham-fisted additions made by the nineteenth-century Jesuits, who decided that the ceiling showed far too many naked female bodies and helpfully added what look like fur suits to the paintings in order to protect the morals of their students.

In 1765 the small villa was joined by a bigger town house, which is still undergoing restoration. The original house was then extended with an additional room at the back, later to become the physics theatre, where James Joyce lectured to the "L & H" (the "Literary and Historical Society") and which features in his *Portrait of the Artist as a Young Man*. The new house was built by Richard "Burnchapel" Whaley, a virulent anti-Catholic who swore never to let a Papist across his threshold and earned his sobriquet by burning chapels in County Wicklow. His son, "Jerusalem" Whaley, was a founder of the Hellfire Club. Legend tells that he threw a crucifix through the front window on Maundy Thursday, and ever afterwards on the same day its image is still to be seen there. The newer house is characterized by lighter, airier plasterwork (the main staircase, decorated with musical instruments and flowers, is particularly beautiful) and is to be restored to its mid-nineteenth-century appearance, with some of the interventions made by the university prelates.

Next door, **University Church** is an amazingly prolix Byzantine fantasy of 1854–56, its ornate interior decorated with coloured Irish marble: the pale brown quarried in Armagh and Laois, the black from Offaly and Kilkenny, the rich red marble from Cork, as well as the famed green marble from the better-known quarries of the far west, Mayo and Connemara. The church is rarely used for services but has, of late, become a very popular venue for chic Dublin weddings

West of the Green

Harcourt Street, leading off from the southwest corner of St Stephen's Green, is a graceful Georgian street that has survived relatively unscathed. There's nothing much to do here (though there is a good Celtic bookshop), but it's worth strolling down a little way to admire the graceful proportions and elegant town planning.

On the west side of the Green is the **Royal College of Surgeons**, which during the events of Easter Week in 1916 was held by the Irish Citizen Army with Constance Markiewicz as second-in-command; the facade is still pocked with stray bullet-marks. Interrupting the skyline around St Stephen's Green is the shopping mall on the corner with Grafton Street, its white wrought-iron detailing intended, presumably, to echo the Georgian balconies of Merrion and Fitzwilliam squares. In the years since it was built in 1809, its flashy architecture has made its peace extraordinarily well with its surroundings, something perhaps not so surprising, given that the famous good taste of Georgian building conceals much the same kind of boom-time, get-rich-quick expansionism.

The Shaw birthplace

A short walk up Harcourt Street, which heads south from the southwest corner of St Stephen's Green, will bring you to Harrington Street. Turn right, then left into Synge Street, a modest street of patchy Georgian houses, for the **birthplace of George Bernard Shaw** (May–Oct Mon–Sat 10am–1pm & 2–5pm; £2.40/€3.04). For playwright Shaw (see the box below) this house, where he lived until he was 10, was not

GEORGE BERNARD SHAW

Born in Dublin in 1856, **George Bernard Shaw** was technically a member of the privileged Ascendancy, but his father's failed attempt, after leaving the civil service, to make money as a grain merchant, meant that Shaw grew up in an atmosphere of genteel poverty and, by the age of 16, he was earning his living in a land agency. When his mother left his father for her singing teacher and took her two daughters with her to London, Shaw soon joined them and set about the process of educating himself. Subsidized by his mother's meagre income as a music teacher, he spent his afternoons in the British Museum's reading room and his evenings writing novels. He also became a vegetarian, a socialist, and a public speaker of some note.

Shaw's novels were unsuccessful, but his plays were a different matter entirely: in a way that perhaps underlined the flamboyant young man's wholehearted involvement with his new London environment, he was acclaimed the most important British playwright since the eighteenth century. However, Shaw recognized his foreignness as being a big part of his success: "the position of foreigner with complete command of the same language has great advantages. I can take an objective view of England, which no Englishman can." In the 1890s, influenced by the new drama represented by Ibsen, he began to write plays hinged on moral and social questions rather than romantic or personal interests. In play after play – his best-known dramas include *Man and Superman*, *Caesar and Cleopatra*, *Major Barbara*, *St Joan*, and, of course, *Pygmalion*, from which the musical *My Fair Lady* was adapted – he expounds a progressive view of humanity. For Shaw, the "life-force" is evolving toward an ever-higher level, and his plays successfully mix the accompanying moral fervour with high social comedy. As well as a dramatist, he was an active pamphleteer, critic, journalist and essayist, on subjects ranging from politics and economics to music. After the ecstatic reception of *St Joan*, Shaw was awarded the Nobel prize for literature in 1925 – which he initially refused as he didn't want money or recognition but relented and donated the money to the newly formed Anglo-Swedish Literary Foundation. In his old age, he was famous almost as much for his dandified persona as his work. He died in 1950.

exactly a cause for celebration; Shaw remembered that "neither our hearts nor our imaginations were in it" and recalled the "loveless" atmosphere. You certainly get a vivid impression of the claustrophobic surroundings of the house and its tiny, neat garden. The terse inscription on the facade "Bernard Shaw, author of many plays", is as Shaw wished.

Merrion Square and Georgian Dublin

East from St. Stephen's Green stand Merrion and Fitzwilliam Squares which, along with the surrounding streets, form the heart of what's left of the city's **Georgian heritage**. Representing the latest of the city's Georgian architecture – decrepit Mountjoy Square and Parnell Square, north of the river, are almost all that's left of the earlier Georgian city – their worn, red-brick facades are a brilliant example of confident, relaxed urban planning. The overall layout, in terms of squares and linking streets, may be formal, but there's a huge variation of detail: height, windows, wrought-iron balconies, ornate doorways, are all different, but the result is a graceful meeting of form and function that's immensely beguiling.

The apogee of the Georgian area, imbued with an atmosphere of grandeur and repose, **Merrion Square**, built around 1770, has been home to a lot of well-known people including Daniel O'Connell, the Wildes, W.B. Yeats, and Nobel prize-winning physicist Erwin Schrödinger. However, it hasn't always been an area devoted to gracious living: during the Famine, between 1845 and 1849, the park in the centre of the square was the site of soup kitchens to which the starving and destitute flocked. Today, the buildings are mainly occupied by offices, but the square still retains a residential feel, and a core of people still live here. The park railings are used on Saturdays and Sundays by artists flogging their wares, and the area is also a centre for most of Dublin's private galleries. On the northwest corner of the square is a statue of Oscar Wilde lounging insouciantly on a rock, while opposite are two marble plinths displaying many of the wit's epithets. Looking along the south side of the square, you experience one of the set pieces of early nineteenth-century Dublin's architecture: the hard outlines, pepperpot tower, Ionic columns and pediment of St Stephen's Church.

The National Gallery

At the northwest side of Merrion Square, alongside the back of Leinster House – its country-house facade – is Ireland's **National Gallery** (Mon–Wed, Fri & Sat 9.30am–5.30pm, Thurs 9.30am–8.30pm, Sun 12–5.30pm; *www.nationalgallery.ie*). The gallery is a place that has a real energy about it, not only because of the number of enthusiastic visitors, but also thanks to the many Dubliners who lunch at the excellent restaurant housed in the atrium on the ground floor. The museum is divided into three main sections exhibiting more than two thousand paintings of Irish, European and British art: the Milltown, the Dargan and the North Wing, with the new Millennium Wing, on Clare Street, due to open summer 2001.

The best place to start a tour is in the **Milltown Wing**, where rooms one to six house Irish art, a great deal of which is by artists working in England; the most significant of the artists of this section being Nathaniel Hone the Elder, whose caustic painting *The Conjurer*, in room one, satirizes the former president of the Royal Academy, Joshua Reynolds. Many of the works in rooms two and three illustrate a tendency towards the romanticization of the lives of the rural poor: Joseph Haverty's *Blind Piper* and Augustus Burke's *Connemara Girl* are classic examples. Also in room three is Edwin Hayes' sentimental depiction of an emigrant ship, bathed in a warm twilight glow, leaving Dublin harbour. In contrast to these are the more politicized representations of Irish peasant life: the emotive sculpture of a lost, bare-footed child, *The Homeless Wanderer*, by John Henry Foley, and the most obvious indictment, *Ejected Family*, by the Scottish painter,

Erskine Nicol, who skilfully depicts the horrors of a peasant eviction. Rooms five and six feature Irish works from the early twentieth century; of special note are Paul Henry's beautifully executed representations of the west of Ireland. Room six culminates in a portrait of **Lady Lavery**, by her husband Belfast-born painter John Lavery. An American heiress and leading socialite of her time, her face appeared on banknotes following Independence in 1921 as the female personification of Ireland. Turning to the left brings you to room seven, where the historical or thematic context on any painting can be gleaned from one of the excellent multimedia consoles; though entries have not been updated since the gallery's extension, and many of the maps are now out-of-date.

Room seven leads you into the ground floor of the **Dargan Wing**, and the new **Yeats Room**, dedicated to the famous artistic family as a whole, but most especially to Jack B. Yeats (brother of poet W.B. Yeats), whose exuberant canvasses line the room. As well as the vibrant colours of Jack's work, the room also features the more sober portraits executed by his father, John B. Yeats, two of which are of his sons, Jack and W.B.. The Yeats Room gives way to the grandiose **Shaw Room**, with its splendid Waterford Crystal chandeliers, dominated by the magnificent 1854 *Marriage of Princess Aoife of Leinster and Richard de Clare*, by Daniel Maclise. The painting was commissioned to satisfy the nineteenth-century fascination with the Celts and, consequently, Maclise chose the symbolic event of the marriage of the daughter of a Celtic chief and the first Anglo-Norman invader in 1170 as his subject; the depiction of the defeated Celts has erroneously been interpreted by nationalists as a subtle critique of English involvement in Irish affairs.

At the opposite end of the foyer to the Shaw Room is Room 32, the most interesting of the ground floor section of the **North Wing**, where the famous portraits of James Joyce, by Jacques Blanche, and Sean O'Casey, by Augustus John, are displayed. The rest of this section, rooms 33 to 36, is dedicated to the works of British artists, most notably Reynolds and Gainsborough. Rooms 23 and 24 on the second floor of the North Wing display a fine selection of altarpieces and early Renaissance paintings, including an exquisite panel by Fra Angelico, while rooms 26 to 30 contain Flemish, German and Dutch art. Room 31 houses the gallery's impressive collection of Spanish art including works by Goya, Murillo and Velasquez.

Room 24 leads to the central **Milltown Wing** where the focus is on Italian painting featuring masters such as Titian and Tintoretto; however, pride of place must go to the stunning *The Taking of Christ* by Caravaggio, which hung on the living room wall of a Jesuit house in Leeson Street before being discovered and moved to the Gallery in the late 1980s.

If, at this stage, your cultural – but not your physical – appetite has been satisfied, you should retrace your steps to the atrium on the ground floor to enjoy the superlative *Fitzer's* **restaurant**.

No. 29 Lower Fitzwilliam Street

At the opposite end of Merrion Square, at **no. 29 Lower Fitzwilliam St**, is what's billed as a "faithfully recreated Georgian family home" (Tues–Sat 10am–5pm, Sun 2–5pm; £2.50/€3.17). Recreated is the word – the house fell down and has been rebuilt, brick by brick, by the Electricity Supply Board, whose offices adjoin it at the back. Considering that since the Board was responsible, in the 1960s, for knocking down 26 Georgian houses and destroying the longest unbroken row of period houses then surviving, this act of homage is perhaps the least that could be demanded of it. If you want a postmodern take on the Georgian, this is it, furnished in a notional style of between 1790 and 1820. Viewing the house is an extraordinary experience, there's little feeling that you'd have anything in common with the people who once lived here: rather you're left with the impression that they "only drank wine and beer" and that the women "did nothing but write letters to themselves". Georgian life is turned into a cabinet of curiosities, a weird kind of sideshow which does, admittedly, have its fascination. For an idea of "real" eighteenth-century Dublin life, Newman House is far superior(see p.82); but if you have a taste for kitsch and can overlook the obvious irony, then you may find some pleasure at no. 29.

Fitzwilliam Square, south of Merrion Square along Fitzwilliam Street, is another elegant example of a late Georgian square – it was built between 1791 and 1825 – with some of the city's finest Georgian doors and fanlights. The dwindling number of residents still hold keys to the central garden.

Baggot Street and the Grand Canal

Running east from Grafton Street and across Fitzwilliam Street, **Baggot Street** – with its multitude of lively pubs – starts out Georgian, but the street plan is pretty soon broken by the great black metal-and-glass bulk of the Bank of Ireland building, enlivened only by a few brightly coloured metal constructivist sculptures. Just beyond the bank, you reach the Grand Canal, one of Dublin's two constructed waterways – the other, the Royal Canal, runs through the north of the city. True Dubliners, or "Jackeens", are said to be those born between the two waterways.

The **Grand Canal** was the earlier and more successful of the two waterways: started in 1756 and reaching the Shannon by 1803, it carried passengers and freight between Dublin, the midland towns and the Shannon right up to the 1960s, despite competition from the railways. Its total length, including stretches of the rivers Barrow and Shannon, was 340 miles. The potential for tourism in re-opening the canals has only recently been realized; consequently some patches are clean, free-flowing and beautiful while around the bend the vista is a picture of economic decline. Perhaps the best stretch of the canal to visit is the section around Baggot Street Bridge, where the water is fringed by trees. Baggot Street and a Dublin institution, the late, lamented **Parson's bookshop**, were haunts of many of Dublin's celebrated writers in the 1950s, including the poet Patrick Kavanagh and the playwright Brendan Behan. Kavanagh lived in a flat nearby in Pembroke Road and produced a "journal of literature and politics" entitled *Kavanagh's Weekly* and written largely by himself (with a few contributions from Behan and Myles na Gopaleen, aka Flann O'Brien). It ran to a total of thirteen issues before folding, with pieces about anything and everything – professional marriage makers, visits to the bookies, weeks when nothing happens.

The Grand Canal reaches the River Liffey at Ringsend (about a mile northeast of Baggot Street Bridge), through its original locks, constructed in 1796. You can find out more about the history and use of all of Ireland's canals and waterways at the Waterways visitors centre, a little upstream from the Grand Canal Dock.

Ballsbridge

If you walk for just over half a mile west of Baggot Street Bridge (buses from the centre of town: #5, #6, #6A, #7A, #8, #10, #46 and #46A) you'll get to **Ballsbridge**, a respectable, essentially Victorian suburb with some pleasant guesthouses (see "Accommodation", p.69, as well as many of the foreign embassies and smarter hotels – and, for soccer and rugby fans, the essential Lansdowne Road Stadium.

The showgrounds of the **Royal Dublin Society** are also here (off the main Pembroke/Merrion Road) – the first of its kind in Europe, founded in 1731 to promote improvements in agriculture, stock breeding and veterinary medicine. The Society was highly instrumental in the development of Dublin as a modern metropolis, and encouraged the foundation of the National Museum, the National Library, the National Gallery and the Botanic Gardens. If you're in town for the Spring Show in May, don't pass it by; the **Dublin Horse Show** (usually in August) is even more impressive – its international showjumping draws the horsey elite (human and equine) from both Ireland and Britain. Details and tickets from the Royal Dublin Society, PO Box 121, Ballsbridge, Dublin 4 (☎669 2386).

Temple Bar

The main thoroughfare west from College Green is **Dame Street**. Immediately north, the area between the modern Central Bank and the Liffey is known as **Temple Bar**. Until the dissolution of the monasteries in 1537, the land on which Temple Bar stands was the property of the Augustinian order. Originally built on marshy land reclaimed from the Liffey, Temple Bar owes its name not to the friars, as you might expect, but to a seventeenth-century owner, Sir William Temple. During the eighteenth century, the place was a centre for Dublin's low life, in the shape of brothels and pubs (the pubs are still there), while in the nineteenth century it attracted the small businesses and tradesmen who gave it its character.

Bought up in the 1960s by CIE (formerly the state transport company), which wanted to build a new central bus terminal to replace the one on the other side of the river, it suffered for many years from a benign sort of planning blight. Even after the bus station idea was abandoned in the 1980s, shops, studios and offices in the area continued to be rented out on short leases and as a result the streets were full of art galleries, restaurants and cultural centres. However, over recent years the area has been extensively redeveloped and has lost much of the bohemian and anarchic feel that was its appeal to begin with. All the same, Temple Bar still remains one of the liveliest and most interesting parts of town, often compared with Covent Garden in London or Les Halles in Paris. With its emphasis now firmly placed on the bacchanalian – although stag and hen parties have now been banned – it's not surprising that the area really comes to life at night, as revellers spill out from bars onto the narrow streets for impromptu street parties, while others head to nightclubs such as the U2-owned *Kitchen* to hear some of the finest dance music in town. For those of a more sedate disposition, the super-cool Irish Film Centre is recommended for movies, eating, or people-spotting. You can bone up on the more official side of Temple Bar life at the **Temple Bar Information Centre**, Eustace Street (June–Aug Mon–Fri 9am–6pm, Sat 11am–4pm, Sun noon–4pm; Sept–May Mon–Fri 9am–6pm, Sat 11am–4pm; ☎671 5717), which publishes a *Temple Bar Guide* with a useful map; or consult *In Dublin* for a more general guide to what's on.

One of the best places to see work by contemporary Irish artists is **Temple Bar Gallery and Studios**, 5–9 Temple Bar (Mon–Sat 10am–6pm, Sun 2–6pm); consisting of thirty studios in all and two exhibition spaces, it is the biggest complex of its kind in the country. Next door is the Original Print Gallery where both Irish and international prints are displayed. Walking away from the river and onto Crow Street, you can't fail to notice **The Green Building**, an experiment in energy-efficient building in a dense urban area. The roof is made up of propellers and solar panels, while the facade is decorated with artworks on the theme of recycling and includes balcony balustrading by James Garner, made from disused bicycle frames. Tracing your steps back down Crow Street, Curved Street, off Temple Lane, is home to **Temple Bar Music Centre** (Mon–Fri 10am–5.30pm; ☎670 9202, *www.tbmc.ie*), a major concert venue and showcase for new Irish musical talent. The building consists of recording studios in the basement, a 340-seat venue on the ground floor, an information centre on the first and second floors and a music school on the third. Curved Street leads on to Eustace Street where you'll find **The Ark Children's Cultural Centre** (Tues–Fri 9am–4pm; ☎670 7788, *www.ark.ie*), a theatre specially designed for children with a child-size auditorium, child-height windows and a stage backed by a vertically revolving wall that opens out onto Meeting House Square to allow for outdoor performances.

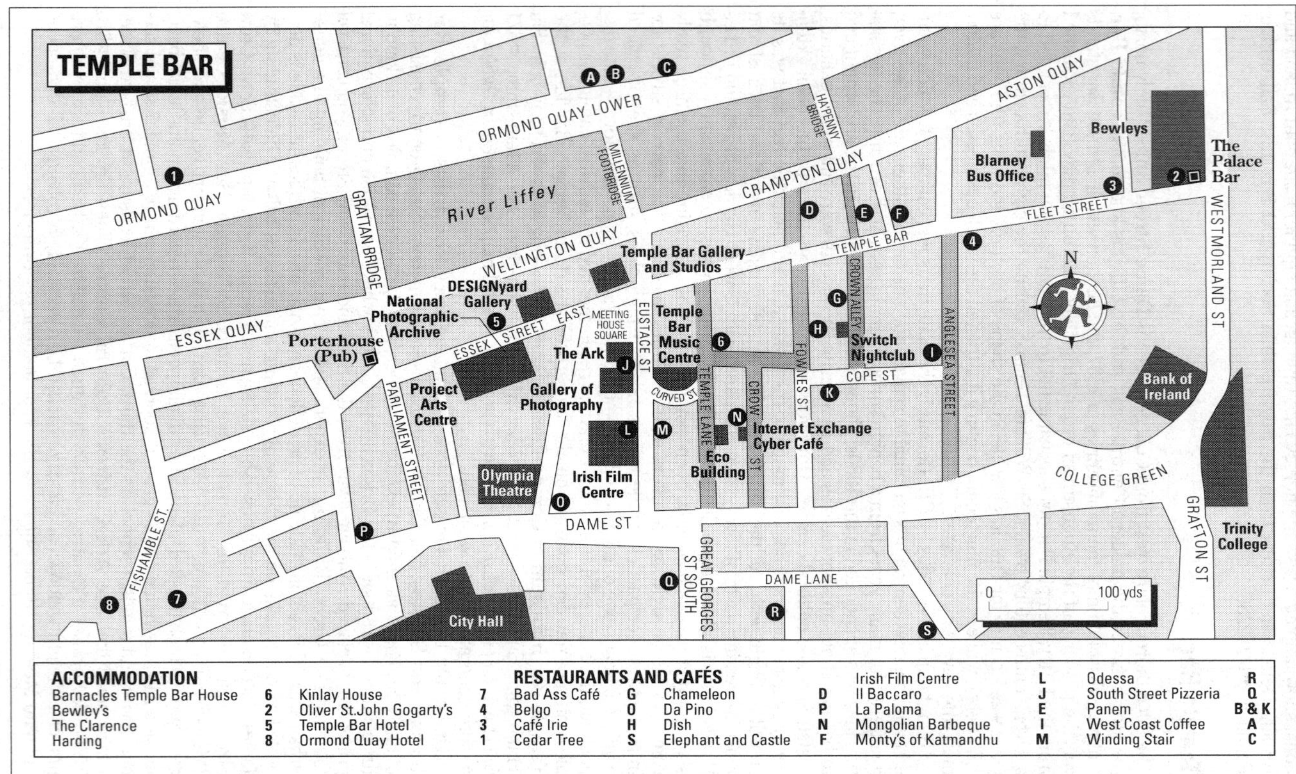

ACCOMMODATION			
Barnacles Temple Bar House	6	Kinlay House	7
Bewley's	2	Oliver St.John Gogarty's	4
The Clarence	5	Temple Bar Hotel	3
Harding	8	Ormond Quay Hotel	1

RESTAURANTS AND CAFÉS							
				Irish Film Centre	L	Odessa	R
Bad Ass Café	G	Chameleon	D	Il Baccaro	J	South Street Pizzeria	Q
Belgo	O	Da Pino	P	La Paloma	E	Panem	B & K
Café Irie	H	Dish	N	Mongolian Barbeque	I	West Coast Coffee	A
Cedar Tree	S	Elephant and Castle	F	Monty's of Katmandhu	M	Winding Stair	C

At the back of Eustace Street, **Meeting House Square** is the second of the main squares in the Temple Bar area and is surrounded by cultural centres. At the south end stands the **Gallery of Photography**; its main exhibition space is reached via an opaque-glass stair tower, and on top there's a roof terrace with views over the square. At the other side you can access the **Irish Film Centre** (*www.fii.ie*), but, if you want to really appreciate the building, it's best to retrace your steps and use the entrance on Eustace Street. The IFC was, in many ways, the inspiration for much of the architecture in the area, and is a coolly minimalist conversion of an old Quaker meeting house. Inside is a courtyard with a film bookshop, an excellent restaurant and bar, plus two screens where you can catch an interesting repertory of art-house movies. The National Film Archive and Film Base, an independent co-operative of Irish film-makers, is also housed here. A worthwhile introduction to Irish film is screened every afternoon. Taking the Sycamore Street exit from the IFC and walking towards the river, you'll come to the **DESIGNyard**, a space for showing contemporary Irish jewellery, furniture and interior design. The building itself is a converted eighteenth-century china warehouse, and the mosaic-patterned floor is designed to represent the River Poddle which flows beneath the building.

The elegant, arching pedestrian bridge that leads from Temple Bar to the north bank of the Liffey is known as the **Ha'penny Bridge**, from the toll which was charged until the early 1900s. Close by, on the northside of the river, is The Winding Stair at 40 Lower Ormond Quay, a kind of northerly outpost of the anarchic spirit of Temple Bar as it used to be before the money-men arrived. Here you'll find an excellent secondhand bookshop with plenty of good remaindered paperbacks, and a café where you can sit and stare peacefully through the grimy windows while the Liffey oozes past the Ha'penny Bridge.

Dublin Castle and around

Dublin Castle (Mon–Fri 10am–5pm, Sat & Sun 2–5pm, tours every 15min; *www.historic-centres.com*; £3/€3.81) is just a short walk along Dame Street. Once inside the castle precinct, you're confronted with a real pig's ear of architectural styles: an ugly modern tax office stands to your left, an over-precise Gothic fantasy of a church of 1803 adorns the ridge straight ahead, and to your right is the worn red brick of the castle itself.

The castle dates from King John's first Dublin court of 1207, so it's a surprise to find that today it has the appearance of a graceful eighteenth-century building, with only the massive stone **Record Tower** giving the game away – although, in the nineteenth century, this too was heavily rebuilt. Originally there were four such towers – the base of the Bermingham Tower, to the southwest, also survives – but the castle later became more of an administrative than a military centre. After the Act of Union at the beginning of the nineteenth century the castle continued as the Viceroy's seat, and as the heart of British rule, the place stands as a symbol of seven hundred years of British power in Ireland.

Sometimes the intended symbolism is subverted by Dublin humour: the figure of Justice that stands at the top of the **Bedford Tower**, on the northside of the yard, turns her back to the city, illustrating, it was said, just how much justice Dubliners could expect from the English. Furthermore, the scales she holds used to tilt when it rained; to ensure even-handedness, the problem was solved by drilling holes in the scale-pans.

The castle hosted the European Parliament in 1990, and massive amounts of EU funds were spent on refurbishing it in honour of the occasion. The **State Apartments** are now used by the president to entertain foreign dignitaries (so at times they will be closed to visitors). It's these, including the **State Drawing Room** and the **Throne Room**, that you'll see on the official tour. The grandeur of the furnishings takes a bit of adjusting to; for instance, all the rooms have Donegal hand-tufted carpets mirroring the eighteenth-century stucco-work, which although superb examples of craftsmanship really are quite overpowering. This opulence must always have been in stark contrast to the surrounding reality of the city: the high wall that you'll notice at the end of the castle's garden is said to have been built to shield the delicate sensibilities of Queen Victoria from the appalling condition of the slums on St Stephen Street.

Excavations for the new conference centre built in 1990 revealed perhaps the most interesting part of the tour, the **Undercroft**. Here you can see remains of an earlier Viking fort, part of the original thirteenth-century moat plus the base of the Powder Tower, a section of the old city wall and the steps that used to lead down to the Liffey. It's unfortunate that similar care for the city's past was not practised two blocks north of the castle on **Wood Quay**, the site of Viking and Norman settlements that yielded amazing quantities of archeological finds (on show in the National Museum Annexe). The excavations were never completed and there's undoubtedly more to be discovered on the site, but despite a lot of argument the corporation of Dublin was able to go ahead and put up two massive Civic Offices, known to one and all as "The Bunkers", destroying what may have been the most important early Viking archeological site in Europe.

The castle is also home to the **Chester Beatty Library and Gallery** (May–Sept Mon–Fri 10am–5pm, Sat 11am–5pm, Sun 1–5pm; Oct–April Tues–Fri 10am–5pm; *www.cbl.ie*; free), created by Sir Alfred Chester Beatty, an Irish-American mining magnate who settled in Dublin in 1950 and gave his remarkable collection of oriental art to the nation. Its superbly crafted *objets d'art* range from Chinese rhino-horn cups to life-size Burmese Buddhas, while the manuscripts include the oldest surviving examples of Egyptian love poetry.

In front of the castle on Lord Edward Street is **City Hall** (Mon–Sat 10am–5.15pm, Sun 2–5pm), one of the finest examples of late Georgian architecture in the city. Built between 1769 and 1779 as a financial centre, the building's sumptuous interior reflects the power and prestige felt by eighteenth-century Dublin's merchant class. One of the most striking features of the building is the exquisite plasterwork by stuccodore Charles Thorpe which decorates the gently lit dome above the building's rotunda. To the right of the entrance is an eighteen-foot-high statue of Daniel O'Connell, created by John Hogan in 1843, where "the Liberator" is represented in the classical oratorical pose he may have adopted in 1800 when he made his first public speech in this building.

St Werburgh's Church

Werburgh Street (left as you come out of the castle, and then left again) was the site of Dublin's first theatre; today, it's home of *Leo Burdock's*, the legendary fish-and-chip shop (see p.111) as well as **St Werburgh's Church**. Reputedly, by origin, the oldest church in Dublin, its plain exterior, with peeling paint in motley shades of grey, conceals a flamboyant and elegant 1759 interior built in the height of Georgian style, which is well worth seeing. Unfortunately, as with a lot of Dublin's Church of Ireland churches, you'd better resign yourself to the fact that it nearly always seems to be closed; except for services on Sundays (at 11am). Lord Edward Fitzgerald, one of the leaders of the 1798 Rebellion (see p.671), is buried in the vault; Major Henry Sirr, who captured him for the British, is interred in the churchyard. Also, John Field, the early nineteenth-century Irish composer and pianist who is credited with having invented the nocturne, later developed by Chopin, was baptized here, and in the church records there is mention of one "Molly Malone, fishmonger" who died in 1734.

The cathedrals

The area west of Dublin Castle is the site of the **original Viking settlement** and represents the most ancient part of the city: the old Tholsel, or town hall, used to stand here, as did the original Four Courts. Today, this historic place is remarkable for its strange combination of urban desolation and renewal (generous tax concessions are ensuring that there's plenty of new building), and the massive, over-restored grey bulks of not one but two **cathedrals**. Both date originally from the twelfth century: Christchurch from 1172 and St Patrick's, designed to supersede it, from 1190. The reason why both have survived appears to be that Christchurch stood inside the city walls, and St Patrick's outside. Both cathedrals remain dedicated to the Church of Ireland, their great forms once a symbol of the dominance of the British, but now manifestations of what is very much a minority religious denomination.

Christchurch Cathedral and around

Christchurch (daily 10am–5pm; £2/€2.54 donation suggested) stands isolated by the traffic system. Like St Patrick's, it suffered at the hands of Victorian restorers, but is still very much a resonant historic site. Dublin's first (wooden) cathedral was founded here by Sitric Silkenbeard, first Christian king of the Dublin Norsemen, in 1038; that church was demolished by the Norman Richard de Clare – Strongbow – who built the new stone cathedral in 1172. This building didn't fare very well, either: it was built on inadequate foundations on a peat bog, and the south wall fell down in 1562. The building you see now is the result of an 1870s restoration; even the purely ornamental flying buttresses are a figment of the imagination of its architect, G.E. Street. Despite all this, the building remains a monument to that first serious British incursion into Ireland in the twelfth century. Strongbow himself is interred here (or part of him), underneath an effigy which quite possibly depicts an Earl of Drogheda.

Like many of Dublin's larger monuments, Christchurch keeps drawing in the crowds with multimedia evocations of history. Styling itself as "a bridge to the medieval past", **Dublinia** (Feb & March Mon–Sat 10am–4.30pm; April–Sept daily 10am–5pm; last admission one hour before closing; ☎679 4611, *www.dublinia.ie*; £3.95/€5.00, includes admission to Christchurch), offers a series of presentations of medieval Dublin, including Strongbow's arrival, a full-size reconstruction of a merchant's house and a grotesque depiction of the Black Death. The Viking and Norman artefacts dug up at nearby Wood Quay are also on display here.

Close by, the augustly monumental **St Audoen's Church** (entry is on Sunday mornings), the oldest of Dublin's parish churches, was founded by the Normans. Today, it's a strange hybrid: the original one, part of which dates from the twelfth century, is now a Protestant church which is grafted on to a much larger, nineteenth-century, Catholic structure. The arch beside it, dating back to 1215, is the only surviving gate from the old city walls.

Not all is as old as it seems hereabouts; for all its air of authenticity, the pub, *Mother Redcap's* (a little further west on Back Lane, off High Street), is a modern creation amid the open spaces left by the clearance of the inner-city slums. Nearby, however, the **Tailors' Guild Hall** (1706) is the city's last surviving guildhall, with an assembly room that includes an eighteenth-century musicians' gallery where Wolfe Tone and Napper Tandy spoke to the revolutionary "Back Lane Parliament" in the run-up to the 1798 Rebellion. Tailors' Hall is now the headquarters of An Taisce (pronounced *On Tashka*) a pioneering conservation organization which has done much to raise awareness of the city's need to preserve its rich architectural heritage.

St Patrick's Cathedral

South down Nicholas and Patrick streets from the Guild Hall is **St Patrick's Cathedral** (April–Oct Mon–Fri 9am–6pm, Sat 9am–5pm; Nov–Mar Mon–Fri 9am–6pm, Sat 9am–4pm, Sun 10am–4.30pm; £2.30/€2.92; bus #50, #54A, #56A from Eden Quay) the national cathedral of the Church of Ireland and a much more elegant place inside than the grey tank-like exterior leads you to expect. Legend has it that St Patrick baptized

JONATHAN SWIFT

Best known for his satires, including the classic *Gulliver's Travels*, **Jonathan Swift** (1667–1745) was born at Hoey's Court, close to St Werburgh's Church. He could read by the age of 3, and at 15 got a place at Trinity College where he studied Latin, Greek and Aristotelian philosophy. On graduating, he worked in England for the diplomat Sir William Temple, after whom Temple Bar is named, and subsequently for the Church of Ireland in the small parish of Kilroot, Co. Antrim. He was appointed Dean of St Patrick's in 1713, where he remained until his death.

In 1704, while in London, Swift began publishing political pamphlets and was forced to return to Ireland because his pen secured him some enemies among the Whigs. Over the next couple of decades, both his commitment to Ireland and his social conscience grew. He was among those who advocated Irish economic independence: in 1720 his *Proposal for the Universal Use of Irish Manufactures*, published anonymously, suggested that the Irish burn everything English except its coal. More notorious is *A Modest Proposal* of 1729, a bitter satire in which he suggested that the Irish could solve their problems by selling their babies to the English for food.

Swift's presence is everywhere in the cathedral, giving hints of both his often vitriolic interventions in Dublin's public life and his own mysterious and contorted private life. Immediately to the right of the entrance are memorials to both him and Esther Johnson (1681–1728), the "Stella" with whom he had a passionate, though apparently platonic, relationship. Stella was the daughter of Sir William Temple's housekeeper; in 1701, after Temple's death, Swift brought her to Dublin and lived near her for the rest of her life.

Within the cathedral there's a tribute to Swift from the sharp-quilled English poet Alexander Pope:

Let Ireland tell how Wit upheld her cause,
Her Trade supported and supplied her Laws
And leave on Swift this grateful verse engraved
"The rights a Court attack'd a Poet sav'd."

The two men were good friends and used to plan sharing a home in retirement (the correspondence – which appears in *The Correspondence of Jonathan Swift* – between them is an interesting one, particularly for the gentle light it casts on Pope), although this plan never came to fruition.

The north pulpit contains Swift's writing table, chair, portrait and death mask. He died aged 78 after years of agony from an ailment, unidentified at the time, whose symptoms of giddiness and deafness terrified him with the possibility that he might be going mad. It's thought that his malady was Méunière's disease, a degenerative disease of the middle ear that was finally identified in 1861. He left money to build Swift's Hospital, now St Patrick's, close to the Royal Hospital Kilmainham for the insane. When it opened in 1757 it was one of the first psychiatric institutions in the world.

Swift's epitaph, which he wrote himself, appears in Latin in simple gold lettering on a plain black slab above the door to the Robing Room in the Cathedral. The English translation hangs beside the door:

Here is laid the body of
Jonathan Swift, Doctor of Divinity,
Dean of this Cathedral Church,
Where fierce indignation can no longer
Rend the heart
Go, traveller, and imitate, if you can
This earnest and dedicated
Champion of liberty.

converts within its grounds; however, its most famous association is with the writer Jonathan Swift, who was dean of St Patrick's in the eighteenth century (see box on opposite).

At the west end of the church is the former chapter door of the south transept with a hole roughly hewn into it. Local legend has it that, in 1492, the feuding earls of Kildare and Ormonde met here, and with Ormonde's supporters barricaded inside the cathedral, Kildare, eager to end the struggle, cut a hole in the door and put his arm through it, inviting Ormonde to shake hands. He did, peace was restored, and the phrase "chancing your arm" was born.

There are plenty of interesting tombs and memorials in the cathedral. One of the most elaborate, at the west end of the church, is a seventeenth-century **monument to the Boyle family**, earls of Cork, which is teeming with painted figures of family members. The tomb originally stood beside the altar, but only a year after being installed in 1632 it was moved. Thomas Wentworth, Earl of Strafford and the British Viceroy in Dublin, had objected that churchgoers were forced to pray "crouching to an Earl of Cork and his lady... or to those sea nymphs his daughters, with coronets upon their heads, their hair dishevelled, down upon their shoulders." This was not the end of the argument, and it was the Earl of Cork who won: he later had Wentworth executed. Robert Boyle – who, as the only son, has pride of place in a niche of his own in the centre of the lowest tier – went on to become a scientist who established the important relationship, still known as Boyle's Law, between the pressure, volume and temperature of a gas.

At the east end of the church a series of three Elizabethan brasses tells the plaintive stories of some of the early English settlers in Ireland. There's a small, plain monument in the north transept to one Alexander McGee, a servant of Swift, erected by the dean in what was clearly an unusual gesture as all the other tablets are to people of property. Finally, near the entrance, it comes as a surprise, among all the relics of the Anglo-Irish, to find an inscription in Irish dedicated to Douglas Hyde, founder of the Gaelic League, first president of Ireland and son of a Church of Ireland clergyman. The plaque commemorates him by using his Gaelic pen name "An Craoibhín Aoibhinn" meaning "the delightful little branch".

Archbishop Marsh's Library

Just outside the main entrance of St Patrick's Cathedral is a compact Georgian building, faced in brick at the front but, tactfully, in the same unrelenting grey stone as the cathedral on the side that faces the church. This is **Archbishop Marsh's Library** (Mon & Wed–Fri 10am–12.45pm & 2–5pm, Sat 10.30am–12.45pm; £1/€1.27 donation is expected), Ireland's first public library, built in 1701 (by Sir William Robinson, who also designed the Royal Hospital Kilmainham) and given to the city by the wonderfully named Archbishop Narcissus Marsh. Inside, the tiny reading cubicles and the dark carved bookcases carrying huge leather-bound tomes – some 25,000 of them, most dating from the sixteenth to the eighteenth centuries; the earliest a Latin manuscript of 1400 – can hardly have changed since the library was built. The library was peppered with bullets during the 1916 rising, and some of the seventeenth-century volumes are marked by British Army bullets intended for the nearby Jacob's factory which was a rebel stronghold. The single most important collection in the library is that of Edward Stillingfleet, Archbishop of Worcester. His 10,000 books were bought for £2,500 and include works from some of the earliest English printers, including Berthelet, Daye and Fawkes. Archbishop Marsh – of whom Swift remarked that "no man will be either glad or sorry at his death" (the dean believed that it was Marsh's fault he had not risen higher in his ecclesiastical career) – was responsible for the preparation of the first translation of the Old Testament into Irish, and two of the volumes survive in the library. The chains that once protected the books from theft are long gone, but three lock-in cages for readers of rare books survive; although today it's more likely you'll sit in the main office under the watchful eye of the librarian.

The Liberties, the Guinness brewery and Kilmainham

Two blocks northwest of the library is the area known as **The Liberties**, which was once outside the legal jurisdiction of the city and settled by French **Huguenot** refugees escaping religious persecution in their own country. They set up home and poplin- and silk-weaving industries in the southern part of The Liberties known as the Coombe (there is now a street named after it). The ten thousand Huguenots who arrived between 1650 and the early eighteenth century had a great civilizing effect on what was then a small and underdeveloped city: they founded a horticultural society and encouraged the wine trade. The Liberties have maintained the characteristics of self-sufficiency that the Huguenots brought with them, and there are families able to trace their local roots back for many generations. In the nineteenth century, local rivalries frequently erupted into violence between the Liberty Boys, the tailors and weavers of the Coombe, and the Ormond Boys, butchers who lived in Ormond Market (to the north of the Liffey at Ormond Quay). Today, The Liberties are still a hotchpotch of busy streets full of barrows and bargain and betting shops, but Government tax incentives and low property prices have encouraged speculators to build blocks of high-security luxury apartments, which sit oddly among the urban jumble.

The main road leading west of Christchurch (High Street leading to James's Street), is interspersed with grim corporate housing and deserted factories, and dominated by the **Guinness brewery**. The brewery was used as one of the sets in Fritz Lang's *Metropolis*, with huge dark chimneys belching smoke and tiny figures hurrying along grimy balconies. For all the seediness of its surroundings, however, Guinness is one of Ireland's biggest commercial successes. Founded in 1759, the St James's Gate brewery covers 64 acres and has the distinction of being the world's largest single beer-exporting company, exporting some three hundred million pints of the famous stout a year; 2.5 million pints are brewed here every day. Unfortunately, you can't go round the brewery, but the former Guinness Hop Store on Rainsford Street houses an exhibition centre containing a replica brewery, pub, restaurant, gift shop and various exhibition rooms (Mon–Sat 9.30am–5pm; ☎453 3645, *www.guinness.ie*; £5/€6.35; buses #21A, #78, #78A and #78B from outside the Virgin Megastore opposite O'Connell Bridge). The best of the exhibition rooms are on the upper floors of the airy, four-storey building, and feature displays on Guinness advertising from the animal cartoons and painful puns of John Gilroy to the more obscure modern masterpieces. The upper floors are also given over to exhibitions of contemporary art and offer fine views over Dublin. The self-guided tour ends with what is arguably the best Guinness in Dublin – arguably because the honour traditionally went to *Mulligan's* in Poolbeg Street (northeast of College Green near George's Quay, see p.116), which still has its devotees.

The Royal Hospital Kilmainham and the Irish Museum of Modern Art

If you get off the bus (#21A, #78, #78B, #79 and #90) where James' Street joins Bow Lane, you'll walk past Swift's Hospital, now known as St Patrick's, on your way to the **Royal Hospital Kilmainham** (just five minutes' walk further west). The hospital was extensively and well restored between 1980 and 1984, and the result is that Ireland's first Classical building – its date is 1680 – is a joy to look at, from the outside at least. The name doesn't imply a medical institution of any kind: it was built as a home for wounded army pensioners, like Chelsea Hospital in London or Les Invalides in Paris. The plan is simple: a colonnaded building around a central courtyard, erected with cool restraint so that the sober stone arcading creates a lovely, unadorned rhythm.

Initially the use of the hospital to house the **Irish Museum of Modern Art** (Tues–Sat 10am–5.30pm, Sun noon–5.30pm; free), which opened in 1991, caused a great deal of controversy. This was not least because its inside was depersonalized and painted white to provide gallery space of the correct, "modern" kind of conversion, which led one commentator to quote the Flann O'Brien story about a man born at the age of 25 with a consciousness but no history. As the gallery evolved, acquiring a permanent collection and thus a character and "history" of its own, most of the criticism dissipated and the former hospital has proved to be a very successful and popular exhibition space. There are no permanent exhibitions in the museum (consult *In Dublin* for current exhibitions), which so far owns few works of its own, but instead has a regularly changing collection of works mainly borrowed from European collections that hang alongside Irish ones. In the basement under the north wing is an excellent restaurant.

Kilmainham Gaol

Outside the hospital, a small formal garden runs down to the Liffey, and a long, tree-lined avenue leads out to the front gates, beyond which looms the grim mass of **Kilmainham Gaol** (April–Sept daily 9.30am–4.45pm; Oct–March Mon–Fri 9.30am–4pm, Sun 10am–4.45pm; £3/€3.81; Heritage Card). Built in 1792, the jail was completed just in time to hold a succession of Nationalist agitators, from the United Irishmen of 1798, through Young Irelanders, Fenians and Land Leaguers (including Parnell and Davitt) in 1883, to the leading insurgents of the 1916 Easter Rising – Pádraig Pearse and James Connolly were executed in the prison yard. Éamon de Valera, subsequently three times prime minister and later president, was the very last prisoner to be incarcerated here; he was released in July 1924.

The complex is a great introduction to the history of Republicanism in Ireland, though don't expect any revisionism here, as the history has a real green tint. Not all the prisoners were political: an indication of the severity of punishments is given by a document recording a sentence of seven years' transportation for stealing a piece of printed calico. The **guided tours** (included in admission price) give an emotionally coloured impression of the place, climaxing in the low lighting of the chapel, where, on May 4, 1916, Joseph Plunkett, one of the leaders of the Easter Rising of 1916, was married by candlelight to Grace Gifford while twenty British soldiers stood to attention, bayonets fixed. They were married at 1.30am; he was executed at 3.30am, after just ten minutes in his wife's company. Until the executions of most of the leaders of the Easter Rising, the insurrection commanded little popular support in Dublin. The rebels had held notable buildings, among them the General Post Office (see p.96) and the Jacob's factory, for five days until British artillery pounded them into submission. It was only after the leaders of the rebellion, most especially James Connolly, already almost mortally wounded, were executed at Kilmainham (he had to be tied to a chair so they could shoot him) that a wave of support gathered behind the Nationalist cause – leading, ultimately, to the withdrawal of British troops, the partition of Ireland, and civil war.

The northside: O'Connell Street and around

Crossing over O'Connell Bridge you reach O'Connell Street, the northside's main thoroughfare and once the most grandiose of Dublin streets. However, before wandering up what is still the city's busiest, although less salubrious, centre for shopping, it's worth taking a detour eastwards along Eden Quay to the famous **Abbey Theatre** and the elegant **Custom House**.

The Abbey Theatre

Not far along Eden Quay, turn left up Marlborough Street to the Abbey Theatre on the corner of Abbey Street Lower. Ireland's national theatre, it was opened in 1904 (nearly twenty years before Independence), with co-founders and Celtic literature revivalists W.B. Yeats and Lady Gregory as its first directors. The Abbey soon gained worldwide prestige for its productions of Irish playwrights such as Sean O'Casey, J.M. Synge and W.B. Yeats, but at home it also generated great controversy – even riots. Indicative of how much the theatre in Ireland has always been a platform for political dialogue, O'Casey's *The Plough and the Stars* (1926), which questioned the motivations of the by-now haloed martyrs of 1916, so undercut and discredited the romanticized vision of Ireland that Yeats had helped to create – and the Nationalists had encouraged – that Dubliners took to the streets to protest. Today the new Abbey (its predecessor was destroyed by a fire in 1951) holds two theatres, the main one devoted to the Irish classics and new works by writers such as Brian Friel and Frank McGuinness, while the smaller Peacock Theatre often shows new experimental drama. For details of what's on, see *In Dublin*.

The Custom House

It's easy enough to overlook the **Custom House**, lying in the shadow of the metal railway viaduct that runs parallel to O'Connell Bridge, east along the river. But, as one of the great Georgian masterpieces built by James Gandon, it's an impressive reminder of the city's eighteenth-century splendour. It is principally Gandon's public buildings that put Dublin ahead of other great, and better-preserved, Georgian cities such as Bath and Edinburgh. The Custom House was the first of them, completed in 1791 (the Four Courts, although started in 1786, were not completed until 1802, and the King's Inns were designed in 1795). It burned for five days after it was set alight by Republicans in 1921, but was thoroughly restored (and has recently been refurbished again), and now houses government offices.

The best view of the building is from the other side of Matt Talbot Bridge, from where you can admire the long, regular loggia, portico and dome, all reflected in the muddy waters of the Liffey. This elegance conceals a story of personal ambition and dirty tricks. The building was originally planned by John Beresford, chief commissioner of revenue, and his friend Luke Gardiner. A large stone in the bed of the Liffey was preventing some boats from reaching the old customs point, further upstream, and this was ostensibly the argument for building a new one; Beresford and Gardiner's prime reason for backing the scheme on the other hand was that it served their own purposes to shift the commercial centre of the city east from Capel Street to the area where O'Connell Street now stands. Their plans were opposed through parliamentary petitions, personal complaints, even violence, and the hostile party was delighted to discover that the site for the new building was the muddy banks of the Liffey where, they thought, it would be impossible to build foundations. Gandon, however, confounded the scheme's critics by building the foundations on a layer of pine planks – which seems to have done the job.

O'Connell Street

Most things of historical interest on O'Connell Street –now lined by fast-food restaurants, shops, cinemas and modern offices – have long since been submerged under the tide of neon lights and plate glass, but one major exception is the **General Post Office** (Mon–Sat 8am–8pm, Sun 10.30am–6.30pm), which stands at the corner of Henry Street. It was opened in 1818, and its fame stems from the fact that almost a century later it became the rebel headquarters in one of the most significant battles in the fight for Independence in 1916 (see box opposite). The entire building, with the exception of the facade, was destroyed in the fighting; it was later restored and reopened in 1929. From the street you can still see the scars left by bullets: inside the reconstructed marbled halls are also worth a look. In the window is one of the finest sculptures anywhere

THE EASTER RISING

The **Easter Rising** of 1916, which resulted in pitched battles in the streets of Dublin, is remembered as one of the key events leading to Irish self-government. In fact, at the time, it seemed to most Nationalists a botched and inconclusive event. Leaders of the **Irish Volunteers**, a Nationalist group that had been founded in 1913, secretly planned a nationwide uprising for Easter Sunday 1916. The insurrection was to be staged with the help of a shipment of arms from Germany which were to be picked up by Sir Roger Casement (a British official who became a fervent Nationalist supporter; see p.566). Things began to go wrong almost immediately: the arms arrived a day too early, and the British apprehended Casement and hanged him.

So secret had the preparations for the uprising been that the Irish Volunteers' leader, Eoin MacNeill, knew nothing of them. A week before Easter, the extremist plotters, led by **Pádraig Pearse**, showed MacNeill a forged order, purporting to come from the British authorities at Dublin Castle, for the suppression of the Irish Volunteers. MacNeill consented to give the order for the uprising. Then, the day before it was due to happen, he learned that the document was a forgery, and placed advertisements in the Sunday papers cancelling the insurrection. Pearse and his allies, however, pressed ahead in Dublin only the next day: Easter Monday. They took, among other public buildings, the General Post Office (GPO) in O'Connell Street, and Pearse walked out onto the steps of the GPO to read the historic Proclamation of the Irish Republic (see p.674). Fighting continued for five days before being suppressed by the British authorities.

It was not the rising itself, but the British reaction to it, that was significant for the Republicans. The authorities executed a total of fifteen leaders of the rebellion, including Pearse and another patriot, James Connolly, at Kilmainham Gaol (see p.95). The result in the eyes of the public, however, was to turn these men into martyrs to the Nationalist cause. When, a year later, the British attempted to introduce conscription to the trenches of World War I, the public mood turned sharply away from any form of compromise with British rule and towards demands for full independence, which was finally achieved in 1921.

in the city – *The Death of Cúchulainn* by Oliver Sheppard. The exquisite bronze sculpture was commissioned in 1935 and represents the moment when the raven rests on the shoulder of Cúchulainn, the mythical warrior, before he finally dies. O'Connell Street itself is reputedly one of Europe's widest, and there's a paved stretch down the middle with a series of **statues**. Until 1966 one of them, directly in front of the GPO, depicted Nelson on top of a column; it was blown up by IRA sympathizers in March 1966 (you can inspect the statue's head in the Civic Museum (see p.79). The city's millennium year saw a notoriously expensive new addition: an angular recumbent woman bathed by a fountain representing Joyce's Anna Livia, the personification of the river Liffey, and quickly nicknamed "the floozie in the Jacuzzi", or "the whore in the sewer" (this rhymes in a Dublin accent). The site will soon be home to another contentious statue, the *Monument of Light*, a huge illuminated stainless steel spike said to represent the city's hope for the new millennium; Dubliners have been outdoing each other yet again to devise a suitable sobriquet with "the stiletto in the ghetto" proving to be the most popular so far.

Two areas of interest lie either side of the GPO. On Abbey Street Lower, a couple of streets south towards the river, is one of the city's newest exhibitions: **The Hot Press Irish Music Hall of Fame** (daily 10am–7pm; ☎878 3345, *www.imhf.com*; £6/€7.61). The exhibition traces the history of Irish music from traditional to, by far the most interesting section, pop and rock music, following the latter's progress from the sublime Gary Moore to teeny idles such as Boyzone and B*witched. All manner of memorabilia from Bob Geldof's stained Live Aid T-shirt to Sinéad O'Connor's family album catches your eye. Audio guides help to orientate you through the exhibition by cleverly picking up on a signal in each room, though this can result in some annoying overlap. While the exhibits are well presented and there are plenty of good music samples, it's hard to justify the exorbitant entrance fee, though if you are a fan of Irish music you may find it worth the extra cost. Beside the GPO, Henry Street leads to **Moore Street Market**, where you'll find some of the disappearing street life that people are apt to get misty-eyed about. The truth is that the same activities continue to flourish in the less romantic settings of the Illac shopping centre, round the corner, or in the new mall on St Stephen's Green; that doesn't alter the fact that Moore Street's brightly coloured stalls and banter are a lot of fun. On the opposite side of O'Connell Street is Cathedral Street, which leads to the Greek Revival **St Mary's Pro-Cathedral** (1816–25), Dublin's most important Catholic church. Due to fears that the originally planned position on O'Connell Street would incite anti-Catholic feeling among the English, the cathedral is hidden away here. Consequently, getting a good view of its six Doric columns – based on the Temple of Theseus in Athens – is nigh on impossible. Inside, every Sunday at 11am, you can hear the famous Palestina Choir; the Choir was established in 1902. John McCormack, the respected and popular tenor, began his career here in 1904.

The final statue at the top of O'Connell Street commemorates the nineteenth-century politician Charles Stewart Parnell (see p.672), quoting his famous words "No man has a right to fix the boundary to the march of a nation. No man has a right to say to his country, Thus far shalt thou go and no futher...".

Parnell Square to Mountjoy Square

At the top of O'Connell Street, behind Parnell's statue in the square named for him, stands the **Rotunda Maternity Hospital**, built in 1752. This was the very first purpose-built maternity hospital in Europe. The barber-surgeon Bartholomew Mosse funded the enterprise by organizing events including fancy dress balls, recitals and concerts – one of these was the first performance of Handel's *Messiah*, which took place on April 15, 1742. There's a superb chapel with a stucco ceiling by Bartholomew Cramillion, and the Rotunda Room itself houses The Ambassador cinema (see p.119). Part of the remainder of the building is still a maternity hospital, while another section – the old Assembly Rooms – houses the **Gate Theatre**, which was opened by the legendary actor Micheál MacLiammóir and Hilton Edwards in 1929. Behind the Rotunda, bordering on Parnell Square, is all that remains of the pleasure gardens, yet another of Dr Mosse's successful fund-raising ventures. This little open space is now a **Garden of Remembrance** for all those who died in the Independence struggle, with a sculpture by Oisín Kelly of the *Children of Lir* (see p.203). **Parnell Square**, originally called Rutland Square, was one of the first of Dublin's Georgian squares and still has its plain, bright, red-brick houses, broken by the grey-stone mass of the **Hugh Lane Municipal Art Gallery** (Tues–Fri 9.30am–6pm, Sat 9.30am–5pm, Sun 11am–5pm; free; buses passing from the centre include #10, #11, #13, #16 and #22). Originally the town house of the Earl of Charlemont, built for him by the Scottish architect Sir William Chambers in 1762, it was the focus of fashionable Dublin – the northside of the square was known as Palace Row – before the city centre moved south of the river. Chambers was also the architect of the delightful Casino, built to embellish the aesthetic Lord Charlemont's country house a few miles away at Marino (see p.107).

The house works well in its revised role as an art gallery, with plenty of good lighting and an intimate scale that complements the pictures. The gallery was set up in 1908 with funds donated by Sir Hugh Lane (nephew of Lady Gregory of Abbey Theatre fame), who died when the *Lusitania* was torpedoed in 1915. He left his collection – centred around the French Impressionists – to "the nation", and with Ireland's independence the problem arose of which of the two nations he might have meant. In 1960 the two governments agreed to exchange halves of the collection every five years, but in 1982 the British government put in a claim for the lot. The matter has recently been settled, with half the collection permanently in residence at Hugh Lane. It makes interesting viewing, with work from the pre-Raphaelites onwards added to by more modern Irish painters such as Jack B. Yeats and Paul Henry; of particular note is a stained glass window by Harry Clarke, who was also responsible for the Birds of Paradise window in the Westmoreland Street *Bewley's* (see p.111). At the time of writing, plans were well advanced for a new wing devoted to Irish-born artist Francis Bacon; the contents of his studio were recently donated to the gallery. There are sometimes free recitals on Sunday lunchtimes (see *In Dublin* for details), and downstairs there's a good-value café/restaurant.

Two doors down, at nos. 18 and 19, a pair of modest Georgian houses are the home of the **Dublin Writers' Museum** (Mon–Sat 10am–5pm, Sun 11.30am–6pm; ☎872 2077; £3.10/€3.93, £4.70/€5.96 including Shaw's birthplace or the James Joyce Tower in Sandycove). There's certainly plenty of material to draw on: apart from its three Nobel laureates – George Bernard Shaw, W.B. Yeats and Samuel Beckett – Dublin nurtured a host of other writers, including Joseph Sheridan le Fanu, Jonathan Swift, Sean O'Casey, Brendan Behan and, of course, James Joyce. However, the exhibits are on the dull side – there's a predictable range of memorabilia, including Brendan Behan's typewriter – and the free audio guide does little to enliven the proceedings. The exhibition begins with a reference to early Irish poetry and the English poet Edmund Spenser's *Faerie Queen*, weaves rapidly through Jonathan Swift's *A Modest Proposal* of 1729 and the romantic fiction of the mid-nineteenth century to Oscar Wilde and the playwright George Bernard Shaw. Joyce shares a cabinet with Sean O'Casey – this really is a whistle-stop tour – and the exhibits wind up with material on Samuel Beckett, Brendan Behan and the comic writer Flann O'Brien. Upstairs is a fine 1760s library with rather oppressive colour added in the nineteenth century, now somewhat sententiously dubbed the Gallery of Writers. A good bookshop stocks an intelligent selection of books, including contemporary authors, and a café offers a modest selection of salads; the restaurant below the museum is excellent, and if you are in the area, you could do worse than try their pre-theatre menu. Next door is the **Living Writers' Centre**, with work rooms, a couple of apartments, a lecture room, and an on-going programme of literary lectures and seminars: ring the museum for further details.

Mountjoy Square

As you head northeast along Denmark Street toward Mountjoy Square, the streets, although a little run-down, are being slowly regenerated. Appropriately enough given the presence of the Writers' Museum, the area also has plenty of **literary associations**: Belvedere College in Great Denmark Street is where James Joyce went to school; Sean O'Casey wrote all his plays for the Abbey Theatre – *The Shadow of a Gunman, Juno and the Paycock, The Plough and the Stars* and *The Silver Tassie* – at 422 North Circular Rd (a few streets north of the square); and Brendan Behan grew up nearby at 14 Russell St.

Mountjoy Square itself is Dublin's earliest Georgian square, now in an advanced state of decay. Although there are some signs of revitalization, there's little left of the elegance described by Thomas Cromwell in his *Excursions through Ireland* in 1820 "Taste and opulence have united to embellish; the streets in the vicinity are all built on a regular plan; the houses are lofty and elegant; and neither hotels, shops, nor warehouses, obtruding upon the scene, the whole possesses an air of dignified retirement – the tranquillity of ease, affluence and leisure. The inhabitants of this parish are indeed almost exclusively of the upper ranks."

JAMES JOYCE

Author of *Ulysses* (1922), the ultimate celebration of his native city, **James Joyce** – who spent most of his adult life in voluntary exile from Ireland – was born in 1882. After an impoverished childhood, he went to University College, a place of learning then staffed by Jesuit priests, where he led a dissolute life and began to experiment with writing short pieces of prose which he called "epiphanies". In 1904 he started writing the short stories that were eventually published as *Dubliners*. On June 10 of that year, Joyce met Nora Barnacle, and, on their next meeting, June 16, he fell in love with her; it's on this day that the entire epic narrative of *Ulysses* is set. They finally got married some 27 years later.

With the exception of two brief visits to Dublin in 1909, when he attempted to set up a chain of cinemas, and a final visit in 1912, Joyce never again lived in Ireland. All the great works, including *A Portrait of the Artist as a Young Man* (1916) and his late masterpiece, *Finnegans Wake* (1939), were written in various European cities – Zurich, Paris, Trieste – where Joyce and his family eked out a penurious existence supported mostly by donations from rich patrons. At the time of Joyce's death in 1941, *Ulysses* was banned in Ireland, condemned as a pornographic book; it wasn't published in the Republic until the 1960s.

Joyce once remarked that he was "more interested in the street names of Dublin than in the riddle of the universe", and boasted that Dublin could be rebuilt from scratch using the information contained in his books. The **Bloomsday** pilgrimage, held every year on June 16, draws people from all over the world to meet in Dublin where they retrace the action of the novel. It starts at the Martello Tower at Sandycove (see p.105) and progresses through the streets of Dublin, stopping at *Davy Byrne's* pub (see p.115) where Leopold Bloom's lunch of a glass of burgundy and a gorgonzola-and-mustard sandwich is served, followed by the National Library, the *Ormonde Hotel* (Ormond Quay, north Dublin) and all the other locations made iconic by this great novel.

For serious Joyceans, the **James Joyce Centre** at 35 North Great Georges St (Tues–Sat 10am–4.30pm, Sun noon–4.30pm; ☎873 1984; £2/€2.54), not far from the Irish Writers' Centre, has a museum with documents of his life and work, and an excellent bookshop. The centre also has information on lectures, walking tours, and Bloomsday events.

Croke Park GAA Museum

Half a mile east of Mountjoy Square, just outside the boundary formed by the Royal Canal, is Ireland's premier sports stadium, **Croke Park**, home of the Gaelic Athletic Association (May–Sept daily 9.30am–5pm; Oct–April Tues–Sat 10am–5pm, Sun noon–5pm; £3/€3.81). The stadium is intended for use exclusively for the playing of Gaelic games (hurling and gaelic football), though it has in the recent past, much to the horror of cultural traditionalists, hosted pop concerts. One such concert was almost cancelled when a band attempted to fly the flags of the world, because, included amongst them, was a Union Jack. This mixture of sport and politics is at the heart of the GAA (which still bans British security force members from playing its games) but is understandable when one considers its history. Croke Park was the scene of one of the bloodiest atrocities in modern Irish history when, on November 11, 1920, the notorious Black and Tans entered the ground during a match and opened fire on the players and the crowd killing twelve, including Tipperary hurling captain Michael Hogan after whom one of the stands is named. The **museum** is situated under the impressive New Stand, and the exhibition as a whole, most especially the fascinating film *National Awakening*, reflects the political and cultural as well as the sporting history of the organization. There is plenty of interactive entertainment for kids; although anyone will struggle to master the intricate skills of hurling on their first attempt. The tour ends with the exhilarating film *A Day in September*, which captures the excitement, colour and passion, both on and off the field on All Ireland finals day; anyone visiting Dublin at this time should make a trip to the ground to sample the revelry.

The King's Inns, St Michan's and the Four Courts

Leaving Parnell Square at the northwest corner and following Gramby Row round brings you to the **Black Church** (or St Mary's Chapel of Ease) in St Mary's Place – a sinister, brooding building with spiky finials. Legend has it that St Mary's and other similar massive Protestant churches built during the 1820s were designed so that they could be turned into defensive positions should the Catholics attack. As you walk down Dorset Street and into Bolton Street, everything speaks of urban deprivation: rubbish blowing in the gutters, broken glass, barred shop windows. Running off Bolton Street is Henrietta Street; dowdy as it is now, it was once the most fashionable street in Dublin and was one of the first sites of really big houses in the city, two of which (numbers 9 and 10, at the far end) were designed by Sir Edward Lovett Pearce. These adjoin the impressive **King's Inns** – home of the Irish Bar – designed by James Gandon, architect of the Four Courts and the Custom House. During the daytime you can walk through the courtyard to the Inn's garden from which the grandeur of Gandon's building can be truly appreciated. At the west end of the garden is the exit to Constitution Hill. It was from here that St Patrick admired the city he had just converted to Christianity, though the great saint's view was not blocked by the tower blocks that litter the modern day hill. Walking along Constitution Hill into Church Street you reach St Michan's Church.

St Michan's Church

Though it doesn't look much now – only the tower and a few other fragments are original – **St Michan's Church** (Mon–Fri 10am–12.45pm & 2–4.45pm, Sat 10am–12.45pm; £1.50/€1.90), founded in 1095, is the oldest building on the northside. The reason it's on the tourist trail is that the crypt's combination of dry air and constant temperature, together with methane gas secreted by rotting vegetation beneath the church, keeps corpses in a state of unnatural, mummified preservation: some of the "best" are on display, with skin, fingernails and hair all clearly identifiable, sometimes after three hundred years. Depending on the mood of the guide, different crypts are opened, and among the dead are a nun, a crusader and a thief – this last identified as such because of a missing hand, amputated as penance for an earlier offence. One of the crypts contains the death mask of United Irish leader, Wolfe Tone, and the bodies of two of his compatriots, the Sheare brothers. None of the bodies was originally stored in the church, and how this odd collection of corpses got here is still a mystery. St Michan's also boasts an early eighteenth-century organ, still with its original gilding on the case, which Handel played and admired during a visit to Dublin.

The Four Courts

Towards the river and one block east of St Michan's Church are the Four Courts, another of Gandon's majestic architectural pieces. A solid example of Georgian architecture and urban planning, the **Four Courts** (Mon–Fri 9.30am–5pm), were designed between 1786 and 1802 as the seat of the High Court of Justice of Ireland and a chambers for barristers. From the outside the Four Courts have a grim perfection. Inside, the courts – Exchequer, Common Pleas, King's Bench and Chancery – radiate from a circular central hall. The building holds particular historical significance in that it was here that former comrades turned their guns on one another following the 1921 treaty; it was completely gutted and legal documents dating back to the thirteenth century destroyed, when shelled by pro-treaty forces led by Michael Collins, who received the unwelcome reassurance from Winston Churchill that "the archives of the Four Courts may be scattered, but the title deeds of Ireland are safe."

Smithfield and around

A short walk west along Arran Quay from the Four Courts takes you into the cobbled expanse of **Smithfield**, a traditional public space where, for over three hundred years, horse fairs have taken place. In the 1980s the area became infamous as the meeting point for prostitutes and their clients until the idea was mooted to develop the square as Dublin's next cultural centre. Seemingly quixotic at the time, these plans have in many ways been realized by the building of the complex on its eastern edges known as **Smithfield Village**, which includes **Chief O'Neill's Hotel** (see "Accommodation" p.65), **The Old Jameson Distillery**, the **Ceol Irish Traditional Music Centre**, and the **Jameson Chimney Observation Tower**.

The square itself cast off its former scruffy image when architect Garry Ní Eanaigh's visionary plans were realized: the 400,000 cobbles were lifted, hand cleaned and replaced, and the square is now lit by twelve imposing 26-metre-high braziers which cast a two-metre flame skyward. Below these futuristic icons, on the first Sunday of the month, the travelling community's traditional horse sales still take place. A load of horse boxes carrying filthy ponies are brought together, and deals are finalized by spitting into the palm and clapping the hands together. There's nothing remotely glamorous about this entirely male activity, but the event does possess a certain fascination. Most of the buyers and sellers are travellers, once known as itinerants, and before that gypsies: people who speak their own dialect, known as shelta. In fact, shelta has nothing to do with Romany (the most common theory is that the travellers are of purely Irish origin, and took to the roads at the time of the Famine), but the travellers do share with gypsies an impressive knowledge of horses. After the sales you'll see scraggy ponies being ridden away bareback by equally scraggy young boys towards the grim northern suburbs, where impromptu pony races are held. There's great concern, however, that the sales, which date back to 1664, may not form part of the vision for the square, and at the time of writing, the traders were seeking assurances from the High Court that their traditional fair will be allowed to continue unhindered.

The Old Jameson Distillery

Housed in the former distillery of Ireland's favourite whiskey, the tour around the **Old Jameson Distillery** (daily 10am–5.30pm, tours every 30min; ☎807 2355, *www.irish-whiskey-trail.com*; £3.95/€5.00) extols the virtues of Irish whiskey or *uisce beatha* (pronounced ishke baha) in Irish, literally translated as "the water of life", from which the English word whiskey is derived. The exhibits explain the modern-day malting, fermenting and maturing processes, while claiming that it is not only the Scotch spelling of the word (whisky, without the "e") but the product itself that is a corruption of the real (Irish) whiskey. It is alleged that the famous "peaty" taste of Scotch is caused by their use of cheaper fuel and that Scotch is only distilled twice, while the purer, smoother, life-giving water from Ireland is distilled three times. The blatant plugging of the Jameson product and the fact that whiskey is not actually distilled here (the rich aroma which pervades the building is, in fact, synthetic) can be forgiven at the end of the tour when you get to test a tot or two from around the world and compare them with the excellent Jameson product.

Ceol Irish Traditional Music Centre

Housed within the *Chief O'Neill's Hotel* complex is the excellent new **Ceol Irish Traditional Music Centre** (Mon–Sat 9.30am–6pm, Sun 10.30am–6pm; ☎817 3838, *www.ceol.ie*; £5/€6.35) devoted to Irish traditional music (*ceol* is Irish for music). The exhibition eschews the ersatz folksiness that usually surrounds this subject by presenting challenging, bold and progressive multimedia displays. The chrome touch-screen consoles provide a wealth of information on the subject (although there is a limited archive of recorded music, resulting in a certain amount of repetition), while an interactive element is added to the children's room where the young, and young-at-heart, can follow the dance steps of a tune to the sound of the uileann pipe or accordion on floor-panel sensors. The tour ends in a state-of-the-art surround-screen cinema with a thirty-minute film showing the finest traditional musicians in Ireland in full swing, which ultimately leads to the souvenir shop which stocks an impressive range of traditional music.

Jameson Chimney Observation Tower

Directly outside the entrance to *Chief O'Neill's Hotel* stands the old 170-foot chimney of the old Jameson Distillery, on top of which is the **Jameson Chimney Observation Tower** (Mon–Sat 9.30am–6pm, Sun 10.30am–6pm; £5/€6.35 tickets from the Ceol) a two-level glass pod. From this impressive vantage point you can take in this architectural hotchpotch of a city from the huge expanse of green that is Phoenix Park (see below), to the regular, maze-like streets of nearby Stoneybatter, and eastward to the grey-blue waters of the docks where the Liffey finally spews into the Irish Sea. As no maps are provided it's advisable to take your own.

Collins Barracks

A few roads west of Smithfield towards Pheonix Park stand **Collins Barracks**, a series of imposing grey-stone buildings formerly known as the Royal Barracks. Founded in 1704, their chief claim to fame is as the oldest continuously occupied purpose-built barracks in the world, and they now act as an **annexe of the National Museum** (Tues–Sat 10am–5pm, Sun 2–5pm; free). The eclectic collection ranges from the exotic to the mundane, and highlights are the excellent Curator's Choice room where museum curators from throughout Ireland have submitted items of particular interest, and the Irish Silver Room which demonstrates the craftmanship of early Irish silversmiths. To the north is **Arbour Hill Cemetery** (Mon–Sat 9am–4.30pm, Sun 9.30–noon; free) where fourteen of the executed 1916 leaders are buried, while to the south of here is a railed-in plot of grass known as **Croppies Acre** where a monument marks the spot where the executed rebels of 1798 are buried.

Phoenix Park

If you have walked through the urban confusion of the northside, the open spaces of **Phoenix Park**, Dublin's playground – which begins a few-minutes walk west of Collins Barracks – will come as a welcome relief. The name is a corruption of the Irish *fionn uisce* (or "clear water") as a fresh water stream flows through its grounds. A series of pillars stand across the road and suddenly you're surrounded by grand, clipped hedges and tended flowerbeds in what is one of the largest city parks in the world – it's more than twice the size of London's Hampstead Heath or New York's Central Park. The park originated as priory lands, which were seized after the Reformation in the seventeenth century and made into a royal deer park. The Viceroy's Lodge – now *Áras an Uachtaráin*, the president's residence – is here, as well as a 205-foot obelisk erected in 1817 in tribute to the **Duke of Wellington**. Wellington was born in Dublin, but was less than proud of his roots – when reminded that he was Irish by birth, the Duke replied tersely "being born in a stable doesn't make one a horse."

In the northwest corner of the park, near the Ashtown Gate exit, is the **Phoenix Park Visitor Centre**, which incorporates the recently restored **Ashtown Castle** (daily: April–May 9.30am–5.30pm; June–Sept 9.30am–5pm; £2/€2.54). Set in the stables of what was the home of the Papal Nuncio, this is an interesting, if uninspiring diversion. While the exhibits in the centre are a little dull, there is a good video on the history of the park and an interesting tour of the castle (a seventeenth-century tower house), which had been concealed in Papal Nuncio's residence, the top floor acting as a private chapel. It is from here that free tours of **Áras an Uachtaráin** (President's Residence) leave on Saturdays every hour between 10.30am and 4.30pm (come early in summer as there are a limited number of places). The old duelling grounds, or **Fifteen Acres**, are also to be found in the park – now the venue for gaelic football, cricket, soccer and, occasionally, polo – as well as a race course where a **flea market** is held every Sunday from noon onwards. The quality of what's available can vary tremendously, and there seems no way of knowing what it will be like until the day.

The park was also the scene of two politically significant **murders** in the late spring of 1882, when two officials of the British parliament, Lord Frederick Cavendish, the chief secretary, and T.H. Burke, the undersecretary, were killed by an obscure organization known as "The Invincibles". At first it seemed that the motivation for the crime – long-standing bitterness over the landlord-and-tenant relationship in post-Famine Ireland – was directly connected with the Anglo-Irish politician Charles Stewart Parnell's ongoing agitation for reform on behalf of the Irish tenancy (see p.672). It seemed to Parnell that he would have to withdraw from public life due to the implication – however ill-founded – that he was connected with these murders, but his obvious sincerity in denouncing them, and the effect that the event had on British policy regarding the tenancy issue, was in fact to make his position in Ireland stronger than ever.

Phoenix Park also contains Dublin's **zoo** at the southeast corner of the park (Mon–Sat 9.30am–6pm, Sun 11am–6pm; adults £5.50/€6.98; buses #10, #25, #26), the second oldest in Europe – it was opened in 1830. Its claim to fame used to be that this is where the MGM lion was bred; the zoo now has a programme for breeding endangered species for subsequent release into the wild.

The outskirts

Even without going as far as the Wicklow Mountains, whose unlikely, conical outlines you encounter every time you look to the south, there are a number of rewarding trips beyond the city centre which are well worth making time for. The best of these are out along Dublin Bay, using the frequent DART services. These trains will take you southwards to **Sandycove** – a mile beyond **Dún Laoghaire** – and the James Joyce Tower; to the pretty village of **Dalkey**, with its incongruously continental atmosphere; and to between Dalkey and **Killiney**, where the views across Dublin Bay are magnificent. Although the journey north on the DART is nothing like as spectacular as the southward trip – once the industrial city ends, it gives way to suburbia, and it's only when you get as far as **Sutton** (a much sought-after address) that you even see the sea – it takes you to the popular seaside resort of Howth (the DART terminus at the northern end of Dublin Bay), with its rugged hill and long views south. Further out, Malahide and its castle and the charming villages of Donabate and Skerries are accessible both by commuter train and bus. For the worthwhile stops closer in to the city – **Glasnevin**, **Marino** and **Dollymount Strand** – it's easier to take the bus.

Dún Laoghaire and Sandycove

Taking the DART south out of Dublin, you very quickly have the feeling that you're leaving the grime of the city far behind. Almost immediately, the track starts to run

THE JAMES JOYCE TOWER

The reason the **Martello Tower** at Sandycove has become a place of pilgrimage for Joyce fans is not so much the association with the author's life – the 22-year-old writer spent barely a week here with his friend Oliver St John Gogarty in August of 1904, a month before he left the country with Nora Barnacle – as the fact that it features so prominently in the opening chapter of *Ulysses* (for more on Joyce and Bloomsday, see p.100). Joyce's stay wasn't a particularly happy one: Gogarty's other guest was one Samuel Chenevix Trench who, on their sixth night, had a nightmare, grabbed a gun and let off some shots into the fireplace of the room where they were sleeping. Gogarty then seized the gun and shot a row of saucepans that were hanging above Joyce's head, shouting "Leave him to me!" Joyce left the following morning.

The tower was opened as a museum in 1962 by Sylvia Beech, who first published *Ulysses*. The exhibits inside amount to little more than a collection of memorabilia – the author's guitar, cigar case and cane are on display – which, with one or two exceptions, offer no great insights into his life. Perhaps most interesting are the letters, including a plaintive note to Nora Barnacle on September 10, 1904, accusing her of "treating me as if I were simply a casual comrade in lust"; there's also a delicious edition of *Ulysses* illustrated by Henri Matisse. But it's the atmosphere of the place that really makes it worthwhile, particularly when you climb up the narrow staircase to the open top of the tower where stately, plump Buck Mulligan performs his ablutions at the beginning of *Ulysses*.

along the coast, past **Booterstown Marsh**, a designated bird sanctuary and out to **DÚN LAOGHAIRE**, where the Stena Line car ferries come in from Britain. At this distance, Dún Laoghaire manages to retain some of its flavour as a superior kind of Victorian resort, full of wide, tree-lined avenues, promenades and wedding-cake architecture. Its port is still the base for Irish lightships and the biggest Irish centre for yachting (call the National Sailing School for details; ☎284 4195). This aspect of its history is chronicled in the National Maritime Museum, Haigh Terrace (☎280 0969), housed in the Mariners' church and containing, among other things, a longboat sent by the French in support of the United Irishmen, two years before the 1798 Rebellion.

A mile south of Dún Laoghaire, the **Martello Tower** (April–Oct Mon–Sat 10am–1pm & 2–5pm, Sun 2–6pm; £2.40/€3.04) is **SANDYCOVE**'s most prominent feature (see box above). James Joyce spent some time here with his friend Oliver St John Gogarty, whom he later transformed into Buck Mulligan in *Ulysses*. The tower itself is on the seafront and is a quick and pleasant walk from the station: opposite the station entrance take Islington Avenue down to the seafront where the tower stands next to an extraordinary bit of 1930s modern seaside building – "Geragh", a house built by Michael Scott, architect of Busáras (see p.61), and some of the small number of Dublin's other modernist buildings. On the seaward side of the tower is the Forty Foot Pool – named not for its size but because the 40th Foot Regiment of the British army used to be stationed in a battery above it. For many years it was a men-only swimming hole where nude bathing was the rule; now that women are allowed, although you seldom see them, it's strictly "togs required – by order", as the notice says. The hardier swimmers use this rocky, natural swimming pool all year round, and the hardiest of them all at the traditional Christmas-morning dip. Sandycove is also good for canoeing, wind-surfing and water-skiing. For all water-sports, check out Oceantec, 10–11 Marine Terrace (☎280 1083), a diving equipment shop that will also arrange local diving. By far the best place for **food** is the excellent seafood restaurant, *Cavistons*, on Glasthule Road (just down the hill from the station) which now has an outlet in the city centre (see p.111) and has long been regarded by locals as the best place in the city to enjoy the fruits of the sea.

Dalkey and Killiney

Further south along the coast lies the little town of **DALKEY**. Immortalized, if that's the word, in Flann O'Brien's satirical *The Dalkey Archive*, Dalkey (pronounced *Dawkey*) is nowadays a charming, prosperous seaside town, and nothing much besides. Its origins as a walled medieval settlement and important landing place for travellers from England are evident though, especially in the massive Archibold's Castle which dominates the main street. There are narrow lanes with fine, bourgeois residences and, back in the main street, a really excellent new and secondhand bookshop, with plenty of recent review copies. John Dowland, the melancholy Elizabethan lutenist and composer, may have been born here, and George Bernard Shaw certainly lived at Torca Cottage on Dalkey Hill: he later claimed to be "a product of Dalkey's outlook". When the sun is shining, Dalkey has an almost Mediterranean holiday atmosphere, and it's thoroughly pleasant just to stroll about and drink it all in.

In the summer you can rent a boat to take you out to **Dalkey Island**, where you'll find a bird sanctuary; another in the series of Martello towers that were built to defend the coast from Napoleonic attack; and the ruins of the early Irish St Begnet's Church. A curious ritual involving the "King of Dalkey", complete with crown and sword, was once enacted here: originating in the eighteenth century, it started out as a student joke, but became increasingly political until it was stamped out by Lord Clare in 1797. *Finnegans*, Sorrento Road (daily noon–3pm; ☎285 8505), has a fine lunchtime menu, usually featuring **seafood** freshly caught from nearby Coliemore Harbour served in a beautiful mahogany lounge bar (if you miss lunch, you can dine on the excellent Guinness). If you fancy something a little more exotic then down the hill from *Finnegans* and the DART station is the *Thai House* restaurant (☎284 7304), regarded as one of the best Thai restaurants in the country. *Munkberry's* on Castle Street, serving predominantly Mediterranean cuisine, is becoming popular with Dalkey's discerning locals; Sunday brunch, served to a backdrop of live jazz, is especially recommended.

From Dalkey Hill a ridge leads to the public park on **Killiney Hill** (pronounced *Kill-eye-nee*), with terrific views of Dublin Bay and the Wicklow Mountains. The best way to reach this is to walk along Sorrento Road (the first right down the hill from the station), crossing the small bridge at the end of the road and ascending the steep Knockaree Road. After the old British postbox (now painted green) are the Gorse Hill Gates through which is a pleasant walk along the ivy-clad walls of the old castle, leading to Torca Cottage: the former home of George Bernard Shaw and now a private residence. Running alongside the cottage is the path to Killiney Hill Park from which the landscape opens out before offering you an overwhelming view of the sweep of the bay with the blue sea on one side and the weird bulk of the Sugarloaf Mountain on the other. It could well have been these very hills that inspired Shaw to write "Men of Ireland are mortal and temporal, But her hills are eternal". Continue to follow the castle walls and the path leads down Killiney Hill to the beach and Killiney station. Alternatively there are good views from the DART which stops right on the beach in **KILLINEY** itself.

The entire coastline from Dún Laoghaire to Bray is good for **fishing**. Off Dalkey Island the dominant catches are conger, tope, pollock, skate and coalfish; further out, on the Burford and Kish banks, turbot, brill, dab and plaice are common. Fishing from the rocks and piers at Dún Laoghaire is free, and you can rent boats at Bullock and Coliemore harbours.

Glasnevin, Marino and Dollymount Strand

The suburb of **GLASNEVIN**, a couple of miles north of O'Connell Street (take bus #13, #19 and #19A, or from Abbey Street Middle #34 and #34A), has two attractions to recommend it. The **National Botanic Gardens** (March–Oct Mon–Sat 9am–6pm, Sun

11am–6pm; Nov–Feb Mon–Sat 10am–4.30pm, Sun 11am–4.30pm; free), founded in 1795, is a quiet open space with a couple of large greenhouses dating from the mid-nineteenth century designed by Richard Turner, who also constructed the glasshouse at Belfast's Botanic Gardens and the magnificent Palm House at Kew Gardens in London. Ireland's mild climate makes it an excellent place for growing exotic species – witness all those palm trees you see in front gardens along the seafront – and the Botanic Gardens were the first place in the world, in 1844, to raise orchids from seed, and the first place in Europe to grow pampas grass and the giant lily successfully.

Close by is **Prospect Cemetery** (daily 8.30am–4pm; guided tours late May–Sept Sun 11.30am; free), which started out as a burial place for Roman Catholics in 1832. Its jungle of patriotic iconography – shamrocks, high crosses, and harps – are eerily surveyed by the watchtowers in the walls from which sentries would endeavour to deter body snatchers in the nineteenth century. The Prospect is, in many ways, a good place to end a trip to Dublin as so many of the city's important historical figures are buried here: the politicians Daniel O'Connell (see p.671), who died in 1847 but whose body was brought here in 1869; Charles Stewart Parnell (see p.672); Sir Roger Casement, who was executed as a traitor by the British government in 1916; and the Independence fighter Michael Collins. Countess Markievicz and Maud Gonne MacBride were also both laid to rest here, as was the poet Gerard Manley Hopkins. After a trip to the graveyard, drop in for a pint at nearby *Kavanagh's* (commonly known as *The Gravediggers*), one of Dublin's finest old pubs, where mourners have sought solace since 1833.

Marino

MARINO, just off the Malahide Road three miles north of the city centre (#20A and #24 bus from Eden Quay), is the home of the eighteenth-century Casino, one of the most delightful pieces of Neoclassical lightheartedness you could hope to see anywhere. The bus will let you off next to some playing fields, from where the Casino, exuberantly decorated with urns and swags of carved drapery, is clearly visible to the left.

Needless to say, the **Casino** (mid-June to Sept daily 9.30am–6.30pm; Oct daily 10am–5pm; Nov & May to mid-June Wed & Sun only noon–4pm; last admission 45 minutes before closing; £2/€2.54; Heritage Card) has nothing to do with gambling. Commissioned by Lord Charlemont (whose town house in Parnell Square is now the home of the Municipal Art Gallery), it was designed in the 1750s by Sir William Chambers, the leading Neoclassical architect of the day, to accompany a villa which would in turn house some of the priceless works of art he had brought home from his grand tour of Europe. Marino House – the building of which spared no expense, and is said to have crippled Lord Charlemont's estate – was demolished long ago, but the Casino, restored in 1984, survives in perfect condition, crowded with witty and unlikely architectural features: the urns, for example, conceal chimneys.

As you go back into town, try to sit upstairs on the left-hand side of the bus. As it turns from the Malahide Road into Fairview, you can see Marino Crescent, an elegant row of Georgian town houses, once nicknamed "Ffolliot's revenge" after a painter who built the crescent out of spite to block the view from Marino House to the sea. Ffolliot's final twist of the knife was to make the backs of the houses, which faced Marino House, an unsightly jumble of chimneys, ill-placed windows and sheds.

Dollymount Strand

Immediately north of Dublin Harbour, **DOLLYMOUNT STRAND**, or Bull Island (bus #30 will take you out here, up the Clontarf Road), is one of the seaside areas most readily accessible to Dubliners. Designated, like Booterstown Marsh (in the south bay), a UNESCO Biosphere Reserve, Dollymount Strand is a spit of low sand dunes linked to the shore by an early twentieth-century wooden bridge. Apart from holidaying

Dubliners, it's host to thousands of wintering wildfowl and wading birds and provides a stopping-off point for Arctic migrants. Birds are not the only interesting wildlife of Dollymount Strand: just a couple of miles from the centre of Dublin, there are foxes, shrews, badgers and rabbits, as well as a wide range of grass and plant species. You can find out more at the new **interpretative centre**, where the causeway road meets the island.

Howth

HOWTH (the name derives from the Danish hoved, or "head", and is pronounced to rhyme with "both") lies at the northernmost point of both Dublin Bay and the DART line. Arriving in Howth, turn right out of the DART station for the castle, left for the village, abbey and cliff walks. You can also get here on the #31 bus, picking up from the centre.

Howth Head is a natural vantage point giving views right across Dublin Bay to the Wicklow Mountains and at times, so they claim, even as far as the distant mountains of Mourne in the north and those of Wales across the Irish Sea. Not surprisingly, it has been a strategic military point for centuries, and its history involves a long line of fearful incumbents on the lookout for raiders. The legendary copper-mining Parthalons and Firbolg were the first to come, later conquered by the Gaelic chieftain Criomthain, whose grave is reputedly marked by a cairn on the summit. The Gaels, in turn, were ousted by the Vikings in the eighth century, and they were overthrown by the technologically and strategically superior Normans, led by Sir Almeric Tristram. His descendants, bearing the surname St Lawrence, continue to live at Howth Castle today.

Howth is a popular day-trip destination for Dubliners, and it has the happy and bracing air of a seaside resort, even off-season. There's a **harbour** on the northside, dating from the days when it, rather than Dún Laoghaire, was the main packet station for Dublin. At the jetty at the end of the West Pier you can see the footprint of King George IV, who landed here in 1821 instead of at Dún Laoghaire (which was expecting to rename itself Kingstown in honour of the event; he made up for it later by going home that way). It was from the same jetty, in July 1914, that the Irish Volunteers succeeded in landing 900 rifles and 25,000 rounds of ammunition from Erskine Childers' yacht *Asgard*, which you can see at Kilmainham Gaol. The harbour, full of working boats, is nowadays sited alongside a marina crowded with less practical craft. You can fish from the harbour pier, and, if you're in Howth on a Thursday evening, it's worth staying to see the spectacle when the herring boats come in. *Beshoff's* (renowned for their fish-and-chip shops throughout the city) has a fishmongers on the west quay, selling the freshest and cheapest seafood in the Dublin area.

Opposite the harbour, the rock-encrusted island is **Ireland's Eye**. A bird sanctuary, this uninhabited expanse of scrub grass and ferns sports yet another Martello Tower and the ruins of a sixth-century monastic church, St Nessan's. In summer, you can cross by boat with Frank Doyle & Sons (☎831 4200; return trip £5/€6.35) to explore the island.

Much of the interior of Howth Head is built up, but a **footpath** runs all the way round the coast. There are impressive cliffs and amazing views: south past the mouth of the Liffey to the Wicklow Mountains, and beyond, north to the flatlands of the Boyne. To get to the cliffs, either carry straight on along the shore road, or take the #31B bus up to the summit and cut down from there.

Howth village itself is a slow, suburban place full of steep streets and sudden views. Its one monument, on a quiet site overlooking Ireland's Eye, is the ruined Howth Abbey, the first church founded by Sigtrygg, Norse king of Dublin, in 1042. In one of the later phases of a chequered history, it was used by smugglers for storing contraband. The abbey is kept locked, but it is possible to get the keys from the caretaker

(☎840 1979). Just below the abbey is the *Abbey Tavern*: bare, stone-walled, with stark wood furniture, turf fires and gas lighting. While the old-world ambience can seem a little over-the-top it's well worth visiting, as long as you don't mind the tourist bus-trip approach to Irish wit and music. The *Abbey Tavern* **restaurant** specializes in fish (best to book; ☎839 0307) while the adjoining pub serves hearty lunchtime fare. The small lane and steep steps beside the pub lead to the excellent *Big Blue* café/restaurant, a tastefully restored building overlooking the abbey where you can lounge in a deep-blue sofa and enjoy a coffee, while taking in views of the abbey ruins below, and beyond to the harbour and Ireland's Eye. The other good eating place, if you've money to burn, is the excellent *King Sitric's Tavern*, East Pier (☎633 5235) with expensive but fabulous main courses of fresh seafood, while at the opposite end of the market, opposite the west pier (nearest the train station), is another outlet of the excellent *Beshoff's* fish-and-chip shops.

To get to **Howth Castle**, turn right out of the station along Howth Road towards Dublin and, after a couple of hundred yards, it's signposted on the left. The castle itself isn't open to the public, but there's a small **transport museum** which is (daily: June–Aug 10am–5pm; Sept–May noon–5pm; £1.50/€1.90). It's an impressive building, even from the outside – a true, battlemented castle, partly ruined, partly inhabited – and one that architects from Francis Bindon to Edwin Lutyens have had a hand in restoring. The gardens are famous for their azaleas and rhododendrons, which bloom from May to June.

Malahide

The easiest way to get to **MALAHIDE** from the centre of town is to take the suburban train service from Connolly Station (you can also take the #42 bus from Talbot Street or the #47 bus from Marino Casino). Either way, **Malahide Castle** makes for an enjoyable day out (April–Oct Mon–Sat 10am–5pm, Sun 11am–6pm; Nov–March Mon–Sat 10am–5pm, Sun 2–6pm; park open daily Feb & March 10am–6pm, June 10am–9pm, July & Aug 10am–8pm, Oct 10am–7pm, Nov–Jan 10am–5pm; £3.15/€4.00). When the last Lord Talbot died in 1973, his family home was taken over by the state. Much of the grounds has since been given over to playing fields but, unpromising as these look, the castle itself is terrific. If you're in need of refreshment pay a visit to the excellent **tea room**. For miniature-train buffs, Malahide also has the Fry Model Railway, a working O-gauge layout (April–Oct Mon–Sat 10am–5pm, Sun 2–6pm; £2.90/€3.68).

Dating in parts from 1174, when a marauding Norman, Richard Talbot, seized the lands and made it his fortress, the castle has been added to haphazardly over the ensuing centuries to make it look just how you think a castle ought to: turrets, Gothic windows, battlements and all. As well as being satisfyingly picturesque, what's fascinating about Malahide Castle is that you can follow its progress from a simple defensive tower – the first room you see inside, with amazing black carved panelling, and within the original square tower – to the addition of embellishments such as battlemented walls and turrets and, later still, its transformation into a country house, all fortifications now strictly decorative, with a mock-Gothic entrance. Inside, a remarkably successful attempt has been made to show the best Irish furniture and pictures in good period settings; much of what you see is on loan from the National Portrait Gallery of Ireland. It's indicative of the complex history of the Anglo-Irish, that the rich and powerful Anglo-Norman Talbot family didn't actually turn Protestant until the eighteenth century. The castle even passed out of the hands of the family for ten years during the Cromwellian wars. In the dining room is a large picture of the Battle of the Boyne; as Catholics, the Talbots fought not for Prince William but on the losing side. It's said that of the fourteen members of the family who sat down to breakfast in the dining room before setting out to fight, not one returned alive.

Malahide village, which must once have been little more than a crossroads at the gates of the castle, has long since outgrown its estate village status. It's a delight, one of those places where there's nothing much to write about, but which for some reason is really pleasant to be in: just a few grandish houses, some more modest colour-washed ones, the most spick-and-span train station you've ever seen and quiet streets sloping gently down to the golden strand and wild sea beyond.

Donabate and Skerries

A stop northward from Malahide on the commuter train (or the #33 and #33B bus from Dublin) is **DONABATE**, another trim town, worth visiting for **Newbridge House** (April–Sept Tues–Sat 10am–1pm & 2–5pm, Sun 2–6pm; Oct–March Sat & Sun 2–5pm; £3/€3.81), signposted from the station, at the end of a twenty-minute ramble through woodlands, or a short car journey from the main road. Built in 1737 for the Cobbe family, who came to Ireland in 1717 and rose rapidly through the Church of Ireland, it's a solid Georgian mansion whose main draw is the extraordinary **Museum of Curiosities**, a rare and marvellous family museum, started in 1790 and almost intact. Decorated with elegant representations of the "labours of China", it includes everything from exotic weapons and fish to an African chief's umbrella and the mummified ear of an Egyptian bull. The house remained without electricity until the 1960s, when it was wired up for the filming of *The Spy Who Came in from the Cold*, which starred Richard Burton and Clare Bloom. A cosy **coffee shop** serves soup and cakes, and the courtyards have been converted into a traditional farm with wandering goats and publicity-shy pigs.

SKERRIES, on the coast a few miles further north on the rail line, is close enough to Dublin to have a prosperous suburban hinterland, but the long main street, and the brightly painted huddle of houses on the spit of land that forms the harbour, preserve the romantic air of a remote fishing village. Atmospheric when it basks in the westering sun, and yet more so when the rain lashes down, this is a place to hole up and write your masterpiece – and, if your publisher's advance is big enough, to enjoy the **seafood** at the *Red Bank Restaurant and Guesthouse* in Church Street (☎849 1005 or 1006).

Cafés and restaurants

Dublin may not be the gastronomic capital of the world, but there's plenty of choice – nearly all of it south of the Liffey – for both lunchtime and evening eating. **Café society** has reached Dublin in a big way in recent years, providing a new range of chic and trendy locations – in and around Grafton Street and Temple Bar – for all-day eating and drinking, and on Sundays many more places open up for sustaining brunches. At least once, you should experience one of the three *Bewley's* coffee houses: try the table-service section on the second floor of the Grafton Street branch for elegance and potted palms. At lunchtime, Dublin's many **pubs** usually offer the best value: you can usually get soup and sandwiches and often much more substantial, traditional meals. The cheapest **fast-food** outlets – everything from *Pizzaland* and *Wimpy* to cheap Chinese and the ubiquitous kebab houses – are centred around O'Connell Street, but are generally, with one or two exceptions such as *Beshoff Ocean Foods*, pretty missable.

In the evening there's no shortage of **restaurants** either; although on the northside, places where you'll want to spend any time are thin on the ground. The spectrum of cuisines on offer is impressively wide, ranging from Egyptian, Lebanese, Russian and Cajun to the more familiar French, Italian and Chinese. Several restaurants offer **traditional Irish** fare, and there's also a number of good **seafood** places and plenty of **vegetarian** options. The cheaper, livelier restaurants are concentrated around the

Temple Bar area, between Dame Street and the Liffey, while more expensive establishments are scattered throughout the city, with a concentration around St Stephen's Green.

Cafés

Alpha Café, first floor, corner of Clarendon and Wicklow streets. Traditional fare at a great price served by waitresses that remind you of your favourite auntie.

Aya, 48 Clarendon St. Next door to the *Alpha*, but miles away both gastronomically and socially, is this temple of urban cool. The first revolving sushi bar in the city with traditional Japanese food available (excellent *yakitori*), this is one of the chicest eateries in the city. If all the self-reverence of the other diners is too much, grab one of the excellent bentos (lunch boxes) and head for nearby St Stephen's Green.

Bad Ass Café, 9 Crown Alley, Temple Bar (☎671 2596). Once the hippest of Dublin's pizza joints. Sinead O'Connor was waitressing here when she cut her first disc with *Ton Ton Macoute*; now distinctly unhip for adults, but great fun for kids. Daily 11am–11pm.

Beshoff Ocean Foods, 14 Westmoreland St and 7 Upper O'Connell St. Superior fish and chips, with bistro-type decor. Daily 11am–3am.

Bewley's, 78 Grafton St (daily 7.30am–7pm); 12 Westmoreland St (daily 7.30am–7pm). A Dublin institution, serving everything from drinks to sticky buns and full meals, and its delicious, renowned potato soup, in an elegant ambience.

The Bite of Life, corner of Patrick Street and Bull's Alley. Small café with great toasted ciabatta sandwiches.

Caviston's, Food Court, Liffey St. A new outlet for the Caviston family, this is a modern seafood bar which serves delicious and generous helpings of chowder.

Café Irie, Fownes St. Possibly the best sandwiches in Dublin served by staff so laid back, they're virtually horizontal.

Cobalt Café, North Great George's St. Good food in a café-cum-gallery. The space is light, the displays are exemplary, all of which makes this one of the most pleasant places to enjoy a coffee in the city. If you visit the James Joyce centre or stay in the *MEC Hostel* opposite, this café is a must.

Cornucopia Wholefoods, 21 Wicklow St (☎677 7583). Vegetarian shop and café. For anyone who has pigged out on one traditional Irish breakfast too many, *Cornucopia* offers a vegetarian alternative, including vegetarian sausages, between 8am and 11am. Café open daily until 9pm.

The Globe, 11 South Great George's St. A bar by night (see p.115), this is a buzzing café by day, serving cappuccinos and herbal teas.

Govinda's, 4 Aungier St. Vegetarian restaurant featuring mostly Indian-inspired veggie fare; plenty of dhal with heavenly lassis at down-to-earth prices. Mon–Sat 11am–9pm.

Harveys, 14 Moira House, Trinity St. Good-value breakfast, excellent coffee and exceptional if pricey sandwiches: including the decadent avocado and mozzarella bagel. Mon–Sat 8am–7pm, Sun 11am–5pm.

The Hugh Lane Gallery, Parnell Square. A decent café, good for relaxing in after the delights of the gallery.

Juice, South Great George's St. This chic vegetarian eatery serves imaginative macrobiotic food blending oriental and Californian cuisine. Daily 8am–11pm.

Leo Burdock's, 2 Werburgh St. Dublin's legendary fish-and-chip shop, now modestly wondering whether its fish and chips are the best not only in Dublin, but maybe in the world. Carry-out only. Mon–Fri 12.30–11pm, Sat 2–11pm.

Odessa, 13–14 Dame Court. Exotic snacks and outré decor make this one of the trendiest new cafés; downstairs is good for gossiping on big squashy sofas. Noon–midnight daily; breakfast served noon–4pm.

Panem, 21 Lower Ormond Quay/Anglesea St. Dubliners' famous loquacity has meant that what was once the city's best-kept secret is now one of its most talked-about subjects. *Panem* deserves all the attention it gets, and if you manage to find a space between the barristers and their *Irish Times* newspapers you will be treated to the finest, filled focaccia and savoury croissants in town.

Simon's Place, South Great George's St beside George's Arcade. With possibly the friendliest staff in the city, this is a great hang-out serving cheap but substantial sandwiches to a loyal clientele.

Steps of Rome, Chatham Court, Chatham St. Tiny café serving, by far, the best pizzas in town.

Trí D, Dawson St. Irish-speaking café run by Gael Linn, an organization that promotes the use of the ancient tongue.

West Coast Coffee Company, 20 Lower Ormond Quay. Opposite the new millennium footbridge this is a bright, relaxed place with large windows and sumptuous sofas, offering a good choice of healthy, reasonably priced sandwiches with good vegetarian options.

Winding Stair Café, 40 Lower Ormond Quay. This vast, secondhand book emporium also has a café serving soup, salads, sandwiches and cakes. Sit by the window and watch the Liffey ooze by. Open daily till 6pm only.

Internet cafés

Global Internet Café, 8 Lower O'Connell St (☎878 0295, *www.globalcafe.ie*). Just to the north of O'Connell Bridge this is the best Internet café in town: modems are fast, the service is friendly and the Belgian hot chocolate divine. Internet access £3/€3.81 per hour; student reductions available. Mon–Sat 8am–11pm, Sun 10am–10pm.

Internet Exchange, Crow St, Temple Bar (☎670 5601, *www.internet-exchange.co.uk*). This is one in a chain of excellent Internet cafes popping up throughout the city, charging members 3p/€0.40 per minute from 8am–noon, 7p/€0.90 per minute from noon–8pm, and 5p/€0.60 per minute from 8pm–11pm; non-members are charged 12p/€0.15 per minute at all times (although membership is free). Daily 8am–11pm.

Planet Cyber Café, 23 South Great George's St (☎679 0583, *www.irelandsweb.ie*). Beside the market arcade on South Great George's St (in the basement below Laser Video) this was one of the first Internet cafes in the city, and although the food has deteriorated the café's hardware has been updated, allowing for speedy access. Internet access £3/€3.81 per hour; student reductions available. Mon–Wed & Sun 10am–10pm, Thurs–Sat 10am–noon.

Restaurants

Dublin has, of late, developed a **restaurant** scene on a par with most European capitals, and while a range of international cooking is widely available, it is the new Irish cuisine, where young chefs experiment with traditional Irish ingredients, that is the most exciting. Many of the restaurants specializing in this are based in the Temple Bar area, but can be both overcrowded and a little overpriced. Dublin's elegant, more established restaurants are mostly centred in the Georgian southside, while the few outlets north of the river tend to give the best value in town.

MODERATE (MAIN COURSES UNDER £10/€12.70)

Bangkok Café, 106 Parnell St (☎878 6618). This restaurant has become fashionable among the city's trendy set, daring to venture into dingy Parnell Street. The restaurant itself, however, is unselfconscious and its unfashionable location, wobbly tables and slightly tacky decor are testament to its owner/chef's devotion to food rather than image. Daily 5.30–10.30pm.

Belgo, 17–19 Sycamore St. Fun restaurant with copious amounts of Belgian food and beer, suited to a group party rather than a romantic night out. Try the beat-the-clock promotion where your bill matches the time you sit down, though their *pièce de résistance* has to be the wonderful mussels. Mon–Thurs noon–3pm & 5–10.45pm, Sat noon–midnight, Sun noon–10.45pm.

Blazing Salads II, Powerscourt Town House Centre, Clarendon St (☎671 9552). Marvellous vegetarian food in a Georgian town house turned shopping centre. Open Mon–Sat.

The Cedar Tree, 11 St Andrew's St (☎677 2121). A dazzling array of Lebanese meze dishes with plenty of vegetarian options, served in a lively restaurant – especially at weekends when the renowned belly dancers make an appearance. Open Mon–Sat 5.30–11.45pm, Sun till 11.30pm.

The Chameleon, 1 Fownes St (☎671 0362). Award-winning and highly regarded Indonesian on the northern edges of Temple Bar. Tues–Sun 5–11pm.

Da Pino, 38 Parliament St (☎671 9308). Marvellous fresh pasta and huge pizzas at low prices. Daily noon–11.30pm.

Elephant and Castle, 18 Temple Bar (☎679 3121). Cross between a New York diner and a brasserie serving anything from a drink to dinner. Some main courses can be pricey, while burgers are pretty standard rates. Popular for Sunday brunch, but make sure you book. Open Mon–Thurs 8am–11.30pm, Fri till midnight, Sat 10.30am–midnight, Sun noon–11.30pm.

Fitzer's, 51 Dawson St (☎660 1644). Cool, airy café/restaurant serving a Californian-style, new-wave menu of soulful food, including pasta, salads, seafood and chargrills, or you can just drop in for a coffee. There's outdoor seating on busy Dawson Street, and other branches in Temple Bar Square and National Gallery. Open Mon–Sat 8am–11pm.

Il Baccaro, Diceman's Corner, Meeting House Square, Temple Bar. As you descend the steps into this cavernous eatery you get the feeling you're entering an illicit shebeen or speakeasy. The mood inside matches as upbeat patrons wash back hearty, traditional Italian dishes such as Sicilian aubergine stew with house wine served by the carafe. Open till late.

Irish Film Centre, 6 Eustace St (☎677 8788). Coolly minimalist designer bar and restaurant in what used to be a Quaker meeting house. Serves delicious food – including highly sinful cakes and pastries – all day. Plenty of vegetarian choice on an eclectic menu: vegetable pâtés, burgers, chicken, jambalaya with bananas. Open according to programme.

La Paloma, 17B Temple Bar (☎677 7392). Saturated yellows and hot pinks offer a suitably un-Irish backdrop for good, cheap tapas with a pricier evening menu. The descriptions of the meals, however, are so over the top the food can only be an anticlimax. Open daily noon–midnight.

Mao Café and Bar, 2–3 Chatham Row (☎670 4899). The communist chic theme has really taken off in Dublin and nowhere more successfully than *Mao*. The dishes are rice- or noodle-based, the vegetables as fresh as you get and the service is first rate. Highly recommended. Daily 9.30am–10.30pm.

Milano, 61 Dawson St (☎677 8611). First venture of the British *Pizza Express* chain in Ireland – swish surroundings with the familiar and affordable range of pizzas. Daily 6.30–11pm.

Mongolian Barbeque, 7 Anglesea St (☎670 4154). The Genghis McKhan jokes aside this can be a fun place for a group party. You choose your meats, noodles and sauce and the chefs cook them in front of you on a large grill. Mon–Fri noon–3pm & 6–10pm, Sat noon–10pm, Sun 1–10pm

Monty's of Katmandhu, 28 Eustace St (☎670 4915). The window of this restaurant boasts pictures of Bono and Quentin Tarantino, two of the more famous celebrities to enjoy classic Indian/Nepalese cooking in this quiet Temple Bar establishment. Daily noon–2.45pm & 6pm–midnight.

Pasta Fresca, Chatham St (☎879 2402). Ireland's first fresh pasta shop. Its restaurant is consistently busy so get there early or book ahead. If you can't secure a table try the take out from the excellent deli. Mon–Fri 11am–11.30pm, Sat 10am–midnight, Sun 12.30–10pm.

Romano's, 12 Capel St. Excellent Italian, though somewhat overlooked, being on the "wrong" side of the river. Main courses are very reasonable and there's a great three-course lunch special. Mon–Sat 12.30–10pm.

South Street Pizzeria, South Great George's St (☎475 2273). Great pizzas in a relaxed and friendly atmosphere. Look out for the excellent lunchtime specials. Daily noon–8pm.

Tosca, 20 Suffolk St (☎679 6744). Excellent new-wave Italian cooking in a cool halogen-lit interior guarantees this restaurant's continuing fashionability. There are piles of newspapers for slow browsing during the day, but it can get quite hectic at night. Daily noon–3.30pm & 5.30pm–midnight, Fri & Sat till 1am.

Wagamama, King St South. Clean air and healthy food served in a restaurant resembling a Japanese *ezakiya*. Although the food is generally of a very high standard – ramen is particularly good – the atmosphere is a little sterile making this more a place for quick lunch than an evening meal. Daily noon–midnight.

Yamamori Noodles, 71–72 South Great George's St (☎475 5001). Popular Japanese restaurant; the sushi is fine, teriyaki great but avoid the tempura. Mon–Sat 12.30–2.30pm & 5–11pm, Sun 5–11pm.

MODERATE TO EXPENSIVE (MAIN COURSES £10–15/€12.70-19.05)

Dish, 2 Crow St (☎671 1284). Distinctive international cuisine by two young Dublin chefs in this bistro-like restaurant in Temple Bar. Daily 12.30–11.30pm.

Jacob's Ladder, 4–5 Nassau St (☎670 3865). Finest Irish food with some Mediterranean variations and a good selection of New World wines. One of the best dishes on the main menu is the roast breast of duck with caramelized chicory, stuffed potatoes and honey and ginger syrup. Tues–Sat 11.30am–2pm & 6–11pm.

Kilkenny Design Centre Restaurant, first floor, 6 Nassau St. Great place for lunch but always packed, so be prepared to queue. Mon–Sat 9am–5pm.

101 Talbot, 101–102 Talbot St (☎874 5011). One of the very few good restaurants north of the Liffey. This spacious dining room, close to the Abbey Theatre, is worth visiting for its excellent, eclectic menu and relaxed conviviality. Pasta bar open daily noon–11pm; main restaurant Mon–Sat noon–3pm & 6–11pm.

EXPENSIVE (MAIN COURSES AT £15/€19.05 AND OVER)

Chapter One, Parnell Square (☎873 2266). A classy establishment located in the basement of the Dublin Writers' Museum. The pre-theatre menu is good value for three courses. Tues–Fri 12.30–2.30pm & 6–10.30pm.

Cooke's Café, 14 South William St (☎679 0536). Accomplished cooking in cool, terracotta surroundings. Very fashionable, very new wave. Mon–Sat 10am–5pm, Sun 11am–4pm.

Imperial Chinese Restaurant, 12A Wicklow St (☎677 2580). Popular with the Chinese community and that should be recommendation enough for anyone. If the prices are prohibitive then try the Sunday brunch. Daily 12.30pm–midnight.

L'Ecrivain, 109A Lower Baggot St (☎661 1919). Exclusive French restaurant a short walk fom St Stephen's Green. The stylish interior and exquisitely crafted food attracts a small but faithful clientele from the city's wealthiest set. Traditionalists should avoid this restaurant as the style incorporates *haute cuisine par excellence*. Mon–Thurs 6.30–10.30pm, Wed 12.30–2pm, Fri & Sat 7–11pm.

Lord Edward Fitzgerald, 23 Christchurch Place (☎454 2420). Around the corner from *Leo Burdock's*, the legendary chippie, the *Lord Edward* represents the other end of the scale. Located above a very ordinary pub, it's been going for decades and is a Dublin tradition with a terrific reputation for simple cooking using the very freshest fish. Open Mon–Sat 12.30–3pm & 6–10.45pm.

The Old Dublin, 90–91 Francis St (☎454 2028). Superb Russo-Irish food amid the dusty junk shops and markets of The Liberties area serving delicious borscht, gravadlax (*The Old Dublin*'s definition of Russia seems to include most of Scandinavia), coupled with hearty Irish meat and veg. Cheap menu early evenings. Booking advisable. Open Mon–Sat 12.30–2pm & 6–10.30pm; no Sat lunch.

Trocadero, 3 St Andrew St (☎677 5545 or 679 2385). Pleasant and friendly trattoria with excellent food, including a very popular pre-theatre menu. It's one of Dublin's oldest Italian restaurants, and the walls are hung with plaudits in the form of signed photographs of visiting showbiz luminaries. The place really comes into its own late at night when it fills up with theatre folk. Daily 6pm–12.15am.

The Unicorn, off Merrion Row, in an unpromising little courtyard that leads off to the right a few paces down from St Stephen's Green (☎676 2182). Plain, no-nonsense interior and an extensive Italian menu including pasta and pizzas as well as the standard meat-and-sauce dishes. With *Doheny and Nesbitt*'s pub (see opposite), across Lower Baggot Street, it forms a focus for the more intellectual side of Dublin life, frequented by journalists, economists, campaigners and musicians. Daily noon–3pm & 6–11pm.

Pubs and music

Pubs are an integral part of Dublin's social life and an essential part of any visit. The charm of most of Dublin's older pubs derives from the fact that they're simple, no-nonsense places, the better ones unchanged for decades, where you can get a good pint of Guinness and the people are friendly. There are over 800 pubs and bars in the city, so what follows doesn't try to be anything like a comprehensive, or even a representative, guide. Instead it's a small – and very personal – selection of Dublin's traditional pubs and new drinking places, with some indication of where you're likely to find music and other entertainment.

The **music scene** is volatile, though, so if you're after something in particular – jazz, folk, traditional – the best place to check is the fortnightly listings magazine *In Dublin*. *Hot Press*, the national music paper, is another useful source of information. For traditional music, contact the traditional music society, Comhaltas Ceoltóirí Éireann (also known as Cultúrlann) at 32 Belgrave Square, Monkstown (☎280 0295). Their offices are, in any case, worth a visit almost any night for their programmes of traditional music and theatre.

It's worth knowing that pubs in Dublin tend to be fairly male preserves, but if you're a woman don't be put off – you're unlikely to be made to feel uncomfortable, even if you're alone. And many Dublin pubs have snugs, or small private rooms, which can be the cosiest places to drink if you're in a group. There's nothing exclusive about these – just go in and stake your claim if you find one empty – and drinks cost the same as in the main bar.

Pubs and bars

The Baggot Inn, 143 Lower Baggot St. Ageing rock clientele congregate to hear rock music nightly.

Café en Seine, 40 Dawson St. Cavernous, lively and hip café/bar with extraordinary Celtic/Art Nouveau murals. Good place to drop in for a cappuccino or espresso during the day.

Clarence Hotel, Wellington Quay. U2-owned hotel, that is as designedly cool/uncool as its owners and is loved and hated in equal measure. Its bar is well worth a visit, if only to make use of the wood-panelled toilets.

Cobblestone Bar, Smithfield. On the northern end of the square in Smithfield this is the place to find some of the finest impromptu music sessions in the city.

Davy Byrne's, 21 Duke St, off Grafton St (☎677 5217). Here, in *Ulysses*, Leopold Bloom stopped to eat a gorgonzola sandwich and quaff a glass of burgundy; and here, on Bloomsday (June 16) every year, numerous pilgrims stop to do exactly the same thing. Now decked out in tasteful shades of lemon and grey, *Davy Byrne's* no longer looks exactly Joycean.

Doheny and Nesbitt, 5 Lower Baggot St. Archetypal Dublin pub – the tiny, atmospheric, smoke-filled room looks as if it has hardly changed since the beginning of the century. Always packed, cosy snugs. Upstairs is a slightly less hectic lounge for those who can't stand the pace. Much frequented by *Irish Times* hacks.

The Front Lounge, Parliament St. The spacious interior is always full of the city's most beautiful people. Gay-friendly, great cappucinos, but can get very crowded at weekends.

The Globe, 11 South Great George's St. Mecca for the terminally hip, this is a big airy bar that pulls in large numbers of young drinkers for a pre-club beer.

Grogan's, 15 South William St. Smoky haunt of literary types down through the years where conversation dominates. Good drinks at relatively reasonable prices, this is the place if you like your beer without the frills.

The International Bar, 23 Wicklow St. Another great drinking establishment that has changed little over the decades. Upstairs hosts comedy, music and theatre in a small room that can get very hot in the summer.

The Irish Film Centre, 6 Eustace St, Temple Bar. This designer bar is one of the places to see and be seen. Open according to programme (also see pp.113 & 119).

Kavanagh's, Glasnevin. Also known as *Gravediggers*, this bar has a delightful wooden interior and benches to match.

Keogh's, 9 Anne St South, off Grafton St. Wonderful snugs for those who want to curl up in comparative privacy to sip their pint.

Life Bar, Irish Life Centre, Liffey St. Stylish café-bar in an ugly building near the Custom House and the Abbey Theatre. Popular post-work and pre-club drinking spot with the city's twenty-somethings looking to dispose of some of their newly acquired wealth.

The Long Hall, 51 South Great George's St. Victorian pub with an astonishing array of antiques on show.

McDaid's, 3 Harry St. A literary pub, this is where Brendan Behan used to drown his talent in Guinness – there's a photograph of him with a tiny typewriter wedged between two glasses of the black stuff, one full, one empty.

Morrisson, *Morrisson Hotel*, Ormond Quay. Draconian bouncers with a pathological hatred of "runners" (trainers) guard this bastion of cool from the advances of the hoi poloi. Inside things are a little more relaxed but definitely not a place to let your guard, never mind your hair, down.

Mulligan's, 8 Poolbeg St. Mulligan's traditionally served the best Guinness in Dublin; many people now acknowledge that honour to have passed to Guinness's own visitor centre, but *Mulligan's* still has its partisans.

The Palace, 21 Fleet St. Wood-and-glass interior, crowded and friendly pub much loved by Dubliners.

The Porter House, 16–18 Parliament St. Given its location among bars marketing themselves as "traditional" despite being little more than ten years old, the *Porter House*, is an admirable attempt to present the pub in a modern form. It brews its own drinks and attracts a transitory crowd, more interested in the concept and design of the place, than aficionados of its various beers.

Pravda, Lower Liffey St. The design motif is communist chic and this huge bar has been a great success since securing a fashionable beachhead on the city's formerly run-down northern quays. The top floor, decorated with Russian Orthodox iconography, is immersed in daylight and has great couches conducive to daytime coffee and chat.

Ryan's, Parkgate St, across the river from Heuston Station. Another pub famous for its cosy, wood-lined snugs; considered the finest Victorian pub in Dublin.

Sackville Lounge, Sackville St, off O'Connell St. Quiet watering hole if you need a pint and a chat while north of the river. Becomes lively later in the evening when it attracts a post-theatre crowd.

Stag's Head, 1 Dame Court, a tiny turning off Dame Street almost opposite the Central Bank. Hard to find – a mosaic set in the pavement on Dame Street alerts you to the tiny alleyway it's located in – but worth it when you get there: inside it's all mahogany, stained glass and mirrors. Good pub lunches, too, and friendly atmosphere.

Thomas Read's, 79 Dame St. Trendy pub with good food at lunchtime; a lively though very crowded spot in the evenings.

Toners Victorian Bar, 139 Lower Baggot St. Dark, cosy pub with a refreshingly plain interior. Snugs, with glazed partitions, for making and breaking confidences.

Pubs with music and music venues

Brazen Head, 20 Lower Bridge St. Possibly the oldest pub in the city, the *Brazen Head* is situated on the road that leads downhill from Christchurch to the river. It is said to be the last place Robert Emmet had a drink before his abortive rebellion and some drinkers have sworn to have met the former patriot's ghost after a long night. Its courtyard makes a great place to have a beer on a summer's evening. The traditional music played here is generally tourist oriented.

Hughes', 19 Chancery St. If you're in the vicinity of the Four Courts this is a great place for a drink. If you stay until the day wears off then you could find yourself in the midst of as fine a music session as you're likely to come across in the city.

The International Bar, 23 Wicklow St. Great singer-songwriter nights most Tuesdays when young Dubliners cut their musical teeth.

The Merchant, Lower Bridge St, opposite the *Brazen Head*. Traditional music most nights with impromptu sessions in between.

The Modern Green Bar, 31 Wexford St. A stylish bar on Wexford Street featuring live DJs playing ambient jazz, funk and soul.

Mother Redcap's Tavern, Back Lane, off High St. Traditional and country music – Ireland's other folk tradition – in an old shoe factory in one of the oldest parts of Dublin. A pint of Guinness here, fried fish and a poke of chips from *Leo Burdock's* famous fish-and-chip shop around the corner (see p.111), and your night's made. Big-name billing on Fri and Sat nights for a £6 cover charge.

The Norseman, 29 Essex St, Temple Bar. Formerly a popular haunt of Dublin's bohemia, now more of a tourist hang-out, the *Norseman* has traditional music some evenings.

O'Donoghues, 15 Merrion Row. Seen by many as the home of Dublin folk music. Get here early, get a seat and a pint and the fun will soon follow.

Oliver St John Gogarty's, Anglesea St. "Traditional" music every night though it's a bit of a tourist trap.

The Olympia, 74 Dame St, off Temple Bar. When the evening performance ends in this tinselly ex-music hall on Fri and Sat nights, the theatre closes down for half an hour; at 11.30pm the doors open and the late-night music spot, *Midnight at the Olympia*, begins. As a music venue it's a strange place – you sit in plush theatre seats and dance in the aisles – but it's unbeatable for its line-up of both up-and-coming and established performers. Bar open till 2am.

Slattery's, 129 Capel St. Good drink and great music are the two essential ingredients for a night's *craic* and *Slattery's* provides both in abundance.

Whelans, 25 Wexford St. Very lively pub with bands and bar extensions most nights; an eclectic line-up of acts, sometimes Irish traditional or "world music".

Clubs

Clubs are by nature volatile, so you should check the latest *In Dublin* listings to see which club nights are still in operation. There are two distinct club scenes in Dublin. The first (and the one listed here) is an eclectic collection – including the new, much talked-about chic clubs – scattered around the city centre, many of which offer special interest and theme nights. Most are hard to get into – that's part of their cachet – and expensive at the weekends. The second, and distinctly less appealing, is based in and around Leeson Street, southeast of St Stephen's Green. The clubs here do, however, serve a purpose: a string of basement places that are busy after everything else has shut, these are the clubs to hit at two or three in the morning if you're really desperate to go on partying. Most have no entry fee but serve very expensive drinks – they're at their dubious best Thursday to Sunday from around 1am till dawn.

Break for the Border, Lower St Stephen's St. The music here only provides a soundtrack to the courting rituals. If you want to meet a Dubliner of the opposite sex, drink lots of beer and have a laugh, this may be the place for you. Open daily.

Club M, *Blooms Hotel*, Anglesea St, Temple Bar. Music is pretty mainstream, and the clothes are generally minimalist. Open Wed–Sun.

Club Mono, 26 Wexford St. Relatively new club and bar. Downstairs plays funky techno and deep progressive house, while upstairs features progressive house, with local and international DJs. Open Wed–Sun.

The Gaiety Theatre, South King St. This old theatre promotes various nights such as *Planet Reggae* on Thursday, *Salsa* on Friday and *Soul Stage* on Saturday which attracts an older though no less energetic crowd.

HQ at the Hall of Fame, 57 Middle Abbey St. Excellent venue for concerts with a very late bar, which can be a curse as well as a blessing as the club can get crowded with the heavily imbibed late at night. Thursdays is a swing night, Fridays soul while Saturdays has a Latin feel. Open Thurs–Sun.

The Kitchen, East Essex St, Temple Bar. Worth getting to this club – that's owned by U2 – early to check out the interior design where the curved walls and dipping ceiling gives a premature feeling of intoxication. Be warned that entry can be difficult but if you do get in expect to hear some of the best dance music in the city. Open daily.

Lillie's Bordello, Adam Court, Grafton St. Wannabe stars pose amongst the velure in this club. A strict door policy means that you may find it difficult to get in but the best advice is to get there before pub closing time. Open daily.

The POD, 35 Harcourt St. Formerly the place to go dancing in the city, though it's losing its grip a little. A draconian door policy looks for sartorial smartness rather than trendiness. It's more relaxed on Thursdays when the music is a little softer too with jazz, funk and reggae. Open Wed–Sun.

Rí-Rá, South Great George's St (☎677 4835). Compared to other clubs in town the doormen are almost courteous, the music is variable and the crowd fun. Look out for Monday nights with Strictly Handbag, by far the best retro night in the city. Like most clubs, don't expect to get in if you stagger up to the door after pub closing. Open daily.

Sirens, *Ormond Quay Hotel*, Ormond Quay. Weekend club with funky house on Thursdays and Fridays, while Saturdays are a three-floor affair with, as well as house, first-rate soul and funk. Entrance may be a problem as the doormen are a little capricious.

The Sugar Club, 8 Lower Leeson St. A new club that is rescuing Leeson Street from its seedy reputation. Doors open early – but few make their way here before midnight – and live salsa, jazz and blues plus DJs. Open Wed–Sun.

Switch, Crown Alley Temple Bar. In a dark basement in Temple Bar is *Switch*, featuring nights promoted by the city's two leading dance promoters: DI and Bassbin. The DJs are first rate but are let down by the poor sound and overzealous security. Open Wed–Thurs.

The Temple Bar Music Centre, Curved St, Temple Bar. The venue here holds 650 people and has acoustics which are unrivalled in the city. Thursday nights host an excellent indie club, Friday is fun hip-hop and R&B, while on Saturdays it's high-tempo dance. Open Thurs–Sat.

Temple Theatre, St George's Church, Temple St. Housed in an enormous restored church this club has suffered from its unfashionable location. It promotes a funky Seventies retro night on a Friday, while Saturday features guest DJs playing high-tempo house. Open Fri & Sat.

Vicar Street, 99 Vicar St (off Thomas St). Another of the city's newer venues hosting the excellent *Velure* on Friday and Saturday nights, a long established rhythm and soul club (formerly held in the *Gaiety*) popular with a discerning older crowd.

Theatre and cinema

As seems fitting for a city with Dublin's rich literary past, **theatre** flourishes. The traditional diet of Irish classics at the "establishment" theatres is now spiced up by experimental or fringe programmes at newer, smaller venues; tickets are cheap – averaging around £10/€12.70 – and drama is accessible, and popular.

Dublin has a large number of **cinemas** – almost all of them on and around O'Connell Street – showing mainstream films. All Dublin's cinemas operate an enlightened policy of cheap seats before 5pm (6.30pm in some cases), seven days a week. The peculiarities of the film distribution system mean that new movies are often released earlier in Ireland than in Britain. There are two art-house cinemas, both showing a changing repertoire of films.

You'll find details of all theatre performances and cinema programmes in the fortnightly listings magazine, *In Dublin*.

Theatre

Abbey Theatre, Lower Abbey St, just off O'Connell St (☎878 7222). The grim concrete building housing the famous Abbey Theatre gives little away about its illustrious past (see p.95). On its rebuilding in 1952, however, Patrick Kavanagh was scathing, writing in his eponymous *Kavanagh's Weekly*: "The Abbey Theatre is the opposite of what it set out to be. The Abbey Theatre was never much good. The life it portrayed was not Irish, but a convention invented by Synge mainly." The theatre is still known for its productions of older Irish plays (by playwrights such as Boucicault and Richard Brinsley Sheridan), but does encourage younger writers. One of the most acclaimed productions of the 1990s was Brian Friel's *Dancing at Lughnasa*. In addition to the main auditorium, the building houses the smaller Peacock Theatre, which sometimes has more experimental shows.

Andrews Lane Theatre, Andrews Lane (☎679 5720). Theatre and studio, just off Dame Street in what appears to be the middle of a car park, concentrating on the latest Irish writing. One of Dublin's new performance spaces, under the same management as the remarkable Gate Theatre (see opposite).

City Arts Centre, Moss St, off George's Quay (☎677 0643). A venue that usually features community-based drama.

Civic Theatre, Tallaght. This is a modern theatre in the suburbs of Tallaght. Despite its excellent facilities it is struggling to attract either a local audience or theatre goers from other areas of the city.

Crypt Arts Centre, Dublin Castle (☎761 3387). In the crypt of the Chapel Royal, this venue has an eclectic mix – from drama to rock concerts – and is used by Amharclann na Hide, the Irish language theatre group.

Focus Theatre, 6 Pembroke Place, off Upper Pembroke St (☎676 3071). This small venue theatre was founded by Deirdre O'Connell of the Actors Studio in New York and normally produces powerful modern pieces from Europe and America.

Gaiety Theatre, South King St (☎677 1717). Dublin's oldest theatre stages a mix of musical comedy, revues, occasional opera, and, every now and then, something really worth seeing.

Gate Theatre, Cavendish Row, next to the Rotunda (☎874 4045 or 674 6042). Another of Dublin's literary institutions, it stages more modern Irish plays and can be lively and atmospheric.

International Bar, Wicklow St. The small room above this excellent bar acts as a theatre venue for small independent productions.

Lambert Puppet Theatre, 5 Clifdon Lane, Monkstown (☎280 0947). A favourite with children this is Dublin's only puppet theatre, producing puppeteering of the highest standards on Saturdays and Sundays.

Olympia Theatre, Dame St (☎677 8962 or 8147). Formerly Dan Lowry's Music Hall, and that's exactly how it looks: raffish, down-at-heel, with an air of faded, once tinselly glamour. It now puts on (no surprises) vaudeville, comedy, ballet and drama, sometimes packing in two completely different shows in one evening with a late-night music spot to round things off.

Peacock Theatre, Lower Abbey St (☎878 7222). The Abbey's smaller sibling features more progressive theatre and acts as a springboard for some of the country's best talent.

Project Arts Centre 39 East Essex St, Temple Bar (☎671 2321). After spending two difficult years in a temporary venue the Project has returned to its old (though impressively renovated) venue in Temple Bar. Despite its flashy new home the company is still committed to producing experimental or politically sensitive work.

Tivoli Theatre, Francis St (☎454 4472). A modern theatre near The Liberties that doubles as a rock venue.

Cinemas

Mainstream cinemas include: The Ambassador, 1 Parnell Square (☎872 7000; one screen); The Savoy, O'Connell St Upper (☎874 6000; five screens); and UGC (formerly Virgin), Parnell St (☎872 8400; nine screens). Art-house cinemas include those listed below.

Irish Film Centre, 6 Eustace St, Temple Bar (☎679 5744). Art-house cinema with two screens and an excellent restaurant (see p.113), as well as a film-related bookshop and dance-club nights on Fridays and Saturdays (see p.115). Films shown include new, low-budget Irish work plus seasons of world, gay and children's cinema; a worthwhile survey of Irish film-making is shown every afternoon.

The Screen, D'Olier St (☎671 4988). Shows a less commercial selection than most Dublin cinemas and has good afternoon prices.

Gay life

Although Ireland's celebrated gays include Oscar Wilde, Somerville and Ross, Eva Gore-Booth and, contemporarily, TV host Graham Norton, prejudice against the gay community remains considerable in the country. In 1988 the European Court of Human Rights decreed that Ireland's anti-gay law contravened the European Convention on Human Rights, and in 1990 the law was repealed and the age of consent lowered to 17. The result is that, despite the hegemony of the Catholic Church, gay voices are increasingly making themselves heard in public debate, and Dublin now has a visible gay scene. A good starting point for any gay travellers to Ireland is *Outhouse*, 6 South William St (☎670 6377) which has a gay community centre and a café/restaurant. Alternatively, you can ring Gay Switchboard Dublin (Mon–Fri & Sun 3.30–6pm &

8–10pm; ☎872 1055) or the 24-hour information and events line (☎1550/122 345). Lesbian travellers may wish to contact Lesbians Organizing Together, which has a drop-in centre at 5 Capel St (Mon–Thurs 10am–6pm, Fri 10am–4pm; ☎872 7770). It's also a good idea to get a copy of the excellent freebie *Gay Community News* – which you can pick up at the Temple Bar information centre or Books Upstairs.

Gay and mixed meeting places include, *The Globe*, *The Front Lounge*, *Pravda* and *Hogans* (see "Bars", p.115). A lot of mainstream venues have themed nights and gay events, and many of the city-centre pubs have a very mixed clientele. More specifically gay places include:

Front Lounge, Parliament St. More a mixed than an exclusively gay venue, its atmosphere is certainly camp which appeals to quite a large gay crowd.

The George Bar and Bistro, 89 South Great George's St (☎478 2983). Three bars in total at this gay venue: the *Loft* disco, trendy bar with music and a quiet bar. From Wednesday to Sundays there's also a lively and vibrant club open until 2.30am, with a "no effort, no entry" dress code.

Hogans, (*The Globe and Hogans*; see p.115), 11 South Great George's St. Busy and stylish mixed crowd.

Molloy's, High St, Christchurch, Dublin 2. This is the venue for Dublin's most popular lesbian night, *Stonewaltz*, on Friday nights.

Out on the Liffey, 27 Upper Ormond Quay. More relaxed than the *George*, this pub is popular with gays and lesbians alike.

Shopping

Around Grafton Street and O'Connell Street, the business of buying and selling rates second only to pub life for vigour, humour and sheer panache. Although many of the store chains – Next, Marks & Spencers, Waterstones – will be familiar to British visitors, the relatively small size of the city means that shopping in Dublin is as much about seeing, being seen and socializing as it is about actually purchasing anything, making it both a spectator and participant sport of the highest order. The **O'Connell Street** area represents the more ordinary, high-street end of the market, with cut-price shops, chain stores, and a boisterous street market concentrated on nearby Henry Street. Clery's, the august department store, and Eason's bookshop are two of the highlights; the Ilac centre, behind Moore Street, is probably the nadir.

South of the river are the smarter outlets and the tourist shops, as well as the kaleidoscopic and rapidly changing range of "alternative" boutiques that characterizes the fashionable **Temple Bar** area (the place to go for club gear and street fashions). Pedestrianized **Grafton Street** contains Dublin's swankiest department store, Brown Thomas. Just off Grafton Street, the two hundred-year-old Powerscourt Town House has been converted into a covered mall, with plenty of expensive clothes shops.

As a visitor, you'll find it difficult to escape the range of shops touting "typically" **Irish goods** aimed at tourists, mainly wool, ceramics and crystal. You may well come away with the impression that these are universally depressingly overpriced, but there are some exceptions, and you can occasionally pick up some real bargains.

Antiques

Sullivan Antiques, 43 Francis St in The Liberties, is one of the best established antique shops specializing in *objets d'art* and furniture. Shops in Molesworth Street – including Alexander Antiques at number 16, which has a wide range of antique clocks, pictures and period furniture – South Anne Street and Kildare Street are all worth a browse. The **Antiques Gallery** in the Powerscourt Centre has a number of outlets selling jewellery, porcelain and silverware while an antiques collectors' fair takes place every fortnight at Newman House (see p.82) on Sundays from 11am to 6pm (☎670 8295).

Bookshops

General bookshops include Eason's, 40–42 Lower O'Connell St (beside the GPO); Waterstones at 7 Dawson St; and Ireland's leading independent bookstore Hodges Figgis, nearby at 56–58 Dawson St, which has a particularly extensive stock of **Irish books**, a good remainder bookshop downstairs and a pleasant café on the first floor. Probably the best place to try for specialized Irish books, however, is Cathach Books, 10 Duke St (☎671 8676), which also has many rare first editions. The excellent Fred Hanna's, 29 Nassau St, has been taken over by the Eason chain and is now elegantly housed in the former bank building on the corner of Nassau and Dawson streets. Dublin Bookshop, 24 Grafton St, is one of the better mainstream bookshops, while Books Upstairs, 36 College Green (just outside the gates of Trinity College), is still Dublin's major alternative bookshop and has a good selection that includes feminist and gay fiction, women's studies, poetry and cinema, magazines and reviews. Greenes, 16 Clare St, an academic, topsy-turvy secondhand bookshop is also worth a look, and The Winding Stair, 40 Ormond Quay, is an excellent and pleasantly shabby secondhand bookshop with an unhurried café where you can peruse your finds, before or after purchase. If it's sci-fi, fantasy or horror you're after then Forbidden Planet, 36 Dawson St is the place to find it, while Connolly Books, 43 East Essex St, stocks a wide range of books on the political sciences.

Clothes

Brown Thomas, Grafton Street, offers smart designer wear from Irish labels such as Paul Costelloe, Louise Kennedy and John Rocha, while the Irish Fashion Design Centre (Powerscourt Town House), Clarendon St, has a changing range of stalls by young designers who work mainly in natural materials such as linen, silk and wool. For secondhand clothes, Flip, Shorts Ville and The Real McCoy, all at 4 Fownes St, specialize in Americana, jackets, shirts and jeans; at Eager Beaver, The Crown Alley, and Sé Sí Progressive, Fownes St Lower, Temple Bar, you can find a wider range of good-quality used clothing. You could also try the George's Street Market Arcade, off South Great George's St, which has a range of stalls selling secondhand clothing (plus jewellery and records).

Irish goods

Kilkenny Design Centre, 6 Nassau St, originally set up by the government to promote good design, is now privately run and stocks high-quality Irish goods: clothes (mainly linen and knitware), crystal and ceramics, which come significantly reduced in price at sale-time. Exquisite tweed and linen is also available at An Táin, 13 Temple Square North, Temple Bar. For knitted clothing made only from natural fibres, try Cleo Limited, 18 Kildare St (☎676 1421). A range of jewellery and Irish ceramics can be found in the new Duck Lane shopping arcade in Smithfield village, while The Blarney Woollen Mills, College Park House, Nassau St, offers a more traditional range of Irish crystal and china, plus the obligatory woolly pullovers and linen blouses; again, some bargains if you are prepared to sift. House of Ireland, also in Nassau Street, has fancy Irish crystal ranging from Belleek to Waterford, as well as the sweetly sentimental Lladro ceramics. At 41 Lower Ormond Quay, The Dublin Woollen Company sells a huge range of cut-price Irish knitwear, tweeds and lace. If cashmere is your thing then Monaghans in Grafton Arcade is the place to go. Talented local jewellers showcase their work at the DESIGNyard, 12 Essex St, Temple Bar, where you can also commission works, and if the jewellery on display there fails to impress, the stunning collection on display at Angles, 10 Westbury Mall, off Grafton Street (☎679 1964) surely will. Weir and Sons, 96 Grafton St, has antique silver and jewellery plus a good selection of Irish crystal. If you are keen on genealogy, Clans of Ireland, 2 Kildare St, is able to trace the location and significance of most Irish family names.

Music

Claddagh Records, 2 Cecilia St, Temple Bar, stocks a good range of traditional Irish and "world music". Both Celtic Note, 12 Nassau St and Ceol, Smithfield, stock an impressive range of traditional music. Back in Temple Bar, Comet Records, 5 Cope St, sells new indie CDs and secondhand records, and dispenses useful information on current bands and where to see them; Freebird, 1 Eden Quay, specializes in secondhand indie. For local dance music check out the new D1 store on Parnell Street which promote DJs on its independent label. Both HMV, 65 Grafton St, and Virgin Megastore, 14 Aston Quay, offer mainstream sounds.

Listings

Airlines Aer Lingus, 41 Upper O'Connell St and 13 St. Stephen's Green (☎886 8888, *www.aerlingus.ie*); British Airways, 60 Dawson St (☎1800/626747, *www.british-airways.com*); British Midland, Merrion Centre (☎283 8833; Dublin Airport ☎677 4422, *www.britishmidland.com*); Ryanair, 3 Dawson St (☎669 7800 *www.ryanair.ie*).

Banks Banking hours are Mon–Fri 10am–4pm, except Thurs when they stay open until 5pm. Main high-street banks are the Allied Irish and Bank of Ireland; branches throughout the city centre. ATMs are widely available throughout the city.

Bicycles Bicycles can be hired from: Bike Store, 58 Lower Gardiner St (☎872 5399); Dublin Bike Tours, 3 Mornington Rd, Ranelagh (☎679 0899); Track Cycles, 8 Botanic Rd, Glasnevin (☎850 0252).

Car rental Budget at the airport (☎844 5150 or 874 5919), in the city (☎837 9611 or 9802); Dan Dooley Kenning, 42–43 Westland Row (☎677 2723); Thrifty Rent-a-Car, 14 Duke St (☎679 9420); Windsor Car Rentals (☎1800 515 800, *www.windsor.ie*); plus all the usual desks at the airport.

Counselling Rape Crisis Centre, 70 Lower Leeson St (☎661 4911 or ☎1800 77 88 88); Samaritans, 112 Marlborough St (☎872 7700); Well Woman's Centre, 73 Lower Leeson St (☎661 0083).

Departures Buses to the airport set off from Eden Quay (not all of them go into the airport compound, so check with the driver). For the ferries, take the DART service to Dún Laoghaire; or a bus (#53 or #53A) to Dublin Port from Eden Quay. Buses to all parts of the country (Bus Éireann) leave from Busáras or the streets immediately around (Eden Quay, Abbey Street, Talbot Street); enquiries all handled at the information office located at 59 Upper O'Connell St, opposite the main tourist information office (Mon–Fri 9am–5pm, Sat 9am–1pm; ☎836 6111). Officially approved private buses are generally cheaper: ask to see the bus information file at the tourist office. Unofficial buses may be cheaper still; they leave from various points around the city, especially on Friday and Sunday evenings. Check the *Evening Herald* for advertisements – weekend buses generally need advance booking. Trains to the limited parts of Ireland served by the national train system leave from Heuston Station (still sometimes known by its old name of Kingsbridge) on the southside (Cork, Waterford, Limerick, Killarney, Tralee, Athlone, Galway, Westport, Ballina, Claremorris) or Connolly Station (aka Amiens St Station) on the northside (Belfast, Derry, Portadown, Dundalk, Sligo, Arklow, Wexford, Rosslare Harbour). Mainline commuter trains serving coastal towns north and south of Dublin call at Connolly, Tara Street and Pearse Street stations. For train information call ☎836 6222.

Embassies Australia, Fitzwilton House, Wilton Terrace (☎676 1517); Canada, 65 St Stephen's Green (☎478 1988); Denmark, 121 St Stephen's Green (☎475 6404); France, 36 Ailesbury Rd (☎269 4777); Netherlands, 160 Merrion Rd (☎269 3444); Norway, 34 Molesworth St (☎662 1800); Sweden, Sun Alliance House, Dawson St (☎671 5822); UK, 31–33 Merrion Rd (☎269 5211); United States, 42 Elgin Rd, Ballsbridge (☎668 8777).

Exchange American Express Foreign Exchange in Dublin Tourism's main office, Suffolk St (Mon–Sat 9am–5pm) and Thomas Cook, 118 Grafton St, give a fair rate; although the best exchange rates are given by banks (see opposite).

Ferry companies Irish Ferries, 16 Westmoreland St (☎661 0511); Isle of Man Steam Packet Co. (☎1800 551743); Merchant Ferries (☎819 2999); Stena Line, 15 Westmoreland St (☎204 7777).

Gaelic football All the major games of the season are played at Croke Park (☎831 2099). The championship season runs from mid-February, culminating in the All Ireland finals on the third Sunday in September. Prices reflect the status of the match, with stand tickets starting from £20/€25.40 for semi-finals and £25/€31.75 to £50/€63.50 for finals. For more on gaelic football see "Sports and Activities" in Basics on p.47.

Gay Switchboard (☎872 1055). Also see "Gay life" p.119.

Horse racing You shouldn't leave Dublin without experiencing Irish horse racing (and betting). Many of the bigger races are run out in Co. Kildare (see p.142), but check out more local events at Leopardstown (☎289 3994); its major jump-race festival is held on the four days after Christmas, while in early February its most prestigious steeplechase, the Hennessy Gold Cup, is run. Dublin Bus (see p.61) run a special service to Leopardstown on race days, leaving an hour and a half from Busáras before the first race (£3/€3.81 return). Tickets to the races range in price from £8/€10.16 to £10/€12.70, with an extra £5/€6.35 to £7/€8.89 for admission to the enclosure.

Hospitals northside: Mater Misericordiae Hospital, Eccles St (☎830 1122); southside: Meath Hospital, Heytesbury St (☎453 6555). Dial ☎999 for an ambulance.

Hurling As with gaelic football (see above for ticket prices) the important games are played at Croke Park; the championship season which begins in early summer finishes with the All Ireland final on the first Saturday in September. For more on hurling see "Sports and Activities" in Basics on p.47.

Laundry EXEL Launderette, 12 Main St, Donnybrook (☎269 7172); Nova Launderette, 2 Belvedere St, just off Dorset St (☎855 6736); Powder Launderette, 42a South Richmond St (☎478 2655); Shirley's, 141 Rathmines Rd (☎962 2228).

Left luggage There are left luggage offices at Busáras (Mon–Sat 8am–8pm, Sun 10am–6pm), Connolly Station (Mon–Sat 7.40am–9.30pm, Sun 9.15am–1pm & 5–9pm) and Heuston Station (Mon–Sat 7.15am–8.35pm, Sun 8am–3pm & 5–9pm).

Legal advice Free Legal Advice Centre, Administration office, 49 South William St (☎679 4239).

Pharmacy O'Connell's, 55 Lower O'Connell St (☎873 0427), is open till 10pm daily.

Phones At least half of Dublin's public phones now operate on CallCards, available from newsagents and garages. International payphones are available in the GPO.

Photography One Hour Photo, 110 Lower Grafton St (☎677 4472), or 5 St Stephen's Green (☎671 8578).

Police The main metropolitan Garda station is on Harcourt Street, just off St Stephen's Green (☎873 2222). In an emergency dial ☎999.

Post office General Post Office, O'Connell St (Mon–Sat 8am–8pm, Sun 10.30am–6.30pm; ☎705 7000).

Rugby The big games – the Six Nations Championship matches held between January and March – are played at the Lansdowne Rd Stadium in Ballsbridge (☎668 9300).

Travel agents CIE Tours, 35 Lower Abbey St (☎830 1888), is the biggest internal tour operator, if you want a bus trip around Ireland; Thomas Cook, 118 Grafton St (☎677 1721), and Trailfinders 4–5 Dawson St (☎677 7888, *www.trailfinders.com*), for general travel services; USIT, 19–21 Aston Quay, O'Connell Bridge (☎679 1600), are experts in student/youth travel.

travel details

Trains

Dublin Connolly to: Arklow (4 daily; 1hr 45min); Belfast (6 daily; 2hr 15min); Derry (5 daily; 5hr); Dundalk (9 daily; 1hr–1hr 30min); Portadown (6 daily; 1hr 50min); Rosslare (3 daily; 2hr 50min); Sligo (3 daily; 3hr 15min); Wexford (3 daily; 2hr 30min).

Dublin Heuston to: Athlone (7 daily; 1hr 40min); Ballina (3 daily; 3hr 40min); Claremorris (3 daily; 3hr); Cork (9 daily; 3hr); Galway (4 daily; 3hr); Killarney (4 daily; 3hr 30min); Limerick (11 daily; 2hr 15min); Tralee (4 daily; 4hr); Waterford (4 daily; 2hr 30min); Westport (3 daily; 3hr 40min).

Buses

Dublin to: Belfast (6 daily; 3hr); Cork (4 daily; 4hr 30min); Derry (4 daily; 4hr 25min); Donegal (4 daily; 4hr 15 min); Galway (9 daily; 3hr 45min); Limerick (6 daily; 3hr 30min); Waterford (6 daily; 2hr 45min); Westport (3 daily; 5hr).

In addition to Bus Éireann, scores of private companies connect Dublin with the rest of the country. Routes are too numerous to detail here – we've listed the most useful in the text of the relevant chapters.

CHAPTER TWO

WICKLOW AND KILDARE

Kildare and Wicklow, close to Dublin, provide a welcome respite from the capital's urban bustle. As central counties of the Pale region (the area of land around Dublin most successfully controlled by the Anglo-Normans and then the British, see also p.667), each is heavily resonant with the presence of the Anglo-Irish, yet

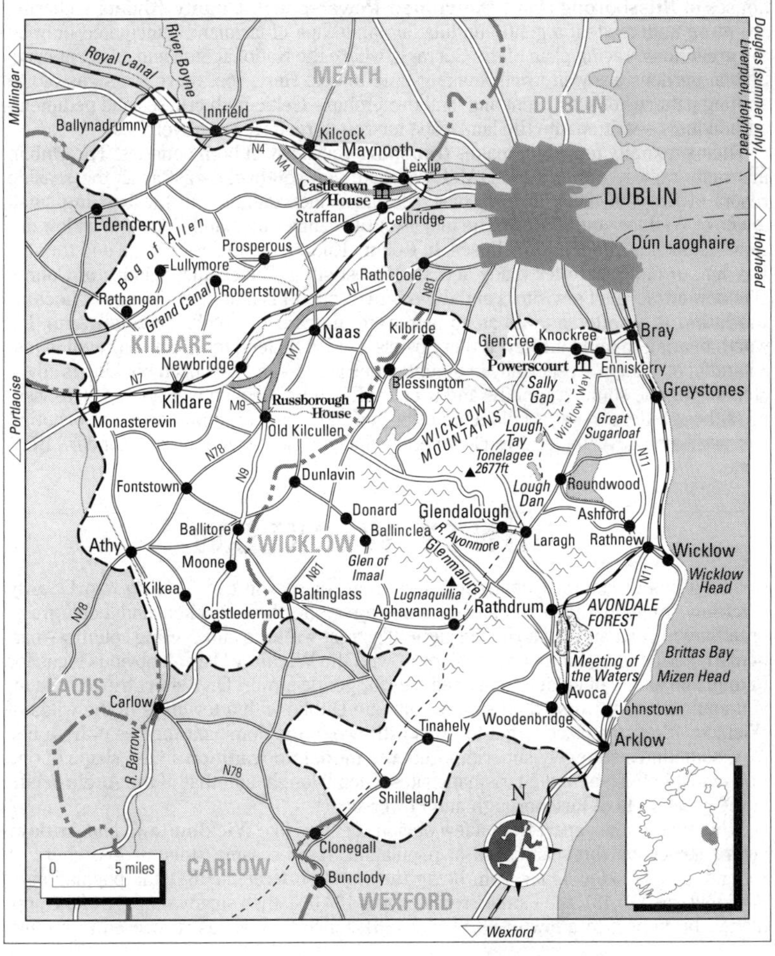

ACCOMMODATION PRICE CODES

Throughout this book, prices of hotels, guesthouses and B&Bs have been graded with the codes below, according to what you can expect to pay for a double room in high season. For more details on accommodation, see p.34.

① Under £26/€33.01	④ £40–55/€50.79–69.84	⑦ £90–110/€114.28–139.67
② £26–33/€33.01–41.90	⑤ £55–70/€69.84–88.88	⑧ £110–130/€139.67–165.07
③ £33–40/€41.90–50.79	⑥ £70–90/€88.88–114.28	⑨ Over £130/€165.07

scenically they are in complete contrast. **County Wicklow** has some of the wildest, most spectacular mountain scenery in Ireland, as well as some impressive monuments: the early Celtic monastery of Glendalough and the Neoclassical splendours of the great houses of **Russborough and the ruined Powerscourt**. **County Kildare**'s charms are more understated: a gently undulating landscape of farmland punctuated only by the great horse-racing plain of the Curragh, where the National Stud and adjacent ornamental gardens are well worth making time to see. Here, too, there are signs of the shifting patterns of settlement and land ownership – Celtic high crosses and pedimented buildings – written into the landscape for you to read as you travel.

Their proximity to Dublin makes **transport** very easy in both counties. The Dublin inner-city railway network, or DART, will take you southwards as far as the seaside resort of Bray on the Wicklow coast; the main line continues to the bustling small towns of Wicklow and Arklow. The major tourist centres in inland County Wicklow are served, albeit infrequently, by buses. In County Kildare the major N7 road and the railway line to Limerick offer ready access to most sites. The scenic beauties of County Wicklow attract a lot of visitors and the positive spin-off is that a good range of **accommodation** is on offer, as well as an increasing number of excellent **restaurants**. It's worth bearing in mind, however, that hostels and B&Bs tend to be concentrated in just a handful of villages – especially in mountainous areas – and advanced booking is advisable during the summer months and over bank holiday weekends. Kildare is less visited, although here too a few pioneers offer good food and accommodation in beautiful surroundings; nevertheless, you'll generally find yourself relying on the standard B&B trade.

COUNTY WICKLOW

Get on a bus in central Dublin, and in an hour or so you can be deep into **County Wicklow**, high in the mountains among gorse, heather, bracken and bent grass, breathing in clear air with no one in sight. It's great **walking** and **cycling** country – particularly challenging for mountain bikers – with the **Wicklow Way** an obvious focus for hiking, and plenty of golden sandy beaches for gentle strolls. On a short trip to Ireland, you could do a lot worse than simply combine Dublin with a few days in the wilds of Wicklow. It's also a place to get to grips with two of the dominant themes of Irish history, sometimes strangely superimposed: the **monastic tradition** in the shape of one of its most important and charismatic sites, Glendalough; and that of the **Anglo-Irish**, at the great seats of Russborough and Powerscourt.

Wherever you go, apart from a few obvious centres like **Wicklow** town and **Arklow**, you're struck by the sparseness of population. It's the same story as elsewhere in Ireland, and Wicklow is far from being the worst sufferer: in 1841 the population of Wicklow was 126,431, the Famine reduced it to 100,000, then steady seepage of the population brought it to a low of 58,473 by 1961. Since then it has recovered to around

100,000, partly through the development of commuter towns, as first the railway, then the suburban DART service have penetrated further into the county.

Heading out from Dublin you could follow the **coast**, but a far more attractive option is to head for the hills, stopping off at **Powerscourt House** and **Enniskerry** en route. If you have transport, you could continue on into the valley and join the **Wicklow Way** at the An Óige hostel at **Knockree**, or continue a couple of miles further into the valley for a stopover at similarly isolated **Glencree** hostel.

Alternatively **Glendalough** and **Laragh** are both accessible by public transport from Dublin by St Kevin's bus service (☎01/281 8119; see p.130), and make excellent bases from which to explore the mountains. If you only have a day to explore the area, it's worth considering a **tour** – the Wild Wicklow Tour leaves Dublin daily (☎01/280 1899; £22/€27.93).

The Wicklow Mountains

The **Wicklow Mountains**, so clearly viewed from Dublin, are really round-topped hills, ground down by the Ice Ages, with the occasional freakish shape like the Great Sugarloaf Mountain, where a granite layer has arrested the weathering. Despite their relatively modest height – Lugnaquillia, the highest peak, only just tops 3000ft – they're wild and uninhabited, with little traffic even at the main passes. Given this, and their proximity to Dublin, it's hardly surprising that they were traditionally bandit territory, and that the last insurgents of the land agitation that spread all over Ireland following the French invasion of County Mayo in 1798 hid out here; the mountains were virtually inaccessible until after the ensuing uprisings, when the army built a road to enable them to patrol effectively. This you can still follow, from Rathfarnham in the Dublin suburbs to Aghavannagh, high in the mountains; the **Wicklow Way** partly follows the road, too.

Along with offering some of the east's most wild and desolate landscapes, the Wicklow Mountains shelter a number of powerful historic monuments. The medieval monastic site at **Glendalough** evokes a sense of the sequestered lives of the Early Christian monks who lived there. Stately **Powerscourt House**, with its grand facade and its charred yet glorious interior, stands as a fitting symbol for the passing of the Anglo-Irish Ascendancy, and **Avondale House**, in the intensely pretty wooded valley to the southeast of the mountains, tells the story of one of Ireland's greatest nineteenth-century statesmen, Charles Stewart Parnell.

Enniskerry and Powerscourt House

The little village of **ENNISKERRY**, twelve miles south of Dublin, forms a popular stopping-off point for visitors heading for Powerscourt House, just a mile or so to the west (daily 9.30am–5.30pm, winter times may vary; *www.powerscourt.ie*; £1.50/€1.90). It was here, in the heart of the Pale, that the Anglo-Irish were at their most confident and relaxed. Powerscourt is a particularly bold statement of a theme repeated all over Ireland: big houses with adjoining tied villages. But in Powerscourt's case, the 14,000-acre estate stands as a sort of metaphor for the passing of the power of the Ascendancy. For Powerscourt is an estate without a heart, the shell of a house, designed in 1740 by the German architect Richard Castle and burnt out in 1974 on the eve of a big party that was to have celebrated the completion of an extensive programme of renovation. From afar, the Palladian mansion still looks impressive, set in its rolling parklands. Inside, however, only shadows of its former glory remain. There's fresh hope that it will be fully restored once more, and you can at least get some sense of its past grandeur from the smoky brickwork remains of the double-storey ballroom. Fortunately, photographs of the room before the fire, with its classical columns and lavish gilt decoration, survive and are on display in the attendant **exhibition**. The exhibition also includes some interesting material on Powerscourt's strategic importance from the twelfth century onwards and its role in the constant struggle between the Anglo-Irish and the local Irish clans.

The famous **gardens** attached to the house (same hours as exhibition; £4/€5.08; exhibition and gardens £5/€6.35) are mid-Victorian, but echo earlier European classical gardens. The designer of the upper terraces was one Daniel Robertson, an individual with a relaxed approach to his job. Robertson had himself trundled about the gardens in a wheelbarrow, clutching a bottle of sherry; when this was exhausted his creative powers waned and he finished work for the day. However unorthodox his working methods, the end result was fine: formal gardens with stepped terracing leading the eye down to a lake, with the weird whipped-cream peak of the **Sugarloaf Mountain** as a backdrop. This set piece aside, there's plenty of diversity: neat walled gardens, a pet cemetery, and a very fragrant Edwardian **Japanese garden**. The terrace **café bar** and counter-service **restaurant**, overlooking all of this, makes an ideal spot from which to enjoy both house and gardens and offers excellent food at very reasonable prices.

The spectacular 400ft **Powerscourt waterfall**, lies three miles from the house: turn right out of the main gate and follow the signs along the road (daily: summer 9.30am–7pm; winter 10.30am–dusk; £2/€2.54).

Practicalities

To get to Enniskerry from Dublin, take the #44 bus from Hawkins Street or the DART **train** to Bray and then the #185 bus. There are a couple of places to stay on the square in Enniskerry village: the *Powerscourt Arms Hotel* provides comfortable **accommodation** (☎01/282 8903, fax 286 4909; ⑤), while *Ferndale B&B* (☎01/286 3518; ④) is a lovely, relaxed alternative with antique furniture and a great breakfast menu.

Although there are very few **places to eat** in the village itself, *Poppies Country Kitchen* serves tasty homemade lunches, pies and puddings, and is open until 7pm in summer. Eighteenth-century *Johnnie Fox's Pub*, three miles from Enniskerry at **Glencullen**, is a time-honoured watering hole and worth negotiating the back roads to find. Daniel O'Connell was a regular here when he lived in the village and fliers of considerable historical interest decorate the walls. From chowders to Russian beluga caviar, the seafood available suits all purses; if you want to be sure to eat here, book a table (☎01/295 5647).

Glencree

Lying about six miles west of Enniskerry, the tiny village of **GLENCREE**, with its eponymous valley stretching away southeast to the Wicklow Way, is a quiet place with wonderful views of the Sugarloaf mountains. The only reason you're likely to be here is to stay at the An Óige **youth hostel** in Glencree, *Stone House* (book through the Dublin office ☎01/ 830 4555); a cosy stone house dating from the construction of the military road in 1798. Note that only basic provisions are available in the village and there is no pub. As an alternative, *Lackan House* An Óige **hostel** (☎01/286 4036; book through Dublin office ☎01/830 4555), halfway up the valley at **Knockree**, three miles west of Enniskerry, is less inviting, but in a much better position for joining the **Wicklow Way**, which passes through its grounds. Glencree was once famous for its **oak woods**, but the small one behind the hostel was actually planted in 1988, in sad commemoration of the fact that broadleaved woodlands now cover barely one percent of the country. Further down the valley a dense conifer plantation has been designated a place for walks, with the misleading name of Old Boley Wood.

THE WICKLOW WAY

Knockree is one of the better places to pick up the **Wicklow Way**, Ireland's first officially designated long-distance walk. Following a series of sheep tracks, forest firebreaks and bog roads – above 1600ft for most of the way – the walk leads from Marlay Park in the Dublin suburbs up into the Dublin mountains, skirts the end of Glencree, cuts across the bleak, boggy hillside below Djouce Mountain, and pushes on to Glendalough and Aghavannagh; it finally ends up 82 miles later at Clonegall on the Wexford border. It's not particularly well organized – one of its chief attractions for many hikers – but the whole route can be walked comfortably in five to six days.

Marlay Park is accessible via the #16A bus from O'Connell Street, Dublin city centre, for those who want to walk the whole route. If you're short of time, the best part to walk is probably the three-day section between Enniskerry and Glendalough; the path reaches its highest point at White Hill (2073ft), from which you can get a view of the mountains of North Wales on a fine day. Take the #44 bus from Hawkins Street, Dublin to Enniskerry, and pick up St Kevin's bus service at Glendalough for the return journey.

Low as they are, the Wicklow Mountains are notoriously treacherous, and even if you're planning on spending no more than a day **walking**, it's well worth investing in *The Wicklow Way Map Guide*, by Barry Dalby, which includes very detailed local maps and is available in Glendalough or from the publisher (*www.http://hompage.tinet.ie/eastwest*; £4.50/€5.71). The OS maps (Nos. 50, 56, 61 and 62) are also very useful, though some sections of the Wicklow Way have changed recently so first-rate map-reading skills are essential if using these. Advice on routes and conditions is available from the Wicklow Mountains National Park **information point** in Glendalough (see p.131). All the customary warnings about mountain walking apply and if you don't have any great experience of map reading, you'd do best to follow the yellow way-marking arrows. Trail walking is fairly new in Ireland; consequently, the paths are far less crowded than their counterparts in, say, Britain. Be aware that bad weather can close in rapidly, making the going dangerous and frightening if you're far from a road or house.

There are three An Óige **hostels** along the way – Knockree (see opposite), Glendalough (see p.131) and Glenmalure (see p.132), plus plenty of other places to stay around Glendalough, so accommodation shouldn't be a problem, although it may be wise to book ahead in high season. For these hostels and the one at Ballinclea (see p.133) – not actually on the Wicklow Way but in the locale – advanced booking is through the main An Óige office in Dublin (☎01/830 4555, fax 830 5808; *anoige@iol.ie*).

Above Glencree the military road ascends through dark, sinister terrain towards one of the two main mountain passes, the **Sally Gap**. Close to the source of the Liffey, the area has been heavily invaded by Dubliners seeking peat – a further depredation inflicted upon the landscape. The most spectacular route from here is to continue south along the military road down to Laragh and Glendalough, which runs over rough country until it joins the **Glenmacnass River** – at this point there's the extraordinary, extended Glenmacnass waterfall. The R759 heading southeast of here takes you past Lough Tay as it winds its way down to Sraghmore, a couple of miles north of Roundwood.

Dramatic, inaccessible **Lough Tay** – whose scree sides plunge straight into the water – is owned by Garech a'Brún, a member of the Guinness family who is also the man behind Claddagh Records in Dublin. Access to **Lough Dan**, south of here, with its gentler woodlands, is also barred and visitors are made to feel unwelcome by numerous signs warning against trespassing on private land.

Roundwood

The swifter, less mountainous route, to Glendalough from Dublin or Bray is via **ROUNDWOOD** (one of the stops on the St Kevin's bus service, see. p.130); a pleasant enough village, though not in the heart of the mountains. It's just a mile from the Wicklow Way as it passes south of Lough Dan and, Glendalough and Laragh aside, is one of the few places to get a range of food and accommodation in this part of the county.

You can get **B&B** accommodation here at *Tochar House* (☎01/281 8247; ③), a good, central option, which also has pleasant dorm bunks in an annexe catering for hikers and cyclists (£15/€19.05). Slightly further out are two other B&B options: *Woodside* (☎01/281 8195; ③), a mile and a half along the Dublin road, and *Ballinacor House* (☎01/281 8168; ②), a mile along the road towards Glendalough. The village also has a **campsite** (☎01/281 8163; closed Oct–Easter). Your **eating** choices in Roundwood are limited: there's one fast-food outlet; bar food at *The Coach House*; or you might try *The Roundwood Inn* (☎01/281 8107), a seventeenth-century coaching inn which is noted for its excellent, but pricey food in the restaurant (for which you'll need to book), and great bar meals. However, for a wider range of accommodation, and for readier access to lonelier and more impressive scenery, your best bet is probably to head on down to Laragh, six miles southwest of here (see p.132).

Glendalough

GLENDALOUGH – the valley of the two lakes – is one of the standard and very popular bus tours out of Dublin. Its famous monastic site is one of the most important in Ireland and, despite the huge number of visitors, the place has an amazing, quite tangible, quality of peace and spirituality. Access to the site is free, and there are numerous pleasant walks from here into the mountains. **Transport** to Glendalough from Dublin is easy – use the St Kevin's bus service (☎01/281 8119), which leaves twice daily from the Royal College of Surgeons on St Stephen's Green, and returns from the Glendalough Visitor Centre car park. The bus passes through Bray, where you can pick up the train to continue your journey south.

Glendalough is amply equipped to receive its many sightseers, with acres of car parking and a huge, modern **visitor centre** (daily: mid-March to end May & Sept to mid-Oct 9.30am–6pm; June & Aug 9am–6.30pm; mid-Oct to mid-March 9.30am–5pm; £2/€2.55; Heritage Card). This has an excellent exhibition and a video show that sets Glendalough in the context of the monastic ruins elsewhere in Ireland. The admission charge to the centre includes the video show, exhibition and a guided tour.

The monastery

The **monastery** at Glendalough was founded by St Kevin, a member of the royal house of Leinster, during the sixth century. As a centre of the Celtic Church, it became famous throughout Europe for its learning, and despite being sacked by the Vikings in the ninth and tenth centuries and by the English in the fourteenth century, it was patiently restored each time, and monastic life continued tenaciously until the sixteenth century.

All the following buildings are clustered between the visitor centre and the **Lower Lake**, and you'll be shown all of them unless it's raining hard, in which case the tour gets truncated. The **cathedral**, dating from the tenth and twelfth centuries (it was built in two phases), has an impressively ornamental east window, and the remains of a Late Romanesque doorway in the north wall. To the east of the cathedral, **St Kevin's Cross** is a massive slab of granite, carved in the eighth century, in the Celtic form of a cross superimposed on a wheel. It may have been left unfinished, since the "halo" formed by the wheel has not been pierced. The doorway of the **round tower** is ten feet above the ground. The traditional explanation for this raised entrance, and the one that the guide will undoubtedly give you, is that this design was adopted so that monks could pull up the ladder in times of trouble, turning the tower into an inaccessible treasury and refuge; however, more recent thinking suggests that the reason may be structural. The twelfth-century **Priest's House**, partially reconstructed 700 years later, got its name from being used as a burial place for local priests during the suppression of Catholicism. The carving above the door, so worn as to be indecipherable, possibly shows St Kevin between two ecclesiastical figures.

Perhaps the most famous building here is **St Kevin's Church**, a solid, barrel-vaulted stone oratory, also known as St Kevin's Kitchen. Although it may well date from St Kevin's time, the round-tower belfry is an eleventh-century addition, and the structure has clearly been altered many times.

The lakes and surrounding attractions

The real delights of Glendalough lie beyond what you get to see on the tour of the monastery. As you climb above the monastery complex, landscape and architecture combine in a particularly magical way, and you could spend days walking the footpaths that crisscross the upper valley, drinking it all in. The scenery is at its most spectacular at the **Upper Lake**, where wooded cliffs and a waterfall plunge vertically into the water. Also here is the Wicklow Mountains National Park **information point** (see below), where you can get details of some of the many **local walks**. *Twelve Walks in Glendalough*, by Paddy Dillon, is a useful walking guide to the area, detailing walks of varying difficulty, and is available locally.

There are plenty more antiquities connected with the monastic life among the cliffs around the upper lake, many of them formerly pilgrim shrines. The site of St Kevin's original church, the **Temple-na-Skellig**, is on a platform approached by a flight of stone steps, accessible only by boat. **St Kevin's Bed** is a rocky ledge high up the cliff, where it's said the holy man used to sleep in an attempt to escape from the unwelcome advances of a young girl. Eventually she found his hiding place and, waking up one morning to find her beside him, he reacted with the misogyny characteristic of the early Church fathers – and pushed her into the lake.

Practicalities

There's a small **tourist information** kiosk in Glendalough (June–Sept Mon–Sat 10am–1pm & 2–5.30pm; may be subject to variation; ☎0404/45688) offering a limited range of general information, but no booking service. The Wicklow Mountains National Park **information point** (May–Aug daily 10am–6pm; April & Sept Sat & Sun 10am–6pm; ☎0404/45425 summer, 0404/45338 winter) is located about a mile from the village at the head of the Upper Lake, and is accessible by following the road west from the *Glendalough Hotel*, or by walking along a pleasant track from the monastic site. Here you can pick up information on the landscape and wildlife of the surrounding area.

Accommodation in Glendalough itself is limited and it's advisable to book up in advance: *Luganure*, Lake Road (☎0404/45563; ④) offers comfortable B&B in a great location overlooking the tranquil scenery between Glendalough and the lakes; the large Victorian *Glendalough Hotel* (☎0404/45135, *www.glendaloughhotel.ie*; ⑦) occupies a similarly scenic location – while the lobby and bar can be busy and smoky, bedrooms are well-furnished and offer lovely views. For budget travellers, the newly refurbished An Óige hostel, *The Lodge* (☎0404/45342; ②) is a haven of comfort and can provide breakfast and evening meals; four-bed rooms are available and cost £50/€63.49, while dorm beds are £11/€13.97. They can also arrange **fishing** rod rental with licences for around £15/€19.05 a day. Unless you are staying in the hostel, the only place to **eat** in Glendalough is in the hotel, which serves bar food. Only a limited range of supplies are on sale in the hostel, so if you plan to use it as a base and want to cook for yourself, it's a good idea to bring food with you.

Laragh

Offering more amenities, the little village of **LARAGH**, just over a mile east of Glendalough, also makes a good place to **stay** (see below). Places to **eat** are thin on the ground though: *Lynham's*, a lively bar with roaring fires, is probably one of the best places; *The Wicklow Heather* is a moderately expensive family restaurant offering steaks, chops and stews; *Anne's* coffee shop (Easter–Oct daily; weekends rest of year) serves hot lunches, snacks and cakes; and the tea rooms at *The Woollen Mills*, about half a mile out of Laragh on the Rathdrum road, occupy a particularly pretty location and serve scones, desserts and open sandwiches (closed Nov to March).

If you need guidance on how to exploit the **sporting opportunities** of the area, check out the rock-climbing, mountaineering, canoeing and kayaking courses offered by the Tiglin Adventure Centre (☎0404/40169), about eight miles east of Glendalough near Ashford.

Accommodation

Derrybawn House, about half a mile out of Laragh on the Rathdrum road (☎0404/45134). An elegant late eighteenth-century house tucked into the hillside in extensive wooded grounds. ⑤.

Glen Ailbhe, (☎0404/45236). A family B&B, in the village itself, offering good-quality accommodation in brightly coloured rooms, all en suite. ③.

Glendalough River House, tucked away off the Rathdrum road, about half a mile out of Laragh. (☎0404/45577). Comfortable B&B in a converted mill house, occupying a superb riverside location with fabulous views and tranquility. ④.

Peter and Maura McGrath's, No. 4 Laragh (☎0404/45444). A modest family home, welcoming and right in the centre of the village. ②.

Tudor Lodge, half a mile from the village on the Rathdrum road (☎0404/45554). Spacious modern B&B offering comfortable accommodation in a beautiful spot. ④.

The Wicklow Way, (☎0404/45398 or 45345). A very basic hostel right on the Wicklow Way; close to the pub. There's a possibility of work on the hostel, so things may improve.

Woodview, No. 2 Laragh (☎0404/45485). A modest B&B with brightly decorated rooms, all en suite; reductions for children. ③.

Glenmalure and the Glen of Imaal

Northwest of Glendalough, the main road takes you over the Wicklow Gap, whence there's a tolerably tough climb up to the top of **Tonelagee** (2677ft), and beyond here there's the option of following the R756 west out of the mountains towards Blessington. South and west of Glendalough, the country rises, becoming wilder and more desolate, dominated by **Lugnaquillia**, the highest mountain in the Wicklow range at 3039ft. The military road offers a scenic route continuing southwest from Laragh; experienced walkers and map-readers have the option of trekking to the head of Glendalough, through the forest and down into the next glen.

Whether on foot or by car, you'll arrive in dark and lonely **GLENMALURE**, half of which is off limits as an army firing range. Perhaps appropriately, Glenmalure was the scene of a decisive victory by the Wicklow Irish under Fiach MacHugh O'Byrne over the English under Elizabeth I. One of the 1798 barracks, now ruined, stands at the point where the military road hits the glen. It's a symbol of decay that somehow sets the tone for the entire valley, with its enclosed, mysterious feel and steep scree sides which scarcely afford a foothold to the heather. The road eventually peters out in a car park, but a track continues up to the extremely basic An Óige Glenmalure **youth hostel** (June–Aug daily; Sept–May Fri & Sat only; book through the Dublin office ☎01/830 4555), which stands at the head of the valley just above the point where the river rushes over a weir. With no other buildings in sight, it's an unspoilt setting. From here it's possible to follow a track further up the valley, over the Table Mountain, and down into the Glen of Imaal.

By comparison with Glenmalure, the **Glen of Imaal** is almost inviting. Again, it's dominated by the impressive summit of Lugnaquillia, and, likewise, half of it is reserved as an army shooting range. Altogether, it's as wild and desolate as you could wish for, though more open and lighter than Glenmalure. There's an An Óige **youth hostel** at **BALLINCLEA** (closed Dec–Feb; ☎045/404657), just over two miles southeast of Donard.

At **DERRYNAMUCK**, on the southeast side of the valley, stands a cottage where Michael O'Dwyer, one of the last insurgents of 1798, took refuge when trapped by the British, and subsequently escaped because Samuel McAllister drew the enemy's fire and died in his place. It's now run as a **folk museum**: the Dwyer McAllister Cottage (mid-June to mid-Sept daily 2–6pm; free).

Avondale House and The Vale of Avoca

South of Laragh, the **Vale of Clara** leads to **RATHDRUM**, a quiet village on the Dublin–Rosslare railway route and the Dublin–Arklow bus route. Here the *Old Presbytery* **hostel** (IHH; ☎0404/46930; ①) offers comfortable accommodation in twin rooms and dorms. As so little budget accommodation in this area exists this is a handy stopover; cyclists in particular may find it a useful place to stay if the Glendalough hostel is fully booked. The hostel is well equipped with gym, sauna and full disabled access, and it caters for groups, so phoning ahead is advisable. About a mile and a half south of Rathdrum lies Avondale where you can visit **Avondale House** (mid-March to Oct daily 11am–6pm; grounds open daily all year; £3/€3.81 house). Home to one of Ireland's most influential and important politicians, **Charles Stewart Parnell**, born here in 1846, was hailed as the "uncrowned king of Ireland" until his career – and his campaign for home rule – was brought to an end by the scandal of his love for a married woman, Kitty O'Shea (see p.672 for more on Parnell).

The **house**, designed in 1779 by the celebrated English architect John Wyatt, is a modest, box-shaped building. Inside, there's a delicate, Wedgwood-like blue dining room with plasterwork by the famous Lanfranchini brothers, a striking vermilion library (Parnell's favourite room), and, in the entrance hall, an elegant minstrels' gallery from where Parnell, a nervous orator, used to practise his political speeches.

The Avondale estate has been in the possession of the Irish Forestry Board since 1904, and the grounds are used for silvicultural experiments. As a result, they're filled with rare tree species. There's a coffee shop, and plenty of picnic tables in the estate.

The scenic **Vale of Avoca**, two miles south of Avondale, can be excessively crowded with coach tours heading for the mills. Nevertheless, don't be put off: its beauty – once you leave the fertilizer plant behind – is genuinely rewarding, with thickly wooded slopes on either side of the river, culminating in the **Meeting of the Waters**, the confluence of the Avonmore and Avonbeg rivers.

The Meeting has attracted its fair share of coffee shops, and there's a pleasant pub, but for excellent daytime **food**, among other things, you're better advised to stop a mile or so downstream at the pleasantly unassuming village of **AVOCA** with its hand-weaving mill (May–Sept Mon–Fri 8am–4.30pm, Sat & Sun 9am–5pm; Oct–April Mon–Fri 8am–4.30pm, Sat & Sun 10am–4.30pm; ☎0402/35105; free). The weavers are housed in a group of whitewashed buildings with steep grey roofs, where the fly-shuttle looms that caused mass unemployment when they were introduced in 1723 appear as picturesquely traditional. There's an excellent, inexpensive lunch room which serves sandwiches, soup and cakes, and a shop selling good quality crafts and knitwear.

The Wicklow coast

County Wicklow's most outstanding scenery is chiefly inland. Nevertheless, the coast offers a handful of pleasant, if unassuming, towns and some very fine beaches. For bracing walks, **Wicklow** and **Bray** are probably the best of these and, along with **Arklow**, offer plenty of accommodation.

Travelling south from Dublin along the **Wicklow coast**, the N11 takes you to **Bray**, the first major town which, although very much a dormitory suburb, retains something of its Victorian resort character. From here the coastal road runs south down to **Rathnew**, where you join the main road again. By train, the **DART service** from the capital runs as far as Bray; to get to Wicklow town or Arklow, catch the Wexford train. Alternatively you could take the Wexford bus, which also runs to Wicklow town but then takes you on a scenic detour inland via the heavily wooded Vale of Avoca to Arklow.

Bray

BRAY, originally a Victorian resort developed in the 1850s when the railway was extended south of Dún Laoghaire, welcomes hordes of visitors from Dublin at the weekends. With a seafront full of hotels, video arcades, B&Bs and fast-food shops, Bray has lost some of its genteel charm. Nevertheless it does boast a superb sand and shingle **beach** and there are excellent walks to be had up around Bray Head, a knob of rock pushing into the sea, where a massive cross, erected to mark the holy year of 1950, serves as a reminder that you are still in Catholic Europe. In the shadow of the head are a few secluded coves where you can swim.

Besides its fine setting, Bray's chief claim to fame is that James Joyce lived here from 1889 to 1891. The main visitor attraction, the **Bray heritage centre** (June–Aug Mon–Fri 9am–5pm, Sat 10am–1pm & 2–4pm; Sept–May Mon–Fri 9.30am–1pm & 2–4pm, Sat 10am–1pm & 2–4pm; ☎01/286 6796; £3.50/€4.44), is currently undergoing major renovation work, while details have not yet been finalized, the newly enhanced displays are likely to focus on local history and include a folklore room and also a presentation on the engineer William Dargan (1799–1867), the man who brought the railway to the town, and who is thus considered the founder of modern Bray. You'll also find the **tourist office** (same hours) here. The other attraction of note in Bray, is the **National Sea-Life Centre** (daily 10am–6pm; £5.50/€6.98), a large aquarium with a great range of sea-life, including sharks and the blue ring octopus. **Bicycle rental** in Bray is available from Bray Sports Centre, 8 Main St (☎01/286 3046; £10/€12.70 per day), and **horse riding** can be arranged with Brennanstown Riding School (☎01/286 3778).

Outside Bray, **Killruddery House** and its **garden** are worth seeing (gardens open April–Sept daily 1–5pm; house May, June & Sept daily 1–5pm; £4.50/€5.70, gardens only £3/€3.80), and are reached by bus #184 from Bray. Laid out in the seventeenth century, Killruddery's gardens are among the earliest that survive in Ireland. Home of the Brabazon family since 1618, the house was remodelled by Richard and William Morrison in the 1820s.

Wicklow

There's nothing much to **WICKLOW**, seventeen miles south of Bray, but it is the first place that wholly escapes the influence of Dublin as you go down the coast. It's a pleasant, ramshackle town with plenty of entertainment, one or two good, cheap places to eat, a couple of smarter places on the fringes of the town, and walking and swimming, too. It has none of the presence you might expect of a county town and comes across as a happily disorganized kind of place, full of people chatting on pavements, cars parked on double yellow lines and solidly built houses in bright marine pastels.

Two minor squares form the town's core: Fitzwilliam Square, where you'll find the tourist office (see below); and Market Square, where a spirited memorial to the 1798 rebel Billy Byrne grabs your attention. Byrne, born into a wealthy Catholic family, led rebels from south and central Wicklow during the 1798 Rebellion, but was eventually executed at Gallow's Hill in Wicklow town (for more on the rebellion see p.671). Around fifty yards from Market Square on Kilmantin Hill stands **Wicklow's Historic Gaol**, originally built in 1702 to hold prisoners under the repressive penal laws, and now converted into a tourist attraction (April–Sept daily 10am–6pm; *www.wicklow.ie/gaol*; £4.20/€5.33) offering a very lively re-creation of the life of the prison. The gaol looks at the part it played in the lives of those involved in the 1798 Rebellion, and those transported from here to the Penal Colonies.

Just outside town on the seaward side, a knoll encrusted with some knobbly piles of stone constitutes all that's left of **Black Castle**: one of the fortifications built by the Fitzgeralds in return for lands granted them by Strongbow after the Anglo-Norman invasion of 1169, and all but demolished by the O'Byrnes and O'Tooles in 1301. **Wicklow Head** really is spectacular, and you can walk all the way round (there are two tiny swimming beaches) accompanied by exhilarating views of the open sea and, northwards, the weird silhouettes of the Great and Little Sugarloaf mountains. There's also sociable, if unglamorous, swimming near the harbour breakwater closer to the centre of town.

Practicalities

Wicklow, along with Arklow and Bray, provides a convenient point of entry to the hinterland. A minibus service operates from Wicklow to Glendalough from June to mid-September, departing twice daily from Bridge Street – contact the tourist office for details. The **tourist office** is on Fitzwilliam Square (June–Sept Mon–Sat 9am–6pm; Oct–May Mon–Fri 9.30am–1pm & 2–5.30pm; ☎0404/69117).

A good range of **accommodation** is on offer in Wicklow and the surrounding area (see below), and you can **camp** near the beach at Silver Strand, about two miles south of town (☎0404/67615; closed Oct–May). Options for **eating** in Wicklow are fairly limited. *The Bakery Restaurant and Wine Bar*, Church Street, just off Fitzwilliam Square, is one of the best places, offering a varied menu of Mediterranean and Modern-Irish cuisine in a cosy bistro-style setting (☎0404/66770). During the day their café serves homemade soups, salads and patisserie. There are other coffee shops serving lunch which are located around Fitzwilliam Square. *The Opera House*, Market Square, is a pleasant inexpensive Italian restaurant, and several pubs serve food – *Phil Healy's* on Fitzwilliam Square is especially good for carvery lunches. For top quality – and expensive – modern Irish cuisine, make a reservation at *The Old Rectory* or *Hunter's Hotel* (see p.136). Wicklow has a handful of decent **pubs**: *Philip Healy's* is a genial bar on the Square; for traditional music try *The Bridge Tavern*, Bridge Street on Tuesdays, and *The Bayview Hotel* on Thursdays.

Accommodation

Bayview Hotel, The Mall (☎0404/67383). Although the lobby is fairly unappealing, and the service minimal, the recently refurbished bedrooms are large and pleasant. The lively hotel bar has traditional Irish music on Thursdays, and assorted live music at weekends. ④.

The Grand Hotel, Abbey St (☎0404/67337, *www.grandhotel.ie*). A large, traditional three-star hotel in the town centre. Cosy fires in the lobby and comfortable bedrooms: all en suite with TV, and tea- and coffee-making facilities. Reduced rates for short breaks. ⑥.

Hunter's Hotel, Rathnew, around two miles from Wicklow town (☎0404/40106, *www.indigo.ie/~hunters*). Comfortable en-suite rooms in this lovely old coaching inn, furnished with antiques that was once a haunt of the nineteenth-century politician Charles Stewart Parnell. Today it's particularly renowned for its excellent restaurant serving lunch, afternoon tea and dinner, and for the riverside gardens. ⑧.

Kilmantin House, Kilmantin Hill (☎0404/67373). A centrally located B&B, right next door to Wicklow's Historic Gaol. Bright, cheery rooms with stripped-pine floors and airy colour schemes. All en suite with TV. ④.

MacReamoinn Town House, Summerhill (☎0404/61113). A pleasant B&B on the edge of town offering en-suite accommodation and generous breakfasts. Quiet location and an easy stroll into the centre of town. ④.

The Old Rectory (☎0404/67048; closed Jan & Feb). A delicate pink mansion in a tranquil location up a lane off the Dublin road, five minutes' walk from the town centre. Rooms are en suite, welcoming and decorated with fresh flowers. The hotel is noted for the organic food and edible flowers of its gourmet restaurant. Extensive facilities include a sauna and fitness suite. ⑦.

Wicklow Bay Hostel, Marine House (IHH; ☎0404/69213 or 61174; closed mid-Nov to Jan) A big, breezy, hostel close to the town centre, overlooking the sea. The hostel is well run by friendly staff. Dorms, four-bed and twin rooms are available: linen included. Bike rental is also on offer here. ①.

Brittas Bay and Mount Usher Gardens

Heading south of Wicklow towards Arklow on the R750, you'll come to a string of white-sand **beaches**. The one at **Brittas Bay**, just north of Mizen Head, is particularly good – don't be put off by the caravan site, there's plenty of seclusion to be found.

Horticultural enthusiasts should also know about **Mount Usher Gardens** (mid-March to Oct daily 10.30am–6pm; £3.50/€4.44), a few miles inland near Ashford, where rare trees, shrubs and flowers grow in profusion in a narrow strip next to the road. For others, the gardens' main attraction may be the miniature suspension bridges where you can see engineering principles at work as they sway and bounce under your weight.

Arklow

If the poetry and passion of Van Morrison's *Streets of Arklow* have brought you here, you may well be disappointed. While it's an ideal point from which to access the intensely pretty Vale of Avoca, the town itself is chiefly a commercial centre wrapped around an old port. **ARKLOW** has a long and prosperous history based on fishing, shipbuilding and the export of copper ore, pyrites and even gold, mined further up the valley. While no longer a major port, shipbuilding continues to be important – *Gypsy Moth IV*, Sir Francis Chichester's prize-winning transatlantic yacht now moored at London's Greenwich, was built at John Tyrrell's yard here. For a grip on the past, stop off at the **Maritime Museum** in St Mary's Road (summer Mon–Sat 10am–5pm; £1/€1.27). A delightfully haphazard collection of local finds, it claims a history for Arklow going back to Ptolemy's celebrated second-century map. It also emerges that Arklow was a major centre for arms-smuggling during the upheavals of 1798. The museum houses such curiosities as a whale's tooth and eardrum and a model ship made with 10,700 matchsticks.

Arklow's **beach**, white sand like the rest of this part of the coast, is sandwiched between the docks and a gravel extraction plant – you may prefer to head north to Brittas Bay, or, if you have transport, five miles south to the sheltered sandy **Clogga Beach**.

Practicalities

The **tourist office** (May Mon–Fri 10am–1pm & 2–5.30pm; June–Sept Mon–Sat 10am–1pm & 2–5.30pm; closed rest of year; ☎0402/32484) is located in the Coach House on Upper Main Street. **Accommodation** should be easy enough to find, with plenty of B&Bs – try *Vale View*, Coolgreany Road (☎0402/32622; ③–④), or for a peaceful stay in a fine country setting there's *Plattenstown House*, Coolgreaney Road, about two and a half miles out of town (☎ & fax 0402/37822; ④). *Avonmore House* **hostel**, Ferrybank (IHH; ☎0402/32825), a handy short walk from the town centre, offers decent budget accommodation and a field for **camping**. Places to **eat** are thin on the ground, but you'll find a good range of inexpensive grills and roasts at *Riverwalk Restaurant*, River Walk, off Main Street, and decent bar meals at *Christy's*. There are lots of **pubs** – most of which seem to have some kind of entertainment on offer, including traditional Irish music, discos and the odd pub quiz: *Christy's* and *The Mary B* are are both worth trying.

Russborough House

Russborough House and its impressive **art collection** (May–Sept daily 10.30am–5.30pm; April & Oct Sun & bank holidays 10.30am–5.30pm; 45min tour; £4/€5.08) in west Wicklow ranks alongside Powerscourt House and the monastic site at Glendalough as a great cultural landmark. Designed, like Powerscourt, by the German architect Richard Castle (with the assistance of Francis Bindon), Russborough is one of the jewels of the Pale. A classic Palladian structure whose central block is linked to two wings with curving arms, its design was subsequently repeated throughout Ireland, as a result of Castle's influence and its own suitability as a kind of glorified farmhouse.

In Russborough's case, it's very glorified indeed. The house was constructed for Joseph Leeson, son of a rich Dublin brewer and MP for Rathcormack in the days of the semi-independent Irish parliament: he was created **Lord Russborough** in 1756. Russborough House epitomizes the great flowering of Anglo-Irish confidence before the Act of Union deprived Ireland of its parliament, much of its trade and its high society (thereafter, the rich Anglo-Irish spent much of the year in London). No expense was spared. Not only were the fashionable architects of the day employed, but the plasterers, the Francini brothers, were also of the best. The plaster ovals in the drawing room, for instance, were made to order to fit the four Joseph Vernet marine paintings that still occupy them.

The **lake** in front of Russborough provides the house with an idiomatically eighteenth-century prospect. The impression is a false one, however – it's actually a thoroughly twentieth-century reservoir, created by damming the Liffey, which provides Dublin with twenty million gallons of water a day.

The art collection

Impressive though Russborough is, the chief reason why it is so firmly on the tourist trail is its collection of **paintings**. The German entrepreneur Alfred Beit (1853–1906) was a co-founder with Cecil Rhodes of the De Beer Diamond Mining Company, and he poured the fortune he derived from that enterprise into amassing works of art. His nephew, Sir Alfred Beit, acquired Russborough in 1952, which explains why such an extraordinary collection of famous pictures is kept in this obscure corner of County Wicklow. Whatever you may feel about their irrelevance to the site or the source of the wealth that made the acquisitions possible, there are some marvellous paintings by Goya, Murillo, Velázquez, Gainsborough, Rubens and Frans Hals, to name but a few.

Russborough has been burgled twice: in 1974, when Bridget Rose Dugdale stole sixteen paintings to raise money for the IRA – although her booty, worth £18 million, was recovered undamaged from a farmhouse in County Cork a week later; and in May 1986 – some of the paintings taken in the second heist have since been retrieved in The

Netherlands. Nowadays security is tight, and visitors are herded around the house in groups, with little chance to study the paintings – or anything else – in detail.

Practicalities

Getting to Russborough is no problem – **BLESSINGTON**, the pleasant coaching town it adjoins, is forty minutes from central Dublin on the Waterford **bus**. There's a central **tourist office** (June Mon–Fri 10am–5pm; July & Aug Mon–Fri 10am–6pm, Sat 11am–5pm; ☎045/865850), which has information on possibilities for **outdoor pursuits**. A wide range – including canoeing, sail-boarding, pony-trekking and hill-walking – is available at Blessington Land and Water Sports (☎045/865092). Blessington's marvellous **location** close to the shining waters of the **Blessington lakes** and, beyond them, the spectacular heights of the Wicklow Mountains, should make it a good base for exploration; however, accommodation and places to **eat** are rather limited. The informal *Courtyard Restaurant* (closed Wed) is a good spot for snacks, lunches and evening meals; *O'Connor's* serves excellent bar food. A few miles out of town, there's the An Óige *Baltyboys* **hostel**, on the wooded shores of the lake (☎045/867266; closed weekdays Dec–Feb; limited access between 10am–5pm).

COUNTY KILDARE

County Kildare, in the heart of the Pale, forms part of the hinterland of Dublin. Although it lacks the spectacle of the Wicklow Mountains, or the extraordinary range of ancient monuments of the lush Boyne Valley to the north, it has a quiet charm of its own. The **landscape** is a calm one of rolling farmland for the most part, with open grasslands and rough pasture, just touching the drab stretches of the monotonous Bog of Allen in the northwest. This is ancient countryside, marked by a string of **Celtic crosses** at Moone, Old Kilcullen and Castledermot. But you're also constantly made aware that you're in Pale country – with big, stone, estate walls bordering many of the fields and Georgian proportions in the buildings, as well as more obvious attractions such as the magnificent **Castletown House** with its model village at Celbridge; the **Grand Canal**, which traverses the county and has a walkable towpath; and the pin-neat **National Stud** at Kildare town with its fabulous horses and ornamental gardens.

Because of its proximity to Dublin, there's no problem about transport in County Kildare although it's worth avoiding driving between Dublin and Kildare during rush hour on weekdays as delays are common. The main **buses** to Limerick ply up and down the N7 trunk road, with the **rail** line running close beside it for most of the way. **Accommodation** is less easy – you're reliant on B&Bs, many of them the more expensive kind, catering for business travellers rather than tourists.

Maynooth, Castletown House and around

There really isn't all that much to detain you in **MAYNOOTH** – due west of Dublin on the M4 – (pronounced *Ma-nooth*, with the stress on the second syllable), pretty though it is. A handful of worthwhile attractions lie near to Maynooth including, four miles west, the intriguing **Larchill Arcadian Gardens** – a monument to the eccentricities of the eighteenth-century landowners who first developed them. **Castletown House**, outside Celbridge, is perhaps Ireland's most splendid Palladian mansion and combines a perfect eighteenth-century Classicism with follies to rival the idiosyncracies of Larchill. Around four miles west from Castletown House, the village of Straffan is home to a steam museum and a butterfly farm. Maynooth itself is renowned chiefly for its seminary, **St Patrick's College**, which, in addition to training priests, now houses two universities. Fans of Victoriana will be especially interested in the square here, which is by

Pugin in Gothic Revival style. The ruins beside the entrance to the college are those of the thirteenth-century **Maynooth Castle**, one of the two main strongholds of the Anglo-Norman Fitzgerald family who ruled Kildare and, effectively, most of Ireland from the thirteenth century until the coming of the Tudor monarchs (their other castle is at Kilkea, in the south; see p.146). Maynooth's formal town planning is made sense of by Carton House, a Georgian gem by Richard Castle which lies at the other end of the main street.

Castletown House

Few places give a better impression of the immense scale on which the Anglo-Irish imagination was able to work than **Castletown House** (Easter–Sept Mon–Fri 10am–6pm, Sat & Sun 1–6pm; Oct Mon–Fri 10am–5pm, Sun 1–5pm; Nov Sun 1–5pm; £3/€3.82; Heritage Card) designed in 1722 for the Speaker of the Irish House of Commons, **William Conolly**, by the Italian Alessandro Galilei. You enter the grounds through the village of Celbridge, around four miles southeast of Maynooth, planned to lend importance to the house itself. Exhibiting the strictest Classicism the house faces out over the Liffey, giving little away except for a rigidly repeated succession of windows. It's the only thing about it that is restrained, though, for Castletown, from the very beginning, was built for show.

William Conolly, who commissioned it, was a publican's son from Donegal who – like many others – owed his success to the changed conditions after the Battle of the Boyne, making his fortune by dealing in forfeited estates. Member for Donegal in the Irish parliament since 1692, he was a staunch supporter of the Hanoverian cause and was unanimously elected Speaker of the Irish House of Commons in 1715. In 1717 the ambassador at Florence noted Conolly's intention to bring to Ireland "the best architect in Europe", a move of some significance to national self-esteem. A letter to the famous metaphysician, Bishop Berkeley, states "I am glad for the honour of my country that Mr Conolly has undertaken so magnificent a pile of building. Since this house will be the finest Ireland ever saw, and by your description fit for a Prince, I would have it as it were the epitome of the Kingdom, and all the natural rarities she affords should have a place there." Although plans for the house were magnificent, work proceeded in a haphazard way. The cellar vaults, begun before the design of the house was finalized, still bear little relation to what's above ground, and the house interior remained unfinished – lacking, for instance, a main staircase – until the end of the long life of William's wife, who preferred building follies.

The fruits of old Mrs Conolly's imagination are most obvious in the **grounds**, where what appears to be a 140foot monument to chimney-sweeping closes the vista to the north, while the **Wonderful Barn** (a bizarre ornamental folly) lies to the east. Both projects were set up to provide relief work for estate workers hard hit by the famine-ridden winter of 1739. Mrs Conolly's sister, for one, disapproved "My sister is building an obleix to answer a vistow from the bake of Castletown house… It will cost her three or four hundred pounds at least, but I believe more. I really wonder how she can dow so much and live as she duse", she wrote of the folly. Incidentally, it seems that the ground on which the obelisk stands did not belong to Castletown, not that this bothered Mrs Conolly. The Wonderful Barn can be visited most weekends, but it's worth phoning ahead to check that someone is there (☎01/624 5448).

Mrs Connolly had no children and the house was inherited in 1752 by her grand-nephew who married Lady Louisa Lennox in 1759 when she was only 15. The **interior** decoration of the house was the inspiration of Lady Louisa Lennox. The newlyweds might have lived in London (Louisa's brother-in-law described her as wanting "to buy every house she sees"), but the fact that Louisa's elder sister, Lady Emily Kildare, had settled at Carton, close by at Maynooth, decided matters. (The life of the Lennox sisters is vividly chronicled, through their letters and diaries, in Stella Tillyard's novel

Aristocrats). Although little of the furniture at Castletown is original to the house, you can see some of the results of Louisa's efforts. It was she who, with her sister Lady Sarah Bunbury, created the print room on the ground floor, commissioned the Lanfranchini brothers to produce the hall's extraordinary plasterwork and ordered the long gallery at the back of the house, which she considered "the most comfortable room you ever saw, and quite warm; supper at one end, the company at the other, and I am writing in one of the piers at a distance from them all". Apparently, she ordered the magnificent Murano glass chandeliers on a journey to Venice, but when they arrived they were found to clash with the room's blue, Pompeiian-style decor: it was too late to redecorate, so both decor and chandeliers are still there.

Straffan Steam Museum and Butterfly Farm

About four miles southwest of Castletown, housed in a neat Victorian church that's been brought stone by stone from Dublin, the **Straffan Steam Museum** (Easter–May & Sept, Sun 2.30–5.30pm; June–Aug Tues–Sun 2–6pm; *www.steam-museum.ie*; £3/€3.81) offers a benign view of the driving force behind the Industrial Revolution. There are miniature models of steam trains and four – amazingly quiet – working steam engines, plus a series of wall panels offering a rather rose-tinted account of how steam advanced the way forward to our modern world. They also reflect Ireland's uneven industrialization – in 1838 the North had more steam horsepower than the rest of Ireland put together.

A big hit with children is nearby **Straffan Butterfly Farm** (May–early Aug daily noon–6pm; £3.25/€4.11): huge exotic butterflies fly freely, while giant insects, reptiles and tarantulas remain safely behind glass.

Larchill Arcadian Gardens

Larchill Arcadian Gardens (May–Sept daily noon–6pm; £3.50/€4.44) at **KILCOCK**, four miles west of Maynooth off the N4, are an extremely rare example of a ferme *ornée* (literally an "ornamental farm"), which were popular amongst rich landowners during the second half of the eighteenth century after a fashion set by Marie Antoinette at Versailles. It's an absolute must for anyone interested in the development of landscape gardening during this period. A circular walk links recently discovered Classical and Gothic follies, ten in all, most notably the island folly "Gibraltar" and the "Foxes' Earth". The latter was built on the instruction of a Mr Watson, a dedicated fox-hunter, who was convinced he would be reincarnated as a fox as retribution and wanted to be sure of a bolt-hole from the hounds in the next life. It appears today as a knobbly grass-covered mound with Gothic tunnels for escape, topped by a cluster of rubble-rough columns. Rare breeds of farm animals are kept in the new *ferme ornée* in fascinating buildings with turrets and ramparts, and interesting material on the conservation project is to be found in the pleasant tearoom.

Kildare town and the Curragh

The main Dublin–Limerick road, the N7, is a relatively swift – rush hour aside – but rather dull drive from Dublin to **Kildare town** and the **Curragh**; additionally, there's a new stretch of motorway, the M7, which runs from before Naas for about ten miles, rejoining the N7 near Kildare town. Either way, it's best to avoid rush hour: traffic along the N7 can be particularly bad heading out of Dublin on a Friday afternoon and evening, and also into Dublin on Sunday and bank holiday Monday evenings. The chief attraction at **NAAS** (pronounced Nace) is **Punchestown race course**, whose main meeting is the three-day steeplechasing event in late April, when the race course itself is greatly celebrated for its flowering gorse; a close second is **Mondello Park** motor-racing circuit (☎045/860200), which holds races most weekends. If you're not content with simply spectating, for around £129/€163.80, you can experience the thrill of driving a racing saloon around the track. The town has little in the way of accommodation, but there's a welcoming **B&B** at *Setanta Farmhouse*, four miles away at **Castlekeely** (☎045/876481; ③).

Newbridge, a nineteenth-century town which grew up around the British barracks here, is similarly unmemorable. But after Newbridge the road heads over the grassy, unfenced stretches of the Curragh, and you're into racing country proper.

Kildare town

KILDARE town is a delight: a solid, respectable place centred on a sloping triangular square, dominated by the massive, squat Church of Ireland **Cathedral of St Brigid**, who founded a religious house here in 490. The present structure dates originally from the thirteenth century, though the north transept and choir were burned to the ground in the Confederate War of 1641, and the Victorian reconstruction of 1875 is pseudo-medieval. Its round tower, probably twelfth century, has a particularly elaborate doorway twelve feet up; nineteenth-century battlements conceal the original conical roof – which you find yourself standing on once you've climbed to the top. The views from here are fine – rolling farmland to the south, the Bog of Allen to the north and the Curragh race course to the east.

The **tourist office** (May Mon–Fri 10am–1pm & 2–5.30pm; June–Sept Mon–Sat 10am–1pm & 2–5.30pm; ☎045/522696) is sited in the nineteenth-century Market House right in the middle of the main square. **Accommodation** is limited to a hotel, the *Curragh Lodge*, Dublin Street (☎045/522144, fax 045/521247; ⑦), and a handful of **B&Bs** – good central options include the comfortable *Singleton's* at 1 Dara Park, Station Road (☎045/521964; ③), and *Fremont*, Tully Road (☎045/521604; ③). For **eating**: *Jimmy Bean's* café on the square serves decent lunches and open sandwiches; *Georgio's*, a few doors down, serves moderately priced pizza and pasta, and the *Silken Thomas* does good bar food and has a restaurant alongside. The *Silken Thomas* takes its name from a member of the ruling Fitzgerald family, whom the growing powers of the Tudor monarchy provoked into rebellion in 1536, the uprising was unsuccessful, and a bloody massacre followed at Maynooth, later known, ironically, as "the pardon of Maynooth". In the square beside the cathedral, you'll find *Nolan's*, an old **bar** with cosy snugs; it hosts traditional music three or four nights a week.

The Curragh and the National Stud

The Curragh, just south of Kildare, is the centre of the Irish racing world, for the race course itself and dozens of stud farms. First thing in the morning you can see strings of slim racehorses exercising on the six thousand acres of grassland. Breeding and training them is one of Ireland's major money-spinners, and much of it is centred on the Curragh. For an idea of the scale of the operation, Goff's Kildare Paddocks at Kill, which sells over half of all Irish-bred horses, processes an annual turnover of around £50 million/€63 million.

Security considerations mean that none of the working stud farms are open to the public. The best place to see the perfectionism that attends the breeding and training of these valuable horses is the **National Stud**, just outside Kildare, signposted from the centre of town (mid-Feb–mid-Nov daily 9.30am–6pm, last admission 5pm; guided tours on the hour from 11am in high season, and according to demand at other times; ☎045/521617, *www.irish-national-stud.ie*; £6/€7.62). You can easily walk out to it from the town, though the entrance is not the obvious one (through the main gates that you pass on the road from Dublin) instead, follow the signs from the centre for the stud.

A DAY AT THE RACES

You don't have to know anything about horses to enjoy a day at the races. Irish race-going is quite unlike its English counterpart: there's none of the snobbery attached to who's who or who's allowed in the enclosure, and it's not as expensive – around £8–12/€10.16-15.24. It's also different in that there's just as much excitement attached to steeplechasing as flat racing – steeplechasing, in fact, despite its smaller prize money, is often regarded as the better sport.

The major Irish classic meets are all held at the Curragh: the Entenmann'f Irish 1000 Guineas in May; Goffs £100,000 Challenge in June; the Budweiser Irish Derby and the Kildangan Irish Oaks in July; and the Irish St Leger in September. Punchestown is also famous for a three-day jump-race meeting in late April. Details of race meetings can be found in all the daily papers or in the specialist press: *Irish Field* (published Saturday morning) and the *Racing Post* (daily). Bord Fáilte publishes an annual information sheet with the dates of the current year's meetings; you should also be able to get schedules from local tourist offices.

You can take special bus and train services to get to the Curragh (March–Oct; ☎045/441205, *www.curragh.ie*), which are scheduled to fit in with all major meetings; ring Irish Rail for details (☎01/836 6222).

Access to the adjacent St Fiachra's Garden and the Japanese Garden (see below) is included in the price of the ticket.

The National Stud itself consists of neat white buildings set in green lawns as close-cropped and well groomed as a Derby-winner's coat: a spick-and-span monument to the greater glory and perfectability of horses. Established in 1900 by Colonel William Hall Walker, who believed that horoscopes affected horses' form, the stud enjoyed a marvellous record of success, and in 1915 was bequeathed to the British Crown, which rewarded Walker by creating him Lord Wavertree. When transferred to the Irish State in 1943, it became the National Stud.

Colonel Hall Walker's belief in the stars is reflected in the **stallion boxes**, built in the 1960s according to his astrological principles, with lantern roofs allowing moon and stars to exert their influence on the occupants. There's a brass plaque on each door giving the stallion's name and details of his racing career. The National Stud's **museum** is an enjoyably chaotic account of the history of horses and horse racing which contains, among other bizarre exhibits, the skeleton of the 1960s champion racehorse, Arkle. The high point of the visit though has to be the **horses** themselves: you can admire top stallions at close quarters, stroll between perfect paddocks of grazing thoroughbreds, and, between February and June, watch mares with their foals.

Within the grounds of the National Stud are two highly distinctive gardens: the Japanese Garden and St Fiachra's Garden (both with the same opening hours as the National Stud). The rather bizarre **Japanese Garden** was laid out on a drained bog, between 1906 and 1910, by Colonel Hall Walker and two Japanese gardeners. Part of the Edwardian craze for all things Japanese, they're planned to represent the "life of man" – man, emphatically, it has to be said, rather than woman. In a weird kind of enumerated metaphysical joyride, you're led from birth to death via the Tunnel of Ignorance (no. 3) and the Parting of Ways (no. 6), where you're invited to choose between a life of philandering bachelorhood or marriage. Choosing marriage, you step across stepping stones to the Island of Joy and Wonder (no. 7) and meet your wife at the engagement bridge (no. 8; easily confused with the Red Bridge of Life, no. 17) and so on. Finally you pass through the Gateway to Eternity (no. 20), and it's time to go.

The nearby **St Fiachra's Garden** is similarly engaging. St Fiachra was a sixth-century Irish monk of noble birth who travelled throughout Ireland and Scotland before founding a hermitage at Breuil in France. Fiachra urged his followers to undertake manual labour, cultivate gardens and aid the poor; after his death he became the French patron saint of gardeners. St Fiachra's Garden seeks to present some sense of the natural environment which inspired the spirituality of the sixth- and seventh-century monastic movement in Ireland, through a series of motifs gleaned from that history. The resulting landscape of still pools and rushing water, monumental limestone and sculpted grassy banks makes for a suitably peaceful place. At the centre of the ensemble stands a re-creation of the stone monastic cells found on Skellig Michael, off the Kerry coast (see p.328); once inside you can make up your own mind about the hoarde of twinkling Waterford Crystal embedded in the floor, which is claimed to be "like the delicacy of the human soul, pure and undefiled". All in all, St Fiachra's Garden is a tranquil place to wile away half an hour or so and makes the perfect contemporary counterpoint to the old style New-Age philosophizing of the Japanese Garden nearby.

The Bog of Allen

The Bog of Allen, six miles to the north of Kildare around the village of Rathangan, marks the beginning of what was a great belt of bogland stretching westward across the country to Shannon and beyond. It's figured in Irish history and legend since prehistoric times, though these days only small pockets of it remain. **LULLYMORE**, five miles northeast of Rathangan, at the foot of the Hill of Allen, site of the legendary Finn MacCool's palace, offers a good opportunity to get to grips with the life of the bogs, past and present. The place – its name means "great dairy pasture" – is an island in the bog where St Patrick reputedly appointed Eve, an early convert, to run a training college for monks.

Peatland World (April–Oct Mon–Fri 9.30am–5pm, Sat & Sun 2–6pm; Nov–March Mon–Fri 9.30am–5pm; £3/€3.81), housed in the eighteenth-century stable block of Lullymore House, provides a comprehensive introduction to Irish bogs and includes

ALL ABOUT BOGS

Ten thousand years ago, after the last Ice Age, the melting glaciers and ice sheets left central Ireland covered by shallow lakes. As time went by the lake and lakeside vegetation grew and died and partly decomposed in a continuing cycle that changed these lakes to fens, and eventually into domed bogs. Ireland now has the finest range of peatlands in Europe.

Bogs have been cut away and used for fuel for centuries, and there are plenty of songs and stories that bear witness to the importance of the bog in folk history. Estimates of the amount of raised bog that has been lost over the centuries vary widely, from 300,000 to 600,000 hectares. Today there are only 300,000 hectares of raised bog remaining, making it an endangered habitat. It was during the 1930s in particular that depletion rates began to accelerate as the work of the newly founded Turf Development Board got under way. Whatever the exact statistics though, it is likely that the large commercial bogs will be exhausted within fifty years.

It is only recently that the Irish have awoken to the great natural importance of the boglands. Not only are they home to rare plants, from mosses to bilberries, but they provide a habitat for birds. The bog gases also act as preservatives, and the bogs of Ireland have yielded archeological evidence of botanical and human history up to nine thousand years old in the form of pollens and plant remains, gold and silver artefacts, dug-out canoes and human bodies.

To see a raised bog of international importance, go to **Mongan Bog** in County Offaly, situated on the banks of the Shannon. And if the bog bug really bites, head for the **Peatland World** in Lullymore. For more on bogs, see "Contexts" p.686, or visit the Irish Peatland Conservation Council's Web site at *www.ipcc.ie*.

exhibitions on conservation, energy production, and plant and animal life, together with a history of the area and the estate itself. Bear in mind, though, that the project is supported by both Bórd na Móna (the Irish Peat Board) and the Electricity Supply Board, whose attitudes to bogland conservation may not necessarily coincide with your own.

Further insights into the area's history are provided by the nearby **Lullymore Heritage and Discovery Park** (Easter–Oct Mon–Fri 9am–6pm, Sat & Sun noon–6pm; Nov–Easter Mon–Fri 9am–4.30pm; £3.50/€4.44), set in wooded parkland, with reconstructions of a Mesolithic campsite, a Neolithic farmstead, an exhibition on early Christian history, and displays covering social history from the eighteenth century onwards. The entrance fee also includes access to crazy golf and a children's playground.

Canal country

Monuments to eighteenth-century confidence in Irish trade, the **Royal and Grand canals** flow from Dublin through County Kildare and on into the Irish heartland. While Ireland had experienced a minor industrial revolution in the mid- to late-eighteenth century, when mines, mills, workshops and canals were created, the Act of Union precluded further development. By walking along the towpaths, or cruising on the Grand Canal, you can see how industrialization affected – and failed to affect – the eighteenth-century landscape.

The **Grand Canal** was a monumentally ambitious project, running from Dublin to Robertstown, where it forks. The southern branch joins the River Barrow at Athy, effectively extending the waterway as far south as Waterford, while the western branch runs up to Tullamore in County Offaly and on to join the great natural waterway of the Shannon at Shannon Harbour. As late as 1837 the Grand Canal was carrying over 100,000 passengers a year; it continued to be used for freight right up to 1960. These days narrow boats can be hired in Tullamore (contact Celtic Canal Cruisers ☎0506/21861); from where you can explore the Grand Canal west to meet the River Shannon, or east and then south to join the River Barrow.

The **Royal Canal** runs past Maynooth and Mullingar before joining the Shannon, many tortuous meanderings later, at Cloondara, north of Lough Rea, for access to the northwest. With the recent reopening of the Shannon–Erne Waterway (see p.466), these southern waterways are linked once more with the Fermanagh Lakes in the North, as they were in the nineteenth century.

Robertstown and Monasterevin

Two locations are particularly evocative of canal life. **ROBERTSTOWN**, due north of Kildare, where the ways divide – the canal arrived here in 1785 – is no more than a village, yet it boasts a canal stop complete with the *Grand Canal Hotel* (☎045/870005; no accommodation), which serves **bar food** and arranges leisurely **barge tours** (summer Sun 2–6pm). There are pleasant walks along the towpath from here: pick up *Towpath Trails* from a regional tourist office if you are interested in exploring these pleasantly undeveloped routes. If you want to navigate the waterways yourself, **cruiser rental** is available from Canalways in Rathangan, six miles northwest of Kildare (☎045/524646, *www.canalways.ie*).

MONASTEREVIN, west of Kildare along the N7, follows the set pattern of an Irish Pale town: a big house, in this case **Moore Abbey** (once the home of the Irish tenor John McCormack), a church and the town itself – a street of eighteenth-century houses, their gardens sloping down to the river. A couple of features merit a pause as you pass through: a fine sculpture commemorating the English Jesuit poet and master of sprung rhythm, Gerard Manley Hopkins – at the side of the road opposite the houses

– and an eighteenth-century aqueduct that takes the Grand Canal over the River Barrow.

South Kildare: ancient remains

At **Old Kilcullen**, seven miles south of Naas, three **high crosses** set in green, rolling farmland attest to ancient histories. It's the site of an early Celtic monastery, and nearby stands an evocative round tower damaged during the 1798 Rebellion. Further south along the N9, there are more monuments to Ireland's ancient heritage at Moone and Castledermot, and northwestwards on taking the R418 at Kilkea; but first it's well worth stopping off at the village of Ballitore about seven miles south of Old Kilcullen.

Ballitore

BALLITORE is an old Quaker village where the eighteenth-century Anglo-Irish political philosopher **Edmund Burke** (1729–97) was educated in the school run by Quaker Abraham Shackleton – a good example of the religious toleration that it seems the British government was prepared to grant anyone but Catholics. Born in Dublin of a Catholic mother and Protestant father, Burke went on to attend Trinity College, and, moving to London in 1750, he kept company with some of the leading figures of the time, among them Oliver Goldsmith (also a Trinity graduate), Samuel Johnson and Joshua Reynolds. His most important works are *A Philosophical Enquiry into the Origin of Ideas of the Sublime and the Beautiful*, an essay in aesthetic theory that is still studied by art historians, and *Reflections on the Revolution in France*, published the year after the event in 1790, in which he argued strongly against Jacobinism and for counter-revolutionary conservatism.

The **Ballitore Quaker museum** (June–Sept Wed–Sat noon–5pm, Sun 2–6pm; Oct–May Tues–Sat noon–5pm; free) above the village library, which is housed in the old Friends Meeting House, gives a vivid picture of what Quaker life was like here: each member of the industrious community plied a trade, and their sober, business-like approach made Ballitore a model village by comparison with the general squalor and poverty of surrounding places. But the dominant impression given by the copperplate handwritten letters on show is the sheer boredom of life in a place where any stranger was cause for excitement. Up towards the main road is the walled **Quaker graveyard**, whose plain, dignified tombstones seem suitable monuments to the qualities of the dead. *Griesmount* (☎0507/23158; ④), a fine Georgian house a little way from the village centre, offers a place to **stay** amidst Ballitore's peaceful simplicity.

Signposted from the centre of the village is **Crookstown Mill** (Easter–Sept daily 10am–6pm; Oct–Easter by appointment 11am–4pm; ☎0507/23222; £2.50/€3.17). Built in the 1840s and still functioning, it contributed to an independence from the potato that, along with the industries introduced by the Quakers, meant that there was strikingly little emigration or starvation here during the Famine.

A mile or so further south is the **Irish Pewtermill** (☎0507/24164); although you can see pewter being worked, the place is primarily a retail experience – fine if you're into the Claddagh rings and ancestral crest type of export Irishness.

From Moone to Kilkea

Back on the N9, the small village of **MOONE**, three miles south from Ballitore, once formed a link in the chain of monasteries founded by St Columba, and the garden of Moone Abbey contains the ruins of a fourteenth-century Franciscan friary and a ninth-century **cross**. The cross is particularly interesting; rich in naive and strangely orderly carving. The east side depicts Daniel in the lion's den, the sacrifice of Isaac, Adam and Eve, and the Crucifixion; on the west are the twelve apostles, the Crucifixion and St John; and on the north, other carvings – including a number of figures and animals. The *Moone High Cross Inn* (☎0507/24112; ④) is a friendly, rambling old pub here, serving a good range of bar food, plus a more ambitious menu in the restaurant.

Five miles further south at **CASTLEDERMOT** there's more to see: two tenth-century granite high crosses, plus a bizarre twelfth-century Romanesque doorway standing by itself in front of an ugly modern church and a truncated round tower. Castledermot also has a thirteenth-century Augustinian abbey, an example of how the European monastic orders muscled in on the indigenous Irish church. Its substantial remains give a completely different feel to what might otherwise be merely a roadside stop.

Kilkea Castle, the Fitzgeralds' second Kildare stronghold (after Maynooth), stands a couple of miles up the Athy road (R418) from Castledermot. It's impressive looking: originally built in 1180, it was modified in the seventeenth century, and most of it is a mid-nineteenth-century restoration. Massively refurbished again in the 1980s, it's now a luxury **hotel** (☎0503/45156, fax 0503/45187, *kilkea@iol.ie*; ⑨) boasting a leisure centre and sauna. There's a more reasonably priced **B&B** option at *Kilkea Lodge Farm* (☎0503/45112; ⑤), a stone-built farmhouse with a riding centre attached, and it does dinner for around £20/€25.70.

Athy

On the border with County Laois, five miles north of Kilkea, close to the point where the Grand Canal meets the River Barrow, sits **ATHY** (rhymes with sty, emphasis on the last syllable), one of those places where a bucketful of imagination is required to envisage it as it once was: prosperity has turned a formerly handsome Georgian town with a fine main square into something much more ramshackle. Georgian fanlights sit oddly with a bizarre modern church: the latter is apparently supposed to make reference to a dolmen, although the Sydney Opera House seems a stronger influence. Athy's designation as a heritage town, however, is bringing its historical resonances to life. By the riverside stands the square tower of the fifteenth-century **White's Castle**, built by Sir John Talbot, Viceroy of Ireland, to protect the ford across the River Barrow and the inhabitants of the Pale from the dispossessed Irish beyond. The early eighteenth-century town hall houses a **heritage centre** (March–Oct Mon–Sat 10am–6pm, Sun 2–6pm; Nov–Feb Mon–Sat 11am–5pm; £2/€2.54), with a comprehensive exhibition covering the Famine, the 1798 Rebellion, the part played by Athy men in World War I, and the life of Antarctic explorer Sir Ernest Shackleton, who came from nearby Kilkea. The town hall is also where you'll find the **tourist office** (same times). Aside from some leisurely **strolls** along the Grand Canal and visiting the heritage centre, the town's unlikely to detain you for too long – except to **eat** or **stay** at *Tonlegee House* (☎0507/31473, *tonlegeehouse@eircom.net*; ⑥; restaurant closed Sun & Mon), signposted off the Kilkenny road, a solidly built mansion that surveys the countryside just beyond Athy's suburban sprawl and has a restaurant noted for its imaginative menu.

travel details

Trains

Arklow to: Dublin Connolly (3–5 daily; 1hr 20min).

Bray to: Dublin Connolly (approximately every 10–20min; 25min).

Kildare to: Dublin Heuston (20–30 daily; 30min).

Maynooth to: Dublin Connolly (5–15 daily; 30min).

Wicklow to: Arklow (3–4 daily, 30min); Dublin Connolly (3–5 daily; 50min); Enniscorthy (3 daily, 1hr 20min); Rosslare Europort (3 daily, 2hr 20min)

Buses

Bus Éireann

Arklow to: Dublin (12–13 daily; 2hr 30min).

Kildare to: Cashel (3 daily; 1hr 45min); Dublin (26–28 daily; 1hr 30min).

Wicklow to: Avoca (1–2 daily, 45min); Dublin (5–8 daily; 1hr 30min); Wexford (2 daily; 2hr 15min).

St Kevin's bus service

Glendalough to: Dublin (2 daily; 1hr 30min).

CHAPTER THREE

LAOIS AND OFFALY

If you've come to Ireland for the scenery, the wild remote places, or the romance of the far west, then the central counties of Laois and Offaly probably don't hold a great deal to entice you. But this quiet and unremarkable part of the country between Dublin and the Shannon is an excellent place to get to know another Ireland, one not yet much hyped by the tourist authorities. Its gentle, verdant farming land bears the marks of a complex pattern of settlement: the Celtic Church, Viking invaders, the arrival of the Anglo-Normans and, very strongly in these twin counties, the planted settlements with which the British sought to keep their base in the Pale secure. It's a subtle, detailed, rural landscape which, as a result of the Act of Union in 1801 and the subsequent destruction of Ireland's foreign trade, remained untouched by the Industrial Revolution and thus virtually unchanged over the past two hundred years.

Getting around Laios and Offaly is straightforward – the main N7 trunk road and the main railway line to Limerick slice straight through Laois, while the industrial centre of Tullamore makes an obvious transport centre, by both road and rail, for Offaly. There's an increasing number of **accommodation** possibilities – some comfortable, mid-price hotels and even the odd hostel – but, with the exception of the Celtic monastery at Clonmacnois, the area remains lightly touristed, and it's wise to plan overnight stops in advance.

COUNTY LAOIS

Laois, or Leix in the more old-fashioned orthography (it's pronounced *Leash*), is in many ways Ireland's least-known county. Most people know it only for the maximum security jail at Portlaoise, or as an ill-defined area you go through on the way to Limerick. While most Irish counties have a strong identity, Laois seems oddly accidental. To the east it's more or less bordered by the **River Barrow**; to the north, it forms a large part of the **Slieve Bloom** mountain range (though some of that is in Co. Offaly); but to the west and south, with no distinct geographical features to mark its borders, Laois quietly gives way to its more prominent neighbours Tipperary and Kilkenny. Laois smarts from an image problem that's summed up by the adage that its landscape is like the local accent – flat and boring. That unjust reputation seems at last to be fad-

ACCOMMODATION PRICE CODES

Throughout this book, prices of hotels, guesthouses and B&Bs have been graded with the codes below, according to what you can expect to pay for a double room in high season. For more details on accommodation, see p.34.

① Under £26/€33.01	④ £40–55/€50.79–69.84	⑦ £90–110/€114.28–139.67
② £26–33/€33.01–41.90	⑤ £55–70/€69.84–88.88	⑧ £110–130/€139.67–165.07
③ £33–40/€41.90–50.79	⑥ £70–90/€88.88–114.28	⑨ Over £130/€165.07

ing, as its quiet charms and proximity to Dublin attract a variety of people escaping the pressures of life in the capital.

Some history

Until the mid-sixteenth century, Laois remained under its traditional chiefs, the O'Mores, FitzPatricks, O'Dempseys and O'Dunnes, and posed an increasing threat to the British in the Pale. In 1556, a new county was carved out of these tribal lands, settled – or "planted", in the terminology of the time – and named Queen's County (to Offaly's King's County). A new town, **Maryborough**, named after Mary Tudor, was established at what is now Portlaoise. None of this passified the O'Mores, but eventually transplantation succeeded where mere plantation had failed. The troublesome clans of Laois were exiled to County Kerry and Laois was left free for the colonizers. Because Laois came under British control so early, there are none of the huge estates that were later dished out by Cromwell and Charles II to loyal followers in the far west. Rather, there are smaller landholdings and planned towns, interspersed with some settlements of dissenting religious groups – such as the Quakers and French Huguenots. These groups, unlike the Catholic population, which was being persecuted at the time, were able to find the freedom of worship they desired here. All this makes for an intimate – if unspectacular – landscape, epitomizing a history of colonialism as real as anywhere else in the former British Empire.

Portlaoise and around

PORTLAOISE is best known for its top-security **jail** and mental hospital – they're both on the same street, known to locals as Nuts 'n' Bolts Road. The prison was founded in 1547, when the O'Mores held the fortress of Dunamase to the south, as a fortification under the name of Fort Protector. The town itself is pretty unremarkable, though it does have a useful **tourist office** James Fintan Lawlor Ave (May–Sept Mon–Sat 10am–6pm; open sporadically at other times; ☎0502/21178) offering information on the whole county; reached by car by taking the bypass and stopping at the car park beside the new shopping mall, or, more easily, on foot by walking along Main Street and turning right down the small alley beside *Dowling's Café*. There's an adequate **hotel**, *O'Loughlin's*, on Main St (☎0502/21305, *oloughlins@eircom.net*; ④); though it's advisable to continue to Abbeyleix where the accommodation is generally of a higher standard. You'll have no trouble finding somewhere to **eat**, however: possibilities range from the hospitable home-cooking and open fires of the *Kitchen* café/restaurant (☎0502 62075) in Hynds Square (a small courtyard off Main St), to the excellent *Kingfisher Indian* restaurant, a little further down Main St (☎0502 62500), in a fine converted redbricked building that once acted as the town's bank. Drinking options are vast as the town boasts 22 pubs in all. You could also head a few miles out of town on the Dublin Road to the thatched *Treacy's*, supposedly the oldest family run pub in Ireland (founded in 1780), which now sits somewhat uncomfortably on an island between a motorway and a main road but still fulfils its role of serving travellers on the long haul from Dublin to the west.

The most impressive site in the local vicinity, not only physically but also historically, is the **Rock of Dunamase**, two or three miles east on the Stradbally Road (N80) – the easiest way to reach it is by car; follow the signs from the roundabout at the end of the cobbled Main Street. An extraordinary, knobbly mound encrusted with layer upon layer of fortifications, it's a great place for gazing out, beyond the flat surrounding countryside, to the Slieve Bloom hills to the north and the Wicklow Mountains in the east. There are suggestions that Dunamase was known to Ptolemy under the name of *Dunum*, and to the Celts as *Dun Masc*, it was valuable enough to be plundered by the Vikings in 845. Today, the hill is crowned by a ruined castle of the twelfth-century king of Leinster, Dermot MacMurrough. He invited Strongbow to Ireland to marry his daughter, Aoife, and included Dunamase in her dowry. The castle was taken back into Gaelic control by the bellicose O'More family at the end of the fourteenth century, though they surrendered their lands to the Cromwellian forces under Charles Cook in 1641. In 1645 Dunamase again fell into Catholic hands for a brief period before its destruction by Cromwell's army in 1650. The earthworks five hundred yards to the east of the fortress are still known as Cromwell's lines.

STRADBALLY (literally "street-town"), a few miles southwest of Dunamase, is notable chiefly for the **narrow-gauge railway** at Stradbally Hall, where a nineteenth-century steam locomotive, formerly used in the Guinness brewery in Dublin, runs six times a year. Of most interest in the town is the **Steam Museum** (Mon–Fri 11am–1pm & 2–4pm; £1.50/€1.90) recently renovated and restored by the Irish Steam Preservation Society. Enthusiasts will be in steam heaven among the plethora of related exhibits, though many of the mechanical artefacts will be of interest to non-steam buffs too. In August, Stradbally is a must for the steam engine rally that attracts all manner of steam-operated machinery and vintage cars from throughout the country (call the tourist office in Portlaoise for further details ☎0502/21178). On weekends a lively traditional music session can be found in *Dunne's* bar, while you can **stay** in solid comfort at *Tullamoy House*, a stone-built nineteenth-century farmhouse set in its own parkland, three miles east out of town on the Athey road (closed Nov–April; ☎0507/27111, *tullamoy@indigo.ie*; ③).

Once a busy halt on the Grand Canal, **VICARSTOWN**, four miles north of Stradbally on the R427 (about ten miles from Portlaoise) is now just a few houses and some crumbling stone warehouses clustered round a humpback bridge, although it's showing new signs of life with rented barges and boats mooring along its quays as a result of the increased use of the canal. It's chiefly remarkable for the spirited **traditional music** sessions on Monday nights in *Turley's* bar (aka *The Anchor Inn*) – be there by nine and sit tight. Accommodation is available on the other side of the water at *Crean's*, officially known as *The Vicarstown Inn* (☎0502/25189; ③). The green beside *Turley's* is a good spot for camping and this stretch of the canal is ideal for a pleasant stroll.

The South: Abbeyleix and around

The south of County Laois consists of lush farmland, dotted with estate towns and villages. The largest of these and well worth a visit is **ABBEYLEIX**, about ten miles from Portlaoise on the N8, named after a Cistercian abbey founded here by a member of the O'More family in 1183. In one of those periodic bursts of enthusiasm that seem to be a mark of the Ascendancy, Abbeyleix was entirely remodelled by Viscount de Vesci in the eighteenth century and relocated on the coach road away from the old village to the southwest. The place has been designated a heritage town, and has an excellent **heritage centre** (☎0502/31653, *www.laois.local.ie/abbeyleix*), housed in the old National School Building just off Main Street, which has exhibits on the town's history and examples of the craft of carpet weaving that once was an important part of the local economy. Unfortunately, the attractive pedimented eighteenth-century Abbeyleix House (designed by James Wyatt) isn't open to the public, and the gardens are open just two Sundays a year. In the village, the famous **Morrissey's Bar**, an enormous grocer's shop and pub combined, probably hasn't changed in fifty years, with pew seats and a brazier and old advertisements for beer and tobacco that seem to have been forgotten by time. It's a great place to sit and soak up the atmosphere. If you prefer to stimulate rather than relax your senses then head across the road from *Morrissey's* to the Dove House Convent where you'll find the **Sensory Gardens**. Inside the convent's ivy-clad walls, the gardens not only provide a sanctuary from the busy street, but promote awareness of the senses by devising walks around beds of flowers that are visually striking, and which exude an arresting and at times intoxicating combination of smells.

Accommodation is plentiful in the area: the friendliest **B&B** is offered at Ms Peverell's *Olde Manse* (☎0502/31423; ③), while next door is the Dowling's creeper-covered B&B *Preston House* (☎0502/314332; ④), which boasts good-quality rooms and excellent home-cooking in the adjoining restaurant. Just out of town on the main Cork road is the comfortable, though characterless, modern *Manor Hotel* (☎0502/30111, *info@abbeyleixmanorhotel.com*; ⑤); and the fine *Hibernian Hotel* (☎0502/31252; ④) is back in town on Lower Main Street. If you have a few hours to spare, it's worth considering a short excursion to the tiny village of **Timahoe**, seven miles northeast of Abbeyleix, on the R428. The village is the site of a twelfth-century monastery, of which all that now remains is a round tower, its entrance framed with unusual carvings of human faces.

About three miles southeast of Abbeyleix is **BALLINAKILL**, itself a pretty Georgian village on a sloping main street, and just north of the town, the gardens of **Heywood House** (mid-June to mid-Sept Mon & Fri–Sun 1–6pm) are worth a look for their re-creation of a distant Italianate idyll. The house was burned down early last century, but the gardens, drawn up by the English garden designer Gertrude Jeckyll and architecture – complete with gazebos and sunken terraces – by Sir Edwin Lutyens, architect to the Empire, have been fully restored.

DURROW, back on the N8, about six miles south of Abbeyleix, is yet another planned estate town, grouped around a green adjoining **Castle Durrow**, which is – its medievalized gateway notwithstanding – the first great Palladian house to be built in this area (1716). It's now a convent, but you can walk up the drive and see it from the outside. The town was owned by the Duke of Ormond, who had it adopted by County Kilkenny; it took an act of parliament to get it returned to what was then Queen's County in 1834. The *Castle Arms* (☎0502/36117; ④), facing the green, is one of the few places to **stay**, while sturdy **home cooking** can be found at the *Copper Kettle*, two doors up.

The extreme **southwest** corner of County Laois consists of quiet farming land punctuated by small villages such as Cullahill, Rathdowney and Erill, full of neat colourwashed houses. **Cullahill**, about four miles southwest of Durrow, and its castle, up the road opposite the *Sportsman Inn*, are of little interest in themselves, but if you walk through the farmyard next to the castle and look at the stone protruding high up on the south wall, you'll see a fine example of a Sheila-na-Gig (an ancient fertility symbol, see also p.208). The unassuming village of **BALLACOLLA**, about two miles northwest of Durrow, has few sights to speak of but offers some cosy, and reasonably priced, accommodation options. Excellent **hostel** accommodation (IHH; ☎0502/34032) is available in a converted grain loft on a working farm just outside the village itself; take the right at the bottom of the village (R434) to the family-friendly farm where owner Marty Farren takes great care of his guests. Nearby is Sean Hyland's *Foxrock Inn* (☎0502 38637, *www.foxrockinn.com;* ③) where you will find a hearty welcome in the convivial pub and fine B&B accommodation; to get here follow the R434 to Ballacolla, taking a right in the middle of the village and from there follow the *Foxrock* signposts to the small hamlet of Clough. About eight miles west of Durrow (take the R434 then the R433), **Rathdowney** is altogether a more metropolitan sort of place, with a raffish pride that gives it a continental flavour. The *Central* bar on the main square does B&B (☎0505/46567; ③), plus breakfast, tea and dinner.

Just north of Rathdowney, **DONAGHMORE**'s **Workhouse and Agricultural Museum** (daily 2–5pm; £2/€2.54) gives some idea of the less picturesque aspects of the area's past. The austere building, formerly the parish workhouse (at some distance from the village itself), is evocative of the lives of the poor – its very size indicates the scale of the problem of rural poverty, even if the exhibits themselves, a selection of mainly agricultural machinery, seem a bit random. Families were frequently broken up on admission and no one was allowed to leave the premises; on average two of the eight hundred inmates died every week, to be buried in the mass grave behind the workhouse. The buildings functioned as a workhouse between 1853 and 1886, and the museum exhibits take up the story again with a series of documents relating to the Donaghmore Co-operative, which was founded in 1927. Unfortunately, many of them – one of the cases has an order for sandwiches at a hotel in Birr – are of little more than local interest. The museum practises a strenuous self-censorship over the intervening period, during which the buildings were used as a British army barracks, at one stage housing the notorious Black and Tans – something the authorities deem as wiser not to address.

Donaghmore itself – three pubs, a Protestant church and a mill – is a clear statement of the inability of these little settlements to ride out the economic turbulence of the nineteenth century. A glimpse of the other end of the social spectrum can be gleaned from a visit to **Balaghmore Castle** (appointment only, call ahead on ☎0505 21453; £3/€3.81) on the Laois/Tipperary border (take the R433 north to where it meets the main N7 road and the castle is on the right, two miles after the town of Borris-in-Ossory. Formerly guarding the outer reaches of the Fitzpatrick lands the castle has been single-handedly renovated by its owner, Ms Pym, and is now open to the public to view and rent; it's best to call the owner before visiting as opening times can vary. As with many of the castles in the area, a Sheila-na-Gig can be found three quarters of the way up its southern wall.

Slieve Bloom and North Laois

North Laois is dominated by the **Slieve Bloom Mountains** – Bloom is an anglicized version of Bladhma the name of a Celtic warrior who once sought refuge in the area. The mountains bring some welcome variation to this flat county, although the highest point, the Arderin Mountain, in the southern half of the range, only reaches to 1735ft, they're ruggedly desolate enough to give a taste of real wilderness, even if you follow the **Slieve Bloom Way**. The Way, a little over 31 miles in length, takes you on a complete circuit of the mountains – across moorland, woods and bog, along part of one of the old high roads to Tara and through the bed of a pre-Ice Age river valley. Along the way dense conifer plantations attempt to survive, with a little help from the taxpayer, way above the natural tree line. If your time is limited and you have a car, the best place to start is probably at the northern end of the range at **Glen Barrow's** car park (three miles west of Rosenallis). Skirting the mountains, the road from Mountmellick (R422), as it passes through Clonaslee and Cadamstown (strictly speaking in Co. Offaly), offers easy access to some pleasant walking, particularly at Cadamstown. Here a waterfall's icy waters are used for bathing by hardy locals, with the tweely named *My Little Tea and Craft Shop* (actually the front room of a cottage) open for a revitalizing feed afterwards. If you don't have a car, you can catch the Dublin–Portumna **bus** at Birr or Portarlington and start walking at Kinnitty, a couple of miles south of Cadamstown, a delightful upland village, which has an excellent pub, *The Slieve Bloom*, with a pretty beer garden (at the time of writing a new restaurant was also being completed). A part of the Slieve Bloom Way skirts Arderin Mountain, the summit of which offers a breathtaking panorama of the midland counties; the old custom of trekking to the summit in summer has recently been revived so, if you're here on the last Sunday of July, ask around for details. John Feehan's *The Landscape of Slieve Bloom* is a good read and is highly relevant to the area, while Bord Fáilte's *Holiday Guide to County Laois* details many excellent walks in the mountains; both are available in tourist offices throughout the country.

Excellent **accommodation** options in this area include: the fine, stone *Victorian Ard More House*, as you enter the village (☎0509/37009; ③), whose old-fashioned comforts and fine home-cooking are designed to energize even the weariest hill walker. Comfort and style can be had in **Kinnitty Castle**, on the road between Kinnitty and Cadamstown (☎0509/37318, *kinnittycastle@tinet.ie*; ⑨), a unique Gothic Revival castle standing in 650 acres of parkland in the Slieve Bloom foothills. There is also an unregistered hostel (☎0509/37034), on the opposite side of the road to the castle, which is as basic as the castle is luxurious and used mostly on specialist walking excursions. If none of the above suit, you may want to base yourself in Birr (see p.160) or you could head for the Slieve Bloom's southeastern foothills. Here, in **COOLRAIN**, accommodation can be found at *Pine House Farm*, Annaghmore (☎0509/37029; ③), an ideal base for walking, while the *Village Inn* is good for traditional music. Alternatively, for a real treat, check in at **Roundwood House** (☎0502/32120, *roundwood@eircom.net*; ⑥), just outside Mountrath, a mid-eighteenth-century Palladian mansion now run as a guesthouse. Built by a Quaker who had made his fortune in America, it's a doll's house of a building decorated in vibrantly authentic Georgian colours, with a double-height hall boasting a Chippendale Chinese-style staircase. It's a relaxed, unceremonious sort of place that seems devoted to the virtues of good food, conversation and alcohol: you are likely to find yourself sitting by the turf fire after an excellent dinner, debating tirelessly with other guests about anything and everything.

Mountmellick, Portarlington and around

Mountmellick and Portarlington are typical of the few little settlements that grew up independently of the great houses, and both were communities of outsiders. **MOUNTMELLICK**, about six miles north of Portlaoise on the N80, was founded in the seventeenth century by Quakers and still has a spacious eighteenth-century feel to it. You need imagination to see the houses as the elegant buildings they must once have been, but Mountmellick in its heyday was undoubtedly both cultured and prosperous – it had 27 industries, including brewing, distilling, soap- and glue-making and iron foundries. It was also famous for **Mountmellick work**, white-on-white embroidery that used the forms of flowers and plants to create elegant designs. Displays on this, and on the town's Quaker heritage, can be found in the renovated Codd's Mill which now acts as the town's **heritage centre** (daily 9am–5pm; ☎0502/24525); take the first right after Market Square to the Portlaoise Road, and the centre along with the fine *Old Mill* restaurant are on the right.

PORTARLINGTON, six miles northeast of Mountmellick along the R423, was founded in 1667 by Sir Henry Bennett, Lord Arlington, and settled by a group of Huguenot refugees in the late seventeenth century. They built elegant Georgian houses with spacious orchards and gardens, which once grew exotic fruit such as peaches and apricots; particularly fine mansions are to be seen in Patrick Street. Testimony to the town's French heritage can be seen in some of the French inscriptions on the tombstones of St Michael's Church, still known as the French Church, where names such as Champ and Le Blanc survive. The town's elegant Huguenot menfolk used to sit outside the Tholsel, or Market House, in Market Square, sipping the exotic new beverage, tea, from porcelain cups. This idyll had its darker side though: a channel was dug to encircle the town, already surrounded on three sides by the River Owenmass, with water to protect it from the displaced Irish, who had gone to live in the bogs. Today, the town's heritage is celebrated in a French week – complete with snail-eating competition – in July. The **People's Museum** (Sun 11.30am–1pm & 3–5.30pm; free) in the Catholic Club on Main Street, has exhibits ranging from four thousand-year-old axe-heads to twentieth-century artefacts.

There are few eating options in the town but for a quick **snack** try *Matthews* café/homebakery on Main Street, which as well as serving good coffee has a fine collection of books and pamphlets relating to local history.

Set on the banks of the tranquil River Barrow, between Portarlington and Monasterevin, the ruins of **Lea Castle** are an impressive sight. The best way to reach the castle is to leave Portarlington on the main Dublin road where, after one mile, there is a sign for Killenard on the right, while the road to the castle is shortly afterwards on the left; to access the castle walk through the farmyard near the road or, alternatively you can head along a pleasant river walk beginning in the village of Monasterevin four miles to the east. The castle dates back to the thirteenth century when it was the stronghold of Maurice Fitzgerald, a member of the powerful Anglo-Norman family who controlled this area. In 1315 it was burned by Edward Bruce (brother of King Robert Bruce of Scotland), who had been invited to Ireland by the Irish chieftains to create trouble for the Anglo-Normans. The castle later provided refuge for Silken Thomas, another Fitzgerald, after he rebelled against Henry VIII, and in 1650, like most castles in the area, it fell foul of Oliver Cromwell's forces after they had taken Dunamase.

One of the few really big estates in County Laois is **Emo Court**; take the R419 from Portarlington (or if approaching from Portlaoise turn off the N7 at New Inn). Designed by James Gandon for Sir Henry Bennett around 1790, but not finished, and not entirely according to Gandon's plans, until the mid-nineteenth century. It's a massive domed building which has been impressively restored by its present owner after years of neglect when it was run as a Jesuit seminary. The **house** is now administered by the

Office of Public Works, and open for guided tours (mid-June to mid-Sept Tues–Sun 10.30am–5pm; £2/€2.54; Heritage Card). You can also wander through the extensive **grounds** during daylight hours. The nearby **Coolbanagher Church** is a modest and graceful building also designed by Gandon, but unfortunately is only open for services).

COUNTY OFFALY

From the Bog of Allen in the east to Boora Bog in the west, **County Offaly** is dominated by the stuff. It's a low-lying region bounded to the northwest by the meandering Shannon and its flood plain, and only in the south does the land rise at all into the foothills of the Slieve Bloom range. The **Bog of Allen**, intensively exploited for peat, has been turned into vast swathes of brown desert. **Boora Bog** is entirely different: it's smaller and less unremittingly flat and bare, and is also the site of an archeological find that proves that there was human life here nine thousand years ago. Western County Offaly is also the location of **Clonmacnois**, the greatest monastery of early Celtic Ireland, on the great, watery flood-plain of the Shannon.

The Bog of Allen only really becomes overpowering after **Edenderry**, which traditionally marked the edge of the Pale. But even in Edenderry, after miles of dark bogland, it's a distinct relief to reach somewhere with lots of people and an air of prosperity: its single wide street is lined with cheerfully painted houses. Pushing on along the Dublin–Portumna bus route towards Tullamore, you pass through Daingean, formerly Philipstown, the provincial capital in the days when Offaly was known as King's County (both county and capital were planted in Mary Tudor's reign and named after her husband, Philip II of Spain).

Tullamore

Coming from either direction, from the Bog of Allen to the east or Boora Bog to the west, the bright lights and solid buildings of **TULLAMORE**, astride the Grand Canal, seem welcoming. The town's Victorian ambience makes it look more English than Irish, a result of moving the capital from Philipstown to Tullamore in 1834, following decades in which the British pushed the boundaries of King's County ever further westwards. Tullamore is worth a short visit but has none of the attractions of nearby Birr which makes a much better base for exploring the county. One aspect of its history that Tullamore is attempting to exploit is its whiskey, Tullamore Dew, which was once distilled here – though the factory has since moved to Clonmel. The story behind the smoothest of Irish whiskies is celebrated in a **heritage centre**, which also houses the tourist office, on Bury Quay (May–Sept Mon–Sat 9.00am–6pm, Sun 12–5pm; Oct–April Mon–Sat 10am–5pm, Sun 12–5pm; £3.50/€4.44). The centre is set in a fine, converted warehouse and has a pleasant basement bar and café, though the exhibition itself is painfully dull and doesn't justify the entrance fee, despite the fact that the price includes a complimentary whiskey.

The main reason for visiting Tullamore, however, is **Charleville Forest Castle** (April–May Sat & Sun 2–5pm; June–Sept Wed–Sun 11am–4pm; Oct–March by appointment on ☎0506/21279; £3.50/€4.44), an extraordinary Georgian-Gothic mansion built in 1779 to the designs of Francis Johnston. The surrounding estate is wonderfully spooky, with a Gothic element suggestive of a horror movie – castellated turrets, shady trees and clinging ivy – while the house in the centre of the estate, surrounded by a second wall topped by urns, is a secretive, eerie place. With its splendid old trees, leafy walks and even a grotto, the place has plenty of diversions. To get there, take the Birr road out of Tullamore (the N52), and Charleville's gates are on the right as you leave the town – about ten minutes' walk.

Practicalities

Tullamore's **tourist office** (June–Aug Mon–Fri 10am–5pm; ☎0506/52617) is on Bury Quay; to get there from the main street, walk down Rahan Road, turn right and head towards the canal. If you want to **stay**, you could try one of the numerous B&Bs in town, such as the comfortable and friendly *Oakfield House*, Rahan Rd (☎0506/21385; ③), and *High House* (☎0506/51358; ③), which serves decent food at reasonable prices. You can feast on baked loin of marinated venison at the more upmarket *Tullamore Court Hotel* (☎0506/46666, *www.tullamorecourthotel.ie*; ⑥), while traditional hospitality and hearty cuisine are available at the excellent *Beechlawn Farmhouse* (☎0506/53099; ③) in Daingean, a little way out of Tullamore along the canal. Tullamore's location makes it a good starting-point for exploring either the Shannon or Barrow rivers by **boat** – it's linked to both by the Grand Canal – although if you're headed for the Shannon, it's worth considering basing yourself among the quieter charms of Banagher; cruisers can be rented from Celtic Canal Cruisers (☎0506/21861). **Bike rental** is available from Buckley Cycles, Brewery Lane.

Durrow Abbey

Four miles north of Tullamore on the N52, beyond some handsome wrought-iron gates to the left of the road, lies the site of **Durrow Abbey** (daily 9am–1pm; free), one of the monasteries founded by the energetic St Columcille (better known as St Columba), and the place where the *Book of Durrow* – an illuminated late seventh-century copy of the Gospels, now exhibited in Trinity College Library, Dublin – was made.

A long avenue leads you to a typically Irish juxtaposition: a grand Georgian mansion next to a medieval church, which stand on the site of the monastery. A notice at the main gates gives directions to the high cross and tombstones, and ahead of you are the well-tended grounds of the house. Within the disused churchyard is a rather eerie atmosphere: the masonry is strangled with ivy and gravestones lean crazily on uneven ground as if the earth has opened and disgorged their contents.

Along The Shannon: Clonmacnois to Banagher

Western Offaly is dominated by the bogs of Allen and Boora and the **Shannon**, the first two virtually impassable, the other for centuries a means of transportation and communication. Exploring the *esker* ridges (raised paths above the bog) of this drowsy, bog-and-water landscape has a quiet appeal if you hit good weather. Equally appealing, and increasingly popular, are boating trips, with visitors following the gentle flow of the meandering Shannon downstream to Clonmacnoise, Banagher and further west to the sea. It's excellent **cycling** country too, and, although they may be a little difficult for the untrained eye to identify, the romantic ruins that dot the landscape offer plenty of food for the imagination, and following roads that have for centuries been the only passages through the bog has a resonance of its own.

Although the monastery at **Clonmacnois** has made it onto the bus-tour itinerary, visitors to it generally climb straight back on board their buses and head for the west. In general the area remains pleasantly unfashionable and untouristed. That said, there's an increasing range and number of places to **stay** in the area as the Shannon-based tourist industry expands, with the best base located in the relaxed Georgian town of **Banagher**, basking on the banks of the river. Alternatively, you could stay in the busier town of **Birr**, further south, with its elegant Georgian architecture and impressive Big House (see p.160).

Clonmacnois

Of all the ancient sites along the Shannon, **Clonmacnois**, early Celtic Ireland's foremost monastery, in the northwest of the county, is by far the most important. Approaching from Shannonbridge to the south, the first evidence of its whereabouts is a stone wall leaning precariously towards the Shannon. This is actually a remnant of a thirteenth-century Norman **castle**, built to protect the river crossing, and has nothing whatever to do with the monastery.

The **monastic complex** (daily: mid-March to May & mid-Sept to Oct 10am–6pm; Nov to mid-March 10am–5pm; £3.00/€3.81; Heritage Card) – a huddle of wind- and rain-swept buildings on an open plain on a bend of the Shannon – can feel swamped at times by the volume of tourist traffic being processed by the new visitor centre. It's advisable to stay nearby and visit the complex in the evening, when the tourist traffic recedes and the site exudes the sense of tranquillity which must have attracted its monastic founders to begin with. This was not just a monastery, but a **royal city** and burial place for the kings of Connacht and Tara, including the last high king of Ireland, Rory O'Conor, who was buried here in 1198. It stood at what was then the busy junction of *Escir Riada*, the great road from Dublin to the west, and the Shannon; and – as the bookshrines, croziers and other richly decorated artefacts on show in the National Museum in Dublin testify – it was also an artistic centre of the highest order. The twelfth-century *Book of the Dun Cow*, now in the Royal Irish Academy Library in Dublin, is only one of many treasures made here. Founded by **St Kieran** around 548, the monastery was largely protected by its isolation: surrounded by bog, Clonmacnois could only be reached by boat or by one road that ran along the *eskers*. It withstood Irish, Viking and Norman attacks, but in 1552 the English garrison at Athlone looted the monastery and left it beyond recovery. However, plenty remains: a cathedral, eight churches, two round towers, high crosses, grave slabs and a thirteenth-century ring fort.

The admission fee to the complex includes an audio-visual presentation and a guided tour, as well as access to the interpretative centre, exhibition, and cosy coffee shop. Clonmacnois is still a pilgrimage site – St Kieran's festival is in September – and the video is a rather romantic hagiography, detailing the saint's peregrinations through ancient Ireland before he settled at Clonmacnois.

More important is the **exhibition**: all the site's carved crosses – it has the richest collection in Ireland – have been moved inside to protect them from County Offaly's incessant wind and rain. The early tenth-century **Great Cross**, over twelve feet high, is unusual in that it includes a secular scene representing the monastery's foundation and scenes from the passion; it is believed to commemorate King Flann and Abbot Coman. The **South Cross**, dating from the ninth century, is decorated with flower and animal motifs.

Seeing any significant differences between these small, gaunt, grey buildings takes a trained eye. The **cathedral**, scarcely bigger than its companions, was built in 904 by King Flann and Abbot Coman Conailleach and rebuilt in the fourteenth century by Tomultach MacDermot; the sandstone pillars of the west doorway may have been incorporated from the earlier church.

Not everything at Clonmacnois, however, is as simple as it seems: to the right of the cathedral is **Teampall Doolin**, the temple which carries the elaborate coat of arms of Edmund Dowling of Clondarane, who restored the building in 1689. **Teampall Hurpan**, adjacent, was actually added in its entirety in the seventeenth century. **Teampall Kieran**, on the other side of the cathedral, is the reputed burial place of the founding saint, as well as the place where he allegedly built the site's first church; the ruined **Teampall Kelly** is probably twelfth-century.

Away from the main group of buildings is **O'Rourke's Tower**, a round tower sixty foot high, erected just after the cathedral and blasted by lightning in 1134. On the outer boundary of the site, by the Shannon, are the **Teampall Finghin**, with another round tower dating from 1124, and the **Teampall Conor**, which was founded early in the eleventh century by Cathal O'Connor and used as a parish church from around 1790.

The **Church of the Nunnery**, away from the main enclosure, is signposted but difficult to find, and most people lose heart before they reach it. Follow the path across the site and bear left along the lane and you'll find the church a little further along on the right, complete with two lovely Romanesque arches in a field by the Shannon, exuding a feeling of peace. If your arrival at Clonmacnois does happen to coincide with a bus party, this is certainly the place to come.

Practicalities

Next to the monastery is the Clonmacnois **tourist office** (daily: March–May & Aug–Oct 10am–6pm; June & July 9am–7pm; ☎0906/74134). Comfortable B&B **accommodation** offering en-suite rooms and a friendly midland welcome can be found a mile from Clonmacnois on the Shannonbridge Road at *Kajon House* (☎0905/74191; ③), while nearby a picturesque nineteenth-century cottage painted white, with red windows and a peat roof, has been restored and is now rented out by the Claffeys (☎0905/74149; £10/€12.70 per person per night). To reach the **camping** spot nearby, take the winding road from the monastery (follow signs for the Transport Museum), where, near Clonfalough Church, you'll find the tranquil Glebe Camping Park (☎090 230277).

The **boats** you'll see moored at Clonmacnois, incidentally, are all private; to rent a craft, you'll have to go downstream to Banagher or Athlone. About five miles east of Clonmacnois, just off the main N62 Athlone–Roscrea road, the An Dún **Transport and Heritage Museum** (daily 10am–6pm; £2/€2.54) has a small collection of lovingly tended vintage cars, plus agricultural vehicles and an odd assortment of butter churns, televisions and typewriters. There's also a pleasant coffee shop.

Shannonbridge and Shannon Harbour

From Clonmacnois, the road south skirts the Boora Bog to **SHANNONBRIDGE**. The road leading into the tiny village has a set of traffic lights where it meets the Shannon, as the narrow sixteen-span bridge can only accommodate single lane traffic. Upstream, the wetlands of the Shannon open up; downstream a power station signifies the exploitation of the boglands. This is the point where counties Offaly, Roscommon and Galway meet and the River Suck joins the Shannon: hence the strategically placed and massive artillery fortification dating from Napoleonic times. There are a couple of **B&Bs** here, including *Racha House* right in the middle of the village (☎0905/74249; ③); and *Laurel Lodge* (☎0905/74189; ③), a mile out of town towards Banagher, both of which rent out bikes and boats. The *Shannonside Diner* does snacks and light **meals**; there's a music **pub** – *Killeen's Tavern* – on the main street.

Just outside the town on the Tullamore Road (the R357), at the Irish Peat Board, Bord na Mona's Blackwater power-generating plant, you can join a tour that explores the bog on the **Clonmacnois and West Offaly Railway**, which will take you on a five-mile circular tour on narrow gauge through the Blackwater Bog. Unlike Clara Bog (see opposite) Blackwater Bog is being exploited hell-for-leather; you can't miss the power station with its thin chimneys belching brown smoke into the air. The irony of touring the bog under the auspices of the organization that's itself helping to destroy it won't be lost on anyone "A few hundred years from now", says the publicity material, suavely, the bog "will be an integrated tapestry of fields, woodlands and wetlands. The landscape never stands still." The tour, which lasts some 45 minutes, leaves every hour on the hour (April–Oct daily 10am–5pm; £3/€3.81) and is preceded by a 35-minute video on the flora and fauna you're about to see.

Also nearby, and of particular interest if you have children to entertain, is the **Ashbrook Open Farm and Agricultural Museum** (April–Sept daily 10am–7pm; £2/€2.54), with plenty of farm animals, donkeys, rare birds and farm implements.

About five miles further south (take the R357 and turn at Clonony), **Shannon Harbour** is where the River Brosna and the Grand Canal meet the Shannon after their journey right across Ireland. As you walk down to the junction, there comes a beautiful point where the entire landscape seems to become water. **Clonony Castle**, a mile or two further inland, is a ruined sixteenth-century tower house with a nineteenth-century reconstructed barn – to the side of which are buried Anne Boleyn's sisters, Elizabeth and Mary – and which was extensively restored in the seventeenth century by an entrepreneurial German, Matthew de Renzi.

Banagher and around

Another couple of miles downstream from Shannon Harbour, **BANAGHER** consists of one long street sloping down to the Shannon, fortified on the Connacht side by a Martello tower. With the construction of a new marina, it's rapidly turning itself into a relaxed and elegant tourist centre for the Irish Midlands, as it once was in the nineteenth century when Anthony Trollope was sent here as a Post Office surveyor in 1841, and wrote his first book, *The Macdermots of Ballycloran*; Charlotte Brontë spent her honeymoon here.

Cloghan Castle, two miles out of town and signposted from the centre, is a massive Norman tower house with Georgian additions, inside an equally massive enclosure (May–Sept Wed–Sat 2–6.50pm; £4/€5.08; ⑥). Inhabited continuously for more than eight hundred years, it packs a wealth of history, starting with a seventh-century monastery founded by St Cronan on the site. You can also **stay** here and eat breakfast in the magnificent dining hall, warmed in winter by a massive fire. The Thompsons, who own Cloghan, have another pile, **Emmell Castle**, thirteen miles to the south, which is not open to view but you can rent it. A sixteenth-century keep with a Georgian house attached, it sleeps seven and costs from £400/€508 to £500/€635 a week, and £300/€381 for a three-day weekend. When visiting Cloghan Castle, you can also take in Lusmagh Pet Farm (summer daily 2–6pm; £2/€2.54) for some therapeutic patting of pigs and sheep, and interaction with geese and ostriches.

Close to the castle, and also signposted from Banagher, is **Victoria Lock**, a local beauty spot, where the Shannon runs into two separate channels. Trollope's biographer, James Pope-Hennessy, found the vegetation "so rich and wild, so tangled and impenetrable", that he was moved to compare it, in unreflective colonial tones, to Jamaica or Dominica. It's certainly a beautiful place; beneath the lock, released from artificial constraints, the river spills over once more across its floodplain.

There's a wayward local variant on Classical architecture: two houses on the main street have pepperpot towers, inside which everything curves – doors, fanlights, pediments, the lot. One of these, dated around 1760, has been transformed into a first-rate **hostel**, *Crank House* (IHH; ☎0509/51458). It also houses a **tourist office** (March–Oct Mon–Fri 9.30am–8pm, Sat & Sun 9.30am–5pm) as well as the regional offices of Crann, an organization dedicated to the preservation of Ireland's woodlands, and a fine **coffee shop** (daily 7am–9pm). There's B&B **accommodation** across the road at the startlingly pink *Old Forge* (☎0509/51504; ③) and a comfortable friendly hotel, *The Brosna Lodge* (☎0509/51350; ③).

Banagher also provides a good base for exploring **Clara Bog**, a large (665 hectares) and relatively unspoiled tract of raised bog. Bord na Mona planned to develop it for industrial-scale peat-cutting and began draining the eastern section in the early 1980s, but in 1987 public pressure resulted in its takeover by the Office of Public Works. In the bog you can find rare species of lichen, moss and the uniquely adapted plants that are able to survive in the intensely acid environment – including, in the hollows and pools, the carnivorous sundews and bladderworts that like to supplement their diet with unwary insects. Check the Banagher tourist office for more information on walks into the bog or the Shannon floodplain.

The range of **eating** and **drinking** places reflects the extra visitors the town is getting. For daytime eating, *The Water's Edge* offers coffee and snacks – and a fine view of the pitch 'n' putt course on the opposite bank. *The Vine House* **restaurant** and music bar, close to the river, has a courtyard garden and reasonably priced, elegantly hearty menu with an emphasis on seafood. *The Brosna Lodge*'s restaurant, *Snipes*, has a good, if slightly pricier, menu – try the excellent potato and nettle soup. There's a handful of **bars** – the *Shannon Hotel*, on the main street, often has music and also has a pleasant garden where you can sit outside in good weather; *J.J. Hough's*, on Main St, is a good old singing pub where drinkers are openly encouraged to take the mike. You can **rent bikes** from K. Donegan in the main street (☎0509/51178), and **canoes** from Shannon Adventure Canoeing Holidays (☎0509/51411). **Boats** are also available for rent from Carrick-Craft (☎0509/51189) to cruise up the Shannon: a Clare Class cruiser, which will sleep up to eight, costs between £800/€1016 and £1500/€1905 per week, although smaller boats are available from £250/€317.50. Short cruises on the river are available on Thursdays and Sundays on board the *River Queen*, an enclosed launch with a full bar (☎0509 51112; £4/€5.08).

Birr

BIRR is a perfect example of a mid-sized town planned round a great house – in this case, Birr Castle, home of the Parsons family (the town used to be known as Parsonstown), later elevated to the Earls of Rosse. Here, eighteenth-century urban planning has resulted in a truly delightful Georgian town, with wide, airy streets and finely detailed, fan-lit houses. After decades of neglect the potential of Birr's heritage has been realized, and although it has enjoyed some cosmetic pampering, it still retains the earthy vitality of a busy county town. Birr's claim to be the centre point of the country is not unwarranted and the town is highly recommended as a base for exploring the wetlands of the Shannon and the Slieve Bloom Mountains or simply as a stopover to break up a journey south or west. Habitation at Birr dates back to the sixth century, when there was a monastery here; an Anglo-Norman castle was succeeded by an Irish stronghold of the O'Carrolls and then, after the place was granted to Sir Laurence Parsons in 1619, it became an English garrison town. The development of the Georgian town dates from the time of another Laurence, who succeeded to the title in 1740 and immediately began to "improve" the town, fired by the architectural enthusiasm he'd gained on his Grand Tour.

The Town

Birr is now a heritage town, and there are plans to open one of its Georgian houses on John's Mall to the public, followed perhaps by a pub, school and shop, to illustrate the realities of eighteenth-century life beyond its elegant Georgian facade. Already open is the local **heritage centre** on the refined John's Mall (Mon–Sat 2.30–5.30pm, Sun 3–5pm; £1/€1.27), housed in an impeccably elegant miniature Greek temple, which will fill you in on the town's architectural and social background. In the grounds is a small standing stone, mentioned by Giraldus Cambrensis in the twelfth century as the "navel of Ireland" and used in the early nineteenth century, when it had temporarily migrated to County Clare, for secret celebrations of the Mass.

By far and away Birr's greatest attraction (and fast becoming one of Ireland's) is **Birr Castle and Historic Centre** (daily 9am–6pm; *www.birrcastle.com*; £5/€6.35) which allows visitors a glimpse into the life and home of one of Ireland's most interesting, intelligent and eccentric families, The Earls of Rosse, who still live within the castle's grounds. The greatest attraction on display is the impressive **Rosse Telescope**, built in 1845 by the third earl, it was then, and remained for three-quarters of a century, the largest telescope in the world – a reflector with a diameter of 72 inches. The instrument was used by the fourth earl to make the first accurate measurement of the temperature of the moon and to catalogue the spiral nebulae. The telescope has been restored and a replica of the six-foot mirror in the mirror box has been installed. Visitors can experience this telescopic goliath at work at regular intervals in the castle's gardens. This scientific marvel forms the basis of the recently opened historic centre, housed in the Stable Block of the Demesne, which celebrates the scientific achievements of other family members; there is the Lunar Heat Machine invented by the fourth earl (his younger brother, Charles, invented the steam turbine) and an early darkroom used by the photographer, Mary Rosse, wife of the third earl. The family's talent for invention had its downside though when a family friend and talented microscopist, Mary Ward, became the first motor fatality in Ireland when she was run over in the grounds by an experimental, steam-powered car.

While the formal gardens boast the largest box hedges in the world, a visit to the **demesne** is highly recommended. It offers acres of wild-flower meadows with over one thousand species of shrubs and trees from all over the world, punctuated by a large man-made lake and a crystal-clear river spanned by a charming suspension bridge. Visitors are free to explore the gardens at their leisure until dusk. The centre also has a pleasant coffee shop, *Little Space Cafe*, in the courtyard of the stable block.

Practicalities

Birr's **tourist office** is presently housed in the basement of a converted warehouse, near the castle, and opposite the new development around *Malting's Guest House*. Just across the road are the brightly painted doors of the five Georgian houses that form *Spinner's Town House* (☎0509/21673, *www.spinners-townhouse.com*; ③); the best place to stay in town, *Spinner's* is an elegant **B&B** carved out of old warehouse buildings grouped around a courtyard. Accommodation is in cosy rooms with bare wooden floors, and the rate includes a delicious, cooked breakfast which can be eaten either in a private dining room, or, on a summers morning, in the elegant enclosed courtyard. Almost opposite is the modern *Maltings Guest House* (☎0509/21345; ③) a large complex with en-suite rooms. *Dooly's Hotel* in Emmet Square (☎0509/20032, *www.doolyshotel.com*; ⑤), recently refurbished and extremely pleasant, is one of the focal points for the town's social life. *Dooly's* is where the Galway Hunt acquired the nickname of the Galway Blazers after a hunt in 1809, when their overenthusiastic celebrations resulted in the gutting of the building by fire.

Spinner's Bistro (☎0509 21673), almost opposite the castle entrance, is a quirky bistro with an eclectic menu, with good vegetarian options, that changes regularly and always features fresh local ingredients. You'll get sturdy evening **meals** at *The Stables*, Oxmantown Mall (☎0509/20263; also B&B; ③). Good, if mega-rich, food is served at *The Thatch* (☎0509/20985), a bar and restaurant a little way south out of town at Crinkill – take the Portumna road from Market Square and it's signposted at the split in the road. The walls of *The Thatch* are hung with some fascinating photographs of the military architecture of the old British army barracks at Birr that were blown up in 1922. An alternative is the *Riverbank Restaurant and Coffee Shop*, which overlooks the Little Brosna river and the old stone bridge that will take you over into County Tipperary – again take the Portumna road from Market Square but follow the signposts for

Portumna itself. For something more exotic, there's a good Chinese restaurant, *Kong Lam* (☎0509/21253), in Bridge St. As for **pubs**, you'll get a friendly welcome at *Craughwell's*, in Castle St (just down from *Spinner's Town House*), which often has music and barbecues; or try *Kelly's*, where you can sit outside on the street and watch the world go by.

Excursions

If you're thinking of doing some **walking**, a mile out on the Roscrea Road (the N62), is the Slieve Bloom Interpretive Centre (daily 10am–6pm), which offers some rather dry background on the hills' flora and fauna, land use, architecture and legend. It's also the Birr Outdoor Education Centre (☎0509/20029), which runs courses in canoeing, windsurfing, rock-climbing and so on. For **horse-riding**, ring the Birr Riding Centre (☎0509/20551). You can rent **bikes** from P. Dolan & Sons on Main St.

Finally, there's a little excursion for ghostbusters. A few miles southeast of town beyond **Clareen**, as the land rises towards the Slieve Bloom Mountains, the fifteenth-century **Leap Castle** fortifies the valley between Leinster and Munster. Before it was destroyed in 1922, it enjoyed the sinister reputation of being the most haunted house in Ireland, and was particularly famous for an unusual, smelly ghost, which was described both by Yeats and his contemporary Oliver St John Gogarty.

travel details

Trains

Portlaoise to: Cork (9 daily; 2hr); Dublin (8 daily; 1hr); Limerick Junction (13 daily; 1hr).

Tullamore to: Dublin (8 daily; 55min); Galway (5 daily; 1hr 45min).

Buses

Birr to: Athlone (1 daily; 50min); Cork (1 daily; 3hr 30min); Dublin (2 daily; 4hr).

Portlaoise to: Abbeyleix (2 daily; 20min); Dublin (6 daily; 1hr 45min); Durrow (1 daily; 30min).

Private Buses

For more information on private bus routes contact the following companies who operate in this area: J.J. Kavanagh (☎056/31106), Paddy Kavanagh (☎0902/74839), Kearns Coaches (☎0509/22244).

J.J. Kavanagh

Abbeyleix to: Dublin (5 daily; 1hr 30 min).

Mountrath to: Dublin (5 daily; 1hr 30 min).

Monasterevin to: Dublin (5 daily; 1 hr 30 min).

Portlaoise to: Dublin (5 daily; 1hr 45 min).

Paddy Kavanagh

Athlone to: Clonmacnoise (1 daily; 30min).

Kearns Coaches

Banagher to: Dublin (1 daily; 3hrs).

Birr to: Dublin (2 daily; 2hrs 20min).

Tullamore to: Dublin (2 daily; 1hr 40min).

CHAPTER FOUR

LOUTH, MEATH, WESTMEATH AND LONGFORD

Stretching from the borders of County Dublin to the frontier with the North, and from the coast to the heart of Ireland, the four counties of Meath, Louth, Westmeath and Longford epitomize green and rural Ireland, yet provide a total contrast to the west of the country. It's a region neglected by most visitors, whose impression is one of monotonously similar countryside. Pass through at speed, as most people do, and you'll probably share that impression. But if you slow down and target a small area for more detailed exploration, you'll discover far more. In the east there's a wealth of remains of an exceptionally long, rich history, including the great ritual landscapes flanking the River Boyne, and one or two great beaches on the coast. Further west, you're into the lush, green, agricultural heart of Ireland; it's not spectacular country, but as dense in historical resonance as anywhere else, and largely untouristed, with a slow pace and plain style of living that have a steady charm of their own.

In practical terms, you'll find it easy enough to get about, with most of the sites conveniently strung along major roads well served by public transport. Accommodation is less easy, with only a handful of hostels throughout the four counties, and B&Bs only in the major centres. Still, if you base yourself strategically you'll find that a surprising amount can be seen in a short time.

County Louth, the smallest of the Republic's 26 counties stretches northwards along the coast. Here you'll find the only two towns of any real size in this chapter, **Drogheda** and **Dundalk**. Inland, hilly drumlin country hardens in the northeast to real mountains. Here, on the **Cooley Peninsula**, lies the most exciting part of the coast between Dublin and the border. The peninsula is also the setting of one of the richest

ACCOMMODATION PRICE CODES

Throughout this book, prices of hotels, guesthouses and B&Bs have been graded with the codes below, according to what you can expect to pay for a double room in high season. For more details on accommodation, see p.34.

① Under £26/€33.01
② £26–33/€33.01–41.90
③ £33–40/€41.90–50.79
④ £40–55/€50.79–69.84
⑤ £55–70/€69.84–88.88
⑥ £70–90/€88.88–114.28
⑦ £90–110/€114.28–139.67
⑧ £110–130/€139.67–165.07
⑨ Over £130/€165.07

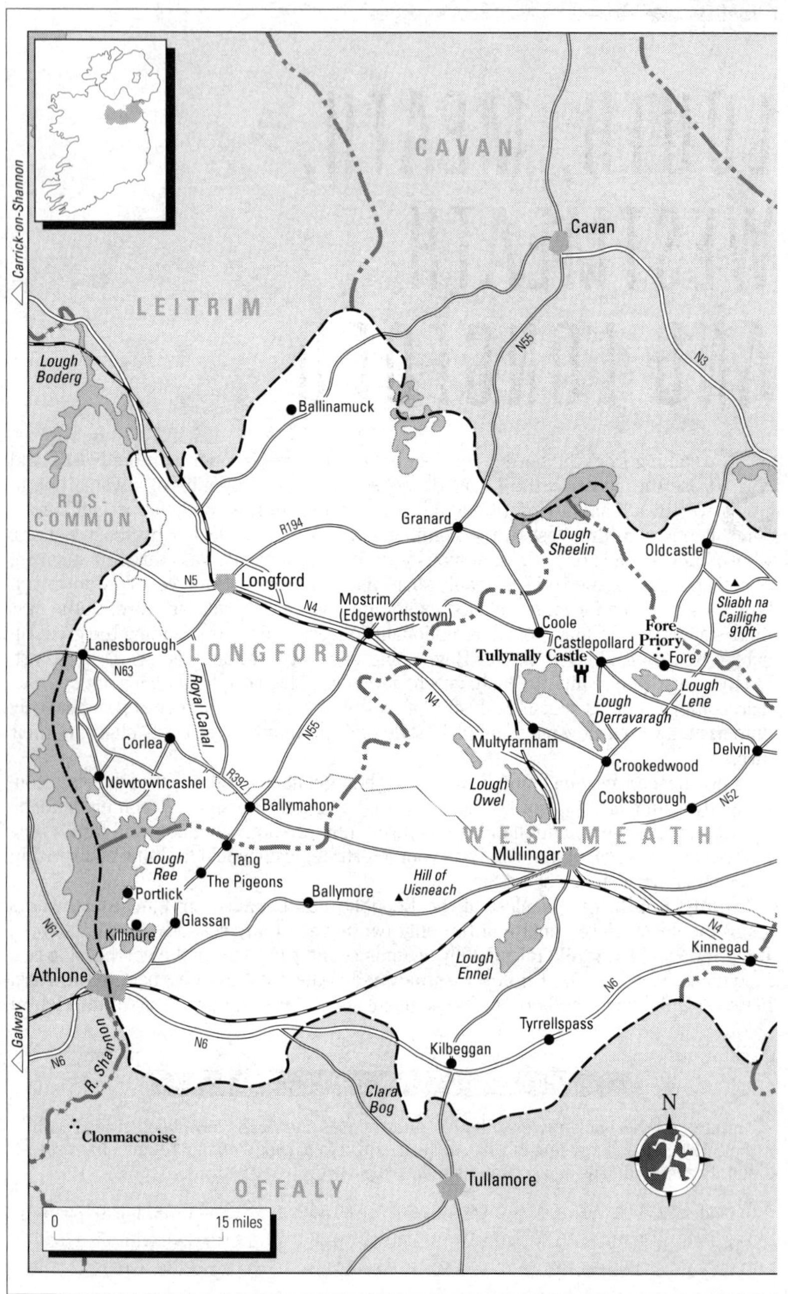
CAVAN
Cavan
LEITRIM
Carrick-on-Shannon
Lough Boderg
Ballinamuck
N55
N3
ROS-COMMON
Granard
R194
Lough Sheelin
Oldcastle
N5
Longford
N4
Mostrim (Edgeworthstown)
Sliabh na Caillighe 910ft
Coole
Fore Priory
Castlepollard
Tullynally Castle
Fore
Lanesborough
LONGFORD
N63
Royal Canal
Lough Lene
Lough Derravaragh
N4
N55
Multyfarnham
Corlea
Delvin
Crookedwood
Newtowncashel
R392
Lough Owel
Cooksborough
N52
Ballymahon
WESTMEATH
Mullingar
Tang
Lough Ree
The Pigeons
Hill of Uisneach
Portlick
Ballymore
N61
Glassan
Killinure
N4
Kinnegad
Lough Ennel
Athlone
N6
Galway
Tyrrellspass
N6
R. Shannon
Kilbeggan
N6
Clara Bog
N
Clonmacnoise
OFFALY
Tullamore
0
15 miles

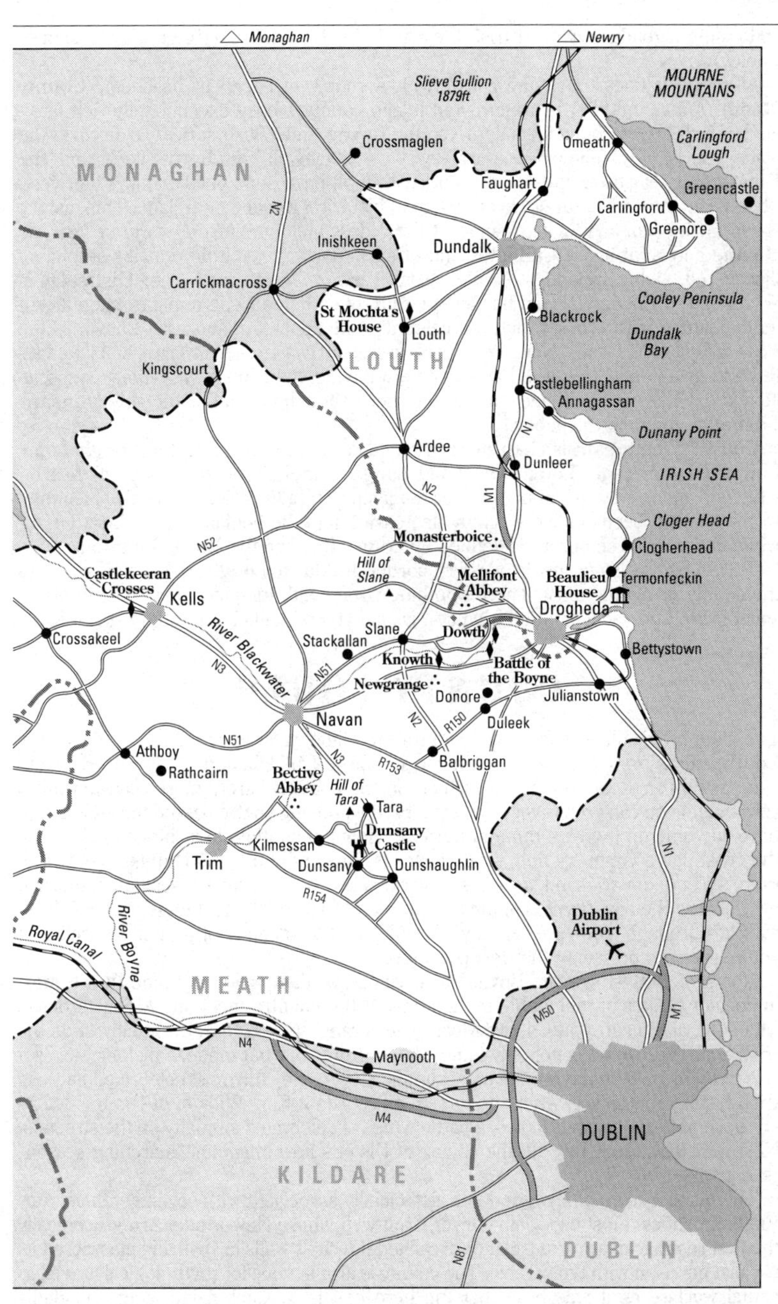
Monaghan
Newry
Slieve Gullion 1879ft
MOURNE MOUNTAINS
Carlingford Lough
Omeath
Crossmaglen
MONAGHAN
Faughart
Greencastle
Carlingford
Greenore
N2
Inishkeen
Dundalk
Carrickmacross
Cooley Peninsula
St Mochta's House
Louth
Blackrock
Dundalk Bay
LOUTH
Kingscourt
Castlebellingham
Annagassan
N1
Dunany Point
Ardee
Dunleer
IRISH SEA
N2
M1
Cloger Head
Monasterboice
N52
Clogherhead
Hill of Slane
Mellifont Abbey
Beaulieu House
Termonfeckin
Castlekeeran Crosses
Kells
Drogheda
River Blackwater
Slane
Dowth
Crossakeel
Stackallan
Bettystown
N3
N51
Knowth
Battle of the Boyne
Newgrange
Donore
Julianstown
Navan
N2
R150
Duleek
N51
Athboy
N3
Balbriggan
R153
Rathcairn
Bective Abbey
Hill of Tara
Tara
Dunsany Castle
Kilmessan
Trim
Dunsany
Dunshaughlin
N1
R154
River Boyne
Royal Canal
Dublin Airport
MEATH
M50
M1
N4
Maynooth
M4
DUBLIN
KILDARE
N81
DUBLIN

and oldest legendary tales of Irish literature, the **Táin Bó Cúailnge** (Cattle Raid of Cooley).

Although it does touch the coast (with a couple of excellent beaches), **County Meath** (*Midhe*, middle) is primarily an inland county, whose exceptionally rich farmland unfurls lazily around its major river, the **Boyne**, and its tributaries. To discover the place you simply follow these waterways – above all the Boyne itself and the **Blackwater** – as thousands of years of civilization have done before. Along its rivers, Meath can boast by far the richest bounty of historical remains in Ireland. This history starts in the Stone Age, with some of the oldest buildings in the world at **Brú na Bóinne** and **Sliabh Na Caillighe**, and other important Neolithic remains still being discovered. Celtic Ireland was ruled from **Tara**, in Meath, and from **Uisneach** in Westmeath. Christian Ireland has left a wealth of early monastic remains, magnificent tenth-century high crosses, and the celebrated illuminated manuscript known as the *Book of Kells*. The largest Norman fortress in Ireland can be seen at **Trim**, and later castles and mansions – from the Plantation period when the county was wholly confiscated and extensively developed – are everywhere, though only a few (notably **Dunsany Castle**) are open to the public.

County Westmeath is characterized by its lakes – **Lough Sheelin**, **Lough Lene**, **Lough Derravaragh**, **Lough Owel** and **Lough Ennel** cut down through its heart – which go a long way to compensate for the falling off in historical or scenic splendour. In the south it becomes increasingly flat, easing into the bogland of northern Offaly, while in the west the border is defined by **Lough Ree** and the **River Shannon**.

The Shannon also forms the western border of **County Longford**, which is about all the county has going for it. There's nothing wrong with the place in a dull and placid sort of way, but placid and dull is what it is, and you're unlikely to want to stay long.

COUNTY LOUTH

The main N1 Dublin–Belfast road, and the train line, provide rapid access to **County Louth** and its principal town, Drogheda, and on to Dundalk and the North. En route you pass through County Meath, which on the coast is barely more than ten miles across, and you can cross over into Louth hardly noticing you've passed through. If you have any time on the way, though, there are some delightful old-fashioned resorts on the coast and a couple of fine, sandy beaches. Biggest of them is **Bettystown**, where there's plenty of dark sand, a campsite, various B&Bs and a superb seafood restaurant overlooking the bay, *Bacchus at the Coastguard* (☎041/982 8251). Pleasant as it is, however, it's probably not somewhere you would want to spend a lot of time, especially if you're going to be seeing the west coast too.

North of Bettystown the Boyne river, whose verdant valley is home to the most important cluster of megalithic monuments in the country including Monasterboice, Mellifont, and, nearby in County Meath, Newgrange (see p.184), eventually finds the Irish Sea. The **Boyne** is not only important in prehistory but modern history too, as it was here, in 1690, that if not the most significant certainly the most celebrated battle in Irish history took place, when the forces of Protestant King William of Orange defeated those of Catholic King James; a battle which is celebrated annually on the streets of Northern Ireland on July 12, the climax of Ulster's now infamous "marching season" (see p.182).

The historic town of **Drogheda**, is also closely associated with seventeenth-century English politics, most especially Oliver Cromwell whose New Model Army (ironically the first republican army in Ireland) breached the city's walls in 1649 and massacred its royalist garrison with typical zeal. The county is also famous for mythological as well as actual warfare as it was here that the hero of Ulster, Cúchulainn, single-handedly defeated the forces of the rest of Ireland in the great Irish epic the Táin Bó Cúailnge (the Cattle Raid of Cooley); much of the county, from the inland town of **Ardee** where Cúchulainn eventually killed his best friend Ferdia, to the Cooley mountains where most of the battles took place, are closely associated with the story. **The Cooley mountains** cover much of the Carlingford peninsula, the furthest point north on the Republic's eastern seaboard, and from here it's hard to believe that the towns of Rostrevor and Warrenpoint on the other side of the lough are, in fact, in another country. This sense of Louth as a crossing point between Leinster and Ulster (since 1922 Southern and Northern Ireland) is most keenly felt in the town of **Dundalk** which, despite the peace process, still exudes the slightly forbidding air of a border town and is seen as the home of hawkish republicanism.

Drogheda and around

DROGHEDA, clustered on either side of the river and tightly contained between two hills, is an enjoyable place in its own right: easily accessible and surprisingly unused to tourism. The precise grey stone of which the town is built, combined with its post-industrial decay, give it a slightly forbidding air, but it has a vitality that suits it well. The architectural legacy of successive civilizations forms the main attraction. The ancient **Millmount mound** and the Boyne itself echo the early habitation you'll see further upstream, but the history of Drogheda as a town really began with the **Vikings**, who arrived in 911 AD and founded a separate settlement on each bank. By bridging the ford between these two, the Danes gave the place its name – *Droichead Átha*, the Bridge of the Ford. By the fourteenth century, the walled town was one of the most important in the country, where the parliament would meet from time to time; remnants of **medieval** walls and abbeys lie like splinters throughout the town. As ever, though, most of what you see is from the **eighteenth century** or later, reflecting the sober style of the Protestant bourgeoisie after the horrific slaughter of Drogheda's defenders and inhabitants by Cromwell. The important surviving buildings of this age – the Tholsel, courthouse and St Peter's Church – have mellowed romantically and stand among the **nineteenth-century** flowering of triumphal churches, celebrating the relaxation of the persecuting stranglehold on Catholicism, and the riverside warehouses and huge rail viaduct that welcomed the industrial boom years. More recent development, with riverside laneways and suburban housing estates, has affected the flavour of the place very little: the past somehow seems stronger here than the present.

Arrival, information and accommodation

Drogheda is an easy place to find your way around. The **Bus Éireann** depot is on Donore Road, on the south bank of the river, and is also where you'll find the **tourist office** (June to mid-Sept Mon–Sat 10am–6pm; ☎041/983 7070). The **train** station is also on the south side, a short way east of town just off the Dublin Road. **Taxis** line up in the centre on Lawrence Street.

B&B accommodation is available at *Mrs Caffrey*, 69 Maple Drive (☎041/983 2244; ③), though book early as this house is very popular; the *Europa Hotel* on the Dublin Rd (☎041/983 7673; ⑥) with large comfortable rooms which is popular with northerners journeying south; and the elegant Victorian *Boyne Valley Hotel*, Dublin Rd (☎041/983 7737, *www.boyne-valley-hotel.ie*; ⑥). Mary Friel's *River Boyne House* (☎041/983 6180; ③) offers good service two miles out of town in an isolated rural location near the Boyne Battlefield. Drogheda's lack of hostel accommodation has been filled by the *Green Door Hostel*, Dublin Rd (☎041/983 4422, *www.greendoorhostel.com*; ②), a friendly place with comfy bunks and double rooms just across from the bus

station at the end of a row of colourfully painted stone cottages. Alternatively there is also a fine, farm hostel a little way out in Slane (see p.187). If you want to **rent a bike** try Bridge Cycles, 4 North Quay or P.J. Carolan, 77 Trinity St.

The Town

The Meath side of town, south of the river, is probably the best place to start exploring Drogheda. Standing on **Millmount hill**, you can enjoy an unimpeded panorama, with the bulk of the town climbing up the northern hill-slope opposite. From this viewpoint, it's clear how the tight-fitting street pattern of the medieval town gave scant room for expansion over succeeding centuries. The backs of the houses stagger down to the River Boyne in a colourless wash of daubed mortar. Millmount's **Martello Tower** also offers an excellent overview, both in a literal sense and through the excellent display in the local museum sited here. The tower (key from the museum) was severely damaged by bombardment during the 1922 Civil War (there's a large picture of the attack in the museum), but in any event it is the earthen mound on which it stands that gives the place its real importance. The strategic value of the site was recognized from the earliest times: in mythology the mound is the burial place of **Amergin**, the poet warrior, one of the sons of **Mil** of the Milesians who are reckoned to be the ancestors of the Gaels. He arrived in Ireland from northern Spain around 1498 BC and later defeated the Tuatha Dé Danann at Tailtiu (Telltown). Another belief is that the mound houses a passage grave. However, the tumulus has never been excavated to find out which story – if either – is true. Not surprisingly, the Normans chose the same strategic eminence for their motte in the twelfth century, and later a castle was built, standing until 1808 when it was replaced by the tower and military barracks you see today. The quickest way up here on foot is via the narrow flight of steps by Dina's corner shop, directly opposite **St Mary's Bridge**. This is near enough the spot where the original bridge was built by the Danes.

Next to the fort is the barracks square whose eighteenth-century houses now shelter arts and crafts enterprises, and, best of all, **Millmount Museum** (Tues–Sat 10am–5.30pm, Sun 2.30–5pm; £1.50/€1.90), one of Ireland's finest town museums, in the best chaotic style of the genre. Within a glass cabinet in the **foyer** hangs a topographical quilt showing much of Ireland's east coast – note the two thousand or so grains of French knots that depict the sandy shores. Next to this is a quilted cummerbund of the Georgian houses in Fair Street, very pleasing and precise in its eighteenth-century detail. When you get out into the town you'll find that the area depicted (Fair Street, along with William, Lower and Upper Magdalene streets and Rope Walk) is still rich in period buildings and architectural detail. The **Guilds Room** follows, hung with three large drapes (the only surviving Guilds' banners left in the country) celebrating the broguemakers', carpenters' and weavers' trades. The broguemakers' banner – in effect an early advertisement – is particularly wonderful. It depicts St Patrick, who in legend rid the country of snakes, standing with his foot on a serpent: even the saint needs some protection, however, so he is sturdily shod in a pair of good Irish brogues. King Charles I also has a bit part, hiding up an oak tree to symbolize both the use of oak for tanning the leather and the security offered by a good pair of shoes (Charles escaped from Cromwell's troops in 1651 by hiding in an oak tree). The carpenters' and weavers' banners are more straightforward, the former depicting compasses and blades, the latter with shuttles clasped in leopards' mouths. In the next room there's a similar theme, with the trade banners of fishermen, labourers and bricklayers. The bricklayers' shows the **barbican at St Lawrence Gate** as their proudest achievement. This, again, is something worth seeing once you get out into the town: still standing and perfectly preserved its two round towers flank a portcullis entry and retaining wall. It is the most significant part of the town walls to have survived (part of the West Gate also exists, and a buttress and embrasure can be seen just south of the gate), and arguably the finest such surviving structure anywhere in Ireland.

Heading down the museum stairs you come to a series of displays of a more domestic and industrial nature. The last heavy manufacturing industry left Drogheda in 1986. The exhibits record the sources of its former prosperity: linen and alcohol – at one time the town had sixteen distilleries and fourteen breweries. Next to a case charting the history of the linen trade and a painting of the ship that used to ply between Drogheda and the English coast is a vessel from a much earlier period in the town's long history: a **Boyne coracle**, a recent example of the type of circular fishing boat in use from prehistoric times right up to the middle of the twentieth century. This one has a framework of hazel twigs and a leather hide taken from a prize bull in 1943. There's also a fully equipped **period kitchen**, pantry and scullery. Among the artefacts displayed are an 1860 vacuum cleaner (a man would wind the suction mechanism from outside the house); a tailor's hen and goose irons (clothes irons named for their various shapes and sizes), which would be heated in the fire (hence the phrase "too many irons in the fire"); a settle bed (preferred by the Irish peasant because it would be next to the warmth of the dying embers and could sleep two adults lengthways and four or five children acrossways). A vast array of other everyday miscellany is also displayed, including an eccentric collection of geological samples gathered by a Drogheda resident whose wife finally insisted he should give them to the museum.

On the **top floor** are a small picture gallery and some rooms devoted to the Foresters and Hibernian societies, both nineteenth-century benevolent institutions set up to provide sickness benefits, burial expenses and the like for the poor. Perhaps ironically, given Drogheda's manufacturing history, the temperance movement was strong here, and one of the banners carries the exhortation "Hibernia be thou sober".

A little further down Mary Street is St Mary's Church, which now houses the recently opened **Drogheda heritage centre** (Mon–Fri 10am–5pm, Sat noon–5pm, Sun 2–5pm; ☎041/9831153; £2.50/€3.17). The centre caused a furore locally on its opening by displaying the death mask of the town's arch-nemesis, Oliver Cromwell, whose forces breached the city's walls right at this point. While the exhibits are far from inspiring, the low-budget video does offer a surprisingly revisionist account of the town's traumatic history and there is a fine coffee shop attached.

The northside

The steep streets of the town's northside run up the hill which is topped by the fifteenth-century **Magdalene Tower** – formerly the belfry tower of an extensive Dominican friary, founded in 1224 by Lucas De Netterville, Archbishop of Armagh. The tower rises above a Gothic arch where the transept and nave would have met; inside, a spiral staircase reaches up into its two storeys, but since it is railed off from public access it's probably seen to best advantage from a distance. In March 1395, **Richard II**, King of England, received within the priory the submission of the Ulster Chiefs; and later Thomas, Earl of Desmond, a former Lord Chief Justice, was found guilty of treason and beheaded here in 1467 (with him expired his Act of Parliament for a university in Drogheda).

Lower down, the spire that leaps out from the centre of town belongs to the heavily Gothic-styled nineteenth-century **St Peter's Roman Catholic Church** on West Street, the town's main thoroughfare. It's an imposing building, with a grand double flight of steps, but it's the presence of a martyr's head, on view in a tabernacle-like box that forms part of a small shrine down the left-hand aisle, that transforms the place into a centre of pilgrimage. The severed head is a searing reminder of the days of religious persecution. It once belonged to **Oliver Plunkett**, Archbishop of Armagh and primate of all Ireland in the seventeenth century, when Drogheda was the principal seat in Ireland. On July 1, 1681, Plunkett was executed in London for treason: as the Lord Chief Justice of England explained, "the bottom of your treason was your setting up your false religion, than which there is not anything more displeasing to God." His head and mutilated members were snatched from the fire but were not brought back to Ireland until 1721, a time when persecution had somewhat subsided. Plunkett was canonized in 1975, after miracles were said to have been performed in his name in southern Italy.

Walking east along West Street and turning up Peter's Street you'll find the town's other St Peter's Church (this time Church of Ireland). The original church on the site was a thirteenth-century wooden structure and it is said that many of the town's inhabitants perished here in a fire as they sought refuge from Cromwell's forces. The present church was erected in 1753, and a porch and spire, designed by the eminent Irish architect Francis Johnston, were added in 1793.

Heading south of here towards the docks, the back alleys and stone warehouses, once relics of the short-lived Industrial Revolution and of the local brewing and milling trades, are being done up by a new breed of entrepreneur to cater for the housing demands of Irish yuppies, known locally as "Celtic Cubs", who are profiting from the "Celtic Tiger" economy. The docks themselves are beginning to show evidence of new life, too, though the depleted commercial shipping fleet anchored on the lethargic Boyne are a far cry from the sixty Viking ships which are said to have wintered here. The docks do, however, boast one of the finest old pubs in the country, **Mrs Carbery's**. A local, family-run institution for over a century, in the evening or early morning (it is allowed to open at 7.30am to cater for the dockers and the men off the boats) the faint orange glow from the lanterns or fire inside the pub makes a welcome landmark and sign of life.

Eating, drinking and entertainment

While many of Drogheda's **restaurants** serve traditional fare, some new establishments are bringing an international flavour to the town. *Weavers* on West Street is an excellent pub for a cheap lunch, and is always crowded; *Jalapeno*, a few doors down, serves filling sandwiches and is also good value. *The Swan House* on West Street is a good Chinese restaurant, with cheap takeaway and sit-down meals; while *La Pizzeria*, on Peter Street, is very popular with locals (daily 6–11pm except Wed; ☎041/983 4208). The *Westcourt Hotel* on West St (☎041/983 0965) does a good early-bird menu, while the *Buttergate Restaurant* in Millmount Square (Tues, Wed & Sun 12.30–2.30pm, Thurs–Sat 7–11pm; ☎041/983 4759) is a little more expensive, but is worth it for its fine French cuisine. Near the docks are two of the town's trendier hangouts, *Monks Espresso Bar/Café*, and the *Keyside Bar/Café* both of which serve excellent coffee and well-prepared, if overpriced, food. On the outskirts of town, on the Dublin road, is the *Black Bull Inn* which has excellent bar food and a good delicatessen next door, while on the opposite side of town, a short way out on the old Slane Road, is Drogheda's new Italian restaurant, *Borzalino's*, which serves traditional Italian meals.

As far as entertainment goes, check out the **pubs**, many of which are rich in character. *Carbery's* on the North Strand is probably the best-known gathering place on this part of the east coast, especially for the traditional sessions on Tuesday nights (from 9pm) and Sunday lunchtimes (12.30–2.30pm). To get a seat on Sunday make sure you're there by noon. *Clarkes*, on the corner of Fair and Peter streets, is quiet and old-fashioned during the week, popular with the local literary set, but on Saturday nights is a fashionable meeting place. *The Pheasant Pub* on Duleek Street often has traditional music, as does *The Rock* on George's Street. *Peter Matthews* on Lawrence Street (known locally as *McPhail's*) is frequented by a younger crowd and has lots of toffee-brown woodwork, partitions and cubicles, and a back room for music.

Entertainment outside the pubs is limited. Your best bet is to check out what's happening at the Droichead Arts Centre (☎041/983 0188) in Stockwell Lane off West Street, which regularly hosts plays, poetry readings and exhibitions. There's a **cinema** in the Abbey shopping centre; weekend **discos** at *Earth* nightclub in the *Westcourt Hotel*; and a fairly trendy dance venue at No. 4 on the opposite side of the road. *Fusion* nightclub on George Street attracts a young crowd, playing disco to funk while older dancers tend to head to *Lucianos* in the *Boyne Valley Hotel*, and also *The Place* in the *Rosnaree Park*, each a couple of miles out of town.

Beaulieu House

Downstream from the town's docks, the **viaduct** carrying trains on the Dublin–Belfast line spans a 200ft-deep gorge. It's an impressive feat of nineteenth-century engineering by Sir John MacNeill, and you can examine it at close quarters if you feel like extending your visit to *Carbery's* pub (see above) into a stroll a mile or so east along the Baltray Road. Beyond the viaduct and cement works you reach some pleasant woodland. Part of this belongs to **Beaulieu House**, a private domain that claims to have been Ireland's first unfortified mansion, built between 1660 and 1665 after Cromwell's departure, when the land was confiscated from the family of Oliver Plunkett and given to Sir Henry Tichbourne, whose descendants reside there today. The house has a hipped roof in the artisan style and an almost perfectly preserved interior. Most rewarding of all is a fabulous picture gallery, with a collection ranging from contemporary portraits of William and Mary on tall canvases by the court painter Van der Wyck to an intense collection of early twentieth-century Irish art. Unfortunately the house is strictly private, but the owners do open their doors to tours by the Drogheda Historical Society, so it's worth checking at the museum (see p.169) to see if your visit coincides with one of these.

Mellifont and Monasterboice

A few miles north of Drogheda, lie two of the great historical sites which characterize this part of the country: the **monasteries of Mellifont and Monasterboice**. Both are easily reached from Drogheda and can be visited on your way to or from the sites of the lower Boyne Valley.

To get to Mellifont from Drogheda (about five miles), turn off the road to Collon at Monleek Cross; alternatively turn off the Slane–Collon road at the signpost. There is no direct bus service to Mellifont, but Mullens taxis (☎041/983 3377) will take you for £8/€10.16 each way. Monasterboice, six miles from Drogheda, can be reached from the main N1 Dublin–Belfast road, or by continuing up the Drogheda–Collon road and following the signs to the right.

Mellifont Abbey

Mellifont (May to mid-June & mid-Sept to Oct daily 10am–5pm; mid-June to mid-Sept daily 9.30am–6.30pm; £1.50/€1.90; Heritage Card) was, in medieval times, one of the most important monasteries in Ireland, the Motherhouse of the Cistercian Order and a building of exceptional beauty and grandeur. The ruins you see today in no way do justice to this former glory, but they're pretty impressive even so.

At its foundation in 1142 – the inspiration of St Malachy, Archbishop of Armagh, who did much to bring the early Irish Church closer to Rome – Mellifont was the first **Cistercian monastery** in Ireland. Malachy's friend St Bernard, then abbot of the Cistercian monastery at Clairvaux, did much to inspire the work, and sent nine of his own monks to form the basis of the new community. The abbey took fifteen years to build, and you can gauge something of its original size and former glory by imagining the gargantuan pillars that once rose, finishing high among a riotous sprouting of arches and vaulted ceilings, from the broad stumps remaining today. For nearly four hundred years Mellifont flourished, at its peak presiding over as many as 38 other Cistercian monasteries throughout the country, until in 1539 all of them were dissolved by Henry VIII.

One hundred and fifty monks fled from Mellifont, and the buildings were handed over to Edward Moore, ancestor of the Earls of Drogheda, who converted the place into a fortified mansion. In 1603 the last of the great Irish chieftains, **Hugh O'Neill**, was starved into submission here before eventually escaping to the Continent in the Flight of the Earls. Mellifont, meanwhile, went into gradual decline. It was attacked by Cromwellian forces, and then used as William's headquarters during the Battle of the Boyne, before eventually falling so far as to be pressed into service as a pigsty in the nineteenth century.

The ruins

Today the remains rarely rise above shoulder height, with the striking exception of the Romanesque octagonal **lavabo**, built around 1200, whose basins and water jets provided washing facilities for the monks.

The rest of the ruins can be easily identified on the map provided, their ground plan almost perfectly intact. You enter through the **north transept**, which originally had five chapels, three in its eastern and two in its western aisle. Two of the three on the eastern side had apsidal ends, an unusual feature in medieval Ireland, seen here presumably because of the French influence on the builders. The chancel area, or **presbytery**, has the remains of an ornate arch and sedilia where the priests celebrating Mass would sit. The entire **nave** would have been paved in red and blue tiles, some inscribed with the words "Ave Maria" and others decorated with the fleur-de-lis emblem; the **pillars**, too, would originally have been painted in brilliant colours and topped with flowery capitals. At the river end of the nave is a **crypt** – an unusual position which served to level the site on which the church was built. The **chapter house**, beyond the south transept, was once the venue for the daily meetings of the monks. It now houses a collection of medieval **glazed tiles**, moved here from around the site for safety.

Behind the lavabo is the south range, where the **refectory** would have been, and back towards the road you'll find the **gatehouse**, the only surviving part of a high defensive wall that once completely ringed the monastic buildings. Also within the grounds are another ruined church up on the slope (converted to a Protestant one in 1542) and a building that was converted by An Óige into a youth hostel. This is now permanently closed, a shame since the setting is delightful, with the River Mattock gliding through gently wooded country.

Monasterboice

Monasterboice (*Mainistir Buite* or "Buite's monastery") is a tiny enclosure, but it contains two of the finest high crosses (both dating from the tenth century) and one of the best round towers in the country – the site is open to all during daylight hours. As you enter, the squat cross nearer to you is reckoned the finer of the two, and certainly its high-relief carving has worn the centuries better. It is known as **Muiredach's Cross** after the inscription in Irish at the base of the stem – *Or do Muiredach i Chros*, "A prayer for Muiredach by whom this cross was made." The boldly ornate stone picture panels retell biblical stories and were designed to educate and inspire the largely illiterate populace. Some of the subjects are ambiguous and open to a certain amount of conjecture (William Wilde, father of Oscar, argued that many relate as strongly to events associated with Monasterboice as to the Bible), but most have been fairly convincingly identified.

The story begins at the bottom of the **east face** of the cross, nearest the wall, with Eve tempting Adam on the left and Cain slaying Abel on the right. Above this, David and Goliath share a panel with King Saul and David's son Jonathan. The next panel up shows Moses striking the rock with his staff to conjure water while the Israelites wait with parched throats, and above this, the Wise Men bear gifts to the Virgin Mary and baby Jesus. The centrepiece of the wheel is the scene of the **Last Judgement**, with the multitudes risen from the dead begging for entry to Heaven, their hands holding one another in goodwill and the trumpets playing loudly. Below Christ's foot the Archangel Michael is seen driving a staff through Satan's head after weighing the balance of good and evil in one individual's favour. At the very top, St Anthony and St Paul are seen breaking bread.

The **west face** of the cross is largely devoted to the **life of Christ**. At the bottom is his arrest in the Garden of Gethsemane, with Roman soldiers and the treacherous kiss of Judas. This is followed by three figures clutching books – thought to represent the dispelling of the doubts of St Thomas. The third panel shows the Risen Christ returned to meet St Peter and St Paul, their faces bowed in shame at ever having doubted the truth. The hub of the wheel shows the Crucifixion, with soldiers below, angels above and evil humanity to the sides. This is surmounted by Moses descending from Mount Sinai with the Ten Commandments. The flanks of the cross are also decorated. On the **north side** are St Anthony and St Paul again, Christ's scourging at the pillar, and the **Hand of God** (under the arm of the cross) warning mankind. On the **south side** is the Flight of the Israelites from Egypt and also possibly Pontius Pilate washing his hands. All this is capped at the top as if under the roof of the church and surrounded with abstract or uninterpreted embellishment.

The **West Cross**, the taller of the two and near the round tower, is made up of three separate stone sections, all of them much more worn. The **east face** shows David killing the lion, then Abraham ready to sacrifice his son Isaac, with the ram which became the last-minute substitute. Above this is the worship of the golden calf, with Moses coming down from Mount Sinai to catch his people red-handed in idolatry. The panel shows them trembling for forgiveness. The other three panels, before Christ seated in Heaven at the end of the world in the centre of the wheel, are hard to identify, though on the right arm of the wheel you can see the upside-down Satan being speared again by St Michael. The **west face** begins with the **Resurrection**, and the **Baptism of Christ** is shown on the second panel. The four three-figure panels before the wheel are again hard to identify, although the central figure looks a strong candidate for Christ. Again the **Crucifixion** dominates the wheel, with Christ tied to the Cross by rope; the left arm shows him being blindfolded and ridiculed, while the right arm has Judas' kiss of betrayal.

The round tower and two churches

Behind the West Cross stands possibly the tallest **round tower** in Ireland, 110ft tall even without its conical peak. Round towers were adopted between the ninth and eleventh centuries by monks throughout the country as a defence against continued Viking attack. They needed no keystone that enemies could pull out for speedy demolition; their height created a perfect look-out post; and the entrance would be several feet from the ground, allowing a ladder to be drawn in when under attack. The only drawback was that if a lighted arrow were to pierce the inner floorboards the whole column would act as a chimney, guaranteeing a blazing inferno. Sadly, you can't go into the tower, which has been closed for safety reasons.

Finally within the enclosure are two thirteenth-century **churches**, the north and the south church. They probably had no real connection with the monastic settlement, which had almost certainly ceased to function by then, and there's little of great interest within their ruined walls.

North to Dundalk

The main reason to head northwards into County Louth, apart from reaching the border, is to get to the mountains of the **Cooley Peninsula**. You have three routes to choose from: the main Drogheda to Belfast road, the N1, is the fastest, speeding directly towards the border and passing Monasterboice early on, but with little other reason to stop. An alternative inland route is to head towards Collon on the less busy N2 and north to Ardee, the scene of the heroic battle between Cúchulainn and Ferdia, then north to Louth town and St. Mochta's House, and on to **Dundalk** from there. These roads give excellent, unhindered cross-country views of County Louth, especially the drumlins rising inland towards counties Cavan and Monaghan. The final, more scenic option, suitable if you want to dawdle along or if you're cycling, is to take the bay road out of Drogheda and follow the coast north through the villages of **Termonfeckin**, **Clogherhead**, **Anagassan**, joining the main N1 road once again in the attractive village of Castlebellingham.

Termonfeckin

TERMONFECKIN (*Tearmann Feichin* or "St Feichin's sacred land") is a placid country village lying in a wooded dip half a mile from the shore. The village has a small tower house **castle** and a tenth-century **high cross** in the graveyard of St Feckin's Church. The castle (keys from Patrick Duff in the bungalow across the cul-de-sac) dates from the fifteenth and sixteenth centuries and has as its most unusual feature a corbelled roof – notably less well constructed than the four-thousand-year-older one at Newgrange. There have been reports of car theft in the area, so if you're visiting the castle be sure to remove all valuables from your car.

For **accommodation**, try Mrs Kitty McElvoy at *Highfield House* (☎041/982 2172; ③; closed Oct–April), where you can also have a hearty breakfast for £3/€3.81. You can get some of the best **food** in the county at *The Triple House* restaurant (☎041/982 2616) whose Italian/French menu offers five courses for £18.50/€23.49, or four courses for £12.95/€16.44 before 7.30pm.

The coastal road: Termonfeckin to Blackrock

Heading north from Termonfeckin, you pass through the glum beach resort of **CLOGHERHEAD**, from where the road takes you north to **PORT ORIEL**, a tiny fishing harbour tucked hard into the coast's rockface that enjoys good mackerel fishing off the pier in summer. It's only a little way beyond here, as you approach the village of **ANAGASSAN** (*Áth na gCasán* "Ford of the Paths") that the signposts designating the "scenic route" (the coastal road) begin to earn their keep, with the mountains of Cooley and Mourne, one range south of the border, the other north, spectacularly silhouetted against the sky. *The Glyde Inn* in Annagassan has food (of sorts) and is a nice reclusive spot to take time out for "a small drop of medicine". There's little else to see around the village, although local archeological explorations have provoked controversy by claiming to have revealed the first permanent Norse settlement in Ireland, predating even Dublin. Continuing northwards across the hump-back stone bridge, you've a watercolourist's idyll of rowing boats laid out along the bulging ramparts of the canalized river as it meets the sea.

Inland from these villages, just off the M1 motorway on the N1 road, lies the village of **DUNLEER**, formerly a traditional stop on the Belfast to Dublin route. The town has little to offer in terms of tourist attractions, except for **White River Mill**, a traditional water mill, where wheat has been ground for at least three hundred years (enquire at the house beside the mill to view). B&B **accommodation** is available at the red-bricked *Bramble Lodge* (☎041/685 1565, *mcondra@esatclear.ie*; ③). For **food** you could follow the locals to the *Grove* restaurant where you can get a substantial meal for less than a fiver.

Travel a further five miles north on the N1 and you will arrive at **CASTLEBELLINGHAM**. Despite the main Dublin–Belfast road blundering right through the middle, Castlebellingham remains a pretty village. You can take refuge from the traffic down by the **mill**, now converted into a restaurant, where there's a turning gable-end water wheel powered by the River Glyde. Further upstream stands the *Bellingham Castle*, a sugary, castellated hotel, that serves good two-course bar lunches and is also the only place to stay in Castlebellingham (☎042/937 2176; ⑤). Moving northwards again, the next significant turning off the N1 (right) takes you to Blackrock and later allows you to bypass most of Dundalk. Blackrock itself (the *Claremount Arms* can have good Saturday-night traditional music sessions) is an overstretched ribbon of Victorian seaside villas along a mudflat beach. It does, though, offer a handsomely crystalline view across **Dundalk Bay** and on to the Cooley Peninsula, by now looming very close.

Ardee to Dundalk

The inland route that follows the N2 from Collon to Ardee is far less travelled, and there's less to see along it. Without transport of your own you'll have difficulty getting along here, unless you're prepared for some very leisurely hitching. Nonetheless, it has its rewards, mostly in this lack of traffic or population; a rural tranquillity unrivalled even on the west coast.

Almost exactly halfway between Drogheda and Dundalk, **ARDEE** (*Baile Átha Fhirdia* or "Ferdia's Ford") recalls the tragic legendary duel between Cúchulainn the defender of Ulster and his foster brother Ferdia, a battle brought about through the trickery of Medb, Queen of Connaught. Ardee is named after the ford where this great battle was fought and there is a fine bronze statue depicting this battle at the beginning of the town's pleasant riverside walk.

Today, Ardee reeks far more strongly of the Plantation era, with fortified buildings along the main street and a memorial **statue** to a landlord erected by his thankful tenants in 1861. The thirteenth-century **castle** on the main street, currently being turned into a museum, was built here mainly because the town was at the northern edge of the Pale, and from here the Anglo-Irish made forays into Ulster, or were themselves periodically forced onto the defensive.

For a quick sandwich or coffee Caffrey's bakery is the best bet, while *Gables Restaurant* (☎041/685 3789) does an immensely filling set dinner for around £20/€25.40. For **B&B** accommodation try Magennis' *Carraig Mór*, one mile south of Ardee on the N2 road, a comfortable, family-run house (☎041/685 3513; ③), but if you want something a little special then head to Linda Connolly's *Red House* (☎041/685 3523; ⑥), a country house with indoor swimming pool, sauna and tennis courts.

An interesting short diversion from Ardee takes you to the so-called **Jumping Church** at Kildemock. To get there head east from the junction at the southern end of Ardee's main street and turn right after about a quarter of a mile – the small, ruined church lies a mile further down this road. It gets its name from its end wall having shifted three feet from its foundations, which, according to local lore, it did to exclude the grave of an excommunicated person. Less romantic accounts tell of a severe storm taking place in 1715 at around the time the wall jumped, but either way it's a remarkable sight, with the wall shorn clear of its foundations yet still standing (albeit at a 35-degree angle). In the graveyard are simple, foot-high stone markers, some of the earliest graveslabs for the poor.

Ardee is a major road junction, and moving on you could head northeast to Dundalk, northwest to Carrickmacross or west to Kells. If you want to go on heading north, however, a more interesting route is along the minor roads to **LOUTH VILLAGE**: keep on the left fork at the northern end of Ardee and take an immediate right towards Tallanstown, where you'll need to turn right again for Louth. The village isn't much in itself (and certainly doesn't seem to deserve sharing a name with the county), but it does have one thing well worth seeing in **St Mochta's Church** – turn left towards Carrickmacross and immediately right onto the Inniskeen Road. According to legend the church was built in a night to give shelter to its founder, **St Mochta**, who died in 534. Originally part of a monastery, and dating probably from the late twelfth century, it has a high, vaulted roof – beautifully crafted – and reached by a constricted stairway. In its early years the church was plundered many times; these days they obviously feel safer, since the church is left open to any passing visitor. The fourteenth-century **Louth Abbey** is accessible through the graveyard back up the road, from where, if you look west, you'll notice a motte on the nearby hill.

Dundalk

Although **DUNDALK** has a reputation as a tough border town, home to uncompromising Republicanism, it still has enough interest to justify a visit. Starting life in legendary prehistory as a fort guarding a gap in the mountains to the north (*Dún Dealga,* the "Fortress of Dealga"), it became in turn a Celtic, Norse, Anglo-Norman, Jacobean and finally Williamite stronghold. This hard tradition seems still to hang over the town, and it never seems a place where you – or for that matter the locals – can feel fully at ease (having said that, the town has some excellent pubs; see below).

As far as sights go, the outstanding one is the nineteenth-century Neoclassical **courthouse**, whose open Doric portico leads in to an airy, classically proportioned interior. In the plaza outside, the Guardian Angel or motherland statue is unequivocally dedicated to "the martyrs in the cause of liberty who fought and died in the struggle against English Tyranny and foreign rule in Ireland" – a far cry from the monument of gratitude in Ardee. **St Patrick's Cathedral** in Francis Street is also worth a look while you're here: its cornucopia of embellished towers, turrets and crenellated walls is a reasonably successful imitation of King's College Chapel, Cambridge. Inside are some rich mosaics using gold pieces in abundance to depict biblical stories.

Louth County Museum (Tues–Sat 10.30am–5.30pm, Sun 2–6 pm; £2/€2.54), in a warehouse on Jocelyn Street (beside the tourist office), uses a variety of artefacts and documents to tell the stories of local industries, from coopering to cigarettes. The museum is an uneasy mix of high-tech display and poorly labelled exhibits, but there is a wealth of material here. During the 1960s, Henkel bomber cockpits were sent over to Dundalk to be made into bubble cars – you'll find a 1966 model on the first-floor landing. The top two floors have recently been set aside to house a new exhibition that focuses on the area's rich Stone Age history.

Should you wish to see, a well-designed and well-maintained Irish Modernist building, head for the 1970 **Carrolls tobacco factory**, designed by Scott Tallon Walker. A mile south of Dundalk on the Dublin road (N1), it is fronted by a striking sculpture by Gerda Froemmel reflected in an artificial lake, and contains an impressive collection of **modern Irish art**.

Practicalities

The regional **tourist office**, which also hosts touring art exhibitions, occupies a restored tobacco warehouse on Jocelyn St (July & Aug Mon–Sat 9.30am–1pm & 2–5.30pm; Sept–June Mon–Fri 9.30am–1pm & 2–5.30pm; ☎042/933 5484). The Council Arts Office in the Market Square (Mon–Fri 9am–5pm; ☎042/933 2276) provides up-to-the-minute details of music and theatre. **Bikes** can be rented at the Cycle Centre, opposite the shopping complex.

A small number of **places to stay** are available both in and around town. Among the best of the town's numerous B&Bs are *Glenn Gat House* (☎042/932 8266; ③) at the top of Stapleton Place, off the Dublin road, and *Pinewoods* (☎042/932 1295, *olmurphy@eircom.net*; ③) a few miles out of town on the main Dublin road. While the central *Imperial Hotel* (☎042/933 2241, *info@imperialhoteldundalk.com*; ⑤) is not as bad as its drab facade would suggest, it is advisable to head out of town to the modern *Fairways Hotel*

(☎042/932 1500, *www.fairways.ie*; ⑥), or the excellent *Ballymascanlon Hotel* (☎042/937 1124, *www.globalgolf.com/ballymascanlon*; ⑥) on the fringes of the Cooley peninsula. **Eating** well and cheaply is not a Dundalk speciality, but there are plenty of fast-food places around the centre of town; try *Connolly's* on the ground floor of the shopping centre. Better fare can be had at *McKeowns Pub* and *Quaglino's* (☎042/933 8567), both on Clanbrassil St, or at *La Cantina* (☎042/932 7970) off Park St (evenings only). **Pubs** that are well worth visiting include *Toal's* on Crowe St, a sawdust-on-flagstone hide-out and a venue where you can sometimes catch traditional music. *McManus's* pub near the library in Seatown is self-described as "simply a great pub" – there are old-fashioned snugs to drink in, excellent-value soup and sandwiches, guitar folk music on a Sunday night and more bluesy stuff on Monday. *McArdles* on Anne St hosts *Ceolteóirí* every Thursday night. *Café Metz* on Francis St is the new fashionable place in town, while there are a couple of more old-style pubs on Park St: *Mr Ridley's*, *Tara* and *McDaids*.

Faughart

From Dundalk, the border lies just eight miles on up the N1. Opposite the turning for the Cooley Peninsula, a couple of miles outside Dundalk, is a lesser road that leads a short distance inland to **FAUGHART**. A small place of little modern interest, Faughart nevertheless has several older associations worth mentioning.

Cúchulainn was born at Castletown Hill on the edge of the plain of Muirthemne, which stretches away towards Armagh in the north, and in the legendary account he was sent a false offer of peace by Medb asking him to meet her at Faughart. Instead, fourteen of Medb's most skilful followers awaited him: fourteen javelins were hurled at him simultaneously but Cúchulainn guarded himself so that his skin, and even his armour, was untouched. Then he turned on them and killed every one of the "Fourteen at Focherd".

Faughart is also said to be the birthplace of **St Brigid**, patron of Ireland, whose four-armed rush-cross is often to be found on the walls of rural Irish households. In the local churchyard you can see her holy well and pillar-stone, as well as the grave of **Edward Bruce**, who was defeated here in 1318 after being sent to Ireland by his brother (Robert the Bruce) to divert the English away from the Anglo-Scottish border. There is a stone nearby which in legend was used for his decapitation.

The Cooley peninsula

You come to **Cooley**, east of Dundalk, for the raw beauty of its mountains, to walk and to experience a life where the twenty-first century intrudes only rarely. Indeed when you get up among the bare hilltops the peninsula's links with legend seem at least as strong as its grip on modern reality. For above all this is country associated with the **Táin Bó Cúailnge** ("Cattle Raid of Cooley"), and in the mountains many of the episodes of the great epic were played out. Its plot (set around the first century AD) concerns the Brown Bull of Cooley (*Donn Cúailnge*) which is coveted by Medb, Queen of Connaught, in her envy of her husband Ailill's White Bull (*Finnbenach*). In their efforts to capture the bull, Medb and Ailill, who come from the west, effectively declare war on the east in general, and Ulster in particular. All the men of Ulster – save one, Cúchulainn – are struck by a curse which immobilizes them through most of the tale, leaving our hero to face the might of Medb's troops alone. The action consists largely of his (often gory) feats, but the text is also rich in topography and placenames, many of them still clearly identifiable.

A single road runs around the peninsula, leaving the N1 to trace the southern slopes of the Cooley Mountains and then cutting across country to Greenore, **Carlingford** and **Omeath** on the north shore. It is here, facing the mountains of Mourne across **Carlingford Lough**, that the most beautiful scenes lie, with forested slopes plunging steeply towards the lough. The southern slopes are gentler and lazier, making a far more sedate progress to the water's edge. The exact location of the border, visible on the map as a dotted line bisecting the lough, has been in dispute since 1922. Once, it was continually patrolled by British army helicopters; now, there is little evidence of army presence.

Before you reach any of this, however, only about a mile down the peninsula road, there's a short and rewarding detour. From the back of the *Ballymascanlon Hotel*, a footpath leads to the **Proleek Dolmen** (from *Proilig*, meaning "Obscure") whose massive capstone balances with far more elegance than its 46 tons ought to allow; to reach the Dolmen take the path that runs from the hotel car park through the courtyard of whitewashed cottages along the fringes of the hotel's new golf course. On the path just before the dolmen, a Bronze Age wedge-shaped **gallery grave** can be seen, though be aware when visiting it of stray balls from the golf tee behind.

Omeath

Aside from being the more scenic, the peninsula's north shore is also the best place to base yourself for **hill-walking** and the easiest for finding food and a bed. Here, at **OMEATH**, the lough has narrowed dramatically, so that the sedate towns of Warrenpoint and Rostrevor on the Mourne Mountain slopes across the border seem only a handshake away. In summer there's a handy passenger **ferry service**, which also takes bikes, between Omeath and Warrenpoint (July & Aug daily till about 6pm, tides permitting; 5min; £2.50/€3.17 return). Staying in the Republic, you can rent **jaunting cars** for short trips out of town; they run mostly to the open-air **stations of the cross** at the Rosminian Fathers' School down the road. As a village, Omeath, with its widely scattered dwellings, is far from typical of the east coast – it was until recent years the last remaining *Gaeltacht* village of any significance in this part of the country.

You can **stay** cheaply at *Delamore House B&B* (☎042/937 5101; ③), or in slightly more comfort at *Omeath Park* (☎042/937 5116; ④), half a mile out on the other side of town at the end of a long driveway up the hillside. Around the crossroads that mark the centre of town are grouped a few grocery stores.

Carlingford

CARLINGFORD, a former fishing village five miles or so down the lough from Omeath, makes a considerable contrast to its neighbour, both for its neatly ordered network of narrow, whitewashed, terraced streets, often with naive murals, at the foot of the Sliabh Foye Mountain, and in its development as an upmarket resort. Although the development may take a trained eye to detect – it's discernible perhaps mainly as a sprinkling of craft shops – the place retains real charm as well as some excellent places to eat and drink.

Carlingford is also an historic place. St Patrick is said to have landed here briefly on his way to introduce Christianity to Ireland (he finally ended his journey further north, in County Down), and the settlement is ancient enough to have been raided by the Vikings. But the oldest visible remain is the D-shaped ruin of **King John's Castle**, down by the main road on the water's edge. King John is said to have visited in 1210, and the Anglo-Norman castle, guarding the entrance to the lough, may be even older than that. It has its counterpart across the water at Greencastle. The village in general retains a distinctly medieval feel, and there are a couple of solid fifteenth-century buildings: the **Mint**, in a narrow street off the square, is a fortified town house with an impressive gate tower; **Taafe's Castle**, which stood on the shore when it was built but

LEGENDARY WALKS

You can walk almost anywhere in the mountains behind Carlingford and Omeath, and once you're up there the heather-tuffeted ground on top offers some of the most beautiful hill-walking imaginable, the setting for many episodes from the *Táin Bó Cúailnge*. It's at its best in the afternoon, with the light bringing out the colours of the Mourne Mountains across the water – in the morning the sun tends to get in your eyes. The road up behind the former youth hostel, a mile or so south of Omeath, a few yards off the main road behind the *Ranch Pub and Restaurant*, offers the best approach, switchbacking its way into the hills with the climb ever increasing the drama of the fjord below. At about 1200ft there's a car park where a map table marks out the major sights, and there's a long spiel on the formation of the lough: a valley gouged out by a glacier which was flooded at the end of the last Ice Age.

With a little imagination, it's not hard to translate the gaps, boulders and fording points of rivers up here into the scenes of Cúchulainn's epic battles. And some of the places are clearly identified. From **Trumpet Hill** (*Ochaine*) he slew a hundred men of Medb's army with his sling on three successive nights as they rested in a plain to the west. This forced Ailill, fearing that his entire force would be destroyed, to offer up champions in single combat. Between Ochaine and the sea Cúchulainn slew the first of these warriors, **Nadcranntail**, by letting his spear fly high into the air so that it dropped down onto Nadcranntail's skull and pinned him to the ground. Then he sprang onto the rim of Nadcranntail's shield and struck his head off and then struck again through the neck right down to the navel so that he fell in four sections to the ground.

From **Slievenaglogh** (*Sliab Cuinciu*) Cúchulainn swore to hurl a sling stone at Medb's head – no easy task as she never moved without her army in front holding a barrel-shaped shelter of shields over their heads. Then one of Medb's bondmaids, Lochu, went to fetch water and, thinking it was Medb herself, he loosed two stones, killing her on the plain in the place known as *Réid Locha*, Lochu's level ground. In fact, when he had the chance, Cúchulainn couldn't bring himself to kill Medb. During the final battle an earthy episode is inserted in which Medb suddenly gets a gush of blood that makes her need to urinate. Fergus, her chief warrior and lover, is furious at her bad timing and takes his place in the army of shields raised to protect her while she relieves herself, creating three great channels known as *Fual Medba*, Medb's foul place. Finding her in this delicate position, Cúchulainn was too honourable to kill her from behind (though he seems happy enough to kill everyone else whenever and wherever he can).

Fual Medba is not clearly identified, but you can find the scene of an earlier episode, the **Black Cauldron** (*Dubchoire*), where Medb divides her armies to search for the white bull, which has last been seen here: it's a recess north of the Glenngat Valley (the valley above Ballymackellet). When the spoils are brought back and the cattle have to be driven over the mountain at the source of the Big River (the *River Cronn*), Fergus decides that they will have to cut a gap in the hills to get the cattle. This is the *Bernas Bo Ulad*, today known as **Windy Gap**. It's also the point in the story where Fergus and Medb hang back behind the army to make love, and where Ailill, aware of their tryst, sent a spy to take Fergus's sword, thus acquiring proof of his unguarded weakness and providing the basis of a phallic joke which recurs throughout the story.

Windy Gap is also the setting of a far later tale, the tragic legend behind the **Long Woman's Grave**, marked by a pile of stones at the roadside. The story concerns two sons at their father's deathbed: the elder promised to give his younger brother a fair share of the estate, saying he would take him up to a high place in the mountains and give him all he could see. He kept his word, but the place where they stood was Windy Gap, where if you look around you see nothing but the immediate hills rising on all sides. The younger son instead became a trader, and on one trip wooed a Spanish beauty to whom he gave the same promise, tempting her hand in marriage. When he brought her home and took her up to the Windy Gap to show her his estate she dropped dead on the spot from shock. Thus the Long Woman's Grave for the tall Spanish beauty is explained.

is now some way from it, is impressively crenellated and fortified but sadly not open to the public. The best and safest **beaches** in the area are at Gyles Quay and Shelling Hill.

Practicalities

Carlingford has a small **tourist office** (Mon–Fri 10am–7pm; ☎042/937 3888) behind *O'Hare's* pub. To find it, turn left at the castle as you enter the village from Dundalk. If you want to **stay**, try the *Viewpoint* B&B on Omeath Rd, whose modern, motel-like flatlets enjoy good views from a little way up the hill (☎042/937 3149; ③). *Mourne View* (☎042/937 3551; ③) is a friendly place right at the foot of the mountains, signposted from the main Dundalk road. For views alone, *Barnave B&B* (☎042/937 3742; ③) on the shores of the lough, is difficult to fault. *McKevitt's Village*, Market Square (☎042/937 3116; ⑤) provides a little more luxury, while *Jordan's* on Newry St (☎042/937 3223; ⑥) is a real treat. The IHH-run *Carlingford Holiday Hostel*, Tholsel St (☎042/937 3100; closed Dec–Jan) caters for the cheaper end of the market, but, as this is part of the **Carlingford Adventure Centre**, you may have to book early as it is often group-booked.

Jordan's pub-cum-bistro is easily the best of the places to **eat and drink** in Carlingford. The menu includes some perhaps over-sophisticated variations (mango sauce) on excellent local ingredients, but the food, especially the fish, is good and excellent value; you'll need to book, weekends especially (daily: summer 12.30–2.30pm & 6–10pm; winter 12.30–2.30pm & 7–9.30pm; ☎042/937 3223). There's a small room at the back of the pub which sometimes acts as a pre-dinner theatre. *O'Hare's* (aka *PJ's*), on the corner near the Mint, is an old grocery store and bar and the most entertaining place to drink – its publican has a considerable local reputation as a raconteur of tall tales; they also serve pub grub and oysters in season, which here seems to mean most of the year round. Nearby is the blue- and yellow-fronted *Oystercatcher Bistro* (☎042/9373922), which serves delicious seafood. *Ghan House*, a fine Georgian mansion down near the crab-clawed pier, is yet another place where you can get a meal and a drop to drink.

COUNTY MEATH

The sweeping, green pastures of **County Meath** illustrate that this is one of Ireland's richest areas of farmland. Bisected by the **River Boyne**, the county consists to the south of a fertile plain bordered by the Royal Canal and the Bog of Allen, and to the north, the drumlins and lakes of Cavan and Monaghan. The large, prosperous farms and solid houses which pepper the countryside are from the era when Meath was, from the twelfth century, one of the most settled areas of Ireland. The most important legacy of this period are its castles, most especially the imposing Anglo-Norman edifice, **Trim Castle**, whose impenetrable walls were used in the film *Braveheart*. Most of Meath's other major sites are found in the **Boyne Valley**, and, while the river's name is synonomous with the eponymous battle fought on its northern banks in the seventeenth century, it's the architectural heritage of a period four and a half thousand years earlier that first occupies your attention. Found in the bend in the river between the towns of Drogheda and Slane, is the area known as the **Brú na Bóinne** complex, where some of Europe's finest prehistoric remains can be found. The whole Boyne Valley, in fact, has been populated from earliest times, evidence of which can be found in the megalithic monuments of **Sliabh na Caillighe** in the north to the **Hill of Tara** in the centre, the traditional seat of the Celtic High Kings.

Before exploring the sites along the northern shore of the Boyne – and especially as there is no river crossing between Drogheda and Slane – you might want to take in **Donore** and **Duleek** south of the river, easily reached from Drogheda (or if you're heading up the N2 from Dublin).

THE BATTLE OF THE BOYNE

For all the significance attached to it now (including big Protestant celebrations in the North on July 12), the **Battle of the Boyne** was just one skirmish – and arguably not the decisive one – in the "War of the Kings" between James II of Ireland and William of Orange, King of England. It took place at Oldgrange, west of the River Boyne in County Meath, on July 1, 1690 (the change of date came with the switch to the Gregorian calendar in the eighteenth century). The deposed James II, retreating southwards, took up defensive positions on the south bank of the river, with some 25,000 men (including 7000 well-equipped French troops, but largely Irish irregulars) holding the last major line of defence on the road to Dublin. William's forces – around 36,000 – occupied a rise on the north bank from where they forced a crossing of the river and put their enemies to flight. In terms of losses, the battle was a minor one – some 1500 Jacobites and 500 of William's men – and James's forces were to regroup and fight on for another year. But in political terms it was highly significant and can legitimately be seen as a turning point. In the complexities of European struggle, the Protestant William was supported by the pope and the Catholic king of Spain, both fearful of the burgeoning power of James's ally, the French King Louis XIV. Although the victory on the battlefield was small, the news gave heart to William's supporters in Europe while making Louis fearful of extending further aid to the Jacobite cause. At the same time, it gave William a breathing space to establish his control back home: in the long run, Protestant ascendancy was assured.

The location of the **battlefield** is directly opposite the turn-off from the N51 to Tullyallen, a couple of miles out of Drogheda. Here a stepped path leads to a viewing point on the site occupied by William's troops before the battle. It's only a slight elevation, but it nevertheless commands a broad swathe of the valley and it's not too hard to conjure up a picture of the armies battling it out in front of you. A panoramic plan marks out the various positions of the opposing forces.

Donore and Duleek

A couple of miles southwest of Drogheda, **DONORE**'s chief interest, apart from having been King James's base at the time of the Battle of the Boyne, lies in its **ten-pound castle**. In 1429 Henry VI promised a grant of £10 to every one of his subjects who, in the next ten years, built a castle 20ft long, 16ft wide and 40ft high within the counties of Meath, Louth, Kildare and Dublin – the area known as the Pale (the tract of land around Dublin under English control). The three-storey castle here is built almost exactly to these measurements, though unfortunately it seems to be permanently locked up.

DULEEK (*An Damh Liag*, "The Stone Church"), a few miles further south, on the River Nanny, is an historic little place of considerably more interest. The south-of-the-Boyne equivalent of Kells, it was founded by St Patrick who settled St Ciaran here to build the first stone church in Ireland and found a monastic settlement; it was also an early bishopric. Much later, the Jacobite forces withdrew to Duleek after the Battle of the Boyne and spent the night here, while James himself fled to Dublin and then on to France. The ruined **St Mary's Priory** you see today was probably founded in the twelfth century, and was abandoned after Henry VIII's dissolution of the monasteries: there are some fine tombs in the roofless building, and nearby a squat, tenth-century **high cross**. In the town square is a **wayside cross** of a different nature, erected by Genet de Bathe in 1601 as a memorial to William, one of her husbands, and one of the finest examples of a type of cross that crops up all over the place.

Good, reasonably priced B&B **accommodation** and home-produced food are available at the historic house of Annesbrook, a short, well-signposted distance out of town (closed Oct–April; ☎041/982 3293, *hugh.mce@oceanfree.net*; ④). William Thackeray in his *Irish Sketchbook* (1842) wrote uninspiringly about Annesbrook, but its most striking asset, the Ionic pedimented portico, has an interesting tale attached. The stately entrance is said to have been hastily affixed onto the box-shaped house when its owner was told to expect a visit from George IV, the first king to arrive from England after the departure of William and James. The portico was felt a necessary addition to bring the house up to the standards expected by royalty. The north wing, housing a Gothic dining room, was also built in the king's honour, but he preferred to dine in the garden.

Brú na Bóinne

The area known as **Brú na Bóinne** comprises a landscape made up of a group of forty or so related prehistoric monuments caught in a curve of the river five miles west of Dundalk between the villages of Tullyallen and Slane. The three most important of them, Dowth, Knowth and Newgrange, are what are known as **passage graves** – high round mounds raised over stone burial chambers. They predate the pyramids by several centuries, and although there's no comparison in terms of size or architecture, there are certain parallels. Just as the fertility of the Nile floodplain helped create the great Egyptian culture, so the lands of the River Boyne and its watershed have been proved to have had some of the richest soil in Europe (and considerably higher temperatures than today) around 3000 BC. On the banks flourished what seems to have been the most advanced Neolithic civilization in Europe. Physically, the tombs' size and solidity are what impress most; beyond the massive, bare stones there's not much to be seen, but there's plenty of scope to try and disentangle the various theories about these structures, to work out who built them, where they came from and where they went.

Access to the site is via **Brú na Bóinne Visitors' Centre** on the southern side of the river. It's signposted from Slane town centre and is on a minor road off the N2. From the **visitors' centre** (daily: March, April & Oct 9.30am–5.30pm; June to mid-Sept 9am–7pm; May & mid- to end Sept 9am–6.30pm; Nov–Feb 9.30am–5pm; ☎041/982 4488) – a well-organized place that provides background information on the construction, artwork and religious significance of the tombs and also contains a reconstruction of a passage grave – tour buses run to Newgrange and Knowth. The third site, Dowth, remains closed to the public while lengthy excavations are carried out. A ticket which includes entrance to the visitors' centre and a shuttle bus to Newgrange costs £5/€6.35 while the same for Knowth is £4/€5.08 (both include a guided tour). Tickets for both Newgrange and Knowth cost £7/€8.68.

It would be an understatement to say that the visitors' centre is controversial and there has been much argument about how best to preserve the tombs. One of the main arguments for building the centre was that, with the increase in numbers visiting the site, a scheme had to be devised to protect it from destruction; however, since its opening and the intense marketing of Brú na Bóinne the amount of visitors has increased enormously, though the number of people allowed to visit the Newgrange tomb is limited to six hundred per day. Consequently, long delays for the Newgrange tour are common, especially in high season, a problem further compounded by the fact that you can't book a tour in advance of your arrival. While the sites themselves, especially Newgrange, are extremely impressive, the overcrowding and slight theme-park approach tends to detract somewhat from a true appreciation of their significance. The best advice is to come as early in the day as possible, book a place on one of the later tours and, if you have transport, spend the intervening time exploring the surrounding area. If you want to visit a comparable yet unexploited site head north to the Sliabh na Caillighe complex (see p.192).

Newgrange

The **Newgrange tumulus** has an average diameter of around 338ft and is some 30ft high at its centre point. It has been so completely restored that at first sight it resembles a grounded, 1950s sci-fi flying saucer. But once you get over the initial shock, the sparklingly new appearance of it all serves only to heighten the wonder. The quartzite retaining wall is glisteningly white and gives some hint (not revealed at other sites where everything is grey and moss-covered) of the power this particular stone must have had for the builders. The nearest natural source is in the Wicklow Mountains, south of Dublin. You'll notice that the wall is bossed with small, round granite stones, the purpose of which no one knows. Speculation is not helped by the fact that they are probably not in their original positions: during the most extensive of the renovations (1962–75) the original photographs were lost and their placement was therefore a matter of educated guess. Other non-original features worth noting are: the front and most ornate kerbstone was originally placed by the entrance tunnel (it was moved to prevent damage by visitors); the entrance tunnel itself was closed by a standing slab; and the concave wall at the entrance is designed to accommodate some 100,000-odd tourists each year – originally the wall would have continued directly up to the sides of the spirally decorated kerbstone. It is also believed that an obelisk once stood at the top of the mound, to mark it out from afar.

NEWGRANGE – MYTH AND SUPPOSITION

The name Newgrange derives from "new granary", simply because that was its function at one stage in its history. This hardly seems an adequate description for one of the most important Stone Age sites in Europe, however, and an alternative derivation, "the Cave of Gráinne", is considerably more satisfying, if less accurate. The site has many associations with **myth**. First among these concern the **Tuatha Dé Danann**, the first Irish gods who descended from the sky and inhabited the land before the Celts. Dagda (chief of the gods) gained possession of the mound by making love to Boand (the white cow goddess who later deliberately drowned herself at the source of the Boyne so as to invest the river with her divinity), first tricking her husband Elcmar by sending him on an errand for a day which took him nine months. From their union **Oengus** was born and called *ac ind Oc* (The Youthful Son). In ancient literature Newgrange is *Brugh Mac ind Oc*, the Brugh of Oengus. Oengus also appears later in the **Fenian Cycle** as the succourer of Diarmuid and Gráinne, carrying the fatally wounded body of Diarmuid to Newgrange "to put aerial life into him so that he will talk to me every day". Other legends make the local mounds the tombs of the Kings of Tara although radio-carbon dating, pinpointing the third millennium BC, disproves this fairly convincingly.

What does emerge is just how little concrete information there is on the people who created Newgrange. Perhaps the most tempting of the more off-beat **theories** regarding the meaning of the monuments is that of the American Martin Brennan in his book *Stars and Stones* (1983). He claims that the scrollwork, lozenges and lines on the stones, which most archeologists see as abstract decoration, perhaps with religious significance, are in fact all part of a single incredibly involved **astronomical chart** which includes not only Newgrange itself, but the rest of the Brú na Bóinne complex and even sites as far-flung as Loughcrew and those in the Curlew Mountains in south County Sligo. In his book he claims that the scrollwork all relates to a calibration system based on the diameter of the earth. Brennan insists that the Newgrange monument is not only the largest but also the oldest such system in the world: predating and far outranking in sophistication the instruments of the Greek astronomers. It is not a theory you are likely to find espoused by your guide, but it does have its convincing aspects. In the end, though, you have to ask why, if they were so sophisticated, is this the only evidence that survives?

The outer ring of **standing stones**, of which only twelve uprights now remain, was a feature unique among passage grave tombs, and it may have been the addition of a later civilization. None of the standing stones is decorated, and many show signs of being eroded by water, which suggests that they may have been hauled up here from the river. There is an inner ring of 97 **kerbstones** all placed on their sides and touching each other, engineered one supposes as a support for the layers of sod, loose stones, shale and boulder clay (20,000 tons of it) that were laid over the chambers.

Perhaps the most important feature of Newgrange – again unique – is the **roof-box** several feet in from the tunnel mouth. This contains a slit through which, at the **winter solstice**, the light of the rising sun begins to penetrate as soon as its full disc appears above the horizon. The rays edge their way slowly up the passage tunnel and, narrowed into a single shaft, eventually find the back of the cruciform chamber. In minutes the chamber becomes radiant with a glow of orange light which fades as suddenly as it has blazed. The sun actually rises at about 8.20am above a hill known as the Red Mountain: it reaches the chamber a couple of minutes before 9am, and fifteen minutes later the whole thing is over. The guided tour includes a "re-creation" of the phenomenon which involves a flash of orange electric light.

The entry passage, about three feet wide, leads into the **central chamber** where the finest of the work is to be found. Its corbelled roof creates a space some 20ft high, and on the stones everywhere are carved superbly intricate decorations, apparently abstract but perhaps with some more precise meaning (see the box opposite). On the way out, beware the last roof-slab – on which most tall people will graze their heads.

Knowth

Visited as part of the same tour as Newgrange from the Brú na Bóinne visitor centre (see p.183), **Knowth** is the lesser known, though historically the most important of the complex. Major excavations have been going on at the Knowth site since 1962 and the discoveries here have already surpassed what was excavated at Newgrange, because unlike Newgrange, the site was continuously inhabited until the fourteenth century, and archeologists have been able to explore four distinct phases of settlement. Because of the excavation work it is only possible to visit the exterior of the site.

Several periods of occupation by different cultures have been identified: the original **Neolithic** one (3000–2000 BC); the **Beaker people** (2000–1800 BC), so called because of a distinctive beaker left with each of their dead; a **Celtic** settlement in the early centuries AD; early **Christian** occupation (eighth to twelfth centuries); and finally **Norman** usage (twelfth and thirteenth centuries) that brought an extensive settlement and a glut of souterrains (underground passages and chambers), some bored into the Neolithic mound itself. The main passage tomb is about twice the size of that at Newgrange – with a tunnel over 100ft long leading to the central chamber – and even more richly decorated. At Knowth there is also, so far uniquely, a second, smaller passage tomb within the main tumulus, and up to seventeen **satellite tumuli**. Both main tombs are aligned east–west. In construction the mound is basically the same as Newgrange, with a cruciform chamber, high corbelled roof and richly decorated stones, but here there is also evidence of settlement around the mound. Probably the two were created by two distinct communities of the same culture: a supposition backed by carbon dating that places the Knowth mound some five hundred years earlier than Newgrange. At Knowth alone, about two hundred and fifty decorated stones have been found: over half of all known Irish passage grave art. The most recent discovery is a series of large post-holes arranged in a circle, suggesting the existence of some form of wood-henge.

Dowth

The **Dowth mound** – roughly 50ft high and 200ft in diameter – is closed for conservation work at the time of writing, but you can wander about and see the outside. It's reached by taking the first left off the N51 after the battlesite, a minor road which trails the north bank of the river. Just before you reach the cairn you'll see the tower of **Dowth Castle** on the left, adjoining a rambling red-brick Victorian mansion. John Boyle O'Reilly, a Fenian patriot transported to Australia, who later became editor and part-owner of the *Boston Pilot*, was born in the castle in 1844. At the back of the neighbouring ruined church there's a monument to him that forms the heart of a small **commemorative festival** every year on the Sunday closest to August 10.

When you get to the site, the signs of earlier excavations and of pillaging (in the nineteenth century some of the stones were removed for road-making) are immediately apparent, having left a crater in the top of the mound and a large chunk burrowed out of the side. Around one hundred **kerbstones**, perhaps half of which can be seen today, originally marked the edge of the tumulus. Inside are two **passage tombs** and an early Christian chamber. The passages are similar in construction to those at Newgrange, as is the decoration of the standing stones which form the walls of the passage, and the ten-foot-high corbelled roof. One distinction between the two sites, however, are the **sill stones** placed across the passage floor and at the entrance to the chamber.

The name Dowth derives from the Irish for "darkness", and the main chamber faces west to the setting sun (the minor chamber looks southwest, directly towards Newgrange). In myth, the site was built when the Druid Bresal, attempting to build a tower that would reach heaven, contracted all the men of Erin for a single day. His sister worked a spell so that the sun would not set until the mound was built, but the two then committed incest, destroying the magic and causing the sun to set: thereafter the sister declared "Dubad (darkness) shall be the name of that place forever". Today, as the sun sets at the winter solstice, its rays enter the tomb (at about 3pm), lighting up the tall stone slab at the back and then moving across to illuminate a recess in which is a decorated stone precisely angled to catch this moment, before finally sinking below the horizon (see p.185).

Close to the site, with its fine views over the Boyne Valley, is the *Glebe House* which offers **B&B** (☎041/983 6101; ③), as well as afternoon tea.

Slane and around

SLANE village, set on a steep hillside running down to the Boyne a mile or so west of Knowth, is an enchanting little place which packs a surprising amount of interest. The scene is set at the village centre, where four three-storey eighteenth-century houses stand at the four corners of a crossroads, each virtually identical (with arched entrance courtyards to the side) and built of rough-cut grey limestone. The story goes that they were built by four spinster sisters who wanted to keep an eye on one another's comings and goings.

Down by the river, the Georgian theme is continued in the fine **mill**, built in 1766, across the road from which stands a large Gothic gate to Slane Castle, whose lands stretch out westward along the river. **Slane Castle** suffered an enormous fire in the spring of 1992 and is strictly out of bounds to the public. Some restoration work has been completed but it's a painstaking and expensive task and it seems as if the castle will remain closed to the public for the forseeable future. During the reconstruction period, the owners have appealed to tourists not to enter the grounds at all, for their own safety. Approximately once a year, however, the castle does open its gates to half of young Ireland for massive, open-air rock concerts promoted by the entrepreneurial

Henry Conyngham, Lord Mountcharles, who has a warm relationship with Ireland's rock business – including U2, who recorded *The Joshua Tree* in one of the rooms at Slane. The only other way of getting a glimpse of the castle grounds is to go to the tiny **nightclub** held in the castle basement every Saturday night (☎041/982 4207).

On a more traditional level, the castle is the seat of the **Conyngham family** and is a classically ordered mass of mock battlements and turrets with a neo-Gothic library. The best architects of the day – Wyatt, Johnston and Gandon – were involved in the design, and the grounds were laid out by Capability Brown. Inside, there's a substantial art collection and many mementos of King George IV, who is said to have spent the last years of his life involved in a heady liaison with the Marchioness Conyngham: some claim that this relationship accounts for the exceptionally fast, straight road between Slane and Dublin.

Further out in the castle grounds, and not for public consumption beyond a glimpse from the river towpath, is **St Erc's Hermitage**. Lord Mountcharles recently gave this to the nation, but it will be some time before it opens to the public.

Walking north from the crossroads, uphill, you can climb to the top of the **Hill of Slane**, where **St Patrick** lit his Paschal Fire in 433 AD, announcing the arrival of Christianity. This was in direct defiance of Laoghaire, High King of Tara, who had ordered no fire-making until Tara's own hillside was set alight. Fortunately for St Patrick, Laoghaire was promptly converted, welcoming the new religion throughout the country. The summit commands magnificent views of the whole Boyne Valley. Near the top, the ruined **Friary Church** (1512) and separate college building are worth investigating. The church has a well-preserved **tower**, with a very narrow and steep flight of sixty-odd steps: if you make it up you're rewarded with a broad panorama of the eastern counties, though Slane itself is all but hidden from view. In the graveyard there is a very unusual early Christian tomb with gable-shaped end-slabs. This is supposed to be the final resting place of **St Erc**, Patrick's greatest friend and servant whom he made Bishop of Slane. The **college** was built to house the four priests, four lay-brothers and four choristers there to serve the church; assorted pieces of carved stonework can be found if you mooch round its ruins.

Practicalities

Slane has an exceptionally friendly **tourist office** on Main St (April–Oct daily 9am–6pm; Nov–March Mon–Fri 9.30am–5pm; ☎041/982 4010). B&B **accommodation** is offered at *Ye Olde Post House* on Main St (☎041/982 4090; ③) which also has a fine coffee shop and restaurant attached; and *Boyneview* (☎041/982 4121; ③), one of a row of stone cottages overlooking both the river and the grandiose entrance lodge of the castle. Handily placed just opposite the tourist office, the stone fronted *Conyngham Arms Hotel* (☎041/982 4155, *conynghamarms@tinet.ie*; ⑥) has comfortable rooms and also serves reasonably priced lunches and evening **meals**. Comfortable budget accommodation, especially suitable for families, can be found at *Slane Farm Hostel*, which is well signposted both from the village and opposite the castle gates (☎041/9884 985; ①). Inexpensive though delicious food is also served at *Boyle's Tea Rooms* on Main St. You can get to Slane by bus from Dublin; the journey takes forty-five minutes.

The Ledwidge Museum

A mile or so east out of Slane is the **Francis Ledwidge Museum** (daily: April–Sept 9am–1pm & 2–7pm; Oct–March 9am–1pm & 2–4.30pm; £2/€2.54). This stone-built labourer's cottage was the birthplace, in 1887, of the local poet Francis Ledwidge, who died on a battlefield in Flanders on July 31, 1917. His poems were written on a small scale, and the museum reflects this: a modest, almost spartan house with the poetry daintily hung in miniature picture frames. The lines inscribed on a stone plaque outside the cottage were written when Ledwidge heard of the death of his Irish poet friend Thomas MacDonagh, who was executed by the British for his involvement with the Easter Rising of 1916 – it's an echo of MacDonagh's own poetic translation of Cathal Buidhe's *Mac Giolla Ghunna* (The Yellow Bittern):

He shall not hear the bittern cry
In the wild sky, where he is lain,
Nor voices of the sweeter birds
Above the wailing of the rain.

Upstream to Navan

In its course **upstream to Navan**, the Boyne runs past the grounds of several great houses. You can't visit any of them, but if you follow the river – a distance of some eight miles – you get a real sense of an all but vanished world. The old towpath switches sides from time to time, with no obvious means of crossing: the solution to this apparent mystery is that the horse would step onto the barge and be poled across to the other side. It is just about possible to walk all the way if you're prepared to crash out your own path some of the time, but it's a great deal easier to walk as far as you can from this end, then travel to Navan by road and do the same from the other end.

After Slane Castle itself, on the opposite side of the river, comes **Beauparc House**, the mid-eighteenth-century mansion also owned by Lord Mountcharles. A little further on you pass the remains of **Dunmoe Castle** (signposted off the N51, but accessible from there only by a nightmarish potholed lane), high on the northern bank. All that remains are two sides of a four-storey castle which was square in shape with large rounded turrets at the four corners. Inside, you can still see parts of the vaulted ceilings of the lower storeys. Better than the crumbling structure, though, are the views it commands: in the river a diagonally dividing weir breaks the water into a stretch of rapids and another of calm, while on the opposite bank, there's a delightful red-brick mansion with a stretch of garden steps worthy of Versailles breaking through the wooded thickets to reach the river. Finally, shortly before Navan and right by the side of the main road, you pass the **Domhnach Mór** (Great Church), site of a superbly preserved round tower above whose arched doorway is carved a relief figure of Christ.

Navan and around

At **NAVAN** the River Blackwater meets the Boyne. It's an historic crossroads – important in the days when the waterways were the chief means of transport – and also a modern one. The N3 comes up from Dublin to follow the course of the Blackwater to Kells and to the Loughcrew Mountains in the northwestern corner of Meath; the N51 arrives from Drogheda to continue into Westmeath, its interest diminishing rapidly as you go; and to the south you can take the N3 to Tara (see p.193), Dunsany and then go eastwards on minor roads to Bective Abbey and Trim (see p.197).

Although it offers access to a lot of places and has a **tourist office**, located behind the local library on Railway St (Mon–Sat 10am–5pm, Sun 10am–1pm; ☎046/21581), Navan itself has little to detain you. There are a couple of hotels here and a number of fairly simple B&Bs not far away, should you wish to **stay**, such as *Lios na Greinne* in the Athlumney area a twenty-minute walk from the centre (☎046/28092; ③); *Dunlair House*, Old Rd (☎046/72551; ③); or the excellent *Athlumney Manor* (☎046/71388, *pboylan@eircom.net*; ③), less than a mile out of town on the Duleek road. A good upmarket option is the modern *Newgrange Hotel* on Bridge St (☎046/73732, *www.newgrangehotel.ie*; ⑥) with a fine restaurant, *The Bridge Brasserie*, which does an excellent tourist menu for £14.50/€18.41. You'll find a good cheap **lunch** at *Susie's Cookhouse*, centrally placed on the Market Square, or at *The Loft* on Trimgate St which has a fun, relaxed ambience. A little more upmarket is *Hudson's Bistro* (☎046/29231) on Railway St which has an eclectic menu with good vegetarian choices. *Peter Kavanagh's* on Trimgate St is a good, old-fashioned **pub**. *Molloys* on Bridge St, opposite the infirmary, hosts **traditional-music** sessions on a Thursday, as does the *Lantern*, Watergate St every Wednesday; the *Lantern* also hosts poetry readings once a month.

Athlumney Castle

One local sight worth going out of your way for is **Athlumney Castle**, about a mile's walk from the centre of town – head over the bridge, then turn first right following the signs. Just as you come up to the ruin, veer right into **Loreto Convent** (once the castle's outbuildings) where you can pick up the keys. In the convent grounds you should immediately spot the twelfth-century motte (now surrounded by a ring of trees) that would have had a *Bretesche*, or wooden tower, built on it. This was purely defensive, and the owner would actually have lived closer to the river.

The castle you see now is a fifteenth-century tower house to which a Jacobean manor house was added in the early seventeenth century. The **Tower House** has four floors in excellent condition, the first of which has a secret chamber down the stairs in the wall. The last occupant of the mansion was Sir Lancelot Dowdall, a Catholic who, on hearing of the defeat of James II, decided to set his home alight rather than see it fall into the hands of William's army. According to the story, he crossed the river and stood all night watching it burn before heading into permanent exile. The interior shows large gaping fireplaces and a horseshoe stone-oven on the bottom floor which would have been the area of the kitchens (the heat from which would rise to warm the living quarters above). It once had a gabled roof within which the servants were housed, and it still has many impressive mullioned windows as well as a magnificent oriel window overlooking the modern road.

If you head back to the bridge you can take the steps down to the **ramparts**, then a pleasant walk follows the canalside all the way to Stackallen, though a certain amount of building work may disrupt your way to begin with. A mile or so northeast of Navan on the Slane road is a fine 100ft-high round tower at Donaghmore. This stands on an early Christian site, reputedly founded by St Patrick.

Kells and around

Following the Blackwater upstream from Navan, the obvious place to make for is **Kells**, ten miles up the N3 Dublin–Cavan road. En route, you'll pass the site of the **Tailteann games** (on the hill above Teltown House), a little over halfway. Here, games and ancient assemblies sacred to the god **Lugh** took place in the first days of August. As late as the twelfth century the games were still being recorded, and right up to the eighteenth century a smaller celebration took place, in which locals rode their horses across the river for the benefit of the sacred qualities of its waters. Christianity eventually put paid to most of the rituals, but there is still talk of what was known as the **Teltown marriages**, where young couples would join hands through a hole in a wooden door, live together for a year and a day, and then be free to part if they so wished. Today only a few impressions in the soil remain, and certainly if you have visited Tara, or intend doing so, there's little to be gained in stopping here.

Kells

KELLS itself is a place of history and monastic antiquities – several high crosses, an eleventh-century oratory, a round tower and an ancient square bell tower – but it is most famous for what is not here, the magnificent illuminated manuscript known as the **Book of Kells**, now housed in Trinity College, Dublin. The **monastery** was founded by St Columba in the sixth century, and from about 807 it became the leading Columban monastery in Ireland, when the monks from the original foundation on the Scottish island of Iona fled here from repeated Viking raids. It is probable that the *Book of Kells* was actually made on Iona and that they brought it with them when they moved. The new home was little safer than the original one and was attacked time and again by Danes and later the Normans: in the twelfth century the monastic order's headquarters moved on to Derry, and by the time of the Dissolution there was little left to suppress. So most of what you actually see is eighteenth century or later, though the town's layout still etches out the concentric ridges of the early monastery's plan, on what little survives is well worth making the effort to see.

When you arrive, head for the spire of the **bell tower** that stands within the grounds of the modern church where most of the relics are to be seen. In the church itself (if it's not open you can get the key from the gate-lodge outside working hours, otherwise search for the priest) there's a facsimile copy of the *Book of Kells*, and up in the gallery you'll find a small exhibition of blown-up photos of some of its pages. The **Round Tower** in the churchyard is known to have been here before 1076, for in that year Murchadh Mac Flainn, who was claiming the High Kingship, was murdered within the tower. It's a little under 100ft high, with five windows near the top, and missing only its roof.

Near the tower is the **South High Cross**, the best and probably the oldest of the crosses in Kells, carved as ever with scenes from the Bible. On the south face appears: Adam and Eve, Cain and Abel, the three children in the fiery furnace, and Daniel in the lions' den. On the left arm of the wheel Abraham is about to sacrifice Isaac, and on the right are St Paul and St Anthony in the desert; at the top is David with his harp and the miracle of the loaves and fishes. There are two other complete crosses in the churchyard, and the stem of a fourth (behind the church back-entrance door) with the inscription *Oroit do Artgal* "A Prayer for Artgal". This has several identifiable panels; the near side shows the baptism of Christ, the marriage feast at Cana, David with his harp again, the presentation in the Temple, and others too worn to make out. On the other side are a self-conscious Adam and Eve, Noah's ark, and others hard to identify accurately. There are sculptured stones embedded in the walls of the bell tower.

St Colmcille's House, probably built by the Columban community, can be found just outside the churchyard walls at the north end – coming out of the main gates take a sharp left uphill, but first obtain the keys from the chocolate-brown house just after the stop sign. It's a beautifully preserved building – thick-walled and high-roofed – and peculiarly in character with the terrace of nineteenth-century workers' houses alongside which it stands. A modern entrance has been broken in at ground level, when originally the door would have been about eight feet off the ground in the west wall (reached, for security, by a removable ladder); you can still see the intended way in round to the left from where you enter now. Inside is a space about 19ft by 16ft, where you emerge into a vaulted room that would have once had two levels (with the present ground floor as a basement). Above were three tiny attic rooms, reached now by a metal ladder, which were probably where the residents slept and also a hideout in times of trouble. Underground tunnels link the oratory and the Round Tower, supposedly running beneath *O'Rourke's* pub on Castle Street.

In the central **market square** the replica of a fine **high cross** will be erected in the summer of 2001. The original cross, which was said to have been placed there by Jonathan Swift, was substantially damaged when a local reversed into it in her car. One of the more macabre episodes in the history of the original cross was during the 1798 Rebellion when it was used as the gallows from which local rebels were hanged. At the time of going to press the original cross was being repaired and plans are afoot to make it the star attraction in a new heritage centre.

Practicalities

Buses pick up outside *O'Rourke's* lounge in Castle Street – an Expressway bus from Dublin is £10/€12.70 return and takes around an hour. Kells' **tourist office** is in Headfort Place behind the town hall. For **accommodation**, the *Headfort Arms* hotel (☎046/40063; ⑤) at the beginning of the Dublin road is a reasonable choice. Kells' **hostel** (IHH; ☎046/49995) is part of the *Carrick House* pub, at the top of Carrick Street, a steep street of pastel-coloured flat-fronted houses that leads out of the centre of town. You'll get very tasty **food** during the day at *Penny's Place*, a café/lunch room at the bottom end of Market Street (closes 6pm), but in the evenings there's not much choice outside the pubs. *Magee's* on Farrell Street serves fine snacks, but otherwise good **pubs** are surprisingly scarce. One that's definitely worth a visit, however, is *O'Shaughnessy's* on Market Street (running along the bottom of the church plot), which has Irish ballads and old-time music on Friday, Saturday and Sunday nights at 9pm. The song *The Isle of Inishfree* was written here by D. Farley, the former owner who was also once superintendent at Dublin Castle.

The Castlekeeran crosses

From Kells the N3 follows the Blackwater northwest into County Cavan. A considerably more interesting route takes the Oldcastle Road or R163 (the one that passes alongside the round tower) towards the Loughcrew cairns (see p.192). Only a mile out of Kells a very worthwhile short detour takes you up a winding road to the right that leads, after about another mile, to the **Castlekeeran crosses**. Entry is signposted through the yard of a creamy-orange farmhouse and across a field which will take you into the old monastery enclosure.

Hardly anything of the monastery, known as **Díseart Chiaráin**, or the Hermitage of Ciaran, has survived, although you can pick out a partially earth-covered arch. The high crosses here, three of them plus a fourth in the middle of the river, are older than those at Monasterboice and Kells and far simpler. But their greatest charm lies in the fact that you'll probably be quite alone as you contemplate their history. The only decoration on the crosses are some simple fringing patterns and boss protruberances in the "armpits" and tops and wheel centres. The story of the cross in the River Blackwater tells how St Columba was caught red-handed by St Ciaran as he carried the cross off to his own monastery. In his shame he dropped the cross where he stood and fled back to Kells.

There is also an **early Christian grave slab** in the graveyard, and a very good example of an **Ogham stone**. Ogham was an early Irish script which was widely used from around the fourth to the seventh century AD, after which it was gradually replaced by Latin script. Even at the height of its popularity Ogham co-existed with Latin writing: it was used primarily on stones and monuments such as this, while Latin script was found in manuscripts. It is thought that the script was once used for secret communication, part of a signalling or gesture system for magical or cryptic purposes; it can also be found in parts of Devon, Wales and Scotland. As late as the nineteenth century some isolated peasant communities still used Ogham script if they needed to write anything down – it had the advantage that no one from outside would be able to interpret it. On stones like this, the edge is used to help define the characters. Five strokes above the line give you five letters; five below another five letters. Five strokes that cross the line make five more letters and five oblique strokes five more: to these a few less obvious symbols are added to make up the alphabet. The inscription here reads *covagni maqi mucoi luguni*, but although the letters can be made out nobody seems to know what these words actually mean.

Sliabh Na Caillighe

Sliabh Na Caillighe, the Mountain of the Sorceress (910ft), is the highest part of the **Loughcrew Mountains**, whose two-mile east–west stretch virtually cuts off the furthest tip of County Meath. From the top there's a wonderfully disparate view, with the Cavan lakelands in one direction and the undulating flow of earthy Meath in the other, blending in the far distance into the mountains of Wicklow and Slieve Bloom. Three major groupings of **Neolithic cairns** were constructed on these summits, no doubt chosen to be seen from afar. The first group (coming from the east) is known as the **Patrickstown cairns** and has been so thoroughly despoiled, largely for building material in the nineteenth century, that no significant trace remains. The other two summits have one major cairn each: **Cairn T on Carnbane East** and **Cairn L on Carnbane West**. Each has a handful of satellite mounds, though these represent only a fraction of what must once have been here. The sites are not easy to get to – you'll need your own transport and still face a hefty walk at the end – but they are well worth the effort. Little known as they are, the Loughcrew Cairns are almost as impressive as the Newgrange mounds (certainly when you take into account the sheer number) and you'll almost certainly be free to explore them entirely alone, and with as much time as you want. Bring a torch if you want to appreciate what lies inside.

The Oldcastle Road runs beneath the northern flank of the mountains, and about four and a half miles before Oldcastle you'll see a broken signpost pointing off to the left. Follow this road for a mile and then take the right turn (signposted) that clearly heads towards the hill complex. From May to September the complex has guides on site, and a tour costs £1/€1.27.

Carnbane West

Half a mile up the road – a steep climb – you'll come to a small clearing where a stile leads into a field: this path heads to the **Carnbane West** grouping. On your way across you'll notice **Cairn M** off to your left on a high peak – except for its astronomical involvement with Cairn L, this hasn't much of interest and it's not really worth the hike. **Cairn L**, with its wide ring of kerbstones, should be obvious to you immediately. It was most recently explored by Martin Brennan in 1980, after years of relative neglect by archeologists. It is Brennan's astronomical theories which are in part set out below. They are far from being generally accepted, but in the absence of other explorations they do at least attempt to answer some of the questions about the sites.

Cairn L has an asymmetrical chamber unique among the Loughcrew cairns, with a white **standing stone**, over 6ft high, positioned at the back right. It is probable that the mound was built as a majestic housing for this one special stone. According to Brennan its function is found in the rising sun on the cross-quarter days November 8 and February 4 (the days halfway between the solstices and the equinoxes). On these days a flash of light enters the tomb from the rising sun at about 7.40am and catches the top of the standing stone. The lower edge of the light is formed by the shadow of Cairn M, and other standing slabs in L further shape it so that the ray marks out only the standing stone. If you have a torch, then study the decorated slab by the basin to the left of the stone, facing away from the entrance. There are many designs carved into the various stones, but at the bottom of this one, according to Brennan, you can see a pictorial representation of this astronomical event.

Brennan sees **Cairn H** as a warning of the November cross-quarter day. The rising sun begins to penetrate its chamber from mid-October onwards, with the backstone being touched come November, and then from about the third onwards the sun leaves Cairn H and moves on to Cairns M and L for November 8. **Cairn F**, with several examples of decorative grooves, kicks off another alignment series. The sun begins to enter in late April, ready to mark another cross-quarter day on May 6, when the rays of the setting sun centre on **Cairn S**. Cairn S is also aligned for the final cross-quarter day, August 8. By August 16 they enter F again, and from there move on to **Cairn I** to warn of the autumn equinox. If Brennan's theories are correct (critics tend to claim that if you look long enough, and pick enough times and days, you can prove almost anything this way), then cairns I, T, F and S form the longest such sequence of alignments known.

Carnbane East

To get to **Carnbane East**, return to the hill road and carry on until you reach a large car-parking space where a path leads up the hill to the mounds. If you lose the path, which is vague at times, just keep climbing steeply, steering left if there's any doubt; towards the top follow the barbed wire round and enter by the kissing gate which will put you on the threshold of Cairn T. At Carnbane East Brennan sees three mounds functioning as solar dials. **Cairn T** deals with the spring and autumn equinoxes (March 23 and Sept 22). In its cruciform chamber is a large backstone liberally patterned with chevrons, ferns, petals and moon and sun signs. At the spring equinox a shaped patch of light passes across a passage stone, and various of the other designs, to focus on the large radial sun sign in the centre of this stone. At the autumn equinox the sun makes a more leisurely progress, rising at about 7.11am, and strikes the backstone just over half an hour later. Once again it crosses the sunwheel emblem. Of the satellite mounds, neither of which has a roof any more, **Cairn S** is said to mark the cross-quarter days on May 6 and August 8, while **Cairn U** is synchronized with Cairn L to mark November 8 and February 4. Cairn S has lots of sun emblems, while Cairn U has a variety of more unusual (and less identifiable) markings. Whatever you make of Brennan's theories in the end, he has at least opened an important new area of exploration; and in the undeniable light of Newgrange's connection with the equinox there are few people any more who would contend that these structures were simply tombs and nothing more.

Tara and around

South from Navan down the Dublin–Navan road (N3), there's a trio of places well worth seeing. The first is one of the most famous historic and mythical sites in Ireland, **Tara**, and its eponymous hill; moving south you'll come across **Dunsany Castle**, where you'll find an interesting art collection; and not far northwest of the castle, the remains of **Bective Abbey** are beautifully located on the River Boyne and make a pleasant stop on the way to Trim (the R161 from Navan to Trim is just by the abbey).

Tara

TARA, the home of the High Kings of Ireland and source of so many of the great tales, looks nowadays like nothing so much as a neatly kept nine-hole golf course: a gently undulating swath of green marked out by archeological plaques. Imagining the palace, whose wood-and-wattle structures have entirely disappeared, leaving only scars in the earth, isn't easy. But it's an effort worth making, for this was a great royal residence, already thriving before the Trojan Wars and still flourishing as late as the tenth century AD. The origins of the site are lost in prehistory, but it originally probably had a religious significance, gradually growing from the base of a local priest-king to become the seat of the High Kings. Its heyday came in the years following the reign of the legendary Cormac Mac Art in the third century AD – when five great highways converged here: this was a ritual, rather than a residential, centre – and by the time of the confrontation of St Patrick with King Laoghaire in the fifth century, its power was already declining. The title of High King was not, on the whole, a hereditary one: rather the kings were chosen, or won power, on the battlefield. So they were not necessarily local, or even permanently based here, but all evoked the spirit of Tara as the basis of their power.

In later history, there was a minor battle at the site during the 1798 Rebellion, and in 1843 **Daniel O'Connell** held a mass "Monster" meeting – said to have attracted as many as a million people (a quarter of Ireland's population today) – as part of his campaign against union with Britain.

You'll find the **site** signposted just off the N3. From the car park it appears as a wild meadow on a table-top hill, no more than 300ft above the surrounding countryside; just beside the car park is the *Banquet Hall Café,* (daily 9.30am–6pm). There is a plan near the entrance, which will help you to identify the various mounds. The path to the site leads through the yard of the old Church of Ireland, which is now used as a **visitor centre** (May to mid-June 9.30am–5pm; mid-June to mid-Sept 9.30am–6.30pm; mid-Sept to Oct 10am–5pm; £1.50/€1.90), with a romantic but reasonably sophisticated audio-visual show that gives some background to Tara's history and also, more valuably, shows a number of aerial views that do a lot to make sense of the design. The **church** itself, dating from 1822, is a modest grey building typical of the Anglican churches found all over Ireland; somehow it seems fitting that it should find a role participating in the re-enhancement of a more ancient landscape that its builders once attempted to dominate. The church's only remarkable feature is a bright stained-glass window by the well-known Dublin artist Evie Hone, which was installed in 1935 to commemorate the 1500th anniversary of the visit of St Patrick to the site and thus the coming of Christianity to Ireland. St Patrick challenged the then High King at Tara, Laoghaire, by lighting his paschal (Easter) flame on the nearby Hill of Slane in defiance of the holy fire at Tara – thereby demonstrating the ritual sympathies of the new religion with the old. Once you are on top of what is actually very rich pasture, the power of the setting immediately becomes clear, with endless views that take in whole counties, their patchwork fields and a huge sky.

The Banquet Hall

Teach Miodhchuarta, the **Banquet Hall**, is on the northern hill slope and consists of two parallel banks between which runs a long sunken corridor. Its length is about 750ft and the breadth 90ft. An account of it in the medieval book known as the *Dinnshenchas* reads:

> *The ruins of this house are situated thus: the lower part to the north and the higher part to the south; and walls are raised about it to the east and to the west. The northern side of it is enclosed and small; the lie of it is north and south. It is in the form of a long house, with twelve doors upon it, or fourteen, seven to the west, and seven to the east. It is said that it was here the* Feis Teamhrach *was held, which seems true; because as many men would fit in it as would form the choice part of the men of Ireland. And this was the great house of a thousand soldiers.*

Easy as it is to imagine the five ancient highways thronged with people on their way to crowd the hall for the great *Feis,* all this is now known to be fantasy. There was no banqueting hall, and the meaning of the banks remains unclear; they may perhaps have been part of a ceremonial entrance to the site.

Gráinne's Fort and the Sloping Trenches

Northwest of the hall is a smaller group of earthworks, the first of which is **Ráth Gráinne** (Gráinne's Fort). It is surrounded by a fosse and bank and has a low mound at its centre, probably once a burial mound or maybe a house site. It is here that the tragic love tale of the *Pursuit of Diarmuid and Gráinne* begins, although, as a much later invention – it wasn't originally associated with the mound. Gráinne was the daughter of Cormac Mac Art, who had arranged to marry her to his aged commander-in-chief, Finn Mac Cool. Instead, she fell in love with Diarmuid, one of Mac Cool's young warriors, and the two of them fled together, relentlessly pursued by the spurned Mac Cool. Their various hiding places lie strewn throughout Ireland, marking practically every geological oddity in the country.

Further west lie the **Claoin-Fhearta**, or Sloping Trenches, created, according to the legend, when Cormac Mac Art as a youth in disguise corrected the judgements of the then king, Lugaid MacCon. (Mac Art was also something of an Irish Solomon figure.) The consequence of his justice was that half the house where the false judgements had been given slipped down the hill, creating the sloping trenches. The southern part of the trenches witnessed the murder of the princesses of Tara, some thirty of them, in a massacre whose total casualties were said to have been three thousand, by Dúnlaing, King of Leinster, in 222 AD.

The major mounds

South of the Banquet Hall lies the main group of mounds, the most prominent of which is the triple-ringed fort known as the **Rath of the Synods**: so called because of the various church synods said to have been held here by St Patrick, St Brendan, St Ruadhan and St Adamnan, although little archeological evidence has been found relating to this function. Two gold torques (flat strips of gold soldered and twisted together rope-like into a necklace) were found here in 1810. Much of the rath, which appears to have originally been a ring fort defended by three concentric banks, has been destroyed over the years. Partly by the graveyard which encroaches on it, but more especially by a group of British Israelites who earlier this century rooted around trying to find the Ark of the Covenant. More serious archeologists have discovered four stages in the rath's construction, starting with a flat-topped mound in the centre known locally as the **King's Chair**. There were timber palisades on the banks, and in the middle a house where five burnt bodies were found, along with Roman artefacts which suggest trading links between Tara and the Romans in Britain or Gaul.

The **Mound of the Hostages** (*Dumha na nGiall*) is the most prominent of the mounds and also the most ancient. It contained a passage grave to which entrance is now barred, though you can look in to see the markings on the upright slab at the threshold. About forty Bronze-Age cremated burials were found inside, many in large urns which were then inverted over the remains. Eating vessels and knives had been left with them, and an elaborate necklace of amber, jet, bronze and faience was found round the neck of a 15-year-old boy, the only body not cremated. A wealth of goods from the passage-grave culture (carbon dated 2000 BC) were also discovered, making it the most comprehensive find rescued from any tumulus in Ireland. The mound, once again, is associated with Cormac Mac Art: here he is said to have imprisoned hostages taken from Connacht, who subsequently died within the chamber.

The **Royal Enclosure** (*Ráth na Ríogh*), immediately to the south, is a large area surrounded by a bank and ditch, within which are two earthworks: the **Forradh** (Royal Seat) and **Teach Cormaic** (Cormac's House). Both, though they're not contemporary, are typical ring forts, with a central raised area for a rectangular house – Cormac's has two protective fosses and banks, the Royal Seat only one. In the centre of Cormac's House are a grotesque, lichen-scabbed **statue of St Patrick**, entirely inappropriate to the site, and the **Lia Fáil** (Stone of Destiny), a standing stone moved from elsewhere on the site and re-erected here in memory of those who died in 1798. It is marked with a cross and the letters RIP. According to one tradition this stone was the original Jacob's pillow, brought to Ireland by the Milesians from the Island of Fal. It is also said to be the stone used in the inauguration of the High Kings, which would roar three times to signify its approval of the coronation.

The final remaining rath on the site is named after High King Laoghaire, who made the historic meeting with St Patrick when he lit his challenging fire on the Hill of Slane.

For accommodation at Tara, there's a modern bungalow **B&B**, *Seamróg*, right next to the site (☎046/25296; ③).

Dunsany Castle

Dunsany Castle (July & Aug Mon–Sat 9am–1pm; tours can only be organized through the Drogheda tourist office ☎041/983 7070; £3/€3.81) is only a few miles south of Tara, just outside the village of Dunsany. This is still a private residence, owned by the Plunkett family (under the title Lord Dunsany) who have lived here since the sixteenth century. The last Lord Dunsany who died in 1957 established a dual reputation as an author; he wrote witty sketches of London clubland and also bizarre dream-fantasy tales that influenced such American writers as H.P. Lovecraft. It's worth going to the trouble of arranging a visit, for this is one of the finest, most thriving examples of an Irish castle you're likely to see, and packed with a wealth of art.

The castle was originally built in the twelfth century by Hugh de Lacy as another of his fortresses defending the Anglo-Norman possessions around Dublin. It has been much altered and added to since, but it's still a magnificent building, with grounds to match. Among the family relics kept here – and quite apart from the superb private art collection and the furniture that you'll see on the tour – are the ring and other reminders of Patrick Sarsfield, second-in-command of the Jacobite forces in Ireland and successful defender of Limerick for over a year, and possessions and a portrait of St Oliver Plunkett, who was hanged in London for treason (his offence: being Catholic). The Dunsanys, in fact, seem to have made a habit of being on the wrong side in Ireland's conflicts, and it's remarkable that they have held on here so long.

Neighbouring **Killeen Castle** belonged to another branch of the Plunkett family (when the estate was divided, the boundaries were supposedly set by a race; the wives of the inheritors ran from their castles, and the border was set where they met), and during the long years of Catholic suppression it was kept in trust for them by the (converted) Protestant Dunsanys.

In the grounds of Dunsany Castle is a fifteenth-century **church** built by and for the family on the site of a still older one. There are some fine family tombs in here and a beautiful carved fifteenth-century font, with representations of the Twelve Apostles and the Crucifixion. You'll need to call the Drogheda tourist office if you want to visit.

Bective Abbey

Northwest along the minor roads from Tara or Dunsany is **Bective Abbey**. A beautiful example of medieval Cistercian architecture, it is also set in flawlessly idyllic surroundings by an old bridge over the river. The abbey was once a considerable power in the land, and its abbot held a peer's seat in the English Parliament – one of only fifteen granted to the whole of the Pale. At this time the Church as a whole owned as much as a third of the county of Meath. The buildings you see date from a variety of different periods, sometimes bewilderingly so, but its basics are clearly identifiable.

Of the original abbey, founded in 1146 by **Murcha O Maelechlainn**, King of Meath, nothing at all survives. In the late twelfth century, the abbey was completely rebuilt, perhaps in time to accept the disinterred body of **Hugh de Lacy** in 1195 (see opposite). By 1228 it was decided that Bective should sever its ties with Mellifont and go under direct rule from Clairvaux in France. Of this second abbey you can still see the **chapter house** with its central column, part of the **west range** and fragments of the cruciform **church**. In the fifteenth century, this church was shortened on the west side, its aisles were removed, new south and west ranges were built inside the lines of the old cloister and a smaller cloister erected. Both the south and west sides of this latest cloister remain. The **tower** at the entrance over the porch is in excellent shape, and you can also see the layout of the fortified mansion that was built after the abbey's dissolution in 1543.

Trim and around

Five miles southwest of Bective Abbey, **TRIM** (*Baile Átha Troim*, "Town of the ford of the elder tree"), marks the final architectural masterpiece (a medieval one this time) along the banks of the River Boyne. The town can boast the remains of the largest Anglo-Norman castle in Ireland, ruins of various abbeys and a host of other medieval remains. Yet it remains surprisingly little visited and somewhat downbeat in atmosphere. Nonetheless, it's worth stopping here, with plenty to see in and around the town.

The obvious place to start exploring is the **castle** (May–Sept 9.30am–5.30pm £1/€1.27 to enter the lower grounds, £2.50/€3.17 for guided tours of the lower grounds and the keep) – ironically used as a location for Mel Gibson's 1995 film *Braveheart* – right in the centre of town and approached either from the riverside walk or via the gate at the end of a modern causeway off Castle Street. The first castle on the site was a motte-and-bailey construction put up by **Hugh de Lacy** in 1173 after he had been granted the lordship of Meath by Henry II. Within a year this was attacked by Rory O'Connor, King of Connacht, and destroyed. A new castle was begun in the late 1190s, too late for Hugh de Lacy who, in the meantime, had been beheaded with an axe by an Irish labourer in Durrow. It was this second attempt that eventually grew to become the finest, and largest, Anglo-Norman castle seen in Ireland.

The stronghold became known as **King John's Castle** after John spent a day or two in Trim in 1210 – though in fact he didn't even lodge there – but it has stronger associations with Richard II, who incarcerated his ward Prince Henry of Lancaster (later Henry IV) here for a time. In look and feel this is very much an English medieval castle, with a 486-yard **curtain wall** enclosing some three acres, ten D-shaped **towers**, various **sally gates** (small openings in the wall for surprise sorties) and, most impressive of all, a massive, square, 70-foot-high **keep** with its walls running at a thickness of a solid eleven feet. The keep is named after Geoffrey de Joinville who, along with Walter de Lacy, was responsible for its construction from 1220 to 1225. De Joinville spent many years on the Crusades (his brother Jean was the companion and biographer of St Louis, King of France), and finally became a monk in the Dominican "Black Friary" which he built at the northern end of Trim (currently undergoing excavation). One unusual, and not altogether successful, feature of the keep was the addition of a side chamber on each face (three out of four survive): an experiment not repeated elsewhere as it greatly increased the number of places which could be attacked, and hence which had to be defended. Here, though, it hardly mattered given the solidity of the outer wall. Hardly anything is left inside the keep, but you can make out the outlines of two great halls and, above these, the main bedrooms. The entrance door was in the east tower on the second floor.

Outside, the curtain wall runs round only three sides of the keep – on the fourth, the deep-running river was relied on as adequate cover. As you walk around, take in especially the **Dublin gate**, with its well-preserved barbican and two drawbridges, and the impressive section of the wall between here and the river, near the end of which is an underground chamber thought to have been used as a **mint** in the fifteenth century.

Across the river

On the opposite bank of the river from the keep stands **Talbot's Castle**, a beautiful three-storey fortified manor house. It was built in 1415 by the Lord Lieutenant of Ireland, Sir John Talbot, on the site of an Augustinian abbey; remains of the earlier building are incorporated into the lower floors of the castle. Queen Elizabeth I formulated a plan to convert it into Ireland's first university, but instead it was established as a Latin school whose most famous scholar was Arthur Wesley, later (having changed his name to Wellesley) the Duke of Wellington. Wellington entered parliament as MP for Trim and, despite his contempt for his Irish roots, was responsible as prime minister for passing the Act of Catholic Emancipation.

Behind Talbot's Castle rises the **Yellow Steeple**, so called because of the glint of its stone in the sunset. This is the only surviving part of **St Mary's Abbey**, and its ruined state owes more to Cromwell's attack in 1642 than the ravages of time. The abbey itself once housed **Our Lady of Trim**, venerated by pilgrims for the miraculous cures it performed. The wooden statue was burnt in front of Commander Croot, Cromwell's general, as he lay recuperating from wounds received in the attack on Trim. An artist's impression of this lost treasure can be seen at the roadside by the junction of the Dublin Road and New Dublin Road. Near the Yellow Steeple, **Sheep Gate** is the only remaining piece of the fourteenth-century town walls.

Also on this side of the river, and easiest reached from Trim Castle by heading out of Dublin Gate, along the Dublin Road and across the river by the sign, are the ruins of thirteenth-century **St Patrick's Cathedral** and its cemetery. The cathedral burned down over five hundred years ago, but its remains preserve a surprising amount that is worth seeing, especially in the cloister. The wall also acts as a soundpost to create a natural echo that is eerily brilliant in its clarity and closeness. In the cemetery, look out for the famous tomb of the **Jealous Man and Woman**, Sir Lucas Dillon and his wife Lady Jane Bathe, their effigies separated by a sword (Lady Jane Bathe is said to have had an affair with her husband's brother). The rusty pins you'll see left in the stone tresses are thanksgiving offerings to the rainwater caught here that is reckoned to cure warts.

Taking the next left turn off the Dublin Road, about a mile out of town, will take you to the ruins of Newtown, to which Simon de Rochfort, first Norman bishop of Meath, moved his seat in 1210. The cathedral he built here was the biggest in Ireland. Close by is **Crutched Friary** (key from the tourist office), yet another fine medieval ruin. This was a hospital run by the so-called Crutched (or Crossed) Friars, the *Fratres Cruciferi*, whose habits were marked with a cross on recognition of the fact that they had tended the Crusaders. Next to it is a gorgeous old **Norman bridge**, reckoned to be the second oldest in Ireland, and still very much in use (*Marcy Regan's*, at the other end of the bridge, similarly claims to be the **second oldest pub** in the land).

Practicalities

Buses stop on Haggart Street outside Tobin's newsagents on the north side of the river. The **tourist office** is next to the town's heritage centre in Mill Street close to the river (May–Sept 9.30am–6pm; ☎046/37111). The **heritage centre** (April–Sept daily 10am–6pm; £2/€2.54; ☎046 37227) houses an informative audiovisual display on the town's medieval history; however, at the time of writing plans were afoot to move the display to the castle complex.

For B&B **accommodation** try *Brogan's* on the High St (☎046/31237; ③), which also has a bar open to the public, or, just out of town, *Finnegan's* solid country house (☎046 31635, *crannmor@iol.ie*; ③). A more upmarket option serving up hearty cuisine, can be found at the *Station House* (☎046/25239, *stnhouse@indigo.ie*; ⑤), an old cattle-loading bay station roughly six miles to the east in Kilmessan, and almost equidistant from Tara, Bective and Dunsany. The town's **hostel** (☎046/31848) is near the tourist office off Bridge Street and apart from communal accommodation has a couple of good-value private rooms (②). You can get excellent wholefood snacks from the Salad Bowl Delicatessen on Market Street, or more substantial **meals** at *Brogan's*, as well as a range of hefty bar snacks. **Pubs** are as plentiful as ever, but one you should definitely sample is *Marcy Regan's*, a tiny, ancient place – but remember not to order a pint, for the pub is too old to cope with draught.

Laracor and Rathcairn

A couple of miles south of Trim is **LARACOR**, the place where Jonathan Swift lived during his association with Esther "Stella" Johnson and where he was rector (with very little rectitude) from 1699 to 1714. No trace of his time here survives, however. Two miles further is **Dangan Castle**, the family home of the Duke of Wellington, now no more than a shell and again with little trace of its past. Ambrosio O'Higgins, father of Bernardo O'Higgins, liberator of Chile, was born here.

Perhaps of more interest as an excursion is the Irish-speaking community of **RATHCAIRN**, near Athboy, eight miles northwest of Trim, where traditional Irish entertainment may well be taking place. The community was uprooted from Connemara by the Land Commission between 1935 and 1940 and replanted here in Meath as a *Gaeltacht*. The population is about three hundred and fifty and increasing, a unique statistic as most other Irish-speaking communities are rapidly decreasing in numbers. Not far away, in a field beside the Athboy–Navan road, is the **Rathmore Church and Cross** (*An Ráth Mhór Teampall agus Cros*). The church, built by the Plunkett family in the fifteenth century, is a fine example of the flowering of an Anglo-Norman culture sympathetic to the native Irish which the Tudor conquest succeeded in eradicating, and is full of interesting stone carvings which are worth leaving the road to take a look at. There's an octagonal shaft from a baptismal font, a violated Norman sarcophagus in the fortified tower, a decorated altar stone, the stalk of an ancient cross and other stonework. Note the corbelled roof in the other tower, now trapped as a pigeon-cote.

WESTMEATH AND LONGFORD

Heading west, leaving the Boyne valley behind, historical interest diminishes rapidly as you cross into **Westmeath**. Topographically similar to Meath, Westmeath consists of rich pastures used primarily for beef and dairy farming. **Mullingar**, the central town, is a traditional stopover for people on their way west. If you wish to spend a night in the county, however, it is advisable to journey further to the historical town of **Athlone**, where the main road across the country meets the River Shannon as it flows through Lough Ree on its long journey south. While Athlone is the centre for cruising the Shannon, the main attractions of Westmeath lie in its lakes to the northeast, around **Castlepollard**, an area definitely worth visiting.

Although **County Longford** has little to offer in terms of either dramatic scenery or conventional tourist attractions, its rolling, fecund countryside does have a certain modest charm, and the area is beginning to attract young, affluent Dubliners who are buying up and renovating the county's many abandoned cottages (the result of generations of emigration). The main route into the counties is the N4, following the Royal Canal, and the borders of counties Meath and Kildare, out from Dublin to **Mullingar** and then **Longford town**. As the road enters Westmeath the N6 turns off, to cut across the south of the county to Athlone. Heading out from Meath, roads from Navan and from Kells converge at Delvin, to run on together towards Mullingar.

Mullingar and around

MULLINGAR, the chief town of Westmeath, is a raucous, wheeling-and-dealing provincial capital, constantly choked with traffic – the sort of thing most people come to Ireland to escape. While it's the centre of a rich cattle-rearing area and its preoccupations essentially rural, Mullingar is a far cry from the sleepy towns further west, and you get the impression that this big trading centre is on a short lead from Dublin. In 1951 Mullingar hosted a traditional music festival which evolved into the annual celebration of Irish music, the **Fleadh Cheoil** (Festival of Music), which only took place once again in the town, in 1963, and now moves from town to town throughout the country. You're unlikely to be bowled over by the beauty of the place, but Mullingar is a good base for exploring the county and a convenient stopover on the journey west.

One of the town's few points of interest is the **cathedral**, an uninspiring Neoclassical structure whose tapering twin towers, which look like melting candles, are visible from the south of town. Inside, behind the side altars of St Patrick and St Anne, are two well-known mosaics by the Russian artist Boris Anrep. To get into the **Ecclesiastical Museum** – whose contents include many wooden penal crosses and the vestments of St Oliver Plunkett – ask for the key at the parochial house, on the right (June–Sept Wed, Sat & Sun 3–4pm; guided tours £1/€1.27).

The Military Museum

Mullingar's only real tourist attraction is, however, the **Military Museum** (☎044/48391) at the Columb Barracks (unfortunately at the time of going to press the future of the museum is uncertain); going southwards, turn right after the bridge over the canal, then swing left and it's 200 yards up on the left, easily walkable. The collection, in the **Old Guard Room**, has a surprisingly broad range of interest. There's all the weaponry you'd expect, of course, with plenty of World War I and II firearms, and uniforms and flags from all over the world. But more intriguing are the sections devoted to the **"old" IRA** ("old" is used to disassociate them from the "new" IRA, or Provisional IRA, who have been active in Northern Ireland since the late 1960s) with various local bands' uniforms and the tunic of Dan Hogan, Chief of Staff after 1929, who was shot by the FBI in 1941. There's also the uniform of Giles Vandeleur, whose role in World War II was portrayed by Michael Caine in the film *A Bridge Too Far*, and a pistol said to be that of **Michael Collins**, who was Chief of Staff throughout the War of Independence and the Civil War – though it's well known that Collins rarely carried a weapon.

Miscellaneous items on display include long, canoe-like boats of bog-blackened oak dredged up from the surrounding lakelands; first thought to be of Viking origin, they have been carbon dated well into the first millennium AD. Similar boats are still being dredged up today, especially in Lough Derravaragh, but are as quickly being wrapped up again in peat and resunk in the middle of the lake. One of the stranger curios is the **military cycling handbook** that was in use until at least 1964. The book instructs the young cadet as to where to put his left foot and where his right and, with even more disciplinary stringency, orders him not to twist the handlebars without the officer's permission. While the layout is somewhat chaotic, it also has a certain charm and there is usually someone around to help you make sense of it all.

Practicalities

Mullingar is on the main Dublin–Sligo **train** line; **buses** arrive and depart from beside the *Druid's Chair* pub on Austin Friars Street to Dublin, Sligo, Athlone and Galway. The **tourist office** occupies Market House on Pearse St (daily 9.30am–1pm & 2–5pm; ☎044/48650). There are plenty of places to **stay** In Mullingar: the best central B&B is Gladys Buckley's *Grove House*, Grove Ave (☎044/41974; ③); and *Hilltop* (☎044/48958, *hilltophouse@eircom.net*; ③), a mile or so out on the Navan Rd, is also good. You can **camp** at the *Lough Ennel Caravan and Camping Park* (☎044/48101), three miles out on the Tullamore Rd. Hotels in town include the traditional *Newbury* on Main St (☎044/42888; ⑤), and friendly *Austin Friar's* (☎044/45777, *www.globalgolf.com*; ⑥), on Austin Friar St. Slightly more luxurious accommodation is offered in the *Greville Arms* on central Pearse St, where they also serve good food (☎044/48563; ⑥); a wax effigy of James Joyce stands in the foyer, a reminder of a mention of Mullingar somewhere in *Stephen Hero*.

There's no shortage of **eating** places: *Gallery 29* on Oliver Plunkett Street is probably the best café in town, while *Canton Casey's* café/wine bar on Pearse Street, next to the Market House, has filling portions of spaghetti bolognese, nachos and baked potatoes at rock-bottom prices; the popular *Oscar's* Italian restaurant, 28 Oliver Plunkett St has a good local reputation, as does *Austin Friar's* hotel restaurant. If you have transport you could consider travelling a little out of town for both food and accommodation: *Woodville House* (☎044/43694; ④) has fine rooms and excellent country cooking – take Lynn Road past the greyhound track and then the first left after O'Brien's garage.

Congenial **drinking** places include *Hughes's* on Main St, *Caffrey's* on Mount St, with traditional music sessions, and the more upmarket *Danny Byrne's*, Pearse St, with good food as well.

Cooksborough

COOKSBOROUGH, a hamlet of a few houses strung together about eight miles east of Mullingar on the Delvin Road (N52), has an unusual beehive-shaped tomb, which might tempt you as a short detour. Neither Cooksborough nor the tomb is signposted but you can find it by looking out for the sign to the *Bee Hive Nite Club*: about thirty yards past this, in the direction of Delvin, enter by an old gate and cross the field to a church and graveyard smothered in bramble, weed and grass. The tomb, which looks like a stone missile warhead poking out of its silo, is that of **Adolphus Cooke** and his nurse Mary Kelly. A famous local eccentric, Cooke was convinced that he would be reincarnated as a bee and so made sure he was prepared for the event. During his life he was similarly convinced that one of the turkeys scratching around in his yard was his father reincarnated. He also had the windows of his house made into the shape of spoon-backed chairs, in order to reflect the furniture within.

Lough Ennel and Belvedere House

Lough Ennel, with its low-lying, rushy shoreline, is not an especially dramatic expanse of water, but it is an easy place to go bathing, boating or fishing, especially if you base yourself at the holiday camp immediately outside Mullingar, or in any of the B&Bs that cluster around the lough – one secluded and rather stately establishment close to the water is *Lynnbury*, a few miles out on the Tullamore road (☎044/48432; ③).

If you do stay here, you'll be well placed for making the short trip to **Belvedere House and Gardens** (May–Oct Mon–Fri noon–4.30pm, Sat & Sun noon–6pm; £1/€1.27), further out on the Tullamore Road just before the turning to the campsite. Note that you're not meant to cut across the fields from the campsite – the way lies across private land. Belvedere House was built by **Lord Belfield**, the first Earl of Belvedere, in 1740, and conceived by him as a fishing villa. Much of Belfield's life seems to have been spent feuding with his younger brothers, George and Arthur. In 1736 he married the 16-year-old Mary Molesworth, daughter of the third Viscount Molesworth. Within a few years of building Belvedere House he accused her of having an affair with Arthur, and virtually imprisoned her for 31 years at another of his houses. She was eventually released by her son on his father's death in 1774, still protesting her innocence. Meanwhile Arthur had fled to Yorkshire, but when he returned to Ireland in 1759 the earl sued him for adultery and Arthur, unable to pay, spent the rest of his life in jail. An argument with his other brother was responsible for one of the first sights you'll come across in the gardens south of the house, the **Jealous Wall**. This folly is said to be Ireland's largest purpose-built ruin, and was constructed to block the view of Tudenham House, where George lived, from the earl's own home. Considerable expense went into the construction, including the employment of an Italian architect to design the authentic-looking Gothic facade.

The interior of the **house** is still in the process of renovation, a job which shortage of funds looks certain to make a long one. However, the **rococo plasterwork** of the drawing- and dining-room ceilings is well worth a look, as is the curved balustrade **staircase** in the entrance recess. Otherwise, the **gardens** are the main attraction. In front of the house three terraces run down to the lake's shore and, behind, woodland stretches along the northeast shore of Lough Ennel. There's also the aforementioned Jealous Wall to see, and a walled garden, gazebo, ice house and stables, where there is a **coffee shop** for refreshments.

Kilbeggan and Tyrrellspass

At **KILBEGGAN**, south of Lough Ennel, and heavily advertised for miles around, is **Locke's Distillery Museum** (April–Oct Mon–Sat 9am–6pm, Sun 10am–6pm; £3.25/€4.12). The mill-wheel is still working and the entrance fee includes a free sample which certainly enhances the tour. The building is suffused with a tantalizing malty smell and there is a small bar that sells some exceptional *uisce beatha* – the Irish for whiskey – which literally means "the water of life"; try either the Locke's single malt or the Connemara single malt for a real treat. The building that looks like a small coal-tip is actually a whiskey warehouse reputedly modelled on a Syrian palace. A pleasant restaurant adjoining the museum serves reasonable food in front of an open fire.

If you need to break your journey on the haul back to Dublin on the N6, you could head for **TYRRELLSPASS** – a tiny cluster of high Georgian and vernacular buildings around a green – just to bask in its delicious prettiness. The *Village Hotel* (☎044/23171; ④), right on the green, is the place to **stay**. The impressive tower house at the other end of town has a museum and a café that does a range of bar-type lunches for around £5/€6.35. **St Sinian's**, a Gothic Revival church on The Crescent, has some elaborate Belvedere tombs. One of the simplest commemorates Jane, a countess "gifted with a masculine understanding".

Northern Westmeath

A good portion of the interest of Westmeath lies in the northeast, around the Fore Valley, Lough Lene and Lough Derravaragh. Certainly this is the most beautiful part of the county by some way. It's easily approached from Meath, from the area of Oldcastle and the Loughcrew cairns, or from Mullingar. Coming from Mullingar you'll pass through **CROOKEDWOOD**, near the scenic lower end of **Lough Derravaragh**, set among steep wooded hills that stand out immediately in such flat country. There are two main attractions to detain you here: an excellent restaurant (see below) and a fine church, **St Munna's**. This beautifully restored fifteenth-century tower-fortified church lies a mile and a half up the road to the right of the village pub; fifty yards before is a butterscotch-coloured bungalow on the left belonging to Seamus O'Simon, who has the key. From the church you can spot a motte on the hill slope, behind which is the Georgian house whose rustic cellar contains the superlative **restaurant**, *Crookedwood House* (closed Mon & Sun eve; ☎044/72165; ④), which is far better than you would normally hope to find in such an obscure location, and which also offers equally impressive accommodation.

While in the area, it's worth visiting the village of **MULTYFARNHAM** (*Muilte Farrannáin* "Farrannan's Mills") where there is a Franciscan friary and two excellent pubs, *Weir's* and *Conor Mutagh's*, both of which have music sessions most weekends. B&B **accommodation** can be found at the *Schoolhouse* (☎044/71153; ③); follow the signs out of the village, take a right at the fork and turn left at the T-junction. The village's **restaurant**, *An Tintain* ("the fireplace"), is a restored, cut-stone cottage that offers a good menu and homely accommodation (main courses around £10/€12.70; ☎044 71411; ④).

Castlepollard and Tullynally Castle

Towards the northern end of Lough Derravaragh, **CASTLEPOLLARD** is the most convenient base from which to explore the whole area, handily placed right in the middle of all the attractions. It's not the most exciting of villages, although it clearly sets great store by its picturesqueness, with a vast triangular green surrounded by carefully tended eighteenth- and nineteenth-century dwellings. Many of the visitors are here for the fishing – mainly roach, pike and trout – on Lough Derravaragh. There are a number of **B&Bs**, of which the *Pollard Arms* (☎044/61194; ⑤) is probably the most attractive.

The biggest draw in the immediate vicinity is **Tullynally Castle** (mid-June to mid-Aug daily 2–6pm; £4.50/€5.71; gardens May–Sept daily 2–6pm; £3/€3.81; ☎044/61159), whose entrance can be found half a mile from Castlepollard down the road to Granard (alongside the gable of the *Derravaragh Inn*). From the gatehouse a drive leads across another half-mile of rolling parkland to the castle itself. The home of ten generations of the Anglo-Irish Pakenham family – the Earls of Longford – it's one of the largest and most romantic of castles in Ireland, a vast conglomeration of architectural styles (largely Gothic Revival) with four towers and a long stretch of battlements.

Three hundred years ago the castle was no more than a tower house set amidst the ancient oakwoods which grow around Lough Derravaragh. The park was first laid out in 1760, very much along the lines you see today, by the first Earl of Longford; his wife founded the family **library** of more than eight thousand volumes which features on the tour. Their son returned from the French wars to greatly expand the castle to the Gothic designs of **Francis Johnston**, whose work crops up throughout Ireland. The

THE CHILDREN OF LIR

You'll find continually throughout Ireland that physically atmospheric places are the setting for ancient tales or myths, and Lough Derravaragh is no exception. In this case the legend is that of the **Children of Lir** (*oidheadh cloinne Lir*), one of the most tragic of all Irish fables.

Lir had married the daughter of Bodb Derg, King of Connacht. Her name was Aebh and she bore him twins, Fionula and Aodh, and then two more children, Fiachra and Conn. Aebh died and Lir then married her sister, Aoife, who very quickly became jealous of Lir's love for her sister's children. She took them to Lough Derravaragh, and with the help of a druid changed them into swans, condemned to spend three hundred years on Derravaragh, another three hundred years on the Sea of Moyle, the waters between Ireland and Scotland, and a final three hundred on Inis Glóire off Erris Head, County Mayo. In a last-minute pang of remorse she granted them one mercy: that they could have human voices and make the most beautiful music for all humans to hear. When Lir learned of what had happened, he was enraged and changed Aoife into an ugly grey vulture. Meanwhile the sons of Bodb Derg, Fergus and Aed, set out to search for the Children of Lir with a host of the *Tuátha Dé Danann*. They eventually found them suffering on the Sea of Moyle, but were helpless to save them from the spell. Left to their destiny the children flew towards Inis Glóire, stopping on the way to search for their father's palace on the plains of Armagh, but finding that only earth mounds remained as they were now six hundred years on in their own lives. At the end of the allotted span they died, finally returning to a very aged human form for their last few breaths, and were buried at the onset of the Christian era on Inis Glóire.

second earl's other claim to fame is to have refused his daughter Kitty's hand in marriage to the young man later to become the Duke of Wellington – they eventually married regardless. One of Kitty's brothers, Edward, fought as Commander-in-Chief of the British Army in America in 1814, and died leading his troops in the attack on New Orleans. His body was sent home pickled in a barrel of rum. In 1840 the third earl added a further 600ft of battlements, a servants' hall for forty, and an immense **Victorian kitchen** which will also make up part of your tour. Later Pakenhams have been less militarily inclined than their forebears: one, Charles Pakenham, forsook the army in the nineteenth century to found the Irish Passionist order of priests; and the present Lord Longford is well known in Britain for his liberal writings and involvement in prison reform.

In the grounds in front of the castle, a **garden walk** leads to a spacious demesne on the left, and the flower garden, River Sham pond and walled gardens off to the right. Passing further to the right, between two stone sphinxes, is the **kitchen garden**, one of the largest in the country and still resplendent with its row of Irish yews. Slightly further afield, the most rewarding walk of all is a forest path which takes you around the perimeter of the spearhead-shaped demesne, with excellent views back onto the castle.

The Fore Valley

East of Castlepollard towards the Meath border, the **Fore Valley** is an area of exceptional natural beauty. It's easy hiking country with a wealth of small-scale interest, especially in the **Seven Wonders of Fore**. There are moves afoot to convert these into some kind of tourist trail, but so far there are few visitors, and the local tradition, strengthened by an early Christian legacy in stone, still seems close to the surface. The wonders are all based on ordinary things which you can find in the valley, and in this perhaps lies the lasting strength of their reputation. They are: the water that will not boil; the wood that will not burn; the monastery built on a quaking sod; the mill without a race; the miraculous emplacement of the lintel stone above the door of St Fechin's Church; the water that flows uphill; and the Anchorite's Cell in the Greville-Nugent family vault.

The village of **FORE** sits at the eastern end of the valley and is the best place to start, discovering the wonders as you walk west. There's a tiny ancient cross on the tiny village green, and a couple of pubs are worth visiting. You'll need to pop into the *Seven Wonders* pub anyway to pick up the key for the **Anchorite's Cell**: the *Abbey* pub next door has seven old murals depicting the wonders, worth contemplating over a pint. There's usually plenty of ready advice in here for anyone planning to head down the valley.

A handy base nearby, for some gentle rambling, is the B&B **accommodation** available at *Hounslow House* (☎044/61144; ③; closed Nov–March), which is well signposted.

The Seven Wonders

On the valley plain you'll immediately spot the ruined Benedictine priory built on reclaimed bogland (the third wonder), and en route to it you'll pass the first two. The **wood that will not burn** consists of a dead branch of a tree, landscaped into a viewing spot as part of the creation of the tourist trail (from the picture in the *Abbey* pub you'll remember it looking more lively than this); the idea of piercing its bark with coins is also a recent invention. The **well of unboilable water** is handily close by.

The **priory** was founded by the De Lacys around 1200, and its remains are the most substantial reminder of the Benedictine Order left in Ireland. It was fortified in the fifteenth century; the towers also served as living quarters. There's a plan in the cloister of the various periods' additions, and some subtly sensitive restoration has been undertaken so that although it's very much a ruin, there's a strong monastic feel to the walls and halls. If you intend to ascend the **tower** at the chancel end, beware that its spiral staircase seems to wind around the diameter of a dinner plate and above all that the steps finish in midair; it should certainly not be attempted in poor light.

On the far hillside from here, the lower of the two buildings is the tenth-century **St Fechin's Church**, which marks the site of the original monastery founded in 630 by St Fechin himself, at one time housing over three hundred monks. Note the rare Greek cross on the massive **lintel stone** (which weighs over two tons and was only moved by the miraculous intervention of the saint, hence wonder five), resting on two boulder-sized jambs. Within the ruin is a very weatherbeaten font to your left, a cross slab pinned next to the wall in the chancel at the far end (the chancel was a thirteenth-century addition) and a few other stone slabs, the engravings on which are not clear. From here a ridged path takes you up to the tiny, fortified church known as the **Anchorite's Cell** (wonder seven), decoratively hugged by a low-lying, castellated perimeter wall. The most famous hermit who lived here was Patrick Beaglan, who broke his neck trying to climb out of the window in 1616, thereby fulfilling his vow to stay in the cell till his death. The Romanesque doorway leads into a barrel-vaulted, sandstone interior.

The **water that flows uphill** (wonder six) refers to another of St Fechin's miracles; and the river flowing out of Lough Lene up at the head of the valley does look as if it's flowing upwards. The **mill without a race** (wonder four) is signposted two hundred yards downstream from here.

The heart of Ireland: Uisneach to Athlone

As you head west from Mullingar towards Athlone on the R390, you'll approach the middle of Ireland, a spot traditionally identified as the **Hill of Uisneach**. About a mile before Killare (ten miles or so from Mullingar) there are two signposts pointing off the road up to the hill. Follow the second, more westerly one, climb the hill steeply, veering a little to the left, and after crossing a few fields you'll come to the **Catstone** (so called because it resembles the poise of a pouncing cat). More historically known as the *Ail na Mearainn* (the "Stone of Divisions"), it's a massive boulder (now fragmented a little) set into a circular indentation in the hillside. The stone was said to mark the very centre of Ireland and the division of the five provinces of old. A further and longer walk up the slope will bring you to the summit of a flat-topped hill, barely 250ft above the neighbouring land yet able, on a clear day, to command a view of parts of twenty of the thirty-two counties of Ireland.

Here, it is recorded, the palace of **King Tuathal Techtmar** stood in the second century AD, and here some claim that the High Kings of Ireland ruled for the two centuries preceding the arrival of St Patrick in 433 AD, when the seat moved back to Tara. On the hill there are two spurs with traces of earthworks, but these are neither easy to find nor to make out if you do, so it's probably easier to accept the history without evidence. Excavations were made here in the late 1920s, but came up with surprisingly little. No pottery was found, nor any significant trace of permanent occupation. Instead there were great **beds of ashes** which suggested that the place was used for elaborate feasts and ceremonials rather than for defence or peaceful habitation. This accords with the tales of the great pagan festival of *Bealtaine* (Bel's Fire) that was said to be held here in the opening days of the month of May, when vast fires were lit and cattle sacrificed. It was both a religious festival and a market, where traders from the Mediterranean would arrive with their silks and spices in exchange for Irish tools and materials. *Bealtaine*, incidentally, is now the Irish word for the month of May.

As you continue towards Athlone, look out for the tenth-century **Twyford Cross** on a hillside to the left about four miles before you arrive. It was re-erected here after being found sunk in a bog.

Athlone and around

The Hill of Uisneach may be the traditional centre of Ireland, but the busy, thriving town of **ATHLONE** is a more convincing modern contender. Here, east meets west and north meets south at the midpoint of the River Shannon. This position is its greatest asset, with access by boat upstream to the islands and shores of **Lough Ree** (see p.209), and downstream to the magnificent early Christian site of Clonmacnois (see p.156). Either of these trips can easily be done in an afternoon: ask for details at the tourist information office.

Not surprisingly, perhaps, given its position, Athlone has quite an interesting history attached, and at least one important legend. The name *Áth Luain*, the Ford of Luan, came from (or may perhaps have inspired) the **Snám Dá Én** ("Swim of Two Birds"), a tale that tells of Estiu, wife of Nár. She had a lover called Buide who used to come and visit her in the form of a bird with his foster-brother Luan. The magic of their song lulled all around to sleep, allowing the lovers to enjoy their trysts undisturbed. Nár, however, questioned a druid about the coming of the birds and on learning the secret he set out for the place on the Shannon (near Clonmacnois) where Buide and Luan could be found and shot both of them with one cast of his sling. Buide was killed instantly, but Luan managed to fly as far north as the ford that marks Athlone today, where he dropped dead from the sky. An alternative derivation of the name comes from the *Táin*, which describes how the remains of the white bull (*Finnbennach*) were deposited throughout the countryside as he died. His loins were left at a place that came to be known as *Áth Luain*, the Ford of the Loins.

In straight historical terms, this ford of the Shannon has always been strategically important. The first castle was erected in 1129 by Toirdelbach Ó Conchobhair, King of Connacht, and replaced in 1210 by the **Norman castle** which, still stands today. It saw action many times, above all in the seventeenth century in the Cromwellian Wars and the Jacobite invasion. The former put a swift end to the predominantly Catholic nature of the town, placing most of the land and political power in the hands of Protestants. The later battles of 1690 to 1691 saw probably the most vicious fighting in the **War of the Kings**, as the Williamites captured first the Leinster part of town and, after 12,000 cannonballs had reduced much of it to rubble, the Connacht side.

The Town

Aside from the castle the few really distinguished old buildings that survive can be found off Church Street in the **Court Devenish** area. Finest of them is **Court Devenish House**, a seventeenth-century Jacobean mansion now resting ruined in private grounds. Nearby the ruins of the likewise seventeenth-century **abbey** offer perhaps the most peaceful spot in town, and there's an intriguing corridor of tombstones leading off the Abbey Road into its graveyard.

The one place really worth visiting, if only briefly, is the **castle museum** by Market Place (Mon–Sat 10am–4.30pm; the ticket includes entrance to the Visitors' Centre, £2.50/€3.17), housed in the two storeys of the circular keep. On the upper storey is a section devoted to **folk history**, an Aladdin's cave of rustic implements used in threshing, seeding, ropemaking, harnessing, milking and the like. There's a beautiful article on milking, telling how a few squirts were always dropped first on the grass for the fairies and at the end the sign of the cross made on the teat to bless its consumption. You'll also come across a pair of pony boots that were used when rolling the lawn, to prevent any hoof marks. Downstairs is a more regular collection on local history and prehistory and two fine examples of **Sheila na Gig** sculptures (see box on p.208).

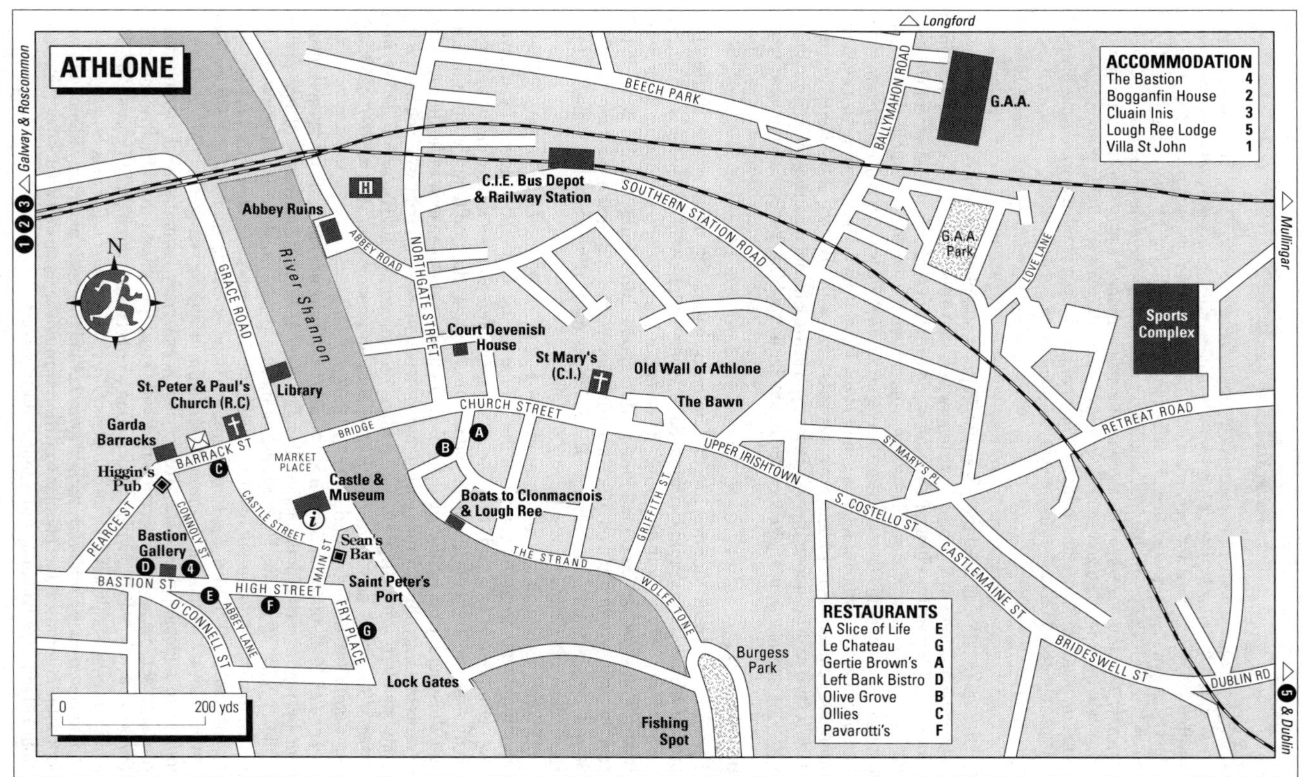
ATHLONE
ACCOMMODATION
The Bastion 4
Bogganfin House 2
Cluain Inis 3
Lough Ree Lodge 5
Villa St John 1
RESTAURANTS
A Slice of Life E
Le Chateau G
Gertie Brown's A
Left Bank Bistro D
Olive Grove B
Ollies C
Pavarotti's F
Longford
Mullingar
5 & Dublin
1 2 3 Galway & Roscommon
N
BEECH PARK
BALLYMAHON ROAD
G.A.A.
C.I.E. Bus Depot & Railway Station
SOUTHERN STATION ROAD
G.A.A. Park
LOVE LANE
Sports Complex
Abbey Ruins
ABBEY ROAD
NORTHGATE STREET
GRACE ROAD
River Shannon
Court Devenish House
St Mary's (C.I.)
Old Wall of Athlone
The Bawn
St. Peter & Paul's Church (R.C)
Library
CHURCH STREET
BRIDGE
RETREAT ROAD
Garda Barracks
BARRACK ST
MARKET PLACE
UPPER IRISHTOWN
ST MARY'S PL
Higgin's Pub
Castle & Museum
Boats to Clonmacnois & Lough Ree
S. COSTELLO ST
CASTLE STREET
CONNOLY ST
PEARCE ST
Bastion Gallery
Sean's Bar
GRIFFITH ST
THE STRAND
CASTLEMAINE ST
MAIN ST
BASTION ST
HIGH STREET
Saint Peter's Port
WOLFE TONE
O'CONNELL ST
ABBEY LANE
FRY PLACE
Burgess Park
BRIDESWELL ST
DUBLIN RD
Lock Gates
0
200 yds
Fishing Spot

SHEILA NA GIG

Sheila na Gig sculptures (the term itself is thought to be a corruption of the Gaelic *síla na gcíoch* – "Sheila of the teats") are nude female figures, generally represented face on with their legs splayed and hands placed behind the thighs, the fingers opening grossly oversized vulva. They were thought to be either the symbol of a fertility cult or used to ward off the evil eye, though quite how they managed the latter is not explained. They mainly appear in the walls (usually near the main entrance door) of castles and churches, built between 1200 and 1600. To a lesser extent they are also found in round towers and on standing stones and bridges. They are also known in other parts of the British Isles, and even France, but the majority of them by far are in Ireland.

On a quite different level there's an old 78rpm gramophone on which you can request your choice of one of the best lyric tenors ever recorded. The gramophone was John McCormack's own, travelling all over the world with him so that he could use it to test out the quality of his new releases. He is said to have been born in the Bawn area, the old market quarter up behind Devenish Gate Street, and in 1928 he was rewarded for his work for Catholic charities by being made a Count of the Papal Court. The one song that even the youngest generations in Ireland are able to associate with his voice is his *Panis Angelicus* – the record may be among the pile. Before you leave, look out for an early Christian grave slab with carvings as beautifully ornate as any high cross that you're likely to have seen.

Practicalities

The **bus** and **train stations** are on Southern Station Rd, north of the centre. The **tourist office** (May to mid-Oct Mon–Sat 9.30am–5.30pm; ☎0902/94630) is in the castle in Market Place. Both the **post office** and a **laundry** are situated on Pearce St. Boats of all sizes can be rented locally. Much good rod **fishing** can also be done just past the weir, where you'll often see a line of anglers; rod and reels are for rent from the Strand Tackle Shop in the Strand (£5/€6.35 per day). **Bike rental** is available from Hardiman's, 48 Connaught St (☎0902/78669).

Athlone has one budget **accommodation** option: *Lough Ree Lodge* (☎0902/76738), a ten-minute walk from the centre on the Dublin Rd, opposite the college. If you have a few extra pounds to spend then *The Bastion*, situated above a trendy clothes shop on Bastion St (☎0902/94954, *bastion@iol.ie*; ③) is a must: the traditional wooden interior and idiosyncratic decoration give the place a slightly bohemian feel, while the breakfast of croissants, freshly ground coffee and various cheeses and fruit is a welcome relief from standard fried B&B fodder. Other recommended B&B's are *Villa St John* (☎0902/92490; ③) and *Bogganfin House*, both on Roscommon Rd (☎0902/94255; ③), and *Cluain Inis* on Galway Rd (☎0902/94202; ③).

The *Left Bank Bistro* on Bastion St (☎0902/94446; closed Sun), café by day and restaurant by night, serves imaginative, flavoursome Mediterranean **meals** at low prices, while *A Slice of Life* on High St dishes up cheap pasta dishes. In the same street, *Pavarotti's* Italian restaurant has a cosy wine bar and serves excellent pizzas (Thurs–Sun 11pm–2am); and there's good lunchtime bar food at *Gertie Brown's*. The *Olive Grove* (☎0902/76946) restaurant on the east side of the bridge serves excellent Mediterranean food at reasonable prices – the Greek salad is especially recommended. If you want a romantic setting and aren't concerned with cost, investigate the varied menu at *Le Chateau* (☎0902/94517), which is located in a converted church on St Peter's Port. For a quick, cheap sandwich the place to go is *Ollies*, a tiny café on Barrack St.

The best **pub** is *Sean's Bar*, tucked away behind the castle and easily identified by its four Ionic columns. It has popular **traditional music** sessions on a Tuesday (pipes and violin), Thursday (violins), and Sunday (open session).

Lough Ree

Try to make time for one of the excellent **cruises** along the River Shannon while you're in Athlone. An enjoyable cruise north to Lough Ree (ask for the islands of Inchclearaun and Inchbofin) is on the *MV Ross* (☎0902/72892), which departs from the Strand (on the opposite side of the river to the castle) at noon and 3.30pm weekdays in summer, the tour lasts ninety minutes and costs £5/€6.35. Both the island of **Inchclearaun** and **Inchbofin** (especially Inchclearaun), have several churches and early Christian grave slabs. Inchclearaun (*Inis Clothrand*) took its name from Clothru, who was murdered by her sister Medb so that she could wed and bed Clothru's husband Ailill and rule Connacht from the island. Medb, goddess of war and fertility, is the most famous of all the legendary and historical characters and a source of continual argument as to which branch of study (legend or history) she truly belongs to. Her life was to end in the waters by the island when Clothru's son Furbaide hurled a piece of cheese from his sling that entered Medb's forehead and struck her dead while she was bathing, thus avenging the murder of his mother.

Another enjoyable option (especially for a family) is to take Rossana Cruise's (☎0902 73383) replica longboat south to the monastic settlement of Clonmacnoise (see p.156); the excellent tour departs from the Strand at 10am on Wednesdays and Thursdays throughout summer, lasts four hours (including an hour at the sight itself) and costs £10/€12.70.

Goldsmith country

The N55 rushes north from Athlone along the eastern shore of Lough Ree, crossing the Royal Canal into the area known as **Goldsmith country,** which straddles western Westmeath and southern Longford. The area gets its name from its geographical associations with the works of the eighteenth-century poet, playwright and novelist, Oliver Goldsmith (see p.210). It's pretty, small-scale countryside, gently rolling and ready-made for cycling through landscaped villages and along aromatic fuschia-lined lanes that run off the N55 down to various small boating points such as **Killinure**, Kileenmore and Muckanagh on the lough shore. While **Longford** offers little in terms of conventional tourist attractions, the elegant **Carriglas Manor** is worth visiting, and in early summer and autumn the county attracts fishermen from across Europe to its lakes and rivers.

Glassan and around

Ironically enough, **GLASSAN** – identified as "Sweet Auburn", the subject of Goldsmith's celebrated anti-enclosure poem *The Deserted Village* and described as "the village of the roses" – owes its orderly layout of creamy-grey pebbledash cottages to enclosure: it was built by the neighbouring Waterstown estate to provide accommodation for the artisans needed to tend the massive estate with its ten-acre formal garden. The estate was divided by the Land Commission in the 1920s, and the house, designed by the eighteenth-century architect Richard Castle, was sold for scrap. As you head north towards Ballitore, there's a profusion of brown "Goldsmith country" signs. Only the front and end walls of Goldsmith's childhood home, the parsonage at Lissoy, remain, and still less of the school he attended, or of the "busy mill" that may be the one mentioned in the poem. **Forgney Church**, where Goldsmith's father worked as curate until 1730, was rebuilt in 1810 and is usually locked. Goldsmith's supposed birthplace at **Pallas** has a rather spooky shrine erected by members of the Oliver Goldsmith Society in 1974: a larger-than-life statue of the writer enclosed behind bars in a sort of grotto-prison, as if his poetic spirit is too dangerous to be let out into the world. It's curious to imagine what Goldsmith's mocking soul would have made of such funereal pomposity. At present, there's little to see of the Goldsmith collection, but the interpretive centre in the old school building can provide some information on the poet's relationship with the area.

Glassan is probably the best **place to stay** to explore this part of Lough Ree and Goldsmith country. There's a scattering of **B&Bs** – try *Carraun View* in the village (☎0902/85391; ③); or the good, rather elaborate *Village Restaurant* (☎0902/85001). *Grogan's Pub* is a popular local watering hole and does fine, bar food, while next door is a craft shop that also does teas and sandwiches – in short, a whole range of creature comforts you're unlikely to find further north in the county. Heading back down the road to Athlone you'll find the excellent *Wineport* restaurant on the shores of Lough Ree (summer daily from noon; rest of year evenings only; ☎0902/85466).

From Glassan, you could do worse than follow the waymarked **Lough Ree tour**, especially if you're cycling. Leaving the village, this takes you down winding lanes for **PORTLICK**, the "local Killarney", set in romantically wooded country and farmland sloping down to the loughside, but without the crowds of Kerry. Portlick's fifteenth-century Gothic castle gazes wistfully across the lake, crumbling but still inhabited.

At **KILLINURE** there's a fine marina from where you can take boats out to the islands of Inchmore or Inchbofin; boats can be rented from the local pub *Manto's*, a mile away in the townland of Killeenmore. *Manto's* also does B&B (☎0902/85204; ③), with camping and self-catering apartments available too. The *Wineport Sailing*

OLIVER GOLDSMITH

Best known for his prose, including the comedy *She Stoops to Conquer* and the novel *The Vicar of Wakefield*, **Oliver Goldsmith** (1728–74), the son of a Church of Ireland parson, was probably born in Pallas, ten miles north of Glassan in County Longford. When he was 2, he and his family moved to the parsonage at Lisson, just a couple of miles north of Glassan. Goldsmith was also active as a poet, and in travelling through this depopulated landscape, his epic anti-enclosure poem, *The Deserted Village*, conjures up the reality of the short-lived heyday of the Anglo-Irish society of which he was a part:

Sweet was the sound, when oft at evening's close
Up yonder hill the village murmur rose;
There, as I passed with careless steps and slow,
The mingling notes came softened from below.

But now the sounds of population fail,
No cheerful murmurs fluctuate in the gale,
No busy steps the grassgrown foot-way tread,
For all the bloomy flush of life is fled.

The poem is a protest against an oppression of the rural poor all over the British Isles, not just Ireland; whether it can really be traced to Glassan village is uncertain, but its mood of nostalgic regret for a golden childhood past undoubtedly gives it some points of contact with the local landscape. The treasure-hunt for locations mentioned in the poem, all signposted and almost all in ruins, can prove oddly evocative of an absent population – removed not by enclosure but by much more recent economic pressures. The poem also points out some of the internal contradictions of the self-confident Georgian building mania: Goldsmith's lament is for a landscape that disappeared with the building of the great Georgian houses – many of which, like Waterstown at Glassan itself, have now disappeared.

A Goldsmith summer school is held in the area each June, when academics gather and discuss his works, details of which can be obtained from Sean Ryan (☎043/41030 or 46493).

Centre, signposted from Killinure (☎0902/85466), rents out boats and has a loughside restaurant.

North to Lanesborough

Halfway up Lough Ree, Goldsmith Country seeps into **County Longford** through the uninspiring village of Ballymahon (where his mother lived) and across to Pallas (near Abbeyshrule) where he was born. Following the R392 north from Ballymahon to Lanesborough, you'll pass **CORLEA**. On the edge of the Bog of Allen, it's worth stopping here for the **Corlea Interpretive Centre** (May–Sept daily 9.30am–6.30pm; for winter hours, call the Office of Public Works on ☎01/661 3111 ext 2386; last admission 45min before closing; £2.50/€3.17), a low, mustard-coloured cruciform building, aligned with a buried *togher*, a trackway of oak planks discovered by turf cutters in 1985. Some of this has been excavated and preserved in an air-conditioned chamber, while the rest still lies beneath the bog. The bog dates from 147 BC, and its evolution and the way of life in the bog is examined in a number of displays, while the guided tour includes a walk outside in the bog and a video of the archeological dig.

Alternatively, if you turn off the main road north of Ballymahon (before Corlea) and follow the more minor roads up the lough to the rather nondescript Newtowncashel, you'll pass the workshop of the bogwood sculptor Michael Casey, whose raw material is timber many thousands of years old. The wood is dug out of the bog and left for a few years to dry out. On the road north from Newtowncashel to Lanesborough stands **Rakish Paddy's Pub**, worth a visit above all on a Tuesday night for its traditional music session: look in for a drink anytime, though, and you can see the three superb modern metal sculptures by local sculptor John Mahan of a seated fiddler, boy and girl dancers and a wooden-flute player evidently playing the well-known reel called Rakish Paddy.

LANESBOROUGH itself, at the head of Lough Ree, is another place to stop off for the boating or fishing (the last bungalow before the bridge has boats for rent) but for no other reason.

Longford

Heading northeast from Lanesborough on the N63 brings you to the county town of **LONGFORD**, which has little of special interest but makes a good base for visiting the county's main attraction, **Carriglas Manor**. East of the manor **Edgeworthstown** celebrates the county's other famous author, nineteenth-century novelist Maria Edgeworth, while, in August, Longford's traditional musicians gather in the town of **Granard** for the famous harp festival.

There's a **tourist office** (Mon–Thurs 9.30am–5.30pm, Fri 9.30am–5pm; ☎043/46566), and **accommodation** is plentiful, including the recently renovated *Longford Arms* on Main St (☎043/46296, *longfordarms@tinet.ie*; ⑥), which does good food. There are also numerous B&Bs, most of them on Dublin Road, such as *Tivoli* (☎043/41569; ③), though it may be worth travelling a few miles out of town to the hamlet of Newtonforbes to stay in the comfort of Mandy Etherton's *Olde Schoolhouse* (☎043 24854; ③).

Carriglas Manor

Chief of the surrounding attractions is **Carriglas Manor** (June, July & Sept Mon, Thurs & Fri 1.30–5pm; Aug Mon, Thurs & Fri 1.30–6pm; 40min tours on the hour beginning 2pm; ; house £7/€8.89; gardens and costume museum only, £3/€3.81). Situated just three miles out of Longford on the R194 to Granard, it's the seat of the descendants of Huguenot Lefroys. As you go up the avenue, the stables with their classically pedimented and rusticated archways (designed by James Gandon of O'Connell Bridge and Dublin Custom House repute) are on the left. They now house a **costume museum** and tearoom. The yard and buildings are being restored at the moment, but you're free to wander around it and the parkland, within the hours listed above. The costumes in the museum date mainly from the mid-eighteenth century and were found going mouldy in trunks in the castle.

The castle itself is perhaps best described as Tudor-Gothic Revival, and extremely handsome it is, too. It was built in 1837 by Chief Justice Thomas Lefroy, possibly the model for Darcy in *Pride and Prejudice*, as at one stage he enjoyed a romantic liaison with Jane Austen. The **tour** of the building is directed by the present Lefroys, who have succeeded in restoring the place to a state which reflects its former majesty. It takes in the dining room, with its set of 1825 Waterford glasses and original ironstone china; the drawing room with its Dutch furniture, one cabinet of which contains an original tea and breakfast set of 1799; a fastidiously well-stocked library; and family portraiture on virtually every wall. All this is explained and expanded on in detail by the present occupier.

Granard and Edgeworthstown

Continuing on the N4, you'll reach **GRANARD**, about fifteen miles from Longford. A famous **harp festival**, originating in 1781, took place here and was revived in 1981. Nowadays it spreads over the second weekend of August, starting on the Friday afternoon with competitions, street entertainment, *seisiúns* and *ceilidhs*. Lessons on the harp can be arranged on the spot and usually start on the Friday morning. Two **campsites** are set up for visitors (during the festival only); or you can stay at *Houricans Hotel* on Main St (☎043/86041; ③), though for genuine rural hospitality head a mile out of town to *Toberphelim House* (☎043/86568; ③). The biggest Norman **motte** in Ireland is sited at Granard, with yet another statue of St Patrick on top. The site is said to date back to 5 AD, and to Cairbre, eldest son of Niall of the Nine Hostages.

Finally, it's worth noting a couple of Longford's other literary connections, centred on Mostrim or **EDGEWORTHSTOWN**, about ten miles southeast of Longford town on the N4. The town takes its name from the family name of Maria Edgeworth (1767–1849), who, in her day, was an extremely famous author. *Castle Rackrent*, perhaps her most famous book, was written just before the Act of Union of 1801. Although its caricatures of both the Irish and Anglo-Irish can veer uncomfortably close to stage Irishry, it's a hilariously ironic and oddly prophetic insight into a chaotic Anglo-Irish lifestyle that was disappearing even as she wrote. The town now is little more than a crossroads and **Edgeworthstown House** is used as a nursing home. Maria's father, Richard, was a keen inventor and the house had a water pump which dispensed coins to beggars in return for a stint at the handle. It also boasted central heating, and at one time was the only house to have it in this part of Ireland. The Edgeworth family vault can be seen in the graveyard of St John's Church, on the N4 south to Mullingar. Oscar Wilde's sister Isola is also buried here, and one of his most touching poems, *Requiescat*, was written in her memory.

travel details

Trains

Athlone to: Dublin Heuston (11 daily; 1hr 30min); Galway (4 daily; 1hr 10min); Westport (3 daily; 2hr).

Longford to: Dublin Connolly (4 daily; 2hr 15min); Sligo (3 daily; 1hr 15min).

Mullingar to: Dublin Connolly (4 daily; 1hr 15min); Sligo (3 daily; 2hr 15min).

Buses

Athlone to: Dublin (13 daily; 2hr); Galway (9 daily; 1hr 45min); Sligo (2 daily; 2hr 30min); Westport (4 daily; 2hr 45min).

Kells to: Dublin (36 daily; 1hr).

Longford to: Dublin (3 daily; 2hr 15min).

Mullingar to: Athlone (2 daily; 1hr); Dublin (10 daily; 1hr 30min); Galway (2 daily; 3hrs); Sligo (3 daily; 2hr 30min).

Trim to: Dublin (15 daily; 1hr 15min).

CHAPTER FIVE

WEXFORD, CARLOW AND KILKENNY

The southeast of Ireland is not the most obvious of areas to visit, especially if this is your first time in the country. There are none of the wild wastes of rock, bog and water, nor the accompanying abandoned cottages that tell of famine, eviction and emigration, so appealing to romantic tastes. It is, however, Ireland's sunniest and driest corner, and what the region does have to offer – whether you're spending a couple of days passing through, or if you simply haven't the time for more distant wanderings – is worth savouring. On the whole, the region's attractions are frustratingly widely scattered, but its medieval and Anglo-Norman history is richly concentrated in the ancient city of **Kilkenny** – the region's only heavily touristed town – and the lush countryside around it shelters some powerful medieval ruins. **Wexford** town's conviviality makes up for its disappointingly scant traces of a vigorous Viking and Norman past; **Carlow** town, sadly, doesn't. While the extreme east is dull and low-lying, and the Blackstairs Mountains open and empty, the southeast is characterized overall by a quality of rich cultivation, as much to do with its history as its natural fertility.

Inland, the region is shaped by three majestic rivers: the Nore, the Barrow and the Slaney, and by the empty Blackstairs Mountains which form a rough natural boundary between the counties of Wexford and Carlow. The rivers roll through rich, lush pastures and pretty wooded valleys, past medieval Christian ruins and little towns and villages, whose history belongs to the trade these waterways brought inland. This landscape is at its prettiest in the hills and valleys of the **Nore** and **Barrow**, just north of New Ross, and south of Kilkenny town, perfect countryside for leisurely cycling and easy **walking** – an option made all the more attractive by the hostels at New Ross and Kilkenny. The signposted **South Leinster Way** meanders through the heart of this countryside to some of the choicest spots, before heading northeast to the less intimate country of Carlow and the Blackstairs Mountains.

Head for **the coast** and, to the east, superb sandy beaches stretch practically the entire length of County Wexford. While the south coast is less suitable for swimming, its sand banks, shallow lagoons and silted rivers offer great opportunities for **wildlife**

ACCOMMODATION PRICE CODES

Throughout this book, prices of hotels, guesthouses and B&Bs have been graded with the codes below, according to what you can expect to pay for a double room in high season. For more details on accommodation, see p.34.

① Under £26/€33.01	④ £40–55/€50.79–69.84	⑦ £90–110/€114.28–139.67
② £26–33/€33.01–41.90	⑤ £55–70/€69.84–88.88	⑧ £110–130/€139.67–165.07
③ £33–40/€41.90–50.79	⑥ £70–90/€88.88–114.28	⑨ Over £130/€165.07

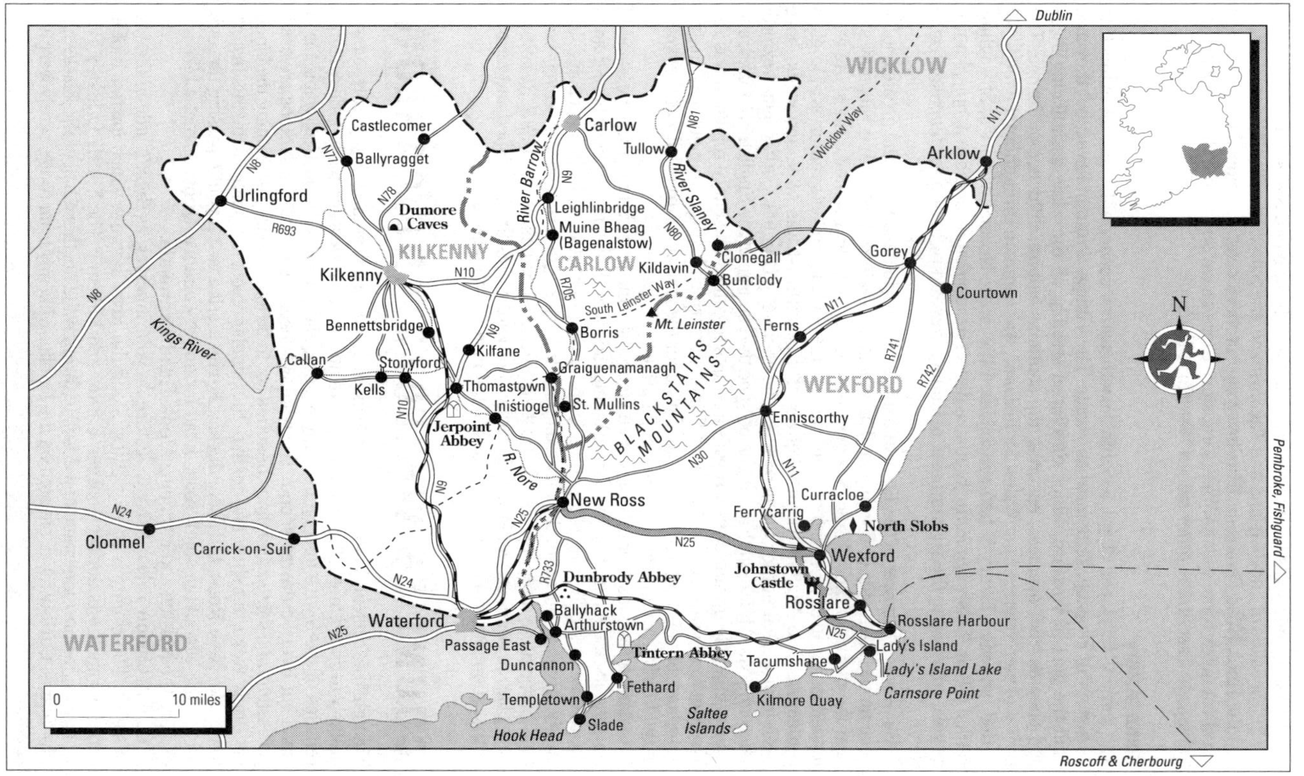
Dublin
WICKLOW
Wicklow Way
N11
Arklow
Castlecomer
Carlow
Tullow
N81
N77
Ballyragget
N8
Urlingford
R693
N78
Dumore Caves
River Barrow
N9
Leighlinbridge
Muine Bheag (Bagenalstow)
River Slaney
N80
Clonegall
KILKENNY
CARLOW
Kildavin
Bunclody
Kilkenny
N10
R705
South Leinster Way
Mt. Leinster
Gorey
Courtown
N11
Ferns
Bennettsbridge
Borris
Kings River
Kilfane
BLACKSTAIRS MOUNTAINS
R741
R742
Callan
Stonyford
Graiguenamanagh
WEXFORD
Kells
Thomastown
N10
Inistioge
St. Mullins
Enniscorthy
Jerpoint Abbey
N30
R. Nore
N9
N11
Curracloe
New Ross
Ferrycarrig
North Slobs
N24
Clonmel
Carrick-on-Suir
N25
N25
Wexford
Pembroke, Fishguard
R733
Dunbrody Abbey
Johnstown Castle
N24
Rosslare
Ballyhack
Waterford
Arthurstown
Rosslare Harbour
WATERFORD
N25
Passage East
Tintern Abbey
N25
Lady's Island
Duncannon
Tacumshane
Lady's Island Lake
Fethard
Carnsore Point
0
10 miles
Templetown
Kilmore Quay
Saltee Islands
Slade
Hook Head
Roscoff & Cherbourg

enthusiasts: prime spots for **birdwatching** include the Wexford Slobs (around the town itself), the lakes of Lady's Island and Tacumshane, the Saltee Islands off Kilmore Quay and the Hook Head Peninsula. This low-lying southern coastal region also provides an excellent quick route west to Waterford, since there's a car ferry from Ballyhack across to Passage East on the other side of Waterford Harbour.

Some history

The settled, developed character of this southeastern corner of Ireland owes much to its history of invasion, settlement and trade. The Vikings wrought havoc, but they also built the port of Wexford, which developed steadily, all the while assimilating ideas and peoples from overseas, ensuring the continual cultural influence of Europe. The arrival of mercenaries from Wales, for instance, was common throughout the medieval period, and after Henry II had consolidated the Anglo-Norman victories, Strongbow settled fellow Welshmen in the region: a dialect descended from these people, known as yola, survived in the far southeast of County Wexford right into the nineteenth century.

But it was the power of the English Crown that was to have by far the greatest influence on the character of the region. The towns of Wexford, Carlow and Kilkenny still bear the marks of their **Anglo-Norman** past in city walls and ruined castles; the well-tended farmland of rich surrounding countryside similarly reflects centuries of English settlement. The Anglo-Norman takeover of the southeast was swift, and would have been total were it not for the fiercely Gaelic enclave of counties Carlow and Wexford. There the MacMurrough Kavanaghs became the scourge of the English in Ireland, and they continually thwarted the Crown's attempts to control the entire region. It was Art MacMurrough who defeated Richard II in battles which lost the king not only control of Ireland, but his English throne, too. Only after the arrival of Cromwell was the power of the MacMurroughs broken once and for all.

Colonization was thereafter pursued vigorously: the proximity of the Pale – and of England itself – meant that the Crown's influence was always far stronger here than in the remote west. The English found this area easier to control and administer, and during the growing unrest of the eighteenth century the region remained relatively tranquil. Surprisingly then, by far the most significant uprisings of the **1798 Rebellion** took place in counties Wexford and Carlow. For nationalists the bloodshed and heroics of that summer form the region's most fêted history and legend.

COUNTIES WEXFORD AND CARLOW

Though the ancient Viking town of **Wexford** bills itself as a tourist centre, you're unlikely to spend more than a day or so here unless you have a car. Sadly, little evidence remains of the town's long and stormy history, and the place is most enjoyable for its small but **lively cultural scene**. The wildfowl **reserves** of the North Slobs are easily accessible, and some marvellous **beaches** are to be found nearby, stretching the length of County Wexford's shoreline north to the popular resort of Courtown. Inland, historic towns like **New Ross**, **Enniscorthy** and **Ferns** merit a visit if you're passing through. To see the best of the south coast, head for quaint **Kilmore Quay**, or rent a bike and explore the isolated and intriguing **Hook Head Peninsula**.

County **Carlow** is less likely to feature on your itinerary, as there's little in the way of sights. The county is at its prettiest along the River Barrow, which for much of its length forms the boundary between Carlow and Kilkenny. The **South Leinster Way** trudges at its most lonesome and desolate through the northern half of the Blackstairs Mountains; **Carlow** town, situated on the Dublin–Kilkenny train route, barely warrants attention.

Wexford town

Apart from the Viking legacy of narrow, quirky lanes, **WEXFORD** town retains few traces of its past, and only the quays suggest that it was once an important trading centre. In fact, the harbour, in business from the ninth century, has now silted up, and Wexford has lost its trade to its old rival Waterford. That's not to say, though, that the town's history stopped with the fall of the Vikings. Settled by the Normans in the twelfth century, it became an English garrison town, brutally taken by Cromwell in 1649 (who had 1500 Wexford citizens put to death). In the 1798 Rebellion, the town saw brave, rebel fighting against the English Crown (backed by a mainly Protestant yeomanry), which was fearful that the port might be used as a landing place by the French. The uprising lasted longer in Wexford than in most places, but the rebels were finally put down, and the Crown was quick to exact retribution. Wexford, though, plays down its contribution to Republicanism and has emerged as a positive, forward-thinking place. It is internationally famous for its prestigious **Opera Festival**, while a more mainstream draw are the town's estimated 93 **bars**, reason enough to give Wexford at least a night.

Arrival, information and accommodation

Wexford's **train** and **bus** stations (☎053/22522) are in Redmond Place at the north end of the quays, just past the bridge over the estuary – which, if you crossed, would take you out to the campsite, the wildfowl reserve (see p.219) and the beaches of the county's east coast. **Bike rental** is available nearby at The Bike Shop, 9 Selskar St (☎053/22514; £8/€10.16 per day). Wexford town centre runs southeast from Redmond Place, parallel to the estuary. The **tourist office** (April, May & Sept Mon–Sat 9am–6pm; July & Aug Mon–Sat 9am–6pm & Sun 11am–5pm; Oct Mon–Sat 9.30am–5.30pm; Nov–Jan & March, Mon–Fri 9.30am–1pm & 2–5.30pm; ☎053/23111) is located towards the south end of town in a break in the quays known as The Crescent. The Viking Shuttle Bus (☎053/21053) to Johnstown Castle and Kilmore Quay departs from outside the tourist office. **Harbour trips** run throughout the summer (£5/€6.35) and can be booked at the Kirwan House hostel (see below). Pádraig's Launderette is right next door to the hostel. **Internet access** is available at Bridge IT, 87 North Main St (☎053/42880).

Wexford has a good range of **accommodation** on offer, although bear in mind that rooms all over town are at a premium during the Opera Festival (see p.219). You can **camp** at *Ferrybank Camping and Caravan Park* (closed Nov–Easter; ☎053/42987), immediately over the bridge from Commercial Quay – and there's a swimming pool next to the campsite.

Bilrene, 91 John St (☎053/24190). A cosy, welcoming family home offering B&B in standard rooms only. ③.

The Blue Door, 18 Lower George's St (☎053/21047, *bluedoor@indigo.ie*). Beautifully kept, spacious Georgian house just off Main Street offering very good en-suite B&B accommodation. Despite its central location, rooms are very quiet. ④.

Kirwan House, 3 Mary St (☎053/21208, *kirwanhostel@eircom.net*). A fairly small, well-organized IHH hostel run by a convivial crowd. Two twin rooms are available (①), and dorms are mixed; linen is included. Bikes for hire and harbour trips can be booked here; launderette next door.

McMenamin's Townhouse, 3 Auburn Terrace, Redmond Rd (☎053/46442). A very cosy B&B near the station noted for its excellent breakfasts; rooms are en suite and no smoking. ④.

St Aidan's Mews, Lower John St (☎053/22691). Plain, unpretentious B&B run by a friendly family offering standard rooms only; inexpensive single rooms available. ③.

Talbot Hotel, Trinity St (☎053/22566, *www.talbothotel.ie*). A very pleasant three-star hotel, tastefully decorated with original modern art, while maintaining a warm and traditional atmosphere.

Facilities include a leisure club and pool. Located at the end of the quays; some bedrooms overlook the mouth of the bay. It's worth enquiring about special weekend and midweek deals. ⑦.

Westgate House, Westgate (☎053/22167). The elegant sitting room of this B&B is furnished with elaborately carved antiques and crystal chandeliers; the rooms too are pleasantly decorated. It's a handy place for the train station. ④.

White's Hotel, George St (☎053/22311, *www.wexfordirl.com*). A comfortable three-star hotel right in the centre of town. Although many of the bedrooms occupy a fairly characterless modern extension, the hotel itself is well run and welcoming. ⑦.

The Town

Set on the south side of the broad, featureless Slaney estuary, Wexford town sits behind its quays, which drag on relentlessly. A waterfront promenade and marina are planned to cheer things up, but at the moment, the only relief is **The Crescent**, where a statue of **John Barry**, a local who founded the American Navy during their War of Independence, strides against the buffeting wind with cloak billowing. Parallel to the quays runs Wexford's lengthy Main Street, lined with bright shopfronts and creaking bars, a narrow and winding route that gives some idea of the medieval town's layout, and a place of some charm. Once you've seen it, there is little else left to explore. A monument to the 1798 Rebellion briefly draws your attention to the **Bull Ring** (part of Main Street), also scene of a massacre by Cromwell that left all but four hundred of the population dead. A lane up behind *The Cape Bar*, famous for being both pub and undertakers, leads to the Cornmarket and the parallel streets of the small town centre.

The **Westgate**, built around 1300, is the sole survivor of the medieval walled city's original five gates, and is now designated as West Gate Heritage Tower (run on a voluntary basis with no set opening hours, enquire at the tourist office; £.1.50/€1.9); you can watch a short film here of the town's history. Nearby are the remains of **Selskar Abbey** (wrecked by Cromwell), where Henry II spent an entire Lent in penitence for the murder of Thomas à Becket in Canterbury Cathedral.

Eating and drinking

There's no shortage of places to get a decent meal in Wexford. The town boasts a vast selection of **pubs** and bars, many featuring live music on one or more days of the week. For after-hours drinking and dancing try *The Backroom* (Thurs–Sat; £3–6/€3.81–7.62) behind *The Centenary Stores.*

Restaurants

Asple's, The Crescent. Big airy pub attracting a mixed sociable crowd. The bar food is a cut-above-average and this is one of the few places to get an inexpensive meal early evening. The tasty grilled salmon with lemon butter sauce is especially good.

Cappuccino's, 23 North Main St. Cheap and jolly café cramming as many varieties of Mediterranean-inspired snacks on its menu as it does customers on its two small floors. Hot ciabatta melts, filled pittas, omelettes, burgers and baguettes are amongst the reasonably priced dishes on offer.

Dragon Heed, Redmond Place (☎053/21332). Generally considered the best Chinese restaurant in town, with a friendly, family atmosphere. Also does takeaways.

Heaven's Above, 112 South Main St (☎053/21273). Exquisite food makes this place a firm favourite; even though the seating is not especially comfortable for the price bracket. A varied menu encompassing pan-fried salmon with ginger and sun-dried tomatoes, steaks, suckling pig, a handful of vegetarian options, and around 350 wines. Closed Sunday.

Mange 2, 100 South Main St (☎053/44033). Stylish yet cosy restaurant sporting abstract art on blood-red walls, and offering an eclectic contemporary menu. Closed Monday.

La Riva, Crescent Quay (☎053/24330). Lovely, intimate restaurant serving great food. Typical main courses include rack of lamb with roasted vegetables; prawns with garlic, chilli and ginger; and baked monkfish with parmesan and cream sauce.

The Sky and the Ground, 112 South Main St. One of Wexford's most popular pubs, full of character and serving excellent bar food prepared by the same kitchen that's responsible for *Heaven's Above*.

Tim's Tavern, South Main St. A regular local pub/restaurant with a lived-in feel and a bar menu which offers staples such as liver and bacon, and beef and Guinness casserole, while the restaurant is noted for cutlets, stews and steaks.

Pubs and bars

The Cape, The Bull Ring. Bar-undertaker run by an affable family, and as good a place as any to raise the spirits.

The Centenary Stores, Charlotte St. A lively pub attracting a young crowd, and a great spot to catch traditional music on Monday and Wednesday evenings, and Sunday morning, with a folk/blues mix on Tuesdays.

The Crown Bar, Monke St. A pleasant bar, dating from 1841, tucked down a peaceful side street. A good spot for a quiet pint five nights a week; live rock music on Thursdays and easy listening on Tuesdays.

The Sky and the Ground, 112 South Main St. Immensely popular bar favoured by tourists and locals alike. The interior's kitted out with old enamel ads for beer, baccy and booze. You could be forgiven for thinking that this bar has been here for years. Great atmosphere and traditional music every night except Saturday.

The Thomas Moore Tavern, Cornmarket. Traditional bar with a good fire in the corner. Named after the poet who, in 1836, came here "in the zenith of his imperishable fame to render honour to the mother he venerated and loved", as an inscription outside will tell you. Things haven't really revved up much since then and this place is another ideal choice for a quiet pint.

Opera, theatre and art

The long-established and hugely successful annual **Wexford Opera Festival** lasts for three weeks every October and draws people from all over the world. Each year the festival rescues three lesser-known operas by famous composers and presents them in the intimate setting of the Theatre Royal. Seasoned opera lovers find the festival a delight because of the sheer energy of the enterprise: a world-class festival on a shoe-string budget flowing through the narrow lanes of this friendly little town. Alongside the three major pieces are lunchtime recitals, choral and orchestral concerts, theatre, traditional music and immensely popular "Opera Scenes" in which well-known operas are presented in ninety-minute versions, with the principal characters accompanied by a pianist. It's advisable to book months in advance for tickets: the box office usually opens in June and you can get information on ticket availability and programmes from the festival office at any time (☎053/22400, *www.wexfordopera.com*).

Even out of festival time, Wexford has a lively cultural life, largely generated by a couple of **theatre** venues: the Theatre Royal on High St (☎053/22144), and the Wexford Arts Centre (☎053/23764) housed in an eighteenth-century market house and town hall in Cornmarket. The Theatre Royal hosts visiting companies including light opera and touring theatre groups, and the Wexford Arts Centre offers a healthy turnover of exhibitions and hosts performance artists, dance groups, drama and music. It's also worth calling in to *Abstract Studios*, 90 South Main St (up a little laneway), a small **gallery** which promotes the work of emerging artists, local and otherwise.

Around Wexford town

Within a few miles of Wexford lie plenty of attractions to justify staying around for a day or so. Some, like the wildfowl reserves at the endearingly named **North Slobs**, are of specialist interest. Others, though, could claim anyone's time – not least the excellent sandy beaches as near as Curracloe, five miles to the north, or the resort town of Rosslare to the south. The mud flats sheltered behind the sea walls of the Slaney estuary, known as the North Slobs, are home to the Wexford Wildfowl Reserve. The Slobs are the main wintering grounds for a third of the world's population of Greenland white-fronted geese, Bewick's swans, pintails and blacktailed godwits; you can also see spotted redshanks, gulls and terns. At the reserve there's a **visitor centre** (daily: mid-April to Sept 9am–6pm; Oct to mid-April 10am–5pm), a wildfowl collection, a research station, hides, lookout towers and identification charts, all freely accessible.

To reach the North Slobs, take the Gorey road (the R741) north out of Wexford over the bridge, and it's signposted on the right after about two miles.

Just two and a half miles inland from Wexford, the **Irish National Heritage Park** at **FERRYCARRIG** (March–Oct daily 9.30am–6.30pm, last admission 5pm, closing times may vary; £5/€6.35) plots nine thousand years of social change using full-scale models of settlements, homesteads and burial places, from the Stone Age through to Norman times. It's a great place to clarify your knowledge of Ireland's **ancient history**, and helps make sense of the numerous archeological remains dotted throughout the country. The park is also being developed as a **nature reserve**, and the environment has been carefully nurtured to provide the appropriate settings. It works well, so that as you walk through the Mesolithic campsite, the shaggy lichen covering on the hazel trees, the mud and the reeds all help evoke a primeval bog, while the Viking shipyard nestles convincingly on the estuary's banks. Access by public transport is very difficult, but a taxi there from Wexford costs around £4/€5.08, or you could always rent a bike.

Irish Agricultural Museum

Four miles southwest of Wexford, off the Rosslare Road, the **Irish Agricultural Museum** (April, May, Sept & Oct Mon–Fri 9am–12.30pm & 1.30–5pm, Sat & Sun 2–5pm; June–Aug Mon–Fri 9am–5pm, Sat & Sun 11am–5pm; Nov–March Mon–Fri 9am–12.30pm and 1.30–5pm, closed Sat & Sun; £2.50/€3.17) is set in the gardens of Johnstown Castle, a Gothic Revival castellated mansion. The museum, which is signposted "Research Centre", has good, clear displays on all aspects of rural life, encompassing domestic objects, farming machinery, carts and carriages, reconstructed workshops, and much on dairy farming. In addition, the grounds have mounds of rhododendrons, ornamental lakes, hot houses, dark woodland and walled gardens – all very spruce and well maintained. Three Viking Shuttle buses to Johnstown Castle depart daily from outside the tourist office.

The beaches

The southeast has more sunshine than any other part of Ireland, and as the entire coastline of the county to the north of Wexford town is made up of safe and sandy **beaches**, the region is a popular spot in summer for families and caravanners.

From **CURRACLOE**, five miles northeast of town (take the R742), superb, sandy dunes stretch away into the far distance, and it was here that Steven Spielberg shot the epic World War I film *Saving Private Ryan*. Curracloe makes a good point from which to access the Wexford Coastal Path. Though the little villages roundabout are overloaded in July and August, the sands themselves aren't. Unfortunately, without your own transport you'll be reliant on the Bus Éireann services from Wexford to Curracloe, which run highly infrequently.

Roughly six miles southeast of Wexford is the huge sandy beach at **ROSSLARE**, the county's other main seaside resort, not to be confused with Rosslare Harbour, another five miles further south. Right on the edge of the beach, the best hotel in the southeast, *Kelly's* (☎053/32114; ⑨), has excellent sporting facilities, outdoor hot tubs, and an

ROSSLARE HARBOUR TRAVEL INFORMATION

Rosslare Harbour is the arrival point for ferries from Pembroke and Fishguard in Wales, and Cherbourg and Roscoff in France. It's worth noting that the train station here is called Rosslare Europort.

Bus Éireann (☎053/22522). For local and national bus services, with direct links to Cork, Dublin and Limerick, see "Travel Details" at the end of this chapter.

Irish Ferries (☎053/33158, *www.irishferries.ie*). Services to Cherbourg (April–Jan 1–2 weekly; 19hr); Pembroke Dock (year round, 2 daily; 4hr); and Roscoff (April–Jan 1–3 weekly; 16hr 30min).

Irish Rail (☎053/33114). Rosslare Europort to Dublin (3 daily; 3hr 30min) and Wexford (3 daily; 30min).

Stena Line (☎053/33115, *www.stenaline.co.uk*). Ferry service to Fishguard (year round, 2 daily; 3hr 30min); Lynx catamaran to Fishguard (year round 3–4 daily; 1hr 40min).

impressive collection of Modern Irish art. Campers can pitch their tents among the caravans at *Burrow Holiday Park* (mid-March to early Nov; ☎053/32190).

Rosslare Harbour

ROSSLARE HARBOUR serves ferries to Cherbourg and Roscoff in France, and Fishguard and Pembroke Dock in South Wales. There's a **tourist office** at the harbour terminal (May–Sept open to meet all sailings except the 6.30am sailing; ☎053/33622), or, especially handy if you are driving, there's the Rosslare Kilrane tourist office, just over a mile from the ferry along the N25 (April–Sept daily to meet all sailings, except the 6.30am; Oct–March Tues–Sun restricted opening hours; ☎053/33232).

Ferries aside, there's not much to the place, but if you do need to stay, St Martin's Road, the village's main street, is dotted with several decent **B&Bs**: *Ailsa Lodge* (☎053/33230; ④), *Clifford House* (☎053/33226; ③), *Oldcourt House* (☎053/33895; ③) and *Rock Villa* (☎053/33212; ②) – all of a similar standard. You'll find an An Óige **hostel** nearby in Goulding St (☎053/33399) where a dorm bed costs £9/€11.43 in high season. You can **camp** for free down in the dunes by the beach or travel the three miles to Kilrane for *The Holiday Inn Caravan and Camping Park* (closed Oct–late May; ☎053/31168).

The south coast

In the southeast corner of Ireland, the sea has made inroads into an otherwise flat region, forming small lagoons popular with wind-surfers, at **Tacumshane** and **Lady's Island**, both venues for bird enthusiasts. Lady's Island itself sits mid-lagoon at the end of a causeway and has been a place of religious devotion for centuries: an annual pilgrimage to our Lady is still made here on August 15. On the island are the remains of an Augustinian priory and a Norman castle, both built in the thirteenth century, but the spirit of the place has been destroyed by a large, modern church building that has been tacked onto the side. West of here lies the quaint fishing village of **Kilmore Quay**, a good choice for accommodation and the departure point for trips to view the colonies of puffins on the **Saltee Islands**. The **Hook Head Peninsula**, around twenty miles further west, offers fine beaches, bracing walks and atmospheric castle and abbey ruins. There are few eating options for travellers in the area, but *The Lobster Pot* bar and restaurant at **Carne** is a great exception, serving delicious seafood meals.

Kilmore Quay and the Saltee Islands

KILMORE QUAY comes as a real surprise after the largely dull countryside which precedes it. A small fishing and holiday village of thatched cottages and whitewashed walls, with a good sandy beach, it's attractively situated around a stone harbour wall, looking out at the nearby Saltee Islands. County Wexford's **Maritime Museum** is housed in an old lightship alongside the marina (May–Sept daily noon–6pm; April & Oct Sat & Sun noon–6pm; £2/€2.54).

The village hosts a **seafood festival**, usually in the second week of July – a fine excuse to eat plenty of seafood. One of the most popular seafood restaurants and only a short walk from the harbour is *The Silver Fox* (☎053/29888). The village also has a handful of good bars, including *Kehoe's*, right in the middle of the village opposite the church, which has excellent barfood year round and singalongs during the summer. *Walkers*, down by the harbour, is probably one of the best fish-and-chip shops in Ireland.

Kilmore Quay is also the point of departure for visiting the uninhabited **Saltee Islands**, one of Ireland's most important bird sanctuaries, especially for puffins, razorbills, cormorants, shags, gannets, kittiwakes and auks. In the nesting period of late spring and early summer, there are thousands of them; by the end of July they have all left – so time your trip carefully. **Boat trips** to the islands may be available during the summer – contact Declan Bates of *The Saltees Princess* (☎053/29684) or Dick Hayes (☎053/29704), who organizes deep-sea angling trips at around £15/€19.23 per day.

B&B accommodation can be found at the quaint, thatched *Curlew Cottage* (☎053/29772; ②); and *Harbour Lights* (☎053/29881; ③), a short walk from the harbour. For a smart guesthouse there is *Quay House* (☎053/29988, *kilmore@esatclear.ie*; ④), conveniently situated on the road into the village. An **hostel** and **camping** are available at *Kilturk Independent Hostel* (IHH; closed Oct–April; ☎053/29883), a quiet spot about a mile outside the village on the R739.

The Hook Head Peninsula

Heading west from Kilmore Quay, the R736/R733 will take you to the **Hook Head Peninsula**, which forms the eastern side of Waterford Harbour. Only when you reach the peninsula does the flat coastline begin to undulate and the scenery become more attractive. Just five miles from the evocative ruin of **Tintern Abbey** is **Arthurstown**, the first village on the peninsula that you'll encounter, and about half a mile further on is the pretty **Ballyhack**, a tranquil spot beside the estuary and the place to catch the ferry across to county Waterford. South of both lies the popular seaside town of **Duncannon**, but it is really beyond here, on the head of the peninsula, that the eerie, windswept character of the Hook is best enjoyed.

Arthurstown and Tintern Abbey

ARTHURSTOWN, on the estuary near the neck of the peninsula, is a tiny village offering a handful of good **B&Bs**, namely *Clogheen* (☎051/389110; ②), the comfortable *Arthur's Rest* (☎051/389192; ③) and spacious *Glendine House* (☎051/389258; ④). There's also an An Óige **hostel** (closed Oct–May; ☎051/389411) in the old coastguard station – ring ahead to book. The *Waterfront Restaurant* (☎051/389534) has a good reputation.

About five miles east of Arthurstown (take the R733), near the muddy Bannow Bay, scene of the first Norman landing in 1169, stand the ruins of **Tintern Abbey** (mid-June to late Sept daily 9.30am–6.30pm, though times may vary; call ☎051/562650 if you want to be sure; £1.50/€1.90; Heritage Card), built in 1200 by William Marshall, Earl of Pembroke. Another fine Cistercian edifice, it owes its existence in this unprepossessing spot to a vow made by the earl while he was caught in a storm off the south coast. Praying that he might be saved, he promised to build an abbey wherever his boat came ashore. The presbytery is based on the foundation's more famous namesake in Wales.

Ballyhack and Dunbrody Abbey

Just half a mile to the north of Arthurstown lies the little village of **BALLYHACK**. From here a useful year-round **car ferry** service runs regularly across the harbour to Passage East in County Waterford, taking just ten minutes (see p.247). Setting off the picturesque scene is **Ballyhack Castle**, a fine five-storey, sixteenth-century tower house. You can climb about halfway up the tower and enjoy a strong sense of its stout proportions (June–Sept Mon–Fri 10am–1pm & 2–6pm, Sat & Sun 10am–6pm; £1/€1.27). The village's upmarket **seafood restaurant**, *The Neptune* (☎051/389284), is held in high regard, while *Byrne's* is a pleasant quayside spot for a drink.

The magnificent ruin of **Dunbrody Abbey** (daily: April–June & Sept 10am–6pm; July & Aug 10am–7pm; £1.50/€1.90) stands at the widening of the Barrow estuary, to the northeast of town off the R733. A thirteenth-century Cistercian foundation, it was altered in the sixteenth century after the Dissolution of the Monasteries, when the large central tower and adjacent buildings were added.

Duncannon to Slade

Unfortunately, the pretty, wooded coastline south of Ballyhack, down to Duncannon, is privately owned, and you can't walk along it. **DUNCANNON** itself is a holiday town, pleasant enough, with a rocky coast to the south that protects its big, sandy Blue Flag beach. Up on the headland, eerie **Duncannon Fort** (June–Sept daily 10am–5.30pm; £2/€2.54) dates back to 1586, when the Spanish Armada was expected to attack. Constantly added to since then, one of its grislier sights is the reputed dungeon of the Croppy Boy – tortured for his part in the 1798 Rebellion and hero of a well-known rebel song. Facilities in Duncannon are minimal: for **accommodation**, try *Shayanne B&B*, in a great location beside the beach (☎051/389250; ③). If you're **camping**, ask to use a local field. A couple of **bars** serve sandwiches and burgers, and *The Strand Seafood Bar* does an all-day menu.

From Duncannon, the countryside opens out and gives way to the strange emptiness of the peninsula which is quite magical. Little sandy bays lie concealed behind low cliffs, and there are lovely views across to the broad and beautiful Waterford coastline. Although the Hook Head Peninsula promotes itself as a tourist area, caravans and kids mostly keep to the areas around Duncannon and Fethard to the east, and there are plenty of isolated spots to be found. A couple of particularly fine, **sandy beaches** are Booley Strand, two miles south of Duncannon, and beyond that the smaller Dollar Bay.

At the peninsula's tip the shoreline is rockier, the limestone rich with fossils, and the land, flat and desolate, just slips away into the sea. The extremity is marked by a **lighthouse** (open to the public daily in summer 9.30am–5.30pm) said to be the oldest in Europe – the first on this site was built in the twelfth century. This part of Hook Head is favoured by ornithologists who come to watch the bird migrations, and if you're lucky you can sometimes spot seals. Crashing spray and blow-holes make it a dangerous and dramatic place in a storm – and you certainly shouldn't swim here at any time. For a bracing coastal walk, pick your way east along the coast as far as Slade (see p.224), about one and a half miles away.

The nearest shop to Hook Head is three and a half miles away at the Texaco petrol station at the Fethard–Duncannon junction. Taking the Duncannon road, *The Templars*

Inn (☎051/397162) in Templetown, about three miles from the tip, has a **restaurant** and bar food. The *Hotel Naomh Seosamh* (☎051/397129; ④) in Fethard, is the real hub of social activity in the area, serves great food both in the bar and restaurant, and has decent **accommodation**.

Tucked away on the east flank of the peninsula, the evocatively crumbling harbour of **SLADE** is a quiet, beautiful place: fishing boats cluster around its quays and slipways, stacked lobster pots lean against a fifteenth-century **castle**, and the whole place is built from stone a nutty-brown colour: rich, rusty and warm. To look around the castle, take the lane that runs alongside it and ask at the farm.

New Ross

First impressions of **NEW ROSS,** twenty-one miles west of Wexford on the N25, are not encouraging: a glamourless old port of grubby wharf buildings. However, the place isn't without character, thanks mostly to the river that has long given access to the heart of the Wexford and Kilkenny countryside, and the clutter of narrow lanes that do much to preserve the human scale of the place. In addition, the quayside itself will be greatly enhanced from spring 2001 by the presence of the tall-ship *Dunbrody*, a magnificent reconstruction of the original *SS Dunbrody*, a three-masted famine ship which took thousands of emigrants to new lives in America and Canada. On board will be an interactive visitor centre and a comprehensive database of all Irish immigration into the US from 1820 to 1920 (call ☎051/425239 or the tourist office for details; the ship might not remain in port all year round). It's worth climbing the steep back alleys to the top of town for views over the river and hills, and exploring the thirteenth-century ruins of St Mary's Church, with its graceful, Gothic windows and medieval tombstones in the chancel.

New Ross's **tourist office** (mid-June to Aug Mon–Sat 10am–6pm; ☎051/421857) is located on the quays. Bus Éireann buses to Waterford leave from outside the *Mariner's Inn*, also on the quays. Options for **accommodation** include the comfortable *Riversdale House*, Lower William St (☎051/422515; ③); a short walk from the centre of town. The friendly *MacMurrough Farm Hostel* (IHH; ☎051/421383, *machostel@eircom.net*) is a comfortable cottage **hostel** in a beautiful setting a couple of miles out of town; it makes a particularly good base for cyclists from which to explore the Nore and Barrow river valleys (see p.233 and p.234). To get there, ask for directions to Kelly's Statoil petrol station on the ring road; the hostel is signposted down the lane alongside.

Down on the quays, *John V's* has an excellent reputation for midday and evening **meals**, while good-value bar food is also served at *The Ship* on North Street, and there's no shortage of coffee shops along South Street. For something different, reserve a table on the *Galley Cruising Restaurant* (☎051/421723), which, from Easter to October, runs **boat trips** up the Barrow and Nore as far as Inistioge and St Mullins and along the Suir to Waterford.

You can sometimes catch live bands at *Crosbies*, while traditional **music** can be heard on a Friday night during summer at *Mannion's,* a cheerful country pub, about a mile out from the centre along the N30 Enniscorthy road.

The **arboretum**, five miles south of New Ross, known as the J.F. Kennedy Memorial Park (daily: April & Sept 10am–6.30pm; May–Aug 10am–8pm; Oct–March 10am–5pm; £2/€2.54; Heritage Card), contains a collection of around five thousand species of trees and shrubs and affords expansive views of the surrounding countryside. Kennedy's great-grandfather was born close by in Dunganstown, so the place is often frequented by Americans in search of presidential roots. The road south of here will take you to the coast and the Hook Head Peninsula (see p.222).

Enniscorthy and North Wexford

The market town of **ENNISCORTHY**, fourteen miles north of Wexford on the N11, is well worth visiting for the **National 1798 Visitor Centre** (Mon–Sat 9.30am–6pm, Sun 11am–5pm; *www.1798centre.com*; £4/€5.08), arguably the best interactive centre in Ireland and a must for anyone with an interest in the history of the eighteenth century and the political complexities of contemporary Ireland. Drawing on a rich array of audiovisual techniques, the exhibition brings to life the events surrounding the 1798 Rebellion in Ireland, and sets it in the wider context of revolution in France and the struggle for independence in America. One of the highlights is a tremendously effective audiovisual dramatization of a debate between the English radical Thomas Paine and the Anglo-Irish conservative Edmund Burke.

For a more traditional presentation of the events of 1798 and for material on the 1916 uprising, call in at **The County Museum** (March–Sept daily 10am–6pm; Oct–Feb Sun 2–5pm; £3/€3.81), housed in a Norman castle overlooking the town. It's crammed with a wonderful mixture of local objects, from an ogham stone to a sedan chair. Across the river, covered in mustard and yellow gorse, lies **Vinegar Hill**, the site of the rebels' main encampment during the 1798 Rebellion – and the scene of their final slaughter by Crown forces. Enniscorthy hosts the enjoyable week-long "Strawberry Fair", usually held over the last week of June, or, the first week of July (☎054/33256), which combines music and street entertainment with the pleasures of soft fruit. The modern *Enniscorthy Holiday Hostel*, Railway Square (IHH; ☎054/37766) offers family **rooms**, doubles (②), dorms and bike hire.

The uplands to the north and west of Enniscorthy are bald and spartan. There's little in the way of sights on this side of the Blackstairs Mountains, though if you're heading north, **FERNS**, seven miles from Enniscorthy, makes a good lunch stop. One-time seat of the kings of Leinster, it's now a little scrap of a village, top-heavy with history: it was here that Dermot MacMurrough was attacked by Tiernán O'Rourke – whose wife he had abducted fourteen years earlier. MacMurrough sought help from Henry II in France, who lent him Richard Fitzherbert de Clare (Strongbow), and thus an adultery led to the Norman invasion of Ireland. An **abbey** was founded in Ferns in the sixth century, and you can see its remains in St Edan's churchyard and the adjacent field. Most impressive, though, are the ruins of the thirteenth-century **castle**, with its pair of towers – which you can climb – and two curtain walls (opening times and admission charges to be confirmed; ☎01/647 2453; Heritage Card). When you're feeling peckish, head for *The Courtyard* in the village, which does superb bar food. Decent budget accommodation and camping are to be found at **BUNCLODY**, about twelve miles north of Enniscorthy, at *The Bunclody Hostel* (closed Oct–Feb; ☎054/76076). The village itself is pretty unremarkable, but it is on the Dublin–Waterford bus route, and just three miles from **CLONEGALL** at the southerly end of the Wicklow Way – the hostel will pick you up from here on request.

Quite the nicest family **seaside town** in the area is **COURTOWN**, around 25 miles north of Wexford (turn off the N11 onto the R742 at Gorey) and plumb in the middle of another excellent, long stretch of sand. A short walk from the beach is *Harbour House* (☎055/25117; ④), a well-run **B&B**.

GOREY, four miles inland from Courtown, is the main shopping centre for the north Wexford coast, a very cheerful place of brightly coloured stores and plenty of interesting bars. Whether you're stopping here or not, you're likely to get caught up passing through Gorey as it's a notorious traffic bottleneck jammed with the heavy traffic travelling from Rosslare Harbour and Wexford to Dublin.

Carlow

For centuries, the town of **CARLOW** was an Anglo-Norman stronghold at the edge of an otherwise fiercely Gaelic county. As such, it has a bloody history, with its most terrible battle during the 1798 Rebellion, when over six hundred rebels were slaughtered. Today there's nothing to suggest its former frontier status, and this small, busy town is distinguished only by a fine Classical courthouse with a portico modelled on the Parthenon, an elegant Regency Gothic cathedral – one of the first Catholic churches to be built after Catholic Emancipation in 1829 – and the remains of the once proud Norman **castle**, which lie beside the river at the west end of town. Otherwise, there's plenty on local military, religious and folk history in the **museum**, housed in the town hall (Tues–Fri 11am–5pm, Sat & Sun 2–5pm; £1/€1.27).

You can get more local information, including a free map and historical guide, from Carlow's **tourist office** at the lower end of the large car park off Kennedy Ave (May–Sept Mon–Sat 9.30am–5.30pm; Oct–April Mon–Fri 10am–5.30pm; ☎0503/31554). **Bike rental** is available during the summer from A.E. Coleman, 19 Dublin St (☎0503/31273; £5/€6.35 per day) and you can rent a Canadian **canoe** from Charlie Horan (☎0509/31307 or 087/529700; two-person canoe £30/€38.09 per day) to paddle down the River Barrow. Those interested in getting to grips with the intricacies of **celtic brewing techniques**, should book in for a tour of The Carlow Brewing Company, lodged up beside the train station. The beers produced here are based on traditional Celtic recipes and include a wheat beer, red ale and, of course, stout. The short tour explains the process and offers the chance to sample a glass or two; it's best booked the day before as opening times vary (☎0503/34356; £3/€3.81).

B&Bs in Carlow include *Westlow*, Green Lane (☎0503/43964; ③) and *Redsetter House*, 14 Dublin St (☎0503/41848; ④), both of which are a good standard. Several more accommodation options are out on Kilkenny Road; one of the best of these is *Barrowville Town House* (☎0503/43324; ④), an elegant Regency building set in a mature garden, just a short walk from the town centre. Nearby lies *Ottersholt Riverside Lodge* (IHH; ☎0503/30404), a rambling old hostel offering budget accommodation in dorms and twin rooms (①), and **camping** down by the river.

You'll find the best places to **eat and drink** on Tullow Street: *Tully's* is an appealing bar and a handy spot for lunch, and *Buzz's*, across the street, offers hearty home-cooked lunches and manages to combine laid-back stylishness with a no-nonsense lived-in atmosphere. Coffee shops serving light lunches, also in Tullow Street, include *Bradbury's* and *Muffins*. Both *Buzz's* (late closing Thurs–Sat till 1am) and *Tully's* are lively spots during the evening, and *Teach Dolmen*, at 76 Tullow St is the best place to catch impromptu traditional music sessions on Thursdays.

Two miles east out of town on the R726 road is arguably County Carlow's most impressive sight: the **Browneshill dolmen**. It's enormous, possibly the largest Neolithic stone formation in Europe, dating from 2500 BC, and the burial place of a local king or prince.

Seven miles south of Carlow on the N9 lies **LEIGHLINBRIDGE**, a pretty riverside village. A good place to stop for lunch here is *The Lord Bagenal Inn*: an old bar of some character popular for its **bar food** and family atmosphere.

Borris and the South Leinster Way

Ten miles south from Leighlinbridge, along the R705, is tiny **BORRIS**, which you're most likely to visit if you're travelling through the county by car or walking the South Leinster Way. It's not especially attractive aside from its fresh air and one broad (fast) main road, the R705, that sweeps down towards a striking backdrop formed by the ash-mottled Blackstairs Mountains, but it's as good a place as any to stop in the area. Mrs Susan Breen in Church Street does decent, inexpensive **B&B** (☎0503/73231; ③) and *The Step House*, 66 Main St (☎0503/73209; ⑤) is a fine Georgian guesthouse. You can camp by the disused train line and get your provisions from *O'Shea's bar and shop*.

The Green Drake Inn serves snacks and lunches every day till 6pm, and more expensive **meals** until 9.30pm. Considering its size, there's a lot going on in Borris, with **live music** several nights of the week, mostly in the singalongs and ballads category: try *The Green Drake Inn* (Wednesday is Irish night, Sunday for music and dancing), *O'Connors* or *O'Shea's*. This last doubles up as a hardware store so you can sup your pint leaning on a bacon slicer, keeping a weather-eye on the hacksaws and sink plungers dangling from the ceiling.

East of Borris, the **South Leinster Way** leaves the intimate landscape of the valleys, crossing the open farmland of south Carlow and eventually skirting the bleak height of Mount Leinster. The way finally descends to the lonely cluster of houses which makes up Kildavin, six miles or so from Mount Leinster on the main Carlow–Enniscorthy road.

COUNTY KILKENNY

County Kilkenny offers the finest of the southeast's countryside. Mostly it's intensely pretty, rich farmland, especially to the north of New Ross around the confluence of the Nore and Barrow rivers. **Medieval ruins** are scattered all over the county, but they reach their richest concentration in ancient **Kilkenny city** – a quaint but really bustling favourite. The delightful surroundings make it ideal for biking around the river valleys and their medieval ruins, most notably **Kells Priory** and **Jerpoint Abbey**. The cycling is easy: off the main roads there's little traffic, and the minor roads that stay close to the rivers are especially scenic. Alternatively, the heart of this rich, historical farmland can be crossed on foot. As they head south, the Nore and Barrow rivers flow through gentle valleys of mixed woodland. The **South Leinster Way** provides unstrenuous walking, passing through pretty **riverside villages** – Inistioge, Graiguenamanagh, and nearby Borris and St. Mullins – before heading north towards the **Blackstairs Mountains**. To access the area from Kilkenny hitching is probably your best bet, as there's just one bus a week, on Thursday, from Kilkenny to Inistioge. Alternatively, you could see the region from the **cruises** that operate from the river port of New Ross (see p.224).

Kilkenny

KILKENNY is Ireland's finest medieval city. Above the broad sweep of the River Nore sits the castle, while a pretty, humpbacked stone bridge leads up into narrow, cheerful streets laced with carefully maintained buildings. Kilkenny's earliest settlement was a monastery founded by St Canice in the sixth century, but all that remains from those days is the round tower which stands alongside the cathedral. The city's layout today owes more to its medieval history. Following continual skirmishes between local clans, the arrival of the **Normans** in 1169 saw the building of a fort by Strongbow on the site of today's castle. His son-in-law, William Marshall, consolidated Norman power in Kilkenny, maintaining the fortified city and keeping the indigenous Irish in an area of less substantial housing, beyond its walls – of which only the name "Irishtown" remains. In 1391, the Butler family acquired Kilkenny Castle and so ensured the city's loyalty to the English Crown.

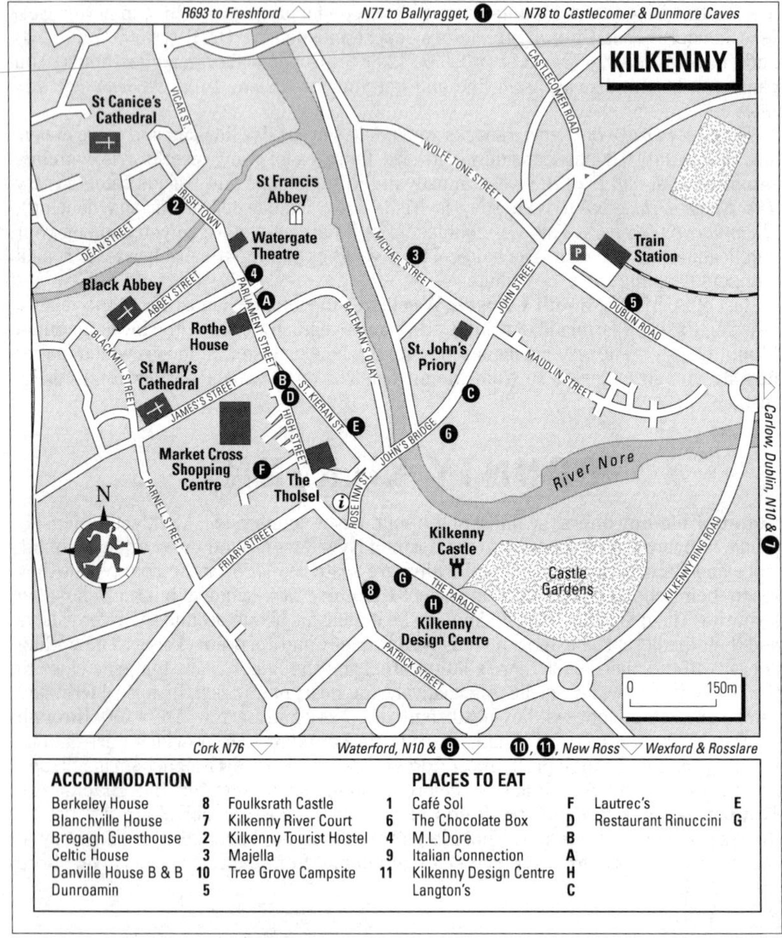

In the mid-seventeenth century, Kilkenny virtually became the capital of Ireland, with the founding of a parliament in 1641 known as the **Confederation of Kilkenny** (see p.669). This attempt to unite resistance to the English persecution of Catholics was powerful for a while, though its effectiveness had greatly diminished by the time Cromwell arrived – in his usual destructive fashion – in 1650. Kilkenny never recovered its former prosperity and importance. The disgrace of the Butler family in 1715, coupled with English attacks upon the rights of Catholics through the Penal Laws, saw the city decline still further, though the towering mill buildings on the river banks are evidence of a considerable industrial history.

Enough medieval buildings remain to attest to Kilkenny's former importance, however, and in a place brimming with civic pride, there's been a tasteful push towards making the town a major tourist attraction. Kilkenny is sometimes known as "the marble city" because of the limestone mined locally, which develops a deep black shine when polished. Echoing this, the town's bar and shop signs all gleam with black and brown lacquer, the names cut in deeply bevelled, stout gold lettering.

Arrival, information and accommodation

The **train** station (☎056/22024) lies just off the north road out of the city on Dublin Street. Bus Éireann services (☎056/64933) depart from both the train station and Patrick Street; privately operated **buses** generally depart from The Parade outside Kilkenny Castle. Note that in Irish the city is called *Cill Chainnigh*, and this is what it says on the front of buses. You can get free maps of the city and plenty of other information from the **tourist office** in Rose Inn St (May & June Mon–Sat 9am–6pm; July & Aug Mon–Sat 9am–7pm, Sun 11am–1pm & 2–5pm; Sept 9am–6pm, Sun 11am–1pm & 2–5pm; Oct–April Mon–Sat 9am–5pm; ☎056/51500).

Kilkenny is well served by **B&Bs**, although in the summer the city gets crowded, and at festival time (see p.232) you'll need to book in advance. *Tree Grove Campsite* (mid-Nov to Feb by prior arrangement only; ☎056/70302), about a mile south out of town along the R700, is a well-equipped and well-run site if you want to **camp**.

Berkley House, 5 Patrick St (☎056/64848). Comfortable guesthouse in generously proportioned period town house, right in the centre of town. All rooms are en suite with TV and tea and coffee making facilities. ⑥.

Blanchville House (☎056/27197, *www.blanchville.ie*). Fine Georgian house set in rich farmland, about five miles east out of town. Comfortable rooms with private bathrooms also offer lovely views of the surrounding countryside. There's a tennis court and billiard room for guests to use. Dinner is available but you need to book before noon. Closed Nov–Feb. ⑥.

Bregagh Guesthouse, Dean St (☎056/22315). Large, detached family house set back from the road, right in the town centre. All rooms are en suite. ④.

Celtic House, 18 Michael St (☎056/62249). Beautifully decorated, spic and span B&B offering spacious rooms, all of which are en suite. Quiet location, yet only five minutes walk from the town centre. ④.

Danville House, New Ross Rd (☎056/21512) A delightful eighteenth-century mansion set in beautiful gardens of grassy lawns and mature trees; located about one mile south of town along the R700 and next door to the Tree Grove Campsite. The house is full of interesting antiques and the rooms are pleasant and airy. ③.

Dunroamin, Dublin Rd (☎056/61387). Wonderfully welcoming B&B in a nineteenth-century family home. All rooms are en suite. ④.

Foulksrath Castle, Jenkinstown (☎056/67674). An Óige hostel located eight miles north of town along the N77. Buggy's buses run from Kilkenny Castle to Jenkinstown; call Buggy's for timetable details (☎056/41264) or ask at the tourist office. The setting – a sixteenth-century fort in lush meadows – makes up for the inconvenience of getting out here. Dorm-room accommodation only is available.

Kilkenny River Court Hotel, John St (☎056/23388, *www.kilrivercourt.com*). Comfortable, traditionally styled accommodation, superbly situated on the banks of the river; some of the deluxe rooms have views of the castle. Facilities include pool, gym and riverside bar. ⑨.

Kilkenny Tourist Hostel, 35 Parliament St (☎056/63541, *http://homepage.eircom.net/~kilkennyhostel/*). Right in the town centre and run by a friendly crowd, this IHH hostel is by far the nicest budget accommodation in town. There's a bright, airy kitchen and sitting room; clean and spacious dorms and private rooms (①) are available.

Majella, Waterford Rd (☎056/21129). Welcoming B&B in a modern bungalow about half a mile from the city centre. Good breakfasts, pleasant interiors and non-smoking rooms are available. Open May–Oct. ③.

The City

Kilkenny is focused on the hill and its **castle**. Climbing from the river up Rose Inn Street brings you to the tourist office (see above), housed in the sixteenth-century

Shee Alms House, one of the very few Tudor almshouses to be found in Ireland. A walking tour of the city leaves from here six times a day (£3); enquire at the tourist office for exact times. At the top of Rose Inn Street to the left is the broad stretch known as **The Parade**, which leads up to the castle. Formerly used for military and civic ceremonies, it now serves as a bus park in summer. To the right, the High Street, graced with the eighteenth-century **Tholsel**, once the centre of the city's financial dealings, and now the town hall, soon becomes the busy main thoroughfare of Parliament Street, then continues, crooked and intriguing, with little medieval slips and alleyways ducking off it, through Irishtown towards the **cathedral**.

Of all the surviving buildings from the prosperous Tudor commercial period, the finest is **Rothe House** on Parliament St (April–June, Sept & Oct Mon–Sat 10.30am–5pm, Sun 3–5pm; July & Aug Mon–Sat 10am–6pm, Sun 3–5pm; Nov–March Mon–Sat 1–5pm, Sun 3–5pm; £2/€2.54). Home to the **Kilkenny Archeological Society museum**, and a **costume** gallery of waistcoats, bonnets and gowns from the eighteenth century onwards, the building itself is a unique example of an Irish Tudor merchant's home dating back to 1594, and comprises three separate houses linked by interconnecting courtyards. There is also a genealogical research centre here for those wanting to trace their roots locally.

Also on Parliament Street you can visit **Kilkenny Brewery** (June–Aug Mon–Fri at 3pm). Although you won't get a tour, they do at least show a video of the production process, followed by tasting in the cellar bar. It's free, but only fifty tickets are available each day; these can be picked up in advance at the security gate.

Kilkenny Castle

It's the **castle** (April–May daily 10.30am–5pm; June–Sept daily 10am–7pm; Oct–March Tues–Sat 10.30am–12.45pm & 2–5pm, Sun 11am–12.45pm & 2–5pm; guided tours only; £3.50/€4.44), an imposing building standing high and square over the river, that really defines Kilkenny. Dating originally from the twelfth century, it was much added to in the seventeenth and nineteenth centuries. While the furnishings and paintings suggest a civilized wealth and domesticity, the scale and grandeur of the rooms, with their deeply recessed windows and robust fireplaces, signify a much cruder political power. The biggest surprise is the flimsy wooden hammer-beam roof of the picture gallery, covered with the folksy, pre-Raphaelite decoration of John Hungerford Pollen – plenty of gold and burnt umber plant life smudging its way across the ceiling.

Also within the castle is the **Butler Gallery**, housing exhibitions of modern art, and a tearoom (summer only), in the castle's former kitchen – you don't have to pay the castle entrance fee to visit either the Butler Gallery or the tearoom. The eighteenth-century stables, opposite the castle, have been converted into The Design Centre, an outlet for high-quality Irish crafts, and an excellent café.

The cathedral, round tower, churches and brewery

The other must in Kilkenny is **St Canice's Cathedral** (Easter–Sept Mon–Sat 9am–1pm & 2–6pm, Sun 2–6pm; Oct–Easter Mon–Sat 10am–1pm & 2–4pm, Sun 2–4pm). It was built in the thirteenth century, and the purity and unity of its architecture lends it a grandeur beyond its actual size. Rich in carvings, it has an exemplary selection of sixteenth-century monuments, many in black Kilkenny marble, the most striking being effigies of the Butler family.

The **Round Tower** next to the cathedral (same hours; £1/€1.27) is all that remains of the early monastic settlement reputedly founded by St Canice in the sixth century; there are superb views from the top – ask anyone working in the church or churchyard for access (if you want to climb the tower during June, July and August be there before 5.30pm; arrangements are more flexible at other times).

Kilkenny is littered with the remains of other medieval churches. The **Black Abbey**, founded by Dominicans in 1225, has been carefully restored and contains some unusual carvings and sepulchral slabs. On the other side of town, **St John's Priory** has only a roofless chancel, a fine seven-light window and a medieval tomb. Thirteenth-century **St Francis' Abbey** stands in ruins by the river.

Eating, drinking and entertainment

Kilkenny is a very lively small city, and while there's not a huge number of places to **eat**, there is at least a reasonable range. **Bars** are as alluring in Kilkenny as anywhere in Ireland, you won't be hard pushed to find some kind of **music** here either, and in June it hosts the fabulous comedy festival, **The Cat Laughs**. It's a small enough town to enjoy sampling a few bars before choosing your favourite; if you want to check out pubs and entertainment generally it's worth taking a look at *www.kilkennycraic.com* an informative **Web site**.

Cafés and restaurants

Café Sol, William St (☎056/64987). Arguably the best place to eat in Kilkenny, whether you want a quick lunch or a leisurely evening meal. The emphasis is on fresh, local ingredients; there's plenty of fish on the menu and always some good vegetarian options. Closed Sun year round and Wed evenings in winter.

The Chocolate Box, High St. Hand-made fudge and chocolate shop that has a little café serving inexpensive homely favourites such as scrambled egg on toast, shepherds pie, apple pie and muffins.

Italian Connection, Parliament St (☎056/64225). A firm favourite for inexpensive pizza and pasta in a convivial atmosphere.

Kilkenny Design Centre, The Parade. The centre's café serves excellent homemade soups, salads and quiches.

Langton's, 69 John St (☎056/65133). Large, briskly run bar noted for its award-winning bar meals: homemade burgers, grilled cutlets and vegetarian stir-fry are typical evening fare.

Lautrec's, 9 St Kieran St (☎056/54400). Bustling, friendly bar-bistro serving good pizza and pasta dishes.

M.L. Dore, 65 High St. Café serving inexpensive salads and hot dinners. Open daily from breakfast till 10pm, Sun till 9pm.

Restaurant Rinuccini, The Parade (☎056/61575). Excellent, and expensive, Italian-Irish restaurant specializing in fish, game and homemade pasta dishes. Not especially spacious, but nevertheless generally considered the classiest place in town.

Bars and music venues

Anna Conda, Parliament St. Cosy, friendly little pub attracting locals and visitors alike. The atmosphere is relaxed, except for Saturdays when it tends to be hectic. Traditional music is played here on Mondays, Wednesdays & Saturdays.

The Cat Laughs, Dean St. Newspapers, chess, coffee and croissants give this pub something of a cosmopolitan air. It's a venue for occasional theatre and comedy acts.

John Cleere's, Parliament St. Traditional Irish and folk music on Mondays; an open jam session on Wednesdays; occasional bands at weekends; and a tiny theatre where they sometimes lay on drama and comedy.

Kyteler's Inn, St Kieran St. A pub which is something of a tourist attraction, but a must if you've an interest in all things medieval. It was once the home of Dame Alice Kyteler, a woman accused of witchcraft and rumoured to have murdered four husbands. She escaped to France, but her maid, the unfortunate Petronella, was burned at the stake in her place.

Maggie Holland's, St Kieran St. An old-style bar with a good atmosphere, and excellent traditional/folk sessions most of the year on Wednesdays and Thursdays.

Pumphouse, Parliament St. A cosy old pub with a nice fire in the winter and a very lively atmosphere during the summer. Traditional music from Mondays to Wednesdays; rock bands during the summer at weekends.

Ryan's, Friary St. A laid-back, friendly spot with great traditional music sessions on Thursdays.

Tynan's Bridge Bar, beside John's Bridge. A quaint little old pub and a pleasant spot for a quiet pint.

Widow McGrath's, Parliament St. Hosts live music at weekends and can be very lively indeed. Sit out in the beer garden in summer to enjoy the barbeques held on Tuesdays.

Entertainment – Arts Week and The Cat Laughs

Other entertainment is fairly easy to come by in summer. *The Kilkenny People*, published on Wednesday, lists what's on in the city and the surrounding villages; and it is worth checking out the Watergate Theatre, Parliament St (☎056/61674; *watergate theatre .homepage.com*), which hosts a wide range of touring companies, including theatre, ballet and music. One event to try to coincide with is the **Kilkenny Arts Festival**, a ten-day event, usually run over the last two weeks in August(☎056/63663). The emphasis is on classical music, but alongside this is a fringe festival of literary readings, art exhibitions and jazz and folk sessions. **The Cat Laughs**, a comedy festival held at the beginning of June, brings together comedians from all over the world – many of them trying out new material before heading for Edinburgh in August. Events are held in pubs, clubs and theatres. The programme comes out a month beforehand and is available from tourist offices, while information is available on the Web site: *www.thecatlaughs.com*. It's worth booking ahead by calling the organizers directly on ☎056/63416.

Listings

Bank Allied Irish Bank, 3 High St. *M.L. Dore* restaurant, will cash travellers' cheques, personal cheques and currency, and operates Western Union till 10pm daily. Ulster Bank have an ATM upstairs in the Market Cross Shopping Centre.

Bike rental J.J. Wall, Maudlin St (☎056/21236). Rental is £7/€8.86 per day, £30/€38.46 per week.

Books For Irish-interest books, maps and guides, try Dubray Books, Market Cross Shopping Centre or The Book Centre in the High St – the latter also has a wide selection of foreign newspapers.

Camping supplies Kilkenny Camping and Watersports, Kilkenny Arcade (upstairs), High St (☎056/64025).

Hospital St Lukes, Freshford Rd (☎056/51133).

Internet access Compustore, Unit 12, Market Cross Shopping Centre, off High St (*cstorekk@iol.ie*).

Laundry Bretts, Michael St (☎056/63200).

Pharmacy Boots, 36 & 37 High St; Michael O'Connell; High St.

Police ☎056/22222.

Post office High St (Mon–Sat 9am–5.30pm, Tues opens 9.30am).

Swimming pool Michael St (☎056/21380 for opening times).

Trains Irish Rail ☎056/22024.

Travel agent Mannings Travel, High St (closed 1–2pm; ☎056/22950).

The Dunmore Caves

The main points of local interest are undoubtedly the **Dunmore Caves** (mid-March to mid-June & mid-Sept to Oct daily 10am–5pm; mid-June to mid-Sept daily 10am–7pm; Nov to mid-March Sat, Sun & public holidays 10am–5pm; check opening times with the tourist office; £2/€2.54), situated seven miles north of Kilkenny (take the N77 then the N78) on an isolated limestone outcrop of the Castlecomer plateau. Alternatives to driving there include renting a bike in Kilkenny, or taking Buggy's bus from The Parade.

In 1967, Viking coins and the skeletons of 46 women and children were found among the stalactites and stalagmites. It's thought that the Vikings attacked the native Irish, and the women and children hid in the caves for protection. The plan obviously failed, but the fact that the skeletons showed no broken bones suggests that the victims starved to death, were lost or that the Vikings tried to smoke them out.

The Nore and Barrow valleys

Two rivers, the **Nore** and the **Barrow**, flowing magnificently through rich countryside, have long been of immense importance to the southeast. Formerly they were the chief means of communication, bringing prosperity to the heart of the region: the Nore brought trade to medieval Kilkenny, the Barrow to Carlow. Today they are treasured for their considerable beauty and are a real treat for anglers. The surrounding countryside is extremely pretty, perfectly enjoyed on bike or on foot – the South Leinster Way dips down into some of the choicest spots. Plan a leisurely route, and you can meander through picturesque ancient villages and take in exceptional medieval ruins. There's a concentration of high-quality craft workshops here too – including those of Jerpoint Glass and the potter Nicholas Mosse – pick up a leaflet on the Kilkenny Craft Trail from the tourist office for further information.

The Nore Valley

The **Nore Valley** is deservedly renowned for its beauty, the river rolling through lush pastures and past some engaging ruins. It is perhaps at its finest as it broadens to the south of Kilkenny, where, along the tributary King's River eight miles south of the city (take the R697 or the N10 and turn off at Stonyford), sits medieval **KELLS**. Set amidst lush pastureland, the tiny village is an unexpected sight: its broad bridge is majestically out of scale, an ancient stone water mill stands on the river bank, and the encompassing deep hollow is flecked with mallows, marsh marigolds, docks and irises. Hard by, the magnificent ruin of **Kells Priory** – founded in 1193 – sits like a perfect scale model of a medieval walled city, a clean iron-grey against the surrounding green fields. The ruins consist of a complete curtain wall with square towers and fortified gatehouse, and the remnants of the fourteenth- and fifteenth-century church form one of the most impressive and largest medieval sites in Ireland. This town has nothing to do with the *Book of Kells*, which is associated with Kells in County Meath, though ironically enough the remains at that far more famous site are considerably less exciting than these.

Signposted from Kells, two miles south, are **Kilkree Round Tower** – just one of the many round towers scattered around this part of the country – and the nearby high cross, decorated with much-eroded biblical carvings. Alternatively, you can take the road east out of Kells and past Stonyford to placid **Jerpoint Abbey** (daily: March to May & mid-Sept to mid-Nov 10am–5pm; June to mid-Sept 9.30am–6.30pm; last two weeks of Nov 10am-6pm; £2/€2.55; Heritage Card). The abbey follows a typical Cistercian layout around an elegant, cloistered garden, and is built of warm, oat-coloured stone, and is generally visited for its tombs and twelfth-century carvings – especially the animated figures in the cloister.

You can **stay** at the very pleasant *Abbey House* guesthouse (☎056/24166; ⑤), which is directly opposite the abbey, or at the *Nore Valley Park* (closed end Oct to Feb; ☎056/27229), about two miles south of Bennettsbridge, which is a neat, family-oriented campsite with a farm alongside.

Thomastown and Inistioge

A mile north of Jerpoint is **THOMASTOWN**. Formerly a medieval walled town of some importance, it's now simply a picturesque country town on the Kilkenny–Waterford train line. Minimal ruins of the walls, a castle and a thirteenth-century church (with some weathered effigies) remain, and in the Catholic church you'll find the high altar from Jerpoint.

A restored medieval tower, *The Tower House*, on Low St (☎056/24500; ④) offers good quality **B&B**, as does *Belmore*, Jerpoint Church, an eighteenth-century hunting lodge a mile south of town in a picturesque spot (☎056/24228, *teesdale@trailblazers.ie*; ④). Several places serve pub **lunches**, and *The Watergarden* tearoom, run by the local Camphill Community, makes a refreshing place for a break combining a delightful, small ornamental garden with a craft workshop. There's also a couple of interesting little bars tucked away on Logan Street – *Carroll's* and *O'Hara's*.

Heading north, it's worthwhile stopping off to visit **Kilfane Glen** and its **woodland garden** (April–June & Sept Sun 2–6pm; July & Aug daily 11am–6pm; £3/€3.81), a steep glen, complete with cottage *orné*, waterfall and hermit's grotto. It's an example of the Romantic craze for constructing "wild" landscapes in the back garden, although it's something of a rarity in Ireland. To get to the glen, turn right two miles north of Thomastown on the N9 (before you get to Kilfane), then right again, following the signposts. In **KILFANE** itself, a ruined church holds the fourteenth-century **Cantwell Effigy**, an impressive piece of stone-carving of a knight in full armour.

INISTIOGE, a few miles southeast of Thomastown on the R700, boasts a tree-lined square beside a fine stone bridge. The village is dotted with crumbling stonework, and little eighteenth- and nineteenth-century houses climb the steep lane that twists away from its centre. The grounds of the local estate, Woodstock, are open to the public if you fancy a stroll overlooking the neighbouring countryside, but the house itself was burnt down in 1922 after it had been occupied by the Black and Tans (see p.674). Alternatively, there's a very pleasant walk along the riverbank signposted from the centre of the village.

For **accommodation**, the beautifully situated *Kookaburra House* B&B is on Rock Rd (closed Sept–May; ☎056/58519; ②) – head over the bridge towards New Ross, turn left, and follow the lane for just under a mile. *The Circle of Friends* (☎056/58800) – named after the film starring Minnie Driver that was shot in the village – is a fairly formal **restaurant** with an interesting menu, they also have a good café downstairs serving homemade snacks, cakes and sandwiches.

The Barrow Valley

The Barrow River flows through some of the most picturesque spots in the south east, which makes it particularly popular with boating enthusiasts; narrow boats can be hired in Graiguenamanagh from Valley Boats, Barrow Lane (☎0503/24945). For walking, the stretch of the South Leinster Way northeast from Inistioge is particularly pretty and offers a couple of pleasant places to rest up. The dusty little market town of **GRAIGUENAMANAGH** (you can also reach here by road from Inistioge and Thomastown) stands in a lovely spot beside the River Barrow, with herons fishing in the rushing weir. The town's great age is indicated by the central **Duiske Abbey** which dominates Graiguenamanagh. Founded in 1204, it was the largest Cistercian abbey in Ireland at that time, and although much has been altered and added outside (including a nineteenth-century clock tower and pebble-dashed walls), the thirteenth-century interior has been lovingly preserved. Besides some original fleur-de-lis tiling and a fine effigy of a knight in chain mail, most impressive is the superb Romanesque processional doorway to the right of the organ – heavily decorated and one of the best to have survived the Reformation. In the churchyard, near the steps outside the south transept, stand a couple of ninth-century stone crosses, and a sixth-century font from Ullard stands outside the north wall of the chancel. The **Abbey Centre** nearby (June–Aug Mon–Fri 10am–1pm & 2–5pm, Sat & Sun 2–5pm; Sept–May Mon–Fri 10am–1pm & 2–5pm) displays interesting contemporary religious art exhibitions.

Graiguenamanagh is also a good point from which to walk up **Brandon Hill** (1703ft). The walk is along forest tracks for much of the way, none of it particularly steep, opening out onto a heathery summit and wonderful views. Follow the South Leinster Way route from town, and when you reach the hill follow the route which is waymarked as the Brandon Way. Alternatively, for a more sheltered and leisurely walk, you can follow the Way north from here along the Barrow to Borris (see p.226).

The best place to **stay** and **eat** in Graiguenamanagh is the plush *Waterside* B&B and restaurant (☎0503/24246, *info@waterside.iol.ie*; ⑥), a beautifully restored stone building overlooking the river. More modestly priced B&B accommodation is offered at *The Anchor Bar* (☎0503/24207; ③), which also serves food daily; and also at *Woodside*, Ballynakill (☎0503/24765; ③), about a mile out on the New Ross road. An extensive dinner menu and good, inexpensive daytime snacks are available in *Monks Refectory Restaurant* (closed Mon & Tues; ☎0503/24988).

St Mullins

Five miles south down the towpath along the River Barrow from Graiguenamanagh, or the R729, and into County Carlow, is **ST MULLINS** tucked away among wooded hills, with the open heights of the Blackstairs Mountains beyond. Strolling through the village, you'll come across the scant remains of a monastery, founded in 696 AD by St Moling, Bishop of Ferns and Glendalough, and alongside them in the churchyard are the base of a round tower and a very worn stone cross. Down beside the stream, at the back of the ruins, a path leads to St Moling's Well, while near the centre of the village stands a defensive earthwork, looking like a sturdy pudding just shaken from its bowl.

Blanchfield's **pub** does regular soup and sandwiches and *Teac Moling* offers **B&B** in a very pretty spot beside the river(☎051/424665; ④). The nearest shop is at Glynn, one and a half miles away.

travel details

Trains

Carlow to: Dublin (5 daily; 1hr 15min); Kildare (5 daily; 30min); Kilkenny (4 daily; 45min).

Kilkenny to: Carlow (4 daily; 30min); Dublin (4 daily; 1hr 45min).

Rosslare Harbour/Europort to: Dublin (3 daily; 3hr 15min).

Wexford to: Dublin (3 daily; 2hr 30min–3hr); Rosslare Harbour/Europort (3 daily; 30min).

Buses

For more information on privately run bus routes contact the following companies who operate in this area: Buggy's (☎056/41264); J.J. Kavanagh (☎056/31106); Viking Shuttle Bus (☎056/21053).

Buggy's and Bus Éireann

Carlow to: Dublin (7 daily; 1hr 30min).

Kilkenny to: Clonmel (6 daily; 1hr); Dublin (6 daily; 2hr).

New Ross to: Dublin (3 daily; 2hr 45min).

Rosslare Harbour to: Cork (3 daily; 4hr); Dublin (9 daily; 3hr 15min); Limerick (4 daily; 4hr 15min); Waterford (6 daily; 1hr 15min).

Wexford to: Dublin (7 daily; 2hr 45min); Rosslare Harbour (3–11 daily; 30min).

J.J. Kavanagh's

Kilkenny to Dublin: (2–5 daily; 2hr).

Viking Shuttle Bus

Wexford to: Johnstown Castle (Mon–Sat 3 daily; 15min), Kilmore Quay (Mon–Sat 3 daily; 30min).

CHAPTER SIX

WATERFORD, TIPPERARY AND LIMERICK

Fertile, rolling farmland typifies the landscapes of **Waterford**, **Tipperary** and **Limerick** generating prosperity, but offering a fairly bland experience for the visitor. There are, however, a handful of notable exceptions and these, along with some exceptional historic sites, are well worth making time to explore. Arrive in Ireland at Shannon Airport and Limerick city makes a good first stopover; arrive via Rosslare Harbour in the south east of the country and you are likely to pass through County Waterford if you are heading for the scenic splendours of Cork and Kerry, and through all three of the counties on this chapter if you're making your way to the music of Clare.

County Waterford has a great deal more to offer than it is generally given credit for. All along the Waterford coast, rolling green hills spread down to a fine shore of cliffs interspersed with expansive bays and secluded beaches. Inland rich farming country gives way to the desolate, boggy Comeragh and Knockmealdown mountains, offering good opportunities for easy scenic walking. The county even boasts its own tiny *Gaeltacht* (Irish-speaking) community at **Ring**, one of the best areas on the south coast to hear traditional Irish music. Waterford city is perhaps most famous for the high quality crystal that is made there, but the city's prime draw has to be Waterford Treasures, a superb new museum with a wealth of Viking and medieval artefacts.

Straddling Waterford's border with **County Tipperary**, the **Knockmealdown Mountains** offer attractive walking opportunities, as do the **Galtees**, and the landscape reaches its most sumptuous in the velvety slopes of the **Glen of Aherlow**. Scenery aside, Tipperary's farming towns have little to offer the visitor. At the very heart of the county, though, is a site of outstanding interest – the **Rock of Cashel**. A spectacular natural formation topped with Christian buildings from virtually every period, it's effectively a primer in the development of Irish ecclesiastical architecture. The historic sites at **Cahir** and **Carrick-on-Suir** are also well worth taking in.

In **Limerick** you've arrived in the west of Ireland, but the county still has relatively little to tempt you. Industrial and depressed, **Limerick city** has a luckless reputation.

ACCOMMODATION PRICE CODES

Throughout this book, prices of hotels, guesthouses and B&Bs have been graded with the codes below, according to what you can expect to pay for a double room in high season. For more details on accommodation, see p.34.

① Under £26/€33.01	④ £40–55/€50.79–69.84	⑦ £90–110/€114.28–139.67
② £26–33/€33.01–41.90	⑤ £55–70/€69.84–88.88	⑧ £110–130/€139.67–165.07
③ £33–40/€41.90–50.79	⑥ £70–90/€88.88–114.28	⑨ Over £130/€165.07

Nonetheless, recent efforts to regenerate the city do seem to be teasing out strands of elegance and interest in its weather-worn Georgian streets and there's a renewed vibrancy to its cultural life. More importantly, Limerick is home to the **Hunt Museum**, arguably Ireland's most important collection outside Dublin, and the town is notable too as the setting for the international bestselling novel, *Angela's Ashes*. Inland, the rich pasture of Tipperary continues into County Limerick, and perhaps its greatest attraction is the exceptional number of **medieval castles** and towers that dot the landscape; immaculately preserved **Castle Matrix** in the west is one of the finest in the country. There's also an extremely important Neolithic site at **Lough Gur**, in the heart of the county, and the famously quaint village of **Adare**. In the end, though, Limerick is somewhere you go through to get to counties Clare and Kerry.

COUNTY WATERFORD

Photographs rarely do justice to the beauty of **Waterford**. In the **south**, grand hills rise gradually from coast and valley, their slopes cloaked with plantations of fir trees. The smoothly sculpted **coastline** is one of bold dimensions with low cliffs giving views over large, open bays. The **mountains** in the **north** rise gently above the prettiness of their wooded valleys, offering long walks with stupendous views over the plains of Tipperary. Central to the county, Waterford's **river valleys** are luxuriant and fertile, the finest being that of the **Blackwater**, which rolls through rich farmland with a real majesty. Here, it's easy to see why the county was so attractive to foreign invaders – Viking, Norman and English. The influence of wealthy colonists is clear, their opulence reflected in the remains of elegant, cultivated estates.

The county of Waterford and it's namesake city and port developed quite separately. **Waterford city** was initially a Viking settlement that became a Norman stronghold and thrived as an independent city-state with a major share of Ireland's European trade. While the city prospered as a mercantile centre, the surrounding county lived off farming and fishing, retaining much of its Celtic identity. The Vikings and Normans were not the first newcomers to leave their mark: the area of **Old Parish** around Ardmore gets its name as the arrival point of St Declan in the first half of the fifth century, supposedly the very first of Ireland's proselytizing Christians, preceding St Patrick. The region's early Christian foundations became influential across the country, the most important being that at **Lismore**, founded in 636. It flourished first as a centre of ecclesiastical learning, and later as a secular power rivalling that of Waterford city itself.

Today the distinctions between urban and rural remain marked. Alongside thriving, modern Waterford city, pockets of ancient cultures and histories survive, such as the tiny Irish-speaking community of **Ring** and the historic ecclesiastical foundations of **Ardmore** and **Lismore**. An air of prosperity pervades the county as a whole, in farmland enriched by centuries of cultivation and in the renewed commercial importance of the historic port of Waterford city. The coast offers **sandy beaches**, a handful of quaint fishing harbours and some great seascapes. It's easily accessible, too – notably good main roads serve city and county, good for long-distance **cycling**.

Waterford

WATERFORD's appearance from the river is deceptively grim: the bare and open stretch of water with its ugly grey wharves and cranes of the working port holds no suggestion of the lively city that lies beyond its dull quays. This is the commercial capital of the southeast, and yet it retains buildings from Viking and Norman times,

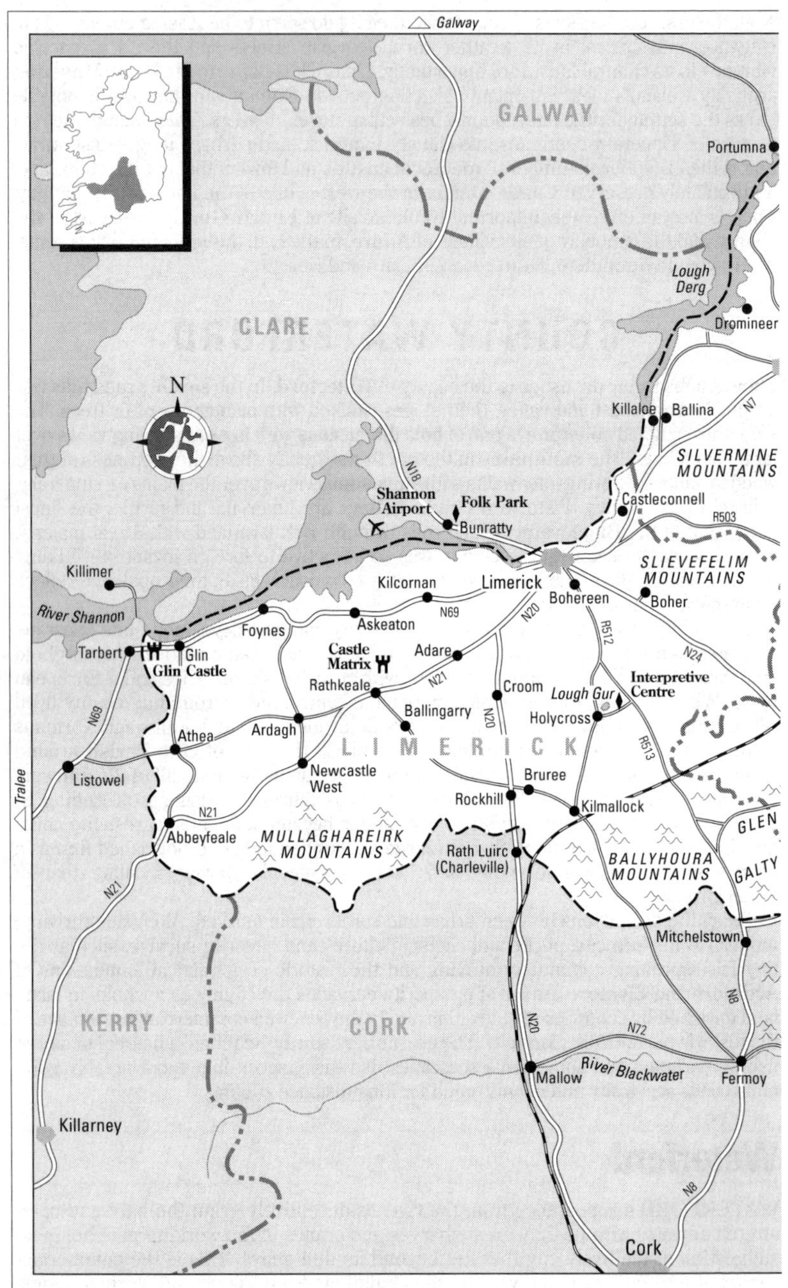
Galway
GALWAY
Portumna
CLARE
Lough Derg
Dromineer
N
Killaloe
Ballina
N7
SILVERMINE MOUNTAINS
N18
Shannon Airport
Folk Park
Bunratty
Castleconnell
R503
SLIEVEFELIM MOUNTAINS
Killimer
Limerick
Kilcornan
Bohereen
Boher
River Shannon
Askeaton
N69
Foynes
N20
R512
Tarbert
Glin
Glin Castle
Castle Matrix
Adare
N24
Interpretive Centre
Rathkeale
N21
Croom
Lough Gur
N69
Ballingarry
Holycross
N20
Athea
Ardagh
LIMERICK
R513
Listowel
Newcastle West
Bruree
Tralee
Rockhill
Kilmallock
GLEN
N21
Abbeyfeale
MULLAGHAREIRK MOUNTAINS
Rath Luirc (Charleville)
BALLYHOURA MOUNTAINS
GALTY
N21
Mitchelstown
N8
KERRY
CORK
N20
N72
Mallow
River Blackwater
Fermoy
Killarney
N8
Cork

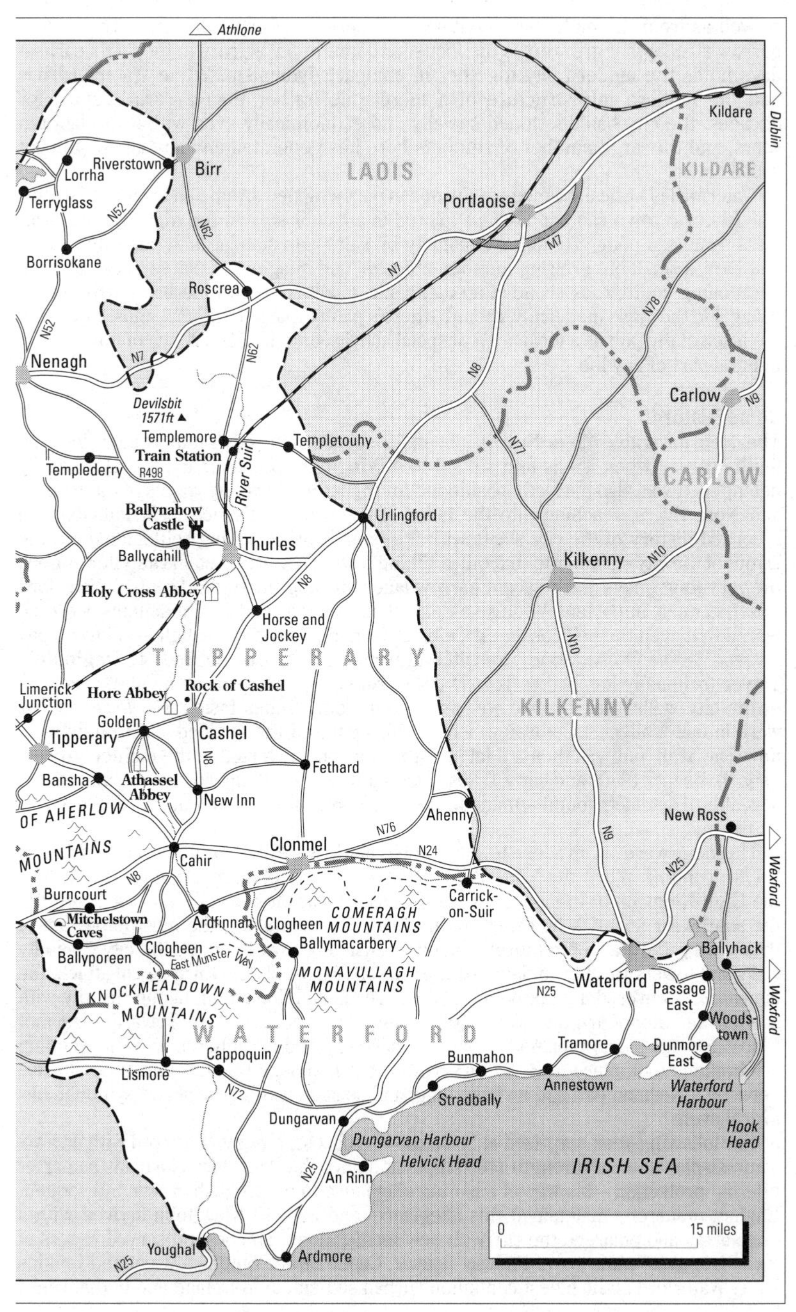
Athlone
Dublin
Kildare
KILDARE
LAOIS
Birr
Riverstown
Lorrha
Terryglass
Borrisokane
Portlaoise
Roscrea
Nenagh
Devilsbit
1571ft
Templemore
Train Station
Templederry
Templetouhy
River Suir
Carlow
CARLOW
Urlingford
Ballynahow Castle
Ballycahill
Thurles
Kilkenny
Holy Cross Abbey
Horse and Jockey
TIPPERARY
Limerick Junction
Hore Abbey
Rock of Cashel
KILKENNY
Golden
Tipperary
Cashel
Fethard
Bansha
Athassel Abbey
New Inn
OF AHERLOW
Ahenny
New Ross
MOUNTAINS
Cahir
Clonmel
Wexford
Burncourt
Carrick-on-Suir
Mitchelstown Caves
Ardfinnan
Clogheen
COMERAGH MOUNTAINS
Ballymacarbery
Ballyporeen
East Munster Way
Ballyhack
MONAVULLAGH MOUNTAINS
Waterford
Passage East
KNOCKMEALDOWN MOUNTAINS
Woodstown
WATERFORD
Tramore
Dunmore East
Cappoquin
Bunmahon
Lismore
Annestown
Waterford Harbour
Stradbally
Dungarvan
Hook Head
Dungarvan Harbour
Helvick Head
IRISH SEA
An Rinn
0
15 miles
Youghal
Ardmore

as well as from the eighteenth century – all periods of past eminence. The web of narrow streets that grew up as the focus for commercial activity in the city's earliest days holds the modern city together in compact dynamism. While Waterford has had the modern infrastructure of a mercantile, rather than a rural, centre for decades, the city has developed socially and economically even within the last ten years, and the large number of students here has generated an increasingly upbeat social scene.

Waterford is basically a modern European port wrapped around an ancient Irish city. The **historic town** can happily be explored in a day or so, and the **nightlife** also warrants some sampling. Though a small city by European standards, it has some excellent bars, a small but growing number of decent and imaginative places to eat, and the burgeoning youth/rock scene of an optimistic, albeit small-scale, urban environment. Alongside the city's modernity, though, there's plenty that's traditional, most obviously the place of the pub as a focal point of social activity, and the persistence of music as an integral part of city life.

Some history

The deep, navigable **River Suir** has been the source of the city's importance since the tenth century when it was first settled by **Vikings**; deep inland, and therefore easily defended, it was also perfectly positioned for the internal trading routes of the Barrow and Nore rivers, reaching into the heart of the southeast's rich farmland. Reliable recorded history of the city starts with the tenth-century Viking settlement, and the layout of the city – similar to that other Viking town, Wexford – retains its Viking roots, the very long quays and adjacent narrow lanes forming the trading centre. Waterford was the most important Viking settlement in Ireland, and its inhabitants were so feared that even the bellicose local Celtic Déisí had to pay them tribute – failure to pay *Airgead Sróine* (Nose Money) resulted in having your nose chopped off. **Reginald's Tower** (originally Ranguald's Tower) dates from this time, as do some of the remains of the city walls. Nearby, two well-preserved stone arches inside *The Reginald* bar were in fact "sallyports", through which ships entered the fortified city from what is now The Mall, but was then a tidal pool that was only diverted in the eighteenth century. In the late 1980s and early 1990s, over a fifth of the Viking city was excavated and a wealth of artefacts found – many of them are now on show in Waterford Treasures on the quays.

The next wave of invaders to leave their mark were the **Anglo-Normans** in the twelfth century. When the King of Leinster, Dermot MacMurrough, made his bid for the High Kingship of Ireland, he knew Waterford was strategically vital for control of the southwest. In 1170, he called on his Anglo-Norman allies, the most important of these being the Earl of Pembroke, known as **Strongbow**, to attack the city. The city walls and towers were formidably strong, but on August 25, the third day of attack, the Normans discovered a weak point, made a breach and flooded in, taking the city with scenes of bloodcurdling violence. Strongbow received his reward: Dermot MacMurrough's daughter Aoife's hand in marriage, and her inheritance. The wedding celebrations took place in Reginald's Tower; the marriage was the first such alliance between a Norman earl and an Irish king, and as such was a crucial and symbolic historical event.

The following year, surprised at Strongbow's success, **Henry II** arrived with an awesome display of naval strength (400 ships) and gave the Waterford Normans a charter offering protection – his way of ensuring allegiance to the English crown. Subsequent English monarchs maintained this allegiance, and in 1210 King John arrived with a huge army and enlarged the city with new fortifications. The best-preserved towers of these **Norman walls** are at Railway Square, Castle Street, Stephen Street and Jenkins Lane. Waterford is the oldest continuous urban settlement in Ireland and in that sense

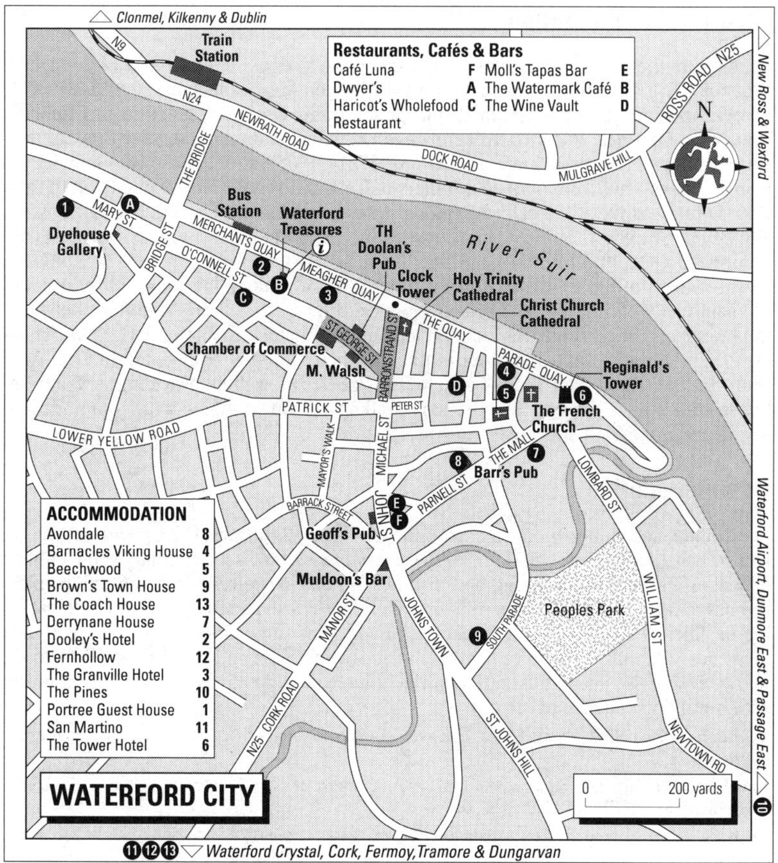

can be considered its oldest city. Its proximity to Europe made it a prime port for the important wine trade and it enjoyed royal patronage from the medieval period onwards. In the late fifteenth century it reaped further royal favour through its part in bringing to ground two would-be usurpers threatening Henry VII: first Lambert Simnel in 1487, then Perkin Warbeck eight years later.

Waterford flourished as an important European **port** into the sixteenth and seventeenth centuries, **trading** with England, France, Spain and Portugal, and Newfoundland during the eighteenth and early nineteenth centuries, as well as maintaining its inland commerce. It was the only city in Ireland to withstand **Cromwell**, though his forces returned under the command of General Ireton, who took the city without the usual scenes of carnage, giving its citizens honourable terms. Abundant testimony to the city's eighteenth-century prosperity is evident in both ecclesiastical and secular architecture. However, Waterford is nowadays most famous for its **crystal**, first produced here in 1783. The factory closed in 1851 but reopened in 1951 and is now one of the city's major employers, as well as being a popular draw for tourists.

Arrival and information

Roads from the north and the east converge on the river at the **train station**, on Dock Rd (☎051/873401); the city – and the **bus station**, on Merchants Quay, (☎051/879000) lie over the bridge to the south. Regular daily trains connect Waterford to Clonmel, Tipperary, Limerick, Wexford, Kilkenny and Dublin. In addition to regular Bus Éireann services, Rapid Express Club Travel (☎051/872149), operates a cheap **bus service** to Dublin; buses leave from outside the Bank of Ireland, Parnell Street. Scheduled **flights** from London arrive at Waterford Regional Airport in Killowen eight miles south of the city (☎051/875589). There's no bus between the airport and the city: a taxi will cost you around £10/€12.70.

The **tourist office** is in The Granary, roughly midway along the quays that run along the south side of the river and effectively form the city's northern boundary between the bridge across the River Suir and the nineteenth-century clock tower (Jan–March & Oct–Dec Mon–Fri 9am–5pm; April–June & Sept Mon–Sat 9am–6pm; July & Aug Mon–Sat 9am–6pm, Sun 11am–5pm; ☎051/875823); as well as providing a wealth of information about the city and the surrounding region, it offers an accommodation booking service for a small fee.

Accommodation

For **hostel** accommodation, head for the IHH-run *Barnacles Viking House*, Coffee House Lane, Greyfriars (☎051/853827, *www.iiol.ie/~lalco*), a welcoming, well-run hostel just off Parade Quay offering beds from £9/€11.39 in twelve-bed dorms and doubles rooms from £16.50/€20.89. Price includes light breakfast, and there are good self-catering facilities, a spacious lounge, bike lock-up and an email kiosk. If the *Viking House* turns out to be full, and you're contemplating staying in any other hostel in Waterford, we *strongly* advise you to talk to the tourist office before booking. There's no **campsite** within walking distance of the city.

Avondale, 2 Parnell St (☎051/852267). A very comfortable city-centre B&B in a Georgian town house. ④.

Beechwood, 7 Cathedral Square (☎051/876677) Standard B&B in a centrally located family home overlooking Christ Church Cathedral. ②.

Brown's Town House, 29 South Parade (☎051/870594). A pleasant Victorian town house decorated with modern Irish paintings and located in a quiet residential street. ⑤.

The Coach House, Butlerstown Castle, Butlerstown (☎051/384656; *coachhse@iol.ie*). Comfortable B&B in a converted coach house, around three miles from Waterford, off the N25. ⑤.

Derrynane House, 19 The Mall (☎051/875179). Inexpensive, simple B&B in the city centre. The Mall can be noisy, so ask for a room to the rear. ③.

Dooley's Hotel, 30 Merchants Quay (☎051/873531, *www.dooleys-hotel.ie*). Well-appointed, comfortable three-star hotel in a prime city-centre location overlooking the river. ⑧.

Fernhollow, Cork Rd, Ballinaneeshagh (☎051/358128). Pleasant and comfortable B&B around two miles out of the centre, just past the glass factory. ③.

Foxmount Farm, Passage East Rd (☎051/874308). Four miles from town, off the Dunmore Road, this farmhouse B&B also does excellent evening meals. ⑤.

The Granville Hotel, Meaghev Quay (☎051/855111). Grandiose, historic hotel whose former guests include Daniel O'Connell and Charles Stewart Parnell. Swish, elegant interiors and a prime location on the quays make it one of the most prestigious hotels in town. ⑨.

Mrs O'Brien's, 2 New St (☎051/875764). Inexpensive accommodation in a city-centre family home; breakfast not provided. ②.

The Pines, Knockboy, on the Dunmore Road (☎051/874452; *bjackman@tinet.ie*). Clean, comfortable B&B serving excellent breakfasts. Around two miles from the city centre. ③.

Portree Guest House, Mary St (☎051/874574). Comfortable central guesthouse in a quiet side street offering en-suite rooms. Close to the bus and train stations. ④.

San Martino, Ballinaneeshagh (☎051/374949). Decent no-smoking B&B just past the glass factory. ③.

The Tower Hotel, The Mall (☎051/875801, *www.towerhotelgroup.ie*) Large, modern three-star hotel right in the centre of town; facilities include leisure centre and pool. ⑨.

The City

Waterford is centred on a wedge of Georgiana, between the eighteenth-century shops and houses of **O'Connell and George streets**, which run behind the modern quays, and the faded splendour of **Parnell Street** and **The Mall** with their fine doorways and fanlights. The city's prime attraction is **Waterford Treasures**, which stands on Merchants Quay, housing an extraordinary collection of Viking and medieval artefacts. Head east along the quays from here for about half a mile and you'll pass a clock tower and a turning into Barronstrand Street, which runs through the city's main shopping area and through a number of changes of name to John Street, with its great concentration of fast-food joints and bars. Continue along the quays from the clock tower and after about half a mile you will reach **Reginald's Tower**, the most impressive remaining medieval building in Waterford. The area of tangled laneways between here and The Mall contains some of the city's finest juxtapositions of medieval and eighteenth century architecture, including **Christ Church Cathedral**, which dates from 1770. The splendours of that era are remembered too at **Waterford Crystal**, the world-famous glass factory about one and a half miles from the city centre, a trip to which is vigorously promoted throughout the region.

Waterford Treasures

The Granary, on Merchants Quay, is a nineteenth-century warehouse that has recently been converted to hold the tourist office and, behind this, the city's chief visitor attraction – **Waterford Treasures** (daily: May & Sept 9.30am–6pm; June–Aug 9.30am–9pm; Oct–April 10am–5pm; £4/€5.08). This first-rate museum covers the history of the city from the Viking period to the present day through a variety of audio-visual presentations, and a superb array of Viking artefacts and early royal charters. **Viking finds** include elaborately carved antler combs, intricately fashioned bracelets, lathe-turned wooden bowls, weaponry, ceramics and leather footwear. The twelfth-century kite brooch is a work of breathtaking intricacy and there are gold and silver needles and pins of a similar age. There's plenty from the **Anglo-Norman period** too, including a mid-thirteenth-century yew bow stave – the only complete medieval bow in the British Isles; and a late fifteenth century cannon – the oldest in Ireland – which clearly shows the hooped construction typical of the time. Also on show is the city's magnificent collection of medieval, Tudor and Stuart royal charters. One of the highlights here is the extraordinary Great Charter Roll of 1372, Ireland's most important late medieval decorated manuscript, rich in illustrations of English monarchs, governors of Ireland, medieval mayors and the earliest known depiction of an Irish city.

The collection is rich in content and it's well worth getting to grips with the audio guide in order to dip in and out of the areas you want to learn about in depth. Refreshingly, the interpretation on offer has a markedly contemporary and international perspective, debunking commonly held notions that the Vikings were little more than marauding hooligans and presenting a balanced picture of just how beneficial Waterford's relationship with the English Crown was.

Reginald's Tower and the French Church

Waterford's most historic building is **Reginald's Tower** (daily 10am–5pm; £1.50/€1.90; Heritage Card), around half a mile east along the quays from Waterford Treasures. A large cylindrical late twelfth- or early thirteenth-century tower, its design is similar to the Scottish broch, with a concealed stairway built within its massive wall; the original Viking tower which stood here was built in 1003. It was the most substantial of the seventeen defensive towers that encircled the city in medieval times. Inside a display details its history and that of the powerful Waterford Vikings, their struggles with the Anglo-Normans, and the subsequent arrival of the English Crown. Much of this material is covered in a far more lively manner in the Waterford Treasures exhibition, but it's still worth visiting Reginald's Tower to absorb some sense of the raw power of its various former incumbents.

Wander up Bailey's New Street, just behind Reginald's Tower, and you soon come to Waterford's other important medieval building, the **French Church**, on Greyfriars (key from Reginald's Tower). Founded by Franciscans in 1240, the church served as an almshouse in the sixteenth century, and from 1693 to 1815 was used as a place of worship by French Huguenot refugees, whom the city sheltered in their exile from persecution at home. It's now a solid, roofless ruin with a complete tower and fine east triple-lancet window. Stones at the base of the outer windows are decorated with comic carved figures, and the church contains some interesting carved burial slabs, including that of Sir Neal O'Neill, who accompanied James II in his flight from the Battle of the Boyne.

The old church that stands nearby is scheduled to hold the **Waterford Municipal Art Collection** from 2001, featuring work by major twentieth-century Irish painters, including Jack Yeats, Louis Le Brocquy, Paul Henry, Lamb and Keating; for latest details, contact the tourist office.

Christ Church and Holy Trinity cathedrals

The Church of Ireland **Christ Church Cathedral**, a short stroll up Bailey's New Street from the French Church, forms the prime architectural landmark of Georgian Waterford. Built in the 1770s by John Roberts, who did much work in Waterford for both Catholics and Protestants, it's a nicely proportioned building with a fine steeple, a spacious interior and an elaborate stucco ceiling; it stands on the site of a Viking church which was enlarged during the medieval period and survived up until 1770. The monuments inside the cathedral are worth a look, in particular that of James Rice (one-time Lord Mayor of Waterford), dating from 1482, a gruesome effigy of a corpse in an advanced state of decay, with various creatures crawling in and out of the carcass. The story of Waterford city from the time of the Norman invasion to the present day is relayed in a 45-minute sound and light presentation (April, May, Sept & Oct Mon–Fri at 11.30am, 2.30pm & 4pm; June–Aug Mon–Sat at 9.30am, 11.30am, 2.30pm & 4pm, Sun 2.30pm & 4pm; £2/€2.54).

If you want to see more of Roberts' work, visit Holy Trinity Cathedral in Barronstrand Street off Parade Quay, and St Patrick's Church off George's Street. Originally built in 1793, **Holy Trinity Cathedral** was greatly altered during the nineteenth century to become the swirling, ornate extravaganza it is today. That the same architect could work on the Protestant and then the Catholic cathedral is evidence of the measure of religious tolerance enjoyed by Waterford's citizens at the time. This is further borne out in the little church of **St Patrick's**, tucked away up a lane off George's Street. Built in the mid-eighteenth century, it remained a Catholic church throughout penal times and as such is unique. It seems that mercantile strength gave Waterford considerable cultural independence, and Catholics were allowed to hold services here – in stark contrast to the suppression that went on in the rest of the country. Funding came from the sons of Waterford merchants who settled in Spain during the eighteenth century, and dark and dolorous paintings hang either side of the altar, revealing a strong Spanish influence.

City Hall, Georgian architecture and Waterford crystal

Christ Church apart, it's in the city's secular architecture that the best of the eighteenth century is realized. Christ Church Cathedral looks down over The Mall, with its **City**

Hall (Mon–Fri 10am–5pm), built in 1788 by the ubiquitous John Roberts. Its spacious entrance hall was once used as a meeting place and merchants' exchange; if you are interested in seeing the Waterford crystal chandeliers in the council chambers and the Waterford Room, ask at the desk. By far the finest eighteenth-century architectural detail in the city, though, is the oval staircase inside the lilac-coloured **Chamber of Commerce** in George Street (Mon–Fri 9am–5pm; access by appointment only, call ☎051/872639). Built in 1785, with a beautiful cantilevered staircase and fine decorative stucco-work, it, too, is the work of John Roberts.

If you want to find out more about Waterford crystal (which is for sale all over town), you should make a trip out to the **Waterford Crystal Glass Factory** for one of its **guided tours** (April–Oct daily 8.30am–4pm; Nov–March Mon–Fri 9am–3.15pm; £3.50/€4.43) around the glass-cutting and blowing workshops. This is interesting if you've never seen the process before, and a fair way to work up an appetite on a wet day, but not the "absolute must" the publicity tends to suggest. The factory is located about a mile and a half from the city centre on the N25 towards Cork; check at the tourist office for times of buses from the city centre.

Eating and drinking

Finding something to **eat** in Waterford is unlikely to prove a problem. There's no shortage of **bar food**: try *Dooley's Hotel*, Merchants Quay; *T.H. Doolan's*, also a live music venue (see below), on George's Street; or *Egan's* on Broad Street. For late-night cafés and fast food, head for John Street. The following listings cover the range:

Café Luna, 53 John St. A popular spot for inexpensive ciabatta, baguettes, croissants and hot specials. Mon–Wed 10am–midnight, Thurs–Sat 10am–3am, Sun noon–3am.

Dwyer's, 8 Mary St (☎051/877478). Despite a rather uninspiring exterior and location, this is one of the best restaurants in Waterford. It offers classic French cooking using the best local produce. Closed Sun.

Haricot's Wholefood Restaurant, 11 O'Connell St. Cheerful, inexpensive café with the a cosy country-kitchen atmosphere. This long-time favourite guarantees a varied menu of flavoursome and satisfying meals. Mon–Fri 9am–8pm, Sat 9.30am–6pm.

Moll's Tapas Bar, 54 John St. Mellow wine bar serving bangers and a very tasty Savoy-cabbage stir fry as well as tortilla, squid and mussels. Around £5/€6.35. Daily 12.30–3pm & 6–10pm.

The Watermark Café, The Granary, behind the tourist office and occupying the same building. Stylish café with a wine licence and a relaxed atmosphere. Serving huge and inexpensive Caesar salads, sandwiches, homemade burgers, noodles and much more. One of Waterford's best spots for snacks and lunches. Mon–Sat 9am–9pm.

The Wine Vault, High St (☎051/853444). Classy and moderately priced bistro-restaurant, with a warm, convivial atmosphere, serving excellent contemporary Irish food. Mon–Sat lunch & dinner.

Drinking and live music

Waterford has a fair sized student population and, not surprisingly, there is no shortage of lively **bars**, many with live **music** on offer, from traditional through rock to the astonishing array of tribute bands on the circuit.

Barr's, Mayor's Walk. Cosy little pub attracting a discerning, off-beat clientele; space to think while you drink.

T.H. Doolan's, 31–32 George's St. Big pub full of old carved fireplaces and dusty folk memorabilia. A good spot to catch traditional music, which is played here most nights.

Geoff's, John St. The place to catch up on what's happening around town. Antiquated wooden benches and lots of space for the mixed, predominantly young, crowd.

Jack Meades Pub, Halfway House. Despite being about four miles out of town along the road towards Cheekpoint, this is a very popular bar, noted for its traditional music.

Kitty Kerin's, Barrack St. A pleasant, regular bar and a good spot to catch traditional Irish music four or five nights a week.

Muldoon's, on the corner of Manor and Parnell streets. Large pub, popular with locals for the late bar (till 1.30am), its upstairs disco and varied entertainment – from excellent traditional music (Sun) to tribute bands (midweek).

Preachers, John St. The club behind the *Pulpit Bar*. Arguably the liveliest club in town and certainly the most bizarre with its lavish Gothic-fantasy interior. Generally, the music is mainstream chart stuff aimed at the under-25s. Entry fee £5/€6.35. Closed Mon.

Rhythm Room, on the corner of Manor and John streets. Fairly casual club, playing mainstream chart and dance music, that is popular with students during the week and locals at weekends.

M.Walsh, 11 Great George's St. Ancient, old-fashioned bar with a grocery shop fronting the street stocked with pop bottles, sweets and an off-licence.

Theatre and the arts

The Garter Lane Arts Centre (Mon–Sat 10am–6pm; ☎051/855038), housed at 5 and 22a O'Connell St, has a theatre showing both drama and film, and a good current events notice board. It's the place to catch a performance by the Waterford-based Red Kettle Theatre Company as well as various other touring companies. The centre also hosts painting and sculpture exhibitions of contemporary Irish artists. Waterford's other theatre is the **Theatre Royal**, on The Mall (☎051/874402), which stages the city's **Light Opera Festival** in September, an international competition for amateur musical societies. The Regional Technical College on the main Cork Road is used for **classical music** recitals, generally advertised in the tourist office.

The city's municipal **art** collection is scheduled to be housed in an old church on Greyfriars (see p.244); the small commercial **Dyehouse Gallery**, Dyehouse Lane (Mon–Sat 11am–6pm; ☎051/878166, *www.dyehouse-gallery.com*) offers an interesting collection of contemporary Irish and international art – chiefly prints and paintings – and there's a pottery showroom alongside.

Listings

Bike Rental Wright's Cycle Depot, 19–20 Henrietta St, off Parade Quay (☎051/874411; £12/€15.24 per day).

Dental emergencies South Eastern Health Board, Community Care, on the Cork Road (Mon–Fri 9am–5pm; ☎051/876111).

Hospital Waterford Regional Hospital, Dunmore Road (☎051/873321).

Internet café *Voyager*, Parnell Court, Parnell St (*voyager@iica.net*).

Laundry Duds & Suds, Parnell St (Mon–Sat 7.30am–9pm).

Left luggage at the train station (Mon–Sat 7.15am–9pm; £1/€1.27).

River cruises Galley River Cruises offers trips to New Ross, including lunch, afternoon tea or evening meal (June–Aug; ☎051/421723; £7–22/€8.89–27.93).

Travel agents USIT Youth and Student Travel Office, 36–37 George's St (☎051/872601).

The Waterford coast

Waterford's coastline offers good sandy beaches and some breathtaking coastal walks. The open grandeur of bays like Dungarvan is offset by the intimacy of hidden coves and scenic fishing ports. The best of the **beaches** are at **Woodstown, Dunmore East, Tramore, Annestown** and **Ardmore** – where you'll also find the vestiges of early Christian history. Major seaside towns are connected to Waterford by regular bus services; Suirway buses provide a limited service to some of the choicest spots, but you may well find that the best are walked, cycled or slowly hitched to. The coastal area also offers some of the best traditional music in the southeast of Ireland, most notably at **Ring**, home to a small Irish-speaking community.

Passage East, Cheekpoint and Woodstown

Immediately east of Waterford city, at the neck of its long harbour, the pretty ferry village of **PASSAGE EAST** nestles under craggy hills, the estuary slopes aflame with wild gorse. The **ferry** here connects with Ballyhack in County Wexford (Passage East Car Ferry ☎051/382488) – a particularly useful route east for cyclists, especially if you're making for Rosslare or want to stay with the coast. If you want **to stay**, try the *Cois Abhann* (☎051/382190; ③). Across the water, less than a mile from Ballyhack, there's an An Óige **hostel** at Arthurstown (closed Oct–May; ☎051/389411). The tiny fishing village of **CHEEKPOINT**, to the north of here, sits at the confluence of the rivers Suir, Nore and Barrow, its chief draw the excellent **seafood** at the *Suir Inn*. Coastal paths south of Passage East afford views over the estuary to the Hook Head, County Wexford. The long sandy beach flanked by deep woodland at **WOODSTOWN**, just over two miles south of Passage East, takes some beating if you're looking for a quiet stroll or a gentle dip.

Dunmore East

Further around the Waterford coast, **DUNMORE EAST** settles snugly between small, chunky sandstone cliffs topped by masses of rambling golden gorse. The main street follows a higgledy-piggledy contour from the safe, sandy cove beside which the east village sits, towards a busy harbour full of the rippled reflections of brightly coloured fishing boats and cradled by the crooked finger of the harbour wall. From here, the ruddy sandstone cliffs make bold ribs around the coast. This is still a very active fishing harbour, but has also cashed in on its picturesqueness, with obviously new-thatched houses sneaking in alongside the originals.

Quaint as it is, Dunmore East has become very much a playground for affluent Waterford people, and there are three large **hotels** to cater for them – including the *Haven* (☎051/383150; ⑥). More moderately priced accommodation is offered by a number of **B&Bs**, including *Church Villa* (☎051/383390; ③) and *Copper Beech* (☎051/383187; ③), both on Dock Road. For seaviews stay at *Carraig Liath* on Harbour Road (☎051/383273; ④). For **camping**, there's *Strand Caravan Park* (June to mid-Sept; ☎051/383174).

Eating is expensive here, and the café down by the beach is just about the only place where you'll get a cheap meal. Good **pub food** is available at *The Ocean Hotel,* by the sandy beach in the east village (☎051/383136). *The Strand Inn*, also beside the beach, has a very good fish restaurant and serves good, more moderately priced bar food; while the upmarket *Ship* restaurant serves excellent meals (☎051/383141).

For **canoeing** and **wind-surfing** contact The Adventure Centre (☎051/383783). The Centra supermarket on Dock Road operates a **bureau de change**.

Tramore to Dungarvan

Nine miles west of Dunmore East, **TRAMORE** caters for a different type of holidaymaker and a different kind of bank balance. It's a busy, popular seaside resort serving families from Waterford and Cork, and has plenty of amusements, caravans and a huge sandy beach. **B&Bs** are concentrated along Tivoli Road: try the hospitable *Sea Court*

(☎051/386244; ③) or the smart *Tivoli House* (☎051/390208; ③). *O'Shea's* is probably the liveliest and most popular **bar** in Tramore, with plenty of MOR bands and good bar food.

The wild and splendid **coast** west of Tramore is one of tussocky grassland, hidden coves and sheer cliffs. Really just a handful of houses, **ANNESTOWN**, six miles from Tramore, is famous for being the only village in Ireland without a pub. It's said that there were once numerous bars catering for the local barracks, but that such was the brawling, the local landowner decided that enough was enough and took away all the licences. There's a cosy **B&B** at *Wee Bluin* (☎051/396344; ②), or you can enjoy fabulous views at *Annestown House,* a fine early nineteenth-century building where you can expect cosy log fires and excellent breakfasts (☎051/396160; ⑥).

Seven miles further along the coast you'll come to the neat, pretty village of **STRADBALLY**. A road leads one mile from here through deep deciduous woods to the fabulous **Stradbally Cove**, a secluded sandy beach flanked by craggy oak and ash-covered slopes. Rather more popular, **CLONEA STRAND**, four and a half miles further along the coast and two miles east of Dungarvan, is a broad sandy beach with plenty of space for the holidaymakers at *Casey's Caravan and Camping Park* at its west end. For more comfort, try the nearby *Clonea Strand Hotel* (☎058/42416, *www.amireland.com/clonea*; ⑦), the pool and bar of which are also open to non-residents.

DUNGARVAN, the major coastal town of County Waterford, has a confident, buoyant air and enjoys a magnificent setting. A wonderful view over the grand, broad bay opens up as you descend to the town, the open heights around topped by pine forests that seem to have been poured on like thick syrup. The **tourist office** on the Square (June–Aug Mon–Fri 9am–9pm, Sat 9am–1pm & 2–6pm, Sun 2–5pm; rest of year Mon–Fri 9am–6pm, Sat 9am–1pm & 2–6pm; ☎058/41741) can help with **accommodation** and you'll find some decent pubs and restaurants on the square and along the quays. You may well come across first rate traditional **music** too: *Bridgie Terries* at a spot known as The Pike, four miles out of town on the N25 towards Waterford, is especially recommended. On the whole, though, the area of greater interest and charm lies immediately to the west.

Ring (An Rinn)

RING, or *An Rinn* as it is known in Irish, is a pocket of Irish tradition hidden away on the modern Waterford coast, signposted off the N25 about six miles outside Dungarvan. It's a tiny **Irish-speaking community** of about 1500 that has somehow survived in what is otherwise one of Ireland's more developed counties, and all the more remarkable given the "West Brit" flavour of much of the county's coast. The language survives healthily, as do other traditions, notably music and set dancing.

Like many Irish-speaking areas, the community consists of farms and a handful of bars spread over a wide area, with no real centre. This can be frustrating if you don't have transport, as you have to rely on hitching to and from some of the best bars – the real draw here, as there's little to see, other than the way of life. *Mooney's* is the first pub on the way into Ring if you are travelling from Dungarvan. It's a great spot for traditional music, and the owners will let you **camp** in their field. Other bars for traditional music are *The Seanachie,* just off the N25, about six miles west of Dungarvan (Thurs & Sat), and nearby *The Marine Bar* (summer daily, except Wed; rest of year Mon, Sat & Sun only). The **Oyster Festival** over the first weekend in August is a real high point in Ring's music calendar: book accommodation in advance over this period or take a tent. At other times, you should have no trouble finding a bed at the pleasant little **hostel**, *Ceol na Mara* – the owners also offer **B&B** in their spacious nineteenth-century house (☎058/46425, *desibeau@eircom.net;* ③). Other options include the welcoming, well-run

Aisling, Gurtnadiha, Ring (☎058/46134; ③), in a fabulous spot overlooking Dungarvan Harbour, or *Helvick View*, Ring (☎058/46297; ③).

When the tide's out, you can walk a few miles west of the quayside towards Dungarvan, and out along a sand spit. Alternatively, you could walk along the cliffs at **Helvick Head** to gain splendid views of the sculpted coastal cliffs and of the mountains inland.

Ardmore

The delightful village of **ARDMORE**, fourteen miles southwest of Dungarvan is steeped in history and full of character. The fifth century saw the arrival here of St Declan, at least thirty years before St Patrick arrived in Ireland, and the surrounding area of **Old Parish** is so called because it's supposedly the oldest parish in Ireland. In Ardmore itself, a medieval **cathedral** and **round tower** stand on the site of the saint's original monastic foundation, commanding stunning views over Ardmore Bay. The long, low twelfth-century cathedral has massive buttresses, its stoutly rounded doors and windows confirming the proud – albeit now roofless – Romanesque solidity of the building, while the slender round tower, tall and fine with a conical roof, stands alongside in poignant contrast. Inside, there are stones with early ogham inscriptions, but the most exceptional carvings are on the west external wall. Here, Romanesque arcading, originally from an earlier building, has been set beneath the window, with boldly carved scenes showing the weighing of souls, the fall of man, the judgement of Solomon and the adoration of the magi: truly impressive, and unique in quality and design. **St Declan's Oratory**, supposedly his burial site, also stands in the graveyard. Earth from the saint's grave is believed to protect against disease.

The village down below – busy in summer – consists of a pleasant row of cottages, a few pubs, a shop and a handful of cafés, with a couple of excellent sandy beaches nearby. Myth has it that when St Declan arrived here from Wales, his bell and vestments were magically carried by the large stone that now sits on the **beach**. This would explain why the boulder is completely different geologically from the surrounding land – though the Ice Age seems a more likely, if comparatively mundane, explanation. Another improbable tale is that crawling under the stone cures rheumatism. It looks unlikely that a fit person could squirm under it, let alone an invalid.

Walking through the village to the east, up the hill you come to a path which leads to the ancient **St Declan's Well** and a steeply gabled **oratory**. It's an atmospheric spot, with fresh water springing beside three primitive stone crosses where pilgrims used to wash, and a stone chair. From here, there's a fine walk around the headland along rocky cliffs for five miles or so, as far as Whiting Bay, a quiet spot with a small sandy beach; alternatively there's a waymarked path that takes you over three miles and brings you back down by the round tower. For longer rambling you can take **St Declan's Way**, a 55-mile route which links Ardmore with Cashel in County Tipperary.

Ardmore has one, small **hotel**, *The Round Tower* (☎024/94494, *www.waterfordtourism.org*; ⑤); **B&B** can be had at *Byron Lodge* (☎024/94157; ③), and there's an excellent little **hostel**, *Ardmore Beach Hostel* on Main Street (☎024/94501), with dorms and family rooms. The **caravan** and **camping** site is just beside the beach, and there's a **laundry** on Main Street. The welcoming *Paddy Mac's* pub does good **bar food**, and has occasional traditional music sessions during the summer. For inexpensive but filling meals there's the cosy *Cup and Saucer* café; nearby *The White Horses Restaurant* (May–Sept daily, except Mon lunch; Oct–April Fri–Sun only; ☎024/94040) serves good-value lunches and evening meals.

Cappoquin, the Blackwater Valley and around

Typical of the outstanding beauty of inland County Waterford is the stretch of the Blackwater Valley around Cappoquin, 38 miles west of Waterford city and 19 miles north of Ardmore, where the river makes a sharp westward turn towards County Cork, describing as it goes the southerly limit of the Knockmealdown Mountains (see p.255). **CAPPOQUIN** itself is prettily situated on a wooded hillside overlooking the river. Despite this beautiful location, the village seems strangely neglected, and there's little attempt to cater for visitors beyond a few B&Bs used mainly by a handful of fishermen at holiday times: if you want to **stay**, try the friendly *Riverview House* (☎058/54073; ③), which is a good, central option. You'll get inexpensive home-cooked **food** at *The Saddlers Teashop* (Mon–Sat 8am–6pm), including marvellous breads baked in *Barrons'* Victorian ovens next door. *Richmond House* (☎058/54278; ⑨), on the way to Lismore, is the place for a more extravagant meal (dinner from about £27/€34.28) and luxurious B&B.

Although there's little to detain you in the village, the surrounding countryside is lovely. Walk half a mile east, take the right fork by the statue of the Virgin, and you come to the **Glenshelane river walk**. This follows the minor River Glenshelane through its deep valley banked by pine trees and, after about three miles, brings you to **Mount Melleray**, a Cistercian monastery that welcomes visitors in search of solitude. The trail eventually opens out, affording great views of the Knockmealdown and Galtee mountains of Tipperary. The walk's a good taster for the varied terrain of the major long-distance walk just north of here in County Tipperary, the East Munster Way (see p.252).

Lismore

Set in the lovely broad plain of the Blackwater Valley, three miles west of Cappoquin, **LISMORE**, recently designated a heritage town, has a significant ecclesiastical history. There's not much sign of this rich history today, but nevertheless the town does somehow manage to preserve a quiet reverence for its past. The town is dominated by the romantic towers and battlements of **Lismore Castle** (not open to the public), whose pale, white-grey stone, set with mullioned windows, rises magnificently on the hill from glorious woodlands and sumptuous **gardens** (May–Sept daily 1.45–4.45pm; £3/€3.81). The castle itself is a successful mid-nineteenth-century imitation of a Tudor castle, remodelled by Joseph Paxton (designer of London's Crystal Palace) around the remains of the medieval fort that originally stood here. Its long occupation by the Anglo-Irish aristocracy (and less permanent colonists, including Sir Walter Raleigh) explains why so much of the layout of the park and farmland around here is reminiscent of wealthy English shires.

However, it is to a much earlier period than the castle's for which Lismore owes its reputation. In 635 AD St Carthage founded a **monastic complex** for both monks and nuns in Lismore, and the place so flourished as a centre of learning that in the next century, under the influence of great teachers such as St Colman, it became an important **university city**. This growth continued into the twelfth century, despite three hundred years of sporadic pillage by first Vikings then Normans. Lismore held great political as well as religious power, and the rivalry between the sees of Lismore and Waterford, which epitomizes the split histories of Waterford city and county, was only resolved in 1363 when the two were united.

Invaders continued to attack the city and in the late sixteenth century the medieval cathedral was almost totally destroyed by Queen Elizabeth's army. Its site is now occupied by the Church of Ireland **St Carthage's Cathedral**. Although built in 1633, its overall appearance is early nineteenth-century neo-Gothic, the tower and ribbed spire having been added in 1827 by James Pain and the windows of the nave reshaped at the same time. It's a lovely building, sitting in a cobbled churchyard of ancient yews and pollarded limes. Inside is some interesting stonework, including the McGrath family tomb (1548), which has carvings of the apostles, mystical beasts and skulls. The chunky carving of a bishop holding an open book set in the back wall is probably from the ninth-century monastic settlement. In the south transept, just on your left as you enter, there's some striking stained glass by Burne-Jones, the English pre-Raphaelite.

Practicalities

Lismore's main street sits on the south side of the river, and it's here that you'll find the **tourist office**, in the heritage centre in the courthouse (mid-March to Aug daily 9.30am–6pm; Sept & Oct Mon–Sat 9.30am-6pm, Sun noon–5.30pm; Nov to mid-March Mon–Sat 9.30am–5.30pm; ☎058/54855). There's **B&B** in the centre of town at *Alana* in Chapel Street, just up behind the tourist office (☎058/54106; ②); *Ballyrafter House Hotel*, Vee Road (☎058/54002, *www.ballyrafter*, ⑦), a fine Georgian house set in mature gardens; or *Beechcroft*, Deerpark Road, half a mile out of town (☎058/54273; ③). Converted Georgian coach-houses provide **hostel** accommodation at Kilmorna Farm (☎058/54315); breakfasts and evening meals are served on request, and they also have room for **camping**.

Eating places are limited to a few pubs along the main street: *Madden's* serves fresh modern-Irish dishes; for more traditional pub grub try *Eamonn's*. As for drinking, the town has some fascinating ancient **bars**, a delight to explore in themselves, though there's not much beyond this trip into the past by way of entertainment. Try *Foley's*, *O'Brien's* – or *Madden's*, once the "local" for castle guests, such as Fred Astaire.

Towards the Comeragh Mountains

The road north from Lismore towards Cahir is typical of this area's gorgeous river valleys, stuffed with rhododendrons, bracken, beech trees and oaks, and feathery pines. The walls are covered with spongy mosses and young ferns. About three miles along the road you can pick up a path leading to higher ground and more open spaces scattered with sheep and fir trees. The path goes through the **Knockmealdowns**, round the huge peat-covered mound of Sugarloaf Hill and after five miles leads to a viewing spot known as **The Vee**. From its steep, heathery V-shaped sides there's a tremendous view of the perfectly flat vale below with its patches of fields and of the town of Cahir at the foot of the Galtee Mountains. If you want to stop off at this point you can follow the road down to Clogheen and hitch to one of two **hostels** in Cahir, County Tipperary; for the independent one, see p.256), the An Óige one is called *Mountain Lodge*, at Burncourt (closed Oct–Feb; ☎052/67277). To press onwards, you can pick up the **East Munster Way** at The Vee. From here it descends to Clonmel, County Tipperary, around seventeen miles further on, taking in the scenic wooded **Nier Valley**.

At their most scenic from the Nier (also spelt "Nire") Valley, the **Comeragh Mountains**, which form the county's central uplands, appear for the most part as heathery, boggy open moorland. The Nier Valley runs from below Knockaunapeebra west to **BALLYMACARBERY**. Walks into the mountains take you up to a fine series of corrie lakes, encircled by high cliffs. Ballymacarbery makes a good base from which to explore the area: *Clonanav Guesthouse* (☎052/36141; ④) offers **B&B**, and there's traditional music at *Melody's* **bar** (generally Tues & Wed). The village is also a good stopover for walkers on the **East Munster Way** (see p.252), which crosses the Nier three miles west of Ballymacarbery.

COUNTY TIPPERARY

Tipperary is the largest of Ireland's inland counties, and also the richest. The county's wealth comes from the central **Golden Vale**, a flat limestone plain shared with eastern Limerick that's prime beef and dairy cattle territory. This enormous stretch of farming land is abutted on most borders by crops of mountain ranges, the most beautiful of which are the **Galtee Mountains** and the **Glen of Aherlow**. These are all in the south of the county, and it's this area, without doubt, that packs in the most excitement. The curling course of the **Suir**, Tipperary's principal river, sweeps by most of what there is to see. But for many, Tipperary's attractions hang on one site alone. The **Rock of Cashel** is the county's most dramatic feature by far, its limestone sides rising cliff-like 200ft above the level ground, crowned with the high walls and towers of some splendid medieval ecclesiastical architecture.

Tipperary often has a vaguely familiar ring, thanks to the World War I marching song *It's a long way to Tipperary*. The county was actually picked for the song simply for the rhythmic beat of its name, which dashes the romance somewhat. In fact, Tipperary isn't particularly far from anywhere in southern Ireland, and this is probably its greatest advantage: you can catch the few worthwhile sights on your way through, and still be on the south or west coast within a few hours.

Carrick-on-Suir and around

Tucked in Tipperary's southeast corner, at the foot of the mountain slopes of neighbouring County Waterford, **CARRICK-ON-SUIR** may well be the first place you see in Tipperary, a slight country town raised a cut above the rest by what is perhaps Ireland's most beautiful Elizabethan mansion: similar examples abound in England but are a rarity here. Set at the very eastern end of the main street, **Ormond Castle** (guided tours mid-June to Sept daily 9.30am–6.30pm; £2/€2.54; Heritage Card). was built by Thomas, tenth Earl of Ormond ("Black Tom"), in anticipation of a visit from Queen Elizabeth I – and tributes to her are incorporated in the decoration throughout: above all in a fresco over the entrance way and in the superb stucco work of the long gallery. A stunning mansion, with mullioned windows running the length of the building, it's the only major example in Ireland of a completely unfortified dwelling to date from the sixteenth century. It adjoins the remains of an earlier castle built in 1309; the two rectangular towers, currently undergoing renovation, date from the mid-fifteenth century. There's a collection of magnificent royal charters here, too: the oldest dates from 1661 and granted

THE EAST MUNSTER WAY

The **East Munster Way** runs from Carrick-on-Suir for 43 miles west to the village of Clogheen, eight miles south of Cahir. The first stretch is easy walking alongside the River Suir as far as **Clonmel**. From here the Way climbs the heathery, wooded slopes of the Comeraghs, to descend three miles west of Ballymacarbery and the Nier Valley (see p.251). The path soon follows the flank of the Knockmealdown Mountains, affording fine views of the plain below, and winds up at the tiny village of Clogheen, six miles west of Ardfinnian. The walk involves long distances rather than steep, dramatic inclines, and for most of the way you're within a mile or so of habitation. Nevertheless, solitary walkers should bear in mind that much of the route is out of sight of the lowlands, and distress signals won't be noticed. The relevant Bord Fáilte Information Sheet, giving route guidelines for this section of the way, is Carrick-on-Suir–The Vee, Information Sheet no. 26J, and you'll need OS **maps** nos. 74 and 75, 1:50,000.

James Butler the title of Duke of Ormond. Some historians also claim that Anne Boleyn was born here. Regardless of the mansion's splendours, however, it is as the birthplace of the champion cyclist **Sean Kelly** that the town is most proud – and the tiny main square at the west end of the main street has been renamed in his honour.

Tourist information (Mon–Fri 10am–5pm, Sat & Sun 9.30am–5pm, though weekend opening hours may vary in winter; ☎051/640200) can be found in the heritage centre, just off Main Street. **Accommodation** is fairly limited: in the centre of town are *The Bell and Salmon Arms Hotel*, 95–97 Main St (☎051/645555; ⑤), and *Fatima House* B&B, John Street (☎051/640298; ③). There's also B&B at *Hillcrest*, (☎051/640847; ③), a mile out on the N24 opposite the Sean Kelly Sports Centre. You can **camp** at *Carrick-on-Suir Caravan and Camping Park*, Ballyrichard, Kilkenny Road (closed Nov–Feb; ☎051/640461), one mile out of town. Cyclists heading for the hostel outside Clonmel (see p.254) are better off leaving the main road at Carrick-on-Suir and heading across country via Rathgormuck.

You'll find good **bar food** at *The Carraig Hotel* on Main Street (daily till 9.30pm). As for **entertainment**, *The Bell and Salmon Arms Hotel* has a bright modern bar attracting a young crowd, with open Irish sessions (Mon & Wed), live rock and pop bands (Sun), and discos (Fri & Sat in summer). For a quiet pint, try the bar of the *Carraig Hotel*.

Five miles north of Carrick, **AHENNY** has two beautiful high crosses in its graveyard. They're thought to be eighth century, and are excellent examples of the transitional style between the early Christian plain shaft crosses and the highly ornate didactic crosses of Monasterboice and Kells.

Clonmel and around

CLONMEL, thirteen miles upstream from Carrick-on-Suir, is far and away Tipperary's prettiest centre. It's a strangely genteel kind of place and retains something of its flavour as an early coaching town. It was the birthplace in 1713 of Laurence Sterne, philosopher and literary comic genius, and it's not at all difficult to imagine Shandyesque shenanigans in the fine Georgian inns around town. A hundred years later Clonmel became the principal base for Bianconi, the most successful coach business in the country. The company's founder, Bianconi, came from Lombardy in Italy and ran his so-called Bians from what is now *Hearn's Hotel* on Parnell Street.

The town is a beautiful place to breeze through: you can't miss Clonmel's finest building, the sorely dilapidated **Main Guard** sagging at the eastern end of O'Connell Street. The oldest public building in Ireland, built in the classical style, it predates Dublin's Royal Hospital, it is now undergoing full renovation. The facade visible today was built by James Butler, first Duke of Ormond, as a courthouse for the Palatinate of the County of Tipperary, and it bears two panels showing coats of arms dated 1675. The Main Guard is set to open some time during 2001 as a heritage centre.

Other examples of period architecture include the nineteenth-century **St Mary's Roman Catholic Church**, with ziggurat tower and portico, in Irishtown, out past the Tudor-style nineteenth-century West Gate; the Greek Revival-style **Wesleyan Church** on Wolfe Tone Street; and the **Old St Mary's** Church of Ireland church with its octagonal tower and tower house. All of these are impressive from the outside; none offer much if you venture in. The **County Museum** in Emmet Street (Mon–Fri 10am–5pm, Sat 10am–1pm & 2–5pm; free) records local history in a collection of maps, newspapers, postcards and prints of Bianconi's coaches; it also has a small gallery of fine paintings and hosts temporary exhibitions.

At Richmond Mill, opposite SuperQuinn supermarket, there's a **Museum of Transport** (Mon–Sat 10am–6pm; £2.50/€3.17) housing two rooms of gleaming nostalgia, including Rolls, Jags and Fords from the 1930s on and a 1965 VW Karman Ghia.

Practicalities

Clonmel's **tourist office** is in the Chamber of Commerce building on Nelson Street down by the quays (July & Aug Mon–Sat 9.30am–5.30pm; May, June & Sept Mon–Fri 9.30am–5.30pm; Oct–April 9.30am–1pm & 2–5.30pm; ☎052/22960). There are a few **B&Bs** in the centre of town and plenty more further out. Central *Mr Bumbles*, Kickham Street (☎052/29188; ④), offers travel-lodge style accommodation, and *Fennessy Hotel*, Gladstone Street (☎052/23680; ⑤), a traditional, but newly refurbished **hotel** with bright, comfy rooms and a good breakfast menu. For B&B's outside the centre, follow the Cork Road out of town for about one mile and you'll find several signposted up a road that forks to the left, including *Benuala* (☎052/22158; ③) and *Hillcourt* (☎052/21029; ③). Worth the extra journey is the welcoming farmhouse B&B at *Ballyboy House* (☎052/65297; ④), five miles south on the R671 at Clogheen (not to be confused with the town of the same name further west). The nearest **hostel** is *Powers the Pot* at Harneys Cross, five and a half miles up the slopes of the Comeragh Mountains (☎052/23085). It's popular with **campers**, and there's a cosy **bar** on site. At 1200ft this claims to be the highest house in the country, and it's certainly on the threshold of excellent hill-walking country.

There are several good places to **eat** in Clonmel. At lunchtime *Angela's* on Abbey Street (Mon–Sat till 6pm), off behind the Mainguard, serves excellent good-value vegetarian meals, and *Niamh's* deli and coffee shop on Mitchell Street, is a good spot for light snacks. For **pub lunches** there's the hugely popular *Mulcahy's* on Gladstone Street – they serve on into the evening, and there's a restaurant attached if you don't want to eat in the bar. *Tom Skinny's*, also on Gladstone Street (noon–midnight) is a cheerful place serving excellent pizzas, while *Mr Bumble's* on Kickham Street is one of Clonmel's more stylish and informal restaurants (☎052/29188).

Good **pubs** for music include *Kitty O'Donnell's* near the station, and *Lonergan's* on O'Connell Street. *Fennessy's Hotel* has a cosy bar with occasional sessions. Good for a quiet pint are *Chawke's* on Gladstone Street, and *Phil Carroll's* "antique bar" on Parnell Street, both full of character.

Keen anglers will be interested to hear that **fishing** off the quay is free; otherwise you can get salmon and trout licences from Kavanagh's Sports Shop, Westgate. The river is said to be very good for the late run of the salmon in early September, and trout stocks have risen recently. If you want to find out about **walks** in this lovely area, head to the tourist office who can offer you tips as well as sell you OS maps and a copy of the *East Munster Way Map and Guide*.

Fethard

Leaving Clonmel, you could either head southwest to the plain between the Knockmealdown and Galtee mountains (see opposite); or north for Cashel, in which case the route via **FETHARD** is the most rewarding. A touchingly plain place to travel through, and rarely sought out by tourists, Fethard has a number of forgotten medieval remains, set at the back of the town towards the river. One of these is a ruined **Templars' Castle**, access to which is through the *Castle Inn* (contact the publican, Mr Keogh). Other remains of old friaries and Iron Age raths can be found in the surrounding land. There's also a **Folk Farm and Transport Museum** at the beginning of the Cashel Road (Sun noon–6pm, otherwise by appointment; ☎052/31516; £2/€2.54). For refreshments, *P.J. Lonegan's* home-cooked **lunches** are worth stopping off for and *McCarthy's* is a good place for a **drink** and also has a good restaurant alongside.

The Knockmealdown and Galtee mountains

Of the mountain ranges in southern Tipperary, the **Galtees** make up one of the most scenic inland ranges in the country and are well worth discovering – the Glen of Aherlow makes an excellent base in the heart of it all (see p.261). The **Knockmealdowns** are less interesting, but offer easier hill-walking. The valley plain between the two mountain ranges, which runs for about ten miles east of Mitchelstown (itself over the border in County Cork, see p.256), is not much in itself, but the *Mountain Lodge* An Óige hostel is a good overnight stop for hikers, and the **Mitchelstown caves** are well worth a visit. Starting from Clonmel you've a choice of two routes west: the main roads via **Cahir**, or the lesser R665, which cuts straight across to Mitchelstown.

Cahir

You're unlikely to miss **CAHIR**. The town sits on a major crossroads on the routes between Clonmel, Cork, Cashel and Tipperary. Its **castle** (daily: mid-March to mid-June & mid-Sept to mid-Oct 9.30am–5.30pm; mid-June to mid-Sept 9am–7.30pm; mid-Oct to mid-March 9.30am–4.30pm; £2/€2.54; Heritage Card), set on a rocky islet in the River Suir, beside the road to Cork, is Cahir's outstanding attraction – even the name Cahir means "fort". In essence the building is Anglo-Norman, and goes back to the thirteenth and fifteenth centuries, though the virgin appearance of the outer shell is deceptive, with a good deal of the brickwork dating back to the eighteenth and nineteenth centuries. The Irish chieftain Conor O'Brien was the first to build a fortress on the rock; but it was the Anglo-Norman Butlers, the Earls of Ormond, who made this into one of the most powerful castles in the country. The Earl of Essex showered the castle with artillery fire in 1599; it got off lightly during the Cromwellian and Williamite invasions, and gradually fell into ruin until rejuvenated, along with other town buildings, by the Earl of Glengall in the mid-nineteenth century. In modern times, the interior has been uniformly whitewashed and spartanly furnished.

Entrance to the castle is along the side rampart, bringing you into the confined space of the **middle ward**, dominated by the three-storey thirteenth-century **keep**. The keep itself consists of a portcullis, vaulted chambers and a round tower containing a prison, accessible through a trap door. Down to the left, you pass through a gateway topped by machicolations, musket loops to either side, where sixteenth-century invaders could have been bombarded with missiles or boiling oil. Beyond is the much larger **outer ward** and, at its far end, the cottage built by the Earl of Glengall. The cottage now houses a **video theatre** where a twenty-minute film enthuses rhapsodically on the antiquities of southern Tipperary.

In the **inner ward**, two corner towers overlook the road to Cork. The larger was probably designed to be independently defensible once the keep had fallen, and it dates from a mixture of periods – straight, thirteenth-century stone stairs; fifteenth- to sixteenth-century stone vaulting over the ground-floor main room; and nineteenth-century renovation work in the Great Hall, whose stepped battlements reflect sixteenth-century style. The smaller, square tower at the other end of the ward and the curtain wall date from the nineteenth century, though with medieval bases. Just to the left of this second tower, steps lead to the bottom of the well tower, where the castle could safeguard its water supply during a siege. The informative **guided tour** of the castle is well worth taking.

One further building worth seeing is the **Swiss Cottage** (mid-March & mid-Oct to Nov Tues–Sun 10am–1pm & 2–4.30pm; April Tues–Sun 10am–1pm & 2–6pm; May to mid-Oct daily 10am–6pm; £2/€2.54; Heritage Card), a pleasant one-mile walk along the river from the castle or a short drive out of Cahir on the Clonmel Road. Probably designed by John Nash, it was built in 1810 to provide the Earls of Glengall with a lodge of romanticized – and fashionable – rustic simplicity from which to enjoy their hunting, shooting and fishing. With its thatched roof and ornate timberwork it certainly looks the part, and its status as a unique period piece makes it a popular attraction.

Practicalities

Buses from Waterford and Dublin drop you off outside the *Crock of Gold*, across from the castle, while those from Cork and Limerick stop outside the tourist office; there's a timetable posted in the window. The **tourist office** is in the car park beside the castle (May, June & Sept Mon–Sat 9am–6pm; July & Aug also Sun 11am–5pm; ☎052/41453). From the castle you can see another castellated mansion on the hill further along the Cork road: the *Carrigeen Castle* (☎052/41370; ④), once the town prison – though rather a picturesque one – and now a **B&B**. More conventional alternatives are signposted off the N24 Clonmel road, a short walk from the centre: *Killaun* (☎052/41780; ③) and *Silver Acre Guesthouse* (☎052/41737; ③). Basic budget accommodation and camping are available at the welcoming IHH-run *Lisakyle Hostel* (closed Nov–Feb; ☎052/41963), one mile out of Cahir beyond the Swiss Cottage. Most secluded of all is An Óige *Mountain Lodge* hostel (see p.251). For walkers, its handy location, a ten-mile hike from the *Ballydavid Wood* hostel in the Glen of Aherlow, six miles out of Cahir (see p.261), makes it a popular base. There's **camping** among the fruit trees at *The Apple Farm* (closed Oct–Easter; ☎052/41459), four miles out of Cahir along the Clonmel road.

Standard **café** fare is served at the coffee shop above the *Crock of Gold*, opposite the castle, and at *Roma's Café*, on the Dublin side of the square. You can get pasta, pizzas and Irish food at the *Italian Connection*, open every day till 11pm. For good **pub lunches** try the *Galtee Inn* on the square or *The Castle*, opposite the castle. **Traditional music** is minimal, but sometimes takes place at *Morrissey's*, opposite the castle, while *Irwin's*, on the Square, has a mix of traditional music and ballads (Thurs); the tourist office will know of the most likely place any given day.

Ardfinnan to the Mitchelstown Caves

Along the minor road from Clonmel to Mitchelstown, is **ARDFINNAN**, where a beautiful fourteen-arched stone bridge crosses the Suir and a private castle stands on the hillside opposite. Follow the foot of the Knockmealdowns for several miles and you'll come to Clogheen, where there's the best turn-off route into the mountains, towards the terrific scenic point known as The Vee (see p.251).

Continuing along the R665, you'll come next to **BALLYPOREEN**, a wide-streeted crossroads turned ghost town, whose moment of glory came on June 3, 1984, when **Ronald Reagan** made a prodigal return – his great-grandfather was supposedly born here in 1810. You can read all about it and look at photos of the visit in a specially built centre at the crossroads, opposite the *Ronald Reagan* pub.

Eight miles from Mitchelstown itself, the massive pre-glacial underworld of the **Mitchelstown Caves** (daily 10am–6pm; £3.50/€4.44) – signposted north from Ballyporeen down the interlacing lanes of the valley, or south off the N8 – are, aside from walking, the main attraction in the area. By far the most extensive and complicated cave system in Ireland (a couple of miles in all), they have remained, considering their scale, very uncommercialized. The whole underground system was discovered in 1833, when a labourer lost his crowbar down a crevice, though there are records from much earlier of one cave being used as a hiding place, most famously to shelter the Earl of Desmond after his unsuccessful rebellion in 1601.

The caves were formed by the action of rainwater on the limestone over millions of years, and the fantastical stone formations grew out of the calcium carbonate (dissolved limestone) deposited by the dripping water, hardening as it evaporated into gigantic encrustations of stalactites and stalagmites. The temperature in the caves is around 54°F – this can feel chilly in summer, so bring a sweater. The **tours** only take in a few of the major caves but are nonetheless worth taking.

Cashel and around

Just eleven miles north of Cahir on the road to Dublin, **CASHEL** grew around, and is completely dominated by, the spectacular **Rock of Cashel**, a limestone outcrop topped by a splendid array of medieval buildings. No tourist bus will bypass the site – so an early-morning or late-afternoon visit will make an important difference to your first impressions. In deep contrast to the ecclesiastical splendour of the Rock is the tiny **Bothán Scóir** – a unique one-roomed peasant dwelling. For antiquarian book-lovers the **GPA Bolton Library** is a must, and the museum at **Cashel Folk Village** will appeal to anyone interested in Irish social history.

A view of the Rock in the dwindling light of dusk is one of Ireland's most memorable sights; consider this along with the town's position around 95 miles from the ferry ports at both Dublin and Rosslare Harbour and there's a very strong argument for stopping over in Cashel if you are heading to the west coast.

The Rock of Cashel

Approached from the north or west, the **Rock of Cashel** (daily: mid-March to mid-June 9am–5.30pm; mid-June to mid-Sept 9am–7.30pm; mid-Sept to mid-March 9am–4.30pm; £3.50/€4.44; Heritage Card) appears as a spectacular mirage of fairytale turrets, crenellations and walls rising bolt upright from the vast encircling plain. It's a tour operator's dream: on one piece of freak limestone outcrop stands the most beautiful and complete Romanesque church in the country, a gargantuan medieval cathedral, a castle tower house, an eleventh-century round tower, a unique early high cross and the exquisite fifteenth-century Hall of Vicars – medieval Irish architecture wrapped up in a morning's investigation. Two more medieval priories lie at its feet.

In **legend** the Rock was formed when the Devil, flying overhead with a large stone in his mouth, suddenly caught sight of St Patrick standing ready to found his new church on the site, and in his shock dropped the rock (in the northeast of the county, a striking gap in a mountain range is known as the "Devil's Bit"). The Rock is also the place where St Patrick is supposed to have picked a shamrock in order to explain the doctrine of the Trinity – God the Father, Christ the Son and the Holy Ghost as three beings of the one stem – since which time the shamrock became Ireland's unofficial emblem.

The Hall of the Vicars

Approaching the Rock from Cashel town, you come first to the **Hall of the Vicars**, built in the fifteenth century to cater for eight vicar *meistersingers*, who assisted in the cathedral services but were later dispensed with because of growing resentment over the power and land that their privileged office entailed. The upper floor of the building is divided between the main hall, with screens and a minstrels' gallery, and what would have been the dormitories. The ground floor, a vaulted undercroft, today contains the original **St Patrick's Cross**, a unique type of high cross. It once stood outside, where there's now a replica. Tradition has it that the cross's huge plinth was the coronation stone of the High Kings of Munster, the most famous of whom was Brian Boru, killed in his tent by a fleeing Viking at the Battle of Clontarf. The cross is simpler than other high crosses, with a carving of Christ on one side and St Patrick on the other. It has an upright supporting its left arm and is without the usual ring-wheel in the centre. It may be that originally the upright and its missing counterpart represented the two thieves crucified with Jesus, and it is also possible that it was never intended as a freestanding cross in the first place, but for erection on a wall.

Cormac's Chapel

Cormac's Chapel, built 1127 to 1134, is the earliest and most beautiful of Ireland's surviving Romanesque churches, and the intricacies of its decoration are as spectacular as they are unique. The architecture has clear continental influences – the twin square **towers**, for example, were probably engineered by monks sent from Regensburg, Germany. The **tympana**, or panels, above the grandiose north door (more than likely the original entrance, now leading blindly into the flank of the cathedral) and south door (today's entrance), are also rare in Irish church architecture. Above the north door is depicted a curious carved scene of a large beast ensnaring a smaller one, itself on the point of being speared by a macho centaur in a Norman helmet. The north door is set in six orders of pillars, creating a tunnel-vaulted **porch**, which is sheltered by an outer stone roof porch. Each arch is crowned with capitals, human heads, fantastic beasts, flutings and scallops.

The small size of the chapel is typical of Irish architecture of this period, as are the lack of aisles and the steeply pitched stone roof – you'll find similar-looking buildings at Glendalough and Kells, though Cormac's chapel is larger than these. The wall opposite you as you walk in has a tall triple arcade, in the centre of which is a large round-headed **window** that would once have lit up the whole interior, illuminating all the painted colour – of which a little remains up at the altar and just above the chancel arch. The **sarcophagus** at the foot of this wall, although fragmented, has an exquisite Scandinavian Urnes design of interlacing serpents and ribbon decoration. It's said to have been the tomb of King Cormac, and is certainly old enough to be so.

The cathedral and round tower

The **cathedral** was begun a century or so after Cormac's chapel. Although Anglo-Norman in conception, with Gothic arches and lancet windows, this is a purely Irish-built endeavour. A graceful limestone building, it features a series of tall, high-set lancet **windows**, and also some good examples of quatrefoil, or four-petalled, windows, especially above the lancets in the choir space. You'll notice that some of the lancets have been shortened – probably as a measure of fortification. The **choir** is longer than the nave and both are without aisles: the nave was shortened to make room for the **castle tower**, built most obviously for refuge, and also as an archiepiscopal residence. A wooden-floored hall would once have been above the nave (the corbels are still apparent), accessible from the castle tower.

The **central tower**, at the meeting of the transepts, is also on a grand scale and, typically, did not appear until the fourteenth century. It's supported by four Gothic arches rising from very wide piers, their shafts sweeping beautifully into the concave bottom. Access to the tower is by winding stairs from the south transept (this may not be open to the public, so ask). **Passages** also ran through the nave and choir walls, supposedly for the outcasts or lepers of the community, so that they could watch the holy ceremonies without being seen themselves. The **transepts** have shallow chapel altars with some tomb and piscina niches. In the north transept, panels from sixteenth-century altar-tombs survive – one with an intricately carved retinue of saints, the others more broken but just as beautiful.

Some 92 feet high, the nearby **Round Tower** is the earliest building on the Rock. Its tapering features have led to suggestions that it dates from as early as the tenth century, though the officially accepted date is early twelfth century. It's not a typical tower; the entrance door was originally twelve feet above the ground, and various levels of windows ensnare viewpoints in all directions.

Around the Rock

From the grounds of the Rock you can look down at **Hore Abbey** on the plain below, and it's an easy enough walk down, over the fields and jumping the road wall. But there's little to be gained in doing this, beyond escaping the sightseers – you can see just as well from the Rock. The thirteenth-century abbey was the last Cistercian daughter monastery of Mellifont to be completed before the Reformation, and was probably built by those working on the Rock's cathedral. Originally a Benedictine foundation, it converted after its abbot had a wild dream that his Benedictine monks were plotting to cut his head off; he expelled them and donned the Cistercian habit in 1269. There's yet another abbey ruin, **St Dominic's**, down the south side of the Rock in the town, but this has even less to offer in terms of things to see.

A path known as the **Bishop's Walk** leads from the Rock's rampart entrance down into town through the back garden of the **Palace Hotel**. The Palace was built in Queen Anne-style by Archbishop Theophilus Bolton in 1730 as a mansion for the archbishops of Cashel (hence the Bishop's Walk to the Rock). It has a simple, red-brick front and a cut-stone rear. Cashel owes much to this particular archbishop; it was he who saw the value of Cormac's chapel and put his wealth into its restoration at a time when the Rock's antiquities were degenerating rapidly towards irrevocable ruin. A further legacy is the **GPA Bolton Library** (late May–Sept daily 11am–4.30pm; £2/€2.54), opposite the hotel and set in the grounds of the slender-spired eighteenth-century St John's Protestant Cathedral. Its manuscripts (from as early as the twelfth century), rare maps and wealth of literary treasures were principally Bolton's own bequest when he died in 1744. A selection of the books and maps are on display, changing bi-monthly and well worth viewing.

Also well worth seeing is the **Bothán Scóir**, a one-roomed peasant dwelling dating from around 1600, the only one of its kind in Ireland. To get there, walk up the street past the tourist office, turn first right and look out for a tiny cottage about half a mile up on your right Bothán means "hut", scóir is "score", referring to the score notched up on a tallystick as the peasant worked the 180 days of the year demanded by the landlord in payment for rent of the cottage and a patch of land. The soot-black thatch, the chimneyless roof, the half-door and the jamb wall – layer upon layer of authentic detail – tell a history of systematic oppression and thorough misery. All this is wonderfully articulated by your guide, Albert – a man with an inspiring passion for the history of the common people; it proves a wholly memorable experience. If you find no one at the cottage, go to 6 Ard Mhuire, the first cul-de-sac on the right as you head back down the hill towards town, and ask for Albert Carrie.

If you have the time to delve further into Cashel's social history, **Cashel Folk Village** (March & April daily 10am–6pm; May–Oct daily 9.30am–7.30pm; £2/€2.54), in a lane behind the tourist office, is well worth a visit. Crammed with interesting exhibits, the collection includes a gruesome traditional butcher's shop guaranteed to turn you vegetarian and a fascinating museum of Republican history.

Arrival, information and accommodation

Buses set down in the main street. Cashel's **tourist office** (May, June & Sept Mon–Sat 9.15am–6pm; July & Aug daily 9.15am–6pm; ☎062/61333) sits in the market house in the middle of the main street. The Cashel of the Kings **heritage centre** alongside gives an overall picture of the history of the town, in particular its ecclesiastical buildings.

There are several central **B&Bs** to choose from, a handful of more spacious establishments can be found out along the Dulla road, and the tourist office can suggest others in the area. For **hostel** accommodation, you could try one of two IHH-run places: the excellent and very central *Cashel Holiday Hostel* at 6 John St (☎062/62330; *cashelho@iol.ie*), or the equally impressive, but more rural *O'Brien's Farmhouse Hostel* (☎062/61003), located in a converted stone barn a short walk from Cashel. To get to the latter, turn right at the bottom of Main Street and follow the road towards Dundrum; it's signposted off here. *O'Brien's* also offer excellent **camping** facilities with superb views of the Rock.

Abbey House, 1 Dominic St (☎062/61104). Centrally located B&B in a quiet street near St Dominic's Friary. All rooms are en suite. ④.

Georgesland on the Dulla road (☎062/62788). Spacious modern farmhouse in a rural setting, within a mile of town. All rooms are en suite and non-smoking, and the beds are very comfortable. ④.

Maryville, Bankplace (☎062/61098; *maryvill@iol.ie*) Welcoming B&B right in the centre of town with gardens adjoining the thirteenth-century abbey. All rooms are en suite and non-smoking. ④.

Rahard Lodge on the Dulla road (☎062/61052). Spacious modern farmhouse, just a mile out of town with en-suite bedrooms and no-smoking policy. ③.

Rockview House (☎062/62187) B&B in a family home situated up a steep lane off the top of the main street, with views of the Rock from rooms. ③.

Rockville House (☎062/61760) Another decent B&B near St Dominic's Friary, a short walk from both the Rock and the centre of town. En-suite rooms; quiet location. Closed Nov to mid-March. ③.

Thornbrook House on the Dulla road (☎062/62388; *thornbrookhouse@eircom.net*) Spacious B&B in an antique-furnished, large and modern bungalow, within a mile of town. Room are all non-smoking, and some are en suite. ③, ④ en suite.

Eating and drinking

You'll have no trouble finding places to **eat** in Cashel. There are several coffee shops on Main Street and good-value meals are served at *The Bakehouse*. For **pub food** try *Kearney's Castle Hotel*, or *Hannigan's*, both on Ladyswell Street, the top end of the main road. *Spearman's,* 97 Main St, serves good, wholesome meals, but if you feel like splashing out, head for *Chez Hans* (closed Sun & early Jan; ☎062/61177) which serves top-notch meals in the unlikely setting of a former Wesleyan chapel.

A great deal of **music** is laid on in the summer – from rock, through country and western, to singalong and traditional Irish. This last tends to move around, but Cashel is a very small town, so if there's something going on, it won't be hard to find. Likely spots worth checking out include three on Main Street: *Feehan's, Con Gleeson's* and the cosy *Dowling's.*

Tipperary town and around

Twelve miles from Cashel and less than five from the border of Limerick, stands **TIPPERARY** town, at the northern side of the Glen of Aherlow. Like many of these namesake county towns, Tipperary is much less important than it sounds. If you've already visited Clonmel, it will come as something of a shock – compared to Clonmel's yuppy prosperity, Tipperary feels somewhat down at heel. The town has bold statues sculpted in granite here and there, most notably one to its literary local son, Charles J. Kickham, entitled *Poet, Novelist but above all Patriot.*

You might want to stop over briefly to take in the small and intriguing **museum** (Mon–Sat 9.30am–5pm; free) hidden away in the foyer of the town swimming pool, by the Cashel Road exit. A tiny store of memorabilia, it exhibits photos, letters and weaponry from the warring years of 1919 to 1923, especially relating to the old IRA. Tipperary was a particularly hot spot during the Anglo-Irish and Civil War strife, especially through its most remembered son, **Seán Tracey**, whose battalion fired the first shots of the Anglo-Irish War (1919–21). There are letters he wrote to his family from prison, some talking about the honour the British had bestowed on him by taking the trouble to get him captured, others of a more domestic nature. A violin belonging to **Joseph Mary Plunkett** (one of the poets executed in the 1916 rising) hangs beside revolvers, pistols and land mines. Most striking of all, perhaps, are the photographs of the young officers shown clenching their revolvers, either posturing a rebel's stance of defiance or slightly abashed, with innocent-looking smiles.

Practicalities

Tipperary is a small town and you won't have any trouble finding your way around. **Buses** from Limerick will drop you in Abbery Street, right in the centre of town. The **tourist office** is on James's Street (May–Sept Mon–Sat 9.30am–5.30pm; ☎062/51457). If you plan to **stay** in town, try *Central Accommodation*, 45 Main St (☎062/51117; ②), a B&B run by a friendly family. If this is full, there are several pleasant alternatives about one mile out of town on the Galbally road, including *Clonmore House* (☎062/51637; ③) and *Riverside* (☎062/51219; ③).

Places to **eat** are very much geared up to cater for locals working in town, though there's decent **bar food** at *Kiely's Bar* and *The Kickham House*, both on Main Street. *The Kickham House* is the best place to look for traditional **music** (Tues); other watering holes include *Corney's* on Davitt Street, which has a mix of traditional and country and western music at weekends, and *The Churchwell Tavern*, also in Davitt Street, where you can sometimes hear rock bands.

The Glen of Aherlow

Tucked away four miles south of Tipperary town off the R664, the luxuriant and majestic **Glen of Aherlow** runs for eight miles beneath the northern slopes of the Galtee Mountains, a breathtaking place to drive through. One of the nicest places **to stay** in the glen is *Ballinacourty House* (closed Dec & Jan; ☎062/56230; ③), offering accommodation in converted seventeenth- and eighteenth-century haylofts that look out over an extremely pretty, cobbled courtyard; there's also a wine bar, a moderately priced restaurant and a **campsite** within the grounds. Alternatively, you could try *Homeleigh Farm House* (☎062/56228; ③), which offers welcoming B&B and **pony trekking**; or nearby *Aherlow House Hotel* (☎062/56153; ⑦) which makes a fine place to stay, offering comfortable rooms in one of the most scenic locations in the county – non-residents can enjoy soups and sandwiches and stunning views from their **terrace bar**. For **walkers**, there's the An Óige **hostel**, the *Ballydavid Wood* (closed Dec–Feb; ☎062/54148); try to arrive in daylight for this one, for although meticulously signposted, the route has enough twists and turns to get you lost. It's a short day's trek from the *Mountain Lodge* **hostel** (closed Oct–Feb; ☎052/67277), a spacious, Alpine-style old shooting lodge, offering the bare necessities (including gas lighting) on the southern slopes of the Galtee Mountains, ten miles south of here. The forest trail between the two is not waymarked and little used, but if you do want to walk here, its advisable to contact the hostel manager about your estimated time of arrival.

Thurles and around

North of Cashel, both the Suir itself and the attractions along its banks wane. The river passes through the larger towns of **Thurles** and Templemore, though its source in the Devil's Bit Mountain falls short of the little town of **Roscrea**. Thurles is on the main

Limerick–Dublin train line; Roscrea is more easily accessed by bus, being on the main bus route between those two cities.

THURLES is of very little interest in itself, but if you're passing through and in need of refreshment you might want to check out the *Dwan Brewery & Restaurant* in The Mall off Liberty Square, a modern micro-brewery, giving the town's social scene something of a lift, and offering a markedly contemporary barfood menu. Just four miles south of town, **Holy Cross Abbey** sits beside a broad stretch of the Suir and is well worth a visit. Founded in 1180, restored significantly in the fifteenth century and then left derelict for four hundred years, the abbey was totally restored between 1971 and 1985 and is now a thriving parish church as well as a tourist attraction. You really need to see photographs of the period before restoration to appreciate the significance of this – they suggest that every other ruin you've seen could as easily be so converted. Holy Cross always had singular importance as a centre of pilgrimage, however, claiming to possess a piece of the **True Cross**. The splinter was reckoned to have been given to Murtagh O'Brien, King of Munster, by Pope Paschal II in 1110. At the turn of the seventeenth century both O'Donnell and O'Neill, the Ulster chiefs, stopped off to venerate this relic on their way to Kinsale to meet the French – no doubt hoping they'd be rewarded with a victory over Elizabeth I.

The **interior** of the church has been fully restored, though here there's been no particular attempt at period accuracy; virtually every wall and pillar has been whitewashed, and all the pews have been varnished. Nevertheless, it's rewarding to see the stone ribbing of the vaulted roofs and most particularly the undamaged fifteenth-century **sedilia** in the chancel area, the finest in the country. The sedilia, recessed stone seats for the celebrants of the Mass, is of a hard limestone shaped into cusped arches and crowned with crockets, showing decorative friezework as well as the English royal crest and the escutcheon of the Earls of Ormond. In the transept to the left of the nave, you'll find one of Ireland's rare medieval **frescoes**, this one showing a Norman hunting scene painted in browns, reds and greens. The exterior of the church has a startling full-length slate roof, which reaches down to the cloister pillars. Though the church itself is open year-round, the clositer and its ranges have limited opening times (mid-April to Oct Mon–Sat 10am–6pm, Sun 11am–6pm). There's an informal **tourist information centre** with variable opening hours, a coffee shop and a religious crafts shop within the abbey complex.

Ballynahow Castle

If you're cycling or driving north towards Thurles you might also think of taking in **Ballynahow Castle**, a circular castle tower built by the Purcell family in the sixteenth century. To get there from Holy Cross, take the road directly opposite the Protestant church, not the Thurles route (even though the signpost says so). From Thurles itself, it's out on the Nenagh road, right at the Jet petrol station, and after another mile the castle stands next to a farmhouse – *Ballynahow Castle Farm* where you can pick up the key; the farm also offers **B&B** from March to October (☎0504/21297; ④). You enter the castle at the lowest of its five storeys, the circular design giving the feel of entering into an igloo, with the corbelled roof curving round almost to the floor. There are many little rooms hidden within the walls and, although undecorated and entirely bare (and quite dark), most of it is in an excellent state of preservation and very atmospheric.

Roscrea

ROSCREA sits on a low hillock between the Slieve Bloom Mountains to the northeast and the Devil's Bit to the southwest. It's a charming place, with streets running down the hill slopes and a certain conscious lack of worldliness. However, where the rest of Ireland has secluded river sites and spacious countryside for its abbey ruins, Roscrea has the main Dublin–Limerick road roaring through the middle of **St Cronan's Monastery**. On one side of the road is the round tower, with a garage shed built into the side of it and the top third removed by the British in 1798. Immediately opposite, virtually on the pavement, is the west gable of **St Cronan's Church**, its yellow sandstone carved out in a twelfth-century Romanesque style reminiscent of Cormac's Chapel in Cashel. The rest of the church was pulled down in the nineteenth century and the stone used as building material elsewhere. **St Cronan's Cross**, just to the right of the gable, must have been a beauty once, but now it's severely weather-beaten and hacked. Up by the centre of the town is a large, sturdy-looking **Gate Tower Castle** dating from the thirteenth century across the courtyard stands the imposing eighteenth century Damer House, a good example of pre-Palladian architecture, which has been restored and now displays an exhibition on the history of the house. **Tours** of both house and castle are available (May–Sept daily on the hour from 10am, last tour 5pm; £2.50/€3.17; Heritage Card). Backed by a polygonal curtain wall, it now houses a **heritage centre** where there's an exhibition on the imposing eighteenth-century Damer House, which stands on the south side of the courtyard; the tour takes in the Palladian-style house and the castle.

Nenagh

NENAGH is usually jam-packed with heavy traffic trying to plough its way through on the main Dublin–Limerick road. It has one singular historical remain, a colossal round **castle keep** with walls 20ft thick, its five storeys reaching a height of 100ft and topped with nineteenth-century castellations. Totally gutted within, this final retreat tower was originally one of five round towers which, linked by a curtain wall, formed a Norman stronghold. Founded by Theobald Walter, a cousin of Thomas à Becket, it was occupied by the Butlers, then captured in turn by the O'Carrols of Eile, Cromwell, went back to James II and then to and fro between Ginckel (King William's chief general) and O'Carrol in the Williamite war. And there the fighting stopped until many centuries later when a farmer, wanting to get rid of a nest of sparrows that were feeding on his crops, stuck some gunpowder in the walls of the keep and blew another hole in the fortress. A few reinforced concrete steps help you to get near the top, but there's little to be seen.

Across the road from the keep, the Nenagh **heritage centre** (Easter–Oct Mon–Fri 9.30am–5pm; £2/€2.54) is set in the old jail, now a Convent of Mercy school. Housed in the octagonal Governor's House, up the driveway, it has a display room housing temporary exhibitions, a mock-up of an old schoolroom with a four-foot mannequin nun, and a re-created old post office, bar and telephone exchange. In the basement are the usual agricultural items and a faithfully reproduced but clinical-looking forge. Back at the entrance arch, the cells of the jail have their original hefty iron cell doors, and you can also see the former exercise yard, tiny and cluttered.

Buses from Dublin and Limerick stop right in the centre of town, some also stop at the **train station**, which is on the Thurles side of town, a short walk from the town centre. **The tourist office** is on Connolly Street (mid-May to mid-Sept Mon–Sat 9.30am–1pm & 2–5.30pm; ☎067/31610). There's reasonably priced **B&B** at *Sun View*, on Ciamaltha Road (☎067/31064; ③), quite close to the bus and train stations, and you can get excellent home-cooked **meals** at *Country Choice Deli & Coffee Bar*, 25 Kenyon St; the shop stocks superb Irish cheeses.

COUNTY LIMERICK

To an even greater extent than Tipperary, everyone passes through **County Limerick**, and hardly anyone stays. Once here, you're tantalizingly close to the much more rewarding counties of Cork, Kerry and Clare, and frankly you're not likely to linger. Urban, industrial Limerick has none of the breezy west-coast spirit so appealing just about everywhere else along this seaboard. Nevertheless, it is well worth making time to visit the superb **Hunt Museum** which has collections to rival that of the National Gallery in Dublin, and this, along with a handful of good restaurants and bars, makes the city worth considering as a stopover. Around the county are a number of points of interest, the best of which lie close to two main routes that run southwards from Limerick city. **Castle Matrix**, an authentic, lavishly restored and renovated tower house stands beside the N23 Limerick to Killarney road; **Lough Gur** lies thirteen miles south of the city, a Mesolithic-to-Neolithic lake and hill enclave of preternatural beauty, well worth making a detour off the N20, the road to Cork. Both can be reached by public transport.

For **cyclists**, Limerick's terrain is more variable than it's usually given credit for. In its western-to-southwestern corner, the upland bears a likeness to barren stretches of Donegal, whereas the northern estuary stretch is indeed only a slightly bumpy flatland. The centre and east bow in contour towards the eastern frontier of the Tipperary Golden Vale's rich dairy land, but not without gently rising mounds for hills and broadish trickles for rivers. More so than any other county, the land in Limerick is dotted with an array of **tower castles**, some inhabited but most in ruins or no more than stumps.

Historically, Limerick's most notable period arrived with the Norman strongholds, the most dominant family being the Fitzgeralds, also known as the Earls of Desmond – virtually all of Limerick's significant ruins were once this clan's power bases. They quickly became Gaelicized and ruled as independent monarchs, pulling very much away from English rule. The inevitable confrontation with Britain came to a head at the end of the sixteenth century, when in 1571 the Geraldine uprising against Elizabeth I sparked off a savage war, which brought about their downfall and destroyed in its wake much of the province of Munster.

Limerick city

Squarely on the path of all the major routes across the country, and situated pretty much at the head of the Shannon estuary, the city of **LIMERICK** seems a logical place to make for, but it's a disappointment. Though it's the Republic's third city, and heavily industrialized, it somehow falls significantly short of being a metropolis, yet also lacks the attractions of a typically relaxed western seaboard town. Unemployment and eco-

SPORT IN LIMERICK: THE GARRYOWEN

Even more than most of Ireland, Limerick seems obsessed with sport; horse racing, hurling, gaelic football, soccer and rugby are all avidly followed, and hurling and rugby have particularly strong local traditions. In rugby, the region has passed into immortality with the invention of the **Garryowen** – named after a district of Limerick city which also lent its name to one of Ireland's finest rugby clubs. The move, a high kick upfield pursued by a charging team who hope to hit the opposition as they catch the ball, the equivalent of Rugby League's "up-and-under", is said to have been invented here in the 1920s.

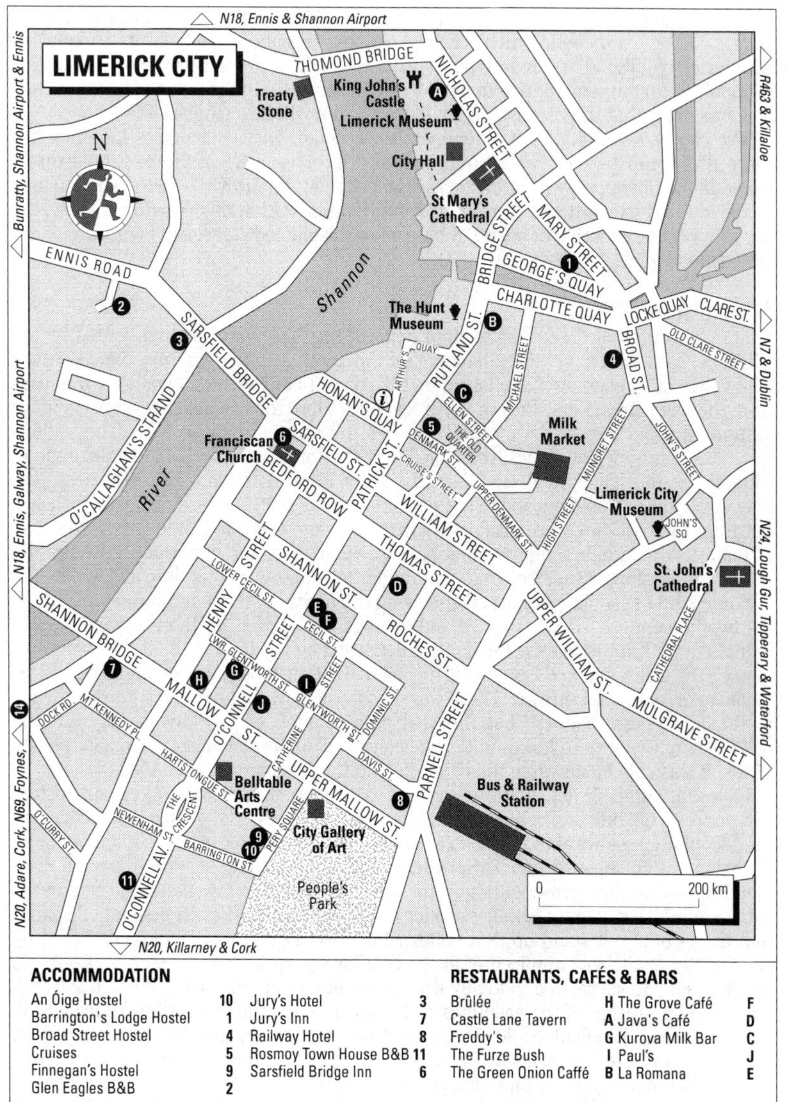

nomic hard times have left their mark, it doesn't always seem a friendly place and certain areas can feel positively intimidating at night. Even so, recent efforts to clean up Limerick's image are starting to pay off. On a fine day the area around **King John's Castle** affords some sense of the city's medieval history and the Georgian Custom House is home to the excellent **Hunt Museum** – reason enough to give Limerick some time.

The city is famous too as the setting for Frank McCourt's international best-seller *Angela's Ashes* – a memoir which received a mixed reception locally for its portrayal of a Limerick childhood of grinding poverty. Lively walking tours are proving increasingly popular with tourists wanting to tap into the experiences at the heart of the book, and it seems likely that the reconstructed heritage slum will be a similar draw.

The city you see today is predominantly Georgian, but nevertheless Limerick has three distinct historical areas: **Englishtown**, the oldest part of the city, built on an island in the Shannon with the castle as its focal point; **Irishtown**, which began to take shape in the thirteenth and fourteenth centuries; and within this **Newtown Pery**, the modern centre, a jumble of beautiful but rather dilapidated Georgian terraces and garish fast-food joints.

Some history

Limerick, located at the lowest fording point of the Shannon, was first settled by the **Vikings**, who sailed up the Shannon in the tenth century to *Inis Sibhton* (now Kingstown in Englishtown), an island by the eastern bank formed by a narrow bypass from the main stream now known as Abbey River. Here they established a port, and for a hundred years war after war raged between them and the native Irish. The Vikings were frequently defeated and were finally crushed nationally in 1014 at the Battle of Clontarf, at the hands of Brian Boru, the High King of Ireland. Limerick itself was attacked soon after and burned to the ground. Most of the Vikings didn't actually leave, but from then on they were gradually assimilated into the Gaelic population. The fate of Limerick itself didn't improve much, however, as over the next hundred years the Irish fought amongst themselves, burning the town to the ground time and again.

Some kind of stability was established with the arrival of the **Normans** at the end of the twelfth century. They expanded and fortified the town; King John arriving in 1210 to inaugurate King John's Castle, one of his finest. High walls were built that were now to keep the Gaels out, and because of this exile the first suburb across the Abbey River began to grow into **Irishtown**. There was trouble again with the visits of Edward Bruce in the fourteenth century; but the real emasculation of the city began with the onslaught of Cromwell's forces under the command of his son-in-law, Ireton, in the late 1640s. It was concluded when the city rallied to the Jacobite cause in 1689.

Following James II defeat at the Battle of the Boyne in 1690, most of his supporters surrendered quickly – except for the ones at Limerick. As the Williamites advanced, the Jacobite forces within Limerick castle resolved to fight it out under the command of their Irish champion **Patrick Sarsfield**, Earl of Lucan and second in overall command of the Jacobite army. Although the walls of a medieval castle had little hope of withstanding seventeenth-century artillery (one of James's French generals declared that they would not stand up to a bombardment of apples), Sarsfield gained time by sneaking out, with five hundred of his troops, for a surprise night attack on William's supply train. He succeeded in totally destroying the munitions, while William sat waiting for them in front of the castle walls. However, when the Williamites returned the following year, Sarsfield could finally hold out no longer, and he surrendered on October 3, 1691, to the terms of a **treaty** that's so sore an historical point that it's still stuck in the minds of most Limerick people today.

The treaty terms were divided into military and civil articles. Militarily, Jacobite were allowed to sail to France, which most of them did, along with Sarsfield himself (he died on the battlefield at Landon in Belgium, two years later); the civil agreement promised Catholics the religious and property rights they'd once had under Charles II. Within a couple of months the English reneged on this part of the treaty, and instead enforced extreme **anti-Catholic measures**. There followed civil unrest on such a scale that the city gates were locked every night for the next sixty years, and the betrayal has never been forgotten – it alone may explain the roots of today's element of Republican support in the city. The concordat was supposedly signed upon the **Treaty Stone** that rests on a plinth at the western end of Thomond Bridge. For many years, although this was used as a stepping stone for mounting horses, small pieces continued to be gouged out as souvenirs; one fragment set into a ring is said to have fetched £1000 in the US.

It was not a promising start for the modern city, and there are those who claim that festering resentment has stunted Limerick's growth ever since. Being also lumbered with a geographical setting that gives it the Irish name *luimneach* ("a barren spot of land") has not helped. One redeeming factor has to lie in its humour; how else could its corporate motto read *An ancient city well studied in the arts of war.*

Arrival and information

Limerick is the nearest big city to **Shannon Airport** (☎061/471444; see p.348) – ten miles away off the Ennis Road. Airport buses (£3.50/€4.43) run approximately every thirty minutes in the morning, hourly in the afternoon and irregularly after 6pm; a taxi costs around £12–15/€15.24–19.05 (☎061/313131). The **train** (☎061/315555) and **bus** (☎061/313333) stations are next door to each other on Parnell Street in Newtown Pery; however, some buses arrive at Penney's Store on the corner of Lower Cecil Street and Henry Street rather than the bus station.

The excellent **tourist office** (May, June, Sept & Oct Mon–Sat 9.30am–5.30pm; July & Aug Mon–Fri 9am–7pm, Sat & Sun 9am–6pm; Nov–April Mon–Fri 9.30am–1pm & 2–5.30pm, Sat 9.30am–1pm; ☎061/317522) is at Arthur's Quay, near where the river branches merge and you cross over into Englishtown: most easily found by following O'Connell Street north towards the Custom House. The tourist office's city map also has useful information and phone numbers. **Walking tours** of the city are organized by St Mary's Action Centre, 44 Nicholas St. Their Historic Walking Tour (daily 11am & 2.30pm; £4/€5.08) focuses on Englishtown; it's a colourful account steeped in murder, treachery and passion, and really does bring this, the oldest part of Limerick, to life. Alternatively, the **Angela's Ashes Walking Tour** (departs daily from the tourist office at 2.30pm; £4/€5.08) takes in some of the same area in an account of slum life in early twentieth century Limerick, lavishly embellished with extracts from Frank McCourt's book, full of humour and pathos. Phone in advance to arrange a place on either tour in low season (☎061/318106).

For **bike rental** try Emerald Cycles, 1 Patrick St. **Internet** access can be gained at Websters on Thomas Street.

Accommodation

There is a good range of **accommodation** in Limerick, particularly for budget travellers. If you have a car, secure parking in the centre is a consideration, as Limerick is a modern city with all the problems that go with that. Some areas of town are far better lit than others at night; for women travelling alone the following places are probably the most appealing: *Barrington's Lodge and Hostel*, the *Sarsfield Bridge Inn*, *Cruises House* and the B&Bs on the Ennis Road.

Hotels, B&Bs and inns

Cruises House, Denmark St (☎061/315320). Pleasant and functional city-centre guesthouse. All rooms have TVs and are en suite. ④.

Glen Eagles, 12 Vereker Gardens, off the Ennis Road (☎061/455521). A short walk from town, this B&B is in a family home on a quiet cul-de-sac. ③.

Jurys Hotel, on the Ennis Road (☎061/327777, *www.jurys.com*). A small four-star hotel a short walk from the city centre with a gym, pool and tennis courts. Ask for a room away from the main road. ⑨.

Jurys Inn, Lower Mallow St (☎061/207000, *www.jurys.com*). Smart, comfortable and inexpensive accommodation for families and groups, though not in the most inspiring part of town. £53/€67.30 per room sleeping up to two adults and two children or three adults. Ask for a room away from the road.

Railway Hotel, Parnell St (☎061/413653). A comfortable, family-run hotel, but located in a rather lacklustre part of town opposite the train station. ④.

Rosmoy Town House, 1 Alexander Terrace, O'Connell Ave (☎061/314556) Good value central B&B offering en-suite rooms. ④.

The Sarsfield Bridge Inn, Sarsfield Bridge (☎061/317179). Pleasant, modern inn accommodation. The price includes self-service continental breakfast, though guests can also cook their own food. Some of the rooms have excellent views of the castle and there's a secure car park. ④.

Hostels

An Óige Limerick Hostel, 1 Pery Square (☎061/314672). Easy-going youth hostel in a large Georgian house in a quiet location near the train station.

Barrington's Lodge and Hostel, Barrington House, George's Quay (☎061/415222). Very well run IHH place with secure parking. There's a large number of twin and four-bed/family rooms available.

Broad Street Hostel, Broad St (☎061/317222). Crisp budget accommodation with good facilities and secure car park, although their book-ahead service could be better. Facilities for wheelchair users.

Finnegan's Holiday Hostel, 6 Pery Square (☎061/310308). Another IHH-run hostel with beautiful, huge Georgian rooms and relaxed, studenty atmosphere; dorms are very big, so its worth considering paying extra for either a four-bed or twin room.

The City

The sometimes incongruous blend of old and new in Limerick is testimony to a city discovering itself after years of neglect. Renovations and new building programmes stand alongside buildings – and indeed whole districts – that seem barely touched by the last fifty years. The best **views** of the city are to be had walking along the banks of the Shannon, especially around Arthur's Quay and the City Hall, or alternatively from the top of King John's Castle. Although virtually all the sights are in the old parts, **Englishtown** and **Irishtown**, the modern centre of the city is **Newtown Pery** – where the shops, pubs and restaurants congregate – an area of broad parallel streets scattered with fine, if neglected, Georgian buildings. O'Connell Street is the chief artery of this part of the city, and it's worth wandering down here, checking out the side streets with their characterful pubs and shops. Getting around the centre is easiest on foot.

Englishtown

Englishtown, which still has the narrow curving streets of its medieval origins, if few of the buildings, is the oldest part of the city, north of the modern centre. Crossing Matthew Bridge, the first things you'll see are St Mary's Cathedral ahead of you and the City Hall to your left. If you look down to the embankment of George's Quay on the right, your eye should just catch two very fine but armless torsos, metal-sculpted and set upon tall plinths facing one another some forty paces apart. This twentieth-century grotesquerie of war from within and without takes you by surprise – it's an unusually strong statement for Limerick.

The Church of Ireland **St Mary's Cathedral** (Mon–Sat 9.15am–5pm) was built at the end of the twelfth century, but only the Romanesque doorway facing the courthouse, the nave and parts of the transepts remain from this period. The chancel, windows and the rest of the transepts date from the fifteenth century. The cathedral's unique feature is its **misericords**, the only set in Ireland: made of black oak with reptilian animals – cockatrice, griffins, sphinx and wild boar – they are carved in bold relief. The area around St Mary's has had a very successful face-lift in recent years. As you leave the cathedral, walk down to the courthouse and stroll around City Hall – a modern affair of glass and pink tubing – to appreciate the rushing river and Limerick's buoyant new civic pride. Follow the Shannon up towards Thomond Bridge and just before you get there you'll find yourself diverted up **Castle Lane**, a reconstruction of an "authentic" eighteenth- and nineteenth-century Irish streetscape – bound on the north by the outer wall of King John's castle. The buildings to your right are actually all new, but create an attractively 'historic' atmosphere as you progress to Nicholas Street. Housed in one of these buildings is **Limerick Museum** (Tues–Sat 10am–1pm & 2.15–5pm; free), which holds the city maces, civic sword, charters granted by Charles I along with pieces of local lace work. Also on show are coins which date as far back as the Viking period; historic maps showing the old walled towns of Englishtown and Irishtown; memorabilia of various Fenian uprisings (notably a Pádraig Pearse letter from the 1916 rising); and Stone, Iron and especially Bronze Age implements. Many of the Mesolithic items (circa 7000–4000 BC) are from the Lough Gur area, and it's worth looking at the excavation photographs of this site before you visit it.

Nearby, on Nicholas Street, overlooking the river at Thomond Bridge, stands **King John's Castle** (daily: mid-April to Oct 9.30am–5.30pm; Nov to mid-April 10.30am-4.30pm; £4.40/€5.58). Don't be put off by the newly built entrance hall, a senseless addition of overwhelming vacuity that tends to negate any sense of power as you approach what is in fact one of the most impressive Anglo-Norman castles in Ireland. Built in the early thirteenth century, the castle was originally a five-sided fortress with four stout round towers; these were shortened at a much later stage to accommodate artillery positions – though one was actually replaced as a bastion in 1611. Inside, instruments of medieval siege warfare enliven the castle yard; here, you can climb the battlements for superb views, or watch an interesting twenty-minute film of the history of Limerick, and a much more detailed history of the Normans in Ireland in the "stand-and-read" **interpretive centre**. Beneath all of this are the foundations of pre-Norman dwellings – the finds of recent excavations. Despite all this, the castle is probably most impressive from the outside, as you stare up at the cliff-like immensity of its walls alongside Thomond Bridge.

The famous **Treaty Stone** stands opposite the castle, on the far side of Thomond Bridge, on Clancy Strand on the west bank of the Shannon. In recent years it has been moved – only about twenty yards – and sandblasted clean. This, if you want to read symbolic significance into it, can be seen as an attempt to loosen a burden that was preventing the city from developing.

Irishtown

Cross Matthew Bridge to reach **Irishtown** and the bustle of the modern city centre along Rutland Street and then Patrick Street. Without doubt the most distinguished building in this part of town is the **Custom House**, an eighteenth-century structure of harmonious classical balance, and home to the excellent **Hunt Museum** (Mon–Sat 10am–5pm, Sun 2–5pm; £4.20/€5.33). This astonishing collection – spanning nine thousand years, from the Stone Age through to the twentieth century – is the personal collection of John Hunt (1900–76), an English antiques dealer who went on to become an expert on medieval art, advising on internationally important collections such as those of William Burrell in Glasgow and the Aga Khan. One of the highlights of the collection is the bronze and enamel Antrim Cross, one of Ireland's most important examples of ninth-century early Christian metalwork and thought to be a precursor of the high cross designs at Monasterboice and Kells. Other highlights include the eleventh-century Beverley crosier, made of exquisitely carved walrus tusk; the dazzling fifteenth-century O'Dea mitre and crosier; and the late Bronze Age Ballyscullion cauldron. Many of the artefacts are kept in drawers which visitors are free to open and include a thirteenth-century Limoges enamel and drawings by Giacometti.

A series of lanes – Ellen Street, Denmark Street and Cruises Street – run off the main thoroughfare, Patrick Street, just a couple of hundred yards from the museum, worth exploring for their sprinkling of contemporary design shops and fashionable café-bars. The back streets beyond here are somewhat less appealing, the only feature of note being **St John's Cathedral**, a nineteenth-century Gothic Revival monstrosity which boasts the tallest spire in the country (280ft). Outside stands a memorial to Patrick Sarsfield, unsuccessful Jacobite defender of the city.

Patrick Street soon becomes **O'Connell Street**, Limerick's main, busy, but run-down commercial street, with its shops and bars. Further south along it, however, the Georgian buildings are better preserved and the Crescent at the far end of the street is rather fine, especially when lit up at night. To the east of here lies more examples of Limerick's Georgian architecture, and the interior of one such elegant home can be explored at **2 Georgian Pery Square** (summer: Mon–Fri 10am–1pm & 2–4.30pm, Sat & Sun 2–4.30pm; rest of year Sat & Sun only, by appointment; £2/€2.54, with "Angela's Ashes" £3.50/€4.44), along with an exhibition on the history of Limerick and, in the stable block to the rear, a reconstruction of the damp, cramped slum-home that Frank McCourt detailed so vividly in *Angela's Ashes*.

Eating, drinking and entertainment

A welcome sign of Limerick's regeneration is the rate at which good new cafés and pubs are appearing. The following list will give you some useful starting points. There's an abundance of bars, and in recent years Limerick has revived its reputation as a musical centre – particularly for contemporary and rock music. Again, a selection of **bars** and places to hear **music** can be found below. *The Belltable*, and the *City Gallery of Art* are good places to make contact with the Irish **arts scene**.

Cafés and restaurants

Brûlées Restaurant, 21 Henry St (☎061/319931) A converted Georgian town house given a crisp, contemporary look. The menu includes such delights as warm rabbit salad to start followed by roast guinea fowl stuffed with goats cheese and fresh herbs. Set dinner menu £25/€31.65. Tues–Sat 6.30–10.30pm.

Castle Lane Tavern, off Nicholas Street. Solid bar food is served at this popular pub (see "Bars" opposite).

DuCartes Restaurant, The Hunt Museum, Custom House basement, Rutland Street. A stylish spot overlooking the river and extremely popular for its excellent, inexpensive home-cooked lunches, teas and snacks. Opening hours same as museum.

Freddy's Bistro, Theatre Lane (☎061/418749), down an alley off Lower Glentworth Street. Expensive bistro serving steaks and seafood. Tues–Sun 5.30pm till late.

Furze Bush Café Bistro, corner of Glentworth and Catherine streets. Delightful bistro serving delicious crêpes, sandwiches and salads. Lunch only Mon–Wed, closed Sun.

The Green Onion Café, Rutland St (☎061/400710). Funky jazz-café/restaurant with an imaginative and reasonably priced menu offering such dishes as Moroccan spiced vegetables with pulses, Italian spicy sausage with tagliatelle, and numerous off-beat sarnie combos. Daily till 10pm.

The Grove, Cecil St. Health-food shop that does good bar-stool lunches and takeaways.

Java's, 5 Catherine St. Little café with bags of atmosphere. Hot lunches, all-day breakfasts plus bagels, baguettes and butties all generously stuffed with tasty homemade fillings. Good value. Mon–Wed 9am–midnight, Thurs–Sat 9am–3am, Sun 11am–midnight.

Kurova Milk Bar, 3 Ellen St. Trendy late-night wine bar offering baguettes, tortillas and sandwiches.

La Romana, 36 O'Connell St (☎061/314994) Warm, convivial and unpretentious Italian restaurant. The food is moderately priced and a notch better than you might expect from the location. Flavoursome and satisfying Italian standards.

Paul's, 59 O'Connell St (☎061/316600). Mouthwatering Italian menu going way beyond the usual pizza brief. Main courses from around £8. Lunch only on Mondays, and evenings only at weekends.

Bars and music venues

An Síbín, *Royal George Hotel*, O'Connell St. Traditional music and country singalongs during the summer.

Castle Lane Tavern, off Nicholas Street. Brand new pub cunningly disguised as a medieval hostellry. Purpose built to cater for tourists visiting the castle, it's generally full of locals. On a warm evening the grassy slope to the rear is worth considering as a place to enjoy the fading light over the Shannon.

Doc's The Granary, Bank Place. Upbeat bar in brick-vaulted granary courtyard; generally attracts a studenty crowd.

Dolan's, 3–4 Dock Rd (☎061/314483). Limerick's top traditional-music venue, with sessions most nights. On Sundays music starts at around 6pm and goes on until closing time.

Dolan's Warehouse, 4 Alphonsus St, behind Dolan's bar (☎061/314483, *www.dolans-pub.ie*). A great venue for live bands – from soul and R&B, to traditional Irish and tribute bands. There's also a big screen for viewing major sporting events. Doors open at 9pm.

James Gleeson, *The White House Bar*, 52 O'Connell St. Ancient ale house, full of character – and characters; packed, but warm and friendly.

The Locke, George's Quay. Head for the pleasant old bar with its easy sociable atmosphere, rather than the larger bar that's been added alongside. A good spot to catch traditional Irish music (Sun & Mon) and ballads and folk (Tues). Particularly pleasant on a fine evening, as you can sit outside.

Kurova Milk Bar, 3 Ellen St. Trendy late-night bar playing Latin jazz sounds; especially popular at weekends, when the sets go on into the early hours. Mon–Wed & Sun 11am–11pm, Thurs–Sat 11am–4am.

Nancy Blake's, Upper Denmark St. Lively pub with traditional music (Mon–Wed & Sun) and a pleasant beer garden.

The Outback, at the back of *Nancy Blake's*. A great venue for live bands, chiefly rock.

The Works, Bedford Row. Popular club playing mainly charts, dance and indie music until 2am.

Art, theatre and classical music

The following are the main venues for exhibitions, theatre and classical concerts. For full, current listings, pick up a copy of *Limerick Corporation Arts Calendar* at the tourist office.

Belltable Arts Centre, 69 O'Connell St (☎061/319709). Interesting mix of performances, including local and international touring companies. The gallery space shows a similarly diverse range of contemporary art with twelve exhibitions a year.

City Gallery of Art, Pery Square. Situated in the People's Park, a short walk from the train station, this place puts an emphasis on international contemporary art, with a lesser focus on Irish work. It also houses the city's permanent collection of paintings from the eighteenth century to the present day, and includes work by Yeats and Sean Keating. Open Mon–Fri 10am–6pm, Thurs until 7pm, Sat 10am–1pm.

National Self-Portrait Collection, Limerick University (Mon–Fri 9am–5pm; free) Small but absorbing collection of Irish self-portraits; the Watercolour Society of Ireland Collection is also housed here. To find the university, head out along the Dublin Road; after a few miles, take a left turn immediately after the petrol station for Plassey; follow the road round for another third of a mile and the entrance is on the left.

University Concert Hall, Limerick University (☎061/331549). The largest purpose-built concert hall in Ireland and the best place to catch classical music; pick up their events listings at the tourist office. Directions as for the National Self-Portrait Collection.

The Clare Glens

The **Clare Glens** on the Limerick–Tipperary border is a beautiful area of flowing falls, parts of which you can swim in: it makes a great day's excursion for cyclists. Head for Moroe (sometimes spelt Murroe), about ten miles east of the city; Clare is two miles north of this. A circular ride of some twenty miles could take this in, along with **Glenstal Abbey** and the village of **CASTLECONNELL**, a well-known Irish-music and Irish-language centre in a scenic setting on the banks of the Shannon some seven miles from Limerick. **Coillte Forest Park**, sixteen miles west of the city, has a well-equipped **campsite**, the *Curragh Chase Caravan and Camping Park* (closed mid-Sept to March; ☎061/396349), picnic site, arboretum and the ruins of the home of poet Aubrey de Vere. To the south, it's not much further to Lough Gur (see below) and Adare (p.274).

Lough Gur and around

Leaving Limerick city for Cork the main route is the N20, a fast and efficient but rather dull route south. If you have time to stop along the way, the smaller R512 road has considerably more to offer – above all **Lough Gur**, site of a wealth of Neolithic finds and one of County Limerick's chief attractions. Seventeen miles south of Limerick city, the lough looks as though its waters have been accidentally spilt onto the Limerick soil. It's the only significant lake in the county, and comes as a rare treat in the midst of an otherwise lustreless terrain. The area that surrounds the lake has been an extremely rich source of archeological finds – though what exists now is often an extremely frugal sketch of what took place five thousand years ago. The lake is C-shaped, with a marshy area to the east that would complete the full circle.

In the middle of this circle is a small rise known as **Knockadoon**, whose slopes are studded with faint remains of earthworks showing ring forts and hut foundations dating from 3500 to 1000 BC. The length of its less secure marshy side is naturally forested and guarded at either end by two medieval tower houses, Bouchier's Castle and Black Castle. Mary Carbery's nineteenth-century book, *The Farm by Lough Gur*, gives a vivid contemporary account of life by the lough – the farm still stands up the road from the Neolithic huts known as the Spectacles.

Lough Gur must have been the perfect setting for a **Neolithic settlement**. The lake provided fish, and the gentle hillsides produced berries, nuts and trappings for animal hunting, as well as protection from the elements – and detection. When the lake was partly drained in the middle of the nineteenth century, and its level dropped by three yards, prehistoric artefacts were found in such quantities that stories tell of whole cartloads being hauled away. This may not be such an exaggeration; visit museums across the world today, and you'll discover some find from Lough Gur on display. The most famous discovery was a bronze shield from 700 BC, perfect in its concentric rings of bosses but for a hacking in two places by the reedcutter who discovered it. The finds here pair well with the Neolithic discoveries made in Meath; this was once a Neolithic living commune, where the Brú na Bóinne site is concerned with ritual and burial. Today there's abundant **birdlife** on the lake; the grazing cattle, antlered goats and lack of modern buildings give you a strong intimation of the life of five thousand years ago.

The interpretive centre and stone circle

The simplest approach to Lough Gur is to come off the R512 at Holycross. Follow the road to the northernmost section of the lake, keeping an eye out for a wedge-shaped **gallery grave**. The grave, typically, shows a long gallery space where the bodies of eight adults and four children from around 2000 BC were found. The gallery has parallel double walls of stone slabs filled in with rubble and what's called a septal slab at its back. The road then circles on round the marsh to an **interpretive centre** (mid-May to Sept daily 10am–6pm £2.20/€2.79). Housed in replica Neolithic huts, the centre attempts to give some idea of what life was like for the early inhabitants. From it, the chief attractions on Knockadoon are easily accessible on foot.

A quarter of a mile north of the Holycross turn-off, the first thing you'll see is a gargantuan **stone circle** close to the main road, the most substantial of the area's prehistoric remains. Possibly the grandest example in the country, it has a ring of standing stones marking out an almost perfect circle. A posthole was found at the centre which must have held a stake, from which, with a length of cord attached, the circle could be struck. Some of the stones are massive and are bolstered within their earth sockets by smaller boulders, which were then covered. Flints, arrowheads, blades and bowls were found within the enclosure, but little has been learned about the site's exact function. A circle of this size clearly demanded a good deal of social organization and a strong sense of purpose; the obvious conclusion is that this was a great centre for religious rituals, and frustratingly little else can be said.

The castles and Knockadoon

If you're walking, an alternative approach to Knockadoon is across the stone causeway that leads from near the gallery grave to **Black Castle**. Possibly thirteenth century, the castle is now weighed down by a swarthy camouflage of nettles, brambles and trees. It was once quite extensive, with a high curtain wall and square towers, and acted as a principal seat for the Earls of Desmond. The pathway north to Bouchier's Castle has three **Neolithic hut** remains at various degrees up the hill slope. If you're intent on seeing them, you'll have to forage around among the wooded thickets. **Bouchier's Castle** itself. is a typical fifteenth-century Desmond tower house of five storeys; but it's still privately owned and can't yet be visited (in any case, there's a better example at Castle Matrix; see p.275).

Turning westwards from the Black Castle towards the lakeshore, you'll see various ring forts and hut traces on the bare grassy slopes. It's not much, but even this scant evidence is enough to conjure up a thriving Stone Age community on **Knockadoon**. Rather than continue round along the bank of the lake, it's best to take this opportunity to cross back along the hilltop centre, where, from a point known as **M**, you can get penetrating views into Kerry and Cork, with Limerick spreading towards them in a swath of low hills. **Crock** and **Bolin islands** in the lake are both *crannógs* which the mainland has now caught up with. They were built by laying down a ring of boulders, then the inner space was filled with earth and brushwood. **Garret Island** is a natural island with some stone remains of another Desmond castle.

Kilmallock

Eight miles further down the main road from Lough Gur, **KILMALLOCK** has some good Norman remains: a tower castle, a town gate, a Dominican friary and a medieval stone mansion on the main street. **St John's Tower Castle** stands in the middle of the street and was the town citadel – to look inside, you need to get the key at the bungalow across the road, but there's little to see here. Turn instead down the lane opposite and you'll find a tiny **museum** (Mon–Fri 1.30–5pm; otherwise contact T. Bohan, Lord Edward St; free) which won't take a minute to get through, unless you lend an ear to the homemade audiovisual history of the town.

Bruree

Four miles west of Kilmallock, **BRUREE** was the childhood home of **Eamon De Valera**, founder of the Fianna Fáil (Soldiers of Destiny) party in 1926 and familiarly known as the "big man" or "Dev" to a population for whom he's been the most influential political instigator since the birth of the Free State in 1922. After founding Fianna Fáil, he acted as premier of Ireland from 1932 to 1948, 1951 to 1954 and 1957 to 1959, and assumed the honorary role of president from 1959 to 1973. This makes up a sizeable chunk of the Republic's history, and his grip on the nation has left an ambivalent attitude to his worth and integrity.

De Valera was the only leader of the 1916 Easter Rising to survive. His initial death sentence was commuted to imprisonment because of his American dual nationality – he was born in New York, and at this time the British were sensitive to American neutrality in World War I. He escaped from prison in England and was unconstitutionally elected the first president of the Irish Republic in 1919; his almost miraculous survival had marked him out as the man to lead Ireland out of seven hundred years of British domination. The Republic immediately declared war on Britain, and when two years of struggle forced the British to negotiate, De Valera's was the leading rebel voice against the signing of the Anglo-Irish Treaty in 1921. He wanted to hold out for an all-Ireland Free State, rather than accept only 26 counties out of 32, as was laid down in the Treaty. This stance divided the Irish and provoked the Civil War of 1921 to 1923. The one war he succeeded in keeping the Irish out of was World War II, at the end of which he had the gall to send official commiserations to the Reichstag on Hitler's death, so profound was the bitterness of his battle with the British.

De Valera was brought up just outside Bruree in a small cottage, which has now been turned into a modest memorial of the family's household possessions, including a bulky trunk that was used for their return from exile in New York. The cottage is signposted nearly a mile down the road to the right at the eastern end of Bruree village – get the key from the house on the right, a hundred and fifty yards further down the road. At the western end of Bruree village itself is the old schoolhouse, which has been turned into a **museum and heritage centre** (Tues–Fri 10am–5pm, Sat & Sun 2–5pm; £3/€3.80), stocked with memorabilia of the ex-premier and president, plus a few rural items of general interest.

South and west of Limerick

The road southwest to Killarney is by far the most interesting route out of Limerick, catching the prim English beauty of thatched cottages in **Adare** and, of much more interest, taking in **Castle Matrix**, a Desmond tower house that has been brilliantly restored and gives a unique insight into life as it might have been lived in these castles. The road west to Tralee, the N69, is the least interesting of the three major routes across County Limerick. It runs parallel to the Shannon estuary but mostly through flat alluvial land, without the compensation of having the waters alongside except for the last few miles into Glin.

Adare

Famously picturesque **ADARE** has cultivated nearly as many antiques shops as pubs. In peak season, it will more than likely be infested with tourists taking photos of the wayside cottages that sit in a neat row, their quaint deep-brown thatch hanging in low fringes. The cottages represent the nineteenth-century ideal of romanticized rusticity, as realized by the third Earl of Dunraven (1812–71), landlord and master of Adare

TIM HALL/AXIOM

View along the Liffey River, Dublin

PAUL QUAYLE/AXIOM

St Patrick's Day Parade, Dublin

MICHAEL JENNER

Fitzwilliam Square, Dublin

CHRIS COE/AXIOM

Bray, Co. Wicklow

MICHAEL JENNER

Newgrange (passage tomb), Co. Meath

Tower houses flourished between the fifteenth and seventeenth centuries, especially in these southern counties. They provided a robust enough mini-fortress for the shift in the times; Anglo-Norman confidence was increasing, resulting in an expansion of settlements. The big Irish estates were being broken up owing to the fall of the old Gaelic chiefs, and more towns were cropping up, with land being cultivated in hitherto uninhabited areas. Tower houses took on a uniform plan, usually of four or five floors, the top floor being the living quarters, the bottom windowless and usually used for storage. Castle Matrix has a tiny chapel re-created on its top floor and a medieval bedroom on another floor. It's stocked with exciting *objets d'art*, including a jewel-encrusted nineteenth-century Gaelic harp made by Fall of Belfast; an ebony writing bureau imported by the Southwells from China and finally donated back to Matrix some years ago, now sitting in the Oriental Room; documents referring to the Wild Geese (Irish officers who fled to the Continent at the beginning of the seventeenth century); and the most remarkable item of all to return home – the original deed of the Southwells (the Earls of Desmond), which Seán O'Driscoll came across accidentally in London's Portobello Road.

The castle derived its name from the *matres*, a Celtic sanctuary, on which it stands. The scattering of destroyed cashels and raths in the surrounding area give substance to the idea of an ancient sanctuary here. An annexe of the castle offers luxury **B&B** (☎069/64284; ⑥). A slightly cheaper alternative in the village is *Rathkeale House Hotel* (☎069/63333; *rhh@iol.ie*; ⑥), which also does food, and there is top quality B&B at *The Willows* (☎069/63157; ④), just along the road to the castle from the village.

Newcastle West

Between Rathkeale and Newcastle West a signpost points to Ardagh, the ring fort where the wonderful Ardagh Chalice was found in 1868 (it's now in the Dublin National Museum). The site here is unimpressive, however, and it's not worth dragging yourself off the main road. Press on, instead to **NEWCASTLE WEST** to look at the **Desmond Banqueting Hall** (mid-June to mid-Sept daily 9.30am-6.30pm, £1/€1.27). The hall is on the main square and very little fuss is made of it; but it's part of a scattered and hidden complex of ruined buildings – a keep, a peel tower, a bastion and curtain wall. Even though this was once the principal seat of the Fitzgeralds, the town hasn't harnessed its history to its advantage. The hall is in a near perfect state of preservation, and ready for an inspired restoration. At present, apart from a marriage fireplace said to have been imported from Egypt, it's all bare.

There are several small **B&Bs** in town – try Mrs Burke on Bishop Street (☎069/62287; ③); you can also get food and rooms at the *Courtney Lodge Hotel* (☎069/62244; ⑥).

Glenquin Castle is another well-preserved but entirely deserted tower house, about five miles south of Newcastle West, just outside the village of Killeady. To find it follow the N21 from Newcastle West towards Abbeyfeale; the road to the castle is signposted after a few miles on the left by a petrol station. It has very good views of the countryside, but is really only worth a stop if you're passing by anyway. If you have children in tow, you might prefer to visit **Springfield Castle Deer Centre** (summer daily 1–6pm) outside Dromcollogher, about ten miles south of Newcastle West. There are pets for children to handle, and a tractor trailer takes you on a tour past herds of deer, so tame they feed from your hand.

Celtic Theme Park and Gardens

Beyond here, a good mile off the N69 at Kilcornan, is the **Celtic Theme Park and Gardens** (mid-March to Oct daily 9.30am–6pm; £3/€3.81). Don't let the words "theme

Manor and an eternal improver of circumstances for his tenants. Given that Adare is now probably regarded as the prettiest (and, it must be added, prissiest) village in Ireland, it's hard to believe that before the earl's improvements it was one of the grottiest. The cottages today are pure upmarket thatch, with pricey restaurants and craft shops.

Adare Manor House, to the north of the village, is a huge, near fanatical assembly of castellations and turrets in limestone, built by the earl to Gothic Revival designs in 1832. This castle has only recently passed into private hands as a grand **hotel**, the *Adare Manor* (☎061/396566; ⑨), which offers luxurious accommodation, a swimming pool and a golf course. The River Maigue flows by the estate a little further up, at the head of the village, and although an exciting-looking triumvirate of **medieval buildings** beckons, a golf course steers its course next to all of them, inhibiting any snooping around you might want to do. It may not be worth the effort anyhow, for the Desmond castle – interesting as it looks to explore – is completely bricked up and deemed unsafe. The fifteenth-century friary appears far better preserved, but it was extensively restored as late as the mid-nineteenth century. These are perhaps easiest viewed from the bridge.

Back in the village there are ecclesiastical sites, too, starting with an **Augustinian Priory** just by the bridge. Beautifully preserved, the priory still serves as the local Church of Ireland church, its interior as close as any to the old medieval model. The **Trinitarian Abbey**, halfway down the main street, was founded in 1230 for the Trinitarian Canons of the Order of the Redemption of Captives, and is the only house of this order in Ireland. Today, it's Adare's Catholic church, with one of its turrets at the back a deserted columbarium.

Buses from Limerick stop in the main street. Adare's **tourist office** (Mon–Fri 9am–7pm, Sat & Sun 9am–6pm; ☎061/396255) is in the main street alongside the **heritage centre** (same times; £3/€3.81). There are numerous **B&Bs** in the village, including *Berkeley Lodge* (☎061/396857; *berlodge@iol.ie*; ④); *Avona* (☎061/396323; ④) and *Church View House* (☎061/396371; ③), all situated on Station Road. You can get decent meals at *The Arches Restaurant* on Main Street; for snacks try the café in the same building as the tourist office. *Bill Chawke's* and *Collin's Bar* both have **traditional-music** sessions one evening a week during the summer.

Five miles southwest of Adare, the pleasant village of **BALLINGARRY** has an excellent IHH **hostel**, *Trainor's* (closed mid-Oct to Feb; ☎069/68164). The village is also home to an upmarket **restaurant** of some renown, *The Mustard Seed* (closed March; ☎069/68508), which offers imaginative country-house cooking using plenty of organic and local produce

Rathkeale and Castle Matrix

About eight miles on from Adare along the N21, **RATHKEALE** was once an important Geraldine town, and the main source of interest here is their one-time stronghold, **Castle Matrix** (mid-May to mid-Sept daily 11am–5pm; £2/€2.53). To get there, turn right at the south end of the exceptionally long main street, just after the bridge: the castle lies half a mile down the road, on the right. Castle Matrix is a fifteenth-century tower house built by the seventh Earl of Desmond, and would inevitably have met with the same ruinous fate as virtually all the other 427 tower houses that once existed in Limerick, or the 2700 that once stood throughout the country – but for the brilliant restoration work of current owner Seán O'Driscoll, an Irish-American military enthusiast. With his army expertise, he understood the design of the fortifications and realized that measurements needed to be within an inch for the battlements on the parapets to be effective (in contrast, the ornamental battlements at somewhere like Bunratty in County Clare wouldn't have lasted long in a fifteenth-century siege).

IAN CUMMING/AXIOM

Ardigeen River Estuary, Timoleague, Co. Cork

IAN CUMMING/AXIOM

Hurling sticks for sale, Macroom, Co. Cork

LUKE WHITE/AXIOM

Religious ornament

IAN CUMMING/AXIOM

Kinsale harbour, Co. Cork

MICHAEL JENNER

Jerpoint Abbey, Co. Kilkenny

B. GARRETT/TRAVEL INK

Rock of Cashel, Co. Tipperary

MICHAEL JENNER

Russborough House, Co. Wicklow

park" put you off – there's not a drop of moulded plastic in sight. The hour or so stroll through the park takes in a string of features associated with ancient Ireland – a stone circle, dolmen, holy well and twelfth-century church. While some are replicas, others, most notably the lake dwelling and the (unexcavated) ring fort, are original, and overall this is a very sensitive blending of ancient landscape with imitation. Back up by the tearoom, there's an attractive formal garden, with fine scented flowers, a tranquil lily pond and walkways between silver birch and blackthorns.

Back on the N69, the road passes a few more tower houses on the right and the **Curraghchase Forest Park** (see p.272) on the left before reaching **ASKEATON**. Here, there's an Anglo-Norman **friary** next to the River Deel, just off the main road at its second entry to Askeaton from the east. The friary was founded by the fourth Earl of Desmond, Gerald the Poet, in 1389. It now seems particularly hidden away, and has one of the loveliest cloisters you'll come across and some excellent window tracery. From the dormitory above, you can pick out the towering remains of the **castle**, penned in towards the centre of the town. Worth a quick scout around, it has a large banqueting hall, very similar to the better example in Newcastle West, its vaulted ground-floor chambers remaining just within the walls. A very dodgy-looking fifteenth-century end tower stands upon a rock in the centre of what was once an island in the River Deel. The castle's present decay does little to suggest its one-time Anglo-Norman prominence, when it flourished in the hands of the Earls of Desmond, until their fall to the Earl of Essex during the sixteenth century.

FOYNES is a moderately busy seaport, with a **flying boat museum** (April–Oct daily 10am–6pm; £3.50/€4.44) which celebrates the town's past as an aviation centre. In the late 1930s and early 1940s, Foynes, as Limerick's only seaport, was the terminus for a transatlantic flying-boat service. Moving on, the afforested hillsides that now appear mark a pleasant route along the estuary as far as Glin on the Limerick–Kerry border.

travel details

Trains

Limerick to: Cahir (Mon–Sat 1 daily; 1hr 15min); Carrick-on-Suir (Mon–Sat 1 daily; 2hr); Clonmel (Mon–Sat 1 daily; 1hr 35min); Dublin (8–13 daily; 2hr 40min); Rosslare Harbour/Europort (Mon–Sat 1 daily; 3hr 50min); Tipperary (Mon–Sat 1 daily; 50min).

Waterford to: Dublin (3–6 daily; 2hr 45min); Limerick (Mon–Sat 1 daily; 3hr).

Buses

Bus Éireann

Cahir to: Waterford (6–8 daily;1hr 15min).

Cashel to: Cahir (4–5 daily; 15min); Cork (4 daily; 1hr 35min–2hr); Mitchelstown (4 daily; 45min).

Limerick to: Cahir (6–7 daily; 1hr 35min); Cork (14 daily; 1hr 50min); Dublin (13 daily; 3hr 30min); Shannon Airport (frequent service; 45min); Tipperary (6–10 daily; 50min); Waterford (6–7 daily; 2hr 5min).

Nenagh to: Dublin (13 daily; 2hr 40min); Limerick (13 daily; 1hr 20min).

Roscrea to: Dublin (10 daily; 2hr 20min); Limerick (13 daily; 1hr 15min).

Waterford to: Dublin (7–10 daily; 3hr 30min); Tramore (frequent service; 25min).

Rapid Express (☎051/872149)

Waterford to: Dublin (9 daily; 3hrs)

Suirway (☎051/382209)

Waterford to: Dunmore East (3–4 Mon–Sat, July & Aug 3–4 daily; 30min); Passage East (1–4 daily, 30min); Woodstown (1–4 daily; 30min),.

CHAPTER SEVEN

COUNTY CORK

Cork, Ireland's largest county, is the perfect place to ease yourself gently into the exhilarations of Ireland's west coast. **Cork city**, the south's self-proclaimed cultural capital manages to be at one and the same time a relaxed and a spirited place. There are no spectacular sights, but Cork is one of Ireland's most pleasurable and accessible cities. Always a port, and with an island at its core, Cork nestles well inland on the estuary of the River Lee, which sustains the city with that same clear, soothing atmosphere that characterizes most of the county, and in particular its coast and rivers. In the east of the county maritime history is still more richly distilled, in the small ports of **Cobh**, **Youghal** and – most of all – **Kinsale**, all suggestive of a prosperity that Ireland could have had throughout the eighteenth and nineteenth centuries were it not for the strangulation of its overseas trade by Britain. On the other side of this coin are the riches of the Anglo-Irish legacy, most in evidence at **Bantry House** with its outrageously sumptuous art treasures.

In the main the charms of the Cork countryside are those of a gently rural backwater, but as you head west along a fabulously indented coastline of hidden bays and coves to the wild peninsulas of the extreme southwest, or through the ravine of Gougane Barra high above **Glengarriff** and **Bantry Bay**, the soft contours of a comfortable and easy prettiness slip away to reveal beauty of a more elemental kind. There's not as much of this as you might find in, say, Kerry, but in the **Caha Mountains** careering north from Bantry Bay, the scintillating cliffs of **Mizen Head** or the seascapes of **Sherkin** and **Clear islands**, teeming with birdlife, Cork has scenery as exciting and dramatic as you'll find anywhere.

Public transport around the county is fairly extensive if infrequent. **Bus Éireann** covers the whole of Cork except for the extreme west of Mizen Head and the Beara Peninsula. Major towns have daily connections – though there's only one bus a week along Sheep's Head and one linking Kenmare with Castletownbere. Small towns and villages off the main roads are served less frequently, so if you are relying on public transport it's worth taking details of times and days of services you are likely to want while in a major bus station. Ask about return fares – often they are as cheap as single tickets if used on certain days. On certain routes private buses provide the only transport: see "Travel Details" at the end of this chapter for details. The intricate landscape of west Cork, in particular, is best explored at a slow pace, making it ideal country for touring by **bike** or **hitching**. The N71 is the main coastal road, but it's much more

ACCOMMODATION PRICE CODES

Throughout this book, prices of hotels, guesthouses and B&Bs have been graded with the codes below, according to what you can expect to pay for a double room in high season. For more details on accommodation, see p.34.

① Under £26/€33.01	④ £40–55/€50.79–69.84	⑦ £90–110/€114.28–139.67
② £26–33/€33.01–41.90	⑤ £55–70/€69.84–88.88	⑧ £110–130/€139.67–165.07
③ £33–40/€41.90–50.79	⑥ £70–90/€88.88–114.28	⑨ Over £130/€165.07

rewarding to meander off along the minor roads through remoter areas, past sandy coves and small communities.

If you have a tent, you can **camp** almost anywhere along the coast if you ask permission first, though the Beara Peninsula and the Caha Mountains are very rocky. The few official campsites are listed in the text.

Cork city

Old **CORK** city – the second city of the Republic – is built on an island, the two channels of the River Lee embracing it either side while nineteenth-century suburbs sprawl up the surrounding hills. This gives the city centre a compactness and sharp definition. It's a place of great charm, with a history of vigorous intellectual independence, and approached from rural Ireland, it has a surprisingly cosmopolitan feel to it.

Evidence of Cork's history as a great mercantile centre is everywhere, with grey stone quaysides, old warehouses and elegant and quirky bridges spanning the river. Many of the city's streets were at one time waterways: St Patrick's Street had quays for sailing ships, and on the pavement in Grand Parade you can still see moorings dating from the eighteenth century. Important port though Cork may be, however, it doesn't feel overridingly commercial, and the Lee is certainly not the river of an industrial town. The all-pervading presence of its waters reflects and seems to double any light, so that even on the cloudiest of days there is a balmy, translucent quality to the atmosphere which effects a calm on the visitor. Cork is a welcoming, friendly place. While it has the vibrancy to enliven and excite, the pace is always Irish and somehow the island breathes enough space for all temperaments.

Some history

Cork (*Corcaigh*, meaning "marshy place") had its origins in the seventh century when St Finbarr founded an abbey and school on the site where the impressive nineteenth-century Gothic St Finbarr's Cathedral stands today. A settlement grew up around the monastic foundation, overlooking a marshy swamp where the city centre now stands. In 820 the Vikings arrived, bringing their usual violence and destruction, and wrecked both abbey and town. They built a new settlement on one of the islands in the marshes and eventually integrated with the native Celts. The twelfth century saw the Norman invasion and Cork, like other ports, was taken in 1172. The new acquisition was fortified with massive stone walls, which survived Cromwell but were destroyed by Williamite forces at the Siege of Cork in 1690. From this time the city began to take on the shape recognizable today. Expansion saw the reclamation of marshes and the development of canals within the city, and waterborne **trade** brought increasing prosperity. Evidence of this wealth survives in the form of fine eighteenth-century bow-fronted houses and the ostentatious nineteenth-century church architecture decorating the city – sharp, grey and Gothic, much of it by the Pain brothers. Traces of the great dairy trade of that period can still be seen in the Shandon area.

More recently, Cork saw much violence and suffered greatly during the Anglo-Irish and Civil wars: the city's part in **Republican** history is well documented in the local museum. The **Black and Tans** reigned here with particular terror, destroying much of the town by fire, and were responsible for the murder of Thomas MacCurtain, the mayor of Cork, in 1920. Cork's next mayor, Terence MacSwiney, was jailed as a Republican and died in Brixton prison after a hunger strike of 74 days. He was a popular hero, and his hunger strike remains one of the longest achieved in the history of the IRA. One of his colleagues in Cork prison, Joseph Murphy, achieved the longest fast on record, going 76 days without food.

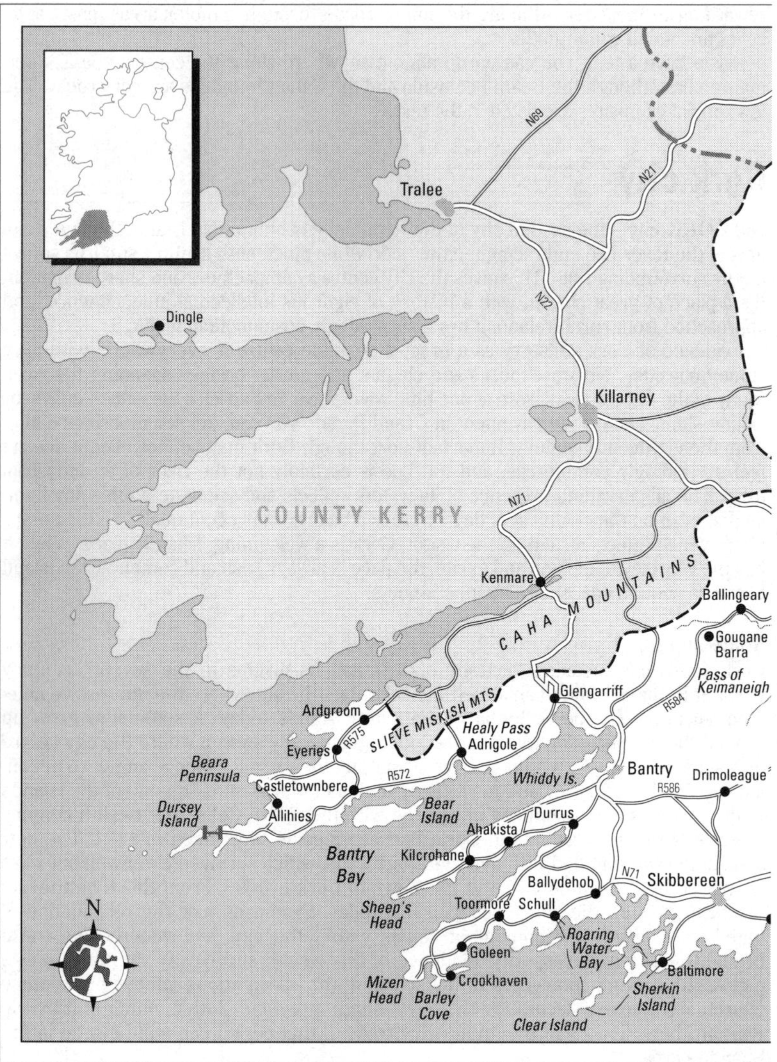

As part of the Republic, Cork has continued to develop – as a port, a university city and a cultural centre – and to assert its independence from Dublin.

Arrival and information

One of the joys of Cork is the fact that its scale is human: most of what it has to offer can be explored on foot. **Buses** to the suburbs and outlying towns and villages all go

from the **Bus Éireann** station at Parnell Place alongside Merchant's Quay, and most of these also pick up from the more central St Patrick's Street. The Bus Éireann station also operates an extensive nationwide bus service, while the **train station** is less than a mile out of the city centre on the Lower Glanmire Road. Irish Rail's travel centre is located at 65 Patrick St. **Private buses** operate from various central points, mostly along St Patrick's Street and from outside *Mulligan's* on Parnell Place. If you arrive by **ferry** you'll be at Ringaskiddy, some ten miles out of town, from where you can catch a connecting bus into the centre. Coming in by **plane** you can easily pick up local bus #226 for the twenty-minute journey into town. A taxi to the airport will cost around £8/€10.16, £10/€12.70 to the ferryport. If you're driving remember that, as in all the major cities, a disc parking system is in operation: discs can be bought from newsagents or the tourist office.

The **tourist office** on Grand Parade supplies the usual wide variety of information and can also book accommodation (June & Sept Mon–Sat 9am–6pm; July & Aug Mon–Sat 9am–7pm, Sun 10am–5pm; Oct–May Mon–Sat 9.15am–5.30pm; ☎021/427 3251). Cork is a great city for **festivals**, the biggest of which are the **film festival** in early October and the **jazz festival** towards the end of October – for more on both see p.289. For information on theatre and music performances, ask at the tourist office or consult the *Irish Examiner*, available in newsagents, or the free *Whazon*, available in cafés and arts venues around the city.

Accommodation

Cork's **hotels** are at the top end of the market; the mid-range, however, is more than adequately covered by the numerous **B&Bs**, mainly concentrated near the university along Western Road, and at the opposite end of town on Lower Glanmire Road, near the train station. If you are planning your stay to coincide with one of the October festivals, advance booking is advisable, and prices tend to rise during this period. Cork also has plenty of good budget accommodation, including a number of **hostels**.

Hotels

Clarion Hotel, Morrison's Island (☎021/427 5858, *morrison@iol.ie*) Ugly exterior, but inside the style is fresh and contemporary. Comfortably appointed rooms with ensuite baths, TVs and Internet access. Suites of rooms including galley kitchen also available. Quiet yet central; good weekend deals. ⑨.

Imperial Hotel, South Mall (☎021/427 4040, *imperial@iol.ie*). Cork's oldest hotel. The foyer retains glimmers of the grand Victorian era in chandeliers and portraiture, and the hotel is noteworthy, too, as the place where Michael Collins spent his last night. Worth checking out their lower-rate offers out of season. ⑧.

Jurys Hotel, Western Road (☎021/427 6622, *www.jurys.com*) A well established formal hotel within walking distance of the city centre that manages to be both smart and welcoming. Good weekend rates available. ⑨.

Metropole Ryan Hotel, MacCurtain St (☎021/450 8122, *www.ryan-hotels.com*). Pleasantly refurbished grand Victorian hotel. Residents have full use of a gym, pool and saunas; there are also supervised creche facilities. If traffic noise bothers you, ask for a room away from MacCurtain Street. ⑨.

Guesthouses and B&Bs

Antoine House, Western Rd (☎021/427 3494, *antoinehouse@eircom.net*). Regular B&B, all rooms en suite with satellite TV; private parking. ⑤.

Auburn House, 3 Garfield Terrace, Wellington Rd (☎021/450 8555). Beautifully kept B&B with TVs in all rooms, in a quiet location within ten minutes' walk of city centre. ④.

The Blarney Stone, 1 Carriglee Terrace, Western Rd (☎021/427 0083). TVs in all rooms, off-street parking, non-smoking bedrooms. ④ & ⑤.

Clare D'Arcy, 7 Sydney Place, Wellington Rd (☎021/450 4658). Worth paying a little more to stay in this beautiful Georgian town house. ⑤.

Clon Ross, 85 Lower Glanmire Rd (☎021/450 2602). All rooms have TVs; it's also handy for the train station. ④.

Garinish House, Western Rd (☎021/427 5111). Good quality guesthouse offering an impressive breakfast menu, including porridge with Irish whiskey and spiced grapefruit with cinnamon toast; some rooms have a Jacuzzi. Off-street parking. ⑥.

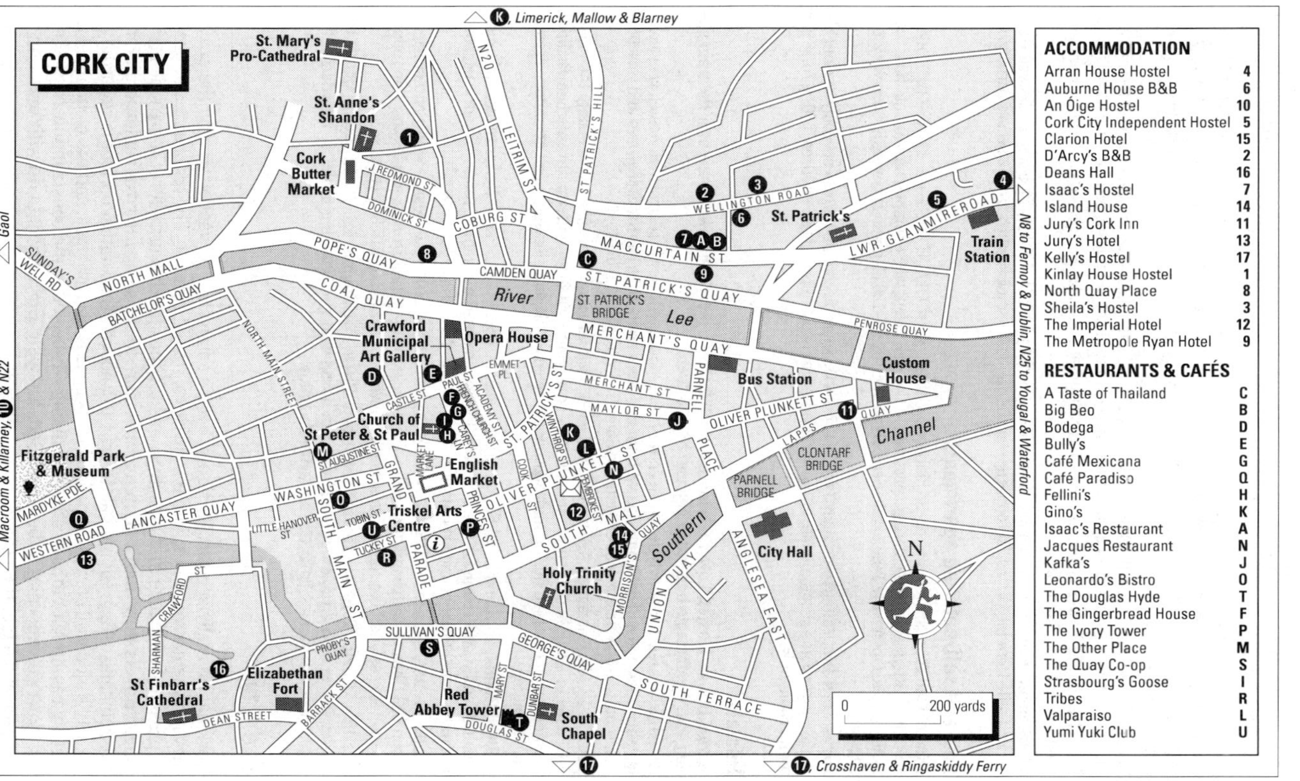
CORK CITY
K, Limerick, Mallow & Blarney
N8 to Fermoy & Dublin, N25 to Yougal & Waterford
17, Crosshaven & Ringaskiddy Ferry
Macroom & Killarney, 10 & N22
Gaol
St. Mary's Pro-Cathedral
St. Anne's Shandon
Cork Butter Market
St. Patrick's
Train Station
Crawford Municipal Art Gallery
Opera House
Bus Station
Custom House
Church of St Peter & St Paul
English Market
Triskel Arts Centre
Fitzgerald Park & Museum
City Hall
Holy Trinity Church
St Finbarr's Cathedral
Elizabethan Fort
Red Abbey Tower
South Chapel
River Lee
Channel
Southern
0 200 yards
ACCOMMODATION
Arran House Hostel 4
Auburne House B&B 6
An Óige Hostel 10
Cork City Independent Hostel 5
Clarion Hotel 15
D'Arcy's B&B 2
Deans Hall 16
Isaac's Hostel 7
Island House 14
Jury's Cork Inn 11
Jury's Hotel 13
Kelly's Hostel 17
Kinlay House Hostel 1
North Quay Place 8
Sheila's Hostel 3
The Imperial Hotel 12
The Metropole Ryan Hotel 9
RESTAURANTS & CAFÉS
A Taste of Thailand C
Big Beo B
Bodega D
Bully's E
Café Mexicana G
Café Paradiso Q
Fellini's H
Gino's K
Isaac's Restaurant A
Jacques Restaurant N
Kafka's J
Leonardo's Bistro O
The Douglas Hyde T
The Gingerbread House F
The Ivory Tower P
The Other Place M
The Quay Co-op S
Strasbourg's Goose I
Tribes R
Valparaiso L
Yumi Yuki Club U

Kent House, 47 Lower Glanmire Rd (☎021/450 4260). B&B in a family home offering en-suite and standard non-smoking rooms. Handy for the train station. No car parking. ④.

Number Forty Eight, 48 Lower Glanmire Rd (☎021/450 5790). Comfortable, smart B&B in a Victorian town house on the busy Cork–Dublin road. Early breakfasts available. No parking. ④.

Oakland, 51 Lower Glanmire Rd (☎021/450 0578). Regular B&B offering both standard and en-suite rooms. ④.

Seven North Mall, 7 North Mall (☎021/439 7191). Good quality guesthouse in an eighteenth-century town house, centrally located beside the river. Excellent breakfasts; secure car park. ⑤.

Tara House, 52 Lower Glanmire Rd (☎021/450 0294). Regular B&B with standard and en-suite rooms; TVs throughout. ③.

Westbourne House, 2 Westbourne Villas, Western Rd (☎021/427 6153). Pleasant, traditional B&B about a mile from the centre; all rooms are en suite and non-smoking throughout; secure parking. ④.

Inns and self-catering apartments

Deans Hall, Crosses Green, nr St Finbarr's Cathedral (☎021/431 2623, fax 431 6523). Student accommodation let as self-catering apartments. Central, clean, well-equipped apartments hold four to six people. Open early June to mid-Sept. £80–95/€101.58–120.63 per night; weekly rates work out cheaper.

Jurys Cork Inn, Anderson's Quay (☎021/427 6444). Smart accommodation, especially reasonable for families; rooms accommodate either three adults or two adults and two children. £60/€76.18 per night, room only.

Hostels

Aaran House Hostel, Lower Glanmire Rd (☎021/455 1566). Small town house near the train station with comfortable bunks, kitchen and bike lock-up.

An Óige Hostel, 1–2 Redclyffe, Western Rd (☎021/454 3289). Newly refurbished hostel; very comfortable, spacious and well-run. Bus #8 from the bus station or St Patrick Street; two and four-bedded rooms also available with en-suite facilities. Twin room £32.50/€40.63.

Isaac's, 48 MacCurtain St (IHH; ☎021/450 8388, *www.isaacs.ie*). This place is certainly the plushest hostel in town, but if you are intending to cook your own food, note that the kitchen facilities become pretty cramped during high season; inconvenient daytime lock-out of all dormitory accommodation, too.

Kelly's Hostel, 25 Summerhill South, off Douglas St (☎021/431 5612, *kellyshostel@hotmail.com*). Small, friendly and colourful hostel. Cable TV dominates the common room. Laundry facilities. Dorm, twin and three-bedded rooms available. Rooms £15/€19.05 per person.

Kinlay House, Shandon (IHH; ☎021/450 8966, *kincork@usit.ie*). Very clean, friendly and efficiently run USIT hostel, with laundry facilities. Price includes breakfast. Dorms, singles and twin rooms. Internet access and bike rental also available. Twin rooms £12.50/€15.88 per person.

Sheila's Cork Tourist Hostel, Belgrave Place, Wellington Rd (IHH; ☎021/450 5562; *sheilas@iol.ie*). A central, friendly and well-run hostel with good cooking facilities, a garden to the rear, breakfast, sauna, bike rental and email facilities.

The City

Cork has no really spectacular sights, but it's a fine place to wander: around the quays, through the narrow lanes, into the markets, up to Shandon. The ambience and sense of place are enjoyable in themselves, and for those with a taste for it there's plenty of nineteenth-century Gothic church architecture to see along the river banks, and evocative remnants of a great mercantile past to uncover. Exploration on foot is rewarding – the city's medieval core is embedded in its central narrow lanes, and the meshing of its history can be felt embodied in its buildings, reflected in the constant flow of the Lee. But don't go expecting to be astounded. Enjoying Cork city is to do with tuning in to the pace and life of the place.

The island

The **city centre** is essentially the island, with its quaysides, pretty bridges, alleyways and lanes, plus that segment to the north of the River Lee that has MacCurtain Street as its central thoroughfare, and the lanes leading up to Shandon. **St Patrick's Street** and **Grand Parade** form the modern commercial heart, with a healthy smattering of the modish amenities generally associated with much larger European cities. Not that you are ever engulfed by commercialism; aggressive multinationals barely dominate, and major chainstores exist alongside modest traditional businesses. It is in such immediate contrasts that the charms of the city lie. To the north of St Patrick's Street run the narrow laneways of **French Church Street** and **Carey's Lane**, busy with restaurants and cafés; tucked away to the south are the densely packed stalls of the covered English Market.

The eastern, downstream, end of the island is the more clearly defined: many of its quays are still in use, and it's here that you get the best sense of the old port city. In the west the island peters out in a predominantly residential area. Heading in this direction, though, you can follow the signs off Western Road for **Fitzgerald Park**, home of the **Cork Public Museum** (July & Aug Mon–Fri 11am–1pm & 2.15–6pm, Sun 3–5pm; rest of year Mon–Fri 11am–1pm & 2.15–5pm, Sun 3–5pm; closed bank holidays; £1/€1.27), about a mile out of the city centre, easily combined with a trip to Cork Gaol (see below). Primarily a museum of Republican history, it has an excellent commentary on the part played by nationally significant local characters and events in the Republican movement. There are exhibits of local archeological and geological finds, too, and a section on the history of the dairy trade.

Shandon

North of the River Lee is the area known as **Shandon**, a sadly neglected reminder of Cork's eighteenth-century status as the most important port in Europe for dairy products. To get there head up John Redmond Street, or simply aim for the giant fish atop the church tower. The most striking survival is the **Cork Butter Exchange**, stout nineteenth-century Classical buildings recently given over to rather quiet craft workshops. The old **butter market** itself sits like a generously proportioned butter tub in a cobbled square, and now houses the Firkin Crane Theatre. Despite the air of dereliction, this part of town is worth a visit for the pleasant Georgian church of **St Anne's Shandon** (1750), easily distinguishable from all over Cork city by its weather vane – an eleven-foot salmon. The church is perhaps most famous for its bells, which feature in the verse of *Father Prout*, a nineteenth-century fictional character devised by an ex-Jesuit to satirize the church. You can climb its tower (daily: June–Sept 9.30am–5.30pm; Oct–May 10am–3.30pm; £3/€3.81) for excellent views and ring the bells – a good stock of sheet tunes is provided.

To the west of here is an area known as Sunday's Well, and **Cork City Gaol** (daily: March–Oct 9.30am–6pm; Nov–Feb 10am–5pm; £3.50/€4.44). It's a good thirty minutes' walk from the city centre, up the hill from North Mall. A lively taped tour takes you through the prison, focusing on social history in a way that is both engaging and enlightening. It's occasionally threaded with characters of national importance, all vividly brought to life by a dramatic audiovisual finale. The gaol also houses the **Radio Museum Experience** (same times; £3.50/€4.44, combined ticket £6/€7.62) which uses similarly engaging techniques to convey the tremendous importance of the development of the wireless. When an audiovisual character in role as Marconi begins with a passionate "what is jolly about science is this: it encourages one to go on dreaming...to think [the] way to the truth of things" he takes you with him all the way. The museum also has a large collection of early radios, a wealth of popular archival recordings and a strangely affectionate and evocative reconstruction of the first radio station in Cork. There's a pleasant walk from here to Fitzgerald Park: turn right as you leave the prison, left, right and then left down a flight of steps and over the Shaky Bridge.

The stark precision of nineteenth-century Gothic which is repeated time and again in the city's churches may not be to everyone's taste, but here it undeniably gives the city a rhythmic architectural cohesion. Both Pugin and Pain are very much in evidence, Pugin in the brilliant Revivalist essay of the Church of St Peter and St Paul on Friar Matthew Quay, with its handsome lantern spire, and Pain in St Patrick's Church on Lower Glanmire Road. Best of all is William Burges' **St Finbarr's Cathedral** (built 1867–79), obsessively detailed, with its impressive French Gothic spire providing a grand silhouette on the southwesterly shoulder of the city.

Eating

Cork doesn't have a wide range of cuisines for you to choose from – the main influence is Mediterranean – but it does have a high standard of food on offer; several cafés and restaurants serve dishes made from organic local produce, and there are plenty of seafood and vegetarian options. Places like the *Ivory Tower*, *Café Paradiso*, *Isaac's* and, above all, *Ballymaloe House* at the Crawford Gallery epitomize the creativity of Cork's culinary scene, and the influence of these places permeates many of the more affordable places to eat around the city. Alongside the more conventional eating places, **The English Market** located between Grand Parade and Princes Street, with entrances off both, is a wonderful place to share in the city's enthusiasm for all things culinary. Here, the cosmopolitan rubs shoulder with the decidedly unpretentious; stalls specializing in the finest olive oils and cheeses jostle for space among the rakes of tripe and bacon.

Cafés and budget places

Bia Beo, Thompson House, MacCurtain St. Breezy art gallery/café serving inexpensive wholesome snacks and lunches. Stir frys, pastas and filled pancakes for around £5/€6.35, plus delightful cakes.

Bodega, Coal Quay. Cork's most stylish bar, worth calling in for its wonderfully bold interior alone; Mediterranean-influenced menu.

The Crawford Municipal Art Gallery Café, Emmet Place (☎021/427 4415). The gallery's café is an affordable offshoot of *Ballymaloe House* restaurant near Cloyne, famous for taking traditional Irish cooking to new heights (see p.292).

The Douglas Hyde, Douglas Street. The pun should give it away – the most civilized bar in Cork, with fine art on the walls, clean and comfy furniture, laid-back ambience and top-notch bar food: filled crêpes, fabulous fish cakes, smoked salmon and beautiful fruit tarts. Meals here start at around £6/€7.62.

The Farm Gate Café, upstairs in The English Market, Princes St. Great for affordable lunches and teas: lots of Mediterranean salads, savoury tarts, and plenty of seafood, with the emphasis on using fresh, local produce; in line with tradition, they also serve tripe and *drisheen* (a kind of black pudding). Listen to the pianist as you eat and watch the market below. Closed Sun.

Fellinni's, Carey's Lane. Comfortably dishevelled café atmosphere with papers to read and seating inside and out; soups, filled pittas for around £5/€6.35, coffees and teas. One of the few places open all day on a Sunday.

The Gingerbread House, Paul St. Great café for soaking up the Paul Street scene. Tasty baguettes, tartlets, soups and coffees and breakfast until 3pm Sunday. Daily till 10pm.

Gino's, Winthrop St. Good cheap pizzas and homemade ice cream.

Kafka's, 7 Maylor St. Great veggie and non-veggie breakfasts, and a huge range of tasty baguettes, burgers, sandwiches and coffee. Handy for the bus station. Closed Sun.

The Other Place, 8, South Main St. Offshoot of *The Quay Co-op*; cheap vegetarian café and gay meeting place. Open Mon–Sat 9am–9pm.

The Quay Co-op, 24 Sullivan's Quay (☎021/431 7026). Delicious, large vegetarian and vegan meals, soups, puddings and teas, all in surroundings of wonderfully faded elegance. Self-service. Closed Sun.

Tribes, Tuckey St. Smoky coffee bar for trendy diehards. Over thirty varieties of coffee, and many herbal teas. Closed Sun.

Yumi Yuki Club, Triskel Arts Centre, Tobin St, off South Main St (☎021/427 5777). Oriental offshoot of the inimitable *Ivory Tower* (see below), offering sushi and saki in a playful club setting. Two-course lunchtime specials for around £7/€8.89; expect to pay around £15/€19.05 for three courses in the evening.

Restaurants

Bully's, 40 Paul St. (☎021/427 3555) Moderately priced wine bar serving pizzas, fresh pasta and fish; popular with families.

Café Mexicana, Carey's Lane. Mexican-themed restaurant with a party atmosphere. Main courses for around £12/€15.24.

Café Paradiso, 16 Lancaster Quay, Western Rd (☎021/427 7939). Busy, informal restaurant with arguably the best vegetarian/vegan menu in town: gleefully high fat. Inexpensive lunches; expensive dinner menu. Not the place for a quiet evening out. Closed Sun & Mon.

Isaac's Restaurant, MacCurtain St (☎021/450 3805). Deservedly popular restaurant. Light, delicious food with a good range of salads, fresh breads, cheeses, seafood and pasta. High emphasis on local and organic produce.

The Ivory Tower, The Exchange Buildings, 35 Princes St (☎021/427 4665). The place to go to treat yourself: adventurous menu specializing in wild and organic food. Exquisite. Five-course set menu £30/€38.09. Closed Mon & Tues.

Jacques Restaurant, Phoenix St (☎021/427 7387). Imaginative restaurant with excellent reputation; mouthwatering food with a Mediterranean influence. Earlybird two-course menu for around £13/€16.51; dinner around £22/€27.93. Closed Sat lunch & all Sun.

Leonardo's Bistro, 97 South Main St (☎021/427 9969). Informal bistro-restaurant with a convivial atmosphere serving a good range of pizza, pasta, tortillas, enchilladas, steaks, fish and fajitas. Lunches from around £6/€7.62, main courses in the evening from around £8/€10.16.

Strasbourg's Goose, 17–18 French Church St (☎021/427 9534). Lively, informal restaurant popular with a mixed young crowd; casual, pavement café atmosphere, and absolutely no anxieties about serving chips and beer with all sorts of dishes, including steaks, fish and homemade burgers. Set lunch menu from £10/€12.70, main courses in the evening from around £12/€15.24.

A Taste of Thailand, 8 Bridge St (☎021/450 5404). Authentic Thai cuisine; earlybird three-course special £11/€13.97.

Valparaiso, 115 Oliver Plunkett St (☎021/427 5488). Huge range of dishes taken from a broad sweep of Spanish cuisine. Main courses around £12/€15.24; earlybird menu (not available Tues or Sat) for around the same price.

Pubs, nightlife and the arts

There are plenty of good watering holes in the city, and if all you want is a drink, you won't need a guide to find somewhere – though a couple of the city's older bars (mentioned below) are worth seeking for their atmosphere. Many bars have **music**, traditional or otherwise, and the following list should give some good pointers on where to find the best of this. Cork also has a strong **club scene**; as with any large city, venues and session nights change: pick up *Whazon*, available free in cafés, shops and arts venues around town, for detailed what's-on information and look for fliers in *The Quay Co-op*, *The Other Place* and *The Phoenix* pub. Wherever you end up, this is not a difficult town in which to enjoy yourself.

Pubs and bars

An Bodhrán, 42 Oliver Plunkett St. Chance midweek sessions of traditional music in summer, rock at other times.

An Crúiscín Lan, Douglas St. Small bar with traditional music (Thurs) and Blues (weekends).

An Spailpín Fánach, 28 South Main St. Traditional Irish music sessions on Tues, Wed, Thurs & Sun in summer.

Bodega, Coal Quay. A friendly, mixed and, for the decor, surprisingly unpretentious crowd. See "Cafés" on p.286.

The Corner House, 7 Coburg St. Popular, young bar with a mixture of mainly Cajun, folk and Irish music (Sun–Wed).

The Douglas Hyde, 63 Douglas St. Laid-back bar with a refreshingly unpretentious contemporary interior and a friendly atmosphere.

Franciscan Well, 12A North Mall. Micro-brewery on the site of a thirteenth-century Franciscan monastery. Lager, ale, stout and wheat beer produced on the premises, and there's a good selecton of bottled beers too. No-frills beer yard to the rear is a pleasant option on a summer evening.

Fred Zeppelin's, 8 Parliament St. Live gig venue for indie, ska, hip-hop and hardcore; it has the touch of a bikers' hangout, but attracts a mixed clientele.

Gable's, 32 Douglas St. Regular bar with traditional music and singing on Wed and Thurs.

Loafers, 26 Douglas St. Friendly bar with pleasant beer garden, attracts a bohemian clientele; probably the most relaxed place for gays to drink in the city.

The Lobby, Union Quay (*www.lobby.ie*). This is one of Cork's top traditional venues and a great spot to catch live music year round. Free traditional sessions (Tues & Fri) and acoustic (Mon) take place in the bar; with further traditional sessions, plus folk and rock upstairs (Wed, Thurs, Sat & Sun), for which there's a cover charge.

The Long Valley, Winthrop St. Excellent traditional bar; something of a one-off and a locals' favourite; the place also does good substantial sandwiches.

The Ovens, 18 Oliver Plunkett St. A great little old bar, serving up traditional music (every night except Fri & Sat), that gets packed to the gills.

The Phoenix, Union Quay. Busy, boisterous and traditional, this place offers blues and folk downstairs (Mon & Wed); the bar upstairs attracts a younger crowd into heavy metal.

The Vineyard, on Market Lane, off Patrick St. Stylish, airy interior decorated with iconic Irish characters from Beckett to Bacon; also serves light Italian meals (except on Sun).

Clubs

City Limits, Coburg St. Mixed crowd at this fun and unpretentious club; plays salsa, acid jazz, world music and disco (Fri & Sat). Comedy from 10pm on Fridays and Saturdays followed by dancing – anything from ska to Blondie, James Brown to Sinatra.

The Half Moon Theatre, in the back of the Opera House (☎021/427 2680). A theatre and club venue; early evening drama productions followed by bands midnight–2am.

The Other Place, 8 St Augustine St. Gay club every Friday and Saturday; closed at other times.

Sir Henry's, in the *Grand Parade Hotel*, South Main St. Cork's top club and winner of Best Dance Club in Munster award. Four rooms and six DJs mixing dance, disco and jazz. Open Wed–Sat.

Yumi Yuki Club, Triskel Arts Centre, on Tobin St, off South Main St. At midnight the sushi ends and live acts (and the bar) become the focus of attention; expect DJs, singer/songwriters or jazz.

Art, theatre, film and festivals

The hub of artistic activity in Cork is the Triskel Arts Centre, found down the narrow and dingy Tobin Street, off South Main Street (☎021/427 2022, *www.iol.ie/triskel*). It has changing exhibitions of contemporary art, a film theatre, a continuous programme of performance art, poetry reading, contemporary music, and the *Yumi Yuki Club* café-bar (see p.287). It is also an excellent source of information about what's on in the city.

Considering the amount of painting and sculpture generated around the county, Cork city is poorly served in terms of the visual arts. **Fine art** has a high profile in cafés, restaurants and private houses, but good galleries are in short supply. Worth a visit, however, is the Crawford Municipal Gallery in Emmet Place (Mon–Sat 10am–5pm), which has a permanent collection of Irish and European painting and usually an interesting contemporary exhibition. The Cork Arts Society, 5 Father Matthew Quay, off South Mall, is a good commercial gallery, with exhibitions of contemporary works. The Blackcombe Galleries, 44A MacCurtain St (above the antiques shop), is a pleasant space, showing eighteen contemporary exhibitions per year.

The Cork Opera House in Emmet Place (☎021/427 6357), offers a full programme of **drama**, concerts both **classical** and popular, **ballet**, **opera**, review and variety, though very rarely anything at all out of the mainstream. Classical concerts are also held at Triskel, the School of Music, on Union Quay, and the City Hall, Anglesea Street. The Everyman Palace, MacCurtain St (☎021/450 1673), and Cork Arts Theatre (CATs), in Knapps Square, off Camden Quay, both offer a range of local small-scale productions. The Firkin Crane, Shandon (☎021/450 5103) is the best place to catch classical and contemporary dance. Cork has a very popular **international jazz festival**, one of the last two weekends in October. With music bursting out of every doorway, you don't need to go and see the big names to enjoy yourself. There's also an important **film festival** in early October (*www.corkfilmfest.org*) with films screened at Triskel and the Opera House, while the excellent **art house cinema**, Kino, on Washington Street (☎021/427 1571) screens films throughout the year. Mainstream films are on offer at the new Gate Multiplex Cinema (☎021/427 9595) at the corner of Batchelor's Quay and North Main Street. Finally, the **International Choral Festival** is held in May (☎021/430 8308), and there is a **folk festival** during September (☎021/431 7271).

Listings

Airlines Aer Lingus (☎021/432 7155); British Airways (☎1-800/626747); Ryanair (☎01/609 7800).

Airport Information ☎021/431 3131.

Banks Branches of the Allied Irish Bank and Bank of Ireland on Patrick St, North Main St, Bridge St and Western Rd.

Bike rental Aidann Quinlan, 55 Barrack St (☎021/431 3133); CycleScene, 396 Blarney St (☎021/430 1183).

Bookshops Collins, Carey's Lane; Eason's, 113/115 Patrick St; Keogh's Books, 6 MacCurtain St; Liam Russell, Oliver Plunkett St; Mercier Bookshop, 4 Bridge St; Waterstones, 69 Patrick St.

Bureau de change At the tourist office and at *Sheila's Hostel*.

Buses Bus Éireann station, Parnell Place, alongside Merchant's Quay (☎021/450 8188) for local and intercity buses. Several private bus companies also operate from Cork: see "Travel Details" at the end of this chapter.

Camping equipment The Tent Shop, Rutland St, off South Terrace, offers camping gear for sale or rent.

Car rental Car Rental Ireland, Monahan Rd (☎021/496 2277); Great Island Car Rentals, 47 MacCurtain St (☎021/450 3536 or 481 1609).

Ferries to France operate from Ringaskiddy, about ten miles from Cork. Brittany Ferries, 42 Grand Parade (☎021/427 7801), sail to Roscoff (April–Oct once weekly); Swansea–Cork Ferries, 52 South Mall (☎021/427 1166), operates a ten-hour crossing, four–six days a week according to season. Ringaskiddy Ferryport: Brittany Ferries (☎021/437 8401); Swansea–Cork (☎021/437 8036).

Gay information Linc, 34 Princes St, above *Rossini's* restaurant (☎021/422 2773, *www.explode.to.corklesbians*): Cork's lesbian resource centre, with a drop-in night on Thurs (8–10pm), and discos on first Saturday of the month. *The Other Place* café, 8 South Main St: gay café and bookshop.

Hospital Cork University Hospital, Wilton Rd (☎021/454 6400).

Hurling and gaelic football For fixtures phone ☎021/496 3311.

Internet access *Plaza 2000*, 65 North Main St (☎021/427 2344, *plaza@iica.net*); *Jumpin' Jack's Cellar Bar*, Sheres St (☎021/427 3000, *leevale@indigo.ie*); *Sheila's hostel* (*sheilas@iol.ie*). webworkhouse.com, 8 Winthrop St (☎021/427 3090, *mail@webworkhouse.com*).

Laundry 14 MacCurtain St, next door to the Everyman Palace theatre (Mon–Sat from 9am, last wash 8pm).

Left luggage At the Bus Éireann station (May–Sept daily 9am–6pm; Oct–April Mon–Fri 8.35am–6.15pm, Sat 9.30am–6.15pm).

Music The Living Tradition, 40 MacCurtain St (☎021/450 2040), sells a great range of Irish and world music on CD and cassette, as well as sheet music and traditional instruments such as *bodhráns* and tin whistles.

Pharmacy Denis O'Leary, 8 Grand Parade (☎021/427 4563); Phelan's Late Night Pharmacy, 9 Patrick St (☎021/427 2511).

Post Office Oliver Plunkett St and MacCurtain St.

Swimming pool Douglas Swimming Pool, Douglas Rd (☎021/429 3073).

Taxis ABC (☎021/496 1961); Blue Cabs (☎021/439 3939); Taxi Co-op (☎021/427 2222).

Trains Iarnród Éireann's travel centre is at 65 Patrick St. For all enquiries, call ☎021/450 6766.

Travel agents USIT have two offices in Cork: at 10–11 Market Parade (☎021/427 0900), and UCC Student Travel, near The Boole Library, University College (☎021/427 3901).

East of Cork

East Cork has none of the scenic splendour of the west, but there are points of interest as you pass through, and a couple of spots that make a good day trip from Cork city if you don't have the time or means to venture further afield. A trip across the harbour to **Fota**, with its wild animals and eighteenth-century Classicism, and **Cobh** with its watersports, will allow you to get back in the evening early enough to take advantage of Cork's nightlife. On the way further east to the quaint port of **Youghal** – with its colourful maritime history and scenic location – there are a string of places worth a brief stop, including **Midleton**, the home of Jameson whiskey. The beaches at **Ballycotton** and **Garryvoe** can't compete with those to the west of Cork, but are pleasant enough.

Fota and Cobh

A visit to Fota House Wildlife Park and the pretty harbour town of Cobh can be managed in a day on a return train ticket from Cork. Going by train really is the best option, taking you across the mudflats of an estuary teeming with birdlife. Both are situated on islands in the mouth of Cork harbour.

Fota Wildlife Park (mid-March to Sept Mon–Sat 10am–6pm, Sun 11am–6pm; Oct to mid-Dec & Jan to mid-March Sat 10am–6pm, Sun 11am–6pm; £4.80/€6.09) is a small, pleasant park with apes, cheetahs, giraffes, red pandas and zebras, among others, all wandering about the landscaped eighteenth-century estate of Fota House. The **house**, originally an eighteenth-century hunting lodge, but much enlarged in 1820, is no longer open to the public, though this situation may change. You can, however, visit

CORK COAST ROUTE

If you want to head west from Cobh along the coast, or you want to cut around twenty minutes' driving time off your return to Cork city, you can take a five-minute ferry to Glenbrook from Carrigaloe, a couple of miles north of Cobh as you head back up towards the N25. Cross River Ferries services start at 7.15am from Carrigaloe and run about every ten minutes till 12.20am. Car £3/€3.81 return, £2.50/€3.17 single; adult 60p/€0.76 each way; bikes carried free.

the estate's **arboretum** (same times as park; free): one of the most important in Europe, with a great variety of rare and exotic flowering shrubs and trees.

Rejoining the train from Fota takes you out to the pretty little town of **COBH**. It is held in a quaint cup of land with steep, narrow streets climbing the hill to the Pugin cathedral. This neo-Gothic monster dominates the town, its entrance giving marvellous views out across the great curve of the bay to Spike Island. Thanks to its fine natural harbour, Cobh has long been an important **port**: it served as an assembly point for ships during the Napoleonic wars and was a major departure point for steamers carrying emigrants to America during the nineteenth century and convicts to Australia. The first-ever transatlantic steamer sailed from here in 1838, and the *Titanic* called in on her ill-fated voyage. Cobh was also the last port of call for the *Lusitania* before she was sunk off the Old Head of Kinsale (p.296); many of the victims' bodies were brought back to Cobh and lie buried nearby and a monument to the dead stands in Casement Square. Cobh's dramatic maritime history is retold at its excellent heritage centre, **The Queenstown Story** (daily 10am–6pm; £3.50/€4.44). Today the port is still used by a substantial fishing fleet. From September to February, when it is awash with fishermen, the town's character changes completely.

First and foremost, though, Cobh is a holiday resort, itself an historic function. Ireland's first yacht club was established here in 1720, and from 1830 onwards the town was a popular health resort, imitative of English Regency resorts like Brighton, a style reflected in its architecture. The main square is flanked by brightly painted Victorian town houses, and the place has a robust cheerfulness – though none of the cosmopolitan flavour of harbours further west. It attracts Irish holidaying families and offers pitch and putt, tennis, swimming and a stony beach. The **International Sailing Centre** on East Beach (☎021/481 1237) runs courses in sailing, canoeing and wind-surfing. There's a **regatta** weekend in mid-August, and for enthusiasts, the third week in July sees the exciting **Ford Yacht Week** across the harbour in Crosshaven (alternate summers; for latest details, check with the tourist office); best observation points are reckoned to be Ringabella, Fennel's Bay, Myrtleville or Roche's Point. Any other time in the summer you can at least take a **harbour boat trip** (Marine Transport Services, Atlantic Quay (☎021/481 1485; £3.50/€4.44)).

Cobh's **tourist office** is housed in the old yacht club, in the town centre (Mon–Fri 9.30am–5.30pm, Sat 11am–5.30pm, Sun 1–5pm; ☎021/481 3301), and has maps and local information – it also hosts art exhibitions. Pick of the **B&Bs** include *Atlantic*, 8 West Beach (☎021/481 1489; ③), *Ardeen*, 3 Harbour Hill (☎021/481 1803; ③); and *The Ship's Bell*, 1 East Beach (☎021/481 1122; ④).

Midleton to Garryvoe beach

The cheery market town of **MIDLETON**, about ten miles east of Cork, is best known for being the home of Jameson Irish whiskey. The **Jameson Heritage Centre** tour is a highly polished promotional affair, taking you through the distillery and culminating in a whiskey-tasting session (March–Oct daily 10am–6pm, last admission 4pm; Nov–Feb Mon–Fri tours at noon & 3pm only; £3.95/€5.02). The best place to eat is *The Farm Gate*, Coolbawn (☎021/463 2771), a deli and restaurant selling and serving fresh local produce (closed Mon–Thurs eve & all Sun). For accommodation, try the **hostel** *An Stór* (IHH; ☎021/463 3106), a converted mill on Drury's Lane.

Four miles to the south is the sleepy, historic village of **CLOYNE**. One of Ireland's earliest Christian foundations, the monastery of St Colman, was established here in the sixth century. In medieval times the village that grouped up around it continued to be of religious importance with the establishment of the see of Cloyne, a diocese which extended well into County Limerick. Reminders of this era, though, are few. There's a fine tenth-century **round tower**, from whose top, 100ft up, there are superb views (key from Cathedral House; £1/€1.27), and you can also visit **St Colman's Cathedral**, a large building of warm, mottled stone originally built in 1250 but disappointingly restored in the nineteenth century. Inside are the grand and grim seventeenth-century Fitzgerald of Imokelly tomb and the alabaster tomb of George Berkley, the famous philosopher who was bishop here from 1734 to 1753. An Egyptian tau cross and the St Anthony's cross on the cathedral doorway are faint traces of earlier Mediterranean influences. Off the Cloyne–Ballycotton road, *Ballymaloe House* (☎021/465 2531, *www.ballymaloe.ie*; ⑨) is an exceptional **restaurant**, one of the most famous in Ireland; a meal here will cost you around £32/€40.63. Accommodation is in a large seventeenth-century manor house set on a four-hundred acre farm.

Five miles on from Cloyne, **BALLYCOTTON** is a pleasant enough spot, with a little quayside, fine cliff walks for miles to the west, and a beach half a mile away. There's fine guesthouse **accommodation** at *Spanish Point Restaurant* (☎021/464 6177; ④): bright and airy, it's in a terrific spot and has a beautiful conservatory/dining room overlooking Ballycotton Bay. *The Cliffstop Café* (closed Mon & Tues, plus Sept–May) is worth the steep climb to the west of the village for good pizzas, seafood and salads, and views over the rock-island lighthouse. Not far away to the north are the holiday villages of Shanagarry and **GARRYVOE**. Garryvoe **beach** is very long and sandy, but it's beset by caravans advancing upon the shore and very busy during high season. To the east of here the bay is flat and of interest only to birdwatchers, its reed-infested estuary now a protected **bird sanctuary**. Here a river sidles its way, smooth and khaki, through the mudflats to the sea.

Youghal

YOUGHAL is an ancient port at the mouth of the River Blackwater, where the counties of Cork and Waterford meet. In a small way it combines the richness of the Blackwater towns with the prettiness of Kinsale and Cobh. A picturesque town, popular with holidaying Irish families, Youghal has a colourful history and some fine architecture to remember it by; even if you're en route elsewhere, it's worth stopping off to take in some of the character of the place.

Youghal's walls were first built by the Norman settlers who established the town, but those which stand today were erected by Edward I in 1275. From medieval times the town prospered as one of Ireland's leading ports, trading with the Continent – particularly France – and with England. Political disturbances and trade restrictions imposed on Irish ports by the English Crown, however, meant the town's growth began to slow in the mid-sixteenth century. It fell into the hands of the Earl of Desmond, and in 1579 the "Rebel" Earl (rebelling against Elizabeth I) sacked and burned the place. After Desmond's death, Youghal was part of the 40,000 acres granted to Walter Raleigh during the Munster Plantations, with which Elizabeth hoped to control Ireland. Raleigh, though, had little interest in Ireland, and spent most of his time composing poetry in an attempt to curry favour with the queen. In this he was abetted by Edmund Spenser, another local colonist, author of *The Faerie Queen*. Spenser proved to be capable of both great poetry and of barbarism in his dealings with the Irish: they eventually repaid him by burning down his castle, Kilcolman, near Buttevant. Raleigh himself spent little time in Youghal, selling his land to Richard Boyle, the "Great" Earl of Cork (and father of the scientist), who then greatly developed the town as he did all his newly acquired land.

When Cromwell reached New Ross in 1649, the English garrison at Youghal went over to the Parliamentarian side, and so the town escaped destruction. Nonetheless, the importance of the port continued to diminish through the seventeenth century. Still, the decline was only relative to its former stature, and there is enough fine eighteenth-century architecture to make it clear that a small but affluent class of merchants still prospered. Today, Youghal is a quiet seaside resort, and the history preserved in its buildings continues to suggest prosperity earned through centuries of vigorous commerce, and offers an insight into the privileged lives of the early colonists.

The Town

Youghal's most famous landmark is the **clock tower**, which bridges the long, curvy main street. A superbly proportioned Georgian structure of warm, plum-coloured stone, it was used as a prison a century ago; more recently it served as a museum, but it's now closed indefinitely. Steps leading off the tower climb the steep hill through little lanes to the top of the town, where the walls and turrets of the old defences still define the shape of the compact harbour.

The most charming buildings lie, in the main, on the landward side of North Main Street and in the lanes that run behind it. On North Main Street itself the **Red House**, built in 1710, is a fine example of domestic architecture, clearly showing the Dutch influence of the original merchant owner. Here, too, are seventeenth-century almshouses, built by Richard Boyle to house Protestant widows. Lanes off to the west of this end of Main Street lead to the Elizabethan **Myrtle Grove**, known as "Raleigh's House", since it was once part of the extensive estates granted to him by Elizabeth I, one of the oldest unfortified houses in Ireland but, sadly, no longer open to the public.

Nearby, you'll find the **Collegiate Church of St Mary's**, a large, simple, thirteenth-century building, one of the few of such age still in use in Ireland. The building has been greatly altered over the centuries, but still has interesting medieval tombs and effigies. Particularly notable are the thirteenth-century monuments in the south transept (entrance is by a little door to the left as you walk up towards the church, or by the main door when open). Wrecked when the town was sacked by Desmond's men in 1579, they were later restored by Boyle, with the addition of effigies in seventeenth-century costume. Heading out of town towards Waterford, you pass the ruins of North Abbey, a thirteenth-century Dominican priory of which little remains.

On the east side of North Main Street is **Tyntes Castle**, a fifteenth-century tower house that is now sadly dilapidated (and, by the look of it, rapidly deteriorating). Edmund Spenser's widow married a former resident of the house, Robert Tynte. Lanes off this side of the street lead to the **quayside**. Here it's all very quaint: warehouse buildings warm with the patina of age surround the harbour; yucca palms decorate the walkways, and the cultivated fields of Waterford across the water look very near.

There is an interesting **walking tour** of the town, which sets off from the tourist office (1hr 30min; June–Aug Mon–Sat at 11am; at other times, tours for groups of four or more can be arranged; £3/€3.81). Signposted from here too is **Fox's Lane Museum** (July & Aug Tues–Sat 10am–1pm & 2–6pm, Sun 2–6pm; rest of year open by prior appointment, call ☎024/91145; £2/€2.54), which displays with illuminating clarity and imagination a collection of domestic gadgetry – everything from sausage makers to petrol-fuelled irons and cucumber straighteners – all mapping the dogged march of progress from the nineteenth century.

Practicalities

The **tourist office** is on Market Square, just behind the harbour (June–Sept Mon–Fri & Sun 9.30am–6pm, Sat 9.30am–1pm & 2.15–6pm; Oct–May Mon–Fri 9.30am–1pm & 2–5.30pm; ☎024/20170). You'll find plenty of **B&Bs** along the main streets and around the quayside – try *Avonmore House* (☎024/92617; ④) or *Attracta* (☎024/92062; ③) both on South Abbey or *Roseville* on New Catherine St (☎024/92571; ③). There are plenty more out on the Cork Road, including *Shalamar* (☎024/93398; ②), about two miles out of town. **Hotel** accommodation is available at *The Devonshire Arms Hotel*, Pearse Square (☎024/92827; ⑥), and *Aherne's*, on North Main St (☎024/92424, *www.ahernes.com*; ⑧), both in the centre of town. The latter is also renowned for its seafood restaurant (☎024/92424). The other hotel in the area is *The Hilltop Hotel* (☎024/92911; ⑤), a mile and a half along the road towards Cork. The **International Busking Festival** during the first weekend in August offers £3000 prize money – and suddenly **camping space** is available everywhere.

There's no shortage of **places to eat** in Youghal. *The Coffee Pot*, on North Main St, just near the clock tower, serves good-value meals; nearby the bistro-style *Perfect Blend* serves moderately priced Irish, Italian and vegetarian dishes. For good bar food, try *The Devonshire Arms Hotel*, Pearse Square at the west end of the town centre.

You'll find **music** of some sort in Youghal's bars several nights a week during the summer, and at the weekends throughout the year. *The Nook* on Main Street and the *Walter Raleigh Hotel* are a couple of likely places to find traditional music and ballads, and *The Clock*, 56 South Main St, has rock and pop bands. If you just want a quiet pint, head for the *Moby Dick* **pub** on the quays – Youghal was used as a location for the film of the same name, and inside you'll find memorabilia and photographs from the making of the film.

To the west of town, clean sandy **beaches** stretch for miles.

Inland Cork

Although most people head straight for the coast, **inland Cork**, aside from providing a quick route west, does have its merits, and, unless you yearn for the sea, it's just as beautiful. The main tourist attraction is the famous historic town of **Blarney**, close to the scenic Lee Valley; it makes a pleasurable stop on your way westwards or an easy day-trip from Cork city. Further inland, the **Boggeragh Mountains** and the route from Macroom to Bantry provide opportunities for gentle walking.

Blarney

BLARNEY is an easy six miles from Cork city; buses leave the bus station every half hour. The town itself functions chiefly as a tourist service centre and, naturally, there are plenty of places to eat here: try *The Muskerry Arms* or the bar of *Christy's Hotel* for pub food. *Blair's Inn*, about four miles west of Blarney (on the R579), is difficult to reach without your own transport, but is especially noted for its barfood and a lovely riverside location. The **Blarney Woollen Mills**, one of Blarney's original industries, is the place to find quality Irish goods – especially clothing – in traditional wools and linens. Alongside is a **tourist office** (July & Aug Mon–Sat 9am–7pm, Sun 10am–5pm; ☎021/438 1624).

The **castle** (daily: May & Sept 9am–6.30pm; June–Aug 9am–7pm; Oct–April 9am-6pm; £3.50/€4.44), a fine stronghold, built in 1446 by Dermot McCarthy, King of Munster, is sadly now synonymous with the whole "Blarney phenomenon". The **Blarney Stone** has been kissed by visitors for over a hundred years, the legend being that to do so gives you the gift of eloquent and persuasive speech. The most famous story of how the legend came about tells of one McCarthy – King of Munster and Lord of Blarney – who, supposedly loyal to the colonizing Queen Elizabeth I, never actually got around to fulfilling any of the agreements between them, always sidetracking her emissaries with drinking, dancing and sweet talk. He was said to be able to talk "the noose off his head". In her frustration the queen is said to have eventually cried out "Blarney, Blarney, what he says he does not mean. It is the usual Blarney." And so the word entered the English language.

The stone itself is a four foot by one foot limestone block set in the battlements 83ft above the ground, so kissing it requires a head for heights. If you want to, you'll have to join the queue (it can take an hour) in the castle keep from which you can watch everyone else (one at a time) being dangled backwards by the shins over the battlements aided by two strong men. This also gives you time to consider whether or not you really want to join in. According to a less challenging legend, the stone is half of the Stone of Scone on which Scottish kings were crowned, given to Cormac McCarthy by Robert the Bruce in gratitude for the support of 4000 men at the Battle of Bannockburn (the rest is at Edinburgh Castle). Views from the top of the castle are superb.

In the castle grounds, **Rock Close** is a nineteenth-century folly, a rock garden supposedly built around druidic remains. It is a pity that myths, authentic or not, are such big business around here, because without the hype these ancient yews and oaks could create a potent atmosphere.

Macroom and the route west

The secondary roads west of Cork city run up the Lee Valley, through scenic countryside and a number of small villages. **MACROOM**, the only place of any size on the N22 between Cork and Killarney, serves as a stopping-off point for tourists and music enthusiasts heading west. Several bars offer meals – the *Castle Hotel* on Main Street is a good option and serves up until about 8pm. The **Boggeragh Mountains** to the north of the Lee Valley appear as high, rolling moorland, unspectacular compared with other ranges in Cork and Kerry but particularly rich in archeological remains: stone circles, standing stones, wedge tombs and ring forts. A leaflet, *Antiquities of the Boggeragh Mountains*, is available from the tourist office in Cork city – of great value in locating these sites.

The stretch of road beyond Macroom west to Bantry Bay is a far quieter one than the route out of Cork; it leads into the mountains and to one of the county's last remaining *Gaeltacht* regions. Fine scenery accompanies you all the way: the little village of **INCHIGEELAGH** sits beside a ribbon lake, which the road passes as it heads for the tiny village of **BALLINGEARY**. Beyond here the route west takes you through the dramatic glacial valley of Gougane Barra and down to Bantry Bay (see p.312 & p.309).

Alternatively, taking the road south of Cork city to Bandon and then west to **DUNMANWAY** brings you to very promising country of deserted hills and lakes. Dunmanway is a plain country town, but just outside it the excellent IHH-run **hostel**, *Shiplake House Mountain Hostel* (☎ & fax 023/45750), is in a beautiful setting and also has gypsy caravans for couples and families (£12.50/€15.87), **camping** and delicious vegetarian food. To find it take the Castle Road next to the Market Diner out of town, follow it for two and a half miles in the direction of Coolkelure (the road to Kealkill) and turn right at the hostel sign. Bus Éireann runs at least two daily **buses** from Cork to Dunmanway, and a bus from Dunmanway to Bantry and Glengarriff.

Kinsale

KINSALE has retained much of the flavour of its rich maritime history and has much in common with the formerly affluent ports of Youghal, Cork and Cobh. The eighteen-mile road south to here from Cork city travels through gentle rolling farmland and alongside an estuary. This easy, meandering coast is a favourite for fishing and bird-watching – indeed, it's so alive with birdlife that it's rewarding even for the uninitiated. At Kinsale the **harbour** is broad, and cormorants and shags skim across its gentle waters. A tongue of land curls from the west into the centre of the harbour, protecting the town from harsh winds, and on this promontory are the ivy-clad ruins of **James Fort**, a ruddy castle built by the English James I.

With its pretty harbour, the opportunities it offers for watersports, and its reputation as the gourmet centre of the southwest, Kinsale is an extremely successful tourist town. For the most part development has been tasteful, though the pace of change is swift and a garish scar of pastel-coloured apartments disfiguring the hillside illustrates the threat commercialism poses to Kinsale's historic character. Still, despite the crowds and the cars, there is plenty of interest in the life, landscape and history to keep you here.

Some history

Originally a fishing town, Kinsale's sheltered harbour has made it a place of strategic importance in Irish, and English, history. The town received its first royal charter from Edward III in 1333, but it was of little importance up until the **Battle of Kinsale** in 1601, a disastrous defeat for the Irish which signalled the end of the Gaelic aristocracy as a power for the English to reckon with. A Spanish fleet stood in the bay ready to support the Irish cause against Elizabethan forces, but was unable to make useful contact with O'Neill and O'Donnell attacking from the north. So the battle was lost, and although resistance to English rule continued, six years later came "the flight of the Earls" – when the Irish nobility fled to the Continent, giving up the fight for their own lands.

It was also at Kinsale that **James II** landed with French support in an attempt to regain his throne in 1689, and it was later the port of his final departure from Ireland after the Battle of the Boyne. The town was an important naval base for the English Crown in the seventeenth and eighteenth centuries, and the sixteenth-century tower house in Cork Street – Desmond Castle – became known as "The French Prison" when it was used to hold as many as six hundred French prisoners during the Napoleonic wars.

It was off the Old Head of Kinsale that the ocean liner, the **Lusitania**, en route to Liverpool from New York, was torpedoed by a German submarine in 1915, killing 1198 people. It remains a controversial incident: Germany claimed there was ammunition on board; the US said it contained only civilians. Whatever the truth, it has been seen as a catalyst for America's entry into World War I.

The Town centre

The town's history is recorded in the **museum** (irregular hours – check with the tourist office; £1/€1.27), bang in the centre of town above the old market (1600) with its Dutch-style facade (1704). It's an intriguing jumble of stuff, including memorabilia from the *Lusitania* disaster, sixteenth-century royal charters and maps, local craftwork, personal effects of the eighteenth-century giant of Kinsale and a variety of bizarre local inventions that never got further than the local museum. Here, too, is the musty old courthouse that had remained much the same from the eighteenth century up until 1915, when the inquest into the sinking of the *Lusitania* was held here and Kinsale suddenly became the focus of the world's press; after the inquest it was decided that the courtroom should be left as a memorial.

Desmond Castle (mid-April to mid-June Tues–Sun and bank holidays 10am–6pm; mid-June to early Oct daily 10am–6pm; £2/€2.54; Heritage Card) offers little to see beyond its simple, sturdy structure, although the tour is worth taking since the guides are instructive and entertaining. Here, too is a small **wine museum** (10am–6pm; £1.50/€1.90) which details the history of the "wine geese", those families that fled Ireland after both the Battle of Kinsale in 1601 and also those who left after the departure of James II in 1690, and who went on to establish vineyards and wine trading routes around the world. Nearby **St Multose Church** has traces of a medieval structure, and in the church porch are the town stocks dating back to the eighteenth century.

Around the harbour

Beyond the town's centre, situated on the hummocky fist of land that curls into Kinsale Harbour, **James Fort** (1601) is fun to clamber over, and during the summer you can take a ferry out to it from the *Trident Hotel* marina, a short walk west of town (summer only: every hour; 5min, £1/€1.27 each way).

Better preserved is **Charles' Fort** (1677), two miles out of town at **SUMMERCOVE** (mid-April to mid-June & mid-Sept to mid-Oct Mon–Sat 9am–5pm, Sun 9.30am–5.30pm; mid-June to mid-Sept daily 9am–6pm; £2/€2.54; Heritage Card). There's a very pleasant walk out here from Kinsale that takes you alongside the harbour: to find it, follow the minor coast road east for a quarter of a mile to *The Spaniards* pub at Scilly, and look out for a path down towards the sea. The outer walls of Charles' Fort, barely touched by weather or gunfire, seem pretty innocuous, but they conceal a formidable war machine. Within is an awesome system of barracks, ramparts and bastions, impressive testimony to the complexity and precision of seventeenth-century military science. The barracks were occupied until 1922, when the British left and handed the fort over to the Irish government. Today they remain largely intact, with only the barracks' missing roofs to give the place an eerily deserted feel.

The Bulman pub at Summercove serves very good **barfood** and makes the ideal place to recharge the batteries before making the pleasant stroll back into town.

Arrival, information and accommodation

The **tourist office** is next to the bus depot and cinema in the centre of town (July & Aug Mon–Sat 9am–7pm, Sun 10am–6pm; Sept–June Mon–Sat 9.15am–1pm & 2.15–5.30pm; ☎021/477 2234); when it's closed, tourist information is readily available at Peter Barry's, opposite *The Spaniards* pub in Scilly, on the eastern coast road out of town. There are numerous ways to get out onto the water at Kinsale and the tourist office can give you plenty of information about these: Castlepark Marina Centre (see "Accommodation" below), just under two miles out of town, offers **deep-sea angling**, **scuba diving** and **harbour trips**. There's a lovely sandy beach two minutes' walk away from the centre where you can rent **wind-surfing equipment**, **dinghies** and **canoes** at very reasonable prices (contact the Outdoor Education Centre in advance ☎021/477 2896, *www.oec.ie/kinsale*). **Bike rental** is available at The Hire Shop, 18 Main St (☎021/477 4884; £8/€10.16).

There are plenty of good places to **stay** in Kinsale, but even so you're strongly advised to book ahead during July, August and the gourmet festival (see p.298). There are a couple of **hostels** to choose from: *Dempsey's Hostel* on Eastern Rd (IHH; ☎021/772124), is a reasonable option offering a very laid-back atmosphere and the benefits of being located a short walk from the centre of town. Alternatively there's *Castlepark Marina Centre* (closed Nov to mid-March; ☎021/477 4959, *maritime @indigo.ie*), about a mile and a half out of town in a beautiful location overlooking the harbour. It's clean, comfortable, well-run and offers basic cooking facilities. There's a pub, *The Dock*, next door, and a lovely sandy beach two minutes' walk away. The centre also offers deep sea angling, scuba diving and harbour trips. To get there head out of Kinsale along Pier Road, cross over the new bridge and take a sharp left; alternatively, in summer, take the ferry from the *Trident Hotel* (see above).

You can **camp** at *Dempsey's Hostel* or at Ballinspittle, seven miles southwest of Kinsale.

Guesthouses and B&Bs

Hilltop B&B, Sleaveen Heights (☎021/4772612). Comfortable modern bungalow overlooking the town and harbour. All rooms en suite, with tea and coffee, TVs and hairdryers in rooms. Two minute's walk into the centre; the B&B is signposted off the R600 to Cork. Good parking. ④.

The Lighthouse, The Rock (☎021/477 2734). Cosy B&B in a flurry of antique lace and Victorian furniture; no smoking en-suite bedrooms. A steep walk up the hill behind the museum. ⑤.

The Little Skillet B&B, 47 Main St (☎021/477 4202). Pleasant rooms above a restaurant of the same name in the centre of town. All en suite, with TVs and tea and coffee making facilities; parking nearby. ④.

Long Quay House, Long Quay (☎021/477 4563). Beautiful, creeper-clad Georgian house in the centre of town offering good quality B&B. All bedrooms have en suite facilities; many have baths. ⑤.

Old Bank House, 11 Pearse St (☎021/477 4075; *http://indigo.ie/~oldbank*). Top quality guesthouse: the lounge and drawing room are furnished with antiques, while prints and illustrations decorate the walls. Highly comfortable throughout; all bedrooms have en-suite bathrooms. Extensive breakfast menu including kippers, smoked mackerel, scrambled eggs. Quiet despite central location. ⑧.

Pier House, Pier Road (☎021/477 4475). Comfortable B&B in a good central location; some bedrooms have balconies overlooking a pleasant garden. All en suite. ④.

Seagull House, Cork Street (☎021/477 2240). A plain old-style B&B, next door to Desmond Castle. En-suite double rooms; there is one standard single room available. Closed Nov–Feb. ④.

Eating

Kinsale is a well-known **gourmet centre** – it even has a **gourmet festival** which is generally held during the first and second week in October (if you plan to stay – or eat – here, then, book well in advance) and has numerous good – and expensive –restaurants. Details can be obtained from the tourist office, but actually this quaint town is small enough to make wandering the streets and browsing the menus in the windows an attractive proposition. Kinsale also has two excellent delis: The Quay Food Co. on Market Quay stocks organic produce, Irish cheeses, coffee, preserves and olives, and *Kinsale Gourmet Store* (see below) is similarly enticing. More mundane eating options are available at the fast-food outlet opposite the tourist office and in the well-stocked supermarket on Pearse Street.

Café Kokopelli, Guardswell. Stylish, inexpensive brunch and snacks served throughout the day.

Crackpots, 3 Cork St (☎021/477 2847) A fairly informal bistro-restaurant with plenty of interesting artwork and – as the name suggests – ceramics. Varied menu that might offer fragrant Indian spiced pork, rack of lamb with mango and passion fruit sauce or a roast vegetable filo bake. Dinner from around £20/€25.70; early bird menu £15/€19.05 until 7.30pm.

Kinsale Gourmet Store, Guardswell. Deli and fishmongers with a no-nonsense café interior and one of the best places to enjoy a great range of fresh seafood – including mussels, crab, lobster and cray fish – mostly for under £10/€12.85. Open daily till 4pm.

1601, Pearse St. Unpretentious pub serving good bar food: their ploughman's lunch comes with Milleens and Cashel Blue cheeses, they do fine open crab-meat sandwiches, and in the chillier months offer warming stews.

The White House, The Glen. Excellent, inexpensive bar food such as chicken stuffed with Irish brie, and celery sauce and salmon smoked in white wine feature alongside the Irish stew.

Drinking

Kinsale has the complement of convivial **bars** that you might expect in an historic town turned tourist centre and the place is so compact that most of them are within a couple of minutes' walk of each other. *The Grey Hound*, just off Market Square, is especially appealing and has a quaint old interior which originally came from England. *The Shanakee* in nearby Market Street, *The Lord Kinsale* on Market Quay and *The Tap Tavern* on Guardswell are all worth calling in if you are looking for music. *The Spaniards* pub in Scilly, a mile away, is a welcoming bar which also has plenty of live sessions – the walk out there is a pleasant one along a minor road that dips down beside the shoreline. *Acton's Hotel*, Pier Road, usually has live jazz on Saturday evenings and Sunday lunch times; it makes sense to call into the very helpful tourist office to check out what else is on around town.

The Seven Heads Peninsula

Between Timoleague, around thirteen miles west of Kinsale, and Clonakilty, six miles further on, lies the **Seven Heads Peninsula**, a delightful area with a pretty indented shoreline and, in summer, a wonderfully balmy atmosphere. While the peninsula has none of the drama of landscapes further west, it does have a quiet, understated charm that can be quite disarming after the hectic tourism of Kinsale. It's a fine place too for birdwatching and leisurely cycling. Both the town of **Clonakilty** and the village of **Timoleague** make good bases from which to explore this part of the county; the little coastal village of **Courtmacsherry** offers a quieter option still.

Timoleague and Courtmacsherry

TIMOLEAGUE is a small village, set inland on the muddy estuary of the Ardigeen River. It is dominated by the extensive remains of a **Franciscan abbey** which was sacked in 1649. The much advertised **Castle Gardens** include a beautiful walled garden, but the ruins of Timoleague Castle itself are negligible and not worth the entrance fee. Timoleague is only a small place, but it boasts a handful of good bars, including *Charlie Madden's* and *The Mill House Bar* – you stand a good chance of finding some sort of live music in one of these at weekends – and *Dillon's*, which serves excellent food in the evenings (expect to pay from around £10/€12.70). Nearby *Lettercollum House* guesthouse and **restaurant** serves exquisite food (dinner around £24/€30.47) and offers good-quality accommodation in a spacious nineteenth-century house set in wooded grounds (☎023/46251, *www.clon.ie/letterco.html*; ④–⑤). If you want to stay in the village itself, try *Panorama B&B*, Chapel Hill (☎023/46248; ④), which offers very comfortable accommodation and excellent views. There's also good **camping** around two miles out of Timoleague along the R600 towards Clonakilty at *Sexton's Camping* (☎023/46347).

At the broad mouth of the estuary, the village of **COURTMACSHERRY** is a safe, quiet family resort. It's certainly tranquil – when asked what happens here one local reckoned "the tide comes in and the tide goes out again". That's slightly exaggerated – if you're feeling rich you can go **deep-sea angling** or **shark fishing** (Courtmacsherry Sea Angling Centre; ☎023/46427), and **horse riding** can be arranged through the pleasant, family run *Courtmacsherry Hotel* (☎023/46198; ⑨). For B&B, *Travara Lodge* (☎023/46493; ④) is a good option, or you could head a few miles south to *Sea Court* (8th June to 20th Aug; ☎023/40151 or 40218; ④; dinner £22.50/€28.57 by reservation), an eighteenth-century mansion, furnished with antiques in the tiny village of **BUTLERSTOWN**.

Clonakilty

The busy little town of **CLONAKILTY** makes a good base from which to explore the Seven Heads Peninsula and the beautiful shoreline to the south of here. The town itself is a pleasantly unassuming place, distinguished chiefly by the **traditional music** on offer in some of its bars. It is perhaps most famous as the birthplace of the Republican leader Michael Collins (see p.674) and what remains of the house he grew up in has been preserved in his memory.

Pubs and music aside (see p.300), the recently excavated Lisnagun Christian **ring fort** might appeal, especially if you have young children in tow. It's the only one in

Ireland to be reconstructed on its original site, with defensive walls, a thatched central house, souterrains, replica weapons, utensils and clothing – all of which create a vivid picture of tenth-century life. Your ticket includes entrance to a small **animal park** nearby, where you can encounter reindeer along with the more predictable chickens and rabbits (June–Sept daily 10am–5pm; £2/€2.54, children £1/€1.27). Just over a mile north of town are the remains of the Templebryan **stone circle** – four of the original nine stones still stand, along with a central white quartzite pillar; to find it head out of town up MacCurtain Hill. Michael Collins aficionados may also want to visit the memorial to the man about four miles west of town on the N71 towards Rosscarbery. Here you can see the scant remains of his home, which was burnt out by the Black and Tans in 1921.

Clonakilty makes a good base from which to explore the crazily indented coastline roundabout, which is especially enjoyable by bike. Quiet, low-lying roads follow the shore offering tranquil cycling and plenty of opportunities for birdwatching with numerous waders searching for food in the sand. Inchydoney **beach**, about two and a half miles south, is especially fine, though check that the red flag isn't flying before swimming as there can be strong currents here. Around three miles south of Inchydoney the impressive ruins of the eighteenth century Castle Freke mansion make a good focus for a walk. The surrounding demesne is varied with oak, beech and conifer woodland and walks here offer fine views over Rosscarbery Bay.

Arrival, information and accommodation

There's a **tourist office** in the town centre at 25 Ashe St (March–June & Sept to mid-Nov Mon–Sat 9.15am–1pm & 2.15–5.30pm; July & Aug daily 7am-7pm; ☎023/33226). **Camping** is available a mere 500 yards' stagger from the pubs at *Desert House*, near the shore (May–Sept; ☎023/33331); head east out of the village and turn right at the roundabout. For **bike rental** try MTM Cycles, 33 Ashe St (☎023/33584).

Recent years have seen an increase in the range of accommodation on offer in Clonakilty, particularly at the top end of the price range. B&Bs and hotels are listed below. Excellent **hostel** accommodation is available at the *Clonakilty Old Brewery Hostel*, Old Brewery Lane (IHH; ☎023/33525) in a quiet yet central location off Emmet Square; private rooms are available, along with facilities for wheelchair users.

Bay View, Old Timoleague Rd (☎023/33539). Very welcoming B&B at the east end of town. Bright and cheerful decor; all rooms en suite. ③.

Clonakilty Town House, 22 Strand Rd (☎023/35533). Very smart, very comfortable and stylish modern guesthouse; bedrooms have en-suite baths. Smoking is permitted in the lobby only. ⑤.

Nordav, Western Road (☎023/33655). Comfortable B&B in a detached house with pleasant gardens. Both standard and en-suite rooms available; some have self-catering facilities. ④.

O'Donovan's Hotel, Pearse Street (☎ & fax 023/33250, *www.iol/~odhotel*). Traditional town-centre family-run hotel, and the hub of much social activity during the summer months. Previous guests include Marconi, Parnell and Michael Collins. ⑥.

Quality Hotel and Leisure Centre, on the road towards Rosscarbery (☎023/35400, fax 35404). Modern hotel on the edge of town; facilities include leisure centre and pool. ⑦.

Wytchwood, off Emmet Square (☎023/33525). A Georgian house with a walled garden offering welcoming, comfortable and tranquil B&B right in the town centre. No smoking bedrooms; both standard and en-suite accommodation available. Cycle hire and route information. ④.

Eating, drinking and nightlife

The town has several decent **places to eat**: for inexpensive breakfasts and lunches check out *Russwurm's* deli, 38 Ashe St. *An Súgán*, 41 Wolfe Tone St, does good bar food. *Fionnuala's*, 30 Ashe St, is an inexpensive and cosy Italian restaurant, while the nearby *Druid's Table*, 12 Ashe St, offers its customers an imaginative menu of seafood, lamb and vegetarian dishes (☎023/33310; dinner from around £12/€15.24). Clonakilty is noted for its **black puddings** (a sausage made from the blood of pigs with a warm peppery flavour), and you may well find it dished up at breakfast in your hotel or B&B; if you're self-catering, and fancy giving it a go, it's well worth it – you'll be able to get some at any one of the local butchers.

Finally, there are plenty of excellent old **bars**: for music *De Barra's* on Pearse Street is probably the most popular place, with traditional or rock music more or less every night. *An Teach Beag* (behind *O'Donovan's Hotel*) has traditional music every night during July and August, and at weekends throughout the year. *O'Donovan's Hotel* hosts live bands every night during July and August – anything from rock 'n' roll and ceilidhs to ballroom dancing; look out too for their gigantic 130-year-old polyphon – a kind of proto-jukebox, which still works.

West to Skibbereen

The **coastline** west of Clonakilty is a beautiful stretch of little bays and creeks, sandy coves and tidal loughs. There are tiny lagoons here and there, isolated along the shore from the main body of the sea, providing placid contrast to the furling white ocean spray. Each place has its own special charms – **Rosscarbery**, **Glandore**, **Leap** and **Union Hall**. If you take the main N71 you're never far from these places, all lie just a couple of miles south of the main drag west – with easy access by foot as well as car.

The broad bay at **ROSSCARBERY** has lost a great deal of its ethereal beauty since the building of the ugly, modern and hideously large *Celtic Ross Hotel* (☎023/48722; ⑨; facilities include pool). Still, their Irish theme bar does serve good food. If you want to stay in more discreet surroundings, try the family-run *Curraheen Lodge* (☎023/48498) **hostel** about one mile west of here – it offers quiet camping too; to find it, turn left opposite the pleasant *Courthouse Bar*, and then take the second lane on the left. Rosscarbery's pretty village square is tucked up a lane behind the main road, and here you'll find a handful of **bars** as well as *O'Callaghan Walshe* (weekends only during the winter; ☎023/48125), an intimate **restaurant** renowned for its fresh seafood. A particularly atmospheric place to stay in the area is *Castle Salem* (☎023/48381; ③) two and a half miles away, a seventeenth-century farmhouse in an extraordinary setting of deep green rolling fields; it's signposted off the N71 after about one mile from Rosscarbery. There's plenty of history too – the house adjoins a fifteenth-century **castle**, accessible via a doorway off the main stairs, and **William Penn**, founder of Pennsylvania, is known to have stayed here.

Heading on from Rosscarbery, take the minor R597 and look out for signs to the **Drombeg stone circle**. Dating from the Bronze Age, the seventeen stones that make up this circle are particularly impressive for their fine location – overlooking fields that fall to the sea. Nearby is a **fulacht fiadh** – a cooking site from the same era, where troughs of cold water would have been heated by hot stones thrown into them from a fire. Back on the R597, about a mile before Glandore, the road passes the neat little *Meadow* **campsite** (☎028/33280), where there are laundry facilities and a wet weather room.

There's a fleeting outrageous glamour to **GLANDORE** with its turquoise-blue waters and deep-green slopes, and there can be no better way to absorb the scene than with a plate of seafood and a cool drink from *Hayes* bar overlooking the bay. Accommodation is thin on the ground, but *Bay View* is a pleasant **B&B** (☎028/33115; ②). The nearest **hostel** is the one just outside **UNION HALL**: *Maria's Schoolhouse* (IHH; ☎028/33002) is a bright and cheery place, with comfy armchairs and big log fires; excellent – but expensive – vegetarian and non-vegetarian meals are readily available, and the hostel also organizes **sea kayaking** and **bike rental**; at the time of writing, *Maria's* was up for sale, so it's worth phoning ahead to check that it's still open and offering the same facilities.

Just over a mile inland from Glandore, **LEAP**, a small village straddling the N71, is best known for *Connolly's* bar, arguably the best **live music venue** in west Cork, with a great range of bands year round: rock, reggae, traditional, bluegrass – just about anything that makes it out of Dublin will be on here. For the latest, details check out *Connolly's* Web site (*www.connollysofleap.com*). For those looking to say in the village, *Highfield* B&B is the best place to try (☎028/33273; ③).

Skibbereen and around

Cheerful **SKIBBEREEN**, smartly painted and set on the River Illen, is the main service and administrative centre for the south of west Cork. This traditional role is still remarkably alive: on Wednesdays the cattle market still operates, drawing crowds from the surrounding country, and every Friday afternoon there's the regular country market. For travellers, it's a good place to stock up or to stop over – there are plenty of supermarkets, a smattering of health-food shops and delis, and plenty of pubs.

The **West Cork Arts Centre** on North Street (Mon–Sat 10am–6pm) is worth checking out. It hosts monthly exhibitions which can be first-rate, stages occasional music and dance performances, and has a reference and slide library through which you can locate local artists. The **heritage centre**, on Upper Bridge Street (July to mid-Sept daily 10am-6pm; £3/€3.81) displays two very different exhibitions: "The Great Famine Commemorative Exhibition" offers a vivid and sobering account of the Famine of the 1840s: Skibbereen was particularly affected by the Famine and around 10,000 famine victims lie buried nearby. The second of the two exhibitions celebrates the abundant marine life of nearby Lough Hyne (see opposite) and sets out to explain the survival of a range of species – from corals, anemones and sea-squirts to goby-fish and sea slugs – this last found only here and in the Mediterranean Sea.

The **tourist office** (June–Aug Mon–Sat 9am–7pm, Sun 10am–1pm & 2.15–6pm; Sept–May Mon–Fri 9.15am–5.30pm; ☎028/21766) is on North Street and will help with accommodation. For **B&Bs** *Ilenroy House*, 10 North St(☎028/22751; ⑤) and *The Ivanhoe* (☎028/21749; ③), further along at no. 67 are a couple of comfortable, central options. There's a good IHH **hostel**, *The Russagh Mill Hostel*, a mile out on the Castletownshend Road, (closed Dec to mid-March; ☎028/22451), a beautifully renovated mill house. Mick Murphy, the hostel manager, is happy to talk to visitors about his Everest climb in 1993, and leads **hillwalking**, **canoeing** and **sail-boarding** activities most days (£8–10/€10.16–12.70 per day).

You can get **Bus Éireann** information from O'Cahalanes in Bridge Street, and **rent bikes** from N.W. Roycroft and Son in Ilen Street (☎028/21235; £7.50/€9.52).

There are a handful of decent places to **eat** in town: *Yin Yang*, 12 Bridge St, is a wholefood shop and café that serves tasty, nutritious and cheap lunches, soups and teas; you can tuck into good budget meals at *The Stove* café on Main Street, and *Bernard's* on the same street serves good pub food (till 9pm). *Kalbo's Bistro*, 48 North St (☎028/21515), has an informal café atmosphere and is something of a favourite, offering inexpensive filled pittas and home-cooked lunches and a moderately priced, varied and enticing evening menu. There's no shortage of bars: *Baby Hannah's*, 42 Bridge St, is a lively young place and occasionally has rock music; for traditional music there's *Sheehy's* on the square, or you might try *The Corner Bar*, 37 Bridge St.

Castletownsend and Creagh Gardens

Around five miles southeast of Skibbereen at the end of the R596 lies **CASTLETOWNSEND**, a delightful little village worth making a quick detour to see. The village clings to a steep lane, a tree in the middle of the road sending what traffic there is gingerly either side, and ends abruptly at a tiny stone quay. It's an eerie, twee place, and appropriately enough was once the home of Edith Somerville of Somerville & Ross fame, authors of the *Irish RM* stories. Their graves are to be found in St Barrahane's churchyard. There's little else to see here, but there is good seafood on the bar menu at *Mary Ann's*, an attractive little pub worth seeking out. Less than four miles southwest of Skibbereen along the Baltimore Road, the **Creagh Gardens** (March–Oct 10am–6pm; £3/€3.81) are a delightful place to unwind. They are ostensibly traditional – with woodland glades, lawns running down to the estuary and a Regency walled kitchen garden – but the late owner's desire to create a garden based on the richness of tone and colour found in Rousseau's jungle paintings was less conventional and is achieved here by a dense, textured build-up of lush vegetation and exotic palms. If you head back a little way up the road and take the turning on your right, you'll soon find **Lough Hyne** (pronounced *Ine*), a land-locked salt lake, linked to the ocean only by a very slender channel down which the receding tide returns to the sea. The lough, surrounded by hillsides dripping with lush, moist greenery, is a unique phenomenon, of great interest to marine biologists (see Skibbereen heritage centre, opposite). From the head of the lake steep slopes, easily climbed, rise to panoramic views: eastwards along the coast to Kinsale, west across the length of the Mizen Peninsula, and out across to Sherkin and Clear islands.

Baltimore and the islands

The approach to **Baltimore** takes you through a landscape that is disarmingly low-key. Instead of some dramatic climax at this, the most southerly point of all Ireland, the land seems simply to be fading away: rocky terrain and scrawny vegetation accompany the windy, listless estuary, untidy with lumps of land that seem to have been tossed at random towards the sea. The whole ragged effect is as if the country is running out of substance; the landmass, already moth-bitten, is now fraying, too. But as the ocean comes into full view this tailing off is put into spectacular context: the whole weight of Ireland is behind you, while ahead are dots, wracks and scraps of islands, petering out across the great open expanse of water to **Sherkin and Clear islands**.

Baltimore

For all the development of holiday homes jostling around **BALTIMORE**, the quayside at the heart of the place still retains the engaging bustle and spirit of an old fishing harbour, the sixteenth-century O'Driscoll stronghold visible above the new houses. Combining traditional fishing activities with tourism, Baltimore makes a good base from which to explore this part of the coast. It's popular too with the yachting crowd and the port is particularly busy during the **regatta** held on the last two weeks in July and the first weekend in August. Baltimore also serves as the departure point for **ferries** to **Sherkin** and **Clear islands**, as well as **Schull** on the Mizen Peninsula (p.307).

Arrival and information

There's a **tourist information hut** down by the quay (May–Aug Tues–Thurs, Sat & Sun 1–5pm). As well as the scheduled Bus Éireann, there is a private service that operates from the harbour to Skibbereen at around 10–10.30am – check the exact schedule locally. For **changing money**, *Declan McCarthy's* by the harbour has a bureau de change; and if you've arrived under sail and are looking for **showers**, these are available at *Bushe's Bar* nearby. Information about ferry schedules are posted up around the harbour and is also available from the **ferry companies** (for Baltimore–Sherkin Island

☎028/20125; Schull–Sherkin Island ☎028/28138; Baltimore–Clear Island ☎028/39153; Clear Island–Schull ☎028/28278; most routes cost £6/€7.62 one-way, £9/€11.43 return; trips to Sherkin Island cost £4/€5.08 one-way, £8/€10.16 return).

Accommodation

Baltimore is a small and attractive place **to stay**, so that, while there is a good range of accommodation on offer, it is nevertheless advisable to book in advance if you want to stay during July and August or over bank holiday weekends. Hotels and B&Bs are listed below. *Rolf's* **hostel** is signposted to the left off the main road as you head into Baltimore, around half a mile after *Casey's Hotel* (IHH; ☎028/20289; twin rooms £12.50/€15.87, family rooms £35/€44.44). It's something of a favourite with its cosy cottage atmosphere; dorms are basic, but twin, four-bedded and family rooms are top-notch. *Rolf's* also offers **bike rental** (£8/€10.16 per day), laundry facilities and Internet access.

Baltimore Bay (☎028/20600) Good quality guesthouse accommodation right by the harbour, with weekend special deals available. ⑤.

The Baltimore Harbour Hotel (☎028/20361, *info@bhrhotel.ie*). Comfortable, modern hotel overlooking pleasant gardens and the bay. All rooms have en-suite bathrooms and TVs; self-catering suites are also available. Facilities include a pool, gym and steam room. Good discounts for midweek and weekend breaks. ⑦.

Bushe's Bar (☎028/20125) Comfortable, simple accommodation. Some rooms overlook the harbour, and all have en-suite baths and TVs. A continental self-service breakfast is provided in the bedrooms. Rooms at the front are more expensive. ② & ③.

Casey's Hotel, About a mile from the harbour on the main road out to Skibbereen (☎028/20197, *caseys@eircom.net*) A tremendous small, family-run hotel: the comfortable rooms are decorated with original artwork; all come with en-suite baths, TV, radio, and tea- and coffee-making facilities. The very pleasant residents' lounge affords views over a tranquil inlet. Lively bar and very good seafood restaurant. ⑦.

Channel View (☎028/20440) Comfortable B&B accommodation in a spacious bungalow overlooking the bay. Standard and en-suite rooms available. ③ & ④.

Fastnet House B&B (☎028/20515) The house was built in 1820 and the new owners have set about renovating it in an attractive rustic style, complete with stripped floors, open fires and bare-stone walls. Comfortable B&B accommodation; all rooms have en-suite facilites. Closed Nov–Feb. ④.

Eating, drinking and entertainment

For its size, Baltimore offers a very good range of places to **eat**, and you can expect the quality to be high. For excellent barfood there's *Bushe's Bar*, by the harbour, and *Casey's* about a mile out on the main road; the latter also has an excellent restaurant noted for its seafood (dinner around £25/€31.74). *Café Art* (☎028/20289; closed Oct–March), alongside *Rolf*s hostel, encourages relaxed dining: tasty pastas, Mediterranean salads, stir frys and similar fare are on offer, and no one minds if you sit down for a full meal or take just one course; the garden is an especially nice place to eat in fine weather. *La Jolie Brise*, right down by the harbour, is a café serving inexpensive breakfasts, excellent pizzas and Sherkin Island oysters. The Australian-run *Customs House Restaurant* (☎028/20200) specializes in seafood and organic produce and has an excellent reputation.

Baltimore has a lively **pub scene** during the summer: *Declan McCarthy's* and, again, *Bushe's Bar* are a couple of lively spots overlooking the harbour; *McCarthy's* hosts traditional, folk and ballad sessions several nights a week in summer. Around a mile from the quays, and well worth considering if you are staying up that end of town, is *Casey's*, a cosy characterful place with traditional music on Saturdays and during the summer on Sundays, too.

Sherkin Island

Tiny **Sherkin Island** is a delightfully pretty place: the considerable remains of a fifteenth-century Franciscan friary nestle down by the quayside, and little fuchsia-spattered lanes lead across the island to fine sandy beaches in the west. There are the remains of an O'Driscoll stronghold, too, and the annual O'Driscoll clan gathering in June is a hectic five-day event spread between Sherkin Island, Clear Island and Baltimore.

The place can get busy with day-trippers on bank holidays and during July and August. If you want to stay you can get **B&B** at *Cuina House* (☎028/20384; ③) and *Island House* (☎028/20314; ②) – both closed in winter. If these are full, it's worth asking at the *Jolly Roger* **pub** for alternatives. The *Jolly Roger* does **bar food** during the summer: at other times you can buy supplies at the post office.

Clear Island

Clear Island (*Oileán Chléire*), also known as Cape Clear, offers rather more to do, and it would be worth visiting for the ferry trip alone, though it can be a topsy-turvy, stomach-churning ride. There's an important ornithology station here, and on the 45-minute boat ride out to the island, it becomes obvious that the place is paradise for **wildlife** enthusiasts: the bay is alive with seabirds – guillemots, cormorants, auks and storm petrels – and with luck you may see seals and, in warm weather, basking sharks. With even more luck you might find your boat raced by a playful dolphin or two, dodging around the bows and leaping out of the ocean to crash back down right alongside the ferry.

The hilly, rocky island seems to have been pinched in the middle where two inlets, **North Harbour** and **South Harbour**, almost meet. In the south, steep and inaccessible cliffs rise from the water; the North Harbour is perfectly sheltered. Roads climb up from here through hills covered in the coarse grass that seems to spread over everything, including old walls and houses long derelict. Sea pinks cling to rocky outcrops, and honeysuckle clambers wherever it can. The island's high points give spectacular views back across the archipelago to the mainland.

The **bird observatory** at North Harbour has been here since 1959 and has complete records going back to that time. When it was set up, by an amateur group, this station was a pioneer of the constant observation of seabirds, and its work has done much for the knowledge of migratory patterns. Clear Island is one of the most important places for seabirds in Ireland, including some genuine rarities – especially plentiful are storm petrels, shearwaters, black guillemots and choughs. If you are new to birdwatching, but fancy learning more, call in at the observatory and see what's happening, though bear in mind that late spring, August and October are the best times for birdwatching.

Clear Island is also an isolated remnant of the **Gaeltacht** and Irish is still spoken by about one hundred and thirty islanders. During the summer, Irish youngsters are sent here to practise the language and each October the island holds a traditional **festival** of drama, music, art and dance, the *Féile Shamhna Chléire* (call ☎028/39153 for details). The island also prides itself on being the birthplace of **St Kieran**, who supposedly preceded St Patrick by thirty years, but the holy well and stone that are attributed to him stand in a sadly unromantic spot by the road at North Harbour. By far the best of Clear Island's historic ruins is **Dún an Óir** ("Fort of Gold"), an O'Driscoll fort, impressive on a high, narrow splinter of rock which is now an island at high tide – sadly inaccessible, though you can see it as you walk down the hill from the heritage centre, or from the 200ft cliffs to the south. The **heritage centre** (June–Aug daily 2–5.30pm; £1.50/€1.90), a steep, one-mile walk from North Harbour (follow the sign for the church), is a tiny museum of the whole domestic, fishing and seafaring history of the island.

If you intend **to stay** anytime between July and October, you would be advised to arrange accommodation before sailing. There are a number of **B&Bs**: *Cluain Mara*, North Harbour (☎028/39153; ③) is good value and run by a friendly family; alternatively, you might try *Ard na Gaoithe*, the Glen, up the steep laneway behind the youth hostel (☎028/39160; ③), or, beyond here, *Fáilte*, at Glen East, up by the lighthouse (☎028/39135; ③). The An Óige **hostel** at South Harbour (closed Dec–Feb; ☎028/39198) is fairly basic, but the staff are friendly and it does offers kayaking (£7/€8.89), archery (£6/€7.62) and snorkelling (£5/€6.35). Finally, there is **self-catering accommodation** at the bird observatory (book in advance, ☎028/39181, *stevewing@eircom.com*; £9/€3.17), though this is likely to be full in late spring and in August and October. In summer, **camping** is available a short walk from the ferry terminal; if you bring food over from the mainland, bear in mind that the island has difficulties in dealing with refuse, so avoiding bringing (and leaving) glass and plastic containers is helpful.

The island has three **pubs** within five minutes' walk of each other: *The Club*, beside North Harbour, where you may well find music in the summer months, *The Night Jar*, a short walk from here, and *Ciaran Danny Mike's*, just at the brow of the hill overlooking South harbour, which serves very good home-cooked **meals** and has a **restaurant** alongside. *An siopa beag* beside North Harbour is the island's one grocery store; inside is a **coffee bar** serving drinks, filled rolls and, in the evenings, takeaway pizzas.

Mizen Head

The Mizen Head Peninsula is a beautiful, remote finger of land poking its way west, offering superb sandy beaches and cliff scenery, getting wilder the further west you go. It's an area rich in **archeological sites**, from Bronze Age wedge graves contemporary with the first copper mining of Mount Gabriel, through Iron Age and early Christian ring forts, down to medieval castles – pick up a copy of the leaflet *Antiquities of the Mizen Peninsula* from the tourist office in Cork city if you want to locate these sites. Finally, while out exploring, be aware that great care should be taken at the **Mizen cliffs**, as the land ends abruptly and without warning.

The most spectacular scenery along this stretch of coast is at **Mizen Head** itself – sheer, vertiginous cliffs, with an offshore lighthouse linked by a little suspension bridge, and accessible if you visit the Mizen Vision **heritage centre** (mid-March to May & Oct daily 10.30am–5pm; June–Sept daily 10am–6pm; £2.50/€3.17). Standing at this exhilarating spot it takes little effort to imagine the great number of ships that have been wrecked in Dunlough Bay to the north. A walk round to **Three Castles Head** brings in sight the curtain wall and two turrets of an O'Mahoney stronghold, one of twelve that were built along this peninsula in the fifteenth century. The setting makes this one truly spectacular. The whole of the peninsula's wild and empty northern coast, in fact, is one of sheer cliffs and stupendous views – an impossible route for hitching, but great for those with transport.

The south coast of the peninsula is more travelled, with small towns at **Ballydehob**, **Schull** and **Crookhaven**, and lovely sandy **beaches**. The best of these is the long and sandy strand at **Barley Cove**, whose rolling breakers make it a favourite with **surfers**. Highland and Harbour offer **pony trekking** through this wild, beautiful countryside (☎028/35416). The only public transport along the peninsula is run by Bus Éireann as far as Goleen.

Ballydehob

BALLYDEHOB, a small town of brightly coloured streets at the neck of the peninsula, was once known as the hippie capital of the west because it was said to have more "blow-ins" than locals. Heavily colonized in the 1960s, it still has traces of their influence, like health-food shops and resident artists, and remains a liberal place compared to others of its size. For all this, it's a sleepy town with just a handful of craft and antique shops worth exploring and a large number of pubs.

If you want **to stay**, try the pleasant *Dun an Oir* (☎028/37272; ③) or *The Old Crossing* (☎028/37148; ③), which enjoys fantastic views of the surrounding countryside – follow the lane alongside *Levi's* bar on Main Street to find it. There's a **campsite** just a couple of hundred yards down the road towards Durrus, and a **laundry** in the centre of the town. *Annie's Restaurant* (closed Sun & Mon; ☎028/37292; £23/€29.20 for dinner), on Main Street, is renowned for its seafood, and the same people serve lunches during the day at *The Bookshop Café* on Main Street. Interesting old **bars** include *Levi's*, a bar-grocery store opposite *Annie's*, and *O'Sullivan's*, a few doors up from *Annie's*.

Ballydehob's nearest **beach** is three miles away at Audley Cove: a secluded pebbly cove, with lovely views of the islands.

Schull and beyond

SCHULL, as well as being the place from which to catch the ferry for Clear Island, Baltimore and Sherkin Island (see p.305), is perhaps the most obvious place to stay on the peninsula, an attractive seaside market town with plenty of cheery amenities aimed at holidaying families and the yachting fraternity. Schull's sheltered, bulb-shaped harbour looks out over Carbery's Hundred Islands, while **Mount Gabriel** rises to 1339ft to the north, offering wonderful views. To make this walk from Schull (9 miles there and back) head up Gap Road past the convent and you'll find a clear track all the way. From the top you can continue around the north side of the mountain, to return through Rathcool and Glaun. The domes at the summit of Mount Gabriel are aircraft-tracking stations. As you walk, beware of unguarded mine shafts: this rough and rocky land was heavily mined for copper in the nineteenth century, and is still dotted with Cornish-style mining chimneys.

Schull is at its liveliest during its **sailing events**. The international sailing festival for children is usually held the second week in July, when the town is awash with nautical teenagers, and the yachting set proper swamp the town for the regatta held in Calves week (following the August bank holiday weekend, usually the first week of the month). At these times accommodation can be difficult, and phoning ahead is advisable.

Practicalities

There are a couple of inexpensive **B&Bs** on Main Street: *O'Regan's* (☎028/28334; ②) and *Adele's* (☎028/28459; ③), and *Stanley House*, about half a mile north of the village, offers comfortable and welcoming B&B (☎028/28425; ③). Five minutes' walk from the village centre is *Schull's Backpackers' Lodge* (IHH; ☎028/28681), an attractive wooden **hostel** surrounded by trees, where you can also **camp**. **Ferries** run from Schull to Baltimore, Sherkin and Clear Island (see p.303) and Karycraft operates **cruises** around the Fastnet Rock (July & Aug Wed 7pm; June & Sept by arrangement, call ☎028/28138 or 28278; 2hr 30min; £10/€12.70). If you fancy taking to the water yourself, contact Schull Watersports Centre, The Pier (☎028/28554), who organizes **sea-angling trips**, **dinghy rental**, **wind-surfing** and, for the experienced only, **diving. Horse riding** can be arranged with *The Colla House Hotel* on Colla Road (☎028/28105). **Bike rental** is available from Cotter's Yard on Main Street (☎028/28165).

As for **eating**, *Adele's Coffee Shop* in Main Street does very good and moderately priced homemade lunches and evening meals, and also has an excellent – though expensive – bakery. *The Courtyard*, on Main Street, serves tasty, inexpensive lunches and has a good deli selling fresh bread from its brick-built steam oven, as well as local cheeses, oils and pickles. You can get superior fish and chips at *George's Grapevine*, Main Street, and very good **bar food** at the *Bunratty Inn*. For a wholly memorable meal, make a reservation at *Island Cottage*, Heir Island (closed Mon & Tues; ☎028/38102; set menu only; meals for around £19/€24.16), a delightful cottage restaurant specializing in duck, lamb and fish accessed by small boat.

Schull's pubs have **music** year round – look out for posters around town, or check out *The Courtyard, The Bunratty Inn, The Galley* or *Arundel's*. If you just want a relaxing pint, try *Hackett's*. The town also has a **bank**, and Fuschia Books on Main Street (secondhand only) is good place to while away a rainy afternoon.

Goleen and Crookhaven

South of Schull, and beyond the settlement of Toormore, is **GOLEEN**. Here, you'll find the delightful upmarket **restaurant** and **B&B**, *Heron's Cove* (☎028/35225; ④), where if you don't want a full meal you can still enjoy chowder, cakes and creek life. Beyond lies **CROOKHAVEN**, the nearest resort to Barley Cove with a large caravan and **camping park** on the Goleen–Crookhaven road; unless you want the facilities, though, there is no real need to use this – there are plenty of remote spots where you can pitch a tent for free.

Sheep's Head

The peninsula north of Mizen, **Sheep's Head**, has an ancient feel to it: barren land almost entirely devoid of people. There are only a couple of tiny villages here, and traffic is sparse – the sole weekly bus runs on Saturday – so don't try to hitch if you're going to need to return in a hurry. It's an ever-changing landscape, where surges of harsh granite rise from sweet green fields, fuchsias and honeysuckle scramble over greystone walls, gorse and heather colour wild heathland, and at every twist of the road plantlife, rock and water fall together to describe some new magic ideal. Whichever way you head down to the Sheep's Head, the scenery is superb. The north coast looks down on the magnificent Bantry Bay, backed by the wild Caha Mountains and offers cyclists a wonderful descent towards Bantry. There are also fabulous panoramic views over County Cork, the Beara Peninsula, and County Kerry from the top of **Seefin**, Sheep's Head's highest hill (1136ft). All of this can now be enjoyed by walking the **Sheep's Head Way** a 55-mile circuit of the peninsula; it's relatively easy walking, clearly signposted, and marked on the Discovery Series OS map number 88.

DURRUS, little more than a handful of pubs and shops at the head of the peninsula, is the largest village here. If you want to stay, try the pleasant **B&B** at *Avoca House* (☎027/61511; ③); the *Long Boat Bar* nearby serves inexpensive **meals**. *Dunbeacon* **campsite** (☎027/61246; wet-weather hut), is three miles back down the road towards Crookhaven, and is a relaxing, low-key affair. Midway down Sheep's Head, minuscule **AHAKISTA** has a narrow slip of sandy beach backed by a showering of trees. *The Ahakista Bar* serves soup and sandwiches and has a gorgeous lush beer garden that runs down to the water's edge. For directions to the only place selling **basic provisions**, ask at the bar. One and a half miles beyond the Ahakista is *Reenmore* **B&B** (☎027/67051; ③). At **KILCROHANE**, three and a half miles southeast of Ahakista, there's a **post office**, a **bar** serving sandwiches, and basic **accommodation** at *Carbery View Hostel* (☎027/67035). A summer **café** with erratic opening times can be found right at the end of the peninsula.

Bantry

The beauty of **BANTRY** is its setting at the head of ever-turbulent Bantry Bay, which stretches thirty miles from the town to the ocean. The deep, churning blue waters of the bay, backed by the dramatic heights of the Beara's Caha Mountains and cowering, usually, under a notoriously changeable sky, form as dramatic a backdrop as any in Ireland. If the tide's out, it's well worth taking a short stroll along the stony shore from the north end of the harbour to fully appreciate all of this. Alternatively, take the steep road that runs up to Vaughan's Pass from the back of the town, as this also affords spectacular views over the bay.

Some history

For centuries **Bantry Bay** attracted attempts from abroad to overthrow English rule. Once inside its shelter, ships were protected from attack by the rugged mountains of the peninsulas on either side. In 1689, a French fleet sailed up the bay to assist James II, but was forced to return after an indecisive battle with Williamite forces. A century later, in 1796, **Wolfe Tone** arrived with another French fleet – and this time with revolutionary ideals – to try to overthrow the Protestant Anglo-Irish. Channel storms, however, had already reduced the fleet from 43 ships to sixteen by the time it arrived, and the remaining vessels spent six days in the bay unable to land, even though, as Tone said, "we were close enough to toss a biscuit on shore". After this failure they were forced to turn back. Richard White, a local landowner, was rewarded for his loyalty to the English Crown at the time of the invasion by being made Baron Bantry. **Bantry House** (1739) still belongs to the same family and constitutes a major reason to visit the town. Along with its fabulous interior (see p.310), there's some irony that it also houses the 1796 French Armada Exhibition so that you can ponder the exhilarating ideals of revolution in the lavish, aristocratic setting that Tone would have swept away had the venture been successful.

Arrival, information and accommodation

Bus Éireann **buses**, connecting with Cork, Skibbereen, Glengarriff, Killarney and the Mizen Head Peninsula, leave from outside *Murphy's Bar* (information inside)on the quays. Private buses leave from Wolfe Tone Square (usually just referred to as The Square). This building also houses the **tourist office** (May–Sept Mon–Sat 9.15am–5.30pm, Sun 10am–1pm & 2.15–6pm; ☎027/50229). **Bike rental** is available at Kramer's, Glengarriff Road (☎027/50278; £8/€10.16).

There's a good, if small, range of **accommodation** in Bantry and the surrounding area and it's advisable to book ahead during July, August and during the classical music festival generally held at the end of June. The **hostel**, *Bantry Independent Hostel*, is on Bishop Lucey Place (IHH; ☎027/51050), a short signposted walk from The Square. It's a friendly, welcoming hostel with a big garden and the kind of atmosphere that makes you want to linger; children are welcome. **Camping** is also available at the hostel, along with Internet access, and a laundry service. Camping is also available at Ballylickey, four miles from Bantry along the road towards Glengarriff: *Eagle Point Caravan and Camping Park* (closed Oct–April; ☎027/50630) is a superbly situated site right on the edge of the bay; you can swim from their pebbly beach and there are excellent wild mountain walks roundabout. It's well worth calling in at Manning's Emporium nearby, an excellent deli with a huge range of Irish cheeses.

Bantry House (☎027/50047, *www.hidden-ireland.com/bantry*). One of the finest stately mansions in Ireland in a superb loation overlooking the bay, yet still a family home. The interior is furnished with antiques and works of art, and musical concerts are often held here. Dinner is available (enquire when booking). Closed Nov–Feb. ⑨.

Blackrock House B&B, 1 Blackrock Terrace (☎027/50432, *www.cork-guide.ie/blackroc.htm*) A mid-nineteenth century house with an elegant, antique-filled dining room offering rooms with en-suite showers – some also with en-suite baths. Excellent location on a quiet lane in the town centre. ④.

Dunauley, Seskin (☎027/50290). Located just under a mile out along the steep road towards Vaughan's Pass, this very comfortable and welcoming B&B offers some of the most spectacular views in Cork. The excellent breakfast menu includes smoked salmon and scrambled eggs, stewed fruits and Irish cheeses. Rooms with views are slightly more expensive than those without, but are well worth the extra money. ④.

The Mill, Newtown (☎027/50278). Half a mile along the Glengarriff road, this spacious bungalow is comfortably furnished, with stripped pine floors and every inch of wall covered with vibrant paintings; all bedrooms are en suite and non-smoking. Closed Nov–March. ④.

Sunville (☎027/50175) Modern bungalow B&B about half a mile out on the road towards Glengarriff. Standard and en-suite rooms available; non-smoking bedrooms. Closed Nov–March. ③.

Westlodge Hotel (☎027/50360, *www.westlodgehotel.ie*). *Westlodge* was purpose built and opened in 1970 with over 100 bedrooms. The majority of its rooms have en-suite baths and all have TVs, radios and tea- and coffee-making facilities. The high season rates are expensive for the standard, though there is a leisure centre, with pool, tennis and squash courts are the major draw. The hotel is located about a mile out of town on the southbound N71. ⑧.

The Town

Bantry sits around a long square focused at the head of the bay, distinguished by a pretty Regency Gothic church, a statue of St Brendan staring out to sea, and a rather refined one of Wolfe Tone further inland. In the immediate surrounds are lush wooded slopes – a safe haven indulged between the ravages of the sea and the wilds of the rocky mountains. The **Sheep's Head Way** starts here, passing through the grounds of Bantry House before heading west for the low hills of the Sheep's Head Peninsula (see p.308). The town itself is the chief fishing port and commercial centre for the area, and the traditional market is held on the first Friday of every month.

Bantry House (March–Oct daily 9am–6pm; house, armada exhibition and gardens £6/€7.62, gardens only £2/€2.54), nowadays provides an elegant vision of the rarefied life led by the Anglo-Irish aristocracy. Sumptuously decorated and packed with art treasures, it deserves some time. Much of the furniture is French Napoleonic, and there are Gobelin tapestries and Aubusson carpets; but what makes this house such a gem is the sheer variety of artefacts that have been collected, many of them during the second earl's European wanderings in the nineteenth century. The setting is superb: ordered landscaped gardens look down over the bay, calmly asserting the harmony of the aristocratic order, unruffled by the ruggedness of the surroundings. **The Bantry 1796 French Armada Exhibition Centre** (June–Aug daily 11am–4pm; this may change and it is advisable to phone ahead or check with the tourist office; ☎027/51796), housed in one of the courtyards, gives a blow-by-blow account of Wolfe Tone's failed mission. You can see artefacts recovered from the wreck of the frigate *La Surveillante*, scuttled on Whiddy Island in 1797 and excavated in 1982.

Another aspect of the past is remembered with relish by the ladies who run the **Bantry Museum**, behind the fire station on Wolfe Tone Square (June–Aug Tues & Thurs 10am–1pm, Wed & Fri 2–5pm; 50p/€0.68). The museum is the collection of the local history society – domestic paraphernalia, old newspapers and everyday trivia of every sort – which the curators willingly demonstrate with an entertaining blend of history and gossip. The modern library, at the top of Bridge Street, was built in 1974 and, at first glance, looks like some sort of spaceship, though the design was in fact inspired by a prehistoric dolmen: as adventurous a piece of public architecture as you'll find in the west of Ireland, it's let down by a white facade that already seems thoroughly tacky.

One final thing worth going out of your way to see is the fine, early Christian **Kilnaruane Pillar Stone** just out of town. Its worn carvings depict four men rowing, an apostle and the cross; two of the men are thought to represent SS Paul and Anthony, and the boat is considered to be an early representation of a currach. Follow the main road south out of town and take the first turning on the left past *The Westlodge Hotel*: the stone is in a field 500 yards further on the right.

Eating, drinking and entertainment

There are just a handful of decent places to **eat** in Bantry and it has to be said that if the weather's fine and the tide's out, getting together a picnic and heading out around the northern shoreline is a good option. This aside, *The Snug* on the square serves excellent cheap **bar food** (last orders 8.30pm daily); *The Pantry Bistro* (☎027/52181) on New Street, above a butcher's shop and opposite the supermarket, has a welcoming, informal atmosphere and a good spot for a varied menu that might include pasta, burritos and salads during the day and moderately priced Mediterranean-style meals in the evening. *Ó S'ocháin*, in Bridge Street, is a cheery café serving hearty lunches and seafood platters and *The Brick Oven*, on the square, is a café serving pizza, pasta and steaks. For more upmarket evening meals in a comfortable and relaxed setting you might try the French and Italian food at *Claret's Bistro* (☎027/52187) on the corner of Barrack and Marino streets.

Regular **pubs** are plentiful: *The Anchor Bar* is a convivial place to start, with a good, friendly mix of locals and visitors. Bantry is a small town, and entertainment is a matter of getting involved in whatever's going on. You're as likely to enjoy a handful of **rock music** or **ballad** sessions in the bars as anything else: try *The Anchor Bar*, *The Bantry Bay* or *Vickery's Inn*, New Street, a rather low key bar, but with folk or traditional music on a Monday night. *Bantry House* hosts the **West Cork Chamber Music Festival**, a ten day classical music festival usually held during the last week in June (☎027/52788, *www.westcorkmusic.ie*), a great time to be in town; along with the full programme of events at Bantry House there are classical fringe events in *Vickery's Inn*, serving as a platform for young musicians, and there's a literary fringe too with readings by Irish writers. Finally, Bantry's **mussel festival** over the second weekend in May brings with it music, late bars and plenty of seafood.

BOWLING

One local sport worth looking out for is **bowling**, a game peculiar to west Cork and played around Bantry on Sundays. A 28oz iron ball is thrown along country roads, and the winner of the game is the person who moves the ball over a prescribed distance (usually two and a half miles) with the fewest throws. Undoubtedly, a fair amount of betting goes on too. If you come across handfuls of grass that have been dropped along a lane at intervals, it generally means a game has been or is being played along that route – clumps of grass are used as markers.

Glengarriff and the mountains

Whichever way you travel out of Bantry, the scenery is magnificent. Heading east, the road to Dunmanway and its fine independent hostel (p.295) takes you through fabulous empty mountains, while the Pass of Keimaneigh further north leads through a steep, rocky ravine up to Ballingeary, **Gougane Barra** and a corrie lake, the source of the River Lee. An island on this lake was the site of St Finbarr's hermitage before he founded his monastery at Cork city downstream. The remains on the island are, however, eighteenth century. It's an area famous for its beauty, popular for day-trips, and there's a bar that does teas and sandwiches beside the lake. Gougane Barra also has a forest park with nature trails (£2/€2.54).

Glengarriff

Around nine miles north on the main road from Bantry and cradled between the Caha Mountains and Bantry Bay, **GLENGARRIFF** is an oasis of greenery. South-facing and sheltered by rugged mountains, it has a peculiarly gentle climate; oak and holly woodlands hug the shoreline while occasional palms flourish in hotel gardens. This picturesque juxtaposition has been exploited since the nineteenth century, when sensitive Victorians became alerted to the beneficial effects of the uniquely mild atmosphere in this pocket of lushness. Unfortunately, recent exploitation has resulted in a barrage of billboarding; ads for gift shops and boat trips have destroyed virtually all of the village's former character.

Yet, despite the commercialism, Glengarriff is a great place to stay if you want to explore some of Cork's and Kerry's wildest and most beautiful countryside. The surrounding mountains are wonderfully rugged; huge areas of barren rock show odd patches of scrawny, rough vegetation, and then the occasional seam of brilliant deciduous woods. There is a real exhilaration up here as you watch the constantly changing patterns of weather over the mountains and the bay, with squalls of rain and pools of sunlight bowling across the landscape. Pick up a leaflet of suggested walks at the **tourist office** (June–Aug Mon–Sat 10am–1pm & 2.15–6pm; ☎027/63084) in the main street. They will also help with accommodation. Comfortable **B&Bs** include *Conimar* (☎027/63405; ③) and *Rockwood House* (☎027/63097; ④). For traditional hotel accommodation try *Casey's* (☎027/63010; ⑤) in the centre of the town. *Murphy's* (IHH; ☎027/63555) is a central, well-run and cheerful **hostel**; if this is full, the tiny *Hummingbird Rest Hostel* (☎027/63195), about half a mile along the road towards Kenmare, is a reasonable alternative. You can camp here, too, or at *O'Shea's* **campsite** (closed mid-Oct to mid-March; ☎027/63140), a beautiful little site, about a mile out of Glengarriff on the Castletownbere Road (R572).

Places to eat are limited. Your best bets are the bars at *Casey's Hotel* and *The Eccles Hotel* or the café at *Murphy's Hostel* (closed Oct–April), which serves good-value wholesome lunches and snacks. Glengarriff's **bars** are very lively during July and August; there's usually music at *The Blue Loo*, *Bernard Harrington's* or *Johnny Barry's*.

Garinish Island

Walking down the street in Glengarriff you'll inevitably be hassled sooner or later by a stage-Irish boatman trying to sell you a ticket for **Garinish Island**. The island trip is quite something, although massively overpriced. In 1910, the owner of Garinish conceived a plan to turn his island – then bare rock – into a floating oasis of exotic plantlife. All the topsoil had to be imported and the resultant growth delicately nurtured for years. The end product is undeniably impressive: flowers and shrubs from all over the world flourish here, and through much of the year the place is ablaze with colour, in vibrant contrast to the desolate mountains of the Beara a stone's throw across the water. If you decide to take the ten-minute trip out there past basking seals, be warned that the price you pay the boatmen (£5/€6.35) does not include **admission to the island** (March & Oct Mon–Sat 10am–6.30pm; April–June & Sept Mon–Sat 10am–6.30pm, Sun 1–7pm; July & Aug Mon–Sat 9.30am–6.30pm, Sun 11am–7pm; £2.50/€3.18; Heritage Card).

The Beara Peninsula

The **Beara Peninsula**, barren and remote, seems to have an energy all of its own, bounding in great ribs of rock thirty miles out into the ocean. In good weather it can be outrageously beautiful, especially in the extreme west, but the weather is notoriously changeable and when the mists roll in and the wind rises there are precious few places to shelter from it all. It is a fine place for tough cycling and energetic hiking, though you need to be prepared: careful planning of routes, particularly the descent, is vital. Alternatively, you could try the **Beara Way**, a signposted, long-distance walk (125 miles) following old roads and tracks, stretching from Glengarriff west along the southern side of the peninsula to Dursey Island, along the north side to Kenmare and back down to Glengarriff (route guides available locally; OS 1:50,000 Discovery map 84). Everywhere along the peninsula you are accompanied by fine views of the mountains and the sea, and there are occasional sandy beaches on either side; take local advice before swimming, as currents can be treacherous.

In practical terms, there are just enough hostels and B&Bs to make lengthy exploration a viable proposition, but it's worth bearing in mind that a sparse population means there's little traffic of any sort – don't rely on being able to hitch back if you're in a hurry. If you're planning to **camp**, be aware that though there is no shortage of open land, a lot of it is very rocky. **Private buses** connect the Beara communities with Glengarriff, Bantry and Cork several days a week. See "Travel Details" at the end of the chapter. Bus Éireann connects Castletownbere with Kenmare during the summer.

Adrigole

The first settlement along the coast, about fifteen miles west of Glengarriff, is **ADRIGOLE**, a handful of houses stretching over a couple of miles with no real centre. Just to the west of the junction for the Healy Pass is a shop, a pub and a basic IHH **hostel** *Hungry Hill Lodge* (☎027/60228) with good **camping** – phone ahead to check they are open; three miles to the east you'll find a couple of old-style **B&Bs**: *Bayview Farmhouse* (☎027/60026; ②) with standard rooms and lovely views of the sea, and the nearby *Beechmount* (closed Nov–Feb; ☎027/60075; ②). It's all wild and wonderful walking country. **Hungry Hill** rises to 2251ft, a good climb rewarded by fabulous views, hidden lakes and waterfalls, while the steep road through the **Healy Pass** leads north to Lauragh, County Kerry, where there is an An Óige **hostel** at Glanmore Lake (closed Oct–Easter; ☎064/83181).

Castletownbere

Beara communities have always relied heavily on fishing; **CASTLETOWNBERE**, the peninsula's main town, is no exception. Set on Ireland's second largest natural harbour, it's periodically awash with Spanish and Portuguese sailors. To serve them there's a handful of cafés, well-stocked shops, a chip shop and some enjoyable pubs (see opposite). Essentially, the town serves as a useful place to pick up provisions or rest up if you're travelling through the area. It's also the point of departure for **ferries** to Bere Island (July & Aug 3–5 daily; by arrangement at other times; ☎027/75009; car £15/€19.05 return, foot passenger £4/€5.08), which shelters the harbour.

The **stone circle** a mile from town is worth seeing. A coastal walk west from Castletownbere takes you to the ruins of **Dunboy Castle** – where an Irish and Spanish force was besieged and overcome by the English in 1602 – and **Puxley's Castle**, the eerie, dilapidated shell of a Victorian Gothic mansion. This was the home of the Puxley family, who made their money out of copper-mining; their story, and that of the mines, was used by Daphne du Maurier in her novel *Hungry Hill*. The castle itself was burnt down by the IRA in the 1920s, but its setting is idyllic: a placid inlet behind Castletownbere harbour fringed by rich woodlands, with stunning views of the wild mountains – expect to be charged £2/€2.54 to enter the grounds.

There's a useful **tourist information** hut on the square (☎027/70054). For information about private **bus services** to Glengarriff, Bantry and Cork contact either Harrington's (☎027/74003), O'Donoghue's (☎027/70007) or Peter O'Sullivan (☎027/74168); see Travel Details at the end of this chapter. There are several **B&Bs**: options at the west end of town include the pleasant *Old Presbytery* (☎027/70424; ④), hung with some interesting paintings by Allihies artists, and *Knockanroe* (☎027/70029; ③). *Murphy's* (☎027/70244; ②), Main Street (above the café) offers decent budget B&B, and at the east end there's *Ár d'Teachna* (☎027/70071; ③), a family home that also has inexpensive single rooms. You can **camp** at nearby *Beara Hostel* (☎027/70184), two miles west of Castletownbere on the road towards Allihies, a clean hostel with laundry facilities and bike rental. The alternative for **campers** is *Berehaven Camper Amenity Park* (☎027/70700), about one mile east of town, a well developed site for tents and camper vans. One of the best inexpensive places to **eat** is *The Old Bakery*, West End; serving excellent home-cooked food, it's a welcome refuge on a rainy day with plenty of art books and board games to while away the time. Seafood features prominently on the reasonably priced menu at *Niki's*, on Main Street. Provisions are available at all hours from *MacCarthy's* shop-cum-bar – one of the nicest places to drink.

There is a **laundry** on Main Street. **Bike rental** is available from the Supervalu supermarket. If you want to explore this coastline from the water, try **sea kayaking** with Beara Kayaks (☎027/70692).

On to Allihies and the tip of the peninsula

Moving on from Castletownbere you can head down to the remote, tiny villages at the end of the peninsula, a few houses, a shop and a pub being the typical set-up. This extreme of the peninsula saw some development in the nineteenth century when copper was mined, but little remains beyond the unguarded shafts; beware of these if you're walking. Signposted to the left off the road around five miles west of Castletownbere (then about another half a mile on) is the remote **Garranes Farmhouse Hostel** (☎027/73147), clinging to a beautiful, ravaged coastline. The hostel is next to the **Buddhist Dzogchen Beara Retreat Centre** (same number), and hostellers are welcome to join meditation classes. Phoning ahead is advised since the hostel can be full of people on retreat at any time of the year. Note that the nearest shop is one mile away towards Allihies and stocks only basic provisions; the nearest pub is six miles away.

Tiny **ALLIHIES**, formerly a major mining centre, nowadays has simply four pubs, a shop, a sandy beach, a handful of places to stay and, in fine weather, superb views. For

B&B *Sea View House* (☎027/73004; ③) in the main street offers very comfortable rooms, as does *Sea Haven Lodge* (☎027/73225; ③) in a fabulous spot overlooking the beach. There are a couple of **hostels**: the comfy, central *Village Hostel* (IHH; closed Nov–March; ☎027/73107) is a delightful place and has a good bookshelf, but you'll need to book ahead in the summer; the An Óige hostel (closed Oct–May; ☎027/73014) is about a mile from the centre and is rather more basic, though adequate nonetheless – and beautifully secluded; follow the **Beara Way** signs from the south end of the village if you are walking. You can **camp** by the beach – either rough or on a small site. There's **barfood** in *O'Neill's*, and you may come across some kind of folk music either here or in any of the three other pubs.

Perhaps the quietest of the islands to be visited off the coast hereabouts is **Dursey Island**, situated at the very tip of the peninsula and fringed by high cliffs. Dursey's attractions include fabulous views, solitude and the thrill of taking a very dodgy-looking cable car across the narrow and treacherous sound. You can walk up its hills for endless views westward over the ocean, with three great lumps of rock in the foreground: the Cow, the Calf and the Bull. For a day-trip, you need to get to the very end of the R572 in the morning. The **cable car** has no regular schedule, but during July and August you can usually get to the island Monday to Saturday at 9am, 10.30am, 2.30pm, 4.30pm and around 7pm. Sunday times vary slightly. There is a **B&B** near the cable car station: *Windy Point House*, Garrish (closed Nov–March; ☎027/73017; ③, plus evening meals available), which also serves tea and snacks in the summer. If you want to stop over you'll need to pitch a tent, as Dursey Island has just a few houses, none offering B&B – the islanders claim to occupy the most westerly habitation in Europe – and there's no pub or shop.

Heading along the northside of the Beara Peninsula towards Kenmare, the fine scenery continues, with peerless views of the Kerry mountains to the north. About four miles west of Eyeries you can get simple **hostel** accommodation at Urhan post office (☎027/74005 or 74036). Phoning ahead is strongly advised, especially in July and August. There's nothing here but a shop, a pub, a little beach and fabulous views to enjoy. **EYERIES** itself is a brightly painted village with some pleasant pubs and the friendly little *Ard Na Mara* **hostel** (closed Oct–April; ☎027/74271), a spacious bungalow in a beautiful spot overlooking the sea, where you can also **camp** – to find it walk around half a mile along the road east from the pubs and it's signposted off to the left. Phoning ahead is strongly advised. There is **B&B** in the village at *Coulagh Bay House* (☎027/74013, ③), high on the main road.

Four miles north of here, the small village of **ARDGROOM** also enjoys beautiful scenery, backed by the Slieve Miskish mountains and set beside a rushing river. It makes a very pleasant stopover if you're walking the **Beara Way** or want to fish for brown trout in nearby Glenbeg Lake. **B&B** is available at *O'Brien's* (☎027/74019; ② & ③) in the main street, and you can get bar food at *The Village Inn*.

travel details

Trains

Cork to: Cobh (7–16 daily; 25min); Dublin (7–8 daily; 3hr 10min); Fota (7–16 daily; 15min); Rosslare Harbour (Mon–Sat 1 daily; 5hr).

Buses

Bus Éireann

Cork to: Bantry (3–4 daily; 1hr 50min–2hr 20min); Cork airport (4–16 daily; 20min); Killarney (5–8 daily; 2hr 30 min); Kinsale (3–12 daily; 40 min).

Castletownbere to: Kenmare (late June–early Sept Mon–Sat 2 daily; 1hr 20min).

Harrington's Buses

Castletownbere to: Cork (1 daily except Thurs; 2hr)

O'Donoghue's Buses

Castletownbere to: Bantry (1–2 daily except Wed; 1hr 10min); Cork (Thurs 1 daily; 2hr 45min); Glengarriff (1–2 daily except Wed; 40min).

Ferries

Baltimore to: Clear Island (1–3 daily; 45min); Sherkin Island (4–8 daily; 10min).

Schull to: Clear Island (late May–mid-Oct 1–3 daily; 45min); Sherkin Island (June–Aug 1–3 daily, 1hr).

CHAPTER EIGHT

COUNTY KERRY

If you've come to Ireland for the scenery and the remoteness, you'll certainly find them in **County Kerry**: miles and miles of mountain-moorland where the heather and the bracken are broken only by the occasional lake; smooth hills whose fragrant, tussocky grass is covered with sea pinks, speedwells, thrift and red campion, and that fragment into jagged rocks as they reach the sea. The ocean looks enormous,

ACCOMMODATION PRICE CODES

Throughout this book, prices of hotels, guesthouses and B&Bs have been graded with the codes below, according to what you can expect to pay for a double room in high season. For more details on accommodation, see p.34.

① Under £26/€33.01	④ £40–55/€50.79–69.84	⑦ £90–110/€114.28–139.67
② £26–33/€33.01–41.90	⑤ £55–70/€69.84–88.88	⑧ £110–130/€139.67–165.07
③ £33–40/€41.90–50.79	⑥ £70–90/€88.88–114.28	⑨ Over £130/€165.07

and you can stand in the sunshine and watch a storm coming in for miles before you have to run for cover. The only catch is that a good part of the county is very much on the tourist trail. However, the plus side of Kerry's long tradition of welcoming tourists is that it's very easy country to travel in, with plenty of accommodation and food in all price brackets, and, during the summer at least, transport is pretty good – though with some notable exceptions.

Broadly speaking, Kerry divides into four areas: the Dingle Peninsula; the Iveragh Peninsula, encircled by the Ring of Kerry, with Killarney in its hinterland; the Kenmare River, bordered to the north and south by the Iveragh and Beara peninsulas; and northern Kerry, from Tralee to the Shannon. Each section is quite distinct and has its partisans. By far the most visited area – indeed the most visited in the whole of Ireland – is **Killarney and the Ring of Kerry**. Deservedly famous for the beauty of the adjacent lakes and mountains, this region is, predictably, geared up for tourism, and the principal roads and sights are often overburdened with visitors. Luckily, however, the real wilds are never far away, and whether you head for the mountains or the sea you can soon lose yourself and feel remote from modern civilization. The **Dingle Peninsula** is on a smaller scale than Iveragh, but equally magical: peppered with monastic remains, it has a contemplative atmosphere that makes you understand why people talk about the mystic quality of the west. Around **Kenmare** things are different again, with a tamed feeling about the scenery; one half of the Beara Peninsula belongs to more cultivated, genteel County Cork. To the **north**, flat, fertile farming land makes for less exciting scenery, but in contrast to the rest of the county there are many signs of Anglo-Norman settlement.

Killarney and around

Although **KILLARNEY** has been commercialized to saturation point and has little in the way of architectural interest, the real reason for coming here is without doubt the surrounding landscape. Its three spectacular **lakes**, Lough Leane (the Lower Lake), Muckross Lake (the Middle Lake) and the Upper Lake, are only the appetizer. Behind them loom **Macgillycuddy's Reeks**, which have a grandeur out of all proportion to their height: rarely exceeding 3000ft, they're still the highest mountains in Ireland. Much of this wonderful scenery is contained within the huge **Killarney National Park**.

Arrival, information and accommodation

Kerry's **airport** (☎066/976 4644) is about a mile outside the village of Farranfore, eight miles north of Killarney on the N22 Tralee road. It is served by direct flights from Stansted and connecting flights from Dublin. Farranfore village is on the Killarney to Tralee trainline. A taxi into Killarney centre will cost around £12/€15.24. Killarney's

train station off East Avenue Road, and **bus station** on nearby Park Road, are both pretty central. Even if you're not planning to bike round the Ring of Kerry, cycling is a great way of seeing Killarney's immediate surroundings, and makes good sense because local transport is almost non-existent. **Bike rental** is available at O'Sullivan's Cycles, Bishop's Lane, New St (☎064/31282; £7/€8.89 per day) or at several of the hostels. The post office and banks can be found on New Street, and, off the same street down a lane next to Dunnes Stores, you'll also find Killarney's laundry. Fishing licences for Killarney are available at O'Neill's, 6 Plunkett St (☎064/31970). Although there's plentiful accommodation of all sorts, the town gets very crowded in high season and it's worth visiting the extremely helpful **tourist office**, on Beech Rd (June & Sept Mon–Sat 9am–6pm, Sun 10am–6pm; July & Aug daily 9am–8pm; Oct–May Mon–Sat 9.15am–1pm & 2.15–5.30pm; ☎064/31633) or better still calling ahead to make advance bookings. The tourist office also offers a wealth of information about Killarney and the surrounding area, a good stock of local guides and maps for sale, a foreign exchange and Western Union money transfer (☎1800/395 395), and is a good place to make bookings for a number of bus and walking tours including trips to the Dingle Peninsula, the Gap of Dunloe and around the Ring of Kerry. There are a number of options for **camping** nearby: *Fleming's White Bridge* (☎064/31590) is just a mile east of Killarney – follow the N22 Cork road turning right for Ballycasheen; *Flesk Muckross Caravan and Camping Park* (☎064/31704) is a mile south from Killarney on the N71 Kenmare road and handy for both the Kerry Way and Muckross House; and *White Villa Farm* (☎064/32456) is a small site about two miles east of town on the N22 Cork road.

An Óige Hostel, Aghadoe Rd (☎064/31240). A large, well-run hostel that has been recently refurbished. About three miles northwest of town towards Killorglin it's located in beautiful countryside, and is well situated for walking in the mountains. Dorms sleeping up to eight are available, and there are comfortable twin (①), and four-bedded rooms (£14/€17.78). A free shuttle bus service to and from the bus and train stations, and bike rental are available here.

Arbutus Hotel, College St (☎064/31037, *arbutus@tinet.ie*). One of Killarney's oldest, this is a charming, traditional hotel with a spacious antique-furnished lobby and a homely atmosphere. Some of the bedrooms have canopy beds, and all offer TV, video, and tea- and coffee-making facilities. There's also a laundry service. ⑧.

The Copper Kettle, Lewis Rd (☎064/34164). Comfortable B&B accommodation with rooms that have pleasant, rustic-styled interiors; one room has an en-suite Jacuzzi bath. ⑤.

Fair View House, Lewis Rd (☎064/34164). Good-quality guesthouse in the centre of town that offers a range of standard and en-suite rooms. All rooms have TV, video and hairdryers. ③–⑤.

Killarney Royal Hotel, College St (☎064/31853, *www.killarneyroyal.ie*). A family-run traditional hotel with a warm welcome. All the rooms have excellent furnishings and en-suite bathrooms, and there are some superior suites available. The generously proportioned sitting room has an elegant fireplace with a turf fire. ⑨.

Neptune's, Bishop's Lane, off New St (IHH; ☎064/35255, *neptune@eircom.net*). A friendly hostel which manages to successfully combine size with intimacy and offers lots of information and discounts for tours in the area. Family rooms, twins, doubles (①) and dorms are available.

Orchard, Fleming's Lane, off High St (☎064/31879). A very pleasant, centrally located B&B, tucked down a quiet alleyway. ③.

Peacock Farm Hostel, seven miles out of town, signposted off the road to Muckross (☎064/33557). A relaxed hostel with lovely airy rooms that overlook a stunning, rugged mountain location; an ideal place to unwind. Breakfast is available, but bring your own food to cook in the evening. Free lifts to and from Killarney are available. Closed Oct–March.

Súgán Hostel, Lewis Rd (IHH; ☎064/33104). Small, cosy, cottage-style hostel right in the centre of town. The owner is a musician who welcomes others who want to play, and sessions take place frequently in the summer. Dorms are cheerful and small, and one private room is available. You can rent bikes from here and there is plenty of information about what's on around town. Discounts can be arranged on local tours.

The Town

The town is essentially one main street – High Street which runs into Main Street – and a couple of side roads full to the brim with souvenir shops, cafés, pubs, restaurants, B&Bs and guesthouses. Pony traps are lined up against walls, while their weather-beaten owners talk visitors into taking trips through the surrounding countryside. These can be expensive and you might want to consider taking a combined pony and trap and boating trip as an alternative (see p.323).

The town's Irish name *Cill Áirne* (which means Church of the Sloe) doesn't imply a settlement of any great antiquity, and the Cromwellian Survey of 1654 found no town or village of that name in existence. By 1756, however, a burgeoning **tourist trade**, fed by the growing Romantic attraction to lakes and mountains, had created Killarney: "A new street with a large commodious inn was designed to be built here, for the curiosities of the neighbouring lake have of late drawn great numbers of curious travellers to visit it," said a contemporary survey. The local landowner, Lord Kenmare, quickly spotted commercial opportunities and granted free leases for new inns and houses, building four major roads to connect his creation with the outside world. That said, the town doesn't look particularly planned, and the only building of any distinction is the high Gothic Revival **cathedral**, built by Augustus Pugin in 1855. A particularly florid Victorian interpretation of medieval architecture, the cathedral inspires respect or derision, but is certainly worth seeing. During the Famine, when building work ceased for five years, the covered area served as a hospital for victims of starvation and disease.

Eating, drinking and entertainment

Places to **eat and drink** are thick on the ground in Killarney, and the only time when you might need to book ahead is over bank holiday weekends. Given the number of visitors to Killarney, it's not surprising that there's plenty of **entertainment** laid on, particularly throughout the summer. Although the widely publicized "traditional" Irish music can seem pretty spurious when you are surrounded by bus loads of other tourists, it sounds great nonetheless. All the pubs listed below have some form of music several nights a week during the summer months; in winter this dies down to weekends and Monday nights only in some instances, with the exception of the *Grand Hotel*. If you just want a quiet pint, you'll need to ask at the bar whether or not there is likely to be music later in the evening because Killarney is a lively town and sessions tend to move around.

In May, July and October there's **racing** at Killarney's race course on Ross Road, which, like any Irish race meeting, is well worth a detour. The tourist office can give details of **gaelic football** matches; Killarney is a top team and feelings run high. The Rally of the Lakes brings hordes of motor fanatics to Killarney over the first weekend in May. Rally drivers roar along the roads around the lakes, so if you want to enjoy the mountains in peace, this is probably a weekend best avoided.

Restaurants and cafés

The Bean House, 8 High St. This is a pleasant café which serves all the usuals: toasted sandwiches, BLTs, cakes, herb teas and coffee.

The Bricín, 26 High St (☎064/34902). A reliable coffee shop serving good-value home-cooked lunches; à la carte menu in the evening offering traditional Irish food, steaks and chicken dishes.

The Caragh, 106 New St (☎064/31645). A restaurant and bar whose winning combination of filling hot dinners of roast lamb, Irish stew and pan-fried trout, served up with delicious pints of stout, make it extremely popular with families.

The Cooperage, Old Market Lane (☎064/37716). A stylish, modern interior and contemporary menus make this popular with a fashion-conscious young crowd and one of the more interesting places to eat in Killarney; noise levels can be high. Closed Sun lunch.

Cronin's, 9 College St. A bright and cheerful café offering great-value filling meals such as shepherds pie, lasagne, and smoked salmon on brown bread with chips.

Gaby's Seafood Restaurant, 27 High St (☎064/32519). One of Killarney's best seafood restaurants, with a warm and welcoming atmosphere. Lobster and wild salmon dishes feature prominently. This place is very popular and booking is advised. Closed Sun.

Bars and music

The Bean House, 8 High St. A coffee bar with a relaxed atmosphere that hosts singer/songwriters sessions and contemporary folk and poetry evenings on Tuesday and Thursday.

Buckley's, College St. A comfortable and traditional bar catering for all age groups, this is a great spot for traditional music.

The Danny Man, New St. A cavernous bar catering for the hordes of tourists who arrive in town looking for traditional Irish music. The bands who perform here tend to be heavily amplified, and a lively holiday atmosphere is guaranteed.

The Grand, Main St. A very touristy bar with nightly live entertainment: ballads or traditional music between 9 and 11pm, with Celtic rock and a club after 11pm (cover charge after 11pm of £3–4/€3.81–5.08). On Wednesday there's set dancing from 10pm to midnight.

The '98, High St. A little bar with a fresh modern interior but still hosting live music. On Thursday and Friday evening and Sunday afternoon there are singer/songwriters sessions.

O'Connor's, High St. A quaint old-style bar attracting a good mix of locals and tourists. Look out for Tea Theatre performances (a one man storytelling show) here.

O'Meara's, 12 High St. Lively traditional bar attracting a fairly young, bohemian crowd. Live music is performed here (five nights weekly during summer, and weekends in winter) ranging from rock and blues through to the occasional traditional session.

Knockreer Estate and Lough Leane

Oddly enough, given its origins as a tourist town, Killarney turns its back on the grand scenery to the west and south, hunching itself inwards so that you'd hardly guess at the delights that await you. But the gates of the old Kenmare Estate – now known as the **KNOCKREER ESTATE** – are just over the road from the cathedral, and a short walk through the grounds takes you to the banks of Lough Leane. The Browne family, Earls of Kenmare, were unusual among the Irish peerage in that they never renounced their Catholic faith. Given lands confiscated from the O'Donoghues in the seventeenth century, they were subject in the eighteenth century to the penal laws which decreed that every Catholic landowner had to divide his property among his male heirs. The

THE LANDSCAPE AROUND KILLARNEY

It was the last Ice Age that formed the Killarney landscape. Glaciation left its mark on the contorted limestone valleys of the Lower and Middle lakes, and the nearby Devil's Punch Bowl and Horses' Glen show other signs – huge rocks smoothed to sucked-sweet shapes, and improbably teetering boulders. The lower slopes of the mountains are covered with what is often virgin **forest**; a joy to see in a country that has cut down almost all its trees. Almost all flora seems to thrive in the local climate of high rainfall and humidity. In the woods you'll find a rich mixture of oak interspersed with bilberry, woodrush and woodsorrel, plus mosses, liverworts and lichens (sensitive organisms whose continued survival testifies to the clean air here). As elsewhere in the west of Ireland the **vegetation** here includes a number of plants generally found in quite different parts of Europe. The famous arbutus, or strawberry tree (so called from its bright-red, and non-edible, fruit), generally grows only in Mediterranean countries and Brittany, and some saxifrages and the greater butterwort, with its fleshy purple flowers and sickly green leaf rosettes, are otherwise found only in northwest Spain and Portugal.

Brownes' estate remained intact quite simply because there was only one son in each generation.

At **Lough Leane**, the scenery is magnificent: tall wooded hills plunge into the water, with the mountain peaks rising behind to the highest, **Carrauntoohil** (3411ft). Ireland's last wild wolf was killed here in 1700, and when the weather's bad (as it often is) there's a satisfying similarity to early Romantic engravings. The main path through the Knockreer Estate leads to the restored fifteenth-century stronghold of **Ross Castle** (April daily 10am–5pm; May & Sept daily 10am–6pm; June–Aug daily 9am–6.30pm; Oct Tues–Sun 10am–5pm; closed Nov–March; £3/€3.82, Heritage Card), the last place in Munster to succumb to Cromwell's forces in 1652. The story goes that General Ludlow, having learned of a tradition that Ross Castle would never be taken from land, brought ships from Kenmare and sailed them up from Castlemaine, whereupon the defenders – whom nothing else had budged – immediately surrendered. It houses examples of sixteenth- and seventeenth-century furniture; somehow the interior lacks a sense of it's medieval history. Near the water you can make out copper workings, last used during the Napoleonic Wars and thought to date back four thousand years.

From Ross Castle you can **tour the lake** in large glassed-over boats like the bateaux-mouches that ply the Seine in Paris (£6/€7.62; trips last one hour); an alternative is to get a fisherman to take you out in a little craft with an outboard motor, or rent one yourself. This way, you can land on and explore the island of Inisfallen. (If you're navigating yourself, look for a limestone outcrop in the water. Inisfallen is the island to the left, about a mile out.)

Inisfallen

Of the thirty-odd small islands that dot Lough Leane, **INISFALLEN** is the biggest and the most enchanting. The monastery founded here in the seventh century was an important scholastic centre for a thousand years. Brian Boru, the eleventh-century High King and victor over the Vikings at Clontarf in 1014, was reputedly educated here, and the twelfth-century Annals of Inisfallen, now in Oxford's Bodleian Library, are an important source document for early Irish history. Wandering round the island is a delight: heavily wooded, it's also scattered with monastic buildings – nothing from the original seventh-century foundation, but there's a small Romanesque church and a ruined twelfth-century Augustinian priory. Eighteenth-century tourists were clearly aware of Inisfallen's charms: Lord Kenmare used to give parties for his influential friends here, and the gap in the wall of the Romanesque church is where he installed a bay window when the building was converted into a banqueting house. The picturesque ruin you see now is the result of further tinkering, around 1840.

Muckross Estate and the lakes

The road from Killarney to the **MUCKROSS ESTATE** passes through unlovely territory dominated by huge modern hotels, and though jaunting cars from the centre of Killarney will take you out to Muckross (cars are prohibited on the Muckross Estate), it's more fun to rent a bike. Take the earliest turning right into the park that's available, to escape the busy main road. The first place to head for is **Muckross Abbey** (mid-June to early Sept daily 10am–5pm; free), not only for the ruin itself – one of the best preserved in Ireland, part Norman, part Gothic, though sadly despoiled by Cromwell's troops – but also for its calm, contemplative location, and the fact that it, like Ross Castle, hints at something predating Killarney's tourist history. Founded as a Franciscan institution by Macarthy Mor in the mid-fifteenth century, it was suppressed by Henry VIII; the friars returned again, but were finally driven out by Cromwell's army in 1652.

Back at the main road, signposts direct you to **Muckross House** (daily: mid-March to June 9am–6pm; July & Aug 9am–7pm; Sept & Oct 9am–6pm; Nov to mid-March

9am–5.30pm; £4/€5.09, Heritage Card; joint ticket including farms £6/€7.64; gardens free), a solid, nineteenth-century neo-Elizabethan mansion designed by the Scottish architect William Burn. Some rooms are given over to material on Kerry folk life – craftspeople demonstrate their trades (Mon–Fri) both in the basement, where you can watch weavers, and in the nearby craft centre, where there's more weaving, along with potters and a bookbinder; there's a well-stocked shop alongside – and there's a **traditional working farm** too where you can watch a blacksmith at work (mid-March to April & Oct Sat, Sun and bank holidays 1–6pm; May daily 1–6pm; June–Sept daily 10am–7pm; £4/€5.09; joint ticket including the house £6/€7.64; Heritage Card). The excellent **tea shop** provides a good refuge from the rain, but the **gardens** (open all year; free) – well known for their rhododendrons and azaleas – are the place to be when the weather is fine.

The estate gives access to well-trodden paths along the shores of the **Muckross Lake**, and it's here that you can see one of Killarney's celebrated beauty spots, the **Meeting of the Waters**. Actually a parting, but highly picturesque nonetheless, it has a profusion of indigenous and flowering subtropical plants – eucalyptus, magnolia, bamboo and an arbutus, or strawberry tree, on the left of the Old Weir Bridge. Close by is the massive shoulder of Torc Mountain, shrugging off the spectacular 60ft **Torc Waterfall**; the climb up the side of the mountain is worth doing, if only for the view across to Macgillycuddy's Reeks. On a good day, the Slieve Mish Mountains on the far side of Dingle Bay are visible.

About two miles south of here is the **Upper Lake** which is also incredibly beautiful, although it too is still firmly on the tourist trail. The main road running along one side up to **Ladies' View** is where many queue up to admire the scenery – which is, in fact, truly amazing, including the Gap of Dunloe and the wild and desolate Black Valley beyond the lake.

The Gap of Dunloe

Although the **Gap of Dunloe** – a narrow defile formed by glacial overflow that cuts the mountains in two – is one of Killarney's prime tourist attractions, it's possible to find a modicum of solitude if you're willing to use your legs. **Jaunting cars** continually run here from Killarney's centre, a fact which, as the drivers tout loudly for business, you're not likely to miss. They tend to be expensive, but the Gap of Dunloe is just about the most scenic jaunting car ride on offer. Castlelough Vintage Tours, 17 High St (☎064/32496) offer a splendid full-day tour, which takes you by bus to the starting point of Kate Kearney's Cottage, from where you transfer to a jaunting car for the ride through the Gap, then after a lunch stop at Lord Brandon's Cottage you take a boat ride through the three lakes to Ross Castle, and finally a bus brings you back into town.

At the foot of the road leading to the Gap of Duloe stands **Kate Kearney's Cottage**, a pub and restaurant which caters for the large number of tourists who climb down from pony and trap rides here during the summer months. Moderately priced meals and sandwiches are on offer, and this is the last place for food and water before **Lord Brandon's Cottage** (open approximately June–Aug), seven miles away over the other side of the Black Valley, which serves teas, scones and sandwiches. The best time to walk the four and a half miles from the cottage up the valley is late afternoon, when the jaunting cars have gone home and the light is at its most magical. The road, which is closed to motor traffic, winds its way up the desolate valley between high-rock cliffs and waterfalls – Macgillycuddy's Reeks is to your right, and to your left is the Purple Mountain, so called because in late summer it's covered in purple heather – past a chain of icy loughs and tarns, up to the top, where you find yourself in what feels like one of the most remote places in the world: the **Black Valley**. Named after its entire population perished during the potato famine, and now inhabited by a mere handful of families, the Black Valley makes you begin to feel that you've left mass tourism behind. The fact that it was the very last valley in Ireland to get electricity is some measure of its isolation, and there are no pubs or shops here. There is, however, a **hostel** run by An Óige (closed Dec–Feb; ☎064/34712), where you can also get meals. Moving on, you can either carry on down to the Upper Lake or pick up the Kerry Way (see box below).

The Ring of Kerry

The 110-mile Ring of Kerry, which encircles the Iveragh Peninsula, can be driven around in a day, and most tourists view its spectacular scenery without ever leaving

THE KERRY WAY

The **Kerry Way**, 133 miles long, is part of a long-distance footpath that goes through Macgillycuddy's Reeks then right around the Iveragh Peninsula through Glenbeigh, Cahersiveen, Waterville, Caherdaniel and Kenmare – a sort of walkers' Ring of Kerry. More than most of Ireland's long-distance footpaths, it's resonant of the culture, as well as the nature, of the area and consists largely of green roads, many of them old drovers' roads or "butter roads" (along which butter was transported) and routes between Kerry's ancient Christian settlements. Whichever section you choose to walk, you'll need the relevant 1:50,000 OS map – numbers 78 and 83 respectively.

The Kerry Way starts inauspiciously in **Killarney**, threads down through the Muckross Estate and alongside the Upper Lake – road walking, most of it – before heading up to meet the Black Valley (see above). From the Black Valley, it heads on towards **Cloghernoosh** via a stony path that becomes a green road. After the footbridge over the stream running out of Curraghmore Lake, there's a stretch of bridleway, and from here on you're among the peaks, with exhilarating views of Carrauntoohil to the north.

Next, the footpath follows the Lack Road, zigzagging up to a saddle point at the top, then skirting the side of **Lough Acoose** before reaching the Glencar Valley (and the first tourist accommodation since the Black Valley). No longer traversing really high ground, the rest of the way into Glenbeigh is less exciting, although the stretch on Seefin Mountain above Caragh Lake is still spectacular. From here the Way runs around the peninsula, is especially scenic between Waterville and Caherdaniel and eventually leads back to Killarney.

All the usual precautions need to be taken seriously in a region where gales blowing in off the Atlantic can make the weather change rapidly. Bring waterproofs, walking boots and food.

You should really fix up **accommodation** beforehand. There's an An Óige hostel in the **Black Valley** (see above), roughly eight hours' walk from Killarney; hitching isn't recommended, since the nearest road seeing any traffic is eight miles from the start of the valley. Next stop is the *Climbers' Inn* (weekends only Nov–March; ☎066/976 0101; ④), offering both B&B and hostel accommodation, hidden among woodlands at **Glencar**; meals are available in the bar, decorated with a church pulpit, and there's a shop and advice on local walks and climbs; check they have hostel accommodation in advance if you don't want to end up paying for B&B. For accommodation in **Glenbeigh** see p.326. Nine miles from Killarney, the *Mountain Rest Lodge* (☎064/44272), Carnahone, **Beaufort**, is close to the main approach to Carrauntoohil. About one mile along the N72 west of the Beaufort turn-off there's camping at *Riverside Park*. If you do plan to scale Ireland's highest mountain, you should really get some local advice first: try John Walsh at the *Climbers' Inn*, Glencar, or phone Eileen Daly of Killarney Mountaineering Club on ☎064/34677. Alternatively, pick up a copy of the excellent *Walk Guide: South West of Ireland* by Seán Ó Súilleabháin (pub. Gill and Macmillan), which details 47 walks in and around Kerry, including walks up Carrauntoohil.

their bus or car. Consequently, anyone straying from the road or waiting until the buses knock off in the afternoon will be left to experience the long, slow twilights of the Atlantic seaboard in perfect seclusion. Part of the excitement of travelling round the Kerry coast comes from the clarity with which its physical outline stands out against the vast grey expanse of the Atlantic. Every gully, bay, channel and island is as distinct as it is on the map, giving a powerful sense of place amidst the isolation.

If you really are limited to a day's exploration of the wild coastal scenery, it could be worth heading for Dingle, the next peninsula north, instead: its intimacy of scale means you can see a lot more without having to rely upon buses or cars. **Cycling** the Ring itself takes three days (not counting any diversions), and a bike will let you get on to the largely deserted mountain roads; just be sure your machine has lots of gears, and you have plenty of energy – the combination of gradients and strong winds can be gruelling. **Buses** serve the entire circuit from late May to mid-Sept only (2 daily); the rest of the year buses from Killarney only go as far as Waterville (Mon–Sat 1 daily) – but during summer, flotillas of tourist buses ply the Ring. You can get details of tours from the tourist office and for an extra charge some companies will drop you off somewhere along the way and pick you up the next day. Hitching is unreliable as traffic simply may not exist away from the main roads.

Killorglin to Glenbeigh

By travelling the Ring of Kerry **anticlockwise**, you get a gradual introduction to the wild grandeur of the coastline scenery, with the Dingle Peninsula and the dim shapes of the Blasket Islands visible in the distance.

The first stop on the way out from Killarney is the pleasantly unexceptional hillside town of **KILLORGLIN**, whose main claim to fame is the **Puck Fair**, held over three days in mid-August, a bacchanalian event with a wild goat captured and enthroned, plenty of dancing and drinking, plus a cattle, sheep and horse fair. These rituals honour the wild goats which, stampeding through the town, warned residents of the approach of Cromwell's army. The fair's pagan origins, however, date back to the Celtic festival of Lughnasa, three days of feasting and ritual sacrifices to celebrate the beginning of harvest.

For B&B **accommodation** the comfortable *Riverside House* on Ballykissan Rd (☎066/976 1184; ③), or the homely *Fáilte Towers*, Iveragh Rd (☎066/976 1155; ③) are good options. Inexpensive hearty bar **food** is served at the pleasant *Kerry's Vintage Inn*, Upper Bridge St (till 9pm in summer), and the hugely popular, but pricey, *Nick's Restaurant* (☎066/976 1219) comes recommended. For such a small town, Killorglin has some excellent **bars**: the lively *Kerry's Vintage Inn* holds traditional music sessions on Thursday, Friday and Saturday evenings during the summer; *The Old Forge Inn* is

SOUTH KERRY AND THE FIANNA

Many legends of the **Fianna**, a band of warriors led by **Finn Mac Cool** who served the High King in the third century, are set in South Kerry. One of them tells of how, near Killarney, Niamh, a golden-haired beauty on a white horse, persuaded Finn's son Oisin to come away to her kingdom. Where the magical wave Tonn Toime roars between Inch and Rossbeigh, they galloped out across the sea to Tír na nóg, the Land of Eternal Youth. After a blissful three hundred years, Oisin borrowed Niamh's magical horse to visit his homeland, with a warning not to dismount. Unable to find any of the Fianna in Kerry, he rode north to Dublin and found a band of puny men trying to shift a boulder. Leaning down to help, he broke a girth and landed on the ground a very old man. Before he died, St Patrick persuaded him to convert to Christianity.

an atmospheric old bar on the steep main street, attracting a young crowd; and *Coffey's*, at the bottom of the main street beside the bridge, is a plain old bar with traditional music on Thursday.

In **GLENBEIGH**, eight miles southwest along the N86 from Killorglin, almost everything is given over to tourism – despite plenty of accommodation, the town illustrates the disadvantages of sticking rigidly to the Ring. However, there are wonderful views all along the coastline and across to Dingle, and a spectacular seven-mile long Blue Flag beach just a mile away. For **accommodation**, try the family-run *Village House* B&B in the main street (☎066/976 8128; ④), or the tiny *Horseshoe Hostel* (closed Nov–March; ☎066/976 8606) at the end of the main street, catering for walkers and cyclists, and offering dorms and private rooms (①). *Sweeney's* and *The Towers* are a couple of lively **bars**; both serve good bar **food**, and the latter has a good deal of rock and traditional music at weekends. By taking the road up past **Caragh Lake**, you'll find some of Kerry's best mountain scenery, full of deep silences and the magical slanting light of the west. If you're on a relaxed budget and are looking for comparative luxury, you could stay at the *Glendalough House*, a mid-nineteenth-century country house on the shores of Caragh Lake (☎066/976 9156; ⑦). Alternatively, you could carry on up to the three small lakes of Coomnacronia, Coomaglaslaw and Coomasaharn (good trout fishing, but you'll need a licence). The lack of trees that contributes to the feeling of austerity in this area was not an original feature of the landscape; Sir William Petty, Cromwell's surveyor general, had an iron mine at Blackstones and felled the forests to fuel a smelter.

Cahersiveen, Portmagee and Ballinskelligs

At **Kells Bay**, eight miles west of Glenbeigh, the road veers inland for **CAHERSIVEEN**, giving you an opportunity to take a detour. On the way you'll pass *Caitín Baiters* pub, beside which is the clean and bright *Kells Ring of Kerry Hostel* (closed Nov–Feb; ☎066/947 7614). Any of the turnings right will lead eventually to the sea, past bright fuchsia hedges, with little or no traffic. "One wonders, in this place, why anyone is left in Dublin, or London, or Paris, when it would be better one would think, to live in a tent, or a hut, with this magnificent sea and sky, and to breathe this wonderful air, which is like wine in one's teeth," wrote J. M. Synge of the Kerry landscape; and here, for the first time, you begin to understand how the Ring inspires such hyperbole.

Cahersiveen (*Cathair Saidhbhín*; pronounced *Caher-sigh-veen*, stress on the last syllable) was said by Daniel O'Connell, its most famous son, to be the only town established in Ireland after the Act of Union. It is a long, narrow street of a town and the main shopping centre for the western part of the peninsula, giving itself over cheerfully to the tourist trade in summer. A laid-back, unremarkable place, it has more relaxed attitudes to shopping hours than anywhere else on the peninsula. Worth having a look at is the community-funded **Barracks heritage centre** (June–Sept Mon–Sat 10am–6pm, Sun 1–6pm; ☎066/947 2777; £3/€3.81), which contains a concise history of the town and a gallery of paintings and sculptures by local artists. The **tourist office** (June to mid-Sept Mon–Fri 10am–6pm; ☎066/947 2589) is also in the heritage centre. Not far from here is the magnificent **Daniel O'Connell Memorial Church**, highly unusual in that it is dedicated to a statesman rather than a saint, an indication of the high regard in which the liberator was held (for more on Daniel O'Connell see p.671).

On Valentia Road you can get **B&B** at *Castleview* (☎066/947 2252; ③) or *San Antoine* (☎066/947 2521; ③). If you also fancy galloping along a beach or trekking through the countryside, try *The Final Furlong Farmhouse Accommodation and Riding Stables* (☎066/947 2810; ③), just over a mile out on the Glenbeigh road. There are two small independent **hostels**, the cosy *Sive Hostel*, 15 East End (IHH; ☎066/947 2717), with camping facilities, and the laid-back *Mortimer's*, West Main St (☎066/947 2338). As for **food**, you can get all-day breakfasts at *An Cupan Eile* and bar food at *The Town House*. For good, though expensive, evening meals, try *O'Donoghue's* fish restaurant. There are plenty of friendly **bars**, such as *The Anchor Bar* or *Mike Murt's*, both of which are full of character. *The Cudgel Stout* has music sessions during the summer, as do *Cráineen's* and *The Skelligs Rock*.

REENARD POINT, three miles west of Cahersiveen, is the departure point for the ten-minute ferry crossing to Knightstown on Valentia Island (☎066/947 6141; cars return £4/€5.08; cyclists return £3/€3.81; last sailing from Reenard Point 10pm, last sailing from Knightstown 9.50pm). It's also a departure point for trips to the **Skelligs** (see box on p.329), and there's excellent, reasonably priced seafood here at *The Point Bar* – it's hugely popular, so you may well have to wait to be served. If you need **B&B**, *Sea Breeze* (☎066/9472609; ③) has stunning views over the island.

Beyond Cahersiveen, the main road takes the bulk of the traffic inland again towards Waterville, giving you an opportunity to explore the quiet lanes that lead out to Valentia Island and the peninsula's end. **PORTMAGEE** nestles beside a small harbour, its handful of bars and coffee shops providing welcome refuge on a blustery day. The village's much-hyped Skellig heritage centre (March–Oct daily 10am–6pm; £3/€3.81) provides information on Celtic monastic life, lighthouses and lighthouse-keeping, seabirds and aquatic life, and an audio visual show on Skellig Michael, which is interesting enough, though no substitute for a visit to the rock itself. The often single-track, and very steep, road south of here signposted the **Ring of Skellig**, affords spectacular views out to the Skelligs and Puffin Island, and eventually winds down to the tiny village of **BALLINSKELLIGS**. Monks from the Skellig Islands retreated to Ballinskelligs Abbey in the thirteenth century; today the place is a focus of the Kerry *Gaeltacht* (Irish-speaking area), drawing large numbers of schoolchildren and students of Irish in the summer. The village is tiny – there's a pretty basic An Óige **hostel** (closed Oct–Easter; ☎066/947 9229) and shop, a similarly basic pub, which seems to be full at any time of the day or night, and a lovely sandy beach with fabulous views across Ballinskelligs Bay to the Kerry Mountains. Trips to the Skelligs can be arranged from here (see p.329).

Valentia Island

VALENTIA, an island now linked to the mainland by bridge, is Europe's most westerly harbour, and standing at Bray Head on the island's tip, there's nothing but ocean between you and Newfoundland, 1900 miles away. Valentia's significance is out of all proportion to its size: the first ever transatlantic telegraph cable was laid from here in 1857 – though permanent contact wasn't established until 1866 – and for years it had better communications with New York than with Dublin.

In contrast to the endless vistas west, the island itself is small, and consequently every scrap of land has been cultivated, forming a rolling patchwork of fields stitched with dry slate walls. Valentia's position in the Gulf Stream gives it a mild, balmy climate, and the abundance of fuchsias grown by the inhabitants in local hedgerows enhances its domesticated atmosphere. It's a homely, tame place to stay, though from July onwards the peace is disturbed by tourists.

Arrival and accommodation

Access by ferry is from Reenard Point (see above) to Knightstown, or via the Maurice O'Neill Bridge, Portmagee, at the south end of the island, thirteen miles from the main coast road and a difficult hitch. Once on the island, there's no public transport at all. Accommodation is at a premium during the summer season. **B&Bs** include homely *Walsh's* (☎066/947 6115; ②) and *Spring Acre* (☎066/947 6141; ③), both in Knightstown, and *Glenreen Heights*, Knightstown Rd (☎066/947 6241; ③), about a mile away towards Chapeltown. The An Óige **hostel** has space for forty at the Coastguard Station in Knightstown, though services are spartan (closed Oct–May; ☎066/947 6141). The island's other hostel, the independent *Ring Lyne Hostel* (☎066/947 6103), lies midway between the bridge and Knightstown at Chapeltown.

The island

KNIGHTSTOWN is the focal village on the island and, facing Cahersiveen across the Portmagee Channel, affords fine panoramic views of the Kerry Mountains. A pretty harbour front with sprucely painted fishers' cottages is dominated by the Victorian *Royal and Pier Hotel*; now rather dilapidated and something of a white elephant, it's currently being run as an independent hostel. Tolerating rather than encouraging tourists, Knightstown is deeply old-fashioned, and if there are more than three in your group, you could feel something of an intruder. About a thousand houses cluster around a slate church hidden within a dark rookery. The main street has a few well-stocked shops, a post office offering a good selection of Irish literature and free maps of the island, and a couple of bars – one of which, *The Boston Bar*, serves **bar food**.

From Knightstown, take the Kilmore Road down towards the lighthouse, where there's a fine view of Valentia's empty harbour, the Beginish Islands and tiny **Church Island**. This mere rock supports the ruins of an eighth-century cell, once inhabited by a solitary monk, a soulmate of the brotherhood on the nearby Skellig Islands, whose only company was the seabirds. On a clear day you can also make out the sheer cliffs of the Blasket Islands west of the Dingle Peninsula.

Continuing west, the foreshore is an imposing clutter of megalithic slabs hurled together by the waves, with deep, limpid pools left by the winter storms. A couple of miles further on, a cove, great for swimming, combines intimacy with the grandiose, sheltered by lush, deciduous woods, with the whole of Kerry as its scenic backdrop. This adjoins the incongruously exotic gardens of **Glanleam House** (May–Oct daily 11am–5pm; £2.50/€3.17), former seat of the local magnate, the Knight of Kerry.

The fervour with which locals urge you to visit the **Grotto**, at the north end of the island, is misplaced. A gaping slate cavern, it boasts a crude, municipal bath-blue statue of the Virgin (erected 1954) perched 200ft up, amidst monotonously dripping icy water. Nevertheless, this is the highest point on the island and a good walk for a clear day. But more exciting by far is the cliff scenery to the northwest, some of the most spectacular of the Kerry coast.

The Skellig Islands

From Valentia you get a tantalizing view across a broad strip of sea to the **Skellig Islands** (*Na Sceilig*), apparently no more than two massive rocks. **Little Skellig** is a bird sanctuary, home to 40,000 gannets, and landing isn't permitted, but you can visit Great Skellig, or Skellig Michael as it's also called, and climb up to the ancient monastic site at the summit.

There are several **departure points for the Skelligs** around the Kerry coast (see box opposite); the trips are not cheap at around £25/€31.74 but, if the weather's good they make a fascinating and dramatic voyage. Once at sea, boats are followed by wheeling seagulls and, if you're lucky, puffins, too, from the nature reserve of Puffin Island, further north. You'll also pass the huge, jagged arch of rock that forms Little Skellig, where gannets with six-foot wingspans career overhead or make headlong dives into the sea for fish.

Skellig Michael looms sheer from the ocean, a gargantuan slaty mass with no visible route to the summit. From the tiny landing stage, however, you can see steps cut

SKELLIG FERRIES

A trip to the Skelligs really demands fine weather; if it looks changeable be prepared for a very rough ride. Either way, boats need to be booked the night before – and it's not uncommon to have to wait several days before the boats will sail. Bear in mind too that it is possible to get stranded on the island if the weather breaks. The trip is only feasible if you are able-bodied since landing on the island involves climbing a vertical ladder up onto the quay. It's advisable to take warm clothing, walking shoes, waterproofs and some kind of picnic as there is nowhere to get any food or drink. Ferries operate between May and September from the following points around the Kerry coast: Ballinskelligs – Joe Roddy (☎066/947 4268) Knightstown, Portmagee, Reenard Point – Seán Murphy (☎066/947 6214 or 087/236 2344).

into the cliff face, formerly a treacherous monks' path. Nowadays there's also a broad path leading to Christ's Saddle, the only patch of green on this inhospitable island. From here, it narrows and leads on to the arched stone remains of **St Fionan's Abbey** (560 AD). Among the ruins are six complete beehive cells – drystone huts that have survived centuries of foul weather. The island is dedicated to St Michael, guardian against the powers of darkness and patron of high places, who helped St Patrick drive the last of the venomous serpents over the 700ft cliffs to perish in the sea. Contrasted with Valentia, it's a wild, cruel place, an awesome sanctuary of devotion, even if the monks didn't remain here all year round to feel the violence of the elements. The Viking invasion of the island in the ninth century lived long in folk memory, inspiring a Skellig monk to write:

Bitter and wild is the wind tonight
Tossing the tresses of the sea to white
On such a night as this I feel at ease
Fierce Northmen only course the quiet seas.

Waterville and around

WATERVILLE may be touristy, but it manages to avoid being tacky. Popular as a Victorian and Edwardian resort and angling centre, it still has an air of consequence that sits oddly with the wild Atlantic views. Its few bars and hotels aside, the town is chiefly notable as the best base on the Ring for exploring the coast and the mountainous country inland. There's B&B **accommodation** at *Ashling House*, Main St (☎066/947 4247; ③) and at *The Smuggler's Inn*, Cliff Rd (closed Nov–Feb; ☎066/947 4330; ⑥). The *Butlers Arms Hotel* (closed late Oct–March; ☎066/947 4144, *butarms@iol.ie*; ⑨) offers seaviews and a welcoming atmosphere. *Peter's Place Hostel*

WATERVILLE IN LEGEND: NOAH'S CHILDREN IN IRELAND

Waterville and Ballinskelligs Bay form the setting for one of the more wayward Irish legends. When the biblical flood was imminent, so the story goes, Noah's son **Bith** and his daughter **Cessair** found that there was no room for them in the ark. So they and their retinue set sail for Ireland which, Cessair was advised, was uninhabited, free of monsters, reptiles and sin, and would therefore escape the flood. However, although 49 women survived to land along with Cessair in 2958 BC, only two men besides Bith made it. The three men divided the women between them, but when Bith and Ladra, the pilot, died, Fintan, the last man, was overwhelmed and, to his eternal shame, ran away – upon which Cessair, who loved him, died of sorrow.

(no phone), on the seafront at the south end of town, is small and cosy, and its jovial owner may rustle you up a meal, and you can also camp. Most of the bars and hotels do food, one of the best being *The Lobster Bar*, and for inexpensive home cooking, try the welcoming *An Corcán*, at the north end of the main street (till 10pm in summer).

From Waterville, it's a long haul by bike or on foot up to the **Coomakista Pass**, but the effort is well worth it for the breathtaking views over the mouth of the Kenmare River, all greys and blues, the three rocks called the Bull, the Cow and the Calf, and beyond them the Beara Peninsula – most spectacular when the weather's good; when it rains you can see the squalls being driven in across the ocean. Unfortunately you can't hope to avoid lots of other tourists here.

Derrynane to Sneem

Tucked away on a little promontory of its own between the Ring of Kerry and the sea, and about six miles south of Waterville, is **DERRYNANE** (pronounced *Derrynaan*), home of the family of Daniel O'Connell, the Catholic lawyer and politician who negotiated limited Catholic emancipation in 1829. Derrynane itself is a pleasant place, with wide, flat sand beaches, two miles of dunes, good swimming and rocks glistening black with mussels. Although fun in the daytime, like everywhere along this western seaboard it's most atmospheric at sunset, when the long twilight lingers; the Gaels believed that sunset and sunrise were points of transition (like stiles and gates) where it was possible to slip from the real world into the faerie one, and here you can see their point.

Derrynane House (April & Oct Tues–Sun 1–5pm; May–Sept Mon–Sat 9am–6pm, Sun 11am–7pm; Nov–March Sat & Sun 1–5pm; £2/€2.55; Heritage Card), remodelled by Daniel O'Connell himself, is absolutely simple – a square slate tower and roughly elegant rooms with the slanting sea-light a constant presence. The O'Connells were an old Gaelic family who'd made their money trading and smuggling – the west of Ireland had a long tradition of trade with Europe in wine, spices and silks. Daniel O'Connell's uncle bequeathed him a fortune, giving him the financial independence necessary to devote himself to politics. Discrimination against Catholics was widespread and closely experienced by Daniel: another uncle was shot dead because he would not give up his fine horse, as the law demanded of Catholics.

The touristy *Scarriff Inn* (☎066/947 5132, *www.caherdaniel.net*; ④), right on the N70 just east of the Beenarourke viewing point, is a focal point for the area and offers rooms with seaviews and good bar **food** to the hordes of coach parties passing by. The steep lane down behind here leads to a couple of pleasant **B&Bs** with spectacular views: *Harbour View*, Farraniaragh (closed Nov–March; ☎066/947 5292; ③) right on the Kerry Way; and down by the bay, *Skellig House* (☎066/947 5129; ③), who also arrange trips to Skellig. From here you can pick your way east for around three miles along a beautiful Mass Path to the beach in front of *Derrynane House*.

The little village of **CAHERDANIEL**, around three miles east of the *Scarriff Inn*, makes a very good base and there's excellent **hostel** accommodation right in the centre at the *Traveller's Rest Hostel* (☎066/947 5175). Most other accommodation is on the main road west: nearby is *O'Sullivan's* **B&B** (☎066/947 5124; ③); *Derrynane Bay House* (☎066/947 5404; ③) is about a mile from Caherdaniel, and the pleasant *Carrigbeg Hostel* (IHH; ☎066/947 5229) is about two miles away. For **camping** head a mile south of the village for *Wave Crest Caravan Park* (☎066/947 5188), a fabulous spot overlooking the sea. Caherdaniel has a small shop, a petrol station and a couple of lively **pubs**: *Freddy's* and *The Blind Piper* – in the latter you can get very good food at the bar or in the upstairs restaurant and there's fine traditional music in the summer on Wednesday and Saturday evenings.

The immediate area has plenty of ancient forts and standing stones. Continuining east around the Ring of Kerry towards Sneem, there's a sign on the left for **Staigue**

Fort; after two-and-a-half miles up a rough lane (some of it part of the Kerry Way), you'll come to a very well-preserved ring fort, possibly created as early as 1000 BC, and probably a residence of the Kings of Munster. Back on the N70, the road winds on towards Sneem, past hedgerows blossoming with fuchsia and hydrangea, and there's good **swimming** along the way, particularly at White Strand.

Spectacularly set against the mountains, **SNEEM** (*An tsnaidhm*), is dominated by the 2245ft Knockmoyle; but the village has lost something by selling out to tourism. Sneem's houses are washed in different colours – reputedly so that drunken residents can find their way home – and their picture-book prettiness juxtaposed against tourist shops and cafés has a touch of the surreal. Good local fishing is advertised by the salmon-shaped weathercock on the Protestant church. You'll probably want to push on to more interesting Kenmare, but if you do decide to **stay** here, you could try *Avonlea House* (☎064/45221; ③), *Old Convent House* (☎064/45181; ③) or *Rockville House* (☎064/45135; ③).

The approach to Kenmare along the estuary is unexciting, seemingly more in character with the Beara Peninsula opposite than with wild Iveragh, and you'll have a more scenic journey back to Killarney if you take the mountain road direct from Sneem. The two routes join up again at the spectacular **Moll's Gap**, north of Kenmare.

Kenmare and around

With its delicatessens and designer boutiques, **KENMARE** feels like a prosperous foreign enclave, and you're more likely to hear English or German tones here than Irish. Neatly organized on an X-plan (laid out by the first Marquess of Lansdowne in 1775), the town is pleasantly cosmopolitan: besides the resident foreigners, it's the natural crossing-over point for everyone travelling up from Cork.

Kenmare was founded by **Sir William Petty**, Cromwell's surveyor general, to serve his mining works beside the River Finnihy. Petty was extremely active in (and benefited greatly from) the dealings in confiscated properties that went on after the Cromwellian wars. Many soldiers were paid by the impecunious government in land, but not all of them wanted to settle in Ireland and so sold their land to dealers – such as Petty. His acquisition of land all over Ireland, including roughly a quarter of Kerry, was surely helped by his commission to survey the country on behalf of the government, when he investigated two-thirds of the Irish counties in the amazingly short period of fifteen months. Petty's other achievements were no less remarkable: a professor of medicine at Oxford at 27, he was also a professor of music and founder member of the Royal Society in London; an early statistician, economist and demographer; and politically astute enough to get yet more land and a knighthood out of Charles II, even though he had earlier served Cromwell faithfully. In Kerry, he laid the foundations of the mining and smelting industries, encouraged fishing, and founded the enormous Lansdowne estate which once surrounded the town; many of its buildings still remain today.

Evidence of a much more ancient settlement are the fifteen stones which make up the **stone circle** just outside the centre of town on the banks of the river; go up by the right of the market house that faces the park, and past some estate houses. Then walk up the lane at the cul-de-sac sign, and a few yards after it meets another lane coming in from the left you'll find the circle, behind a high ditch.

Practicalities

Buses stop in Main Street which runs down to the square where you will find the **tourist office** (April–May & Sept to mid-Oct Mon–Sat 9.15am–1pm & 2.15–5.30pm;

June–Aug Mon–Sat 9am–6pm, Sun 9.15am–1pm & 2.15–5.30pm; ☎064/41233). The **heritage centre** next door (April, May & Sept to mid-Oct Mon–Sat 9.15am–1pm & 2.15–5pm; June–Aug Mon–Sat 9am–5.30pm, Sun 9.15am–1pm & 2.15–5pm) has a wealth of detail on the history of Kenmare, particularly on the lace-making industry that was introduced here by the Church during the nineteenth century. Rather less engaging is the photograph of Margaret Thatcher that grimaces at you on the way in – apparently the former British Prime Minister is fiercely proud to have descended from a Kenmare washerwoman.

Bike rental is available from the *Fáilte Hostel,* Finnegan's on Henry St, and White's on Killarney Rd. If you want to see Kenmare from the water, Seafari River Cruises (☎064/83171) depart from the pier three times a day in high season.

Accommodation

Plenty of good **accommodation** is available in the Kenmare area, but only a limited amount in the centre of town, so if you're travelling in high season or on a bank holiday it's worth booking in advance. The Ring of Kerry Caravan and **Camping** Park is located at Reen (☎064/41648) three miles west of town towards Sneem.

D'Arcy's, Main St (☎064/41589). The en-suite rooms of this town-centre guesthouse are quite tired and plain, but nevertheless this is a pleasant and convenient place to stay. Breakfast is served in the spacious restaurant which is more interestingly decorated with some very lively artwork. ④.

Druid Cottage, a mile out on the Sneem road (☎064/41803). A solid nineteenth-century house, which has been pleasantly renovated and offers excellent hospitality. En-suite and standard rooms are available. ③.

Fáilte, Shelbourne St (IHH; ☎064/42333). Large, clean and well-run hostel right in the town centre. There are twin (①) and family rooms as well as dorms. Closed Nov–March.

Hazelwood, Killaha, about a mile and a half out of town towards Castletownbere (☎064/41420). This excellent-value B&B is set in a stunning location overlooking the Kenmare river. The atmosphere is relaxed and the vegetarian and traditional Irish breakfasts are superb. There's a delightful woodland walk to a private beach, and they can arrange horse riding at £12/€15.24 per hour. ②.

Park Hotel, at the top of Main St (☎064/41200, *www.parkkenmare.com*). A famous, and phenomenally expensive, luxury hotel built in the late nineteenth century in a fabulous location overlooking the Kenmare estuary. The extensive facilities include tennis and croquet. ⑨.

Silver Trees, Kilowen Road (☎064/41008). A friendly, efficient and rather plush B&B, five minutes' walk from the centre, opposite the golf course on the road towards Kilgarvan. Rooms, which all have their own bathroom and TV, are spacious and comfortable, and the breakfast, whether Continental or a full Irish fry-up, is definitely worth getting up for. Closed Nov–March. ④.

Eating and drinking

Kenmare is an affluent tourist town and, while this means there's a good range of **places to eat**, prices – particularly for bar food – do tend to be more expensive than elsewhere. You will have no problem finding a decent pub to **drink** in and catch some traditional Irish music: *The Square Pint*, on the Square, is one of the best spots for traditional music in Kerry, and others worth trying include *The Wander Inn* on Henry Street, and *Moeran's*, off the top of Main Street.

An Leath Phingin, 35 Main St (☎064/41559). Excellent Italian-Irish restaurant with a cosy cottage interior, serving fresh pasta, stone-oven pizzas, and oak-wood fired barbecued meats.

The Bean and Leaf, 4 Rock St, off Main St. Charming bookshop and café serving good coffee and pastries, which also offers Internet access. Closed Sun & Mon and Nov–March.

Café Indigo, The Square, above *The Square Pint* (☎064/42356, *www.cafe-indigo.com*). Contemporary, eclectic menu including delicious dishes such as roast sea scallops on a herb and asparagus risotto, and lamb cutlets with herb polenta.

The New Delight, Henry St. A warm and welcoming vegetarian café serving inexpensive wholesome snacks such as filled pittas and baguettes, open sandwiches and soups, along with more substantial meals such as lentil koftas and aubergine bake. Organic wine and herb teas quench your thirst.

The Purple Heather, Henry St. A traditional pub that serves good bar food. The interesting menu includes homemade chicken liver paté with cumberland sauce, crab salad and Cashel blue cheese sandwich with walnut salad.

The Square Pint, The Square. This very pleasant bar has a contemporary interior, and offers great bar food which comes from the *Café Indigo* kitchen upstairs. Try the chargrilled chicken with Parmesan shavings and roasted pine kernels.

The Wander Inn, 2 Henry St. A large and popular pub serving traditional pub meals such as bacon and cabbage, roasts, homemade burgers and pizzas.

Wharton's Chipper, Main St, no sign, but located two doors up from *An Leath Phingin*. A good-value fast-food option – with seating upstairs – open till 2 or 4am. Traditional fish and chips; the fish is fresh and the chips homemade.

The Beara Peninsula

Cross the river from Kenmare and you're on the **Beara Peninsula**, which Kerry shares with Cork. Beara has its followers, but after the wildness of the rest of Kerry, it can at first seem over-lush and polite, with more of the flavour of Cork. Even along the River Kenmare, though, the scenery is attractive enough and curiously, once you actually cross into County Cork, the Beara becomes far wilder (see p.313).

Turn right after the bridge out of Kenmare, and the road runs through heavily wooded country alongside the Kenmare estuary; after about seven miles there's a signpost to the left for **Inchiquin Lake**. Following this, you soon quit the luxuriant vegetation as the bumpy road ascends rapidly to the lake, affording exhilarating views of the countryside left behind. A waterfall tumbles down from a second lake, and on the far side of Inchiquin Lake is **Uragh Wood**, one of the last surviving remnants of the ancient sessile oakwoods that once covered most of Ireland. The entire valley is packed with **plants**: large-flowered butterwort covers the meadows in spring, and you can find Irish spurge, saxifrage, arbutus and other flora specific to the southwest here. At the lake itself, the surrounding hills seem to act as some kind of intensifier focused on a tiny stone circle by the side of the water – bringing to mind the theory that these prehistoric monuments indicate earth forces. There's salmon, sea trout and brown trout fishing in both lakes, but, as always, check the licence position before you start.

Lauragh

Following the main road for **LAURAGH**, twelve miles southwest of Kenmare, you're still in the enormous estate once owned by Petty. The gardens at **Derreen House** (April–Sept daily 11am–6pm; £2.50/€3.17), for a long time one of the Irish residences of Petty's descendant, the Marquess of Lansdowne, are open to the public and stocked with plants that clearly luxuriate in the mild sea climate, including such exotica as tree ferns and bamboo, plus rhododendrons and camellias. Yet despite its magnificence, it doesn't compare with the wild and windswept grassy uplands. Head westwards from Lauragh and you're soon over the border into Cork; south, the road climbs spectacularly above Glanmore Lake to the Healy Pass – again, the county border – giving amazing views in both directions. There's the fairly basic An Óige *Glanmore Lake* **hostel** beside the lake (closed Oct–Easter; ☎064/83181).

The Dingle Peninsula

The **Dingle Peninsula** is a place of intense, shifting beauty. Spectacular mountains, long sandy beaches and the staggering splinter-slatted mass of rocks that defines the extraordinary coast at Slea Head all conspire to ensure that, remote though it is, the Dingle Peninsula is firmly on the tourist trail. The mountain scenery is at its most dramatic at **Mount Brandon**, which rises to 3119ft and affords splendid opportunities for hiking.

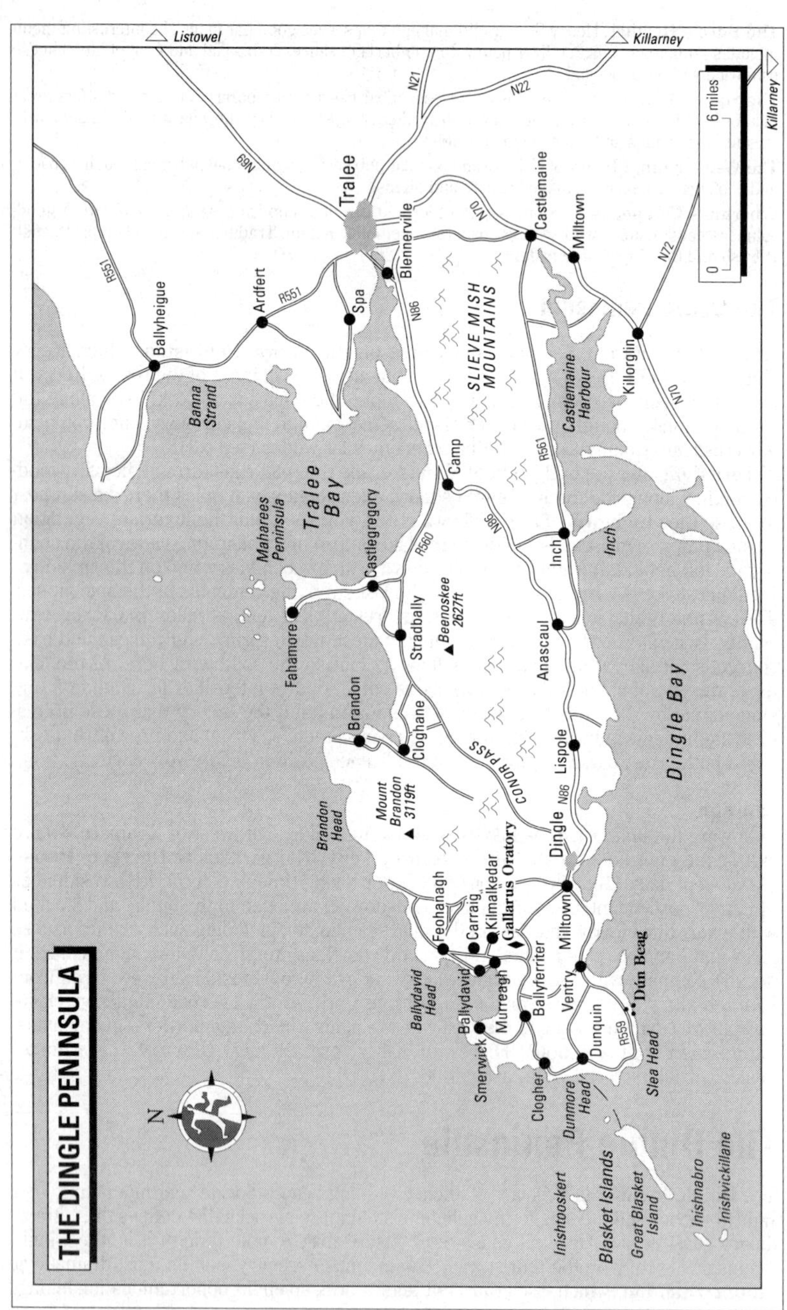
THE DINGLE PENINSULA
N
Listowel
Killarney
Killarney
0
6 miles
N69
N21
N22
Tralee
R551
R551
Ballyheigue
Ardfert
Spa
Blennerville
N70
Castlemaine
Milltown
N72
Killorglin
N70
SLIEVE MISH MOUNTAINS
Castlemaine Harbour
Banna Strand
Tralee Bay
Maharees Peninsula
Castlegregory
Fahamore
N86
Camp
R560
R561
N86
Inch
Inch
Beenoskee 2627ft
Stradbally
Anascaul
Brandon
Cloghane
Lispole
Dingle Bay
CONOR PASS
Mount Brandon 3119ft
Brandon Head
N86
Dingle
Feohanagh
Carraig
Kilmalkedar
Gallarus Oratory
Milltown
Dún Beag
Ballydavid Head
Ballydavid
Murreagh
Ballyferriter
Ventry
Smerwick
Dunquin
R559
Slea Head
Clogher
Dunmore Head
Blasket Islands
Inishtooskert
Great Blasket Island
Inishnabro
Inishvickillane

HORSE-DRAWN CARAVAN HOLIDAYS ON THE DINGLE PENINSULA

The ultimate Irish tourism cliché it may be, but a horse-drawn caravan holiday is a great way to unwind and to absorb the breathtaking beauty of the Dingle Peninsula. What's more, you're likely to have a very sociable time, the caravan's theatricality provoking plenty of conversation. You can also expect to develop a strong relationship with your horse – one way or another.

Slattery's Travel, 1 Russell St, Tralee (☎066/718 6240; freephone from the UK ☎0800/515900 for brochure) rent out caravans for three-day weekends (£180/€228.55 low season only) and week-long breaks (£290/€368.22 low season, £590/€745.15 high season); additional costs include £8/€10.16 per night stopover fee, £5/€6.35 per day insurance and £12/€15.24 per week horsefeed. Slattery's will tell you no previous experience of handling horses is necessary, but it certainly helps – as do height and brute strength. Before setting off, however, friendly stable-workers take you through the basics of catching, harnessing, driving, watering and feeding your horse. Slattery's also supply a map of the peninsula with a range of routes and stopover sites; most sites are fields alongside pubs, so you can have a drink beneath the stars and still keep an eye on the children.

Caravans have one double bed, a small single, and a couple of extra fold-down bunks – with bedding. In theory there's room for five people, though in fact any more than three adults may well find it a bit cramped, and if there are more of you, it's a good idea to have a small tent. The caravans also come equipped with a small stove and cooking utensils.

The steep Conor Pass road that runs south of here between Dingle town and the peninsula's northern coast is much-loved by cyclists determined to prove their stamina. There are very fine beaches all around the peninsula: at the tiny village of **Inch** three miles of sand stretches out into the ocean; **Castlegregory** on the **Maharees Peninsula** acts as a magnet for surfers; and, as you travel west both the inland and coastal scenery intensifies, with superb beaches at **Ventry** (the best place for safe swimming), the Blasket Islands, **Murreagh** and Ballydavid, to name but a few. There's plenty of myth and history too: the peninsula has one of the greatest concentrations of Celtic ruins in Ireland. Ring forts, beehive huts, oratories and stone crosses are prevalent here and the vigour of the Christian culture that set out from here to evangelize and educate the rest of Europe is almost palpable. The best of these ancient monuments lie west of Dingle town and include **Dún Beag**, just outside the tiny village of Ventry; the early Christian **Gallarus Oratory** and the medieval church of **Kilmakedar** are both further west still. The now uninhabited **Blasket Islands** once generated a wealth of Irish literature, and indeed the area at the far west of the peninsula remains a *Gaeltacht* region (Irish-speaking), with the language still very much alive in and around the little villages of **Ballydavid** and **Ballyferriter** – both of which offer a handful of places to stay and eat and are within easy reach of fabulous sandy beaches. As if all this were not enough, the peninsula has a place in film history too: *Ryan's Daughter* was filmed here, as were parts of *Far and Away,* starring Tom Cruise. For all its popularity as a tourist destination, the Dingle peninsula remains magical. On a fine day exhilarating views stretch out as far as the monastic settlement on Great Skellig, off the Iveragh Peninsula to the south; but it can be more exciting still in the rain, when the cloud shifts down over the land and you find yourself in a white mist through which the dim shapes of oratories and beehive huts loom.

Inch and Anascaul

Though most of the peninsula's delights are to the west of Dingle town, there are a few notable stopping points on your way to Dingle town from the east. First of these is *The*

Phoenix Organic Vegetarian Restaurant & Farmhouse Accommodation (Oct–Easter by appointment only; ☎066/976 6284; accommodation from £13/€16.51), three miles west of **Castlemaine** village on the Killarney–Dingle road, providing hostel **accommodation** with a difference: rooms are decorated with furnishings from Bali, India and Egypt and the restaurant's menu strikes a similarly exotic note. You can also camp here, and there's Irish music and set dancing in *The Anvil* pub, about one mile away. There's a break in the shoreline at **INCH**, where a long, narrow sandbar pushes out into Dingle Bay. In the eighteenth century, the beach was used by wreckers who, on stormy nights, would tie a lantern to a horse's head and leave the horse grazing; mariners mistaking the bobbing light for another ship steered their vessels aground on the strand. There's B&B accommodation about a mile east of here at *Waterside B&B* (☎066/915 8129; ③). For hostel accommodation, as you head west take a sharp right after *Foley's* pub; after about three miles turn right for the *Bog View Hostel*, situated midway between Camp and Anascaul (IHH; closed Sept–May; ☎066/915 8125). Back in Inch, you can hear lively traditional music sessions at *Foley's* pub (Saturday year round, summer on Wednesday).

The road turns inland, five miles further west, towards **ANASCAUL** (*Abhainn an Scáil*), a single street of brightly painted houses, pleasant enough but with a curiously safe, inland feel considering the proximity of the wild Atlantic coast. Two pubs here have famous associations: the magician Dan Foley's shocking-pink bar, familiar from a host of postcards, and the *South Pole Inn*, so named by local man Tom Crean, a veteran of Scott's Antarctic expedition. There are several **B&Bs**: *The Anchor House* (☎066/915 7382; ③) and *Brackluin House* (☎066/915 7145; ③), both centrally located, and slightly further out on the road to Dingle, *Four Winds* (☎066/915 7168; ③). In addition there's a **hostel**, *Fuchsia Lodge* (IHH; ☎066/915 7150), about two miles east of the village, where it is also possible to **camp**. Heading northwards, along a string of increasingly rough tracks, you'll reach Anascaul Lake, overshadowed by the scree slopes of Stradbally Mountain: a secretive place, with plenty of wilder country beyond.

Dingle town

DINGLE (*An Daingean*) doesn't offer a huge amount to see, but the town is a pleasant place to stay, devoted to fishing and tourism, and certainly makes the best base for exploring the peninsula. There are plenty of opportunities to get out onto the water from here and many fine walks accessible from the town centre; the Kerry Way actually passes right through the centre. Though crammed with pubs, little restaurants and B&Bs, Dingle somehow never feels too crowded, and even if you don't like the way the place has geared itself up for tourism, you'll be glad when the weather's bad – which it often is – that there are plenty of places to hole up. The town services the tiny communities west of here, so if you are heading on it makes good sense to stock up on supplies.

Arrival and information

Getting to Dingle is easy by **bus** from either Tralee or Killarney. Travel west of Dingle town is less straightforward – buses leave Dingle for Dunquin Monday and Thursday three times daily, and during the summer months they depart Monday to Saturday twice daily and go via Slea Head. The Mountain Man, Strand St (☎066/915 2400), runs a minibus from Dingle to the ferry at Dunquin where you can go on to Blasket Island. **Bikes** can be rented from Foxy John's in Main St (£6/€7.62 per day).

The **tourist office** in Strand St (March–May & mid-Sept to Nov Mon–Sat 9.15am–1pm & 2.15–5.30pm; June & early Sept Mon–Sat 9am–6pm, Sun 10am–1pm & 2.15–6pm; July & Aug Mon–Sat 9am–7pm, Sun 10am–1pm & 2.15–6pm; ☎066/915 1188) has an accommodation service and plenty of information on the surrounding area; perhaps the only drawback is the very long queues that you can expect during high season. Dingle's **Internet café** is *The Dingle Web* on Lower Main St (*info@dingleweb.com*), where Internet access costs £5/€6.35 per hour.

Accommodation

Dingle offers a very good range of hostels, B&Bs and hotels. It is advisable to book ahead during July and August, either directly or through the very helpful tourist office.

Ballintaggart House, Racecourse Rd, one mile east of Dingle (IHH; ☎066/915 1454, *info@dingleaccommodation.com*). This hostel is one of the best around, boasting huge roaring fires, plenty of space and wonderful views. Private rooms (①) have excellent en-suite power showers. Camping is available and there's a regular free pick-up service from town.

Benners Hotel, Main St (☎066/915 1638, *benners@eircom.net*). A traditional town centre hotel where the lobby has a pleasantly lived-in feel, and the bedrooms are newly refurbished in a warm rustic style. ⑧.

Boland's, Goat St, at the top of Main St (☎066/915 1426). A well-run B&B in a central location. All rooms are en suite with phones, TV, hairdryers and tea- and coffee-making. ④.

Brosnan's, Cooleen (☎066/915 1146). A B&B located just a short walk from the centre of town down the laneway opposite the Esso station. Bedrooms are pleasant, with stripped floors and en-suite facilities, although there's no use of the sitting room. ③.

Dingle Skellig Hotel, (☎066/015 1144, *www.dingleskellig.com*). A large and modern four-star hotel situated right down by the bay. Facilities include a pool, gym, kids' club and crêche. Enquire about the good weekend deals which are available. Closed mid-Jan–mid-Feb. ⑨.

Grapevine, Dykegate St (☎066/915 1434). A friendly, welcoming and well-run hostel in the centre of town.

Greenmount Guesthouse, Upper John St (☎066/915 1414). This spacious and award-winning guesthouse is set in a great location overlooking the harbour. All rooms are en suite and also have TVs. ⑥.

Kirrary B&B, Avondale St (☎066/915 1606). Pleasant B&B in a very central spot which offers a homely atmosphere and has a lovely garden. Rooms are either en suite or with shared bathroom. ④.

Lovett's Hostel, Cooleen (☎066/915 1903). A small and clean family-run hostel found down the laneway opposite the Esso garage.

O'Coiléain B&B, Holyground (☎066/915 1937). A congenial family home, in an excellent central location, with fresh, contemporary interiors and a lovely garden. All rooms are en suite. ③.

The Sleeping Giant, Green St (☎066/915 2666). Clean, well-run and central hostel accommodation with the use of a small kitchen.

The Town

Essentially just a few streets by the side of Dingle Bay, the town has a hugely impressive natural **harbour** where the boats come in and **Fungi the dolphin** likes to play; half-tame Fungi is one of Dingle's main tourist attractions. It may sound silly, but there are people who talk of their meetings with this solitary, 663lb maritime mammal in the terms of a religious conversion, and others travel hundreds of miles just to see him. If you want to go for an early-morning dip with him, check out Flannery's beside the tourist office (☎066/915 1967; two-hour boat trip £10/€12.70, wet suit hire £14/€17.78) – boats depart at 8am and you will need to be measured for a wet suit the day before. Flannery's also offer boat trips out to see him (☎066/915 2626). Alternatively, you can walk down to the coast via the lane alongside the *Skellig Hotel* and watch him from the shore – Fungi often comes in this far. There are plenty of other ways to get out onto – if not into – the water from Dingle, including Eco archeological boat trips, which head along the coast, the guide explaining the flora, fauna and history of the peninsula as you go (2–2hr 30min; ☎087/285 8802; £15/€19.05). All trips depart from the quays throughout the summer; the length of the season depends on the weather.

The solidity of the town's colour-washed houses suggests this was a place of some consequence, and Dingle was indeed Kerry's leading port in the fourteenth and fifteenth centuries. It later became a centre for smuggling, and at one stage during the eighteenth century (when the revenue from smuggling was at its height) even minted its own coinage. Contemporary reports describe the stone houses with balconies and oval windows, imparting a Spanish feel to the town. In the nineteenth century, Dingle was the focus of a uniquely successful attempt to woo the Kerry Catholics from their faith, when in 1831 the Protestant curate T. Goodman began preaching in Irish, establishing schools on the peninsula and building houses as inducements for converts; these still stand at the edge of town.

Eating and drinking

For its size, Dingle has a high proportion of upmarket restaurants, a number of them noted for seafood. More affordable meals are available in several pubs and a handful of cafés.

Adam's, Main St. Characterful old-style bar with an up-beat atmosphere serving inexpensive and delicious homemade soups, open sandwiches, and fresh crab salads.

An Cafe Liteartha, Dykegate Lane. Wholly unpretentious bookshop-café that stocks both Irish and English language editions (politics and local interest are both well represented) to the gentle sounds of pleasant Irish music. The no-nonsense food focuses on delivering very cheap tea, coffee, scones and sandwiches (ham, cheese, beef).

The Chart House, The Mall (☎066/915 2255). Informal, upmarket restaurant with a fine reputation for its imaginative menus, which might feature cajun-spiced monkfish, saffron roast turbot with sun-dried tomato mash and salsa verde, or pan-fried guinea fowl. Call ahead for a reservation. Closed Tues.

Doyle's Seafood Restaurant, John St (☎066/915 1174). There's great seafood to be had all around the Kerry coast, and in Dingle *Doyle's* is the most famous place to sample the delights of the deep. Evenings only.

The Global Village, Main St. True to the name, the menu revolves around a wide-ranging mix of influences gleaned during the proprietor's world travels. Breakfasts are tasty, lunches are light and inexpensive. Evening meals are a little pricey. The laid-back atmosphere makes this a great place to chill.

Máire de Barra's, Strand St. Regular smoky pub catering for tourists, and generally very busy. Plenty of filling pub grub, including beef casserole, lasagne and chips, and homely puddings like rhubarb pie to satisfy sweet cravings. Food served till 9pm in summer.

The Oven Doors and Dingle Tea Rooms, Holyground. Handy café and pizza restaurant right in the town centre serving tea and scones, salads and fabulous cakes along with its inexpensive pizza menu. Open till 8.30pm, depending on business.

Nightlife and entertainment

Life in the evenings is centred on Dingle's many **pubs**, which between them offer **traditional music** sessions on just about any night you choose during the summer, and at weekends during the winter. *An Droichead Beag* at the bottom of Main St is probably the best place to start at any time with music most nights year round; *O'Flaherty's* in Bridge St is well worth checking out too and *Máire de Barra's* has traditional, folk or ballads just about every night in summer. **Special events** here include the compulsive Dingle Races in early August, the Dingle Regatta later in the month and *Féile na Mara* in September, when the entire fleet sails out in procession to the mouth of the harbour to be blessed by the bishop; visit the tourist office for details.

Ventry and ancient monuments

The first village of interest west of Dingle is tiny **VENTRY** (*Ceann Trá*) five miles further on, once the main port of the peninsula and another fine natural harbour: a wide curve of sandy beach beneath the enormous, gnarled shoulder of Mount Eagle, dropping almost sheer to the sea with only a precarious ledge for the road.

It's in the inhospitable surroundings on the stretch out from Ventry to Slea Head that the main concentration of **ancient monuments** can be found. What follows here can only be an introduction to the major sites; the minor ones alone could take weeks to explore. A good local **map**, such as the one available at the tourist office, is essential for exploring minor sites, while several excellent guides to the peninsula exist for real enthusiasts (available at bookshops in Dingle town).

First off there's the spectacular **Dún Beag** (dating from the eighth or ninth century AD), a scramble down from the road towards the ocean about three to four miles out from Ventry (entry £1/€1.27). A promontory fort, its defences include four earthen rings, with an underground escape route, or souterrain, by the main entrance. It's a magical location, overlooking the open sea and the Iveragh Peninsula, the drama of its setting only increased by the fact that some of the building has fallen off into the sea.

Between Dún Beag and **Slea Head**, the hillside above the road is studded with stone beehive huts, cave dwellings, souterrains, forts, churches, standing stones and crosses – over five hundred in all. The beehive huts can be deceptive – they were still being built and used for storing farm tools and produce until the late nineteenth century, so not all of them are as old as they look. But once you're standing among genuinely ancient buildings like the signposted **Fahan group** (entry £1/€1.27) and looking south over a landscape that's remained essentially unchanged for centuries, the Iveragh Peninsula and the two Skellig Islands (see p.328) in the distance, you get a strong sense of past lives.

Ventry itself consists of a sprinkling of houses with, at the east end of the bay, a shop, post office, pub and a few **accommodation** options. Up the lane past the post office are *Ceann Trá Heights* (☎066/915 9866; ④) and *The Plough* (☎066/915 9727; ③), two B&Bs which are worth trying. The very comfortable *Bally Beag Hostel*, signposted from the main road at the turning for Ballyferriter (☎066/915 9876), has dorms, family and twin rooms (①), and offers bike rental, laundry facilities and also gives lifts to and from Dingle. *Penny's Pottery Café* (summer only) is a good spot for inexpensive coffee, cakes, crumbles and baguettes. At the west end of Ventry is *Páid Ó Sé's*, a **bar** noted for traditional music sessions which also serves **food**.

Just west of Ventry is the **Celtic and Prehistoric Museum** (May–Sept daily 10am–5.30pm; phone at other times; ☎066/915 9941; £3/€3.81), a small up-beat family-run museum which boasts a large nest of dinosaur eggs, beautiful Celtic jewellery and the only woolly mammoth skull fossil in Ireland – complete with huge curling tusks and affectionately named Milly. Try and take one of their personalized tours in which your enthusiastic guide will encourage you to handle Neolithic flint axes and will tell tales of local mythology. There's a pleasant tea room on site here too.

The Blasket Islands

At Slea Head, five miles west of Ventry, the view opens up to include the desolate, splintered masses of the **Blasket Islands** (*Na Blascaodaí*), officially uninhabited since 1953, though there are still summer communities on the islands. The weather in Blasket Sound can be treacherous – two of the Armada's ships were shattered to matchwood when they came bowling round the Head in September 1588 – but inhospitable as they seem, the islands were once the home of thriving communities. The astonishing body of **Irish literature** that emerged from these tiny islands (Maurice O'Sullivan's *Twenty Years A-Growing*, Peig Sayers's *Peig* and Tomas O'Crohan's *Island Cross-Talk*) gives a vivid picture of the life of the islanders which, although remote, was anything but unsophisticated. Ironically, these literary works describe life among people who could neither read nor write, yet their oral tradition emerges as far from primitive. Locals are less than enamoured of the ugly interpretive centre, **Ionad an Bhlascaoíd Mhoír**, at Dunquin (Easter–June & Sept–Oct daily 10am–6pm; July & Aug daily 10am–7pm;

£2.50/€3.18; Heritage Card), but nevertheless the material it holds on the lives and literature of the islanders is very interesting, and there's a good **café** for lunch too.

In the summer, boats bound for **Great Blasket** (*An Blascaod Mór*) leave the pier just south of Dunquin every half hour between 10.30am and 5pm for around £12/€15.24 return (May–Sept in good weather; ☎066/915 6422, *www.blasketferries.com*). Whether or not you choose to stay over, Great Blasket's delights are simple ones: sitting on the beaches and staring out to sea, tramping the many footpaths that crisscross the island, or trying to spot a seal. If you want to swim be careful as currents are very strong – and the water will be icy. One of the old houses has been renovated and turned into a **hostel** (summer only; ☎086/848 6687); evening meals are available. If you want to **camp** on the island you'll need to be prepared – take food (there's no shop, just the café mentioned below), water carriers for the well, and bags to carry refuse home. Good cheap dinners are available at the island café (noon–5pm). It's advisable to check the longterm weather forecast with the boatmen in advance, as it's possible to be stranded for days if the weather breaks.

There's a comfortable An Óige **hostel** on the mainland at **DUNQUIN** (*Dún Chaoin*), with plenty of dorm, twin (①) and four-bed rooms and a drying room (☎066/915 6121); breakfast is available. Although there isn't a shop in Dunquin, the hostel stocks a very limited range of food stuffs. *Kruger's* **pub** (closed Oct–Feb; ☎066/915 6127; ②) is the hub of local activity, with food and traditional music in summer, and **B&B**. Across from here *An Portán* **restaurant** (☎066/915 6212; ③) enjoys a good reputation and also offers B&B. About a mile up the hill from here is *Gleann Dearg* (☎066/915 6188; ③), a cosy B&B with lovely views, and further up lies the *Dunquin Pottery Café*, one of the best places in Dunquin for daytime eating (the other being the heritage centre) which affords spectacular views out across the Blaskets and, behind these, a mass of mountain laced with a network of stone dykes. *Tig Áine* (☎066/915 6214), about two miles north of Dunquin at An Ghráig, is a laid-back café and weaver's shop where you can enjoy soups, sandwiches, omelettes and stir-frys overlooking the sea and a delightful garden.

Ballyferriter

A couple of miles north round the headland from Dunquin, largely Irish-speaking **BALLYFERRITER** (*Baile an Fheirtearaigh*) is a lively little village during the summer, though it can be bleak out of season. Its beach, the beautiful Wine Strand, is a great spot for swimming in fine weather. The little lanes running northwards from the village lead to impressive 500ft hilltop walling at Sybil Head and the Three Sisters rock (with the Norman ruins of Castle Sybil built within an older promontory fort); and to Smerwick Harbour and **Dún an Óir** (the Golden Fort). In September 1580 at Dún an Óir, a band of Italian, Spanish, English and Irish supporters of the rebellion in Munster, backed by papal funds in support of Catholic Ireland against Protestant England, were defeated by the English. The rebels were massacred – men, women and children – as a warning to others.

In Ballyferriter itself **Corca Dhuibhne Regional Museum** (April–Sept daily 10am–5.30pm; other times by appointment; ☎066/915 6100, *www.corca-dhuibhne.com*; £1.50/€1.95), for all its modest means of presentation, has excellent material on the geology and archaeology of the Dingle Peninsula and is an ideal place to make sense of the surrounding landscape. In addition to providing plenty of information on local prehistoric sites it also has fine examples of cross slabs bearing *ogham* inscriptions. There's a good café at the museum too.

Also in the village centre are various **accommodation** and **food** options, all within a stone's throw of each other. *Tigh Pheig* is a genial place which serves good bar food, and the only upmarket restaurant here, *Tig an Tobair* (open May–Sept, closed Mon;

☎066/915 6404) offers contemporary Irish cooking. Very pleasant en-suite B&B accommodation is available at *Murphy's Bar* (☎066/915 6224; ④), and the *Dun an Oir Golf Hotel* (☎066/915 6133; ⑦) offers comfortable rooms and a swimming pool. Hostel accommodation is available at *An Cat Dubh* (The Black Cat), just outside Ballyferriter on the road to Dunquin (closed Oct–April; ☎066/915 6286), which also has a grocery shop attached.

The Gallarus Oratory, Kilmalkedar and Mount Brandon

The single most impressive early Christian monument on the Dingle Peninsula is the **Gallarus Oratory**, around three miles east of Ballyferriter, signposted off the road to Murreagh. The most perfectly preserved of around twenty such oratories in Ireland, it looks almost too good to be true, though apparently it hasn't undergone any great restoration programmes. Though the oratory can't be dated with any great certainty, it's thought to have been built between the ninth and twelfth centuries (Christian architectural activity dates from the late sixth or early seventh century, but it wasn't until the ninth century that churches began to be built of stone rather than wood), and to represent a transition between the round beehive huts elsewhere on the peninsula and the later rectangular churches. The problem with this construction (and the reason why so many similar buildings have fallen down) is that the long sides tend to cave in – if you look carefully at the Gallarus Oratory, you can see it's beginning to happen here, too.

The next architectural stage can be seen a mile to the north of here in the rectangular church at **KILMALKEDAR**. Its nave dates from the mid-twelfth century, and the corbelled stone roof was a direct improvement on the structure at Gallarus. The site marks the beginning of the Saint's Road, dedicated to **St Brendan**, patron saint of Kerry, which leads to the top of **Mount Brandon** – the route taken by pilgrims to St Brendan's shrine. If you want to follow this tough but historically resonant route up the mountainside, it's marked on the Ordnance Survey map number 70. Alternatively, there's a less challenging hike that skirts around the south of the mountain and leads to **CLOGHANE**, eight miles west of Stradbally, a tiny village flanked by lovely beaches. There's good bar **food** in the pubs, and you can stay at *O'Connor's* (☎066/713 8113; ④) or at *Mount Brandon House* **hostel** (☎066/713 8299; all year) which has a family room as well as small dorms and space for camping.

Carraig and Ballydavid

The tiny village of **Murreagh**, three miles from Ballyferriter, lies at the north end of a fabulous sandy beach; take the road towards **CARRAIG**, half a mile away, and you will come to *Ard na Carriage* (☎066/915 5295; ③), a very comfortable and welcoming **B&B**. There are a number of other places to stay in Carraig itself: *Tigh a Phóist* **hostel**, beside the church and a well-stocked shop (IHH; closed Nov–Feb; ☎066/915 5109), offering dorm and private rooms (①), and nearby *Nic Gearailt* B&B (☎066/915 5142, ③) which offers decent accommodation and a splendid breakfast menu that might include smoked salmon, mackerel and pancakes, evening meals also available. The nearest pubs from Carraig are about two miles away, in Ballydavid or north of the village towards Feohanagh, but there's **music and set dancing** at Teach Siamsa (Wed & Fri) during the summer.

Around the coast from Murreagh lies **BALLYDAVID** (*Baile na nGall*), backed by the mass of Mount Brandon and offering fine walks. A couple of bars stand at Ballydavid pier overlooking the magnificent sweep of the bay: *Begley's* (☎066/915 5123; ②) which offers fairly basic **B&B**, and the cosy *Tigh TP* (☎066/915 5444) which has a good range of **meals** on offer both in the bar and in the restaurant alongside. Ballydavid also has a post office and a small shop. **Brandon Creek** (signposted *Cuas*), just east of Ballydavid Head, is one of a number of contenders for St Brendan's sixth-century departure point, when he sailed off to discover the Islands of Paradise in the western ocean and, arguably, America.

The Conor Pass and the Maharees Peninsula

The interior of the Dingle Peninsula is dominated by two mountains, Mount Brandon and Beenoskee Mountain, separated by the steep **Conor Pass**. This mountainous terrain is excellent walking country; not only are there countless relics of the Celtic church and earlier to explore, but the area is dotted by a series of lakes that give the tussocky landscape some focus. There's a **hostel** at the foot of the pass on the northern side, the *Conor Pass Hostel* (IHH; closed Dec–mid-March; ☎066/713 9179) in **Stradbally**, where you'll find good sandy beaches for swimming.

The **Maharees Peninsula**, stretching north from Stradbally, is an exposed spit of land fringed by long sandy beaches, affording plenty of opportunities for surfing, windsurfing, canoeing and water-skiing – all of which can be arranged through the **Castlegregory Visitor Information Centre** in Strand St (summer only; ☎066/713 9422).

Tralee and around

TRALEE (*Trá Lí*) has had quite a facelift of late, and chief among its new attractions is the excellent **Kerry County Museum** in the Ashe Memorial Hall, Denny St (daily: mid-March–July; Sept & Oct 10am–6pm; August 10am–7pm; Nov & Dec 2–5pm; £5.50/€6.98), which uses interactive media and lifesize models in tracing Irish history back to 5000 BC. Other attractions include the **Tralee to Blennerville Steam Railway** (May–Oct; daily £2.75/€3.49; occasional closures so call ahead to check ☎066/712 1064), which is part of the famous Tralee–Dingle line (1891–1953), and the largest working windmill in Ireland and Britain, the **Blennerville Windmill**, about half a mile southwest of town along the N86 (April–Oct; daily 10am–6pm; £3/€3.81), which has its own exhibition, craft workshops and the usual tourist trinkets.

The **bus** station (☎066/712 3566) and **train** station (☎066/712 3522) are located next to each other, about a five-minute walk northeast of the town centre. The helpful **tourist office** (May, June, Sept & Oct Mon–Sat 9am–6pm; July & Aug Mon–Sat 9am–7pm, Sun 9am–6pm; Nov–April Mon–Fri 9am–1pm & 2–5pm; ☎066/712 1288) is in the Ashe Memorial Hall. Tralee has innumerable **B&Bs**, among them *Denton* (☎066/712 7637; ③) and *Ardroe House* (☎066/712 6050; ③), both on Oakpark Road in the centre. There's no shortage of **hostels** either: try the friendly and cosy *Lisnagree Hostel* (☎066/712 7133), out towards the general hospital, or *Finnegan's Hostel* on Denny St near the tourist office (IHH; ☎066/712 7610), which also rents out bikes. If you want to **camp**, *Woodland Park*, Dingle Rd (☎066/712 1235) is a short walk from the centre of town. You can **rent bikes**, including mountain bikes, from Tralee Gas Supplies in Strand St (☎066/712 2018), part of the Raleigh rent-a-bike scheme.

Finding a cheap place to **eat** in Tralee isn't a problem: for bar food try *The Mall*, *Kirby's Brogue Inn*, Rock St, which also serves seafood and steaks, or *Val's*, Bridge St which also does good bar food at lunchtime and inexpensive bistro meals in the evening. Tralee is a lively town and there are plenty of **pubs** which form the hub of evening entertainment; for **traditional music** try *McDaide's*, Castle St (every night, year round), *Baily's Corner*, Ashe St (Tuesday), *Seán Og's* on Bridge St (four nights in summer, weekends in winter) or, for a mix of ballads and folk, *Kirby's Brogue Inn* (almost every night in summer, weekends in winter) on Rock St – the tourist office will also have plenty of other suggestions.

The **Folk Theatre of Ireland** has its home at the Siamsa Tíre Theatre beside the tourist office (☎066/712 3055), though their excellent performances don't draw the same crowds as the **Rose of Tralee International Festival**. Held in the last week of August, with much accompanying merriment, this is a beauty contest in which women, including foreigners who can demonstrate some credible Irish connection, compete for the dubious honour of being Rose of Tralee; details are available from the Festival Office, Ashe Memorial Hall, Denny St (☎066/712 1322).

Ardfert and Banna Strand

More worthy of your time than anything in Tralee itself is the ruined thirteenth-century cathedral at **ARDFERT**, five miles to the northwest. In a landscape littered with ruined ring forts, castles and churches, Ardfert was the site of a monastery founded by St Brendan in the seventh century, and later became the centre of the Anglo-Norman church in Kerry. As well as some interesting monastic remains, there's a **Franciscan friary** and two smaller fifteenth-century churches.

It's also worth taking the road out to **BANNA STRAND** for the spectacular view over Tralee Bay, and its association with Sir Roger Casement, to whom there's a monument. In April 1916, on the eve of the Easter Rising, Casement was captured by local police as he attempted to land at Banna Strand from a German submarine. He was tried and executed for high treason in 1916, and his body was returned from England to Ireland in 1965 to be reinterred with full military honours (for more on Casement see p.566). You can carry on round the cliffs of **Kerry Head** for more great vistas – south over Tralee Bay, north across the mouth of the Shannon.

Castleisland and Crag Cave

The faster route – the N21 – to Limerick runs east inland via Newcastle West from Tralee. On this road **CASTLEISLAND** offers shops, and places to stop for a drink or a bite to eat. Nearby **Crag Cave** (March–May & Sept–Nov daily 10am–6pm; June–Aug daily 10am–7pm; £3/€3.81) is an impressive limestone cave system extending a couple of miles underground. If you're passing, the thirty-minute guided tour is enjoyable, with plenty of weirdly sculpted stalactites and stalagmites to keep you amused.

North Kerry

The Banna Strand coastal road aside, **North Kerry** is unexciting – undulating farmland rolling up to the Shannon. The main road from Tralee heads up through **LISTOWEL**, a workaday Irish town that does, however, have a degree of literary distinction, boasting a number of fine writers and a four-day festival of literary workshops and meetings, usually held around the end of May or the first week of June. Arguably, the town's most famous writer is John B. Keane, especially known for his *Man of the Triple Name*, an amusing account of North Kerry matchmaking during the 1930s and 1940s. The new **Kerry Literary and Cultural Centre** in the town square includes information on a number of local writers, including John B. Keane, Brian McMahon, Maurice Walsh, George Fitzmaurice and Brendan Kennelly and will act as a venue for Irish music and storytelling (☎066/22212). Throughout the summer there's also free literary entertainment in the *John B. Keane* pub, with performances of his plays and humorous commentary on his work.

The time when Listowel – and surrounding places as far away as Tarbert and Ballybunion – really come to life, however, is for the annual **Listowel races**, in the third week of September, when farming people from far and wide, their harvest in, take time off to eat, drink and lose money on the horses. Further information can be had from the **tourist office**, on the square (June–Sept Mon–Sat 10am–1pm & 2–6pm; Oct–May

Mon–Fri 9.30am–1pm & 2–6pm; ☎068/22590). There's plenty of **accommodation** here, ranging from the comfort of the *Listowel Arms* (☎068/21500; ⑧) to simpler B&Bs such as *The North County House*, 67 Church St. (☎068/21238; ④), and *Ashford Lodge*, Tarbert Rd (☎068/21280; ③).

Northbound from Listowel the main road continues to **TARBERT** on the Shannon estuary, and from there trails the river inland (through County Limerick) towards Limerick and Shannon Airport. There's a **hostel**, *The Ferry House*, on the square (IHH; ☎068/36555). Immediately north of the town, the **car ferry** across the estuary provides a useful short cut into County Clare; there's no other river crossing west of Limerick (April–Sept Mon–Sat 7.30am–9.30pm, Sun 9.30am–9.30pm; Oct–March Mon–Sat 7.30am–7.30pm, Sun 10am–7.30pm; sailings on the half-hour, return from Killimer on the hour; ☎065/53124; car £7/€8.89 single, £10/€12.70 return; foot passenger/cyclist £2/€2.54 single, £3/€3.81 return).

Turning westwards at Listowel, **BALLYBUNION** lies about ten miles away on the coast at the mouth of the Shannon. It does have a kind of charm – it's the sort of sleepy resort that most people remember with a mixture of affection and horror from childhood holidays, and there are good sandy beaches – but unless you're beguiled by nostalgia you're unlikely to want to stay long. If you do, in addition to the complement of cheerful tat, pubs and amusement arcades, there are two golf courses, the caves under the cliffs and the seaweed baths to occupy you. One of the cliff caves, the **Seven Sisters cave**, is named after the seven daughters of a local chieftain, who tried to elope with seven Norsemen he was holding prisoner. When the plan was discovered, their father had them thrown through the roof of the cave.

Perhaps the town's most intriguing feature is its **seaweed baths**. In Ballybunion, great store is set by the restorative powers of seaweed: in the past, local people would take to the sea at the end of the summer, to ease joints aching from the exertions of the harvest, and there are two bathing houses – dating back to the 1920s – perched above Ladies' Strand. Collins' and Dalys' seaweed baths both consist of a series of private bathrooms, supplied with hot salt water from a constantly stoked boiler and seaweed gathered from the Black Rocks beyond the headland each morning. After your soothing, slithery soak you can take a tray of restorative tea and apple tart onto the beach.

B&Bs in this holiday resort tend to be expensive (and full) in summer. A couple worth trying are *Invergordon*, Cliff Rd (☎068/27246; ②), and *Doon House*, Doon Rd (☎068/27411; ④), but you'll save a long walk around the "No Vacancy" signs by checking out possibilities first at the **tourist office**, which operates in season out of a mobile caravan: check at the local post office for details of its whereabouts. Visit **BALLYHEIGUE** further down the coast, for a quieter option, where there's **camping** at *Casey's Caravan & Camping Park* (closed mid-September to Easter; ☎066/713 3195).

Allow yourself to be beguiled by the flatlands of the **Shannon estuary**, if you've time to spare on your onward journey, whose quiet plains are bathed in the oblique light of the west and dotted with monasteries and castles. The ruined fifteenth-century **Carrigafoyle Castle** rises miraculously from the water, joined to the land by a causeway; close by, a road separates two sheets of water, the land it's built on long since submerged.

travel details

Trains

Killarney to: Cork (3–4 daily; 2hr 15min); Dublin (2–4 daily; 4hr); Tralee (4–6 daily; 45min).

Buses

Dingle to: Dunquin (summer Mon–Sat 2 daily, winter Mon & Thurs 3 daily; 45min).

Killarney to: Cahersiveen (summer 2–5 daily, winter Mon–Sat 1 daily; 1hr 30min); Dingle (2–5 daily; 1hr 45min–2hr 30min); Kenmare (summer 2–3 daily, winter Mon–Fri 1 daily; 45min); Ring of Kerry (summer only 2 daily; 4hr 45min); Tralee (8–12 daily; 40min–1hr); Waterville (summer 2–3 daily, winter Mon–Sat 1 daily; 1hr 45min).

Tralee to: Cork (5–10 daily; 2hr 15min–2hr 45min); Dingle (2–8 daily; 2hr 30min); Limerick (7–8 daily; 2hr 15min).

CHAPTER NINE

COUNTY CLARE

Physically, County Clare is clearly defined, with Galway Bay and the Shannon estuary to the north and south, massive Lough Derg forming its eastern boundary, and the Atlantic to the west. Strangely, although plenty of people visit, the county is sometimes glossed over by travellers as simply land between the magnificent scenery of Kerry and Galway. It's true that it doesn't have the scenic splendour of either of these, and for many, the north of the county is too bleak to be attractive. Nonetheless, Clare has a subtle flavour that, once tasted, can be addictive.

Clare has earned itself two epithets: "the banner county" and "the singing county". It was called "the banner county" originally because of the part played by its men in the battle of Ramilles and more recently because of its courageous political history, particularly in the fight for Catholic emancipation. The second epithet reflects the strong musical traditions that are still very much alive in the county and constitute a major reason for coming here. Throughout the summer you will find sessions in pubs and in *teach cheoils* (pronounced *chuck key 'ole*), the latter more sober entertainments, with tea and brown bread rather than stout for refreshment, and very fine musicians too. To find out what's going on, pick up a copy of the *Shannon Region Traditional Irish Music Pubs* leaflet from any tourist office or check out *The Clare Champion*, and, above all, ask around. Pub sessions very often start late in the evening, so don't give up on a bar just because it's half nine and still nothing is happening. A great session can seemingly spring from nowhere, and is liable to prove a wholly memorable experience. Don't underestimate the popularity and excitement of Clare's festivals either. If you have yet to experience "the craic", you are sure to find it here.

Both Clare's titles, "the banner county" and "the singing county" – the strong and the gentle – suggest something of the character of the place and are echoed in the contrasts of the landscape.The **Burren** heights in the north are startlingly stark and barren, while **Ennis**, the county's capital, is surrounded by low, rolling farmland. Fabulous cliff scenery stretches for miles round Clare's southern extreme at Loop Head and is spectacularly sheer at the **Cliffs of Moher**, further north. In between are small seaside towns and villages and wonderful sandy beaches, most dramatic at **Lahinch** – famous for surf. In the east, **Lough Derg** affords opportunities for watersports, and there are panoramic views from the slopes of the Slieve Bernagh and Slieve Aughtie mountains across to the mountains of Tipperary.

ACCOMMODATION PRICE CODES

Throughout this book, prices of hotels, guesthouses and B&Bs have been graded with the codes below, according to what you can expect to pay for a double room in high season. For more details on accommodation, see p.34.

① Under £26/€33.01
② £26–33/€33.01–41.90
③ £33–40/€41.90–50.79
④ £40–55/€50.79–69.84
⑤ £55–70/€69.84–88.88
⑥ £70–90/€88.88–114.28
⑦ £90–110/€114.28–139.67
⑧ £110–130/€139.67–165.07
⑨ Over £130/€165.07

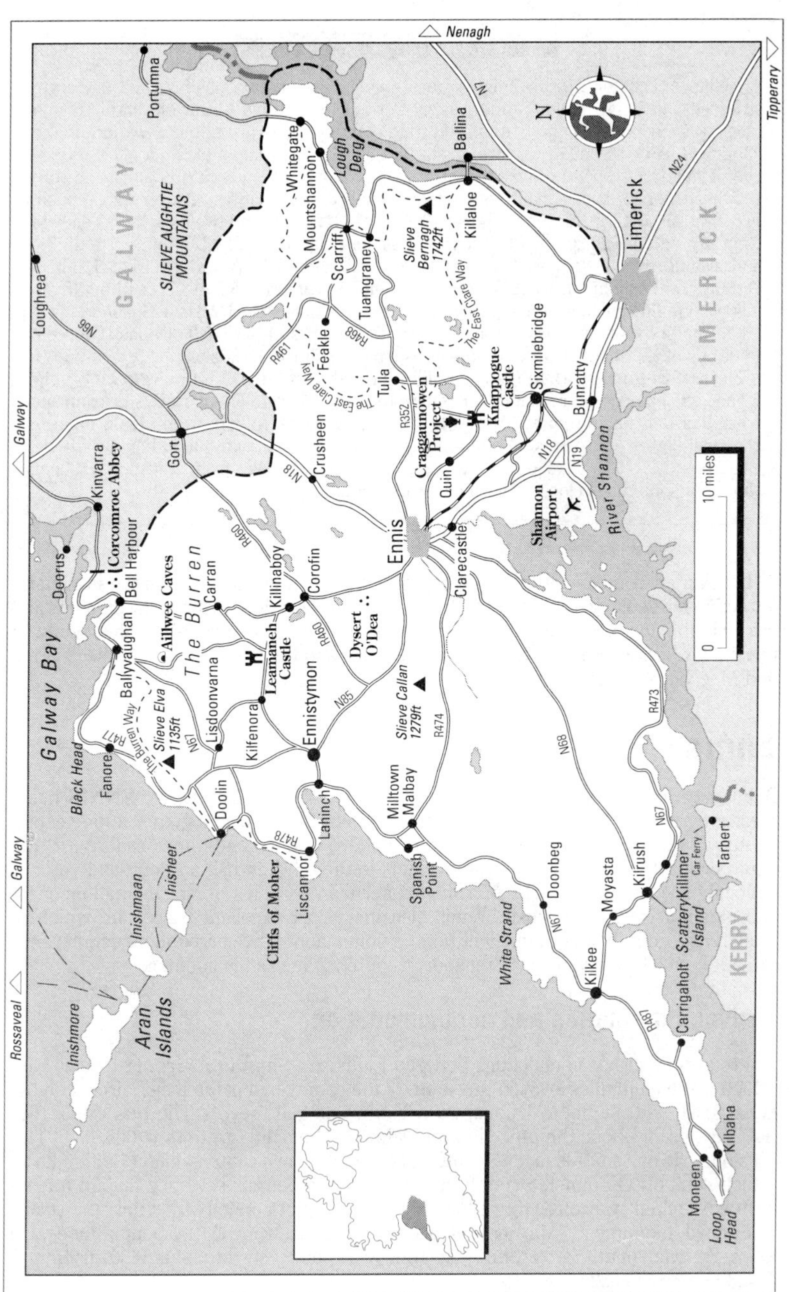
Nenagh
Tipperary
Galway
Galway
Rossaveal
GALWAY
SLIEVE AUGHTIE MOUNTAINS
LIMERICK
KERRY
N
Portumna
Loughrea
Whitegate
Mountshannon
Lough Derg
Scarriff
Tuamgraney
Ballina
Killaloe
Slieve Bernagh 1742ft
Limerick
Feakle
Tulla
Sixmilebridge
Bunratty
Knappogue Castle
Craggaunowen Project
Quin
Gort
Crusheen
Kinvarra
Corcomroe Abbey
Bell Harbour
Doorus
Aillwee Caves
The Burren
Carran
Killinaboy
Corofin
Ennis
Clarecastle
Shannon Airport
River Shannon
Dysert O'Dea
Leamaneh Castle
Ballyvaughan
Lisdoonvarna
Kilfenora
Ennistymon
Slieve Elva 1135ft
Slieve Callan 1279ft
Galway Bay
Black Head
Fanore
The Burren Way
The East Clare Way
Doolin
Lahinch
Liscannor
Cliffs of Moher
Milltown Malbay
Spanish Point
Doonbeg
White Strand
Moyasta
Kilrush
Killimer
Car Ferry
Tarbert
Scattery Island
Kilkee
Carrigaholt
Kilbaha
Moneen
Loop Head
Inisheer
Inishmaan
Inishmore
Aran Islands
N66
N18
N19
N7
N24
N85
N67
N68
R461
R468
R352
R460
R474
R473
R477
R478
R487
0
10 miles

SHANNON AIRPORT

Arriving at Shannon International Airport – where Irish coffee was invented to placate stranded passengers – you're most likely to want to head for **Limerick**, barely fifteen miles away, where you can get bus and train connections to just about anywhere in the country. **Ennis**, a similar distance, is also easily accessible and a pleasant place to stop over if you plan to spend some time in County Clare or want to break your journey before you head north. Alternatively, Bunratty is worth considering as an overnight option. From the airport Bus Éireann **buses** (☎061/313333) run around twenty services daily to Bunratty (20min; £2.20/€2.79), around fourteen daily to Ennis (45 min; £3.70/€4.74) and around twenty daily to Limerick (45min; £3.70/€4.70). A **taxi** (☎061/471538) to Bunratty will cost about £9/€11.43, and to Ennis or Limerick about £17/€21.59. If you just want to find a bed for the night, you could stay at one of the **B&Bs** in Shannon town, all around a five-minute drive from the airport. Try *Mrs Lohan*, 35 Tullyglass Crescent (☎061/364268; ③), or *Avalon*, 11 Balleycaseymore Hill (☎061/362032; ③).

The airport **tourist office** (daily for all major flights; ☎061/471664) is extremely helpful and will book accommodation for you for the usual charge. There's a Bus Éireann and Irish Rail information point (April–Oct), and an **airport information desk**, open to serve all flights – if there's no one there, pick up the phone and dial 0. For Aer Lingus enquiries call ☎061/471666. The **airport bank** is open daily from 6am until 5.30pm, though it sometimes closes early if there are no flights.

This varied countryside holds plenty of specialist interest. The Burren is a major attraction for geology and botany enthusiasts, and is also rich in ring forts, dolmens and cairns in the north. The legacy of later communities is found throughout the county, in the thickly sprinkled medieval monastic remains and the tower houses of the O'Brien and MacNamara clans.

Ennis

A bustling market town and the commercial capital of County Clare, **ENNIS** has a pleasantly inconsequential air. Its handful of central lanes lace together a nineteenth-century cathedral, a stout monument to Daniel O'Connell and a medieval friary. You could probably walk from one side of Ennis to the other in half an hour, and you can certainly see all it has to offer in a single afternoon – but it's worth staying longer for the plentiful traditional music. Ennis also makes an excellent base from which to explore the church ruins and tower houses dotted about the surrounding countryside, although you'll need your own transport as public transport is minimal.

Arrival, information and accommodation

There are direct bus connections between Ennis and **Shannon Airport** (see above), which is thirteen miles away in the south of the county and is the major airport on the west coast, with flights to Dublin, the UK, Europe and the US. The **bus** (☎065/682 4177; if closed, phone the office in Limerick) and the **train stations** (☎065/684 0444) sit alongside one another, a ten-minute walk from the town centre – follow Station Road, which runs off O'Connell Street from beside the cathedral. The very helpful **tourist office** is tucked away on Arthur's Row, signposted off O'Connell Street near the Daniel O'Connell monument (May & Oct Mon–Sat 9.30am–1pm & 2–5.30pm; June–Sept Mon–Fri 9am–6pm, Sat & Sun 9am–1pm & 2–6pm; Nov Mon–Fri 9.30am–1pm & 2–5.30pm; ☎065/682 8366).

For a small town, Ennis has a good range of **accommodation**. The following should be a good starting point, and the tourist office can direct you to many more.

The Abbey Tourist Hostel, Harmony Row (☎065/682 2620). This large and well-run hostel is situated in a prime location, just across the river from the Friary. Private rooms (①) are also available.

Avonlea, Francis St (☎065/682 1632). A pleasant B&B which is only a short walk from the town centre. All rooms are en suite. ③.

Cloneen, Clon Rd (☎065/682 9681) A welcoming B&B that's just a five-minute walk from Ennis, offering standard and en-suite accommodation in a comfortable non-smoking house. ③.

Glenfarne, 10 Ard Aoibhinn, Clare Rd (☎065/684 4922). Comfortable B&B in a family home in a quiet cul-de-sac off the Ennis to Limerick road, about half a mile out of town. TV and tea- and coffee-making facilities in each room. Closed November to February. ③.

Newpark House, Tulla Rd (☎065/682 1233, *newparkhouse@tinet.ie*). Located about half a mile out of Ennis on the R352, turn right opposite the *Roselevan Arms*. A welcoming B&B in a striking seventeenth-century mansion set in wooded grounds. ⑤.

Old Ground Hotel, O'Connell St (☎065/682 8127, *oghotel@iol.ie*). This is one of Ennis's oldest hotels and has a beautiful ivy-clad entrance, pleasant gardens and plenty of traditional character. The rooms have been recently refurbished, and there's an elegant dining room and a welcoming bar. Good weekend rates are available too. ⑧.

Rockfield, Station Rd (☎065/682 4749). A decent budget B&B in a central location, a short walk from Ennis cathedral, offering some en-suite rooms and some with shared bathrooms. ②.

The Temple Gate Hotel, Arthur's Bow, The Square (☎065/682 3300, *templegh@iol.ie*). A comfortable, new town-centre hotel which is styled around the gothic architecture of the old convent it partially occupies. All rooms have TV, tea- and coffee-making facilities and are en suite. ⑦.

The West County Hotel, Clare Rd (☎065/682 3000, *www.lynchotels.com*). A comfortable and modern hotel about three quarters of a mile south of the centre. Facilities include three pools, a gym and a children's playcentre. ⑧.

The Town

The finest monument in town, **Ennis Friary**, lies right in the historic centre (guide/information service daily late May to late Sept 9.30am–6.30pm; ☎065/682 9100; £1/€1.27; Heritage Card). It was established by the O'Briens, Kings of Thomond, in 1242, but most of the existing building dates from the fourteenth century. At that time, it had three hundred and fifty friars and over six hundred pupils and was considered the finest educational institution in Ireland for the clergy and upper classes. In parts it remains striking: graceful lancet windows fill the east end of the chancel, while adjacent convent buildings include cloister ruins and a stoutly barrel-vaulted chapter house. There is good sculpture, too: look out for the small square carving on the jamb of the arch between the nave and transept, which shows a half-length figure of Christ with his hands bound; the relief of Saint Francis with cross-staff and stigmata at the east end of the nave; and the carved corbels beneath the south tower showing the Virgin and Child and an archbishop. The real sculptural highlight, however, is the fifteenth-century **MacMahon Tomb** (now incorporated in the Creagh Tomb), embellished with fine alabaster carvings of the Passion.

Despite the beauty of the friary, Ennis today seems more proud of its later history, as capital of the unyielding "banner county" and a bastion of Nationalism. A monument to **Daniel O'Connell** solidly dominates the old, narrow streets that meet in O'Connell Square. In 1828, County Clare returned O'Connell to Westminster by such a huge majority that he had to be allowed to take his seat, despite the fact that he was a Catholic, which should have barred him at the time; he went on to force through parliament the Catholic Emancipation Act. It was in Ennis, too, that **Parnell** made his famous speech advocating the boycott in the land agitations of the late nineteenth century. **De Valera** was TD for the county from 1917 to 1959 (and Taoiseach for much of that time) and is remembered in a memorial outside the courthouse.

As for other things to search out, the new **Clare Museum** alongside the tourist office on Arthur's Row (June–Sept daily 9.30am–5.30pm; Oct–May Mon–Fri 9.30am–1pm & 2–5.30pm; ☎065/682 3382; £3/€3.81) is well worth a visit, housing a large number of antiquities on loan from the National Museum in Dublin. A permanent exhibition entitled the Riches of Clare illustrates the story of this remarkably diverse county, encompassing weaponry from the Bronze Age through to the IRA, Clare's links with the Spanish Armada and the development of the submarine, and a number of interesting letters and telegrams from Daniel O'Connell (seeking support in the forthcoming election) and De Valera (the telegram that he sent his wife on being elected to parliament). Also among the exhibits are: a thirteenth-century bell from Corcomroe Abbey (see p.365), and recently excavated material from the Poulnabrone Dolmen (see p.367) including an arrow-pierced human hipbone, arrow heads and beads. Ennis's **cathedral**, a nineteenth-century building with a sharp spire, stands icy and grey at the far end of O'Connell Street, somewhat at odds with the friendly atmosphere of the town. A more enjoyable way to kill time in Ennis, however, is to wander the ancient lanes that run from O'Connell Street to the old market place (where a Saturday vegetable and livestock market is held), and from Parnell Street down to the post office field, a riverside meadow right in the town centre. You could also follow the river a short way up from Woodquay to the newly renovated mill chase. Look out too for the interesting modern sculpture around town. All in all though, once you have seen the friary and museum, the most pressing reason to stick around is to sample Ennis's pubs, renowned for traditional music, or to get out into the Clare countryside.

It's worth considering taking a **tour of the Burren** from Ennis – particularly if you are short of time and without transport. The tour also takes in **Coole Park** (see p.386) and **Kilmacduagh** (p.386), and operates from June to August departing the *Temple Gate Hotel* at 10.15am on Tuesday and Thursday, and returning at around 5pm (☎065/692 8234; £15/€19.05).

Eating and drinking

There are a handful of **places to eat** in Ennis, although it has to be said that most of these have a fairly workaday character. For general provisions, the small O'Connell Street shop front of Dunne's Store's hides an enormous, and well stocked, supermarket behind.

Domaine, River Lane, Wood Quay (off Parnell St). A laid-back wine bar serving light meals such as salads and seafood platters. Closed Sunday.

Henry's Deli, Barrack St. Café serving cheap and tasty sandwiches stuffed with delicious cheeses, relishes and Mediterrean salads. Closed Sunday.

Numero Uno, 3 Barrack St (☎065/684 1740). This tiny, cheap and cheerful pizza café offers eat in or takeaway and is open till late.

Old Ground Hotel, O'Connell St. A traditional hotel bar whose wood-panelled walls hung with oil paintings generate a comfortably conservative atmosphere. Decent bar meals are served here from Monday to Saturday, and typical dishes include stuffed pork, fried fish and braised beef in Guinness. Lighter meals of soup and sandwiches are served on a Sunday.

Punjab, 59 Parnell St (☎065/684 4655). One of the best Indian restaurants in the west of Ireland, and reasonably priced too. Lunchtimes are exceptionally good value.

Ruby Tuesday's, Merchants Square (☎065/684 0474). An inexpensive, family restaurant with a broad range of meals on offer – burgers, pastas, chicken and fish – and a BYO policy.

The Sherwood Inn, Ennis Shopping Centre, Francis St. The place to go when funds are low for a cheap and hearty breakfast or lunch.

Temple Gate Hotel, Arthur's Bow. Spacious medieval theme-bar which offers good-value carvery lunches at midday, and bar meals in the evening.

Nightlife and entertainment

Ennis may not have the best selection of restaurants in the west, but when it comes to music, it takes some beating. The town has two major traditional music festivals, the **Fleadh Nua**, which takes place over the last weekend in May, and the fabulous **Guinness Traditional Music Festival** (*www.clarenet.ie/ennis/novtradfest/index.html*), which is usually held over the second weekend in November and draws top musicians. In fact, Ennis is well served for music any time of the year, and perhaps the best place to start is **Cois na hAbhna**, a centre for local traditional music enthusiasts, located less than half a mile out on the Gort Road. Throughout the summer they have Oíche Ceilidh evenings of song and dance (on alternate Sats), and year round there are informal traditional music sessions and set dancing classes (Wed 8.30pm). Sessions organized by Cois na hAbhna also move around the county, so it's worth watching out for them in smaller towns roundabout; call in to the tourist office for details. The Knotted Chord, Cook's Lane, off O'Connell St, is a music shop specializing in traditional Irish, folk and world music, and there's **what's on** information posted on the wall; it's also worth looking at their Web site (*www.knotted-chord.com*).

For such a small town, Ennis itself has a surprising number of **bars** with **music** sessions. For traditional music try: *Brogan's*, 24 O'Connell St (summer Tues and Wed); *Fawl's Railway Bar*, 69 O'Connell St (Fri); *Micky Kerin's*, Lifford, a short walk along Newbridge Rd (Fri); *P.J. Kelly's* in Carmody St (Sat and Sun); *Cruise's*, Abbey St (Sun lunchtime and every night); and *Ciaran's*, Francis St (Thurs). You might also find traditional music in *O'Halloran's*, High St; *Paddy Quin's*, Lower Market St; and the *Temple Gate Hotel*.

Brandon's, O'Connell St, is one of the liveliest young bars, offering a mixture of traditional (Mon and Wed); a DJ (Thurs); rock, blues or cajun (Fri and Sat); and a varied selection on Sundays. They also have a singers' club upstairs (first and third Wed of every month), where anyone is welcome to do any kind of performance including stand-up. *El Paso's*, Parnell St, is a huge, Western-theme bar with pop, folk and ballads four or five nights a week, and *Alexander Knox*, Abbey St, attracts a young crowd with pop and rock (Mon, Wed, Thurs, Fri). For **clubs**, try *The Sanctuary* located behind *Cruise's* on Abbey St (chart music), or *The Bordwalk*, behind *Brandon's* on O'Connell St (rock, world, cajun mix).

Around Ennis

Ennis sits in a low-lying strip of land that runs from a deep inlet of the Shannon River right up to South Galway. To the east of the town lie lush fields edged by white-grey walls and clumps of wild flowers: pinks, purples and yellows of willow herb and ragwort, the strong white horns of bindweed, and even the occasional orchid. Further out, the land breaks into little lakes and rivers before becoming gently hilly to meet the Slieve Bernagh Mountains. This gentle farmland makes for easy cycling, and your trip can be punctuated by village pubs and plenty of church ruins, castles and visitor attractions. The best of these include the evocative fifteenth century **Quin Abbey**, imposing medieval **Knappogue Castle** and the **Craggaunowen Project**, which includes a reconstruction of a Bronze Age lake dwelling. Northwest of Ennis lies the fifteenth-century **Dysert O'Dea Castle**, and thirteen miles south of the county capital stands **Bunratty Castle**, arguably the most impressive of the region's medieval strongholds. It is worth bearing in mind though that the N18 Galway–Limerick road is horribly busy, a nightmare for cyclists as drivers adopt motorway attitudes on what is in fact quite a narrow road.

Quin Abbey and Knappogue Castle

One of the most pleasant rides is east of Ennis to **Quin Abbey** (May–Oct Mon–Fri 10.30am–6pm, Sat & Sun 11.30am–5pm), the area's best-preserved Franciscan friary, founded in 1433. The main church building is graceful, its slender tower rising clear over the high, open archway between chancel and nave and making a distinct outline against the green of the surrounding pastures. Climb up a floor to the first storey and you can look down on the abbey's complete cloister with its arches and buttresses. For all the uplifting beauty of the tower, the abbey seems to have been built on a human scale, to function as a place in which to live and worship rather than to impress and dominate.

On the other hand, the massive walls of **Knappogue Castle** emanate an awesome sense of power. Leave Quin and continue two miles south on the L31 to reach this huge sixteenth-century tower house (April–Oct daily 9.30am–5pm; £2.90/€3.68). It was built by the Macnamaras in 1467, but they lost it to Cromwell, who then used it as his HQ – thereby, no doubt, saving it from the major damage he inflicted elsewhere. At the Restoration, the Macnamaras managed to regain ownership of the castle and hung on to it until 1800. It's been beautifully restored, and inside are boldly carved sixteenth-century oak fireplaces and stout oak furniture. At odds with the overall flavour of Knappogue, the nineteenth-century domestic additions are furnished in eighteenth-century style: beautifully appointed with Irish Chippendale furniture and Waterford crystal. The main body of the castle is used for medieval banquets.

The Craggaunowen Project

The second left turning, two miles south of Knappogue, brings you to the **Craggaunowen Project**, situated on the edge of a reedy lake under a wooded hillside (April to October, daily 9.30am–6pm; £4.40/€6.28). This is based around another fortified tower house, the ground floor of which houses a collection of sixteenth-century European wood carvings. The project itself aims to re-create a sense of Ireland's ancient history, with reconstructions of earlier forms of homes and farmsteads: a ring fort and a *crannóg*, or artificial island, for example. Young workers experiment with old craft techniques, using replicas of wooden lathes, kilns and other traditional devices, and double up as guides if asked.

The most adventurous, and certainly the most famous, of the working replicas here is Tim Severin's **Brendan**, a curragh (leather-hulled boat) in which he and four crew successfully sailed across the Atlantic in 1976, to prove that the legend of St Brendan could be true. St Brendan's story – he was supposedly the first European to reach America – is recorded in a ninth-century manuscript, and the design of the *Brendan* is based on its descriptions, along with the features of curraghs still used off Ireland's west coast. The result is a remarkable vessel of oak-tanned oxhides stretched over an ash-wood frame. Craggaunowen also has an actual **Iron Age road**, excavated at Corlea Bog, County Longford and moved to this site. Made of large oak planks placed across runners of birch or alder, it must have formed part of an important route across difficult bog. For refreshment, there's also a nice **tea shop** here, serving delicious home-made cakes.

Bunratty

Bunratty Castle (daily 9am–4pm; combined ticket for castle and Folk Park £6.50/€8.25), thirteen miles south of Ennis and handily situated on the N18 Ennis–Limerick Road, stands on what was once an island on the north bank of the Shannon. The Vikings of Limerick recognized the site's strategic importance for protecting trade, and so they fortified it – you can still see the moat. The first castle on the site was built by Normans, but they lost control and, in 1460, the Macnamaras built the castle that stands today. It's exceptionally impressive: the fine rectangular keep has been perfectly restored and now houses a large collection of furniture, tapestries, paintings and ornate carvings from all over Europe, spanning the fourteenth to the seventeenth centuries. In the castle grounds stands **Bunratty Folk Park** (daily: June–Aug 9am–5.45pm; Sept–May 9.30am–5.45pm; combined ticket for castle and Folk Park £6.50/€8.25, Folk Park only £4.10/€5.20) a complete reconstruction of a nineteenth-century village. Although extremely touristy, both castle and folk village are well worth taking time over, and you can break up your visit in the excellent tearoom or the pub within the Folk Park.

The nearby *Durty Nelly's* is a favourite tourist bar, regularly overrun by bus parties, and *Kathleen's Irish Pub*, in *The Bunratty Castle Hotel* (☎061/364116; *info@bunratty-castlehotel.iol.ie*; ⑦), offers comfortable accommodation in traditional-style rooms and serves excellent bar food, though again coach parties can mean a long wait to be served. Follow the Lower Road, which runs between Bunratty Castle and *Durty Nelly's*, for *Bunratty Caravan and Camping Park* (closed Nov–March; ☎061/369190), a serviceable site, or for one of numerous good-quality **B&Bs** – *Bunratty Villa* (☎061/369241; ④) is a handy ten-minute walk from the castle; further along are *Innisfree* (☎061/369773; ④), *Bunratty Heights* (☎061/369324; ③); and, about a mile from the castle, the friendly *Castleside* (☎061/369390; ③).

Three miles east of Bunratty, the village of **CRATLOE** is renowned for its oak-wooded hills overlooking the Shannon and Fergus estuaries and is a particularly lovely spot for walking.

Dysert O'Dea

Alternative routes from Ennis can take you north through low-lying country fretted with rush-bordered lakes, their banks dotted with O'Brien strongholds. Seven miles north is **Dysert O'Dea**, the site of the ancient monastic foundation of St Tola (d. 737) and the scene of an important battle in 1318 when the O'Briens defeated the de Clares of Bunratty, thus preventing the Anglo-Norman takeover of Clare. To get there, take the road to Ennistymon out of Ennis, then after two miles take the right fork for Corofin and it's up a road to the left. At the site you can wander around the remains of a twelfth- to thirteenth-century Romanesque church with a richly carved south doorway and carvings of grotesque animal heads and human faces. Of particular interest is the twelfth-century White Cross of Tola, with carvings of Christ and a bishop in high relief, Daniel in the lion's den, as well as intricate patterning. The **O'Dea Castle** nearby houses an **archaelogical centre** (May–Sept daily 10am–6pm; £3/€3.81) from where a history trail starts out that takes in the high cross, ring forts and an ancient cooking site. Travelling north of Dysert O'Dea, you'll come across an abundance of little lakes, offering good fishing.

Lough Derg

The west bank of **Lough Derg** is a seam of beautiful countryside set between bald, boggy mountains and the great expanse of the lake. It forms the county's eastern boundary and, isolated by the empty heights of the Slieve Bernagh and the Slieve Aughtie mountains, has a different character from the rest of Clare. The waterway's wealth of fish and bird life, and the quaint villages on either shore, have long made Lough Derg popular with a wealthy Lough-cruising set, whose exclusive brand of tourism means villages are fairly conservative and well kept. The hunting, shooting and fishing crowds are well catered for and tend to dominate the character of local pubs; but the historic town of **Killaloe** and the village of **Mountshannon** make attractive bases, offering accommodation, bars and opportunities for watersports. There are also pockets renowned for their traditional music sessions, notably the tiny villages of Feakle and Ogonnelloe. attracting predominantly local crowds.

The main road north varies the scene, at times clinging to the lake shore, at others gaining higher ground and panoramic views over the lough, its islands and the mountains of Tipperary. It connects the historic, picturesque towns of **Portumna** in County Galway (see p.387), at the head of the Lough, and Killaloe at its southerly tip, and laces together a handful of little villages.

Access to the area is via Limerick. Bus Éireann runs a very limited service: from Limerick to Killaloe, Scarriff, Tuamgraney, (Mon to Sat only), Mountshannon and Whitegate (Sat only). For timetable information, phone Limerick ☎061/313333. Hitching isn't such a good idea in the Slieve Bernagh and Slieve Aughtie mountains to the west where roads are empty, and this isn't ideal cycling country either, as the roads are deceptively steep and unsheltered. However, if you are keen to cycle, you can arrange bike rental through Killaloe tourist office.

Killaloe

At **KILLALOE**, the Shannon narrows again after the Lough for the final stretch of this great river's journey to the sea. An old stone bridge still spans the waters at this traditional crossing point. The old part of Killaloe centres on **St Flannan's Cathedral**, and the narrow lanes that run up the steep slopes to the west suggest the town's ancient origins. The cathedral itself is a plain thirteenth-century building, impressive in its solid simplicity, with a low square tower and straight, strong buttresses. Just inside the entrance is a heavily decorated Romanesque doorway from an earlier church, and alongside it the huge **Thorgrim Stone**, unique in its *ogham* and runic inscriptions (*ogham* is a form of the Latin alphabet associated with early Christianity; the runic forms are Scandinavian in origin), which is probably the memorial of a Viking convert.

THE EAST CLARE WAY

The East Clare Way is a recently mapped long-distance walking route through a less touristed – but for some tastes no less scenic – part of the county. It passes through a green and rugged corner of Clare, taking in rivers, lakes, woodlands and boglands. It's a circular walk and the latter stages can be broken up with boat trips out onto Lough Derg from Mountshannon, or, in fine weather, swimming from the lakeshore (ask locally about currents). The circular route begins at Killaloe and goes through Broadford, O'Callaghan's Mills, Tulla, Feakle, Flagmount, Whitegate, Mountshannon, Ogonnelloe and back to Killaloe. The longest stage is Flagmount to Whitegate – some 21 miles.

Access: There is a limited bus service from Limerick to Killaloe and Scarriff (Mon–Sat). A bus service operates Saturdays only from Limerick to Mountshannon, Whitegate, Broadford and O'Callaghan's Mills; buses to Tulla from Limerick run on Wednesday.

Accommodation: B&Bs at Killaloe, Tulla and Ogonnelloe, and hotel accommodation in Feakle and Mountshannon; these are small communities, so it makes sense to book accommodation in advance.

Overall distance: 112 miles.

Highest point: Cragnamurragh, 1729ft.

Maps and guides: *East Clare Map Guide*, available from the tourist office in Ennis; OS map Nos. 58 & 65, 1:50,000 (1.25 inches to 1 mile).

In the churchyard the stout Romanesque **St Flannan's Oratory** dates from the twelfth century and is complete with barrel-vaulted roof. Well signposted just over a mile north of town, on the western shore of Lough Derg, stands the earthern fort **Beal Boru**, possibly the site of Brian Boru's palace "Kincora", which was either here or in Killaloe itself. The best way to spend your time in Killaloe, though, is to get out onto the water; see below for details of cruises and boat rental.

Practicalities

The **tourist office**, in Lock House on The Bridge (May–Sept daily 10am–6pm; ☎061/376866), can help with accommodation. Alternatively you could opt for one of the central **B&Bs**, such as *Kincora House*, Church St (☎061/376149; ④), a lovely old town house with antiquated furnishings, or *Lyon's B&B* (☎061/376652; ③), just next door. For something more luxurious, check in at *The Lakeside Hotel* (☎061/376122; ⑦). **Camping** beside the lake is possible at the *Lough Derg Holiday Park* (closed late Sept–April; ☎061/376329), just three miles north of Killaloe along the Scarriff Road.

One-hour **lough cruises** on the *Derg Princess* leave from beside the tourist office (May–Sept daily noon & 2.30pm; £5/€6.35), and the *Spirit of Killaloe* departs from the pier at Ballina, across the bridge in Tipperary (July & Aug daily 1pm, 2.30pm & 4pm). To **rent boats** with outboard engines, that can take up to four adults, call in at Whelan's Foodstore, Main St (☎061/376159; £10/€12.70 first hour, £5/€6.35 additional hours, £30/€38.09 a day). You can rent wind-surfs, canoes, wetsuits and dinghies from Killaloe Activity Centre (☎061/376622), situated two miles out along the road towards Scarriff.

You'll find a few pubs serving decent **food** both in Killaloe and across the bridge in Ballina: *Crotty's Courtyard Bar*, Bridge St, Killaloe, is a popular spot with a fabulous collection of old signs, a cheery beer-yard, and bar food till 10pm in summer; across the bridge *Gooser's* is a rather pricier place for good-quality bar food; the nearby *Simply Delicious* café serves cheap meals that are just that.

Many pubs have some kind of **music** at weekends during the summer – usually a traditional/country mix. For set dancing and traditional music head for *The Anchor Inn*, Bridge St (Wed summer); *Molly's*, across the bridge in Ballina, usually has traditional music (Thurs summer). In **OGONNELLOE**, two and half miles north of Killaloe, *The Piper's Inn* (☎061/375544; ②) is noted for its traditional music sessions on weekends and also offers reasonably priced B&B. The village is also on the East Clare Way (see box opposite).

Scarriff, Mountshannon and around

The villages along the scenic road north of Killaloe are all very small. Wealthy tourists into hunting, shooting and fishing tend to stay in fancy hotels, and amenities for other visitors are sparse. That said, it's still very beautiful countryside, especially the lakeside area up as far as Mountshannon. Traditional music here is very much alive, and there are some excellent opportunities to get out onto the water.

SCARRIFF is a little farming town set high up in rough, open country overlooking the lough. It's a handy place to pick up provisions. There's a Bank of Ireland here and a couple of pubs serving bar food. **FEAKLE**, about six miles to the west, is another small village, but has a far busier social calendar. There are excellent **traditional sessions** throughout the year in *Pepper's* bar (Wed) and *Lena's* (Thurs), and Feakle also has an International Traditional Music Festival (☎061/924288), which is usually held during the second weekend in August. **Accommodation** can be problematic and unless you bring a tent and ask to **camp** at a farm, your choices are limited to: *The Smyth Country Lodge Hotel* (☎061/924000, *www.welcometo/Smythshotel*; ⑦), which offers cosy log fires, comfortable rooms and is popular with people on fishing holidays, or *Laccaroe House* (☎061/924150; ④), a B&B with en-suite rooms, located about a mile from *Pepper's* along the road to Scarriff.

Around nine miles southwest of Feakle sits the similarly quiet village of **TULLA**. You are most likely to be here if you are walking the East Clare Way, or if you want to sample some of the traditional music to be had in *Torpey's* bar (Sun). Accommodation is limited to a few **B&Bs**: *Cragville* (☎065/683 5110; ②) in the village and the welcoming *Toonagh House* (☎065/683 5316; ②), two and half miles away, off the Ennis road.

The best spot to stay right by the lake, Killaloe and Portumna aside, is **MOUNTSHANNON**, about five miles north of Scarriff. It's among the prettiest of the villages and has a couple of cosy pubs and some good **places to eat**. Good bar food, and sometimes traditional music in the summer, arc to be had at *Cois na hAbhna*, while meals are served all day at *An Cupán Caífé* (☎061/927275), a relaxed, small bistro with a cosy atmosphere. **Places to stay** include the *Mountshannon Hotel* (☎061/927162; ⑥), and, slightly further out heading north of the village, *Derg Lodge* (☎061/927180, or 927319; ②) and *Oak House* (☎061/927185; ③), which has its own private beach. **Watersports** enthusiasts will find reasonably priced canoeing, wind-surfing, sailing and motor boat rental, from May to October, at the nearby *Lakeside Watersport Caravan and Camping Park* (☎061/927225).

Southwest Clare

The southwest of the county has glorious sandy beaches, stunning cliff scenery and a couple of popular family holiday resorts. Arguably the best of the resorts is **Kilkee**, a traditional holiday town full of character, with a superb beach and within easy reach of the spectacular cliff scenery of the **Loop Head peninsula**. **Kilrush**, the only other place of any size, can't compete in terms of setting, but it does offer plenty of opportunities for watersports and boat trips to **Scattery Island**, with its medieval round tower and monastic ruins. North from Kilkee stretches a varied coastline of inaccessible cliffs interspersed with fine beaches, especially good near Doonbeg and Quilty; north of here lies the village of **Milltown Malbay**, famous for traditional music. Inland doesn't look so promising. Southwest from Ennis the country flattens out and becomes scrubby and barren: bog, marsh, the odd bit of cotton grass here, the occasional lump of thistles there, with only sporadic pockets of cultivated land. The bald flank of Slieve Callan is to the north and the outline of the Kerry hills to the south across the Shannon.

Kilrush, Scattery Island and Killimer

The best reason to stop in **KILRUSH**, twenty-six miles from Ennis, is for a trip across the broad Shannon estuary to Scattery Island (see below). The town itself has a busy marina and one very broad main street; at the top of the street stands the old market house and a statue of the Maid of Éireann (see box opposite). In Toler Street, just off the main street, the spacious **St Senan's Catholic Church** is worth looking in for a view of the Harry Clarke stained glass windows.

SCATTERY ISLAND lies about a mile offshore from Kilrush in the exposed Shannon Estuary. It was last inhabited in the late 1970s, and, as you land, you'll notice that the quay before you is dotted with overgrown derelict cottages. Walking up the lanes, spongy with moss and bracken, you disturb the burrows the island is riddled with, and rabbits pop out madly all over the place. St Senan founded a **monastery** here in the sixth century, and at one time there were seven monastic settlements. The community suffered greatly from Viking raids, but there are still the remains of several churches dating from between the ninth and the fifteenth centuries.

THE MANCHESTER MARTYRS

Statues of the Maid of Éireann, commemorating the **Manchester Martyrs**, are scattered around Ireland. In Manchester, England, in 1867, a band of Fenians blew open the back of a Black Maria in an attempt to rescue some of their leaders, who had been arrested after an armed uprising. A police sergeant was killed in the explosion, and three Fenians were hanged as a result. The executions provoked demonstrations throughout England and Ireland, since many considered the sergeant's death to have been an accident and the trials rigged: these monuments are testimony to the strength of those feelings.

Wherever you wander on Scattery, you feel as though you're stepping back into a timeless past, a mythical world protected by its isolation in the Shannon estuary. But Scattery's most impressive feature has to be the **round tower**, perfect in form, the stone made a warm mustardy yellow by the lichen that covers it. Unusually for a round tower, the doorway here is at ground level, as opposed to the more typical high-up entrances reached by a ladder that could be withdrawn to make the tower impregnable.

Those with children in tow will find a visit to Fortfield Farm, **KILLIMER**, five miles from Kilrush and just a mile before the ferry terminal (see box below), very worthwhile. Fortfield Farm is a small **farm zoo** (May–Sept Mon–Sat 10am–6pm, Sun 2–6pm; £2/€2.54) with llamas, red deer, pot-bellied pigs, numerous breeds of rabbits and other domesticated rare animals. It's run by a friendly crowd who encourage children to handle the animals. The farm also does **B&B** (closed Nov–Feb; ☎065/905 2533; ③); and access to the zoo is free if you are staying there.

Practicalities

The **tourist office** in Kilrush is housed in the old market house in the main square (late May–Sept Mon–Sat 10am–1pm & 2–6pm, Sun noon–4pm; ☎065/905 1577); ask here for assistance with Bus Éireann information for **buses** to Ennis and around the coast throughout the year, and to Galway and Cork during the summer. The town's **heritage centre** (June–Aug, Mon–Fri 9.30am–1pm & 2–4pm; ☎065/905 1047; £2/€2.54) is also housed in the old market house and town hall, and is, for the most part, a stand-and-read display telling the eighteenth- and nineteenth-century economic and social history of the town. The town has two **banks**: Allied Irish Bank and Bank of Ireland, which are both on Frances Street. You can rent out **bikes**, for £7/€8.89 a day, and get camping Gaz from Gleesons, Henry St (☎065/905 1127).

There's no shortage of **B&Bs** in the town centre. Recommended are: *Crotty's* (☎065/905 2470; ③) on the square; Mrs Hynes' *Hillcrest*, Doonbeg Rd (☎065/905 1986; ③); and *Bruach na Coille*, about half a mile out of Kilrush on the Killimer road (☎065/905 2250; ③). *Katie O'Connor's* **hostel**, Frances St (IHH; closed Jan & Feb; ☎065/905 1133), is a decent place, while superior hostel and B&B accommodation is

THE FERRY TO KERRY

You can cut out many miles and the mental congestion of Limerick city, particularly if you're cycling or driving, by heading for Killimer, five miles from Kilrush, and taking the **car ferry** to Tarbert (April–Sept Mon–Sat 7am–9pm, Sun 9am–9pm; Oct–March Mon–Sat 7am–7pm, Sun 10am–7pm; peak season half-hourly sailings from each side, off-peak sailings every hour on the hour from Killimer, return from Tarbert on the half-hour; £9/€11.43 single car, £13/€16.51 return; pedestrians/cyclists £2/€2.54 single, £3/€3.81 return; ☎065/905 3124).

available at *Kilrush Creek Lodge and Adventure Centre*, Cappa Rd, just beside the marina (☎065/905 2595; ③–④), where dorms cost £11.50/€14.60 and include breakfast, and standard and en-suite rooms are also available. They have an **adventure centre** alongside where you can enjoy kayaking, canoeing, sailing or wind-surfing (multi-activity half day £15/€19.05, full day £25/ €31.74; wet suits are provided). Though primarily for caravans, *Aylevarroo Caravan and Camping Park* (closed mid-Sept to April; ☎065/905 1102), also caters for **campers** – you'll find it on the N67 Killimer Road, less than two miles from Kilrush.

In Henry Street, just off the square in Kilrush, good pub **food** is available at *Kelly's* and *The Haven Arms*. For coffee, cakes and sandwiches there's *The Quayside* on Frances Street. For evening meals, try *Kelly's* mid-range restaurant, above the bar, probably the best alternative to the fast-food outlets around the square. Kilrush is a quiet town, but *Crotty's*, on the square, is a great old **bar**, with traditional sessions every night during the summer, and *Éigse Mrs Crotty* is a **concertina festival** that's usually held around the third weekend in August. Other spots for traditional music include *The Island House*, Henry St, and *Gallagher's* (also known as *The Way Inn*), Vaudeleur St (Sun year round). *O'Looney's*, John St, just off the square, is the place to head for rock music (Fri).

Access to Scattery Island is by small boat (£4.50/€5.71), trips take about half an hour and are restricted by tides. Enquire at the **Scattery Island Centre** down by the marina (mid-June to mid-Sept daily 10.30am–6.30pm; ☎065/905 2139), where an exhibition recounts Scattery's monastic history. For excursions to the island at other times, and for details of **dolphin-watching** trips, contact the Griffin family (☎065/905 1327; island trips £5/€6.35; two hour dolphin-watching trips £9/€11.43).

Kilkee and around

KILKEE, over on the Atlantic coast and eight miles northwest of Kilrush, is a small, busy, seaside holiday town with all the amenities you'd expect: cheap cafés, restaurants, amusements and nightlife. Popular with the bucket-and-spade brigade, the town comes as a healthy piece of normality if the offbeat romanticism of the west coast has become too much. The westerly tip of the town's magnificent golden beach, set in dramatic cliff scenery, meets an apron of laminated rock strata known as the Duggerna Rocks, which protects it from the ravages of the Atlantic. Here, when the tide is out, deep, clear pollock holes form, filled with colourful marine life.

The area is a favourite for scuba diving and snorkelling, but even without equipment, exploration is rewarding. There are exhilarating walks for miles along the cliffs both to the north and, more spectacularly, to the south round **Loop Head**, where you can walk for sixteen miles along the cliff's edge past stack rocks, puffing holes (where the sea spouts up through crevices in the rock) and the natural Bridges of Ross. The other good way to see this peninsula is by **bike**; you can rent them from Williams', Circular Rd (☎065/905 6041; £7/€8.89 per day).

In the little church at **MONEEN**, near Kilbaha at the tip of the peninsula, you'll find a nineteenth-century curiosity known as **The Little Arc**. In penal times, Catholics were forced to be both ingenious and secret in the practice of their faith. Here they were not allowed to worship on land, and so built a little hut on wheels which was kept on the beach and wheeled down below the high-water mark between tides, beyond the legal grasp of the local Protestant landowner. The priest would then say Mass in it while the congregation knelt around it on the beach. A couple of pubs at the tiny village of Cross are handy for breaking your explorations of Loop Head, but better by far is the unspoilt fishing village of **CARRIGAHOLT**, which has a slither of beach beside the quays, a ruined castle overlooking the harbour and some very welcoming pubs: *The Long Dock*, for example, does good pub **food** and has music several nights a week in summer.

Carrigaholt is also an excellent place to see Ireland's only known resident group of bottlenose **dolphins** – they're sometimes visible from the shore, but the best way is to take a boat trip with Dolphin Watch (☎065/905 8156; 2hr boat trip; advance booking essential; £10/€12.70).

Practicalities

The **tourist office** in The Square (mid-May to early Sept daily 10am–1pm & 2–6pm; ☎065/905 6112) is very helpful with accommodation, but it's worth bearing in mind that Kilkee is a popular resort and often booked out in August. *Kincora* (☎065/905 6250; ③) on The Square and *Bay View* (☎065/905 6058; ④) on O'Connell St, are good bets for **B&B**. Alternatively, you could try *Purtill's Guesthouse*, O'Curry St, a solid, newly refurbished place (☎065/905 6771; ④), or *Dunearn House*, West End (☎065/905 6545; ④). The cheapest decent accommodation is at *Kilkee Hostel*, O'Curry St (IHH; closed Nov–Feb; ☎065/905 6209), a friendly, family-run **hostel** right in the centre of town. If you need to **camp**, try the large *Cunningham's Holiday Park* (closed mid-Sept to Easter weekend; ☎065/905 6430), reached as you approach town from Kilrush by taking the first left after the petrol station.

The **Bank** of Ireland and the Allied Irish Bank are in O'Curry St. As for **sport**, the choice includes: pitch and putt at the west end, golf at the eighteen-hole championship golf course (☎065/905 6048), scuba diving (Kilkee Diving and Watersports Centre ☎065/905 6707) and pony trekking (☎065/905 6635). **Kilkee Waterworld**, at the north end of the beach (June daily noon–8pm; July & Aug daily 11am–9pm; phone at other times; ☎065/905 6855), is a popular family attraction, with geysers, gushers and an exhilarating sixty-one-metre tower slide, and is particularly worth a visit if you are travelling with children, though in fine weather there can be few better places to swim than in the safe waters of the Blue Flag beach. **Bus Éireann services**, departing from outside Neville's just along the Lahinch Road, link Kilkee with Ennis and other towns along the coast.

Lodged in among the bars and chippies you'll find a handful of good **places to eat**, including *The Strand Restaurant* (closed Tues; ☎065/905 6177) on the seafront, a popular spot for seafood; *The Pantry*, on O'Curry St, which does café-style home-baking during the day and restaurant fare in the evening. On the same street, you'll get good bar food at *Myles' Creek*. Kilkee has no shortage of **pubs**. *O'Mara's*, O'Curry St, is a great old bar, with traditional and folk music (Mon, Wed, Fri & Sun in summer). A younger crowd frequent *Myles' Creek* (rock and pop five nights a week in summer, weekends in winter, traditional Mon). Finally, *The Greyhound* in O'Curry St is arguably the cutest bar in Clare; closed for over forty years, it was reopened a couple of years ago, had the dust blown away and a fresh fire laid.

Miltown Malbay and Spanish Point

The coastline north of Kilkee is one of fine cliffs and sandy beaches, though not all of them are accessible. Those which are include Doonbeg, a relaxing spot where you might see seals and otters, and about a mile further north the beautiful White Strand – both of which are Blue Flag beaches and ideal for swimming. Doughmore beach near Quilty, about eight miles north of Doonbeg, is excellent for experienced surfers, though swimming is not advised here. *Strand Camping* (☎065/905 5345) is a small family-run site located right by the beach at Doonbeg at the mouth of the Doonbeg River.

The Victorian resort of **MILTOWN MALBAY**, eighteen miles north of Kilkee and situated some way inland, comes alive for the Willie Clancy Summer School, held here usually during the first or second week in July, when it's packed with traditional music enthusiasts from all over the world (and booking accommodation well in advance is essential). *Clancy's* and *O'Friel's* (also known as *Lynch's*) **bars** are likely to be lively any time during the summer, and *The Crosses of Annagh*, about two miles south of Miltown Malbay on the road towards Mullagh, has excellent music sessions (Thurs summer; Sat year round). For **B&B**, there's *An Gleann* (☎065/708 4281; ③) and *Malone's*(☎065/708 4246; ②), both on the Ennis road, or you could try *The Station House* (☎065/708 4008; ③), on the Lahinch road.

Two and a half miles away you'll find an excellent sandy swimming beach at **SPANISH POINT**, so called because it was here that survivors from wrecked Armada ships swam ashore, only to be executed by the High Sheriff of Clare. It's a holiday spot for nuns, and appropriately enough has a very quiet **campsite**, *Lahiff's Caravan and Camping Park* (closed Oct–March; ☎065/708 4006). Other places to stay include *Atlantic Star* (☎065/708 4782; ③), a spacious, modern **B&B** just across from the golf course on the main N67, and a couple of new **hotels**: *Armada Hotel* (☎065/708 4110, *www.iol.ie/~armada/index.htm*; ⑥) and the *Bellbridge House Hotel* (☎065/708 4038; ⑥).

To the east of Spanish Point, **Slieve Callan** rises beside the main road to Ennis. Taking this road you pass Knocknalassa, where there's an impressive wedge-shaped gallery grave, known as Diarmuid and Gráinne's Bed (after the Irish version of the Tristan and Isolde story). It's quite tricky to find: five miles along the road from Miltown Malbay you will pass a house with a thatched little barn alongside; the grave is about half a mile further east from here, tucked out of sight behind a hummocky rise to the left of the road. Follow the cows – it's worth seeing.

Lahinch and Ennistymon

LAHINCH, eight miles north of Spanish Point, is a busy family holiday resort with a fabulous broad sandy beach. Families aside, Lahinch attracts golfers and surfers, a weird hybrid well served by the town. To get a round at Lahinch **golf** course you will need to book well ahead (☎065/708 1003); **surfing** is there for the taking. You can hear good **music** in the bars, especially in the summer months.

B&B accommodation is available at *Seafield Lodge* (☎065/708 1594; ③) and *Mulcarr House* (☎065/708 1123; ③), both close to the centre on Ennistymon Road. Slightly further out, but offering wonderful views of the bay are *Le Bord De Mer*, Cregg (☎065/708 1454; ③) and *Nazira*, School Rd (☎065/708 1362; ③). The resort has several traditional **hotels** including: *The Aberdeen Arms* (☎065/708 1100; ⑦) and *The Atlantic* (☎065/708 1049; ⑥) both on Main Street. At the other end of the scale, the *Lahinch Hostel* (IHH; ☎065/708 1040), next door to the church, is a decent budget option, with laundry facilities and bike rental. You can **camp** at *Lahinch Camping and Caravan Park* (closed Oct–April; ☎065/708 1424), an orderly family site that has a laundry for service washes and a wet-weather shelter. The mighty **meals** served in the bar of *The Shamrock Hotel*, Main St, will satisfy post-surf hunger. Other bars good for food include the seafront *O'Looney's* and nearby *The Spinnaker Bar*, both frequented by a lively young crowd. *The Nineteenth Bar* and *Galvin's*, both on Main Street, have a great atmosphere and music most nights during the summer. For seafood, good vegetarian food and fine views head for *The Barrtrá* (☎065/708 1280), signposted off the road two miles south of Lahinch.

About two miles east of Lahinch, the old market town of **ENNISTYMON**, with its low shop-fronts and great old bars tucked away in the most unlikely of places, has a life, albeit a leisurely one, regardless of tourism. Its people enjoy **traditional music** and ballads in the bars year round. Try *Phil's Bar*, *Daly's Bar*, *Eugene's* or *Cooley's House*, all on Main Street. The church at the end of Main Street has been converted into a *teach cheoil* (ceilidh house) where you can catch evenings of traditional music. The town's Traditional Singing Festival is usually held over the first weekend in June. Ennistymon's setting is surprisingly green; signposted off the main street is the

Cascades Walk which takes you a short way alongside the River Cullenagh as it rushes over slabs of rock through the heart of the little town. Ennistymon's eighteenth-century church stands on a hill above the town, from where you can see the blue river snaking its way out of the woods and beyond to the sea at Liscannor. Central **B&Bs** include the welcoming *Station House*, in Ennis Rd (☎065/707 1149; ③).

The Burren

The Burren (*Boireann*, or "rocky land") is a huge plateau of limestone and shale that covers over a hundred square miles of northwest Clare, a highland shaped by a series of cliffs, terraces and expanses of limestone pavement, with little to punctuate the view. Bleak and grey, the northern reaches of the Burren can come as a shock to anyone associating Ireland with all things lush and verdant. It's an extraordinary landscape of stark rock, fading lower green fields, and above all the sky and the ocean. Its cliffs and terraces lurch towards the sea like huge steps of wind-pocked pumice. Bone white in sunshine, in the rain the rock becomes darkened and metallic, the cliffs and canyons blurred by mists. A harsh place, barely capable of sustaining human habitation, it was aptly summed up in the words of Cromwell's surveyor Ludlow: "savage land, yielding neither water enough to drown a man, nor a tree to hang him, nor soil enough to bury". There are no sweet rolling fields here, but stick with it and its fascination emerges – cruel and barren as it is, there's a raw beauty about the place with its exceptional combination of light, rock and water.

GEOLOGY AND FAUNA

The Burren has an austerity of almost mythical dimensions, suggesting ancient privations. The pavementing that stretches before you is a floor of grey rock, split by long parallel grooves known as grykes. Throughout the Burren, rainwater seeps through the highly porous rock and gouges away at the many underground potholes, caves and tunnels. The only visible **river** is the Caher at Fanore, but there are a multitude of underground waterways, and there are **lakes**, known as turloughs, that are peculiar to this landscape; they appear only after heavy rainfall, when the underground systems fill up, and vanish once again after a few dry days.

The panorama is bleak, but close up, **wild flowers** burst from the grooves in specks and splashes of brilliant colour. A botanist's delight and enigma, the Burren supports an astounding variety of **flora**, with Arctic, Alpine and Mediterranean plants growing alongside each other. The best time to see the flowers is late spring, when the strong blue, five-petalled spring gentians flourish. Here, too, are mountain avens, various saxifrages and maidenhair fern. Later in summer, the magenta bloody cranesbill and a fantastic variety of orchids (considered rare elsewhere) bloom: bee orchids, fly orchids and the lesser butterfly. More common flowers look stunning by sheer force of quantity: bright yellow birdsfoot trefoil and hoary rockrose, and milkwort. Obviously flowers must not be picked.

Nobody knows exactly how these plants came to be here, nor why they remain. It has been suggested that some of the Mediterranean flowers have been here since Ireland had a far hotter climate, but how they survived is a source of speculation: it may be the peculiar conditions of moist warm air coming in from the sea, the Gulf Stream ensuring a mild, frostless climate, and very effective drainage through the porous limestone. It's also thought that the bare rock absorbs heat all summer and stores it, so that the Burren land is appreciably warmer in wintertime than areas of a different geology. There's more on the Burren's geology in the **Burren Display Centre** in Kilfenora and at the Whitehorn Visitor Centre, Ballyvaughan.

In recent centuries, the Burren has supported a sparse population, living, like most of the west of Ireland, in harsh poverty. It was to this land, west of the Shannon, that Cromwell drove the dispossessed Irish Catholics after his campaign of terror. Few could survive for long in such country. The area's lack of appeal to centuries of speculators and colonizers greedy to cream the fat off Ireland's lusher pastures has meant that evidence of many of the Burren's earlier inhabitants has remained. The place has over sixty **Stone Age** (3000–2000 BC) burial monuments, the most common types being wedge-shaped tombs, cairns and dolmens; over four hundred Iron Age **ring forts** (500 BC–500 AD), which were defensive dwellings; and numerous Christian churches, **monasteries**, round towers and high crosses. Amongst the most evocative of the Christian ruins is Corcanroe Abbey, just outside Bell Harbour, and there are fine high crosses at Kilfenora.

You can get to the area by taking a Bus Éireann connection from stations at Galway, Limerick or Ennis. There's a direct **bus** service from Limerick and Galway to Doolin and in summer at least one bus a day from Limerick passes through Ennistymon and Lisdoonvarna, and at least one a day connects Galway with Lisdoonvarna. To see the Burren's archeological and ecclesiastical sites, it's best to go by car or bike (bike rental is available in the main centres of Doolin and Ballyvaughan); to get to know its landscape and flowers, go on foot. For either of these, the excellent Tim Robinson **map**, *The Burren* (available in tourist offices, good bookshops or directly from him at Roundstone, County Galway) is usefully detailed and will make finding sites easy, though it does not show contours. For walking, the Ordnance Survey map number 51 (1:50,000) is ideal – and also covers the Aran Islands. There are two north–south routes across the Burren that are of particular **archeological interest**; these run from Bell Harbour to Killinaboy and from

THE BURREN WAY

The Burren Way runs through countryside which is quite unlike the rest of the west of Ireland; made up of bare limestone, treeless and exposed, this remarkable area has a weird beauty all of its own. Although the Burren Way is marked on maps as starting at Liscannor, this first stretch is currently closed and walkers now have to start at the Cliffs of Moher. From here, the path runs parallel to the coast a little way inland; much of this section, however, is close to the road, which is always very busy in high season affording spectacular views across to the Aran Islands and, on a fine day, the mountains of Connemara. The way then descends to Doolin and picks up a gradual ascent past Ballynalacken Castle and on across open fields around the shoulder of Slieve Elva. There are no really steep climbs and as the path descends to the Caher River, a valley of classic Burren scenery opens up all around, with stark grey limestone hills and barely a tree in sight. At this point there is the tantalizing option of wandering two and a half miles down the valley to stop over in Fanore, from where you have access to other great walks. The Burren Way itself follows the quiet road southeast through the valley, round past medieval Newtown Castle and down to the silvery shoreline of Ballyvaughan Bay. It's a gentle walk from here into Ballyvaughan, accompanied by fine views across the great expanse of Galway Bay.

Access: It is possible to take the bus from Ennis to Doolin and from Ballyvaughan to Galway, Lisdoonvarna and Doolin.

Accommodation: There are numerous B&Bs and hostels in Doolin, a few B&Bs and a fine little cottage hostel at Fanore, and B&B accommodation at Ballyvaughan.

Overall distance: 22 miles.

Highest point: Slieve Elva (flank) 980ft.

Maps and guides: The Ordnance Survey map No. 51 (1:50,000) is quite sufficient; *The Burren Way Map and Guide* is available in tourist offices.

Ballyvaughan to Leamaneh Castle. If you're doing a lot of walking, a compass is a good idea as there's a shortage of easy landmarks. You're allowed to walk more or less where you want, though do be aware that there are a large number of bulls in the fields. A good start might be to follow the Burren Way (see box opposite for more details).

Liscannor and the Cliffs of Moher

Once a tiny village, **LISCANNOR** has been swept along by the tide of development that surges around Ireland's west coast. Still, as a base for exploring Clare's most famous tourist spot, the Cliffs of Moher, it makes a good alternative to the busier tourist centre of Doolin. The village has a few nice bars, a caravan site which accepts tents, a supermarket and a post office. The area is famous for **Liscannor Flag**, a durable stone used for paving, cladding, fireplaces and, traditionally, the roofs of dwellings. Liscannor Stone, St Brigid's Well (about one mile along the road as you go out of the village towards the Cliffs of Moher) is an interesting diversion: an audiovisual display tells the story of the stone, and its shop is worth visiting for its dazzling display of exotic crystals and fossils. Be aware that the sandy stretches south towards Lahinch, near the mouth of the river, are unsafe due to quicksand.

Accommodation is mostly at the cheaper end of the scale and includes the *Village Hostel* (IHH; closed Nov–Feb; ☎065/708 1550), located right next to the bars, and a number of B&Bs: the budget *Cahilly Lodge* (☎065/708 1749; ②); the modern, spacious *Sea Haven* (☎065/708 1385; ③); and *Seamount* (☎065/708 1367; ③), which offers en-suite rooms. *The Mermaid Café* is open for very good, albeit fairly expensive, evening meals (☎065/708 1076).

Circling north round the Burren from Liscannor, you arrive almost immediately at the **Cliffs of Moher**. At their highest, they tower 660ft above the Atlantic, and standing on the headlands that jut over the sheer, ravaged cliffs with their great bands of shale and sandstone, you can feel the huge destructive power of the waves. At points, the battering of the water has left jagged stack rocks standing, continually lashed by white spume. Erosion is constant; during a storm some years ago a section of the cliff fell, taking a picnic table with it. The cliffs have to be seen – ideally on a summer evening, when the setting sun is full on them – but be prepared for the oppressively commercial **visitor centre**, where readily changed money and travellers' cheques are quickly spent on coffee, cakes and souvenirs. Do see the cliffs, though – you can soon walk away from the crowds in either direction, after checking there are no bulls in the field to the north. The cliffs actually stretch for five miles, from Hag's Head, just west of Liscannor, to a point beyond **O'Brien's Tower** – a superfluous viewing point with telescope – some four miles south of Doolin.

Doolin

The village of **DOOLIN**, four miles north of the Cliffs of Moher and marked as "Fisherstreet" on some maps, is for many the music mecca of the "singing county", and in fact of Ireland's west. By the time you get here, you'll no doubt already have met a good few traditional music enthusiasts on their way from across northern Europe, and there are extra buses laid on to bring them here. This said, it is not necessarily the best place for top traditional sessions – these tend to move around – but you are guaranteed to find some kind of merriment in each of Doolin's three pubs (*O'Connor's, McGann's* and *McDermott's*) every night throughout the year. The music varies enormously and you may come across anything from a bunch of amplified performers doing a medley of Eurovision classics to the kind of fabulous session you'll remember for the rest of your life. Bearing this in mind, the key to getting the best out of Doolin is to remember that if you stumble into a poor session, there are two other bars nearby.

Without the music, Doolin would be a rather forlorn and desolate place, lodged as it is beside a treacherous sandy beach at the tail end of the coast that climaxes with the Cliffs of Moher. Bold shelves of limestone pavement step into the sea by the pier, from which a **ferry** (☎065/707 4455) runs to **Inisheer** (mid-April to late Sept 1–6 daily; single £10/€12.70, return £15/€19.05) and **Inishmore** (mid-April to late Sept 1–2 daily; single £10/€12.70, return £20/€25.70), and to **Inishmaan** (mid-May to Aug 1–2 daily; return £18/€22.86). If you want more than a couple of hours on the islands – and this is a very good idea – then day trips are only really feasible to Inisheer. It is possible to sail from Doolin to all three islands and then on to Galway or return to Doolin (£20/€25.70; bikes £2/€2.54). See p.391 for more on the Aran Islands.

Music may be Doolin's *raison d'être*, but the village is now ruthlessly geared to providing accommodation for as many visitors as it's possible to squeeze into the place's three pubs. There's plenty of **B&B** accommodation on offer in Doolin; all are reasonably priced and offer a decent standard. *Seacrest* (☎065/707 4458; ③) is located towards the pier, offering wild, blustery views of the coast, as is *Atlantic View* (☎065/707 4189; ④). A couple of smart, and fairly new, B&Bs are behind *O'Connor's* pub: *Fisherman's Rest* (☎065/707 4673; ③) and *Lane Lodge* (☎065/707 4747; ②). Other good options are found along the road between the three pubs, including: *Riverfield House* (☎065/707 4113; ③), *Doolin House* (☎065/707 4259; ③), *The Horseshoe* (☎065/707 4006; ④), *O'Connor's* itself (☎065/707 4314; ③), and just behind the *Aille River Hostel* (see below), *Doolin Cottage* (☎065/707 4762; ①).

Despite their number, the **hostels** do get packed in July and August, so ringing ahead is essential. *Paddy's Doolin* hostel is near *O'Connor's* pub (IHH; ☎065/707 4006), and is an efficiently run option; further north along the same road is *The Rainbow Hostel* (IHH; ☎065/707 4415), a welcoming and well-run place. Other hostels include the friendly and laid-back *Aille River Hostel* (IHH; ☎065/707 4260), and *Flanagan's Village Hostel* (IHH; ☎065/707 4564), a family-run hostel with excellent facilities, comfy beds and great views, five minutes' walk north out of the village. There's **camping** down by the pier at *Nagle's* (closed late Sept to April; ☎065/707 4458) – a great spot to absorb the drama of the landscape – and near the *Aille River Hostel* at *Riverside Camping* (closed Oct–April; ☎065/707 4314).

You'll find a fair selection of **places to eat** here besides the pubs, which all do filling, good-value bar meals. *The Magnet*, near *O'Connor's Bar*, serves tasty filled crepes, though the service is painfully slow; nearby is a shop selling filled rolls and other picnic provisions. At the far north end of the village, beyond *Flanagan's* hostel and down a road to the right, is the *Doolin Craft Shop* and the adjacent café with its delightful garden is a good spot to unwind, serving fresh salmon sandwiches, smoked salmon platters and fine cakes (closed Oct–Easter). For evening meals there's the moderately priced *Lazy Lobster* (☎065/707 4390) specializing in fish; the similarly priced *Doolin Café* which has a trendy atmosphere; and, a quieter choice, the upmarket *Bruach Na haille*, next door to *McGann's* pub (☎065/707 4120), noted for its seafood and vegetarian meals.

Fanore to Bell Harbour

North of Doolin, the coast remains spectacular but bleak and empty. The first place to stop is **FANORE**. A number of excellent Burren walks are easily accessible from here, the best of which is the magnificent walk up to the Caherdoonfergus ring fort and the heights of Dobhach Bhrainin and Gleninagh – a round walk of nine and a half miles. If you decide to use Fanore as a base, you'll find pleasant B&B at *Monica's* (☎065/707 6141; ③) or cosy hostel **accommodation** at *Bridge Hostel* (closed end Oct to Feb; ☎065/707 6134), which also does camping and evening meals; it only has eighteen beds, so in July and August it's best to ring ahead. **Horse riding** is available at The

Burren Riding Centre (☎065/707 6140; one and a half hours £20/€25.79, three hours £40/€50.79).

Beyond, the scenic coast road to Black Head and Ballyvaughan is well worth taking. Beautifully poised between Galway Bay and the Burren, **BALLYVAUGHAN** is an attractive village with a quay of neat grey blocks. Its significance as a trading centre has dwindled into tourism, but it makes a calm haven from which to explore the Burren hills, and it's also the northerly limit of the Burren Way (see p.362). At the **Whitethorn Visitor Centre**, on the Galway road east out of the village, Burren Exposure (April–Oct daily 10am-6pm; ☎065/707 7277; £3.50/€4.44), a 35-minute audiovisual display on the geology, history and flora of the Burren, is shown. It gives a good overview and the aerial photographs of ring forts are particularly interesting. There's also a restaurant and a craft shop at the centre. Further along this road (about one and a half miles from the village centre), a signposted lane leads to the tranquil and sandy Bishop's Quarter beach. **B&Bs** in the centre of the village include: the comfortable *Gentian Villa* (☎065/707 7042; ③) and the luxurious and welcoming *Ballyvaughan Lodge* (☎065/707 7292; ④). About half a mile east along a quiet green road, there's *Dolmen Lodge* (closed late Oct to mid-March; ☎065/7077202; ④), while a short walk beyond *Monk's* pub will take you to *Oceanville* (☎065/707 7051; ③). For a secluded Burren location try *Merrijig Farmhouse* (☎065/707 7120; ③), three miles inland; head out along the Lisdoonvarna road and take the right fork towards Lismacsheedy Cliff Fort; it's on the right after about a mile and a half. Bicycle rental is available at J. Connole Laundrette.

Whitethorn Restaurant & Crafts (☎065/707 7044; mid-March to Oct daily 9.30am–6pm, July & Aug open for dinner Fri & Sat), located in the Whitethorn Visitor Centre, is worth calling in on for its stunning setting and offers inexpensive, tasty self-service **meals** during the day and formal à la carte dining in the evening. *Monk's* bar does good seafood and the bar meals at *Hyland's Hotel* cater for hearty appetites. You can get tea and snacks at *An Féar Gorta Tearooms* in an attractive setting down by the quays. **Traditional music** is played several nights a week during the summer in *Hyland's Hotel* and *Monk's* bar.

From Ballyvaughan, interesting routes strike south through the heart of the Burren. Within three miles of Ballyvaughan lie Newtown Castle and the Aillwee Caves, both signposted off the Lisdoonvarna Road. Although the newly restored sixteenth-century **Newtown Castle** is nothing more than a fortified tower house, the guided tour is interesting, telling of the medieval law and bardic schools of the surrounding area. The mile-long guided Newtown Castle Trail takes one hour and covers folklore, botany and history (April–Oct daily 10am–6pm; castle £2/€2.54; castle and trail £3.50/€4.44). The well-lit tour through the two-million-year-old **Aillwee Caves** (daily: March–Oct 10am–5.30pm, July & Aug 10am–6.30pm; Nov–Feb 11.30am–4pm; *www.aillweecave.ie*; £4.75/€6.03) will take you past amazing caverns of stalagmites and stalactites and spectacular rock formations.

All along this coast, east of Ballyvaughan, where the Burren borders Galway Bay, short stretches of well-tended farmland reach from the foot of the hills to the shoreline, and water glints through gaps in the high stone walls, while way over Galway Bay the muted cobalt mountains of Connemara lie hazy in the distance. There's a wealth of **birdlife** along these shores: cormorants, guillemots, terns, herons, grebes, fulmars, mallards, teals and swans, as well as sea-otters and seals. Heading towards Galway on the coast road, you pass through **BELL HARBOUR** (*Beulaclugga*), at the southern tip of Muckinish Bay, where the road towards Killinaboy sets off, soon passing the placid **Corcomroe Abbey** signposted on your left. A twelfth-century Cistercian foundation, its considerable remains are beautifully set in a secluded valley.

NEW QUAY, around seven miles east of Ballyvaughan, signposted off the main Galway road, is famous for *Linnane's* seafood bar – in fact there is little else there. It's a cosy bar serving delicious seafood year round and is renowned for its traditional music sessions on Friday.

Lisdoonvarna and the heart of the Burren

LISDOONVARNA, nine miles south of Ballyvaughan and five miles inland from Doolin, is most notable for its month-long **matchmaking festival** held annually in September. The origins of the festival lie with the farmers who would come down after the harvest from the hills to spend their hard-earned cash and look for a wife in a festival of singing, dancing and drinking. It remains popular with a middle-aged crowd who come along for all manner of merry making, so if you want to be here in September, book your accommodation well ahead.

On the whole Lisdoonvarna is probably best enjoyed in spring and early summer as it serves as one of the handiest spots from which to explore the Burren. It's renowned for it's **spa** too: the spring waters here contain magnesia, iodine and iron, and reputedly have restorative qualities. The town's principal sulphur spring is in the Spa Wells Health Centre (June–Sept daily 10am–6pm; ☎065/707 4023), where you can take the waters in the pumphouse, or have a sulphur bath (June–Sept Mon–Fri 10am–6pm, Sat 10am–2pm), a sauna, a shower or a massage. Generally full of elderly holiday-makers, the centre offers an invigorating afternoon for weary cyclists and walkers. The whirlwind tour of **The Burren Smokehouse** (daily 9am–7pm), right in the centre of town, will fill you in on all there is to know about traditional methods of smoking fish: frankly, there's not much to it, but it's worth taking for the banter and the sliver of smoked salmon thrown in to tempt you to buy more.

Recommended **B&Bs** here are *St Joseph's*, Main St (☎065/707 4076; ②) and *Ballinsheen House* (☎065/707 4806; ③). When it comes to **eating**, plenty of pubs serve food; especially good is *The Roadside Tavern* (until 8.30pm). All of the pubs have music most nights during July and August, some of it pretty mixed, but *The Roadside Tavern* is a good starting point.

The Ballyvaughan road leads you northbound through a brief area of dank forestry and out onto the **corkscrew hill**, a famous winding descent with fabulous views between grey hills to the broad expanse of Galway Bay – a visual treat and an especially exhilarating release for cyclists after the long steady climb.

Kilfenora

The tiny village of **KILFENORA**, about four miles southeast of Lisdoonvarna, is a great spot for **traditional music** and is renowned for its year-round music pubs: *Linnane's* and *Vaughan's*. Kilfenora's music festival, held over the October bank holiday weekend, is a wonderful and strictly traditional event. The village is also home to the much-publicized **Burren Display Centre** (April, May & Oct daily 10am–5pm; June–Sept daily 9.30am–6pm; £2.50/€3.17). The centre explains clearly the basic geography and geology of the Burren with the aid of a landscape model and a film. The tearoom makes a good refreshment stop.

Next door stands **Kilfenora Cathedral**, certainly worth a visit for its high crosses, the finest of which is the **twelfth-century Doorty Cross**, showing three bishops and what is probably Christ's entry into Jerusalem, with beautiful Celtic patterning. Nearby in the churchyard are remains of two other twelfth-century high crosses, one near the northwest corner, one opposite the church door. Wander through the gateway behind the church and you'll see a fourth cross, with a decorated Crucifixion, in the field to the west. The cathedral itself was built in 1190 and altered in the fifteenth century. It has a roofless chancel with a finely carved triple-light east window and two effigies of bishops, possibly fourteenth century.

For **B&B**, try *Mrs Murphy's*, Main St (☎065/708 8040; ②). Alternatively, you can stay at *The Cottage Hostel*, Lissylisheen, four and a half miles north of here – it's tricky to find so ask locally for directions. It's a small, charming place and also offers camping (☎086/801 5566).

Leamaneh Castle and Carran

Heading east from Kilfenora you pass **Leamaneh Castle**, a fifteenth-century O'Brien stronghold, adjoining which is a four-storey building with mullioned and transomed windows (circa 1640). The area north of here is littered with ancient remains. Take the Ballyvaughan road north at Leamaneh Castle and you will pass the **Poulnabrone Dolmen**, the most famous of the Burren's portal dolmens, dating from 2500 BC. It's a marvellous place at dusk, when the fading light turns the surrounding fields of stone a vibrant lilac. Alternatively, continue east from Leamaneh Castle and take the left turn north just before Killinaboy. The lane rises steeply through hazel hedgerows and brings you up to a limestone plateau. You will pass two signposted wedge tombs on your left and, after another mile or so, come to **Caher Commaun**, a ninth-century triple ring fort. You may have to pay a small fee to walk across the farmer's field. From here, you can wend your way north through a tangle of roads to minuscule **CARRAN**. The hamlet's prime feature is a turlough: in summer it appears as a meadow, in winter a lake. Overlooking the turlough are *Clare's Rock*, a comfortable new **hostel** (closed Oct–April; ☎065/708 9129), and *Croide na boirne* bar and restaurant (☎065/708 9109), which serves probably the only Burren-themed bar food in the world. Look out for their speciality, *burren mionáin*, organically reared kid. From Carran the road north leads down to Bell Harbour (*Bealaclugga*) and nearby Corcomroe (see p.365).

Killinaboy and Corofin

Follow the road east from Leamaneh Castle and you'll reach **KILLINABOY**, where a ruined eleventh- to fourteenth-century church has a striking Sheila-na-gig over the doorway – a carving of a naked woman with grotesquely exaggerated genitalia (sheila means "femininity", and gig "breast") which was probably some kind of fertility symbol. They're more usually found above castle doorways, and it may be that its siting here was intended as a warning against the sins of the flesh. There are a handful of pleasant **B&Bs** in the area, of which *Fergus View* (☎065/683 7606; ④) is a welcoming option two miles north of Corofin on the Kilfenora road.

From Killinaboy the road winds down into the more substantial village of **COROFIN**, consisting of a handful of houses and a string of cheerful pubs. It makes an excellent base from which to explore the Burren or to enjoy fishing in the abundance of little lakes hereabouts. Lough Inchiquin is particularly scenic and a detour around the lake and up Clifden Hill affords spectacular views – you'll need your own transport for this. The village is also home to the **Clare Heritage Centre** (April–Oct daily 9.30am–5.30pm; Nov–March Mon–Fri 9am–5pm; ☎065/683 7955, *www.clareroots.com*), which portrays the traumatic period of Irish history between 1800 and 1860 and fills in the horrors that the Bunratty Folk Park omits: famine, disease, emigration and the issue of land tenure. It also has a genealogy service for those with origins in the county and holds details of over half a million people, McMahon, Macnamara, Moloney and O'Brien being the most common names. If you want to research your roots in detail, write to or email the centre a few months before your trip and find out as much as possible before you visit (names, dates, marriages, deaths, location, occupation, parish for example). An initial search costs around £40–60, a full one £100–150. Alternatively, the new library here is freely available: a morning spent poring over records will probably convince you just why it's worth paying a trained genealogist to do it for you.

You can stay here at the friendly, family-run *Corofin Village Hostel* (IHH; ☎065/683 7683; the hostel may close, so phoning ahead is advised), with its pleasant **campsite**. Traditional music is dished up with tea and brown bread in summer at the village's pleasantly relaxed *teach cheoil* (music house) in the main street (July & Aug Thurs

9pm; ☎065/683 7706; £3/€3.81), in a lively evening suitable for families, with set dancing. There is also bound to be **music** on in one of the pubs most nights during the summer. *Bofey Quinn's* does good **bar food** – try their Corofin Smokies, a kind of smoked fish and potato hotpot. **Boats** can be hired from Burke's shop.

travel details

Trains

Ennis to: Dublin (1–2 daily; 3hr); Limerick (1–2 daily; 1hr).

Buses

Bunratty to: Shannon Airport (20 daily; 20min).

Doolin to: Galway (summer 2–4 daily; 1hr 30min).

Ennis to: Doolin (1–3 daily; 1hr 15min); Galway (12 daily; 1hr 30min); Kilkee (1–3 daily; 1hr 15min); Lahinch (1–3 daily; 45min); Limerick (8–19 daily; 45min); Lisdoonvarna (summer 1 daily; 1hr 15min); Shannon Airport (14 daily; 45min).

Galway to: Lisdoonvarna (summer 2–4 daily, mid-Sept–mid-May Mon–Sat 2–4 daily; 1hr 20min).

Limerick to: Doolin (1–3 daily; 1hr 40min–2hr 20min); Ennis (15 daily; 1hr); Ennistymon (1–3 daily; 1hr 15min); Killaloe (Mon–Sat 1–2 daily; 45min); Lisdoonvarna (1–5 daily; 1hr 55min); Mountshannon (Sat only 1 daily; 1hr 25min); Shannon Airport (20 daily; 45 min).

CHAPTER TEN

GALWAY, MAYO AND ROSCOMMON

Galway, Mayo and Roscommon mark a distinct change in the west of Ireland scene. Coming from the south, County Galway may at first seem a continuation of what has gone before in Clare and Kerry. And Galway city is in some ways the west coast town par excellence – an exceptionally enjoyable, free-spirited sort of place, and a gathering point for young travellers. But once you get beyond the city things start to change. The landscape is dramatically harsher and far less populous, and there are fewer visitors, too.

Lough Corrib, which divides Galway in two, delineates another dramatic split in the landscape of the county, this time between east and west, inland and coast. To the east of the lake lies tame, fertile land which people have farmed for centuries, while to the west lies **Connemara**, a magnificently wild terrain of wind and rock and water. The **Aran Islands**, in the mouth of Galway Bay, resemble Connemara both in their elemental beauty and in their culture; the Galway *Gaeltacht* – areas where Irish is still spoken – comprises the islands, Iar-Chonnacht and some scattered communities in north Connemara and Joyce country (north of Lough Corrib). While it can't compete with the rest of the county, **east Galway**'s medieval monastic sites are well worth taking in as you pass through. Again, **Galway city** straddles the divide. A bridging point both physically and culturally, it's a fishing port, an historic city and the focus of an energetic social and artistic scene.

Further up the coast is **County Mayo**, where the landscape softens somewhat but is still relatively free of tourists. The pilgrimage centre of **Knock** and the attractions of historic towns like **Westport** aside, it's the coast which is once again the main draw. Physically, it's as exciting and rugged as any in the Republic, and far less exploited, though the downside is that facilities for travellers are relatively thin on the ground. An exception is **Achill**, the largest Irish offshore island and popular holiday resort, which provides both some of the most spectacular cliffs in the country and caters well for travellers.

County Roscommon is entirely landlocked and less visited still. There are few real excitements, and the land is for the most part flat and low lying; nevertheless, the fine

ACCOMMODATION PRICE CODES

Throughout this book, prices of hotels, guesthouses and B&Bs have been graded with the codes below, according to what you can expect to pay for a double room in high season. For more details on accommodation, see p.34.

① Under £26/€33.01
② £26–33/€33.01–41.90
③ £33–40/€41.90–50.79
④ £40–55/€50.79–69.84
⑤ £55–70/€69.84–88.88
⑥ £70–90/€88.88–114.28
⑦ £90–110/€114.28–139.67
⑧ £110–130/€139.67–165.07
⑨ Over £130/€165.07

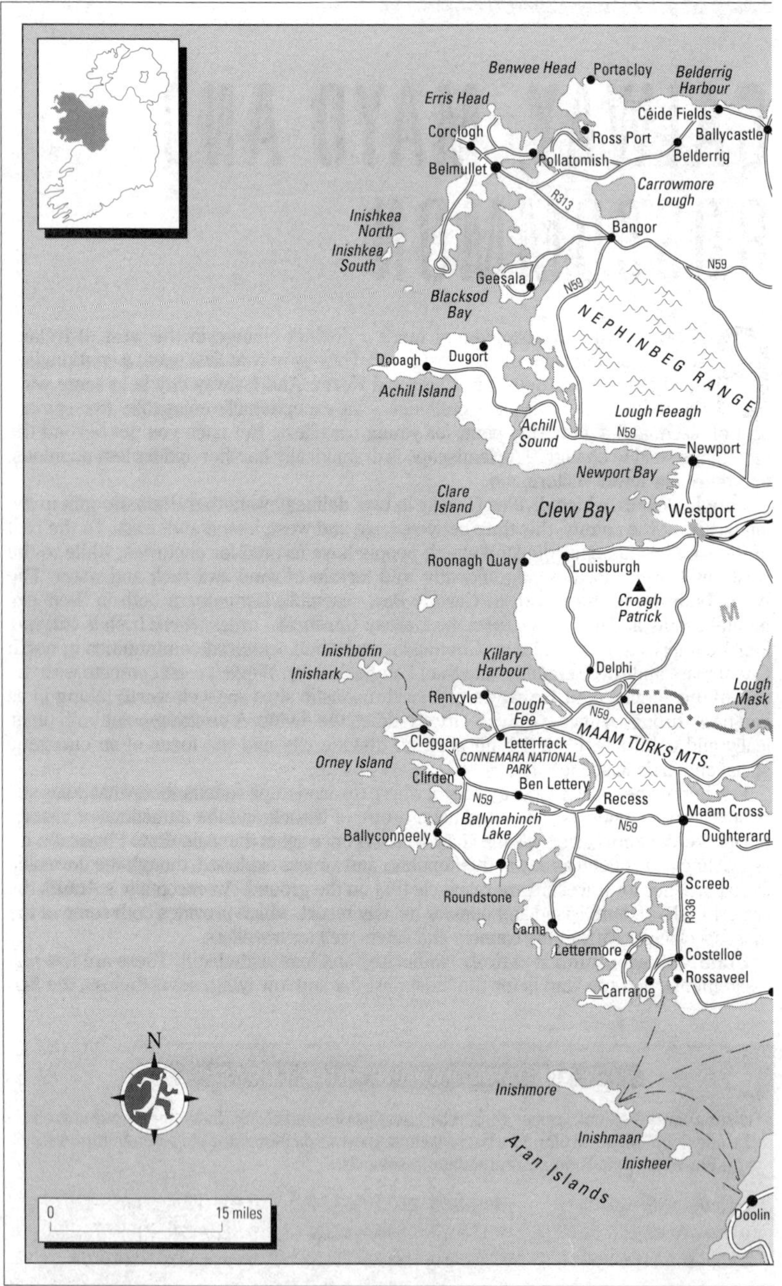
Benwee Head
Portacloy
Belderrig Harbour
Erris Head
Céide Fields
Corclogh
Ross Port
Ballycastle
Pollatomish
Belderrig
Belmullet
R313
Carrowmore Lough
Inishkea North
Inishkea South
Bangor
N59
Geesala
Blacksod Bay
NEPHINBEG RANGE
Dooagh
Dugort
Achill Island
Lough Feeagh
Achill Sound
Newport
Newport Bay
Clare Island
Clew Bay
Westport
Roonagh Quay
Louisburgh
Croagh Patrick
Inishbofin
Inishark
Killary Harbour
Delphi
Lough Mask
Renvyle
Lough Fee
Leenane
Cleggan
Letterfrack
MAAM TURKS MTS.
CONNEMARA NATIONAL PARK
Orney Island
Clifden
Ben Lettery
Recess
Maam Cross
Ballynahinch Lake
Oughterard
Ballyconneely
Screeb
Roundstone
R336
Carna
Lettermore
Costelloe
Carraroe
Rossaveel
N
Inishmore
Inishmaan
Inisheer
Aran Islands
0
15 miles
Doolin

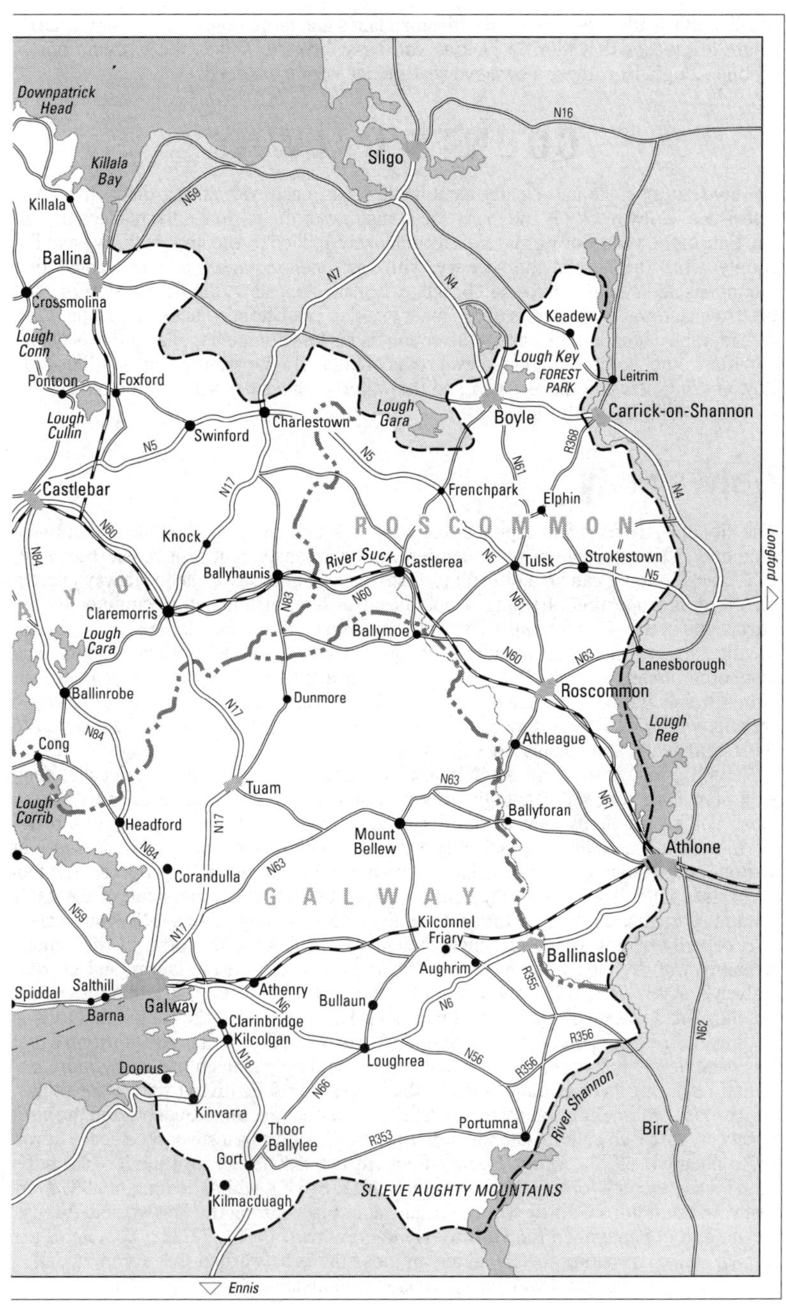
Downpatrick Head
Killala Bay
Killala
Ballina
Crossmolina
Lough Conn
Pontoon
Foxford
Lough Cullin
Castlebar
Swinford
Charlestown
Lough Gara
Sligo
N59
N7
N4
N16
Keadew
Lough Key
FOREST PARK
Leitrim
Boyle
Carrick-on-Shannon
R368
N61
N5
Frenchpark
Elphin
ROSCOMMON
N4
Longford
N17
N60
Knock
N84
Ballyhaunis
River Suck
Castlerea
Tulsk
Strokestown
MAYO
Claremorris
N83
Lough Cara
Ballymoe
N63
Lanesborough
Ballinrobe
Dunmore
Roscommon
Lough Ree
Cong
Athleague
Tuam
Lough Corrib
Ballyforan
Headford
Mount Bellew
Athlone
Corandulla
GALWAY
Kilconnel Friary
Ballinasloe
Aughrim
R355
Spiddal
Salthill
Barna
Galway
Athenry
N6
Bullaun
Clarinbridge
Kilcolgan
N18
Loughrea
N56
R356
N62
Doorus
N66
Kinvarra
River Shannon
Thoor Ballylee
Portumna
Birr
R353
Gort
Kilmacduagh
SLIEVE AUGHTY MOUNTAINS
Ennis

detail of this landscape, scattered with small lakes and large houses, has a slow charm. There are places that merit a look as you pass through, and in the extreme north, around **Lough Key**, there's some very attractive scenery indeed.

COUNTY GALWAY

County Galway splits into clearly identifiable areas, each with strong distinctive characteristics. **Galway city** is the great social magnet of the region, a lively place to visit any time of the year. **Connemara** – a term loosely applied to encompass the west of the county – has the best of the scenery, with vast open expanses of bog, exhilarating mountains and superb white-sand beaches. Equally appealing, the **Aran Islands** combine raw landscape with some of the most exciting pre-Christian sites in Europe – and considerable legends. The east of the county is far less compelling; flat and less inspiring, it nonetheless does hold medieval ruins of interest. The area around south Galway Bay, nestling between the **Burren** and the water, at times has some of the tantalizing, ethereal quality of north Clare.

Galway city

The city of **GALWAY**, folk capital of the west, has a vibrancy and hedonism that make it unique. People come here with energies primed for enjoyment – the music, the drink, the "crack" – and it can be a difficult place to leave. University College Galway guarantees a high proportion of young people in term time, maintained in summer by the attractions of the city's festivals. This youthful **energy** is an important part of Galway's identity, and the city's mix of culture and fun attracts not only disaffected bohemians from other areas of Ireland but folksy young Europeans who return each year with an almost religious devotion. Galway sees itself in many ways as the capital of Gaelic Ireland, where traditional aspects of Irish society, primarily music and language, are most confidently and colourfully expressed.

As is the case with many other Irish cities, Galway has, for the past decade, been experiencing a surge of economic growth. Constant renovation is in progress in the small and crowded city centre, and during the summer it has the energy of a boom town, with an expanding number of shops and restaurants to cater for the increase in visitors and students. The downside of this is the huge amount of property development galloping ahead in the city centre, threatening to take away some of the city's unique character, though, for the time being at least, Galway retains its human scale.

Prosperity allows a vigorous independence from Dublin, mirrored in the artistic dynamism of the city. It's a focus for the traditional **music** of Galway and Clare – Galway's status as an old fishing town on the mythical west coast adding a certain potency – and there's strong interest in drama. This renewed sense of civic and artistic optimism is reflected not only in conventional arts but in the vibrant **street theatre** that has become the hallmark of the city. At no time is the dynamism of Galway more evident than during its **festivals**, especially the **Galway Arts Festival** (☎091/583800) during the last two weeks in July, when practitioners of theatre, music, poetry and the visual arts create a rich cultural jamboree. In April the city hosts a festival specifically devoted to poetry itself, the **Cúirt Poetry Festival** (☎091/565886), in June it's film buffs who invade the city for the **Film Fleadh** (☎091/751655), while the king of all Galway festivals, the riotous **Galway Races** usually takes place during the first week in August. At the end of September, the **Galway Oyster Festival** (☎091/527282) completes the annual round. If visiting the city at any of these times be warned that accommodation will be at a premium, and you'll need to book well in advance.

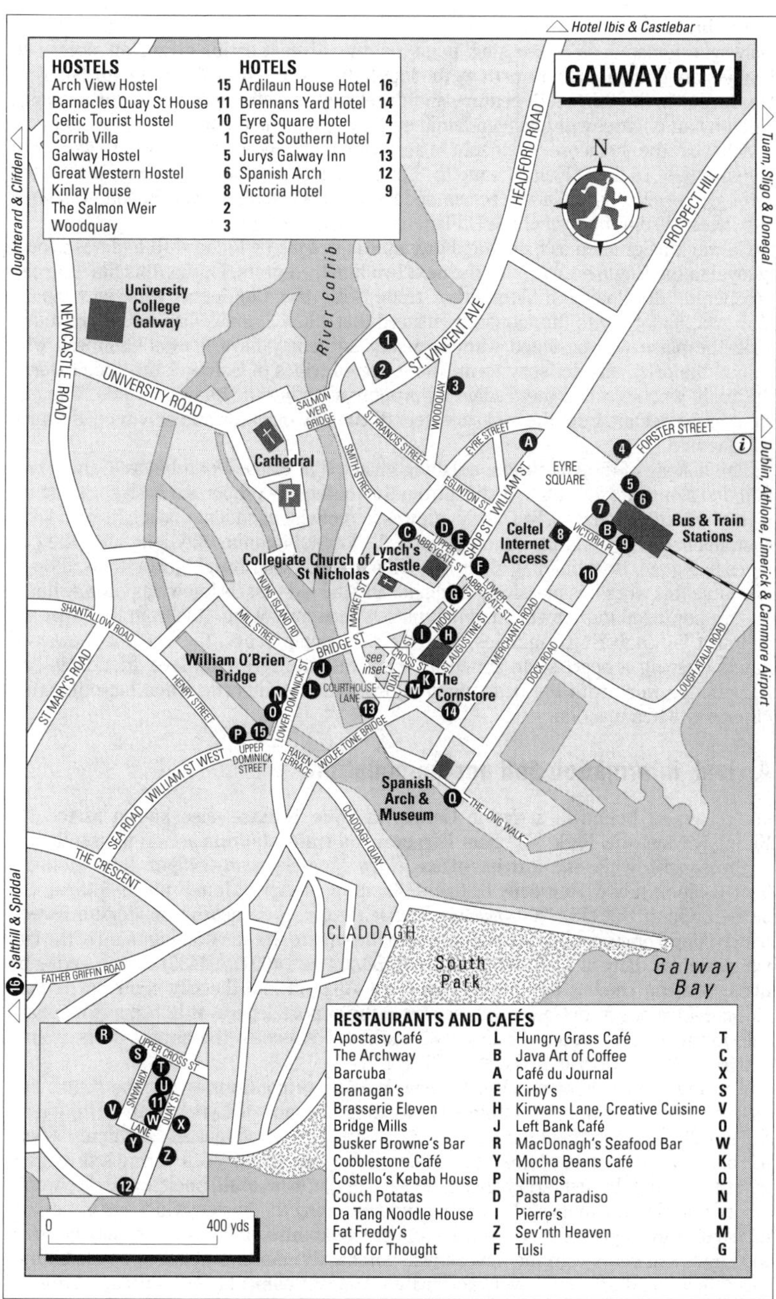
GALWAY CITY
HOSTELS
Arch View Hostel 15
Barnacles Quay St House 11
Celtic Tourist Hostel 10
Corrib Villa 1
Galway Hostel 5
Great Western Hostel 6
Kinlay House 8
The Salmon Weir 2
Woodquay 3
HOTELS
Ardilaun House Hotel 16
Brennans Yard Hotel 14
Eyre Square Hotel 4
Great Southern Hotel 7
Jurys Galway Inn 13
Spanish Arch 12
Victoria Hotel 9
RESTAURANTS AND CAFÉS
Apostasy Café L
The Archway B
Barcuba A
Branagan's E
Brasserie Eleven H
Bridge Mills J
Busker Browne's Bar R
Cobblestone Café Y
Costello's Kebab House P
Couch Potatas D
Da Tang Noodle House I
Fat Freddy's Z
Food for Thought F
Hungry Grass Café T
Java Art of Coffee C
Café du Journal X
Kirby's S
Kirwans Lane, Creative Cuisine V
Left Bank Café O
MacDonagh's Seafood Bar W
Mocha Beans Café K
Nimmos Q
Pasta Paradiso N
Pierre's U
Sev'nth Heaven M
Tulsi G
Hotel Ibis & Castlebar
Tuam, Sligo & Donegal
Dublin, Athlone, Limerick & Carnmore Airport
Oughterard & Clifden
16, Salthill & Spiddal
N
University College Galway
River Corrib
Headford Road
Prospect Hill
St. Vincent Ave
Woodquay
Newcastle Road
University Road
Salmon Weir Bridge
Cathedral
St Francis Street
Smith Street
Eyre Street
Eyre Square
Forster Street
Eglinton St
William St
Shop St
Upper Abbeygate St
Lower Abbeygate St
Victoria Pl.
Celtel Internet Access
Bus & Train Stations
Collegiate Church of St Nicholas
Lynch's Castle
Market St
Nuns Island Rd
Mill Street
Shantallow Road
St Mary's Road
Henry Street
Middle St
St Augustine St
Merchants Road
Dock Road
Lough Atalia Road
Bridge St
see inset
Cross St
Quay St
William O'Brien Bridge
Lower Dominick St
Courthouse Lane
The Cornstore
Wolfe Tone Bridge
Upper Dominick Street
Raven Terrace
William St West
Sea Road
Spanish Arch & Museum
The Long Walk
Claddagh Quay
The Crescent
Claddagh
South Park
Galway Bay
Father Griffin Road
Upper Cross St
Kirwans Lane
0
400 yds

Some history

Galway originated as a crossing point on the River Corrib, giving an access to Connemara denied further north by the lough. It was seized by the **Norman** family of De Burgos in the thirteenth century and developed as a strong Anglo-Norman colony, ruled by an oligarchy of fourteen families. They maintained control despite continual attacks by the bellicose Connacht clans, the most ferocious of which were the O'Flaherties. To the O'Flahertie motto "Fortuna Favet Fortibus" (Fortune Favours the Strong), the citizens of Galway responded with a plea inscribed over the long-vanished city gates: "From the fury of the O'Flaherties, good Lord deliver us."

Galway was granted a charter and **city status** in 1484 by Richard III and was proudly loyal to the English Crown for the next two hundred years. During this time the city prospered, developing a flourishing trade with the Continent, especially Spain. However, its loyalty to the monarch ensured that when Cromwellian forces arrived in 1652 the place was besieged without mercy for ninety days. It was Cromwell who coined the originally derisory term "the fourteen tribes of Galway"; this didn't worry the Irish, who returned the disdain by proudly adopting the name as a title. The city went into a decline from the mid-seventeenth century onwards and only recently started to revive.

The history of the **Claddagh**, a fishing village that existed long before Galway was founded alongside it, is quite distinct from that of the city proper. An Irish-speaking village of thatched cottages, the Claddagh was fiercely independent, having its own laws, customs and chief, and it remained a proud, close-knit community long after the cottages had gone. Boat-building skills are still passed down through generations, though of course this work has massively declined, and the old vessels known as Galway hookers are now used more by boating enthusiasts than for fishing. It is from here that the famous **Claddagh ring** originates, worn by Irish people all over the world. It shows two hands clasping a heart surmounted by a crown and represents love, friendship and respect. It's worn with the heart pointing towards the fingertip when betrothed, the other way when married.

Arrival, information and accommodation

You're almost bound to arrive in Galway at **Eyre Square**, also known as the J.F. Kennedy Memorial Park. The **Bus Éireann** and **train stations** are off the south side of the square, while the **tourist office** (May Mon–Sat 9am–5.45pm; June Mon–Sat 9am–6.45pm; July & Aug daily 8.30am–7.45pm; Sept–April Mon–Fri 9am–5.45pm, Sat 9am–12.45pm; ☎091/537700, *www.irelandwest.travel.ie*) is nearby on Forster Street, which runs from the southeastern corner of the square. It runs walking tours of the city which depart daily at 11.30am and cost £3.50/€4.44 (☎091/794435). If you arrive by plane you can catch a bus from **Carnmore Airport** into the city centre at 1.25pm (Mon–Sat); a bus from Galway bus station to the airport departs at 12.50pm (Mon–Sat). The journey costs around £2.25/€2.85 each way. A taxi to the airport costs around £10/€12.70 with Corrib Taxis (☎091/564444).

Accommodation is plentiful in Galway. **B&Bs** are concentrated in the centre and eastern side of town, most within easy walking distance of Eyre Square. The tourist office will make your booking for a £1/€1.27 fee – not a bad idea at peak times. There are also a large number of **hostels** in Galway, but they get very full during festival time and throughout August – ring ahead, arrive early or, best of all, book ahead. We would advise ignoring the touts at the station, and only using the hostels which are either listed here or are approved by the tourist office. The number of **hotels** in the city has doubled in recent years with the new arrivals forcing the more established hotels both to raise their standards and lower their prices. You can **camp** at *Ballyloughane Caravan*

Park on Dublin Road (closed Oct–April; ☎091/55338) and at several in Salthill, the most pleasant being *Hunter's Silver Strand Caravan and Camping Park*, about four miles west on the coast road (closed Oct–Easter; ☎091/92452 or 92040).

Hotels

Ardilaun House Hotel, Taylor's Hill (☎091/521433, *www.ardilaunhousehotel.ie*). Although this hotel is close to the centre on the Salthill Road the fact that it is set in five acres of woodland gives it the feel of a country retreat. The hotel has been renovated and boasts all manner of leisure-related extras including a Jacuzzi, sauna and gym. The bedrooms are spacious, and the fine dining room overlooks extensive gardens to the rear. It's worth enquiring about special weekend deals that are offered periodically. ⑥.

Brennans Yard Hotel, Lower Merchants Rd (☎091/568166). This is an excellent-value option housed in a unique stone building (formerly a warehouse) near the Spanish Arch. The comfortable bedrooms match the characterful nature of the hotel with their antique-pine furnishings and other tasteful Irish craft items. The staff are courteous and the hotel has a family friendly policy, allowing children under 12 to stay for free. ⑦.

Eyre Square Hotel, Forster St, off Eyre Square (☎091/569633). New hotel that attracts mostly a business clientele. The rooms are modern and comfortable and while it is busy during the week, weekends can be quiet and excellent rates are often offered. ⑦.

Glenlo Abbey Hotel, Bushy Park (☎091/526666, *www.glenlo.com*). Two miles out of Galway on the Clifden road stands the city's finest hotel, *Glenlo Abbey*. Set in a 138-acre estate on the edges of Lough Corrib this former country residence offers total comfort in the most atmospheric and tranquil surroundings. ⑦.

Great Southern Hotel, Eyre Square (☎091/564041, *www.gsh.ie*). Rambling Victorian establishment built as a railway hotel in 1845, which preserves much of its original style and charm. Taking up almost one side of the city's central square this hotel combines its old-world style with modern facilities such as a rooftop pool, and while all the rooms are elegant and spacious, those to the front are preferable for their views of the square. ⑦.

Hotel Ibis, Headford Rd (☎091/771166, *www.ibishotel.com*). Modern hotel, a little way out of the centre, that is a good option for families or groups travelling together because of its excellent flat room rates: rooms sleep two adults and two children. ⑤.

Jurys Galway Inn, Quay St (☎091/566444, *www.jurys.com*). Ideally located on the banks of the River Corrib near the Spanish Arch this hotel shares all the qualities associated with the *Jurys* chain. The rooms are large and comfortable, sleeping up to four people, thus making their flat room rate very attractive to those with a family or on a budget. ⑥.

Spanish Arch, Quay St (☎091/569600, *emcdgall@iol.ie*). A hotel right in the heart of the action with individually designed, period-theme rooms, though those facing onto the street can be noisy. ⑦.

Victoria Hotel, Eyre Square (☎091/567433, *bookings@victoriahotel.ie*). Almost opposite the tourist office, this elegant new hotel is a good option around Eyre Square. The modern rooms, while not luxurious are certainly comfortable and like many central hotels the *Victoria* offers excellent weekend specials when its business reservations are down. ⑦.

B&Bs

Abbey House, 113 Upper Newcastle (☎091/524394, *johndarby@eircom.net*). Excellent option for those travelling by car as this house has good, secure parking and is on the road to Connemara, a few miles out of the city. The owners are extremely helpful and rooms are bright, clean and comfortable. ④.

Ardawn House, 31 College Rd (☎091/568833, *ardawn@iol.ie*). A friendly red-bricked house ten minutes' walk from the city centre in a quiet part of town. The rooms are well furnished and breakfasts well prepared by the attentive hosts. ④.

Crookhaven, 96 Father Griffin Rd (☎091/589019). The best choice amongst the cluster of accommodation on this road; this is a fine place with en-suite rooms and TVs. ③.

Dungaire, 8 Lurgan Park, Murrough, Dublin Rd, Galway City East (☎091/757043, *ccawley@tinet.ie*). A friendly place to the east of the city opposite the *Corrib Great Southern Hotel* (follow the signs to Galway City East). The house offers two en-suite and two standard rooms all of which are comfortable, and also does good reductions for families and single travellers. ③.

High Tide, 9 Grattan Park, Coast Rd (☎091/584324, *hightide@iol.ie*). Two miles out of the city on the road to Salthill is this fine house offering four bright, comfortable en-suite rooms overlooking the bay. ③.

Mandalay By The Sea, 10 Glentian Hill (☎091/524177, *mandaly@esatclear.ie*). This large, distinctive balconied house, overlooking Galway Bay three miles outside the city in the coastal village of Salthill, is a very comfortable option indeed. The rooms are large and airy, and the food excellent. ④.

Marless House, Threadneedle Rd, Salthill (☎091/523931, *marlesshouse@eircom.net*). This is a large, modern Georgian-style house in Salthill, on the coast two miles from the centre of the city. The cosy rooms are large by B&B standard, all are en suite and the hosts welcome children and will do special family deals. ③.

Petra, 201 Laurel Park, Newcastle Rd (☎091/521844). This friendly modern house is a short distance out of the city centre in the Newcastle area of town (buses #4 and #5 from Galway centre), and has two en-suite and two standard rooms. ③.

St Martin's, 2 Nuns Island Rd (☎091/568286). This is one of the few central B&Bs in Galway. The rooms are comfortable, the food is good and the owners could not be more obliging. The location is ideal with the Corrib River running through the house's pleasant garden. ③.

Hostels

Arch View Hostel, 1 Upper Dominick St (☎091/586661). Has seen better days and some of the bedrooms and the common room are a little dowdy. Having said that the atmosphere is good and it's close to the excellent *Roísin Dubh* bar (see p.382).

Barnacles Quay Street House, 10 Quay St (☎091/568644, *qshostel@barnacles.iol.ie*). A brightly painted, well-run, security-conscious hostel right in the centre of town. This is the place to come if you want to take in Galway's nightlife. Don't come here looking for a good night's rest: if the nocturnal comings and goings of the other guests don't waken you, then the hostel's incredibly loud doorbell will. Dorm beds cost from £10/€12.70.

Celtic Tourist Hostel, Queen St (☎091/566606). Around the corner from the tourist office, this IHO hostel has few frills but it does have a large kitchen and often has beds when all the other hostels are full.

Corrib Villa, 4 Waterside (☎091/562892). A large old-style IHO hostel located right on the river. The hostel itself is a little dowdy, but it has the advantage over others in that parking can be found in the area.

Galway Hostel, Frenchville Lane, Eyre Square (IHO; ☎091/566959). A good, friendly budget option opposite the station, which also offers twin (②) and four-bed rooms.

Great Western Hostel, Frenchville Lane, Eyre Square (IHH; ☎091/561139, *shaungwh@iol.ie*). Also opposite the station, this hostel offers many luxuries while missing out on the basics: it has a sauna, but no adequate security lockers, and breakfast isn't served until after 9.30am, in the adjacent café by surly staff. Having said that, the rooms are fine with twin, double, four-bed and family rooms also available. There's also a laundry, bike shed and TV rooms. The hostel accepts credit cards, and dorm beds cost from £10/€12.70.

Kinlay House, Merchants Rd, Eyre Square (IHH; ☎091/565244). Purpose-built hostel, with double rooms available; clean and efficiently run. (try to secure one of the rooms to the back of the building as those to the front suffer from street noise in the morning). Prices include continental breakfast, bed linen and towel, and start from £10/€12.70 for the eight-bed dorm.

The Salmon Weir Hostel, St Vincent's Ave, Woodquay (☎091/561133 or 522653). A small, friendly, comfortable hostel with a relaxed, convival atmosphere suited to those travelling alone who wish to meet up with other people. The hostel has few luxuries but has good laundry facilities and a bike shed.

Woodquay Hostel, 23–24 Woodquay (☎091/562618). A tiny, friendly place near to town, though it is incredibly cramped and can be very warm and stuffy in summer.

The City

Galway's centre is defined by the **River Corrib**. Issuing from the lough, it thunders under the Salmon Weir Bridge and wraps itself round the full body of the city, meeting the lively **Shop and Quay streets** area at Wolfe Tone Bridge, where it flows into the bay. The quaint old shops and bars that give Galway its villagey appeal are being squeezed on all sides by ugly postmodern facades and bone-headed business development; the area around the bridge has to be one of the most architecturally abused spots in Ireland. Still, Galway is a robust city and somehow its charm pulls through. Over the bridge is the Claddagh, and about a mile and a half west of that is **Salthill**, Galway's commercial seaside town. The **Claddagh** now appears as a small area of modest housing, strangely flanked by a crusting of luxury apartments, but it's worth getting to know for some of its excellent bars and cheap eats. From any of the bridges you can wander beside the pleasant walkways of river and canals, checking out the industrial archeology, watching salmon make their way upstream, anglers fly-fishing in the centre of the city and cormorants diving for eels, while gawky herons splash through watery suburban back gardens. At the harbour, a walk out around the stone pier places the city in its impressive setting, with a level coastline stretching to the west and the eerie Burren hills washed and etched in half-tones across the bay.

Eyre Square is an almost inevitable starting point. This small park, set in the middle of a traffic interchange, is one of the places to which everyone seems to gravitate, the other being the Shop and Quay streets area. It's used as a performance space during festivals, and outdoor music sessions can start up here at any time, the relaxed atmosphere lending itself to improvisation. Visually, though, the place is a mess. A sentimental statue of the writer Pádraic Ó Conaire, a seventeenth-century doorway, a couple of cannon from the Crimean War and a clutter of disused flagpoles all detract from what should form the focus of the square: Eamonn O'Donnell's splendid sculpture, whose arcs of rusted metal and gushing white fountains evoke the sails of a Galway hooker and the city's nautical history. The distinctive **town houses** of the merchant class – remnants of which are lightly littered around the city – also hark back to the prosperity of maritime Galway and its sense of civic dignity, with their finely carved doorways, windows and stone slabs bearing armorial carving. The **Browne doorway** in Eyre Square is one such monument, a bay window and doorway with the coats of arms of the Browne and Lynch families, dated 1627. Before you leave the square, it's worth calling into the **Eyre Square Centre**, as the building of this shopping mall in the late 1980s revealed impressive sections of medieval city walls, and these are preserved within the complex.

Just about the finest medieval town house in Ireland is **Lynch's Castle** in Shop Street (leading off from the southwest of the square), now housing the Allied Irish Bank. The Lynchs were Galway's most prominent family for three hundred years from the late fifteenth century. A local story relates that in 1493 James Lynch Fitzstephen, mayor of the town, found his own son guilty of the jealous murder of a Spanish visitor, and that such was the popularity of the lad that no one in the town would take on the job of hangman – so the boy's father did it himself. The house, dating from the fifteenth century, has a smooth stone facade decorated with carved panels, medieval gargoyles and a lion devouring another animal. The front of the bank has been preserved, so step inside and pick up a leaflet for a detailed history of the building and its heraldry. The similarly styled **Lynch's Window** is on Market Street (further down Shop Street and to the right) just outside the **Collegiate Church of St Nicholas**. The largest medieval church in Ireland, it was built in 1320 and enlarged in the next two centuries. The building – dedicated to St Nicholas of Myra, patron saint of sailors – is also decorated with finely chiselled carvings and gargoyles. Continuing south along Market Street, and turning off into Bowling Green Lane, you'll come across the house that **Nora Barnacle**, wife of James Joyce, lived in. It's now been converted into a small museum (May–Sept Mon–Sat 9am–5pm; £1/€1.27) and contains, among other Joycean memorabilia, copies of the couple's letters. For arguably the best sense of medieval Galway make your way through the punters and the pints up to the top floor of **Busker**

Browne's Bar, Cross Street (a short walk south from Nora Barnacle's house). The upper room was the meeting place of the tribes of Galway, and the building has served as a barracks and a Dominican convent.

Down by the harbour stands the **Spanish Arch**; more evocative in name than in reality, it's a sixteenth-century structure that was used to protect galleons unloading wine and rum. Behind it is a fine piece of medieval wall, and next door is the uninspiring **Galway Museum** (May–Sept daily 10am–1pm & 2.15–5.15pm), where the only things of real interest are old photographs of the Claddagh and a few examples of sixteenth- and seventeenth-century stone carving from around the city. From the Spanish Arch you can take a pleasant walk north along a riverside path and across the Salmon Weir Bridge to the **Cathedral of Our Lady Assumed into Heaven and St Nicholas**. Commissioned about thirty years ago and in hideous contrast to the Collegiate College, its copper dome seeps green stains down ugly limestone walls. Inside, the horrors continue in a senseless jumble of stone, mahogany and Connemara marble. It's so remarkably awful that it demands attention, and viewed from a distance its sheer bulk does achieve a grandeur of sorts. Nearby, across the bridge, the clean lines of the Neoclassical courthouse are mirrored in the municipal theatre opposite – an assured symbol of contemporary Galway's civic pride, and surprisingly conservative for a post-colonial nation.

On the road behind the cathedral is **University College Galway**, a mock-Tudor imitation of an Oxbridge college, which was opened in 1849 at a time when the majority of people in Connacht were starving. The university has the dubious distinction of having conferred an honorary degree on Ronald Reagan. More importantly, it is now UNESCO's base for an archive of spoken material in all Celtic languages, and summer courses in Irish for foreign students are held annually in July and August.

The river

If you want to get out onto the water, at nearby **Woodquay** (cross the Salmon Weir Bridge at the cathedral, turn left and walk a little way along Waterside Street) you can either rent a rowing boat (May–Sept) or take the Lough Corrib river cruise (daily 2.30pm & 4.30pm; ☎091/592447; £6/€7.62), which goes five miles up the river through flat countryside punctuated by derelict castles, out into the open expanse of the lough.

Salthill and the beaches

Beyond the Claddagh lies **SALTHILL**, Galway's seaside resort, complete with amusement arcades, discos, seasonal cafés and a fairground – as well as scores more hotels and B&Bs. Salthill's **tourist office** is on the front (June Mon–Sat 9am–6pm; July & Aug daily 9am–8.15pm; ☎091/520500). Alongside the tourist office is the new **Atlantiquaria** (daily 10am–5pm; ☎091/585100; £5/€6.35), which, as the name suggests, is an aquarium showcasing fish found off the shores of Ireland. It makes for a fun diversion for children on a wet day, as does the huge **Leisureland** amusement complex, which, apart from being used as a venue for big concerts, has a swimming pool (summer daily 10am–10pm). **Lower Salthill** has a long promenade with a series of unspectacular but safe and sandy beaches. Even on a hot summer's day it's never so busy as to be oppressive, and its great asset is the view over a glittering expanse of water to the Burren. West of here, **Upper Salthill** is a mess of a suburb that sits around its golf course, despoiled by huge billboards and caravan parks.

Probably the nicest of the sandy beaches immediately west of Galway city is the small one at **Silver Strand**, nestling beneath a grassy headland about three miles out of the centre. Here, in a small inlet backed by a copse, is also the area's most pleasant **campsite**, signposted *Hunters* (see p.375). *The Twelve Pins* pub, around a mile west of the site, is renowned for seafood. Galway's other special beach is **Ballyloughrun**, east of the city; this, too, has a campsite alongside and can be reached by taking the public footpath along by the railway line, or by either the Renmore or the Merlyn Park bus from the station.

Eating and drinking

You'll find a good range of food on offer in Galway – from hot dogs to cajun and Thai – with some particularly upmarket Continental **restaurants** and great seafood. In the listings below, **moderate** restaurants offer main courses for under £10/€12.70, **expensive** restaurants for £10–15/€12.70–19.05. For daytime eating, a plethora of new cafés has appeared recently in the centre of Galway and those listed below are chosen for their atmosphere as well as for their food; plenty of bars also offer good-value meals and snacks.

Cafés

Apostasy, 56 Lower Dominick St. A great alternative to the numerous pubs in the area, with backgammon and chess and walls decorated with quotations from Yeats, Beckett and Joyce. Popular with clubbers as it is open till 4am daily.

Café du Journal, Quay St. Frequented by arty types languishing in the smokey atmosphere, this place serves a wonderful selection of coffees including: Italian, Spanish and cajun. Also does omelettes, croissants and desserts; newspapers are available to read. Open till 10.30pm.

Cobblestone Café, Kirwans Lane off Cross St. Continental-style café with tablecloths and fresh flowers. Try the excellent soups and delicious homemade confectionery.

The Hungry Grass, Upper Cross St. Wholesome, generous baguettes and delicious cheap salads served up amid the hustle and bustle of Cross Street.

Java Art of Coffee, 17 Upper Abbeygate St. Good coffee, great ambient tunes and late hours makes this a perfect place to hang out, especially after late-night dancing.

Left Bank Café, Lower Dominick St. Good sandwiches at reasonable prices, often ideal when you want a quiet spot and other places in the more popular Quay and Cross streets area are full.

Mocha Beans, Lower Cross St. The aroma of rich roasted coffee and home-baked pastries pervades the air of this little place at the bottom of Cross Street.

Moderate restaurants

Barcuba, Eyre Square. Great breakfasts, spicy daytime food and strong coffees distinguish this stylish bar/restaurant. Open 10am–noon for breakfasts, noon–6pm for lunches.

Branagan's, 34 Upper Abbeygate St. Busy restaurant which has a varied menu of cajun, Californian and oriental cuisine; it's a popular party venue. Opens daily 6.45–11pm.

Brasserie Eleven, 19 Middle St. This restaurant specializes in pasta, stir-fry dishes and large salads. Mon–Sat 12.30–10.30pm.

Busker Browne's Bar, Upper Cross St. This restaurant offers original rough medieval stonework, a pitched Gothic roof and floor upon floor of alcoves for comfy eating and drinking (see also "Bars and music" p.381). The bar serves salads and open sandwiches – crab, salmon and oysters – and is always incredibly busy. Food served daily till late.

Costello's Kebab House, Upper Dominick St. A post-pub favourite, this place attracts those requiring the replenishing effects of the generous helpings of char-grilled meat on offer.

Couch Potatas, Upper Abbeygate St. Next to *Branagan's* this place takes cooking the humble spud to a new level.. It claims to show 101 ways to serve a potato, with all manner of sauces and stuffings – and a good selection for vegetarians. Opens noon–10pm daily.

Da Tang Noodle House, Middle St. One of the few authentic noodle houses in Ireland, this is a real treat. Apart from the noodles there are also some excellent soups, and an oriental market has just opened up next door. Open daily 12.30–3pm and 5.30–10pm.

Fat Freddy's, Quay St. Perennially popular place with a buzzy atmosphere, great pizzas, cheap spaghetti; one of the cheapest places to get an evening meal. Open daily noon–10.30pm.

Food For Thought, Lower Abbeygate St. Cheap wholefood and vegetarian snacks, light meals and something that sounds like a misnomer, the "healthy Irish breakfast". Open daily 9am–5pm.

McDonagh's Seafood Bar, 22 Quay St. A must for seafood lovers; nip in for a thick and creamy chowder, or linger for a full meal. Excellent English-style fish and chips are also on offer, and service is extremely friendly. Daily till 12.30am.

Pasta Paradiso, 51 Lower Dominick St. Italian-owned pasta and pizza joint which is very popular locally for its excellent food at affordable prices. Opens daily 11am–11pm.

Pierre's, 8 Quay St (☎091/566066). A haven tucked away within the bedlam that can be Quay Street, this restaurant has a relaxed atmosphere and fine food, and does an excellent pre-theatre menu. Open daily 6pm–11pm.

Sev'nth Heaven, Courthouse Lane, Quay St (☎091/563838). Popular restaurant/bar serving cajun, Tex-Mex, Italian and vegetarian food, including delicious three-course lunches. Daily noon–midnight.

Expensive restaurants

The Archway, Victoria Place. (☎091/563693). This is a quiet place opposite the tourist office where the owner has been making a reputation for himself by cooking perfect interpretations of classic French dishes. Open Tues–Sat noon–2pm and 7–10pm.

The Bridge Mills Restaurant, O'Brien's Bridge (☎091/566231). A relaxed atmosphere pervades in this licensed restaurant and coffee shop set in a beautifully restored mill – complete with working mill wheel. Homemade cakes, chowders, sandwiches and lunches are served during the day, with a continental menu in the evening in summer. All produce is organic and vegetarians are well catered for. Till 10.30pm in summer.

Kirbys, Upper Cross St (☎091/569404). Joined to the excellent *Busker Brownes* bar is its slightly more upmarket sister restaurant. As in the bar this two-storey restaurant offers the best in imaginative contemporary cuisine, using local ingredients where possible. Open daily 1–2pm and 5–10.30pm.

Kirwans Lane, Creative Cuisine, Kirwans Lane, off Upper Cross St (☎091/568266). The popularity of this restaurant (both locally and with tourists) has resulted in a recent extension doubling its seating capacity. The menu is varied, offering a range of international cuisine, and some bold interpretations on traditional Irish dishes. The service is good, and evening dining is formal. Booking is advised. Mon–Sat 12.30–2.30pm and 6–10.30pm.

Nimmo's, Long Walk, Spanish Arch (☎091/563565). An imaginative Continental menu, with plenty of seafood and organic produce, served in a spacious second-floor room above the wine bar. Lunch is served in the bar itself and dinner in the restaurant. Tues–Sun from 12.30–3pm and 6.30–10pm.

Tulsi, Buttermilk Walk, Middle St (☎091/564831). The city's best Indian, slightly hidden in a small street running off Middle Abbey Street, and offering excellent vegetarian food. Daily noon–2.30pm and 6pm–11.30pm, Sun buffet 1pm–4pm.

Nightlife and entertainment

If the "crack" has eluded you so far on your travels, Galway is where you're going to find it. The **bars** are the social lungs of this town, and even the most abstemious of travellers are going to find themselves sucked in. **Traditional music** is performed in many of them; some of it will be depressingly over-amplified, but you can hit a great session on any day of the week and at almost any time of the day during the summer months. The bars of Shop and Quay streets are especially good, as are those over the bridge around Dominick Street. You can't really go far wrong; those listed opposite are popular in the main with a young crowd, but there are plenty more well worth exploring. Look out for *The List*, Galway's weekly free listings magazine, and the *Galway Advertiser* out on Thursday.

There are numerous **clubs** in Galway and Salthill – the latter easy enough to walk back from, though not advisable if you are on your own. As ever, clubs change frequently; to find out what's on look out for flyers round town, and for concessions being handed out in bars. Note, too, that clubs can stop serving at 1.30am, and generally wind down at around 2am. The **gay scene** moves around, so call the information line (see "Listings", p.383) for up-to-the-minute information. Gay clubbing usually happens on Sundays.

Bars and music

Aras na Gael, 45 Dominick St. Irish traditional music and folk theatre run and frequented by Irish-speaking enthusiasts. Admission is usually free, though during the summer it has special programmes costing £3/€3.81.

Barcuba, Eyre Square. Popular new hangout in the centre of town with a relaxed atmosphere, playing tunes with a lively latin beat.

Blue Note, William St West. Excellent bar with a fun crowd partying to live DJs playing funk, soul and acid jazz.

Busker Browne's Bar, Cross St. Frighteningly popular. Traditional Irish music three nights a week during summer; jazz on a Sunday lunchtime.

Calico Jack's, Sea Rd. Another drinker's bar where you could well fall into a lively traditional session.

Cottage Bar, Lower Salthill. A place to find a vibrant music session, with young musicians pushing the boundaries of the canon to its outer limits with boisterous interpretations of traditional tunes.

Crane's, Sea Rd. Busy bar with great traditional sessions, which many regard as the best in the county; the music is especially good on a Sunday.

The Goalpost, Woodquay. A fun bar featuring a mixture of live bands, DJs and traditional music depending on the night.

Hole in the Wall, Eyre Square. Traditional pub formerly popular with local horse-racing enthusiasts in the centre of town that's now drawing in students and tourists for live-band gigs and traditional-music nights.

The King's Head, Shop St. A huge three-storey bar featuring live bands every night of the week. Attracts a young, lively crowd of students in winter and tourists in summer and can be incredibly busy.

Le Graal, Dominick St. A bistro-brasserie with a lively, upbeat atmosphere, and popular with Galway's gay community. Look out for the fun salsa night on Thursdays with salsa dance classes from 7pm.

Lisheen Bar, Bridge St. One of the few good traditional-music bars left this side of the river, the *Lisheen* is well worth a visit, though you may end up staying until closing time. At the time of writing the bar had been bought by the owners of the King's Head (see above) and may soon be similarly renovated.

Mick Taylors, Dominick St. Traditional bar where you might catch the occasional session, though it's more a place to talk than sing.

Monroe's, Dominick St. Good for live bands: rock, blues, cajun, washboards— more or less anything that can pass for rhythm. Worth a visit on Tuesdays for its excellent set-dancing night. Also has the added attraction of serving delicious pizzas till late.

Neachtains, 17 Cross St. The jewel in the Galway pub crown. Unlike other older pubs it has resisted the temptation to remove its traditional interior of small rooms and snugs to maximize profits. If you go there with a group, get there early to commandeer a snug for the night.

Nimmo's Wine Bar, Spanish Arch. Right on the river, this is a fine place to enjoy one of the many fine wines on offer; especially recommended for its Sunday lunches served to a mellow jazz backdrop.

O'Riada's (known locally as the *Front Door*), High Street. A recently converted pub with unusual decor, that's constantly packed by a mixed crowd of students and professionals.

The Quays, Quay St. A traditional bar that's become increasingly popular of late. Best to stop in early in the evening as it is usually heaving by 9.30pm, especially on nights when there is live music.

Queen Street, Victoria St. Purpose-built with the idea of staging jazz and blues concerts, this has proved a popular success and offers bar extensions at the weekend.

Roísin Dubh, 9 Upper Dominick St. This pub is a Galway institution, and has continually hosted some of the best musicians to visit the city over the past decade. Expect all kinds of music from folk and traditional, to cajun and rock.

The Snug, Shop St. Worth checking out at weekends for its traditional music.

Clubs

Alley Nightclub, William St Upper. This is a busy place which attracts an older, more conservative crowd to hear chart and commercial dance music.

Church Lane Club, Church Lane (next to the *Galway Advertiser*). Over-21's flock to this intimate club which plays mostly chart and retro sounds, with some commercial dance music.

Clubcuba, Eyre Square. Large three-storey affair with a lively atmosphere and plenty of pulse-raising beats in the bar section. The club section doubles as a live venue and has a very varied booking policy so it's best to check in local papers or listing magazines (*The List* and *Galway Advertiser*) before going.

GPO, Eglinton St. One of Galway's best. Young, studenty crowd get into 1980s tunes, funk, ska and soul – all highly danceable – plus live bands. Look out for the Sunday night comedy club, acts from 8pm; your £6/€7.62 entrance sees you through to the *JazzJuice* club later.

Liquid, Salthill. Popular club with lots of live music and DJs playing indie on Wednesdays, funk on Thursdays and a mixture of genres, from commercial dance to 1970s disco, on various floors at the weekend.

Vagabond's, Salthill. Popular, busy but relaxed, studenty club with two dance floors. Soul, blues and reggae on offer on Thursday; grunge on Friday; dance music and more grunge downstairs on Saturday; indie bands on Sunday.

The arts

Galway is experiencing a real growth in artistic activity, and it's at its most vibrant during **The Galway Arts Festival** (see p.372). There's plenty to detain you year round too: Galway's the home of the versatile **Druid Theatre Company** (☎091/568617, *info@druidtheatre.com*), in Chapel Lane, off Quay St; a relatively young company, it produces six new plays a year – many of them new works by Irish authors – and undertakes extensive tours. If you're lucky enough to be in Galway city when they're on, book a ticket in advance, as they play to packed houses. The most exciting artistic development of recent years has been the emergence of the local street theatre troupe **Macnas** (☎091/561462, *www.macnas.com*). This internationally acclaimed group have elevated the art of street theatre to new heights; to watch one of their flamboyant street performances is a truly exhilarating experience and should not be missed. **An Taibhdhearc na Gaillimhe** in Middle St (☎091/562024) is an Irish-language theatre that puts on an annual summer show of traditional singing, music and drama. **The Town Hall Theatre**, Courthouse Square, Woodquay (☎091/569777, *www.homepage.eircom.net/~tht*) stages plays from visiting companies most nights of the year.

The **Galway Arts Centre**, Nun's Island, off Mill St, is used as a performance space for dance, theatre and music; for bookings, information and visual arts exhibitions call in at 47 Dominick St (☎091/565886). It's also a good place to find out what's going on in the arts locally. There are a few **commercial art galleries** worth a visit too: The Bridge Mills Gallery, O'Brien's Bridge; The Kenny Gallery, Middle St (☎091/553733, *www.kennysgallery.ie*); and the Logan Gallery in Woodquay (☎091/563635).

Crafts shopping

A hugely successful development in Galway is the **Design Concourse Ireland** (*www.designconcourseireland.com*), down a lane off Cross Street, just near *Busker*

Browne's. Housed in a beautifully restored medieval town house, it stocks the best of contemporary Irish design, including jewellery, furniture and tweed from both the Republic and the North. Dating from the sixteenth and seventeenth centuries, the building once housed a theatre owned by Humanity Dick (see p.402), and it is said that Wolfe Tone performed here.

Further quality contemporary **clothing and craft** can be found in **Design Ireland Plus** housed in the Cornstore (which is also the home of Charlie Byrne's bookstore – see Listings), in nearby Middle Street. A popular local purchase are the chunky woollen **sweaters** people living on the west coast have worn for generations as protection against the notoriously fickle weather. The best places for these are: Faller's Sweater Shop at 25 High St, and **O'Máille's** at 16 High St, which both offer a huge range of colourful Aran ganseys (from the Gaelic *geansaí*).

Galway has become something of an attraction of late for couples wishing to become engaged; if you find yourself overcome by romance and want to pledge your heart with a **Claddagh ring**, the place to go is Dillons on the corner of Cross and Quay streets where there's also a small museum with exhibits on Claddagh village itself and the small symbol of eternal devotion associated with it. Just outside town is the Royal Tara China factory (follow the N6 to *Ryan's Hotel* and take the first left), while a little further along the N6 is the Galway Irish Crystal Heritage Centre (*www.galwaycrystal.ie*).

Listings

Airport/flight enquiries ☎091/755569

Bike rental Europa Bicycles, Earls Island (☎091/563355) opposite the cathedral; £4/€5.08 a day, £6/€7.62 for 24 hours, £30/€38.10 deposit.

Bookshops Charlie Byrne's, The Cornstore, Middle St (☎091/561766), is a good second-hand bookshop; Eason's, Shop St, is a huge general bookshop with foreign newspapers; Hawkins House, Churchyard Lane, includes comprehensive feminist and Irish-language sections; Hughes and Hughes, Galway Shopping Centre (☎091/536904) is a relaxed bookstore with a wide-ranging stock and pleasant coffee shop; Kenny's Bookshop, on High St (☎091/562739), is regarded by many as one of the best antiquarian bookshops in the country and has a small art gallery attached; and Sub City, Corbett Court Centre (☎091/565994) has a good range of comics, videos and posters.

Buses Bus Éireann (☎091/562000) runs 5–8 buses to Dublin daily, from as little as £9/€11.43 single, £11/€13.97 return – check in advance for special deals. Bikes are carried subject to space – £5/€3.81 extra each journey. CityLink (☎091/564163 or 564164) also runs a Galway to Dublin service from £10/€12.70 return. Feda O'Donnell Coaches (☎091/761656 or 075/48114) operates services to Sligo, Donegal and Letterkenny. Nestor Travel (☎091/797144 or 01/832 0094) runs services to Dublin and Dublin Airport from £10/€12.70 return (bikes £3/€3.81).

Camping equipment Great Outdoors, Eglinton St (☎091/562869); Radar Stores, 15 Mainguard St (☎091/568810).

Gay and lesbian line (☎091/566134); gay men Tues & Thurs 8–10pm; lesbians Wed 8–10pm (☎091/564611).

Horse riding Clonboo Riding School, Clonboo Cross, Corrundulla, near Annaghdown (☎091/791362).

Internet Celtel E-centre, Merchants Rd, Eyre Square (☎091/566620, *www.celtel.ie*), a bright modern place with fast access at £1/€1.27 for 15 minutes.

Hospital University College Hospital, Newcastle Rd (casualty ☎091/544338). For emergencies call ☎999.

Laundry The Launderette, Sea Rd (Mon–Sat 9am–6pm); Old Malte Laundrette, Old Malte Arcade, High St (Mon–Sat 8.30am–6pm), does service wash only.

Left luggage *Quay St House Hostel*, 10 Quay St, 50p/€0.63 per bag, or at the train station for £1/€1.27.

Library Galway County Library, Hynes Building, St Augustine St.

Market For more than just fruit and vegetables, try the Saturday market around St Nicholas's Church; stalls sell everything from handmade cheeses to sculptured bog oak. There's also a junk and antiques market beneath the medieval walls inside the Eyre Square Centre (Fri & Sat), and a daily oriental food market beside *Da Tang Noodle House* on Middle Street.

Music Mulligan, 5 Middle St (☎091/564961), for traditional, world music, reggae, country, folk and blues on tape, vinyl and CD; Gimik Records, Lower Fairhill Rd specializes in dance music on vinyl.

Parking Free in front of the cathedral; elsewhere, buy a disc from a newsagent at 20p/€0.25 per hr.

Police Mill St (☎091/563161).

Sailing Galway Sailing Club, Rinville, Oranmore, five miles from the city (☎091/794527).

Taxi Corrib Taxis (☎091/56444); Galway Taxi Coop (☎091/561111); MGM (☎091/757888); and taxi ranks at Eyre Square and Victoria Place.

Train enquiries ☎091/561444 or 564222.

Travel agents USIT, at the New Science Building on the university campus (☎091/524601), is the best agent for youth and student travel; Corrib Travel, in the centre of town in Cathedral Building, Lower Abbeygate St (☎091/563879 or 568318), deals with student flights and youth fares.

Wind-surfing At Rusheen Bay (☎087/605702).

East Galway

East Galway cannot rival the spectacular landscapes of west Galway or County Clare, nor their romantic isolation. Nonetheless, to hurry through east Galway without seeing what the place does have to offer would be a mistake. A lot of the land here is low lying and easily cultivable, attributes which made it attractive to earlier settlers. They've left not only a network of roads and villages, but also a wealth of historic remains, particularly medieval monastic sites. The east of the county has nothing like the strong culture of the west, but towards the south, the musical traditions of County Clare wash over the county boundaries and form an important part of the region's culture. And while the landscape is never exciting, some of it is very pleasant, notably the lakesides of **Lough Derg** at **Portumna** and the delightful southern shore of **Galway Bay**, which becomes particularly special where the heights of the Burren of County Clare become a part of the scene. Added to this is the historical importance of eastern Galway from the walled town of **Athenry** to the village of **Aughrim**, scene of the bloodiest battle in Irish history.

In contrast to Connemara, transport in east Galway is easy. Galway to Dublin **trains** call at Athenry and Ballinasloe (for train information phone Athenry ☎091/544020 or Ballinasloe ☎0905/42105). While Bus Éireann (☎091/562000) serves the surrounding area well, private **buses** offer a faster and cheaper service: Bus Nestor's (☎091/797144) Dublin to Galway service will stop in Ballinasloe, Loughrea and Aughrim on request, as will Citylink (☎091/564163) who will also stop at Athlone and offers a daily evening service direct from Dublin to Tuam. There is plenty of accommodation throughout the area, in the form of B&Bs and independent and An Óige hostels.

Galway Bay and the south

The countryside in the south of the county, around the southern shores of Galway Bay and on towards Clare, is some of the prettiest in Galway, and was greatly loved by Yeats, Lady Gregory and others associated with the Gaelic League. The main N18 road round the bay from the city is a busy one, passing through the villages of Galway's "**oyster country**" – Oranmore, Clarinbridge and Kilcolgan (where the main road leaves the water to head south towards Ennis) – and bringing plenty of visitors, particularly during the **Oyster Festival** over the second weekend in September. The most famous of the oyster pubs are *Paddy Burke's Oyster Tavern* at **Clarinbridge** and *Moran's of the Weir*, in a beautiful waterside setting at **Kilcolgan**. Two miles south of Kilcolgan, off the Kinvarra Road, stands **Drumacoo Church**, a fine stone building dating back to around 1200, with a Regency Gothic chapel of iron alongside, rusting and derelict.

Kinvarra

Set in the southeasterly inlet of Galway Bay, the charming little quayside village of **KINVARRA** (*Cinn Mhara* which means "sea headlands" in Irish) is something of a satellite playground for Galway city. Down at the tranquil harbourside, with its smattering of pubs and restaurants, swans drift across the water to Dunguaire Castle. The **castle** (mid April–Sept daily 9.30am–5.30pm; £2.75/€3.49) was built in 1520 and is a particularly good example of a **tower house**. These tower houses or "castles" were in fact fortified houses, very much a fashion for wealthy landowners from 1450 to 1650, and are found in their greatest concentration in east Clare, east Limerick and south Galway. This is a great one to visit, as the guide delivers a vigorous interpretation of both local history and the political importance of the old building.

Back in the main street, locals are not quite sure what to make of a new landmark: *The Merriman Inn and Restaurant* (☎091/638222; ⑥), which claims to have the largest thatched roof in the country (thatch from Turkey, thatchers from England). It has tasteful interiors, comfortable bedroms, a fine restaurant, a Design Ireland shop and a pleasant bar *M'Asal Beag Dubh*. All in all, Kinvarra's a lively spot and, there's enough variety in the area to warrant a reasonable stay between the rigours of Burren-walking and Galway city-life. In winter you'll need your own transport but in summer bus #50 serves Kinvarra from Galway city. The informative *Kinvarra: A Ramblers Map and Guide*, by Anne Korff and Jeff O'Connell (£1.95/€2.47), is available in the post office and at Dunguaire Castle and is worth buying for exploration of the immediate countryside.

For location, *Cois Cuain* **B&B** (☎091/637119; ③), down by the quays, is hard to beat. Also recommended is *Larkin's Barn Lodge* (☎091/637548; ③), a friendly country house set back off the road, five minutes' drive from the village towards Ballyvaughan. The IHH-affiliated *Johnston's Hostel* on Main St, (closed Sept–May; ☎091/637164; ②) offers good communal accommodation and also caters for campers. To lose yourself in Connemara's rugged beauty, however, it's best to make your way a few miles out of town to the hostel in Doorus (see below). **Bikes** can be rented from McMahon's filling station for £6/€7.56.

Good **places to eat** include *The Café on the Quay*, serving seafood, salads and sandwiches. *The Pier Head Bar and Restaurant* is similarly appealing and has a good reputation locally, while *The Merriman Inn* on Main Street serves bar food till 10pm in summer and also has a formal restaurant. Kinvarra's **bars** are worthy of exploration: *The Auld Plaid Shawl* is a good starting point, with a mixed clientele; *Winkles* can be great fun, especially if you join in the set dancing on a Friday night; *Tully's* is a charming place for a civilized pint; and *The Pier Head* is a lively spot which frequently has music. Kinvarra's early spring **festival**, the *Fleadh na gCuach* (the Cuckoo Fleadh), is held over the May bank holiday weekend, while the *Cruinniú na mBáid* (the Meeting of the Boats) usually takes place over the second weekend in August and involves, along with singing and dancing, the racing of Galway's traditional fishing vessels – Galway hookers – which can often be seen docked in the harbour.

Doorus

In addition to all its other attractions, this part of south Galway is closely associated with the poetry of the literary revival group of Yeats, Lady Gregory, AE and Douglas Hyde; it was in what is now the An Óige hostel in **DOORUS** (out on the peninsula four miles northwest of Kinvarra) that the idea of a national theatre was first discussed – later to become the Abbey Theatre in Dublin. The hostel was then the home of Count Florimond de Basterot, who entertained and encouraged the group (and also the likes of Guy de Maupassant and Paul Bourget); it's easy to appreciate how the group's romantic nationalist and artistic sensibilities were stirred in this serene location. Given the political implications of the Irish literary revival, it's perhaps ironic that Count Florimond's cash came from French estates which his fleeing aristocratic ancestors had somehow hung on to despite the Revolution.

Doorus is on a small peninsula of the same name that was an island until the eighteenth century. The village has only a pub and a shop, and you can stay at the welcoming **An Óige hostel** (☎091/37512), which can be reached on the Galway–Doolin bus (simply ask to be let off at the hostel). You can also camp down by the beach, though you will have to pay a small charge. One of the best **B&Bs** is *Burren Farm View* (☎091/637142; ③) with great views of the Burren hills. The gentle waters to the south are pleasant, tidal backwaters that contrast sharply with the wide sweep of Traught Blue Flag beach to the north, which is stony but safe for swimming and surfing – there's a lifeguard on duty in summer. The beach at Parkmore, to the northeast, however, is dangerous. Along this coast, mussels are free for the picking – ask a local for the good spots. You can walk the coastline from Doorus down to Aughinish or back to Kinvarra, or cycle out to the Martello Tower at Finavarra and around the inlet of Muckinish Bay towards Bell Harbour.

Coole Park and around

Back on the Ennis Road, the N18, two miles to the north of Gort, you'll find **Coole Park** (mid-June to Aug daily 9.30am–6.30pm; mid-April to mid-June & Sept Tues–Sun 10am–5pm; £2/€2.54; Heritage Card), the old demesne of the house of Lady Gregory, much visited by Yeats, and the subject of some of his most famous poetry. All that remains of the house itself are some crumbling walls and a stable yard, but the grounds and the lake are now a particularly beautiful forest park. Sadly, its **autograph tree**, bearing the graffiti of George Bernard Shaw, Sean O'Casey, Augustus John and others, has been railed off to stop the less famous getting in on the act. A pleasant tearoom has been opened by the stables. One mile north of here is the small intersection known as **Kiltartan Cross**, immortalized by W.B. Yeats in his much-quoted poem *An Irish Airman Forsees his Death*, in which the hero of the poem, William Greg, a fighter pilot in World War I, reflects on his role in the war and imminent death:

Those I fight I do not hate, those I guard I do not love
My country is Kiltartan Cross, my countrymen Kiltartan's poor
No likely end will bring them loss, nor leave them happier than before.

The spot is marked by a small **interpretative centre** (daily 10am–5pm; £2.20/€2.79), situated in an unusually designed schoolhouse that was built by Greg's father in the style of those he saw while working in India. A mile further along there are signposts for **Thoor Ballylee** (Easter–Sept daily 10am–6pm; £3.50/€4.44), a sixteenth-century tower house which Yeats bought in 1916, renovated and made his home off and on over the next ten years. A short film tells the story of his life, rare and first editions are on show and readings of his verse are relayed into the spartan rooms of the tower – all best enjoyed if you can avoid clashing with a bus party. Alongside is a very cosy tearoom.

Four miles southwest of Gort, just off the Corofin Road, lie the remains of **Kilmacduagh**, a monastic settlement founded by St Colman Mac Duagh around 632. The sheer quantity of buildings – dating from the eleventh to the thirteenth centuries – is more impressive than any particular architectural detail: a cathedral, four churches, the Glebe House and a round tower 115ft high, all on one site. And the setting, against the shimmering, distant Burren slopes, lends something magical to the ancient grey stone.

Portumna

PORTUMNA, on the north shore of Lough Derg, is a traditional market town and Shannon crossing point, happy to be cashing in on the upmarket tourism that drifts its way on the lough cruisers, yet still retaining a friendly and unpretentious character. Close to the shore stands the ruin of **Portumna Priory**, for the most part a fifteenth-century Dominican building, though its delicately arched cloisters are built around the remains of a much earlier Cistercian foundation. Nearby **Portumna Castle** (Mon–Sat 9.30am–6.30pm; £1.50/€1.90), a fine, early seventeenth-century mansion with Jacobean gables (something of a rarity in Ireland), is currently undergoing renovation. Nobody minds if you take a look via the fields to the rear. The castle's estate is a wildlife sanctuary with a large herd of fallow deer.

There's a **tourist office** (June–Sept daily 9am–9pm; ☎0509/41644) at the entrance to the grounds of the castle and you'll find several good **B&Bs** in the centre: try Mrs Ryan's *Auvergne Lodge*, Dominick St (☎0509/41138; ③), Mrs Finlay's *Cnoc Rua*, St Brendan's Rd (☎0509/41197; ④), or the Dolan's *Shannon Villa*, Bridge Rd (☎0509/41269; ③). The town's **hostel**, *Galway Shannonside Hostel*, St. Brigid's Rd (☎0509/41032; ②) is in a restored nineteenth-century schoolhouse and is one of the finest hostels in the country. There are showers in most of the small dorm rooms, an exceptionally comfortable common room and a generous breakfast of juice, freshly brewed ground coffee, cereal and toast which makes a pleasant change from the frugal offerings of most hostels. It's easy **camping** country, too – just ask a farmer – and during July and August there are **public showers** down by the lough jetty. Swimming is relatively safe in the lake, but not in the river. For **bike rental** and repairs, Tony Cunningham's on Dominick St (☎0509/41070) is the place to go. The Bank of Ireland is on Clonfert Avenue, and the post office is on Abbey Street. There's also a **laundry** – Frank's in Brendan Street.

There are three very friendly places to **eat** in the main street: *An Bialann*, a reasonably priced restaurant serving an impressive and diverse menu; *Clonwyn House*, which does traditional cooked meals at any time; and the *Beehive* which serves exceptional pizzas and is very popular locally. Although small, Portumna has an astounding twenty-one **pubs**, and there's no shortage of ballad sessions – the *Corner House* offers regular nights hosted by owner John Horan. You can catch a traditional **ceilidh** at *Clonwyn House* on Sunday nights, when the old folk come in to do their set dancing.

Clonfert Cathedral

About four miles north of Portumna stands **Clonfert Cathedral**, on the site where a Benedictine monastery was founded around 560 by St Brendan. In subsequent centuries the monastery was pillaged, but towards the end of the twelfth century the church was rebuilt and dedicated to St Brendan. There's a superb Romanesque doorway made up of six arches, each a perfect semicircle and richly carved with heavily stylized plants and animals. The capitals are Romanesque cubes carved with crazy, bold animal heads. The Bishop's Palace beyond the cathedral – now derelict as a result of an accidental fire – was the home of Sir Oswald Mosley after his release from prison in 1949.

Athenry

ATHENRY, thirteen miles east of Galway city, is renowned for the song *The Fields of Athenry*, a poignant indictment of the horrors of the Famine that has mutated into a drunken closing-time song and a football terrace chant. However, the town's history has little to do with the Famine and more to do with its position as a strategic crossing point on the Clareen river (reflected in its Gaelic name *Baile Áth an Rí*, which means "town of the ford of the king"). It was for this reason that the town became so heavily fortified and a base for Anglo-Norman control – so much a feature of east Galway and so conspicuously absent further west. Large portions of its Norman town walls have survived, along with a tower gate, five flanking towers and the bold thirteenth-century **castle** with its stout three-storey keep (daily 9.30am–6.30pm; £2/€2.54), all of which are impressively intact. The narrow streets retain their medieval layout, while the modern town is still contained within the original walls. The centre of town is marked by a rare fifteenth-century **market cross** (indicating permission for a market to be held at that spot), while on the green in front of the castle, close to the river, stands the bird sculpture commemorating the local poet **Pádraig Fiacc**, which was erected by his son. Athenry has a vibrant community spirit expressed most vividly through its support for the local hurling team, which became champions of Ireland in 2000; locals tell tall tales of arch-Unionist and northern Protestant folk-hero, Lord Carson, playing the game here while on holiday.

The town has a good **heritage centre** (May–Sept daily 9.30am–6.30pm; £2/€2.54), housed in an eighteenth-century church, which itself was built amongst the ruins of the thirteenth-century St Mary's Church. **Eating** options are limited, but good bar food can be found in the excellent *Keane's* pub which assuages the conscience of guilty drinkers with a sign over the door claiming that "work is the curse of the drinking classes". For **B&B** try the friendly, comfortable home of *Mrs MacDonagh*, Ballygurrane South (☎091/844579, *mcdhaus@eircom.net*; ③).

Loughrea

LOUGHREA, on the main road to Ballinasloe and ten miles southeast of Athenry, is like Portumna in that it's a lakeside market town. But it's much smaller, and tiny Lough Rea can't compare with the beauty of Lough Derg for a setting. In the thirteenth century, Richard de Burgo founded a **Carmelite monastery** here, and it still stands in an excellent state of preservation. The town also has a late nineteenth-century **cathedral**, whose interior demonstrates the development of the modern Dublin School of Stained Glass – an acquired taste. Much earlier religious art is on display next door in the **Loughrea Museum** (by appointment only; ☎091/841212; free). This small museum includes episcopal vestments and carved crucifixes from the seventeenth century, beautifully simple silver and gold chalices from as early as 1500, penal crosses and a few rare woodcarvings from the twelfth and thirteenth centuries. The Kilcorban *Virgin and Child*, which is also on display here, is the earliest of only three such carvings that have been found in Ireland.

In a field two miles to the north of Loughrea, near Bullaun, stands the **Turoe Stone**. A superb, rounded pillar-stone, this is decorated with the bold swirls of Celtic La Tène art, a style found more typically in Brittany. The finest of its kind in Ireland, it dates from the third or second century BC and was probably a phallic fertility stone, used in pagan rituals. There are a couple of fine **B&Bs** in this area: Mrs Pauline Burke's *Four Seasons*, Athenry Road (☎091/541414; ④), and Mrs Rose Plower's *La Riasc*, Clostoken (☎091/841069; ③), three miles out of town on the Dublin–Galway road. Loughrea also has two fine **hotels**: the cosy well-established *O'Dea's*, a converted Georgian town house on Bride St (☎091/841611, *www.commerce.ie/odeashotel*; ⑥), and the newly renovated *Meadow Court*, two miles out of town on the main Dublin road (☎091/841051, *meadowcourthotel@eircom.net*; ⑥), which has modern, comfortable rooms and a restaurant which serves immaculately prepared traditional meals such as steak and lamb.

Aughrim and Kilconnell Friary

Tiny **AUGHRIM**, fourteen miles from Loughrea and just short of Ballinasloe, makes a good base from which to explore some of the ecclesiastical remains of the area. In 1691, Aughrim was the scene of a key battle in the Williamite Wars in which the Irish and French forces were defeated. The **Battle of Aughrim Interpretive Centre** (Easter–Oct daily 10am–6pm) explains the battle's significance and places the Williamite Wars in the context of seventeeth-century European power struggles. *Hynes* **hostel** (☎0905/73734; ②) which has adequate, small dorm rooms also does camping and is attached to the local pub, which has music at weekends during the summer. It's advisable to book ahead in July and August and also during Ballinasloe's horse fair (see below). The other reason for stopping here is to visit the excellent *Old Schoolhouse Restaurant*, on the other side of the Dublin Road from the village, its adventurous menu featuring such delicacies as tournedos of ostrich with a shallot confit and port and dry plum juice.

Four miles to the northwest lie the very beautiful remains of **Kilconnell Friary**, a Franciscan foundation built near the site of the sixth-century church of St Conall, which gives the place its name. The friary held out successfully against Cromwellian attack in 1651. The ruins are extensive, with additions to the early fourteenth-century building showing that there was increased monastic activity in the later Middle Ages. There's a very pretty arcaded cloister, and in the north wall of the nave are two splendid canopied wall-tombs.

Ballinasloe

Galway's eastern boundary is one of water: Lough Derg, the Shannon and the River Suck. The tourist-geared villages are again catering mainly for the fishing fraternity, but there is enough of historic interest to warrant leisurely exploration. **BALLINASLOE** is the main town in east Galway. Important as a crossing point of the River Suck since 1124 when Turlough O'Conor, King of Connacht, built a castle here – the remains that can be seen today date mainly from the fourteenth century. You're only really likely to be here if you've come for the famous **horse fair**, which starts on the first weekend in October and lasts for eight days. The largest of the ancient fairs left in the country, drawing horse dealers from all over Ireland and England, it gives a fascinating glimpse into a way of life that is slowly disappearing. The bartering is very much a game, though a serious one. Generally, both parties know the value of the horse in question but enjoy the bartering ritual anyway, with its possibilities of outdoing an opponent. The logic seems to be that if you're not up to the bartering, you don't deserve the right price for the animal.

If you intend to visit the fair, you'll have to book accommodation well in advance. The **tourist office**, part of Keller Travel, Main St (July–Aug Mon–Sat 10am–6pm; ☎0905/42131), can give you more information on accommodation around the region and make bookings. The main **hotel** in town is *Hayden's* in Dunlo Street which is good value (☎0905/42347; ⑦); for **B&B** try Angela Lyons' *Nephin*, Portumna Road, Kellygrove (☎0905/42685; ③). **Bike rental** is available from P. Clarke & Sons, Dunlo St (☎0905/42417).

The countryside to the south of Ballinasloe makes a dull setting for a fine piece of ecclesiastical architecture, well worth taking in if you're staying in the area or heading south towards Portumna and Lough Derg. From the R357 road five miles south of town, **Clontuskert Abbey** looks impressive in this open countryside, like some iron-grey battleship adrift on the flat and muddy approaches to the Suck. The church is the only sizeable remnant of the abbey complex, with a perpendicular west door of 1471, carved with figures of the saints.

The east shore of Lough Corrib

The east shore of Lough Corrib provides a gentle route between County Mayo and Galway city, which is less dramatic than the Connemara roads. The lake shore and the many rivers are popular with fishermen (for trout and salmon in summer, pike in winter), and visitors with no taste for field sports have a number of medieval ruins to admire.

Two miles north of Headford, virtually on the border of County Mayo, is **Ross Errilly** (or "Ross Abbey"), the biggest and best-preserved Franciscan abbey in Ireland. It was founded in the mid-fourteenth century, but the bulk of the buildings belong to the fifteenth – the Franciscan Order's greatest period of expansion. The church buildings themselves are impressive, with a battlemented slender tower (typical of Franciscan abbeys) and well-preserved windows, and there's a wonderful tiny cloister, but it's the adjacent domestic buildings and the picture they give of the everyday life of the order that are perhaps the most interesting. Stand in the cloister with your back to the church and you'll see the refectory ahead and to the right, with the reader's windowside desk up in the far northeast corner. Straight ahead is a second cloister (this one without arcading) and behind that the bakehouse. To the northwest of this second courtyard lies the kitchen, where you can see a water-tank used for holding fish and an oven which reaches into the little mill-room to the rear.

Five miles south of Headford, a detour off the main road leads you right down to the lough shore and the ruined Franciscan friary of **Annaghdown** – far less impressive than Ross Errilly – and a nearby Norman castle. It was at this site, after all his voyaging and preaching, that St Brendan finally died, nursed by his sister, who was head of Annaghdown nunnery. The road then loops back to rejoin the main Galway Road.

The road opposite the one that leads to Annaghdown takes you to the townland of Corrandulla, where the seventeenth-century *Gregg Castle* (☎091/791434; ⑦) provides unusual B&B **accommodation**: a place of beautiful faded splendour. Everything is geared towards relaxation (with breakfast till noon) and conviviality: the owners are garrulous traditional musicians and enjoy evenings with guests around the log fire in the Great Hall. Self-catering is also available. Another quality B&B option in the area, with wonderful views over Lough Corrib, is the welcoming *Balindiff Bay Lodge*, Luimnagh, Corrandulla (☎091/791195; ④).

Tuam and around

Northeast County Galway is served chiefly by the small market town of **TUAM** (pronounced *choom*, from the Gaelic *Tuaim* meaning "grave mound"). There's little here to detain you, but should you wish to sniff out the scant remnants of the town's former importance, have a look inside the Church of Ireland **cathedral** on Galway Road. It's primarily a nineteenth-century building, but survivals from the twelfth-century chancel include a magnificent Romanesque arch, showing strong signs of Scandinavian influence, and the accompanying east window. The shaft of an ornamented high cross is set in the wall near the west door. It's a great shame that so little remains of medieval Tuam; a monastery was founded here in the sixth century by St Iarlath, a disciple of St Enda of Inishmore, and in the medieval period Tuam became not only an archiepiscopal seat but also the power centre of the O'Conors of Connacht. The high cross in the town square dates from the twelfth century: it's highly decorated but actually a bit of a patchwork, as the head and the shaft don't really belong together.

The **tourist office** is in the Mill Museum (July–Aug Mon–Sat 10am–6pm; ☎093/25486) and can book **accommodation**. **B&Bs** include: *Gabrielle Hurst*, Dublin Rd (☎093/25934, *thp@iol.ie*; ③), or Mrs O'Connor's pleasant *Kilmore House*, Galway Rd, Kilmore (☎093/28118; ③), half a mile out of town. For **eating** the place to go is *Cré* *na Cille* on High St (☎093 28232), which serves high-quality food at low prices, though it is very popular locally and it's advisable to book ahead.

Dunmore and Knockmoy abbeys

Yet more medieval ruins are dotted roundabout: past Dunmore in the northeast of the county, is **Dunmore Abbey**, an Augustinian priory of 1425, and just to the west of the town, a Norman castle built by the de Berminghams. Alternatively, seven miles south of Tuam off the N63 Galway to Roscommon road, **Knockmoy Abbey** is a Cistercian foundation of 1190 – though the central tower is probably a fifteenth-century addition. The most remarkable feature of the abbey is on the north wall of the chancel, where you'll see one of Ireland's few surviving medieval frescoes. Extremely faint (only the black outlines retain their original colour), it depicts the legend of the Three Dead Kings and the Three Live Kings. Under the dead kings an inscription reads "We have been as you are, you shall be as we are"; the live kings are out hawking. Underneath this is a picture of Christ holding his hand up in blessing and a barely visible angel with scales.

The Aran Islands

The **Aran Islands – Inishmore**, **Inishmaan** and **Inisheer** – lying about thirty miles out across the mouth of Galway Bay, have exerted a fascination over visitors for over a hundred years. Their geology creates one of the most distinctive landscapes in Ireland, the limestone pavement giving the islands a stark character akin to the Burren of County Clare. This spectacular setting contains a wealth of pre-Christian and early Christian remains and some of the finest archeological sites in Europe. And it's not only works in stone that have survived out here: the islands are Irish-speaking, and up until the early part of the last century a primitive way of life persisted, a result of the isolation enforced by the Atlantic.

The most detailed **map** of the islands is produced by Tim Robinson of Roundstone, available on Inishmore and at bookshops and tourist offices in the Galway and Clare area. In fact the Aran Islands are quite easy to explore and the map isn't essential for finding the major sites. It is, however, of great value to those interested in detailed archeology and in Irish placenames. Although it's possible to do a **day-trip** from Galway to Inishmore, and from Doolin (County Clare) to Inisheer, you really need two full days to see the main sites of Inishmore alone, and an overnight stay on Inisheer adds a priceless dimension to a visit. As for Inishmaan, staying the night is the only way to experience its bewitching silence – and to be guaranteed a return journey. For more detailed information on transport to the islands see box on p.392.

Some history

The Aran Islands abound with evidence of their **early inhabitants**: the earliest ring forts possibly date from the Iron Age (circa 400 BC–500 AD), though recent research suggests that some of the larger structures may be even earlier, perhaps Late Bronze Age (circa 700 BC). The next group of people to figure are the **Christians**, who came here to study at the foundation of St Enda in the fifth century and went on to found Iona, Clonmacnois and Kilmacduagh. However, the earliest surviving ecclesiastical remains date from the eighth century.

As Galway's trade grew, so the strategic importance of the islands increased, and in **medieval** times control of them was disputed by the O'Flaherties of Connacht and the O'Briens of Munster, the latter generally maintaining the upper hand. In 1565, Queen Elizabeth resolved the dispute by granting the islands to an Englishman on condition he kept soldiers there to guarantee the Crown's interests. In the mid-seventeenth cen-

TRANSPORT TO THE ARAN ISLANDS

Several ferry companies and one small airline operate between Galway and the Aran Islands. As with any of the ferry services to islands on the west coast, it's a good idea to check on the times of return journeys with the skipper, especially if you are going to Inishmaan or Inisheer as services can be unreliable – during winter, you're at the mercy of the weather, and there's a chance you'll get cut off from the mainland. If you are planning on travelling between the islands check the schedule closely as doing so can be more complicated and time-consuming than you might at first imagine. If you intend to drive to Rossaveel (signposted *Ros an Mhil*) and pick up a ferry from there, bear in mind that it is thirty miles west of Galway and you will be charged £2–3/€2.54–3.81 per day, £10–15/€12.70–19.05 per week respectively to park a car or van. Considering this it may well be worth paying a little extra for the ten-minute journey by air.

Island Ferries, Victoria Place, Eyre Square, Galway (☎091/568903; in the evenings ☎091/561767 or 572273). A return, Galway to Inishmore, costs around £15/€19.05; sailings are daily at 10.30am, 1.30pm and 6.30pm (there are often more in summer) and takes about forty minutes.. Boats to Inisheer or Inishmaan cost around £18/€22.86 return and sail daily at 10.30am and 6.30pm taking around one hour. The ferry company runs a bus to Rossaveel (leaving one and a half hours before the sailing) which costs £4/€5.08, though if you have a bike it's worth noting that often the bus cannot carry them and there is a £2/€2.54 charge to carry bikes on the ferry itself. A B&B-booking service is also offered free of charge and package deals are available. Round trips taking in all three islands are also negotiable.

O'Brien Shipping, tourist office at the junction of Victoria Place and Merchant's Rd, Galway (☎091/567283 or 567676), operates from Galway to Inishmore (1 daily year round), to Inishmaan and Inisheer (4 days weekly). Fare to each island £14/€17.78 return. The fare for trips to all three islands by arrangement. Islands and Doolin (County Clare) return £20/€25.40. Student reductions of £2/€2.54; bikes free.

Doolin Ferry Co, Doolin Pier (☎065/707 4455; in the evenings ☎065/707 4189) sails mid-April to Sept from Doolin to Inisheer (1–6 daily) and to Inishmore (2 daily). Return prices are Doolin to Inisheer £15/€19.05, Doolin to Inishmore £20/€25.40, Doolin to Inishmaan £18/€22.86 (phone confirmation is strongly advised). A trip to all three islands, returning to Doolin or going on to Galway, costs £20/€25.40. Bikes £2/€2.54 return.

Aer Árann (☎091/593034) are based at the airstrip at Inverin, west beyond Spiddal. They offer flights to all three of the islands: at least three flights daily throughout the year and during the summer months a non-stop shuttle service seven days a week. A connecting bus from Galway city meets all flights. The return fare is £35/€44.45, students £29/€36.83 bookable at the Aer Árann desk in the tourist office, where it is also worth asking about fly/sail deals. It is not possible to take a bicycle on the plane. Island airport numbers are: Inishmore ☎099/61109 or 61131; Inishmaan ☎099/73020; Inisheer ☎099/75039.

tury the islands lost their political usefulness; the Cromwellian soldiers garrisoned there simply transferred to the new regime after the Restoration and became absorbed into the islands' traditional way of life.

After the decline of English interest and influence, the islands fell into poverty, aggravated in the nineteenth century by rack-renting. That rents should be levied on this barren rock suggests a cruel avarice and, not surprisingly, Aranmen were active in the **Land League** agitations: acts of defiance included walking the landlord's cattle blindfold over the Dún Aengus cliff edge. Despite this link with the general political movement on the mainland and the islands' use as a refuge for Nationalists during the War of Independence, it is their isolation that has allowed the continuation of a unique and ancient culture that proves so alluring to outsiders in this century.

THE GAELIC REVIVAL
With the burgeoning fascination for all things Gaelic from the 1890s onwards, the Aran Islands, along with the Blaskets, became the subject of great sociological and linguistic enquiry, the most famous of their literary visitors being J.M. Synge. His writings brought the islands to the attention of other intellectuals involved in the **Gaelic Revival**, and the notion of a surviving community of pure Gaels provided fuel for the Nationalist movement. Ironically, this notion may have been misconceived. The distinct physical type found on Aran – the dark skin, large brow and Roman nose – is, some argue, the legacy of the Cromwellian soldiers who were left on the islands. The islands themselves have produced many fine writers: Liam O'Flaherty from Inishmore wrote several acclaimed novels, most notably the *Informer* (1925) and *Famine* (1937), while Gaelic poet Máirtín Ó'Direáin wrote twentieth-century verse describing the hardship of island life *ag coraíocht leis an gcarraig lom* ("wrestling with the bare rock").

In 1934, Robert Flaherty made his classic documentary *Man of Aran*, which recorded the ancient and disappearing culture he found here. (The film can be seen during the summer in Halla Rónáin, Kilronan.) While the **folklore and traditions** recorded in the film have obviously declined, *currachs* – light wood-framed boats covered formerly with hide, now with tar-coated canvas – are still used for fishing and for getting ashore on the smaller islands when the ferry can't pull in, and you may even witness, as in the film, a man fishing with a simple line off the edge of a 200ft cliff. Fishing and farming are still very much a way of life on Inishmaan, while tourism is the major earner on Inishmore and Inisheer. This means that, though their purpose will change, knowledge of these customs will not vanish, and tourism may even help ensure the language survives, as Irish provides the islanders with a curtain of privacy against the visitors.

Inishmore

Although there's some truth behind the attitude that does down **Inishmore** (*Inis Mór*, "Big Island") as the most tourist-oriented and least "authentic" of the Aran Islands, its wealth of dramatic ancient sites overrides such considerations. Increased numbers of minibuses and bicycles can make the main road west along the island pretty hectic in high season, and it's worth taking the low road along the north shore if you want to escape the crowds.

It's a long strip of an island, a great tilted plateau of limestone, with a scattering of **villages** along the sheltered northerly coast. The land slants up to the southern edge, where tremendous **cliffs** rip along the entire length of the island. Walking anywhere on this high southern side, you can see the geological affinity with the Burren of County Clare (see p.361), and visualize the time when these islands were part of a barrier enclosing what is now Galway Bay. As far as the eye can see is a tremendous patterning of stone, some of it the bare formation of the land (the pavementing of grey rock split in bold parallel grooves), some the form of dry-stone walls that might be contemporary, or might be pre-Christian. The textures blur so that it's impossible to make sense of planes and distances, the only certainties being the stark outline of the cliffs' edges and the constant pounding of the waves below. Across the water the Connemara mountains stand in contrast, coloured pink and golden and slatey blue in the evening sun. Up the bay is Galway, now an insignificant speck, and around to the southeast, appearing as just a silvery ridge, are the Cliffs of Moher.

Getting around, information and accommodation

The best way to **get about** Inishmore is by a combination of cycling and walking. You can rent **bikes** from Aran Bicycle Hire, beside the pier in Kilronan, where the ferry docks; Costello's Bike Hire (closed Nov–April; ☎099/61241), opposite the *American Bar* further up the lane; or Mullin & Burke, next to the *Aran Islands Hostel*. The latter

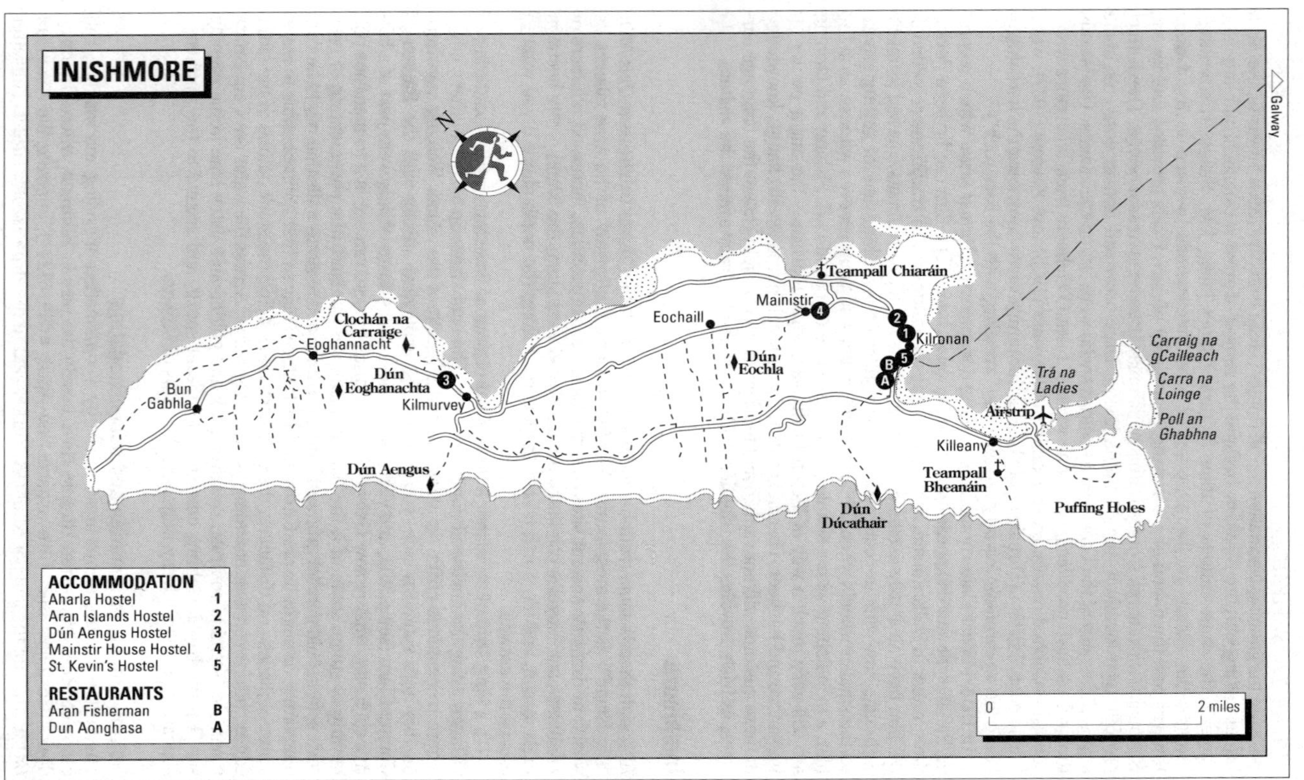
INISHMORE
N
Galway
Teampall Chiaráin
Mainistir
Eochaill
Kilronan
Clochán na Carraige
Eoghannacht
Dún Eochla
Dún Eoghanachta
Bun Gabhla
Kilmurvey
Carraig na gCailleach
Trá na Ladies
Carra na Loinge
Airstrip
Poll an Ghabhna
Killeany
Dún Aengus
Teampall Bheanáin
Dún Dúcathair
Puffing Holes
ACCOMMODATION
Aharla Hostel 1
Aran Islands Hostel 2
Dún Aengus Hostel 3
Mainstir House Hostel 4
St. Kevin's Hostel 5
RESTAURANTS
Aran Fisherman B
Dun Aonghasa A
0
2 miles

will deliver bikes free of charge to B&Bs on the island. **Pony buggies** will take you on a round tour for about £20/€25.40 for a group of four, and **minibuses** ply the length of the island constantly. If you have limited time you can take the public minibus up the island through the villages that stretch over seven miles to the west – Mainistir, Eochaill, Kilmurvey, Eoghannacht and Bún Gabhla – and walk back from any point. The bus leaves Kilronan grocery shop, up behind the hostel, daily every two hours between 9am and 5pm (£2/€2.54 single). The village of Killeany, a mile and a half to the south of Kilronan, has to be either walked or cycled to.

There are five **hostels** on Inishmore, three of which are in Kilronan. The best of these is *Kilronan Hostel* (closed Nov–March; ☎099/61255), it's very near the pier, and is handy if you want to spend the night in the pub below, but noisy if you don't. Between *Tí Joe Mac's* and the Spar supermarket is *St Kevin's Hostel* (summer only; ☎099/61484) which offers adequate dorm beds, while the tiny *Aharla Hostel* (☎099/61305) has two four-bed dorms. Away from the hub of Kilronan, one of the most tranquil spots to stay is the excellent *Dún Aengus Hostel* in Kilmurvey (☎099/61318; ②), an ideally located converted country house, though, at the time of going to press, the hostel's future is uncertain following a fire. On the road to Kilmurvey is the *Mainistir House Hostel* at Mainistir (☎099/61169; ②); this hostel has all the extras – it does excellent vegetarian buffets in the evenings and breakfasts of porridge and freshly baked scones – but unfortunately it tends to ignore basics such as friendly service.

B&Bs can be booked through the **tourist office** (June to mid-Sept daily 10am–6pm), a couple of minutes' walk from the pier in Kilronan, although there will be a small service charge. Try Mrs Gill, *Cois Cuain* (☎099/75106; ③), the large white house facing you as you leave the pier. One mile east of Kilronan is *Tigh Fitz* (☎099/61213; ④) a friendly pub with comfortable rooms above. Towards Kilmurvey the best places to stay are Conneely's *Beach View House* (☎099/61141; ④), overlooking one of the island's idyllic beaches and *Kilmurvey House* (☎099/61218; *kilmurveyhouse @eircom.net*; ④), a solid 150-year-old country house. *Oatquarter House* (☎099/61328; ③), is excellent value and the friendly Irish-speaking family give a welcome as warm as their bright turf fires. If you have a taste for kitsch then you'll enjoy staying at the *Man of Aran Cottages* (☎099/61301; ④), specifically built for the filming of *The Man of Aran* according to what the film-makers thought traditional Irish cottages should look like.

There is a basic **campsite** (no showers) an easy walk from Kilronan: take the lane heading west out of the village and turn right in front of *Joe Watty's* pub. Better equipped though are *Inishmór Camp Site* (☎099/61185) in Mainistir or the campsite at the *Dún Aengus Hostel* (☎099/61318) in Kilmurvey. Alternatively, it's just about possible to pitch a tent down by the idyllic beach at Kilmurvey, a lovely sweep of white sand looking out over to the Connemara mountain range; anywhere else is either bare rock or a treasured piece of cultivated land: finding the owner and asking permission is absolutely essential.

There is a large Spar **supermarket** in Kilronan and a second shop by *Joe Watty's* bar. The village has a **post office**, with a public phone (and cardphone) outside, and the Bank of Ireland opens here Wednesdays (10.15am–12.30pm & 1.30–3pm), plus additional Thursdays in July and August. You can also **change money** at the tourist office, the post office and Carraig Donn, a craft shop selling hand-knitted Aran sweaters by the pier at Kilronan (April–Oct daily) – this last will also advance cash on credit cards.

The island

Inishmore's villages are strung along the main road that runs the length of the northern shore, the hub of activity being **KILRONAN**, where the ferry lands. The Aran Heritage Centre, *Ionad Árann*, on the right of the main road leading out of Kilronan (April–Oct daily 10am–7pm; £2/€2.54), offers a slightly sober introduction to the island's history, geography and geology. There are some great sandy **beaches**: the one at **KILMURVEY** (four miles west of Kilronan) is safe and sheltered, with fabulous views of the Connemara mountains, or you could take the main road to its eastern extreme and then walk north to get to the safe beaches from Carraig na gCailleach, through Carra na Loinge, down to Poll an Ghabhna. Tucked closer to **KILLEANY**, three quarters of a mile to the south, is Cockle Strand, safe for swimming; little over a mile further on, near the airstrip, is Tra na Ladies, which looks nice but where you can get caught by tides or sinking sand. You can **walk** just about anywhere so long as it doesn't look like someone's garden, but be careful when walking on the south of the island in poor visibility, as the cliffs are sheer and sudden.

DÚN AENGUS AND THE FORTS

The most spectacular of Aran's prehistoric sites is Inishmore's fort of **Dún Aengus** (signposted from Kilmurvey, three-quarters of a mile east), a massive semicircular ring fort of three concentric enclosures lodged on the edge of cliffs that plunge 300ft into the Atlantic. The inner citadel is a 20ft-high, 18ft-wide solid construction of precise blocks of grey stone, their symmetry echoing the almost geometric regularity of the land's limestone pavementing and the bands of rock that form the cliffs. Standing on the ramparts you can see clearly the *chevaux-de-frise* outside the middle wall, a field bristling with lurching rocks like jagged teeth, designed to slow down any attack.

The place is tremendously evocative, and it's easy to understand how superstitions have survived on the islands long after their disappearance on the mainland. Visible west of the cliffs of Inishmore under certain meteorological conditions is the outline of what looks like a mountainous island. This is a mirage, a mythical island called *Hy Brasil* that features in ancient Aran stories as the island of the blessed, visited by saints and heroes. Until the sixteenth century *Hy Brasil* was actually marked on maps.

Dún Eoghanachta is a huge drum of a fort, a perfect circle of stone settled in a lonely field with the Connemara mountains as a scenic backdrop. Its walls are 16ft thick, and inner steps give access to the parapets. Inside are the foundations of the ancient drystone huts known as *clocháns*. The stronghold is accessible by tiny lanes from Dún Aengus if you've a detailed map; otherwise retrace your steps to Kilmurvey and follow the road west for just over a mile, where it's (poorly) signposted off to the left.

Dún Dúcathair (the Black Fort) is especially worth visiting for its dramatic location. It's a promontory fort, and what remains is a massive stone wall straddling an ever-shrinking headland precariously placed between cliffs. The eastern gateway fell into the sea early in the last century, leaving the entrance a perilous twelve inches from the sheer drop. Inside are the curved remains of four *clocháns*. It's about a two-mile walk from Kilronan – head south out of the village for three-quarters of a mile, take a turning to the right (signposted to "Cliff House") and follow the lane to the cliffs. If on a bike be warned: the lane becomes extremely rocky, making cycling impossible. Once at the cliff edge you can see the fort on the second promontory to your left.

The **dating** of these forts is tricky: Dún Aengus and Dún Dúcathair have long been considered to date from the first century BC, though recent excavations of the middle enclosure have found pottery fragments from the Late Bronze Age, suggesting a much earlier date of 700 BC. Dún Eoghanachta and **Dún Eochla** (just south off the road to the west of Mainistir) could have been constructed at any time between the first and seventh centuries AD, or possibly earlier. The massive buttresses of Dún Eochla are nineteenth-century additions, but the forts have generally been kept in exceptional condition.

CHURCH SITES AND CLOCHÁNS

From the fifth century onwards, the Aran Islands were a centre of monastic learning, the most important of the eremitic settlements being that of St Enda (*Eanna*). At the **seven churches**, just east of **EOGHANNACHT**, there are ancient slabs commemorating seven Romans who died here, testifying to the far-reaching influence of Aran's monastic teaching. The site is in fact that of two churches and several domestic buildings, dating from the eighth to the thirteenth centuries. Here **St Brendan's grave** is adorned by an early cross with interlaced patterns and, on the west side, part of a Crucifixion carving. There are also parts of three high crosses, possibly eleventh century, and in the southeast corner of the graveyard, alongside the slabs of the Romans, lie several ninth-century slabs incised with crosses and inscriptions.

The most interesting of the ecclesiastical sites on Inishmore, however, is **Teampall Chiaráin**. Take the low road from **Mainistir** (opposite *Joe Watty's* pub), follow the lane parallel to the shoreline, and you'll come to it, a simple twelfth-century church on an old monastic site. Alongside is **St Kieran's Well**, a long U-shaped spring backed by huge blocks of plant-covered stone. It's very pagan-looking – such wells often held sacred significance in pre-Christian times, and were adopted and renamed with the arrival of Christianity. Similarly, some of the tall stones that stand around the site look pre-Christian, even though they have crosses inscribed on them. The one by the east gable has a hole in it that may have held part of a sundial, and nowadays people sometimes pass handkerchiefs through it for luck.

Teampall Bheanáin, on the hill behind Killeany, is a pre-Romanesque oratory dating from around the sixth or seventh century, dedicated to St Benen. It's distinguished by its very steep gable ends and its unusual north–south orientation. In all probability, it used to form part of the great early monastic site that existed at Killeany.

The finest of Aran's *clocháns* is **Clochán na Carraige**, just north of Kilmurvey. This 19ft-long dry-stone hut has a corbelled roof whose arrangement is probably an early Christian design. There are fifty lesser examples of such huts on Inishmore.

Eating, drinking and entertainment

Not surprisingly, **seafood** is the great speciality on the island. *Dún Aonghasa* a five-minute walk west along the coast from Kilronan (closed Nov–Easter; ☎099/61104), with fine bay views, has the most varied menu and is good value for anything from light snacks to full meals, while a similar menu is offered at the *Aran Fisherman* (☎099/61104) plus vegetarian dishes and some cheaper options. Kilronan also has a fast-food restaurant (summer daily until 10pm, later if there is a ceilidh on). *Joe Watty's* bar is good for soups and stews (summer until 8pm), and *Pota Stair* in the heritage centre serves homemade soups and cakes. You can punctuate your cycling or walking with lunch, tea or snacks at *Man of Aran Cottages* in Kilmurvey, used as a set in the eponymous film (June–Sept daily 11.30am–7.45pm); although it is a little expensive the seafood chowder is a must. The film, made in 1934, is shown during the summer in the community centre, Halla Rónáin Kilronan (3pm, 5.30pm & 8pm; £2.50/€3.17).

The **pub** beneath the hostel in Kilronan is convivial enough, but it's still a good idea to wander away from here to sample some of the island's other bars: *The American Bar* in the centre of Kilronan, *Joe Watty's* out of Kilronan to the west, *John Dirrane's* at the top of the road as it slopes down to the beach at Kilmurvey, and *Tigh Fitz* in Killeany, are all worth visiting. In addition to this there are **ceilidhs** in Kilronan parish hall (June–Sept Fri, Sat & Sun; winter Sat; £3/€3.81) and a **disco** on Thursday nights.

Inishmaan

Inishmaan (*Inis Meáin* "Middle Island") is the least visited of the three Aran Islands. Locals go about their lives seemingly oblivious to the trickle of tourists who come over, mostly on day trips from Inishmore. After Inishmore, you're immediately struck by how much greener Inishmaan is. Brambles and ferns shoot from walls, and bindweed clings to the limestone terraces. Here the stone walls are a warm brown and seem almost to glow with yellow moss. They're remarkably high – up to six feet – and form a stone maze that chequers off tiny fields of lush grass and clover. Yet despite this verdancy, the island still feels dour and desolate. Farming here is at subsistence level; farm buildings and cottages are grubby and dull, and soggy thatches sag over low doorways. The only sudden splashes of colour are from tiny cultivated gardens – the bright reds, pinks and oranges of geraniums, gladioli and carnations. The island is shaped something like an oyster shell. It rises in clear levels from the soft dunes of the north, through stages of flat naked rock, up to minuscule green pastures, then again up a craggy band of limestone (along which sit the main villages of the island), eventually levelling out on higher ground to meet the crinkled blowhole-pitted southerly edge. Inishmaan is the least visited, least touched by tourism of the three islands, though it has had visitors since the turn of the century. J.M. Synge stayed here for four summers from 1898, recording the life and language of the people. His play *Riders to the Sea* – which influenced Lorca's *Blood Wedding* – is set here, and his book *The Aran Islands* provides a fascinating insight into the way of life he found. **Synge's Chair**, a sheltered place on the westerly cliffs overlooking St Gregory's Sound, was his favourite contemplative spot. Traces of the **culture** he discovered remain. Some of the women still wear traditional brightly coloured shawls; Irish is the main language, though English is understood; and the islanders get on with what they've always done: farming and fishing. There's no hostility to visitors, but tourism isn't the islanders' concern. If you want to be impressed or entertained, you'll have to look elsewhere.

Forts and churches

One of the most impressive of the Aran forts is Inishmaan's **Dún Conchúir**, situated on elevated ground in the centre of the island and loosely dated between the first and seventh centuries AD. Its massive oval wall is almost intact and commands great views of the island, being built on the side of a limestone valley. (In myth, Conchúir was the brother of Aengus of the Firbolg.) To the east, the smaller **Dún Fearbhaí** stands above the village of Baile an Mhothair and looks out over the little eighth-century **Cill Cheannannach** by the shore near the pier. If you have visited the Hugh Lane Gallery (see p.98) and been impressed by the stained glass windows on display there then you will adore the windows in the modern church on the island from the same workshop of Harry Clarke. Some find his rich purples and turquoise too much but these windows are a real delight, especially since each depicts a scene from the island among the Christian iconography.

Practicalities

Inishmaan's indifference to tourism means that amenities for visitors are minimal. The three **shops** in the main street of the central village have limited provisions: tinned foods, bread and milk. The **pub** is central, too, serving snacks throughout the day during July and August (till 7.30pm); lunches and evening meals are available at *An Dún*, a seasonal café and restaurant just below Dún Conchúir (summer only; ☎099/73068), though at the time of going to press its future was uncertain. The island's other restaurant is beside *Ó'Congaile's B&B* (☎099/73085; ③) which is along the road from the pier. There are few other going commercial concerns on the island: Cniotáil Inis Meáin, the knitwear factory, produces beautifully simple designs in alpaca, linen and wool; it's home, too, to the **museum**, a fascinating photographic archive of island history, largely documented in Irish, and there's a pleasant tearoom. **B&Bs** are cheaper than on the mainland, though if you have an evening meal it may nearly double the price. If you arrive on spec, ask at the pub for some information; the phone number is ☎099/73003. If you want to book ahead, try *Mrs A. Faherty* (☎099/73012; ②) or *Máire Bu Uí Mhaolchiaráin* near the church (☎099/73016; ③), which also offers free camping (campers' breakfast £2.50/€3.17) and guided walks. By far the friendliest place to stay is *Ard Álainn* (☎099/73027; ③) a mile or so up the road to Dún Conchúir, the owner of which cooks possibly the most filling breakfast of any B&B in Ireland and has bikes for rent near the pier. Other advanced-booking accommodation information is available from **Inishmaan Island Co-operative** (☎099/73010). Most farmers will let you **camp**, but remember to ask them – all land belongs to somebody here; it's also worth making sure that the knitwear factory is out of earshot before pitching your tent. There is no chemist or doctor on the island, and **emergencies** are dealt with by a nurse (☎099/73005). A **public phone** is located outside the post office and in the pub, and the Bank of Ireland operates on the second Tuesday of every month.

Inisheer

Inisheer (*Inis Oírr* "East Island"), at just under two miles across, is the smallest of the Aran Islands. Tourism has a key role here; Inisheer doesn't have the archeological wealth of Inishmore, or the wild solitude of Inishmaan, but regular day-trip ferry services from Doolin bring a constant, if small, flow of visitors. This service also makes for a handy route from County Clare to Connemara. Of course tourism threatens the very stuff of its attraction – the purity of traditions and a romantic isolation – but for the moment Inisheer retains its old character, and for some it's a favourite place.

A great plug of rock dominates the island, its rough, pale-grey stone dripping with greenery. At the top the fifteenth-century **O'Brien's castle** stands inside an ancient ring fort. Set around it are low fields, a small community of pubs and houses, and windswept sand dunes. Half buried in sand just south of the beach is the ancient **church of St Kevin**; still in use in the nineteenth century, it is now used only to commemorate him as the patron saint of the island every June 14.

Practicalities

The **tourist office** (June–Sept daily 10am–7pm), in a hut by the pier, will give you a map and a list of **B&Bs**; you may want to try *Uí Chongaile's*, Lioseinee, West Village (☎099/75025; ③). If you need any other information about the island you can also contact Inisheer Island Co-operative (☎099/75008). You should have little trouble finding accommodation unless you arrive in the first weekend of August or at Whit weekend, which are usually booked up well ahead. The *Bru Radharc na Mara* **hostel** (IHH; ☎099/75024; ②) is comfortable, with meals available. The only **camping** is on the official site open May to September.

There are a handful of places to get **food** on Inisheer: *Radharc na Mara*, five minutes' east of the pier (June–Sept until 9pm) serves meals all day, and the *Óstán Inis Oírr*, opposite the pier (closed mid-Sept to Easter; ☎099/75020) does bar meals from 9am to 9pm. *Fisherman's Cottage* restaurant (closed Oct–April; ☎099/75073) uses organic produce, catches its own seafood and caters well for vegetarians. Both the hotel bar, *Tigh Ruairí*, and *Tigh Ned* bar have **music** any time of the week during the summer. There is no bank on the island, but the hotel has a bureau de change.

Connemara

Dominated by two mountain ranges, **Connemara** is exceptionally beautiful. The **Twelve Bens** and **Maam Turks** glower over vast open areas of bog wilderness, while to the southwest the land breaks up into myriad tiny islands linked by causeways, slipping out into the ocean. The whole area has superb beaches, with huge sweeps of opalescent white sand washed by clear blue water. Chance upon good weather here and you feel you've hit paradise; even on the hottest of days the beaches are never crowded.

This is country you visit for its scenery rather than its history. There is little evidence of medieval power in Connemara, either ecclesiastical or secular, beyond a few castles along the shore of Lough Corrib and the occasional one further west. The great exception is the profusion of **monastic remains** dotted over the little islands off the west coast. Mainland settlements up until the nineteenth century were widely scattered, and the area has always been sparsely populated, due to the poverty of the land. There's never been much to attract marauders or colonizers, and any incursions have involved a battle against the terrain as much as against the people. It's easy to see how such a land would remain under the control of clans like the O'Flaherties for centuries, while gentler landscapes bowed to the pressure of foreign rule. In the famine years the area suffered some of the worst of the misery, and a thinly peopled land was depopulated further as people chose to escape starvation by emigration.

Continued economic deprivation and isolation have meant that an ancient rural way of life has continued for far longer here, so Connemara is still Irish-speaking, the largest of the *Gaeltacht* areas. A *Gaeltacht* summer school is held in **Spiddal**, and **Casla** (Costelloe) is the home of *Raidió na Gaeltachta* radio station (556m MW, broadcasting daily 8am–7.30pm). English is spoken too, however, and the only difficulty for the visitor is that the signs on the roads, and on some buses, are often in Irish only.

For all its beauty, the dramatic mountain landscape of west Galway is surprisingly undeveloped in terms of tourism, owing in part to the infamous Irish weather and in part to the fact that walking has not been the popular recreation in Ireland that it is in other, more urbanized European countries. If you're in search of solitude, you won't have to go far to find it.

Practicalities

Bus Éireann services link all villages on major routes between Galway, Oughterard, Roundstone, Clifden and Cong. They are reliable, although infrequent, often with only one service daily, occasionally even less frequently. Timetables can be picked up in Galway bus station (☎091/562000). The area is well served by private buses which can be more flexible and cheaper than Bus Éireann: try Lally's (☎091/562905), O'Neachtain's (☎091/553188) or Hugh Ryan (☎091/555780).

Hostels and **B&Bs** are both in reasonably good supply throughout Connemara, and you can **camp** more or less anywhere, but bear in mind that a lot of the area is bog and therefore very wet. Away from towns and villages, you may have trouble getting hold of water. Gaz canisters are available in Galway city, at Keogh's in Oughterard, Michael Ferron's in Roundstone, Peter Veldon's in Letterfrack, and in Clifden at The Twelve Bens, Stanley's and Miller's. Bord Fáilte-approved **campsites** are listed in the text.

If you intend to go **walking** bear in mind that the mountains here are potentially **dangerous**. There is no organized mountain-rescue service such as you get in European countries that are more developed for mountain sports. The Ordnance Survey 1:126,720 maps are based on surveying done in 1837 and are inaccurate, especially above 1000ft. If you are doing any serious walking, it is worth getting either the *Connemara Map and Guide Booklet* or *The Mountains of Connemara*, a map and guide to eighteen walks, including the Western Way. Both are produced by Folding Landscapes of Roundstone, Connemara, County Galway, and can be obtained in tourist offices in the west of Ireland or by post. **Bike rental** is available at Clifden, Galway, Roundstone and at several hostels (mentioned in the text).

Most of Connemara's more beautiful **beaches** are safe for swimming, including Clifden, Lettergesh, Dog's Bay, Gurteen Bay, Renvyle, Ardmore, Mannin Bay, Aillebrack, Omey, Letterfrack and Spiddal. It is, however, a very varied coast, so, if in doubt, ask about safety locally.

Finally, being the *Gaeltacht*, the area's **signposts** are often in Irish, as are names on buses (even Galway is sometimes *Gaillimh*); where common these are added in parentheses in the course of the guide. Variations in the Irish spellings are common – sometimes the "An" is omitted.

Iar-Chonnacht

Draw a large triangle between Maam Cross, Rossaveel and Galway and you've defined the area known as **Iar-Chonnacht**, an open and bleak moorland of bog. Occasional white-splotched boulders lie naked on the peat that stretches to the skyline; any grass that survives is coarse and windblown, and, but for small pockets of forestation, the bog has no trees. It's difficult and wet walking country, but numerous lanes and *boreens* lead to tiny loughs set in the granite hollows of the hills – these are good for fishing for brown trout, sea trout or salmon. The moorland reaches its highest point near Lough Lettercraffoe on the **Rossaveel to Oughterard Road**, giving fine views down onto **Lough Corrib**, whose green and wooded shores are a vivid foil to the barren west.

To Oughterard and around

If you're heading for the dramatic **walking country** of the mountains, or if you plan to base yourself at Clifden, the road to take from Galway is the N59 through Oughterard. It makes the easiest hitch and the most pleasant cycle ride from Galway, avoiding the boring strip development down to Spiddal and taking you instead along the shore of island-flecked **Lough Corrib**, past crumbling ruins. These include the main sixteenth-century O'Flaherty fortress of **Aughnanure Castle**, two miles south of Oughterard (mid-June to mid-Sept daily 9.30am–6.30pm; £2/€2.54). A six-storey tower house standing on a rock island surrounded by a fast-flowing stream, Aughnanure was one of the strongest fortresses in the country at the time of Cromwell's blockade of Galway during 1652–54.

OUGHTERARD (*Uachtar Árd*, "Upper Height") itself is a small town serving fishing-based tourism, from where you can rent boats on the lough or take a trip to the uninhabited island of **Inchagoill** (boat trip lasts 1hr 30min and costs around £8/€10.16; you can book at the tourist office ☎091/552808 or call Corrib Cruises in Cong ☎092/46029). The island is a magical place, with a couple of evocative ruined churches: St Patrick's and the twelfth-century *Teampall na Naomh* (Church of the Saints), which has interesting carvings and a superb Romanesque doorway. Approached from the east, Oughterard can beguile you into thinking that Connemara is going to be a populated, thriving, developed place, but arriving from the west, it seems a lush, green oasis, the beech trees that line the banks of the river sumptuous and luxuriant after the barren wilds of the bog.

The town's **tourist office** is on Main St (April–Sept daily 9am–6pm; Oct–March Mon–Fri 9am–5.30pm; ☎091/552808). There's no shortage of **B&Bs** in both the centre and the surrounding areas: the popular *Jolly Lodger*, on Bridge St (☎091/552682; ④) is the best option in the centre of town, while on the banks of the Owenriff River is Deirdre Forde's pleasant and comfortable *Camillaun* (☎091/552678; ④). To enjoy the impressive countryside, however, it is preferable to stay in one of the fine houses outside the town, and the best of these include: the elegant *Waterfall Lodge* (☎091/552168; ④), which has private fishing in the grounds and does good child reductions, and *Lakeland Country House* (☎091/552121; ④) just over a mile out of town in Portacarron on the lake shore. There are three fine **hotels** in Oughterard: *Connemara Gateway Hotel* (☎091/552328, *sinnot@iol.ie*; ⑧), which is cosy and welcoming despite its size; the *Corrib House* (☎091/552329; ⑥) whose somewhat basic rooms are more than made up by its warm welcome and open turf fires; and the excellent *Currarevagh House* (☎091/552312; ⑨) set in lush woodland on the Lough Corrib shore. The town's **hostel** *Canrawer House*, signposted from the Clifden end of the main street (☎091/552388; *canrawer@indigo.ie*), is popular with fishermen and travellers alike and is of an impressively high standard; the rooms have en-suite bathrooms, the large well-equipped kitchen is immaculate and the hostel has one of the few Internet points in the area charging £1/€1.27 for ten minutes.

The best place for breakfast is the *Village Rest* on Main Street, a café by day and popular, reasonably priced restaurant by night; a few doors up on Main Street is O'*Fatharta's* which has a similar menu. For an evening meal it's worth trying the excellent **restaurant** beside *River Run Lodge* (☎091/552697); to get there follow Camp Street to the end, turn left over the bridge and the restaurant is on the right.

Oughterard is the starting point of the **Western Way** (approximately 31 miles), which follows the lough shore northwest, heads through the Maam Turks a couple of miles north of Maam and winds up in Leenane. Alternatively, if you want a quick route north, there's a ferry (£12/€15.24 return; same number as for boat trips see p.401) to Cong in County Mayo twice daily during summer.

The main N59 road then takes you through the hamlets of **MAAM CROSS** (*Crois Mám*), where there's a craft shop, petrol station and a pub which serves rather uninspiring **food** all day, and **RECESS**, where all you will find is *Joyce's* bar and shop. Five miles further west, close in under the rugged peaks of the Twelve Bens, is *Ben Lettery An Óige* **hostel**, *Binn Leitrí* Ballinafad (☎095/51136), a cosy haven run by friendly wardens, with a well-stocked shop; its location makes it one of the best spots from which to strike off into the mountains. The nearby castle of **Ballynahinch** was once the home of the land-owning Martin family and is now a hotel with a bar – and food – open to non-residents (☎095/31006, *www.commerce.ie/ballynahinch/*; ⑨). On Ballynahinch lake are the remains of an old O'Flahertie castle, known as Martin's Prison after the use it was put to by Ballynahinch's most famous son, Dick Martin – aka **Humanity Dick** (1754–1834). The story behind the name is that Richard Martin, originally dubbed "Hairtrigger Dick" because of his duelling prowess, spent his adult life campaigning for animal rights, and any tenant he caught causing suffering to animals was thrown into jail in the castle. Dick was known to have fought duels on behalf of threatened animals, and when asked why he did so replied: "Sir, an ox cannot hold a pistol." More constructively, he pushed various acts through parliament protecting farm animals from maltreatment and was instrumental in founding the RSPCA.

West around the coast

The **coast road** is the alternative route west from Galway, passing through the *Gaeltacht* villages of Barna (*Bearna*, "Gap") and **SPIDDAL** (*An Spidéal*, "The hospital"). The Spiddal Craft Centre is a collection of workshops showing high-quality sculpture, ceramics, weaving and jewellery. Spiddal itself can be surprisingly lively for such a tiny, drive-through town. You can catch good sessions in the pubs here; try *Tigh Hughes* or, if you are passing through on a hot day, the beer garden in *An Crúiscán Lán* makes a good place to slake your thirst. Camping is available at *Spiddal Caravan and Camping Park* (*Parc Saoire an Spidéal*); it's off the main road and is well signposted. The *Bridge House Hotel* (☎091/553118; ⑦) is a good upmarket option and there are **B&Bs** aplenty; if you value friendly service and fine food then head straight for *Ardmór Country House*(☎091/553145; ④) where Vera Feeney will take great care of you. Other fine places include *Tuar Beag* (☎091/553422, *tuarbeagbandb@tinet.ie*; ④), *Ard Aobhinn* (☎091/553179; ③), and Maura Ni Chonghaile's *Caladh Gearr Thatch Cottage* (☎091/593124; ③), a pretty, thatched house, three miles out of Spiddal on the road towards Inervin. Travellers looking for budget accommodation here are **strongly** advised to check with the tourist office in Clifden or Galway before booking in at independent hostels in the area.

Beyond **ROSSAVEEL** (*Ros an Mhil*), another departure point for the Aran Islands, the land breaks up into little chains of low-lying islands, linked to one another by natural causeways. These islets, more gentle than the main body of Connemara, make a perfect place to get lost: meandering around the inlets and gullies you experience a happy disorientation.

CARRAROE (*An Cheathrú Rua*) has a strangely suburban feel to it, but the boulder-strewn coast looks across to the Aran Islands, and the beach is made up of tiny fragments of coralline seaweed. *Hotel Carraroe* (*Óstán An Cheathrú Rua*), (☎091/595116; ⑥); is modern and comfortable though a little soulless. For a feel of the place and its people then *Réalt na Maidne* (☎091/595193; ③) which has a bar, a restaurant and **B&B** is a better bet. If this is busy try the modern *Carraroe House* (☎091/595188, *carraroehouse@oceanfree.net*; ③). Near Rosmuc, a speck of a hamlet, is the cottage of the Republican and poet **Pádraig Pearse** (mid-June to mid-Sept daily 9.30am–6.30pm; £1/€1.27; Heritage Card), who signed the 1916 proclamation and was subsequently executed. The cottage is where he wrote short stories, plays and *O'Donovan's Funeral Oration*, and although there is little of real interest inside, its tranquil setting makes it worth a visit. At Carna you can wander out onto Mweenish Island and look out to St Mac Dara's Island, where the remains of a monastery still stand. Such was the former reverence for the saint that fishermen would dip their sails three times when passing the island. A three-day festival, *Féile Mhic Dara*, is still held in July in Carna.

Roundstone

The next place of interest along the coast is **ROUNDSTONE** (*Cloch na Rón*), a fishing village at the foot of the Errisbeg Mountain. Curving its back to the Atlantic, the quaint stone harbour looks across its sheltered waters to the magnificent Twelve Bens of Connemara. Fishing is the main source of income, along with an unobtrusive tourism that makes the most of the unique prettiness of the setting and the glorious beach at Gurteen Bay, one and a quarter miles away to the west. A huge sweep of white sand with lucid blue water, this is really very seductive.

In recent years Roundstone has seen percussionists beating a path to the **workshop** of master **bodhrán maker**, **Malachy Kearns** (May–Oct daily 9am–7pm, Nov–April Mon–Sat 9.30am–6pm; ☎095/35808; free) in the old Franciscan monastery on the edges of the village. The centre shows the techniques Malachy uses to stretch both the 18-inch birch drum frame and the treated goatskin which surrounds it; Malachy's drums are renowned for their perfect tone which produce the haunting, rolling rhythms that form the backdrop to Irish music. There is also a testing room where the uninitiated can happily clamour, while Malachy's wife paints delicate personalized Celtic ornamentations onto the skins of the drum. The centre also has a fine record shop, **craft centre** and coffee shop and is highly recommended. The village itself has several fine craftshops and galleries; look out for the exquisite linen clothes in Dalkey Design Shop or the raw naturalist paintings in the Ivy House Gallery which has a tea room attached.

It's an easy couple of hours' walk from Roundstone up to the top of **Errisbeg** – follow the fuchsia-flooded lane up the side of *O'Dowd's* bar and then the track ahead. The views are panoramic: the frilly coast of isthmuses and islets runs out to the south, while the plain of bog to the north is vast and open, punctuated only by the irregular glinting surfaces of dozens of little lakes. It's through this wilderness that the **bog road** runs, the source of such superstition that some local people will not travel along it at night. Around the turn of the century, two old women, who lived in the road's only dwelling, robbed and murdered a traveller who'd taken refuge with them, and the road is considered to be haunted. From Errisbeg the view across the bog to the Connemara mountain ranges is tremendous. To the west, extensive beaches of white sand scoop their way north – Gurteen, Dog's Bay, Ballyconneely, Bunowen and the coral strand of Mannin Bay – each one echoing the beauty of the last.

There's a **campsite**, the *Gurteen Caravan Site* beside the beach (closed Oct–Feb; ☎095/35882), with laundry facilities, a shop and a tennis court. Several places in the village do **B&B** – try Patricia Keane, *Heather Glen* (☎095/35837, *spkeane@tinet.ie*; ③), or Mrs C. Lowry, *St Josephs* (☎095/35865, *christinalowry@eircom.net*; ③). *Vaughan's House Hotel* (☎095/35864; ⑦) is also a good place to stay. If you don't want to stay in the village itself and feel like splashing out there are two exceptional **hotels** near the village of Cashel, about a fifteen-minute drive away towards Clifden. The first of these is *Zetland House Hotel* (☎095/31111, *www.connemara.net/zetland/*; ⑧), which also has a fine restaurant, but, if you want real indulgence, then follow in the footsteps of Charles de Gaulle and pamper yourself at the *Cashel House Hotel* (☎095/31001, *www.cashel-house-hotel.com*; ⑨), set in award-winning grounds and surely one of the finest places to stay in the country.

For **eating** and drinking while in the village, try *O'Dowd's* which, as well as having a wonderful atmosphere, does fine bar food and has an excellent restaurant attached serving mostly seafood, and *Vaughan's House Hotel* which offers filling bar food. Popular bars are *Connolly's*, *Vaughan's* and *The Hilltop* bar, which has music every night (traditional on Fri & Sat) during the summer. You can buy Camping Gaz bottles and **rent bikes** from Michael Ferron's shop.

Clifden

Because of the dramatic grandeur of the Connemara mountains and the romantic pull of Galway, you expect **CLIFDEN** (*Clochán*, "the stepping stones") – known as the capital of Connemara – to be something special. In fact it's a very small place with only two significant streets. Its great asset is its position, perched high above the deep sides of the boulder-strewn estuary of the River Owenglin. The circling jumble of the Twelve Bens provides a magnificent scenic backdrop, and the broad streets seem consciously to open out to take in the fresh air of the mountains and the Atlantic. Gimlet spires of matching nineteenth-century churches pierce the sky, giving Clifden a sharp, distinctive skyline.

Clifden seems to be trying hard to cultivate the cosmopolitan atmosphere of Galway. Lots of European tourists come here, but, aiming to serve all tastes, the town somehow misses the mark. Bars have loud disco music blaring out onto the streets – exactly the kind of thing most Gaelophile Europeans have come to get away from. It attracts a fair number of young Dubliners, too, revving up the life of this otherwise quiet, rural town. The place is at its most interesting when it's busy being Irish: during the annual **Connemara Pony Show**, for example, on the third Thursday in August. This is for the sale and judging of Connemara ponies, tough, hardy animals that are well suited to a harsh bog and mountain existence, yet renowned for their docile temperament. There's also a community festival in the last week of September.

Arrival, information and accommodation

Clifden is an obvious base if you're hostelling or camping, despite its limitations, and even though the Connemara mountains *look* magnificent from here, they're not at all accessible without transport of one kind or another. Bus Éireann **buses** leave from Market Street, with three buses to Galway daily in the summer and one a day for the rest of the year; Michael Nee Coaches (☎095/51082) also operates a daily service to Galway. The new, well-equipped **tourist office** is part of the development around the old station on the Galway Road (mid-May to June and early Sept to mid-Sept Mon–Sat 10am–6pm; July–Aug Mon–Sat 9am–6pm, Sun 10am–5pm; ☎095/21163).

There's plenty of hotel and B&B **accommodation** in the centre of Clifden, though everything can be very busy in July and August. The best **hotel** in the area is the

Ardagh, Ballyconneely Rd (☎095/21384, *ardaghhotel@eircom.net*; ⑦), a family-run, informal hotel, its relaxed ambience created by candles and scented burners. Other fine hotels include the large, modern *Station House Hotel* (☎095/21699; *station@eircom.net*; ⑥), and *Erriseask House* (☎095/23553, *erriseask@connemara-ireland.com*; ⑥) on the road to Ballyconneely on the shores of Mannin Bay. The best value **B&B** in the area is *Winnowing Hill*, Ballyconneely Rd (☎095/21281; ③), while nearby and also good-value are Maureen Kelly's *Fáilte*, Ardbear, off Ballyconneely Rd (☎095/21159; ④), which does good family reductions, and *Hylands Bay View*, Westport Rd (☎095/21286; ④), which also offers discounts for families and lives up to its name with a sweeping panorama of Streamstown Bay. There are several **hostels** in the centre of town: *The Clifden Town Hostel*, Market St (IHH; ☎095/21076) is by far the best one, and is tastefully decorated with prints by Paul Henry and other well-known Irish artists. Family rooms are available from £35/€44.45 and there is an Internet point in the hostel (£1/€1.27 for 10 minutes). If this is full head back down Market Street where, near the river, is the less comfortable, though adequate, *Brookside Hostel* (IHH; ☎095/21812; ②); the least comfortable option is the independent *Blue Hostel* (☎087/2295654, *tommyrua@aol.com*; ②) at the other end of town near the pier.

There are plenty of places for **bike rental**: try John Mannion, Bridge St (☎095/21160), who also stocks Gaz canisters. There is a Cyberlink **Internet Cafe** (daily 9am–6pm) in the Station House shopping complex off the Galway Road. Clifden's **laundry** is in Main Square. **Pony trekking** is organized at Errislannan Manor (closed Sun; ☎095/21134; £20/€25.40 for one and a half hours), which is about a mile beyond the Alcock and Brown Memorial, south of Clifden on the L102. **Wind-surfing** is available at the boat club, Coast Road. **Dinghy sailing** can be arranged through Clifden Boat Club (☎095/21711 or 087 241 8569; £120/€152.40 for a week-long course) – the setting is superb. The Island House, Market St (☎095/21379, *www.walkingireland.com*), organizes **guided walks** (4–5hr; around £15–20/€19.05–25.40), focusing on the archeology and natural history of Connemara; an excellent way to explore the countryside, especially if you're travelling alone or don't have your own transport.

Eating and drinking

As for **food and drink**, there's no problem getting provisions in Clifden, and the town's two main streets harbour plenty of places to eat. For coffee and home-baked cakes, try either *Walsh's Bakery*, Market Street, or *My Tea Shop* on Main Street. *E.J. King's* pub does cheap soups, salads and conventional bar food and has live music every night throughout summer. Clifden has, of late, gained a reputation for excellent evening dining, due in no small part to the delicious seafood served at *O'Grady's Seafood Restaurant* on Market Square (☎095/21450). *Destry's* (☎095/21722) restaurant/café is a quirky little place with a slightly idiosyncratic menu, though the dishes are immaculately prepared and it's by far the best place for vegetarians to dine.

There are plenty of decent **bars** in Clifden, and several places where you'll find music: for traditional sounds, try *Tom King's*, *Lowry's* or *Barry's Hotel* during the summer, *Mannion's* or *Griffin's* at any time of year. Loud and lively *E.J. King's* on The Square is the likeliest spot for rock 'n' roll and modern folk.

Around Clifden

Clifden offers easy access to some beautiful scenery. To get to the **Twelve Bens** (see p.407) you will need to cycle, hitch or skilfully manipulate the bus service. For more spontaneous walking, take the westward **coast road** out of Clifden (past the *Blue Hostel*) to a fine, sandy beach and a path that follows the shore of Clifden Bay. The shell of a nineteenth-century Gothic castellated mansion that you pass on the way was the home of John D'Arcy, who founded the town. Running north from beside the hostels, what is locally referred to as the **sky road** takes you to more desolate countryside and the long thin inlet of Streamstown Bay. Stick to the road and you'll eventually come down to the little village of Claddaghaduff, where at low tide you can walk across to **Omey Island**. There are excellent beaches here. In the bay three miles north is the little village of **CLEGGAN**, where most people go simply to get the ferry to Inishbofin. However, the village is attractive in itself and may be a better place to stay than the overcrowded Clifden. There are plenty of B&Bs, usually a little cheaper than in Clifden – try *Harbour House* (☎095/44702; ③) or a mile out of town, not far from the beach, is *Cnoc Breac* (☎095/44688; ③).

To the immediate south of Clifden, there's equally pleasant country. A 14ft aeroplane wing carved in limestone sticks out of the bog four miles from Clifden on the Ballyconneely Road, as a melodramatic memorial to the landing of **Alcock and Brown** at the end of their pioneering non-stop transatlantic flight in June 1919. Beyond this is the coral strand of Mannin Bay, excellent for swimming, as is that at Doonlonghan.

Inishbofin

The island of **INISHBOFIN** is a mellow, balmy place, quite different from the mainland. It's more fertile, with sheltered sandy beaches, and there's a general softness to its contours. The only jagged features are the cliffs to the west (the *Stags*), a fine vantage point for viewing seals basking on the shore. Even the high, heathery moorland soon gently descends to the placid **Lough Boffin**, rimmed with rustling water iris and bullrushes. The lough is the scene of the island's most durable **myth**, a story that explains how it got its name. Several versions of the tale exist, but the basic elements are constant. For eons the island lay shrouded in mist under the spell of an enchantment, but one day two lost fishermen came upon it and lit a fire by the shore, thus breaking the spell. As the mist cleared, they saw an old woman driving a white cow along the strand. She hit it with a stick and was instantly turned to rock. Taking her for a witch, the men hit her and they too immediately turned to rock: *Inis Bó Finne* means "Island of the White Cow".

The known **history** of the island starts in the seventh century, when St Colman arrived here from Iona after a quarrel with Rome over the method of calculating the date of Easter. No remains exist of the monastery he founded, but ruins of a thirteenth-century church stand on the original site in a sheltered vale beside the lake in the east. Later the island was taken over by the O'Flaherties, and then Grace O'Malley is supposed to have fortified the place for her fleet. Coming into the island's long protected harbour you'll see the remains of a sixteenth-century castle, low on the hummocky terrain. It was taken and strengthened yet further by Cromwell, who used Inishbofin – and other west coast islands – as a kind of concentration camp for clerics. The most chilling reminder of his barbarity is the rock visible in the harbour at low tide. Known as

TRANSPORT TO INISHBOFIN

You can visit Inishbofin on a day-trip from Clifden, even without a car. Take the bus to **CLEGGAN** (summer Tues & Fri 8am, returning 7.50pm; check with driver). A private bus leaves the square at 11am daily in summer. **Ferry** tickets are available at King's store, Cleggan, Inishbofin Ferry Office on Market Street, Clifden, or Clifden tourist information office for sailings on *The Island Discovery* (April–Sept; £12/€15.24 return), departing Cleggan 11.30am & 6.45pm, with an extra sailing at 10am and 2pm during July and August; departing Inishbofin April to September 9.30am and 5pm, with an extra 1pm sailing in July and August. In winter there's a boat approximately once a week (☎095/44642).

Bishop's Rock, it was here that Cromwell chained one unfortunate ecclesiastic, then let his troops watch the tide come slowly in and drown him.

Practicalities

Both *Day's Bofin House* (closed Oct–Easter; ☎095/45809; ④) and *Doonmore Hotel* (closed Oct–Easter; ☎095/45804; ④) offer standard rooms with magnificent sea views (be sure to secure a south-facing room in *Day's*); both have restaurants open to non-residents, and also serve good **bar food**. If you want to book **B&B**, try *Regina King* (☎095/45833; ②), though book early to secure her en-suite room, or *Hybrazil* (☎095/45817; ③) which has decent rooms with shared bathrooms. The *Inishbofin Island Hostel* (closed Oct–March; IHH; ☎095/45855) is an extremely friendly and well-run place; private rooms are available for £20/€25.40. *Miko's* **pub** is very friendly and has **music sessions** any time of the week during the summer season and at weekends in winter. There's an island shop, with the usual limitations on supplies, and *Miko's* pub will change travellers' cheques.

You can **camp** on any of the open common land. A particularly good spot is at the east end of the island at Rusheen beach, from where you're treated to the glorious sight of the Connemara mountains lurching into the sea. The only places that are dangerous for swimming are at Tra Geall, just beneath Doonmore, opposite the island of Inishark in the west.

The Connemara National Park

The **Connemara National Park** typifies the scenic splendour of west Galway. Its chief functions are to promote the area's natural beauty while conserving this area of bog, heath and granite mountains. The park includes part of the famous **Twelve Bens** range – Benbaun, Benbrack, Bencullagh, and Muckanaght – all of which are for experienced walkers only. Less threatening are the spectacular Polldark River gorge and Glanmore Valley, and the multifaceted granite Diamond Hill – though problems of soil erosion here have led the park to discourage a walk to the top: ask at the visitor centre for the current state of play.

The park's **visitor centre** near Letterfrack (May–Sept daily 9.30am–6pm; £2/€2.54; ☎095 41054; Heritage Card), is an excellent source of information on the fauna, flora and geology of the area; there's an exhibition on ten thousand years of Connemara, which takes in peatland and the changing landscape. It's also the focus for the bogland conservation work that's going on in the area, and the herbarium here is worth looking at if you're interested in botany. The staff can suggest safe hiking routes of varying length and difficulty, and you can leave details of your own route and intended time of return – an invaluable service in this potentially hazardous landscape. The centre has kitchen facilities available for walkers, an indoor "picnic" area and a tearoom. In July and August a botanist leads a guided walk of about two and a half hours, currently leaving at 10.30am on Monday, Wednesday and Friday, though it's wise to ring and check the schedule. As well as offering facilities to outsiders, the centre is doing much to raise local awareness of the value of the area as a tourist amenity.

Letterfrack and around

LETTERFRACK itself is an orderly nineteenth-century Quaker village in a rugged setting. The village is tiny, but there's good **food** (especially wholefood and cheeses), and occasionally music, at *Veldon's* and discos in *The Bard's Den* (Fri & Sat). In the east end of town is the thatched restaurant, *Pangur Bán*, which has an attractive, eclectic menu including delicious tempura, though for a real culinary treat try *Rosleague Manor* (☎095/41101), which serves wholesome and filling traditional food in elegant surroundings. There's also a post office, phone, shop and bureau de change and the lovely, rambling independent *Old Monastery* hostel (IHH; ☎095/41132, *oldmon@indigo.ie*) with **camping**, bike rental and great food; breakfasts of baked scones and porridge are included in the price, and dinners are also available. It makes a perfect base for walking in the national park. **Bog Week** (the weekend leading up to the first Monday in June) and **Sea Week** (the weekend leading up to the last Monday in October) see Letterfrack at its liveliest, when a heady mix of conservationists and musicians descend upon the place for field trips, conferences and sessions.

Two miles east of here, the neo-Gothic towers of **Kylemore Abbey** sit in a rhododendron-filled hollow against lush deciduous slopes. Its white castellated outline, perfectly reflected in the reed-punctured lake, has made it the subject of many a postcard. It's home to Irish Benedictine nuns and houses a girls' boarding school, but the library and entrance hall are freely accessible, and there's an exhibition telling the history of Kylemore (Easter–Oct daily 9am–5.30pm; £3.30/€4.19). A stroll through the woods leads to the Gothic church, a small-scale copy of Norwich Cathedral built in 1868. The abbey also has an impressive heritage shop and restaurant.

Renvyle House, some eight miles northwest of Kylemore Abbey, is of immense interest in Irish literary and political history. At one time it was visited by the great Edwardian comic twosome Somerville and Ross, authors of *Stories of an Irish R.M.*, but the house's most famous owner was Oliver St John Gogarty, the distinguished surgeon, writer and wit. An associate of the Gaelic League, he attended the literary evenings of Yeats, Moore and AE (George Russell), and is immortalized as "stately plump Buck Mulligan" in Joyce's *Ulysses*. *Renvyle House* is now a hotel (☎095/43511 or 43444, *www.renvyle.com*; ⑥) offering facilities – which are also available to non-residents – such as horse riding, wind-surfing and a swimming pool. About a mile west of the hotel lies a ruined O'Flahertie **castle**, superbly positioned overlooking the sea. On Derryniver Bay, one mile west of Renvyle is the Ocean's Alive Aquarium and Visitor's Centre (☎095/43473; £3/€3.81), featuring a reconstructed traditional cottage, a mini farm and a short coastal walk where you can examine old fishing boats.

Killary Harbour and around

The coast road to the east of Renvyle offers magnificent scenery, a great route for the hostel at **KILLARY HARBOUR**, if you are cycling, and some lovely beaches. Inland, the N59 route to Killary Harbour from Letterfrack is faster and similarly beautiful. The lightly wooded shore around Ballinakill Harbour provides a brief luxuriant interlude before the landscape of wild bog and granite reasserts itself with ever increasing austerity. The An Óige **hostel** at Killary (closed Oct–Feb; ☎095/43417), where Wittgenstein finished writing his *Philosophical Investigations* in 1948, has a deeply ponderous setting at the mouth of Ireland's only fjord, a cold dark tongue of water which cuts eight miles into the barren mountains. The hostel, while old fashioned, is warm and friendly and makes a wonderful sanctuary; to get there follow the signposts from the N59, though be warned, it makes for five miles of extremely difficult hitching, so be prepared to walk. There's a shop at the hostel open evenings; otherwise you have to go to Lettergesh shop and post office. From the hostel walk south, past the adventure centre, then take the right turn before the crest of the hill, and keep on for about one and a quarter miles; the shop is the first big house on the left, with a phone box outside. There are good sandy beaches in the vicinity.

Further east, **LEENANE** is most famous as a location for shooting *The Field*, and stills from the film hang on the walls of *Gaynor's Bar*. It's also a finishing (or starting) point for the Western Way. Leenane Cultural Centre (April–Sept; £2/€2.54) explores the history of wool, with spinning and weaving demonstrations and a collection of various sheep outside – if you've an interest, it's very enjoyable, and there's a good tea shop, too. Beside the bright pink, though otherwise unspectacular, *Leenane Hotel* is the *Killary View Coffee House* which does fine coffees and has one of the few Internet points in the area. For **B&B** try Mrs Wallace's *Avondale House* (☎095/42262; ③), or Mrs Roberts' *Sancta Maria* (☎095/42250; ②), while for somewhere a little more expensive there's the superb *Killary Lodge Country Home* (☎095/42276, *www.killary.com;* ⑥), an old hunting and fishing lodge down by the harbour. If you're heading towards Cong in County Mayo (p.426), the desolate road takes you through Maum and on past *Corr na Mona Hostel* on the shores of Lough Corrib (closed Nov–March; IHH; ☎092/48002), just nine miles from Cong.

COUNTY MAYO

Often seen as simply a passage between scenic Galway and literary Yeats country, **County Mayo** is little visited – though it's hard to see why. Like Galway to the south and Sligo to the north, it has a landscape of high cliffs, lonely mountains and bright fuchsia hedges; in the wild, boggy area to the northwest are the vestiges of a *Gaeltacht*; and on Lough Conn there's some of the best fishing in Ireland. The Georgian town of **Westport**, an elegantly urban playground for travellers needing a break from the dazzling lights and landscapes of the wild west, is the only place that's really on the international tourist trail. **Achill Island**, the biggest of the Irish offshore islands and a traditional Irish family holiday resort, has an oddly fly-blown air that won't suit everyone. Some of the most exciting country, however, is the little-travelled northwest. The interpretive centre at **Ceide** holds the key to understanding a landscape that's hardly changed for millennia. The area is easily accessible: the railway will take you right out to Westport, and there's an international airport at **Knock** (with cheap flights designed for pilgrims to the shrine of the Virgin Mary). Furthermore the whole of the county is magical cycling country. Mayo is bound to become busier, but for the moment it remains wonderfully empty.

The Barony of Murrisk and Clare Island

If you're travelling by road, you'll probably enter Mayo from Galway, via the spectacular scenery of Killary Harbour, part of the lobe of land between the Galway border and Westport that's known as the **Barony of Murrisk**. This is country as rugged and remote as anything you'll find in the west, and two ranges of hills, the Mweelrea Mountains and the Sheefry Hills, provide terrain for energetic walking, mountaineering, riding, fishing and canoeing. The coast road passes through the villages of **Delphi** and **Louisburgh** which, along with the deserted **Clare Island**, are closely associated with the belligerent pirate Queen Grace O'Malley (see p.415). Before reaching the lively town of **Westport** the road skirts the foot of **Croagh Patrick** mountain, the scene of an annual pilgrimage honouring the country's national saint.

Delphi and Louisburgh

The road due north from Killary threads along a narrow valley which opens up, briefly, for a famous salmon and sea-trout lough-fishery with the unlikely name of **DELPHI** (in the local pronunciation, *Delph-eye*). The story behind the name involves the first Marquess of Sligo, whose seat, misleadingly, was at Westport. The flamboyant Marquess, a friend of Lord Byron, was caught in the sway of romantic Hellenism and in 1811 set sail for Greece to search for antiquities. He swam the Hellespont with Byron and rode with him overland to Corinth; but when he got to Delphi, he suffered a bout of homesickness, finding that it reminded him of nothing so much as his fishery at home in County Mayo. After numerous adventures, and some pillaging of ancient sites, the Marquess returned home to reminisce. Nowadays, there's an **adventure centre** at Delphi (☎095/42307), offering supervised instruction in anything from wind-surfing and canoeing to abseiling and mountaineering, and **pony trekking** is based at the Drumindoo Stud (☎098/66195). More important for people of a more sedentary disposition, there's also a **hostel** and a comfortable, glassed-in coffee shop where you can sit and gaze out as the cloud creeps down the slopes of Mweelrea and Ben Gorm. Luxurious **accommodation**, excellent cuisine, plus a taste of the area's history, can be had at the *Delphi Lodge* (closed Nov–Dec; ☎095/42211, *www.delphilodge.ie*; ⑤), an 1830s sporting lodge by the lake, built for the Marquess of Sligo in a surprisingly austere Neoclassical style.

North of Delphi, the road runs alongside sombre **Doo Lough**, also known as the Black Lake, and over desolate moorland before reaching **LOUISBURGH** (pronounced *Lewis-burg*). This is one of the few instances where a town this side of the Atlantic has been named after one on the other: it was renamed after Henry Browne, uncle of the first Marquess of Sligo, had taken part in the capture of Louisburgh, Nova Scotia, in 1758. Louisburgh is essentially little more than a crossroads, but its planned buildings give it an incongruous air of importance, and it's a pleasant enough place to stay. The Granuaile Centre (June–Aug Mon–Sat 10am–7.30pm; ☎098/66341; £2.50/€3.17) details the exploits of Grace O'Malley, the pirate queen (see p.415), and has an audiovisual display and local tourist information (it is advisable to call before arriving as the opening hours can be erratic). There is also an exhibition on the Great Famine, as this area suffered heavily from 1845–49: there's a harrowing tale about the march of six hundred starving locals in 1849 to Delphi Lodge to beg, unsuccessfully, for famine relief; many of them, weak and ill-clothed, died on the return journey amid the uncompromising scenery of Doo Lough. This event is commemorated annually in the Great Famine Walk (enquire at the centre for details).

Louisburgh makes a good base for exploring the sandy **beaches** that run along the north coast as far as Murrisk Abbey. One of the best places for **food** is *The River Cafe* in Bridge St (on the left as you cross the bridge from Delphi) which serves tasty home-made soups and salads. There are any number of excellent **B&Bs** around the area; try the excellent, family-friendly *Springfield House* (☎098/66289; ③) or two miles out of town is the modern *Three Arches* (☎098/66484; ③) which also has good family rates. Just outside Louisburgh, at **OLD HEAD** (on the Westport Road), there's a **campsite** with showers and laundry (closed Sept–May; ☎098/66021). Old Head has a good **beach**, though little can compare with the nearby **Silver Strand** beach, claimed grandiosely in the local tourist leaflets to be second only to Florida's Key West; it is, incidentally, the site of a mass Famine burial. You can reach it by turning southwest at the crossroads just outside Louisburgh on the Killary Road along lanes that pick their way through rolling country rich in megalithic monuments, with a clear view out to Clare Island, Inishmore and the smaller islets; it has a couple of **B&Bs** – *Silver Strand House* (☎098/68730; ③) is homely and comfortable and offers evening meals of local seafood.

Clare Island

Follow the road from Louisburgh west along the strand to the land's tip, and you reach **Roonagh Quay**, where a boat leaves three times a day for **CLARE ISLAND**. (The bus from Westport runs at least twice a day and will drop you two miles away in

Louisburgh.) The crossing takes 25 minutes; boats leave Roonagh at 11.00 am, 2.15pm and 6pm. The most reliable place to get information about the ferry is at the *Bay View Hotel* (☎098/26307); fares are £10/€12.70 return. Although it's tiny – only fifteen or so square miles – Clare Island rises to a height of 1522ft in a massive shoulder of land that dominates everything around. There's not much here besides the hills, some ruins and some unfrequented sandy beaches, but there's plenty of walking, and you can go pony trekking, or water-ski, sailboard or fish (see below).

The island is famed above all as the stronghold of **Grace O'Malley** (see p.415). Her massive castle is at the eastern end of the island. Also at the eastern end of the island, she – or a close relative – is buried in a tomb on the north side of the ruined thirteenth-century Cistercian abbey.

You can **stay** overnight on Clare Island, at the *Bay View Hotel* (☎098/26307; ⑤), which also organizes local watersports and operates the ferry.

Croagh Patrick and Murrisk Abbey

The land between Louisburgh and Westport is dominated by the strange, perfectly conical silhouette of **Croagh** (pronounced *Croak*) **Patrick**, which at 2513ft is by far the highest mountain in the immediate area. The sandy beaches of the shore peter out at Bertra Strand, just short of Murrisk and the ruins of **Murrisk Abbey**, a house of Augustinian canons set up on the shore of Clew Bay by the O'Malley family in 1457, less than a hundred years before Henry VIII's dissolution of the monasteries.

Looking out over the hummocky islets of the bay, the abbey is the best starting point if you want to climb the mountain. On the landward side, a little saint's head carved in the wall peers glumly up the slope – it's a very tough **climb**. Still, there's a surprise when you get to the top. The summit isn't conical, as it looks from the bottom, but forms a flat plateau, with a little chapel and a breathtaking view: on a good day you can see right from the Twelve Bens in the south to the mountains of Achill Island in the north, the Nephin Begs east of the island and on to the Slieve League in Donegal.

At the foot of the mountain on the shore side of the road is the national monument to *an nGórta Mór* (the Great Famine); the bronze sculpture, by John Behan, is of a coffin ship headed for America, its rigging made up of the skeletons of the starving and is particularly evocative when lit up at night. For accommodation in the area follow the road beside the statue to *Ceann Cúrsa B&B*, Pier Rd (☎098/64864; ③), which has family rooms and does good vegetarian breakfasts.

A fine place to stop for **refreshments** after a climb up the mountain, barefoot or not, is *Glosh House*, a restaurant overlooking the sea and specializing in seafood and vegetarian dishes. It also does Irish breakfasts and sustaining afternoon teas.

ST PATRICK AND THE SNAKE

In 441, **St Patrick** spent the forty days of Lent on Croagh Patrick in prayer and fasting, and it's from here that he is supposed to have sent the reptiles of Ireland crawling to their doom. Just to the south of the summit is the **precipice of Lugnanarrib**, where he stood, ringing his bell, then repeatedly hurled it over the edge, each time taking with it a stream of toads, snakes and other creepy-crawlies. Luckily he didn't have to go down to the bottom to get his bell back – helpful spirits did the job for him. There's a pilgrimage to the top of Croagh Patrick, which is carried out by some sixty thousand people, some of them in bare feet, every year on the last Sunday of July.

Westport

"The islands in the bay which was of gold colour, look like so many dolphins and whales basking there," wrote the English novelist W.M. Thackeray on a visit to Westport in 1842. Set in a picturesque eighteenth-century landscape on the shores of Clew Bay, **WESTPORT**, is a comfortable, relaxed town, still recognizably Georgian – it was planned by the architects Richard Castle and James Wyatt – with a leafy mall, octagonal square, a canalized river and one of Ireland's great stately homes, Westport House. For the past ten years, it has capitalized on its fine architecture and busy urban buzz to offer some elegant town living in the midst of the wild scenery of the remote west. During summer, the place is tremendously lively, with Irish, British, French and German visitors returning annually to resample its charms, and a couple of excellent festivals.

In its heyday the town was extremely prosperous, fattened by the trade in linen and cotton cloth and yarn. However, like many places throughout Ireland, Westport was hit hard by the Act of Union of 1801. Although local landowners like the first Marquess of Sligo supported the Act in the belief that it would be of economic benefit, the reverse was in fact true: Irish hand looms were no competition for the new spinning jennies in Britain's industrial towns, the national linen and cotton industries declined, and Westport's economy was ruined. Mass unemployment forced a choice between reverting to subsistence farming or starting a new life in America.

Its quiet Georgian beauties and its lively modern streetlife apart, the reason Westport is on the tourist trail nowadays is **Westport House** (June daily 1.30–5.30pm; July & Aug Mon–Fri 11.30am–5.30pm, Sat & Sun 1.30–5.30pm; Sept house only daily 2–5pm; *www.westporthouse.ie*; house £6/€7.62, children's pass for house, animal and bird park and amusements £7.50/€9.52), a mile or so out of town towards Clew Bay. Built on the site of one of the castles of the sixteenth-century pirate queen Grace O'Malley (a direct ancestor of the current owner; see p.415), Westport House was beautifully designed in 1730 by the ubiquitous Richard Castle, with later additions by Thomas Ivory and James Wyatt. This was one of the first Irish houses opened to the public – and it's had a go at any and every way of making money. There's a bird and animal park in the grounds, a water slide, bouncy castle and mini-railway for the kids plus horse-drawn caravans for rent, while the dungeons (which belonged to an earlier house) have everything from a trace-your-ancestor service to ghostly sound-effects; the loos are billed, with some welcome self-irony, "Westport House Toilet Centre". On the plus side, though, the delicate response of the house to its luminous surroundings of land, light and water is undimmed and wonderful if you can ignore the commerce – and feel like shelling out the swingeing admission fee.

Inside the house there's a *Holy Family* by Rubens, a violin which used to belong to J.M. Synge and, on the first floor, a room with lovely Chinese wallpapers dating from 1780. A lot of the mahogany in the house was brought back from Jamaica by the first marquess, who was instrumental in freeing slaves during his time as governor there. On the walls of the staircase, a series of paintings of local views by James Arthur O'Connor, commissioned by the second marquess in 1818 and 1819, shows an idyllic nineteenth-century landscape, an overweeningly romantic version of the dramatic scenery at Delphi and bustling activity as sailing boats are unloaded at Westport Quay. This was wishful thinking – Westport in the 1810s was already overshadowed by the changes in the relationship with England, and by 1825 was finished as an industrial centre.

Further out on The Quay, the Clew Bay heritage centre (Mon–Fri 10am–6pm, Sat–Sun 2–6pm; £2/€2.54) – an engaging but chaotic jumble of old coins, agricultural implements, typewriters, ration books and other detritus – fails to live up to its grandiose title.

Practicalities

The new, informative **tourist office** midway down James St (April–June & Sept Mon–Sat 9am–6pm; July & August daily 9am–6pm; Oct–March Mon–Fri 9am–5.15pm; ☎098/25711) has an abundance of information, a fine selection of local historical and walking books plus a good gift shop. Daytime activities, sightseeing apart, are plentiful. If you're lucky with the weather the best **beaches** are at Bertra, six miles out on the Louisburgh Road, and Mulrany, eighteen miles away on the Achill Road. **Cycling** from Westport is rewarding, if strenuous – there are hills in almost all directions except towards Newport: **bike rental** is from Sean Sammon on James St (☎098/25471; £6/€7.44 per day), or the *Old Mill Hostel* (see below). **Walking** in the nearby Sheefry Hills or Dartry Mountains can be spectacular – pick up Paul Simms and Tony Wyatt's *Northwest Walks* at the tourist office or in any of the local bookshops. **Horse riding**, which will let you get right off the road, is available half a mile out of town on the Castlebar Road at the Drummindoo Equitation Centre (☎098/25616), and also at Westport House. The **sea angling** in Clew Bay is magnificent, and there are also good opportunities for salmon and trout fishing in nearby lakes and rivers – details from the Sea Angling Centre in town. **Sailing** in sheltered waters can be arranged through the Mayo Sailing Club in Rosmoney (☎098/26160) who offer good facilities and lessons for newcomers.

Accommodation

Although you may be put off by the olde-worlde pretensions of the *Olde Railway Hotel* (☎098/25166, *www.anu.ie/railwayhotel*; ⑤), its abundance of Victorian artefacts and its location opposite the canalized river on the leafy Mall, make it the top choice of hotels in the town; of the two central **hotels**, the *Knockranny House Hotel* (☎098/28595, *knockranny@anu.ie*; ④) is the better, though the friendly *Clew Bay Hotel* (☎098/28088; *www.clewbay.anu.ie*; ④) is also worth considering. There are also dozens of **B&Bs**: try Mrs Sheridan at *Altamont House*, Ballinrobe Rd (☎098/25226; ③); *Carrabaun House* (☎098/26196, *carrabaun@anu.ie*; ③), half a mile out of town on the Leenane Road; or *Cedar Lodge*, Kings Hill (☎098/25417, *mflynn@esatclear.ie*; ③). Out at The Quay, the *Helm* bar has pleasant rooms (☎098/26194; ②); make sure to ask for one facing the bay. A terrace of newly built **self-catering cottages** on the quayside blends in very effectively with the eighteenth-century architecture around it (☎098/25511).

For cheap accommodation, you've a choice of one An Óige and three independent **hostels**. The newest and most central is the fine, independent *Old Mill Hostel* on James St, up from the Octagon (IHH; ☎098/27045, fax 21745), converted from part of an eighteenth-century complex of mills and warehouses; bike rental is available here. The large *Club Atlantic*, opposite the train station on Altamont Street, and very close to Fair Green where buses stop (closed Nov to mid-March; ☎098/26644, fax 26241), is affiliated with both An Óige and the IHH and is very well run and maintained. If these two are full you can try either the stone-built *Granary*, past *Ryan's Hotel* on Quay Road just before the road forks (☎098/25903), or the cramped *Slí na hÓige*, on the Fair Green (☎098/26459). For **camping**, try the Westport Estate *Parklands Caravan and Camping Park* (closed Sept–April; ☎098/27766), or there's more camping further out at Old Head.

Eating

There is a surprising variety of **places to eat** in Westport at all ends of the market. *The Lemon Peel* just off the Octagon (☎098/26929), has deservedly gained a good reputation locally by imaginatively improvising with traditional ingredients; the cod steak served on a crab mash with a sweet basil sauce is especially recommended. Two restaurants with similar menus are *Torinos*, through the arch beside Spectrum Video store on Bridge Street (last seating is early at 9.45pm), and *Sol Rios*, also on Bridge Street, opposite *Matt Molloys* pub; both serve pasta and pizza dishes. The *Quay Cottage* (☎098/26412), in a stone building near the harbour, is the place to go for seafood and also has a fine vegetarian menu, while nearby the *Asgard* (☎098/25319) has a delicious bar menu. *Antica Roma*, on Bridge Street, is highly recommended for cheap pizzas and fish and chips. For coffee, homemade soup or fine sandwiches try *Tiley's*, opposite the tourist office on James Street. If you're self-catering, you can find some excellent local produce, much of it organic, at the **Thursday market** at the Octagon.

Festivals and nightlife

Westport is fast developing a real cosmopolitan feel and attracting artistic types from Ireland and beyond. The main focuses for this are the **Arts Festival** at the middle of September, and the public art studios in the redeveloped area of The Quay, by the entrance to Westport House. In the centre, the best **music pubs** are on Bridge Street, where *The West* is hugely popular (arrive early and stay put) and *Matt Molloy's Bar*, owned by the eponymous flautist of *The Chieftains*, features occasional musical celebrities though is incredibly crowded throughout the summer. The *Castle Court Hotel* features dancing on both a Friday and Saturday night, while on a Wednesday it holds a cabaret and ceilidh. The *Towers* pub, overlooking Clew Bay has traditional music most nights. If you want to enjoy a quiet drink then *Conway's* on Bridge Street is the place to go.

Newport

The road north out of Westport, bordered by bright fuchsia hedges, follows the shore of Clew Bay eight miles to **NEWPORT**, a neat, trim little eighteenth-century town unashamedly devoted to tourism and a serviceable base for both the sea and the Nephin Beg Mountains. Newport's main boast is that one of Grace Kelly's ancestors once lived in nearby Drimurla. It's also a centre for sea angling; if you go in the evening to the swanky *Newport House Hotel*, you'll see massive sea trout – caught by guests earlier in the day – laid out for the less energetic to admire.

About two miles outside Newport and signposted off the road to Achill is **Burrishoole Abbey**, a Dominican priory in a peaceful setting, lapped by the waters of the bay – at high tide you have to hop across a stepping stone to get in. Founded in the fifteenth century by Richard Burke – second husband of the pirate queen Grace O'Malley and unfortunately nicknamed "Iron Dick" – who spent the last years of his life here. The abbey has some cloisters still surviving and stands as a symbol of the spread of religious life under the Normans. Another mile or so along the Achill Road, the turning labelled "Carrickanowley Castle" brings you to **Rockfleet Castle**, a perfect fifteenth- or sixteenth-century tower house that stands with its feet in a quiet outlet of Clew Bay – you'll get your feet wet stepping up to the door at high tide. An English attack on it was quelled by Grace O'Malley, who subsequently lived here.

The **tourist office** is on Main St (☎098/41822) and is open weekdays from June to September. For upmarket **accommodation** in Newport, there's the *Newport House Hotel* (☎098/41222; ⑥). *De Bille House* B&B on the main street (☎098/41195; ③) is a handsome stone building which offers generously sized rooms that are a good option for families. The house is named after a Danish sea-captain who was shipwrecked en route for the Danish West Indian Isles in 1782; he and his crew were rescued, but subsequently died of a fever. You can still see the house in which he was nursed in the back yard. There's **self-catering** accommodation at Loch Morchan at Kilbride, just outside Newport (☎098/41221). Good, basic **food** is available from *Kelly's Kitchen* on the main street and *The Black Oak Inn* across the bridge, but for sumptuous dining the only

GRACE O'MALLEY: THE PIRATE QUEEN

There came to me also a most famous feminine sea captain called Granny Ny Mally and offered her services unto me, wheresoever I would command her, with three galleys and two hundred fighting men, either in Scotland or in Ireland. She brought with her her husband, for she was as well by sea as by land well more than Mrs Mate with him.... This was a notorious woman in all the coasts of Ireland.

Sir Henry Sidney, Lord Deputy of Ireland, 1577

Grace O'Malley, or Gráinne Ní Mháille (circa 1530–1600; often corrupted to **Granuaile**), was the daughter of Owen O'Malley, chief of the west coast islands. Through fearless and none-too-scrupulous warfare and piracy, she made herself queen of the Clew Bay area when he died. She effectively controlled the vigorous trade between Galway and the Continent, as well as running a lucrative business importing Scottish mercenaries for chieftains' wars against Elizabeth I and their cattle-rustling and plundering activities. She earned her place in Irish legend by being one of the few Irish chiefs to stand up to the English.

In 1575, she visited the St Lawrences of Howth Castle near Dublin (see p.109), expecting to be made welcome in the Irish fashion. When, instead, she was told that the family was eating and that she would have to wait, she responded by abducting the family's heir. When she met Elizabeth I in London in 1593, she insisted on being treated as her regal equal. However, always a canny tactician, Grace switched sides when she realized she couldn't beat the English, and her son was created first Viscount Mayo. Continually mentioned in sixteenth-century dispatches, her exploits included dissolving her Celtic secular marriage to her second husband, Sir Richard Burke of Mayo, by slamming the castle door in his face and then stealing all his castles. At a time when the old Gaelic world was crumbling around her, Grace ensured the continuation of her own dynasty and something of the old culture.

place is *Newport House* (☎098/41222) which specializes in hearty five-course meals using mostly locally caught fish. **Drinking** itself is best done at *Cowley's Singing Lounge* or at the *Angler's Rest*, which also does traditional music and good food.

Five miles away, high among the powerful outlines of the Nephin Beg Mountains – take the Achill Road and follow the signs – is the An Óige **hostel**, *Traenlaur Lodge* at Lough Feeagh (closed Oct–Easter; ☎096/13272), a hefty climb but well worth it to stay in an unparalleled location at the head of this upland lake – and a perfect base for **walking** in the area (see p.418 for details of the long-distance Bangor Trail); a taxi up here from Newport will cost no more than £5/€6.35 (☎087/220 2123). For **horse riding** and pony trekking the contact is ☎098/36126; permits for **fishing** are available from the *Newport House Hotel*.

The road northwest towards Achill runs, for the most part, too far inland for the glories of Clew Bay to be visible; but it's always worth making detours down the lanes that lead to the water's edge.

Achill Island

More than with most places in the west, you need good weather for **ACHILL ISLAND**. Although it's the part of County Mayo most developed for tourism, this means no more than a few hotels, B&Bs and hostels, and if it rains there's simply nothing to do but pack up and head for Westport or Sligo. Because of a government tax allowance scheme Achill has been blighted by a plethora of tourist developments many of which are modern "cottages" that take no account of traditional architecture or landscape. Against

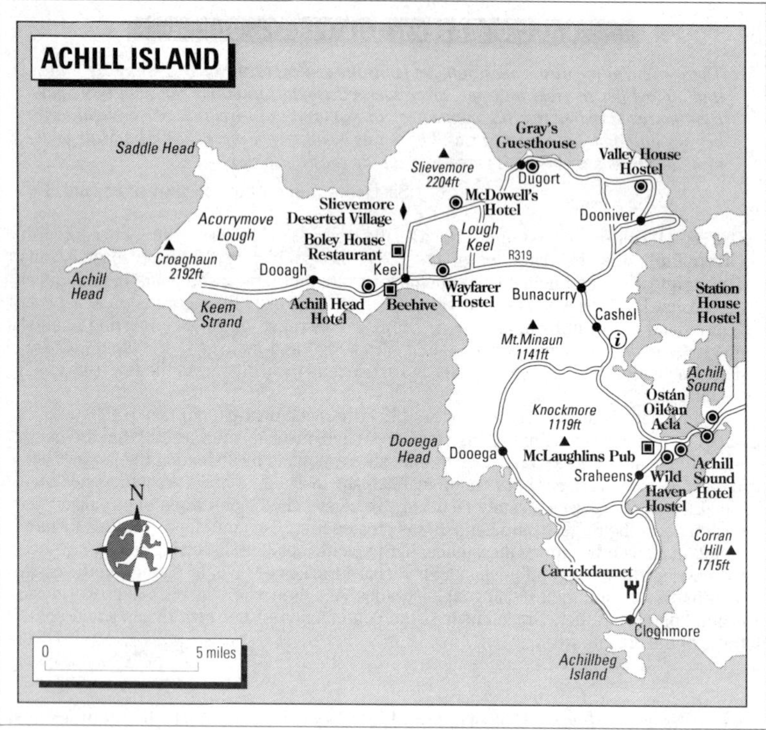

this, however, there's the magnificence of the mountains and cliffs, and in good weather, Achill can be magical, especially for campers who can live at the water's edge. The island's sandy beaches never seem overcrowded, although they attract plenty of (mostly Irish) tourists in high summer. Inland, the bogs and mountains are dotted with ancient relics – standing stones, stone circles and dolmens. The largest of the Irish islands (although it's connected to the mainland by a road bridge), Achill was Irish-speaking until very recently. Tourism here seems to have had an almost entirely beneficial effect, economically at least: before its arrival, islanders subsisted to a very great extent on remittances sent home by emigrant relatives.

Achill Sound

The bridge that crosses to the island will bring you first to **ACHILL SOUND**. It's worth noting though, that on the left before crossing the bridge stands a fine new **hotel**, *Óstán Oiléan Acla* (☎098/45138, *www.achillislandhotel.com*; ⑤) which has an excellent seafood restaurant offering fine views of the bay, and a lively bar that often has traditional music in the evening. Also before the bridge, opposite the Garda Station, you'll find the *Station House Hostel* (☎098/45187), with good rooms, two kitchens and an open fire. On crossing the bridge, faded beachballs and plastic buckets hang forlornly outside a cluster of souvenir shops; there's a post office and bike rental at *Óstán gob A'choire*, aka *Achill Sound Hotel* (☎098/45245; ③) which, like the souvenir shops, has seen better and busier days. Achill Sound really isn't the best base for exploring the island, but if you decide to go no further, it's worth pressing on a few hundred yards for an excellent independent **hostel**, the *Wild Haven* (☎098/45392), which does offer the comforts of warm duvets and an open fire.

Around the island

A combination of **walking** and **cycling** is the most pleasurable way to get to know Achill, although the island can be fairly strenuous going (hitching is a viable alternative, especially in season when the island is full of visitors). The road that encircles the island has now been signposted as the "Atlantic Drive". After a left turn, you'll follow a narrow inlet of the sea for three miles, before coming to **KILDOWNET**, where the well-preserved tower of the fifteenth-century **Carrickdaunet Castle**, once owned by the redoubtable Grace O'Malley, gazes out at the mainland (keys from the house next door). There are also the ruins of a twelfth-century church. As you round the corner of the island, the view of the ocean opens up, and the massive shoulder of **Minaun**, Achill's third highest mountain, appears. The road then winds and undulates its way further west through the villages of **Keel** and **Dooagh** to the strand at **Keem**, whose exotic appearance defies its geography on the north western fringe of Europe. The north of the island is dominated by the imposing **Slievemore** on whose grey slopes a dolmen and a group of standing stones have weathered the Atlantic winds for nearly four thousand years, while nearby is the island's deserted village, once used as a base for summer herdsmen.

Keel and Dooagh

At **KEEL**, there's a wonderful two-mile sandy **beach**, which ends at the twin village of Dooagh. At the Keel end of the strand are the fantastic Cathedral Rocks, eroded into a series of caves and pillars by the wind and water. They are backed by **Minaun**, at 1532ft another mountain worth climbing for the view. A turning off the road into Keel will take you close up to the summit.

West along the strand at **DOOAGH**, one road leads on over the side of the Croghaun to the golden sands and, on a good day, sparkling turquoise waters of **Keem Strand**. Often deserted, it's a rewarding place to make for, with its impressive views over Clew Bay, but if you're on a bike, be warned: it's tough going (and the sheer drop on the seaward side is vertigo inducing). A turning off the Keem Road will take you up to **Acorrymore Lough** – surrounded by scree slopes, and now dammed to supply water locally. It's a bleak, rather than poetic, spot and is the best ascent of **Croghaun**, the island's second highest mountain and just a whisker lower than Slievemore at 2195ft – its seaward side boasts spectacularly high cliffs, the island's highest. This is decidedly tough hill-walking country, so you need to be reasonably experienced even to think of attempting it. Once at the top, however, you're rewarded with a magnificent view of the Belmullet Peninsula and the scattered islands, while the Croagh Patrick and the Partry Mountains rise spectacularly in the southeast.

At Keel there's the *Wayfarer* **hostel**, which is right on the strand (IHH; closed mid-Oct to mid-March; ☎098/43266, *sorchadaly@esatclear.ie*), though it does lack good communal facilities. The **campsite** (closed Oct–May; ☎098/43211) is also on the strand. Dooagh's *Achill Head* **hotel** (☎098/43108; ⑤) has adequate rooms and a nightclub and could make a more lively base. There is also a fine **B&B** in Dooagh, the *West Coast House* (☎098/43317, *achwch@anu*.ie; ③) which is signposted from the Keel Road and offers amazing views of the bay below. The best places for **eating and drinking** in this area are: the *Beehive* in Keel, a relaxed crafts and coffee shop, and the culinary star of the area, and indeed the island, *The Boley House*, signposted from the eastern end of the village (6–9pm; ☎098/43147), which offers modest home-cooking using super-fresh ingredients. For traditional-**music** sessions try the *The Mihaun Pub*. You can rent **bikes** at O'Malley's Island Sports in Dooagh (☎098/43125).

Dugort

While **DUGORT**, a clutch of houses nestling at the base of Slievemore mountain, lacks the arresting open views of the Atlantic on offer at Keel or Dooagh, it does make a more comfortable base, both in terms of accommodation and atmosphere. Follow the signs for the Deserted Village from Keel, and take the Atlantic Drive for Dugort. Half a mile out of Keel, a signposted footpath leads to a mini megalithic tomb set in the hillside where the gorse meets the heather – well worth the climb, if only for the view. A couple of miles further on, some ruined buildings and scattered gravestones are all that's left of a village known simply as **The Settlement**. It was founded in 1834 by a Protestant vicar, the Reverend E. Nangle, who bought up sixty percent of the island and built schools and a printing press in an ultimately unsuccessful effort to evangelize the islanders. Towering to the north is **Slievemore**, Achill's highest mountain at 2205ft – a massive pile of quartzite and mica. Here on its southern slopes stands a **dolmen** with a stone circle at each end and a *booley* village of huts formerly used during summer pasturing – a reminder of a much newer, but equally extinct, transhumant way of life. At the foot of Slievemore, on the seaward side, are the **Seal Caves**, burrowing way back under the mountain; you can visit them by boat from the tiny pier at Dugort.

To get away from the seaside holiday atmosphere that often overtakes Dooagh and Keel (especially on bank holiday weekends), you can **stay** on the southern slopes of the mountain at *McDowell's Hotel* (closed Oct–March; ☎098/43148; ④), which does excellent food, including vegetarian, and has frequent traditional music sessions, while in Dugort itself you can stay in comfort at *Gray's Guesthouse* (☎098/43244; ③) a rambling establishment comprised of several houses, taking up one street of the tiny hamlet. Five miles east, and signposted from all the main roads, is the *Valley House Hostel* (closed Dec–March; ☎098/47204), a handsome, crumbling edifice that was once home to the woman whose story is told in J.M. Synge's *The Playboy of the Western World* – her rejected suitor burned down a barn and tossed her onto the flames. The place now operates as a hostel with four-bed rooms and the luxury of a bar in the courtyard behind the house. Dugort has two **campsites**: the *Seal Caves Caravan and Camping Park* (closed Oct–March; ☎098/43262) and *Lavele's Golden Strand Caravan and Camping Park* (closed Oct–March; ☎098/47232).

North Mayo

Predominantly bogland, **north Mayo** – and especially the northwest – is an area that can seem forbidding in bad weather, but when the sun shines and suffuses everything in a hazy glow, you can forgive all. The long, straight bog road west to **Belmullet** is incredibly bleak and desolate, though the village itself is awash with garish, pastel-coloured buildings. North of Belmullet is the county's most interesting sight, the **Céide Fields**, where prehistoric field patterns have been uncovered beneath nearly seven feet of bog, offering a startling view of the unchanging nature of human habitation here over five millennia. The coast road leading from the Céide Fields to the historically resonant town of **Killala**, scene of the 1798 French invasion, is very dramatic.

Bangor and the walking trail

About 25 miles north from Achill, **BANGOR** (or sometimes Bangor Ennis) is pleasant enough, although its landlocked location makes it less exciting than the seaside places nearby. Bangor marks the start of a spectacular 22-mile hike, the **Bangor Trail**, an ancient route that runs southeast through the **Nephin Beg Mountains** to Newport. As R.L. Praeger, who walked the route in 1937 wrote: "Where else even in Ireland will you find this hundred square miles which is homeless and roadless – nothing but brown heather rising as far as you can see... into high bare hills breaking down here and there in rocky scarps, with the Atlantic winds singing along their slopes?" It is indeed lonely country, with the legacy of the Famine visible everywhere, but the desolation of the landscape can be exhilarating. A couple of fine guides to the route are available from most newsagents in the area: *County Mayo, The Bangor Trail* (£6/€7.62) by Joe MacDermott, and the locally produced *Bangor Trail* by Uinsíonn MacGrath and Theresa ní Ghearraigh.

Belmullet and the peninsula

Heading on from Bangor along the R313 through bleak uninhabited bogland you'll come to **BELMULLET** (*Béal an Mhuirthead*, "mouth of the Mullet"), a functional little village, its streets perpetually mired from the mud of the bogs. Like most Irish towns, it's a planned settlement, founded as late as 1825 by the local landlord, William Carter, to "create a home market for produce that did not previously exist nearer than thirty miles by land". Its success was such that it eclipsed the older landlord village of Binghamstown (*An Geata Mór*), on the peninsula, which was deserted by the late nineteenth century. The attraction of the place lies not so much in its physical charms as in a kind of unpretentious unhurriedness – life goes on, shops stay open until late, and the sun arches slowly toward the horizon over the wide western sea.

There is a small **tourist office** on the left side of the main street as you enter the town (☎097/81500). You can **stay** in the *Western Strands Hotel* (☎097/81096; ④), which has basic rooms, and there are also numerous B&Bs: for good value try *Mill House* in American St (☎097/81181; ②), or *Drom Caoin* (☎097/81195, *dromcaoin@esatlink.com*; ③), which caters well for vegetarians and offers fine views of Blacksod Bay. There are plenty of bars and fast-food joints, so take your pick; the liveliest **bar** is probably the one at the *Western Strands*, where you'll also get a good cheap **dinner**. *Leneghan's*, next to the hotel, has *comhaltas* – traditional **music** – sessions on the third Friday of the month; so does the *Anchor Bar*, which serves local seafood.

A flat slab of land that seems tacked on to the mainland almost as an afterthought, **Belmullet Peninsula** is sparsely populated, but the houses are scattered in the characteristically Irish way (town-dwelling, as well as Ireland's town-planning, was largely an Anglo-Irish invention). Along with this pattern of habitation, you'll also see field-systems not much different from the Stone Age ones uncovered at Céide (see p.420).

The seaward side of the peninsula is raked by Atlantic winds to the extent that almost no vegetation can survive. The landward side, overlooking Blacksod Bay, at the southern tip of the peninsula, is much more sheltered and has some good **beaches**, notably at Elly Bay halfway down. To the east and north the land rises; although the cliffs are not hugely spectacular, there's some rewarding walking. The peninsula is one of the locations where the legendary Children of Lir (see p.203) were condemned to spend their last three hundred years; they are buried, according to legend, on Inishglora, a tiny island off the west coast. The peninsula is rich in historical remains, too: there are promontory **forts** at Doonamo, Doonaneanir and Portnafrankach. The one at Doonamo, on an impressive clifftop site, encloses three *clocháns* and a circular fort. Under the waters of Blacksod Bay lies **La Rata**, the largest of three Spanish Armada galleons that sank in 1588.

In calm weather, Matthew and Josephine Geraghty run boat trips out to the islands of **Inis Gé** (Inishkea North and South) for £12/€15.24 return (☎097/85741) from Belmullet; Millicent Sweeney at Blacksod also arranges them (☎097/85662, or evenings ☎097/85774). You can organize **riding** at the Durham Riding Centre near Blacksod (☎097/85811).

Northeast along the coast to Downpatrick Head

East of Belmullet, the country becomes much wilder: surveyed by the ice-polished shapes of the mountains, it's rough, boggy terrain where many of the remoter villages are still Irish-speaking.

Heading out of Belmullet, ten miles towards Ballycastle, you'll see a signpost for the village of **POLLATOMISH** (*Poll an Tómais*, "Thomas' Hole"), a delightful little place deep in fjord-like country, with a handful of houses and two pubs. By far and away the best place to **stay** in this area is the superb, independent hostel at *Kilcommon Lodge* (☎097/84621, *kilcommonlodge@gmx.net*). The dorm rooms are excellent and there is a reading room, heated by a turf fire with tables with individual reading lamps.

From Pollatomish a single-track roads lead up to Benwee Head; at almost 820ft, this massive cliff has great views of the Donegal cliffs to the northeast and the **Stags of Broadhaven**, a series of seven 300ft rocks, which stand a mile and a half off the coast. **PORTACLOY**, where there's a deeply indented bay edged with golden sand, makes a good starting point for walking on the headland. The **Hackett and Turpin** factory shop is on the road to Rinroe Point at Ceathrú Thaidgh (Carrowteige), the other obvious setting-off point for Benwee Head and an unlikely – not to be missed – outpost of the fashion industry. Here local women work on six hand looms to produce designer knitwear in linen, silk and wool at amazingly low prices. The road descends through intricate interlockings of land and sea to golden beaches and the tiny harbour at Rinroe itself.

Further east, near Porturlin, the waves have carved the rocks into weird, contorted shapes, including the **Arches**, a 30ft opening in the cliff which the brave – or foolhardy – attempt to row through in good weather at low tide.

At **Downpatrick Head**, there are some puffing holes that send up tall plumes of water in rough weather, and a detached stack of rock with a fort perched on it; a plaque commemorates those who were killed in the aftermath of the 1798 Rebellion. There's a profusion of rare birds and grand views over to Céide Fields and the wild country to the west, eastwards to the Sligo mountains, and north across the wide, empty sea.

Céide Fields

In terms of understanding the landscape, the most important site on this stretch of coast is the prehistoric farm that covers some 24 square miles of boggy moorland between Belderrig and Ballycastle. Although signposted from the road, the Belderrig site offers little enlightenment to the untrained eye: for that, carry on another five miles to the main site at **Céide Fields** – pronounced "cajun" without the *n* – (mid-March to May & Oct daily 10am–5pm; June–Sept daily 9.30am–6.30pm; Nov daily 10am–4.30pm; £2.50/€3.17). As Seamus Heaney's poem *Belderg* observes:

They just kept turning up
and were thought of as foreign
one-eyed and benign, they lie about his house
quernstones out of a bog

Under nearly seven feet of blanket bog, archeologists have unearthed the stone walls of a Neolithic farm system and apparently solved the riddle of how the builders of the great megalithic tombs that run across the northern part of Ireland lived. They were, it seems, farming people who joined the original fishers and hunters of Ireland around five thousand years ago and seem to have lived in harmony with them, and each other: the pattern of settlement is dispersed and shows no defensive features. The fields run longitudinally with the slope of the land and appear to have been used for pasture – as in contemporary Ireland, where the largest single contribution to the national economy still comes from grass-raised livestock.

The faint marks left by these ancient farmers don't look like much to the untrained eye, and the **Céide Fields centre** is, inevitably, heavy on interpretation. The building itself is impressively conceived, the pyramidal shape not at odds with the landscape. The interior is a combination of sandstone, oak and glass and in the middle, stretching towards the apex of the pyramid is a huge piece of bog pine. The centre includes an exhibition, a viewing platform an audiovisual theatre (with a romantically voice-overed show giving some of the area's geological background) and an excellent café. The entrance fee also includes a guided tour, usually by one of the archeological workers on the dig.

Ballycastle

The coastal road east from the Céide Fields to Ballycastle is as spectacular as any on Ireland's west coast. **BALLYCASTLE**, in the wide valley of the River Ballinglen, is a tranquil village of just one broad, sloping street, with good swimming beaches.

The **tourist office**, which will be able to offer detailed advice on walking nearby, is based just below the church (Mon–Sat 10.30am–5pm, Sun 1–4pm; closed for long lunches). There are a handful of relaxed **bars** – try the tiny *Lavell's*, or *Barlett's*. The best **restaurant** around is *Doonfeeny House* (☎096/43092) which does five-course meals, while for **accommodation** try the warm hospitality of *The Hawthorns* (☎096/43148; ③) a ten-minute drive from Ballycastle.

Killala and around

KILLALA, overlooking Killala Bay as the coast curves back round towards Ballina, is a must, both for the magnificent local scenery and for its historical connections. Scene

THE FRENCH INVASION

On August 22, 1798, three warships flying British colours anchored at Kilcummin, near Killala. The Protestant Bishop Stock, relieved that they were apparently English and not the rumoured French invasion fleet, sent his two sons and the port surveyor to pay their respects. They were immediately taken prisoner; the **invasion** had begun. After a brief resistance, Killala yielded to the French, and at sunset that evening a French soldier climbed to the top of the Bishop's Palace and replaced the British flag with a green flag with a harp in the centre, bearing the words *Erin go Bragh* (Ireland for Ever).

Wolfe Tone, the inspirational leader of the United Irishmen, had been working since his exile from Ireland in 1794 to secure foreign aid for his planned insurrection against the British. However, by the time the first French expedition of 1100 men under General Humbert reached Killala, the rebellion had already been all but crushed. Not only was there a military mismatch between the French professional soldiers and the few poorly armed Irish novices who joined them, but there were also ideological clashes. The French had expected that liberation from British rule would appeal to Catholics and Protestants alike, and were further confused to find the Irish volunteers greeting them in the name of the Blessed Virgin and apparently having no idea of the significance of the French Revolution.

The rest of the story is sadly predictable. With some heroic fighting, the Franco-Irish army took Killala, Ballina and Castlebar, but on September 8, near the village of Ballinamuck in County Longford, seriously depleted in both numbers and weapons, it was defeated by the united armies of Lord Cornwallis and General Lake. The French were taken prisoner and returned to France; the Irish rebels were hanged. At Rath Lackan, there's a statue to the first French soldier who fell in the 1798 struggle, as well as a wide bay with golden sands looking over to the Sligo mountains.

A month later, sailing with another French force from Brest, Wolfe Tone was himself captured – along with the French fleet – off the coast of Donegal. He was subsequently court-martialled and condemned to death. Despite his insistence that he should be treated with military honour, and therefore shot, he was sentenced to hang. Before that could be carried out, he cut his throat with a pocketknife and died after seven days of agony. He came to personify the tradition of both revolutionary violence and religious tolerance (he was a Protestant) in the cause of an independent Ireland.

The events of 1798 led directly to the Act of Union with Britain three years later, while the land agitation that spread throughout the country laid the foundations for land reform, Catholic emancipation and, eventually, the long process that led to Irish independence.

of one of the most significant events in Irish history – the unsuccessful French invasion organized by Wolfe Tone in 1798 (see box on p.421) – it's a pleasantly run-down seaside town, so small it's difficult to believe it's a bishopric, with lovely, wild sea coasts and some good roads for cycling. As far as sights go, the highlights are an attractive quayside and a fine round tower, but it's the historic atmosphere that's the real attraction here.

Killala's a convivial place with a disproportionate number of **pubs** – *An Gránuaile* and *The Village Inn* are two of the most traditional. **Music** is often available at *The Anchor Bar*, as is local **seafood**. There's a tea shop down on the strand with fine views out to sea. A mile or so north there's a good, sheltered, sandy beach for swimming at Ross Point (signposted from the Ballycastle Road).

There are a few comfortable **B&B** options here: nearest to the centre, though still half a mile out on Crossmolina Road, is *Kevin Munnelly's farmhouse* (☎096/32331; ③); four miles out of town is Mrs Carey's *Rathoma House* (☎096/32035; ③); while *O'Hara's Beach View House* (☎096/32023; ③) is three miles out towards the beach. The **tourist office** (June–Sept 10am–5pm; ☎096/32166) is in the community centre on the road out of town towards Ballina. Most local newsagents sell Bishop Stock's *Narrative* of the events of 1798 – a surprisingly sympathetic account of the uprising.

Ballina to Castlebar

The interior of County Mayo can't match the splendour of its sea coasts, and unless you're keen on fishing or walking, you're unlikely to spend much time here. Like all of Ireland's less touristed areas, however, it has a charm of its own if you stick with it. A region of rough moorland – the foothills of the Nephin Beg and Ox ranges – it's strewn with lakes, giving way in the east to flatter, more fertile country. It's dotted, too, with market towns such as Pontoon, Foxford and Crossmolina, each with its own distinctive architecture and character.

The road from Killala to Ballina runs through flat, farm country. The minor road that runs closer to the Moy estuary is more interesting, with two abbeys on the estuary, **Moyne** and **Rosserk**, both of them founded in the fifteenth century. Rosserk, with a tower at the water's edge, is the bigger and more poetic of the two – and considered the best Franciscan building in the country – but both have good cloisters. Look out for the sixteenth-century graffiti on the wall at Moyne; the place was burned down by Sir Richard Bingham, the English governor of Connacht, in 1590.

Ballina

The busy town of **BALLINA**, clustered around two graceful bridges on the River Moy, makes a good place to stock up on provisions and information; the town is especially vibrant during the two-week street festival that takes place in July. The elegant Victorian and Edwardian pub- and shop-fronts testify to a long history of vigorous trading, and this tradition continues in the rebuilding and energetic business activity that's evident everywhere. Stock up on smoked salmon at Clarke's Salmon Smokery on O'Rahilly Street, which also displays an impressive range of fresh, whole fish in its windows. Keehane's in Arran Street is a reasonable bookshop.

The **tourist office** (April–Sept Mon–Sat 10am–1pm & 2–5.45pm; ☎096/70848) is located between the bridges on the side of the river away from town, and the entrance is guarded by a life-sized picture of Ballina's most famous daughter, former president Mary Robinson. You can **stay** and indulge in some real splendour, with a touch of Gothic-horror excess, at the *Belleek Castle* (☎096/22400; ⑧). Take Pearse Street eastward from the centre, and follow the signs; a left turn will bring you through an imposing stone gateway and to a long drive through dark forest to a neo-Jacobean mansion in forbidding grey stone. The *Bartra House Hotel* (☎096/22200; ④), a cheerful and friendly place, and the modern *Ridgepool Hotel* (☎096/24600, *www.ridgepoolhotel.com*; ⑥) are other pleasant options. The best of the many B&Bs are: *Whitestream House* (☎096/21582; ③), on the Foxford Road, and, four miles out of town, *Jordan's Red River Lodge* (☎096/22841, *dolm@eircom.net*; ③). For **camping** try the well-equipped *Belleek Caravan and Camping Park* (☎096/71533), a couple of miles north of town on the Killala road.

When **eating**, make sure you try the famous Moy salmon. The *River Bar Inn*, on the right bank of the Moy, a little downriver from town, does good seafood as does *Gaughans*, a great old-fashioned pub on O'Rahilly Street. *The Broken Jug* (☎096/72379) – named after John Banville's play – a roomy bar and restaurant at the top of Pearse Street, offers a fine selection of carvery meals. One mile out of town in Quay Village (follow the river to Quay Road and turn left) is *Captain's Table* which, as the name suggests, serves delicious fish dishes. The *Old Bond Store Restaurant and Crafts Shop* in Dillon Terrace, makes a good stop for daytime meals.

Crossmolina and Lough Conn

Five or so miles southwest of Ballina, relaxed, raffish **CROSSMOLINA**, at the top of Lough Conn, has a place to **stay** that's a sight in itself. Not far south on the lakeshore, *Enniscoe House* (☎096/31112; ⑦), a Georgian mansion that does B&B, is a good example of easygoing Georgian attitudes to architecture. Originally built in the mid-eighteenth century as a three-storey house, it was extended in the 1790s (and damaged in 1798 when the French army marched down the back avenue) to include a grand facade overlooking Lough Conn. The result inside is two completely different structures whose floor levels and room sizes don't correspond at all. The nearby **North Mayo Family History Research and Heritage Centre** (☎096/31809, *www.mayo.irish.roots.net/*) is where visitors can trace their north Mayo ancestors and browse around the heritage centre which has mainly agricultural artefacts, with demonstrations of traditional crafts (June–Sept Mon–Fri 9am–4pm, Sat & Sun 2–6pm; Oct–May Mon–Fri 9am–4pm).

There is a **tourist office** in the new Enterprise Centre near the statue that marks the middle of town (May–Oct Mon–Fri 10am–1.30pm & 2–5pm, Sat 10.30am–1pm & 2–4.30pm). The *Dolphin Hotel* (☎096/31270; ⑤) makes for a comfortable alternative to the *Enniscoe*, or for B&B try *Lake View House* (☎096/31296, *lakeviewhouse@oceanfree.net*; ③). You can get good daytime **meals** in the *Tea Room*, or in the lively *Hiney's* pub nearby; there are plenty of other **bars**, most with **music** a couple of nights during the week – *McMorrow's* has traditional sessions on Friday nights, and also sells fishing tackle for anglers bound for the nearby lough.

The main attraction of **Lough Conn** is for fishermen: the lake itself is rich in trout, and the River Moy is a delight for salmon anglers, though the area has plenty of scenic and historical interest to sustain non-anglers. The moorland hills that border the lake are good for gentle **walking**; for a taste of the Nephin Beg wilderness and some more demanding hikes (see p.415) head south from Crossmolina down the west side of the lough and take a right at Lahardaun. The lakesides themselves are scattered with abbeys, castles and megaliths, as well as some hidden sandy beaches.

Pontoon and Foxford

Continuing south along the R315 for Foxford, through rough, peaty terrain strewn with boulders, you reach **PONTOON** after ten miles, on the neck of land that separates Lough Conn from Lough Cullin. The village is a good base for exploring both the lakes' shores and the foothills of the Nephin Beg Mountains to the northwest and the Ox Mountains to the northeast. On either side of Main Street both the *Country Kitchen* and

Anchor Bar serve food though for stylish cuisine (the Sunday lunch is especially recommended) try creeper-clad *Healy's Hotel* (☎094/56443, *healyspontoon@tinet.ie*; ⑤). Originally a lakeside coaching inn and latterly a no-nonsense anglers' **hotel**, it has undergone considerable renovation and is well regarded not only by fishermen but by the many locals who eat at its excellent restaurant, renowned for its wholesome home-cooked Irish food.

FOXFORD, a couple of miles east, is a trim village in the lee of the Ox Mountains which owed its late nineteenth-century survival to the **Foxford Woollen Mill** (April–Oct Mon–Sat 10am–5.30pm & Sun noon–5.30pm; £3/€3.81; includes tour of present-day factory), which now has an elaborate audiovisual presentation to tell its story. There's a gift shop and, upstairs, a pleasant tea shop; rooms are let to local artists and craftspeople. After the 1840s Famine, the potato crop failed again in the 1870s, resulting in evictions and abject poverty for the people of the town and the peat-cutting districts around. Most families led a precarious existence, relying on their own potato crop and, in the absence of significant cash employment in Foxford, the meagre earnings the men were able to bring back from summers working on big farms in Scotland. Such conditions led to demands for land reform – the Land League was founded in 1879 by Michael Davitt, also the bringer of trade unionism to Ireland, whose cottage at **STRADE**, between Foxford and Castlebar, you can also visit (Tues–Sat 2–6pm; 50p/€0.63). The mill at Foxford was founded in 1890 by a far-sighted nun called Marrough Bernard, who called it Providence. At a time when more professionally run mills were failing – so unused were her workers to ideas of productivity that she had to bribe them with cash prizes – the success of the mill could certainly be called providential. Its profits were used to fund schools and a diverse range of cultural activities, of which one, the Foxford Mill brass band, still survives.

The **tourist office**, in one of the mill buildings (Mon–Sat 11am–5pm, Sun noon–6pm; ☎094/56488), has useful details of walking and fishing in the area; the North Mayo Angling Advice Centre, where you can buy licences, is also in the town. There are a few **B&Bs** in Foxford – popular with fishermen is *Mrs M. Gannon's* on Providence Rd (☎094/56101; ③), but on the whole, you're probably better off among the scenic beauties of Pontoon. *Hennigan's* pub has traditional music and ballad nights.

Castlebar and around

CASTLEBAR, although it's the county town of Mayo, offers little reason to hang around. The tree-bordered green is attractive, and the main street has all the facilities you might need conveniently gathered together, but since the demise of the annual rock festival there seems to be little going on. Historically, it's notable for a Franco-Irish victory in 1798, at which General Humbert's army routed a stronger force commanded by General Lake – the event has gone down in history as the "Castlebar Races" because of the speed of the British retreat.

The **tourist office** (Mon–Sat 9.30am–6pm; ☎094/21207) is in the Old Linen Hall – which was the venue for a celebratory dinner after the rout of the British in 1798 – and, with information about the whole of north Mayo, is more than usually useful if you're planning an extended stay; it's particularly strong on walking. In the same building is the Linen Hall Arts Centre, which puts on sometimes imaginative shows (including plenty for children); and, if you are crying out for cappuccinos, you can buy them in the attached café.

You'll find no shortage of **accommodation** here: there's the swanky *Breaffy House* out on the Claremont Rd (☎094/22033, *www.breaffyhouse.ie*; ⑦), a Victorian pile with hideous modern extensions; or, back in town, the friendly and comfortable *Daly's Hotel* (☎094/21961; ⑤), which is ideally situated on the green. **B&Bs** are mainly concentrated on the Westport Road, where you could try *Drumshinnagh House* (☎094/24211, *berniecollins@oceanfree.net*; ③), or *Millhill House* (☎094/24279; ③), both of which allow children to stay for half price. Unfortunately the town's excellent hostel has closed; the nearest **hostel** is *Creevagh House*, six miles away in Ballintubber (see below).

There's a fine fish **restaurant** on Chapel Street, *An Carraig* (☎094/26159), or try the new Indian restaurant, *Tulsi*, on Lower Charles St (☎094/25066), which serves some of the finest Indian cuisine in the west of the country. *Café Rouge* in New Antrim Street does a good range of home cooking for daytime eating, while for a huge breakfast, the *Kitty Sark*, off Main Street is the place to go (walk to the top of Main Street and turn right at the Irish Permanent Building Society). For pub food there's the excellent *Flannelly's* behind the train station, while filling lunches are served at *Daly's Hotel* (see opposite). *McCarthy's Bar* in Main Street has snugs and **traditional music**. *Johnnie McHale's*, opposite the *Welcome Inn* in Upper Chapel Street, is a great old Castlebar music pub, as is the *Irish House* in Thomas Street. *Moran's*, off the green in Spencer Street, has music on Thursday nights.

Seven miles south of Castlebar on the Ballinrobe Road (N84) is **Ballintubber Abbey**. Founded in 1216 by Cathal O'Connor, King of Connacht, it is claimed to be the oldest church in Ireland to have been in continual use. Leaflets on the church are freely available and there is an informative, if rather dated, video showing the local community performing its annual passion play and following pilgrims along **Tóchar Phádraig**, the 22-mile pilgrim route to Croagh Patrick, which starts at the abbey. A mile away is the fine *Creevagh House Farmhouse Hostel* (☎094/30747, *www.creevaghhouse.com*) which is well equipped with small dorms and good showers.

Southeast of Ballintubber Abbey, on the shores of Lough Carra, you can explore the **Doon Archeological Nature Peninsula** (June–Sept 10am–6pm; £3/€3.81). With things to see from standing stones to Norman castles, and a Famine grave, the place opens up the complex human history of this seemingly little-populated area.

About five miles southeast along the N60, **Balla**, a single wide street of pastel-coloured houses, has a short round tower, off the main square, that may be a twelfth-century "fake". The hamlet of **Mayo**, lost in a maze of unsignposted lanes, has only an abrupt right-angle bend in the road to mark the ghostly presence of the Augustinian abbey that gave the place enough importance to make it the county town.

Knock to Cong

East Mayo is dominated by the devotional shrine at **Knock**, which is easy to visit as an international **airport** at nearby Charlestown was built in 1986. However, if you're not a believer, or religious kitsch isn't a strong enough draw, you're best off heading south to the more engaging and historically rich towns of **Cong** and its unique abbey, and **Loughmask** with its big house, once the home of the infamous landlord Charles Boycott.

Knock

Ever since an apparition of the Virgin Mary, accompanied by St Joseph and St John, was seen on the gable of the parish church of **KNOCK** (*Cnoc Mhuire* "Mary's Hill") in 1879, it has been a place of pilgrimage. As a passer-by in Ireland, it's surprisingly easy to forget the all-pervasive influence of the Catholic Church, but at Knock you're brought slap up against it. Whatever you may believe about the possible authenticity of the apparitions, Knock rates for Catholics, along with Lourdes in France and Fatima in Portugal, as one of the leading modern miraculous confirmations of their faith. A massive and ugly church with a capacity of twenty thousand was opened nearby in 1976, and the pope visited the shrine in 1979.

When Monsignor Horan, a local priest, first hatched the plan for the new airport it seemed a crazy and profligate idea, and there were years of bitter controversy over this apparent waste of public funds. In fact it has proved remarkably successful, and as well as bringing in pilgrims to see the shrine, the airport has had the effect of opening up the northwest of Ireland for travellers – to the extent that Mayo is in reach of London for weekend breaks, and house prices in the county are booming as wealthy inhabitants of southeast England buy their second homes. The Lourdes to Knock run is also used by fishers from the southwest of France to reach west Ireland's lake fisheries.

The **airport** (situated three miles south from Charlestown at the junction of the N17 and N5) is open from 9am to 6pm daily, serving many UK airports including Luton, Stansted and Coventry. An Aer Lingus shuttle service to Dublin connects with major international flights. There's a **tourist office** in the airport, open to greet arriving flights (winter closed Tues & Thurs; ☎094/67247), and another in Knock itself (May–Sept daily 10am–6pm; ☎094/88193); ask them for details of transport – most of the time you seem to have to rely on taxis to Charlestown (a major crossroads where you can pick up buses and there are a number of B&Bs) or Knock.

As a place, Knock is nothing much to look at but if you are interested in religion, or the Marian phenomenon in Irish life, it can prove fascinating. The best place to start is the **Museum of Folk Life** (May–Oct daily 10am–7pm; Nov–April daily 10am–6pm; £2.50/€3.17), which contains artefacts relating to the apparition and the miracles associated with it. The scene of the apparitions has been glassed in to form a **chapel**, and pilgrims can be seen there praying at all hours. As you might expect, there is no shortage of kitsch plastic religious souvenirs on sale. There are a couple of basic **hotels**, the *Belmont*, take the turn at *Burkes* pub at the Claremorris end of the village (☎094/88122; ⑥), or the drab *Knock International Hotel* on Main St (☎094/88466; ⑥), and numerous **B&Bs**: try Mrs McGrath's *Bridge House*, Airport Rd (☎094/88205; ③), which does excellent family deals, Mrs Carney's *Burren*, Kiltimagh Rd (☎094/88362; ③), or *Mervue*, overlooking the shrine (☎094/88127; ③).

Ballinrobe

BALLINROBE is probably worth visiting only if you're here in the third week of July, for the **Ballinrobe Races**. This is Irish racing as you've imagined it, with a great atmosphere at a picturesque and compact course; there's excellent viewing and it's all very relaxed and amateur. For accommodation, there are a couple of **B&Bs** – book early for race week – try Mrs Anne Mahon's *Riverside House* in the Cornmarket (☎092/41674; ③).

South of Ballinrobe, on the R334 around Neale, is clustered a sequence of monuments, ancient and not-so-ancient. They range from a series of stone circles, nearer Cong, to a cross and another of the mysterious monuments that abound in Ireland, a massive stone-stepped **pyramid**, with an almost indecipherable inscription, including the name George Browne and some worn Roman numerals, dating it somewhere in the eighteenth century. The Brownes are the family who occupy Westport House; but the reason for the pyramid remains obscure.

Cong and around

CONG, a few miles south of Ballinrobe, lies on the narrow spit of land that divides Lough Mask from Lough Corrib at the point where the dramatically mountainous country of Connemara to the west gives way to the flat and fertile farmland that makes up the east of County Mayo. A picture-book pretty village that caters for plenty of tourists, it's also the site of the ruined **Cong Abbey**, which was founded in 1128 for the Augustinians by Turlough O'Connor, King of Ireland (though it's probably built on a seventh-century monastic site). The doorways represent the transition between the quite different styles of Romanesque and Gothic. The cloisters look just a little bit too good to be true: they were partially rebuilt in 1860. At its height, Cong Abbey had a population of some three thousand, and the practicalities of feeding such multitudes can be glimpsed in the remains of the refectory and kitchen by the river, where a fishing house over the water contains a fish trap beneath the floor. The **Cross of Cong**, a twelfth-century ornamented Celtic cross originally made in County Roscommon for the abbey, gives an indication of the wealth and status of the foundation – it's now on show at the National Museum in Dublin. From the abbey there's a pleasant wander through woods down to the river and the lough, although this runs through the grounds of the local big house, **Ashford Castle**, now a luxury hotel (see below), which charges for admission to its lands (£2/€2.54).

It's also worth taking a look at the **canal**. In the 1840s attempts were made, as a Famine relief project, to dig a canal between Lough Corrib and Lough Mask. The river that links the two, though you can get to it at various points, including the Pigeon Hole, a mile or so north of Cong, runs underground through porous limestone for most of its length. This might have been an indication of what would happen to the canal: the porosity of the rock meant that the water just drained away, and Cong is left with a dry canal, complete with locks.

The town is obsessed with *The Quiet Man*, a film that much of the rest of the world may have forgotten but which, shot here in 1956 and starring John Wayne and Maureen O'Hara, is well remembered here. It's a highly romanticized portrayal of Ireland and is in many ways an expression of the emigrants' notion of Ireland and Irishness.

Practicalities

The **tourist office** in the old courthouse building in Abbey St (May–Sept daily 10am–6pm; ☎092/46542) has many books and leaflets about the area most of which concentrate, predictably, on *The Quiet Man*; in fact guided tours leave the office for the locations used in the film. Undoubtedly the swishest place to **stay** – Ronald Reagan did – is *Ashford Castle* (☎092/46003; ⑧), which stands at the point where the river meets Lough Corrib, and has been converted into a luxury hotel. Although its history goes back to the thirteenth century, what you see now is essentially a Victorian castellated reconstruction. Two other spruce hotels also offer comfortable rooms: pastel green *Danagher's* (☎092/46028; ⑤), by the abbey, and terracotta red *Ryan's*, on the main street (☎092/46243; ⑥). Among the numerous **B&Bs**, half a mile from the village in Drumshiel is Mrs Coakley's *Hazel Grove* (☎092/46060; ③), and, in the same area, O'Connor's *Dolmen House* (☎092/46466; ④). *The Quiet Man* **hostel** (IHH; closed Oct–April; ☎092/46089, *www.quietman-cong.com*) is centrally located on Abbey Street, while the *Cong Hostel* is one mile outside Cong itself in Lisloughery (same phone number). Both hostels rent out **bikes**, as does O'Connor's Garage on Main Street. There's more hostel accommodation and **camping** seven miles to the east in **Cross** at the Courtyard Hostel (IHH; ☎092/46203, *www.dowagh@iol.ie*). You can pitch your tent for nothing on the island of Inchágoill (one of literally hundreds). The *Corrib Queen* does a tour from *Ashford Castle* pier, taking in Oughterard, on the Galway shore of the lough (☎092/46029; return £10/€12.70). The island is the site of two early Christian churches as well as the Stone of Lugha, the tombstone of St Patrick's nephew, which bears the earliest Christian inscriptions in Ireland.

For **eating** in Cong, the fabulous *Echoes* (☎092/46059), offers plenty of delicious fish dishes, and lots of organic vegetables and herbs; if this is booked, *Micilin's*, a few doors along (☎092/46655), also has a fine menu. For a really special meal, in fabulous surroundings, the culinary star is the *Ashford Castle* restaurant (☎092/46003) where meals are served in the stunning Connaught and George V dining rooms. The hotels do good bar food, and the *Quiet Man Coffee Shop* is a friendly place with good home-baking.

Loughmask House

Loughmask House (not open to the public), on the shores of Lough Mask a couple of miles due north of Cong, was the home of the notorious **Charles Boycott**, a retired captain of the British army and land agent to Lord Erne. His behaviour towards the tenant farmers during the Land League unrest of the 1880s – particularly acute in Mayo, where the League originated and many of the "congested areas" were located – made him one of the victims of Parnell's "moral Coventry" policy, subsequently known as "boycotting". As Parnell himself put it in a meeting in Ennis in 1880:

> *You must show what you think of him on the roadside when you meet him, you must show him in the streets of the town, you must show him at the shop counter . . . even in the house of worship, by leaving him severely alone, by putting him into a sort of moral Coventry, by isolating him from the rest of his kind as if he were a leper of old, you must show him your detestation of the crime he has committed.*

COUNTY ROSCOMMON

Roscommon has the unjust reputation of being the most boring county in Ireland. A long sliver of land running from south to north, it's the only county in Connacht without any sea coast, though it is bounded for almost its entire western border by the upper reaches of the Shannon. Although most of the county is either bog or good grassland pasture, the **Curlew Mountains** on the Sligo and Leitrim border rise high and wild. Chances are you'll be approaching the county from the south, which is not its best aspect: the most worthwhile places are **Boyle**, in the far north, for its access to the Curlew Mountains, and **Strokestown** in the east, with its remarkable Georgian mansion and Famine Museum.

Roscommon town

More or less in the centre of the county, there's nothing much to **ROSCOMMON**, but it's an oddly pleasant town to spend time and soak up the atmosphere. Its solid tone is set by heavy, stone buildings – among them the Bank of Ireland, once the courthouse, and the **county jail**, now housing a collection of shops, its serrated top giving the town a characteristic silhouette, identifiable for miles around. The jail was the scene of all public hangings in the county and used to have a woman executioner called Lady Betty, whose own sentence for murder was revoked on condition that she did her gruesome job for free.

Roscommon boasts two impressive ruins: on the Boyle road out of town, the enormous and well-preserved **Roscommon Castle** was built by the Normans in 1269, burnt down by the Irish four years later and rebuilt in 1280. Remodelling clearly continued for some time – there are some incongruously refined windows among the massive walls. The other ruin, in the lower part of the town, is the **abbey**. Roscommon takes its name from a Celtic saint, St Coman, who was the first bishop here and under whom the see became well known as a seat of learning, having close ties with the more famous abbey at Clonmacnois in County Offaly. The priory ruin, however, is Dominican, dating from 1253. Amazingly enough, despite the religious persecution that followed the Reformation and the Plantations, the Dominicans managed to hang on well into the nineteenth century, the last two incumbents, parish priests of Fuerty and Athleague, dying in 1830 and 1872 respectively.

The church in the centre of town houses a slightly higgledy-piggledy **museum** of local history (April–Oct daily 10am–5.30pm; free), the kind of place that museologists are beginning to regard as an endangered species. The building's striking Star of David window was put there by its nineteenth-century Welsh builders in honour of their patron saint.

Practicalities

The **tourist office** is in Harrison Hall in Market Square (May–Sept daily 10am–6pm; ☎0903/26342), which houses the museum. For **accommodation** in Roscommon, there's the central *Royal Hotel* on Castle St (☎0903/26317; ⑥), one of those fine, upstanding inns that still exist in rural Irish towns: comfortable and good fun, with plenty of locals in the bar. Alternatively the *Abbey Hotel* on the Galway Road, just out of town (☎0903/26420, *cmv@indigo.ie*; ⑤), is a comfortable place, and is located in an elegant eighteenth-century manor. There's also a sprinkling of B&Bs to choose from, including: Mrs Campbell's *Westway*, on the Galway Road (☎0903/26927; ③), or, if you have children, the best option is Mrs Carthy's *Hillcrest House* one mile out of town on Racecourse Road (☎0903/25201; ③). *Gleeson's* is a restaurant and B&B (☎0903/26954, *gleerest@iol.ie*; ④) situated in what used to be the manse of the Presbyterian church opposite the old courthouse. For **eating**, the restaurant side of *Gleeson's* (8am–9pm) does everything from breakfast to dinner, with delicious home baking; you can sit outside in good weather. A slightly upmarket option, in the converted jailhouse, is *Restaurant Le Chateau* (☎0903/27616), serving the stylish French cuisine that has proved such a success in its sister restaurant in Athlone (see p.208). There's also a reasonable Chinese restaurant, the *China Palace*, a little further down the hill on Main Street, above the *Lyons Den* bar.

Strokestown

In the east of the county is **STROKESTOWN**, a gem of a planned town whose reason for existence is Strokestown Park House, once the centre of the second biggest estate in Roscommon after Rockingham. The enormously wide main street – reputedly the result of an ambition on the part of an early owner to have the widest street in Europe – ends abruptly in a castellated wall with three Gothic arches, behind which lies Strokestown Park House.

The **St John's Heritage Centre** (May–Sept Mon–Fri 9.30am–1pm & 2–3.30pm, Sat & Sun 2–6pm; £2/€2.54) is located in the elegant St John's church, designed in 1819 in imitation of a medieval chapter house by the fashionable English architect John Nash (who never visited Ireland). There's material on the Ireland of the Heroes, with a focus on the Rathcroghan monuments (see p.431) and also on the epic *Táin Bó Cúailnge*. A genealogical service is available using records to trace Roscommon families back to the seventeenth century.

Accommodation is thin on the ground in Strokestown. Try B&B at *Martin's* (☎078/33247; ③), centrally located near the heritage centre; Mrs Clyne's *Lakeshore Lodge* (☎078/33966; ③), or Mrs Cox's *Church View House* (☎078/33047; ③) both of which are two miles away in the townland of Clooneen.

Strokestown Park House

Strokestown Park House (April–Oct daily 11am–5.30pm) is a graceful Georgian residence designed by Richard Castle on a plan – a central block with two side wings linked by curved arms – whose adaptability as a sort of glorified farmhouse ensures that it turns up again and again throughout Ireland. Sold by the family of the original owners to the local garage in 1979, the house has never gone through an auction and therefore retains everything from furniture to papers relating to the Famine and 1930s school exercise books.

The **house** (£3.25/€4.12) makes a good place to get to grips with the Anglo-Irish tradition. Its story is a fairly typical one. Originally a massive 27,000 acres, the estate was granted to one Nicholas Mahon in reward for his support of the House of Stuart during the English Civil War. The original building, finished around 1696, was fortified but not particularly grand; only one room of it survives, the stillroom in the cellar. As the family became richer and more secure, it made more grandiose additions, and the current house dates essentially from the 1730s, with some early nineteenth-century alterations. In the mid-nineteenth century Major Denis Mahon, who was a particularly nasty piece of work, is believed to have been one of the first landowners to charter less-than-seaworthy vessels (the notorious **coffin ships**) to take evicted tenants to America during the Famine. His activities were reported and censured in contemporary newspapers both in Ireland and abroad. In 1847 he was shot dead on his own estate.

To give a measure of the interconnectedness of Anglo-Irish society even in comparatively recent times, the lady who sold the house to the garage, the redoubtable Mrs Olive Hales Pakenham-Mahon, married the heir to the Rockingham Estate in 1914, thus uniting the two biggest estates in Roscommon, though the land empire set up by this dynastic marriage ceased to exist very soon afterwards, as did the marriage: the Rockingham heir was killed at the front in the first few days of fighting of World War I. Also in the house, in one of the upstairs bedrooms, is a painting of horses and stooks of corn by Woodbrook's Phoebe Kirkwood (see p.435). The interior of the house gives off a feeling of very comfortable living, but not extraordinary opulence; there's a relaxed living room, and a spacious library and dining room, while upstairs you can see the old schoolroom, complete with desks, blackboard and school-books. One of its really extraordinary features is a gallery that runs the length of the kitchen, allowing the lady of the house to watch what was happening there without having to venture in; on Monday mornings she would drop the week's menu down from above.

The **Irish Famine Museum** (£3/€3.81, combined house and museum ticket £6/€7.62) in the stableyards of the Strokestown Estate provides a provocative interpretation of the house and its history and explores wider issues of Famine migration, emigration and oppression in a historical context, aiming, in particular, to break the traumatic silence that surrounds the subject. In 1945, a century after the terrible events, the Irish Folklore Commission noted:

> *I am sorry that this is such a meagre account of what was a dreadful period; but there seems to be very little information or interest left in the minds of the old people about that time. Indeed, it seems there was a sort of conspiracy of silence on the part of their mothers and fathers about it all.*

Informed by a sense of outrage at the attitudes, on the part of the British government and landlords, that allowed this terrible disaster to happen, the exhibition follows the harrowing story of the Famine, juxtaposing it with images of Ascendancy luxury and of present-day famine and emigration. In 1841, Ireland was the most densely populated country in Europe, with a vigorous trading and commercial life. The exhibition shows the tragic results of over-reliance on the potato, which had been introduced into the country in the early eighteenth century; by the 1840s, it was the staple diet of the population. Blight arrived in Ireland in October 1845. In a letter to the British Secretary of the Treasury, a contemporary eyewitness surveyed the devastation:

> *On the 27th of last month I passed from Cork to Dublin and this doomed plant bloomed in all the luxuriance of abundant harvest. Returning on the third instant I beheld with sorrow one wide waste of putrefying vegetation. In many places the wretched people were seated on the fences of their decaying gardens, wringing their hands and wailing bitterly the destruction that has left them foodless.*

The exhibition traces the poverty and hard-heartedness of the Whig government's laissez faire economic response to the crisis. Its callousness in the face of human suffering on a massive scale – as well as its attitude to Irish ways of life – is indicated by Trevelyan's response, as the famine deepened:

The great evil with which we have to contend is not the physical evil of famine but the moral evil of the selfish, perverse and turbulent character of the [Irish] people.

The government resolved to make no official intervention to hinder the operation of private enterprise: relief food imports were stopped. Between 1841 and 1851, about 1.4 million Irish people died and another 1.4 million people emigrated – figures almost entirely attributable to the Famine.

The house and museum – plus a walled garden (£2.50/€3.17, combined ticket for all three £8.50/€10.79) with a spectacular herbaceous border – are geared for group visits, but it can still be a thought-provoking experience, particularly if you arrive between busloads.

West from Strokestown

Heading west from Strokestown, there are a number of historical attractions that may divert you on your way to Mayo, including an extensive ancient Irish settlement near **Tulsk**; **Frenchpark** home of Irish language activist and first Irish president Douglas Hyde; and **Clonalis House**, at Castlerea, the home of one of Ireland's oldest Gaelic families.

Elphin

The trim village of **ELPHIN**, about four miles northwest of Strokestown, has been the seat of a bishopric for 1500 years, ever since St Patrick founded a church on this spot. The **cathedral**, rather unconvincingly restored in part in 1982, contains the tombs both of early bishops and of members of the Goldsmith family – Oliver's birthplace is disputed between here and Pallas in County Longford, which has been doing its best to cash in on the Goldsmith connection (see p.210). Even his famous poem *The Deserted Village* may describe County Roscommon rather than County Longford (and the English claim it's about the *English* enclosures); at any rate, he went to school here.

Tulsk and Rathcroghan

Paganism has been destroyed though it was splendid and far flung… their old cities are deserts without worship.

Oengus the Culdee, early Christian poet

Centred roughly on the village of **TULSK** on the main N5 is a collection of some seventy megalithic monuments that mark one of the great centres of ancient Ireland, plus more than eighty ring forts. Unlike the monuments of, say, County Sligo, they're unmarked and largely unexcavated – most of them are no more to look at than grassy shapes in the fields – and access is generally free and unrestricted. According to legend, the most important of them, the long-barrow of Rathcroghan itself, was built by Eochard Fedleach, King of Connacht and father of Medb – who herself took power by killing her pregnant sister Clothro, who had inherited the title from their father.

In the absence of signposting, the area's monuments are difficult to identify; **Rathcroghan** – or Cruachan – itself, however, lies just beyond the first crossroads on the N5 northwest of Tulsk and is signposted. It's a ring-barrow, traditionally the inau-

MEDB AND EARTH MAGIC

Medb's prodigious appetite for men – she was reported to have thirty lovers a day, "each man in another man's shadow" – reflects her non-historical career as a spiritual symbol: her name links her with the sanskrit *madhu*, a sort of demon, and with Shakespeare's Queen Mab, Queen of the Fairies. She's now enjoying a renaissance in a reincarnation as Gaia, the spirit of earth.

Clothro's unborn child, in one of the gruesome details beloved of those legends, was cut from her womb with a sword and himself grew up to become a warrior. Medb took as a lover the great Cúchulainn of the epic poem *Tain Bo Cúailgne.*

guration place of the kings of Connacht; close by are a cluster of standing stones, cairns and ring-barrows with legendary associations with Medb.

For the rest, it's probably best to rely on inspired guesswork when moving among these unexcavated monuments, knowing that, in this ancient landscape, anything you identify is likely to be at least as old as you think.

Frenchpark

Carrying on along the N5, you'll come to **FRENCHPARK** and the **Douglas Hyde Interpretive Centre** (*Gairdín an Craoibhín*, "Garden of the Little Branch") (May–Sept Tues–Fri 2–5pm, Sat & Sun 2–6pm; donation suggested), housed in an old Church of Ireland church. Hyde (1860–1949), one of the founders of the Gaelic League in 1893 and the leading exponent of the importance of the Irish language and culture in the Nationalist movement, was – like his approximate contemporaries, the poet W.B. Yeats and the playwright J.M. Synge – of Anglo-Irish background. The son of the rector of Tibohine, he was sent home from boarding school when he contracted measles, and was brought up here among Irish-speakers, and later did much to record the rich vernacular tradition, as well as writing in the language – he collaborated with Lady Gregory on a number of Irish-language plays, many of which he published under the pen name An Craoibhín Aoibhinn, "delightful little branch", from which the centre gets its name. Hyde's quixotic aim, to unite all classes in Ireland through the use of Irish language, was bound to end in disappointment and his naive idealism resulted in his disenchantment with the Gaelic League, most especially its espousal of revolutionary violence. After resigning from the Gaelic League, Hyde withdrew from public political life until he was elected as first president of Ireland. With the re-emergence of interest to preserve the language in recent years, there is some sign that Hyde's legacy, which had sometimes seemed a conservative and retrograde form of nationalism, may still be of importance. Hyde is buried in the graveyard of this simple church.

Castlerea

CASTLEREA (*An Caisléan Riabhach*, "The Grey Castle"), south of Frenchpark on the R361, is Roscommon's third most important town after Roscommon and Boyle. It's an unprepossessing place, only worth stopping in to visit **Clonalis House** (June to mid-Sept Tues–Sun 11am–5.00pm; £3.50/€4.44), just outside the town to the west. Clonalis is the ancestral home of the O'Conor clan, which claims to be Europe's oldest family; it is, in fact, one of the few ancient Gaelic families – the O'Conors were traditional Kings of Connacht and last High Kings of Ireland, and can trace their family back to one Feredach the Just in 75 AD – although an even more fanciful family tree preserved in the house goes back to the fifteenth century BC. If you're expecting the house itself to be ancient, however, you're in for a disappointment – it's a Victorian pile, albeit an engagingly Italianate one, of 1878. Unlike most noble Irish families, the O'Conors always remained Catholic and, although their royal past allowed them to hang on to some of their ancestral lands, they weren't in a position to flaunt their wealth – much of it derived from astute marriages to rich heiresses – until the late nineteenth century.

The house, still very much lived in, is a fascinating jumble of furniture, paintings – many of them portraits charting the family's colourful history at home and abroad – and mementos. There's a modest chapel displaying a penal chalice, which unscrews into three parts to make it easy to hide. The manuscript room contains the oldest surviving judgement under the ancient Irish Brehon law system, as well as a number of letters from Douglas Hyde (see opposite). Pride of place, however, goes to the harp of the blind harpist Turlough O'Carolan (1670–1738; see p.715), who numbered the then O'Conor Don among his patrons.

The house aside, there's no need to linger in Castlerea apart perhaps to visit *Hell's Kitchen*, an antiques-packed pub on the main street on the corner of the Boyle Road, describing itself as "the only national museum with a licence".

Boyle

It's disparagingly said that County Roscommon doesn't have any towns. It does, and **BOYLE**, although not the county town, is a fine, upstanding example. It's not a place marked out by particular charm or beauty, but there's enough here to keep you entertained for a one-night stopover, if you're not hurrying to cross the Curlew Mountains into Sligo. Boyle grew up around the greatest estate in County Roscommon, **Rockingham**, and although what remained of the estate was disbanded long ago and the house – in what is now the Lough Key Forest Park – was burned down in 1957, the town is still marked by their ghostly presence.

In Boyle itself, the most charismatic building is the Cistercian monastery, **Boyle Abbey** (Easter–Nov daily 9.30am–6.30pm; out of season, keys available from Abbey House, next door; ☎079/63242; £1/€1.27; Heritage Card), consecrated in 1220 and one of the early results of the arrival of foreign monastic orders in Ireland during the medieval pan-European upsurge in spiritual life. In 1142 a group of monks sent to Ireland by the redoubtable Cistercian abbot St Bernard of Clairvaux, at the instigation of St Malachy, established the great abbey of Mellifont in County Louth. Clonmacnois, the important Celtic monastery on the banks of the Shannon in County Offaly, was quickly abandoned, and within twenty years monks from Mellifont had settled at a site beside the River Boyle here at *Mainistir na Buaille.*

The abbey is small and compact, in very pale stone, well enough preserved to let you see how the monks must have lived. You still go in through the gatehouse (a sixteenth- or seventeenth-century addition), and there's a wonderful twelfth-century church. During the sixty-odd years it took to build the place, the Gothic style arrived in the west of Ireland; in a remarkably playful relaxation of their famous austerity, the Cistercian monks allowed themselves to build Romanesque arches down one side, and the new Gothic down the other. Look out, too, for the fantastically ornate (at least, for Cistercians) column capitals.

Boyle's big house may be gone, but the earlier residence of the King family, **King House** (April & Oct Sat & Sun 10am-6pm; May–Sept daily 10am–6pm; £3/€3.81), in the centre of town, has recently been restored and opened to the public with a range of high-tech exhibitions. An imposing stone mansion built around 1730, King House, with its pleasure grounds across the river, was home to the family for fifty years before they moved to Rockingham, and it represents the heyday of what was aptly known as the Ascendancy. The original Sir John King, a Staffordshire man, had been granted his land for "reducing the Irish to obedience", achieved in part through violent subjugation and by the enforcement of the notorious anti-Catholic Penal Laws. For the King family, establishing themselves in Ireland was a process of determined and successful social climbing: inheriting a baronetcy in 1755, by 1768 Edward King had ensured his elevation to Earl of Kingston.

One section of the exhibition deals with the Famine and recounts a familiar story: Robert King, Viscount Lordon, although not an absentee landlord, did – like many other landlords, after the removal of the corn tariffs flooded the Irish market with cheap grain – find it economic to evict his tenants, transport them to America and use the land for cattle grazing. Other accounts detail the Kings' colourful family history – an eighteenth-century crime of passion and a very public nineteenth-century divorce – and there's a section on the house's use as a base from 1775 for the Connacht Rangers. This details their service to the British Army in such conflicts as the Crimean and Boer wars and World War I, culminating in their mutiny at Jullandar in the Punjab in 1920 in protest at the atrocities being perpetrated by the Black and Tans back home in Ireland. Boyle's civic art collection, with some interesting modern pieces, is housed on the ground floor of the building, and there's a pleasant coffee shop, much frequented by locals at lunchtime.

At the other end of town, down the driveway that leads from beside the bridge, **Frybrook House** (June–Aug daily 2–6pm; £3/€3.81) offers a view of more modest eighteenth-century living – as well as a great place to **stay**. Built around 1752, the house belonged to Henry Fry, an English Quaker (the family may be related to the Cadbury Frys of confectionery fame), who came to Boyle at the invitation of the Earl of Kingston to establish a weaving community in the town. The house has been extensively restored and, although only three pieces of the original furniture remain, it has been sympathetically decorated with items from the same period and there are some fine paintings.

Practicalities

The **tourist office** is at the entrance to King House in Patrick Street, near the bridge (May–Sept 10am–5pm; ☎079/62145); as well as the usual services, it can give you details of the Boyle Arts Festival (☎079/63085), well worth catching for its ambitious programme of concerts, theatre, poetry readings, lectures and exhibitions if you're in town in late July or early August. You can also get information from the Úna Bhán Tourism Co-operative, which is also in the grounds of King House (☎079/63033). Wedged between the rushing river and the abbey, *Abbey House* is a pleasant place to **stay** (closed Nov–Feb; ☎079/62385; ③), as is *Cois Crann* (☎079/62217; ③) directly opposite the Abbey; if neither of these suit try *Forest Park House*, Carrick Rd (☎079/62227, *forestparkhse@hotmail.com*; ③), particularly welcoming to families, while four miles out of town in the townland of Doon is the fine *Hillside House* (☎079/66075; ③). The 250-year-old *Royal Hotel* on Bridge St (☎079/62016; ⑥) is a solid country inn where the river rushes by your window. A little outside the town at Knockvicar is *Riversdale House* (see opposite for details).

You can **rent bikes** (this makes a good starting point for touring the lakelands of northern and southern Sligo) from Brendan Sheerin, on Main Street; if he is closed (as is often the case) try Riverside Cycles (☎079/63777). **Horse riding** is available at the Curlew Trekking Centre (☎079/62764). Places to **eat** include: the restaurant at the *Royal*, which now serves excellent Chinese food at very reasonable prices and has a good coffee shop for daytime eating, as does the *Úna Bhán* restaurant in the grounds of King House. *Bia Beo* ("living food") in the shopping arcade on Bridge Street does fine evening meals, while the best lunches are served at *An Craoibhín* in the Crescent, also an excellent pub. For a genuine **pub** experience try *Kate Lavin's*, one that time seems to have forgotten.

Lough Key Forest Park and Woodbrook

The road west out of Boyle towards the **Lough Key Forest Park**, part of the old Rockingham Estate, leads through the gate of the grounds, itself a Gothic fancy, and past a castellated lodge. The park has been thoroughly and relentlessly amenitized, with a hideous wood-and-glass restaurant at the side of the lake and masses of tarmacked car-parking on the former site of the great house. The latter was designed, in an elegant if fanciful Classical style, by the English architect John Nash, who was also responsible for the Classical mansions in London's Regent's Park. Yet the stable block, church, icehouse and temple – the graces of an eighteenth-century estate – as well as the spine-chilling subterranean passages used to keep the servants out of sight, give an impression of what it must have been like. With boats for rental and plenty of ring forts to explore, it's a pleasant enough place to spend a sunny day.

You can gaze out, too, at the islands on the lake; in a disused castle on one of them W.B. Yeats planned, after his Innisfree days, to base an Irish cult devoted to the occult principles of Theosophy and the Order of the Golden Dawn – the idea was to aid the Nationalist cause by trapping the hidden forces of the land. The **circuit** of the lake is well worth doing, particularly the west side, where the road rises to give you a panoramic view. A possible stop on the way is B&B **accommodation** at *Riversdale House* (☎079/67012; ④), where the River Boyle flows out of the lough – a compact Georgian lodge on a working farm that was once home to Maureen O'Sullivan – where you can also have dinner.

A little further out of Boyle on the Carrick-on-Shannon Road, **Woodbrook** is another old Anglo-Irish house. It's not open to the public, and the reason for mentioning it is that it's the subject of a remarkable book, *Woodbrook*, written by an Englishman, David Thompson, who worked there for most of the 1930s as tutor to the Kirkwood family's two young daughters, one of whom – Phoebe – was a well-known painter. Sometimes naive, sometimes sentimental, it's strong in its evocation of place and in its documentation of the passing of Anglo-Irish culture.

The very north of the county, hilly terrain where farmland gives way to the moors and lakes of the **Arigna Mountains**, is a good introduction to the more spectacular landscape over the county border in Sligo. You can break your journey in the twin villages of **Ballyfarnon** and **Keadue** and, outside Keadue by the ruins of the sixth-century **Killoran Abbey**, visit the grave of the famous blind harpist Turlough O'Carolan (see p.715).

travel details

Trains

Galway to: Athenry (4 daily; 15min); Athlone (4 daily; 1hr); Dublin (4 daily; 2hr 30min–3hr); Portarlington (3 daily; 2hr).

Westport to: Castlebar (3 daily; 15min); Castlerea (3 daily; 1hr 15min); Dublin (3 daily; 3hr 30min); Roscommon (3 daily; 1hr 30min).

Buses

Galway to: Clifden (2–5 daily; 1hr 45min–2hr 15min); Cork (5 daily; 4hr); Donegal (2 daily; 3hr); Doolin (3 daily; 1hr 30min); Dublin (5–8 daily; 3hr 45min); Letterkenny (2 daily; 4hr); Limerick (9 daily; 2hr); Sligo (2 daily; 2hr 15min).

Private Buses

Private bus companies which serve Galway City include: Bus Nestor (☎091/797144), Citylink (☎091/564163), Lally's (☎091/562095) and Hugh Ryan (☎091/555780). O'Neachtains (☎091/553188) and Hugh Ryan (☎091/555780) serve towns and villages in Connemara; and Walsh's (☎098 35165) serves towns and villages in Mayo.

CHAPTER ELEVEN

SLIGO AND LEITRIM

Counties **Sligo** and **Leitrim** pair up well, offering a luscious and gentle scenery that contrasts with the wilder streaks of Donegal and Mayo, yet is equally far removed from the dullness of Longford and Cavan to the east. Leitrim, one of the most neglected counties in the country, is an area of lakelets and low mounds, and presents a singularly withdrawn face to the outside world. Sligo, also underrated, is the more enticing of the two, containing the beautiful mountains of Benbulben and Knocknarea, the lion's share of the enchanting Gill and Glencar loughs, as well as an array of standing stones and other megalithic monuments as dramatic as any in Ireland. Much of the terrain is gently undulating farm land, allowing long cross-country views to the higher outcrops in the county's far corners: the Ox Mountains range to the west, the Bricklieve to the south and the Dartry to the north. At Streedagh and Mullaghmore you'll find some of the country's finest beaches; at Easky and Strandhill some of its finest surf.

COUNTY SLIGO

County Sligo has the greatest concentration of megalithic monuments in Ireland, as well as some of the wildest and most remote country. Especially poetic testaments to the ancient fusion of landscape and human presence are the extensive Neolithic cemetery at **Carrowmore**, to the south of Sligo town, and the large prehistoric village at **Carrowkeel**, on top of the Bricklieve Mountains. The pimple on top of **Knocknarea** is an unexcavated burial mound known locally as Maeve's Lump: legend has it that Queen Medb – Sligo's guardian spirit – is buried there, standing upright and still facing her enemies. This landscape and its culture inspired the great Irish poet **W.B. Yeats**, whose poetry is saturated with the atmosphere of Sligo. Yeats' presence still makes itself felt – above all at places such as the island of **Innisfree** on Lough Gill and **Lissadell House**, north of Sligo.

Sligo town

With a population of 18,000, **SLIGO** is, after Derry, the biggest town in the northwest of Ireland and a focal point for the surrounding area. This engaging place, overshad-

ACCOMMODATION PRICE CODES

Throughout this book, prices of hotels, guesthouses and B&Bs have been graded with the codes below, according to what you can expect to pay for a double room in high season. For more details on accommodation, see p.34.

① Under £26/€33.01	④ £40–55/€50.79–69.84	⑦ £90–110/€114.28–139.67
② £26–33/€33.01–41.90	⑤ £55–70/€69.84–88.88	⑧ £110–130/€139.67–165.07
③ £33–40/€41.90–50.79	⑥ £70–90/€88.88–114.28	⑨ Over £130/€165.07

owed by the presence of Knocknarea and Benbulben mountains, manages to be relaxed and busy at the same time, with a fair dash of the Irish New Age spirit that suffuses much of the west. If you've been too long in the wildernesses, you can soak up something of a city atmosphere. The annual **Yeats summer school** in August, the **arts festival** in May and the **choral festival** in November are indications of Sligo's vitality.

The first recorded mention of Sligo dates from 807 AD, when the town was sacked by the Vikings, and by the thirteenth century it had become the gateway between Connacht and Ulster, with a castle (since destroyed) on what is now Castle Street. The Middle Ages was a period of sporadic violence, most notably between the Anglo-Norman Maurice Fitzgerald and the O'Connells. Thanks to its strong defences, Sligo was the last of the western garrisons to surrender to Williamite forces after the Battle of the Boyne.

The town suffered during the Great Famine, when its population fell by a third through death and emigration, but by the end of the nineteenth century things had picked up to the extent that it was described in guidebooks as "a progressive and busy centre". The upswing has continued to the present day, and in summer the streets are always crowded with visitors – but if you have a chance to look at the photos of old Sligo hanging in the **County Museum** on Stephen Street, you'll appreciate how remarkably constant the look of the town has been with its narrow, tightly packed back streets. Apart from the **Dominican Abbey** there's not much left in the way of sites that recall the town's long history, but the old-fashioned market town atmosphere, the pleasant riverside cafés and the atmospheric old pubs make it an ideal base for exploring the surrounding countryside and sights. Lough Gill, Drumcliff, the megalithic dolmens of Knocknarea and the beaches at Strandhill are all within a five-mile radius of town; Lissadell, Benbulben and Glencar Lough are within ten. If you are without transport, it's worth calling in to the tourist office and checking out details of minibus and walking **tours** of the area to make the most of at least some of these.

Arrival, information and accommodation

The **bus station** (☎071/60066) and **train station** (☎071/69888) are both handily placed on the western edge of town within easy walking distance of almost everything. Feda O'Donnell Coaches (☎075/48114) has two to three buses daily stopping off in Sligo en route between Galway and Donegal – for journeys north, the bus departs from outside *Connolly's* pub on Wine Street; for journeys south, from outside XL Stop & Shop also on Wine Street. Sligo **airport** (☎071/68280) is four miles west of town at Strandhill; a taxi into town costs around £10 (Elliott Taxis; ☎071/41111).

Sligo's main **tourist office**, on Temple Street (mid-June to Aug daily 9am–8pm; rest of year Mon–Fri 9am–5pm; ☎071/61201), is the headquarters for counties Sligo, Leitrim, Monaghan, Cavan and Donegal. They offer car rental, money exchange, Internet access, an accommodation booking service, and also stock *Archaeology in County Sligo*, well worth picking up if you intend on exploring the **archeological sites** of the county in detail. A smaller second tourist office is based in the Yeats Memorial Building, Douglas Hyde Bridge (same times; ☎071/38772) – this is a useful central alternative, although it doesn't have an accommodation booking service. **Bike rental** is available at Flanagan's Cycle Hire, Market Yard (☎071/44477). For **Internet access** there's the tourist office and *Cygo Internet Café*, 19 O'Connell St (Mon–Sat 10am–7pm; ☎071/40082).

Accommodation

Sligo town has plenty of **accommodation** on offer: in addition to the options listed on p.440, there's no shortage of B&Bs along Pearse Road and to the west of town along the main road to Strandhill. *Gateway Caravan and Camping Park*, Ballinode

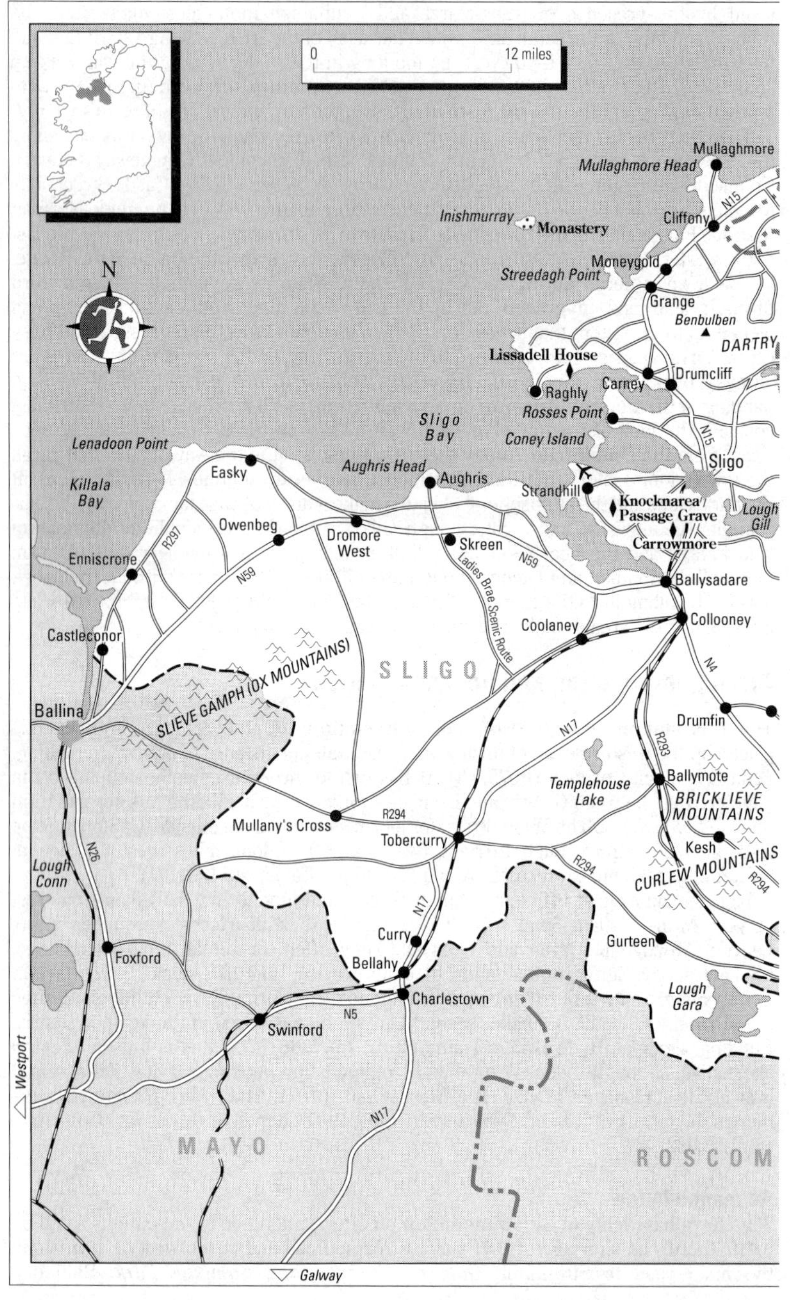
0
12 miles
N
Mullaghmore
Mullaghmore Head
Inishmurray
Monastery
Cliffony
N15
Moneygold
Streedagh Point
Grange
Benbulben
DARTRY
Lissadell House
Carney
Drumcliff
Raghly
Rosses Point
Sligo
Bay
Coney Island
N15
Sligo
Lenadoon Point
Easky
Aughris Head
Aughris
Strandhill
Knocknarea
Passage Grave
Lough
Gill
Carrowmore
Killala
Bay
Owenbeg
Dromore
West
Skreen
R297
Enniscrone
N59
Ladies Brae Scenic Route
N59
Ballysadare
Collooney
Coolaney
Castleconor
SLIEVE GAMPH (OX MOUNTAINS)
SLIGO
N4
Ballina
Drumfin
N17
R293
Ballymote
Templehouse
Lake
BRICKLIEVE
MOUNTAINS
Mullany's Cross
R294
Tobercurry
Kesh
R294
CURLEW MOUNTAINS
R294
Lough
Conn
N26
N17
Curry
Gurteen
Foxford
Bellahy
Charlestown
Lough
Gara
N5
Swinford
Westport
N17
MAYO
ROSCOM
Galway

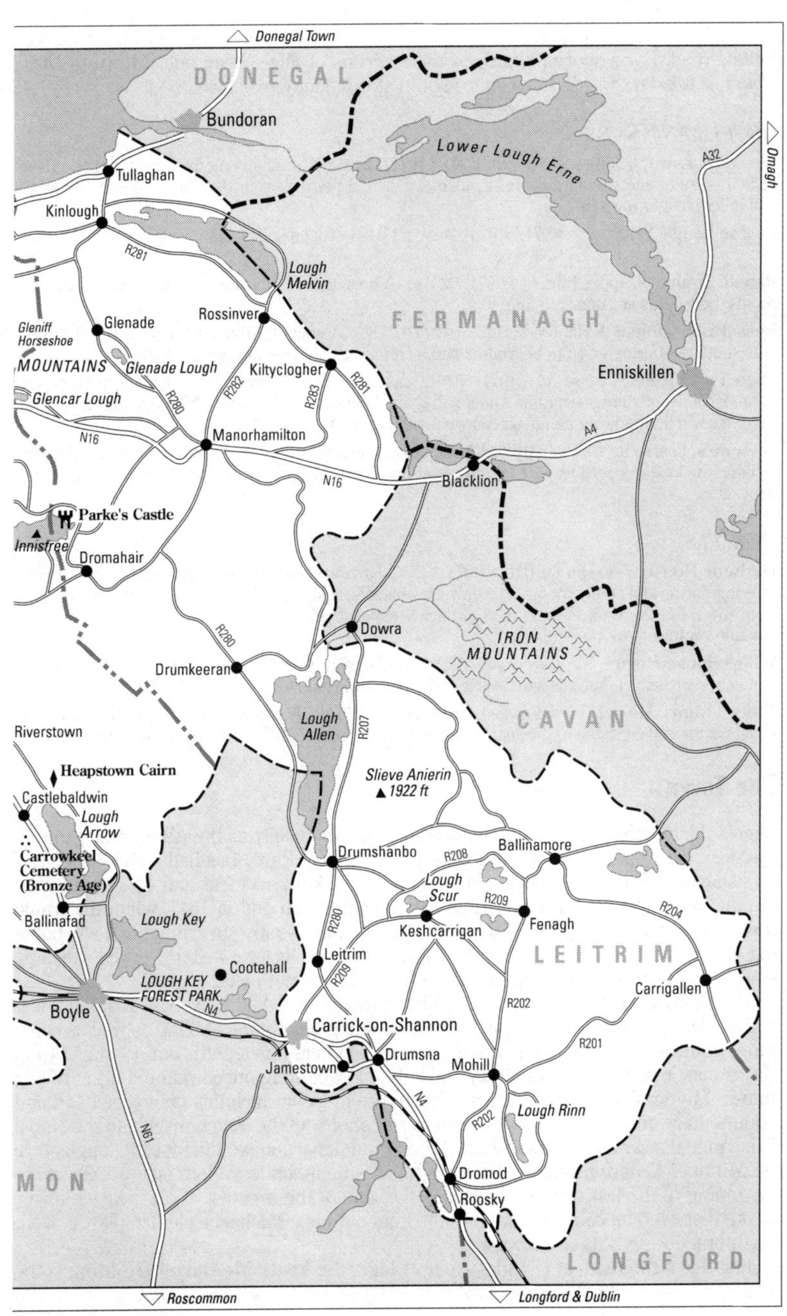
Donegal Town
DONEGAL
Bundoran
Lower Lough Erne
Omagh
A32
Tullaghan
Kinlough
R281
Lough Melvin
Rossinver
FERMANAGH
Gleniff Horseshoe
Glenade
MOUNTAINS
Glenade Lough
Kiltyclogher
R281
R282
R283
Glencar Lough
R280
Enniskillen
N16
Manorhamilton
A4
N16
Blacklion
Parke's Castle
Innisfree
Dromahair
Dowra
IRON MOUNTAINS
R280
Drumkeeran
CAVAN
Lough Allen
R207
Riverstown
Heapstown Cairn
Slieve Anierin
1922 ft
Castlebaldwin
Lough Arrow
Carrowkeel Cemetery (Bronze Age)
Drumshanbo
R208
Ballinamore
Lough Scur
R209
Ballinafad
Lough Key
Keshcarrigan
Fenagh
R280
R204
LEITRIM
Leitrim
Cootehall
R209
Carrigallen
LOUGH KEY FOREST PARK
R202
N4
Boyle
Carrick-on-Shannon
R201
Drumsna
Jamestown
Mohill
N4
Lough Rinn
R202
N61
MON
Dromod
Roosky
LONGFORD
Roscommon
Longford & Dublin

(☎071/45618), is three-quarters of a mile northeast of the centre of town along the N16 Belfast road. For a spot of luxury in the environs of Sligo, head out of town to *Glebe House* or *Markree Castle*, a few miles south at Collooney (see p.453).

HOTELS AND B&BS

Chestnut Lawn, Cummeen, Strandhill Rd (☎071/62781). A spacious modern B&B with well-furnished en-suite and standard rooms available; TVs and hairdryers in bedrooms. About one and a half miles west of town.③.

Pearse Lodge, Pearse Rd (☎071/61090). A smart B&B with en-suite facilities and TVs in all rooms. ③.

Renaté House, 9 Upper John St (☎071/62014). A hospitable B&B offering standard and en-suite rooms; bedrooms are non-smoking. ③.

Ross Brían House, 1 Hanley Terrace (☎071/62186). A small traditional B&B next to the main tourist office offering en-suite bedrooms and a communal sitting room with TV. ③.

Sligo Park Hotel, Pearse Rd (☎071/60291, *www.iol.ie/lee*). A very pleasant modern three-star hotel; facilities include a swimming pool and gym. About one mile south of Sligo along the Dublin road. It's worth enquiring about special weekend rates. ⑧.

St Anne's, Pearse Rd (☎071/43188). Excellent B&B in a beautifully kept, welcoming family home; facilities include a very pleasant sitting room and, surprisingly, an unheated outdoor swimming pool. ④.

HOSTELS

Harbour House, Finisklin Rd (IHH; ☎071/71547, *harbourhouse@eircom.net*) A comfortable hostel offering dorms and family rooms. The only drawback is its location: it's only three-quarters of a mile from town, but the walk to reach it is strangely exposed and desolate. Women may not feel comfortable venturing out there alone.

White House Hostel, Markiewicz Rd (IHH; ☎071/45160). A small hostel close to the town centre. Not especially smart, but nevertheless friendly and well run. Dorms only.

Yeats County Hostel, Lord Edward Street (☎071/46876). A central, well-run hostel with fairly small dorms and a garden to the rear. Safe bike and car parks. Handy for the bus and train stations.

The Town

Sligo's thirteenth-century Dominican **friary**, known locally as the Abbey (mid-June to mid-Sept daily 9.30am–6.30pm; £1.50/€1.90; Heritage Card) has had a chequered history, having been destroyed a couple of times by both accident and design since its foundation. Its life as a religious foundation came to an end in 1641, when the whole town was sacked during the Ulster rebellion. As Sligo's only surviving medieval building, the friary merits exploration; the impressive ruins include well-preserved cloisters, Gothic and Renaissance sculpture and a finely carved high altar.

The **Sligo County Museum** on Stephen Street (Tues–Sat: May–Sept 10am–noon & 2–5pm; Oct–April 2–5pm; free) is full of fascinating old photos of Sligo as well as some more unusual items, including a sequence of excellent nineteenth-century sketches of the monastic ruins on Inishmurray and a double-weight hundred-year-old firkin of bog butter. Memorabilia in the Yeats section of the museum includes photographs of and commentary on his funeral, lots of letters and photos of the man himself and the Nobel Prize medal awarded to him in 1923. Before you depart, make time for the long article on **Michael Coleman**, one of Ireland's most famous fiddle players (see p.709): at the beginning of the last century, Fritz Kreisler, one of the greatest of classical violinists, wrote that even he could not attempt the kind of music Michael Coleman played, were he to practise for a thousand years.

Just down the road, at Douglas Hyde Bridge, the **Yeats Memorial Building** is the headquarters of the Yeats Society (☎071/42693 or 47264; *www.yeats-sligo.com*) and

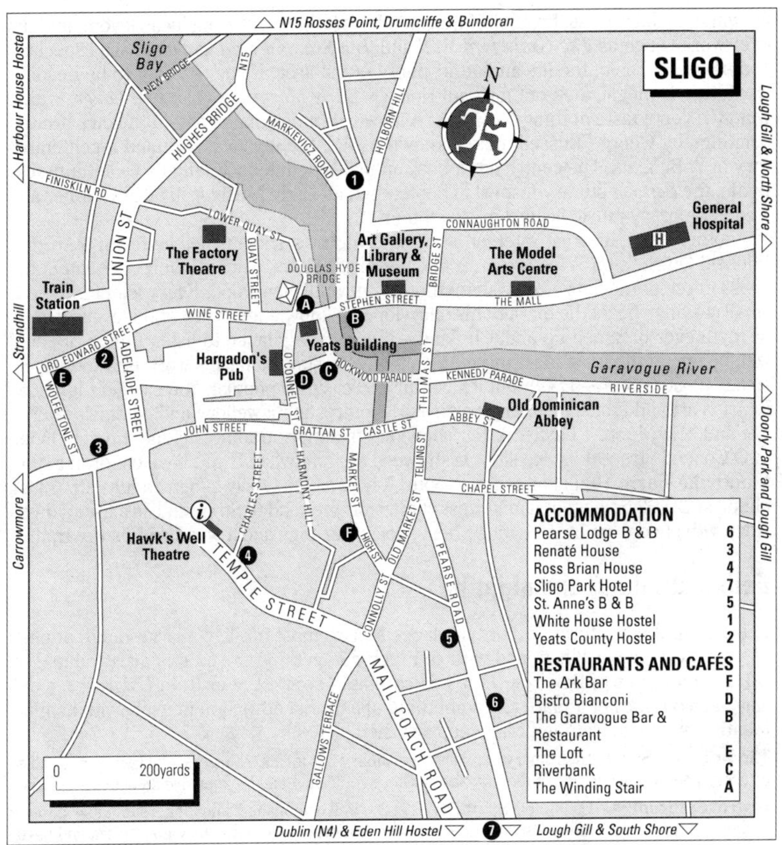

venue for the Yeats International Summer School in August. It has become something of an academic institution, attracting scholars from all over the world. The attendant Yeats Exhibition (Mon–Sat 10am–5pm; £2.50/€3.17) is a fairly small display, including interesting photographic material of the poet, his family, and his influences and associates which include Maud Gonne, Aubrey Beardsley, Ezra Pound and J.M. Synge. There's a short film too, *Yeats Country*, which, despite poor sound and visual quality (it dates from the 1950s), is enjoyable for the spoken verse and as an appetizer for the evocative scenery that lies close at hand. The building is also home to Sligo's second tourist office and the **Sligo Art Gallery** (Mon–Sat 10am–5.30pm; free), which has an extensive exhibition programme showing contemporary, predominantly Irish, work. Outside, the Garavogue River rushes under Douglas Hyde Bridge, and the revamped riverside paths and cafés provide a pleasant focus away from traffic-choked streets. A fifteen-minute walk east along the south side of the river from here leads to Doorly Park and access to the magical **Lough Gill** (see p.443).

For a taste of the northwest's energetic arts scene, head for **The Model Arts Centre** (daily 11am–5pm) on The Mall, housed in an imposing nineteenth-century stone building. It's home to The Niland Collection, which includes paintings and pencil drawings by Jack Yeats, brother of the poet. His work has a strong local flavour, and his later works such as *The Graveyard Wall* and *The Sea and the Lighthouse* are especially potent evocations of the life and atmosphere of the area. If you're going to be heading north into Donegal, look out for Paul Henry's *Early Morning in Donegal Lough*, which will give you a taste of things to come. Also worth more than a passing glance are the paintings by George Russell, better known as AE, the mystical poet and a contemporary of W.B. Yeats. The centre has a busy annual schedule including three autumn **festivals**: the *Scríobh* literary festival in September, an Early Music festival in October and a contemporary music festival in November.

Another place of great interest is an old butcher's shop-turned-**sculpture studio**, Michael Quirke's on Wine Street. A butcher for 31 years, Michael Quirke began in the 1980s to sculpt the figures of Irish mythology in windfallen wood. Every feature of these small carvings bears the mark of his encyclopedic knowledge of just about every legend or myth ever dreamed up about Ireland – if you get a chance to listen to him, it could well be one of the most inspiring moments of your stay. So far his work isn't too expensive (£40–50/€50.79–63.49), but it's getting increasingly popular. You can get high-quality Irish art and crafts, including particularly interesting jewellery and ceramics, at The Cat and The Moon, 4 Castle St. For souvenirs of a more traditional kind, Carraig Donn in O'Connell Street sells excellent Irish tweed and knitwear. If you have children in tow, **Woodville Farm** (June Sat & Sun 2–5pm; July & August daily 2–5pm; adults £3/€3.81, children £2/€2.54), about a mile west of town off the road to Strandhill, is a useful diversion, with sheep, lambs, free-range hens, peacocks, pigs and a woodland nature trail.

Eating, drinking and nightlife

Aside from the scattering of formal places **to eat**, most of Sligo's large range of pubs seem to serve a bar lunch, and with so much competition the food is great value. You can get **picnic supplies** from *Kate's Kitchen* at 24 Market St or from *Cosgrove's*, a delicatessen on Market Square and something of a tourist attraction in itself, with its nineteenth-century interior and craft shop attached.

The Ark, High Street. An ordinary bar serving ordinary bar meals – burgers, chicken, chips, and so on. Very good value and one of the few places where you can get an inexpensive meal in the evening.

Bistro Bianconi, 44 O'Connell St (☎071/41744). Well-established and understandably popular Italian restaurant generating a warm, convivial atmosphere and serving very good pizza and pasta. Open in the evenings every day, and in the summer at lunchtime too.

Garavogue, the rear of 15–16 Stephen St (☎071/40100). Chic and airy bar and mid-priced restaurant with riverside terrace, serving a tantalizing contemporary menu: choice menu options include crab claws in chilli lime butter, fettucine with smoked chicken, olives and sundried tomatoes, and other dishes. Last orders for food daily at 9pm.

The Loft, above *M.J.Carr's*, Lord Edward Street (☎071/46770). Lively, informal railway-themed restaurant, serving moderately-priced Mexican, vegetarian and fish dishes, with carvery lunches in the bar at around midday. Daily 6–11pm.

Riverbank, Rockwood Parade (☎071/71097). Big, cheerful café-restaurant offering good value open sandwiches and filled baked potatoes during the day. In the evenings, the influence is modern Irish and French. Lunches cost around £5/€6.98, evening meals from around £15/€19.05. Mon–Sat 9am–5pm; also Wed–Sat 6.30–10pm.

Winding Stair Bookshop & Café, Wine Street, just near Douglas Hyde Bridge. Airy café with a laid-back atmosphere offering inexpensive and wholesome sandwiches, soups, salads and quiche. Daytime only; closed Sun.

Nightlife and entertainment

When it comes to **pubs**, Sligo does well. *Hargadon's* on O'Connell Street is one of the most enjoyable places to drink and talk. An exclusively male establishment until the early 1980s, it's a fine old pub, with dark recesses and shut-off rooms, and shelves of nineteenth-century earthenware stout jugs. Note the little swivel windows at the far end of the serving bar, where the whiskey could be slipped through with little fuss by either drinker or landlord. *Shoot the Crows*, Castle Street, is a lively bar for an interesting pint, just opposite the Lady of Erin statue.

Furey's, a characterful bar in Bridge Street, is the best spot for **traditional music**, with sessions three or four nights a week plus jazz on Wednesdays. *Early's*, also on Bridge Street is another lively spot (traditional music on Thursdays), while *TD's* on Adelaide Street and *The Leitrim Bar*, across the river on The Mall, both have something happening most nights throughout the year. *McLoughlin's* in Market Street generally has music on a Tuesday, along with impromptu sessions at other times. The *Clarence Hotel* on Wine Street has a live band (Fri & Sat) and a dance floor. Check *The Sligo Champion* for details of other pubs with live music; alternatively *The Sligo Weekender* is a useful free paper with entertainment listings (out on Friday) as is *Sligo's Monthly Gig Guide*, both available in shops and the main tourist office. The big **nightclub** in town is *Toff's* at the Embassy Rooms, John F. Kennedy Parade (Thurs–Sun). *Equinox* on Teeling Street also has discos (Wed–Sun 11pm–1.30am).

The Hawk's Well **theatre** on Lower Quay Street (☎071/61518) stages both amateur and professional drama, and also has musicals and classical music concerts, particularly during the Yeats International Summer School (August) and the Sligo Arts Festival (May). It's also worth checking to see what's on at The Factory Theatre, Lower Gill Street (☎071/70431; *www.blueraincoat.com*), which is home to the movement-based Blue Raincoat Theatre Company; it also acts as a performance space for other cultural events.

Lough Gill

The 24-mile circuit of **Lough Gill**, a broad lake just east of Sligo with luscious woodland covering the small hills that rise off its indented banks, makes a great day-trip by **bike** from Sligo – or you could break the journey midway in Dromahair (see p.444) and allow yourself more time to explore.

A trip out onto the lake – on which sits the isle of **Innisfree**, immortalized by Yeats – is easily accessible from the centre of Sligo: to walk to the lake set off from Bridge Street east along the south bank of the river, until you come after about a mile to **Doorly Park**. Here, short woodland walks give views across the lake and a hint of the beauty that lies beyond. The Wild Rose waterbus from Doorly Park out to Parke's Castle (see below) is a wonderful journey **by boat** across the reed-whipped lake into the heart of Yeats' country (mid-March to May & Sept Sun 2.30pm; June–Aug daily 2.30pm; returns 5.30pm; £8/€10.16; ☎071/64266). From Parke's Castle, they also run trips to the isle of **Innisfree** on the lake (see p.445). Out of high summer, you should phone in advance, or enquire at the tourist office, about their schedule. Alternatively, you could **rent a rowing boat** from the *Blue Lagoon* pub at Doorly Park (☎071/42539) for £15/€19.05 a day, and make your own way onto the water; you'll pass the pub en route to the waterbus jetty.

The northern shore and Parke's Castle

If you have your own transport, head first for **the northern shore**, reached from Sligo by taking The Mall past the hospital, turning onto the R286 at the garage and then following signposts for the **Hazelwood Estate** on the right. A left turn off the road leading into the estate grounds will bring you after half-a-mile to **Half Moon Bay**, where there's a picnic site and a pleasant lakeside walk. Wooden sculptures by various artists are ranged in the woods around – the most stunning is a set piece of chariot and horses, arrayed in its own artificial dell.

THE LEGENDS OF LOUGH GILL

A place of such natural beauty as Lough Gill inevitably features in legend. The story of the lough tells of a warrior called Romra who had a daughter named Gille ("beauty" in Irish). One day Gille was seen bathing by Omra, a friend of Romra. Omra was captivated by the girl – and she wasn't altogether indifferent to him – but when Romra got to hear about it, a fight ensued in which Omra was killed and Romra received wounds from which he later died. Grief-stricken, Gille drowned herself, and the lough was formed from the tears of her doubly grief-stricken nursemaid.

According to another tale, the silver bell from the Dominican Abbey in Sligo lies at the bottom of the lake. Only those free from sin can hear its pealing…

Back on the R286, a left turn soon after the road forks for the "Lough Gill Loop" will take you up to the **Deerpark Forest**, where a magnificent megalithic court tomb surveys the wild country. Ten minutes' walking on an unpaved road brings you to the top of **Cashelgal Mountain**, where you'll find both the tomb and unparalleled panoramic views.

At the eastern end of the lake – which sticks out into County Leitrim – the road begins to skirt the shore on its approach to **Parke's Castle** (Easter–May & Oct daily 10am–5pm; April & May closed Mon except bank holidays; June–Sept daily 9.30am–6.30pm; £2/€2.55; Heritage Card), a romantic-looking seventeenth-century fortress only yards from the water. The castle, built by one Robert Parke in the 1620s, is an evocative example of an early planter building and of the talents displayed by the Office of Public Works for conjuring heritage sites out of virtually nothing. The foundations discovered in the courtyard of the present castle are thought to be those of the moated tower house of the Irish chieftain Brian O'Rourke, prince of Breffni. In 1588, O'Rourke sheltered a Spaniard from the wrecked Armada; arraigned for high treason, he was executed at Tyburn in 1591. It seems that Parke used the simplest (and cheapest) method of making a home for himself, by utilizing the outer walls of O'Rourke's castle – and probably completing the demolition of the tower in the process. The reconstruction is clearly a fairly creative one, but it works well as a focus for the surrounding topography. The entrance ticket also admits you to an **audio-visual show**, which, as a quick introduction to the area's built environment, is also worth seeing.

The southern shore and the isle of Innisfree

From the eastern end of the lough, the signposted Manorhamilton road leads to the modern, uninspiring **Newtown Manor church**; but the journey, a steep climb through the high wild moorland behind the lake, is exhilarating. The main road around the lake winds on through lush woodland to **DROMAHAIR** in County Leitrim, where, at the end of a short walk on the other side of the rushing River Bonet, lies **Creevelea Friary** (see p.462).

Continuing from Dromahair, the road climbs to offer breathtaking views of the mountains opposite. A signposted lane shortly after the Sligo county border will lead you down to the lakeside where you can gaze out at Yeats's tiny "**Lake Isle of Innisfree**" and breathe in the tranquillity:

I will arise and go now, and go to Innisfree
And a small cabin build there, of clay and wattles made
Nine bean-rows will I have there, and a hive for the honey-bee,
And live alone in the bee-loud glade.

And I shall have some peace there, for peace comes dropping slow,
Dropping from the veils of the morning to where the cricket sings;
There midnight's all a glimmer, and noon a purple glow,
And evening full of the linnet's wings.

I will arise and go now, for always night and day
I hear lake water lapping with low sounds by the shore
While I stand on the roadway, or on the pavements grey,
I hear it in the deep heart's core.

The Wild Rose Waterbus runs **boat trips to Innisfree** from Parke's Castle (July & Aug 12.30pm, 1.30pm, 3.30pm, 4.30pm & 6.30pm; April–June & Sept according to demand – phone in advance or check with the Sligo tourist office; ☎071/64266; £6/€7.62). **Inismor**, Innisfree's sister island, was the site of the medieval school of poets to the O'Rourke's; unfortunately, its priceless library of manuscripts was destroyed by fire.

Continuing back towards Sligo, the road winds gently through woods with occasional views of the lough. At **Dooney Rock**, a brief stroll through woodlands brings you to a secluded shore where you can view the island opposite and consider swimming over. The road back into Sligo passes **Cairns Hill Forest Park**, where, from the car park, a path leads to the top of Cairns Hill, with a view across to a second cairn on the peak of Belvoir Hill. These are reckoned to be the tombs of Romra and Omra (see box), though another legend makes them out to be the breasts of a monstrous hag, with Lough Gill as her navel.

North of Sligo town

The countryside **north of Sligo town** is dominated by Benbulben, a foreboding plateau that rises steeply from surrounding farmland, its cold grey-green slopes presenting an extraordinary silhouette against the sky. It was much loved by W.B. Yeats, who asked to be buried beneath its slopes. Yeats' grave at Drumcliff church is something of a place of pilgrimage, and is well worth visiting to absorb the cold magic of the poet's choice and to learn more about his life and work at the nearby visitor centre. Immediately south of Benbulben lies the beautiful Glencar Lough, one of the scenic highlights of the area, while to the west lies Lissadell House, another essential stopping-off point for fans of Yeats that was home to the poet's friends Eva Gore-Booth and Constance Markiewicz.

The countryside along this stretch of coast has none of the drama of the inland scenery, but it does conceal some very fine beaches, most notably at Rosses Point, Streedagh Strand and at Mullaghmore, where the shoreline swings northwards, capturing fabulous views of the Donegal mountains. The island of Inishmurray is a prime draw, a desolate place rich in early Christian remains.

Rosses Point

Leaving Sligo along the coast to the north, almost immediately you have the option of a short detour to **ROSSES POINT** (bus #480 from Sligo), around five miles north of town. This (or Strandhill, see p.450) is the place to go for a day at the **beach**, a perfect picture-postcard scene, with the streaks of **Coney Island** (see p.450) and its neighbour Oyster Island guarding the entrance to the bay and the distinctive beauty of Knocknarea and Benbulben standing behind. A sea marker called the Metal Man marks the deepest part of the channel for Sligo-bound boats; placed there in 1822, it was called by Yeats the "Rosses Point man who never told a lie". The tip of the headland, **Deadman's Point**, took its name from a sailor who was buried at sea here with a loaf of bread thoughtfully provided by his comrades – they weren't sure whether he was really dead but wanted to despatch him quickly so they could make port before the tide turned. Today Rosses Point Blue Flag beach is good for swimming and for reflecting on the works of Jack B. Yeats, W.B.'s brother, who painted the scene here on many occasions.

There are a few **hotels**, including the imposing *Yeats Country Hotel* (☎071/77211; ⑨), which looks out across the Atlantic, and lots of **B&Bs**, too: try *Oyster View* (☎071/77201; ④), pleasantly situated overlooking the bay, or the inexpensive *Allesley* (☎071/43781; ②). You can **camp** at *Rosses Point Caravan and Camping Park* (Easter to mid-Sept; ☎071/77113). For seafood, head for *Austie's Bar & Restaurant* (☎071/77111).

Drumcliff, Benbulben and Glencar Lough

If you stick to the main N15 road out of Sligo you'll bypass the small Rosses Point peninsula, only reaching the sea five miles north of Sligo at **DRUMCLIFF** (bus #480 from Sligo), an early monastic site best-known as the last resting place of **W.B. Yeats**. His grave is in the grounds of an austere nineteenth-century Protestant church, within sight of the nearby Benbulben Mountain, as the poet wished. The grave of W.B. and his wife, George, has a simple headstone bearing the epitaph from Yeats's last poem:

Cast a cold eye
On life, on death.
Horseman, pass by!

In 575, St Columba founded a **monastery** here, and you can still see the remnants of a round tower to the left of the road and a tenth-century **high cross** – the only one in the county – on the right. The east face of the cross has carvings of Adam and Eve, Cain killing Abel and Daniel in the lion's den; the west face shows scenes from the New Testament, including the Presentation in the Temple and the Crucifixion. Local excavations have turned up a wealth of Iron and Bronze Age remains, too. A visit to **Drumcliff Church** (Mon–Sat 9am–6pm, Sun 1–6pm; £2/€2.54) includes a guide to the history of the site, "St Columba and Drumcliff", an accessible film animation portraying the Battle of the Book (see opposite), and access to computer interactives in the nearby visitor centre. These last offer a wealth of material on Yeats, including extracts of poetry along with biographical material and archival film and photography. The visitor centre (Mon–Sat 8.30am–6pm, Sun 1–6pm; free) also houses a good **tea shop** – a welcome refuge on a rainy day. For something more substantial, there's good bar **food** at *The Yeats Tavern*, about a hundred yards further along the main road.

At 1730ft, **Benbulben** is one of the most dramatic mountains in the country, and its profile changes constantly as you round it. According to the Fionn Mac Cumhaill legend, it was here that Diarmuid, the ill-fated young warrior, was killed by the wild boar, its bristles puncturing his heel – his one vulnerable point. Access to the slopes is easy, but you need to take care as there are a lot of dangerous clefts into which the unsuspecting walker can all too easily plunge, especially as the mountain is invariably shrouded in mist.

Around four miles east of Drumcliff is **Glencar Lough**, ten miles northeast of Sligo, squeezed between Benbulben and the range of hills known as the Sleeping Warrior. This secluded lakelet is known for its good salmon and trout fishing. To get there from Sligo, take the Manorhamilton bus, ask to be dropped off at the junction for the lake and walk the remaining two miles. With your own transport, follow the road round the northern edge of the lake, passing the recently reopened barium mine sheds on the left, until you see the "Waterfall" signpost. From the nearby car park a path leads up to the 50ft-high **waterfall**, especially impressive after heavy rain. There are more waterfalls, visible from the road, in the upper reaches of the valley, although none is quite as romantic as this one. For even better mountain walking, continue along the road to the eastern end of the lake, where a track rises steeply northwards to the **Swiss Valley**, a deep rift in the mountain crowned with silver fir.

Cooldrumman and Lissadell House

North of Drumcliff, the first left turn off the main road (signposted "Lissadell") leads to **CARNEY** village, to the north of which is an area known as **COOLDRUMMAN**, where the **Battle of the Book** took place. This battle followed the refusal of St Columba to hand over a psalm book copied from the original owned by St Finian of Moville, in defiance of the High King, who ruled that just as a calf belongs to its cow so every copy belongs to the owner of the book from which it is made. Columba won the battle at a cost of three thousand lives. Repenting the bloodshed he had caused, he then went into exile on the Scottish island of Iona.

In Carney a signpost to the left indicates the way to **Lissadell House** (June–Sept Mon–Sat 10.30am–12.30pm & 2–4.30pm; £3/€3.81), an austere nineteenth-century Greek Revival mansion, the popularity of which is mainly due to its Yeats associations. This was the home of the Gore-Booth family, which produced several generations of artists, travellers and fighters for Irish freedom. During the Famine, Sir Robert Gore-Booth, who built Lissadell, mortgaged the place to feed the local people and doled out rations from the hall. His grand-daughters, **Eva Gore-Booth** and **Constance Markiewicz**, were friends of Yeats and took part in the 1916 rising. Constance was condemned to death by the British for her participation but was pardoned and went on to become the first British female MP and then Minister of Labour in the Dáil's first cabinet. Bathed in Sligo's luminous marine pastels, the house still has an intimacy that makes it easy to imagine how it looked when Yeats used to visit in 1894:

Light of evening Lissadell
Great windows, open to the south,
Two girls in silk kimonos, both
Beautiful, one a gazelle

From *In Memory of Eva Gore-Booth and Constance Markiewicz*

During that year, Yeats was in the throes of his unrequited love for Maude Gonne, and much of his time at Lissadell was spent confessing his problems to the "gazelle" Eva, to whom he also briefly considered declaring his love.

It was not only Constance and Eva who espoused radical ideas; their brother, **Jocelyn**, was drummed out of his club in Sligo for his practical encouragement of the early cooperative movement. He was also one of the first landlords to start selling off land to tenants, retaining no more than 3000 acres of the original 31,000 to run a thriving market garden. Among the more eccentric decorative features of the interior are a series of elongated **mural portraits** of Jocelyn and family retainers and a self-portrait in the dining room, all by Constance's husband Count Casimir Markiewicz. They came into being only because bad weather kept the count from shooting during Christmas 1908. One of the rooms has Constance's name scratched on a window, and a photograph shows her playing Joan of Arc in her husband's theatre company: an appropriate role for a woman whose life was soon to turn so completely to politics and propaganda.

The house went through a difficult period after World War II, when the family lost control of the estate to the government: Sligo newspapers were keenly aware of the irony of the Gore-Booth sisters, nieces of Constance – one of the founders of the Irish Free State – being pursued by the police as they protested against the state's inept administration of the property. The experience has left the family with a distrust of government intervention, even in the form of funding, and although plans for restoration are afoot, Lissadell is likely to retain its air of elegant decay for some time.

Walks around Lissadell: Ellen's Pub

The area around Lissadell has some lovely walks and reputedly the warmest patch of sea on the Sligo coast. Worth seeking out is *Ellen's Pub* at **BALLYCONNELL**, around three miles northwest of Lissadell House, whose cottage-home atmosphere draws people from miles around. Ceilidhs are sometimes held in the back room at weekends, where musicians gather to belt out tunes on fiddles, accordions and banjos. There's a relaxed attitude to the licensing laws – occasionally too relaxed (the pub was closed down for a while in 1986). To find it, follow the road past the turning for the Lissadell Estate, bear right away from Maugherow church, turn left at the pub/grocery store at the crossroads and then take the second right; it's another mile straight on. Hitching is easy, because everyone will assume you're headed for *Ellen's* anyway.

From Raghly Point to Mullaghmore

A couple of miles west of Lissadell is **RAGHLY**, a small harbour with a quiet pier and raised beach from where there are spectacular views of the bay and surrounding mountains. On the way there you'll pass Ardtermon Castle (closed to the public), the seventeenth-century fortified manor house once occupied by Francis Gore-Booth, an ancestor of the Lissadell Gore-Booths. In the early 1990s the place was more or less a ruin, but since then it has been well restored by its German industrialist owner – although, in the absence of documentation of the house's original appearance, the resulting garish yellow is rather more Scottish Baronial than Irish.

The next stop along the coast is sandy **Streedagh Strand**, most easily accessible by taking the main road to Grange (served by 4–6 buses daily from Sligo), and following the signposts from there, as roads on the Raghly Peninsula are hard to disentangle. The beach itself is a fantastic stretch of sand, superb for long walks or horse riding by the waves (there are several stables in the district), though bear in mind that offshore currents can be very strong here. When the tide is at its lowest you can walk round to the **caves** at the southern end to do some fossil collecting. At the very north end of the beach is **Carraig na Spáinneach** (Spaniards' Rock), where three ships of the Spanish Armada foundered; there are numerous anonymous burial stones nearby, said to mark the mass graves of some 1100 sailors who either drowned or were butchered by the British and the locals. There's **B&B** at *Shaddan Lodge* right by the strand (☎071/63350; ③), which also offers various alternative healing therapies.

Grange, Moneygold and Cliffony

At **GRANGE**, five miles north of Drumcliff, there's not much apart from an old boys' bar off to the right, over the bridge. However, if you venture inland past the pub, you'll get a changing perspective of Benbulben as you approach the Gleniff Horseshoe, a scenic road that runs along a glen on the flank of the Dartry range and gives easy access to the top of Benbulben.

MONEYGOLD, a mile north of Grange, offers basic accommodation at the *Karuna Flame Hostel* (☎071/63337; phone ahead during low season or if you want a private room). **CLIFFONY**, about three miles north of Moneygold, is remarkable for the Creevykeel Court Tomb (just past the village by the roadside), one of the most extensive Neolithic sites in the country, comprising two roofless tombs within a stone court. The graves, which were originally enclosed in a barrow, probably date from between 3500 and 3000 BC, and it's easy to see in this ancient evidence of human presence a reflection of a power in the landscape that has gone on working ever since, right down to the poetry of Yeats and beyond. Bundoran, the first town over the county border in Donegal (see p.474), is eight miles northeast along the N15 road.

The Mullaghmore Peninsula

Mullaghmore headland may not have the sense of wild isolation of the other promontories north of Sligo town but it has a charm of its own and, unlike the remoter areas, offers a choice of accommodation and eating places, albeit a limited one. Here the coast faces north, not west, bringing the Donegal mountains into view; Benbulben and the Dartry range are a constant presence behind you.

A left turn at the Cliffony crossroads takes you onto the peninsula, past **Classiebawn Castle** (closed to the public), a construction worthy of Disneyland built by Lord Palmerston. It became the home of Lord Mountbatten shortly before he was killed by the IRA in 1979, when his boat was blown up in the bay.

MULLAGHMORE is a fine village with a peaceful skiff-filled harbour and an excellent, safe Blue Flag sandy beach. It's an exhilarating spot any time of the year, but take care not to walk on the rocky shelves of Mullaghmore Head at the end of the village; the crashing waves can be very dangerous here. If you're wondering what all the nuns are doing in Mullaghmore, it's because the village has a convent holiday home at which they can relax after the rigours of their parishes. Non-ecclesiastical travellers can **camp** in the sand dunes, as long as they're inconspicuous. **B&Bs** are thin on the ground, but *Seacrest* (☎071/66468; ④) is beautifully appointed and has a wonderful location overlooking the beach. A reasonable alternative is *Seawood* (☎071/76671; ③), situated in a quiet spot behind a small copse; to find it look out for a signpost off to the left before you enter the village. Heading more upmarket, there are a couple of comfortable **hotels**: *Pier Head House* (☎071/66171; ⑥) and *The Beach Hotel* (☎071/66103, *beachhot@iol.ie*; ⑥), which has a gym and swimming pool. As you would expect, during the summer **seafood** is available in the bars and restaurants of both hotels, and at *Eithna's Seafood Restaurant* (April–Oct daily; closed Tues during July & Aug; rest of year Sat & Sun only; ☎071/66407).

Inishmurray Island

The island of **INISHMURRAY**, about four miles offshore, has been deserted since the 1950s. It's a wonderfully isolated place that is remarkable for its extensive early Christian remains. The crossing from Mullaghmore takes an hour-and-a-half, and allows for several hours in which to explore, but trips are dependent on the weather and the number of people wanting to go. You should expect to pay around £20/€25.40 per person; book in advance with local boat-owner Rodney Lomax on ☎071/66124.

On the island, the remains of the sixth-century **monastery** of St Molaise stand within a massive stone enclosure and include *Teampall na bFear* (the Men's Church), the much smaller *Teach Molaise* (St Molaise's church) and a fine corbel-roofed building, probably originally an oratory. Also within the enclosure are three altars, one of which features the **Clocha Breaca**, or "speckled stones". Originally prayer stones, they became known as cursing stones; turned anticlockwise they are said to be effective against one's enemies. Numerous engraved slabs stand both within the enclosure and around the shore of the island, and these were used as stations for prayer. To the north of the enclosure stands a corbel-roofed sweat house and to the northwest lies the Women's Church.

West of Sligo town

The major sites of interest directly west of Sligo – off the R292 towards Strandhill – are the ancient remains at the **Carrowmore Megalithic Cemetery** and, on top of Knocknarea Mountain, **Medb's Cairn**. Both make for easy day-trips from Sligo town. The main road south and then westward from Sligo (the N59), flanked by the thrilling outlines of the Ox Mountains and the uninspiring coastline of western County Sligo, is scarcely an enthralling route, yet a few things crop up on the way to Mayo that are worth a mention. If you're not in a hurry, take the road running parallel to, and nearer, the coast.

Strandhill

STRANDHILL, four miles west of Sligo (bus #472), is swiftly becoming something of a city suburb, but does have a wonderful beach and has the dramatic Knocknarea Mountain as an ever-present backdrop. As you head out there, a right turn off the road will lead you down to Sligo Bay, where concrete markers delineate a low-tide crossing to **Coney Island** – venture across for plenty of good birdwatching and tranquil sandy beaches. New York's Coney Island is said to have been named after this dot of land by a homesick sea captain from Rosses Point, the headland opposite.

At Strandhill itself there's a fabulous, wild **beach**, with huge breakers rolling in from the Atlantic. It's a great favourite with surfers, but you do need to be completely confident in your abilities: this is a treacherous beach and **swimming is not advised**. The Sligo Open Surfing Championship is usually held here during the first weekend in August, and should you want tuition, head for the *Perfect Day Surf School* down by the beach (☎071/68464; lessons £15/€19.05). There is an exhilarating **walk** southwest around the headland to the quieter **Cullenamore** strand where you can take a dip: follow the coast until you are walking back around into a broad bay with Knocknarea Mountain in full view. The bay is home to a colony of two hundred **seals**, so your chances of spotting one are good. As the dunes fall to lower fields you can pick your way back towards Strandhill around the back of the golf course (the walk takes a leisurely hour-and-a-half). Another stroll heads east from Strandhill surf beach towards Sligo airport to catch the sight of small planes coming in over the top of Medb's Cairn. At the end of the airstrip stands the tenth-century **Killaspugbone Church** (access across the beach), where St Patrick allegedly tripped on the threshold and lost his tooth. A beautiful casket in which the sacred tooth was enshrined – the Fiacal Pádraig – is now in the National Museum in Dublin, but the whereabouts of the tooth is a mystery. Strandhill village used to be sited here until drifting sand forced the villagers to move a few centuries ago.

Today, Strandhill sprawls over the best part of a mile from the main Sligo road, with its handful of bars and hotels, down to the beach. It also has the **Celtic Seaweed Baths** (daily 10am–9pm; *www.celticseaweedbaths.com*; £10/€12.70) where you can have a steam followed by a seaweedy bath and decide for yourself whether a soak in this slimy organic soup does in fact relieve stress, rheumatism and arthritis. Whatever the claims, it's worth it for the afterglow.

There's an abundance of **B&Bs** to choose from in Strandhill, including *Burma Lodge*, Burma Rd (☎071/68233; ④) and *Knocknarea House*, Shore Rd (☎071/68313; ③), both a short walk to the sea. If you're having to count your pennies, the *Knocknarea Hostel* (☎071/68777) is a reasonable budget option, and you can **camp** at *Strandhill Caravan and Camping Park* (Easter to mid-Sept; ☎071/68111). A more upmarket choice is the pleasant family-run *Ocean View* **hotel** (☎071/68115; ⑥), at the top end of town. Down beside the sea, the cosy fireside of *The Strand* **pub** is the ideal place to satisfy a well-earned appetite with delicious homemade soup and bar meals. Their **restaurant** next door serves an imaginative range of seafood and vegetarian dishes (☎071/68641). Other alternatives are *Shells Café* on the seafront or the restaurant and bar at the *Ocean View Hotel*.

Strandhill is pretty lively during the summer: there is **music** every night in *The Strand* pub (folk, traditional and rock), while *The Venue*, on the main Sligo road, also has its fair share of live music.

Carrowmore Megalithic Cemetery and Medb's Cairn

The **Carrowmore Megalithic Cemetery** lies about two miles southwest of Sligo, signposted off the R292 (May–Sept daily 9.30am–6.30pm; £1.50/€1.90; Heritage Card). A field studded with 45 megalithic dolmens, standing stones and stone circles, this is the largest concentration of such tombs in Europe, and possibly the oldest. Analysis of one of the tombs undertaken in 1998 suggested a construction date as early as 5400 BC; this has caused considerable controversy in archaeological circles since his would indicate that it was built well before the introduction of farming in Ireland. Research is ongoing and recent excavations have found yet more tombs, one of which held a large quantity of burned bone, along with stone and antler jewellery. All in all it's an enthralling place, under the eye of the big mother cairn of them all – **Medb's Cairn**, on top of Knocknarea. The easiest ascent of the mountain is along the path that meets the R292 as it skirts its southern flank (the western slopes are too difficult). The 60ft cairn on the summit is said to be the tomb of Queen Medb of Connaught, but as she was killed elsewhere it's unlikely that she's buried here. There's a rather unhelpful custom of taking a stone away with you, which is resulting in a shrinkage of the cairn; the authorities are trying to promote an alternative tradition that says if you take a stone with you from the bottom of the mountain and put it on top of the cairn, your wish will come true...

Should you want to go **horse riding**, the Sligo Riding Centre is located right opposite the site (☎071/61353).

Aughris and Dromore West

BALLYSADARE, five miles south of Sligo on the N59, is situated at the head of a beautiful bay with striking views back to Knocknarea and Benbulben. It holds the remnants

THE OX MOUNTAINS

Just after **Skreen**, fifteen miles west of Sligo on the N59, comes the turnoff for the Ladies' Brae Scenic Route, one of only two trails across the vast **Ox Mountains** (*Sliabh Ghamh*, or Stony Mountain) into south Sligo. Following the course of a tumbling stream between forests of fir, the road ends not far from **COOLANEY**, a one-street village with accommodation at *The Mountain Inn* (☎071/67225; ④). Nearby is the Hungry Rock: these harsh surroundings were the scene of many deaths during the Famine of 1845 to 1849. **Walking** in the more remote regions of the mountains, where all you'll see are sheep and the odd turf-cutter, can be rewarding – but you need to take care, as the bogs can be treacherous. Much of the Ox range consists of surprisingly undramatic heathery slopes and flat boggy upland, but the second route across the mountains – which starts with a left turn off the road just before Easky – takes you up through the gorgeous setting of **Easky Lough** and then down a dramatic descent of the southwestern face of the range into the area surrounding Tobercurry (see p.455).

of a seventh-century monastery and a pre-Romanesque church, but barely justifies a detour.

About ten miles further west and just after **SKREEN**, you can take a turning south for the route through the Ox Mountains (see box on p.451), or take the lane north down to the coast and the tranquil harbourside village of **AUGHRIS**, home to an early monastic site and a promontory fort. In the fields you can see remains of *booleys*, the temporary shelters built by the old nomadic herdsmen who brought their flocks to graze in these remote coastal areas. There are several good beaches nearby and the little beach at Aughris is safe for swimming. The cliffs west of the pier are good for bird-watching and dolphin-spotting. You can feast on delicious **seafood** during the summer months at *Maggie's Beach Bar & Restaurant*, an eighteenth-century thatched shebeen down by the pier that is also a venue for traditional music. **Accommodation** is in short supply: the *Beach Bar* does **B&B** (☎071/66703; ②) and also has a caravan and **camping** site, or you can stay three miles away at *Ave Maria Farmhouse,* Corkamore, Templeboy (☎071/66674; ③).

At **DROMORE WEST**, about six miles southwest of Aughris, **Culkin's Emigration Museum** (June–Sept Mon–Sat 10am–5pm, Sun 1–5pm; £2.50/€3.17) fills in some of the story behind the deserted buildings that once littered the landscape hereabouts. The museum stands on the site of Daniel Culkin's Shipping and Emigration Agency, which was founded in the nineteenth century and helped many local people on the bitter road to a better life overseas. There's plenty of material on display about emigration and the Famine that fuelled it; most evocative of all is the original shipping agent's shop, a stark reminder of the harsh lives endured by thousands.

Easky and around

Originally a monastic settlement, **EASKY**, about five miles northwest of Dromore West along the coast road, was a vital link in the anti-Napoleon coastal defensive chain, as two nearby Martello towers attest. With its fine reputation for consistent waves, Easky has become something of a **surfers' paradise**; in the summer months the shore fills up with surfers' camper vans. It hosts the Surfing Association's Tiki Cold Water Classic over the last weekend in September and has also staged the national surfing championships. You'll find the Easky Surf and Information Centre in the middle of the village (July & Aug daily 10am–6pm; rest of year Mon–Fri 10am–2pm; ☎096/49020), which can provide information about accommodation in the surrounding area, along with **Internet access**. At the mouth of the salmon-rich Easky river stand the ruins of the fifteenth-century **Rosalee Castle**, with a public **shower block** alongside for the convenience of the many surfers who camp rough nearby; tokens are available in the surf centre and local shops.

There's not much **accommodation** on offer. The *Barr Na Dtonn* (☎088/815 4400) is a well-equipped **hostel** in the centre; *Atlantic 'n' Riverside* (☎096/49001; ③) is a **B&B** which also does **camping**, and there's grander guest accommodation at the *Old Rectory* (☎096/49181; ④), which manages to be both secluded and central.

Easky has a busy, if small, summer pub scene: *McGowan's* has **traditional music**, set dancing and rock music; *The Poitín House* is a convivial spot; and you can expect discos, karaoke and videos at the youth-orientated *The Fisherman's Weir.* **Eating** options take in the café in the surf centre, *The Fisherman's Weir* which serves bar food year-round, and snacks at the other pubs.

This coastline offers magical **walks**; the shoreline east of the village is especially rich in fossils. A mile south of Easky, beside the road, is the extraordinary **Split Rock**, a glacial erratic ten-feet high that's said to have been thrown here by Fionn Mac Cumhaill from the top of the Ox Mountains. Legend also has it that the rock will close on anyone who dares to go through the split three times.

Enniscrone

ENNISCRONE, eight miles southwest of Easky, is a popular, rather ramshackle, seaside resort attracting families during the summer months, with caravan sites hidden away in the sand dunes, and an exceptionally good golf course. There's a sweeping three-mile crescent of **sandy beach** with bath houses, built to exploit the health-giving properties of seaweed and hot seawater. The seaweed bathing tradition continues at the wonderful Kilcullen's Bath House (May & June daily 10am–9pm; July & Aug daily 10am–10pm; rest of year Sat & Sun 10am–9pm; ☎096/36238; bath £8/€10.16, bath and steam £10/€12.70), a strapping Edwardian establishment where you can experience the slightly strange sensation of lying in fronds of slimy seaweed in an enormous glazed porcelain bath of iodine-rich brown water before finishing off with a cold-water rinse. It is extremely popular, and there is a pleasant **tea room** alongside where you can wait for your soak. A similarly exhilarating way to spend time in Enniscrone is to take to the waves, which you can do at Seventh Wave Surf School down by the beach; here you can take **surfing** lessons (☎096/49428; £15/€19.05).

The town is not short of **B&Bs**: try *Central House* on Main Street (☎096/36234; ③) or one of the several good options down Pier Road, such as *Enniscrone Lodge* (☎096/36181; ④) or *Gowan Brae* (☎096/36396; ③). The *Gable End* **restaurant** (July & Aug daily; variable opening for the rest of the year; bar food during the day, and dinner 6.30–9.30pm; ☎096/36110) is one of the very best places to **eat** in this part of Sligo, specializing in seafood.

South Sligo

The key attractions in **south Sligo** are loosely scattered. Passing through Collooney it's worth calling in to witness the Victorian splendour of Markree Castle, now a hotel, before heading south for Lough Arrow and the area's two prime archeological sites: the Neolithic passage tomb of Heapstown Cairn and the superb Bronze Age Carrowkeel Cemetery, magnificently sited high above the surrounding countryside. South Sligo is also noted for its **musical** heritage: the great fiddle-player Michael Coleman came from here and the new heritage centre commemorating him at Gurteen sets out to promote the traditional music of today.

Collooney and Markree Castle

The sight worth stopping for in the village of **COLLOONEY**, five miles south of Sligo where the N4 and N17 separate, is the **Teeling Monument** at the northern entrance to the village, built to commemorate Bartholomew Teeling, hero of the Battle of Carricknagat. The battle was fought nearby during the rebellion of 1798, when a combined Franco-Irish force – on its way from Killala in County Mayo, where the French had landed (see p.421), to Ballinamuck in County Longford – was held up by a single strategically placed English gun. Teeling charged up the hill and shot the gunner dead, turning the tide of the engagement. After their defeat at Ballinamuck the French were treated as prisoners of war, but five hundred Irish troops were massacred. Irish-born Teeling, who was an officer in the French army, was later hanged in Dublin. The monument links Teeling and his fallen comrades with subsequent generations of Irish freedom fighters.

Close to Collooney is the battlemented **Markree Castle**, originally seventeenth-century but with grandiose Victorian extensions, which is still the home of the Coopers, who used to be Sligo's most powerful Anglo-Irish family. It's set in impressive parklands and is now open as a **hotel** (☎071/67800, *www.markreecastle.ie*; ⑨), and also houses an excellent, though expensive, **restaurant**. Midweek, non-residents can wander in for a drink in the bar. Comfort and gastronomic delights at a more affordable level are on offer at *Glebe House* (closed Nov–Feb; ☎071/67787, *www.glebehouse.com*; ⑤), just outside Collooney on the other side of town. A "restaurant with rooms" which is also open to non-residents rather than a guesthouse, this Georgian former rectory is filled with an assortment of heavy, Victorian-and-later furniture – but is attractive not so much for its decor as for its food and the freshness of the ingredients, many of which are grown in the garden outside (restaurant open daily June–Aug; variable for the rest of the year).

Heapstown Cairn and Lough Arrow

The more appealing route south from here, to **Lough Arrow** on the Roscommon border, involves a turn east off the N4 at **DRUMFIN** four miles south of Collooney. You can stay just outside the the sleepy village of **RIVERSTOWN** in a graceful eighteenth-century Big House, *Coopershill* (April–Oct; ☎071/65108; ⑧), which belongs to a branch of the Coopers of Markree. Around three miles south of the village, **Heapstown Cairn** stands beside the road, a Neolithic passage tomb as large as Medb's Cairn and traditionally the last resting place of Aillil, brother of King Niall of Tara. A lot of the cairn stones have been plundered for building material, but even in its diminished state it remains impressive, best appreciated by climbing it and taking in the view from the top. What's most fascinating about the view is the relationship with the surrounding landscape: the cairn takes a perfect central position in relation to the nearby circle of hills, many with cairns on their peaks.

One option from here is to go down the eastern shore of Lough Arrow, whose blue waters are set with ringlets of isles and whose banks are dotted with ancient landmarks, many of them unmarked on the map. When the sun is shining there are few spots to beat it, especially if you can take a rowing boat onto the tranquil lake – keep your eye out for boats lying by the banks and then ask at a nearby house; or try **Lough Arrow Boats** (☎071/65491), which rents out fibreglass boats. The road round the southern edge of the lake goes through **BALLINAFAD**, at the back door of the Bricklieve Mountains. The road into Ballinafad from the south over the Curlew Mountains of Roscommon gives the most stupendous **view** in the whole of Sligo, right up to Benbulben – it's worth backtracking up the hill to get it. **Ballinafad Castle** (left off the road at the top of the village) is a sixteenth-century building remarkable only because its huge circular towers and squat walls are of thirteenth-century design. The charms of the area may well tempt you to **stay** to watch the luminous twilight descend on the lake. You have a choice between the *Rock View Hotel* (☎079/66073; ④), a down-to-earth angler's hotel halfway down the lough (much further than the signs indicate) – the owners will give plenty of advice on trout fishing in Lough Arrow's limpid waters – and the more upmarket *Cromleach Lodge Country House* (closed Nov–Jan; ☎071/65155; ⑨), which is close to the northern end of the water.

Carrowkeel Cemetery and Keshcorran caves

The other route southwards from the Heapstown Cairn takes you back to the N4. Cross the N4 at **CASTLEBALDWIN** and climb the road that forks left behind *McDermot's Pub* for the Bronze Age **Carrowkeel Cemetery** – you can drive all the way up, on dirt roads, or walk: either way, watched over by cairns and (signposted) tumuli, the **panorama** is marvellous, with the whole of County Sligo spread out beneath you. Comprising fourteen cairns, a few dolmens and some fifty-odd pieces of stone foundations, the site is the most important cairn colony west of Sliabh Na Cailllighe in north-west Meath. Several cruciform **passage graves** set in the cairns are still roofed, the smaller ones with great lintel stones, the larger with corbelled vaults. You can actually enter Cairn K, one of the roofed tombs: cruciform in shape, with its dry stone roof intact, it's been compared to Newgrange in County Westmeath (see p.184). Here, however, it's lit by the sun on the year's longest day (June 21).

Also of interest in the area are the **caves** on the hill of **Keshcorran**, the cairn-topped summit that faces Carrowkeel to the west, which you can get to by rejoining the main road across the mountains, then turning left down the hill, taking every descending turning until you reach a major road; take a right here towards **KESH**, and a little further on a fingerpost points right – after a couple of hundred yards you'll spot the line of caves cut into the forehead of the mountain. The caves have no depth at all, but the feeling of isolation is immense at this spot. According to legend, this was one of the places where the lovers Diarmuid and Gráinne lived when they fled the anger of Fionn Mac Cumhaill, and it was here that the baby Cormac Mac Airt, later to be the greatest of all the High Kings who ruled at Tara, was reared by wolves. On the last Sunday in July, in a reflection of ancient pagan rituals, locals still gather by the caves for sessions of prayer.

Ballymote

If, instead of taking the Lough Arrow route from Collooney, you follow the N17 **southwest** for three miles, you can make a diversion along the R293 to the small market town of **BALLYMOTE**, five miles further south. Its fourteenth-century castle, built by Richard de Burgo (the "Red Earl of Ulster"), was once the strongest in Connacht but has associations with major defeats – it was O'Donnell's before he lost at the Battle of Kinsale, and it was James II's possession before he lost at the Boyne. The place has an important and ancient literary connection: it was here, in about 1400, that the Book of Ballymote was compiled, giving the key to the geometrical *ogham* letters that are formed on many standing stones of the fourth and fifth centuries; the name comes from the townland of Ogham, outside nearby Tobercurry, which has plenty of examples of them. Ballymote makes a good centre for both angling and rath-spotting: the low, undramatic countryside all around is covered in ancient ring forts.

For moderately priced **accommodation** you could try *The Millhouse* (☎071/83449; ③), a very pleasant B&B. The most stylish place to stay in the vicinity, however, is *Temple House* (closed Feb & March; ☎071/83329, *www.templehouse.ie*; ⑥), three miles from here on the shores of the lake; take the left fork off the Collooney end of town, and the house is near the N17 towards Tobercurry. Founded by the Knights Templar and expanded in 1560, this is one of the grandest and earliest Anglo-Irish houses ever built in Ireland – the bulk of the house was grandly refurbished in 1864 – on a 950-acre estate, with 97 rooms, five of which are for B&B guests. They also do a good dinner for around £20/€25.40. In the village, *The Stone Park Restaurant* (☎071/83372) serves a good range of inexpensive meals daily, and the village sports a couple of nice old bars, including *Hayden's* which has set dancing (Tues in winter).

Tobercurry and around

The district around **TOBERCURRY** (also spelt Tubbercurry), fifteen miles southwest of Collooney – and indeed south Sligo in general – has a reputation for traditional music: **Michael Coleman**, the greatest of Irish fiddle players, came from here, and it's also where The Chieftains have their roots. Tobercurry itself is a spruce market town, with its most scenic attraction being the lovely **Lough Talt**, around four miles away. Although the town is usually devoid of tourists, **tourist information** is available in *Killoran's Traditional Restaurant*, Teeling Street – don't miss out on their famous fresh salmon from the River Moy (☎071/85111). During the summer months *Killoran's* puts on Irish nights of music and dance. The *South Sligo Summer School* is held in the town during the second week of July, featuring short courses in music and Irish dancing (☎071/85010). **B&B** is available at *The Ox Mountain Lodge*, Teeling St (☎071/85007; ③), which is pleasant and good-value, and also has a café attached (closes 6pm). *Cawley's* hotel in Emmet Street (☎071/85025; ⑤) is a more formal alternative.

Follow the R294 ten miles or so southeast and you'll reach **GURTEEN**, once another thriving centre for traditional music, now a place with something of the atmosphere of a ghost town. The new **Michael Coleman Heritage Centre**, *Ceolaras Coleman* (June–Sept daily 10am–5pm; Oct–May Mon–Fri 10am–5pm; ☎071/82599, *colemanirishmusic.com*) seeks to redress this and promotes the continuation of the living music tradition with evening classes and weekend workshops and puts on shows of traditional music and dance (weekly from April to Oct). The centre also houses a theatre and an audiovisual display on the life of Michael Coleman and a series of touch-screen interactives with detailed information on traditional music, instruments and their manufacture. A few miles west of Gurteen a further group of buildings includes a replica of the fiddler's home and an archive of south Sligo music. Gurteen is also the focus for the **Coleman Traditional Festival** at the beginning of September, and there are a couple of pubs that are likely to have music at other times: *Teach Murray* has a session on Mondays; *Róisin Dubh* has spontaneous music-making throughout the year.

Lough Gara, tucked away in the southernmost pocket of the county, is not as appealing as the map suggests it might be, having a very undramatic surrounding shoreline. **Moygara Castle**, signposted near the lake, is similarly anticlimactic, with just one of its original four towers left intact.

COUNTY LEITRIM

The scenery in **County Leitrim** is far more distinctive than it's normally given credit for, especially the scintillating mountains and glens of the north, though it can't compete with Sligo for historical interest. Leitrim stretches fifty miles from County Longford in the southeast to its slim two-mile coastline at Tullaghan in the northwest, and is neatly split into north and south sections by the vast interruption of **Lough Allen**, the first lake on the River Shannon. The southern half is dominated by the presence of the Shannon, while the lake-peppered terrain to the east of the river, with its characteristic drumlins, or hillocks, also merits exploration. The **mountains** of the northern section are grouped around **Manorhamilton**, and Leitrim shares its most beautiful features – Glencar and Lough Gill – with Sligo.

Carrick-on-Shannon and around

The small county town of **CARRICK-ON-SHANNON**, beautifully positioned on a wide stretch of the Shannon just below Lough Key, is a major **boating** centre, and its marina is full of pleasure boats and Shannon cruisers. The regatta is a lively event, generally held over the first weekend in August. It also makes a good base from which to **cycle** round the southern loop of Leitrim or to investigate Lough Key and Lough Boderg in Roscommon, and there's good **coarse fishing** to be had too.

Carrick's *raison d'être* as a tourist centre received a boost with the reopening of the Ballyconnell–Ballinamore Canal in the summer of 1994. The canal provides the final link in the **Shannon–Erne Waterway**, 239 navigable miles taking in stretches of still-water canal, canalized river and a sequence of lakes before ending up in Belleek, across the border in County Fermanagh. A latecomer to the canal-building boom that swept the country in the eighteenth and nineteenth centuries, the waterway was completed in 1860, and was used for only nine years before being made redundant by Ireland's growing rail network.

The single piece of historical interest the town has to offer is the minuscule **Costello Chapel**, at the top end of Bridge Street. Billed as the second smallest chapel in the world, it was built in 1877 by the fanatically devout businessman Edward Costello as a memorial to his wife, who died young that year. The couple's lead coffins, protected by thick slabs of glass, lie in two sunken spaces on each side of the tiny, beautifully-tiled aisle. Opposite the chapel stands the **Market House Centre** – at the time of writing restoration work was still underway, but once finished it will house, amongst other things, the Leitrim Design House, a showcase for local crafts-people and interior designers. Also worth a visit is Cyril Cullen's pebble-dashed Georgian house and factory shop, **Summerhill**, on the road to St Patrick's Hospital, where he sells porcelain figures and his own distinctive knitwear designs – he breeds his own Jacob sheep for their wool.

Arrival, information and accommodation

The town has good transport connections. **Buses** (☎071/60066) to Athlone, Boyle, Dublin, Mullingar and Sligo leave from in front of *Coffey's Pastry Case* in Bridge Street. The **train station** (☎078/20036), ten minutes' walk southwest of town, is on the main Dublin–Sligo line, with three or four trains a day in each direction.

Carrick's very helpful **tourist office** (Easter–May, Sept & Oct Mon–Fri 9am–5pm; June–Aug daily 9am–6pm; ☎078/20170) is on the quay on the Leitrim side of the river, offering information on all aspects of holiday-making in the area, along with an accommodation booking service. Rental of **bikes** and fishing tackle is available at Geraghty's on Main Street (☎078/21316; bikes £25/€31.74 per week). **Internet access** is available at the small cybercafé at the back of Gartlan's newsagents on Bridge Street.

Michael Lynch's, on the Roscommon side of the river, has **fishing boats** for rent (☎078/20034), and there are numerous companies that rent out **Shannon cruisers** by the week (two- to ten-berth); one is Emerald Star Line (☎078/20234). The locks on the Shannon–Erne Waterway – there are sixteen of them in all – are operated electronically with a swipe-card, so you don't need to be an expert to use the canal. For detailed information on Shannon navigation consult *www.iwai.ie/maps/shannon-erne/contents.html* and to purchase navigation charts call Dúchas, The Heritage Service, in Dublin on ☎01/677 7510. For shorter **excursions**, *Moon River* organizes trips up the river leaving from the bridge (daily 2.30pm & 4.30pm; lasts 1hr 30min; ☎078/21777; £6/€7.62). Another starting point for the waterway is at Ballinamore (see p.460), where you can also rent boats.

Accommodation

There's a fair spread of accommodation in and around the town, including a couple of swanky town-centre hotels and a range of more modest B&Bs. The An Óige **hostel**, *The Bridge* (☎078/21848) is a cosy, well-run place right in the town centre offering a couple of small dorms and one four-bed room.

Aisleigh Guest House, Dublin Rd (☎078/20313). A smart, welcoming B&B about a mile out of town, offering a sauna along with the rather more usual facilities. ③.

Aisling, St Mary's Close, off Main St (☎078/20131). A regular B&B in a quiet, central location. Closed Nov–Feb. ④.

The Bush Hotel, Main St (☎078/20014, *www.homepage.eircom.net/~bushhotel*). Recently refurbished town-centre hotel with a pleasantly traditional character. Rooms vary considerably, but the best are very comfortable indeed. ⑥.

The Four Seasons, Main St (☎078/21333). Another decent town-centre option for inexpensive B&B offering en-suite rooms. ③.

Hollywell, Liberty Hill (☎078/21124). One of the finest places to stay in Carrick-on-Shannon. Grandiose, comfortable, and a short walk from the centre of town. ⑤.

Eating, drinking and entertainment

Carrick has **pubs** to suit most tastes within a short walk down Bridge Street: starting at the top opposite the clock tower is *Flynn's*, an animated bar with lively conversation;

a few paces below here is *Burke's Bar*, a fairly conservative place for a pint, and below here *The Oarsman*, an antique-style bar with live music – generally a mix of pop and traditional – from 10pm on Fridays and Sundays. At the bottom of Bridge Street is *Cryan's*, a bar famous for its traditional sessions. Two miles out of town on the road towards Elphin is *Anderson's Thatch Pub*, another place with an excellent reputation for traditional music all year round. One of the more unusual ways to enjoy a drink and live music in these parts is to take a trip on board *Moon River* (see p.457; Thurs 8.30pm–midnight; £6/€7.62); on Saturdays, *Moon River* acts as a rather civilized floating nightclub. For more details, call into the tourist office.

You can get reasonably priced **food** – lunches and evening meals – at the popular *Cryan's* or *The Oarsman* (see above). Away from the bars, a few other places serve food during the day: try *Coffey's Pastry Case* for light lunches and snacks; the coffee shop of *The Bush Hotel* for good roasts, freshly fried fish and similar meals, or the new *Landmark Hotel* overlooking the river for carvery lunches. If you are self-catering, it's worth calling into Cheese etc on Bridge Street, for just that.

South of Carrick

As with most of Leitrim, there's little of dramatic interest in the area **south of Carrick**, but if you're passing through, there are a couple of places where you could at least slow down a bit and enjoy the leisurely pace of life around the Shannon. **Mohill** stands as the focus of a patch of lovely rolling countryside, laced with rivers, that attracts plenty of interest from angling folk.

Jamestown and Drumsna

The village of **JAMESTOWN**, just over two miles southeast of Carrick off the N4 Dublin road, is a town dating from James I's "plantation" of Leitrim in 1622 – its main road passes through a gate in the old estate walls. The Georgian houses and the wooded riverbanks create a peaceful atmosphere of planned eighteenth-century living. Jamestown makes a good centre for fishing; if you want to stay, try *Weir View* (☎078/24726; ③). *The Arch* is one of a couple of nice **pubs** right in the centre.

At **DRUMSNA**, about a mile or so east of Jamestown, excavations in the summer of 1989 unearthed huge stretches of a Stone Age wall – one of the oldest artificial structures in the world. It's been estimated that it would have taken a labour force of thirty thousand men ten years to build its full length. The village itself is a single street of neat houses leading down to the river. A plaque on the wall of *Taylor's Lounge* claims that Anthony Trollope began his novel *The MacDermots of Ballycloran* here in 1848. The MacDermots were great Catholic landowners during the eighteenth century who were ruined by the anti-Catholic Penal Laws.

Mohill and around

About six miles east of Drumsna lies **MOHILL**, a trim, busy village reached by turning off the main road south of Drumsna. A sculpture on the main street commemorates its most famous son, **Turlough O'Carolan** (1670–1738), the blind harpist and composer. The last of the court bards, he lived by travelling round the chieftains' households playing his new compositions. He was also reputed to have been as great with the whiskey bottle as he was on the harp; it's said that on his deathbed he asked for a cup of the stuff, and finding that he hadn't the strength to drink it, touched the cup with his lip, saying that two old mates shouldn't part without a kiss. Mohill was the site of an abbey founded in the sixth century by St Manachan, but today its associations are entirely secular: it's a **coarse fishing** centre, with fifteen different choices of lake and river in a five-mile radius. You can get B&B **accommodation** on a grand scale at the nineteenth-century stone-built *Glebe House*, set in beautiful parklands a couple of miles north of town on the road to Ballinamore (☎078/31086, *www.glebehouse.com*; ⑤). At a more modest level there's *The Traveller's Rest* guesthouse in the village (☎078/31174; ③). *Fitzpatrick's* **pub** has set dancing on a Tuesday night, country and western at weekends.

Lough Rynn House stands in a fine location on the shores of the lough, and was first acquired by one Nathaniel Clements, a successful Dublin banker and politician, in 1750. The Clements dynasty, earls of Sligo, built the original Rynn Castle – an exact copy of a house in Ingestry in Staffordshire, England – in 1833, and in 1878 extended it to the Scottish Baronial pile you see now. By this time the house was the centre of an estate that encompassed a massive ninety thousand acres, and the grounds include 1840s' farm buildings, the estate office – a picturesque building by the architect Digby Wyatt, who was also responsible for the Senate Chambers in Leinster House, Dublin – a pretty summer house, as well as the ruins of a seventeenth-century castle and a dolmen. The house itself is currently undergoing extensive renovation and is likely to reopen in 2002. In the meantime visitors are welcome to walk around the grounds.

The area around Mohill, rich rolling pasture land crisscrossed by hedged lanes, makes for good cycling. Further east, the terrain becomes rougher and less interesting, but **CARRIGALLEN**, around eight miles northeast of Mohill, is a pleasant enough eighteenth-century town, with excellent fishing all around. It's at a point in Carrigallen parish that the three provinces of Ulster, Leinster and Connacht meet, though nothing about the modest demeanour of the town suggests it.

ROOSKY, just over the border in County Roscommon, straddles the N4 about seven miles south of Mohill. It's a pleasant riverside village catering for holidaying anglers, with B&B at *Shannonville* (☎078/38184; ③), a smart new house set squarely back off the main road, and more upmarket accommodation at the *Shannon Key West Hotel*, a smart and imposing building overlooking the bridge (☎078/38800, *www.keywest.firebird.net*; ⑦). Bar food is on offer at *The Weir Lodge* and you can hear a variety of live music at *Reynold's* bar throughout the summer.

North of Carrick

About four miles **north of Carrick** lies the county's namesake, **LEITRIM** village. It's a tiny one-street place with a lovely canalside setting – best appreciated from the pub on the bank. From just north of here, the elongated **Lough Allen** stretches northwards, almost touching the Cavan border and dividing Leitrim in two. **Drumshanbo** is the most pleasant base from which to get out onto the water, and there's some countryside around and about that's also worth exploring by bike or on foot.

Drumshanbo and around

Though its name translates as "the back of the old cow's arse", **DRUMSHANBO**, eight miles north of Carrick, is a neat, cheerful place with an air of briskness poised at the southern tip of the beautiful **Lough Allen**. The Sliabh an Iarainn Visitor Centre (April–Oct Mon–Sat 10am–6pm, Sun 2–6pm; £1/€1.27) gives some interesting background on local life, including the use of the sweathouse, a sort of sauna, and the tradition of coal and iron mining, especially out towards Arigna. The last of the mines in the area closed in 1990.

In July, the village holds the Joe Mooney Summer School, a week of **traditional music** classes and set dancing. You need to be experienced to join the music classes, but there is set dancing for novices and plenty of sessions in the bars (further details on ☎078/41213). Drumshanbo's **tourist office** is based at *Mrs Mooney's* **B&B** on the corner of the High Street and the Carrick Road (☎078/41013; ②). Other places to stay include *Paddy Mac's* pub and guesthouse (☎078/41128; ④), High Street, and *Fraoch Bán* (☎078/41260; ③), a smart B&B half-a-mile north on the Dowra road, with lovely views over the lake. You can **camp** at Moorlands Equestrian Centre, at the southernmost tip of Lough Allen (☎078/41500; trekking £12/€15.24 per hour). **Meals** are served all day at *The Allendale Restaurant*, Convent Avenue. There are a handful of bars where you might find **music** during the summer: *Conway's*, at the head of the Manorhamilton road, is a cosy favourite, with sessions on Thursdays. Other bars with music worth checking out are *The Mountain Tavern* (Wed), and *Monica's* (Mon).

Music aside, Drumshanbo's finest asset is its proximity to Lough Allen and Slieve Anierin. By car the scenery is not particularly dramatic, but there is plenty of enjoyable walking, cycling and pony trekking. The Leitrim Way from here to Dowra (signposted *Slí Liatroma*, ten miles) affords expansive views across the lake to Corrie Mountain for almost the whole way. You can **rent a bike** for £7/€8.89 from Moran's on Convent Avenue (☎078/41043); a circuit of the lake via Dowra and Drumkeeran is around 25 miles in total. **Horse riding** is available at Moorlands Equestrian Centre (☎078/41500). Fisherfolk are well served too: Lough Allen is noted as having the **best pike fishing** in Europe, and rowing boats can be hired from Lough Allen Angling Services (☎078/41648; £15/€19.05 per day).

EAST TOWARDS BALLINAMORE

The best move from Drumshanbo is to take the R208 southeast and then head **east** along the R209 into the array of lakes that attracts most of Leitrim's tourism. This route makes a pleasant trip on a **bike**, as many of the lanes skirt the shores as they wind between the hills. Two of these hills have legendary names – **Sheemore** and **Sheebeag** (The Hill of Big Fairies and The Hill of Little Fairies; there's a well-known Irish set dance by the same name). As with all such enchanted hills, this pair is supposed to open up on *Samhain* (Halloween), when the fairy folk roam the land.

Sheemore lies on the south side of Lough Scur; unfortunately it's not signposted, so you might have to ask a few of the locals for directions. Topped by a cairn and a St Patrick's Cross, the hill commands the best **view** across Leitrim; the cairn is believed locally to be Fionn Mac Cumhaill's (Finn McCool's) grave. On your way along the south of Lough Scur you'll pass a dolmen by the roadside before reaching Sheebeag, which has a gorse-covered cairn but is less exciting than its bigger brother. To get there follow the road straight on rather than turning left into Keshcarrigan, and take a sharp right up the hill and continue for a mile or so.

KESHCARRIGAN, around five miles southeast of Drumshanbo, is one of the places that has been revitalized by the reopening of the Shannon–Erne Waterway. You can **stay** at *Canal View House* (☎078/42056; ④), an imposing bungalow overlooking the waterway; it also runs a fairly sophisticated **restaurant** (open to non-residents, dinner £15/€19.05). For large portions of excellent, hearty food make for *Gertie's Bar*, an amiably relaxed, child-friendly place, decorated with a chaotic mix of ancient beer ads and road signs, which also puts on traditional music during the summer (Thurs). About four miles east, **FENAGH** has the ruins of a monastery and two churches founded in the seventh century by St Caillain. The key for the ruins is kept in the first house as you turn off the road for *The Old Rectory* (☎078/44089; ③), a beautiful Georgian house in a superb location overlooking Fenagh Lough, just a hundred yards up the Mohill road.

Ballinamore

Three miles northeast of Fenagh lies **BALLINAMORE**, a wide-streeted former coaching town, which has a **heritage-folk museum** in the library building, once the courthouse, halfway down its main street (July–Sept Mon–Fri 10am–1pm & 2–5pm; free).

Highlight of the dull and chaotically organized collection is the "authentic detachable shirt collar worn by executed 1916 patriot Seán MacDiarmada" – and if you don't believe it, there's a photograph of the man to prove it. The library also houses the Leitrim Genealogical Centre. Today, Ballinamore acts as a centre for **angling** in Leitrim's lakes, and for **boating** on the Shannon–Erne Waterway. Canal barges can be rented from Riverside Barge Holidays (☎078/44122), canoes from Thomas Parkes (☎078/44860). Alternatively, you could take a two-hour **river cruise** for £7/€8.89 (takes 2hr; June–Sept only; ☎078/44079).

There's inexpensive **accommodation** at the fine *Ballinamore Holiday Hostel* (IHH; ☎078/44955), located above *Smyth's Restaurant*. One of the nicest **B&Bs** is *Ardnum Lodge* (☎078/44278; ③), on the road towards Fenagh; *Town View* (☎078/44464; ②), on the same road, caters largely for anglers and also does evening meals, while *Mrs Gormley's* (☎078/44082; ④), Main Street, is plain and unpretentious. *McAllister Hotel* (☎078/44068; ④) is central and newly refurbished. Probably the best **place to eat** is the cheerful *Smyth's Restaurant*, Main Street, a good spot for tasty homemade food. During the summer you can hear music in one of the town's numerous bars; *Reynold's* has traditional music on a Thursday.

North Leitrim

The **North Leitrim Glens** offer some breathtaking scenery: rugged mountains fall to ribbon lakes, and the area is quiet and as yet undiscovered. Dromahair is a quiet base from where you can explore the beauty of Lough Gill (see p.443), while on the Donegal border at the northernmost tip of the county sits the peaceful and little-explored Lough Melvin.

Manorhamilton

Focal point of the mountainous area north of Lough Allen is **MANORHAMILTON**, lying in the saddle of five valleys some fourteen miles east of Sligo town. The town was founded on top of a strategic plateau by Sir Frederick Hamilton, a Scots colonist, during the seventeenth century; his Plantation castle was destroyed in the 1650s, but the ruins, on the edge of town, now house the Manorhamilton Castle Heritage Centre (Tues–Sat 11am–6pm, Sun 2–7pm), which tells its bloody and violent history in an audiovisual display. The coffee shop alongside makes a pleasant refreshment stop.

Today, Manorhamilton is a handsome crossroads town, with a sense of self-importance underlined by the sturdiness of its architecture, and makes a good base for **walking** and **potholing** in the surrounding hills, on both sides of the border. Chief among local sights is the well-preserved megalithic tomb at **Cashel Bir**, on the slopes of Benbo. For advice on walking, potholing, caving, fishing and hang-gliding, as well as other local pursuits, go to the Glens Centre, housed in the old Methodist church in the centre of town (summer daily 10am–6pm; ☎072/55833).

The town has a handful of **B&Bs**, including the welcoming *Cill Chiaráin* (☎072/56135; ④) and *Laurel Lodge* (☎072/55018; ③). *Maguire's Bar* (☎072/56053; ③) is more appealing inside than the exterior would suggest. Sturdy **bar meals** can be had from *The Granary*, Main Street, which advertises itself as a bistro and coffee shop, but is actually a straightforward bar. *Maguire's* serves similarly hearty bar lunches; its salmon is excellent.

Dromahair

The R280 southwest of Manorhamilton leads, after ten miles, to the pretty village of **DROMAHAIR**; if you have transport it makes an excellent base from which to enjoy the rugged valleys and the peerless **Lough Gill** and its environs (see p.443). If you want to **stay** in the centre, head for *St Anne's* (☎071/64096; ③) or *Stanfords* (☎071/64140; ④), the latter a quaint creeper-clad little pub with quiet rooms. Light **meals** are served in the *Stanfords* bar, and a set dinner in their restaurant will cost around £18/€22.86.

A short walk from the centre lies **Creevelea Friary**, its ruined east window turned away from the harsh outlines of the mountains and towards the friendly valley below. This Franciscan friary, founded in 1508, was the last to be built in Ireland before Henry VIII's dissolution of the monasteries. It still has some fine sculptures in the cloister arcade: look out for St Francis with the stigmata, and another of him preaching to the birds from a pulpit.

Kiltyclogher

About ten miles northeast of Manorhamilton, **KILTYCLOGHER**, although trim and pretty has little to detain you after you've seen its Seán MacDiarmada statue. The dedicated can visit the three-room cottage where MacDiarmada, executed in Dublin in 1916 for his part in the uprising, was born; it is maintained as a kind of national shrine, a short way out of town and signposted off the Manorhamilton road (summer only, by arrangement; ☎072/53249). There's nowhere to eat in the village, but there's **B&B** at *Meehan's* (☎072/54179; ④). *The Leitrim Lakes Hostel* (IHH; April-Oct; ☎072/54044) is a large, well-run affair, but is often filled by groups; it's advisable to phone ahead to reserve.

Heading south, less than a mile from the village, the road passes a well-preserved **gallery grave**, dated between 2000 and 1500 BC, on a tranquil windblown site among the heather-covered slopes of Thur Mountain, overlooking a tiny lough; it's known locally as Prince Connell's Grave.

Around Lough Melvin

Four miles northwest of Kiltyclogher and just outside **ROSSINVER**, at the southern end of **Lough Melvin**, there's a cool, leafy walk along a river that cascades through its valley in a series of waterfalls – a good outing for the baking hot days that happen sometimes, even in the west of Ireland. Immediately outside the village on the Garrison road, Eden Plants (☎072/54122) is one of the growing band of Irish producers of organic herbs and vegetables, and is open to visitors (Tues–Sun 2–6pm; free). Two miles north of Rossinver on the road towards Kinlough is the Organic Centre which has two of its nineteen acres given over to display gardens which demonstrate the techniques used in domestic and commercial organic gardening. There's also a children's play area and a shop selling plants, herbs and produce.

The route on up to Kinlough, much less spectacular than the country to the west, runs along the eight-mile western shore of Lough Melvin. A few yards from the northern end of the lake is an islet occupied by the ruin of **McClancy's Castle**. It was here that eight survivors from the three Spanish galleons wrecked off Streedagh Point finally found refuge.

KINLOUGH, near the northwestern tip of the lake, is a wholly unpretentious village and has a surprisingly interesting little **museum** at the Manorhamilton end (Mon–Sat 10am–5pm; ☎071/66296; small fee requested); it's currently being redeveloped, but will show rotating displays from the extensive collection of folk and historical memorabilia until it fully re-opens, probably in 2002. *The Courthouse Restaurant* offers both food and accommodation (☎072/42391; ④).

Around three miles north of Kinlough, **TULLAGHAN**, Leitrim's only outlet to the sea, boasts a ninth- or tenth-century **high cross**, standing forlornly askew on a hummock by the roadside – all in all, a rather dreary resort on a dreary strip of coast.

travel details

Trains

Carrick-on-Shannon to: Dublin (3–4 daily; 2hr 20min); Sligo (3–4 daily; 1hr).

Sligo to: Ballymote (3–4 daily; 20min); Boyle (3–4 daily; 40min); Carrick-on-Shannon (3–4 daily; 1hr); Collooney (3–4 daily; 10min); Dublin (3–4 daily; 3hr 20min).

Buses

Bus Éireann

Sligo to: Belfast (2–3 daily; 4hr 15min); Dublin (4 daily; 3hr 15min); Galway (4–5 daily; 2hr 30min).

Feda O'Donnell Coaches

Sligo to: Donegal (2–3 daily; 50min); Galway (2–3 daily; 2hr 10min).

CHAPTER TWELVE

CAVAN AND MONAGHAN

Cavan and Monaghan sit side by side as if one were a physical imprint of the other – Monaghan all small hills, Cavan all small lakes. County Monaghan is renowned for being drumlin country – rashes of rounded hills that diminish as you head west into Cavan where the land breaks up into a crazy pattern of tiny lakes. Both landscapes have their charms, both their practical difficulties. If you're walking or cycling in either county, a compass can be very useful; although the terrain isn't inaccessible or dangerous, you should be aware that there's such a network of winding, crisscrossed roads – the minor ones often riddled with potholes – that you can very easily get lost. In Monaghan, the drumlin hills all look similar, while the myriad lakes of Cavan enforce constant twists and turns. The lakes, however, now offer a more leisurely means of travel; since the reopening in 1994 of an old canal system, you can sail through Cavan along the Shannon–Erne Waterway.

Like County Donegal, Cavan and Monaghan share the peculiar identity of being historically part of **Ulster** yet included in the Republic since Partition in 1921. Not surprisingly, Cavan and Monaghan people (Protestant and Catholic) still share a strong affinity with their northern neighbours. As border counties, they have also sheltered Republican activity during "the Troubles", and, despite the peace process, the communities are still largely polarized along staunchly held political lines.

Although the border has sharpened political and social definitions, there is a sense in which it has also sheltered both of these counties. You'll probably be struck by the old-fashioned feel of the countryside: while slow, rural ways are as prevalent in other Irish counties, the sharp contrast with the industrialization and development over the border makes them more striking here. Uncertainty about the future has left an unhurried rural ordinariness that constitutes much of these counties' appeal. They are not gaily painted for tourists, nor visibly quaint, and there's a dour Scottish severity in many of the villages, particularly in Monaghan – clear evidence of the Ulster planters. But as you explore, you'll find both counties have an understated and quiet charm.

COUNTY CAVAN

Long neglected by most holiday-makers, **County Cavan** is slowly becoming more popular, thanks to the major redevelopment of the old **Ballinamore–Ballyconnell Canal**,

ACCOMMODATION PRICE CODES

Throughout this book, prices of hotels, guesthouses and B&Bs have been graded with the codes below, according to what you can expect to pay for a double room in high season. For more details on accommodation, see p.34.

① Under £26/€33.01	④ £40–55/€50.79–69.84	⑦ £90–110/€114.28–139.67
② £26–33/€33.01–41.90	⑤ £55–70/€69.84–88.88	⑧ £110–130/€139.67–165.07
③ £33–40/€41.90–50.79	⑥ £70–90/€88.88–114.28	⑨ Over £130/€165.07

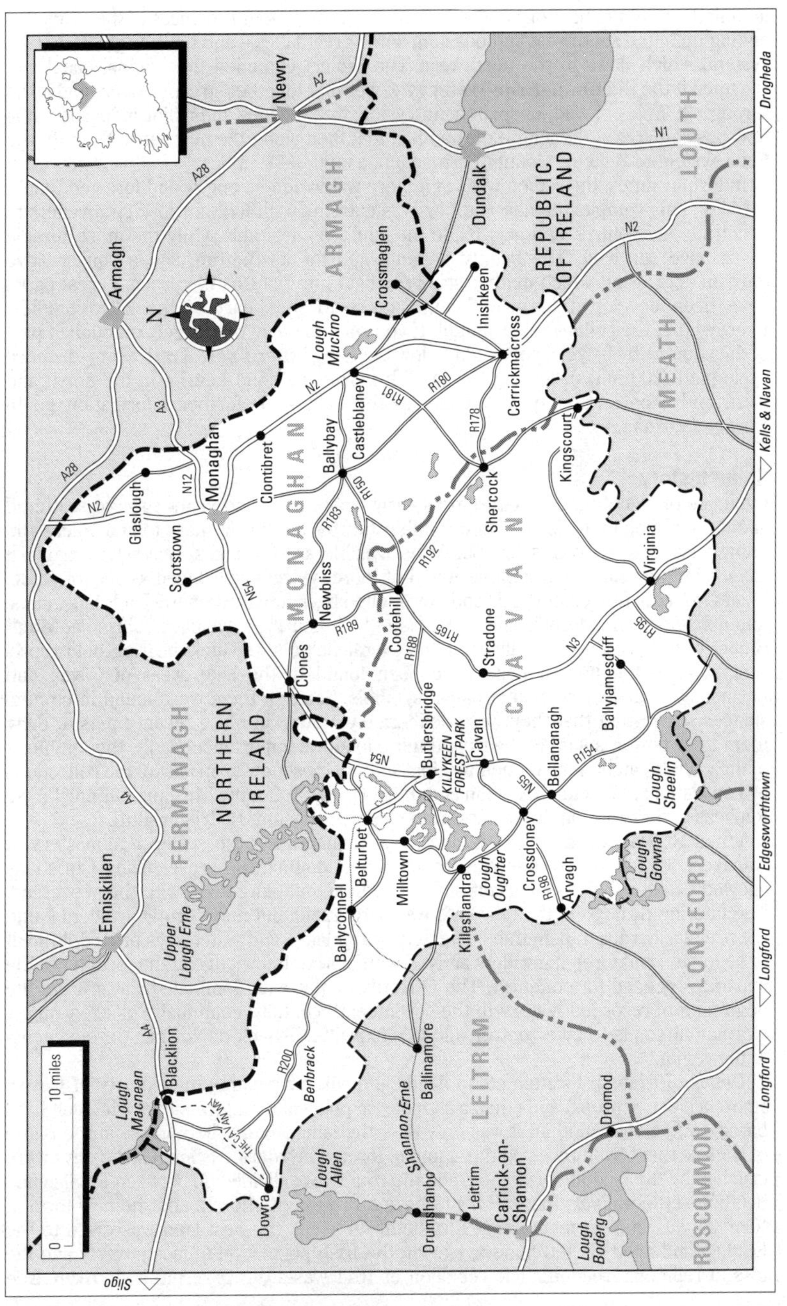
MONAGHAN
CAVAN
ARMAGH
FERMANAGH
NORTHERN IRELAND
REPUBLIC OF IRELAND
LOUTH
MEATH
LONGFORD
LEITRIM
ROSCOMMON
Newry
Armagh
Dundalk
Crossmaglen
Inishkeen
Carrickmacross
Castleblaney
Lough Muckno
Monaghan
Glaslough
Clontibret
Ballybay
Scotstown
Newbliss
Clones
Cootehill
Shercock
Kingscourt
Virginia
Stradone
Ballyjamesduff
Butlersbridge
Killykeen Forest Park
Cavan
Bellananagh
Crossdoney
Arvagh
Lough Sheelin
Lough Gowna
Lough Oughter
Killeshandra
Milltown
Belturbet
Ballyconnell
Ballinamore
Enniskillen
Upper Lough Erne
Blacklion
Lough Macnean
Benbrack
The Cavan Way
Dowra
Lough Allen
Shannon-Erne
Drumshanbo
Leitrim
Carrick-on-Shannon
Dromod
Lough Boderg
10 miles
Sligo
Longford
Longford
Edgesworthtown
Kells & Navan
Drogheda
N1
N2
N3
N12
N54
N55
A2
A3
A4
A28
R150
R154
R165
R178
R180
R181
R183
R188
R189
R192
R195
R198
R200

linking the mighty Shannon waterway, which serves all four provinces of the country – ending up in the southwest and boasting some great lakes – and the **Lough Erne** lake system, which flows to the northwest. The project extended the original canal and renamed it the **Shannon–Erne Waterway,** weaving together streams, rivers and lakes through 39 miles of wild, unspoilt countryside, free of cities and major industries. It is now possible to sail the length of the Shannon, then along the new canal, through the Erne system to Belleek, County Fermanagh, a total of 239 miles.

In former times, the region was even more water-ridden, boggy and forested than it is today. This complex of lake and bog was extremely difficult for foreign invaders to penetrate and control, and also made the land less desirable. Only the most durable relics have survived. The county is renowned for its **fishing**, and a conservative tourism is growing which neither scars the land nor disturbs the peace. Forest parks have been developed to give fishers access to the heart of the lake complex. Everywhere, the stillness is profound. If you want to enjoy this largely untouched part of the country by bicycle, you could follow the **Kingfisher Cycle Trail**, a long-distance cycle path (200 miles), linking Cavan with Fermanagh and Leitrim in the north and west, and Clones, County Monaghan to the east – for further information go to *www.cycleireland.com*.

Some history

Evidence of Neolithic peoples from as early as six thousand years ago are scattered about the region in the form of **court cairn tombs**, but they're hard to find unless you know what you're looking for. Similarly invisible are the lakes' *crannógs* – artificial islands built as early as the Stone Age, but more typically developed as secure settlements from the first century AD and now melted back into the general landscape, indistinguishable from natural islands. The **Celts** had their principal pagan shrine at **Magh Sleacht** near present-day Ballyconnell. Several Celtic stone idols bearing bold representations of the human head have been found in the lake areas of Cavan and Fermanagh, particularly potent pagan symbols. Some of them were found in circumstances suggesting that they were deliberately hidden in more recent times to deny them their power, a sign of their continuing folkloric importance. Sadly, though, none of these idols can be seen in their original setting; most now form part of the collections of The National Museum in Dublin and the Fermanagh County Museum at Enniskillen. Replicas of them are on display at Cavan County Museum, Ballyjamesduff.

When **St Patrick** established his seat at Armagh, he also set up a monastery at Kilnavert. Rather than crudely asserting a new dogma, the proselytizing Christians allowed pagan and folkloric traditions to continue, mingling them with the new creed. The filtering through of the new faith was fairly rapid; but more brutal invaders found the area far harder to penetrate. The network of lakes and waterways proved difficult to negotiate, and foreign invaders arrived with neither knowledge of the terrain nor the apparatus needed for conquest. The **O'Reilly** family, who dominated Cavan from the beginning of recorded history to the seventeenth century, continually blocked Anglo-Norman attempts to take control, and this explains the lack of Norman developments in the region.

Despite Elizabeth I's attempts to divide and rule by creating the **County of Cavan** (more a piece of propaganda than a sign of real political strength) and playing one Irish barony off against another, it was only after the failure of the Irish cause at the Battle of Kinsale that Cavan received the stamp of foreign invaders. Ancient Gaelic ways were crushed by the Jacobite plantation, and the county was divided up between English and Scottish settlers. Every parish was to have a Protestant church, and the new town of Virginia was built in memory of Elizabeth. As usual, the best land was given to the English and Scottish newcomers, leaving the Irish population to face poverty and the loss of religious freedom. The rebellion of 1641 was a direct result, and **Owen Roe**

O'Neill, the Ulster Confederate leader based at Cavan, played an important part, defeating the British General Munro at Benburb to the north of the county in 1646. However, O'Neill failed to follow his victory through, and the Irish Confederates were eventually defeated. After O'Neill's death in 1649, Cromwell quickly took control of Cavan and the resulting confiscation of land and property from the Irish guaranteed the Protestant domination of the county.

Until Partition, Cavan's subsequent history was much in line with the rest of Ulster. In the eighteenth and nineteenth centuries the linen and woollen industries ensured a measure of economic growth – though Cavan was always one of the poorer parts of the province because of the difficulties of the land; and the Famine of 1845 to 1849 brought large-scale emigration. At **Partition**, Cavan was included in the Republic, thus retaining its Irishness; but it shared the fate of Monaghan and Donegal in being torn from its historic and cultural Ulster identity.

Cavan town, Lough Oughter and Ballyjamesduff

CAVAN town grew up around an abbey, but nothing remains of this beyond its memory and an eighteenth-century tower beside the burial place of Owen Roe O'Neill. The town is quite subdued, with only two main streets: Main Street is the principal artery of shops and bars, while Farnham Street has an older character with some very nice stone Georgian houses, a Classical courthouse of warm sandstone and a huge Catholic cathedral, built in the 1940s, that surprisingly succeeds in confirming status and a sense of place without being overbearing.

The **tourist office** on Farnham Street (April–Sept Mon–Fri 9am–5.30pm, Sat 9am–1pm; ☎049/433 1942) will offer information on the county in general; there's little to see in the town itself. The Lifeforce Mill, Mill Road, a renovated nineteenth-century flour mill (May–Sept; ☎049/436 2722), is only open to groups, and building work at Cavan Crystal, Dublin Road, means that tours are unlikely to be available before 2002 (☎049/433 1800). There are a handful of places to stay in and around the town: **B&B** is available at *Oakdene*, 29 Cathedral Rd (☎049/433 1698; ③), and *McCaul's Guesthouse*, 10 Bridge St (☎049/433 1327; ④), and the welcoming *Lisnamandra Farmhouse*, four and a half miles out of Cavan towards Crossdoney, is good value (☎049/433 7196; ③). *The Farnham Arms Hotel* on Main Street (☎049/433 2577; ⑥) provides pleasant and comfortable accommodation, and their bar and restaurant is open to non-residents. Eating options in general are fairly limited, but there are a number of good spots for **bar food**, including *An Síbín*, 86 Town Hall St, the loud and popular *Blackhorse Inn*, Main Street, and *The Imperial Hotel*, which serves excellent, hearty bar meals. There's no shortage of viable watering holes: *An Cruíscín Lán*, 82 Main St, draws a young crowd, as does *An Síbín* (DJ on Friday nights); if you are looking for a bar with character and a mixed crowd, try *Louis Blessings* on Main Street. For rod hire, licences and information on **fishing**, visit *Sports World*, 11 Town Hall St (☎049/433 1812); for bike rental, see p.468. Cavan is very much the transport centre of the county, and Bus Éireann (☎049/433 2533) connects it with all major towns in the Republic and the North. Wharton's private **buses** (☎049/433 7114) also operate a daily service to Dublin, leaving from outside the *Lakeland Hotel*.

Lough Oughter

A major focus of scenic interest in County Cavan is the complex of tiny lakes which riddle the north of the county. They're known collectively as **Lough Oughter** and form part of Upper Lough Erne. The land here is so fretted with water that its very fabric seems to be disintegrating. Contours are provided by very low, unassuming hills while the waters are edged with reeds, spindly silver birch and alder. Everything is on a small scale, but the landscape has a subtle attraction nonetheless, and the roads making their way through the labyrinthine network of lakes are quiet and empty. It makes little sense to head for a particular point in Lough Oughter – it's hard to tell when you've got there anyway – and the best plan is probably just to enjoy the gentle confusion.

The nicest of the little towns serving visitors, especially those interested in fishing, are Cavan town itself and, ten miles north, Belturbet. In between, just four miles north of Cavan, there's also the pretty village of **BUTLERSBRIDGE**, with a popular bar, *The Derragarra Inn* – touristy but serving good food throughout the day, with traditional music (Thurs). **BELTURBET** itself sits prettily on a hill beside the River Erne and is an angling and boating resort with a marina and cruiser station. Weekly **cruiser rental** is available with Emerald Star Line, and you can sail from here and drop the boat off in Carrick-on-Shannon (☎078/20234). *On Yer Bike*, based in Portruan, Belturbet, provides **bike rental** from Belturbet and Cavan town (☎049/952 2219; £7/€8.89 a day). For **B&B**, try *Mrs R. Hughes*, 8 Church St (☎049/952 2358; ③), up behind the library, off the main road.

Heading round the lough there are a few sights of interest. About a mile south of Milltown, you'll find **Drumlane Church and round tower**. A monastery was founded here by St M'Aodhog in the sixth century, and Augustinians from Kells took the place over in medieval times. The church itself is plain and roofless, but its setting beside a lake, and its size in such an intimate landscape, are impressive. The earliest parts of the building are thirteenth century, but it was substantially altered in the fifteenth century, the period from which the carved heads outside the doorways and windows date. The round tower is eleventh century and of good, clean stonework.

Continuing south through **KILLESHANDRA** round the west side of Lough Oughter, bear right at the Arvagh signpost, then first right – it's difficult to reach without transport – to **Mrs Faris's Pighouse Collection**, a quasi-**folk museum** at Corr House, Cornafean (ring ☎049/433 7248 to check that she's in; £3/€3.81). It's a huge accumulation of miscellaneous remnants of the past housed in a series of old barns. Much of Mrs Faris's extraordinary collection, however, is now in the county museum in Ballyjamesduff (see below) and only some of the material here has so far been catalogued – the rest you rummage through and interpret for yourself. There's a vast and fascinating range of stuff here, including clothing from the eighteenth century onwards, coins, domestic utensils and a huge collection of porcelain cheese dishes. Killeshandra is also one of the few places to hear traditional music in the county: the *Shamrock Inn* has a session on a Saturday night and also does **B&B** (☎049/433 4139; ③).

The Protestant cathedral of **KILMORE**, on the R198 three miles southwest of Cavan town, is a modern structure of little interest. However, set in the wall is an impressive Romanesque doorway, removed here from a monastery that stood on Trinity Island, three miles to the west in Lough Oughter. Its deep, chunky carving is superbly intricate and repays detailed attention. Follow the narrow road that runs for about three miles north from here to the hamlet of Garthrotten, and you can enter *Killykeen Forest Park*, a self-catering complex with accommodation in wooden chalets (☎049/433 2541). There is access to woodland walks and fishing, and horse riding is available at Killykeen Equestrian Centre (☎049/436 1707).

Ballyjamesduff

BALLYJAMESDUFF, eleven miles south of Cavan town, just off the N3, is the location for the new **Cavan County Museum** (Tues–Sat 10am–5pm, plus June–Sept Sun 2–6pm; £2/€2.54). The small collection includes replicas of Celtic stone idols dating from the second century BC to the second century AD. Among the exhibits from the medieval period there's the Lough Errol dugout boat (900 AD) and a couple of impressive Sheila na Gigs. Surprisingly, the history of Cavan's emigrants yields Sioux girdles and headdresses, and there's extensive coverage of the GAA footballing history of the county.

West Cavan

To the northwest of Milltown and Killeshandra, west Cavan sticks out like a handle, tracing the line of the border. It's quite different from the rest of the county – wilder and higher, with peat-covered hills, granite boulders and mountain streams. In this inhospitable bleakness, it has more in common with the wilds of Donegal than the more intimate Cavan lakeland.

About six miles from Belturbet is **BALLYCONNELL**, two miles west of which is the county's one independent **hostel**, *Sandville House Hostel* (all year, but advance booking advised Nov–March; ☎049/952 6297; *sandville@eircom.ie*). Housed in an airy converted barn alongside a large Georgian house, it's a tranquil spot, and there are bikes for rent and space for tents. **B&Bs** in the area include *An Crannog*, Cranaghan (☎049/952 6545; ④) and *Rossdean*, Daisyhill (☎049/952 6358; ④).

Right up in the northwestern corner of the county, the Cavan Way is a signposted walk of seventeen miles that takes you through rugged terrain from **DOWRA** to **BLACKLION**, where it meets the southwestern end of the Ulster Way. Small maps of the route can be picked up in tourist offices. From the heights above Blacklion there are spectacular views over Lough MacNean and the Fermanagh lakeland, to the Sligo and Leitrim mountains in the west, and on a clear day to the heights of south Donegal. Along the route, The Shannon Pot is the source of Ireland's mightiest river – the Shannon – and figures heavily in Irish myth, though it's little visited.

Dowra and Blacklion themselves are tiny and remote: the former high on the young Shannon before it fills Lough Allen, the first of many lakes, the latter a border crossing point. Both have very limited facilities indeed. Their B&Bs are almost certain to have space, though it's best to phone ahead and check. In Blacklion there's *Lough Macneann House* (☎072/53022; ④), in Main Street; dinner in their award-winning bistro costs around £30/€38.09 (restaurant open July–Sept Mon–Sat; Oct–June Thurs–Sun). In Dowra, a tiny place with just a few bars and a grocery shop, *The Hi Way Inn* (☎078/43025; ①) is the only option.

COUNTY MONAGHAN

Monaghan is first and foremost **drumlin** country. Drumlins are softly rounded mounds of land left by retreating glaciers at the end of the last Ice Age, and the exceptional number of these small hills packed together in County Monaghan serves as a very good example of what textbooks call "basket of eggs" topography – a reference to the land's appearance from on high; at ground level the soil is poor and the land is broken up into small units which are difficult and uneconomic to farm. The drumlins are grass-covered, and light hedgerows stitch their way across them, marking out the fields. Initially it's a charming scene, but it soon becomes repetitive: the pathways between drumlins are pretty enough, but once you're round or over one small hill the next is much the same. Little lakes provide occasional relief and are excellent for fishing, but they're nothing like as numerous as in Cavan.

The feel of this countryside has been captured in the poetry and prose of **Patrick Kavanagh**, rated by many as Ireland's finest poet after Yeats. He was born in Inishkeen in the south of the county, and his writing evokes the poor quality of peasant life – and also something of the monotony of the rural landscape.

Particularly in the north of the county, the terrain has led to an insane crisscrossing of lanes: a compass is a good idea, as is an up-to-date map. It makes for good walking if you're not in too much of a hurry: in these hilly areas you can wander undisturbed for miles along the labyrinth of ancient tracks and lanes – though it is advisable to avoid the border. If you know what to look for you can seek out the sites of court tombs, forts and cairns from the Bronze Age. Many of them, thanks to the underdevelopment of the land, have remained virtually untouched. The best megalithic sites in the region are the Lisnadarragh wedge tomb, Dún Dubh, at Tiravera, and the Tullyrain triple ring fort near Shantonagh.

Most of Monaghan's towns and villages have very clear origins in the seventeenth and eighteenth centuries. The influence of Scottish planters and English colonists is obvious in the number of planters' Gothic and Presbyterian churches, and in the planned towns and the landscaped estates developed around conveniently picturesque lakes. Stark, stern architecture reflects the character of the hard-working and hard-driving settlers who came here determined to extract prosperity from farming, and from the linen industries which they introduced. Probably the most extreme examples of such discipline are the dour, austere stone cottages of **Glaslough**, cold and orderly in the north of the county. Like Cavan, Monaghan's cultural identity is deeply rooted in Ulster history.

Monaghan town

You're most likely to find yourself in **MONAGHAN** town while on your way to somewhere else, but the actual fabric of the place is quite interesting as you pass through. Monaghan town epitomizes what makes this county very definitely Ulster and yet quite distinct from Cavan. The planning of seventeenth-century settlers, the prosperity of the eighteenth-century linen industry (largely the achievement of Scots Presbyterians) and the subsequent wealth and status of the town in the following century are all very much in evidence.

The Town

Three central squares are linked by a chain of lanes, a layout not, in fact, altogether typical of plantation towns. At the centre is the **Diamond** – the name given to all these Ulster "squares" – in the middle of which stands a grandiose Victorian drinking fountain, the kind of memorial strongly reminiscent of any nineteenth-century industrial British city, yet strangely out of place in rural Ireland. When it was placed here, the earlier seventeenth-century Scottish settlers' cross, with its multifaceted sundial, was shifted a short distance along Dublin Street to Old Cross Square, where it still stands.

Alongside the Diamond is **Church Square**. Here a classical courthouse, a solid Victorian bank and hotel and a very pretty Regency Gothic church, large and spacious, stand together, conferring a strong sense of civic dignity. The town's former importance as a British garrison town is quite clear, and a large obelisk commemorates a colonel killed in the Crimean War. Everything about the place suggests a conscious attempt at permanency, buildings placed with a view to posterity; even the rounded corners of the most mundane buildings and their boldly arched entries – both features unique to Monaghan – suggest strength and pride.

Beyond Church Square, at the top of Market Street, is a pretty, arched **Market House** built in 1792, a solid, graceful building of well-cut limestone, with finely detailed decoration of carved oak leaves and oak apples. In the opposite direction, Dublin Street leads down to **Old Cross Square**. At number ten stands the birthplace of Monaghan's most famous son, **Charles Gavan Duffy** – a Nationalist who was instrumental in the founding of the Irish Tenant League. He was also the co-founder, along with Thomas Davis, of *The Nation*, a paper which was to disseminate politically sensitive ideas. Beyond, high on a hill out of town, **St Macartan's Catholic Cathedral** commands views over the whole town and surrounding countryside. Completed in 1892, it's a Gothic Revival building of hard grey sandstone, with a tall spire and a spacious interior, complete with an impressive hammer-beam roof. As you stand on the steps looking out over the surrounding land you get a real feeling of its era – it's a most successful nineteenth-century statement of religious liberation and pride.

As well as being a busy commercial and administrative centre, Monaghan looks after the county's vigorous and sometimes violent history at the **Monaghan County Museum** on Hill Street (Tues–Sat 10am–1pm & 2–5pm; free). This fine building houses a permanent collection of archeological material, prehistoric antiquities, examples of traditional local crafts, domestic utensils and paintings, prints and watercolours from the late eighteenth century to the present day. The museum's most prized artefact is the **Cross of Clogher**, a processional cross dating from around 1400. Contemporary art exhibitions are also held here. The **heritage centre**, Broad Rd (Mon, Tues, Thurs & Fri 10am–noon & 2–4pm, Sat & Sun 2.30–4.30pm; £1/€1.27), tells the story of the religious order of St Louis, with an intelligent display meticulously put together by one of the sisters; you're guided through it with a cassette recording.

Practicalities

The **tourist office** is in Market House in Market Street (end March–June & Sept–Dec Mon–Fri 9am–1pm & 2–5pm, Sat 9am–1pm; July and August Mon–Sat 9am–6pm, Sun 10am–2pm; ☎047/81122). There are several decent **B&Bs**, including *Ashleigh House*, 37 Dublin St (☎047/81227; ④), and *The Cedars*, Clones Rd (closed Nov–Feb; ☎047/82783; ③). *The Hillgrove Hotel*, Old Armagh Rd, near the cathedral (☎047/81288; ⑥), is smart, spacious and welcoming and offers comfortable rooms.

Several places serve bar **meals**: *Andy's*, 12 Market St, is especially good, *McConnon's Olde Cross Inn*, Olde Cross Square, is another decent option, and carvery lunches are available at *The Hillgrove Hotel*. Otherwise, there is a limited choice of places to eat in the evening: one of the best is award-winning *Andy's Restaurant* at 12 Market St (☎047/82277), and the moderately priced, informal Italian restaurant *Mediterraneo* at 58 Dublin St (closed Tues; ☎047/82335) is also worthwhile.

You won't have to go far to hear **music** in the evenings. In Dublin Street, *McKenna's* has blues bands (3–4 nights a week) and *Mo's Bar* has rock and pop bands (Fri–Sun). *McConnon's Olde Cross Inn* is a good spot for a quiet pint, and on the Diamond *The Squealing Pig* has DJs (Wed, Fri & Sat). For traditional music try *Kavanagh's*, Park Street, just across from the tourist office. Monaghan has some very active local **theatre** groups: check out The Garage Theatre, Armagh Rd (☎047/81597), to find out what's on. There's an international rhythm and blues **festival** over the first weekend in September, usually starting on the Thursday night (☎047/82928 for further information, or visit *www.harvestblues.net*).

Bus Éireann (☎047/82377) links Monaghan with all major towns in the Republic and with Armagh, Belfast, Derry, Omagh and Strabane in the North. McConnon's (☎047/82020) operates a private daily bus service to Dublin, picking up in Church Square (Mon–Sat) and from behind the courthouse (Sun).

Around the county

There are just a few reasons for pushing six miles northeast of Monaghan to the eerie, chill-grey village of **GLASLOUGH**, and the best of these is *Castle Leslie* (☎047/88109; ⑨), a gormenghastian aristocratic pile, crammed with fabulous antiques. Book in and you leave the twenty-first century behind: there are no phones, TVs, or room service, just wonderfully relaxed hospitality and a sense of fading splendour. Previous guests have included Yeats, George Moore, Winston Churchill and Mick Jagger. If an overnight stay is beyond your budget, you can sample some of the atmosphere if you book in for dinner (around £30/€38.09). Back in the village, *The Olde Bar* is a tiny place, similarly seemingly unchanged for decades, open Thursdays and Saturdays only. **B&B** accommodation is available at the *Greystone Equestrian Centre*

(☎047/88100; ⑥), a large Victorian house on the *Castle Leslie* estate, and at the *Pillar House Hotel* (☎047/88125; ③).

Castleblaney

Unless you're heading for Glaslough or the North, there are two main routes out of Monaghan: west to the pleasant town of Clones or south to Carrickmacross. On the latter route you'll pass first through **CASTLEBLANEY**, whose two proud broad streets hinge upon a fine Georgian courthouse at what was once the market square, fourteen miles from Monaghan. Castleblaney was built by English colonists to serve the needs of a large estate, beautifully situated beside Monaghan's largest lake, **Lough Muckno**, and this is still the town's finest asset. When the English picked their spot they knew what they were about: it's a particularly attractive demesne of mixed woodlands and gentle slopes beside placid waters. The estate is now a forest park, with clearly signposted walks around beautiful grounds; access is just behind the courthouse. The Lough Muckno Leisure Park tends to attract families and anglers in search of peace and quiet, but it's also home to an independent **hostel**, *The Lough Muckno Adventure Centre and Holiday Hostel* (☎042/974 6356), where you can hire canoes, sailing dinghies and wind-surfers. It's advisable to ring ahead as the hostel caters mainly for groups. There's more water-based excitement to be had at *Muckno Waterski Club* (☎087/666 0077), and plenty of coarse angling available at Lough Muckno and in the series of small lakes roundabout. **B&Bs** include *Hillview*, just outside town (☎042/974 6217; ②), and the spacious and comfortable *Palm Grove Lodge*, Lough Egish, two miles out on the Shercock Road (☎042/974 5170; ③). There are several **places to eat**: during the day *Joan's Pantry*, Main Street, serves inexpensive, wholesome meals; *The Comet*, Main Street, has good bar food and a restaurant for evening meals; and the location of the down-to-earth *Hope Castle Bar and Restaurant* (☎042/974 9450) takes some beating, overlooking the lake within the grounds of the forest park – they serve generous helpings of pub grub and their evening menu is only a little more expensive. *The Hope Castle* also has the lion's share of **nightlife** around here, with bands several nights a week during the summer months – mainly country, ballads and so forth, plus bluegrass on Fridays. *The Comet* is similarly popular, and in fact pubs in Castleblaney generally seem surprisingly lively given the tranquillity of the daytime rural scene.

Carrickmacross

CARRICKMACROSS, ten miles south of Castleblaney, is the county's second most important town, boosted in the nineteenth century by a prosperous lace-making industry. Still, it's a rather modest place with just one broad main street: a planter's Gothic church stands at one end, and a fine mid-nineteenth century courthouse at the other. In between, lies a bustling array of pubs, shops and Georgian houses, and today's lacemakers have their tiny showcase in the nineteenth-century market buildings at the lower end of the main street. Just outside town, landscaped parkland of sumptuous oaks and beeches surrounds **Lough Fea**. Further out, some three miles down the Kingscourt Road, is the **Dún a Rí Forest Park** with more good wooded walks. The massive *Nuremore Hotel* is very expensive (☎042/966 1438; ⑨), but there are plenty of **B&Bs** near the centre of Carrickmacross, up the Derry Road past the Texaco petrol station: try *Cloughvalley House* (☎042/966 1246; ②), or head for *Eureka* at 27 Ard Rois Ave (☎042/966 2009; ③), a friendly, low-key B&B.

Iniskeen

INISKEEN, six miles east of Carrickmacross, is the birthplace of **Patrick Kavanagh**. There's a small plaque bearing some of his verse in the village, and the house he lived in is well signposted – but you can't go in and it's an entirely uninteresting building.

Kavanagh is buried in the graveyard of St Mary's church. The church is also home to the **Patrick Kavanagh Rural and Literary Resource Centre** (Mon–Fri 11am–5pm; Sat, Sun and bank holidays 2–6pm; ☎042/937 8560; £2/€2.54), which has displays on Kavanagh and his work as well as local history. In a more distant past, Iniskeen was the site of a sixth-century monastic centre: scant remains of the abbey and a round tower survive. The **Folk Museum** (by arrangement only, ☎042/937 8102) deals with local history, folk life and the old Great Northern Railway.

Clones

Around twelve miles southwest of Monaghan, **CLONES** (pronounced *Clo-nez*) is a busy, friendly market town, barely half a mile from the border. Situated on top of a hill, its streets give a good perspective over the surrounding countryside. The town – as it appears today – dates from 1601 when the English took it over and started to develop it. It's very obviously an Ulster town, with large Presbyterian and Methodist churches to rival the usual Catholic and Church of Ireland offerings. The solemn and impressive **St Tiernach's Church** (Church of Ireland) gives out onto the fine Diamond, and there is some evidence of eighteenth-century prosperity in the town's handful of Georgian houses. There are also traces of Clones' earlier identity, the most impressive being the weathered, deeply carved **high cross** which stands in the Diamond. Depicted on it are Adam and Eve, Abraham's near sacrifice of Isaac, Daniel in the lion's den and, on the north side, the Adoration of the Magi, the miracle at Cana and the miracle of the loaves and fishes. Though worn, there's still a strong impression of the richness of the carving. In the sixth century St Tiernach founded a monastery at Clones. It became an Augustinian **abbey** in the twelfth century, and the tumbled-down traces of this can be seen in Abbey Street, along with those of a round tower. Just on the edge of town is an ancient rath (an enclosure used as a dwelling) of three concentric earthworks.

Nowadays, the town's chief claims to fame are as the setting for Patrick McCabe's *The Butcher Boy*, and as the home of Barry McGuigan, the former world-champion boxer – there are a couple of photos of him in *The Lennard Arms Hotel*, which also does **B&B** (☎047/51075; ④). Otherwise there's *Creighton's Hotel* in Fermanagh Street (☎047/51055; ④) and *The Round Tower Bar* in Cara Street, which offers B&B (☎047/51158; ②) and serves good bar food. Just outside Newbliss, around five miles southeast of Clones, is *Glynch House* (☎047/54045; ④), an eighteenth-century mansion offering accommodation.

Ulster Canal Stores provides information and has exhibitions on the area's history, including lace-making and the old Erne–Belfast Canal (July & Aug daily 9am–5pm; Sept–June Mon–Fri 9am–5pm; ☎047/52125). The town is a good point from which to get onto The Kingfisher Cycle Trail; you can rent **bikes** at Snipe Cycle Hire, Ulster Canal Stores (£9/€11.43 a day, £30/€38.09 a week).

travel details

Buses

Bus Éireann

Cavan town to: Belfast (1–4 daily; 2hr 55min); Dublin (4–8 daily; 1hr 40min–2hr).

Monaghan town to: Belfast (2–3 daily; 2hr 45min); Dublin (6–10 daily; 2hr).

Wharton's Buses

Cavan town to: Dublin (1 daily; 1hr 50min).

McConnon's Buses

Monaghan town to: Dublin (1–2 daily; 2hr).

CHAPTER THIRTEEN

COUNTY DONEGAL

Few would disagree with the assertion that County Donegal has the richest scenery in the whole of Ireland. Second only in size to County Cork, it has a spectacular two-hundred-mile coastline – an intoxicating run of headlands, promontories and peninsulas – rising to the highest sea-cliffs in Europe at Slieve League. Inland is a terrain of glens, rivers and bogland hills, of which the best-known parts are the Glencolmcille Peninsula and around Ardara and Glenties in the southern part of the county. The Glencolmcille area attracts more visitors than any other, yet the landscape of northern Donegal is, if anything, even more satisfying, especially the Rosguill and Inishowen peninsulas and the interior region – sometimes called the Donegal Highlands – around Errigal Mountain, Lough Beagh and Lough Gartan. Other noteworthy areas are the Rosses and the Bloody Foreland, which are reminiscent of the more barren stretches of Connemara and make up the strongest *Gaeltacht*, or Irish-speaking districts, in the county.

Donegal's original name was *Tír Chonaill*, which translates as "the land of Conal", who was one of the twelve sons of Niall of the Nine Hostages. After the Flight of the Earls in the early seventeenth century, the English changed the name to that of their main garrison *Dún na nGall* ("the fort of the foreigner") which has a certain irony, because Donegal always eluded the grip of English power, mainly owing to its wild and untillable terrain. Donegal is the most northerly part of Ireland which confuses some into believing that it is part of Northern Ireland. That it is not was due to the Unionists' belief at the time of Partition in 1922 that Donegal's Catholic population would have threatened the stability of the new statelet by voting the county and the whole of the North back into the Republic at a later stage.

Bundoran and around

It's hard to avoid disappointment if **BUNDORAN**, at the southern extremity of the county, is your first sight of Donegal. This popular, though tacky, seaside resort offers no indication of the pleasures which lie beyond. It does have three miles of Blue Flag beaches, packed with holidaymakers in summer, but the town itself provides pretty grim fare. The tiny River Doran separates the more genteel **West End** from the **East End** and its rather down-at-heel Main Street, filled with pubs, B&Bs, eating places, and a headland dominated by a golf course.

ACCOMMODATION PRICE CODES

Throughout this book, prices of hotels, guesthouses and B&Bs have been graded with the codes below, according to what you can expect to pay for a double room in high season. For more details on accommodation, see p.34.

① Under £26/€33.01	④ £40–55/€50.79–69.84	⑦ £90–110/€114.28–139.67
② £26–33/€33.01–41.90	⑤ £55–70/€69.84–88.88	⑧ £110–130/€139.67–165.07
③ £33–40/€41.90–50.79	⑥ £70–90/€88.88–114.28	⑨ Over £130/€165.07

Unless you're fond of golf, Bundoran's chief attraction is a lovely golden-sand beach known as **Tullan Strand**, a bracing stroll along the coastal promenade from the northern end of the town beach. The walk takes in rock formations known as the **Fairy Bridge** and the **Puffing Hole**, with the Atlantic thundering below and appetizing views across to the much more rewarding Glencolmcille Peninsula. Tullan Strand, and the beach just up the coast at Rossnowlagh, are reckoned among the most exciting surfing spots in the world and, in 1997, Bundoran hosted the European Championships at Tullan. Surfing tuition is available from *Donegal Adventure Centre* (☎072/42277, *adventures@donegal-holidays.com*) which also offers body-boarding, horse riding and a range of other activity packages. Far safer waters for swimming are to be found at **Waterworld** (Easter week, April, May & Sept Sat & Sun 10am–2pm & 3–7pm; June–Aug daily same times; £4.50/€5.71), located on the seafront near the river's mouth, a complex of heated pools with wave machine, water slides and seaweed baths.

Practicalities

There's a new **tourist office** by the bridge on Main Street (July & Aug daily 9am–8pm; rest of year Mon–Sat 9am–6pm; ☎072/41350) but you should have no trouble finding **accommodation**. The least expensive place to stay in Bundoran is the *Homefield* **hostel**, Bayview Ave (☎072/41288, *homefield@indigo.ie*), an activity and equestrian centre often full of hearty young groups; to get to it, cross the bridge into the West End and turn left at the church shortly afterwards. **B&Bs** are plentiful, and several in the West End have wonderful views of Donegal Bay: *Avondale*, Bay View Terrace (☎072/41091; ③); *Conway House*, almost next door (March–Sept; ☎072/41220; ②); and *Bayview Guesthouse*, Main St (☎072/41296; ③). Best-known of the numerous **hotels** is the huge old *Great Northern* (☎072/41204; ⑧), dominating the golf course right on the headland. Among other options are the popular *Allingham Arms* (☎072/41075, *allingham @tyrconnell-group.ie*; ⑦) and the *Holyrood Hotel* (☎072/41100, *hrood@indigo.ie*; ⑥) on either side of the bridge. **Bike rental** is available from the Hire and Sell Centre, East End (☎072/41526).

For **eating**, the *Angler's Restaurant* provides a reasonably priced three-course meal. More upmarket, but still not too expensive, is the *Fitzgerald Hotel*, just over the bridge in the West End, and the *Whistling Oyster*, on the main street, serving varied seafood dinners in a bar-room setting. The *Imperial Hotel* in the West End serves good value bar lunches while *La Sabbia* (attached to the *Homefield* hostel) offers a splendid Italian option. There are plenty of simple cafés like the *Kitchen Bake*, in a converted chapel on the main street, for excellent cakes, coffee and snacks. Most **pubs** in Bundoran are pretty ordinary and permanently crowded with northern holidaymakers in high season. For sessions in summer, try *The Bridge Bar* or The *Chasin' Bull* on Main Street. The *Planet Earth* complex on Central Avenue hosts very popular **discos**, with coachloads arriving from all over the county and beyond.

Ballyshannon

The lively town of **BALLYSHANNON**, four miles north of Bundoran at the mouth of the River Erne, was the site of a major battle in 1591 when Hugh Roe O'Donnell drove off the besieging English army, but nowadays its hilly streets become most animated during the **Traditional Music Festival** on the first weekend in August. This is one of the most popular traditional music events in Ireland with performances by major names, such as Donegal's own Altan, along with a multitude of unknown talents. You'll need to book accommodation well in advance, though impromptu space can often be found on someone's floor.

The town stands a few hundred yards upstream from a ford, at the point where the river's fresh waters begins to mingle with the ocean. Most of the interest lies up the

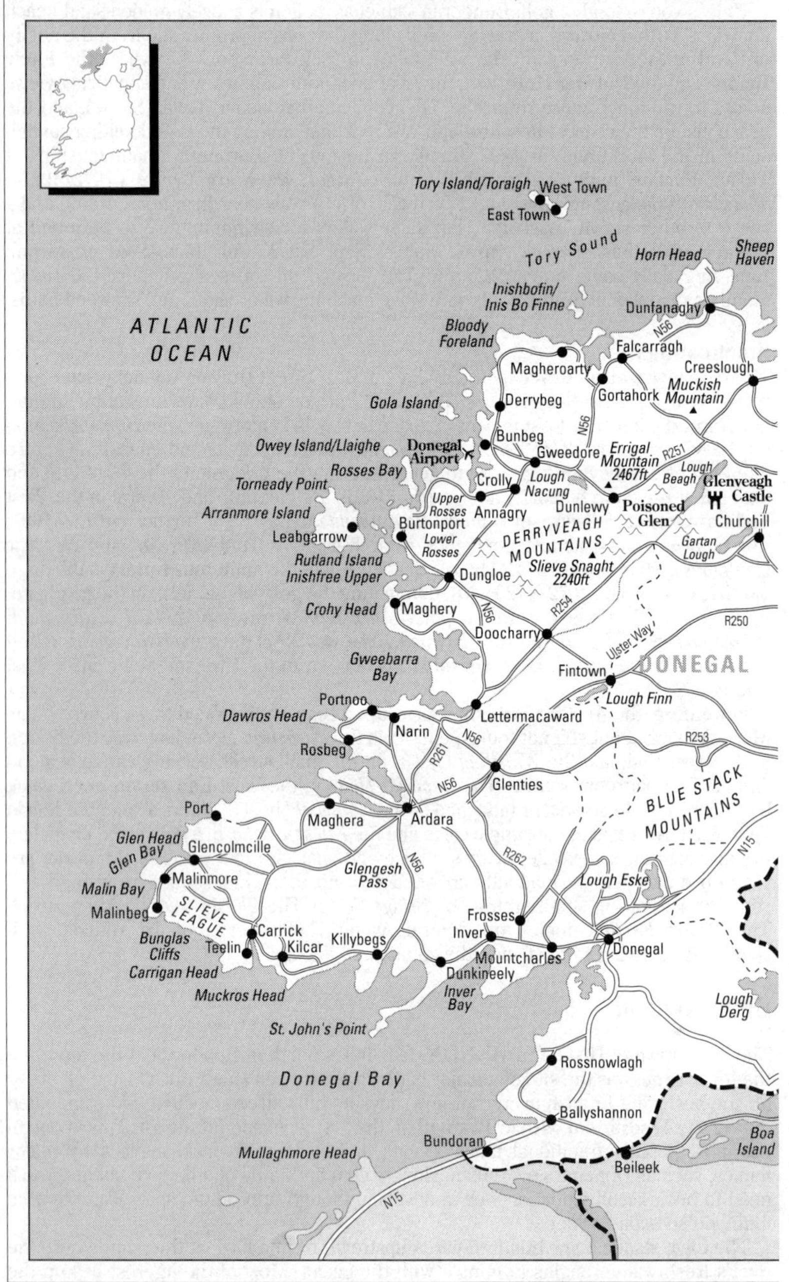

ATLANTIC OCEAN
Tory Island/Toraigh
West Town
East Town
Tory Sound
Horn Head
Sheep Haven
Inishbofin/ Inis Bo Finne
Dunfanaghy
Bloody Foreland
Falcarragh
Magheroarty
Creeslough
Gortahork
Muckish Mountain
Gola Island
Derrybeg
Bunbeg
Owey Island/Llaighe
Donegal Airport
Gweedore
Errigal Mountain 2467ft
Rosses Bay
Lough Beagh
Glenveagh Castle
Torneady Point
Crolly
Lough Nacung
Upper Rosses
Annagry
Dunlewy
Poisoned Glen
Arranmore Island
Burtonport
Churchill
Leabgarrow
Lower Rosses
DERRYVEAGH MOUNTAINS
Gartan Lough
Rutland Island
Inishfree Upper
Dungloe
Slieve Snaght 2240ft
Crohy Head
Maghery
Doocharry
Ulster Way
Gweebarra Bay
Fintown
DONEGAL
Lough Finn
Portnoo
Dawros Head
Narin
Lettermacaward
Rosbeg
Glenties
BLUE STACK MOUNTAINS
Port
Maghera
Ardara
Glen Head
Glen Bay
Glencolmcille
Glengesh Pass
Malinmore
Malin Bay
Malinbeg
SLIEVE LEAGUE
Lough Eske
Frosses
Carrick
Bunglas Cliffs
Teelin
Kilcar
Killybegs
Inver
Mountcharles
Donegal
Carrigan Head
Dunkineely
Muckros Head
Inver Bay
Lough Derg
St. John's Point
Rossnowlagh
Donegal Bay
Ballyshannon
Bundoran
Mullaghmore Head
Beileek
Boa Island
N56
R251
R254
R250
R261
R253
R262
N15

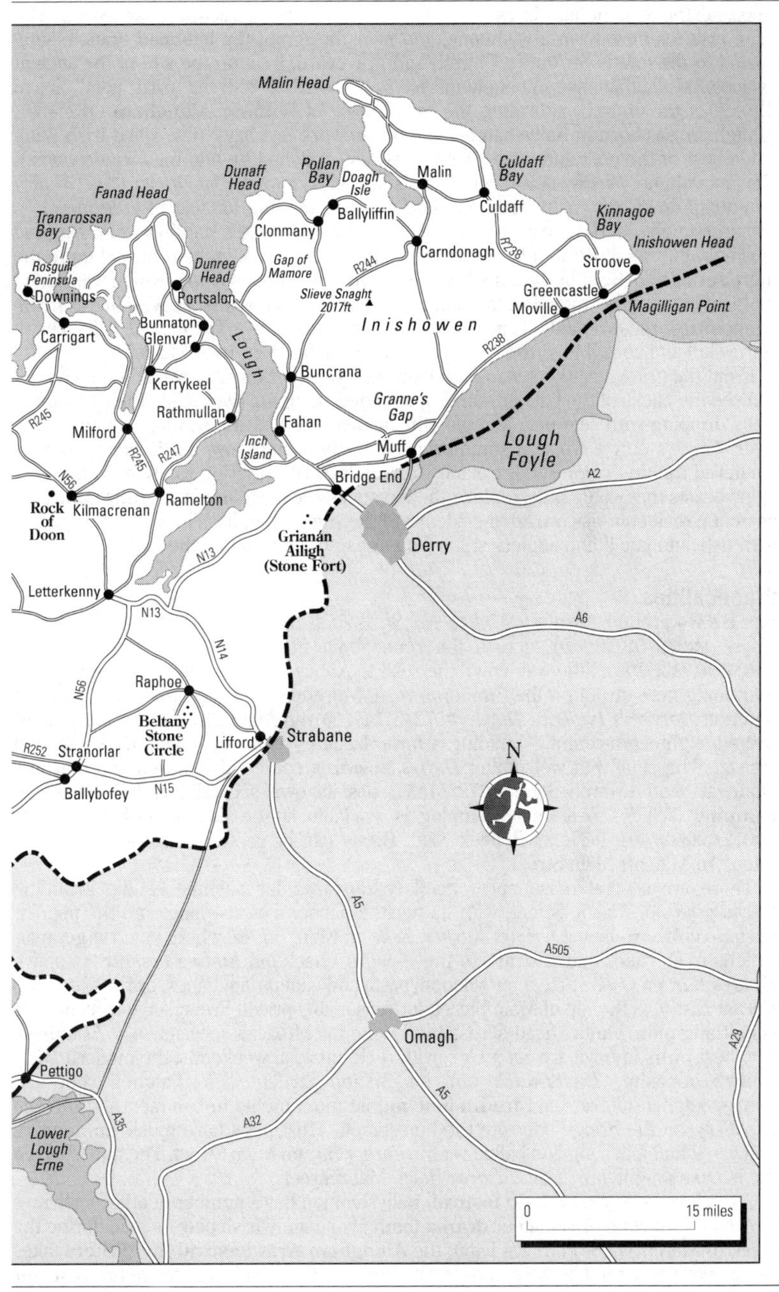

Malin Head
Culdaff Bay
Malin
Pollan Bay
Doagh Isle
Dunaff Head
Fanad Head
Tranarossan Bay
Culdaff
Kinnagoe Bay
Inishowen Head
Ballyliffin
Clonmany
Carndonagh
R238
Stroove
Rosguill Peninsula
Dunree Head
Gap of Mamore
R244
Greencastle
Downings
Portsalon
Slieve Snaght 2017ft
Moville
Magilligan Point
Bunnaton
Carrigart
Glenvar
Inishowen
R238
Lough
Buncrana
Kerrykeel
Granne's Gap
Rathmullan
R245
Milford
Fahan
Inch Island
Muff
Lough Foyle
R245
R247
A2
N56
Bridge End
Rock of Doon
Kilmacrenan
Ramelton
Grianán Ailigh (Stone Fort)
Derry
N13
Letterkenny
N13
A6
N14
N56
Raphoe
Beltany Stone Circle
Lifford
Strabane
R252
Stranorlar
Ballybofey
N15
N
A5
A505
Omagh
A29
Pettigo
A5
A32
A35
Lower Lough Erne
0
15 miles

steep northern slope and is easily combined in a single, straightforward stroll. The main arteries here form a wishbone, and near the top of the left-hand branch, signposted to the left, is St Anne's Church and graveyard, built on the site of the ancient palace of Mullaghanshee. A simple marble slab, inscribed with the word "poet", lies to the left of the church, indicating the burial place of **William Allingham** (1824–89). Allingham was born in Ballyshannon and began work in a bank (the Allied Irish Bank has a bust of the poet and preserves the words scratched by him on a windowpane). His first volume, *Poems* (1850), contains his best-known work *The Fairies* ("Up the airy mountain, down the rushy glen, we dare not go a'hunting for fear of little men..."). Unsurprisingly, such verse attracted him to the pre-Raphaelites: another work, *Day and Night Songs*, was illustrated by Rosetti and Millais, before Allingham moved on to the more serious poetic subject of his homeland. His posthumous *Diary*, which was edited by his wife, the illustrator Helen Paterson, recounts his friendships with literary contemporaries, most notably Tennyson. Allingham was also a fiddler and balladeer of some skill and contributed to Petrie's collections of "Ancient Irish Music".

From the graveyard there's a marvellous view over the town. Down at the quay, you can see the backs of the tall, old warehouses lined along the river bank, their basement walls dripping with seaweed, and also the ancient isle of **Inis Saimer** just out in the river. There's only a wooden summerhouse on the island now, but it claims to have sheltered the first colonists of Ireland, around 3500 BC, offering safety from the ferocious beasts that would have roamed the forests on the mainland. A recently excavated ancient Greek coin has provided evidence of the site's antiquity. The water here teems with fish, and you'll find anglers still trying to bag them well into the night.

Practicalities

For **B&Bs** around town try *Mullac Na Si*, Bishop St (☎072/52702; ③), *Carrickboy House* (☎072/51278; ③), across the roundabout in East Port, or *Channel View* (☎072/51713; ③), a little way down the road to Abbey Assaroe; others are mostly further along here or out on the Bundoran road. More luxurious accommodation can be found at *Dorrian's Imperial Hotel* (☎072/51147; ⑥) on Main Street, a recently refurbished eighteenth-century building whose facilities include a leisure centre and Jacuzzi. The small but welcoming *Duffy's* **hostel**, a couple of hundred yards up the Donegal Road (March–Sept; ☎072/51535) has its own secondhand bookshop and **camping** facilities. Waterside camping is available at the *Assaroe Lakeside Centre* (☎072/52822) off the R230 Belleek road. **Bikes** can be rented from the Erne Cycle Shop, An Mál, off Main Street.

There are several reasonably priced **restaurants** for daytime eating, including *Cúchulainn's* on Castle Street, with its healthy portions of fast food, and the popular upstairs coffee rooms at *Grimes Kitchen Bake* on Main Street, where you can get marvellous fresh cakes and pastries. In the evening, check out *Embers Restaurant*, above *Paddy's Bar*, on Castle Street for seafood, pasta and vegetarian dishes, or try *Shannon's Corner Bistro*, at the top of Main Street, for reasonably-priced French-style cuisine. For something more exotic, head across the bridge for Mexican specialities at *El Gringo*. The best **pubs** in town are *Seán Óg's*, with rock music at weekends, the modern *Dicey Reilly's* opposite, *The Thatch* pub on Bishop Street, with thatched roof and cottage-kitchen interior and **traditional music** most nights in summer, and the *Old Distillery*, on the bridge opposite the bus station. Most pubs have music on Sundays and you'll find folk song and ballads at the *Corner Bar* on Main Street. The hub of **disco** life is *Dino's* nightclub in the *Assaroe Hotel*, Main Street.

As well as its August **music festival**, Ballyshannon has a number of other festivities worth investigating. An amateur **drama festival** of mainly Irish plays is held during the week of March 17 (St Patrick's Day); the **Allingham Arts Festival for Writers** takes place over a weekend at the end of November; and the town's traditional **harvest fair** celebrations around the middle of September draw crowds from the surrounding countryside. The rest of the time you can fill your evenings at the two-screen Abbey **cinema** in the Community Arts Centre, at the north end of town by the Donegal road. At **BALLINTRA**, four miles along the Donegal road, there's **horse racing** in the open fields on the first Monday in August.

Rossnowlagh and around

Instead of taking the main road to Donegal town, you could opt for a left turn by *The Thatch* pub at the top of the hill in Ballyshannon, which takes you along the more pleasant Rossnowlagh road, where a second signposted left turn leads to the sparse remains of **ABBEY ASSAROE**, founded by the Cistercians in 1184. Past the abbey and round to the left, you'll come to a restored **mill** beside a bubbling stream. This makes a pretty picture of millrace and rotating cog wheels, and there's an **interpretive centre**, The Watermills (☎072/51580), explaining the restoration project and the role of the Cistercians in medieval Ireland. The log gate next to the old bridge takes you onto the stream's bank and leads to two artificial **caves**. One is a small grotto known as Catsby's; the other – now around 90ft deep – is said to have once reached all the way under the abbey and run for two miles towards Rossnowlagh. The grotto was once a site for Masses, which had to be held in secret during the enforcement of the penal laws in the eighteenth century, and you'll find in the Rossnowlagh museum the carved stone known as the Monk's Head that once sat above the entrance. A couple of hundred yards upstream are *Eas Aedha Ruadh*, the falls of the chieftain Red Hugh, who reputedly drowned here.

A few yards up the lane from the mill and over a stone stile next to a bungalow a little track runs down to the shore of the **bay**. St Patrick is said to have once stepped ashore here, and today there are several rusted metal crosses perched on small stony outcrops and a tree covered in assorted weather-beaten thanksgiving mementos. The natural **well** here is said to have sprung up at the spot where the saint's foot touched the shore and its waters, when present, have supposed curative powers. Legend also has it that, having arrived, Patrick was driven away by a local leader named Coirbre and responded by cursing the northern side of the river with a barrenness of fish.

Back on the Rossnowlagh road, two miles on, a turning leads to the tiny seaside hamlet of **CREEVY.** It's a tranquil, though lonely spot and a memorial on the pier sadly records the death of three local fishermen in 1988, testament to the sometime ferocity of the waters in the bay. Should you fancy staying, there's the *Creevy Pier Hotel* (☎072/51236; ④) where you can watch the waves from the bar and sample the seafood.

Rossnowlagh

ROSSNOWLAGH lies on the coast away from the main Donegal Road, with good cliffs for walks overlooking a magnificent expanse of beach that is raked by Atlantic surf and is also, sadly, sometimes blighted by boy-racers. Appropriately titled – its name translates as "The Heavenly Cove" – Rossnowlagh has a private surfing club beside the *Sand House Hotel* (☎072/51777, *info@sandhouse-hotel.ie*; ⑧), but one of the many surfing buffs will probably be able to help you out with equipment, or at least advise where else to acquire some. The village is also the site of the only **Orange Order parade** (see p.745) in the Republic, which takes place on the weekend before July 12th. There's a cliff-top **B&B** at *Ard-na-Mara House* (☎072/51141; ④) and nearby, the splendidly situated *Smugglers Creek* inn does excellent food and has music at weekends.

The Franciscan friary nearby on the Donegal road houses a captivating one-room **museum** (daily 10am–6pm; free), run by the Donegal Historical Society and crammed with Stone Age flints, Bronze Age dagger blades, penal crosses, pistols and other local miscellany. This includes a lovely set of *uilleann* pipes with green felt bag and very handsome regulators, a fiddle that belonged to the great piper Tarlach MacSuibhne (himself buried at Magheragallon cemetery, Gweedore) and a seventeenth-century Flemish painting on glass (*The Christ of Pity*) used as a devotion plate. A mile north of Rossnowlagh towards Ballintra lies **Glasbolie Fort**, a huge earthen rampart 20ft high and nearly 900ft round, said to have been the burial place of a sixth-century High King of Ireland.

Donegal town and around

DONEGAL town is not the most exciting of places, but it is making an effort. It's not even the county capital (which is Letterkenny) but, thanks to a new bypass, traffic no longer crams its triangular **Diamond** at the centre, the old market place. A surprising number of tourists visit the town, but the only real reason to stay long is to explore the surrounding countryside, especially the **Blue Stack Mountains** which rise at the northern end of **Lough Eske**.

Arrival, information and accommodation

Buses stop outside the *Abbey Hotel* on the Diamond, with timetables displayed in the helpful and information-packed **tourist office** on the Quay (Easter–June & Sept Mon–Sat 9am–5pm; July & Aug daily 9am–8pm; ☎073/21148). For details of **walks** in the Blue Stack Mountains, just north of Donegal town (see p.483), and in the rest of the county, pick up a copy of David Herman's excellent *Hill Walkers' Donegal* from the tourist office or the Four Masters bookshop on the Diamond. Both also sell Ordnance Survey **maps** of the area.

One advantage of staying in Donegal is that you've plenty of choice of **accommodation**. There are literally dozens of B&Bs scattered around the town, but many of them are very small, so to avoid a lot of walking it's simplest to call at the tourist office. Some **B&Bs** to try include the *Atlantic Guesthouse* on Main St (☎073/21187; ③), *Drumcliffe House* on Coast Rd (☎073/21200; ③) and *Castle View House* (☎073/22100; ②) and *Riverside House* (☎073/21083; ③), both on Waterloo Place across the river from the castle. For something more upmarket, try the comfortable *Abbey Hotel* (☎073/21014; ⑧) or the *Hyland Central Hotel* (☎073/21027; ⑦) both on the Diamond. If you really want to push the boat out, book in at *St Ernan's House* (☎073/21065, *www.sainternans.com*; ⑨), built by Wellington's nephew in 1836 and situated on its own private island, signposted a few hundred yards up the Sligo road.

Hostels include the popular *Donegal Town Independent Hostel* (☎073/22805), half a mile west down the Killybegs road, which has camping and a jovial atmosphere; and the secluded but often busy An Óige *Ball Hill Hostel*, about three miles further west in a former coastguard station on the north side of Donegal Bay (Easter–Sept; ☎073/21174, *mailbox@anoige.ie*), which also offers camping facilities. On the way here you'll pass Ashleigh Riding Stables (☎073/21097) where you can arrange **horse riding**.

Bikes can be rented from the Bike Shop, Waterloo Place (☎073/22515) and from O'Doherty's on Main St (☎073/21119) which also sells **fishing permits** and rents out **tackle**. The owner is a mine of information on the region, including the best angling spots and hiking routes. *Donegal Bay Charters* (☎073/23191, *donegalbay@ireland.com*) offers sea-angling, scuba-diving, whale-spotting and birdwatching trips. Around the Diamond there's good shopping, including the Four Masters **bookshop**, Magee's department store, Foodmarket **supermarket** and Simple Simon's **natural foods**. Dermo's **laundry** (Mon–Sat 9am–6pm) is in the Millcourt Shopping Arcade on the Diamond.

The Town

Donegal takes its name from *Dún na nGall*, and the original "fort of the foreigners" was thought to have been built on the banks of the River Eske by invading Vikings. There's no doubt, however, that the first Red Hugh O'Donnell, king of Tír Chonaill, had a Norman-style tower house, known as **O'Donnell's Castle**, constructed on its site in the fifteenth century. When the English defeated the second Red Hugh in 1603, Sir Basil Brooke was given command of the town and it was he who rebuilt and extended the old castle, retaining the lower parts of the original tower, which had been razed to the ground by Red Hugh to prevent its capture. This well-restored example of Jacobean architecture sits on Tírconaill Street by the Diamond (April–Sept daily 9.30am–6.30pm; last entry 5.45pm; £3/€3.79). It's a fine marriage of strong defence and domestic grace – note the mullioned windows, arches, ten gables and no fewer than fourteen fireplaces, over the grandest of which are carved the escutcheons of Brooke and his wife's family, the Leicesters. Brooke topped the tower with a Barbizon turret and added the mansion on the left, with the kitchens and bakery on the ground floor and living quarters on the floor above. Brooke was highly prolific in Donegal and was responsible for the overall design of the town.

On the stone bridge by the castle on the Killybegs road is a plaque commemorating the town's most famous author, the Reverend Dr John Boyce, better known by his pseudonym "Paul Peppergrass". After ministering for some years in the county, he travelled to America in 1845, concerned for the spiritual welfare of the newly-arrived Irish emigrants. Though largely forgotten now, his most popular work was *Shandy Maguire*, a novel describing the tribulations incurred by the Irish Catholics in defence of their faith. Later dramatized, it became a major success on the American stage.

In the Diamond stands an obelisk in memory of the compilers of the famed **Annals of the Four Masters**. The *Annals* were compiled in Donegal Abbey, on the coast close to Bundoran, and were a systematic attempt to collect all known Irish documents into a history of the land beginning in 2958 BC and ending at the time of writing, 1616 AD.

Down at the **quay** an anchor is on display, retrieved from the sea near Mountcharles in the 1850s and traditionally believed to have belonged to the French frigate *Romaine*, a member of the fleet transporting French troops to support Wolfe Tone's rebellion in 1798. On the left bank of the River Eske, not far from here, stand the few ruined remains of a **Franciscan friary**, built in 1474 by the first Red Hugh and his wife Nuala O'Brien of Munster. It was occupied by the English in 1601 and seriously damaged by the besieging O'Donnell army, being finally abandoned after the Flight of the Earls. On the opposite side a woodland path known as the **Bank Walk** runs out alongside the bay with a pleasant view towards its many sandy islets and stony shoreline. A **Waterbus** (☎073/23666; £6/€7.59) offers a one-hour trip around Donegal Bay starting from the quay.

The County Donegal Railway, which formerly ran from Derry to Ballyshannon, closed in 1959; its history is told at the **Donegal Railway Heritage Centre** at the Old Station House on Tírconaill St (Mon–Sat 9am–5pm, Sun 2–5pm; £2/€2.53). Here you'll find a model of the old railway and lovingly restored railcars and carriages from the age of steam.

Eating, drinking and entertainment

Eating places are plentiful, though it's the pubs as ever that seem to offer most choice. Alternatives include steaks, salmon and pizzas at *The Harbour*, opposite the tourist office, while the restaurant in Magee's store on the Diamond serves light lunches. The carvery in the *Hylands Central Hotel* is hugely popular with locals and the *Abbey Hotel's* restaurant serves equally substantial food. If all you want is a cheap hearty meal make for the *Atlantic Restaurant* or the *Deli-bar* on Main Street and the *Errigal Chipper* offers fresh fish from Killybegs.

Donegal's summer **festival**, one of the biggest in the county, is held in early July. The town also has a lively **music** scene. Many of the town's **pubs** offer traditional entertainment year round and Thursday's *Donegal Democrat* newspaper provides local listings. The *Olde Castle* bar, next to the castle, has an excellent restaurant and a cosy bar. Lively *McGroarty's*, a few doors down, has a Thursday night traditional session and other music at weekends, while the nearby *Central Hotel* is the place for home-grown country and western. Others are mainly out on Main Street: *Zack's* has a young crowd and music most nights; the *Star Bar* is a lively place with sing-songs and live acts at weekends, the *National* has more traditional music in the lounge at weekends, and best of all is *The Schooner*, just past the cathedral, with a nautical interior, an original nineteenth-century bar and music on Fridays and Sundays. In **LAGHY**, three miles south on the Sligo road, *Carlin's* pub has old-time dancing on Tuesday and Irish nights in summer. If all you want is a quiet pint, try *Tírconaill*, an old-time bar on the Diamond. *Nero's*, on Main Street, holds regular **discos**, but the most popular are in the *Abbey Hotel* (Sun 10.30pm–2am; sometimes also on Fridays in summer).

If you're after souvenirs, or simply a way to fill a wet afternoon, then it might be worth heading out to the **Craft Village** (Mon–Sat 9am–6pm, Sun 11am–6pm), three-quarters of a mile south of town on the Sligo road. The workshops are leased to professional craftworkers – including one of Ireland's best-known *uilleann* pipe-makers – whom you can watch in action.

Around Donegal town

Southeast of Donegal town, the corner of the county tucked into a fold in the border is replete with little lakes well stocked for fishing; the largest of these, and a place of pilgrimage, is **Lough Derg**. Less than five miles upriver from Donegal town is another spot of gentle natural beauty, **Lough Eske**, from where you can walk into the wilds of the **Blue Stack Mountains**, which rise to the north.

Lough Derg and Station Island

In the middle of **Lough Derg** (Red Lake) is a rocky islet known as **Station Island** or, more popularly, St Patrick's Purgatory, which has long served as a retreat for Catholics needing rigour and solitude to recharge their faith. A national shrine of pilgrimage since the fifth century, it was described by Girardus Cambrensis in *Topography of Ireland* (1186) as "an island, one part of which is frequented by good spirits, the other by evil spirits." Contemporary scholars have argued that as St Patrick never referred to Lough Derg in his writings he probably never visited the island, but nevertheless it still thrives today as a strong centre for **pilgrimage** (especially from June to August). Participants in the three-day retreats go without sleep and food (apart from black tea and toast) and walk barefoot over rocks, praying at stations of the cross. One-day retreats are less austere. The island cannot be visited for any other reason, though some casual travellers and non-believers do get some sort of stimulation out of passing through this ancient ceremony. Despite the exigencies, it seems particularly popular with Irish students studying for exams – or waiting for the results. *Station Island*, a collection by Seamus Heaney, contains a number of poems dealing with the mystique surrounding this ritual.

If you're interested in participating, contact the Prior (☎072/81518). The island is approached via the R233 from **PETTIGO**, six miles south. A bus from Ballyshannon or Enniskillen will drop you in Pettigo village, where there's a small interpretive centre explaining the island's background (March–Oct 9am–5pm; £2/€2.53). Pettigo also has a remarkable number of pubs for such a small village, suggesting an importance placed on spiritual nourishment of a rather different kind.

IAN CUMMING/AXIOM

Beara Peninsula, Co. Kerry

CHRIS COE/AXIOM

Coonana, Ring of Kerry

CHRIS COE/AXIOM

Kilmacduagh, Co. Galway

CHRIS COE/AXIOM

Torc waterfall, Ring of Kerry

IAN CUMMING

Irish music session, Doolin, Co. Clare

CHRIS COE/AXIOM

Sligo coastline, Co. Sligo

GEOFF WALLIS

Errigal Mountain, Co. Donegal

R. RAINFORD/ROBERT HARDING

Giant's Causeway, Co. Antrim

MICHAEL JENNER

White Island, Co. Fermanagh

CHRIS COE/AXIOM

Malin Head, Co. Donegal

CHRIS COE/AXIOM

White cliffs near Portrush, Co. Antrim

GREG EVANS

Dunluce Castle, Co. Antrim

C. BOWMAN/ROBERT HARDING

Donegall Square, Belfast

CHRIS COE/AXIOM

The Bogside, Co. Derry

Lough Eske

Lough Eske (Lake of the Fish) is no longer a particularly great fishing spot, though it is known as a place to catch char, a tasty nine-inch-long species of the salmon family. They lurk in the depths at the centre of the lake, moving out to the shallower edges around late October where they can be easily fished using worms. The sandy banks of the River Eske are also known for freshwater oysters – some of which are reputed to contain pearls – but they're a protected species so it's illegal to take them. The ruins of an O'Donnell tower, once a prison, stand on one of the small islands. At the southern end of the lough stands *Harvey's Point* (☎073/22208, *harveyspoint@eircom.net*; ⑦), a **hotel** owned by a Swiss millionaire with fine accommodation and one of the best **restaurants** in the county (lunch £12.50/€15.82, dinner £25/€31.64). There's also high-quality **B&B** at *Ardnamona* (☎073/22650, *www.tempoweb.com/ardnamon*; ⑦), set in glorious lough-side gardens planted in the 1880s using many seeds and cuttings from the Imperial Gardens in Peking and palace gardens in Kathmandu.

The most enjoyable way to get to this area of soft beauty is to take the minor road which runs north of the river, signposted "Lough Eske Drive", half a mile out of Donegal town on the Killybegs road. This leads to a forgotten, forested estate, once belonging to the Brooke family but now owned by the Forestry Commission. Circling the lake clockwise from here, you'll pass the western gate of the estate and then a farmyard. A hundred yards or so further on look out for a gap in the hedge on the left, where you'll find hidden a massive cauldron nearly six feet high and six feet round. This is a **Famine Pot**, manufactured in Britain and shipped over to Ireland by English landlords. It would be filled with Indian maize (a substitute porridge) and placed in a field where local people would come during the Famine and fill their own smaller pots to take home.

The Blue Stack Mountains

Carrying on along the western shore of Lough Eske, you'll reach the point where the river flows in at the lough's northern tip. Nearby, a dirt road runs off to the left to take you into the **Blue Stack Mountains**. At the top of the pathway that leads on from the track, there are superb views over the lough and, nearby, the very fine Doonan waterfall. From here you can join the waymarked **Bluestack Way**, which passes Lough Belshade (*Bhéal Seód*, "lake of the jewels"), guarded in legend by a huge black cat. If you're intending to tramp around the mountain range, it's best to keep to the skirts of the hills, for there are many marshy patches on lower ground – and be prepared for misty pockets during bad weather.

West of Donegal town

The most appealing route from Donegal town is the one which heads **west** along the shore of the bay all the way to Glencolmcille. Leaving Donegal town, the first turning off this road will lead you down to **Holmes beach** and the *Ball Hill* hostel (see p.480). Further highlights along this coast include the thriving fishing port of **Killybegs**, while extraordinarily dramatic coastal scenery reaches an apogee in the mammoth sea cliffs of **Slieve League**. The **Glencolmcille peninsula** is a *Gaeltacht*, and the attractive villages of Kilcar, Carrick, Teelin and Glencolmcille itself are rich in both traditional folklore and music.

From Mountcharles to Bruckless

The first sizeable settlement west of Donegal town is **MOUNTCHARLES**, straggling up a steep hillside. Near the top of the hill stands a bright green pump commemorating the birth nearby of the poet and *seanachie* (storyteller) Séamus MacManus. The village is a sea-angling centre and boats can be rented from Michael O'Byrne (☎073/35257).

FROSSES (*na Frosa* – "the showers"), a mile or so inland off the road between Mountcharles and Inver, is a pleasant, crossroads hamlet that has occasional celidhs on Sunday nights in the village hall (dancing begins at 10pm), while *Breslin's* bar hosts traditional sessions on Saturdays. The cemetery here contains the graves of the poet Séamus MacManus and his wife, the very underrated poet, Ethna Carberry. At the end of the nineteenth century, Carberry and Alice Milligan edited the important nationalist literary paper *Shan Van Vocht* (*sean bean bocht* – "the poor old woman", an oft-used euphemism for Ireland).

Continuing west, the secluded seaside village of **INVER** with its small strand, just a few hundred yards off the road, is a tranquil spot and affords good views over Inver Bay. The *Rising Tide* pub is good for a drink (or to hear traditional music on Sat & Sun) and has a ceiling in the shape of the hull of a boat and stone shelves for the spirit bottles. It was also the birthplace of Thomas Nesbitt, inventor of the harpoon gun.

At **DUNKINEELY** there's the *Blue Moon* **hostel** (☎073/37284, *bluemoonhostel @eircom.net*), with space for camping, and Wednesday night traditional sessions in *McIntyre's*. Another deviation left from the main road takes you first past *Castlemurray House Hotel* (☎073/37022; ⑤), noted for its comfortable accommodation and French gourmet **meals** (dinner around £20/€25.32, though you'll need to book ahead), then down a long, narrow promontory to **St John's Point**, where a crumbling castle stands at the tip. As you head south, there are great views over Donegal Bay, especially back towards the narrow entry of Killybegs bay, with **Rotten Island** at its mouth. The waters off the Point are reckoned to offer the best diving in Ireland. If you decide to stay, take advantage of the strategically positioned *Harbour Lights* **B&B** (March–Oct; ☎073/37291; ③).

A little west of Dunkineely, approaching **BRUCKLESS**, you'll spot a magical little lagoon staked out with poles for rearing mussels. On the other side of the lagoon you can see an eighteenth-century Georgian house, *Bruckless House* (☎073/37071, *bruc@iol.ie*; ⑤), which now offers stylish **B&B**. There's also an excellent **hostel** in Bruckless, *Gallagher's Farm Hostel*, Darney (☎073/37057; *homepage.eircom.net /~farmhostel*), with camping. Also here is Deane's Open Farm (April–Sept; ☎073/37160; £2/€2.53) offering **riding** lessons, trekking and a pitch-and-putt course. The village's only pub, *Mary Murrin's*, has recently been splendidly refurbished and provides good-value bar meals, including a children's menu.

Killybegs

Sticking to the coast road west of Bruckless, you'll round Killybegs Bay and arrive in the most successful fishing port in Ireland, **KILLYBEGS** (*na Cealla Beaga* – "the little churches"), where tons of top-quality fish are hauled onto the quaysides daily. This marks the halfway point on the route from Donegal town to Glencolmcille, and also the point at which the scenery changes dramatically for the better: the mile-long approach road around the bay would be idyllic were it not for a fishmeal processing plant interrupting the view. Killybegs itself is perched on a slope above the harbour, its gleaming whitewashed buildings huddled around narrow cramped streets. The town is well served by shops and banks and buzzes with traffic in summer, most of it heading down to the quay, where you can buy fish after watching the fleet come in during the early evening. A huge international **sea angling festival** takes place here in the second half of July but you can go sea angling any time with one of six boats that go out daily – the Harbour Store (☎073/31569) has details and sells all manner of fishing gear. Picturesque though Killybegs is, it isn't exactly overflowing with interest, and most of the pubs are aimed squarely at working fishermen, though students from the local

Tourism College liven the place up in term time. All may soon change, however, as Killybegs is slated to become the service town for the thirty or so **oil rigs** soon to be located off-shore.

If you're staying, it's worth visiting the church at the top of the hill for a glimpse of the sixteenth-century **tombstone** of **Niall Mór MacSweeney**, removed from his grave at Ballysaggart Friary on St John's Point and now covered in Celtic carvings and contained in a glass case to the left of the church door. The MacSweeneys originated from the Scottish Hebridean islands and arrived in Ireland as gallowglasses (*galloglaigh* – "foreign warrior), hired by the O'Donnells to drive the O'Neills from the land around the River Foyle. Receiving land in payment, the MacSweeneys became one of Donegal's ruling families prior to the Flight of the Earls, and Niall Mór was head of one branch of the clan. The **cross** standing on the hillock behind the church is an ugly specimen that serves as a reminder of ugly times – the days of the Penal Laws.

Practicalities

Accommodation possibilities in Killybegs include the elegant *Bay View Hotel* (☎073/31950, *www.bayview.com*; ⑧), overlooking the harbour, and there are rooms in a number of pubs, including *Cope House*, Main St (☎073/31834, *copehouse@ireland.com*; ⑥), and the *Pier Bar* (☎073/31045; ③). The former also has a popular Chinese restaurant. Most of the **B&Bs** are a mile or two out of town on Fintra Road, heading west towards Kilcar.

Melly's Café, by the harbour, is a local institution and the best place for cheap snacks and fast **food**, though the nearby *Galley* restaurant is a pleasant alternative. Otherwise, you can grab a lunch in any of the pubs, including fresh seafood in the *Harbour Bar*; for something slightly more upmarket, try the brasserie at the *Bay View Hotel.* As for evening entertainment, most of the bars have music at weekends.

McGeehan's **buses** (☎075/46150) leave from outside the *Pier Bar* for Ardara and Dublin: enquire at Hegarty's grocery shop by the bus stop.

Kilcar and around

A couple of miles west of Killybegs, signposts point the way to the Blue Flag **Fintragh Beach**. Further on, the road to Kilcar passes *Kitty Kelly's Restaurant*, open in summer (daily 5–9.30pm) for especially good Irish cuisine. Just after the *Blue Haven Restaurant* (Irish dancing on Thurs), the road divides. For the scenic route, take the road to the left, a narrow switchback ride along the coastline with stupendous views over the ocean, especially from **Muckross Head**, and the looming presence of the hills and mountains to your right.

The roads meet again at **KILCAR**, a pleasant village that is a centre for the Donegal tweed industry: there are several small factories open to visitors. The village comes alive during its **sea angling festival** at the beginning of August, followed shortly afterwards by a raucous **street festival. Boats** can be rented from Jim Byrne (☎073/38224), while Paddy Clarke (☎073/38211) offers guided game angling and hill walking. Fishing tackle is available from *McBrearty's*, Main Street. There are five **bars**, including *John Joe's* which stages regular Friday night sessions. *Teach Barnaí* (☎073/38160), across the road, is one of Donegal's best **restaurants**, serving superb evening meals and extremely popular Sunday lunches. McGeehan's **buses** leave from outside *John Joe's* bar daily at 7.40am for Killybegs, Ardara, Letterkenny and Dublin, and at 6.40pm for Glencolmcille.

Kilcar has **B&B** at *Kilcar Lodge*, Main Street (April–Oct; ☎073/38243; ③) or nearby on the coast road to Carrick at *Hillcrest* (☎073/38243; ③) and *Dún Ulún House* (☎073/38137; ②), which also offers **hostel** accommodation. Alternatively, a little fur-

CLIMBING SLIEVE LEAGUE

There are two routes up to the ridge of **Slieve League** (*sliabh leic*, "grey mountain", or *leica*, "flagstone mountain"). Both routes up are **walkable** and very enjoyable, though it's a great deal easier to **drive**.

A less-used back route, known as "One Man's Path", follows the signpost pointing to the mountain just before Teelin and looks up continually to the ridge, while the frontal approach follows the signs out of Teelin to **BUNGLASS** (*bunglas*, "end of the cliff"), swinging you spectacularly round sharp bends and up incredibly steep inclines to one of the most thrilling cliff scenes in the world, the **Amharc Mór**, from which the views are staggering. Bunglass turns out to be exactly what it says, the end of the grass, perched way above a sheer drop. These claim to be the **highest marine cliffs in Europe**, and standing here that seems all too likely. The sea moves so far below that the waves appear silent, and the near-2000ft face glows with mineral deposits in tones of amber, white and red. They say that on a clear day it is possible to see one-third of the whole of Ireland from the summit. A **sightseeing tour** of the cliffs from the waters below is organized from Teelin, weather permitting, by *Smith Campbell* (☎073/39079).

If you want to make a full day of it, you can follow One Man's Path, which leads on to Old Man's Path (so named simply because it's a few inches wider), over the crest of the mountain and down the heather-tufted western slope. The paths are accurately named: in places they are only a few feet wide, and in wet or windy weather they can be **extremely hazardous**. On a fine day, though, it's a wonderful – if terrifying – traverse. Then make your way across towards the verdant headland village of **MALINBEG**, where there's a sublime crescent-shaped golden strand enclosed by a tight rocky inlet. Here, *Malinmore Adventure Centre* (☎073/30123) organizes **diving** – from £75/€94.93 for three dives over two days – and provides other activities, including canoeing and hill-walking. Malinbeg itself is a village of white bungalows, with the land around ordered into long narrow strips. A new **hostel** is due to open here during 2001. On the cliff edge a ruined Martello Tower faces **Rathlin O'Birne Island**, three miles offshore, a place with many folklore associations. There are occasional boats across, but nothing to see beyond some early Christian stone relics and a ruined coastguard station.

Beyond Malinbeg it's relatively easy to extend your walk through **MALINMORE** – where the large *Glencolmcille Hotel* (☎073/3003; ⑤) serves food – and on to Glencolmcille. The whole distance from Teelin can be comfortably completed in six hours.

ther on is *Derrylahan* (☎073/38079, *derrylahan@eircom.net*), run by Shaun McCloskey, set on a working farm and one of the friendliest **hostels** in the country; a shorter approach for walkers involves taking the right-hand of three options just outside the village and following the lane over the hill, though Shaun will pick you up from Kilcar or *The Rock* near Carrick on request. *Derrylahan* is an ideal base for exploring the beautiful countryside around **CARRICK**, especially Teelin Bay and the awesome Slieve League cliffs to the west. In the pretty village of Carrick itself the friendly and atmospheric *Slieve League* **pub** is a must and there are sessions here, at *Enright's* and the *Central* bars. Back on the coast road, Little Acorn Farm (☎073/39386) offers **riding and trekking**.

The road to **TEELIN** (*tigh linn*, "house of the flowing tide") follows the west bank of the River Owenee, whose rapids and pools are good for fishing – licences are available from Teelin Sea Angling Club (☎073/39079). Like most of the peninsula, the village is Irish-speaking and rich in folklore, which has been recorded over the last half-century by Seán Ó'hEochaidh, Donegal's great folklorist. The *Rusty Mackerel* pub (evenings only) is a welcome find, easily spotted by its garish colour and mural painting of one of its old fisherman regulars, and you can **stay** in the village at *Sea Crest* (☎073/39108; ③).

Glencolmcille

As the road approaches **GLENCOLMCILLE** (the Glen of St Columbcille), it traverses desolate moorland that's dominated by oily-black turf banks amidst patches of heather and grass, where not even sheep seem able to subsist. After this, the rich beauty of the Glen, as it's invariably known, comes as a welcome surprise. Settlement in the area dates back to the Stone Age, as testified by the enormous number of megalithic remains scattered around the countryside, especially court cairns and standing stones. There's evidence too of the Celtic era, in the form of earthworks and stoneworks. Traditionally, **St Columba** founded a monastery here in the sixth century and some of the standing stones, known as the *Turas Cholmcille*, were adapted for Christian usage by the inscription of a cross. Every Columba's Day (June 9) at midnight, the locals commence a barefoot circuit of the fifteen *Turas*, including Columba's Chapel, chair, bed, wishing stone and Holy Well, finishing up with mass at 3am in the village church. (Columba and Columbcille/Colmcille are the same person – the latter is the name by which he was known after his conversion, and means "the dove of the church").

In more recent times, widespread emigration left the Glencolmcille area a typical example of rural decay. In 1951, however, a new and energetic curate, Father James McDyer, was appointed and instigated immediate efforts to revitalize the community, while retaining and strengthening its culture. Electricity arrived in the village and road improvements reduced its isolation and allowed new collective enterprises in knitting and agriculture to thrive, simultaneously increasing the area's accessibility to tourism. Thankfully, these developments have not lessened the village's innate attraction. The buildings in Cashel, the village centre, are painted in radiant colours – the village church is lavender, there's a whitewashed semi-detached estate for the newly married, one old pub is a canary yellow and another a Mediterranean sky-blue.

One of McDyer's major initiatives stands in Doonalt down by the beach – the **Folk Village Museum and Heritage Centre** (Easter–Oct Mon–Sat 10am–6pm, Sun noon–6pm; £1.50/€1.90; hourly tours), a clustered *clachan* of replica thatched cottages, each equipped with the particular furniture and artefacts of the era it represents. A new reception building introduces you to the area's history and cultural heritage, including a reputed visit by Charles Stuart ("Bonnie Prince Charlie"). There's free access to the **National School** replica, which has a display of informative photographs and research projects, and a section on the American painter Rockwell Kent, who painted marvellous treatments of the area's landscapes. At **Sheebeen** house, you can try a taster of seaweed wine and other concoctions such as honey, fuchsia and elderberry (most much better than they sound) and then buy a bottle. There's also a tea house and craft shop.

On the way down the main street to the Folk Village is **Foras Cultúir Uladh**, the Ulster Cultural Centre. The centre hosts Tapeis Gael, a group of local artists with an innovative approach to tapestry design, and the many **courses** run by Oideas Gael (☎073/30248, *oideas-gael.com*), including Irish language, painting, *bodhrán* playing, dancing, flute and whistle playing, archeology and hill-walking.

From behind the hostel (see p.488), **cliff walks** steer off around the south side of the bay above a series of jagged drops. Rising from the opposite side of the valley mouth, the promontory of **Glen Head** is surmounted by a Martello Tower. On the way out you pass the ruins of **St Columbcille's Church**, with its "resting slab" where St Columba would have lain down exhausted from prayer. North across this headland you can climb and descend again to the forgotten little cove of **Port** a few miles away, a village deserted since the 1940s. Absolutely nothing happens here – although Dylan Thomas once stayed in the next valley at Glenlough, renting a cottage for several weeks in a doomed attempt to "dry out" in an area replete in poteen stills.

Practicalities

Glencolmcille's **tourist office** (June–Aug daily 10am–6pm; ☎073/30116) is in the *Lace House* craft shop on the main street. **B&B** accommodation is available at *Brackendale* (☎073/30038; ②) and *Corner House* (April–Sept; ☎073/30021; ③), both in Cashel. You can catch the sunset at the beautifully positioned *Dooey Hostel* (☎073/30130, *dooeyhostel@oceanfree.net*) set high above the fine shingle strand at the mouth of the valley; it also offers **camping**. To get there on foot, keep on the village road as far as the Folk Village, and then take a path up to the left; in wet weather the longer route by road may be easier. The tea house at the Folk Village does moderately priced **food**, though the most popular place for lunch and evening meals is *An Bradán Feasa*, part of the Foras Cultúir Uladh complex. Another option is the *Lace House Restaurant* above the shop, with freshly baked bread and evening meals. The **bars** here are often quiet during the week, though tend to come alive at weekends, especially if the superb fiddler James Byrne plays at *Roarty's*, and during the **fiddle festival** at the beginning of August.

Ardara and around

The area around the bustling town of **Ardara** contains some of the most contrasting landscapes in Donegal. Rugged mountains lie to the southwest traversed by the steeply sinuous **Glengesh Pass** and fringed by the unspoiled expanse of **Maghera** strand. Inland to the northeast sits the stately village of **Glenties** while to the north the coastline forms peninsulas punctuated by the **Gweebarra** river which, in turn, leads inland to the tranquil villages of Doocharry and Fintown, virtually surrounded by mountain scenery of an almost lunar quality.

The Glengesh Pass and Maghera

Leaving Glencolmcille you can either retrace your steps along the coast or take the road through the heart of the peninsula towards **Ardara**. This travels through the dramatic **Glengesh Pass** (*gleann géis*, "glen of the swans"), spiralling down into wild but fertile valley land. Just before reaching Ardara, a road to the left runs along the northern edge of the peninsula for five and a half miles to **MAGHERA**, with narrow **Loughros Beg Bay** on one side and steep mountains rising from the road on the other. A mile before Maghera you'll pass the transfixing **Assarancagh Waterfall** and there's a hardy six-mile waymarked walk uphill from here to the Glengesh Pass. Maghera itself is an enchantingly remote place, dwarfed by the backdrop of hills and glens and fronted by an expansive and deserted strand (parking £2/€2.53 in summer) that extends westwards to a rocky promontory riddled with caves. One of the largest of these is said to have concealed a hundred people fleeing Cromwell's troops; their light was spotted from across the strand and all were massacred except a lucky individual who hid on a high shelf. Most of the caves are accessible only at low tide and a torch is essential. Beware the **tides**, however, for even experienced divers have been swept away by the powerful currents. Behind the village, a tiny road, unsuitable for large vehicles, runs up to the Granny Pass, an alternative route to and from Glencolmcille.

Ardara

Traditionally a centre for weaving and knitwear, the bustling little town of **ARDARA**, ten miles or so north of Killybegs on the N56, has recently acquired heritage town status. The European Union grant which accompanied this award has been used to transform the old Law Courts by the bridge into a **heritage centre** (Easter–Oct daily

10am–6pm; ☎075/41262; voluntary donation). Inside, there's a coffee shop and a fascinating exhibition on the history of hand-weaving, Aran knitwear and lots of intriguing photographs and equipment, but the real treat is watching the weaver plying away at his loom and supplying his own anecdotes about the industry. There's **tourist information** in the reception area and the friendly staff can answer most questions about the town. Ardara is an excellent place to buy **Aran sweaters**, sometimes at half the price you'll find further south. Molloy's Tweed Factory, a mile or so beyond the southern end of town, is the biggest outlet, but Kennedy's, at the top of the hill, is handier (its owner is also a mine of local tourist information), and all the stores are well stocked with hand-loomed knitwear and tweeds.

The Catholic church west of the Diamond has a striking stained glass window, *Christ among the Doctors*, by the Modernist-inspired **Evie Hone**, one of the most influential Irish artists of the last century: the authors of the Gospels are depicted symbolically with the infant Christ at the centre and David and Moses above and below. Up the top of the hill, by the Methodist church car park, stands a house once occupied by Jimmy O'Rourke, a notable storyteller and fiddler on whom the Disney film *Darby O'Gill and the Little People* was based.

Accommodation options include the grand old *Nesbitt Arms Hotel* (☎075/41103, *nesbitta@indigo.ie*; ⑥) named after the town's former landlords, which has reopened after major refurbishment, while a mile east of town off the Donegal road is the stylish, seventeenth century *Woodhill House* (☎075/41112, *www.woodhillhouse.com*; ⑥), set in its own extensive grounds. Central **B&B** is available at *Laburnum House* on the Diamond (☎075/41146; ②), *Brae House,* Front St (☎075/41296, *braehouse@tinet.ie*; ③), and *Homeward Bound,* Glenties Rd (March–Oct; ☎075/41246; ③), or, for sea views, try *Greenhaven* (☎075/41129; ③) or *Bay View Country House* (☎075/41145; ③), both up the Portnoo road. There's a small **hostel** on the Diamond too, the *Drumbaron Hostel* (☎075/41200). **Bike rental** is available from Don Byrne, south of town (☎075/41658).

The best place to **eat** is *Woodhill House,* whose restaurant offers an innovative menu that changes daily and is well worth the asking price of £25/€31.65 or so. It's worth a visit even if you're not hungry as there's a bar, often with music. *Nancy's,* just across the bridge, has good value bar meals and snacks, while *L'Atlantique* on Main St (daily 6.30–9.30pm; ☎075/41707) offers splendid French cuisine. Light meals are available at the heritage centre restaurant and *Charlie's West End Café,* Main Street.

Ardara's L-shaped main street is crammed with **pubs**. For a quiet drink, try the ancient *Pádraig MacGiola Dé,* to the west or the renovated *Corner House* bar. For a livelier time, you shouldn't miss *Peter Oliver's,* with traditional music in the front bar (June–Sept nightly) and dancing at the back every Saturday (from 10.30pm or later). *Nancy's,* a cosy 200-year-old pub run by the same family for seven generations, is also excellent, with something happening most nights during the summer. A McGeehan's **bus** leaves for Dublin from outside the post office daily at 8.30am.

Glenties

Set at the foot of two glens, **GLENTIES** lies six miles east of Ardara on the N56, a tidy village of plantation grandeur that is reflected in its elegant Neoclassical courthouse, old lodge and *Highlands Hotel.* It also sports one of the largest **discos** in the northwest, the *Limelight* at the north end of town (Saturday nights), and a host of bars on the main street. Another community attraction is a beautiful modern **church** at the Ardara end of town, designed by the Derry architect Liam McCormack; the vast sloping roof reaches down to six feet from the ground, and the rainwater drips off the thousand or so tiles into picturesque pools of water.

Opposite the church, the **St Conall's Museum and Heritage Centre** (June–Sept Mon–Fri 11am–1pm & 2.30–5pm, Sat & Sun 2.30–6pm; £1/€1.27) houses items from all periods, including an interesting set of pleas submitted to the courts during the Famine and an Edison phonograph that plays *It's a Long Way to Tipperary*. The town's most famous son was **Patrick MacGill** (1890–1963) who was sold by his parents at a hiring fair for servants. He escaped and fled to Scotland, working as a farm-labourer and a navvy, while at the same time writing poems and attempting to hawk them around. He was lucky to attract patronage and ended up working on the *Daily Express*, was wounded in France fighting for the British in World War II, then returned to Ireland before marrying the American author Margaret Gibbons and emigrating to the US. His best-known work is the semi-autobiographical *Children of the Dead End* which brilliantly recounts the wayward lives of migrant navvies, while *The Rat Pit* parallels this in its tale of young Irish women forced into prostitution. A huge **summer school** is held in his honour annually in mid-August, drawing hundreds of people to its exhibitions, seminars and literary debates.

Accommodation in town includes the family-run *Highlands Hotel* (☎075/51111, *highlandshotel@ireland.com*; ④), on Main Street, and, among several **B&B** choices, nearby *Marguerite's* (☎075/51113; ③). Alternatively, outside the village are *Lisdanar House*, Mill Rd (March–Oct; ☎075/51800; ③) and *Claradon Country House*, less than a mile out on the R253 (☎075/51113, *mccafferty@tinet.ie*; ③). Next to the museum is the comfortable *Campbell's Holiday* **hostel** (March–Oct; ☎075/51491, *campbellshostel @eircom.net*). Options for **eating** out are limited, but the excellent *Highlands Hotel*, very much the centre of town life, with traditional-music sessions on Sundays and a small art gallery displaying the works of its landlord, John Boyle, offers a wide range of food – the gargantuan lunches are exceptional value. Alternatives on the main street include *Nighthawk* for pizzas, and *Central Café* and *Jim's Café*. McGeehan's **buses** en route to Letterkenny and Glencolmcille stop outside *Jim's*.

Although there's little in the way of entertainment, there are plenty of places to **drink** – *Wee Joe's Bar* and *McMonagle's Riverside Bar* are both good. For **traditional music**, *Paddy's Bar* has Wednesday night sessions and there's the **fiddlers' weekend** at the beginning of October; otherwise head for the *Glen Inn*, three miles out on the Ballybofey road, beautifully situated by the river at the foot of the Blue Stacks; there are sessions most Wednesday nights. **Fishing** equipment and advice are available at McDevitt's Tackle Shop.

The Dawros Head Peninsula

To the immediate north of Ardara, the **Dawros Head Peninsula** is much tamer than Glencolmcille, with many tiny lakes dotting a quilt of low hills. The terrain of purple heather, fields, streams and short glens makes a varied package for the enthusiastic walker. The first turning to Rosbeg takes you past the **Sheskinmore Nature Reserve**, home to Barnacle and Greenland White-footed geese. The flat sandy coastal plain and patches of short grass are popular too with choughs in late summer and hunted by hen harriers and merlins in winter.

ROSBEG is an isolated village, straggling beside a series of rock-strewn coves, and you can **camp** among the dunes at **Tramore Beach** (☎075/51491, *campbell @eircom.net*). It's even lonelier out at **Dawros Head** itself, but at least there's the welcoming bar at the *Dawros Bay House* to provide succour. In contrast, the caravan and camping sites of Portnoo and Narin, on the peninsula's northern coast, are densely populated with Northern Irish tourists.

Approaching Narin from Ardara, just before the pastel-shaded Kilclooney church on the right is the **Kilclooney Dolmen**, probably the best-preserved portal stones in the country. The capstone is over thirteen feet long and is reckoned to date from around 3500 BC. Continuing onwards, the most worthwhile sight on the peninsula is **Doon Fort**, which occupies an entire oval-shaped islet in the middle of **Lough Doon**. To get there turn left at the Rosbeg/Tramore Beach signpost a mile before Narin, then head right up the lane just after the school. A few hundred yards later you'll see a sign for boat rental leading down to a farmhouse where you can **rent a rowing boat** inexpensively to take you across. The idyllic setting, rarely disturbed by visitors, makes the hassle worth it: although its walls are crumbling, the fort has been untouched for over two thousand years. The walls stand 15ft high and 12ft thick; their inner passages were used in the 1950s for storing poteen. Two other lakes nearby, **Lough Birrog** and **Lough Kiltoorish**, also have ruined castles, both built by later Irish chieftains, the O'Boyles. Their stones, however, have mostly been carted away for house building.

NARIN and **PORTNOO** offer the majority of facilities on the peninsula. The spear-headed two-and-a-half-mile-long **Narin Strand** is a wonderful beach, safe for bathing. At low tide you can walk out to **Iniskeel Island** where St Conal founded a monastery in the sixth century. This has long since disappeared, but there are the ruins of two twelfth-century churches with some cross-inscribed slabs. The villages host a **seafood festival** towards the end of June where you can participate in oyster-opening contests and all the bars offer seafood specials. *Carnaween House* in Narin (☎075/45122; ②) and *Thalassa* in Portnoo (☎075/45151; ③) offer good **B&B**; or you could rent a caravan at *Dunmore Caravan and Camping Park*, by the beach in Narin (☎075/45121; £60–150/€75.95–189.87 a week). The *Lake House* **hotel** in Portnoo (☎075/45123; *www.lakehousehotel.net*; ⑤) offers a great deal more comfort.

Around Gweebarra Bay

The routes north from Ardara and Glenties converge at the village of **MAAS**. The road then twists along the edge of **Gweebarra Bay** before one last turn suddenly brings you to the broad iron bridge spanning the estuary. Until the first bridge was built in 1890 rarely a year passed by without someone being drowned attempting to ford the river, sometimes home-workers bringing wool back from Glenties.

Across the bridge and west of **LETTERMACAWARD**, a signposted scenic route tours the **Dooey Point headland**, a scenically interesting little detour if you have time at hand. The northern shore, on Trawenagh Bay, is the more gratifying, with a fine stretch of beach backed by sand dunes. Classic thatched cottages are the main characteristics. On the southern side is **Cor Strand**, fertile ground for mussels and clams, with a handy bar nearby.

Doocharry and Fintown

A minor road east from Lettermacaward follows the Gweebarra five miles inland to **DOOCHARRY**, a tiny place with just a couple of pubs and a grocery, which acts as the gateway to some of the most dramatic scenery in the county. From Doocharry you can head further upstream northeast along a narrow and tortuous lane past **Slieve Snaght**, through the **Glendowan Mountains** and skirting the southern edge of the **Glenveagh National Park** to **Lough Gartan** (see p.499). The desolate, though beautiful countryside bears little sign of human impact and you'll be lucky to see any life beyond the odd sheep or fluttering bird.

Another road heads five miles southeast from Doocharry through rugged, rock-strewn moorland, streaked by turf banks, to **FINTOWN**. On the way look out for the splendidly set *Glenleighan* **hostel** (☎075/46141, *www.an-tor.de/glenleighan*). Fintown itself is a simple roadside village set at the foot of towering mountains in the Finn River valley where the river broadens to form an elongated strip of lake. Once again, the setting has a mythical background: it was here that Fergoman was attacked by wild boars and cried out so piteously that his sister was driven to distraction and dived into the lake, where she drowned. Running beside the lake for a mile or so is the

Fintown Railway (May–Sept daily 11am–5pm; ☎075/46280; £2/€2.53), a restored stretch of narrow-gauge track along which original rail carriages run. There's little else in the village apart from a few bars and a **traditional music house**, *Teach a' Cheoil* (sessions Thurs and Fri). Roads head southwest to Glenties and off eastwards to Letterkenny or Ballybofey.

The Crohy Head Peninsula

The southern approach to **Crohy Head** curls round the headland's central mountains, looking down to a rocky shelf of coastline from which plumes of spray rise like geysers. As you come round the headland to the final leg, you'll first see the three-storey An Óige *An Chruach* **hostel** (Easter–Sept; ☎075/21950, *mailbox@anoige.ie*), then the domed outline of **Arranmore Island** comes into view, lying close to the Rosses coast. The hillside below the road can be dangerous at points because of a remarkable landslip known as the *tholla brista* (broken earth), but this, and the great sea stack known as *an bríste* (the breeches), make the headland an even more dramatic experience for the walker.

The one-pub fishing village of **MAGHERY** lies at the foot of the north side of the headland. Its most unusual feature is the tall wall that runs by the abandoned mansion house at the far side of the short strand: called the **Famine Wall**, this windbreak was built by the villagers for the landlord, who devised the task so that he could pay them a wage as famine relief.

The Rosses

The **Rosses**, a vast expanse of rock-strewn land and stony soil, is one of the last strong *Gaeltacht* areas. Dotted with over one hundred and twenty tiny lakes, the crumpled terrain stretches from **Dungloe** in the south to **Crolly** in the north, but the forbidding nature of much of the landscape meant most settlements could only survive near the sea, so following the shoreline route around the Rosses is far more rewarding than the more direct road north.

Dungloe

An Clochán Liath is the name you'll see on signposts as you approach **DUNGLOE**, referring to the grey-coloured stepping stones which were once used to cross the town's river. The modern anglicized version comes from *Dún an Ghleo*, meaning "noisy fort", a name you might consider apposite as you stroll down its bustling main street. For most of the year, there's little to detain you except entertainment in the pubs. At the beginning of August, however, the Mary From Dungloe festival, a local, more wholesome variation of Miss World, provides a good pretext for general festivities and late-night drinking. There's no antiquity behind the festival's origins or name – it dates from 1968 and the title comes from a hit single by the Emmet Spiceland band (including the now notable traditional musician Dónal Lunny whose mother hails from the Rosses village of Rann na Feirste).

Dungloe is also synonymous with the rejuvenating work of **Paddy 'the Cope' Gallagher** (1871–1966), who envisaged the salvation of these then poor communities through cooperative ventures, in particular by reducing their dependency on gombeen men (moneylenders). Oddly enough, the enterprise's practical origins lay in Paddy's discovery that the price of manure was reduced when purchased by societies. As a result, he founded the Templecrone Co-operative Agricultural Society (the "Cope") in 1906 and its main branch still stands proudly on Dungloe's main street with branches throughout the Rosses. Copies of his entertaining autobiography, *My Story*, are available in a local edition from the supermarket.

The **tourist office** (June–Aug Mon–Sat 10am–6pm; ☎075/21297) is just off Main Street, to the left as you go downhill towards the bridge. Upmarket **accommodation** is provided by *Ostan Na Rossan*, Mill Rd (☎075/22444, *ostannarossan@iol.ie*; ⑦), with its own leisure centre and pool. On the same road are the **B&Bs** *Roninnis House* (April–Sept; ☎075/21094; ③) and *Sea View* (March–Nov; ☎075/21353) and, in the centre, *Atlantic Bar,* Main St (☎075/21061; ④), which also has a bar and provides meals. *Greene's Holiday* **hostel** (☎075/21021) on Carnmore Road is a modern building with **camping** in its grounds. There's a handy **laundry** nearby on the Gweedore road (Tues–Fri 9am–1pm & 2–6pm).

The popular *Coffee Dock* serves excellent value lunches; other **eating** choices include *Doherty's Restaurant,* a good low-priced grill, with *The Court House* restaurant upstairs and the *Riverside Bistro* near the bridge for more upmarket, though reasonably priced, fare. The *Tírconnaill* **bar** at the top end of the street is a genuine old-timers' bar with not a note of music interfering and a fabulous view of the ocean. *Beedy's Bar* has sessions on Tuesdays and there's assorted entertainment in the *Bayview Lounge* at weekends. The *Central Bar,* in the middle of Main Street, is open during summer only, after more than twenty years in which nothing seems to have been touched – a fascinating old place. **Fishing** tackle and permits for local fisheries are available from Bonner's, Main Street.

Burtonport and Arranmore Island

Passing the smoking funnels of a kelp factory, the coastal route heads off in the direction of **BURTONPORT** (signposted **Ailt an Chorráin**, "curved ravine"), half-a-mile off the main road and the embarkation point for **Arranmore Island** and, if you can find someone to take you out, for other smaller islands. In the late eighteenth century, the English attempted to establish **Rutland Island** as a major trading centre and, consequently, this area became the first English-speaking district in the whole of Donegal. During the 1798 Rebellion James Napper Tandy landed on the island with French troops, but became somewhat inebriated on hearing of Wolfe Tone's capture and had to be carried back on board. More recent English connections have included the Screamers, a post-hippie commune with a belief in primal scream therapy and sexual liberation whose leaders departed some years ago for Colombia, and the Silver Sisters, a trio of apparently demure Victorian-dressed ladies who fled the village once it became clear that the disciplined life they espoused had more to do with sado-masochism than moral rectitude.

Apart from busy activity at the harbour, the village has little to say for itself, but should you want to stay, *Mrs McGinley*, down by the pier, does year-round **B&B** (☎075/42047; ②) and, nearby, there's *Campbell's Pier House* (☎075/42017, *campbellh@boinet.ie*; ④). For **eating**, *The Lobster Pot* specializes in seafood and the *Harbour* provides bar meals. Otherwise you'll have to make do with pies and fish and chips. There's little nightlife here, though the *Skipper's Tavern* offers occasional traditional music. There are plenty of **fish** in the nearby waters and you can rent a boat from Burtonport Sea Angling and Boating Centre (☎075/42077).

Arranmore Island

Arranmore Island Ferry Service (Mon–Sat 5–8 sailings, Sun 3–7 sailings; £6/€7.60 return; car plus driver £18/€22.78; ☎075/20532) operates a year-round **car ferry** for the twenty-minute boat trip from Burtonport to **Arranmore Island**, which passes through the straits between the nearest cluster of islands (Rutland, Inishfree, Inishcoo and Eighter), and then across an open expanse of water to the main village on Arranmore, **LEABGARROW**. There's little **accommodation** on the island apart from the *Glen Hotel* (☎075/20505; ③), and *Bonner's* (☎075/20532; ②) by the pier. The island's permanent population of around eight hundred people is almost entirely concentrated along the eastern and southern coastline. The high centre-ground of bogland and lakes reaches a greater altitude than anywhere else in the Rosses and it's well worth hiking a few hundred yards upland for great views back across the water to Burtonport.

A circuit of the whole island takes only three hours and the terrain isn't especially taxing. Much of it consists of blustery cliff-top views of the Atlantic, but there are a few intriguing spots to investigate or ponder on. The island's greatest tragedy occurred off the very southeastern tip during the stormy night of November 9, 1935, when a sailing ship carrying returning islanders ran aground on the rocks. Nineteen people died, including seven from the same family – the eighth member on board, Patrick Gallagher, was the only survivor. Many ships have foundered in the choppy seas hereabouts, but, in 1983, the lone American yachtsman, Wayne Dickinson, landed on the island's west coast after 147 days at sea in the smallest boat ever to cross the Atlantic. In the cliffs below St Crone's Church on the southern shore is **Uaimh an Áir** (the "cave of slaughter") where seventy hiding islanders were massacred in the seventeenth century by a certain Captain Conyngham, an action which lay somewhat outside his remit from Charles I to rid the Rosses of "rogues and rapparees". Two islanders took revenge by killing the captain in Dunfanaghy. Uninhabited **Green Island**, at the southwestern tip, is now a **bird sanctuary** and rare species have been spotted hereabouts, including the Snowy Owl in 1993. The most dramatic of the several **beaches** is at the northwestern end of the island, on the way to the lighthouse and approached by a set of steps down the side of a perpetually crumbling cliff.

Facilities on Arranmore are limited, but the half-dozen **pubs** are blessed with a 24-hour fishing port licence which is helpful, as there is little nightlife apart from *Boyle's* nightclub, though *Pally's* bar has regular entertainments. A few of the pubs have small shops attached and you can eat at *Bonner's* café or, more expensively, the *Glen Hotel,* while *Phil Ban's* bar serves snacks all day. **Football** (soccer) is the sport here and Arranmore is the only Irish island to have a team playing in a mainland competitive league.

Crolly and around

The road up through the Rosses to Gweedore cuts through a wild and crazed terrain of granite boulders and stunted vegetation. **Cruit Island**, a couple of miles north of Burtonport and accessible by bridge, has beautiful beaches and a cluster of thatched cottages available for rental (☎071/77197; £160–550/€202.53–696.19 per week). A little further along the coast at **KINCASSLAGH** is *Viking House* (☎075/43295, *vikho @indigo.net*; ④), owned by Irish singing star **Daniel O'Donnell**. Another local-born Irish hero is **Packie Bonner**, the goalkeeper who saved a penalty in the 1990 World Cup Finals. Not far away is **CARRICKFINN**, which boasts a fine strand and **Donegal Airport** (2 daily flights to Dublin by Aer Arann; ☎075/48284). About a mile further on, in **ANNAGRY**, *Teac Jack's* pub serves fine food, and, if you wish to spend a little more, *Dannie Minnie's* restaurant (☎075/48201) in the centre of the village offers superb seafood specialities. There's **B&B** in Annagry village at *Bayview House* (April–Oct; ☎075/48504, *jns@eircom.net*; ③), while the Rosses Trekking Centre (☎075/48152) can arrange pony trekking around the local countryside. The local *feile*, one of the biggest in The Rosses, takes place here at the beginning of June.

A short detour north of Annagry leads to **RANN NA FEIRSTE** (Rannafast), a village with an astonishing Irish literary heritage. The oral tradition has always been strong in the Rosses, but its writers only came to prominence once the school system was improved earlier in the twentieth century. Foremost among them were three brothers from Rann na Feirste's **Clann Mhic Grianna**: Séamus Ó'Grianna, the author of 27 books and a popular recent choice for school Leaving Certificate examinations; Seosamh Mac Grianna, whose most famous works are *An Droma Mór* and his autobiography, *Mo Bhealach Féin*; and Séan Bán Mac Grianna, the youngest of the lot and the poet of the family. The village also hosts a large Irish language college. All its pubs were closed to prevent students from undermining their studies.

In the townland of **MEENALECK**, just before Crolly, look out for a sign pointing to **Leo's Tavern**. The proprietors, Leo and Baba Brennan, were both well-known on the dance-band circuit in the 1950s and 1960s, but other family members have achieved greater fame. Two of their children (Máire and Ciarán) are members of the group **Clannad** (a third, Pól, left in 1990) and another is the celebrated singer/musician **Enya** – the pub's walls are decorated with a variety of awards and mementoes. The *Tavern* is hugely popular with tourists, and the nightly singalong sessions, often featuring Leo himself on piano accordion, are usually adapted to suit their tastes. There are regular traditional sessions on Sundays at *Tessie's* bar across the road.

If you take the main N56 road from Dungloe to Crolly, look out for the small signs to your left marked "**Kerrytown Shrine**". In January 1939, some residents of this townland four miles south of Annagry claimed to have witnessed an apparition of the Virgin Mary on a rock and, once the newspapers had reported the story, large crowds began to gather nightly for prayer meetings. Pilgrimages arrived from all over the country and continue to this day, especially on August 15, the Feast of Assumption. A couple of miles further north on the N56 is **LOUGHANURE**, pleasantly set beside the lough from which it takes its name. The local Anglers Club (☎075/48689) has **boats** for rent (£6/€7.60 per day) and fishing permits (£6/€7.60 per day; £12/€15.19 per season), with further information available in the village shop. The thatched *Casad na Tsúgáin* is a popular bar/restaurant with sessions in summer.

CROLLY (signposted *Croichslí*) marks the end of the Rosses and the beginning of neighbouring Gweedore. The large *Teac Paidí Óg* pub has bar food, caravan, camping and laundry facilities and traditional music (Tues & Thurs in summer). For **B&B**, try *Leachrann House* (☎075/32194; ③); failing that, the postmistress in Crolly is a mine of information on accommodation in the area. However, by far the most exciting option is to take the narrow road on the right-hand side, just after the bridge, leading up into the **Derryveagh Mountains** (see p.498). This passes lovely **Lough Keel** and its deserted village before reaching its highest point by an abandoned school and swinging sharply right to return to Dungloe. If you head straight on instead, you'll arrive at the most wonderfully situated **hostel**, *Screag an Iolair* (March–Oct; ☎075/48593), with cosy rooms, open fires, traditional music and lots of advice on walking. Nestling in beautiful semi-wild gardens on the side of **Cnoc na Farragh** mountain, the hostel (whose name means "eagle's nest") provides magnificent views of mountains, lakes, distant Arranmore Island and spectacular sunsets. Hostellers regularly return here for the warmth of the welcome and the congenial atmosphere.

Gweedore and Tory Island

Like its southern neighbour, the Rosses, the interior of the **Gweedore** district is largely desolate and forbidding country and settlements again cling to the shoreline. To the southwest lie the villages of **Bunbeg**, **Middletown** and **Derrybeg**, their cottages sprinkled across a blanket of gorse and mountain grasses. It's a dispiriting kind of landscape and the ruggedness intensifies as it continues up the coast and round the Bloody Foreland to **Gortahork** and **Falcarragh** in the Cloghaneely district. Yet surprisingly, there has been significant house-building across the area and it's said to be the most densely populated rural area in Europe.

BUNBEG has a gorgeous little harbour, packed with smallish trawlers, half a mile from the village along an enchanting rollicking road. There's now a regular year-round **ferry** service to Tory Island (see box), and it's possible to negotiate a boat trip from the pier to other, mainly uninhabited, offshore islands such as Inishinny, Inishmaine, Inishirrer, Umfin, Inishfree and Owey. There are summer boat trips (☎075/31281) to Gola island. The **beach** further up the coast is approached by taking any track off to the left from the road running north from the harbour crossroads towards **DERRYBEG**.

For **accommodation**, there are two luxurious hotels in Derrybeg: *Ostan Gweedore* (☎075/31177; ⑨) and *Ostan Radharc na Mara* (☎075/31159; ⑨). At Bunbeg Harbour, there's excellent **B&B** at *Bunbeg House* (☎075/31305; ④) with pleasant waterside views from its restaurant. You can also **eat** extremely well in Bunbeg at *Mooney's Restaurant*, while nearby *Sergeant Pepper's* is a good place for kebabs and pizzas. The most popular bar is *Teach Húdaí Beag*, by the harbour crossroads, which hosts a famous Monday night traditional session, sometimes involving members of Altan. Both the *Ostan Gweedore* and *Radharc na Mara* hotels hold regular weekend **discos**. Summer **Irish language** courses are run by An Chrannóg in Derrybeg (☎075/32188) and also by *Teac Jack* on the coast road (☎075/31173; ②), which also offers courses in music and dancing and has a restaurant and accommodation.

At **GLASSAGH**, about four miles north of Derrybeg, the road climbs abruptly to the **Bloody Foreland**, a grim, stony, almost barren zone, crisscrossed by stone walls, and so called because of the red hue acquired by its heather from the light of the setting sun. The road turns eastwards at **KNOCKFOLA**, hugging the side of the mountain, with the bogland and its hard-worked turf banks stretching below towards the Atlantic. You should be able to spot the distinctive shape of **Tory Island** far out to sea and, at **MAGHEROARTY**, five miles east of Derrybeg, a road runs down to the pier, where you can pick up a ferry to the island. Nearby are the *Teac Coil* pub and a grocery store – handy if you're waiting for a boat.

Tory Island

With its ruggedly indented shores pounded day and night by the ocean, **TORY ISLAND**, though only eight miles north of the mainland coast, is notorious for its inaccessibility. You can only marvel that anyone should want to inhabit this isolated speck of land and struggle for survival against the ferocity of the elements. Yet despite the odds, the Tory islanders are thriving, a situation no one could have predicted after the events of 1974 threatened abruptly to curtail thousands of years of settlement. During that winter the harshest of storms battered Tory for over eight weeks, severing communications and preventing helicopters from landing. When it finally abated, two dozen families applied for mainland housing, ten of them eventually moving to Falcarragh. It

FERRIES TO TORY ISLAND

Ferries to Tory Island are operated by Turasmara Teo (☎075/31320), whose offices are at the harbour crossroads in **Bunbeg**. There's usually a daily year-round sailing which leaves Bunbeg at 9am and heads back from Tory soon after dropping off. There are also additional sailings from **Magheroarty** (June daily 11.30am & 5pm; July & Aug daily 11.30am, 1.30pm & 5pm) and from **Portnablagh** near Dunfanaghy (July & Aug Wed 2pm). The price of a return trip is £12/€15.19. The company also runs a number of coastal cruises in July and August calling at the island. Note that departure times may be affected by both the tides and the weather, so always call ahead to check. Whatever the weather, be prepared for sudden changes and for a forced overnight stay on the island.

later transpired that Donegal County Council had drawn up a full-scale evacuation plan. As in Glencolmcille (see p.487) the arrival of a new priest, **Father Diarmuid Ó Péicín**, stimulated a transformation. He came on a day-trip in 1980, but ended up staying for four years as the island's pastor. Conditions were poor and the islanders dispirited. Essential amenities such as a water supply, proper sanitation and reliable electricity were lacking. There was no ferry service and, even if there had been, the harbour was unfit to receive it. Rallying the islanders, the pastor began to lobby every possible target, securing support from such disparate characters as the US senator Tip O'Neill and Ian Paisley. The campaign attracted media attention and, despite Ó Péicín's replacement, conditions gradually began to improve with the eventual support of the embarrassed state and the financial assistance of an American philanthropist. Nowadays, around 120 people live permanently on the island and 25 children attend the local junior school, a happy sign of the island's revival (older children spend term times in Falcarragh).

Tory's inaccessibility has long reinforced its remoteness, ensuring the retention of a powerful culture which has almost vanished from the mainland, referred to by islanders as "the country". Only two and a half miles long and less than a mile wide, its openness to the elements means little can grow here, and what does has to be protected from the salty winds behind stone walls. The Irish-speaking islanders have a deep respect for the island and its landscape, both as inspiration for their musicians, storytellers and artists and as powerful sources of myth and legend. Tory was the stronghold of the **Fomorians**, who raided the mainland from their island base (the island's name is possibly derived from *toiridhe*, robber or pirate) and most notable of their number was the cyclops **Balor of the Evil Eye**, the Celtic god of darkness. Intriguingly, the local legend places his eye at the back of his head. The ruins of Balor's Fort lie on the east coast. There's also said to be a crater in the very heart of the island that none of the locals will approach after dark, for fear of incurring the god's wrath. In the sixth century, **St Columba** was helped to land on Tory by a member of the Duggan family. In return, the saint made him king of the island; the line has been unbroken ever since and you're more than likely to meet the present King, **Patsy Dan Rodgers**, who regularly greets arriving ferries. Some monastic relics from St Columba's time remain on Tory, the most unusual of which – now the island's emblem – is the **Tau Cross**. Its T-cross shape is of Egyptian origin, and is one of only two such monuments in the whole of Ireland. It has now been relocated and set in concrete on Camusmore Pier in West Town. There are other mutilated stone crosses and some carved stones lying around, several by the remains of the **round tower**, which is thought to date from the tenth century and is uniquely constructed from round beach stones. Another superstition focuses on the **wishing stone** in the centre of the island, three circuits of which will supposedly lead to your wish being granted. It was utilized to defeat invaders by wrecking their ships: the British gunboat *Wasp*, sent to collect taxes, was caught in a sudden storm that killed all but six of its crew. The islanders have never paid tax since.

Tory islanders are famed for their **painting**, a development which originated in a chance encounter between the English painter Derek Hill and one of the fishermen, **James Dixon**, in 1968. Dixon (now dead) had never lifted a brush before the day he told Hill that he could do a better job of painting the Tory scenery, but he went on to become the most renowned of the island's school of **primitive painters** – Glebe House has a remarkable painting by him; see p.500. You can view the islanders' work and, more than likely, meet the artists, at the **James Dixon Gallery**, the originator's former home, a little way to the east of the harbour.

Tory has two villages, **EAST TOWN** and **WEST TOWN**, and you'll find most of the amenities in the latter. There's a couple of shops, and the *Caife an Chreagáin* serves hearty snacks and meals. Alternatively, there's the restaurant at the *Ostan Thoraigh* which provides comfortable **accommodation** (☎074/35920; ⑤), has one of the only two bars, and organizes a range of summer events, including traditional music, *sean nós*, painting and birdwatching weekends. For **B&B** there's *Graceanne Duffy* (☎074/35136; ②) in East Town. The **Social Club** is one of the hubs of island life, with a bar and regular traditional music and dancing.

The Derryveagh Mountains and Glenveagh

Inland from Gweedore lies some of the most dramatic scenery in Donegal, an area dominated by mountains such as **Errigal** and **Slieve Snaght** and loughs of startling beauty. This is popular hill-walking country, especially along the Poisoned Glen, part of the much-visited **Glenveagh National Park**. Further on, towards Letterkenny, the countryside becomes gentler and increasingly verdant, especially in the environs of **Lough Gartan**, an area rich in assocation with St Columba.

Dunlewy and the Derryveagh Mountains

Heading east on the N56 from Gweedore, the imposing and starkly beautiful mass of **Errigal Mountain** becomes increasingly prominent. From a distance the mountain appears to be snow-covered, but as you skirt the northern shore of **Lough Nacung** it becomes apparent that the white colouration has geological, rather than meteorological, causes. The minor R251 road leads to **DUNLEWY**, where the *An Earagail* An Óige **hostel** (☎075/31180, *mailbox@anoige.ie*) sits by the lough at the foot of the mountain. Here too, in the former *Dunlewy Hotel*, is the independent *Lakeside Hostel* (March–Oct; ☎075/32133). Quite often the area is shrouded in mist, but on a clear day the beauty of Errigal is unsurpassable, its silvery slopes resembling Hokkusai's images of Mount Fuji. A hike up to the top is a must and there's a waymarked trail from the road up the southeast ridge. The climb to the summit is well worth it for the stupendous **views**: virtually all of Donegal, and most of Ulster, is visible and you could easily spend several hours just sitting and absorbing the contrasts provided by coastline, loughs and mountains.

Back down in Dunlewy village, there's a post office, shop and *McGeady's* bar. The lane next to the *Lakeside Hostel* leads to **Ionad Cois Locha/Dunlewy Lakeside Centre** (Easter–Oct Mon–Sat 10.30am–6pm, Sun 11am–7pm; tour of farm and outbuildings £3/€3.80, boat trip £3/€3.80, combined ticket £5/€6.33), an impressive visitor centre on the lough shore. There's an excellent **restaurant** here and a book-cum-craft shop, with maps of the area on sale. It's very child-friendly outside with a small farmyard 'zoo', adventure playground and pony rides on offer. For adults the highlight is the re-creation of the home of the notable local weaver, Manus Ferry. The **boat trip** around the lough is a pleasure for all ages. It's worth keeping a look out for details of the centre's weekly concerts during the summer, as it manages to attract some major names.

Glenveagh National Park

According to legend, the **Poisoned Glen**, east of Dunlewy, is where the cyclops Balor of the Evil Eye was slain by Lugh, poisoning the ground on which his single orb fell. There are many other explanations for the origins of its name, from the darkly conspiratorial (the glen's waters were polluted to kill English soldiers) to the purely botanical (poisonous Irish spurge used to grow here).

To reach the glen, head a little way further east on the R251 and take the signposted lane leading downhill to the right. Just below the ruined church at the eastern end of Lough Nacung turn off to the left and follow the track over the old bridge. The path dwindles away and you should follow the left bank of the river deep into the gorge until it turns sharply left. Cross the water here and climb up towards a granite crest. From here walk beside the small stream through a gully and finally you'll emerge on a ridge. It's not an easy tramp, for a lot of the ground is marshy, but the views are fantastic, with the River Glenveagh flowing into Lough Beagh down below. You're now in the **Glenveagh National Park** and may well see deer hereabouts. If you don't want to retrace your tracks and are prepared for a longer hike, you have a number of options. However, it's vital to follow all the basic rules of hill-walking (see p.49) and essential to keep to the designated roads and paths during the winter deer-culling season (Sept–Feb), or you run the risk of being **shot**. Experienced hill-walkers will probably be tempted by the sight of **Slieve Snaght**, the highest point in the Park, off to the west. Alternatively, if you head downhill to the southeast, the Glendowan road at the bottom leads eastwards to **Lough Gartan** (see below) and westward to **Doocharry** (see p.491). If you take this road east towards Gartan for a short distance, an old disused vehicle track to the left will lead you down the barrel of the glen alongside the river to Lough Glenveagh.

A less arduous approach to Glenveagh is to follow the R251 alongside the mountains until it curves to meet Lough Beagh's northern tip. A little further on is the official National Park **entrance** (Easter weekend & mid-April to Sept daily 10am–6.30pm; Oct same times; closed Fri; £2/€2.53; Heritage Card). The visitor centre has detailed and interactive displays on the area's ecology and geology and there's also a reasonably-priced restaurant. Free minibuses ply between here and **Glenveagh Castle** (same hours; £2/€2.53), built on a small promontory for George Adair in 1870. Adair was the creator of the estate which now forms much of the park and though you might admire the end-product it's impossible to condone the means by which it was achieved. Though some land was obtained through purchase, Adair despicably evicted 244 tenants during the bitterly cold April of 1861 – the **Derryveagh Evictions** – forcing many into the workhouse and others to emigrate to Australia. A second look at the castle might now suggest other reasons why its owner desired to occupy such a fortified construction. The surrounding rhododendron-filled gardens were very much the work of Adair's wife, Cornelia, who also introduced the herds of red deer to the estate. The steep ascent to the viewpoint behind the gardens is more than worthwhile for the wonderful views down to the castle and along the lough deep into the glen.

Lough Gartan and around

The environs of **Lough Gartan** are one of the supreme beauties of Ireland. **St Columba** was born into a royal family here in 521; his father was from the House of Niall of the Nine Hostages and his mother belonged to the House of Leinster. If you walk over from Glenveagh you'll pass his **birthplace** – take the first road right at the first house you see at the end of the mountain track, and you'll come to a colossal cross marking the spot; the site is also signposted by road. Close by is a slab locally known as the **Flagstone of Loneliness**, on which Columba used to sleep, thereby endowing the stone with the miraculous power to cure the sorrows of those who also lie upon it, though nowadays it's bestrewn with copper coins. During times of mass emigration, people used to come here the night before departure in the hope of ridding themselves of homesickness. Archeologically, it's actually part of a Bronze Age gallery tomb and has over fifty cup marks cut into its surface.

Going back to the track leading downhill will bring you to a main country road, where a left turn leads to the remains of a church known as the **Little Oratory of St Colmcille**. It's an enchanting ruin, no larger than a modern living room, with a floor of old stone slabs with grass growing up through the cracks. A holy well is here too and nearby the Natal Stone, where the baby Columba first opened his eyes; to this day pregnant women visit the slab to pray for a safe delivery.

Glebe House and around

Glebe House (Easter week & mid-May to Sept 11am–6.30pm; closed Fri; £2/€2.53; Heritage Card) is a gorgeous Regency building set in beautiful gardens on the northwest shore of Lough Gartan. Richly decorated both inside and out, it owes its fame to the time of its tenure by the artist Derek Hill, though it's now run as a **gallery** by the Office of Public Works. The converted stables house some of Hill's paintings and are used for visiting exhibitions, while the rooms of the house itself display a rich collection of paintings and sketches, including works by Kokoschka, Yeats, Renoir, Braque, Picasso and Degas. The study is decked out in original William Morris wallpaper, and there are Chinese tapestries in the morning room. The kitchen has various paintings by the Tory Island group of primitive painters (see p.497), most remarkably James Dixon's impression of Tory from the sea. It's well worth buying the guidebook and taking the tour.

Moving on round the northeast of the lake, in the direction of Church Hill, a right turn immediately after crossing the bridge will take you down to the modern **Colmcille Heritage Centre** (Easter week & May–Sept Mon–Sat 10.30am–6.30pm, Sun 1–6.30pm; £1.50/€1.90), on the opposite shore from Glebe. The exhibition space is devoted to Columba's life and the spread of the Celtic Church throughout Europe. If you have no interest in ecclesiastical history, there are other intriguing items, including very beautiful stained glass windows of biblical scenes by Ciaran O'Conner and Ditty Kummer and a step-by-step illustration of vellum illumination and calligraphy.

The road to the heritage centre continues a little further on to the **Gartan Outdoor Adventure Centre** (☎074/37032), which runs a range of outdoor activities in the locality and on the Donegal coast, including courses in mountain skills and leadership and sea kayaking (prices start at £80/€101.27 for a mountain skills weekend). Continuing east from here towards Letterkenny, you ascend from the northern shore to **Church Hill**, with superb cross-country views as far north as the peninsulas.

The Rock of Doon and Kilmacrennan

Lying a few miles northeast of Gartan, **The Rock of Doon** and **Doon Well** are signposted off the R255 shortly after the village of **TERMON** on the way to Kilmacrennan. Following the directions will lead you to a rural cul-de-sac right next to the well. A path from here ascends to a large bushy outcrop that is the Rock of Doon. From 1200 to 1603 this was the spot where the O'Donnell kings were crowned standing above a huge gathering of their followers. The inauguration stone on the summit is said to bear the imprint of the first Tír Chonaill king, a mark into which every successor had to place his foot as his final confirmation. Doon, an ancient pagan healing **well**, is still a place of pilgrimage, marked out by a bush weighed down with personal effects left behind by the sick, hoping for a cure. You're meant to take off your shoes as you approach and be well-intentioned before taking the water. You'll probably pick up a story or two of dramatic conversion and miracles effected by the water, which is sent to Irish emigrés all over the world.

KILMACRENNAN is a sweet-looking inland village on the road southeast to Letterkenny. A quarter of a mile down the Ramelton road is yet another site with Colmcille connections, **Cill Mhic n-Eanain**, where Colmcille was fostered and educated by Cruithnechan in around 528. A monastery stood here from the sixth century to 1129 and it was also the site of the O'Donnells' religious inauguration following the rites at Doon. The ruins on the left are of a sixteenth century Franciscan friary, while the Church of Ireland to the right dates from 1622 and fell into disuse around 1845. Back in the village, **Lurgyvale Thatched Cottage** (Easter–Sept daily 10am–7pm; £1/€1.27) is a restored nineteenth-century dwelling with furniture to match. There's a small exhibition of farm implements here, a handy tea room and traditional sessions every Thursday. Both the *Angler's Haven* and the *Village Tavern* **pubs** have reasonably priced food.

The north Donegal coast

Running from the Cloghaneely district which adjoins Gweedore, the **north Donegal coast** holds some of the most spectacular scenery in the whole country, where the battle between the elements is often startlingly apparent. Overshadowed at first by the bleak beauty of **Muckish Mountain** to the south, the main road from **Gortahork** in the west to **Milford** passes through verdant countryside as it meanders around the deep bays and inlets and alongside the glorious and often deserted beaches which punctuate the shoreline. The coast itself is dominated by three contrasting peninsulas: **Horn Head** with its rugged, sea-battered cliffs; **Rosguill**, almost circumscribed by the marvellous Atlantic Drive; and the more sedate **Fanad** for lonely walks and tremendous views across Lough Swilly to Inishowen.

Falcarragh and around

The first place you'll come across in the **Cloghaneely** area to the east of the Bloody Foreland is **GORTAHORK** – both the village and neighbouring area are good for Irish music. *Teac Billie* is an old men's drinking place with Tuesday night sessions, while the Irish College – up to the right after you pass *Whorskey's* on the left – has ceilidhs every night throughout July and August. There are sessions too on Thursdays at *Teach Ruari*, a mile away in **BELTANY**. The newly renovated *Ostan Loch Altan* (☎074/35267, *ostanaltan@esatclear.ie*; ⑤) has snack lunches and a reasonably priced Sunday carvery lunch and there's **B&B** at *Ard Aine* (☎074/35398; ②), a mile out of town in **CASHEL**.

FALCARRAGH is more interesting and better supplied with pubs, shops and other amenities. In the village, there's **B&B** at *Ferndale* (April–Sept; ☎074/65506; ③), while **hostel** accommodation is available at the *Shamrock Lodge* (closed mid-Dec to mid-Jan; ☎074/35859), over the *Shamrock Pub*. There are a few **eating** places in the village: *John's Café*, at the Gortahork end of town or the upstairs restaurant at the *Gweedore* are the best options and the latter has **music** of varying kinds most nights in July and August. The *Shamrock Pub* and *The Loft* also have live music and the *Errigal* runs Friday **discos**. Falcarragh **beach** is reached by following the coast road for a few miles – eventually the dunes will appear behind a car park. This is one of the more beautiful strands on this northwest coast, but a strong undercurrent makes it **unsafe for swimming**.

The road south from Falcarragh to Glenveagh passes through **Muckish Gap**. The slate-grey mass of **Muckish** ("pig's back") **Mountain** dominates the view all the way from Falcarragh; the hillsides are pitted with old workings where quartzite sand was extracted for the manufacture of optical glass. It's a relatively easy climb from the roadside shrine at the Gap up a grassy ridge to the **summit** and, on a clear day from here, the entire coastline from the Bloody Foreland, with distant Tory, to Malin Head is splendidly visible.

Heading east out of Falcarragh, the road to Dunfanaghy opens up a significantly milder landscape, with the green grass beginning to outstrip the ruggedness, and the odd reed-fringed lake with swans sitting prettily alongside the road.

Dunfanaghy and around

The small resort of **DUNFANAGHY**, seven miles east of Falcarragh, is the gateway to the **Horn Head Peninsula**. It's an aristocratically self-conscious plantation town, whose strongly Presbyterian atmosphere contrasts vividly with settlements to the west or south. On the western outskirts of town is the impressive **Workhouse** (March–Oct Mon–Fri 10am–5pm, Sat & Sun noon–5pm; £2.50/€3.16), sympathetically restored as a local history and community centre. It was originally built in 1845 on the eve of the Great Famine and at first had only five inmates, but by 1847, as the Famine intensified, over six hundred people were crowded inside. The Famine story is recounted upstairs, through the tale of one local inmate, 'Wee' Hannah Herrity, who lived until 1926 – though the narrative method (a distinctly dull and disappointing series of tableaux) undermines the power of her story. The centre hosts occasional innovative world- and traditional-**music** sessions and displays work by local artists; alternatively, you can simply sit, sup and chat in the coffee shop. Next door, the former fever hospital houses The Gallery, where you can admire more artwork and consider purchases from a range of crafts.

For accommodation, there are two **hotels**, *Arnolds* (☎074/36208, *arnoldshotel@eircom.net*; ⑦), which also has a riding stables, and *Carrig Rua* (☎074/36133, *carrigruahotel@eircom.net*; ⑥). Both also offer food. There are plenty of **B&Bs**, including *Rushvale* (☎074/36404; ②) and *The Whins* (☎074/36481; ③). As a less expensive, though comfortable, alternative, the excellent *Corcreggan Mill* **hostel** (☎074/36409, *brendanr@eircom.net*) is a mile or so west towards Falcarragh and also has private rooms in a converted railway carriage and **camping**.

As for **places to eat**, there's a fast-food outlet, *Josie's*, as well as *Danny Collins* pub offering soups and pricey but delicious seafood, and the upmarket *Danaa's* (☎074/36150), serving lobster and turbot dishes from £20/€25.40. *McGilloway's Oyster Bar* is light and airy, and a grand place for enjoying a pint, enhanced by the Derry artist John McCandless's tremendous portraits of musicians and writers, from Sinead O'Connor to Brendan Behan. There's occasional live music here, too (from traditional to blues), and sessions also at *Michael's Bar* up the street. *Dan Devine's* is lively and cosy with friendly bar staff and a nightclub, *Roonies*, attached.

Moving east from Dunfanaghy, the road follows the side of **Sheephaven Bay**; signposted turn-offs run to the popular holiday spots Portnablagh and Marble Hill Strand. From the former you can catch the Wednesday **ferry** to Tory Island in summer (see p.496). A little further east, Marble Hill Strand is a vast sweep of sand and is also the location for the *Shandon Hotel and Leisure Centre* (March–Oct; ☎074/36137, *shandonhotel@eircom.net*; ⑦), equipped with pool, tennis courts and pitch-and-putt. You can also learn to wind-surf here or rent boards from Marble Hill Windsurfing (July & Aug only; ☎074/36231) Overlooking the strand, Marble Hill House was once owned by **Hugh Law**, TD for Donegal in the first Irish Parliament of 1922, who entertained all manner of celebrities here, including W.B. and Jack Yeats. Nearby **Ards Forest Park** occupies the former demesne of the Capuchin Friary of Ard Mhuire; a mile-long avenue alongside Lough Lilly takes you into its centre where there are fine walks through the woodland.

The Horn Head Peninsula

Horn Head is magnificent, a 600ft rock face scored by ledges on which perch countless guillemots and gulls. Puffins are also returning in significant numbers. The best view of the cliffs, sea-stacks and caves is from the water, but the cliff road is vertiginous enough in places to give you a good look down the sheer sides. To get there take the slip road at the western end of Dunfanaghy village; it descends to skirt the side of a beautiful inlet before rising steeply to go round the east side of the head. A spectacular vista of headlands opens up to the east – Rosguill, Fanad and Inishowen – but none can match the drama of Horn Head's **cliffs**, their tops clad in a thin cover of purplish heather. Alternatively, you can walk from Horn Head bridge across the dunes to **Tramore Beach** and then follow the sheep track north, passing two small blowholes called the Two Pistols and then a much larger one, **McSwyne's Gun**, so called because of the power of the sonic boom produced by the explosion of compressed air from the cavern. Erosion has occurred over the years, however, and you'll be lucky to hear anything these days. Continuing onwards, you'll come to Pollaguill Bay and the beach. The next wondrous site is the 70ft high **Marble Arch**, cut by the sea through the base of Trawbreaga Head. Horn Head itself soon becomes visible as you ascend the next headland. The walk as far as here takes around three hours from Dunfanaghy and you can either complete the whole circuit of the peninsula or head back by road.

Creeslough and around

The sleepy village of **CREESLOUGH** stands on a slope commanding gorgeous views across the head of Sheephaven Bay. Partway down its main street is a church designed by Liam McCormack, its whitewashed whorl and back-sloping table roof reflecting the thickly set **Muckish Mountain** nearby. You can see the mountain from within the church – it's usually swathed in mist, or what's known locally as the Donegal *smir*. There are pubs and grocery stores in the village, but little to detain you for long.

The coastal road northwards onto the Rosguill Peninsula offers a couple of worthwhile diversions. To the left, just before Lackagh Bridge, **Doe Castle** (currently undergoing works) has been superbly reconstructed. The tall central keep, standing within a *bawn* and rock-cut fosse, was the original fortress of **McSwyney Doe**, whose grave slab is now fixed to its wall, and was the base for the O'Dohertys' raids on Derry in 1608. The carving on the stone is faint, but its intricacy makes it historically important; the seven-speared fleur-de-lis at the top represents the close family connections with Scotland, while other carvings show a fox, cow, dolphin and eagle, as well as Celtic tracery. A walk around the battlements affords a view of the southernmost corner of **Sheephaven Bay**; when the tide is out the whole peaceful expanse looks like a desert, with only a slim channel of water gliding through the sandbanks. If the castle gate is padlocked, a key is kept in the cottage fifty yards back down the approach road where you can also buy a guide pamphlet (£1.60/€2.03).

Lackagh Bridge is an even better viewpoint, the curving silty shoreline lying downstream and a ginger-brown picture of rushes and heather reaching deep into the hills. Immediately after the bridge there's a turnoff which runs for two miles to **GLEN** on a circuitous route to Carrigart that's worth taking for the scenery and the opportunity to drop in at the *Olde Glen Bar*. This is a low-ceilinged place, smoky and atmospheric, with music at weekends and other nights too. If solitude is what you want, this is a good area to explore: apart from Lough Glen, there are several other lakelets in the district, all enclosed in a silent, rocky landscape.

Carrigart

CARRIGART is the back-door entrance to the Rosguill Peninsula. It's a beguiling village, whose **bars** define the essence of the place: *P. Logue's,* at the west end of town, is a welcoming sort of hideaway. **Accommodation** is available in the village at *Hol-Tel Carrigart* (☎074/55114; ⑥) and *Sheephaven Lodge* (☎074/55685; ③), both open between April and September. There are plenty of stores for stocking up on provisions or you can **eat** economically at *Weavers Restaurant.* The only **bank** on the peninsula is in Carrigart (July & Aug Mon–Fri 10am–noon; rest of year Mon, Tues, Thurs & Fri 10am–noon).

The Rosguill Peninsula

The route onto the extremely beautiful and very manageable **Rosguill peninsula** starts by the side of Carrigart church; follow this road for a little, then fork left, and you'll pass the rabbit-infested dunes at the back of a tremendous and usually deserted beach. The three-mile strand runs in a scimitar's curve all the way back round to the southern end of **Sheephaven Bay** – it's a marvellous four-hour walk to Doe Castle, though when the tide comes in, you could have to do a mile or so of the journey on the lanes.

At the top of the strand is **DOWNINGS**, a small and sprightly holiday centre patronized mainly by Northern Irish tourists, with caravan sites hogging the rear end of the beach and holiday chalets creeping up the hillside behind the village. The one **pub** you should be sure to head for is *Downings Bar* (also known as the *Harbour Bar*), uphill at the far end of the village, a welcoming place with an open fire, lots of *craic* and music at weekends. The *Beach Hotel* has occasional summer sessions too. The most luxurious place to **stay** is the *Rosapenna Hotel* (March–Oct; ☎074/55301, *rosapenna @eircom.net*; ⑦), next to its own eighteen-hole golf course. Alternatively, there's the *Beach Hotel* (April–Oct; ☎074/55303; ④), and a couple of B&Bs: *Bay Mount* (April–Aug; ☎074/55395; ③) and *An Crossóg* (May–Sept; ☎074/55498; ③). You can **camp** at *Casey's Caravan Park* (☎074/55301).

Downings' main street runs on round the west side of the headland to become the panoramic **Atlantic Drive**, first passing by the harbour slip road. Just before the pier is McNutt's tweed shop with a daytime coffee shop attached offering superb home baking. The drive runs right round the headland and also makes a stupendous eight-mile walk. The range of views encompasses the essence of Donegal – rugged landscapes in constant tussle with the Atlantic Ocean. About halfway round, a turning leads to **Melmore Head** where you'll find, perfectly placed at **TRÁ NA ROSANN** beach at the northeastern corner of the headland, an Alpine-style An Óige **hostel** (Easter–Sept; ☎074/55374, *mailbox@anoige.ie*). A quicker way to get here is to take the right-hand fork on the way to Downings; it's also quite easy to **hitch** to the hostel, as everyone knows where you're heading.

South of the Melmore Head road you'll pass the congenial *Singing Pub* (traditional music on Sat), sited on a turning up to the left. Opposite this turning and down to the right is **Mevagh Church** graveyard. It has an early Christian cross and an intriguing slab into which some cup-like cavities have been carved. And there's one gravestone that cannot but raise a smile: *Pat MacBride 1910–86, Shoemaker and Philosopher.*

The Fanad Peninsula

The road from Carrigart to the **Fanad Peninsula** passes close to Mulroy Bay before arriving in **MILFORD**, a village with amenities but little attraction, though the *Milford Inn*, out on the Ramelton road, is a popular venue at weekends, usually for country and Irish music (the national adaptation of country and western).

From Milford, the road up the **western** side of the peninsula leads to **KERRYKEEL**, passing on the way the *Mulroy Ballroom*, one of the few remaining 1960s showband ballrooms (June–Aug ceilidhs on Wed night). The *Rockhill Caravan Park* (☎074/50012), opposite the ballroom, provides the only basic **accommodation** in the area. The *Village Inn* at the northern end of the village has a somewhat expensive but wide-ranging menu and *Mr Ed's* serves huge portions of fish and chips. *McGettigan's* Bar has almost nightly entertainment in summer.

From Kerrykeel the road north runs along the water's edge up to **TAMNEY** where there's **B&B** at *Avalon House* (April–Sept; ☎074/59031; ③). Further on, the landscape flattens and the ubiquitous "Fanad fences" begin to appear, agricultural wire barriers which scythe across the countryside and deter adventurous walking. A left turn at the *Fanad Lodge* bar will take you past the large **Ballyhiernan Strand** through hillocks and boulder-strewn terrain to **BALLYWHORISKEY** where a restored pre-Famine cottage houses a small heritage centre (open daily from 2pm), with **boats** for rent. From here you can return to the main road to Fanad Head.

Ramelton and Rathmullan

The road crawling up the **east** side of the peninsula is a much more interesting approach to Fanad Head. It starts at **RAMELTON**, a quaint and sedate little town which sits attractively on the eastern bank of the broad black flow of the salmon-rich River Leannan. The town has heritage status because of its many Georgian houses and there are some fine stone warehouses on the bank side. Wander uphill, however, and you'll encounter boarded-up buildings (including the eighteenth-century *Sweeney's Tavern*) and other signs of decay – fortunately, there are rejuvenation plans afoot. The old Meeting House in Back Lane houses the **Donegal Genealogical Centre**, a must for anyone seeking to verify their local ancestry. *Mirabeau* is a popular **restaurant**, serving steaks and seafood, while the *House on the Brae* coffee shop dispenses home baking. For entertainment, try the *Bridge Bar* (Wed & Fri–Sun), where you can hear R&B, jazz or rock. Should you decide to stay, there's fine **B&B** at *Ardeen* (April–Oct; ☎074/51243, *ardeenbandb@tinet.ie*; ③), overlooking Lough Swilly, and at *Frewin* (March–Nov; ☎074/51246, *flaxmill@indigo.ie*; ⑥), a converted Victorian rectory set in wooded grounds half a mile south of town off the Letterkenny road.

The next stop north, **RATHMULLAN** is a pretty place with its long row of multi-coloured houses facing Lough Swilly. The beach here is classed among the cleanest in Europe – note the Blue Flag at the pier, where **boats** can be rented from Malcolm Bowden (☎074/58282). In 1587 **Red Hugh O'Donnell** was lured onto a British merchant ship here, on the pretext of a merry drink, and ended up in Dublin jail for six years; and in 1607 Rathmullan was a departure point for the **Flight of the Earls**, the event that marked the end of the Gaelic nation. **Rathmullan Heritage Centre** (Easter to mid-Sept Mon–Sat 10am–6pm, Sun noon–6pm; ☎074/58229; £1/€1.27) recounts this event and provides a host of information on local accommodation and leisure activities. In October 1798 the French frigate *Hoche*, with Wolfe Tone on board, was intercepted in the Lough nearby and Tone was captured and taken to Dublin for trial. The view across to Fahan on the Inishowen Peninsula is enticing (a small ferryboat operates in summer), but otherwise the only thing to delay your passing through is **Rathmullan Friary**, one of the better-preserved historical ruins in Donegal. The original part of it was built by Rory MacSweeney in 1508 and then presented to the Carmelites. George Bingham plundered it in 1595 and used it as a barracks, and in 1618 it was further adapted as a castle residence by Bishop Knox. Only the chancel area continued to serve as a church until its eventual abandonment in 1814. Today you can see traces of Gothic doorways and narrow window apertures.

On the way into Rathmullan, there's very good **eating** to be had at the *Water's Edge* restaurant, while gourmets and oenophiles are also catered for by *The Ferry Gate* (Mon & Thurs–Sun, evenings only) on Pier Road. The comfortably old-fashioned *Pier Hotel* (April–Sept; ☎074/58178; ④) serves excellent fresh salmon for a fraction of what you'd pay at the upmarket *Rathmullan House* nearby (closed Jan; ☎074/58188; *rathhse@iol.ie*; ⑧). You can savour the Lough Foyle view over a pint in the friendly *Beachcomber* **bar**. The only other accommodation in the village is offered by the *Fort Royal Hotel* (April–Oct; ☎074/58100, *fortroyal@eircom.net*; ⑨); for less pricey accommodation, you'll need to head to **SALTPANS**, three miles north, where *Carriglough House* (March–Nov; ☎074/58197; ②) provides B&B. The *Pier Hotel* has traditional music on Thursday nights in summer.

Towards Portsalon

Two miles north of Rathmullan, on the coast road, a signpost to the left indicates a little track that leads towards the tenth-century **Drumhallach cross slab**, only four and a half feet high. It has delightful carvings of two figures sitting on the arms of the cross sucking away at their thumbs. This curiosity is linked by local folklore with Fionn Mac Cumhaill, who one day burned his thumb while tending to the salmon of knowledge, and immediately stuck it in his mouth – thereafter doing the same whenever he needed to be wise. The lower figures on this front face are harder to make out but are meant to represent bishops.

Back on the main route, the road climbs to give great views across to **Dunree Head** and the **Urris** range of mountains on the Inishowen Peninsula to the east. About seven miles north of Rathmullan is *Bunnaton House* **hostel** (March–Oct; ☎074/50122, *bunnaton@eircom.net*), sited in an old coastguard station with pleasant views of a small cove with a rocky beach. The hostel can provide details of the great walks nearby, both beside the lough and inland through the Irish-speaking **Glenvar valley** to Kerrykeel on the western side of the peninsula. Further on the road towards Portsalon is the *Knockalla Caravan and Camping Park* (☎074/59108, *knockalla@oceanfree.net*).

Continuing north, the road rises until you're running along the cliff-top approach to **Saldanha Head**. Here you'll witness the most spectacular views on the entire peninsula, looking across to Inishowen and down onto the three-mile stretch of golden sand at Ballymastocker Bay. The tiny village of **PORTSALON**, on the other side of the strand, was once a great holidaying spot, but there's little sign of this now apart from a courtyard full of holiday chalets. The highlight is Rita's Pier Stores by the tiny harbour, with its 1950s-style decor, wooden bar counter and shelves for sweets and bottled drinks. For **B&B** try the award-winning *Croaghross Cottage* (March–Sept; ☎074/59548, *jkdeane@iol.ie*; ④) which also serves excellent dinners. The Portsalon **golf** course (☎074/59459) must have one of the most picturesque settings in the country.

Fanad Head

Though some stretches are forested, most of the five-mile route north from Portsalon to **Fanad Head** is through humpy and barren land, with clusters of granite pushing through marshy ground. By the roadside there's a **Holy Well**, decked out with a crazier than usual collection of mementos. Before reaching the Head, there is one other curiosity worth taking in – the rock formation known as the **Seven Arches**, created by the constant erosive battering of the waters. To get there, follow the signpost on the right of the road, then take the path down to the new house, and finally cross the fields to the rocky strand. Alternatively, there's private access to the arches from Ballydaheen Gardens, a gorgeous six-acre spread of flora, herbs and vegetables (mid-May to Aug; £3/€3.80).

Returning to the main road, you'll find that it leads straight on to **Fanad Head**, where it reaches a dramatically placed cliff-edge lighthouse and its namesake public house, the *Lighthouse Tavern*. The road from here runs on down to the low rocky coast, and a pebble beach.

East Donegal

The rich farming land of **East Donegal** may seem bland in contrast to other parts of the county and, certainly, it's the area's urban communities which offer the greater attractions. **Letterkenny** is Donegal's boom town, seemingly increasing in size and prosperity daily; it's also the hub of the county's public transport network. To its south lie **Ballybofey** and **Stranorlar** (known as "the twin towns"), the border town of **Lifford** and the former ecclesiastical centre of **Raphoe** with its nearby **Beltany stone circle**, one of Ireland's major Neolithic remains.

Letterkenny

LETTERKENNY is the largest town in Donegal and, indeed, the only one with a population in excess of ten thousand. It has been the county's commercial focus ever since

Derry was partitioned into the North and has undergone massive redevelopment in recent years with a refurbished town centre, huge new shopping malls and a growing industrial sprawl beyond its boundaries. Letterkenny's boast is that it is the main place for entertainment in the northwest and there certainly is an ebullient bustle about the place. Although it sits at the mouth of Lough Swilly, there's no water in sight, and the main visual element is the file of shop windows down the main street. The most notable sight is the huge nineteenth-century **St Eunan's Cathedral**, with its intricate stone-roped ceiling, flying buttresses and gaelicized Stations of the Cross. The only other place of interest in town is the **Donegal County Museum** (Mon–Fri 10am–12.30pm & 1–4.30pm, Sat 1–4.30pm; free), housed in part of the old Letterkenny workhouse. Temporary exhibitions occupy the downstairs area while upstairs is a typical display of artefacts from megalithic to more recent times, including the keys and lock of the old Lifford jail, and an account of the old Donegal County Railway which ran to and from Letterkenny. If you're heading west on the R250 Fintown road, look out for the restored **Newmills Corn and Flax Mills** (June–Sept daily 10am–6.30pm; £2/€2.53; Heritage Card), in a pleasant setting by the River Swilly and, naturally, powered by its waters. The mill closed as late as 1982 and much of the old machinery is still present.

Practicalities

Letterkenny's amenable **tourist office** (July & Aug Mon–Fri 9am–1pm & 2–8pm, Sat 10am–2pm, Sun 9am–1pm & 2–5pm; rest of year Mon–Fri 9am–1pm & 2–5pm; ☎074/21160) is a mile east of town on the Derry road. There's a **bureau de change** (daily 11am–6pm), plenty of **banks**, and a **post office** on Main Street.

There are lots of **B&Bs** in the area, but just a few in the centre, including the *Gleneany Guesthouse*, Port Rd (☎074/26088; ⑤); *Oakland*, 8 Oaklands Park (☎074/25529; ②); and *Willow House*, Kilmacrennan Rd (☎074/21871; ③). The central *Gallagher's Hotel*, 100 Main St (☎074/22066; ⑦), is the pick of the more expensive places to stay. Good upmarket alternatives are *Castle Grove Country House* (☎074/51118; ⑧), out of town on the Ramelton road, offering luxury accommodation and a restaurant with prices to match; *Mount Errigal Hotel* (☎074/22700, *info@mounterrigal.com*; ⑦) a mile out on the Derry road with a leisure centre and nightly entertainment during the summer; and the imposing new *Holiday Inn* (☎074/24369; ⑧), further out towards Derry, which has its own 20m swimming pool and sauna.

There are plenty of places **to eat** in Letterkenny, and most are on Main Street. At the top of the hill, *Galfees* has a wholesome daytime buffet and serves excellent coffee. *Pat's On The Square*, 9 Market Square, is an excellent family-run **restaurant** specializing in appetizing homemade pasta and ice cream, freshly ground coffee and desserts to die for; while *Café Rio*, opposite the library, is another grand coffee house. Many of the pubs serve lunches too, including an excellent carvery at *Dillon's Bar* and specials too at *McGinley's* and *The Brewery*. Unquestionably, the current place to be seen is the *Metropolitan*, Lower Main Street, owned by celebrity chef Conrad Gallagher and specializing in 'new world' cuisine. Other choices nearby include *The Lemon Tree* and *The Yellow Pepper*, both specializing in reasonably-priced fish and meat dishes, with several vegetarian options.

There are enough **bars** to defeat even the hardiest pub-crawler; a fair few offer Irish music, too. *McCarry's*, at the corner of the High Road, has music most nights, while the *Downtown Lounge*, on Main Street, has regular Wednesday traditional sessions and other music at weekends; both *McGinley's* and the *Cottage Bar* are popular with students and the latter has a Tuesday session. *Nellie's* currently offers music four nights a week. On Market Square, *The Brewery*, with its striking brass interior, is very popular and has music nightly, including the odd session. Letterkenny also has several **nightclubs**, of which *The Golden Grill* and *Pulse*, both on Port Road, are currently the most popular, attracting up-and-coming and well-established DJs. Currently the hippest place to be is *The Orchard Inn* on High Road whose three floors are usually packed at weekends thanks to music in the lounge and DJs on the top storey. If you just want a quiet pint, then *Blake's* or *McLafferty's* on Upper Main Street will satisfy.

Letterkenny's proudest new development is its new **theatre**, An Granán (☎074/20777), on Port Road, which, apart from an impressive drama programme, has already garnered a reputation as one of Ireland's best music venues (from traditional to classical). There's a four-screen **cinema** nearby, a **bowling centre** out on Ramelton Road and **bikes** for rent from Church Street Cycles (☎074/26204). Letterkenny also hosts two **festivals**: the Donegal International Car Rally in mid-June; and the two-week Errigal Arts Festival in mid-July.

South of Letterkenny

The gently rolling countryside **south of Letterkenny** is probably the least visited of any area in the county. A glance at a map shows a roughly triangular area, delineated by the major roads to and between **Ballybofey** and Strabane, which includes the small town of **Raphoe**, with its striking **stone circle**.

Raphoe and the Beltany stone circle

Almost at the centre of this triangle is the small town of **RAPHOE**, set trimly around one of the largest diamonds in the county. Its erstwhile importance as an ecclesiastical centre is still indicated today by its inclusion in the Church of Ireland Bishopric of Derry and Raphoe, though it was once a see in its own right. The town has had its own **cathedral**, dedicated to St Eunan, since the ninth century, but the present plain Gothic cathedral church dates merely from 1702. Transfixed in the inner wall is a stone block with some peculiar and indecipherable carvings and there's a very impressive and resonant wooden baptismal chapel. The former Bishop's Palace lies in ruins to the rear. The major reason for visiting the area, however, lies two miles to the south – **Beltany stone circle**. To get there follow the signs from the south of the Diamond and eventually you'll arrive at the entrance to a farm. The circle is a quarter of a mile up the bridle path to the right, over a stile and across a field full of sheep. This is one of the best-preserved circles in the country, consisting of approximately sixty stones, varying in height between one and four feet. It's easy to comprehend one of the reasons for its construction as there's a marvellous panoramic view of the local valleys and the distant mountains. Raphoe town makes a pleasant overnight stop, though there's little in the way of **accommodation**, B&B choices being limited to *McGranagan's* (☎074/45144, *info@family-homes.ie*; ③), a Georgian town house on the Diamond, and *Mrs Chambers*, Strabane Rd (April–Nov; ☎074/45410; ③). There are quite a few **pubs** – *Tirconnail House* serves a good pint – and, surprisingly, one of the biggest **clubs** in the county, *Frankie's*, with very popular dance nights. There's **riding** available nearby at the Greenacres Lodge Equestrian Complex, Rooskey Upper, Convoy (☎074/47451).

The Twin Towns and Lifford

Heading southwest towards Donegal town, you're certain to pass through the twin towns of **STRANORLAR** and **BALLYBOFEY**, separated only by a bridge over the River Finn. There's little remarkable about either, though the latter is by far the livelier. **Isaac Butt**, one of the founders of the Irish Home Rule Party, is buried in the Stranorlar church graveyard. Ballybofey is home to Donegal's only League of Ireland football (soccer) team, Finn Harps, and also to the successful and innovative Balor Theatre (☎074/31840) which has its own local company and entertains touring companies from all over Europe. The municipal **tourist office** (Mon–Fri 9am–5pm;

☎074/32337) is inside the Balor Theatre building. Surprisingly, there's some top-notch **accommodation** here at both *Jackson's Hotel*, Ballybofey (☎074/31021, *bjackson@iol.ie*; ⑦) and *Kee's Hotel*, Stranorlar (☎074/31018; ⑦), as well as a **hostel**, *Finn Farm* (May–Oct; ☎074/32261), two miles west of Ballybofey off the Fintown road, which also offers **camping**, horse riding and trekking. There are plenty of bars in both towns; *The Claddagh* in Ballybofey is the current favourite and has music at weekends. Apart from the hotels, the best **eating** place is probably the *Bridgeside Bistro*, in the precinct by McElhinney's department store in Ballybofey.

If you've entered Donegal from Strabane, across the border in County Tyrone, you'll almost certainly bypass the border town of **LIFFORD**, though it does have a couple of sights for which it's worth dallying. The town was formerly Donegal's legal centre and its graceful **Old Courthouse**, dating from 1746, was designed by Michael Priestley. Nowadays, the building houses a **visitor centre** (Easter–Oct Mon–Sat 10am–6pm, Sun 2–6pm; £3/€3.80), which tells the story of the O'Donnell clan and notable events in Donegal's history. The building's former legal use has not been forgotten and models re-enact old trials, including that of Napper Tandy, with the assistance of new technology. Down in the basement cells, there's a pretty gruesome re-creation of the conditions experienced by prisoners. A couple of miles northwest of Lifford off the N14 is **Cavanacor House** (Easter–Sept Tues–Sat noon–6pm, Sun 2–6pm; £2/€2.53), a fine seventeenth-century mansion where James II dined in 1689. It was also the ancestral home of **James Knox Polk**, US president from 1845 to 1849. A small museum reflects on both these notables, but the real treat is the **art gallery** which displays a changing array of work by contemporary painters.

The Inishowen Peninsula

The **Inishowen Peninsula** in the northeast of County Donegal is perhaps the great overlooked treasure of the Irish landscape (and certainly has the longest signposted scenic drive – the "Inishowen 100"). Few tourists come here, perhaps because of its proximity to the North. Yet if you do visit, you'll discover a diverse and visually exciting terrain, where the views usually encompass the waters of the loughs or the Atlantic waves. Virtually every aspect of the landscape is superb – the beaches (especially Fahan, Tullagh and Pollan), the towering headland bluffs (Malin, Inishowen, Dunaff and Dunree) and the central mountain range, with **Slieve Snaght** (*sliabh sneachta*, the "mountain of the snows") at the centre of it all.

The peninsula derives its name from **Eoghán**, who was made First Lord of the island by his father Niall, High King of Ireland. Phases of the peninsula's history before and after Eoghán have left a legacy of fine antiquities, from the **Grianán Ailigh** fort to a host of beautiful early Christian crosses (Cloncha, Mura, Carrowmore and Cooley).

The Grianán Ailigh

The approach to the most stimulating of all Inishowen's sights, the ancient fort known as the Grianán Ailigh, passes the Liam McCormack-designed **Burt Church**, near Bridgend on the N13 Letterkenny–Derry road. This is probably the most beautiful new church in all Ireland, and like other McCormack designs in Donegal, its structure is evocative of the mystical landmark nearby. The seating is set concentrically, under a whitewashed ceiling that sweeps up into a vortex to allow sunlight to beam down directly upon the altar; the allusions in every detail to Neolithic sepulchral architecture (especially Newgrange) are fascinating and very atmospheric.

The origins of the **Grianán Ailigh** (a mile up the hill from the church) date back to 1700 BC and it's thought to be linked to the Tuatha Dé Danann, pre-Celtic invaders. It

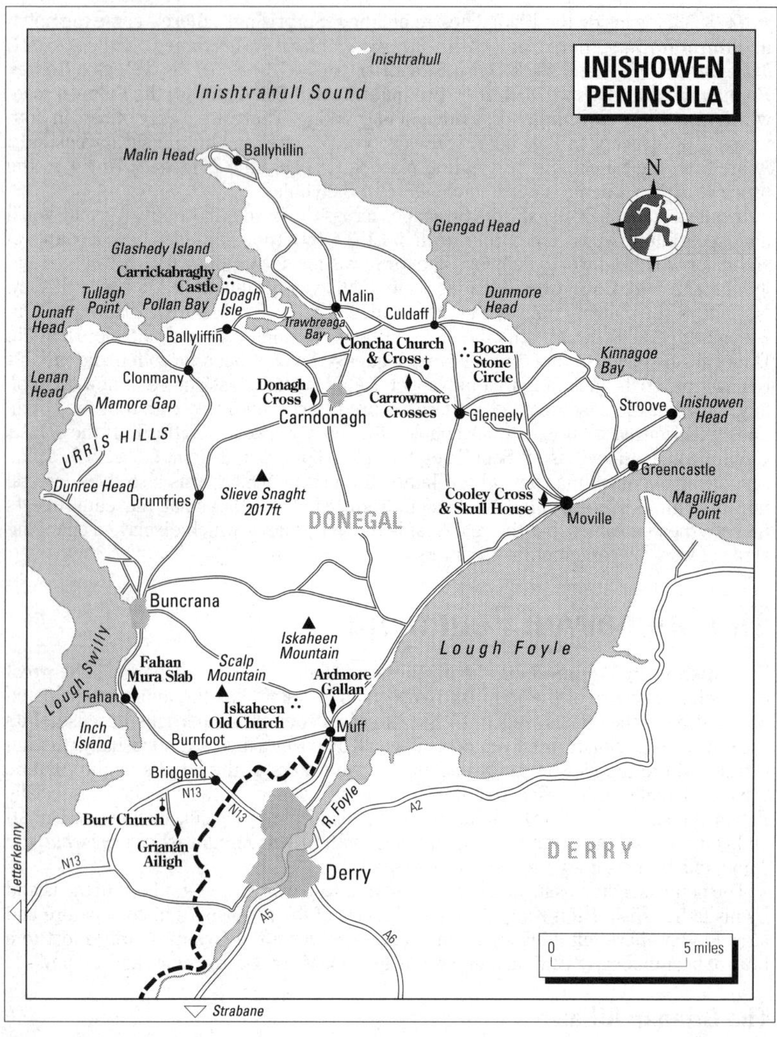

was sufficiently significant to be included by Ptolemy, the Alexandrian geographer, in his second-century AD map of the world, and was the base of various northern Irish chieftains. Here in 450, St Patrick is said to have baptized Eoghán, the founder of the O'Neill clan which ruled the kingdom of Ailigh for more than 500 years. In the twelfth century the fort was sacked by Murtagh O'Brian, King of Thomond, in retribution for a raid on Clare, with the result that a large amount of its stone got carried away. Today's impressive building was largely reconstructed in the late nineteenth century and is the only remaining terraced fort in Ireland. It's enclosed by three earthen banks, but its most stunning asset is the view across the primordial jumble of mountains and hills far away to the west and the loughs to each side of Inishowen immediately to the north. You can discover more about the fort at the **visitor centre** (daily: June–Aug 10am–6pm; Sept–May noon–6pm; £2/€2.53), back on the main road towards Letterkenny, which also contains a superb, innovative **restaurant** (closes 10pm; ☎077/68512), serving Lough Neagh eels and wild boar.

Western Inishowen

The lane on the opposite side of the N13 from the Burt Church leads to **western Inishowen** (or you can head east to Bridgend and turn onto the R238). Whichever you choose, a couple of miles past Burnfoot is a signposted turning to **INCH ISLAND**, connected to the mainland by a causeway. This was once a strategic O'Doherty base, guarding Lough Swilly and the clan heartlands, and has a ruined castle to boot. If you have time for a detour, there are great views of the lough and the Inishowen coastline from the pier, while wetland habitats to the west of the island attract vast colonies of Whooper and Bewick swans and other waterfowl. Inch Island Stables (☎077/60335) organizes **riding** holidays around the Inishowen 100.

The beach at **FAHAN**, next stop on the mainland, is delightful, as are its monastic ruins. The first abbot was St Mura (one of six saints in the same family), and what remains today from his time is the **St Mura cross slab**, a spellbinding example of early Christian stone decoration. Long-stemmed Latin crosses are carved on both faces with typical Celtic interlacing. There's said to be a rare Greek inscription on the edge, but it's hard to locate. *Restaurant St John's*, as you enter the village, offers local seafood specialities, but expect to pay upwards of £20/€25.40, while the *Railway Tavern* cooks its food on an open wood burning firebox and has regular Friday night set dancing.

Buncrana

BUNCRANA, a few miles north of Fahan, is the largest town on the peninsula and its high street is a long cavalcade of shops and bars, many with names saluting one or other of the local clans – Grant, Hegarty, McGonagle, McLaughlin, O'Doherty. The town is packed out during the summer, for this is the Derry people's unrivalled seaside resort, and the streets are especially thronged during the annual **music festival** during the last week of July. To escape the crowds, take the left turn that runs down to the pier at the north end of the main street and you'll reach the coastal path to **Stragill Strand**, a beautiful and isolated stretch of golden sand. The view across **Lough Swilly** here is delightful, as if the waters were those of a large mountain lake. Also well worth visiting is the community-run *Tullyarvan Mill* (May–Sept Mon–Sat 10am–5pm), a mile north of town off the Drumree road, which has a craft shop and café and hosts regular exhibitions and musical events.

Buncrana might have plenty of amenities, but there are surprisingly few places **to stay**. The seasonal **tourist office** (June–Aug Mon–Sat 9am–5pm; ☎077/20020) on the waterfront should be able to help, but rooms are in especially short supply during the July music festival. For **B&Bs**; try *Ross na Rí*, Old Rd (March–Oct; ☎077/61271; ②), or *Kincora*, Cahir O'Doherty Ave (☎077/61174; ②). There are a couple of **hotels**: the *Lake of Shadows*, Grianan Park (☎077/61902; ⑤) overlooking the lough; and, the larger *Inishowen Gateway*, Railway Rd (☎077/61144, *inigatho@iol.ie*; ⑦).

For **eats** in Buncrana, there are the lunchtime specials at the *Cranberry Café* or, for more substantial fare, the more upmarket *Ubiquitous*, also on Main Street. The *Town Clock Restaurant* offers everything from breakfasts to evening meals. *The Drift Inn*, Railway Road, is a popular choice for pub lunches, and *Dorrian's*, Main Street, is another good bet. Buncrana is jam-packed with **pubs**. If you're looking for a plain and unpretentious bar try *Hutton's* or *Roddens*. More upbeat venues include *O'Flaherty's*, which often has traditional music in summer, and *McCallion's* music bar. At the weekends, car- and coach-loads of northerners pour over the border to dance into the small hours at **clubs** such as *Liberty's* or *Club Sands* in the *Inishowen Gateway Hotel.*

North of Buncrana

Perched on a headland overlooking the mouth of Lough Swilly, just past the tiny village from which it takes its name, **Fort Dunree** began life as a Martello Tower and was then enlarged into a fortress. It now has a museum of predictable military memorabilia (June–Sept Mon–Sat 10am–6pm, Sun 1–6pm; £1.80/€2.28; car park £2/€2.53), though the audiovisual display at least provides an insight into the fort's former use. North out of Dunree village the road climbs steeply past a scattering of weather-beaten thatched cottages before crossing a small bridge close to the **Gap of Mamore** (*madhm mór*, "the great mountain pass"), which seems like a chunk bitten out of the Urris Mountains. From here the road spirals steeply downwards, each bend providing an ever-wider and more spectacular view of the flat foreground to Dunaff Head. The mile-long **Tullagh Strand**, to the east of Dunaff Head, is a safe bathing beach, with *Tullagh Bay Camping and Caravan Park* just behind it (☎077/76289 or 76138). *The Rusty Nail* pub, by the roadside, has music at weekends and offers good-value bar food and Sunday lunch. The road from here works its way inland between the mountains to **CLONMANY**, a village of predominantly cream-coloured terraced houses, a few grocery shops and several bars. The backdrop of mountains on all sides shields it from any thought of an outside world.

The holiday village of **BALLYLIFFIN** is more geared to tourism, and has several places **to stay**. The imposing *Ballyliffin Hotel* (☎077/76106; ⑥) has a fine restaurant, while B&B options include *Castlelawn House* (☎077/76600; ③) and *Rossaor House* (☎077/76498; ④). Apart from **golf** – the Glashedy course here (☎077/67119) is reckoned to be one of the toughest in Ireland – the other main local draw is the traditional song **festival** held on the last weekend in March. Should you want to explore the area, **bikes** can be rented from McEleney's Cycles (☎077/76541) on the road to Clonmany.

The minor road heading north from Ballyliffin leads to the entrancing **Pollan Strand**, at the northern tip of which stands the ruin of **Carrickabraghy Castle**, an O'Doherty defence built in the sixteenth century. Weathered by centuries of spray and sea salt, the stones of the tower show colours ranging from the darkest hues through oranges and reds to golden yellows. The strand itself has wonderfully wild breakers, which unfortunately make it dangerous to swim. The castle sits on the western side of **DOAGH ISLE**, another former island, linked to the mainland through centuries of silt accumulation, which you can drive onto by a road a couple of miles east of Ballyliffin. You can't miss the turning, as there's a mannequin pointing the way and, a little further on, a similar male pulling a cart containing a donkey. These direct you to the **Doagh Visitor Centre** (Easter–Oct daily 10am–5.30pm; £3/€3.80 including tea and scones), one man's intriguing attempt to tell the Famine story. You'll discover a re-created farm cottage (including a remarkably small 'kitchen' bed), the fairy house home of Fergus McArt, and more mannequins in various symbolic tableaux. Head out further east for **Trawbreaga Bay** (*trá bréige*, "the treacherous strand"), an exquisite piece of coastline. The mouth of the bay is bewitching: if you walk onto the beach here you'll find the sea has fashioned the rocks into myriad shapes and colours.

Carndonagh

Just before you turn into **CARNDONAGH** town, coming from the Ballyliffin direction, there's a church on the corner against whose wall is the elegantly shaped and decorated seventh-century **Donagh Cross** (*domhnach,* commonly "Sunday", but also "church founded by St Patrick"), with two diminutive pillar stones to its right and left. The pillar stones show figures with rather large heads, while the cross depicts evil little characters jumping out of its Celtic interlacing – all of which harks back to the Druidic religion. A few other decorated stones stand by the entrance.

The buildings of Carndonagh town are stacked up the hillside, near the crown of which stands the omniscient Catholic church. Most of the activity here occurs in the environs of the Diamond and this is the place to stock up on supplies. Near the corner of Chapel Street is the **Inishowen Tourist Office** (Mon–Fri 9.30am–5.30pm; July & Aug also Sat & Sun same times; ☎077/74933) whose friendly staff can supply you with information on the whole peninsula. The town **museum**, in the basement of the Wesleyan church, near the base of the hill as you come from the Ballyliffin direction (July & Aug Mon–Sat 1–5pm; free), has many intriguing folk items. You can rent **bikes** from Bikes and Toys (☎077/74084), three miles northwest of town on the Ballyliffin road – handily, they'll deliver to anywhere on the peninsula.

For **accommodation**, try *Radharc na Coille*, Tiernaleague, left off Church Street then on for a mile (☎077/74471; ②), or *Ashdale Farmhouse* (April–Oct; ☎077/74017; ③), half a mile north on the Malin Road. For **food**, there's the restaurant at *Trawbreaga House* on the Diamond, while on Malin Road, *The Quiet Lady* has extremely good-value lunches and *The Corncrake*'s evening specials are popular enough to warrant booking ahead (☎077/74534). *The Sportsman's Inn*, on the Diamond, does stews and salads and has traditional music in summer. *Bradley's*, on Bridge Street, is an old-time sing-song bar. *Tul-na-ri*, out on the Culdaff road, attracts the crowds to its weekend **discos**. Carndonagh has a **street festival** in the third week of July but it's not one of the more lively ones in the area.

Culdaff and around: the ancient sites

Not far to the east of Carndonagh are a neighbouring set of historical remains – the Carrowmore high crosses, the Cloncha cross, the Bocan stone circle and the Temple of Deen.

To get to the **Carrowmore high crosses**, take the Moville direction out of Carndonagh for four miles, then turn right forty yards after the signposted turning for Culdaff: the two plain crosses are eighty yards up the lane, one on each side, the northern cross undecorated, while its partner has a figure, supposedly of Christ. These and a few meagre building stones are all that remain of the ancient monastery of St Chonas, husband of Dareaca, a sister of St Patrick.

For the **Cloncha cross and church**, return to the Culdaff turning and follow it for a couple of miles until you see a bungalow with a garden hedge of small firs. The site is up a path alongside. This was once the most important monastic foundation in Inishowen, a status reflected in the beautiful designs carved on the cross's stem. Inside the ruined sixteenth-century church are a few more carved stones, the outstanding piece being a tenth-century tombstone.

For the other two sites, continue onwards towards Culdaff, turn right at the church and then first left. The **Bocan stone circle** is through the first field gate on the left. Only seven of the original stones still stand, among a residue of fallen ones; they were all placed here at least three thousand years ago. There's a fine view of the surrounding ring of hills and it's believed that the stones were deliberately aligned on an east–west axis between Slieve Snaght and Jura. On the other side of the main road from the circle is a gallery tomb known as the **Temple of Deen** (go a little further along towards Moville and take a right up as far as the wire barrier – you'll spot it from there). It's nothing special, but it's possible that what is exposed today is only the central chamber of an immense cairn. Unfortunately, there has been no archeological investigation of either this or the stone circle.

CULDAFF is the nearest base for all of these places, a cosy village set around an ancient stone bridge whose nearby **beach** forms a stunning natural crescent. There's a major **sea angling festival** here at the end of July and, in October, a cultural weekend commemorates the eighteenth-century actor, Charles Macklin. However, for the rest of the year, it's *McGrory's* bar which is the centre of attention. It may be hard to credit, considering its isolated location, but the *Back Room* here is one of the best venues in Ireland for **live music** and the bar is decorated with numerous pictures of the stars who've appeared to prove it. You can **stay** here too (☎077/79104, *www.mcgrorys.ie*; ⑥), or at *Ceecliff House* (☎077/79159; ③) or *Culdaff House* (March–Oct; ☎077/79103; ②). Alternatively, there's **hostel** accommodation at *The Pines* (☎077/79060), four hundred yards down the road to Bunagee Pier. Summer **boat trips** to Inishtrahull Island (see below) leave from the pier (☎077/70605).

Malin and Malin Head

Four miles north of Carndonagh, and approached via a ten-arched bridge, is **MALIN** village, tucked picturesquely into the side of Trawbreaga Bay. A planter settlement with a charming grassy Diamond, it has two pubs, *McClean's* and *McGonnigle's*, as well as the recently renovated *Malin Hotel* (☎077/70645, *malinhotel@eircom.net*; ⑤) which hosts a variety of entertainments.

A little way north of Malin a signpost shows the way to **Five Fingers Strand**, across the bay from Doagh Isle – it's worth the diversion to experience the ferocity of the breakers on the beach and the long walks on its sands. Following the "Inishowen 100" signs will next lead you around Knockamany Bens, from which there are tremendous views of the strand and, occasionally at low tide, of the wreck of the *Twilight* which sank in 1889 en route to Newfoundland.

Twelve miles north of Malin village, **Malin Head**, the northernmost extremity of Ireland, might not be as stupendous as other Donegal headlands but is nevertheless excellent for blustery, winding coastal walks – and for ornithologists: choughs, with their glossy black plumage and red legs and bill, inhabit the cliffs and the rasping cry of the rare corncrake can be heard in the fields. The headland's tip is marked by **Bamba's Crown**, a ruined signal tower, built in 1805. The words "S.S. Eire" (*Saor Stát*, "Free State") are written below the tower. Five miles offshore is the now-deserted **Inishtrahull Island**, though boats from the pier at **Bulbinbeg** (a half-mile walk from *Farren's* bar) will take you there in summer. Some say its name translates as the "Island of Yonder Strand", though others claim its meaning derives from a legendary murder – "Island of the Bloody Strand" or even "Shore Grave". Whatever the case, the island is composed of the oldest rock in Ireland, Lewisian gneiss that is two billion years old. Continuing a walk on Malin Head, the western path from Bamba's Crown heads out to **Hells Hole**, a 250ft chasm in the cliffs, which roars with the onrushing tide. Past the *Seaview Tavern* to the east, a path leads to the **Wee House of Malin**, a hermit's cell in the nearby cliff, once the home of St Muirdealach, where there's a "wishing-chair".

B&B places on the headland include *Barraicin* (Easter–Oct; ☎077/70184; ②) and *High View* (☎077/70283; ②), both overlooking the Atlantic. There are a couple of excellent **hostels** here too. The *Malin Head Hostel* (open all year, but advance booking necessary Nov–March; ☎077/70309), just past the post office on the way into Bulbinbeg, is well-equipped and has private rooms, and the owner, who also offers reflexology and aromatherapy, is a mine of information on the area. Alternatively, *Sandrock Holiday Hostel* (☎077/70289, *sandrockhostel@eircom.net*), at Port Ronan Pier – fork left at the *Crossroads Inn* – has dormitory accommodation, wonderful sea views and bikes for rent. The best place to **eat** is *The Cottage* (March–May Sun 1.30–6.30pm; June–Sept Mon–Sat 11am–6.30pm, Sun 1.30–6.30pm), a restored thatched cottage on Malin Head near Bamba's Crown; apart from the fine tea room, with salmon available in season, there's **tourist information** here and traditional sessions in summer. Both the *Seaview Tavern* (with a tiny public bar-cum-hardware shop) and the *Bree Inn* serve meals and have music on Saturdays, while *Farren's* bar is a cosy place to sit and chat to the locals.

Eastern Inishowen

Though still attractive country, the coastline of **eastern Inishowen** holds less interest than the west. Its proximity to Derry also means that it is substantially busier, especially at the weekends when the city's clubbers hit the area's nightclubs. Nevertheless, it's still possible to find isolated spots, especially to the west of Inishowen Head, and there are lots of pleasant places to visit.

Muff and around

The tiny village of **MUFF**, just a few minutes' drive north of the international border, is not quite as moribund as it may at first appear. *Carmans Inn* has Irish music on a Wednesday and another place to try is *The Flough*, a traditional Irish cottage with sessions and dancing to match. There's a lively festival here on the first weekend in August. Lenamore Stables (☎077/84022) offers **riding** and **trekking** in the vicinity and beyond.

The countryside immediately around Muff is scattered with several interesting remains. Uphill from Muff in **ISKAHEEN**, opposite St Patrick's Church, a plaque in the wall of the ruined church in the graveyard marks the burial place of Eoghán, son of Niall of the Nine Hostages. Of greater antiquity is the Bronze Age **Ardmore Gallan** stone, a striking monument heavily carved with symbolic forms. There are forty small cup-dents and a large vertical valley down the middle of one face. To get to it, take a left off the Moville road about half a mile north of Muff, then up the lane at the side of the red-doored house; follow the road straight up, and turn right to the farmyard at the end. The stone is in the far side of the field in front of the yard.

Also to be recommended is the fourteen-mile trip across the mountains through **Gráinne's Gap** and on to Buncrana on the western side of the peninsula (see p.511). There are spectacular views back down onto the Foyle estuary from the gap, and the inland scenery is all trickling burns, heathery boggy slopes lined with turf banks, and rocky granite outcrops.

Moville and around

Set on a gentle hillock beside the Foyle, **MOVILLE** is an agreeable seaside resort and was once a port of call for transatlantic liners, though there's little activity in today's compact harbour. It's handy for a rocky shoreline walk that you can pursue as far as Greencastle without too much difficulty, although at a few points you'll have to walk circumspectly across the bottom of a few private gardens. The village rarely stirs itself to offer anything more than the odd tingle of excitement, except during the late September **Foyle Oyster Festival**, a cross-border event with bucket-loads of entertainment and the chance to devour shellfish galore. There are plenty of places to **stay**. *McNamara's Hotel* (☎077/82564; ⑤) is the grandest and has *Club Max!* attached. For B&B try *Naomh Mhuíre*, Main St (April–Oct; ☎077/82091; ②) or *Iona House*, Gulladuff Rd (☎077/82173; ②). The *Moville Holiday Hostel*, Malin Rd (☎077/82378, *scanvas@iol.ie*) also rents out bikes. *Barron's* café, Lower Main Street, offers economical daytime meals, while *Rosatos*, Malin Road, is the best place for an evening **meal**. There are traditional sessions at *Rawdon's Bar and Grocery* on Fridays. *The Prospect Bar* down on the front by the gaudily blue-painted Temperance Hall has music at weekends. A livelier time is to be had at the *Hair of the Dog* pub by the pier, which promises varied music every night.

The most notable historical remains in the district are the **Cooley Cross** and **Skull House**, approached by taking the left turn just before the petrol station on the way into Moville. Follow the turn-off up the steep hill for about a mile, always bearing right and you'll discover an ancient Celtic wheel-cross, guarding the entrance to a walled graveyard. There are very few examples of this kind of cross with the pierced ringhole in its head – the hole was once a pagan device used to clinch serious treaties, the hands of the opposing parties being joined in amity through it. The Skull House, in the graveyard, is in the form of the beehive huts of early monks and it was once possibly an oratory before becoming an ossuary. Any bones that were stored here have long since vanished.

Greencastle and around

The harbour village of **GREENCASTLE** has a pleasant view across to the extensive golden sands of Magilligan Strand on the Northern Irish side of Lough Foyle. At dusk you'll see the area across the water begin to sparkle with lights like a ship at sea – these are the lights of the prison camp, just hidden behind the dunes. A highlight of village life are the regular visits by cruise ships. Next to the harbour, in the old coastguard station, is the newly-refurbished **Maritime Museum and Planetarium** (June–Sept daily 10am–6pm; £2/€2.53), which recalls maritime travel from a bygone era. Amongst the range of maritime memorabilia, pride of place goes to a nineteenth-century rocket cart used to fire flares to aid survivors of wrecked ships. By the road to Stroove (see below) are the ruins of a fourteenth-century **Richard de Burgo** castle, built on a rocky knoll to allow the Anglo-Normans to guard the narrowest part of the lough. It was briefly captured in 1316 by Edward Bruce of Scotland who had himself crowned King of Ireland. The castle was retaken shortly afterwards and remained in De Burgo's hands until 1333 when his grandson William, the Brown Earl, was murdered and Anglo-Norman control of the northwest ended. Later the castle fell into the hands of the O'Dohertys, but it was badly damaged by an attack by their rival Calvagh O'Donnell. Though there were subsequent attempts at renovation, by 1700 the castle was a complete ruin and has remained so ever since. Nearby is **Greencastle Fort**, a lookout post built during the Napoleonic Wars which unsurprisingly affords good views across the estuary, though nowadays it houses a bar and restaurant with **B&B** (☎077/81426; ⑤). You can also stay right next door to De Burgo's ruin in the *Castle Inn* (☎077/81426; ③), which also has a restaurant and traditional sessions on Fridays, and at *Brooklyn Cottage* (March–Oct; ☎077/81087; ③). As you'd expect, seafood is available in abundance and, in addition to the restaurants above, the place to aim for is *Kealy's*, reckoned to be one of the best in Donegal.

At **STROOVE** (pronounced *Shroove*), the scenery jumps into a more exciting gear, with lovely clambering walks along its coastline to the lighthouse. There you'll have to return to the road to reach the small beach, from where doughtier walkers can resume the clamber as far as the cliffs of the awesome **Inishowen Head**. An easier way to the head is simply to follow the road until it turns left, where you go straight on up the hill; a car can make it up the first couple of miles, but after that you run the risk of getting stuck in a rut. From the head, it's a beautiful but tiring walk to isolated **Kinnagoe Bay**, one of the most secluded sandy beaches around, tucked between the rocky walls of headland against which the waves throw spray as delicate as lace. The alternative route here entails going back to the main road and following it to the right turn by the thatched cottage in Stroove – this will take you along the narrowest of roads over the headland and through two beautiful glens. A plaque by the roadside at Kinnagoe records the sinking of *La Trinidad Valencera* during the Spanish Armada and other ships around the coast. Forty of its crew died in the water and most of the remaining three hundred survivors were killed outside Derry by an English army. The wreckage was recovered and is on display at Foyle College in Derry. *Kinnagoe Bay House* (April–Oct; ☎077/81280, *mconway1@iol.ie*; ③) is a fine place to **stay** with wonderful views of the Bay. Back in Stroove, the *Drunken Duck Seafood Bar* (☎077/81362), offering good **food** and fantastic views, is well worth a visit.

travel details

Donegal has no trains, but there's a plethora of **bus** services, divided here between public and private companies. Apart from express services, few companies operate on Sundays and many services are much reduced in the winter months.

Public bus companies

BUS ÉIREANN covers the south and southwest of the county as well as the road between Donegal town, Letterkenny and Derry (enquiries: Donegal town ☎074/21101; Letterkenny ☎074/21309; Stranorlar ☎074/31008; Dublin ☎01/836 6111; *www.buseireann.ie*).

Ardara to: Donegal (July & Aug 2 Mon–Sat; 1hr 15min); Dungloe (July & Aug 2 Mon–Sat; 1hr 15min); Glenties (July & Aug 2 Mon–Sat; Sept–June Tues, Thurs & Fri; 20min); Killybegs (July & Aug 2 Mon–Sat; Sept–June Tues, Thurs & Fri; 25min); Narin (July & Aug 2 Mon–Sat; 35min).

Ballybofey to: Derry (8 Mon–Sat, 3 Sun; 1hr 10min); Donegal (8 Mon–Sat, 3 Sun; 30min); Letterkenny (8 Mon–Sat, 3 Sun; 25min); Strabane (5 Mon–Sat; 55min).

Ballyshannon to: Bundoran (10 Mon–Sat, 3 Sun; 10min); Sligo (8 Mon–Sat, 3 Sun: 1hr 5min).

Donegal town to: Ardara (July & Aug 2 Mon–Sat; 1hr 15min); Ballybofey (5 Mon–Sat, 3 Sun; 30min); Ballyshannon (5 Mon–Sat, 3 Sun; 20min); Bundoran (5 Mon–Sat, 3 Sun; 30min); Derry (5 Mon–Sat, 3 Sun; 1hr 30min); Dublin (5 Mon–Sat, 3 Sun; 4hr 15min); Dungloe (July & Aug 2 Mon–Sat; 2hr 30min); Glencolmcille (3 Mon–Sat; 1hr 25min); Glenties (July & Aug 2 Mon–Sat; 1hr 30min); Glenveagh (July & Aug 1 Mon–Sat; 1hr 45min); Killybegs (5 Mon–Sat; 45min); Letterkenny (5 Mon–Sat, 3 Sun; 1hr); Sligo (5 Mon–Sat, 3 Sun; 1hr).

Killybegs to: Ardara (July & Aug 2 Mon–Sat; Sept–June Tues, Thurs & Fri; 25min); Dungloe (July & Aug 2 Mon–Sat; 1hr 40min); Glencolmcille (3 Mon–Fri, 4 Sat; 45min), Glenties (July & Aug 2 Mon–Sat; Sept–June Tues, Thurs & Fri; 40min); Malinmore (1 Sat; 1hr).

Letterkenny to: Ballybofey (8 Mon–Sat, 3 Sun; 25min); Donegal (5 Mon–Sat, 3 Sun; 1hr); Lifford (4 Mon–Sat; 50min); Raphoe (5 Mon–Sat; 35min); Strabane (5 Mon–Sat; 55min).

ULSTERBUS operates in the south of the county (enquiries: Belfast ☎028/9033 3000).

Ballyshannon to: Belleek (5 Mon–Wed, Fri & Sat, 7 Thurs, 1 Sun; 15min); Enniskillen (5 Mon–Wed, Fri & Sat, 7 Thurs, 1 Sun; 1hr 10min).

Pettigo to: Ballyshannon (1 Mon–Sat; 45min); Belfast (2 Mon–Fri, 3 Sat; 3hr 15min); Belleek (1 Mon–Sat; 30min); Enniskillen (5 Mon–Sat, 50min).

Private bus companies

LOUGH SWILLY runs services to Inishowen, Fanad and westwards around the coast to Dungloe (enquiries: Derry ☎028/7126 2017; Letterkenny ☎074/22863). Its 'Runabout' ticket gives 8 days' unlimited travel on its services for £18/€22.78.

Buncrana to: Carndonagh via Clonmany and Ballyliffin (4 Mon–Fri, 3 Sat; 50min); Derry (9 Mon–Fri, 13 Sat, 3 Sun; 35min); Letterkenny (3 Mon–Thurs, 4 Fri; 40min).

Carndonagh to: Buncrana via Ballyliffin and Clonmany (4 Mon–Fri, 3 Sat; 50min); Derry (7 Mon, Wed & Fri, 5 Tues & Thurs, 4 Sat; 55min); Malin Head (2 Mon, Wed & Fri, 3 Sat; 30min).

Dunfanaghy to: Derry (5 Mon–Sat; 2hr); Dungloe (2 Mon & Sat, 3 Tues–Thurs, 4 Fri; 1hr 25min–2hr 20min); Letterkenny (5 Mon–Sat; 50min).

Dungloe to: Annagry via Kincasslagh (2 Mon–Sat; 30min); Burtonport (2 Mon–Sat; 10min); Crolly (2 Mon–Sat; 15–45 min); Derry (2 Mon–Fri, 1 Sat; 3hr 10min–5hr 25min); Derrybeg (2 Mon–Sat; 30min–1hr 10min); Dunfanaghy (2 Mon–Sat; 1hr 25min–2hr 20min); Falcarragh (2 Mon–Sat; 35min–2hr); Letterkenny (2 Mon–Fri, 1 Sat; 2hr 15min–4hr 20min).

Fanad to: Letterkenny (1 Mon–Fri, 2 Sat; 1hr 35min).

Letterkenny to: Buncrana (2 Mon–Thurs, 1 Fri; 40min); Derry (10 Mon–Fri, 11 Sat; 30–55min); Dunfanaghy (2 Mon–Thurs & Sat, 3 Fri; 55min); Dungloe (2 Mon–Thurs & Sat, 3 Fri; 2hr 15min–3hr 55min); Fanad (2 Mon–Sat; 1hr 45min); Ramelton (3 Mon–Fri, 4 Sat; 25min); Rathmullan (2 Mon–Fri, 3 Sat; 40min); Portsalon (1 Mon–Sat; 1hr 30min).

Malin Head to: Carndonagh (2 Mon, Wed & Fri, 3 Sat; 30min); Derry (2 Mon, Wed & Fri, 3 Sat; 1hr 25min).

Moville to: Derry (5 Mon–Fri, 6 Sat; 50min); Greencastle (5 Mon–Sat; 10min); Stroove (4 Mon–Sat; 20min).

Portsalon to: Letterkenny (1 Mon–Sat; 1hr 55min).

Ramelton to: Letterkenny (3 Mon–Fri, 4 Sat; 25min).

MCGEEHAN COACHES operates express services to and from Dublin (enquiries: Dungloe ☎075/46150, *mcgeehancoaches.com*). Services listed here operate between June and mid-September, with a reduced frequency midweek during the rest of the year.

Buses run from **Dungloe** daily at 7.45am to **Dublin** via Lettermacaward, Glenties, Ardara, Donegal town, Enniskillen and Cavan. There is an additional service departing Dungloe on Mon–Sat at noon, and on Sun and public holidays at 3pm. Return services depart from the Royal Dublin Hotel, O'Connell St, Dublin daily at 6am and 2pm, with an additional service on Fri at 4pm. Total journey time 4hr 50min.

Buses run from **Glencolmcille** daily at 7.20am to **Dublin** via Carrick, Kilcar, Killybegs, Ardara, Donegal town, Enniskillen and Cavan. There is an additional service departing Glencolmcille on Mon–Sat at 11.40am, and on Sun and public holidays at 3pm. Return services depart from the Royal Dublin Hotel, O'Connell St, Dublin daily at 6am and 2pm, with an additional service on Fri at 4pm. Total journey time 4hr 50min.

JOHN MCGINLEY operates express services between Gweedore, Inishowen and Milford and Dublin (enquiries: Crolly ☎074/35201).

Buses run from **Annagry** daily at 6.45am to **Dublin** (Gresham Hotel) via Crolly, Bunbeg, Gortahork, Falcarragh, Dunfanaghy, Creeslough, Kilmacrennan, Letterkenny, Lifford, Omagh and Monaghan. There's an additional service departing Crolly on Mon–Fri at 3.10pm, and another departing Annagry on Sun at 3pm. Return services depart Dublin's Parnell Square on Mon–Sat at 9.30am and 5.45pm, and on Sun at 12.30pm and 8.30pm, with additional Friday departures at 12.30pm and 4.30pm. Total journey time 5hr 30min.

Buses run from **Moville** on Mon–Sat at 7am and on Sun at 3.30pm to **Dublin** via Cardonagh, Buncrana and Letterkenny. Return services depart Dublin's Parnell Square on Mon–Fri at 5.45pm, and on Sun at 8.30pm. Total journey time 5hr.

Buses run from **Milford** on Mon–Sat at 8am and on Sun at 3.50pm to **Dublin** via Ramelton and Letterkenny. Return services depart Dublin's Parnell Square on Mon–Sat at 5.45pm, and on Sun at 8.30pm. Total journey time 4hr.

Buses depart **Letterkenny** at 8.45am to **Glasgow** (Scotland) – daily in July and Aug, 4 times a week the rest of the year. Return services depart Glasgow at 7.45am. Journey time 7hr 15min.

NORTHWEST BUSWAYS has local services covering Inishowen, and express coaches to Dublin (enquiries: Moville ☎077/86219).

Buses run from **Cardonagh** on Mon–Sat at 7.15pm and on Sun at 3.30pm and 5pm to **Dublin** via Buncrana and Derry; and from **Moville** on Mon–Sat at 7.30pm and on Sun at 3.50pm and 5.20pm to **Dublin**. Return services to both Cardonagh and Moville depart Parnell Square West in Dublin on Mon–Sat at 6am, and on Sun at 2pm, with an additional service on Fri at 3.30pm. Total journey time 5hr.

Buncrana to: Ballyliffin (4 Mon–Sat; 30min); Carndonagh (4 Mon–Sat; 20min); Clonmany (4 Mon–Sat; 35min); Letterkenny (4 Mon–Fri, 3 Sat; 2hr); Moville (4 Mon–Sat; 55min).

Moville to: Ballyliffin (4 Mon–Sat; 30min); Buncrana (4 Mon–Sat; 55min); Carndonagh (4 Mon–Sat; 20min); Clonmany (4 Mon–Sat; 35min); Derry (5 Mon–Sat; 40min); Letterkenny (3 Mon–Fri, 2 Sat; 2hr); Stroove (3 Mon–Sat; 20min).

O'DONNELL runs buses from The Rosses to Belfast (enquiries: Rann na Feirste ☎075/48356).

Buses run from Sweeney's Hotel in **Dungloe** on Mon–Sat at 7.15am and on Sun at 4.30pm to **Belfast**, via Burtonport, Kincasslagh, Annagry, Crolly, Derrybeg, Gortahork, Falcarragh, Dunfanaghy, Creeslough, Kilmacrennan, Letterkenny, Derry, Dungiven and Toomebridge. Return services depart from outside Jurys Hotel, College Square, Belfast on Mon–Sat at 5.30pm, and on Sun at 9.15pm. Total journey time 4hr 30min.

FEDA Ó DONNELL operates buses from Gweedore to Galway (enquiries: Annagry ☎075/48114; *homepage.eircom.net/~fedaodonnell*).

Buses run from **Crolly** on Mon–Sat at 7.20am and 2.45pm and on Sun at 7.20am, 1.50pm and 5.30pm to **Galway** via Gweedore, Gortahork, Falcarragh, Dunfanaghy, Creeslough, Kilmacrennan, Letterkenny, Ballybofey, Donegal town, Ballyshannon, Bundoran, Sligo and Tuam. There's an additional departure leaving Crolly on Fri at 10.20am. Return services depart Galway Cathedral on Mon–Sat at 10am and 4pm and on Sun at 3pm and 8pm (the latter departing from Eyre Square). Additional return services depart Galway Cathedral on Fri at 1.30pm and 5.30pm. Total journey time 5hr 30min.

THE NORTH

On May 22, 1998, the people of Northern Ireland turned out in unprecedented numbers to vote on what had become known as the **Good Friday agreement** (see p.681), the latest inter-governmental attempt to create a political solution to the violence that has afflicted the North since the late 1960s. When the results were declared the following day (which, significantly, was the bicentenary of the 1798 Rebellion), 71.12 per cent had voted in favour of the settlement. Interpretations differed, but most analysts agreed that a majority of both Nationalist/Republican and, more remarkably, Unionist/Loyalist communities had given their support. Simultaneously, electors in the Republic overwhelmingly endorsed the agreement, thus mandating their government to renounce the Irish constitutional claim to the six counties that make up the North. This bilateral ratification was an undoubted triumph for all the agreement's signatories, but, much more momentously, only one possible conclusion could be drawn from the results of the referenda: after almost thirty years

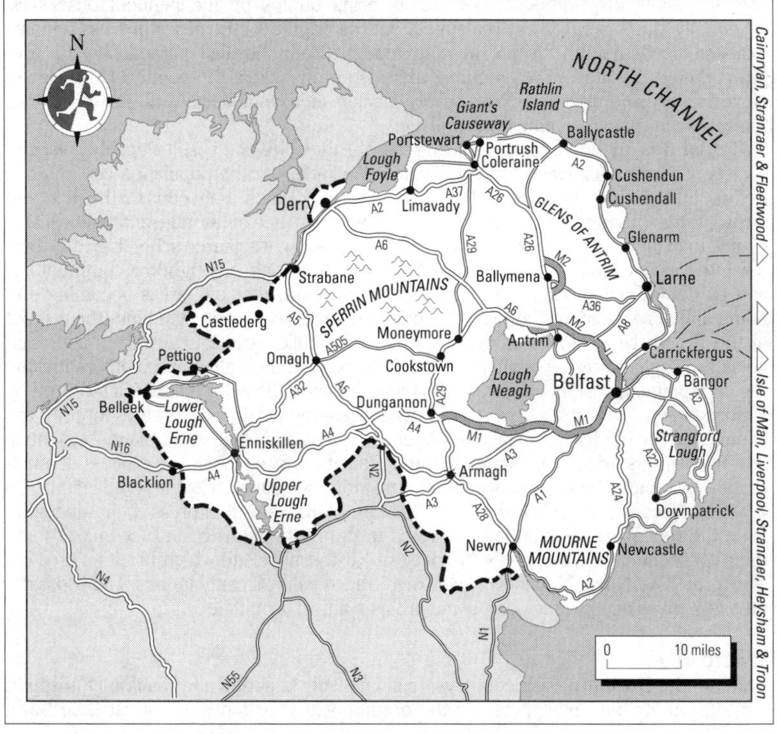

of the "**Troubles**", the people of Northern Ireland had unequivocally expressed their desire for **peace**.

A month later saw the election of the new **Assembly**, the first organization to have (albeit limited) legislative and executive authority over the province since the Stormont Parliament was dissolved in 1972. **David Trimble**, leader of the Ulster Unionists, was appointed First Minister, a position since jeopardized by anti-Agreement factions within his own party, and Seamus Mallon of the Nationalist SDLP became Deputy Minister. However, dissident Republican hardliners expressed their opposition by a series of town centre bombings during the first half of 1998 culminating in a massive explosion in the centre of **Omagh** on August 15 which killed 29 people – the worst single atrocity in the whole history of the Troubles. Frantic and, subsequently, successful efforts were made to deter any Loyalist reprisal and, two weeks later, the dissident Republican faction declared a ceasefire.

Since then three issues have threatened the maintenance of peace. The Patten Commission's proposed disbandment of the **Royal Ulster Constabulary** (RUC) outraged Unionists whose concerns were only partly assuaged by the British government. The contentious issue of **Orange marches** through Nationalist areas has continued to hit the headlines and although the IRA has maintained its ceasefire, its refusal to decommission its weaponry exposed the precariousness of support for the Agreement and saw the Unionists withdraw from the Assembly in February 2000. The British Secretary of State for Northern Ireland, Peter Mandelson, suspended the Assembly and resumed power a mere two months after its inauguration. However, in a surprising development, on May 6, 2000, the IRA declared its intention to put its weaponry beyond use and allow inspection of some of its arms dumps by independent observers. Eventually, the Assembly was reinstated, but the fragility of the peace process remains exposed, most notably by an ongoing feud between Loyalist paramilitary groups. Nevertheless, whatever the outcome, there is no doubt that the political landscape of Northern Ireland has been irrevocably transformed and, despite all the problems, many people remain cautiously optimistic.

Despite this undoubted political progress, Northern Ireland is still a deeply polarized society. Church attendance has significantly declined, but the population continues to define and divide itself along broadly religious lines between **Catholics** and **Protestants** – though this, for many, is now more a matter of heritage and political allegiance than faith. This process is reinforced by a system of separate schooling (there are few integrated schools in the North), which strengthens already tightknit communities, and by demographic shifts which have seen many once 'mixed' areas becoming predominantly Protestant or Catholic. Painting kerbstones red, white and blue (the colours of the British Union Flag) or flying the Irish Republic's tricolour from the telegraph poles are explicit ways by which communities express their allegiance. Others include the very language used to describe Northern Ireland. The word '**Ulster**' is favoured by Unionists and Loyalists, a term which, while geographically inaccurate – three of the counties of the old Irish province of Ulster are not part of Northern Ireland – essentially retains an historical connection with the Plantation (see p.668), the process of immigration by which Protestants became the majority population. Conversely, Nationalists and Republicans may utilize the term "the **Six Counties**" to express their separation from the remaining 26 counties enshrined in the Partition of Ireland (see p.674), and their consequent rejection of the province of Northern Ireland which Partition created. The term "**The North**" is widely used to avoid such political connotations. The Glossary, on p.744, gives an explanation of some of this political terminology.

Where to go

Much of the Northern Irish countryside is intensely beautiful and thankfully unspoilt. Yet, despite its obvious appeal and the promotional efforts of the Tourist Board, the

PHONE NUMBERS

After reorganization in 1999, all **phone numbers** in Northern Ireland now comprise the UK area code **☎028** plus an eight-digit local number. If you're calling within Northern Ireland, simply use the eight-digit number. Calls into Northern Ireland from another part of the UK need the ☎028 area code as a prefix; but if you're **calling from the Republic**, you need to use a different **☎048** code as a prefix to the eight-digit local number. Calls into Northern Ireland from anywhere else in the world need an international access code, then ☎4428, then the eight-digit local number.

number of visitors has declined since the heady days of 1995 when inquisitive tourists, especially from the Republic and Britain, flocked to discover the delights of this neglected corner. Many are still deterred by the uncertainties of the political situation, and the decline in the punt's value against sterling has enhanced the Republic's alternative attractions. As a result, the tourist industry's growth rate has decelerated, though facilities continue to improve and many new hotels and restaurants have opened in the last few years. Despite this, accommodation can still be scarce during peak periods and festivals, especially in Belfast and Derry and the traditional Northern holiday resorts of Portrush and Portstewart on the north coast and Newcastle in County Down in the southeast.

Most of Northern Ireland's major attractions lie at its fringes. To the north are the green **Glens of Antrim** and a coastline as scenic as anywhere in Ireland, with, as its centrepiece, the bizarre black basalt geometry of the **Giant's Causeway**. In the southeast, **County Down** offers the contrasting beauties of the serene **Strangford Lough** and the brooding mass of the **Mourne Mountains**. To the west, the inland counties of **Tyrone** and **Fermanagh** are dotted with megalithic remains and ruined Plantation castles; while Tyrone's main attraction is the wild and desolate **Sperrin mountain range**, Fermanagh has **Lough Erne**, a fabulous place for watersports, fishing and exploring island monastic remains. Elsewhere, near the huge, central **Lough Neagh**, lie the planned towns of the merchant companies who were entrusted with the resettlement of this region in the seventeenth century, and the rolling countryside of **South Armagh** that is almost unsullied but for lingering military installations.

However, to get to grips with the history of the North, a visit to its cities is essential: **Belfast**, with its grand public buildings, was built on the profits of Victorian industry; **Derry** has shed the security barriers and barbed wire that formerly shrouded its medieval walled town; and the cathedral town of **Armagh**, set on seven hills, is where St Patrick established Christianity in Ireland.

The **Ulster Way**, a footpath which loops around Northern Ireland for 500 miles, takes in many of these scenic highlights. Unfortunately, the efficiency of its maintenance and signposting varies from county to county – so you should check with the local tourist offices before setting out on a long walk.

CHAPTER FOURTEEN

BELFAST

BELFAST is the capital of Northern Ireland and its largest city by some way. More than a third of the province's population live within the Belfast conurbation and, consequently, there's a pace and bustle about the place that you'll find almost nowhere else in Northern Ireland. In appearance it closely resembles Liverpool, Glasgow or any other industrial port across the water, and, similarly, its largely defunct

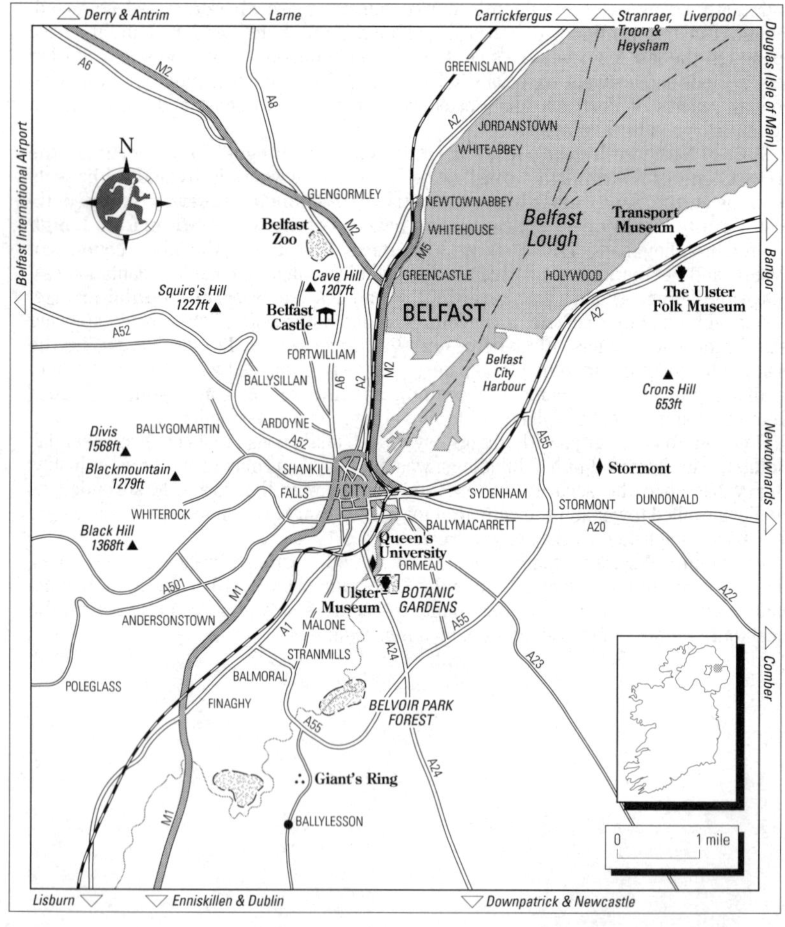

ACCOMMODATION PRICE CODES

Throughout this book, prices of hotels, guesthouses and B&Bs have been graded with the codes below, according to what you can expect to pay for a double room in high season. For more details on accommodation, see p.34.

① Under £26	④ £40–55	⑦ £90–110
② £26–33	⑤ £55–70	⑧ £110–130
③ £33–40	⑥ £70–90	⑨ Over £130

docklands – in which, famously, the *Titanic* was built – are undergoing massive redevelopment. Though the city centre is still characterized by numerous elegant **Victorian** buildings, there's been an enormous transformation here, too, and the streets leading northwards from the hub of Belfast life, **Donegall Square**, are packed with chain stores and new shopping precincts. Yet it is not simply the city's appearance that is changing. Nowhere is the optimism engendered by the peace process more obvious than Belfast at night. Most evenings, the city's bars, clubs and restaurants, especially around the **Golden Mile**, are crammed to overflowing and new venues seem to spring up almost daily. It's almost as though a generation deprived of nightlife by the Troubles has decided to stage a permanent party while it has the chance. Belfast is thriving culturally too: as the tension diminishes, visiting artistes and performers are returning in large numbers and there's been a significant resurgence of homegrown talent. Music, theatre and the visual arts are all flourishing and traditional Irish culture is the subject of rapid rediscovery.

Belfast is a place for getting out and about, and has plenty to experience. This need not take more than a couple of days in the city itself, although Belfast is a good base from which to visit virtually anywhere else in the North. In the centre, concentrate on the glories that the industrial revolution brought: grandiose **architecture** and magnificent Victorian **pubs**. To the south are the lively and influential **Queen's University** and the extensive collections of the **Ulster Museum**, set in the grounds of the **Botanic Gardens**. A climb up **Cave Hill**, to the north, rewards you with marvellous views of the city spread out around the curve of the natural harbour, **Belfast Lough**. Security measures in the city have been considerably relaxed and many of the barriers and controls have been removed. However, the iron blockade known as the **Peace Line** still bisects the Catholic and Protestant communities of **West Belfast**, a grim physical reminder of the city's and country's sectarian divisions.

Some history

Belfast began its life as a cluster of forts built to guard a ford across the **River Farset**, which nowadays runs underground beneath the High Street. The Farset and Lagan rivers form a valley that marks a geological boundary between the basaltic plateau of Antrim and the slaty hills of Down: the softer red Triassic sandstones from which their courses were eroded are responsible for the **bright red** colour of Belfast's brickwork.

Belfast developed slowly at first and, indeed, its history as a city does not really begin until the seventeenth century. A **Norman castle** was built here in 1177, but its influence was always limited, and within a hundred years or so control over the Lagan Valley had reverted firmly to the Irish, under the O'Neills of Clandeboye who had their stronghold to the south in the Castlereagh Hills. Theirs was the traditional Irish pastoral community, their livestock and families spread between the hills and valley plain. Then, in 1604, **Sir Arthur Chichester**, a Devonshire knight whose son was to be the first Earl of Donegall, was "planted" in the area by James I, and shortly afterwards the tiny settlement was granted a charter creating a corporate borough. By the restoration era of

1660 the town was still no more than one hundred and fifty houses in five or six streets, and **Carrickfergus** at the mouth of the lough held the monopoly on trade.

By the end of the seventeenth century, things were looking up. French Huguenots fleeing persecution brought skills which rapidly improved the fortunes of the local linen industry – which, in turn, attracted new workers and wealth. In 1708, the town was almost entirely destroyed by fire, but it was only a temporary setback: throughout the eighteenth century the **cloth trade** and **shipbuilding** expanded tremendously, and the population increased tenfold in a hundred years. Belfast was a city noted for its **liberalism**: in 1784 Protestants gave generously to help build a Catholic church and, in 1791, three Presbyterian Ulstermen formed the society of **United Irishmen**, a gathering embracing Catholics and Protestants on the basis of common Irish nationality. Belfast was the centre of this movement, and thirty Presbyterian ministers in all were accused of taking part in the 1798 **Rebellion**. Six were hanged.

Despite the movement's Belfast origins, the rebellion in the North was in fact an almost complete failure, and the forces of reaction backed by the wealthy landlords quickly and ruthlessly stamped it down. Within two generations most Protestants had abandoned the Nationalist cause, and Belfast as a sectarian town was born. In the **nineteenth century**, Presbyterian ministers like the Reverend Henry Cooke and Hugh (Roaring) Hanna began openly to attack the Catholic Church, and the **sectarian divide** became wider and increasingly violent. In 1835, several people were sabred to death in Sandy Row, and sporadic outbreaks of violence have continued from that day on. Meanwhile, the nineteenth century saw vigorous commercial and industrial expansion. In 1888, Queen Victoria granted Belfast **city** status; the city fathers' gratitude to her is stamped on buildings throughout the centre. By this time the population had risen to 208,000 and, with the continued improvement in both the linen and shipbuilding industries, the population exceeded even that of Dublin by the end of the century.

THE TWENTIETH CENTURY TO THE PRESENT

Although **Partition** and the creation of Northern Ireland with Belfast as its capital inevitably boosted the city's status, decline has been fairly constant over recent years. Bombing in World War II destroyed much of the city, and in the past fifteen years great tracts of West Belfast have been pulled down in a belated attempt to improve living conditions. Nowadays the city is struggling very hard for **revitalization**, and billions of pounds are being poured in from Britain and the European Union, in the hope that economic growth might help to bring about a more hopeful future. The linen industry, which had almost completely disappeared, is undergoing a modest revival in high-fashion clothing, and shipbuilding is also surfacing again after reaching rock bottom.

Arrival, information and transport

Belfast is served by two **airports**. Most flights arrive at **Belfast International Airport**, nineteen miles west of the city in Aldergrove; from here, there are airport buses to Europa bus station (Mon–Sat every 30min 7.10am–11.20pm; Sun hourly 6.50am–11.20pm; £5 single, £8 return). A taxi costs around £25. A handful of carriers use the tiny **Belfast City Airport**, three miles northeast of the centre, from where Citybus #21 runs to City Hall on Donegall Square (Mon–Sat every 20–30min 6am–10.20pm; on Sun the route is served by buses #101 and #102 hourly 9.35am–9.35pm; Mon–Sat 90p, Sun 60p). Alternatively, trains run from Sydenham Halt, a short walk from the City Airport terminal, to Central Station (Mon–Fri every 30min, less frequently at weekends; 90p). A taxi from City Airport to the centre costs around £5.

Ferries from Britain arrive at various dockside termini. The Seacat catamarans from Heysham and Troon, and summer-only boats from the Isle of Man run by Isle of Man

Steam Packet Company all use **Donegall Quay**. From here to the city centre is about a fifteen-minute walk, or a £3 taxi-ride. Stena high-speed ferries from Stranraer dock a little further north at **Corry Road** – a taxi from here will cost around £4 or £5. Norse Irish Ferries from Liverpool dock even further north on **West Bank Road**; expect to pay a taxi fare from here of at least £5. P&O ferries from Cairnryan and Fleetwood, as well as some Stena boats from Stranraer, dock at the town of **Larne**, twenty miles north (see p.560), connected by Ulsterbus to the Laganside Buscentre and by train to Yorkgate and Central stations.

The majority of **trains** call at **Great Victoria Street Station** in the centre, with the exception of trains from Dublin and Larne which terminate at **Central Station** near the Waterfront Hall on East Bridge Street, a little way east of the centre. From Central Station you can hop on a connecting train to Great Victoria Street Station which stops midway at Botanic and City Hospital stations – both of which are useful if you're staying in the university quarter.

Express **buses** arrive at one of Belfast's two stations. The **Europa** bus station, alongside Great Victoria Street train station in Glengall Street behind the *Hastings Europa Hotel*, handles services to Armagh, Derry, west Down, Fermanagh and Tyrone as well as to the Republic, the airports and the ferry terminals. The **Laganside Buscentre** in Queen's Square near the Albert Clock serves Antrim, east Derry and east Down. Both of them are very central and well served by Citybus services.

The **Centrelink** bus runs every twelve minutes on a very useful circular route from and to Central Station, via Donegall Square, the Europa bus station and the Laganside Buscentre.

Information

The **tourist information centre** is at 59 North St (July & Aug Mon–Sat 9.15am–7pm, Sun noon–4pm; rest of year Mon–Sat 9.15am–5.15pm; ☎028/9024 6609, *www.ni-tourism.com*), though at the time of writing it was due to transfer to new premises at 35 Donegall Place during the first half of 2001 – phone or check the Web site to be certain. They stock the usual supply of brochures and maps, as well as providing an accommodation booking service (£1 in the Belfast area, £2 elsewhere). They also take credit-card bookings for accommodation on toll-free ☎0800/404050. There's a 24-hour touch-screen outside the office, which can be a lifesaver if you find yourself bedless late at night. There are tourist offices at both **airports** – Belfast International (daily 24hr) and Belfast City (daily 5.30am–10pm, Sat closes 9pm). **Bord Fáilte**, which supplies tourist information for the Republic, is located at 53 Castle St (Mon–Fri 9am–5pm; March–Sept also Sat 9am–12.30pm; ☎028/9032 7888).

For a guide to entertainment in the city, consult the fortnightly listings freesheet *The Big List*, which is available at the tourist office, pubs, clubs and record shops. The *Belfast Telegraph* evening newspaper or the Tourist Board's own monthly freebie, *Artslink*, are also good sources. The Belfast Visitor and Convention Bureau (*www.gotobelfast.com*) produces the free *Belfast Pocket Guide* and the more substantial *Belfast Visitor Guide* – both free and available at tourist offices.

City transport and tours

Although you can easily **walk** around the city centre, distances to some of the outlying attractions are considerable, and a number of places to stay are also a little way out. The excellent **Citybus** company provides frequent buses to almost every conceivable Belfast destination, while the blue and white long-distance services of **Ulsterbus** – which principally covers Northern Ireland outside Belfast – connect to some of the sights on the city's fringes.

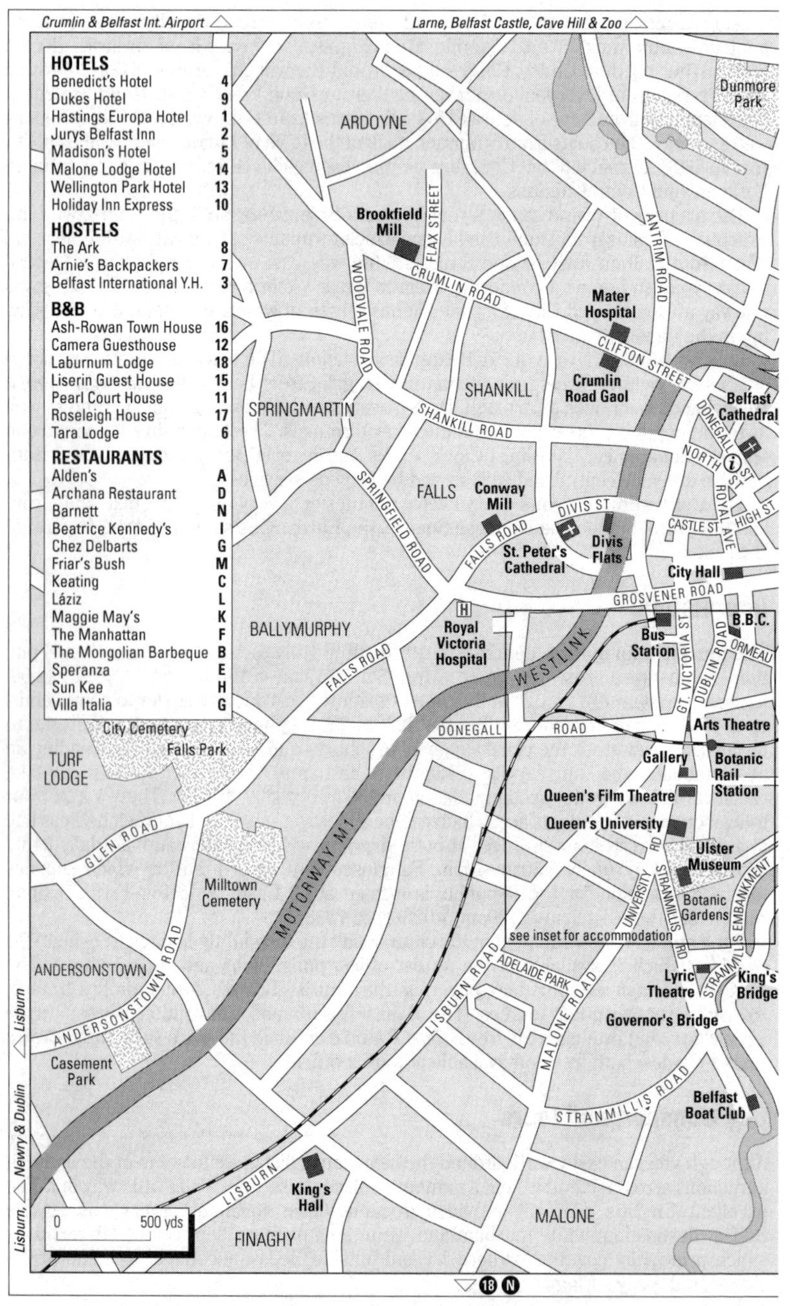

Crumlin & Belfast Int. Airport
Larne, Belfast Castle, Cave Hill & Zoo
HOTELS
Benedict's Hotel 4
Dukes Hotel 9
Hastings Europa Hotel 1
Jurys Belfast Inn 2
Madison's Hotel 5
Malone Lodge Hotel 14
Wellington Park Hotel 13
Holiday Inn Express 10
HOSTELS
The Ark 8
Arnie's Backpackers 7
Belfast International Y.H. 3
B&B
Ash-Rowan Town House 16
Camera Guesthouse 12
Laburnum Lodge 18
Liserin Guest House 15
Pearl Court House 11
Roseleigh House 17
Tara Lodge 6
RESTAURANTS
Alden's A
Archana Restaurant D
Barnett N
Beatrice Kennedy's I
Chez Delbarts G
Friar's Bush M
Keating C
Láziz L
Maggie May's K
The Manhattan F
The Mongolian Barbeque B
Speranza E
Sun Kee H
Villa Italia G
ARDOYNE
Dunmore Park
Brookfield Mill
FLAX STREET
WOODVALE ROAD
CRUMLIN ROAD
ANTRIM ROAD
Mater Hospital
CLIFTON STREET
Crumlin Road Gaol
SHANKILL
SPRINGMARTIN
SHANKILL ROAD
Belfast Cathedral
DONEGALL ST
NORTH ST
ROYAL AVE
HIGH ST
SPRINGFIELD ROAD
FALLS
Conway Mill
DIVIS ST
CASTLE ST
FALLS ROAD
St. Peter's Cathedral
Divis Flats
City Hall
GROSVENER ROAD
BALLYMURPHY
Royal Victoria Hospital
Bus Station
B.B.C.
GT. VICTORIA ST
DUBLIN ROAD
ORMEAU
WESTLINK
FALLS ROAD
City Cemetery
Falls Park
TURF LODGE
DONEGALL ROAD
Arts Theatre
Gallery
Botanic Rail Station
Queen's Film Theatre
Queen's University
Ulster Museum
GLEN ROAD
MOTORWAY M1
Milltown Cemetery
UNIVERSITY RD
STRANMILLIS RD
Botanic Gardens
STRANMILLIS EMBANKMENT
see inset for accommodation
ANDERSONSTOWN
ANDERSONSTOWN ROAD
ADELAIDE PARK
LISBURN ROAD
MALONE ROAD
Lyric Theatre
King's Bridge
Governor's Bridge
Casement Park
STRANMILLIS ROAD
Belfast Boat Club
Lisburn
Lisburn, Newry & Dublin
LISBURN
King's Hall
0 500 yds
FINAGHY
MALONE
18 N

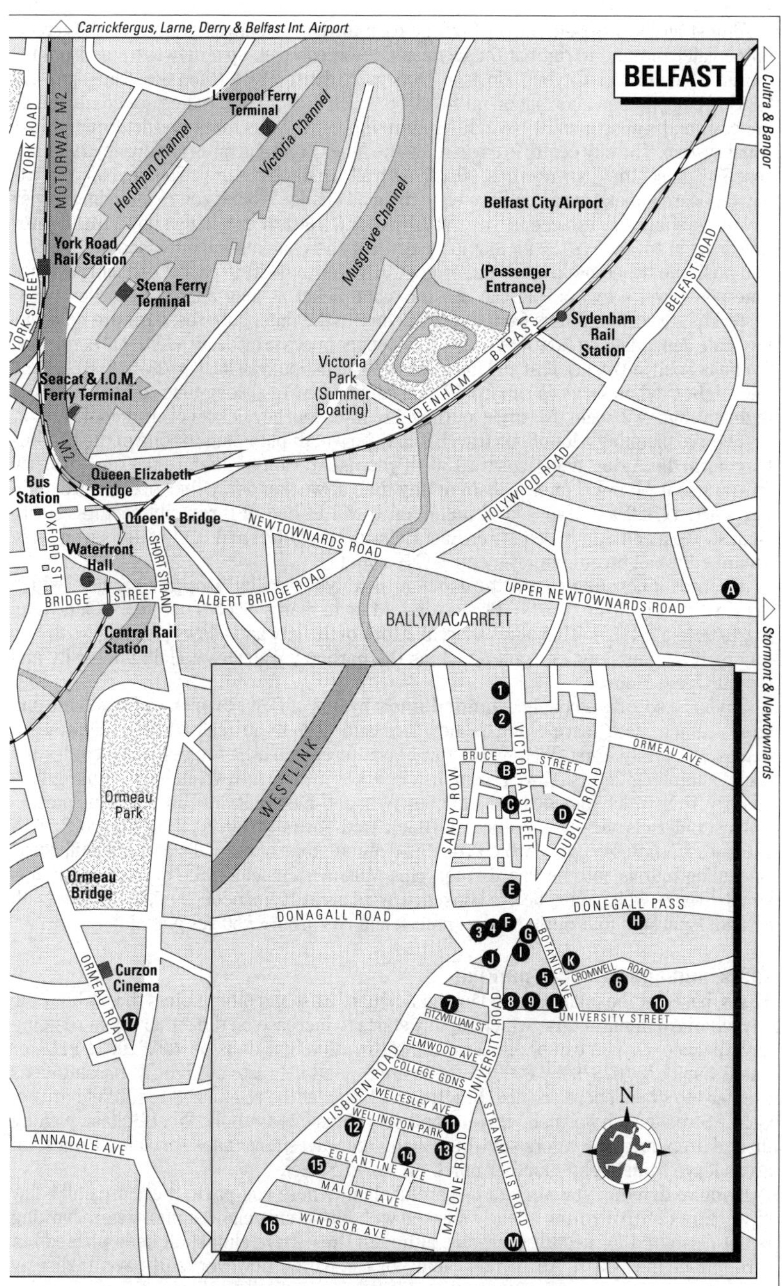
Carrickfergus, Larne, Derry & Belfast Int. Airport
BELFAST
Cultra & Bangor
Stormont & Newtownards
Liverpool Ferry Terminal
Herdman Channel
Victoria Channel
Musgrave Channel
YORK ROAD
MOTORWAY M2
York Road Rail Station
YORK STREET
Stena Ferry Terminal
Seacat & I.O.M. Ferry Terminal
M2
Belfast City Airport
(Passenger Entrance)
Sydenham Rail Station
SYDENHAM BYPASS
BELFAST ROAD
Victoria Park (Summer Boating)
HOLYWOOD ROAD
Bus Station
Queen Elizabeth Bridge
Queen's Bridge
OXFORD ST
NEWTOWNARDS ROAD
SHORT STRAND
Waterfront Hall
BRIDGE STREET
ALBERT BRIDGE ROAD
UPPER NEWTOWNARDS ROAD
Central Rail Station
BALLYMACARRETT
WESTLINK
Ormeau Park
Ormeau Bridge
ORMEAU ROAD
Curzon Cinema
ANNADALE AVE
SANDY ROW
VICTORIA STREET
BRUCE STREET
ORMEAU AVE
DUBLIN ROAD
DONAGALL ROAD
DONEGALL PASS
BOTANIC AVE
CROMWELL ROAD
UNIVERSITY STREET
FITZWILLIAM ST
UNIVERSITY ROAD
ELMWOOD AVE
COLLEGE GDNS
LISBURN ROAD
WELLESLEY AVE
WELLINGTON PARK
EGLANTINE AVE
MALONE AVE
WINDSOR AVE
MALONE ROAD
STRANMILLIS ROAD
N

Almost all local **buses** set off from or pass through Donegall Square or the streets immediately around it, right at the city centre. You can pick up a network map from the tourist office or the Citybus kiosk in Donegall Square West (Mon–Fri 8am–6pm, Sat 8.30am–5.30pm; bus information on ☎028/9024 6485). Note that routes are combined on Sundays and, consequently, have different numbers. Citybus **fares** are determined by a zonal system. The city centre is covered by the Inner Zone and fares for journeys within it cost 50p; most other journeys cost 90p, though all Sunday fares are a flat-rate 60p. You can pay on board – make sure you have enough small change – but if you're intending to visit any of the suburban attractions, you'll save time and a little money if you buy a **multi-journey** ticket in advance (£3.20 for four journeys, from newsagents and other shops citywide). You push the ticket into a machine (or get the driver to do it) to cancel one journey each time you travel – two people can use the same ticket as long as it is cancelled twice. Ulsterbus serves the routes from the city centre to the outer suburbs; fares are on a sliding scale depending on how far you go. Citystopper buses provide an additional service on the Falls Road in West Belfast and the Lisburn Road in South Belfast (#523–538). Weekend **late-night** Citybus services run from Donegall Square West along nine routes (Fri & Sat nights at 1am & 2.30am; £3 single journey, £10 multi-journey ticket covering four trips).

If you're planning a lot of bus travel, it may be worth plumping for one of the Citybus **travel cards**. A **day** ticket costs £3.30 (if you use it Mon–Fri before 9.30am) or £2.60 (if you use it Mon–Fri after 9.30am or any time at weekends). Other options are a **silver card** (£7.50 for seven days' unlimited travel in one of three city sectors: North Belfast, West and South Belfast, or East Belfast) or a **gold card** (£11.50 for seven days' unlimited travel throughout the entire City zone).

A recent innovation to aid the footsore is Citybus's **City Hopper** service, which departs hourly from Castle Place (end May to early Sept Tues–Sat 10am–4pm; ☎028/9045 8484; £5). This takes a circular tour of the city and allows passengers to hop on or off at nine stops en route (such as the harbour, Waterfront Hall, university and Grand Opera House).

Citybus also runs a couple of **guided tours** by bus of Belfast which can save time and shoe leather. Both leave from Castle Place and cost £8.50 (call ☎028/9045 8484 for details). The City Tour (Wed & Sat 1pm) lasts three and a half hours and includes the architectural highlights. More recent history is covered by the two-and-a-half-hour Living History Tour which includes visits to both West and East Belfast (Thurs & Sun 1pm).

West Belfast is one of the features of **Black Taxi Tours** (☎0800/052 3914 or ☎028/9064 2264; *www.belfasttours.com*) which runs a 90-minute tour of the Falls and Shankill roads (including murals and the Peace Line), plus Milltown Cemetery, the docks and the university. Tours, which must be pre-booked, leave daily at 10am, noon, 2pm, 4pm, 6pm (with an additional 8pm tour during the summer), and cost from £7.50 per person.

Taxis, minicabs and car-parking

Taxis, based at the main rank in Donegall Square East and other points throughout the city, charge a minimum £2, which rapidly starts to increase on the meter if you're going any distance. Or you can phone a **minicab** (try Blue Star Cabs on ☎028/9024 3118, or Value Cabs on ☎028/9032 0000) – these are a good idea late at night as passing taxis are hard to grab. There are also **black taxis** based at the revitalized Smithfield area of Castle Street which normally travel along set routes into Catholic West Belfast, picking up and dropping passengers anywhere along the way; similar cabs servicing Protestant areas leave from slightly further north on North Street.

If you're **driving**, you need to be careful about where you **park**: there are still a few city-centre **control zones** (clearly marked with black-and-yellow signs), where parking is not permitted for security reasons, although these have almost all been phased out throughout the North. You'll find plenty of car parks, however, and pay-and-display parking operates in many of the streets. Following a number of recent arson attacks, you'd be strongly advised if you're driving a car with **Republic of Ireland plates** to seek secure, off-street parking at night.

Accommodation

Although tourism has waned in the years following the 1994 ceasefire, the number of places offering **accommodation** has increased, especially at the top end of the range, reflecting continued optimism in the city's future. However, there's still a relative dearth of budget places and it's worth booking ahead in the summer season.

Much of the city's accommodation is concentrated south of the centre in the **university quarter** on Botanic Avenue, Eglantine Avenue and the Malone Road. Many hotels and guesthouses are geared towards business travellers and, consequently, frequently offer significant reductions for weekend breaks.

Hotels

Virtually all these **hotels** have satellite TV and modem points in the rooms.

Benedicts, 7–21 Bradbury Place, Shaftesbury Square (☎028/9059 1999, *info@benedictshotel.co.uk*). Undoubtedly Belfast's funkiest hotel, with excellent rooms featuring king-sized beds and one of the city's most popular club venues. ⑥.

Dukes Hotel, 65 University St (☎028/9023 6666, *www.dukes-hotel.com*). Smart, modern redevelopment featuring 21 elegant bedrooms, a small gym and sauna, popular bars and a restaurant serving Glenarm salmon. ⑧.

Hastings Europa Hotel, Great Victoria St (☎028/9032 7000, *www.hastingshotels.com*). Often bombed in the past, this city-centre hotel near the Opera House has now been grandly refurbished. The bar, with its huge windows overlooking the city's main drag, is a poseur's paradise. ⑨.

Hilton Belfast, 4 Lanyon Place (☎028/9027 7000, *www.hilton.com*). Huge and lavish dockland addition to the Belfast skyline with staggering views across the city and prices to match (a double room here costs almost £200 per night). ⑨.

Holiday Inn Express, 106 University St (☎028/9031 1909, *www.holiday-inn.ireland.com*). Another grand modern hotel with swish decor and all facilities. ⑤.

Jurys Belfast Inn, Fisherwick Place, Great Victoria St (☎028/9053 3500, *www.jurys.com*). A gargantuan 190-bed branch of the Dublin chain, with rooms capable of taking up to 3 adults or 2 adults and 2 children – handily, prices are per room no matter how many stay. ⑤.

Madison's Hotel, 59–63 Botanic Ave (☎028/9033 0040). A plush, economically priced hotel with spacious rooms and a popular bar/nightclub. ⑥.

Malone Lodge Hotel, 60 Eglantine Ave (☎028/9038 2409). Welcoming, completely refurbished hotel near Queen's, with off-street parking and a notable restaurant. ⑦.

The McCausland Hotel, 34–38 Victoria St (☎028/9022 0200, *www.slh.com/causland*) Recently installed in elegant buildings long unused, and ideally situated near the Albert Clock and Laganside Buscentre. The restaurant and bar are excellent, and rooms are spacious and well-furnished. ⑨.

Wellington Park Hotel, 21 Malone Rd (☎028/9038 1111). Comfortable four-star business hotel in the university area, with a bar probably best known as a cruising ground for singles. ⑧.

B&Bs

Ash-Rowan Town House, 12 Windsor Ave (☎028/9066 1983). Grand guesthouse off Malone Road, once home to Thomas Andrews (designer of the *Titanic*); the breakfasts are stupendous. ⑥.

Camera Guest House, 44 Wellington Park (☎028/9066 0026, *malonedrumm@hotmail.com*). Very luxurious and elegantly decorated town house. ⑤.

The Kitchen Bar, 16 Victoria Square (☎028/9032 4901). Cosy accommodation bang in the city centre in one of Belfast's best bars; facilities are self-catering. ④.

Laburnum Lodge, 16 Deramore Park (☎028/9066 5183) Pleasant en-suite accommodation in a quiet street a mile down Malone Road. ⑤.

Liserin Guest House, 17 Eglantine Ave (☎028/9066 0769). A cosy, well-equipped B&B. ③.

Pearl Court House, 11 Malone Rd (☎028/9066 6145). Large house with some family and triple rooms. ④.

Roseleigh House, 19 Rosetta Park (☎028/9064 4414). Deluxe accommodation in a quiet area at the bottom of the Ormeau Road. ④.

Tara Lodge, 36 Cromwell Rd (☎028/9059 0900, *www.taralodge.com*). Swish decor and excellent facilities in this guesthouse off Botanic Avenue. ⑤.

Hostels

The Ark, 18 University St (☎028/9032 9626). Clean, cosy, well-equipped and welcoming terraced house, with 24 beds, laundry and cooking facilities.

Arnie's Backpackers, 63 Fitzwilliam St (☎028/9024 2867). Friendly independent hostel with 22 beds in five-dorm rooms, plus laundry and cooking facilities.

Belfast International Youth Hostel, 22–32 Donegall Rd (☎028/9031 5435). Modern 124-bed hostel (with some double rooms) near the Protestant enclave of Sandy Row; all-year-round 24-hour staffing; no self-catering, but has restaurant. Booking ahead is advisable. From £10.

The Linen House, 18 Kent St (☎028/9058 6400, *www.belfasthostel.com*). New, wheelchair-friendly 130-bed hostel bang in the city centre near the tourist office; also with six private rooms and bike rental.

The City

The physical core of Belfast is **Donegall Square**: in the centre of it stands the City Hall, and buses and taxis depart for every part of the city from the sides of the square. The main shopping area lies a stone's throw north and the main areas for entertainment and accommodation are immediately south. Most of the grand old Victorian buildings which characterize the city are in the north and east, towards the river.

Further out, **North Belfast** boasts Cave Hill, with its castle and zoo, and **South Belfast** is home to the "**Golden Mile**", leading down to the university, Botanic Gardens and Ulster Museum. The River Lagan flows from Belfast Lough along the eastern side of the city centre and offers riverside walks. The riverside is also the focus for the most radical development in the last few years, the Laganside. In **East Belfast**, across the river beyond the great cranes of the Harland & Wolff shipyard, lies suburbia and very little of interest apart from Stormont Castle, the former Northern Irish parliament and home to the new Assembly. Working-class **West Belfast**, by contrast, seems almost a separate city in its own right, divided from the rest by the speeding traffic of the Westlink motorway.

The city centre

Belfast's **city centre** is fairly compact and easy to wander around. The heart of the old city can be found in the narrow atmospheric lanes of the former commercial district, the **Entries**, about five minutes' walk northeast of Donegall Square. On a grander scale, many of Belfast's most handsome buildings, evidence of the city's transformation during the industrial revolution, are concentrated further north and east, between **St Anne's Cathedral** and the River Lagan. Right by the river you'll find the Lagan Weir and a little further south, the huge new Laganside development, currently focused on the **Waterfront Hall**.

Donegall Square

City Hall dominates Donegall Square and the entire centre of Belfast. Completed in 1906, it's a smug-looking building of bright white Portland stone, quadrangular and

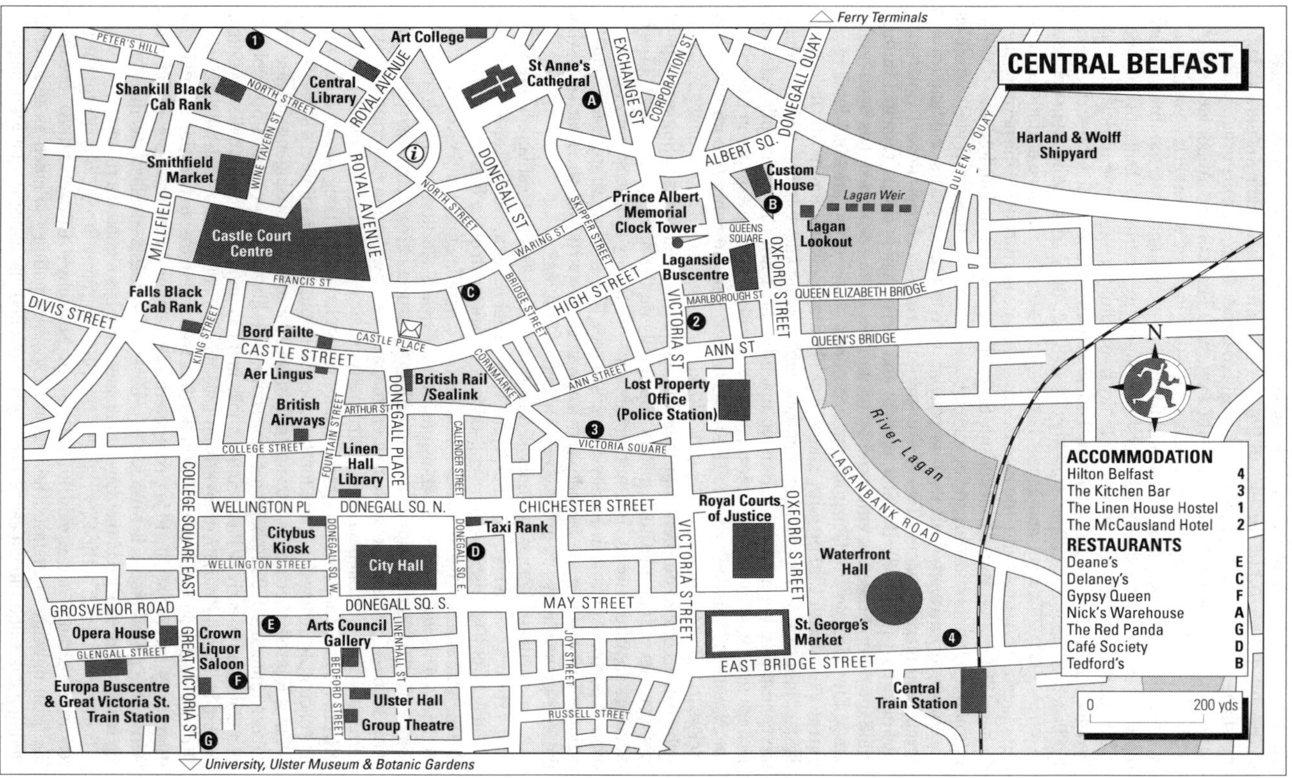
CENTRAL BELFAST
Ferry Terminals
Art College
PETER'S HILL
Shankill Black Cab Rank
NORTH STREET
Central Library
ROYAL AVENUE
St Anne's Cathedral
EXCHANGE ST
CORPORATION ST
DONEGALL QUAY
QUEEN'S QUAY
Harland & Wolff Shipyard
ALBERT SQ.
Custom House
Lagan Weir
Lagan Lookout
Smithfield Market
WINE TAVERN ST
MILLFIELD
Castle Court Centre
ROYAL AVENUE
NORTH STREET
DONEGALL ST
WARING ST
SKIPPER STREET
Prince Albert Memorial Clock Tower
QUEENS SQUARE
Laganside Buscentre
OXFORD STREET
FRANCIS ST
HIGH STREET
BRIDGE STREET
MARLBOROUGH ST
QUEEN ELIZABETH BRIDGE
Falls Black Cab Rank
DIVIS STREET
KING STREET
Bord Failte
CASTLE PLACE
CASTLE STREET
VICTORIA ST
ANN ST
QUEEN'S BRIDGE
N
Aer Lingus
British Rail /Sealink
CORNMARKET
ANN STREET
Lost Property Office (Police Station)
British Airways
ARTHUR ST
FOUNTAIN STREET
DONEGALL PLACE
CALLENDER STREET
River Lagan
COLLEGE STREET
Linen Hall Library
VICTORIA SQUARE
LAGANBANK ROAD
COLLEGE SQUARE EAST
WELLINGTON PL
DONEGALL SQ. N.
CHICHESTER STREET
Royal Courts of Justice
Citybus Kiosk
DONEGALL SQ. W.
City Hall
DONEGALL SQ. E.
Taxi Rank
VICTORIA STREET
OXFORD STREET
Waterfront Hall
WELLINGTON STREET
DONEGALL SQ. S.
MAY STREET
GROSVENOR ROAD
Opera House
GREAT VICTORIA ST
Crown Liquor Saloon
Arts Council Gallery
LINENHALL ST
JOY STREET
St. George's Market
GLENGALL STREET
BEDFORD STREET
EAST BRIDGE STREET
Europa Buscentre & Great Victoria St. Train Station
Ulster Hall
Group Theatre
RUSSELL STREET
Central Train Station
ACCOMMODATION
Hilton Belfast 4
The Kitchen Bar 3
The Linen House Hostel 1
The McCausland Hotel 2
RESTAURANTS
Deane's E
Delaney's C
Gypsy Queen F
Nick's Warehouse A
The Red Panda G
Café Society D
Tedford's B
0
200 yds
University, Ulster Museum & Botanic Gardens

squat, and with its turrets, saucer domes, scrolls and pinnacle pots, is representative of all the styles absorbed by the British Empire. In front of the building stands an imposing statue of Queen Victoria, the apotheosis of imperialism, her maternal gaze unerringly cast across the rooftops towards the Protestant Shankill area. At her feet, sculpted in bronze, stand proud figures representing the City Fathers' world-view: a young scholar, his mother with spinning spool, and father with mallet and boat, the three of them representing "learning, linen and liners", the alliterative bedrock of Belfast's heritage.

The City Hall offers the only opportunity to be shown around one of Belfast's many Neoclassical buildings; guided **tours** last 45 minutes (June–Sept Mon–Fri 10.30am, 11.30am & 2.30pm, Sat 2.30pm; Oct–May Mon–Sat 2.30pm; advance booking necessary on ☎028/9032 0202; free) and access is through a security entrance at the rear, opposite Linenhall Street. Inside, the **main dome**, with its unreachable whispering gallery, arches 173ft above you. Modelled on St Paul's Cathedral in London, the dome is adorned around its rim with zodiac signs, both painted and in stained glass windows. The marbled **entrance hall** itself is palatial, with staircase pillars, colonnades and bronze and marble statues. Two of the statues portray Frederick Robert Chichester, Earl of Belfast (1827–53): the first, upright and stern, stands on the principal landing, while the other, Frederick embraced by his mother on his deathbed, has been hauled out of the rain into the Octagon entrance porch. Also on the principal landing is a **mural**, executed in 1951 by John Luke and celebrating Belfast's now mostly defunct traditional industries – ropemaking, shipbuilding, weaving and spinning. Oddly though, the central position in the picture is occupied by the Town Crier, a cryptic reference perhaps to Belfast having the oldest continuously published newspaper in the world – *The Newsletter*, founded in 1737. The tour also takes in the **robing room**, where the trick is to ask to try on one of the civic cloaks for a snapshot. The building's highlight is the oak-decorated **council chamber** with its hand-carved wainscotting and councillors' pews as well as a visitors' gallery (open only on the first of the month). Council meetings are often stormy, but, in their absence, it's a very urbane scene with a backdrop of portraits of British royalty and aristocracy. The seating arrangement puts the majority Unionists on the far side, with the rest of the parties on the near side, while the ever-present press sit in between as a kind of firebreak.

At the northwest corner of Donegall Square stands Belfast's oldest library, the **Linen Hall Library** (Mon–Fri 9.30am–5.30pm, Thurs until 8.30pm, Sat 9.30am–4pm), established in 1788. The Irish literature collection occupies much of the first floor, and a grand curving staircase sweeps upwards to the second where language and reference books are shelved, as well as what is known as the "Political Collection", a unique accumulation of over 80,000 publications dealing with every aspect of Northern Irish political life since 1966 – a range of literature that encompasses every election poster printed since then, as well as documents ranging from party political ephemera, doctoral theses sent in from all over the world, to prison letters smuggled out of Long Kesh. This radical approach is not a new departure for the Linen Hall: one of the institution's librarians was Thomas Russell, executed in Downpatrick in 1803 for inciting uprising in sympathy with Robert Emmett's 1798 Rebellion down south. The library also contains probably the best collection of early Belfast printed books in the country and has a small selection on display, including *Paddy's Resource*, from 1796, an early collection of Irish patriotic songs. The Linenhall is an independent institution and visitors are free to examine its collection (tours daily except Sat): there is a computerized catalogue on the first floor, use of which is free, though a donation is welcome. The library also boasts excellent facilities for tracing family trees, stocks all the daily newspapers and has a good tea room.

Between the back of the City Hall and the BBC, on Alfred Street, look out for the turrets of the strange and wonderful Catholic **St Malachy's Church** (1844), the finest Victorian building in Belfast. The interior resembles nothing so much as an inverted wedding cake, and the fan-vaulted ceiling is modelled on that of Henry VII's chapel in

London's Westminster Abbey. Other elaborate features are the canopied pulpit and carved marble altar both dating from a 1926 restoration.

The Entries and the High Street

The streets northwards from Donegall Square lead you into downtown Belfast. The main shopping street, **Donegall Place**, continues into **Royal Avenue** and houses familiar chain-store names. Castle Place, off Donegall Place, was once the hub of Victorian Belfast, and the grand old department stores here, in creams, pinks and browns, have only recently been transformed into a plethora of voguish shops, though, happily, only the ground floors have been converted, leaving the lofty grandeur of the storey above undisturbed. New structures, too, have risen swiftly, but they at least tend to reflect the rhythm and sheer bulk of their nineteenth-century forebears. Much of this zone is pedestrianized (though buses go through), and nearly every conceivable shopping need can be supplied in this relatively small area.

The pedestrianized **Cornmarket**, marked by a cap-hooded red bandstand, is a regular gathering place for the city's youth, though most prevalent are the religious ranters. This spot – or near enough to it – is where Henry Joy McCracken was hanged, after leading the Antrim rebels in the ill-fated (and in the North almost farcically unsuccessful) 1798 Rebellion.

Nearby, along Ann Street, and off down any left or right turning, you're among the narrow alleyways known as the **Entries**. You'll stumble across some great old saloon **bars** down here, like *The Morning Star* in Pottinger's Entry, with its large frosted windows and Parisian café-like counter; *The Globe* in Joy's Entry; and *White's Tavern* in Winecellar Entry (off High Street), the oldest pub in the city. Crown Entry was where the "Society of United Irishmen" was born; it was led by the Protestant triumvirate of Wolfe Tone, McCracken and Samuel Nielson. Nielson also printed his own newspaper in this area, the *Northern Star*. Heavily influenced by the French revolutionary ideals of liberty, equality and fraternity, the newspaper's inflammatory material led to him being hounded out of town.

Across the **High Street** to the north, a similar set of Entries used to run through to Waring Street, but were destroyed by bombing in World War II. Still, this end of the High Street, with the River Farset running underground, is the oldest part of the city, its atmosphere in places redolent of the eighteenth century. On Waring Street itself stands the **War Memorial Building**, containing a small exhibition (Mon–Fri 9am–5pm; free) commemorating the role of Northern Ireland in World War II. At the rear is the **Royal Ulster Rifles Museum** (Mon–Fri 10am–12.30pm & 2–4pm), with the usual array of insignia, uniforms and weaponry, as well as Billy, a rather despondent-looking regimental dog, stuffed in 1901. The building at **2 Waring Street** – now a bank – was originally built as a market house in 1769, but is more renowned as the venue for the 1792 Belfast Harp Festival: by the end of the eighteenth century, the old Gaelic harping tradition had reached almost terminal decline and the convention was a deliberate attempt by its organizers, the United Irish Society, to record some of the harpers' airs for posterity. The transcriber, Edmund Bunting, was stimulated to tour Ireland collecting further airs, 77 of which were published in his illustrious collection of 1809.

At the eastern docks end of the High Street stands the **Prince Albert Memorial Clock Tower**, built in 1867–69 and tilting slightly off the perpendicular as a result of its construction upon gradually sinking wooden piles. It's a strange memorial, especially as Prince Albert never had anything to do with Belfast, but it's a handy landmark.

Along the riverfront

North of the Albert Memorial you'll come across a series of grand edifices inspired by the same civic vanity as that behind the design of the City Hall. The restored **Custom**

House on Donegall Quay is a Corinthian-style, E-shaped edifice designed between 1854 and 1857 by Charles Lanyon who was responsible for several of the city's finest buildings. Unfortunately, it's not open to the public, leaving you unable to verify rumours of fantastic art masterpieces stored in its basements – though it is known that Anthony Trollope, the nineteenth-century novelist (and not-so-well-known inventor of the pillar box), once worked here as a surveyor's clerk.

Just beyond the Custom House on Donegall Quay is the ambitious **Laganside** development project, the first component of which to be completed was the **Lagan Weir**, designed to protect the city against flooding. Millions of pounds have been pumped into dredging the river to maintain water levels and revive the much depleted fish population – successfully it seems: there was salmon fishing on the weir's inauguration day.

You can find out more about the weir project at the **Lagan Lookout** (April–Sept Mon–Fri 11am–5pm, Sat noon–5pm, Sun 2–5pm; Oct–March Tues–Fri 11am–3.30pm, Sat 1–4.30pm, Sun 2–4.30pm; £3), a raised circular visitor centre on the riverfront. It also explores the river's crucial role in the successful development of the city as a centre for industries as diverse as linen, tobacco, ropemaking and shipbuilding – a glance across the river to the Harland & Wolff shipyard confirms that the last-named still survives. Windows all round the centre match Belfast landmarks to explanations of their significance, interwoven with fascinating potted histories of local characters.

In summer, **boat trips** on the Lagan (daily 2pm, 3pm & 4pm; £3) leave from opposite the Laganside Buscentre just south of the Lookout. If the sea air's twitching your nostrils, head further north towards the Seacat terminal where you'll find the restored **Harbour Office** and nearby **Sinclair Seamen's Church** (Sun services 11.30am & 7pm; visits Wed 2–4.30pm) on Corporation Square. The latter is yet another Lanyon design, but it's the contents that are most intriguing. Sailors must have felt truly at home among the cornucopia of maritime equipment – an old-fashioned wooden wheel, the bell from *HMS Hood*, assorted navigation lights and a ship's prow for a pulpit.

The most obvious changes to the city's skyline can be seen from almost any river viewpoint: further south along Oxford Street sits the glittering two-thousand-seater **Waterfront Hall** concert venue, a housing development, and a *Hilton* hotel. The gargantuan **Odyssey** leisure complex opened with much pomp in late 2000, featuring a 10,000-seater indoor arena, cinemas, the W5 Science Centre and a complex of bars, restaurants and shops.

St Anne's Cathedral and around

Up Victoria Street, a hundred yards north of the Albert Memorial, you'll hit the eastern end of **Waring Street** and another of Charles Lanyon's designs, the **Belfast Banking Company** building of 1845, now the Northern Bank. Originally containing eighteenth-century Assembly Rooms, it was transformed by Lanyon into a palazzo-style remodelling of Barry's Reform Club in London. Also on Waring Street, you'll come across the **Ulster Bank** (1860), an indulgent Italianate building of rich yellow sandstone, fronted by a spate of fluted pillars and, up on the parapet, decorated Grecian urns flanking an allegorical representation of war maidens. The building is surrounded by intricate wrought-iron railings and a few reassembled stubby, but quaint, Victorian street lamps.

If you head back down Waring Street to the city centre, a couple of hundred yards off to the right (north) up Donegall Street you'll find the most monolithic of all these grand buildings, the Protestant **St Anne's Cathedral**, a neo-Romanesque basilica started in 1899. Entrance is via the huge west door and immediately to the right is an intricately designed representation of the Creation on the baptistry ceiling, consisting of 150,000 tiny pieces of glass. Most significant, however, is its only tomb, marked by a simple slab on the floor of the south aisle and containing the body of **Lord Edward Henry Carson** (1854–1935). His is a name that Ulster has never forgotten: the bodily symbol of Partition, he's seen either as the hero who saved Ulster or the villain who sabotaged the country's independence. A Dubliner of Scots-Presbyterian background, Carson took the decision in 1910 to accept the leadership of the opposition to Home Rule, which in effect inextricably allied him to the Ulster Unionist resistance movement, an association which is about the only thing for which he is remembered. Yet his personality and integrity went far deeper than this. He abhorred religious intolerance, and behind the exterior of a zealous crusader was a man who sincerely believed that Ireland couldn't prosper without Britain and only wished that a federalist answer could have involved a united Ireland. Nonetheless, this was the same man who, as a brilliant orator at the bar, and in the role he loved the most, brought about the humiliating destruction of Oscar Wilde at Wilde's trial in 1895.

Clifton House

As it continues north, Donegall Street becomes Clifton Street, which takes its name from **Clifton House** (built 1771–74). Better known as the "Poor House", or the "Charitable Institute for the Aged and Infirm", it's in handsome Georgian style, of pedimented brick with an octagonal-based stone spire at its rear and symmetrically projecting wings to its sides. This is one of the simpler but more effective buildings that Belfast has to offer, yet was designed by an amateur architect and local paper merchant, Robert Joy, uncle of the hapless Henry Joy McCracken. The Institute was built at a time of much poverty and unrest, brought about by the Donegalls' eviction of tenants when their leases started running out – the very same Donegalls whose name is tagged to so many of Belfast's streets.

A little further along is the **Clifton Street Graveyard** which contains the graves of Robert Joy and Mary Anne McCracken, Henry Joy's sister, along with several United Irishmen, including Dr William Drennan, reputed to have been the originator of the phrase "Emerald Isle".

South Belfast

The university area occupies part of the stretch of **South Belfast** known as "The Golden Mile", which starts at the Opera House on Great Victoria Street and continues south past the **university**, up into the Lisburn, Malone and Stranmillis roads. You're likely to spend much of your time in the area, since it's littered with eating-places, pubs and bars, B&Bs and guesthouses. Near the university are the lush **Botanic Gardens**, within which sits the vast **Ulster Museum**, displaying everything from dinosaur bones to contemporary art.

The Golden Mile

Dozens of restaurants have sprung up along the **Golden Mile** in the last few years, the gourmet explosion said to have been triggered by the refurbishment in 1980 of the grandiose, turn-of-the-century **Grand Opera House**, which sits just a short distance west of Donegall Square at the northern end of Great Victoria Street (not to be confused with Victoria Street out east near the Albert Memorial).

From the Opera House, the Golden Mile storms southwards into the university district. The area buzzes with activity in the evening, even on a weekday (in term time at least). Though cheaper restaurants can be found, the area is moving distinctly upmarket and each week seems to see a swanky new eating house opening its doors, whether on Great Victoria Street itself or further south on Botanic Avenue or Stranmillis Road. There's a plethora of accommodation, too, in amongst the grid pattern of the broad, tree-lined streets surrounding the university campus, much of it in old three-storey Victorian houses.

BELFAST MURALS

As much of a marker of an area's allegiances as painted kerbstones or fluttering flags, the politically inspired **murals** of Northern Ireland are among the most startling sights in the country, and not least in Belfast. This ephemeral art form, which recycles the images and slogans of the Troubles, characterizes the violent struggles of the last few decades. New murals are painted over old ones or the houses which they adorn are demolished; consequently, some of the slogans and murals mentioned here may have vanished by the time of your visit.

LOYALIST MURALS

For most of the twentieth century, mural-painting in Northern Ireland was a predominantly **Loyalist** activity. The first mural appeared in East Belfast in 1908 and, like many of its successors, celebrated **King Billy**'s victory at the **Battle of the Boyne**. Loyalist murals have tended to use imagery symbolic of power, such as the clenched scarlet fist, known as the **Red Hand of Ulster** (Newtownards Road and elsewhere), or flags, shields and other heraldic icons. However, the Loyalist response to the Troubles translated into what is now the most common form of painting, the militaristic mural. If King Billy appears at all, it is often with a guard of balaclava-clad, weapon-toting **paramilitaries**, accompanied by a threatening slogan. Inspired by the desire for "**no surrender**" and preservation of the status quo, Loyalist mural painting is certainly less dynamic and diverse than its Republican counterpart. A typical example, on the Shankill Road, is of two masked gunman kneeling in front of the furled flags of England and Scotland, with a bronze shield between them, the Red Hand at its centre, surrounded by the words "UVF [Ulster Volunteer Force] for God and Ulster". In a mural on the Woodstock Link in East Belfast four gunman guard the UVF badge, captioned simply with "East Belfast 1912–2000". Despite the Loyalist ceasefire there has been no diminution in the production of militaristic images, although in recent years cartoons have been added to the repertoire. A classic example is on Martin Street, off Templemore Avenue in East Belfast – a huge British bulldog in the uniform of a marching band carries a pair of Unionist flags. Another famous example, now removed, had an aggressive Spike the dog grabbing Jerry the cat by the scruff of his Glasgow Celtic football shirt (for more on sectarianism in sport, see p.551).

The greatest concentration of Loyalist murals is to be found on and around the Shankill Road, especially the Shankill Estate, to the right, and Percy Place, off Dover Street, to the left. Nearby Crumlin Road has its fair share too. Other areas are Sandy Row and Donegall Pass in South Belfast, and Newtownards Road, Martin Street and Severn Street in East Belfast.

Standing out among the welter of Golden Mile attractions is one of the greatest of Victorian gin palaces, the **Crown Liquor Saloon**, almost opposite the *Europa Hotel* at the northern head of the street. It's now a National Trust property but is still open for drinking. The saloon has a glittering tiled exterior – amber, carmine, rouge, yellow, green, blue and smoke-grey – resembling a spa baths more than a serious drinking institution. The rich, High Victorian stucco work continues inside, too: the scrolled ceiling, patterned floor and the golden-yellow and rosy-red hues led John Betjeman to describe it as his "many coloured cavern". Once armed with drinks, and if it's not too crowded, grab a snug and shut the door. It's like sitting in a railway carriage compartment, with snatches of conversation floating over from the neighbouring snugs. There's no let-up in decoration here either, what with the painted mirrors, the oak panelling sporting flourishes of frieze-work (like the heraldic beasts guarding each snug entry) and the mounted gun-metal plates provided for striking matches. The push-button bell activates an indicator on a board above the bar, though it's just as much of an experience to order at the bar from the white-aproned and black-bow-tied staff – the bar

REPUBLICAN MURALS

Republican murals were at first limited to simple sloganeering or demarcation of territory, the most well-known example being the long-standing "You are now entering Free Derry" in the Bogside (see p.585). As with much else in Republican politics, however, the 1981 **hunger strikes** had a significant influence. Murals in support of the ten hunger strikers abounded and the (usually smiling) face of **Bobby Sands** – the IRA commander in the Maze prison who led the strike – remains an enduring image. He's there on the Falls Road, sporting a V-necked sweater, accompanied by the quotation "Everyone Republican or otherwise has his/her own part to play". Murals soon became a fundamental part of the Republican propaganda campaign and an expression of the community's current cultural and political concerns, though militaristic images have never really dominated Republican murals as much as they have done Loyalist ones. Prominent themes have been **resistance** to British rule, the call for the **withdrawal of troops** and, most commonly at present, **"Disband the RUC"** (the Royal Ulster Constabulary, Northern Ireland's predominantly Protestant-staffed police force).

A striking crop of Republican murals can be found at the top of Whiterock Road in the Ballymurphy estate in West Belfast. Several of these were the work of Gerry Kelly, who has been responsible for many of the best Republican murals. Redevelopment of the estate offered convenient new canvases for muralists on the fresh brickwork of the houses' gable ends. Of Kelly's murals, one of the most impressive is a 40ft wide by 16ft high piece on the release of prisoners (carried out with the help of painter Spud Murphy). It depicts a prisoner in the foreground standing out against an image of Long Kesh, with two female prisoners on either side and the symbol of **Saoirse** (freedom) to the left. To get there, turn right off the Falls Road up Whiterock Road, passing alongside the City Cemetery wall; once over the brow of the hill, take the next right into Ballymurphy Road, heading towards Springhill Avenue.

More recently, however, Republican muralists have turned increasingly to **Irish legends** and history as their sources of inspiration. Just off the Falls Road is the striking mural commemorating the 150th anniversary of the **Famine**, depicting a crush of anxious women and men waiting for a boat to carry them to salvation in the New World. Near the Cultúrlann MacAdam Ó Fiaich centre, 216 Falls Rd, is the **Children of Lir** mural, an astonishingly colourful image of the mythical offspring forced to wander the earth in the form of swans for nine hundred years before they could regain their human form.

Other main areas where you can find Republican murals are on the Falls Road itself, Beechmount Avenue, Shaw's Road and Lenadoon Avenue in West Belfast, and New Lodge Road and Ardoyne in North Belfast.

counter is a gorgeous S-curve of tile work, with exotically carved timber dividing screens.

Before heading into the university quarter, sidestep off Great Victoria Street into **Sandy Row**, which runs parallel to the west. A strong working-class Protestant quarter (with the tribal pavement painting to prove it), it's one of the most glaring examples of Belfast's divided worlds, wildly different from the Golden Mile's cosmopolitan sophistication, yet only yards away. In Blythe Street and Donegall Road, off to the west, are some of the murals which characterize these sectarian areas (see the box above). Sandy Row used to be the main road south, and although hard to credit today, it was once a picturesque stretch of whitewashed cottages.

The university quarter

Back on the Golden Mile, just past the southern end of Sandy Row (about three-quarters of a mile south of the Opera House), stand three churches – Moravian, Crescent and Methodist – whose distinctive steeples frame the entrance into the **university**

quarter. It's a highly characteristic area; many of the terraces leading up to the university buildings represent the final flowering of Georgian architecture in Belfast. The **Upper Crescent** is a magnificent curved Neoclassical terrace, built in about 1845 but sadly neglected since and now used mainly for office space. The **Lower Crescent**, perversely, is straight.

Queen's University, however, is the architectural centrepiece, flanked by the most satisfying example of a Georgian terrace in Belfast, University Square, where the red brickwork mostly remains intact, with the exception of a few bay windows added in the Victorian era. The terrace now houses various faculty buildings. The Italianate **Union Theological College**, nearby on College Park, was temporarily the site of the Northern Ireland Parliament until Stormont was built in 1932. Both this and **University College** itself are Lanyon designs, the latter built in 1849 as a mock-Tudor remodelling of Magdalen College, Oxford. Across the road from here is the Students' Union, a white 1960s design. A little further south down University Road, the university **bookshop** is especially good for Irish history and politics and, oddly enough, for its collection of Beat poetry.

The Botanic Gardens and Ulster Museum

Just below the university are the popular **Botanic Gardens** (daily 8am–sunset), first opened in 1827 and well-protected from the noise of surrounding traffic. Within the gardens is the **Palm House** (Mon–Fri 10am–noon & 1–5pm, Sat & Sun 2–5pm; Oct–March closes 4pm; free), a hothouse predating the famous one at Kew Gardens in London, but very similar in style, with a white-painted framework of curvilinear ironwork and glass. It was the first of its kind in the world, another success for Lanyon who worked in tandem on this project with the Dublin ironfounder Richard Turner. The nearby **Tropical Ravine** (same hours) is a classic example of Victorian light entertainment – a hundred-year-old sunken glen chock-full of "vegetable wonders" extracted from far-flung jungles and replanted for the delight of the visiting Belfast public.

Also in the Botanic Gardens you'll find the **Ulster Museum** (Mon–Fri 10am–5pm, Sat 1–5pm, Sun 2–5pm; free; admission charged to special exhibitions; buses #69, #70 & #71 from Donegall Square East), re-sited here in 1929 and expanded in 1972 with a concrete extension that subtly matches the original Portland stone. You'll need a fair bit of stamina to get round the museum, since it's a monster of a collection covering over two thousand square feet. Displays run from a dinosaur show through reproductions of early Irish Christian jewellery to the history of the post office in Ireland, water wheels and steam engines, local archeological finds, Irish wildlife, rocks, fossils and minerals. The latest gallery houses the fascinating **Early Ireland** exhibition, tracing the development of the prehistoric population. Among the many explanatory displays you'll find the earliest remains yet discovered (eel bones and burnt waterlily seeds), some remarkable gold lunulae and a couple of polished stone axes dug up on nearby Malone Road. Interesting though this is, the museum's undoubted showpiece is the **Girona exhibition**, treasures from the Spanish Armada ships which foundered off the Giant's Causeway in 1588, salvaged by divers in the 1960s. The top two floors house the **art galleries** and are nowadays dedicated to temporary exhibitions featuring works from both the museum's own extensive collections of national and international paintings and sculptures and from other sources. The bright and airy spaces of the topmost floor are often used for substantial and challenging exhibitions of modern art.

Further south: the Lagan Towpath and the Giant's Ring

Beyond the university area lie the glades of middle-class suburbia. From the Botanic Gardens, a ten- to fifteen-minute stroll south down Stranmillis Road (*struthán milis*, "sweet stream"), turning left into Lockview Road, will take you back to the river and to the start of the **Lagan Towpath**, where the *Cutter's Wharf* pub draws thirsty crowds for Sunday lunch and jazz. From here, follow the signs to the Lagan Meadows. The tarmacked towpath can be tramped for about eight miles south to Lisburn, passing old locks and lock-houses, rapids, woodland and marshes on the way. The waterway opened in the late 1790s, ready to carry the newly discovered coal from Lough Neagh, but its utility declined with the advent of the railway in 1839. Today, it's been harnessed as part of the Ulster Way, for rambling and canoeing enthusiasts. Travelling south under the ring road, you'll pass by **Malone House** (Mon–Sat 10am–4.30pm; free). It's well worth climbing up the hill for the views of the surrounding area and to see the house itself, an almost pristine white bow-fronted late-Georgian mansion, built for William Wallace Legge, a prominent local merchant. The house was rebuilt by Belfast Council following a devastating fire in 1976 and is now mainly used as a conference centre, though you can visit the Higgin Gallery which hosts regular art exhibitions and there's a fine restaurant here too (see p.546). A little further south along the towpath, you'll find the internationally renowned **Mary Peters Track**, part of the Malone Playing Fields, which is just off the Upper Malone Road. Set in what amounts to a natural amphitheatre, with the Castlereagh Hills in the distance, the track, established by Olympic gold medallist Mary Peters, is on the European Grand Prix Athletics Circuit.

Alternatively, if you leave the towpath at Shaw's Bridge (the ring road crossing), it's a mile-long signposted walk along country lanes to the **Giant's Ring**. This colossal, 200-yard-wide earthwork is thought to be a burial ground or meeting place. You wouldn't be far wrong in thinking that its inwardly sloping wall would make an excellent speed-track circuit, for in the eighteenth century it was used for horse racing: six circuits made a two-mile race, with the punters jostling for position on the rampart's top. Most captivating of all is the huge dolmen at the central hub of this cartwheel structure. As a single megalithic remain, it is immediately more impressive than even the great structures of the Irish High Kings at Tara, though here there's little information concerning its origins and usage. The ground chosen for the site, high above the surrounding lowlands (probably once marshy lake), is impressive – there's a powerful feeling that the great dramas and decision-making of the ancient northeast must have been played out here. To save you the entire walk back, you can catch Ulsterbus #13 back to the city; it passes Shaw's Bridge every half-hour or so, and takes you back to Laganside.

East Belfast

The Lagan Lookout near the Custom House (see p.536) is a good position from which to view the world's second- and third-largest cranes, *Goliath* and *Samson*, across the river in **East Belfast**'s Harland & Wolff shipyard. This is the city's proudest international asset: the ill-fated *Titanic* was built here, and the shipyard is nowadays said to possess the largest dry dock in the world – over 600 yards long and 100 yards wide. Unfortunately, the area is very security-conscious, as its workforce has always been predominantly Protestant, and access is impossible without making a formal application.

In fact, there's barely any reason to cross the river into **East Belfast** at all. The only exception are **Van Morrison** fans, who might get a thrill from seeking out his birthplace, a private house at 125 Hyndford Street, and the many streets that feature in his songs (Cyprus Avenue, Castlereagh Road, and others). While here, you might also like to stroll around the area's two pleasant parks.

Four miles east of the centre, off the Newtownards Road, is **Stormont** (bus #16 and #17 from Donegall Square West), the home of the Northern Ireland Parliament until the introduction of direct rule in 1972, and now housing the new Assembly, elected in June 1998. You can't visit the house itself, which is occupied by civil servants, but it's an impressive sight, a great white Neoclassical mansion crowning a rise in the middle of a park at the end of a magnificent long, straight drive. You can wander freely in the grounds, a popular place for a walk. Also here, though obviously not open to the public, is **Stormont Castle**, the office of the British Secretary of State for Northern Ireland.

North Belfast

North Belfast's attractions amount to no more than a castle and the city's zoo, both out on the Antrim Road and conveniently alongside one another on the slopes of Cave Hill, served by a welter of buses (#45–#51) from Donegall Square West.

Belfast Castle (daily 9am–6pm) and its wooded estate are open to the public. The castle was restored and refurbished in 1990 but, sadly, is virtually empty of Victorian period accoutrements, though the cellars have been redesigned in an attempt to re-create a typical Victorian Belfast narrow street and contain a bar and restaurant. It stands on the former deer park of the Third Marquis of Donegall, whose wish it was for the sandstone castle to be built here to the designs of Lanyon and his associates, in 1870. Consequently, the exterior is in the familiar Scottish Baronial style, inspired in part by the reconstruction of Balmoral Castle in Aberdeenshire in 1853, with a six-storey tower, a series of crow-stepped gables and conically peak-capped turrets. The most striking feature of all, however, is the serpentine Italianate stairway that leads down from the principal reception room to the garden terrace below. Upstairs a modest **visitor centre** (daily 9am–6pm; free) is best visited for a look through its remote-controlled camera on the roof.

Adjoining the castle is the Bellevue Estate, the old pleasure gardens laid out by the Belfast Street Tramway Company, but functioning since 1934 as **Belfast Zoo** (daily: April–Sept 10am–5pm; Oct–March 10am–3.30pm, Fri closes 2.30pm; £4.90), set in well-landscaped parkland stretching up towards Cave Hill. After a fifteen-year renovation programme and an investment of £10 million it's looking less like an animal prison. Within, you'll find spider monkeys, Malayan tapirs, penguins and sea lions, and a free flight aviary, where rare species have room to breed.

Castle and zoo aside, though, it's **Cave Hill** itself that should be your target in the area. Several paths lead up from the castle estate to the hill's summit – a rocky outcrop known as "Napoleon's Nose" – which affords an unsurpassable strategic overview of the whole city and lough. From here you can't help but appreciate the accuracy of the poet Craig Raine's aerial description of the city in his *Flying to Belfast*: like "a radio set with its back ripped off". Cave Hill was once awash with Iron Age forts, for there was flint (for weapon-making) in the chalk under the basalt hill-coverings. In 1795, Wolfe Tone, Henry Joy McCracken and other leaders of the United Irishmen stood on the top of Cave Hill and pledged "never to desist in our efforts until we have subverted the authority of England over our country and asserted our Independence".

West Belfast

Like many other cities, Belfast's population expanded dramatically during the nineteenth century as people flocked from the countryside to work in the booming new flax and linen industries. Many of these migrants were crammed into jerry-built housing in the grids of streets which still today define **West Belfast**. Conditions were deplorable and did nothing to ease tensions between Catholic and Protestant residents. There were numerous sectarian riots – the worst was in 1886, during the reading of the Home Rule Bill, when 32 people died and over 370 were injured – leading to the almost inevitable creation of two separate neighbourhoods. In 1968 and 1969, this division was pushed to its limit when sectarian mobs and gunmen evicted over eight thousand families from their homes, mainly in Catholic West Belfast. The Royal Ulster Constabulary, or RUC, called for government assistance and British troops arrived on the streets on August 15, 1969. A month later the makeshift barrier dividing the Catholic **Falls** from the Protestant **Shankill** had become a full-scale reinforced "peace line". British intervention may have averted a civil war, but it failed to prevent an escalation in sectarian conflict. Indeed, the army soon came to be viewed as an occupying force and a legitimate target for a reviving IRA. In return, Loyalist paramilitaries sought to avenge Republican violence, often through indiscriminate acts of aggression. Over the next 25 years, West Belfast remained the major battleground of the Troubles. The busy **Westlink motorway** separates West Belfast from the rest of the city, and at the height of the conflict, the various overhead bridges and roundabouts were used by the police and army as virtual border crossings to control access to and from the area.

Today, however, West Belfast is completely safe for strangers to the city to stroll around in. There's little of architectural note among the mainly residential streets and most of the "sights" are associated with the area's troubled past. Much of the old terraced housing has been replaced in recent years by rows of modern Housing Executive homes, but it's impossible to miss examples of the partisan **mural paintings** which decorate walls and gable ends in both Catholic and Protestant areas (see box on p.538).

The Falls

Two routes lead into the heart of the Catholic **Falls** area: one along Grosvenor Road, the other through Divis Street. The latter is the more infamous and is also the route that carries the main injection of black taxi-cab traffic into the area (see "City transport", p.527). The taxis assemble in ranks at the end of Castle Street, in the Smithfield area; the drivers, incidentally, are said to be Republican ex-prisoners. Smithfield itself used to have a large covered bazaar that has now been replaced by **Smithfield Retail Market** – actually a set of small shop units rather than a traditional open-air market. The area has undergone major redevelopment through the building of the massive Castlecourt shopping centre, though there is a reminder of its old character in Gresham Street, home to several bookshops and junk shops.

Moving on, you enter the **Falls Road** proper, which continues for a further two miles west past Milltown Cemetery (see p.544) and into Andersonstown. Most of the interest is concentrated in the area you've now entered – the **Lower Falls**. While most of the land to your left (south) consists of the recently built red-brick terraced housing estates, the right-hand side of the road is more of a hotchpotch and features some of the local landmarks: the bright blue swimming baths, a new railing-secured shopping plaza, the DSS (the Department of Social Security, known as "the Brew" – a corruption of "bureau") cooped up in an awning of chicken-wire, a weary-looking Victorian library and a Worshippers of Peace convent. Down Conway Street (by the DSS), stands the old **Conway Mill**, revitalized by a concerted community effort, spearheaded by local activist Father Des Wilson. Inside you can buy the wares of the few small businesses that operate from here. All the way along the Falls Road you'll spot, blocking the ends of the streets to the right (north), walls of iron sheeting. These comprise the **"Peace Line"**, and directly behind them is the Protestant working-class district of the Shankill.

Further on, you'll pass the red-brick buildings of the **Royal Victoria Hospital**, at the junction with Grosvenor Road. Since the Troubles began, the Royal, as it's known locally, has received international acclaim for its ability to cope with the consequences of the violence. Just beyond it, in a disused Presbyterian church at 216 Falls Rd, is the **Cultúrlann MacAdam Ó Fiaich**, a cultural centre for Irish-speakers, housing a bookshop, café, school and theatre. This is the best place in Belfast to buy traditional-music

CDs. The Irish language is thriving in Catholic areas of Belfast and throughout the North; the first Irish-speaking primary school is over twenty years old, and the first secondary school was opened in 1991. A year earlier, the Ultach Trust was set up, a group that aims to broaden the appeal of Irish among Unionists. Although you are unlikely to hear any Irish being spoken on the streets or in most pubs, the language has a growing presence in the city.

The **Springfield** area to the northwest is the focus for a massive new £80 million campus jointly run by the University of Ulster and the Belfast Institute, geared towards offering opportunities in further education to the local population.

MILLTOWN CEMETERY

Follow the Falls Road west for another mile and you'll come to **Milltown Cemetery**, the main Republican burial ground in Belfast, situated opposite a fortified RUC station. Enter through the stone arch and you're immediately surrounded by a numbing array of Celtic and Roman crosses. If you're in search of the Republican plots, continue directly on from the entrance for about a hundred yards, then veer right, heading towards a corrugated warehouse shed just outside the perimeter of the cemetery. Along the way are two plots, marked off by a low green border fence. The nearer one holds a large memorial tablet listing the Republican casualties in the various uprisings from 1798 to the present day. The far plot contains a modern granite-block sculpture, and also the graves of Bobby Sands, Mairéad Farrell, Seán Savage and others. Once you start to look, it's not difficult to spot the graves of many other victims of the Troubles, a devastatingly long list of (usually young) men and women.

The M1 motorway lies below, at the bottom of the burial park. It was onto this stretch of road in 1988 that Michael Stone, a solo Loyalist attacker, was pursued after he'd opened fire and hurled grenades at mourners at the funeral of Seán Savage, one of the IRA members (along with Mairéad Farrell and Danny McCann) who were killed that year by a British SAS unit in Gibraltar.

Shankill

The Protestant population of West Belfast lives in the area abutting the Falls to the north, between the **Shankill** Road and the Crumlin Road. As with the Falls, there's little here of especial interest, apart from an array of Loyalist murals and street names familiar from news bulletins. Along the **Crumlin Road**, in particular, are a number of evocative sites symbolizing the worst years of the Troubles. From the Westway you'll pass between the courthouse and the notorious Crumlin Road jail, the two connected by an underground tunnel; the jail is no longer in use, and is set to be developed as a new arts centre. Nearby is the bizarre sight of a completely fortified betting shop, standing in grim isolation in the centre of a patch of wasteland. Further along is an army encampment, set back from the road, with a tentacled iron sheeting corridor and lookout post.

Despite many obvious signs of redevelopment and renovation – the most apparent being the new leisure centre – the area is in decline, its population shrinking in inverse proportion to the Catholic population the other side of the Peace Line. Yet Shankill (*sean cill*, "the old church") does have a rich history, though you'll have to travel almost out of town to learn more about it. A two-mile journey on bus #63 from Wellington Place will convey you to the end of Glencairn Road; a further ten-minute stroll down here will take you to **Fernhill House: The People's Museum** (April–Sept Mon–Sat 10am–10pm, Sun 10am–6pm; Oct–March Mon–Sat 10am–4pm; £2), a re-created 1930's Shankill house. Here you'll find displays on the history of the Shankill district, with particular focuses on the 1886 Home Rule crisis and both world wars. Fortunately, there's a café here to restore your spirits for the return trek.

Eating

Eating out is one of young Belfast's favourite evening pastimes and an astonishing number of fashionable cafés and chic restaurants have sprung up around the city centre during the last few years. Although there's an emphasis on modern Irish and European cuisine, with French and Italian especially popular, you'll find a smattering of Indian and Chinese restaurants too. Standards are generally high and often exceptionally good value for money. The choice is limited for vegetarians, and there's a real dearth of wholefood restaurants, but many more restaurants now include vegetarian dishes on their menu. Bear in mind that restaurants are often fully booked on Friday and Saturday evenings, so you need to reserve a table or be prepared either to eat early or spend a fruitless time trekking around for a free table.

There are plenty of places for daytime eating in the centre and along the Golden Mile, from new cafés to traditional pubs (many of the latter serve excellent lunches); most of the city's well-established restaurants are south of the centre from the Golden Mile outwards.

Cafés

Bewley's, Donegall Arcade. Welcoming branch of the much-loved Dublin coffee house. Mon–Sat 8am–5.30pm, Thurs until 8.30pm.

Bookfinders, 47 University Rd. Secondhand bookshop with a café at the back serving healthy lunches. Mon–Sat 10am–5.30pm.

Bronco's Web, 122 Great Victoria St. Newish Internet café, serving paninis, sandwiches and soup. Mon–Sat 7.30am–10pm.

Café Renoir, 5 Queen St. Unpretentious self-service café with excellent and oversized wholefood dishes and baguettes. Mon–Sat 9am–5pm, Thurs until 8pm.

Café Vincents, 78 Botanic Ave (☎028/9024 2020). Known to all as *Vincents*, this place does excellent breakfasts, value-for-money high teas and plenty of pizzas. Daily 9am–11pm, Fri & Sat until midnight.

Conor's Cafe Bar, 11a Stranmillis Rd (☎028/9066 4714). Opposite the Ulster Museum, a café with an interesting, affordable Mediterranean-style menu in the artist Willie Conor's former studio. Good for brunch. Daily 9.30am–11.30pm.

Equinox, 32 Howard St. One of the new bloom of café society hangouts, at the back of the Equinox interiors shop. As you'd expect, it looks good with food to match. Mon–Sat 9.30am–4.30pm.

Mad Hatter, 2 Eglantine Ave. Fine coffee shop offering excellent breakfasts, home-cooked lunches and afternoon teas with a pleasant garden in summer. Daily 8am–8pm.

Queen's Espresso, 17 Botanic Ave. Good coffee and all sorts of snacks, from toasted sandwiches to tasty salads. Mon–Sat 8am–5.30pm.

Revelations – The Internet Café, 27 Shaftesbury Square (☎028/9032 0337, *www.revelations.co.uk*). Friendly cybercafé with diligent and helpful staff and DTP facilities. Mon–Fri 10am–10pm, Sat 10am–6pm, Sun 11am–7pm.

Roscoff Café, 12–14 Arthur St and 27–29 Fountain St. Modernist interiors, gourmet coffees and, best of all, choice Mediterranean breads. Mon–Sat 7.30am–5.30pm, Thurs until 8pm.

The Upper Crust, 15 Lombard St. Serves homemade pies and bakes, and is guaranteed to be packed with shoppers and office workers at lunchtime. Mon–Sat 9am–4.30pm.

Restaurants

Alden's, 229 Upper Newtownards Rd (☎028/9065 0079). Top-quality fish and seafood menus in this East Belfast outpost, well worth the trek to reach. Mon–Sat noon–2.30pm & 6–10pm, Fri & Sat until 11pm.

Archana, 53 Dublin Rd (☎028/9032 3713). Possibly Belfast's finest Indian restaurant, serving spicy curries and Balti dishes upstairs and vegetarian meals below in its *Little India* offshoot. Mon–Sat noon–2pm & 5pm–midnight, Sun 5pm–midnight.

Barnett, Malone House, Barnett Demesne (☎028/9068 1246). Award-winning, non-smoking restaurant serving grand lunches and afternoon teas (until 5pm) in a sublime setting. Mon–Sat 12.30–3pm.

Beatrice Kennedy's, 44 University Rd (☎028/9020 2290). Ever-changing and innovative cosmopolitan menu at around £20 per head. Daily 5–10.30pm.

Café Society, 3 Donegall Square East (☎028/9043 9525). The downstairs bistro (Mon–Sat noon–9pm) serves inexpensive meals all day, while from the upstairs restaurant (Mon–Fri noon–3pm & 6–10pm) you can feast on more substantial modern and imaginative cuisine and watch the Belfast whirl below.

Chez Delbarts, also known as **Frogities**, 10 Bradbury Place, off Great Victoria St (☎028/9023 8020). Savoury pancakes and mixed kebabs at unbeatably low prices, though you often have to queue. Tues–Sat 5pm–midnight, Sun 5–9.30pm.

Deane's, 38 Howard St. Former Helen's Bay stalwart, now in sleeker city-centre premises with an excellent brasserie (Mon–Sat noon–2.30pm & 5.30–10.30pm; ☎028/9056 0000) and outstanding modern Irish cuisine in the restaurant (Tues–Sat 7–9.30pm; ☎028/9033 1134).

Delaney's, 19 Lombard St. Economical, wholesome food from a restaurant handily placed in the main shopping area. Mon–Sat 9am–5pm, Thurs until 9pm.

Friar's Bush, 159 Stranmillis Rd (☎028/9066 9824). A bit of a walk south, but worth it for the excellent, reasonably priced four-course meals, with wild venison or turbot specials. Tues–Sat 7–10pm.

Gypsy Queen, 13–17 Amelia St (☎028/9024 5489). One of the North's few vegetarian specialists (also serving some vegan options), with excellent GM-free organic soups and meals. Call for opening times.

Keating, 103 Great Victoria St (☎028/9059 4949). Elegant surroundings for an eclectic menu of Modern European delights. Mon–Sat 12.30–2pm & 5.30–11pm, Sun 5–9pm.

Láziz, 99 Botanic Ave (☎028/9023 4888). Superb (and very popular) Moroccan restaurant with tasteful decor, top-quality service and outstanding food. Mon–Sat 7–11pm.

Maggie May's, 45 Botanic Ave (☎028/9032 2662). Huge, economically priced portions with lots of veggie choices. Be prepared to queue and bring your own wine. Daily 7.45am–11pm.

The Manhattan, 23 Bradbury Place (☎028/9023 3131). Cajun specials, plus live music upstairs. Mon–Sat noon–10pm.

Mongolian Barbeque, 73–75 Great Victoria St (☎028/9024 6404). This newly-arrived branch of a Dublin success story satisfies the terminally ravenous with its all-you-can-eat stir-fries. Daily noon–3pm & 6–10pm, Fri & Sat until 10.30pm.

Nick's Warehouse, 35 Hill St (☎028/9043 9690, *www.nickswarehouse.com*). Chic, pricey restaurant upstairs and an atmospheric wine bar and less expensive menu downstairs. Mon 10am–5pm, Tues–Fri 10am–10pm, Sat 6–10pm.

Rajput, 461 Lisburn Rd (☎028/9066 2168). Well south, but handy for the area's B&Bs. A good reasonably-priced Indian restaurant and takeaway. Mon–Sat 5pm–midnight, Sun 5–11pm.

Red Panda, 60 Great Victoria St (☎028/9080 8700). Hugely popular new arrival, specializing in dim sum and other authentic Chinese dishes. Daily noon–3pm (Sun until 4pm) & 5–11.30pm.

Speranza, 16 Shaftesbury Square (☎028/9023 0213). Massively popular Italian restaurant with a very reasonably priced three-course menu; expect to queue. Daily 5.30–11.30pm, Sun until 10.30pm.

Sun Kee, 38 Donegall Pass (☎028/9031 2016). No-frills decor, but nonetheless a superb adventurous Chinese restaurant. Daily 5–11pm.

Tedford's, 5 Donegall Quay (☎028/9043 4000). A piscivore's paradise with fresh seafood, lobsters and king scallops; offers a theatre menu in keeping with its handiness for the Waterfront Hall. Mon–Sat 12.30–3pm & 5.30–11pm.

Villa Italia, 37–41 University Rd (☎028/9032 8356). Queues outside are the best indicator of the quality of the menu at this Italian place. Mon–Fri 5–11pm, Sat 4–11.30pm, Sun 4–10pm.

Drinking, nightlife and entertainment

Until fairly recently, Belfast used to operate as a city under curfew, and unless you were a native, it was difficult to track down just where the best **pubs**, **clubs** and **music** were to be found. Now new bars have appeared and the club scene is booming. Overall, the city centre is far more open and vibrant at night, although Sundays can be quiet with many bars closing early or remaining shut all day. To tap into the pulse of the city, your best bet is to wander down the **Golden Mile**, where you'll find an abundance of pubs and clubs to choose from. For the latest information on what's going on in the city, the fortnightly listings freesheet *The Big List* is essential.

Pubs and bars

As always in Ireland, the **pubs** are the heart of the city. The liveliest are on Great Victoria Street and around the university, and if you start drinking at the famed *Crown Liquor Saloon* (see below) you can manage a substantial pub crawl without moving more than about 100 yards from where you started. In addition to the handful of places mentioned here, there are dozens of pubs around the city that double up as venues for live music of one sort or another; we've listed these separately below.

If you're short of time, you could always join the **Historical Pub Tour**, covering six of Belfast's best-known bars (convenes at *Flannigan's*, above the *Crown Liquor Saloon*; April–Sept Tues 7pm, Sat 4pm; ☎028/9268 3665; £5).

Crown Liquor Saloon, 46 Great Victoria St, opposite the *Europa Hotel*. The most famous and spectacular pub in Belfast with a clientele that thinks itself intellectual (there's no music). Good repertoire of Ulster food – champ, colcannon, and the like – and also Strangford oysters in season, which usually go by early afternoon.

Flannigan's, 19 Amelia St, above the *Crown*'s side entrance. Sedate, cosy alternative to the packed bar below. Closed Sun.

Morning Star, 17 Pottinger's Entry. Fine old-fashioned bar, busy in the day, quiet at night. Its upstairs restaurant is one of Belfast's best.

Robinson's, 38 Great Victoria St. Theme bar spread over four floors and overshadowed by the *Crown* next door. Packed at lunchtimes with local workers taking advantage of the cheap menus.

White's Tavern, Winecellar Entry, High St. Atmospheric old Entries bar, offering enormously popular 'pile your plate' self-service lunches.

Live music

The best Belfast entertainment is **music** in the pubs. The range on offer covers excellent traditional and folk, blues, country, jazz and indie music, and the number of visiting international performers has increased dramatically. The local scene is thriving too and, despite the absence of any real music industry infrastructure, there are always good up-and-coming bands playing in the city, just waiting to get noticed. While traditional music usually comes **free** with your pint, rock venues may charge between £2 and £5 depending on the act's reputation. Pre-booked tickets for the biggest names playing in purpose-built halls will usually cost much more – between £10 and £20. **Classical music** concerts are thin on the ground and almost all take place in the Ulster Hall or Waterfront Hall. **Opera** fans are catered for at the Grand Opera House.

Traditional music

The Hercules, 61 Castle St. Fine city centre bar with food at lunchtime and established sessions (Fri–Sun).

The John Hewitt, 53 Donegall St. Light and airy pub run by the Belfast Unemployed Resource Centre, with newspapers, plus excellent traditional sessions (Mon, Wed & Sun 9pm, Sat 4pm) featuring musicians who used to play at the sadly defunct *Liverpool*. Also healthy, reasonably-priced meals.

Kelly's Cellars, 30 Bank St. According to legend a frequent meeting place for the United Irishmen behind the doomed 1798 Rebellion – Henry Joy McCracken hid under the bar counter from British soldiers. Good lunches (thumping portions of homemade Irish stew and steak pie); weekend sessions, including Sat afternoon.

The Kitchen Bar, 16 Victoria Square. A long, narrow bar and one of the city's finest pubs, featuring superb-value lunches and a brilliant Sunday session.

Maddens, 74 Smithfield. Wonderful, unpretentious, atmospheric pub. Lots of locals drinking in two large rooms, one upstairs, one downstairs. Serves cheap stew and soup and there are excellent traditional sessions (Thurs–Sat).

Pat's Bar, 20 Prince's Dock St, in the north of the city by the docks, off York Rd, most easily reached by taxi. Recently renovated in traditional style, with a choice of two bars (one large, one small) and open fires. Sessions irregular but great when they happen.

Rock, indie, blues and jazz

Aunt Annie's Porterhouse, Dublin Rd (☎028/9050 1660). Large drinking emporium with music on two floors most nights (singer/songwriters downstairs, rock and indie upstairs).

Basement Bar & Grill, 16 Donegall Sq East (☎028/9033 1925). Live blues every Friday night from 9.30pm.

The Botanic Inn, 23 Malone Rd (☎028/9066 0460), opposite the "Eg" (see below). Perhaps inevitably, known as the "Bot". Almost entirely students, and plenty of atmosphere. Thurs–Sun there are DJs; live bands the rest of the week.

Cutters Wharf, Stranmillis Embankment. Excellent Laganside pub with rock bands (Fri & Sat) and a regular jazz session on Sunday afternoons.

The Duke of York, 11 Commercial Court (☎028/9024 1062), off Donegall St. Music most nights, with bands on Saturdays.

The Edge, Laganbank Rd. New waterside development off East Bridge Street near Central Station, featuring a grand, if rather pricey, à la carte menu and music at weekends, including its Sabor Latino club for salsa enthusiasts on Saturdays.

The Eglantine Inn, 32 Malone Rd, opposite the "Bot" (see above). Known to the students who pack it out as the "Eg". Very crowded, with a traditional session on Mondays and a mixture of live bands and DJs the rest of the week.

The Empire Bar & Music Hall, 42 Botanic Ave, just up from the station. Cellar bar in a former church with a boisterous beer-hall atmosphere. Good-value food and bands (Thurs, Fri & Sun) and a "pre-club strut" (Sat). Upstairs the Music Hall hosts salsa lessons (Fri) and occasional gigs.

The Errigle Inn, 320 Ormeau Rd. Live music (Thurs–Sun), including splendid blues and rock gigs run by The Real Music Club.

The Front Page, 106 Donegall St. Packed with journalists from the nearby *Belfast Telegraph* and *Irish News* during the day; there's live music featuring local bands (Thurs & Sat).

Katy Daly's, 17 Ormeau Ave. Singers, indie and rock bands most evenings plus an innovative new film club showing shorts from local film-makers (Sun).

King's Hall, Balmoral Showgrounds (☎028/9066 5225). The city's main stage for the biggest pop and rock gigs.

Lavery's Gin Palace, 14 Bradbury Place. Snazzy outside but a regular pub within. The Back Bar has indie, rock and retro bands (Thurs–Sat) and traditional music (Mon), while the Gin Palace itself hosts soul nights (Mon–Wed), and the Top Bar has the Club Heaven for dancers (Sat).

The Library Bar, Frames Complex, 2–14 Little Donegall St. Popular bar near the *Belfast Telegraph* offices featuring quizzes, karaoke, live music and discos; excellent bar meals too at lunchtime.

McHugh's, 29–31 Queen's Square. Belfast's oldest surviving building features live rock and indie bands (Wed–Sat).

The Menagerie, University St. Near the Ormeau Rd, this retro-kitsch bar, run by escapees from the *Rotterdam*, hosts gigs by some of the North's most innovative up-and-coming bands and musicians.

Mercury Bar & Grill, 451 Ormeau Rd. Hosts a popular Sunday afternoon live jazz band, plus traditional music the same evening.

Morrison's Spirit Grocers, 21 Bedford St. Another city-centre retro pub; go mid-afternoon to sip fruit vodkas and marvel at the hand-painted faux nicotine ceiling. Music most nights – popular on Fridays for its local bands' showcase.

Rotterdam Bar, 54 Pilot St (☎028/90746021). Reopened dockland institution with bands most nights, leaning towards blues, rock, new country and a traditional session on Tuesdays.

The Shenanagan Rooms, 21 Howard St. Pub behind City Hall featuring live rock bands Thurs–Sat, followed by DJs.

Classical music and opera

Grand Opera House, Great Victoria St (☎028/9024 1919). Belfast's most prestigious venue, featuring regular operatic performances.

Ulster Hall, Bedford St (☎028/9032 3900). Most of the city's classical music performances are given by the Ulster Orchestra; the hall is also used for big rock and pop concerts.

Waterfront Hall, Lanyon Place, Laganside (☎028/9033 4455). Hosts classical music and ballet, mainstream jazz and occasional big names from the moribund world of MOR pop and rock.

Whitla Hall, Queen's University (☎028/9024 5133). Stages some professional and amateur classical concerts.

Clubs and discos

Belfast's **club scene** is buzzing – dance culture is big, so are celebrity DJs. Check *The Big List* for who's on when; you'll find most venues run different clubs on different nights. Venues are scattered fairly evenly around the city centre; students – not surprisingly – tend to dominate those closest to the university area. Admission may be free early in the week and as low as £1 or £2 up to Thursday nights, while weekend prices are usually around £4 to £6.

Benedicts Hotel, Bradbury Place (☎028/9059 1999). Bands and/or DJs nightly; strict dress code – no jeans or trainers.

Bob's, Russell Court Complex, 38 Lisburn Rd (☎028/9033 2526) Popular club venue with retro and commercial dance nights (Tues, Wed, Fri & Sat).

Dempsey's Terrace, 45 Dublin Rd (☎028/9023 4000). Popular hangout for the younger set, especially on Fridays for The Loft Club.

The Fly Bar, 5–6 Lower Crescent (☎028/9023 5666). Intensely hip three-storey venue; sport those designer labels at club nights most evenings, but watch out for the appropriate spider and fly decor.

The Limelight, 17 Ormeau Ave. A serious dance club with various club nights covering everything from Britpop to rare groove and sporadic indie gigs.

Madison's, 59–63 Botanic Ave (☎028/9032 0966). Be seen, but wear the right threads at this thirty-somethings' hotel bar and nightclub, the latter featuring DJs at the weekend.

M Club, The Manhattan, 23 Bradbury Place (☎028/9023 3131). Different themes (Mon & Thurs–Sat), such as the Groovy Train 70s retro night on Fridays, flares essential.

Network Club, 118 Lower North St (☎028/9023 8226). Opens at midnight on Saturday for the city's major all-nighter (£10).

Orpheus & The Underworld, University St (☎028/9020 5005). Hugely popular with students, thanks to its low prices, and Thursday club anthems night; more DJs and live acts on Fri & Sat.

Shine, Mandela Hall, Queen's Student Union (☎028/9032 4803). Saturday student bash favouring trance, funk and smoother sounds.

Thompson's, 3 Pattersons Place, Arthur St (☎028/9032 3762). Once a garage owned by aviation freak Harry Ferguson – an addiction commemorated with a mural of an aeroplane in mid-flight. It now hosts a variety of club nights featuring house, garage and Old Skool, "Congress" on Saturday being the big draw.

Theatre, cinema and art

Most of the **theatres** and **cinemas** are concentrated in the south of the city. Although the choice for both is relatively limited, there is enough of a range to please most tastes. Recently, the city has seen a rapid expansion in the number of **art galleries**, and there's now an interesting selection to choose from, showing the best of modern and contemporary Irish art.

Theatres and arts centres

Arts Theatre, Botanic Ave (☎028/9031 6900). Mostly mainstream stuff – often children's specials.

Crescent Arts Centre, 2–4 University Rd (☎028/9024 2338). A focus for much of Belfast's leftfield arts and performance activities and home to the Fenderesky Gallery (see below).

Empire Bar, Botanic Ave (☎028/9032 8110). Transforms into the Comedy Club on Tuesday nights, featuring satire and killing Northern wit that will reveal more about Belfast than a volume of history. Queue early to avoid disappointment; the laughter starts at 9pm.

Grand Opera House, Great Victoria St (☎028/9024 1919). Belfast's most prestigious venue, showing many of London's West End productions in amongst the opera.

Group Theatre, Bedford St (☎028/9032 3900). Tends to be used mainly by local drama companies.

Lyric Theatre, 55 Ridgeway St, Stranmillis (☎028/9038 1081; bus #69). Stages more serious contemporary drama, and gave actor Liam Neeson an early platform.

Old Museum Arts Centre, College Square North (☎028/9023 3332). The place to go for experimental or fringe productions; also hosts regular art exhibitions.

Cinemas

Mainstream **cinemas** showing the usual general-release movies include the monster ten-screen UGC on Dublin Rd (☎0870/155 5176), Belfast Cineplex in the Kennedy Centre, Falls Rd (☎028/9060 0988, *www.filminfo.net*), the Movie House, Yorkgate on York St (☎028/9075 5000), and the Strand, Hollywood Rd (☎028/9067 3500). As an alternative, Queen's Film Theatre, 7 University Square Mews off Botanic Ave (☎0800/328 2811, *www.qub.ac.uk/qft*) has two screens showing art-house movies and late-night shows at exceptionally good prices.

Art galleries

Arts Council Sculpture Park, 180 Stranmillis Rd (☎028/9038 1591; bus #69). Al fresco exhibition of works by local contemporary sculptors.

Eakin Gallery, 237 Lisburn Rd (☎028/9066 8522). A family-run terraced house gallery, which highlights Belfast's star painters.

Fenderesky Gallery, Crescent Arts Centre, University Rd (☎028/9024 2338). Presents important Irish moderns – Barrie Cooke, Patrick Hall, Felim Egan – and the Ireland-based Mexican printmaker Alfonso Monreal.

Ormeau Baths Gallery, Ormeau Ave (☎028/9032 1402). Set in what was once a public baths, this is the hippest venue on the arts scene, with four exhibition spaces spread over two floors. Hosts exhibitions of contemporary Irish and international artists' work.

Ulster Museum, Stranmillis Rd (☎028/9038 1251). Has a wide-ranging collection of international and national art, but increasingly allocates space to temporary, yet ever-absorbing, exhibitions.

Waterfront Hall, Lanyon Place, Laganside (☎028/9033 4455). Regularly mounts shows for viewing while you wait for the main performance to commence.

Spectator sports

Though watching, discussing and betting on **sport** is as much of a pastime in Belfast as anywhere else, you'll find very few locals expressing especially passionate opinions about the city's teams and players, with the notable exception of boxing. Indeed, when people watch sport here, it's usually the televised variety and attendances for most events are relatively small, an indifference which applies equally to the North's national teams. Nevertheless, if you're interested in attending a match of whatever kind, there are plenty of opportunities and the *Belfast Telegraph* usually has the details.

The Northern Ireland **football** (soccer) team has not seen anything approaching glory since its astonishing performance at the 1982 World Cup finals in Spain when it defeated the home country 1–0 in Valencia. Sadly, the superb George Best, the "Belfast Boy", who was the toast of Manchester United in the 1970s, never graced such a stage. Internationals are played at **Windsor Park** (the home ground of the **Linfield** club) near the Lisburn Rd (bus #58 and #59 to Lower Windsor Avenue). The biggest club sides in Belfast – paradoxically enough – are Glasgow's Celtic and Rangers, supported respectively by Catholics and Protestants, as well as Liverpool and Manchester United; the city's pubs are packed out for major televised games. If you'd like to see the local teams in action, bear in mind that Irish League football is a major sectarian bastion. The last regularly successful Catholic side, Belfast Celtic, resigned from the league in the late 1940s after players were assaulted on the pitch, the result of one fulfilled threat too many. More recently, the police refused to allow local amateur side Donegal Celtic to play a cup match against Linfield (whose supporters are known as the Billy Boys) on their own ground for fear of sectarian violence. Other Belfast league clubs and their grounds are **Crusaders** (Seaview, off Shore Rd; bus #7–#11), **Glentoran** (The Oval, Redcliffe Parade; bus #16, #20–#22, #24 down the Newtownards Road to Dee Street) and the surprising 1998 champions, the Catholic-supported **Cliftonville** (Solitude, Cliftonville Road; bus #35).

Since football is the Belfast sport, success at both **hurling** and **gaelic football** has been lacking and County Antrim has never won either All-Ireland Senior Final, although hurling is undergoing something of a revival. You can see both sports most weekends at Roger Casement Park, on Andersonstown Road (bus #14, #15 and #90), where the Ulster Hurling Final is held in July.

Belfast's **rugby** hero was Mike Gibson, Ireland's most-capped player, and top-class games are played by the Malone club at the park named after him off Woodstock Road (bus #33 and #34) and by Collegians at Deramore Park, Malone Road (bus #70 and #71). Major **athletics** meetings take place at the Mary Peters Track (see p.541) and in early May the streets are cleared for the Belfast **Marathon**. For many, Belfast's **boxing** success will always evoke 1980s' memories of Barry McGuigan (actually born in Monaghan); big fights take place at the King's Hall, Upper Lisburn Road.

Listings

Airlines Aer Lingus, 46 Castle St (☎0845/973 7747); British Airways (☎0845/773 3377); British European (☎0870/567 6676); British Midland (☎0870/607 0555); Comed Aviation (☎01253/402661); easyJet (☎0870/600 0000); Gill Airways (☎0191/214 6666).

Airports Belfast City (☎028/9045 7745); Belfast International (☎028/9442 2888).

Banks Most of the major UK banks are allied to the following Northern Irish ones, all of which have city-centre branches: Bank of Ireland, 54 Donegall Place (☎028/9023 4334); Northern Bank, Donegall Square West (☎028/9024 5277); Ulster Bank, 47 Donegall Place (☎028/9024 4112). British cards will work in their cash dispensers.

Bike rental Bike-It, 4 Belmont Rd (☎028/9047 1141); McConvey Cycles, 467 Ormeau Rd (☎028/9049 1163) and Unit 10, Pottinger's Entry (☎028/9033 0322); Recycle, 1–5 Albert Square (☎028/9031 3113).

Books Bookfinders at 47 University Rd has secondhand books; there's also the University Bookshop on University Rd, Waterstones on Royal Ave and Fountain St, and branches of Easons on Ann St and Botanic Ave. No Alibi, 83 Botanic Ave, specializes in crime books, while for antiquarian books try Dublin Roma Ryan's Books and Prints, Dublin Rd.

Buses Citybus enquiries ☎028/9024 6485; Ulsterbus ☎028/9033 3000 for long-distance information. There's also a touch-screen information service at the Europa bus station with full timetables and information on places to visit and accommodation throughout Northern Ireland.

Car rental Avis, Belfast International Airport (☎028/9442 2333) and Belfast City Airport (☎028/9045 2017); there are many other big names at the airports and local firms such as McCausland Car Hire (☎028/9033 3777) which also has a city-centre depot at 21–31 Grosvenor Rd.

Exchange As well as banks try Thomas Cook, 11 Donegall Place (☎028/9055 0030); the Tourist Information Centre, 59 North St, which is due to move to 35 Donegall Place in 2001 (☎028/9024 6609); and the post offices at Castle Place, Donegall Square and Shaftesbury Square.

Ferries Isle of Man Steam Packet Company, Donegall Quay (☎0870/552 3523); Norse Irish Ferries, West Bank Rd (☎028/9077 9090); P&O, Larne Harbour (☎0870/242 4777); Seacat, Donegall Quay (☎0870/552 3523); Stena Line, Corry Rd (☎0870/570 7070).

Festivals Belfast International Festival at Queens University (two to three weeks from late Oct to Nov) claims to be Britain's second-biggest arts festival after Edinburgh. Others are the Belfast Folk Festival (ten days in Sept); Orange Parades on July 12 (and marching season from Easter onwards); Royal Ulster Academy Annual Exhibition (at the Ulster Museum for three weeks in Oct); Belfast Summerfest, featuring plenty of outdoor gigs and entertainment at the end of May; and the Ardoyne *Fleadh Cheoil*, a hugely popular traditional music festival (first week in August), followed immediately by the West Belfast Festival, another week-long music and dance festival – originally a Republican event, this increasingly includes Unionist voices.

Gay and lesbian life The gay scene in Belfast is small and there's much travel back and forth to Dublin. The main city venues are *The Crow's Nest*, 2 Skipper St (☎028/9032 5491), which caters for the older crowd, with quizzes, sing-songs or discos; and *The Parliament Bar*, 2 Dunbar St (☎028/9023 4520), which has events Thurs–Sun, and is especially popular on Saturdays, with dancing to house on table-tops; on Monday nights there's classical music with food, chess and backgammon. Monday sees a livelier time at Forbidden Fruit in *The Milk Bar Club*, Tomb St (☎0707/499 9997). For more information, call Lesbian Line (Thurs 7.30–10pm; ☎028/9023 6668) or Mensline (Mon–Wed 7.30–10pm; ☎028/9032 2023).

Golf Nearest links to the city centre are at Ormeau Park (☎028/9064 1069); weekday fees £12, weekends £14.50.

Hospitals In an emergency, call ☎999. Belfast City Hospital, Lisburn Rd (☎028/9032 9241); Royal Victoria Hospital, Grosvenor Rd (☎028/9024 0503).

Internet access Bronco's Web, 122 Great Victoria St (Mon–Sat 7.30am–10pm); The Linen Hall Library, Donegall Square (Mon–Fri 9.30am–5.30pm, Thurs until 8.30pm, Sat 9.30am–4pm); Revelations, 27 Shaftesbury Square (Mon–Fri 10am–10pm, Sat 10am–6pm, Sun 11am–7pm).

Laundry Duds 'n' Suds, 37 Botanic Ave (☎028/9024 3956).

Left luggage Despite the reduced level of security, there is still, unfortunately, no official place where you can leave your luggage.

Libraries Central Library, Royal Ave (Mon–Fri 9.30am–5.30pm, Mon & Thurs until 8pm, Sat 9.30am–1pm).

Lost property Musgrave police station, Ann St (☎028/9065 0222).

Markets The huge St George's Casual Retail Market (also known as the Variety Market) in May St (Tues & Fri mornings) is the liveliest: the Friday food and variety market is by far the more popular, with about 200 traders taking part; on Tuesday it's more of a fleamarket-type affair, selling new and secondhand clothes and a variety of junk. The Smithfield Retail Market, at the back of the new Castlecourt development on West St/Winetavern St, is also pretty good; it operates from about thirty shop units and sells new and secondhand goods and clothes. For antiques, try the Saturday market at Alexander The Grate, Donegall Pass.

Motoring organizations AA, 108 Great Victoria St (☎0870/550 0600; 24-hr rescue ☎0800/887766); RAC, 14 Wellington Place (☎028/9023 2640; 24-hr rescue ☎028/9082 8282).

Newspapers Two daily newspapers for all of Northern Ireland are published in Belfast, the Nationalist *Irish News* and the Unionist *News Letter*. The city's local daily paper, the *Belfast Telegraph*, has adopted an increasingly liberal, pro-Agreement stance in recent years.

Police In an emergency, call ☎999. Main city-centre police station is in North Queen St.

Post office General Post Office, Castle Place (Mon–Sat 9am–5.30pm).

Shopping hours Mon–Sat 9.30am–5.30pm. Many city-centre stores stay open until 8pm or 9pm on Thursdays and an increasing number open on Sundays (1–5pm).

Tennis Belfast Indoor Tennis Arena, Ormeau Embankment (☎028/9045 8024).

Trains For information call Central Station (☎028/9089 9411).

Travel agents Thomas Cook, 11 Donegall Place (☎028/9055 0030); USIT, Fountain Centre, College St (☎028/9032 4073).

travel details

Trains

Belfast to: Antrim (9 Mon–Sat, 4 Sun; 45min); Ballymena (9 Mon–Sat, 4 Sun; 1hr); Bangor (39 Mon–Fri, 25 Sat, 9 Sun; 35min); Carrickfergus (35 Mon–Fri, 18 Sat, 8 Sun; 25min); Coleraine (9 Mon–Fri, 8 Sat, 4 Sun; 1hr 30min); Derry (7 Mon–Fri, 6 Sat, 3 Sun; 2hr 20min); Dublin (8 Mon–Sat, 5 Sun; 2hr); Dundalk (7 Mon–Sat, 4 Sun; 1hr 15min); Larne Harbour (12 Mon–Fri, 10 Sat, 5 Sun; 55min); Larne town (21 Mon–Fri, 16 Sat, 6 Sun; 50min); Lisburn (41 Mon–Fri, 29 Sat, 12 Sun; 10–20min); Newry (9 Mon–Fri, 8 Sat, 4 Sun; 50min); Portadown (20 Mon–Fri, 29 Sat, 8 Sun; 35–55min).

Buses

Only details of direct services from Belfast are listed. Call Ulsterbus on ☎028/9033 3000 to get details of bus connections for places not given here.

The Antrim Coaster service runs from Belfast to Coleraine via Larne, the Glens of Antrim and Ballycastle; see p.596 for full details.

Belfast (Bridge St) to: Carrickfergus (37 Mon–Fri, 27 Sat, 8 Sun; 30min); Whitehead (11 Mon–Fri, 7 Sat, 4 Sun; 45min).

Belfast (Europa) to: Armagh (13 Mon–Fri, 7 Sat, 4 Sun; 50min–1hr 25min); Athlone (1 Mon–Sat; 4hr 50min); Banbridge (29 Mon–Fri, 28 Sat, 9 Sun; 1hr 5min); Bangor* (3 Mon–Fri; 35min); Bundoran (4 Mon–Sat, 1 Sun; 3hr 45min); Cahir (1 Mon–Sat; 8hr 25min); Cavan (4 Mon–Sat, 1 Sun; 2hr 40min); Cork (1 Mon–Sat; 10hr); Craigavon (19 Mon–Fri, 15 Sat, 3 Sun; 1hr 20min); Derry (19 Mon–Sat, 6 Sun; 1hr 40min); Donaghadee* (3 Mon–Fri, 4 Sat; 1hr 10min); Downpatrick (26 Mon–Fri, 16 Sat, 5 Sun; 1hr); Dublin (7 Mon–Sat, 4 Sun; 2hr 45min); Dublin Airport (6 Mon–Sat, 3 Sun; 2hr 35min); Dungannon (15 Mon–Sat, 7 Sun; 50min); Dungiven (19 Mon–Sat, 6 Sun; 1hr 10min); Enniskillen (10 Mon–Sat, 4 Sun; 2hr 15min); Galway (3 Mon–Sat, 1 Sun; 6hr 40min); Hillsborough (34 Mon–Fri, 29 Sat, 10 Sun; 45min); Limavady (5 Mon–Fri, 2 Sat; 1hr 35min); Lisburn (47 Mon–Fri, 35 Sat; 30min); Monaghan (4 Mon–Sat, 1 Sun; 1hr 45min); Newcastle (19 Mon–Fri, 16 Sat, 11 Sun; 1hr 20min); Newry (17 Mon–Fri, 13 Sat, 5 Sun; 1hr 20min); Newtownards* (9 Mon–Fri, 6 Sat; 40min); Omagh (10 Mon–Sat, 6 Sun; 1hr 30min–1hr 45min); Portadown (13 Mon–Fri, 7 Sat, 4 Sun; 40min–1hr 15min); Portaferry* (2 Mon–Fri, 4 Sat; 1hr 40min); Sligo (3 Mon–Sat, 1 Sun; 3hr 50min).

** more frequent service from Laganside*

Belfast (Laganside) to: Antrim (40 Mon–Fri, 28 Sat, 10 Sun; 35–50min); Ballycastle (3 Mon–Fri; 1hr 30min); Ballymena (32 Mon–Fri, 16 Sat, 5 Sun; 1hr–1hr 20min); Bangor (31 Mon–Fri, 27 Sat, 8 Sun; 45min); Carrickfergus (24 Mon–Fri, 27 Sat, 8 Sun; 35min); Coleraine (6 Mon–Fri, 7 Sat, 5 Sun;

45min); Comber (22 Mon–Fri, 14 Sat, 7 Sun; 30min); Cookstown (4 Mon–Fri, 3 Sat, 1 Sun; 1hr 40min); Donaghadee (22 Mon–Fri, 19 Sat, 9 Sun; 1hr); Holywood (34 Mon–Fri, 27 Sat, 8 Sun; 25min); Killyleagh (8 Mon–Fri, 5 Sat, 1 Sun; 1hr); Larne (13 Mon–Fri, 10 Sat, 2 Sun; 55min–1hr 25min); Magherafelt (5 Mon–Fri, 3 Sat, 1 Sun; 1hr 10min); Newtownards (61 Mon–Fri, 43 Sat, 12 Sun; 40min); Portaferry (14 Mon–Fri, 8 Sat, 4 Sun; 1hr 30min); Portrush (6 Mon–Sat, 4 Sun; 1hr 10min); Portstewart (6 Mon–Sat, 4 Sun; 1hr); Whitehead (10 Mon–Fri, 7 Sat, 4 Sun; 50min).

Belfast (Upper Queen St) to: Lisburn (43 Mon–Fri, 41 Sat, 28 Sun; 25min).

CHAPTER FIFTEEN

ANTRIM AND DERRY

Much of the coastline of counties **Antrim** and **Derry** is as spectacular as anything you'll find in Ireland and, consequently, unlike other parts of the North, it has always attracted an abundance of tourists. On fine days, the Mull of Kintyre and the islands of Islay and Jura are clearly visible across the water, and much of the predominantly Protestant population derives originally from Scotland.

County Antrim's major attractions are the nine **Glens of Antrim** in the northeast corner, green fertile fingers probing inland from high cliffs, almost immediately followed by the weird geometry of the **Giant's Causeway**. Along this part of the coast the **Ulster** and **Moyle Ways** offer great opportunities for short walks and long hikes, and pass some wonderful deserted beaches. As you follow the coast road (A2) further west, you'll come to two of the North's great seaside resorts, **Portrush** and, across the border in County Derry, **Portstewart**, attractive holiday spots with sandy beaches and waves perfect for surfing. Modern **Derry city** sprawls around the old steep, walled town and spills over the banks of the River Foyle. A border town, with a substantial Catholic majority, it was traditionally the starting-point for emigrants from Donegal and around on their journey to the Americas. Derry is a more alternative city than Belfast and its forward-looking council has encouraged the arts with great success.

If you're not driving, **transport** around the coastline can be a problem. **Buses** are infrequent, although there are summer specials to the various sights. **Hitchhiking**, though, is easy enough hereabouts or you can take the **train** which cuts a less interesting **inland** route through bland farming country. Trains from Belfast run to both Larne and Portrush, but most of the stops along the way to Derry are at some fairly grim inland towns: **Antrim**, **Ballymena** and **Coleraine**. The other route inland is the A6 road from Antrim to Derry, passing through and near some of the Plantation towns, and ascending steeply through the northeastern fringe of the Sperrins by means of the **Glenshane Pass**.

If transport is somewhat scarce, then at least finding **accommodation** is usually easy. There are some fine hotels and plenty of unpretentious, reasonably-priced B&Bs where you're generally assured of a friendly welcome and a cup of tea. Hostels are growing in number and improving in quality and there's a fair smattering of campsites. Keep in mind, though, that this is where Northerners also holiday, so accommodation may be hard to come by in July and August and at festival times.

ACCOMMODATION PRICE CODES

Throughout this book, prices of hotels, guesthouses and B&Bs have been graded with the codes below, according to what you can expect to pay for a double room in high season. For more details on accommodation, see p.34.

① Under £26	④ £40–55	⑦ £90–110
② £26–33	⑤ £55–70	⑧ £110–130
③ £33–40	⑥ £70–90	⑨ Over £130

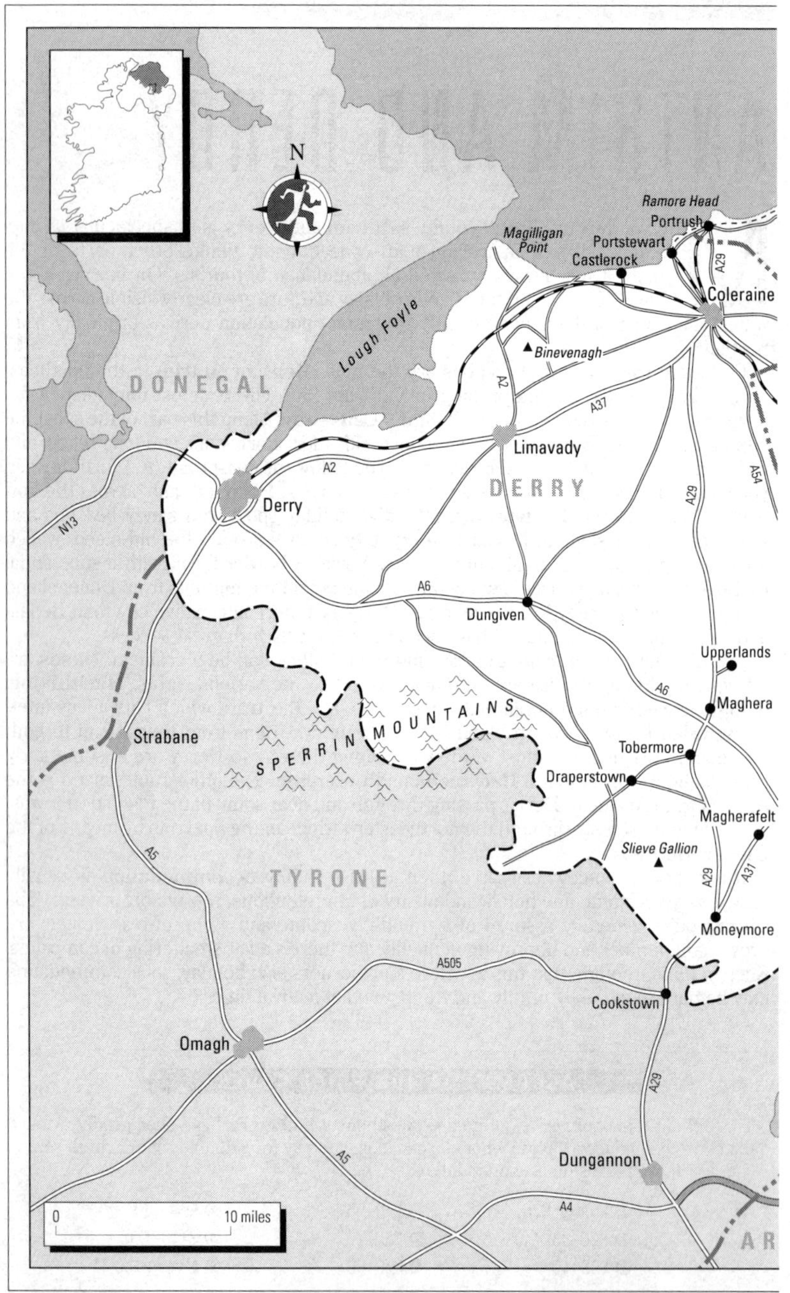
N
Ramore Head
Portrush
Magilligan Point
Portstewart
Castlerock
Coleraine
Lough Foyle
Binevenagh
DONEGAL
A2
A37
A29
A54
Limavady
DERRY
Derry
N13
A6
Dungiven
Upperlands
Maghera
SPERRIN MOUNTAINS
Strabane
Tobermore
Draperstown
Magherafelt
Slieve Gallion
A31
TYRONE
A5
Moneymore
A505
Cookstown
Omagh
Dungannon
A4
0
10 miles
AR

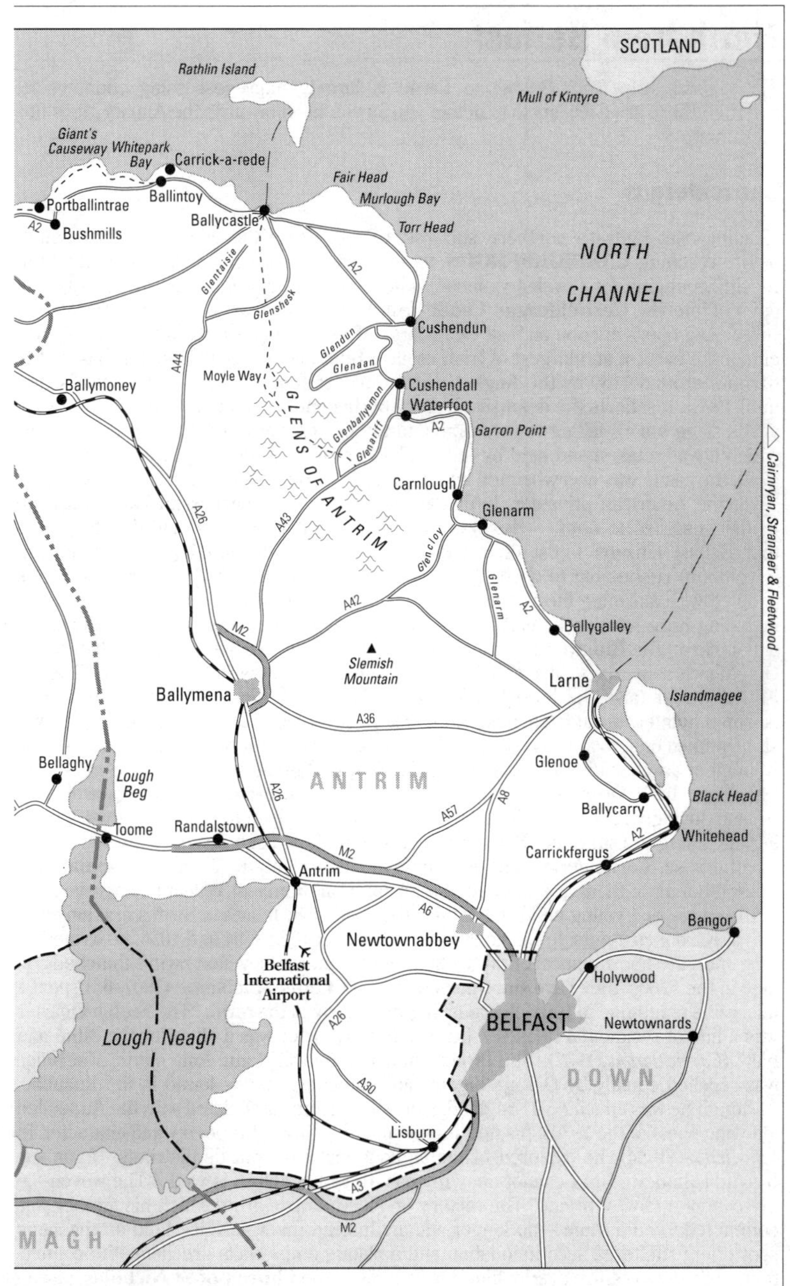
SCOTLAND
Rathlin Island
Mull of Kintyre
Giant's Causeway
Whitepark Bay
Carrick-a-rede
Fair Head
Murlough Bay
Torr Head
Portballintrae
Ballintoy
Ballycastle
Bushmills
A2
NORTH CHANNEL
Glentaisie
Glenshesk
Cushendun
Glendun
Glenaan
A44
Moyle Way
Cushendall
Ballymoney
GLENS OF ANTRIM
Glenballyemon
Waterfoot
Glenariff
Garron Point
Cairnryan, Stranraer & Fleetwood
Carnlough
Glenarm
A26
A43
Glencloy
A42
Ballygalley
M2
Slemish Mountain
Larne
Ballymena
Islandmagee
A36
Bellaghy
Lough Beg
ANTRIM
Glenoe
A8
Black Head
A57
Ballycarry
Toome
Randalstown
Whitehead
Carrickfergus
Antrim
A6
Bangor
Newtownabbey
Belfast International Airport
Holywood
BELFAST
Newtownards
Lough Neagh
A30
DOWN
Lisburn
A3
MAGH

North from Belfast

The coastal strip from Belfast to Larne is largely unprepossessing countryside, although there are a few spots to detain you as you head towards the Antrim glens further north.

Carrickfergus

Heading past Belfast's northern suburbs, the A2 skirts the edge of Belfast Lough before reaching **CARRICKFERGUS**, an unremarkable seaside town (though with a recent reputation for Loyalist violence) whose seafront is dominated by its only real point of interest, **Carrickfergus Castle** (April–Sept Mon–Sat 10am–6pm, Sun 2–6pm; July & Aug opens at noon on Sun; Oct–March Mon–Sat 10am–4pm, Sun 2–4pm; £2.70), one of the earliest and largest of Irish castles. Built on a rocky promontory above the harbour around 1180 by the Anglo-Norman invader John de Courcy (and garrisoned until 1928), it reflects the defensive history of this entire region. In 1315, it endured a year's siege before falling to the combined forces of Robert and Edward Bruce, after which it was retaken and held by the English for most of the next three centuries. In 1760, the castle was overwhelmed by a French force and hurriedly recaptured; and, in 1778, the American privateer, John Paul Jones, fought a successful battle with the British vessel *HMS Drake* – this was America's first naval victory, and the story runs that Belfast citizens (most of the Protestants were sympathetic to the American Revolution) rushed out to cheer the victors. The castle has now been restored and is peopled with alarming life-size figures plucked from various moments of its history – including King John in the garderobe. You can buy a joint ticket (£4.85) for the castle and a trip on the **Knight Ride** (April–Sept Mon–Sat 10am–5.30pm, Sun noon–5.30pm; Oct–March same days till 4.30pm; £2.70), a short walk away in the Heritage Plaza on Antrim Street (also the tourist office, see opposite). A monorail journey in a huge Norman helmet through Carrickfergus history from 581 AD when noble Fergus was shipwrecked on a rock (*carrick)*, the ride bombards you with sound, smells and sights. A smell of another kind hits you at the **Gasworks Museum** (June–Aug Sun 2–5pm; £1.50), on Irish Quarter West, the only complete Victorian coal-fired gasworks in Ireland, lovingly restored by local enthusiasts, which helped to power the town's lighting, including the surviving **Big Lamp** at the end of the High Street.

Otherwise, Carrickfergus and its environs claim plenty of **literary associations**, though not all of them are tangible: the Restoration dramatist William Congreve lived in the castle as a young child (his father was a soldier); Jonathan Swift's first sinecure was at Kilroot, just outside Carrickfergus, where, between 1694 and 1696, he wrote *The Tale of a Tub*. The chemicals firm ICI bought the land and levelled Swift's thatched cottage in the 1960s; they have since moved on. Poet **Louis MacNeice** (1907–63) spent a miserable childhood in Carrickfergus; he says sourly of the town: "The Scotch Quarter was a line of residential houses / But the Irish Quarter was a slum for the blind and halt" (*Carrickfergus*, 1937). The Protestant son of a local Home Rule cleric, MacNeice was repelled equally by Orange bigotry and the complacency found in the Republic. Although he was educated in England, where he became associated with the Auden-led left-wing poets of the 1930s, his upbringing indelibly tinged his poetry and character. In *Valediction* (1934), he explored his ambiguous feelings towards his roots: "I can say Ireland is hooey... But I cannot deny my past to which myself is wed / The woven figure cannot undo its thread." The rectory on North Road – from which his mother was committed to an asylum – no longer stands. Instead the MacNeice Fold on the same spot offers sheltered accommodation and a plaque on its walls proclaims the connection. In the town centre overlooking Market Place, the **Church of St Nicholas**, patron saint of mariners and children, where MacNeice's father ministered (open mornings only), was built by John de Courcy in 1205 – like many of the castles and historic buildings hereabouts – but extensively reworked in 1614. Some interesting features set it apart: a leper's window, a "skew", or crooked aisle, symbolizing Christ's head on the cross falling to the right and, in the porch, a Williamite bomb fired in 1689.

Still, none of these claims to fame is as tenuous as that of the connection with the American president Andrew Jackson, whose parents emigrated from Carrickfergus in 1765. The **Andrew Jackson Centre** (April, May & Oct Mon–Fri 10am–1pm & 2–4pm, Sat & Sun 2–4pm; June–Sept Mon–Fri 10am–1pm & 2–6pm, Sat & Sun 2–6pm; £1.20), two miles north of Carrickfergus on the Larne Road, isn't even their home, but a reconstruction of an eighteenth-century thatched cottage, with a little museum. Next door is something slightly more substantial – the **US Rangers' Centre** (same hours and ticket), which celebrates the formation of the first Battalions of this American Commando force in 1942 from US troops based in the North and trained at Carrickfergus.

One reason to give Carrickfergus a little more time might be the **annual fair**, *Lughnasa*, which is tackily medieval – with wrestlers, archers, minstrels and people dressed up as monks – but great fun nonetheless. It's held at the end of July; check the dates with the **tourist office** at the Heritage Plaza on Antrim Street (April–Sept Mon–Fri 9am–6pm, Sat 10am–6pm; July & Aug also Sun noon–6pm; Oct–March Mon–Fri 9am–5pm; ☎028/9336 6455).

If you do want **to stay**, there's a scattering of hotels around, including the central, family-run *Dobbins Inn Hotel*, 6 High St (☎028/9335 1905; *www.dobbinshotel.co.uk*; ⑤) and the Mediterranean-style *Quality Hotel*, 75 Belfast Rd (☎028/9336 4556; ⑥), while for B&B there's *Langasgarden* on the seafront at 72 Scotch Gardens (☎028/9336 6359; ③) or *The Tramway House*, 95 Irish Quarter South (☎028/9335 5639; ③), a Victorian town house opposite the Marina. The hotels offer the best **eating** options, though other good bets include *Chandler's Wine Bar*, 13 High St, for reasonably priced European cuisine and there's a plethora of cafés, fast-food outlets and inexpensive Chinese and Indian restaurants. This is also **golf** and **fishing** country. Carrickfergus Golf Club (☎028/9336 3713), on North Road west of the town centre, is an eighteen-hole parkland course with great views to Scotland and over the Mourne Mountains. Whitehead Golf Club (☎028/9335 3792), half a mile north of town at McCrea's Brae, also offers distracting views and a challenging course over varied terrain. If you want to go fishing, you can rent boats at Carrickfergus or fish off the rocks and piers along the coast.

Whitehead and Islandmagee

The small coastal village of **WHITEHEAD**, three miles further up the coast, marks the entry point to the narrow peninsula of Islandmagee. There's little to detain you here, apart from a bracing stroll along the promenade or onto the Black Head path and its cliff-top views of the Down coast to the south. However, the village provides a base for visiting the **Railway Preservation Society of Ireland** at the end of Castleview Road. There's a collection of steam locomotives for viewing and riding (Sun afternoons in July & Aug) and the Society runs a number of summer excursions from Belfast Central to Portrush and from Whitehead to Derry (☎028/9333 5367 for details).

Seven miles long and two wide, **ISLANDMAGEE** is a predominantly rural strip of land with the blatant exception of the Ballylumford power station at its northern tip. In the seventeenth century, the "island" was held by the Bissett family in return for an annual payment of goshawks, which breed on the cliffs. The most notable of these cliffs are the **Gobbins**, halfway along the eastern seaboard, and once much visited, though the paths and bridges constructed to guide tourists have long since fallen into disrepair and the cliffs are remembered more for a notorious incident in 1641 when the local inhabitants were hurled into the sea by soldiers from the Carrickfergus garrison. You can approach the cliffs via a gate on Gobbins Road, but much of the path around the cliffs is now decidedly unsafe.

Further north lies the tiny harbour village of **Portmuck**, named after the apparently pig-shaped island it faces (*muc* being Irish for "pig"), and a sandy beach at **Brown's Bay**, where there's a caravan park that allows camping (☎028/9338 2497). At **Ballylumford**, at the tip of the peninsula, you can catch a ferry across the water to Larne (Mon–Sat hourly 7.30am–5.30pm; 60p). On the road to **Millbay** you can spot the 4000-year old Ballylumford Dolmen, known locally as the "Druid's Altar", sitting incongruously in the front garden of a house. There are few bars on the peninsula, but one, the *Millbay Inn*, in Mill Bay, holds regular traditional sessions on Wednesday nights and offers **B&B** (☎028/9338 2436; ④).

Ballycarry and Glenoe

Back on the A2, **BALLYCARRY**, just off the main road, is the site of the remains of the first Presbyterian church ever to be built in Ireland, **Templecorran**, with a memorial to its first minister, who was ordained in 1613. The **church**'s graveyard contains the tombs of some of the supporters of the 1798 Rebellion, including that of James Burns, whose cryptic gravestone can only be deciphered using the following key: the numbers 1, 2, 3 and 4 represent the vowels "a", "e", "i" and "o" respectively, and 5 and 6 the letter "w". Another United Irishman, James Orr – better known as the Bard of Ballycarry, Ulster's answer to Robbie Burns – is also buried here, and some ringing verses in dialect are carved into his tombstone. There's also a grand Masonic memorial of 1831, which bears a patriotic poem about Ireland: "Erin, loved land! From age to age, Be thou more great, more famed and free". The author might not have been impressed by the huge and colourful gable-end mural of William of Orange astride a prancing white horse which adorns one of the village houses.

Five miles along the back road from Ballycarry nestles the picturesque village of **GLENOE**, visited for its pretty waterfall and for Maud's Ice Cream Factory (Mon–Fri 8am–4pm), where you can discover the intricacies of the production process and sample such flavoursome varieties as the award-winning "Pooh Bear and Guinness" in the factory's café.

Larne

Seven or so miles north of Ballycarry, the A2 enters **LARNE**, the last town of any size for a considerable distance on the coastal route. Larne is an important freight centre and is also one of the main ports of entry for visitors to Northern Ireland, served by **ferries** run by P&O (from Cairnryan in Scotland and Fleetwood in England) and Stena Line (from Stranraer in Scotland). Although the town's seaside position is impressive and its main street bustles with shoppers most of the week, it is, in reality, a grim and ugly place, paint-splattered with Loyalist slogans, symbols and insignia. The town's **history** is inextricably linked to its convenience as a landing stage. Norse pirates used Larne Lough as a base in the tenth and eleventh centuries; Edward Bruce, brother of Robert, landed here in 1315 with a force of six thousand men to urge the Irish to overthrow the English; and in 1914, the Ulster Volunteers, opposed to the Irish Home Rule Bill, landed German arms here – one April night, some 140 tons, consisting of an astonishing 35,000 rifles and five million rounds, were unloaded and rapidly distributed to supporters throughout Ulster by a waiting motorcade of several hundred vehicles. The racket was such that local residents believed an invading army had arrived. History apart, though, Larne is not a place to hang around in. The only real landmark is the **round tower**, at the entrance to the port, and even that's an 1888 reproduction – a memorial to James Chaine MP, the driving force behind the develop-

AMANDA M'KITTRICK ROS

In contrast to Larne's lack of vigour is the work of the town's best-known author. **Amanda Malvina Fitzalan Anna Margaret McLelland M'Kittrick Ros** – her signature gives some indication of the embroidery of her prose style – has gone down in history as the world's worst novelist. Born in 1860 in Ballynahinch, twenty miles south of Belfast, she was a true child of the Victorian era. She came to Larne as a schoolteacher and married the stationmaster, Andrew Ros. On their tenth wedding anniversary he gave her a present that generations of fans must be grateful for – the publication of her first fantastical alliterative work, *Irene Iddlesleigh* – and a stream of feverish hyperbole followed. Take, for instance, a passage from *Helen Huddleston* about her heroine:

> *She had a swell staff of sweet-faced helpers, swathed in stratagem, whose members and garments glowed with the lust of the loose, sparked with the tears of the tortured, shone with the sunlight of bribery, dimpled with the diamonds of distrust, slashed with sapphires of scandal and rubies wrested from the dainty persons of the pure...*

Mark Twain and Aldous Huxley swooped on her work with delight and formed appreciative societies, reading circles and dining clubs dedicated to her "unintentional enormities". She became a cult figure, never, it seems, realizing what inspired such devotion. "My works," she said, "are all expressly my own – pleasingly peculiar – not a borrowed stroke in one of them." Quite. She also wrote excruciating verse.

ment of Larne's sea routes to Scotland and the Americas. The other sight is the ruined sixteenth-century **Olderfleet Castle**, which cowers amid the industrial wasteland of the harbour.

The coast around Larne, stretching from Garron Point in the north to Black Head in the south, is of great **geological** interest, with examples of just about every rock formation and period, from the earth's original crust to raised beaches and glacial deposits. At **Curran Point**, just south of the harbour, flint bands, frequently found in the chalk of this coast, provided useful material for Stone Age people, and many arrowheads and other artefacts have been found. Three-quarters of a mile out on the Antrim Coast Road, north of Larne, beyond Waterloo Cottages, stands a large monument to the engineer of this road, William Bald, and his stalwart workers, who blasted their way through, over and round this route in the 1830s. Here, at low tide, bands of fossil-rich Lias clay are exposed – even **dinosaur remains** have been discovered – and beneath the black basalt boulders, the mollusc shell, *Gryphea*, known locally as the Devil's Toenail, is common. Check at the Larne tourist office for geological tours and their useful guidebook to the rock formations of this part of the coast.

Practicalities

If you really have to stay in Larne, the **tourist office** (Mon–Fri 9am–5pm; July & Aug until 5.45pm; Easter–Sept also Sat 9am–5pm; ☎028/2826 0088), in Narrow Gauge Road, will book B&B **accommodation** for you, and there is plenty to choose from. Close to the ferry terminal is the simple *Manor Guesthouse*, 23 Olderfleet Rd (☎028/2827 3305; ②); for more luxury, try the upmarket Victorian *Magheramorne House Hotel*, 39 Shore Rd (☎028/2827 9444; ⑤), just south of town on the A2. There's a **campsite** at *Curran Caravan Park*, 131 Curran Rd, near the harbour (late April to Sept; ☎028/2827 3797), but you're better off at Carnfunnock Country Park on the way to Ballygalley (see p.562). **Ferry information** for P&O services to Cairnryan and Fleetwood is on ☎0870/242 4777, for Stena Line to Stranraer on ☎0870/570 7070; see p.5–7 for fares and further details. For **bus** information, call ☎028/2827 2345.

The Glens of Antrim and Rathlin Island

Northwest of Larne lie the nine **Glens of Antrim**, cutting back from the sea to wild country behind. It's a curious landscape, with enormous contrasts between the neat seaside villages and the rough moorland above, and its well-defined topography gives first-time visitors the strange sensation that they know it well already. The best base for exploration of the area is **Cushendall**, a charming village 26 miles northwest of Larne in the heart of the Glens.

Despite their proximity to the Scottish coast, the Glens were extremely isolated until the completion of the coast road in the 1830s. As a consequence, they were also one of the last places in Northern Ireland where Irish was spoken. **Transport** is still a problem here and the only service to run from one end of this coast to the other is the daily Belfast–Coleraine Ulsterbus express, called the Antrim Coaster (☎028/9033 3000 for times). If you've time, you can dawdle along on a series of local buses; check the times with local tourist offices. **Hitching** is generally fine, but don't expect lifts to take you very far. **Cycling** is heady but strenuous, and don't rely on being able to rent a bike: one of the few places that has some is the Ardclinis Activity Centre (☎028/2177 1340) in Cushendall. One alternative means of getting about is **pony trekking**, which can be a delight in good weather: the main centre is at **Ballycastle**, at the northern extremity of the glen-fractured coast; see p.566.

Ballycastle is also the departure point for the ferry to rugged **Rathlin Island**, Northern Ireland's last inhabited island, in one of whose caves Robert the Bruce of Scotland acquired a legendary lesson in patience from a spider spinning and re-spinning its web.

Ballygalley and Glenarm

The impressiveness of the road builders' achievement becomes apparent the moment you leave Larne's dull suburbs. The view expands to take in the open sea and, beyond it, the low outline of the Scottish coast. **Carnfunnock Country Park** (daily 9am–dusk; car-parking charge related to length of visit) is a good walking stop with a maze in the shape of Northern Ireland, a walled garden, a time garden with a collection of sundials ranging from the simple to the arcane, and a nine-hole golf course. You can also camp here (late April to Sept; ☎028/2826 0088). The first settlement you come to is **BALLYGALLEY**, with a wide, wild bay and a sandy beach embraced by hills. There's something about the sobriety of the architecture that makes it look more like Scotland, an impression heightened by the crow-stepped gables of **Ballygally** [sic] **Castle**, built by seventeenth-century planters. You can call in here for a drink – it's now a **hotel** (☎028/2858 3212; *res@bgr.hastingshotel.com*; ⑥) with, they tell you, a ghost in the dungeon bar – although the building is more impressive from the outside.

The southernmost of the glens, **Glenarm**, is headed by a village of the same name, which grew up around a hunting lodge built by Randal MacDonnell after Dunluce Castle, further up the coast, was abandoned. Glenarm became the major seat of the Earls of Antrim, something that might lead you to expect that **Glenarm Castle** would be worth seeing, but major rebuilding in the eighteenth and nineteenth centuries have left it an architectural mishmash of conflicting styles. **GLENARM** village itself, though, is a delight and very much a taste of what's to follow, with a narrow main street of colour-washed buildings broadening out as it approaches an imposing gateway, the old estate entrance, which now provides access to the glen itself. The lower part of the glen is blighted with Forest Service conifers, but carry on and you reach National Trust land, with far better walking. Back in the village, you'll find a couple of cosy **bars** and a salmon processing plant on the outskirts with a shop where you can inspect the wares.

There's a **tourist office** here in the Community Hall (Mon 1–5pm, Tues, Thurs & Fri 9.30am–5pm, Sat 1–4pm, Sun 1–6pm; ☎028/2884 1087) and a smattering of comfortable and affordable places **to stay**, including *Margaret's House*, 10 Altmore St (☎028/2884 1307; ②), *Riverside House*, 13 Toberwine St (March–Sept; ☎028/2884 1474; ③) and *Nine Glens*, 16 Toberwine St (☎028/2884 1590; ②).

Carnlough and Waterfoot

Shortly after leaving Glenarm, you'll pass through the hamlet of **STRAIDKILLY,** the "sliding village", so named because of the houses' moving about an inch annually towards the sea. Rounding the next bay, you'll arrive at **CARNLOUGH**, standing at the head of **Glencloy**, the "glen of hedges". The village's most striking feature is its sturdy, white limestone buildings: until the 1960s, Carnlough's way of life was linked to its limestone quarries. The shining white stone buildings in the centre of the village were constructed by the Marquess and Marchioness of Londonderry in 1854. Over the main road there's a solid **stone bridge** that once carried the railway bringing material down to the **harbour** – which itself has an impressive breakwater, clock tower and courthouse of limestone. A mile north of the village, in a cottage garden on the Ballymena road, there's an idiosyncratic alfresco "**scrap museum**", consisting of an astonishing range of cleaned up *objets trouvés*, ranging from Roman coins to tin baths, all bedecked with various humorous slogans and philosophical statements from the owner.

Carnlough's **tourist office** inside McKillop's souvenir and ice cream shop on Harbour Road (shop hours; ☎028/2888 5236) can solve any problem, accommodation or otherwise. Almost next door, the solid *Londonderry Arms Hotel* (☎028/2888 5255; *www.glensofantrim.com*; ⑥), once owned by Winston Churchill, is a comfortable **place to stay**; you can sample the smoked salmon fished in Glenarm, or just go for a drink and admire the bizarre collection of mementos of the 1960s' champion steeplechaser, Arkle. For cheaper B&B, try *Harbour View*, 50 Harbour Rd (☎028/2888 5335; ②), *Bethany Guesthouse*, 5 Bay Rd (☎028/2888 5667; ③), or the rooms above the *Bridge Inn* in Bridge Street (☎028/2888 5669; ③). If you're **camping**, the *Bay View Caravan Park* (April–Sept; ☎028/2888 5685) and *Ruby Hill Caravan Park* (March–Oct; ☎028/2888 5692), both on Largy Road, have spaces for tents. *Black's Pub*, on Harbour Road, is the place to head for **music**, with sessions most nights. This is also a good place to attack the **Ulster Way**, with walks up behind the village to forests and waterfalls along the Carnlough River – check first at the tourist office for maps and an update on the state of the paths.

From Carnlough the road skirts round a gaunt shoulder of land and on to **WATERFOOT**, a short strip of houses with a couple of bars that comes to life in the evenings. There's also plenty of **B&B** around including the welcoming and comfortable *Glenhaven*, 38 Bayview Garron Rd (☎028/2177 2839; ④) and farmhouse accommodation at *Dieskirt Farm*, 104 Glen Rd (☎028/2177 1308).

It's **Glenariff**, though, Waterfoot's glen, that is the real attraction. Wide, lush and flat-bottomed, it's abruptly cut off by the sea, while a few miles up the glen is the **Glenariff Forest Park** (daily 10am–dusk; car £3, pedestrians £1.50) which has a **campsite** (☎028/2175 8232; contact the head forester in advance) and a number of waymarked trails. Opt for the Waterfall Trail to see a spectacular series of **waterfalls** skirted by a timber walkway, first built a hundred years ago. You'll pass Altnagowna, the highest waterfall of all, as you travel up the Glenariff road from Waterfoot and you can see some of the others by turning left at the *Manor Lodge* sign and stopping at the restaurant.

To the north, between Waterfoot and Red Bay, there's a series of **caves** with an odd history. The so-called "school cave" was where lessons were conducted for the children of Red Bay in the eighteenth century, a practice made necessary by the oppressive penal laws that outlawed Catholic education. One such pupil was Dr James McDonnell, founder of the Belfast Medical School. The largest of the caves, "Nanny's Cave", 40ft long, was the home of the redoubtable distiller of illicit poteen, Ann Murray, who died, aged 100, in 1847.

Cushendall and around

CUSHENDALL lies at the head of three of the nine Glens of Antrim, a delightfully understated village, its charming colour-washed buildings grouped together on a spectacular shore. The red sandstone **tower** at the main crossroads was built in 1817 by one Francis Turnley, an official of the East India Company, as "a place of confinement for idlers and rioters". Now it's owned by the art terrorist pop band, the KLF. Down the road on Mill Street, sharing premises with the Glens of Antrim Historical Society, is Cushendall's **tourist office** (Tues–Sat 10am–1pm; ☎028/2177 1180), where you can check for details of **dancing and traditional music** in local pubs: *McCollam's,* known to all as *Johnny Joe's,* also on Mill Street, is not to be missed, sessions usually taking place on Tuesday and Friday. Another great session takes place every Wednesday at *The Skerry Inn* in Newtowncrumlin, eight miles southwest off the Ballymena road. Cushendall itself comes alive during the Heart of the Glens **festival** in the middle of August, one of the area's oldest events, replete with traditional music, sporting events and much merriment. **Eating** options are limited to *Gillan's* friendly café on Mill Street during the day, while *Harry's* on the same street offers wholesome, filling meals in both its downstairs bar and restaurant upstairs.

Cushendall is probably the best base for exploring the Glens of Antrim, and accordingly it's well provided with **accommodation**. For B&B, try *The Meadows,* 81 Coast Rd (☎028/2177 1130; *cdda@antrim-glens.demon.co.uk*; ③), friendly and spacious with disabled access too, or the welcoming *Cullentra House*, 16 Cloghs Rd (☎028/2177 1762; ②), a mile northwest of town off the Cushendun road, with its wonderful views. At the time of writing the future of the HINI **youth hostel** was under threat, so it's advisable to call ahead before taking the half-mile uphill trek to Layde Road (head along Shore Street from the tower, go left at the fork, and look out for the youth hostel sign on the wall) (open March to Dec 23; Jan & Feb advance bookings only; ☎028/2177 1344). The *Glenville Caravan Park* (March–Oct; ☎028/2177 1520) is further up the road, and the municipal **campsite** stands on the hill to the north of the town (April–Sept; ☎028/2177 1699). You can **rent bikes** from the Ardclinis Activity Centre, 11 High St (☎028/2177 1340), which also arranges all manner of outdoor pursuits. **Fishing** licences are available from O'Neill's Country Sports on Mill Street.

Layde Old Church and Ossian's Grave

Beyond Cushendall, the land rises sharply and the main road swings away from the coast, which is good news for **walkers**. A cliff-top path, running northwards from the beach, takes you to the ruins of the **Layde Old Church**, chief burial place of the MacDonnells, that originally dates from the thirteenth century. The local historical society has published a catalogue of the gravestones here – an interesting read in itself, but more so if you have Glens ancestry.

The other trip from Cushendall is to **Ossian's Grave**, signposted a couple of miles along the main road to Cushendun. There's a double fake involved here. Ossian, the legendary son of Fionn Mac Cumhaill, was the supposed author of the popular Ossianic cycle of poems, though these were in fact largely fabricated by James Macpherson in the 1760s. The poems inspired the early Romantic movement, particularly in Germany, where Goethe quoted Ossian at length in *The Sorrows of Young Werther*. However, the tomb doesn't actually have anything to do with either legendary or poetic incarnation as it's really a Neolithic court grave. All the same, standing in a sloping field above the valley, with views to Glendun, Glenaan and, in the distance, Scotland, it oozes spirit – as good a place as any to reflect on the shaky origins of the first Celtic literary revival. The stone cairn here commemorates a more substantial literary figure, John Hewitt, known as the poet of the Glens.

Beyond the grave runs **Glenaan**, one of the smallest of the glens, soon petering out to little more than a dip of red reeds and black seams of peat between two hills of heather and cotton grass.

Cushendun to Fair Head

The once fashionable resort of **CUSHENDUN** is an architectural oddity, almost entirely designed by Clough Williams-Ellis, the stylish architect of Portmeirion in Wales, between 1912 and 1925. However, it has nothing of Portmeirion's twee Italianate style that was used famously as the setting for the TV serial *The Prisoner*. Built to a commission from Ronald McNeill, the first (and last) Lord Cushendun, and his Cornish wife, Maud, Cushendun's houses are of rugged, rough-cast whitewash with slate roofs – a Cornish style which clearly weathers the Atlantic storms as efficiently here as in Cornwall. The town was home to Agnes Nesta Shakespeare Higginson (1870–1951), who crafted folksy, sentimental ballads under the far more apposite adopted name of **Moira O'Neill**. Very popular in her day, she's now better known as the mother of Mary Nesta Skrine (d. 1996), who went one better than Agnes and wrote under two pen-names, Molly Keane and M.J. Farrell. *Good Behaviour*, written in her eighties after a thirty-year silence, is a piercingly witty novel of family life in the Big House tradition.

All of Cushendun is National Trust property, and it shows. It's a tiny and well-tended place where tourists – and everyone else – seem peculiarly out of place. The high spot of the village calendar is unquestionably its **festival week** towards the end of July, with plenty of music, competitions and sporting events. Otherwise it's a place for summer strolls and watching the fishing boats. The village is blessed with one of the county's best **restaurants**, *Mary McBride's*, whose homemade chowder and more substantial fish lunches and dinners are well worth sampling, if a touch pricey at around £15 for two courses (excluding drinks). **B&Bs** include the popular *Sleepy Hollow*, 107 Knocknacarry Rd (☎028/2176 1513; ③), and, out towards Torr Head, *Drumkeerin* (☎028/2176 1554; *drumkeerin@ireland-holidays.com*; ③) and *Villa Farmhouse* (☎028/2176 1252; ③). The council caravan park, 14 Glendun Rd (April–Sept; ☎028/2176 1254), has space for **camping**.

The main road from Cushendun northwest to Ballycastle runs inland, traversing some impressively rough moorland and passing **Loughareema**, the "vanishing lake", so termed because of its tendency to drain away completely in hot weather. A mile further on **camping** is available at *Watertop Open Farm* (May–Nov; ☎028/2076 2576), a working farm with pony trekking and fishing available. However, if you take the main road, you'll be missing some of the best of the northern coastline. The **coastal road**, edged with fuchsia and honeysuckle, switchbacks violently above the sea to **Torr Head**, the closest point on the Irish mainland to the Mull of Kintyre. You can also pick up the signposted **Ulster Way** around here, although it swings inland immediately after Cushendun, joining the coast again at Murlough Bay. If you're keen to linger, there's farmhouse **B&B** at *Torr Brae*, 77 Torr Rd (☎028/2076 9625; ③).

Murlough Bay and Fair Head

Perhaps because of the absence of a main road, **Murlough Bay** is the most spectacular of all the bays along the northern coast. From the rugged cliff-tops, the hillside curves down to the sea in a series of wildflower meadows that soften an otherwise harsh landscape. As much as anywhere else on the Irish coastline this is a place for just spending time and drinking it all in.

SIR ROGER CASEMENT

A stone cross in the second Murlough Bay car park commemorates **Sir Roger Casement**, who was, extraordinarily, both a successful administrator for the British and later a martyr for the Nationalist cause. Born in Dublin in 1864, he moved to Antrim following the death of his parents, to live with his guardian and, initially at least, espoused the Loyalist views that characterized his Anglo-Irish upbringing. His brilliant diplomatic career included a stint in the Belgian Congo, where he fearlessly exposed all manner of colonial exploitation, and Peru, which he called the "Devil's Paradise of the Amazon". He was knighted in 1911, but, influenced by his foreign experiences, on his return to Ireland became increasingly involved with the Sinn Féin movement. Believing that World War I offered Ireland the opportunity of achieving independence from Britain, he negotiated military aid from Germany and arranged for a shipment of arms to be landed at Banna Strand on the Kerry coast. His plans were discovered and he was captured before the crucial 1916 Easter Rising and tried.

Seemingly set on martyrdom, at his trial he asserted: "I committed high treason with my eyes open – and for a cause I love above all else. I must some day pay the penalty – I do not mind if I have helped Ireland." However, aside from treason, Casement's homosexuality played a part in his fate. His diaries – the notorious "black diaries", supposedly recording his sexual exploits – were confiscated by the British government after his arrest and circulated unofficially. Their contents were said to be so damning that the chance of a reprieve was out of the question, despite campaigning behind the scenes by Conan Doyle, George Bernard Shaw and others, and he was hanged in Pentonville Prison, London, in 1916. Debate still rages today over the authenticity of Casement's diaries and whether they were a British fabrication designed to sully Casement's reputation as a champion of the colonially oppressed. Whatever the case, it's more likely that Casement's sexuality compounded his treachery in the eyes of the British establishment and made it determined to exact revenge on one of its own. A further twist to the tale has come with the release of once-secret MI5 papers in which Casement admits the futility of the uprising, once Germany had refused to send troops in support, but that he would be branded a coward and traitor to the Irish cause if he did not complete his part in the plan.

The last headland before Ballycastle is **Fair Head**, whose massive 600ft cliffs offer a truly spectacular view across the North Channel to Scotland – the Mull of Kintyre and further to Islay and the Paps of Jura – a proximity which sheds light on the confusion of land ownership between Ireland and Scotland. Nearby Rathlin Island (see p.568) was hotly contested right up to the seventeenth century, while the MacDonnells owned land both here and on Kintyre (which was considered dangerous enough to English interests to be settled, or "planted", with people from elsewhere in Scotland during the seventeenth century, just as Ireland was). **Lough na Cranagh**, one of three lakes in the hinterland behind the cliffs, has an oval island that is actually a *crannóg*, a lake dwelling, encircled by a parapet wall. A walk from the Fair Head car park to Murlough Bay takes about 45 minutes, but muddy paths and changeable weather make walking boots and a waterproof essential.

Ballycastle

The lively market town and port of **BALLYCASTLE** sits at the mouth of the two northernmost Antrim glens, **Glenshesk** and **Glentaisie**, and makes a pleasant base for exploring the Causeway Coast or the glens themselves, especially if you find yourself passing through at the time of the *Fleadh Amhrán agus Rince* three-day music and dance **festival** in June, the cross-community Northern Lights Festival in mid-August, or the **Ould Lammas Fair** held on the last Monday and Tuesday in August. This last event is more than just a tourist promotion: Ireland's oldest fair, it dates from 1606 when the MacDonnells first obtained a charter, and has sheep and pony sales as well as the obligatory stalls and shops. Stallholders do a roaring trade in **dulse**, an edible seaweed, and **yellowman**, a tooth-breaking yellow toffee that's so hard it needs a hammer to break it up. Both of these delicacies feature in a sentimental song that originates locally:

Did you treat your Mary Ann
To dulse and yellowman
At the Ould Lammas Fair in Ballycastle–O?

Ballycastle has a solid, prosperous feel about it that derives from the efforts of an enlightened mid-eighteenth-century landowner, Colonel Hugh Boyd, who developed it as an industrial centre, providing coal and iron ore mines, a tannery, brewery, soap, bleach, salt and glass works. The town's prosperity, though, really depended on its **coal mines**; lignite was mined at Ballintoy, on the coast a few miles further west, an enterprise which came to an abrupt end in the eighteenth century when the entire deposit caught fire and burned for several years. More recently, the harbour area was redeveloped to cater for the now-defunct ferry to Campbeltown on the Mull of Kintyre, though, fortunately, Morton's fresh fish shop has been left intact. Boats leave from here also to Rathlin Island (see p.568).

At the seafront there's a memorial to **Guglielmo Marconi**, the inventor of the wireless, who in 1898 made his first successful radio transmission between Ballycastle and Rathlin. From the seafront, Quay Road leads gradually uphill past houses and shops to the **Diamond**, the town's focus. Up the steeper Castle Street hill, the town's tiny **museum** (July & Aug daily noon–6pm; free) occupies the old eighteenth-century courthouse. Temporary exhibitions are hosted upstairs, while, downstairs in the former cells, there's a small and somewhat poignant collection of artefacts produced by the pre-World War I Irish Home Industries Shop. Pride of place goes to the Glentaisie banner for the first *Feis na nGleann* in 1904.

A little way out of town, on the main road to Cushendall, are the ruins of **Bonamargy Friary**, founded by the dominant MacQuillan family around 1500. One family member, Julia, insisted on being buried in the main walkway, so that she might be humbled by the stepping feet of others even in death. A number of the rival MacDonnell family are also buried here, including the hero of Dunluce Castle, Sorley Boy MacDonnell, and his son Randal, first Earl of Antrim (see p.573). An indication of the strength of the Irish language in these parts is that the tomb of the second earl, who died in 1682, is inscribed in Irish as well as the usual English and Latin: the Irish inscription reads "Every seventh year a calamity befalls the Irish" and "Now that the Marquis has departed, it will occur every year". The **Margy river**, on which Bonamargy Friary stands, is associated with one of the great tragic stories of Irish legend, that of the Children of Lir (see p.203), whose jealous stepmother turned them into swans and forced them to spend three hundred years on the Sea of Moyle (the narrow channel between Ireland and the Scottish coast). Also on the stretch of shore near Ballycastle is **Carraig Uisneach**, the rock on which the mythical Deirdre of the Sorrows, her lover Naoise, and his brothers, the sons of Uisneach, are said by some to have come ashore after their long exile in Scotland (also see p.570).

Practicalities

If you're going to **stay** in Ballycastle, the **tourist office** in Sheskburn House on Mary St (July & Aug Mon–Fri 9.30am–7pm, Sat 10am–6pm, Sun 2–6pm; Sept–June Mon–Fri 9.30am–5pm; ☎028/2076 2024) can point you in the right direction. If your budget is generous, the *Marine Hotel*, at the bottom of Quay Road on the waterfront (☎028/2076 2222; ⑤), is very comfortable. Otherwise opt for the stunning seascape views from comfortable *Kenmara House*, 42 North St (☎028/2076 2600; ④), uphill from the front, the very place where Marconi conducted his tests. Alternatively, there are several **B&Bs** at the harbour end of Quay Road – *Glenluce Guesthouse* at no. 42 (☎028/2076 2914; ③) or *Fragrens* at no. 34 (☎028/2076 2168; *jgreene710@aol.com*; ③) or *Cushleake House* at no. 32 (☎028/2076 3798; ③) which also rents **bikes**. The last house on the left, 62 Quay Rd, incorporates the independent *Castle Hostel* (☎028/2076 2337), while round the corner on North Street is the smaller *Ballycastle Backpackers* (☎028/2076 3612). There are also several **caravan sites** which take tents, but the most pleasant is six miles east of town at *Watertop Open Farm* (see p.565).

The usual range of fast **food** and tea shops can be found around town: both *Donnelly's Coffee Shop* and *Herald's Restaurant* on Ann Street are excellent for daytime meals, and there are good bar lunches at nearby *McCarroll's* and at the *Marine Hotel*, which also has live music on Sundays and hosts *Legends* nightclub for karaoke-style entertainment. *Wysner's* restaurant, 16 Ann St (closed Wed), has an adventurous and inexpensive menu, often including salmon from Carrick-a-rede (see p.570), and is next door to the famous butcher of the same name while *Connolly's Restaurant*, above the Anzac Bar, 5 Market St, has a deserved reputation for its splendid meals. You'll find Ballycastle's **pubs** surprisingly lively – *McCarroll's* has **traditional music** on Thursdays; the *House of McDonnell* (also known as *Tom's*), on the main street, is young and lively with music on Fridays; both *McVeighs's* and the *Central Bar* opposite have sessions on Wednesdays, and the *Boyd Arms* on Fridays; while *The Diamond Bar* is the place for a quiet pint. Down on the seafront, the friendly *Angler's Arms* is a great place to end the evening.

There's **pony trekking** on offer in Ballycastle, at the Loughareema Trekking Centre (☎028/2076 2576), on the Ballyvennaght Road.

Rathlin Island

Northern Ireland's last remaining inhabited offshore island, **Rathlin Island**, lies five miles north of Ballycastle and just twelve miles west of the Mull of Kintyre in Scotland. Caledonian MacBrayne **ferries** (☎028/2076 9299; *www.calmac.co.uk*) make the fifty-minute trip from Ballycastle harbour four times daily between June and September; a return ticket costs £8. Outside these months services are reduced but, in winter, the wreck-filled waters in the race can become too treacherous for the boat to sail at all or make the return trip, so it's worth making sure in advance that you find a bed on the island, as accommodation is strictly limited.

Shaped like a truncated figure seven, Rathlin is an impressive, rugged island, with a coastline consisting almost entirely of cliffs and a lighthouse at each tip. As the island's width is never more than a mile, the sea dominates the landscape and its salty winds discourage the growth of vegetation – wind turbines harness this energy source for electricity generation. The presence of dry-stone walls and numerous ruined cottages indicates a time when the population was far larger than the hundred or so current inhabitants concentrated around **Church Bay**. A stroll around the island will reveal relics of far greater antiquity. Halfway to the West lighthouse is the site of a **Stone Age** axe factory, and, to its north, earthworks known as **Doonmore** (*dún mór*, "big fort"). In the early Christian period the island was a haven for **monks**, who've left evidence of their presence in the form of a sweathouse (a kind of primitive sauna) at Knockans, back towards Church Bay. In 795 AD Rathlin was the first place in Ireland to be raided by the **Vikings**. Subsequent times saw three bloody massacres, one by the Scots and two by the English. In 1575, the mainland MacDonnells sent their women, children and old people to Rathlin for safety from the English, but that didn't stop the invading fleet, under the Earl of Essex (whose soldiers included Sir Francis Drake), from slaughtering the entire population. Later, in 1642, the MacDonnells were again butchered by their Scottish enemies, the Campbells; Rathlin was deserted for many years afterwards. You can discover more about the island's history in the Boathouse, down by the harbour, recently converted to house a **heritage centre** (Easter–Aug daily 11.30am–4.30pm; 50p).

The island's cliffs make superb **birdwatching** country, particularly **Bull Point**, on the western tip, part of a large RSPB nature reserve. The viewpoint at the West lighthouse (April–Aug; contact warden in advance on ☎028/2076 3948) provides wonderful views of Northern Ireland's largest colony of seabirds – a minibus plies between here and Church Bay in summer. The foot of the cliff is riddled with **caves**, many of them accessible by boat only in the calmest of weather, and many also filled with detritus from wrecked ships, brought to the surface by storms.

Bruce's Cave, on the northeast point of the island, below the lighthouse, is a cavern in the black basalt where, in 1306, so the story goes, the despondent Robert the Bruce retreated after being defeated by the English at Perth. Seeing a spider determinedly trying to spin a web gave him the resolve to "try, try and try again", so he returned to Scotland and defeated the English at Bannockburn. You can **rent a boat** to see the cave (see below), but only in calm weather.

Practicalities

There's not much in the way of **accommodation** on Rathlin and booking ahead is always advisable. There's B&B by the harbour at the *Rathlin Guest House* (April–Sept; ☎028/2076 3917; ②) or at the National Trust-owned *Manor House* (☎028/2076 3964; ③), a restored late-Georgian home with its own excellent tea room.. Overlooking Mill Bay ten minutes' walk to the south is the *Soerneog View Hostel* (☎028/2076 3954) which also rents **bikes**. **Campers** can pitch their tents for free on the east side of Church Bay. Life on the island is simple and uncomplicated, but not entirely basic: you'll find a **bar-restaurant**, *McCuaig's*, and a couple of shops at Church Bay. Rathlin is a good place for fishing, and you can **rent a boat** (☎028/2076 3933 or 2076 3935) or get Tom Cecil (☎028/2076 3915) to take you **scuba diving** around one of the many wrecks offshore. Rathlin's two major events are the week-long **festival** in mid-July, with everything from ceilidhs to model yacht-racing, and the **regatta** on the last weekend in August.

The north Antrim coast and northeast Derry

The north coast of County Antrim, west of Ballycastle, is dominated by Northern Ireland's most famous tourist attraction, the strange formation of basalt columns at the mythical **Giant's Causeway**. On the way, around the town of **Ballintoy**, there are several attractions to divert you, not least the precarious rope bridge to **Carrick-a-rede Island**. West of the Causeway, you can sample some whiskey at **Bushmills** and visit the imposing and well-preserved remains of **Dunluce Castle**, the stronghold of the local MacDonnell clan.

The coastline west of Dunluce is another major holiday spot, with the twin resorts of **Portrush** and **Portstewart** filled with tourists in July and August and students the rest of the year. Inland lies the dull manufacturing town of **Coleraine**, which you're only likely to visit en route to the coast.

To Ballintoy and Dunseverick Castle

Heading west from Ballycastle to Ballintoy, there are a couple of places on the way that are worth a stop off. The first of these, **Kinbane Castle**, is a decaying sixteenth-century fortification on a long white headland, built by Colla Dubh, brother of the redoubtable Sorley Boy MacDonnell. The pathway is slippery and badly eroded, but it's worth climbing up to the castle to inspect these Irish defences against the English. (At the time of writing a landslip had closed access to the castle.)

Drawing level with **Carrick-a-rede Island**, not far outside Ballintoy, you'll see the **rope bridge**. Strung 80ft above the sea, the rope-connected planks lead to a commercial salmon fishery on the southeast side of Carrick-a-rede (the name means "rock in the road": the island stands in the path of migrating salmon) – but its main function seems to be to scare tourists, something it does very successfully. Walking its 60ft length, as the bridge leaps and bucks under you, is enough to induce giggles and screams from the hardiest of people. The bridge is up from late April to mid-September, when the salmon fishing season ends; there's a car park – always open (£2) – and a **café** (June–Aug daily noon–8pm). You can **camp** here for one night only at the National Trust's *Larrybane Campsite* (☎028/2076 2178).

BALLINTOY itself has a dramatic harbour, much-loved by artists, with a dark, rock-strewn strand contrasting oddly with the neat pale-stone breakwater. It's lively with boats in the summer, and visitors pack the café, *Roark's Kitchen*, but in winter it's bleak and exposed. The little white church that stands at the top of the harbour road was a replacement for the one where local Protestants took refuge from Catholics in 1641, before being rescued by the Earl of Antrim. A landlord of Ballintoy in the eighteenth century, Downing Fullerton, founded Downing College in Cambridge; the staircase and oak panelling from the castle at Ballintoy were removed when it was demolished and taken to the Cambridge college. In good weather you can rent boats for fishing and trips along the coast. **Sheep Island**, the bizarre rocky column standing just offshore, is home to a colony of cormorants. In the summer, **boat trips** run out from Ballintoy, past Sheep Island, to Carrick-a-rede (£1). If you're tempted to **stay** in the village, try the refurbished *Fullerton Arms*, 22 Main St (☎028/2076 9613; ③), or *Ballintoy House*, 9 Main St (☎028/2076 2317; ②). Hostel accommodation is also available at the recently built and extremely comfortable *Sheep Island View Hostel*, 42a Main St (☎028/2076 9391; *s.mcshane@virgin.net*), which has space for **tents** and rents out **bikes**. Traditional music fans should head for the *Carrick-a-Rede* bar and its Tuesday and Sunday night sessions.

Continuing west along the coast, **Whitepark Bay** is a delight, a mile-long sweep of white sand with a HINI **youth hostel** (open all year; ☎028/2073 1745), which will organize pony trekking, canoeing, pub trips and parties and is the sort of place where you arrive for one night and stay several. A footpath from Ballintoy leads past here to **PORTBRADDAN**, a tiny hamlet of multicoloured houses, next to one of which is St Gobban's, a slate-roofed little church which, at twelve feet by six and a half is, supposedly, the **smallest church** in Ireland. Needless to say, there are other contenders: the ruins of an even smaller one, St Lasseragh's, stand on the cliff above.

Dunseverick Castle

From Portbraddan the coast path leads round a headland, through a spectacular hole in the rock and then, by degrees, up to the cliffs of **Benbane Head**. The road and path almost converge at **Dunseverick Castle**, now no more than the ruins of a sixteenth-century gatehouse. This was once capital of the old kingdom of Dalriada, which spread over north Antrim and Scotland, and the terminus of one of the five great roads that led from Tara, the ancient capital of Ireland. Its location, naturally enough, made it one of the main departure points for the great Irish colonization of Scotland that took place from the fifth century onwards, and the castle was stormed by the **Danes** in the ninth and tenth centuries. Dunseverick also features in one of the great Irish love stories, the ninth-century *Longas mac n-Usnig* or "The fate of the children of Uisneach". Deirdre, the betrothed of King Conor, falls in love with his bodyguard, Naoise. Together with Naoise's two brothers, the sons of Uisneach, they flee to Scotland. Fergus, one of

Conor's soldiers, believes the king has forgiven them and persuades them to return home. Landing at Dunseverick (or, some say, Ballycastle), they take the high road to Conor's court at Armagh, but the king kills the brothers and seizes Deirdre, who dashes her head against a stone and dies. And Fergus, outraged, destroys Conor's palace (though not, apparently, the king himself). Down in postcard-picturesque Dunseverick harbour, there's a tiny **museum** (June–Aug Mon–Sat 10am–4pm; £1), focusing on objects salvaged locally and elsewhere, including lumps of coal from the *Titanic*.

The Giant's Causeway

Ever since 1693, when the Royal Geographical Society first publicized it as one of the great wonders of the natural world, the **Giant's Causeway** has been a major tourist attraction. The highly romanticized pictures of the polygonal basalt rock formations by the Dubliner Susanna Drury, which circulated throughout Europe in the eighteenth century, did much to popularize the Causeway: two of them are on show in the Ulster Museum in Belfast. Not everyone was impressed, though. William Thackeray ("I've travelled a hundred and fifty miles to see *that*?") especially disliked the tourist promotion of the Causeway, claiming in 1842 that "the traveller no sooner issues from the inn by a back door which he is informed will lead him straight to the causeway, than the guides pounce upon him". Although the Causeway is probably less overtly money-making than it used to be, it still attracts hundreds of thousands of visitors annually, filling the architecturally incongruous visitor centre (see p.572) and the minibus which scurries back and forth. However, even in high season, it's easy to escape the crowds by taking to the cliffs.

For sheer otherworldliness, the Causeway can't be beaten. Made up of an estimated 37,000 black basalt columns, each a polygon – hexagons by far the most common, pentagons second, and sometimes figures with as many as ten sides – it's the result of a massive subterranean explosion, some sixty million years ago, that stretched from the Causeway to Rathlin and beyond to Islay, Staffa (where it was responsible for the formation of Fingal's Cave) and Mull in Scotland. A huge mass of molten basalt was spewed out onto the surface, which, on cooling, solidified into what are, essentially, crystals. Though the process was simple, it's difficult, when confronted with the impressive regular geometry of the columns, to believe that their production was entirely natural. The Irish folk versions of their creation (see box) are certainly more appealing.

Undoubtedly, the best way to **approach** the Giant's Causeway is along the cliffs, preferably on a wet and blustery day when you're scared you'll lose your footing along the muddy way. The waymarked **North Antrim Cliff Path**, cut into the cliff side

FIONN MAC CUMHAILL: THE CAUSEWAY LEGENDS

According to the romantic version of the legend, the Causeway is the everyday story of a love affair between giants. The Ulster warrior **Fionn Mac Cumhaill** (Finn McCool) became infatuated with a female giant who lived on the island of Staffa, off the Scottish coast (where the Causeway resurfaces), and built the great highway to bring his lady love to his side. Some have added fanciful embellishments to the story, such as an estimate of Fionn's height calculated on the basis of a large shoe-shaped stone that's known as his boot. A more robust version has Fionn involved in a row with a Scottish giant. He built the Causeway to go over to Scotland for a punch-up, but on seeing the size of the other giant, lost his nerve and fled home. Safe in Ireland, he had his wife tuck him up in an outsize cot. When the Scots giant arrived in pursuit he saw the size of Fionn's "baby" and in turn took fright and fled, never to be heard of again.

alongside the black geometric configurations, runs all along this stretch of coast. **Public transport** to and from the Causeway is well organized in summer: the "open topper" **bus** runs in July and August four times daily between Coleraine (where the stop is opposite the train station) and the Causeway, stopping at Portstewart, Portrush, Portballintrae and Bushmills; you can flag it down anywhere along the way. If you're travelling by **train** from Belfast, the line ends at Portrush, from where you can catch either the open topper or the regular bus #172 towards Ballycastle; for more details phone ☎028/7034 3334. If you want to **stay** close to the Causeway there's the *Causeway Hotel* (☎028/2073 1226; ⑥) near the visitor centre or the *Carnside Guesthouse*, 23 Causeway Rd (☎028/2073 1337; ③), which has superb views.

Visiting the Causeway

The Causeway's **visitor centre** was severely damaged by fire in March 2000, and most of its exhibits were destroyed – though the shop and café survived. At the time of writing tourist information was available in temporary premises (daily: March–May, Sept & Oct 10am–5pm; June 10am–6pm; July & Aug 10am–7pm; Nov–Feb 10am–4.30pm; ☎028/2073 1855; car park £3).

Resist the temptation to follow the crowds on the ten-minute walk along the path straight down to the Causeway (and dodge the minibus that runs every 15min; £1 return); instead take a better route that's a round trip of roughly two miles. Follow the cinder path up behind the visitor centre and round the edge of promontories – among them **Weir's Snout** – from which you can gasp at the Causeway from above, and watch the eider and gannets wheeling across from Ailsa Craig, thirty miles away in Scotland. If you're here in autumn and in luck, you may sight the Aurora Borealis bouncing in the sky northwards. A flight of 162 steps takes you down to sea level and a junction in the path, leading further along to the 40ft basalt columns, known as the **Organ Pipes**. Many of the formations have names invented for them by the guides who so plagued Thackeray and his contemporaries – the Harp, for example – but at least one, **Chimney Point**, has an appearance so bizarre that it persuaded the crew of the *Girona*, a ship of the Spanish Armada, to think it was Dunluce Castle, a couple of miles further west, where they might get help from the MacDonnells: instead, their vessel was wrecked on the rocky shore. Before you reach Chimney Point, **Port-na-Spánaigh** is the place where the ship foundered in September 1588. The treasure it was carrying was recovered by divers in 1968, and some of the items are on show in the Ulster Museum in Belfast. Sadly, extensive cliff erosion prevents any further exploration and prohibitive costs are likely to deter future reparation.

Tucked into the coastline, inaccessible from land, are some spectacular **caves**: Portcoon Cave, 450ft long and 40ft high; Leckilroy Cave, which you can't go into; and Runkerry Cave, an amazing 700ft long and 60ft high. Your best option, if you want to explore, is to persuade a fisherman in Portballintrae (see opposite) or Dunseverick Harbour to take you – £40 is considered a persuasive sum.

If the weather is inclement, you can warm yourself up by playing with the whipping tops and skipping ropes in the museum of the Williams-Ellis designed **Causeway School** (July & Aug daily 11am–5pm; 75p), next to the centre car park, or sit at an ink-splotched desk in the recreated 1920s classroom.

Bushmills and Dunluce Castle

The next stop on the main road beyond the Causeway is **BUSHMILLS**, whose foremost attraction is the **Old Bushmills Distillery**, on the outskirts of town. Whiskey has been distilled here legally since 1608, making it the oldest licit distillery in the world, and it's well worth making the **tour** (April–Oct Mon–Sat 9.30am–5.30pm, Sun noon–5.30pm, last tour 4pm; Nov–March Mon–Fri tours at 10.30am, 11.30am, 1.30pm,

2.30pm & 3.30pm; £3.50). Bushmills whiskey is distilled three times, once more than Scotch; but perhaps the biggest surprise is just how unsubtle a business the industrial manufacture of alcohol is, despite all the lore that surrounds it. The distillery is a massive factory where an extraordinary range of (mostly unpleasant) smells assail your nostrils, making it difficult to imagine that the end product really does delight the taste buds. All the same, at the end of the tour you're offered a tot of the hard stuff. The best bet is the unblended malt, representative of what goes on in Bushmills itself, as the grain whiskey that goes into the blend is almost all distilled in Cork; alternatively ask for a tot of Coleraine whiskey, only a tiny amount of which is still produced. They also serve hot toddies, which may be more in order in winter. To find the distillery follow the signs from the cenotaph in the centre of town – it's barely a quarter of a mile.

Accommodation is mostly out of town. *Ahimsa*, 243 Whitepark Rd (☎028/2073 1383; ②), with an organic garden and good vegetarian **meals**, offers inexpensive accommodation in a modernized traditional cottage. Just about the only cheap place in Bushmills itself is *Ardeevin,* 145 Main St (☎028/2073 1661; ③), on the road out to the distillery. The very best rooms in town are at the *Bushmills Inn*, 25 Main St (☎028/2073 2339; *innkeepers@bushmills-inn.com*; ⑦), a former coaching **inn** with cottage-style interior complete with secret room and peat fires, and a superb **restaurant** which features such delights as beef fillet flamed in (naturally) Bushmills whiskey; allow at least £20 per head. You should at least pop in for a drink in the gaslit **bar** while waiting for the bus (which stops outside). There's more luxury at *Killen's,* 28 Ballyclough Rd (☎028/2074 1536; ⑥), a converted nineteenth-century schoolhouse four miles southwest of town off the Coleraine Road; it's well equipped with swimming pool, sauna and solarium and a **restaurant** with excellent local produce.

A detour westwards along the minor coast road from Bushmills will take you a mile to **PORTBALLINTRAE**, a decorous little place with **accommodation** at the plush *Beach Hotel*, 61 Beach Rd (☎028/2073 1453; *info@beachhousehotel.com*; ⑥), or en-suite B&B at nearby *Bayhead House*, 1a Bushfoot Drive (☎028/2073 2501; ③). There's **camping** at the caravan park on Ballaghmore Ave (April–Oct; ☎028/2073 1478) and good **fishing** from the tiny harbour which you can watch from the conservatory of *Sweeney's Wine Bar*, 68 Seaport Ave (☎028/2073 2405), housed in converted stables dating from the seventeenth century and serving tasty, reasonably priced **meals**.

Dunluce Castle

The main road rejoins the coast a couple of miles west of Bushmills. Here you'll see the most impressive ruin on this entire coastline – the sixteenth-century **Dunluce Castle** (April–Sept Tues–Sat 10am–6pm, Sun 2–6pm; Oct–March Tues–Sat 10am–4pm; March & Oct also Sun 2–4pm; £1.50). Perched on a fine headland, high above a cave, it looks as if it only needs a roof to be perfectly habitable once again. Its history is inextricably linked to that of its original owner, **Sorley Boy MacDonnell**, whose clan, the so-called "Lords of the Isles", ruled northeastern Ulster from this base. English incursions into the area culminated in 1584 with Sir John Perrott laying siege to Dunluce, forcing Sorley Boy ("Yellow Charles" in Irish) to leave the castle. But as soon as Perrott departed, leaving a garrison in charge, Sorley Boy hauled his men up the cliff in baskets and recaptured the castle, later repairing the damage with the proceeds of the salvaged wreckage of the *Girona* and arming the fort with three of its cannons. Having made his point, Sorley Boy agreed a peace with the English, and his son, **Randal**, was created Viscount Dunluce and Earl of Antrim by James I. In 1639, Dunluce Castle paid the penalty for its precarious, if impregnable, position when the kitchen fell off the cliff during a storm, complete with cooks and dinner. Shortly afterwards, the MacDonnells moved to more comfortable lodgings at Glenarm, and Dunluce was left empty.

However, it remains an extraordinary place. The MacDonnells' Scottish connections – Sorley Boy's son continued to own land in Kintyre – are evident in the **gatehouse**'s turrets and crow-step gables and the tapering chimneys of the seventeenth-century **Great Hall**. There's a strange touch of luxury in the **loggia** that, oddly, faces away from the sun. A spectacular scramble, particularly in wild weather, takes you down to the **cave** below the castle which pierces right through the promontory, with an opening directly under the gatehouse.

Portrush

The town of **PORTRUSH**, on the Ramore Peninsula, has sandy beaches backed by dunes, running both east and west, and everything you'd expect from a seaside resort, including summer drama in the Town Hall and plenty of amusements for children. Many students from the University of Ulster at Coleraine live here, and make it a considerably livelier place than you might expect, even out of season. The huge popularity of the local dance scene draws clubbers from all over the North and the town can have a distinctly raucous feel at weekends. The **beach** is long and sandy, ending, towards eastern Dunluce at the **White Rocks**, where the weather has carved the soft limestone cliffs into strange shapes, most famously the so-called "Cathedral Cave", 180ft from end to end.

On a different note, Portrush offers a range of activities and entertainments for children and wet afternoons. There's the all-weather **Waterworld**, by the harbour (June–Aug Mon–Sat 10am–9pm, Sun noon–9pm; Sept Fri 3–9pm, Sat 10am–9pm, Sun noon–9pm; £4.25), with water flumes, slides, sauna, Jacuzzis, aquarium and restaurant; **Fantasy Island** indoor adventure playground on the promenade (Easter–Sept Mon–Sat 10am–8pm, Sun noon–8pm; Oct–March Fri–Sun same hours; £3.25; £2.50 for under-4s); and the summer-only **Barry's Fairground** just behind the seafront. The controversially expensive **Dunluce Centre**, 10 Sandhill Drive (April Sat & Sun noon–5pm; May, June & early Sept daily noon–5pm; July & Aug daily 10am–7pm; £5) houses the tourist office (see below), a viewing tower and a variety of interactive and cinematic experiences. The former bath-house for the well-heeled patrons of the *Northern Counties Hotel* on the seafront is now the **Portrush Countryside Centre** (June–Sept Mon & Wed–Sun 10am–6pm; free), with an indoor sea-creature-filled rock pool, local natural history displays and staff who will happily name your rock samples or flower specimens. There is rewarding **surfing** here off West Strand and White Rocks: you can rent boards and gear at one of the surf shops in Portrush or further along the coast in Portstewart, but first check the safety of the waves (☎028/7082 4596). Safety considerations are seemingly jettisoned during the annual **raft race** at the end of May when participants race each other across the harbour on homemade rafts.

The main sporting attraction is the **Royal Portrush Golf Club** (☎028/7082 2311), which hosted the British Amateur Championships in 1993. The North's premiere club, it boasts one nine-hole and two eighteen-hole courses, though in fact most of the coast seems to be covered in greens and putters – eighty in all – whose vistas offer a welcome distraction from your handicap. Demand is high in the summer, especially in good weather, and it's wise to **book ahead**. A detailed list of green fees, course lengths and standard scratch scores is available from the tourist office.

Practicalities

The friendly and efficient **tourist office** (March & Oct Sat & Sun noon–5pm; April to mid-June Mon–Fri 9am–5pm, Sat & Sun noon–5pm; mid-June to Sept daily 9am–8pm; ☎028/7082 3333) is in the Dunluce Centre on Sandhill Road, a little south of the town centre. **Bikes** can be rented from Thompson's Cycles, 77b Main St (☎028/7082 9606).

Note that **accommodation** fills up quickly in high season and also in May during the "**North West 200**" motorbike road races and July during major golf championships.

Options in town range from the upmarket *Peninsula Hotel*, 15 Eglinton St (☎028/7082 2293; *reservations@peninsulahotel.co.uk*; ⑥) and *Eglinton Hotel*, 49 Eglinton St (☎028/7082 2371; ⑥), both near the station, to dozens of **B&Bs**, most of them very friendly and welcoming. Try, for example, *Glenkeen Guest House*, 59 Coleraine Rd (☎028/7082 2279; ④), which has won tourist board awards, or the Victorian *Harbour Heights,* on the seafront at 17 Kerr St (☎028/7082 2765; ④), beside which are several other options. *Macools* independent **hostel** (☎028/7082 4845) is nearby on Causeway View Terrace. For superb farmhouse B&B, there's the award-winning *Maddybenny Farmhouse* (☎028/7082 3394; *www.maddybenny.freeserve.co.uk*; ④), out of town on Loguestown Road; the breakfasts here are sumptuous and there's an attached **riding school** and self-catering cottages (£250–450 per week). **Campsites** abound in the area, though most of them are actually fairly unattractive caravan parks that also take tents; closest to town are the *Skerries Holiday Park*, 126 Dunluce Rd (☎028/7082 2531) towards Dunluce, and the municipal *Carrick Dhu Caravan Park*, 12 Ballyreagh Rd (☎028/7082 3712), a mile west of town.

At the harbour, the *Ramore Restaurant* (☎028/7082 4313; at least £25 a head; reservations essential) serves good **food**, while its wine bar offers a less pricey menu, or try the excellent Italian *Don Giovanni's*, 9 Causeway St; otherwise there are plenty of cheap cafés and takeaways. The town has a few convivial pubs – the nicest **bar** in town is the *Harbour Inn* – but if you're hoping to hear traditional music your best option is to head to Ballycastle (see p.566). **Nightlife** is quite a serious business here. *Lush!* in *Kelly's Goldlinks Hotel* on Bushmills Rd (☎028/7082 3539) attracts major DJs and, consequently, clubbers from far and wide. There are regular discos at *Burberry's* in the *Magherabuoy House Hotel*, out of town on Magherabuoy Road, which also has a decent modern restaurant.

Portstewart

Across the border in County Derry, **PORTSTEWART**, like Portrush, is full of Victorian boarding houses. Of the two, Portstewart is decidedly quieter and has always had more airs and graces: the train station is said to have been built a mile out of town to stop the hoi polloi from coming. In terms of sheer location, though, Portstewart wins hands down. Just west of the town is **Portstewart Strand** (car £2.50), a long sand beach firm enough to drive on – which the locals delight in doing – with some of the best **surfing** in the country. It's a grand place too, if you hit fine weather and feel like getting out your bucket and spade. The best way to take the sea air is the bracing **cliff-side walk** which runs between the beach and the town, passing battlements and an imposing Gothic mansion, now a Dominican College.

The **tourist office** in the Town Hall (July & Aug Mon–Sat 10am–4pm; ☎028/7083 2286) can help with **accommodation** bookings if you have any problems – there's less choice here than in Portrush. **B&Bs** are mostly along the promenade or nearby. Hotel accommodation is available at the *Edgewater Hotel*, 88 Strand Rd (☎028/7083 3314; ⑦), which has breathtaking views from its lounge bar. There's also the good independent *Rick's Causeway Coast* **hostel** at 4 Victoria Terrace (☎028/7083 3789) and a municipal **caravan park**, *Juniper Hill*, at 70 Ballyreagh Rd (April–Sept; ☎028/7083 2023). *Morelli's*, on the promenade, is justly famous for its ice cream, and also serves snacks and Italian **food** in *Nino's* next door. The busy local haunt *Shenanigans*, 78 The Promenade (☎028/7083 6000), is a mid-priced restaurant on the main drag, while *Ashiana*, 12a The Diamond (☎028/7083 4455), is the best tandoori in these parts and not too expensive. In the evenings, *Nero's* **nightclub**, part of *Nelly's Complex* on Coleraine Road, is the place for late-nighters, and has a pleasant pub attached. The *Anchor* bar is the place to try for traditional music while the Flowerfield **Arts Centre**, 103 Coleraine Rd (☎028/7083 3959), runs a variety of courses and stages occasional exhibitions.

Coleraine

COLERAINE is County Derry's second-largest town, a lively enough manufacturing and shopping centre during the day, but a depressingly empty, pedestrianized wasteland at night. Most of the interesting action here takes place down by the River Bann, where there are pleasant walks and a thriving marina, and at the **University of Ulster** campus with its excellent **Riverside Theatre**.

The helpful **tourist office** on Railway Road by the station (July & Aug Mon–Sat 9am–6pm; Sept–June Mon–Sat 9am–5pm; ☎028/7034 4723) will attempt to convince you of the town's attractions: there's a mildly diverting "Historical Trail" to follow. In summer, it's worth enquiring at the tourist office about the environmental **walks** regularly conducted in the area. **B&Bs** are mostly out of town; try the remarkable *Greenhill House*, 24 Greenhill Rd in Aghadowey (☎028/7086 8241; *greenhill-house @btinternet.com*; ⑥), an award-winning Georgian country house seven miles south of Coleraine on the B66; or *Camus House*, 27 Curragh Rd in Castleroe (☎028/7034 2982; ④), a seventeenth-century listed country house overlooking the River Bann, two miles south of Coleraine. The University of Ulster campus provides cheap rooms during the summer vacation (☎028/7034 4141; ③).

Though Coleraine has plenty of daytime cafés, there are few **eating** choices available at night. *Little Caesars*, 45 Railway Rd (☎028/7032 9991) is a worthwhile Italian option while *The Water Margin* (☎028/7034 2222), on the river, is the best-known Chinese. *Lacy's Wine Bar*, 2 Beresford Court, is the hippest drinking hole, but, otherwise, Coleraine's pubs are particularly dire. There's an **Internet café**, *The Globe*, in the centre at 43 Kingsgate St (Mon–Sat 9am–6pm; £1 for 15min; *www.theglobecafe.co.uk*).

A mile south of Coleraine, on the eastern bank of the river, **Mountsandel** is a 200ft mound, apparently the earliest-known dwelling place in Ireland, though the discoveries in Boora Bog in County Offaly must run a fairly close second. The post-holes and hearths of the wooden houses that once stood here have been dated at around 7000 BC.

The northwest Derry coast and Limavady

West of the Bann estuary, the remaining northern coastline of County Derry sees relatively few visitors, but makes a pleasant detour. There are marvellous beaches here all the way from **Castlerock** to **Magilligan Point** and stunning views from the cliffside **Mussenden Temple** and around **Binevenagh** Mountain. Inland, **Limavady** retains a few relics of Georgian times.

Castlerock and Mussenden Temple

Five miles or so west of Coleraine, at the Castlerock crossroads, is **Hezlett House** (April, May & Sept Sat & Sun noon–5pm; June–Aug Mon & Wed–Sun same times; £1.80), built in 1690 and restored after a fire in 1986. The house is a fine example of cruck-truss construction, an early method of prefabricated building using wooden frames filled with clay and rubble that was common in England but is enough of a rarity here to warrant preservation by the National Trust. The last owner of the house is buried in the graveyard at Downhill, where his gravestone quaintly bears both his own version of the spelling of his name and that of his father, a Mr Hazlett.

Lying almost a mile north, the small resort of **CASTLEROCK** has a long strand reaching eastwards to the Barmouth, where the River Bann's estuary draws flocks of migratory birds and watchers. Unless you're a surfer, there's not much else to tempt you, apart from the renovated but still cosy *Bertha's Bar* (known locally as *Love's*).

Two miles west of the Castlerock crossroads, a pair of huge ornate Pompeian gates alongside the main A2 road mark the main entrance to **Downhill Palace** (April–June & Sept Sat & Sun noon–6pm; July & Aug daily same times; free; grounds open all year), built in the 1780s by **Frederick Augustus Hervey**, Anglican Bishop of Derry and fourth Earl of Bristol. Hervey was an enthusiastic grand traveller, after whom all the many *Hotel Bristols* throughout Europe are named, and was also an art collector and great sportsman, once organizing a pre-prandial race between Anglican and Presbyterian clergy along the strand. His palace, accessed through pleasant gardens, lies in ruins and was last occupied by US troops, billeted there during World War II. Across fields at the back of the house is the diminutive **Mussenden Temple** (same times), which clings precariously to the eroding cliff edge and, naturally, offers stunning sea views. Its classic domed rotunda was apparently modelled on the Roman temple of Vespa and was built by Hervey in honour of his cousin Mrs Frideswide Mussenden, who died aged 22 before it was completed. It was subsequently used as a summer library. Later, with characteristic generosity and a fairly startling lack of prejudice, Hervey allowed a weekly Mass to be celebrated in the Temple as there was no local Catholic church. The inscription on the temple frieze translates rather smugly as: "It is agreeable to watch, from land, someone else involved in a great struggle while winds whip up the waves out at sea." The bishop's other constructions include a **folly** in the grounds of the palace, and the **Bishop's Road**, which runs from Downhill and across Binevenagh Mountain on its way to Limavady.

There's **camping** in nearby Downhill Forest (☎028/7084 8728), across the road from the palace gates. The main A2 road continues down the hill a few hundred yards to **DOWNHILL** hamlet, where you'll find the excellent and spacious *Downhill* **hostel** (☎028/7084 9077) on the edge of the hugely long, car-accessible **beach** which is itself overlooked by Mussenden Temple on the cliff-edge above.

Magilligan Point to Limavady

West of Downhill the road hugs the cliffs, while the seven-mile stretch of beach curves around to **MAGILLIGAN POINT**, passing further **camping** opportunities at the *Benone Tourist Complex* (☎028/7775 0555). The road to the point runs across the dunes, skirting the edge of an open prison (once an army base and later an internment camp) before reaching the tip of the peninsula. Here, at the narrow entrance to Lough Foyle, stands a **Martello Tower**, dating from the Napoleonic Wars, with walls more than nine feet thick. There's the *Point Bar* too (open summer only) to provide succour. One of Ireland's most famous harpist, Dennis Hempson, was from the Magilligan townland and attended the great Belfast harp festival of 1792 where he played the *Londonderry Air*.

From the peninsula the road cuts south alongside the foot of **Mount Binevenagh** before reaching **BELLARENA**. The land around the mountain is now a conservation park, dedicated to the preservation of birds of prey, in particular, falcons and kestrels. In the village itself lies Bellarena House, an old Plantation mansion, dating back in parts to the seventeenth century. This was once the home of Sir John Heygate, a minor novelist now long out-of-print, who achieved some notoriety when he travelled with his more famous Fascist-sympathizing colleague, Henry Williamson (author of *Tarka the Otter*) to pay homage to Adolf Hitler in the 1930s. Unfortunately, the house is no longer open to the public, but it is visible from the common ground banks of the River Roe.

LIMAVADY was once a major settlement, its old site lying two miles further south down the valley of the River Roe. The town was refounded as Newtown Limavady in the early 1600s by Thomas Phillips, speaker of the Irish House of Commons, and promptly spent the next three hundred and fifty years or so in relative obscurity. However, in recent years, Limavady has undergone major economic expansion and most roads to the centre now pass through industrial estates. Although the town's population has consequently increased, there's still relatively little to do or see here. The six-arch bridge spanning the river was built in 1700, and Main Street which runs down from it is still recognizably Georgian. Number 51 Main Street was once the home of Jane Ross who noted down the *Londonderry Air* ("Danny Boy") from a travelling fiddler in 1851. A more modern musical event is the town's excellent jazz and blues **festival** in mid-June. Limavady's only other recent claim to fame is as the birthplace of William Massey, Prime Minister of New Zealand from 1912 to 1925. **Tourist information** is available from the council offices at 7 Connell St (July & Aug Mon–Fri 9am–5.45pm; rest of year Mon–Fri 9am–5pm; April–Sept also Sat 9.30am–5.30pm; ☎028/7772 2226). There are some lively **bars** in the centre of town, including the atmospheric *Owen's* on Main Street, and a few **B&B** options, such as the *Alexander Arms*, 34 Main St (☎028/7776 3443; ④). At **Drenagh**, just outside Limavady, *Streeve Hill* (☎028/7776 6563; ⑥), a Palladian-fronted house dating from 1730, offers superb accommodation and gourmet meals.

The **Roe Valley Country Park**, a couple of miles south of Limavady, preserves Northern Ireland's first hydroelectric power station, opened in 1896, with much of the original equipment intact, as well as a small **weaving museum** and visitor centre (June–Aug daily 10am–8pm, rest of year Mon–Fri 10am–5pm, Sat & Sun 2–5pm; free).

Derry city

DERRY lies at the foot of Lough Foyle, immediately before the border with the Republic. It's a crossroads city in more ways than one; roads from all cardinal points arrive here, but it was also a major point of emigration from the eighteenth century onwards, an exodus which reached tumultuous proportions during the Great Famine. Derry is the fourth-largest town in Ireland and the second-biggest in the North, but it has a markedly different atmosphere from Belfast, being two-thirds **Catholic**. While entrances to the city are now marked by signs in Irish welcoming visitors to Derry, the city still appears as "**Londonderry**" on many road maps and signs, a preference adhered to by the British government, Unionists and television news bulletins, Indeed, it has also acquired the nickname "**Stroke City**" – a reference to the tactful placating of both Nationalist and Unionist traditions by entitling it "Londonderry/Derry" on signs and in radio and television broadcasts. Whatever, the case, locals of both persuasions now generally refer to their city as "Derry". Within Ireland, Derry is highly regarded for both its characteristically caustic humour – best caught in the busier bars and at the football matches at the Brandywell – and its musical pedigree, having produced names as diverse as Dana, Dáithí Sproule (of Altan), Phil Coulter, The Undertones, and many less famous.

Approached from the east in winter twilight or under a strong summer sun, the city presents a beguiling picture, with the spread of the **River Foyle** and the rise of the city's two hillsides, terraced with pastel-shaded houses from which rise the hueless stone spires of the ever-present Church Orders. This scenic appeal apart, at first sight Derry might appear to offer little cause to linger, for all the richness of its history. Yet there are several real attractions, mostly enclosed within the seventeenth-century **walls**, themselves the most significant reminder of the city's past. And four miles or so west of the centre, across the border on the Letterkenny Road, is the unmissable **Grianán Ailigh** (see p.509), a stone fort and the oldest habitation left standing in Ireland.

Outside Ireland, the name of Derry recalls the Troubles of recent years and savage events like the **Bloody Sunday** massacre. Nonetheless, under no circumstances be deterred from visiting, for, unlike Belfast, the cutting edge of violence had receded con-

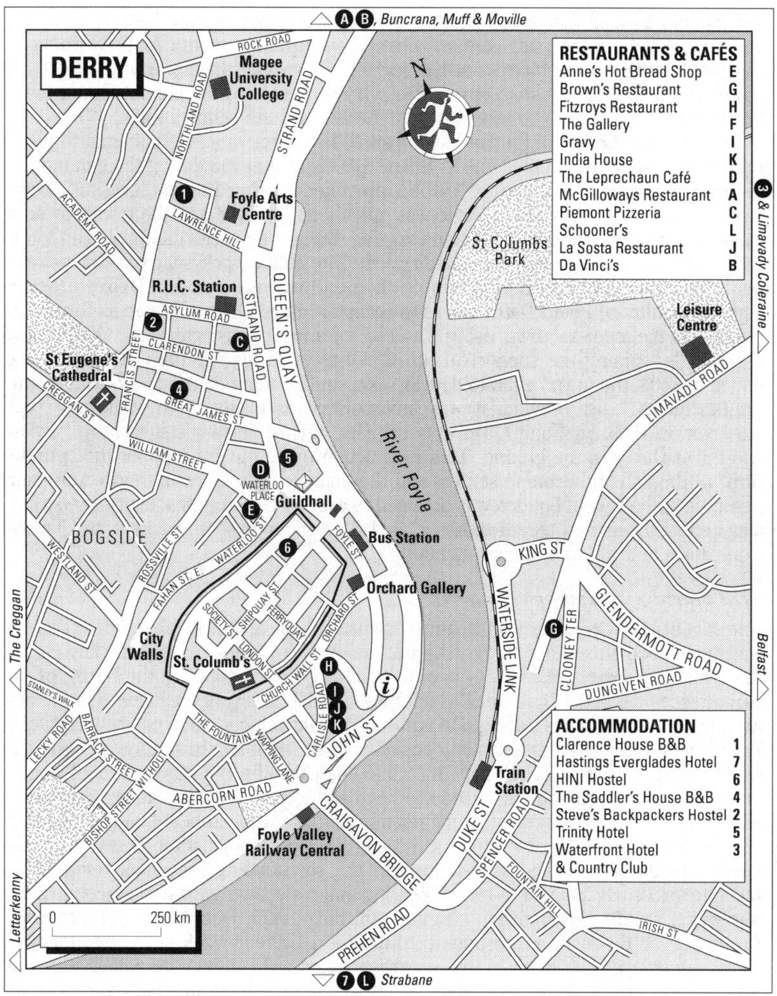

siderably here even before the ceasefires, and the city is still imbued with a real sense of optimism, despite losing much trade to nearby Letterkenny thanks to the declining value of the punt against sterling.

Some history

Derry's original name was *Daire Calgaigh* ("oakwood of Calgach"), given for a warrior who led the Caledonians at the battle of the Grampians. Some time after **St Columba** founded a monastery here in 546 AD, the spot was renamed *Doire Cholmcille*. The monastic settlement must have been relatively unimportant for, although **Vikings** settled around Loughs Foyle and Swilly, only one actual attack was made on *Doire*. By the twelfth century, however, the Mac Lochlainn dynasty, based in Inishowen, had taken control and a small township began to develop. However, decline had set in by the beginning of the fourteenth century when it was granted to the Anglo-Norman de Burgos, builders of the fortress at Greencastle, Inishowen (see p.516). By 1500, the power of the O'Dohertys had spread from Inishowen and they constructed a tower house which was later to be absorbed into the seventeenth-century walls.

In 1566, **Elizabeth I** of England sent a small task force in a failed attempt to pacify such troublesome Irish chieftains as Shane O'Neill, but at the end of the century the uprising of Hugh O'Neill, Earl of Tyrone, provoked another English invasion. *Doire's* strategic position on the River Foyle was quickly appreciated and the town was soon captured and the resident population expelled, though an accidental explosion led to the evacuation of the garrison soon afterwards. The military presence was not restored until 1600 when an English army of four thousand troops under **Sir Henry Docwra** landed at Culmore Point. *Doire* was soon recaptured and Docwra began fortifying the remains of the medieval town, using it as a base for incursions against the O'Neills and O'Donnells, gaining the support of the O'Dohertys in his ventures. When the war ended in 1603, the town began to develop as a small trading centre and *Doire* became **anglicized** as "Derry" when it was incorporated as a city in the following year. However, in 1608, Sir Cahir O'Doherty rebelled against Docwra's successor, Pawlett, and burnt Derry to the ground. This destruction made the city ripe for the "**plantation**" of English and Scottish settlers and the financial assistance of the wealthy businessmen of the City of London was obtained to achieve this. A new walled city was constructed and renamed "**Londonderry**" in 1613 in honour of its backers, the Twelve Companies of the Corporation of London.

THE SIEGE AND ITS AFTERMATH

The **seventeenth century** was the most dramatic phase of the city's evolution. The city walls withstood successive sieges, the last of which (in 1688–89) played a key part in the Williamite army's final victory over the Catholic King James II at the **Battle of the Boyne** (see p.669), the Derrymen's obduracy crucially delaying the plans of James and his ally Louis XIV. James's accession had seen the introduction of a policy of replacing Protestants with Catholics in leading positions in the Irish administration and army. In December 1688, a new garrison attempted to enter the city, but was prevented when a group of young **apprentices** seized the keys and locked the city's gates. Eventually, after negotiation, an all-Protestant garrison under Governor Robert Lundy was admitted. Over the following few months the city's resident population of two thousand swelled to thirty thousand as people from the surrounding area took refuge from Jacobite forces advancing into Ulster. Fearing that resistance against the Jacobite army was futile, Lundy departed; his effigy is still burnt each December by Protestants. Around seven thousand Protestants died during the fifteen-week **siege** that followed (the longest in British history), the survivors being reduced to eating dogs, cats and rats. The suffering and heroism of those weeks still have the immediacy of recent history in the minds of Derry's citizens, who commemorate the siege with a skeleton on the city coat of arms, and the lyrical tag "maiden city", a reference to its unbreached walls.

After the siege, many Derry people **emigrated** to America to avoid harsh English laws, and some of their descendants, such as **Daniel Boone**, achieved fame there. George Farquhar (b. 1678), a Derryman who chose to stay, achieved fame as a playwright. Derry's heyday as a **seaport** came in the nineteenth century, a period in which industries such as linen production also flourished. It was a Derry weaver, William Scott, who established the world's first industrialized shirt manufacturers, cutting the shirts in Derry and sending them to the cottage women of Donegal for stitching. After **Partition**, the North–South dividing line lay right at Derry's back door, and the consequent tariffs reduced much of its traditional trade.

CIVIL RIGHTS AND THE TROUBLES

Though Derry remained relatively peaceful, its politics were among the North's most blatantly discriminatory, with the substantial Catholic majority denied its civil rights by gerrymandering geared towards ensuring the Protestant minority's control of all important local institutions. On October 5, 1968, a 2000-strong **civil rights march** demanding equality of employment and housing, and other political rights – and led by a Protestant, Ivan Cooper, and a Catholic, John Hume, the current SDLP leader – set off on a route through the walled city. Confronted by the batons of the Protestant police force and the notorious B Specials, rioting spilled over into the Catholic **Bogside** district and over eighty people were injured. The clash is seen by many as the catalyst for the modern phase of the Troubles: faith in the impartiality of the Royal Ulster Constabulary was destroyed once and for all, and the IRA was reborn a year or so later.

The Protestant **Apprentice Boys' March** in August 1969 was a further step. The infamous "Battle of the Bogside" ensued when the RUC attempted to storm the area (from where stones were being thrown at the march) which for several days afterwards lay in a state of siege. The Irish prime minister, Jack Lynch, moved units of the army to the border and set up field hospitals for injured Bogsiders. In the mounting tension that ensued, British troops were for the first time widely deployed in the North, and many of the demands of the civil rights movement were forced on Stormont from Westminster. Then, on January 30, 1972, came **Bloody Sunday**. Thirteen people were shot dead when British paratroopers (who subsequently claimed that they had been shot at first) opened fire on another unarmed civil rights march. In 1999, after years of mounting pressure for a full investigation, the British government established the Saville Enquiry which has since conducted its proceedings in Derry's Guildhall.

While 2000 saw the election of Cathal Crumley, the first **Sinn Féin mayor** in Northern Ireland, the city has been controlled for some time by the Social Democratic and Labour Party (SDLP), which attempts to operate in a scrupulously non-sectarian fashion. In this they seem to have been successful (at least in Northern Irish terms), and they also pursue an enlightened policy towards the **arts**, which has succeeded in making this a lively and unexpectedly entertaining place to visit. The city's fabric has also undergone dramatic changes with the construction of huge new developments such as the Foyleside, Quayside and Richmond shopping centres.

Arrival, information and accommodation

Northern Ireland Railways runs about seven **trains** a day from Belfast to Derry (information on ☎028/7134 2228), and there are also frequent **buses** from all parts of the North and the Republic; Ulsterbus (☎028/7126 2261) serves all the main Northern Ireland destinations and Dublin, at frequencies ranging between five daily to Dublin and nineteen most days to Strabane; Bus Éireann (information from Ulsterbus) operates a good network, connecting Derry to such as Galway and Dublin; and Lough Swilly Bus Services (☎028/7126 2017) runs services from across the border in north Donegal. The AIRporter coach service (☎028/7126 9996) runs direct from Belfast International Airport. Good roads enter the city from all directions, making it very straightforward to **hitch**. You can also **fly**: Ryanair and British Airways operate from a range of UK departure points to the tiny City of Derry Airport (☎028/7181 0784), seven miles northeast on the A2 road, connected by regular buses to the train station and the Ulsterbus station on Foyle Street. **Black taxis** run from Foyle Street and most operate in a similar way to those in Belfast, functioning like minibuses to ferry the Catholic community to or from their housing estates. For an ordinary taxi call Co-op Taxis (☎028/7137 1666) or the Derry Taxi Association (☎028/7126 0247).

The **tourist office** is situated in a spanking new building at 44 Foyle St (July–Sept Mon–Fri 9am–7pm, Sat 10am–6pm, Sun 10am–5pm; Oct–June Mon–Fri 9am–5pm;

Easter–June also Sat 10am–5pm; ☎028/7126 7284), which also houses a **Bord Fáilte** office (Mon–Fri 9am–5pm; ☎028/7136 9501) and a **bureau de change**. Grab a free pocket *Visitor Guide* for up-to-date information. The Nationalist *Derry Journal* newspaper (Tues & Fri) is good for entertainment listings. **Walking tours** of the historic centre leave from the tourist office (May–Sept daily 2.30pm; ☎028/7128 9051; £3) while alternative literary and political tours are provided by DAT (☎028/7128 2727).

Accommodation

Although Derry has plenty of **accommodation** at the top end of the price range, finding a more economically priced room in the centre can be difficult, especially in high season. It's worth **booking in advance**, or calling in at the tourist office when you arrive.

HOTELS AND B&B

Clarence House, 15 Northland Rd (☎028/7126 5342). Mostly en-suite, well-equipped guesthouse on a road running parallel to Strand Road. ④.

Hastings Everglade Hotel, 41–53 Prehen Rd (☎028/7134 6722; *www.hastingshotels.com*). Top-of-the-range, high quality accommodation on the banks of the Foyle. ⑧.

The Saddler's House, 36 Great James St (☎028/7126 9691; *lucy@sdn.co.uk*). Elegant Victorian town house B&B very near the city centre, off Strand Road. Its friendly, knowledgeable owners also run the equally grand Georgian *Old Rectory* at 16 Queen St nearby. ③.

Trinity Hotel, 22–24 Strand Rd (☎028/7127 1277; *www.god-group.com*). Bang in the centre of town with its own bistro and popular bar. ⑦.

Waterfoot Hotel & Country Club, 14 Clooney Rd (☎028/7134 5000). Another Waterside location, though somewhat out of town and approached via the Caw roundabout on the Limavady road. Nonetheless well-appointed with restaurant and leisure centre. ⑥.

HOSTELS AND SELF-CATERING

Oakgrove Manor Hostel, 4–6 Magazine St (☎028/7137 2273). Efficient but slightly impersonal 150-bed HINI hostel inside the walls which has an economical restaurant, rents bikes and acts as an unofficial tourist information centre.

Steve's Backpackers, 4 Asylum Rd (☎028/7137 7989). Contrastingly, this friendly independent hostel is based in a small terraced house off Strand Road by the RUC station and offers sixteen beds in smallish dorms.

University of Ulster (Magee College), Northland Rd (☎028/7137 5255; *www.ulst.ac.uk/accommodation*). Accommodation in study bedrooms available from June to mid-September at £14.10 per night or £140 for a week-long stay in a two-bedroom unit.

The City

Since the removal of the security blanket of metal barricades and barbed wire following the ceasefire, it has once again been possible to walk the entire circuit of Derry's **city walls**. One of the best preserved defences in Europe, a mile in length and never higher than a two-storey house, the walls are reinforced by bulwarks and bastions and a parapeted earth rampart as wide as any thoroughfare. Within their circuit, the original medieval street pattern has remained, with four **gateways** (Shipquay, Ferryquay, Bishop and Butcher) surviving from the original construction, albeit in slightly revised form.

You're more than likely to make your approach from the Guildhall Square, once the old quay, east of Shipquay Gate. The neo-Gothic ecclesiastical appearance of the **Guildhall** (Mon–Fri 9am–5pm; guided tours July & Aug; ☎028/7137 7335) belies its true function as the headquarters of the City Council. Inside, the city's history is depicted in a series of stained glass windows. Most of the city's cannon are lined up opposite

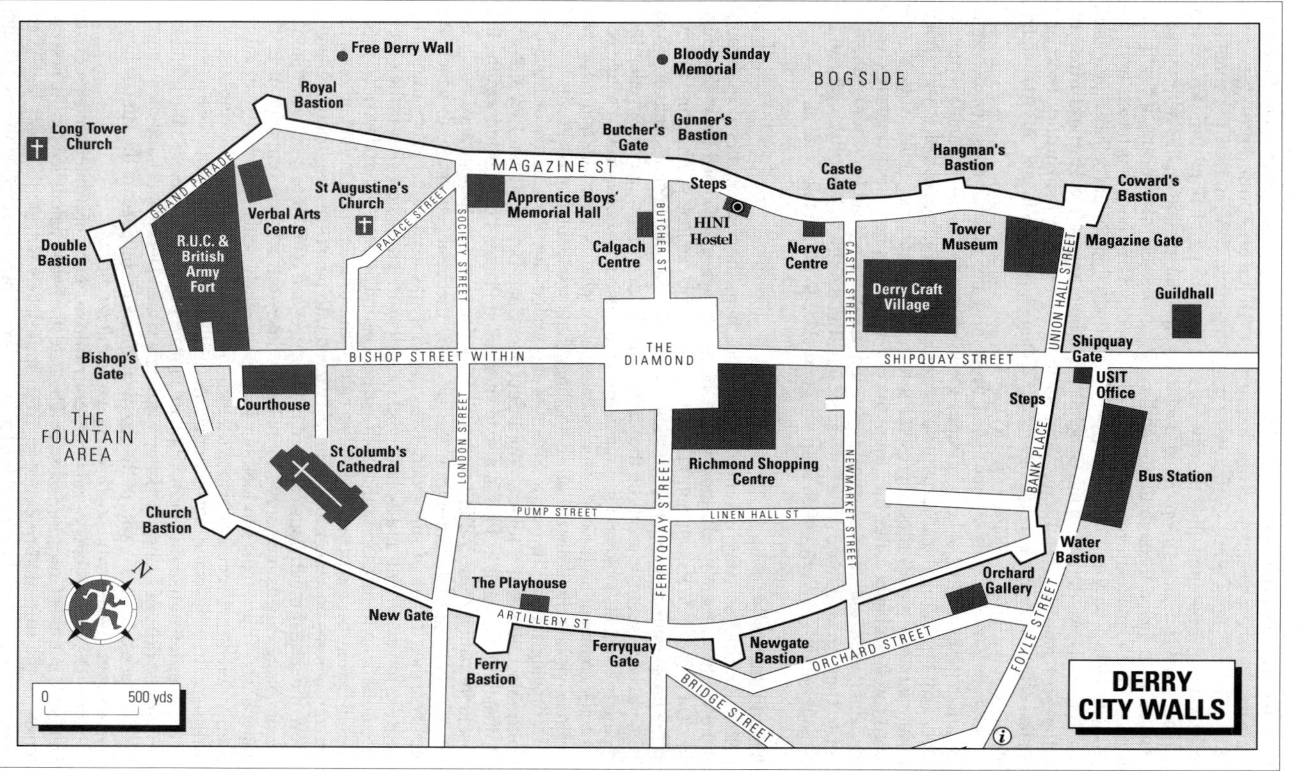
DERRY CITY WALLS
BOGSIDE
THE FOUNTAIN AREA
Free Derry Wall
Bloody Sunday Memorial
Royal Bastion
Long Tower Church
Double Bastion
Bishop's Gate
Church Bastion
R.U.C. & British Army Fort
Verbal Arts Centre
St Augustine's Church
Courthouse
St Columb's Cathedral
New Gate
Apprentice Boys' Memorial Hall
Butcher's Gate
Gunner's Bastion
Calgach Centre
Steps
HINI Hostel
Nerve Centre
Castle Gate
Hangman's Bastion
Derry Craft Village
Tower Museum
Coward's Bastion
Magazine Gate
Guildhall
Shipquay Gate
USIT Office
Steps
Bus Station
Water Bastion
Orchard Gallery
Newgate Bastion
Richmond Shopping Centre
The Playhouse
Ferryquay Gate
Ferry Bastion
GRAND PARADE
MAGAZINE ST
BUTCHER ST
CASTLE STREET
UNION HALL STREET
SHIPQUAY STREET
THE DIAMOND
BISHOP STREET WITHIN
SOCIETY STREET
PALACE STREET
LONDON STREET
PUMP STREET
ARTILLERY ST
FERRYQUAY STREET
LINEN HALL ST
NEWMARKET STREET
ORCHARD STREET
BRIDGE STREET
FOYLE STREET
BANK PLACE
N
0
500 yds

here, between **Shipquay Gate** and Magazine Gate, their noses peering out above the ramparts. A reconstruction of the medieval **O'Doherty Tower** here (June–Sept Mon–Sat 10am–5pm, Sun 2–5pm; rest of year closed Sun & Mon; £3.65) is home to a prize-winning **museum** telling the city's history over the past four centuries. Tableaux and audiovisual displays supplement traditional museum exhibits in this determinedly non-sectarian gallop through time – and, as far as possible, you're supplied with the facts and left to make up your own mind. The upper gallery houses artefacts from the Spanish Armada wrecks, while the basement occupies tunnels and cellars dating back to the siege. Down the side of the Guildhall in Harbour Square, the **Harbour Museum** (Mon–Fri 10am–1pm & 2–4.30pm; free) recounts Derry's maritime history, contains a replica of the thirty-foot curragh in which St Columba sailed to Iona in 563 AD and has an intriguing display of maps of old Derry.

Shipquay Street slopes steeply uphill from the gate. Just off it as you penetrate towards the heart of the old city is **Derry Craft Village** (Mon–Sat 9.30am–5.30pm), an Inner City Trust project in a purpose-built traditional stone village complex, with shops, restaurants and a craft shop representing a range of traditional skills. Though now largely well-established, like the rest of the city, the shops here have been affected by the falling value of the punt against the pound; shoppers instead flock across the border to Donegal, and there are a few vacant lots. But it's still well worth a visit and the elegant *Boston Tea Party* coffee shop is a good place to sit and take it all in.

Around the walls

Left inside Shipquay Gate is **Bank Place**, which hugs the walls as they dogleg round at the southeastern Water Bastion, where the River Foyle once lapped the walls at high tide. On to Newgate Bastion and **Ferryquay Gate**, you can look south across the river to the prosperous and largely Protestant **Waterside district**. Several sculptures have been placed at strategic points on the walls by the English artist Antony Gormley, their gaping eye sockets looking out in diametrically opposite directions from a single body – a frank comment on the city's ideological split. Aesthetics aside, the figures provide welcome visual relief from the office buildings that swamp the immediate view.

Occupying the southwestern corner of the walled city, the Church of Ireland **St Columb's Cathedral** (Mon–Sat: April–Sept 9am–5pm, Oct–Mar 9am–1pm & 2–4pm; £1 donation) was built in 1633 in a style later called Planter's Gothic and was the first post-Reformation cathedral in the British Isles. Displayed in the entrance porch is a cannon shell catapulted in during the siege by the besieging army, to which was attached their terms of surrender. The cathedral was used as a battery during the siege, its **tower** serving as a lookout post; today it provides the best **view** of the old city. The present spire dates from the late Georgian period, its lead-covered wooden predecessor having been stripped to fashion bullets and cannon shot. Inside, an open-timbered roof rests on sixteen stone corbels carved with figures of past bishops. Hanging above the nave, French **flags** captured in the siege, and others brought back from various military expeditions, serve to make the interior a forceful reminder of British imperialism. Other things to look out for are the finely sculpted reredos behind the altar, the eighteenth-century bishop's throne and the window panels showing scenes as diverse as the relief of the city on August 12, 1689, and St Columba's mission to Britain. In the **chapter house museum** (50p) are more relics of the siege, plus the grand kidney-shaped desk of Bishop Berkeley (who only visited Derry once) and mementos of Cecil Frances (1818–95), wife of Bishop Alexander and composer of the famous hymns *Once in royal David's city* and *There is a green hill far away*.

Inside **Bishop's Gate** stands the **courthouse**, built of white sandstone from Dungiven in crude Greek Revival style. The gate itself was remodelled for the first centenary of the siege and reopened in 1789. Immediately outside the walls here is the **Fountain** area, named after the freshwater source that once supplied the city, though there are few remnants of any antiquity here apart from the immediately visible remaining tower of the old Derry jail, jammed up against the grim modern houses. The Fountain is a Protestant housing estate that sticks into the Catholic west bank like a sore thumb, with a single road entrance close to the Craigavon Bridge. It's of interest solely for its Union Jack kerb paintings and huge **murals** which read as direct responses to the more famous Catholic "Free Derry" mural in the next valley. Until recently, the Fountain area had the **oldest mural** in the North. Painted in the early part of the twentieth century by Bobby Jackson, it showed the Siege of Derry and the Battle of the Boyne, and was repainted every year. In the 1970s, when the area was redeveloped, the wall was painstakingly dismantled, moved, reassembled and repainted, but it finally disintegrated in 1994. A replica was painted in 1995 on a special Bobby Jackson memorial wall. Other Loyalist murals are to be found in Fountain and in Bond Street in the Waterside.

Continuing north from Bishop's Gate you reach the **Double Bastion** where the "Roaring Meg" cannon sits. During the siege it was said that "the noise of the discharge was more terrifying than were the contents of the charge dangerous to the enemy". Just by here is **The Verbal Arts Centre** (*www.verbart.demon.co.uk*), a unique project aimed at sustaining and promoting forms of communication and entertainment once central to Irish culture: legend, folklore, *sean nós* – a nasalized and unaccompanied narrative form of singing (see p.707) – and storytelling performed by a *seanachie* (storyteller). The centre, incorporating designs by Louis De Brocquy, commissions works from writers, hosts poetry readings and storytelling and has its own resident *seanachie*. It also visits schools and community centres and has a determinedly non-sectarian ethos, influenced by its understanding of the importance of the oral tradition in all cultures. Every year at the beginning of April, it promotes an international **storytelling festival**; and there are also plenty of events year-round, so drop in and check out what's on the programme.

The nearby **Royal Bastion** was constructed between 1826 and 1828 and used to be topped by a nine-foot high statue of Reverend George Walker, the defender of Derry "against an arbitrary and bigoted monarch" (to quote the still-legible inscription). The statue was blown up in 1973 and the surrounding area remains a significant flashpoint every August 12 when the Apprentice Boys march in Walker's and their predecessors' memory (see box on p.669). The view from here across the Bogside district (see below) is expansive.

Just inside **Butcher's Gate** is Derry's latest attraction, **The Fifth Province** in the Calgach Genealogy Centre, an overblown multimedia "journey" through Ireland's heritage (shows Mon–Fri 11.30am, 12.30pm & 2.30pm; £3). The trip begins in a stone chamber "Departure Lounge" where the actor Richard Harris provides a video introduction to the history of Derry. Next it's off to the module and a trip into space to meet Calgach, founder of ancient Derry, who regales you with tales from the past. Finally, your senses are bombarded with a panoply of images celebrating Irish culture. A little further downhill, on the south side of Magazine Street, is another focus of Derry's dynamic cultural world, **The Nerve Centre** (*www.nerve-centre.org.uk*), which contains all manner of sound, film and video studios and editing suites alongside an arthouse cinema, music venue and coffee bar.

The Bogside

In the valley below the northern city walls is the Catholic **Bogside** district, where, at the start of the Troubles, young Catholics were caught up in an advancing disarray of army and police, who replied to bricks and petrol bombs with tear gas, rubber bullets and careering Saracen armoured cars. The area at the foot of the escarpment has been redeveloped in the form of a dual carriageway, a new estate of tenement flats and empty concrete precincts. But clinging to the opposite hillside is a classic urban landscape, with turn-of-the-century terraces of stucco facades, blue tile roofs and red chimney stacks.

Most eye-catching in this panorama is an isolated wall bearing the slogan "You are now entering Free Derry". The **Free Derry Mural** was originally painted by local man John "Caker" Casey in the aftermath of the attack by Loyalists on a civil rights march in 1968. Since then this signature of the Nationalist camp in Derry has become almost a community notice board, marking events as disparate as Derry's win in the All-Ireland Gaelic Football Final in 1993 and the release of Republican prisoners. A nearby wall carries another well-known mural, with a message to the British Army that you'll also see displayed in many other Catholic areas in the North: *Slán Abhaile* ("good-bye/safe home").

For the first two years of the Troubles, the territory beyond the Free Derry mural was the notorious "no go area", the undisputed preserve of the IRA. This autonomy lasted until 1972, when Operation Motorman was launched; the IRA men who had been in the area were tipped off, though, and got across the border before the invasion took place. Further across to the right of the wall stands the memorial pillar to the thirteen Catholic civilians killed by British paratroopers on **Bloody Sunday**, January 30, 1972 (a fourteenth died later of his wounds). The soldiers immediately claimed they had been fired upon, an assertion that was later disproved, though some witnesses have come forward to report seeing IRA men there with their guns. The bitter memory of the subsequent Widgery Commission's failure to declare anyone responsible for the deaths has festered in Catholic Derry and maintained pressure on successive governments to reopen investigations. A new enquiry was finally announced in spring 1998. To the right of this area once stood the Rossville flats, by far the most infamous part of the Bogside – Derry's equivalent of the Divis flats in Belfast. Other murals visible from the walls include a young Bernadette Devlin speaking at a rally, megaphone in hand; another depicting a member of the women's branch of the IRA; and the powerful "68–96 Nothing Has Changed" mural, decrying beatings by the RUC.

The Railway Centre

The **Foyle Valley Railway Centre**, to the south of the walled city on Foyle Road by Craigavon Bridge (Tues–Sat 10am–4.30pm; free) is more interesting than it might sound and has train rides at weekends. The highlight is a short trip up the Foyle Valley on a steam train (£2.75), but there are also plenty of old engines and models, plus extensive displays on the history of railways in the area, a sad tale of decline that is enthusiastically explained.

Eating, drinking and entertainment

Although **eating out** in the city has improved dramatically over recent years, you still won't be faced with a bewildering choice. *The Galley*, within the walls at 12a Shipquay St, is a good daytime choice with quality pizzas and home baking. Otherwise, try bustling and good-value *Anne's Hot Bread Shop,* 8 William St, open until 2am Mon–Sat, or the very sociable *Leprechaun Café* on the Strand Road. As ever, you can also get lunch in many of the pubs: *Badgers*, in Orchard Street, has recently won awards, but the *Metro* in Bank Place, the *Linenhall* in Linenhall Street and the *Monico Lounge* opposite the main post office are also worth checking out.

All of Derry's more formal restaurants require booking at weekends year-round, and on weekdays as well during the summer. The best modern food is to be found at central *Fitzroys*, 2–4 Bridge St (☎028/7126 6211); *Brown's*, 1 Bond's Hill on the east bank (☎028/7134 5180); or in the southern suburbs of the Waterside at *Schooner's*, 59 Victoria Rd (☎028/7131 1500). Carlisle Road, just south of the walls, has a cosmopolitan selection: *India House* at no. 51 (☎028/7126 0532), is an excellent Indian with main courses for around £7; *La Sosta* at no. 45a (☎028/7137 4817) is the city's best Italian;

and, despite its name, *Gravy* at no. 32 (☎028/7136 0300), is one of the few Derry restaurants offering vegetarian specials. North of the centre is *Piemonte Pizzeria* (☎028/7126 6828) on Clarendon Street, the best pizza place in town, while further north *McGilloway's*, 145 Strand Rd (☎028/7126 2050), whose decor deliberately replicates an old-fashioned chip shop, has quality seafood and an especially good chowder.

Bars and music

What Derry lacks in restaurants, it makes up for, inevitably, in **pubs**. Congenial and conversational places include *The Clarendon Bar*, 44 Strand Rd; *The Anchor Bar*, 38 Ferryquay St; *Badgers*, 18 Orchard St (for an older clientele); and *Mullins* on Sackville Street. The swish *Porters Bar* in *The Tower Hotel* on Strand Road is the place to sit, spot and be spotted. North past Magee College on the Culmore Road is *Da Vinci's*, one of Derry's newer pubs with a restaurant and nightclub.

Traditional music in the city is not as exciting as it once was. The venues that remain are mostly grouped in and around **Waterloo Street**, just outside the northern section of the walls, a mainly Catholic working-class area. The *Dungloe Bar* claims to be the most regular music-making place here, with traditional sessions on Friday and Saturday. Other sessions take place at the *Rocking Chair Pub* and the *Gweedore Bar*, which has a function room upstairs with good music and dancing; it often stays open until 1am and is connected to *Peadar O'Donnell's* next door, a retro pub, which has traditional music most nights in summer. Elsewhere, *J&T McGinley's*, on Foyle Street, offers live music six nights a week, and *Sandinos*, around the corner in Water Street, has a mixed bag, including traditional music and jazz.

For livelier **nightlife**, head for Shipquay Street, where the *Glue Pot* and *Townsman* pubs and the cavernous *Squire's* nightclub all attract a young crowd. Also worth checking out is the *Carraig*, at 113–121 Strand Rd, or the *Delacroix*, on Buncrana Road, where the dancing is more traditional and there's a Wednesday night comedy club. Another popular choice for Friday and Saturday nights is to cross the border, to nightclubs in Letterkenny, Carndonagh and Buncrana.

Arts and other entertainment

Classical music thrives in the city through the Londonderry Arts Association (☎028/7126 4481), with around a dozen concerts a year held in the Great Hall of Magee University College. Orchestral concerts by the Ulster Orchestra are held much less regularly in the Great Hall of the Guildhall. The Playhouse on Artillery Street is a good venue for art, dance, music and drama, while The Rialto in Market Street offers a broad range of populist entertainment. However, **theatre** in Derry since the early 1980s is still associated, despite its current inactivity, with the polemical and hugely controversial Field Day Theatre Company, whose principal members have included, at one time or another, the poet Seamus Heaney (see p.590), the academic Seamus Deane, actor Stephen Rea and playwright Brian Friel. **Film** buffs are catered for by the seven-screen Strand cinema in the Quayside Centre, as well as by The Nerve Centre (see p.585) and the Foyle Film Club at the Orchard cinema in Orchard Street.

The **visual arts** are also attracting a lot of international attention, thanks largely to the highly innovative contemporary art programming of the Orchard Gallery in Orchard Street. A visit there is a must – and watch out for the exhibitions it sometimes arranges in the Foyle Arts Centre, off Lawrence Hill, or at other venues around the city. The Heritage Library, on Bishop Street, occasionally has local artists' work on display.

Several **arts festivals** take place at regular times throughout the year (see "Listings" p.588). In addition, **Halloween** is traditionally an excuse for riotous celebration, with fireworks, fancy dress and partying in the streets. The tourist information office has more details of all events.

Listings

Airlines British Airways (to and from Glasgow and Manchester; ☎0845/773 3377); Ryanair (to and from London Stansted; ☎0870/156 9569).

Banks Principally situated on Shipquay Place, Shipquay Street and Waterloo Place.

Bike rental and repairs Rental at An Mointean, 245 Lone Moor Rd (☎028/7128 7128) and Oakgrove Manor, 4–6 Magazine St (☎028/7137 2273); repairs at Bee's Cycles, 4 Waterloo St (☎028/7137 2155) and Beragh Hill Cycles, 21 Beragh Hill Rd (☎028/7135 8400).

Bookshop Bookworm, 18–20 Bishop St, is one of the best bookshops in Ireland, with superbly comprehensive coverage of contemporary and historical Irish works.

Car rental Desmond Motors, 173 Strand Rd (☎028/7136 0420); Europcar, City of Derry Airport (☎028/7130 1312).

Coach tour Foyle Civic Tour – a one-hour tour of the city (July & Aug Tues 2pm from Foyle St bus station; ☎028/7126 7284; £3.20).

Exchange Available from all banks; the Tourist Information Centre; and Thomas Cook in the Quayside shopping centre (☎028/7185 2500).

Festivals Celtic Spring Festival (March – three weeks of various events, including drama and Irish language festivals); Foyle Film Festival (late April – one of the most prestigious in Ireland); International Jazz and Blues Festival (late May); Two Cathedrals Festival (October – classical music); Halloween Carnival (a week of mayhem with a huge firework display on October 31).

Hospital Accident and emergency department, Altnagelvin Hospital, Belfast Rd (☎028/7134 5171); call this number also for dental emergencies after working hours or at weekends.

Laundry Foyle Dry Cleaners, 147 Spencer Rd.

Library The Central Library, 35 Foyle St, has a good selection on Irish studies and local history.

Market Bottom of William Street – stalls most days, but busiest on Sat.

Newspapers The Nationalist *Derry Journal* (Tues & Fri) has a good run-through of what's on in the city; the Unionist local paper is the *Londonderry Sentinel* (Wed).

Police Main Police Station, Strand Rd (☎028/7136 7337).

Post office Custom House Street (☎028/7136 2563; Mon 8.30am–5.30pm, Tues–Fri 9am–5pm, Sat 9am–12.30pm).

Travel agents Premier Travel, 35 Carlisle Rd (☎028/7126 2261); Thomas Cook, Unit 7, Quayside Centre (☎028/7137 4174); USIT, 4 Shipquay Place (☎028/7137 1888).

Southern County Derry

South of the Derry–Antrim A6 road, the landscape settles down into a pattern more familiar to the Republic: fertile farming land rising to the **Sperrin Mountains**, punctuated by small planned towns. The pattern in the North is subtly different, though, because the grants of land here were not made to individuals but to various London guilds or companies. Consequently, there isn't the strange, late-flowering feudalism that you see in the Republic, with its repeated archetype of Big House and surrounding town, but rather entirely **planned towns**, such as **Magherafelt** and **Moneymore**, often built on green-field sites selected by professionals, who specialized in doing just that. The huge expanse of Ireland's biggest lake, **Lough Neagh**, laps against the county's southeastern corner and here too is one of the must-see sites of the entire North, **Bellaghy Bawn**.

The road to Dungiven

Seven or so miles east of Derry, a turning leads to **Ness Wood Country Park**, a pleasant place to stop and stroll through a mixture of natural and imported woodland. The centepiece is **Shaun's Leap waterfall**, the highest in the North, whose waters cascade into a small glen below a thirty-foot wide chasm, across which the outlaw, Shaun Crossan, is said to have leaped to evade capture. The waterfall featured in the Mills & Boon guide to the *Most Romantic Places in Britain* and, although the scene is undoubtedly picturesque, you might reckon the authors need to get out more in the evenings.

DUNGIVEN, ten miles further on, is a fairly unremarkable town, though it does harbour one or two ruins of interest. Originally an O'Cahan stronghold, Dungiven was given to the Skinners' Company to settle in the seventeenth century. The remains of the O'Cahan fortifications are incorporated into the ruined nineteenth-century **castle**, whose battlemented outline gives Dungiven a particular flavour when approached from the south. This was the scene of the 1971 attempt to set up an independent Northern Ireland parliament.

Dungiven Priory, signposted down a footpath half a mile out of the town towards Antrim, gives a taste of the pioneering life of the early plantation settlers, and of the continuity of tradition. No more than a ruin, the Augustinian priory stands on an imposing, defensible site on a bluff above the river. Founded in 1100 by the O'Cahans, it belongs to the first wave of European monastic orders which arrived in Ireland to supplant the Celtic Church. The church contains what is rated as the finest **medieval tomb** in Northern Ireland, that of Cooey na Gall O'Cahan, who died in 1385: beneath the effigy are six bare-legged warriors in kilts, presumably denoting Scotsmen, who represent the O'Cahan chieftain's foreign mercenaries, from whom he derived his nickname "na Gall", or "of the foreigners". At some point, the O'Cahans added a defensive tower to the west end of the church, and later – when Dungiven was granted to the Skinners' Company, in the person of Sir Edward Doddington – this was enlarged to become a two-and-a-half-storeyed defensive manor house. There's an evocative artist's impression on the site of what that building looked like. Although the church hasn't been used since 1711, Dungiven Priory remains a religious site of sorts. A tree knotted with rags – handkerchiefs, torn-off bits of summer dresses, socks – stands over a deeply hollowed **stone**, originally used by the monks for milling grain and now an object of pilgrimage for people seeking cures for physical illness. There's little to tempt you to stay, although if you fancy a night in a converted stone mill, aim for *The Flax Mill* (☎028/7774 2655), an independent **hostel** three miles north of town and signposted off the Limavady Road.

The ruined **Banagher Old Church**, a couple of miles southwest of Dungiven, was founded in the twelfth century by St Muiredach O'Heney, who is buried in the well-preserved mortuary house built on a sandhill in the churchyard. Banagher sand is said to bring good fortune to the founder's line and perhaps did so to a famous modern bearer of the name, **Seamus Heaney**, who is known to have visited for the explicit purpose. The ruins themselves are sedately impressive, as are the walks around the nearby Banagher Glen **nature reserve** (June–Sept daily 9am–9pm).

The Plantation towns

South of Dungiven, well into the Sperrin Mountains, are more of the **Plantation towns** of the London companies, most of them characteristically planned around a central diamond. **DRAPERSTOWN** is essentially a junction, with well-mannered houses facing each other in a very grand street design. The **Plantation of Ulster Visitor Centre** on the High Street (daily 11am–5pm; *www.workplace.org.uk/plantation*; £3), as its name suggests, recounts the story in more detail, using multimedia technology. At **UPPERLANDS**, ten miles north beyond Maghera, you can get some idea of the impact of the new eighteenth-century technology on the area at the **Old Mill Museum**, a private textile museum owned by the Clark family. In 1740, Jackson Clark dammed the river to provide power and installed linen-finishing machinery here. If you want to look around, phone William Clark & Sons in advance to arrange a guided tour (Mon–Thurs; £1.50; ☎028/7964 3265). *Ardtara Country House* nearby offers a taste both of Victorian elegance and of roast racks of Sperrin lamb (☎028/7964 4490; ⑨).

Heading south, **MAGHERAFELT**, granted to the Salters' Company by James I, has another wide, sloping main street and an increasingly successful Arts Festival in March. The town makes a reasonable base for exploring Lough Neagh and the Bellaghy area and has an amenable **tourist office** (Mon–Sat 9am–5pm; ☎028/7963 1510) in The Bridewell, 2 Churchwell Lane. There's **accommodation** at *Laurel Villa*, 60 Church St (☎028/7963 3228; ④), which also organizes heritage and angling breaks, and at the comfortable new *Hostel 56*, 56 Rainey St (☎028/7963 2096; *www.hostel56.club24.co.uk*), complete with its own roof garden. There's also plenty of **eating** choices, including the grand *Fiolta's Bistro*, 4 Union Arcade, for modern European cuisine; and *Mary's*, an exceptionally pleasant old-time bar on the Market Place.

At one time a real gem, **MONEYMORE**, about five miles further south, is now a rundown, traffic-choked disgrace. Dilapidated but once-graceful pedimented buildings originally constructed by the Drapers (and restored by them in 1817) face each other across a wide main street topped by an Orange Hall; there are plenty of red, white and blue kerbstones here. Moneymore was the first town in the North to have piped water – amazingly enough, as early as 1615. Just outside town, **Springhill** (April–June & Sept Sat & Sun 2–6pm; July & Aug Mon–Wed & Fri–Sun same times; £2.75) is a typical example of the fortified manor houses built by the early planters. Dating from the late seventeenth century, it's a lovely bit of sober whitewashed architecture, housing a good

SEAMUS HEANEY

There was a sunlit absence.
The helmeted pump in the yard
heated its iron,
water honeyed

in the slung bucket
and the sun stood
like a griddle cooling
against the wall
of each long afternoon.

(From *Mossbawn: 1. Sunlight*)

It's impossible to conceive of a contemporary poet, Irish or otherwise, whose works are more evocative of time and place than **Seamus Heaney**. He was born, the eldest of nine children, on the family farm of Mossbawn (itself the title of two poems in his fourth collection *North*), in the townland of Tamniarn, near Bellaghy, on April 13, 1939. Heaney's family background, his Catholic upbringing and his study of Irish at school imbued him with a strong sense of being Irish in a state which considered itself British, a paradox which would form a major motif in his work during the 1970s. While at Queen's University, Belfast, he was further influenced by the literature he discovered in Belfast's Linen Hall library, especially the works of John Hewitt, the Antrim-born "Poet of the Glens", and the English "naturalist" poet, Ted Hughes where he found an "association of sounds in print that connected with the world below". The rural Monaghan setting of Patrick Kavanagh's poetry further echoed his own experience and vision.

Heaney's first poem, *Tractors*, was published in the *Belfast Evening Telegraph* in 1962. His first significant collection, *Death of a Naturalist*, followed in 1966 and was immediately recognized for its earthiness and command of diverse metrical forms. While lec-

costume collection and a delightfully overgrown garden. You can **camp** in the farmyard here (☎028/8764 8210).

Lough Neagh and Bellaghy

East of Magherafelt and Moneymore are the fish-filled waters of the biggest lake in Ireland, **Lough Neagh**. Tributaries flow from every point of the compass: the Lower Bann, which drains the lake and runs north to **Lough Beg** (finally reaching the sea north of Coleraine), contains some huge **trout**, including the rare *dollaghan*, the Lough Neagh trout; best **fishing** is from mid-July to October. Similar to salmon – which are also common – *dollaghan* grow by three pounds every year and can be caught by spinning, worming and fly fishing: the Ballinderry Black and the Bann Olive are famous flies derived from this region. To fish in the lough or the river, all anglers require a Fisheries Conservation Board Rod Licence (call Lough Neagh Tourism; ☎028/9448 1312); however, while this entitles you to carry a rod it doesn't mean that you can fish unless you have a permit from the owner or you're in free water. The angling clubs which control much of the water let day tickets at reasonable rates. For details of licences and permits ask at local tackle shops, the nearest being Heuston's Sport, Main Street, Castledawson (☎028/7966 8282) and Hamilton's Sport, Burn Road, Cookstown (☎028/8676 6541; see p.647).

Like many of the Plantation settlements in the area, **BELLAGHY**, just west of Lough Beg, has a history which reflects the divisions between communities. Indeed,

turing at Queen's, his career expanded into journalism and television and he became increasingly involved in the **Civil Rights movement**. His response to the Troubles saw him seeking for "images and symbols adequate to our predicament" and he began to see poetry as a mode of resistance, but, eventually, the violence so disturbed him that he moved with his family to County Wicklow. Ian Paisley's *Protestant Telegraph* bade farewell to "the well-known papist propagandist" on his departure to his "spiritual home in the popish republic". While his 1970s' collections *North* and *Field Work* had mixed receptions – some saw the strong influence of Robert Lowell on the former – Heaney found himself turning increasingly to his Irish heritage as a source of inspiration, particularly the long medieval poem *Buile Suibhne (The Madness of Sweeney)*, and published his own *Sweeney Astray* collection in 1983. The following year's *Station Island* drew upon his experiences as a participant in St Patrick's Purgatory (see p.482).

The hunger strikes of the early 1980s brought a new urgency to Northern politics and a revival of Heaney's polemicism. Prompted by the staging in Derry in 1980 of Brian Friel's play *Translations*, which showed English surveyors travelling through eighteenth-century Ireland anglicizing all the place names, Heaney co-founded the **Field Day Theatre Company** with Friel, his old friend and fellow-academic Seamus Deane, the actor Stephen Rea and others. While the group's theatrical activities were themselves controversial, it was their publications which engendered the most antipathy. Their pamphlets were criticized as attempts to over-intellectualize the Troubles and the 1991 *Field Day Anthology of Irish Writing* was decried for its under-representation of work by women writers.

Heaney's reputation, however, has remained largely unsullied, maintained not merely by the sheer literary strength of his work and its ready accessibility, but by his undoubted "presence" and a lack of pomposity – his nickname, "Famous Seamus", notwithstanding. In 1995, his abilities were more widely recognized by the award of the Nobel Prize for Literature. Heaney's latest work is a translation of the Anglo-Saxon epic poem *Beowulf*, his dramatic retelling of this tale of monster- and dragon-slaying managing to breathe new life into a work that was long considered too dense and metaphorical for a modern readership.

no less than two of the ten 1981 hunger strikers (see p.595) – cousins Francis Hughes and Thomas McElwee – came from the village, and Orange Parades have been a regular flashpoint. Bellaghy is neatly laid out around a T-junction and, if you wander south, past the whitewashed terraces on Castle Street, you'll come to one of the best examples of a surviving Plantation castle, **Bellaghy Bawn** (June–Sept Mon–Fri 10am–5pm, Sat noon–5pm, Sun 2–5pm; Oct–May Mon–Sat 10am–5pm; £2). The castle was constructed in 1622 by the Vintners' Company. Most of its fortifications were lost in 1641, but it still retains an impressive circular flanker tower. The Bawn is now owned by the Department of the Environment, and has been sensitively restored. Inside you'll find fascinating interpretive displays explaining the 7000-year-old history of the settlements in this area, the Vintners' construction of the village – today's houses still occupy the same original allocated plots of land – and the diverse ecology of the Lough Beg wetland area. The real treasure here, however, is the dedication of much of the Bawn's space to a most notable local man, **Seamus Heaney**, one of the twentieth-century's greatest living poets, who was born and brought up nearby (see box on p.590). Heaney himself is the star of a unique and atmospheric video showing in the Bawn, "A Sense of Place", in which he recounts the influence of his upbringing, local character and landmarks on his poetry. His father, for instance, rented grazing rights on the strand at Lough Beg and, in his poem *Ancestral Photograph*, Heaney recalls helping to herd the cattle that grazed there down Castle Street on their way to market. Prints of other poems are displayed on the walls of various rooms and the Bawn's library contains the ultimate collection of his works, including first drafts and extremely limited editions. The Bawn's helpful curators are very knowledgeable and there's a small **café** here too.

You can see the shimmering Lough Beg from the windows of the flanker tower and a stroll down to the lake is well worthwhile. In summer, the lake's waters recede and **Church Island** becomes accessible from the strand. Besides a walled graveyard, here you'll find the ruins of a medieval church, said to have been founded centuries before by the ubiquitous St Patrick, with a tower and spire added in 1788 by the eccentric Frederick Augustus Hervey, Anglican Bishop of Derry and fourth Earl of Bristol (see p.577), to improve his view from Ballyscullion House on the mainland nearby. He commissioned Lanyon to build a huge replacement for the original, with, apparently, 365 windows, but died abroad before ever moving in. You can view the ruins from one of the *Lough Beg Coach Houses* (☎028/7938 6235; £200–380 per week) which offer good **self-catering accommodation** and run coarse fishing and birdwatching weekends. Bellaghy's only **B&B** is at the tiny, though comfortable, *Bawn Lodge*, 10 Castle St (☎028/7938 6241; ②). Seven buses run daily to Bellaghy from Magherafelt and Ballymena.

South Antrim: Ballymena to Lisburn

South Antrim is unlikely travelling country, being largely rolling and unexciting farmland, with places whose names are familiar because you've heard them so often on the news: Ballymena, Antrim and Lisburn. Still, you're likely to see something of most of these towns since the train from Belfast passes through them on the way to and from the northern coast.

Ballymena and around

BALLYMENA (pronounced *Ballamena*, unless you're a BBC newsreader) is a fine, upstanding, predominantly Protestant town that could have been transplanted straight from the Scottish lowlands. Indeed, most of its plantation settlers came from the southwest of Scotland, and the Ballymena accent still retains traces of Scottish lowlands speech. Like many Northern Irish towns, its prosperity derived from the linen trade, while the alleged tightfistedness of its residents earned it the sobriquet of the "Aberdeen of Ireland". Ballymena is the home base of the Reverend **Ian Paisley**, despite the fact that he originates from Armagh; this demagogic leader of the Democratic Unionist Party, who has dominated local politics since the late 1970s, remains the most outspoken Loyalist opponent to the Good Friday Agreement. Ballymena's Saturday market is a lively affair and its streets are often thronged with shoppers and crammed nose to tail with traffic, but significant redevelopment has left little surviving from the pre-Victorian era. In the summer, there's a **tourist office** in the town hall at 15 Bridge St (Mon–Fri 9.30am–5pm; ☎028/2565 3663); otherwise it's a trek out to the Council Offices, 80 Galgorm Rd (Mon–Fri 9am–5pm; ☎028/2564 4111). Next door to the town hall is the quaint **Morrow's Shop Museum**, 13 Bridge St (Mon–Fri 10am–1pm & 2–5pm, Sat 10am–1pm; free), an erstwhile draper's store complete with original fittings that displays local memorabilia.

A mile and a half west of Ballymena is **GRACEHILL**, a reminder of the curious mixture of religious oppression and tolerance that has characterized Northern Ireland's history: at the same time as Ireland's Catholics were suffering heavy penalties, the country was welcoming dissenting Protestant groups, among them the Moravians (the United Brethren), who founded a model settlement at Gracehill in 1746. The elegant square survives, with separate buildings for men and women, whose main trade was making lace and clocks. Segregated in life, the sexes remained divided in death, and in the graveyard you can walk down the long path that separates the graves of the men from those of the women.

For miles around Ballymena the landscape is dominated by one of County Antrim's most mystical reference points, **Slemish Mountain**, best approached from the village of **Buckna**, eight miles or so east. This extinct volcano is said to be the place where St Patrick herded swine as a slave-boy after being captured and brought to Ireland, and, consequently, is a place of pilgrimage on March 17 – though others claim his writings indicate that the place of his captivity was Killala, County Mayo. Whatever, the mountain's a steep climb of about 700 feet from the car park to the summit, but the **views** are well worth the effort; to the north, you can see the ruins of Skerry Church, the ancient burial place of the O'Neills of Clandeboye.

Antrim town

ANTRIM is a largely undistinguished town whose centre demonstrates all the typical decay that follows the construction of out-of-town shopping developments. Although its population has trebled since the 1970s, it doesn't feel especially fecund with possibilities. If you've time to kill, there's a tenth-century **round tower** in Steeple Park, a mile north of town, indicating the site of an important monastery that flourished between the sixth and twelfth centuries; and a pretty, if unremarkable, eighteenth-century cottage, **Pogue's Entry** on Church St (call ☎028/9442 8000 for times), the preserved childhood home of Alexander Irvine, author of *My Lady of the Chimney Corner* which recalled his boyhood years before the Famine. The tiny **tourist office** nearby at 16 High St (Mon–Fri 9am–5pm; July & Aug Thurs & Fri until 6pm & also Sat 9am–5pm; April, June & Sept also Sat 9am–2pm; ☎028/9442 8331) will let you in. If you pop through the Castle Gate on Dublin Road, you'll find yourself in the pleasant gardens of the old **Antrim Castle**. The building itself was totally destroyed by fire in 1922, but the carriage house and stables now house the **Clotworthy Art Centre** (Mon–Fri

9.30am–9.30pm, Sat 10am–5pm; July & Aug also Sun 2–5pm; free), which is worth a look for its galleries of work by local artists and occasional international exhibitions.

Belfast International Airport is just four miles south of Antrim, but luckily this doesn't mean that you have to stick around – the transport links to Belfast are much better than to Antrim. There's **camping** on the shore of Lough Neagh at *Sixmilewater Marina & Caravan Park* (May–Sept; ☎028/9446 4131), plus daily cruises on the waters. If you've time for a pint, *Madden's* on the High Street is Antrim's liveliest **bar**, while hunger can be satisfied both here and at the wood-beamed *Top of the Town*, Fountain Street, which also has a pleasant beer garden.

West of Antrim, Lough Neagh's northern shores are easily accessible by taking the road from **Randalstown** to **Creeve**. From here a minor road leads down to Churchtown Point and the Lough. The ruins of an ancient Irish church are here and close by is a still-extant **holy well**. This was formerly the site of an annual pilgrimage on May 1 which involved walking barefoot thirteen times around both church and well before drinking the waters and then bathing in them. The Lough's waters are rich in **eels** here and, if you're lucky, you might find a fisherman willing to sell you a few before he takes his catch off to the processing plant at Toomebridge. If not, nearby *Cranfield Inn* serves eel suppers and also runs an equestrian centre (%028/9447 2342). Back in Creeve, the *Creeve House Country Inn*, 115 Staffordstown Rd (%028/9447 2547; b) is a friendly **pub** and **guesthouse** and an ideal base for soaking up the atmosphere of this tranquil spot.

Lisburn

LISBURN, eight miles southwest of Belfast, is the administrative centre of Northern Ireland's second-largest local authority and its busy, pedestrianized shopping streets and packed car parks indicate recent commercial success, perhaps unknown since its days as an important linen town. After the revocation of the Edict of Nantes in 1685, which removed French and Dutch Huguenots' freedom of worship, large numbers of them were persuaded to come to Ulster, where they founded the local linen trade. Bleach greens were set up along the banks of the River Lagan, the first of which started in 1626 at **Lambeg**, a mile downstream from Lisburn. Lambeg has given its name to the big drums which appear in the Orange marches, deriving from the military drums of Prince William's army.

Lisburn's one major attraction is the **Irish Linen Centre and Museum** (Mon–Sat 9.30am–5pm; free), situated in the eighteenth-century assembly rooms in the Market Square. A permanent exhibition, "Flax to Fabric", recounts the industry's history and you can watch weavers plying away in the purpose-built hand-loom workshop. The museum typically collects items and artefacts of essentially local interest. The building's modern annexe contains the **tourist office** (same times; ☎028/9266 0038), plus a café and shops, and there are often art displays and lunchtime recitals. There's been a **Tuesday market** in Lisburn since 1627, but little of architectural note survived a catastrophic fire in 1707. The seventeenth-century **cathedral** opposite the Linen Centre was rebuilt after the fire and you'll find a number of Huguenot graves in its churchyard. Nowadays, the fourteen-screen Omniplex **cinema** on Governor's Road tends to be a more popular draw.

A mile northeast of Lisburn in the village of Hilden, the **Hilden Brewery** (Tues–Sat 10.30am–4pm; tours 11.30am & 2.30pm; £2.50, includes glass of ale) is one of only two real-ale breweries in Ireland (the other is Whitewater in Kilkeel, County Down). It was established in 1981 in the courtyard of a former linen baron's mansion. A visit is an olfactory treat, the whiff of malted barley and hops leaving you eager to slake your thirst with a taste of the amber-coloured ale or the dark, malty Special Reserve. You can lunch here, too, in the attached *Tap Room* restaurant.

THE MAZE

The political prison of **Long Kesh** (or **the Maze**), which lies to the south of Lisburn and is clearly visible from the main M1 motorway, incorporates the notorious "H-blocks" which were the focus of the 1981 **hunger strikes**, in which Republican inmates demanded the reinstatement of political status. The prison, erected on an old airfield soon after the Troubles began, housed hundreds of activists, Loyalist and Republican, interned without trial by the British government. Originally all inmates – convicted prisoners as well as internees – had special category status (a kind of POW status), in accordance with the Emergency Powers legislation under which they had been convicted, but when the British government phased out internment in late 1975, special status went with it. From March 1, 1976, the prison was in the peculiar position of housing the last of these special category prisoners as well as – in the H-blocks – those convicted after this cut-off date, who were now classified, and treated, as ordinary criminals.

The IRA campaign for the reinstatement of status began in 1976 when Kevin Nugent, in refusing to wear prison clothes, initiated what became known as the "**blanket protest**" (quite simply, draping a blanket around himself instead of wearing prison clothes). By 1978, this had escalated into the famous "**dirty protest**", in which Republican prisoners refused to undertake ordinary prison duties such as emptying chamber pots, resorting instead to smearing the cells with their own excrement in order to get rid of it. In 1981, a concerted **hunger strike** led to the deaths of ten men, including Bobby Sands, provisional commander of the IRA men inside the prison, who had, significantly, been elected MP for Fermanagh and South Tyrone six weeks into his fast (Sands popularized the Republican slogan *Tiocfaidh ar lá*, "our day will come"). None of this succeeded in budging the government, which steadfastly refused to back down in the face of what it believed was nothing more than moral blackmail. The motivation for the hunger strikes was made manifestly clear in a piece of contemporary graffiti that appeared in Republican areas:

I'll wear no convict's uniform
Nor meekly serve my time
That England might brand Ireland's fight
Eight hundred years of crime.

Since the hunger strike, the Maze has regularly returned to the headlines, most notably in early 1998 when Billy Wright, the leader of the LVF (Loyalist Volunteer Force), was shot dead in the prison by the INLA (Irish National Liberation Army), an action which led to retaliation killings across the North. The almost universal disgust provoked by the murder of a pair of Catholic and Protestant friends in Poyntzpass was, undoubtedly, a central factor in the resolution of the peace settlement talks in April 1998.

A key and controversial element in the Good Friday Agreement was the **early release of political prisoners**, a process which, by August 2000, had left a mere twelve inmates at the Maze. A couple of months later, as the remaining few prisoners were transferred, the Maze finally closed. Its demolition is to follow, and several proposals for the use of its land are currently under consideration, including, most notably, the construction of a new international football stadium.

travel details

Trains

Antrim to: Belfast (9 Mon–Sat, 4 Sun; 1hr 10min); Derry (7 Mon–Fri, 6 Sat, 3 Sun; 1hr 35min).

Ballymena to: Belfast (9 Mon–Sat, 4 Sun; 1hr 25min); Derry (7 Mon–Fri, 6 Sat, 3 Sun; 1hr 20min).

Carrickfergus to Belfast (34 Mon–Fri, 18 Sat, 7 Sun 25min).

Coleraine to: Belfast (9 Mon–Fri, 8 Sat, 4 Sun; 1hr 50min); Derry (8 Mon–Fri, 6 Sat, 3 Sun; 40min); Portrush (19 Mon–Fri, 16 Sat, 10 Sun; 15min).

Derry to: Ballymena (7 Mon–Sat, 3 Sun; 1hr 20min); Belfast (7 Mon–Sat, 3 Sun; 2hr 40min); Castlerock (8 Mon–Fri, 6 Sat, 3 Sun; 35min); Coleraine (8 Mon–Fri, 6 Sat, 3 Sun; 40min).

Larne to: Belfast (21 Mon–Fri, 17 Sat, 6 Sun; 50min).

Lisburn to Belfast (every 10–15 min; 20min).

Buses

(all Ulsterbus unless stated otherwise)

The Antrim Coaster (Goldline Express Service #252) operates from Belfast all the way around the Antrim coast to Portrush (via Larne, the Glens, Ballycastle and the Giant's Causeway), then calls at Portstewart before terminating at Coleraine. The summer service (last week of May to the last week of September) leaves Belfast Europa Buscentre Mon–Sat at 9am, calling at Laganside Buscentre ten minutes later. A Sunday service operates at the same times in high summer (July–Sept). In winter (November to the third week of May), you must either take a train to Larne to connect with the Mon–Fri 10.15am Antrim Coaster that departs from Larne bus station, or catch the 2pm Antrim Coaster from the Belfast Laganside Buscentre. The return service departs from Coleraine (late May to late Sept Mon–Sat 3.40pm; July to late Sept Sun 9.40am & 3.40pm; Nov–May Mon–Sat 9.40am).

The Bushmills Bus is an open-top service running from Coleraine through Portrush to the Giant's Causeway, weather permitting, from the end of June to the end of August. The bus leaves Coleraine daily at 9.10am, 11.30am, 1.50pm, 4pm & 6.15pm, and returns from the Giant's Causeway at 10.20am, 12.40pm, 2.55pm, 5.10pm & 6.55pm. A day return costs £3.50.

Antrim to: Belfast (40 Mon–Fri, 28 Sat, 9 Sun; 35–55min); Staffordstown (2 Mon–Fri; 25min).

Ballycastle to: Ballymena (6 Mon–Fri, 5 Sat; 50min); Belfast (6 Mon–Fri, 5 Sat; 1hr 50min); Bushmills (8 Mon–Fri, 6 Sat, 4 Sun; 40min); Coleraine (5 Mon–Fri, 4 Sat; 1hr); Cushendun/Cushendall (1 Mon–Fri; 40/50min); Giant's Causeway (7 Mon–Fri, 6 Sat, 4 Sun; 35min); Portrush (7 Mon–Fri, 5 Sat, 4 Sun; 1hr).

Ballymena to: Belfast (26 Mon–Fri, 15 Sat, 7 Sun; 1hr–1hr 20min); Bellaghy (7 Mon–Fri, 5 Sat; 50min); Carnlough (4 Mon–Sat; 1hr); Cushendall (4 Mon–Fri, 3 Sat; 55min); Cushendun (5 Mon–Fri, 4 Sat; 1hr 10min); Larne (5 Mon–Fri, 4 Sat; 50min).

Carrickfergus to: Belfast (34 Mon–Fri, 27 Sat, 8 Sun; 35min).

Coleraine to: Armagh (1 daily; 2hr); Ballycastle (5 Mon–Fri, 3 Sat; 1hr); Belfast (8 Mon–Fri, 7 Sat, 6 Sun; 1hr 45 min); Bushmills (8 Mon–Sat; 25min); Castlerock (9 Mon–Fri, 8 Sat; 15min); Derry (14 Mon–Fri, 6 Sat, 2 Sun; 1hr 15min–2hr); Dublin (1 daily; 4hr 30min); Limavady (14 Mon–Fri, 6 Sat, 2 Sun; 25min–1hr); Portrush/Portstewart (circular service; Mon–Sat every 30min–1hr, Sun hourly; 20/30min).

Derry to: Ballybofey (*Bus Éireann;* 8 Mon–Sat, 3 Sun; 1hr 10min); Belfast (15 Mon–Sat, 8 Sun; 1hr 40min); Buncrana (*Lough Swilly;* 10 Mon–Fri, 12 Sat, 3 Sun; 35min); Cahir (1 Mon–Sat; 8hr 30min); Carndonagh (*Lough Swilly;* 5 Mon–Fri, 4 Sat; 45min); Coleraine (6 daily; 1hr); Cork (1 daily; 10hr 15min); Derry Airport (6 daily; 20min); Donegal (*Bus Éireann;* 5 Mon–Sat, 3 Sun; 1hr 30min); Dublin (5 Mon–Sat, 3 Sun; 4hr 15min); Dunfanaghy (*Lough Swilly;* 2 Mon–Thurs & Sat, 3 Fri; 2hr 10min); Dungiven (25 Mon–Fri, 19 Sat, 6 Sun; 30min–1hr); Dungloe (*Lough Swilly;* 2 Mon–Thurs, 3 Fri, 1 Sat; 3hr 15min–5hr); Enniskillen (7 Mon–Fri, 4 Sat & Sun; 2hr–3hr 30min); Galway (*Bus Éireann;* 3 daily; 5hr 40min); Gweedore (*Lough Swilly;* 2 Mon–Thurs, 3 Fri, 1 Sat; 3hr–4hr 10min); Letterkenny (*Lough Swilly;* 11 Mon–Fri, 12 Sat; 1hr); Limavady (15 Mon–Fri, 11 Sat, 3 Sun; 1hr); Magherafelt (1 Mon–Fri; 2hr 50min); Malin Head (*Lough Swilly;* 2 Mon, Wed & Fri, 3 Sat; 1hr 25min); Moville (*Lough Swilly;* 5 Mon–Fri, 6 Sat; 50min); Omagh (8 Mon–Fri, 5 Sat, 4 Sun; 1hr 15min); Shrove (*Lough Swilly;* 4 Mon–Sat; 1hr 10min); Sligo (*Bus Éireann;* 3 daily;

2hr 40min); Strabane (19 Mon–Fri, 15 Sat, 9 Sun; 25–40min).

Draperstown to: Maghera (1 Mon–Fri; 15min); Magherafelt (8 Mon–Fri, 3 Sat; 30min); Omagh (via the Sperrins; 1 Mon–Fri; 55min).

Dungiven to: Belfast (15 Mon–Sat, 8 Sun; 1hr 10min); Derry (19 Mon–Sat, 6 Sun; 30min); Limavady (8 Mon–Fri, 5 Sat, 3 Sun; 25–45min).

Larne to: Belfast (16 Mon–Fri, 12 Sat, 2 Sun; 55min–1hr 35min); Carnlough (9 Mon–Fri, 7 Sat, 3 Sun; 40min); Cushendall (4 Mon–Fri, 2 Sat & Sun; 1hr 15min); Cushendun (4 Mon–Fri, 2 Sat & Sun; 1hr 30min); Glenarm (9 Mon–Fri, 7 Sat, 3 Sun; 30min).

Limavady to: Belfast (5 Mon–Fri, 4 Sat, 3 Sun; 1hr 40min); Castlerock (7 Mon–Fri, 6 Sat; 45min); Coleraine (12 Mon–Fri, 7 Sat, 3 Sun; 25min–1hr); Derry (15 Mon–Fri, 11 Sat, 3 Sun; 50min); Dungiven (7 Mon–Fri, 4 Sat, 3 Sun; 25min).

Magherafelt to: Antrim (10 Mon–Fri, 8 Sat, 3 Sun; 50min); Bellaghy (7 Mon–Sat, 4 Sun; 15 min); Cookstown (14 Mon–Fri, 13 Sat, 4 Sun; 30min); Toome (1 Mon–Fri, 2 Sat; 30min).

Portrush to: Armagh (1 daily; 2hr 30min); Dublin (1 daily; 5hr); Giant's Causeway (6 Mon–Sat, 4 Sun, plus additional open-top service in July & Aug; 25min).

Whitehead to: Belfast (14 Mon–Fri, 12 Sat, 4 Sun; 1hr); Islandmagee circular service to Millbay, Brown's Bay and Portmuck (4 Mon–Fri, 2 Sat; 20/30/20min).

CHAPTER SIXTEEN

DOWN AND ARMAGH

Counties **Down** and **Armagh** occupy the southeastern corner of Northern Ireland, between Belfast and the border. It's a region where all too many of the place names are familiar from the news, and certainly the border areas, especially South Armagh, have borne more than their share of the Troubles. But it's also very attractive country, especially around the coast, and you're never far away from associations with **St Patrick**, who sailed into Strangford Lough to make his final Irish landfall in County Down, founded his first bishopric at Armagh, and is buried at either Downpatrick or Armagh, depending on whose claim you choose.

Heading south from Belfast, the glowering **Mourne Mountains** increasingly dominate the panorama, and it's in this direction that most of the attractions lie. If you simply take the main roads in and out of Belfast – the A1 for Newry and the border, or the M1 motorway west – you'll come across very little to stop for: it's in the rural areas, the mountains and coast, that the charm of this region lies. Probably the best option is to head east from Belfast around the Down shore – past the **Ulster Folk and Transport Museum**, one of the best in the North, and the blowsy suburban resort of **Bangor** into the **Ards Peninsula** or along the banks of **Strangford Lough**. There are plenty of little beaches, early Christian sites, defensive tower houses and fine mansions to visit on the way towards **Newcastle**, the best base for excursions on foot into the Mourne Mountains. Beyond the Mournes a fine coast road curves around to **Carlingford Lough** and the border.

Inland there's less of interest, certainly in County Down. **Armagh city**, though, is well worth some of your time for its ancient associations, cathedrals and fine Georgian streets. South Armagh has some startlingly attractive country, especially around the peak of **Slieve Gullion**.

COUNTY DOWN

The coast and the **Mourne Mountains** at the southern extremity are the major attractions of County Down. The big towns in the north, **Newtownards** and **Bangor**, are much less appealing, but beyond them the A2 road clings to the coast for much of the way down the **Ards Peninsula** and, via the Strangford ferry, all the way to **Newry**. Other routes follow the shores of **Strangford Lough** towards **Downpatrick** and its

ACCOMMODATION PRICE CODES

Throughout this book, prices of hotels, guesthouses and B&Bs have been graded with the codes below, according to what you can expect to pay for a double room in high season. For more details on accommodation, see p.34.

① Under £26	④ £40–55	⑦ £90–110
② £26–33	⑤ £55–70	⑧ £110–130
③ £33–40	⑥ £70–90	⑨ Over £130

associations with the arrival of St Patrick. There are numerous small resorts around the coast, but **Newcastle** is the biggest, and in many ways the most enjoyable. It's also the ideal place to start your exploration of the mountains.

East of Belfast

Heading east into County Down from Belfast, you've a choice of two routes: the A20 which heads due east past Stormont (see p.541) to **Newtownards**, at the head of Strangford Lough; or the A2, which heads northeast past the excellent Ulster Folk and Transport Museum to **Bangor**.

Newtownards and around

Following the A20, the single interesting sight as you near Newtownards is **Scrabo Tower** (Easter & May bank holidays and June–Sept Sat–Thurs 10.30am–6pm; free), whose looming presence dominates the surrounding area. The tower protrudes from the top of a rocky, gorse-strewn hump of a hill (a long-extinct volcano), but getting to it after you've spotted it is quite a circuit – follow the signs to **Scrabo Country Park** and you'll arrive in the car park just below. The hill itself is pitted with quarries used to extract Scrabo stone, employed for all manner of local building, including Grey Abbey (see p.606). Up close the tower looks like a monstrous rocket in its launcher, hewn out of rough black volcanic rock. It was built in 1857 as a memorial to the third Marquess of Londonderry, General Charles William Stewart-Vane, in gratitude for his efforts on behalf of his tenants during the Great Famine. The spot was originally a Bronze Age burial cairn, probably the resting place of one of the grand chieftains of the area, and there's evidence of a huge hill fort here too. Despite the 122 steps to its top, the tower is now very popular with sightseers, who come mostly for the wonderful **views** across Strangford Lough and the healthy, blustery weather that often curls around the side of the hill. The woodland immediately behind is a country park open to the public (free access); in contrast to the tamed, prosperous countryside round about, Scrabo is the only piece of ground for miles around to feel at all wild.

Scrabo Tower looks down on **NEWTOWNARDS**, a place strong on manufacture but unexciting for the traveller. Despite its name, it's an old town, founded in 1244, though there's little evidence of this beyond the ruined Dominican priory just off Castle Street. The Scrabo stone Market House (1765), now the town hall and arts centre, lords it over a large square filled on Saturdays by market activity. The **tourist office** is near the bus station at 31 Regent St (July & Aug Mon–Thurs 9am–5.15pm, Fri & Sat 9am–5.30pm; rest of year Mon–Fri 9.15am–5pm, Sat 9.30am–5pm; ☎028/9182 6846).

Two miles north on the A21 Bangor road you'll find the **Somme Heritage Centre** (July & Aug Mon–Fri 10am–5pm, Sat & Sun noon–5pm; rest of year closes 4pm & closed all day Fri; Feb, March & Oct–Dec closed Sat & Sun; tours £3.50). The re-created frontline trenches are staffed by guides in battledress who provide a sobering and moving account of the role of the Irish and Ulster Divisions in the futile World War I battle – 5500 men of the 36th (Ulster) Division alone were reported dead, wounded or missing. Across the main road is **Ark Open Farm** (Mon–Sat 10am–6pm, Sun 2–6pm; £2.90), Ireland's first public rare breeds farm, where you can compare Irish Moiled and Kerry cattle and marvel at the sheer ugliness of the Vietnamese pot-bellied pig.

A mile east of Newtownards on the Millisle road stand the ruins of the fifteenth-century **Movilla Abbey**. It's a largely disappointing site, but some ancient grave slabs in its north wall hint at what once was here. In the cemetery next door there's the more recent grave of James Francis, a Greyabbey man who fought in the Irish Brigade on the Union side in the American Civil War. The Brigade suffered heavy casualties during

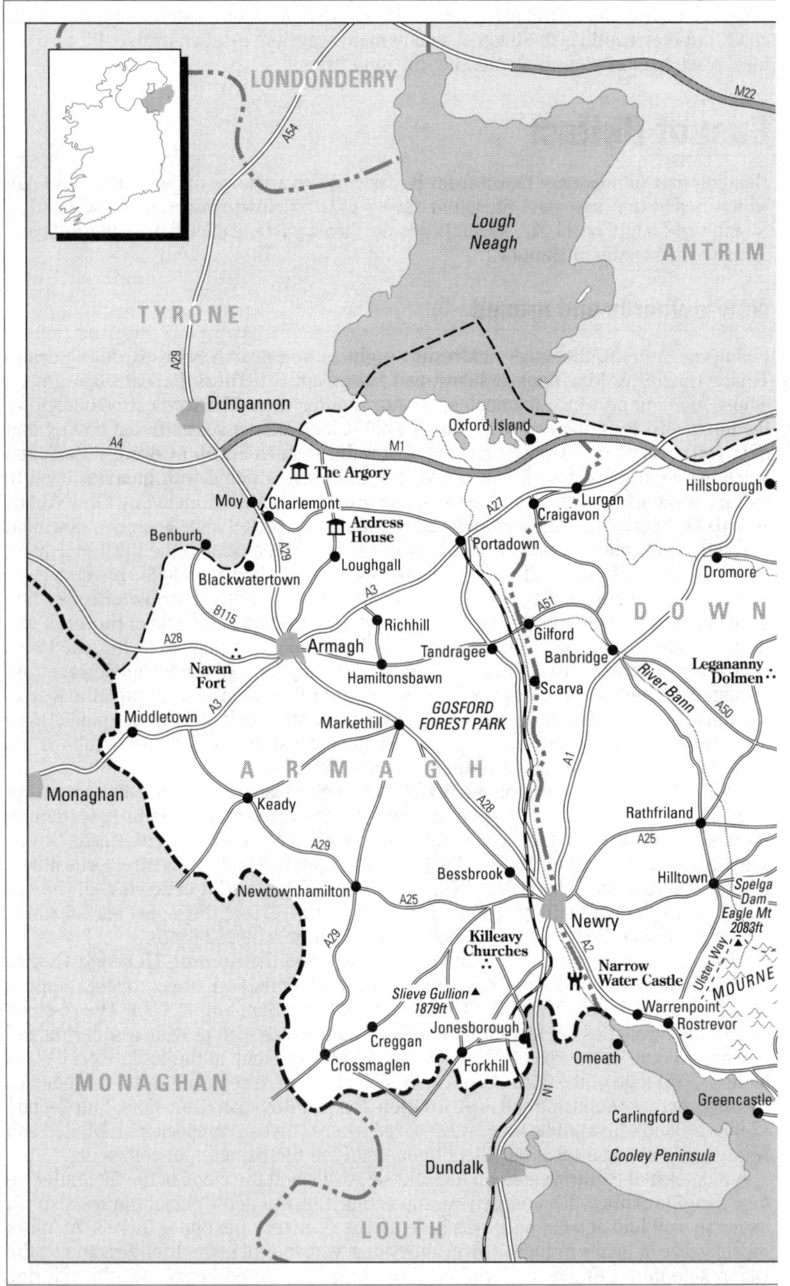
LONDONDERRY
M22
A54
Lough Neagh
ANTRIM
TYRONE
A29
Dungannon
Oxford Island
A4
M1
The Argory
Hillsborough
Moy
Charlemont
Lurgan
A27
Craigavon
Ardress House
Benburb
Portadown
Loughgall
Blackwatertown
Dromore
A3
A51
DOWN
B115
Richhill
Gilford
A28
Armagh
Tandragee
Banbridge
Legananny Dolmen
Navan Fort
Hamiltonsbawn
River Bann
Scarva
A50
A3
GOSFORD FOREST PARK
Middletown
Markethill
ARMAGH
A1
Monaghan
Keady
A28
Rathfriland
A25
A29
Bessbrook
Hilltown
Spelga Dam
Newtownhamilton
A25
Newry
Eagle Mt 2083ft
A29
Killeavy Churches
A2
Ulster Way
Narrow Water Castle
MOURNE
Slieve Gullion 1879ft
Warrenpoint
Rostrevor
Jonesborough
Creggan
Omeath
Forkhill
Crossmaglen
MONAGHAN
N1
Greencastle
Carlingford
Cooley Peninsula
Dundalk
LOUTH

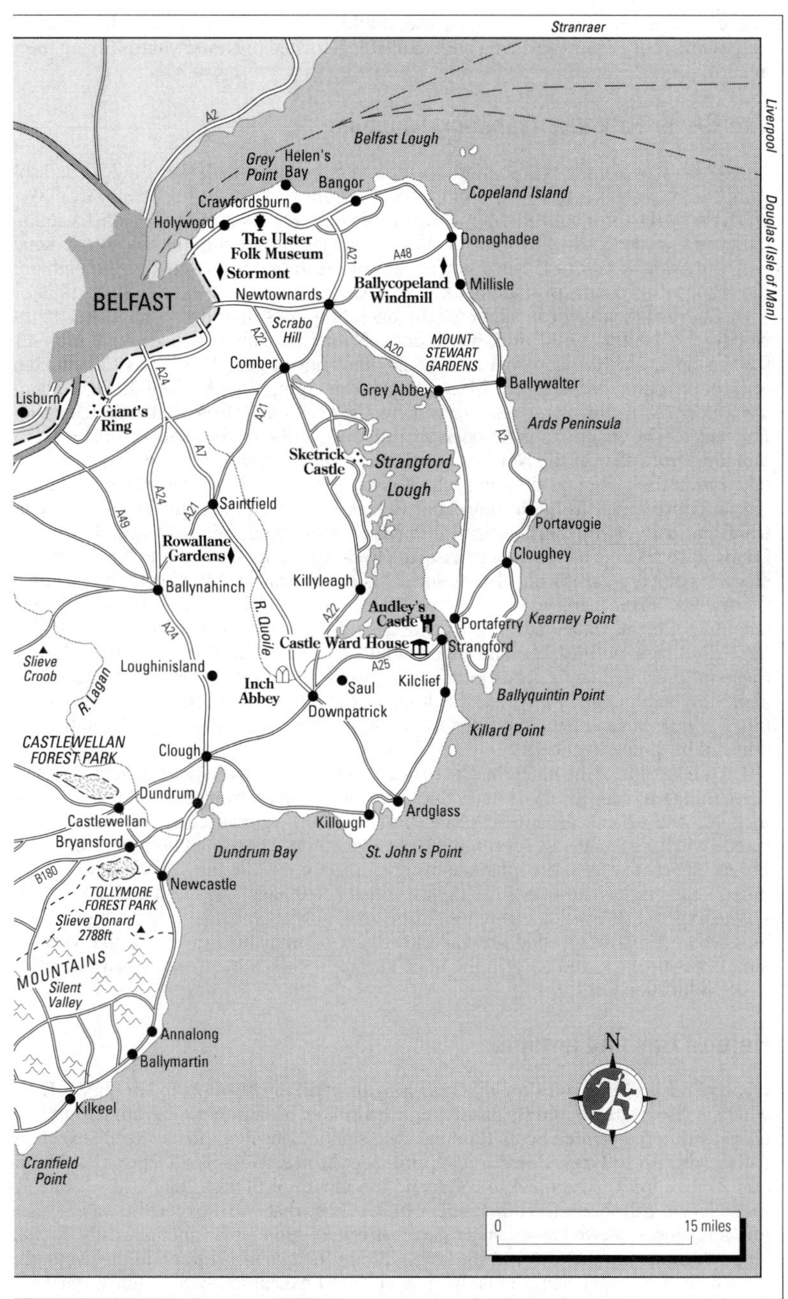
Stranraer
Liverpool
Douglas (Isle of Man)
Belfast Lough
Grey Point
Helen's Bay
Bangor
Copeland Island
Crawfordsburn
Holywood
The Ulster Folk Museum
Stormont
Donaghadee
A48
A21
Ballycopeland Windmill
Millisle
BELFAST
Newtownards
Scrabo Hill
A22
A20
MOUNT STEWART GARDENS
Comber
Ballywalter
Grey Abbey
Lisburn
Giant's Ring
A24
A21
Ards Peninsula
A7
A2
Sketrick Castle
Strangford Lough
Saintfield
A49
Portavogie
Rowallane Gardens
Cloughey
Ballynahinch
Killyleagh
R. Quoile
Audley's Castle
Portaferry
Kearney Point
Castle Ward House
Strangford
Slieve Croob
Loughinisland
A25
Kilclief
R. Lagan
Inch Abbey
Saul
Downpatrick
Ballyquintin Point
Killard Point
CASTLEWELLAN FOREST PARK
Clough
Dundrum
Castlewellan
Killough
Ardglass
Bryansford
Dundrum Bay
St. John's Point
B180
Newcastle
TOLLYMORE FOREST PARK
Slieve Donard 2788ft
MOUNTAINS
Silent Valley
Annalong
Ballymartin
Kilkeel
Cranfield Point
N
0
15 miles

two of the war's bloodiest actions, the Battle of Cold Harbour and the Siege of Petersburg, but Francis survived both and later returned to Newtownards, dying there in 1921.

The Ulster Folk and Transport Museum

The A2 towards Bangor is both more scenic and more interesting than the A20, and still within easy reach of a day-trip from Belfast. There's a lovely fifteen-mile walk from **HOLYWOOD** (pronounced *Hollywood*) to Helen's Bay (see below), along a mildly indented estuary coast with some beautiful silvery sand beaches, especially the small crescent-shaped ones at Helen's Bay itself. The **train** line runs between the path and the road, with a couple of stations where you can pick up services on towards Bangor.

At Cultra station you can alight for the one of the most fascinating museums in the North, the **Ulster Folk and Transport Museum** (April–June & Sept Mon–Fri 9.30am–5pm, Sat 10.30am–6pm, Sun noon–6pm; July & Aug Mon–Sat 10.30am–6pm, Sun noon–6pm; Oct–March Mon–Fri 9.30am–4pm, Sat & Sun 12.30–4.30pm; *www.nidex.com/uftm*; £4) – also served by Ulsterbus #B1 from Belfast's Laganside Buscentre. The main site is an open-air **museum village** where about thirty typical buildings from all over the North, some dating from the eighteenth century, have been taken from their original sites and rebuilt complete with authentic furnishings, including an entire street from Dromore and Belfast terraces. Conceptually, you can walk from one part of Northern Ireland to another, amid appropriate scenes. Traditional **farms** have also been created and assorted livestock roam between the buildings. The starting point is a gallery on Ulster's social history and an introduction to the buildings themselves. From here you walk around the grounds, visiting the various buildings, including a small village street with church and rectory, two schools, various typical farm dwellings, and a forge and other buildings used in light manufacture. Each of these is "inhabited" by a member of staff, garbed in period costume and informative about the building and its origins. Such historical realism is impressive, though sometimes a little disquieting: the Kilmore Church graveyard contains real tombstones donated by family members.

On the far side of the main road, across a bridge, are the **transport galleries**, where the exhibits include every conceivable form of transport from horse-drawn carts to lifeboats and a vertical take-off plane, but especially veteran cars, motorcycles and trams. You'll also meet *Old Maeve*, the largest locomotive ever built in Ireland, and a De Lorean sports car from the infamously defunct factory, while the *Titanic* exhibits documents the origins and fate of the Belfast-constructed liner. The latest addition is "The Flight Experience", which examines the history of aviation through films, models and interactive displays. Outside the galleries there's a miniature railway which runs on summer Saturdays, and back in the main section there's a handy **restaurant**, located in the Education Centre.

Helen's Bay and around

If you're not walking, you should follows a signpost off the A2 to reach **HELEN'S BAY**, which is also a stop on the Belfast–Bangor **train** line. It's a rather twee but restful little place, with a red-painted Scots Baronial-style station. Down at the bay itself, a walking path leads east to **Grey Point Fort** (April–Sept Mon & Wed–Sun 2–5pm; Oct–March Sun 2–5pm; free), positioned to command the mouth of Belfast Lough, along with its sister fort at Kilroot on the other side. The fort has what you'd expect by way of quarters and stores, as well as an impressive battery of gun emplacements, ready to challenge the shipping that entered the lough during the two world wars. In the event, the two six-inch breech-loading guns were never fired except in practice (local residents had to be warned to open their windows and doors to prevent blast damage), apart from one occasion in World War II, when a merchant ship failed to respond to the signal "heave to or be sunk" and received a warning shot across its bows. The guns were sold for scrap in 1957 when the Coast Artillery was disbanded. After the fort was opened to the public in 1987 an identical six-inch gun was relocated here from the prison on Spike Island in Cork harbour. The Battery Observation Post and Fire Command Post are today staffed by dressed-up mannequins, like stills taken from a war movie – though they're now staring straight into a growth of trees that have sprung up to obscure the view. There's also a selection of photos showing the original guns and their positions; but it's really as a viewpoint with an atmosphere of military history, rather than the other way round, that the fort is worth visiting nowadays.

Should you want to stay, there's a classy **B&B**, *Carrig-Gorm*, 27 Bridge Rd (☎028/9185 3680; ④), with equally stylish Mediterranean food in *Carriage Nouveau* (Tues–Sat eves & Sunday lunch; booking required on ☎028/9185 2841).

Crawfordsburn Country Park

The whole short stretch of coast from Helen's Bay, including the fort, is actually part of the **Crawfordsburn Country Park** (April–Sept 9am–8pm; Oct–March 9am–4.45pm), an estate handed down from the Scottish Presbyterian Crawford family, then acquired by Lord Dufferin (whose mother Helen gave her name to the bay) and now in public hands. Its glens and dells are replete with beeches, cypresses, exotic conifers, cedars, the usual burst of rhododendrons and also a Californian giant redwood, but the park's best features are the wildflower meadow and the woodland planted with native species. Perhaps the most scenic walk (well-marked by green arrows) is to follow the pathway back from Grey Point to the top of the bay's beaches and turn inland by the trickle of Crawford's Burn. This will take you up through the best of the woodland, under a fine – and still used – nineteenth-century railway viaduct, and up to a waterfall at the head of the glen. The **Park Centre** (daily: April–Sept 10am–6pm; Oct–March 10am–5pm) has a café and an incredible amount of information on local ecology and wildlife. **Helen's Tower**, which can be seen from a considerable distance, was built by Lord Dufferin in the nineteenth century to honour his mother, and as a famine relief project.

CRAWFORDSBURN village is on one of Ireland's most ancient highways, a track that ran from Holywood to Bangor Abbey (now the B20), and has a nice but (like many things in this part of the world) twee early seventeenth-century **pub**, *The Old Inn*, 15 Main St (☎028/9185 3255; *www.theoldinn.com*; ⑥), a partly thatched coaching inn offering elegant en-suite accommodation and an excellent, if pricey, **restaurant** serving specialities such as Portavogie scampi.

Bangor

BANGOR probably takes its name from its curving bay set between a pair of symmetrical headlands (*beanna chor* – "curved peaks") and its sheltered position made it ideal for exploitation as a holiday resort. The town has been hugely popular with Belfast people since the railway came in the 1860s, but today it's as much a suburb of Belfast as a holiday spot. It still possesses a tawdry charm, stuck in a 1960s time warp with all the appropriate bucket-and-spade paraphernalia – giant swan boats to paddle around a mini-lake in the fun park, a miniature railway and amusement arcades. There's also a 500-berth marina which makes Bangor a good place for stocking up on provisions or exploring the coast, while for the land-based the town is well equipped as a stop-off point for dinner and a stroll along the promenade.

Bangor's period of greatest historical significance was almost entirely associated with its **abbey**, which was founded by St Comgall in 586 AD, and from which missionaries set forth to convert pagan Europe. Though the abbey remained powerful for eight hundred years, there's not a trace of the building left. The only vestige of its fame is the *Antiphonarium Benchorense*, one of the oldest-known ecclesiastical manuscripts, consisting of collects, anthems and some religious poems; the original now lies in the Ambrosian Library in Milan, but you can view a facsimile of it in the **North Down Heritage Centre** (July & Aug Mon–Sat 10.30am–5.30pm, Sun 2–5.30pm; rest of year closes 4.30pm & all day Mon; *www.north-down.gov.uk/heritage*; free), tucked away at the back of the town hall. Other displays trace the rise of the Ward family (see Castle Ward, p.612) who were largely responsible for the town's development and built Bangor Castle (now the town hall). There's also a fascinating collection of Eastern *objets d'art* collected by a local-born diplomat, Sir John Jordan, and a collection of archeological discoveries featuring the Ballycroghan swords, a wonderful pair of Bronze Age weapons, dating from 500 AD.

Practicalities

The only building of any antiquity in Bangor is the seventeenth-century **Old Custom House and Tower** on the seafront, now occupied by the **tourist office** (July & Aug Mon & Sat 10am–7pm, Tues–Fri 9am–7pm, Sun noon–6pm; rest of year Mon 10am–5pm, Tues–Fri 9am–5pm, Sat 10am–4pm; June & Sept same weekday hours, but Sat 10.30am–4.30pm and also Sun 1–5pm; ☎028/9127 0069).

As you'd expect, there are dozens of places to **stay** here. The two most luxurious **hotels** are on Quay Street – the *Marine Court* (☎028/9145 1100; *www.visitcoastofdown.com/marinecourthotel*; ⑧) and the *Royal* (☎028/9127 1866; *TheRoyalHotel@compuserve.com*; ⑦) – but you'll find plenty of less expensive **B&Bs** on Queen's Parade and Princetown and Seacliff roads. The nearest **camping** is at Donaghadee, six miles south along the coast.

Most of Bangor's **restaurants** are dotted along the seafront or up nearby sidestreets. Overlooking the marina, *Genoa's*, 1a Seacliff Rd, is the place for modern European cuisine while *Café Brazilia*, on Bridge Street, serves numerous varieties of espresso plus an imaginative and cheap menu. Further along the esplanade and up Gray's Hill, *Knuttel's Restaurant* – named after and decked out in paintings by the owner himself – offers a good-value four-course dinner. Other relatively inexpensive restaurants are at the *Marine Court Hotel*; the *Green Vegetable*, 6 Hamilton Rd (for vegetarian specials); and the *Back Street Café* on Queen's Parade for fish delights such as fresh turbot.

Most of the **pubs** opt for discos or balladeers with a beatbox, but you'll find regular traditional **music** at Friday night sessions at *Fealty's* (also known as the *Ormeau Bar*) on the High Street. The *Jenny Watts*, also on the High Street, has traditional sessions (Tues & Sun nights) as well as Sunday lunchtime jazz. There are regular **boat trips** (☎028/9145 5321) from the harbour to various destinations, such as the Copeland Islands, and for deep-sea fishing (rods and tackle supplied).

The Ards Peninsula

The **Ards Peninsula** stretches out an arm to enclose the waters of Strangford Lough, with only the narrowest of openings to the sea in the south. The eastern seaboard coast south of Bangor is far from the most attractive hereabouts, but, if you have the time for a detour, there are still some pleasant spots.

Donaghadee

East of Bangor's sprawling suburbs, the first place of any size is **DONAGHADEE**, a small market town whose origins lie in its proximity to the Scottish coast – on a clear day, it's easy to see Galloway across the water, if you climb up the little hill to **The Moat**, the remains of a nineteenth-century folly. From the 1600s until the middle of the nineteenth century, ferries ran between here and Portpatrick in Galloway, the shortest sea-crossing available. Various notables arrived in Ireland by this route, including, in 1818, **John Keats** on his walking tour of the British Isles. He was reputedly so depressed by the poverty he saw on his way to Belfast, and the mockery attracted by his fancy London clothes, that he soon returned to Scotland. *Grace Neill's Inn,* on the High Street, dates back to 1611 and claims to have put up Peter the Great of Russia, during his European tour. Donaghadee's decline began when the ferry service was transferred to Larne in 1849. Nowadays, apart from watching the dulse-gatherers at low tide or fishing activity at the harbour, there's little going on here and the town's only other claim to fame is that its lighthouse received a lick of paint from Brendan Behan when he was employed after the war by the Commission for Irish Lights. More enticing is the possibility of visiting the three **Copeland Islands**, a mile or so offshore and uninhabited since the 1940s. The middle one, Cross Island, is now a bird sanctuary run by the RSPB, who arrange cruises to it (☎028/9049 1547); Nelson's Boats in Donaghadee run regular trips to the other two (☎028/9188 3403).

There are several small **B&Bs** around town, including *Deans*, 52 Northfield Rd (☎028/9188 2204; ③) and *Herdstown House* (☎028/9188 3773; ③), a listed farmhouse on Hogstown Road. **Camping** is available at *Donaghadee Caravan Park* (April–Oct; ☎028/9188 2369) on Millisle Road. *Chick-a-Dee*, on the High Street, is the place for economical breakfasts and lunches, while the bistro in *Grace Neill's* across the road offers a popular upmarket option for **meals**.

South to Ballyquintin Point

Unless you're a caravan devotee, you'll want to give the villages of **MILLISLE** and, further down the coast, **BALLYWALTER**, a complete miss – each is swamped by half a dozen sites. Just about the only piece of interest around here is the late eighteenth-century **Ballycopeland Windmill** (June–Sept Tues–Sat 10am–6pm, Sun 2–6pm; £1), a mile west of Millisle. This claims to be the only windmill in working order in Ireland, though it hasn't ground grain on a regular basis since 1915. An electrical model in the miller's house demonstrates its functions.

If you leave the A2 in Ballyhalbert and stick to the coast road, you'll pass **Burr Point**, the most easterly place in Ireland, before reaching **PORTAVOGIE**, a fishing port famous for its catches of giant prawns, which can be bought ready-peeled in the village. From here the coast road curves inland, taking you around Cloghy Bay and past **Kirkistown Castle**, a tower house built in 1622 by one of the Savage family, the Anglo-Norman landlords of the peninsula; unfortunately it's on private land, so you can't inspect the remains from a closer viewpoint. The next stop, **KEARNEY**, is a charming village, consisting almost entirely of whitewashed cottages and now mostly owned by the National Trust. You can walk from here to **Kearney Point**, an often blustery ten-minute stroll with panoramic views across the Irish Sea. Instead of heading directly to Portaferry from Kearney, choosing the road around **Ballyquintin Point** will take you past the entrance lane to **St Cowey's Wells**, where the faithful optimist is spoilt for choice: there's a drinking well, a wishing well and a well for bathing sore eyes. Look out for the rock nearby – the indentations are supposed to mark the places where the saint's hands and feet rested as he prayed.

Strangford Lough

Ancient annals say that **Strangford Lough** was formed around 1650 BC by the sea sweeping in over the lands of Brena. This created a beautiful, calm inlet, the archipelago-like pieces of land along its inner arm fringed with brown and yellow bladderwrack and tangleweed, and tenanted by a rich gathering of bird life during the warmer months and vast flocks of geese and waders in the winter. It's an attractive haven for small boats and yachts, and several picturesque halts for the land-bound make the road along the lough's western shore the most interesting route leading south from Belfast.

The eastern shore

The eastern edge of Strangford Lough is not as indented as its opposite shore but betters it in having a major road (the continuation of the A20) that runs close to the water virtually all the way down. Also the scenery is delightful, and there are two places to stop off en route to Portaferry – the **Mount Stewart** gardens and **Grey Abbey**.

Mount Stewart

Five miles southeast of Newtownards, served by Ulsterbus #9 and #10 from Belfast's Laganside Buscentre, is the former family home of the Londonderry family, the National Trust-owned **Mount Stewart House and Gardens** (opening times differ, see below; £3.50 for house, gardens and temple; £3 for gardens and temple only).

The 98 acres of **gardens** (March Sun 2–5pm; April–Sept daily 11am–6pm; Oct Sat & Sun 11am–6pm) were laid out by Lady Londonderry, wife of the seventh marquess, in the 1920s – and a thorough job she made of it: among others, there are Spanish and Italian gardens, a Space Garden and the Shamrock Garden (with a topiary harp and an appropriately leaved Red Hand of Ulster). The trees and shrubs here are no more than sixty to seventy years old, but they've grown at such a remarkable rate that they look twice that. The principal reason for this is the unusually warm and humid microclimate: the gardens catch the east coast sun, causing a heavy overnight dew, and the Gulf Stream washes the shores only a stone's throw away. Despite the northerly latitude, conditions here rival those of Cornwall and Devon.

Although the gardens are the highlight, the **house** is also worth viewing (Easter week 1–6pm; April & Oct Sat & Sun 1–6pm; May–Sept Mon & Wed–Sun 1–6pm). The family was a leading member of the Protestant Ascendancy and its members included Lord Castlereagh, who was Foreign Secretary under Pitt the Younger and is best remembered for guiding the Act of Union into operation. Among the splendid (and occasionally eccentric) furniture inside is a set of 22 Empire chairs used by the delegates to the Congress of Vienna in 1815, who included the Duke of Wellington and Talleyrand; the chairs were a gift to Castlereagh's brother Lord Stewart, another high-ranking diplomat of the time. The continental connection is flaunted further in bedrooms named after various historically important cities: Rome, St Petersburg, Madrid, Moscow and Sebastopol (from the time of the Crimean War). The house contains a number of paintings, particularly portraits of Castlereagh's political contemporaries, but the most notable and largest is *Hambletonian* (1799) by George Stubbs, showing the celebrated thoroughbred being rubbed down after a victory at Newmarket.

A little to the east of the house, the octagonal **Temple of the Winds** (April–Oct Sat & Sun 2–5pm) is a remodelling by James "Athenian" Stuart (1713–88), one of the pioneers of Neoclassical architecture, of Athens' Tower of Andronicus Cyrrhestes. The temple is set on a promontory overlooking Strangford Lough, making it a great place for birdwatching.

Grey Abbey

A couple of miles south on the shore road, **Grey Abbey** (April–Sept Tues–Sat 10am–6pm, Sun 2–6pm; Oct–March Sat 10am–1pm & 2–4pm, Sun 2–4pm; £1; Ulsterbus #9 and 10) lies slightly to the east of the village which later developed around it. The abbey was founded in 1193 by Affreca, daughter of Godred, King of Man, and wife of

John de Courcy, as a thanksgiving for having made a safe sea-crossing during a storm. Typical of the **Cistercian** order, of which Mellifont was the mother house in Ireland, the abbey sits in once-remote parkland beside a rivulet, which would have been a source of fresh water and fish – self-reliance was crucial to Cistercianism. Even today, that setting is barely disturbed, and reason in itself to visit, with a substantial set of ruins to complete the picture.

Following the standard design of Cistercian abbeys, it has a church at one end and the living and working quarters of the monks ranged around a **cloister**, a plain structure overall without distracting embellishments. Grey Abbey is unusual for Ireland, though, in showing early Gothic features at a time when late Romanesque work was still common here. Among the best-preserved remains are the **west door**, much of whose carved decoration can still be made out, and the fine lancet windows in the east end. Another unusual feature is that the church is a simple hall, with no aisles. Outside the church there's a re-created "physic garden" and the notes on display help you to imagine the elongated cloister when it was overshadowed on three sides by the chapter house, dormitories and refectory, which are now no more than stumps.

GREYABBEY village is renowned for its numerous **antiques** shops. The *Wildfowler Inn* on Main Street is a popular choice for both its bar meals and **restaurant**. Nearby **B&Bs** are *Brimar*, 4 Cardy Rd (☎028/4278 8681; ④); *Woodview Farm*, 8 Ballywater Rd (☎028/4278 8242; *www.visitcoastofdown.com/woodview*; ②); and, out towards Kircubbin, *Mervue*, 28 Portaferry Rd (☎028/4278 8619; *www.visitcoastofdown.com/mervue*; ③).

Portaferry

PORTAFERRY, at the mouth of the lough, is the home of the **Exploris** aquarium (April–Aug Mon–Fri 10am–6pm, Sat 11am–6pm, Sun 1–6pm; rest of year closes 5pm; *ards-council.gov.uk/exploris.htm*; £3.85), which has a touch tank for the brave to stroke a stingray and an open sea tank where you can view the odd roaming shark and basking seals. However, the town's main attraction is the marvellous **sunset** looking across the "Narrows" to Strangford, a view enhanced by a ten-minute climb to the stump of the old windmill just behind the town. In July the **Galway Hookers Regatta** livens the place up – the traditional boats sail round from Galway to be welcomed by the Portaferry Yacht Club, and every pub has virtually 24-hour music sessions.

Ferries leave every half-hour for the five-minute ride across the lips of the lough to Strangford (Mon–Fri 7.45am–10.45pm, Sat 8.15am–11.15pm, Sun 9.45am–10.45pm; single 85p on foot, £4.20 per car; return £1.40/£6.80). The **tourist office** is in The Stables, Castle St (Easter–June & Sept Mon–Sat 10am–1.15pm & 2.15–5pm, Sun 2–6pm; July & Aug Mon–Sat 10am–5.30pm, Sun 1–6pm; ☎028/4272 9882), next to the ruined tower house. Should you be looking for somewhere to **stay**, the *Portaferry Hotel*, 10 The Strand (☎028/4272 8231; *www.portaferryhotel.com*; ⑥), is relatively luxurious and has a popular **restaurant** specializing in fish meals; or try the brilliantly designed *The Narrows*, 8 Shore Rd (☎028/4272 8148; *www.narrows.co.uk*; ⑥), where every room has a stupendous view across the lough. There's super food here too and all manner of special craft and activity weekends on offer. For good-value **B&B** try *Adairs*, 22 The Square (☎028/4272 8412; ②) or the rooms above the *Fiddlers Green* pub, 10 Church St (☎028/4272 8383; ③). Bear in mind that accommodation may be hard to find during the Castle Ward opera season in June (see p.612). Portaferry also has a HINI-affiliated **youth hostel** called *Barholm*, 11 The Strand (☎028/4272 9598) which offers B&B and self-catering facilities. The nearest **campsite** is *Tara Caravan Park*, three miles south-east on Ballyquintin Road (☎028/4272 8459), by a long, sandy beach.

As for **food**, the *Castle Restaurant* on Castle Street offers ample portions; for coffee and good cakes try the *Harlequin* next door. The **pubs** are good at just about any time of year, with nightly singalong folk sessions led by the landlord and traditional music at the *Fiddler's Green* most nights; another popular session pub is the *Saltwalter Brigg*, six miles north of Portaferry towards Kircubbin, on Friday evenings.

The western shore

Leaving Scrabo Tower just east of Belfast on the A22, you'll pass through **COMBER** – famous for its potatoes – before reaching a turning east to **Castle Espie Wildfowl and Wetland Centre** (March–Oct Mon–Sat 10.30am–5pm, Sun 11.30am–6pm; Nov–Feb Mon–Sat 11.30am–4pm, Sun 11.30am–5pm; £3.25), where admission earnings are ploughed back into conserving the wetlands area for the seven thousand birds that visit it, and the resident population of waterfowl. The centre also has a coffee shop and art gallery. Immediately beyond Castle Espie, you'll see the excellent *Old Schoolhouse Inn* by the roadside – unmistakable, with a fire engine lodged in its front garden. It offers a fair-priced Sunday lunch (otherwise Mon–Sat 7–9.30pm; ☎028/9754 1182).

From Castle Espie, you can wind along the very edge of the lough on a series of minor roads. Travelling this scenic route is enjoyable in itself, but there are a couple of spots worth making for. First of them is **Mahee Island**, named for St Mochaoi, supposedly the first abbot of the island, and reached via a twisting lane and several causeways. Heading past the crumbling remains of Mahee Castle at the entrance to the island, and over the final causeway, you come to the Celtic **Nendrum Monastic Site** (visitor centre open April–Sept Tues–Sat 10am–1pm & 1.30–6pm, Sun 2–6pm; Oct–March Sat 10am–4pm, Sun 2–4pm; 75p), a few hundred yards further on. It's a marvellously isolated spot, surrounded by drumlins and the lough's waterways. Annals and excavations indicate that a sizeable community lived here from the seventh century onwards, but the remaining ruins probably date from the twelfth century at the very earliest. It was clearly a substantial establishment, with church, round tower, school and living quarters all housed in a *cashel* of three concentric wards. Today, the inner wall shelters the ruined church, and a reconstructed sundial uses some of the original remnants. There's an illuminating reconstruction map at the site and a helpful visitor centre.

Back on the road along the lough, follow the signs to Ardmillan, Killinchy and then Whiterock to reach **Sketrick Island** (which itself is not signposted). As with Mahee Island, there's a castle to guard the entrance, now no more than a shattered reminder. *Daft Eddie's Pub and Restaurant*, behind the castle, offers bar snacks as well as a more elaborate restaurant menu. An equally daft competition known as the **Hen Island race** takes place here in October, when craft constructed from oil drums and crates are ridden and paddled between Sketrick and the nearby Hen Island.

The tiny coves and inlets at the feet of little drumlins continue as far as Killyleagh, almost any of them worth exploring. A good way to do this is to take one of the **cruises** organized by Strangford Charter (☎07711/034576), which operate from Sketrick Island at weekends during June to August from noon onwards, and cost £6 per person for a one-hour trip.

Killyleagh

Approaching **KILLYLEAGH**, what looks like a huge Gothic fantasy comes into view, a sight wholly out of character with the area. The **oldest inhabited castle** in Ireland, it was erected by John de Courcy in the late twelfth century, but was rebuilt by the Hamilton family in 1648 and again in 1850 to give it the Bavarian *Schloss* appearance it has today. It's still a private house, and when viewed close up it's much more gaunt, with a squat mixture of crenellations, turrets and cones. The stone outside the castle gates commemorates the town's most famous son, Hans Sloane (1660–1753), physician to King George II and founder of both the British Museum and Kew Gardens – London's Sloane Square is named after him. The gatehouse towers themselves have been adapted for **holiday letting** (☎028/4482 8261; *killyleaghcastle@virgin.net*; £200–350 per week). A little way back down the hill, the *Dufferin Arms* coaching inn (☎028/4482 8229; *www.nova.co.uk/dufferin*; ⑤) offers extremely comfortable **B&B** and organizes a wide range of activity breaks.

Two miles south of Killyleagh is **Delamont Country Park** (daily: April–Sept 9am–dusk; Oct–March 9am–5pm; car £2.50), a pleasant spot with grand views over the lough, a heronry and Ireland's longest miniature railway.

The Lecale region

Jutting into the southern reach of Strangford Lough, the **Lecale Peninsula** is above all **St Patrick** country. Ireland's patron saint was a Roman Briton, first carried off as a youth from somewhere near Carlisle in northern England by Irish raiders. He spent six years in slavery in Ireland before escaping home again and, at the age of thirty, decided to return to Ireland as a bishop, to spread Christianity. Christianity had already reached Ireland a while earlier, probably through traders and other slaves, and, indeed, St Patrick was not in fact the first bishop of Ireland, but he remains easily the most famous. He arrived in Ireland this second time, according to his biographer Muirchú (also his erstwhile captor, converted), on the shores of the Lecale region, and his first Irish sermon was preached at **Saul** in 432. Today the region commemorates the association with sites at Struell Wells and Saul, as well as at **Downpatrick** town.

The **Lecale Trail** is a thirty-mile tour of the peninsula starting from in front of the Down County Museum in Downpatrick (further information and trail maps can be obtained from the town's tourist office). If you've had enough of St Patrick and his seeming connection with nearly every landmark, alternative ways of exploring the peninsula are the **nature rambles** and **horse rides** available at the Quoile Countryside Centre just outside Downpatrick.

Downpatrick and around

DOWNPATRICK, 23 miles south of Belfast, comes to life during its nowadays occasional race meetings, but at other times it seems depressed and rather lethargic, as if awaiting the invigorating kiss of economic revival. A town of little more than ten thousand people, Downpatrick's compact size and the proximity of its rich and well-preserved historical sites makes for an easily negotiable day's visit.

All buses arrive at the **bus station** (☎028/4461 2384) on Market Street; from here it's a half-mile signposted stroll to Downpatrick's **Cathedral** and the **Hill of Down**, at the north of the town. This was once a rise of great strategic worth, fought over long before the arrival of St Patrick made it famous. A **Celtic fort** of mammoth proportions was built here and was called first *Arús Cealtchair*, then later *Dún Cealtchair* (Celtchar's fort). Celtchar was one of the Red Branch Knights, a friend of the then King of Ulster, Conor MacNessa, and, according to the *Book of the Dun Cow*, "an angry terrific hideous man with a long nose, huge ears, apple eyes, and coarse dark-grey hair." The *Dún* part of the fort's name went on to become the name of the county, as well as the town.

By the time the Norman knight **John de Courcy** made his mark here in the late twelfth century, a settlement was well established. Pushing north out of Leinster, and defeating Rory MacDonlevy, King of Ulster, de Courcy dispossessed the Augustinian canons who occupied the Hill of Down to establish his own **Benedictine abbey**. He flaunted as much pomp as he could to mark the occasion, and one of his festive tricks was to import what were supposedly the disinterred bodies of St Brigid and St Columba to join St Patrick, who was (allegedly) buried here. One of the earliest accounts of

Patrick's life asserts that he's buried in a church near the sea; and since a later account admits that "where his bones are, no man knows", Downpatrick's claim seems as good as any.

The Town

Uphill from the centre of town, at the very end of the elegant, spacious Mall, sits Downpatrick's **Cathedral** (daily 9am–5pm). The site of the three graves of Columba, Patrick and Brigid is meant to be just to the left of the tower entrance and is marked today by a rough granite boulder, put there around 1900 to cover the huge hole created by earlier pilgrims searching for the saints' bones. The cathedral built by de Courcy was destroyed in the fourteenth century, and a new abbey erected in the early sixteenth century was even more short-lived. Today's cathedral dates basically from the early part of the last century, though it incorporates many aspects of earlier incarnations. Its most unique feature is the private box-pews, characteristic of the Regency period and the only ones remaining in use in Ireland.

Leaving the cathedral and retracing your steps a little down English Street, which is crowded with Georgian buildings, you come to the eighteenth-century jail, now home to the **Down County Museum** and the **St Patrick Heritage Centre** (June–Aug Mon–Fri 10am–5pm, Sat & Sun 2–5pm; rest of year closed Sun & Mon; *www.downdc.gov.uk*; free). The heritage centre occupies the gatehouse and has a range of displays telling the St Patrick story, principally through words taken from his autobiographical *Confessions* (the short video also provides a handy summary of what the rest of the peninsula has to offer by way of relics of the saint). The three-storey Georgian **Governor's House** in the centre of the walled courtyard houses a local history gallery, which has regular exhibitions. The cell block at the back of the enclosure once held the United Irishman Thomas Russell, who had already survived the 1798 Rebellion but was found guilty of complicity in Robert Emmett's uprising and was duly hanged in 1803 from a sill outside the main gate of the jail.

Turn downhill between the jail and the barricaded courthouse and, inauspiciously tucked behind a secondary school, you'll find the **Mound of Down**, a smaller prominence half submerged in undergrowth. It's in fact 60ft high and inside its outer ditch is a horseshoe central mound of rich grass. Once a rath, or round hill-fort, it was considerably altered and enlarged to create a Norman motte and bailey fortification, with a *bretasche* (a wooden archery tower) at the centre. Its view of the Hill of Down clearly displays the attractions the hill had for its earliest settlers; it's believed by some to be the site of the palace of the Kings of Ulster.

At the rear of the market car park, the **Downpatrick Railway Museum** (July & Aug Sun 2–5pm; £2.50), offers tours of the restored station and workshops and occasional train rides (details on ☎028/4461 7517). A little further along the main drag is **Downpatrick Race Course**, the second-oldest in Ireland and home to the Ulster National. Nowadays, meetings happen here relatively infrequently, so it's best to enquire at the tourist office for dates.

Practicalities

The **tourist office** is at 74 Market St (mid-June to Aug Mon–Fri 9am–6pm, Sat 10am–6pm, Sun 2–6pm; rest of year closes 5pm & all day Sun; ☎028/4461 2233). The best and most central of the **B&Bs** are *Denvir's Hotel*, 14–16 English St (☎028/4461 2012; *www.visitcoastofdown.com/denvirs*; ④), which offers en-suite accommodation in one of Ireland's oldest coaching inns, and *Hillside*, 62 Scotch St (☎028/4461 3134; ②), a listed Georgian town house. Out of town, farmhouse accommodation is available at *Hillcrest*, 157 Strangford Rd (☎028/4461 2583; ③), overlooking the Lough near Castle Ward. The upmarket option is the *Abbey Lodge Hotel* (☎028/4461 4511; ⑤), a mile northwest on the A7 Belfast road. If you're **camping**, your best bet is to go to Castle Ward Park (see p.612), six miles northeast on the A25 towards Strangford.

For **food**, *Denvir's Hotel* serves superb lunches and evening meals and Downpatrick boasts a number of equally fine cafés, including the *Iniscora Tea Rooms* in the Down Arts Centre on Irish Street, for soups, salads and imaginative sandwiches, and *Harry Afrika's*, 102 Market St, a diner popular with students for its phenomenal breakfasts and vast Sunday brunches. Good **pub lunches** are easy to find: try *Brendan's Pub* on Market Street; nearby *Rea's*, which has a big open fire; or the *Forge Bar* on Church Street.. The best **traditional-music** session is on Friday nights at *Speedy Mullan's* on Church Street. There may be occasional performances in the excellent **Down Arts Centre** on Irish Street, which has an art gallery and performance space.

Around Downpatrick

A mile northwest of Downpatrick, on the other side of the Quoile Marsh, lie the remains of the Cistercian **Inch Abbey** (April–Sept Tues–Sat 10am–6pm; Oct–March Sat 10am–4pm, Sun 2–4pm; 75p). The exquisite setting is temptingly visible from the town, but the river's intervention means that the only access is a mile out along the Belfast Road, taking the left turn down Inch Abbey Road just before the *Abbey Lodge Hotel*, followed by another signposted left turn shortly afterwards. The site was once an island, and its early church was replaced by de Courcy in the 1180s with the Cistercian abbey, whose monks were shipped over from Furness Abbey in Lancashire with the intention of establishing a strong centre of English influence. Little of it is now left standing – it was burnt in 1404 and monastic life was completely over by the mid-sixteenth century. Still, its setting, among small glacial drumlins and woodland, is picturesque; and strolling up the valley sides is a very pleasant way to pass time.

On the trail of St Patrick

About four miles west of Inch Abbey (take the B2 to Annacloy and then the first turning on the left), **Loughinisland** is probably the most worthwhile of all the sites in the area associated with St Patrick, and indeed one of the most idyllic spots in County Down. It comprises a reed-fringed lake contained by ten or so little drumlin hills, one of which forms an island in the lake. Here, across a short causeway, are the ruins of three small churches, set next door to each other. The most interesting of the churches is the smallest one, **MacCartan's Chapel** (1636), which has an entrance door no taller than four or five feet. The larger northern church was used by both Catholics and Protestants until they quarrelled on a wet Sunday around 1720 over which camp should remain outside during the service. The Protestants left and built their church at Seaforde instead.

The next St Patrick landmark is at **SAUL**, a couple of miles northeast of Downpatrick off the Strangford Road. St Patrick is said to have landed nearby, sailing up the tiny River Slaney, and it was here that he first preached, immediately converting Dichu, the lord of this territory. Dichu gave Patrick a barn as his first base (Saul in Irish is *Sabhal*, meaning "barn") and the saint frequently returned here to rest from his travelling missions – legend has it that he died here in 461. Today a **memorial chapel** and round tower in the Celtic Revival style, built of pristine silver-grey granite in 1932 to commemorate the 1500th anniversary of the saint's arrival, is open daily to visitors. Two cross-carved stones from between the eighth and twelfth centuries still stand in the graveyard, though there's not a trace of the medieval monastery built here by St Malachy in the twelfth century.

A short distance further south, between Saul and Raholp, **St Patrick's Shrine** sits atop Slieve Patrick, a tract of hillside much like a slalom ski-slope, with the stations of the cross marking a pathway up. This huge Mourne granite statue, clad at the base with bronze panels depicting Patrick's life, was erected in the same year as Saul church. The summit is no more than a twenty-minute climb and offers a commanding view of the county, a vista of the endless little bumps of this drumlin-filled territory.

At **RAHOLP** is the ruined church of **St Tassach**, named for the bishop from whom the dying Patrick received the sacrament. Patrick gave Raholp to Tassach as a reward for crafting a case for Christ's crozier, the *Bachall Isú*, one of Ireland's chief relics until its destruction in 1538. The ruins here were mainly restored in 1915 from the rubble that lay around, but their material is thought to date from the eleventh century. If you're eager for the complete St Patrick experience, it's a mile from the *Slaney Inn* car park in Raholp to the spot on the lough shore where he is believed to have first landed: head towards Strangford, then left down Myra Road; cross the main Strangford road and turn left at the first fork; at the bottom of the hill take the track on the right to the shore.

The easiest way to find the last St Patrick site, **Struell Wells**, is to return to Downpatrick. Take the Ardglass Road southeast, turn left just past the hospital, then right down a narrow track into a secluded rock-faced valley and you'll come to the **wells**. The waters here, believed to be the wells referred to in early accounts of Patrick's mission, have been attributed with healing powers for centuries. In 1744 Walter Harris described the scene: "Vast throngs of rich and poor resort on Midsummer Eve and the Friday before Lammas, some in the hopes of obtaining health, and others to perform penance." Mass is still said here on midsummer night, and people bring containers to carry the water home with them; but if you're not looking for health or penance, there's still the joy of spotting one of the tiny gems of Irish landscape beauty – a hideaway rocky dell with an abundance of yellow-flowering whin, its underground stream rechannelled to run through the wells' purpose-built bath houses.

About two miles northeast of Downpatrick, off the A25 Strangford road, the **Quoile Countryside Centre** (April–Sept daily 11am–5pm; Oct–March Sat & Sun 1–5pm; free) focuses attention on the natural habitats created by the building of a tidal barrier to prevent local flooding. It organizes **nature rambles**, seal watches in Strangford Lough, dawn chorus walks on Quoile River, and even butterfly trips. *Tullymurray Equestrian Centre* on Ballyduggan Road takes **trail rides** to the local big houses – Tollymore, Castlewellan and Castle Ward – or along the coast with beach rides to Newcastle and Tyrella (Mon–Sat; £10 per hour; ☎028/4481 1880).

Strangford and the Lecale coast

If you're following the A2 round the coast of the Ards Peninsula, your arrival on Lecale will be at tiny **STRANGFORD** village, directly opposite Portaferry and linked to it by a regular ferry service (see p.607). The earlier name of this inlet was Lough Cuan (*cuan* being Irish for 'harbour' or 'haven'), but it was renamed Strangfiord by the Vikings over a thousand years ago because of the strong eight-knot current in the narrows. Its small harbour makes a pleasant setting for watching the to and fro of the ferry boats, and the *Lobster Pot* **inn**, on the front, has a welcome pub garden and middle-of-the-range prices for evening meals. The only **places to stay** are the elegantly furnished rooms at *The Cuan* (☎028/4488 1222; *www.visitcountydown.com/thecuan*; ⑤), which has a deserved reputation for its splendid restaurant and equally friendly bar. There's **camping** at *Strangford Caravan Park*, Shore Rd (☎028/4488 1888).

Immediately around Strangford are a few houses and castles worth visiting, the first of them on the road back towards Downpatrick. **Castle Ward** (Easter week 1–6pm; April, May, Sept & Oct Sat & Sun 1–6pm; June–Aug Mon–Wed & Fri–Sun 1–6pm; house £2.60; grounds £3.50 per car) is Ireland's Glyndebourne: for three weeks every June, **opera** enlivens the house and grounds, and *bon viveurs* flock here with picnic hampers, starched napkins and candlesticks (tickets £25–40; for information call ☎028/9066 1090). The house, which was the eighteenth-century residence of Bernard and Anne Ward, later Lord and Lady Bangor, is now owned by the National Trust. It's a positively schizophrenic building, thanks to the opposed tastes of its creators (they later split up): Bernard's half is in the Classical Palladian style, Anne's neo-Gothic, a split carried through into the design and decor of the rooms inside. Outside there are pleasant **gardens** (daily dawn–dusk) and preserved farm buildings. There's also a sixteenth-century tower house (Old Castle Ward) inside the grounds; the fifteenth-century **Audley's Castle** just outside on the lough shore, with a superb view across the lough – though there's a better example of a tower house just south of Strangford at Kilclief (see below); and the **Strangford Lough Wildlife Centre** housed in a restored barn (April–June & Sept Sat & Sun 2–6pm; July & Aug Mon–Wed & Fri–Sun 2–6pm). If you want to stay, you can **camp** in the castle estate (☎028/4488 1680).

South from Strangford to Ardglass

A signposted turning one mile south of Strangford directs you to the **Cloghy Rocks** observation point. The rocks themselves are twenty yards or so out in the lough and, for most of the day look decidedly inconsequential, but, at low tide, you can spot basking **seals**. They're well camouflaged against the seaweed, so a pair of binoculars would be handy.

Further south, **Kilclief Castle** (April–Sept Tues–Sat 10am–7pm, Sun 2–7pm; 75p) is one of Ireland's earliest tower houses, a well-preserved fifteenth-century example that was originally the home of John Cely, Bishop of Down – until he was defrocked and thrown out for living with a married woman.

The next stop is **St Patrick's Well**, set on a wonderful rocky shore between Ballyhornan and Chapeltown. You can get to within a few hundred yards of the well by road, but the best approach is to start from Ballyhornan – where you'll see a narrow strip of water separating the village from Guns Island, accessible at low tide and still used for grazing – and follow the foreshore path for about a mile. The well is easily spotted: it looks rather like a sheep dip with concrete walls, but with a crucifix at its head. Its holy water has turned into something closer to stagnant consommé than an ever-youthful source of new life.

Half a mile or so before you reach Ardglass, the ruin of fifteenth-century **Ardtole Church** is well signposted just a few hundred yards east of the road. It's set on the spur of a hill, which gives it a fine perspective out to sea and back across the undulating flat of Lecale. Once dedicated to St Nicholas, patron saint of sailors, this church was used by English fishermen until a quarrel broke out with the Irish around 1650. The story goes that the fishermen tied a sleeping Irish chief to the ground by his long hair so that he couldn't get up when he awoke. Tradition has it that Swift derived the similar episode in *Gulliver's Travels* from this tale, and certainly the Ardtole region runs amok with tiny drumlins – very much like the description of the Lilliputian mountains.

Ardglass

ARDGLASS is set on the side of a lovely natural inlet. Its domestic buildings, rising steeply from the harbour (*ard glas* in Irish means "the green height"), are interspersed with seven fortified mansions, towers and turrets. These date from a vigorous English revival in the sixteenth century, when a trading company first arrived to found a colony here. The best preserved of the fortifications, and the only one open for visits, is **Jordan's Castle**, next door to the *Anchor* pub on the Low Rd (July & Aug Tues–Sat 10am–6pm, Sun 2–6pm; 75p). The most elegant and highly developed of all the Down tower houses, this has recently been renovated – all whitewashed walls and massive ceiling beams – and has regular exhibitions on local history. The tall, crenellated building with white plaster trimming up on the hill was once **King's Castle**; its nineteenth-century renovation is obvious, as is modern work to turn it into a nursery. The lone ornamental-looking turret on the hilltop is **Isabella's Tower**, a nineteenth-century folly created by Aubrey de Vere Beauclerc as a gazebo for his disabled daughter.

In the nineteenth century, Ardglass was the most thriving **fishing** port in the North; and even today, aside from the prawns, herrings and whitefish brought in by the fishing fleet, there's very good rod fishing to be had off the end of the pier for codling, pollack and coalfish. Even the Spar supermarket on the quay is wonderfully stocked with a vast range of seafood (scallops, monkfish, oysters, salmon, and more), enough in itself to entice a quick shopping visit. It's also sometimes possible to buy direct from fishing boats or from the cannery on the quay. The old **inn**, the *Commercial*, on the main street has a well that is still in use; it's covered over with glass on the lounge floor. You can **eat** well at the popular *Aldo's* Italian **restaurant**, 7 Castle Place, which serves evening meals (Tues–Sun 5–10pm). **Campers** are catered for at *Coney Island Caravan Park* (☎028/4484 1448) and there's **B&B** at *Burford Lodge*, 30 Quay St (☎028/4484 1141; ③), a Georgian building on the seafront; and *The Cottage* (☎028/4484 1080; ②), next door to *Aldo's*.

West from Ardglass to Clough

KILLOUGH, a few miles west of Ardglass, is a tranquil village stretching around a harbour that is much larger than its neighbour's but is now silted up. The A2 passes through Killough's main street – a fine French-style avenue of sycamores with a string of picturesque cottage terraces at its southern end, making an unlikely major thoroughfare. It was the Wards of Castle Ward who built the harbour in the eighteenth century, and there's still a direct road running inland, virtually in a straight line, from Killough to Castle Ward.

From the southern end of Killough you can head out to **St John's Point** – much favoured by birdwatchers – on which lie the ruins of one of the North's best examples of a **pre-Romanesque church**. It's an enjoyable two-and-a-half-mile walk. The tiny west door of the tenth-century church has the distinctive sloping sides, narrowing as the doorway rises, that were a common feature of these early churches. Also still apparent are the *antae*, enclosures created by the extension of the west and east walls to give extra support to the roof. Excavations in 1977 showed up graves that extended under these walls, indicating that an even earlier church existed in the early Christian period, probably made of wood. There's a black-and-gold-striped **lighthouse** on the nail of the point.

From Killough, the A2 heads west past long, sandy beaches at Minerstown and Tyrella Strand – the latter ruined at holiday times by hot dog stands and cars parking (£2) on the beach – before reaching **CLOUGH**, a crossroads village midway between Downpatrick and Newcastle. Tucked behind the petrol station at the northern end of the village is a Norman motte and bailey earthwork **castle**, as pristinely preserved as a carpet of fresh grass, though marred by the remains of a thirteenth-century stone keep stuck in the middle. Despite its low-lying position the site has surprisingly good views across Dundrum Bay inlet towards the Mournes and back over to Slieve Croob in central Down.

It's worth taking a short detour north at Clough on the A24 to the **Seaforde Tropical Butterfly House** (April–Sept Mon–Sat 10am–5pm, Sun 1–6pm; £2.20, or £3.80 including gardens). There's a flight area swarming with hundreds of giant, vividly coloured butterflies, quails running underfoot and a ferocious collection of large and fast-moving insects and reptiles, fortunately kept in glass cases. Best of all, though, is the overgrown walled **garden**, whose maze leads to a rose-covered pavilion that shelters a statue of the goddess Diana. Nearby, *Drumgooland House* on Dunnanew Rd (☎028/4481 1956; *www.visitcoastofdown/drumgoolandhouse*; ④) does a great **B&B**, and offers fishing in its own lake and riding. Loughinisland (see p.611) is three miles further north.

Dundrum

Although it's not officially in the Lecale region, whose inland ending is at Clough, **DUNDRUM**, just a few miles down the Newcastle road, has some quite spectacular ruins of a large Norman **castle** (April–Sept Tues–Sat 10am–6pm, Sun 2–6pm; Oct–March Sat 10am–4pm, Sun 2–4pm; 75p). The town lies beside a hammer-headed tidal bay, with the ruins sitting dramatically above, a steep fifteen-minute walk uphill from the village. The castle has a central circular donjon (with a fine spiral stairway in its walls), a fortified gateway and drum towers, all set upon a motte and bailey. In its time it was described as the most impenetrable fortress in the land, yet it was captured on several occasions and partly dismantled by Cromwell's soldiers in 1652. Some say it was a de Courcy fortress, designed for the Knights Templar, but the circular keep, a rarity in Ireland, is unlike the other fortresses de Courcy built to defend the stretch of coast from Carlingford right up to Carrickfergus. De Courcy's successor, de Lacy, is a more likely candidate – his Welsh connections tie in with the castle's similarity to the one at Pembroke in west Wales.

Dundrum's **B&B** is *Mourne View House*, 16 Main St (☎028/4475 1457; ②). Both the *Buck's Head* and the *Murlough Tavern* serve good **meals** and snacks.

Newcastle and the Mourne Mountains

Newcastle, with its lovely stretch of sandy beach, is the biggest seaside resort in County Down – packed with trippers from Belfast on bank holidays and summer weekends – and, with Slieve Donard rising behind the town, it's by far the best base if you want to do any serious walking or climbing in the **Mourne Mountains**. On busy days the main drag can feel like nothing more than a soulless strip of amusement arcades, fast-food outlets and tacky souvenir stores, but the town's more sedate qualities can be appreciated when the trippers have gone.

The Mournes are a relatively youthful set of granite mountains, which explains why their comparatively unweathered peaks and flanks are so rugged, forming steep sides, moraines and occasional sheer cliffs. Closer up, these give sharp, jagged outlines; but from a distance they appear much gentler, like a sleeping herd of buffalo. The wilder topography lies mostly in the east, below Newcastle, although the fine cliff of **Eagle Mountain** (2083ft), to the southwest, is wonderful if you can afford the time and effort to get there, and the tamer land above Rostrevor has views down into **Carlingford Lough** that can rival any in Ireland.

In summer at least (winters can be surprisingly harsh) there are plenty of straightforward hikes in the Mournes that require no special equipment, with obvious tracks to many of the more scenic parts. For further information, and maps, go to the Newcastle tourist office or to the youth hostel there (see p.617). There are also, of course, more serious climbs: **climbing courses** in the Mournes are run by the Tollymore Mountain Centre in Bryansford (☎028/4372 2158; *www.tollymoremc.com*), but they must be booked well in advance.

Newcastle

NEWCASTLE isn't exactly exciting, but it's well equipped for a range of outdoor activities, including **walking** in the Mourne Mountains southwest of town (see box on p.616), **pony trekking**, and **fishing** on the river. Golfing enthusiasts may be tempted by Newcastle's Royal County Down **golf** course (☎028/4372 3314) which has a reputation as one of the top ten links worldwide.

All buses arrive at the terminus (☎028/4372 2296) on Railway Street at the eastern end of Main Street, which, heading a couple of hundred yards west, becomes the

WALKS IN THE MOURNES

There's little to see in Newcastle itself, but the mountains offer some beautiful walks close to the town, and, for more serious walking, plenty of good hiking routes throughout the range. Before you set off it's worth visiting the **Mourne Countryside Centre**, 91 Central Promenade in Newcastle (Mon–Fri 9am–5pm; June–Aug also Sat & Sun 9am–4pm; ☎028/4372 6493) for information on walks, access and the local ecology.

The climb up **Slieve Donard**, just south of Newcastle, is the obvious first choice. Although at 2796ft it's the highest peak in the Mournes – and in all Ulster – the ascent is a relatively easy one on a well-marked trail that starts three miles out of town on the Annalong road at Bloody Bridge (see p.618) and ends at the massive hermit cell on the summit; from here the views across the whole mountain landscape are quite spectacular.

For more gentle local walking, there are several pleasant **parks**, created from the estates of old houses. The nearest is **Donard Park** (open access) on the slopes of Slieve Donard. There's a good meander along the River Glen from Newcastle town centre to the park, and if you keep following this path uphill you'll emerge on the other side and eventually come to the Saddle, a col between the two mountains of Slieve Donard and Slieve Commedagh. If you want to carry on further into the mountains from here, a good route is via **Trassey Burn** towards the **Hare's Gap**, where minerals have seeped through the rock to form precious and semi-precious stones – topaz, beryl, smoky quartz and emeralds – in the cavities of the **Diamond rocks** (hidden behind an obvious boulder stone on the mountainside). Around this point in spring, you might get the chance to hear the song of the Ring Ouzel, a bird which migrates from Africa to breed in these upland areas.

Two miles inland from Newcastle, along the Bryansford Road, **Tollymore Forest Park** (daily 10am–sunset; car £3.80; pedestrians £2) is considerably bigger and better equipped than Donard, and has a **campsite** (for which, call the ranger on ☎028/4372 2428). The park creeps up the northern side of the Mournes, and its picturesque trails wind through woodland and beside the river. You enter the park by one of two ornate Gothic folly gates – there are more follies in Bryansford nearby – and there's an **information centre** and café in an elaborate stone barn.

Castlewellan Forest Park (same hours and prices) is also inland about five miles further north, outside the elegant market town of Castlewellan. The estate lies in the foothills of the Mournes, and from the highest point in the forest, **Slievenaslat**, you get panoramic views over the mountain range. A wonderful **arboretum**, dating originally from 1740 but much expanded since, is its outstanding feature: the sheltered south-facing slopes of its hills, between the Mournes and the Slieve Croob range, allow exotic species to flourish. There's trout fishing in its main lake and coarse fishing in the smaller lakes. The 1720 Queen Anne-style farmstead and courtyards near the main entrance, *Hillyard House* (☎028/4377 0141; from £17.50), offers hostel-style accommodation, arranges outdoor pursuits, and runs an excellent café (daily 11am–9pm). You can **camp** in the park here, too (call the forest officer on ☎028/4377 8664). Nearby **riding schools** offering trekking through the forest parks include Mount Pleasant Riding and Trekking Centre in Castlewellan (☎028/4377 8651) and Mourne Trail Riding Centre, 96 Castlewellan Rd, a couple of miles out of Newcastle on the A50 (☎028/4372 4351).

If you're planning on more serious hiking in the Mournes, heights worth chasing include **Slieve Binnian**, beyond the Hare's Gap, reached through the Brandy Pad passes by the Blue Lough and Lough Binnian; **Slieve Commedagh**, with its Inca-looking pillars of granite; and **Slieve Bearnagh**, up to the right of the Hare's Gap. Also, try and cross the ridge from **Slieve Meelmore** to **Slieve Muck**, the "pig mountain", descending to the shores of Lough Shannagh, where there's a beach at either end – useful for a dip, though the water's freezing. In the panorama beyond the Hare's Gap, the places not to miss are the eastern slopes of the **Cove Mountain** and **Slieve Lamagan**. If you're sticking to the roads, all you can really do is circle the outside of the range, though there is one road through the middle, from Hilltown to Kilkeel.

Promenade. Here you'll find the very helpful **tourist information office** at 10–14 Central Promenade (Mon–Sat 10am–5pm, Sun 2–6pm; ☎028/4372 2222). There's a wide choice of **places to stay**; the best of the more upmarket **hotels** is the *Hastings Slieve Donard Hotel* on Downs Rd (☎028/4372 3681; *www.visitcoastofdown.com/slievedonardhotel*; ⑥), though it's closely pressed by the *Burrendale Hotel & Country Club,* 51 Castlewellan Rd (☎028/4372 2599; *reservations@burrendale.com*; ⑦). Cheaper central **B&Bs** include *Fountainville House,* 103 Central Promenade (☎028/4372 5074; ③), and *Castlebridge House,* 2 Central Promenade (☎028/4372 3209; ②). Three miles northwest of town, in **BRYANSFORD** village, opposite Tollymore Forest Park, is the cordial and comfortable *Briers Country House,* 39 Middle Tollymore Rd (☎028/4372 4347; *www.visitcoastofdown.com/thebrierscountryhouse*; ④), with a popular restaurant serving wholesome meals at reasonable prices. The only HINI **youth hostel** in this region is in a town house on Newcastle's seafront at 30 Downs Rd, near the bus station (☎028/4372 2133). There are also eleven **caravan and camping sites** around Newcastle, though the best are located in the forest parks (see box).

Mario's Italian Restaurant, 65 South Promenade, on the front towards the harbour is the best place for evening **meals** and Sunday lunches, unless you go out of town towards Castlewellan (take the A50) for the *Burrendale Hotel & Country Club* whose *Vine Restaurant* is extremely popular. The *Donard Hotel* on Main Street also does reasonable lunches. The *Pavilion* on Downs Road does everything from snacks to steaks, while the *Percy French,* also on Downs Road, offers reasonable à la carte. Otherwise there are plenty of cafés, chip shops and fast-food outlets along the Promenade.

For the inevitable rainy day, the town has indoor alternatives at the Newcastle Centre and Tropicana Complex on the promenade (summer only), with swimming pools, water slides and playgrounds. On Dundrum Road, half a mile east of town, is the **Route 66 US Automobile Museum** (Easter & June–Aug daily 11am–5pm; May, Sept & Oct Sat & Sun 2–5pm; £2.50), displaying all the great American cars – Thunderbirds, Cadillacs, Mustangs – and a wondrous collection of jukeboxes. Newcastle has a few literary connections: **Seamus Heaney** was a waiter in the 1950s at the long-gone *Savoy Café*; Brook Cottage (now an hotel), on Bryansford Road, was home to the dramatist and dialect-poet Richard Valentine Williams, better known as Richard Rowley; and, a fountain on the Promenade commemorates the popular Irish songwriter Percy French, composer of "The Mountains of Mourne" and numerous comic songs. Behind the Newcastle Centre a plaque celebrates one of the first powered flights in Ireland, undertaken in 1910 by Harry Ferguson to win a £100 prize – he was later to become famous through the success of the Massey Ferguson tractor.

The landward slopes of the Mournes

The landward side of the Mourne Mountains is a patchwork of fields divided by drystone walls: attractive, especially in the morning light, but with nothing of pressing interest. **HILLTOWN** has a main street extraordinarily well provided with pubs – supposedly because it was once a smugglers' hideaway, where the spoils would be divided – and it's still a crossroads where numerous roads meet. There's a pretty parish church which was founded in 1776, a Georgian market house opposite and a fortnightly market, but most of the time it's quiet as a ghost town. Little over a mile east of Hilltown on the Newcastle Road is the handsome **Goward dolmen**, known locally as "Pat Kearney's big stone". It's well signposted off the road, though the last quarter-mile of track is severely potholed.

Drumena Cashel, two miles southwest of **CASTLEWELLAN** on the A25, is one of the better-preserved ring forts, or defended homesteads, in the area. It has a T-shaped underground chamber intended to give shelter from the Vikings – though this is only twelve yards long and seems better suited to its peacetime function of providing cold storage for food. The stone foundations of a few circular beehive huts (known as *clocháns*) also remain. The puzzling aspect of the *cashel* is its position below the summit of the hill: possibly a compromise between the needs of defence and those of comfort, so there would be some shelter from the harsh winds that curl through the area.

The Mourne coast

The A2 south along the coast from Newcastle is a beautiful drive, trailing the shore around the edge of the mountains. It takes you past the chasm known as Maggie's Leap, after a local woman who jumped to avoid the attentions of an unwanted suitor, and over the Bloody Bridge, reputedly so called because of a nearby massacre during the 1641 Rebellion. Further along the way, the fishing harbour towns of **Annalong** and **Kilkeel** are alternative bases for **walking** or exploring the mountains.

Annalong and Silent Valley

The small fishing harbour of **ANNALONG** – its name in Irish is *Áth na Long*, or "the ford of the ships" – is a pleasantly relaxed seaside town during the summer, with a stony beach and Slieve Binnion providing a grandiloquent backdrop. In the harbour, pleasure craft are tied up alongside the fishing boats and small trawlers; the whiff of their herring catches sometimes permeates the whole town. The village goes about its maritime work in its narrow streets much as it always has done, and it comes as a surprise in this out-of-the-way part of the North to find the grey harbour walls adorned with the familiar ritualized Protestant graffiti – "Ulster 1690", "UVF" and a Union Jack flag. A path from the campsite just off the main road gives immediate access to an early nineteenth-century **cornmill**, still in working order and open for visits (Feb–Nov Tues–Sat 11am–5pm; £1.30), and to a herb garden down by the walled harbour and the beach.

There are a number of small **B&Bs** here, including a former farmhouse, *The Sycamores*, 52 Majors Hill (☎028/4376 8279; ③), and *Kamara*, 106a Kilkeel Rd (☎028/4376 8072; ③). Luxurious country house accommodation can be had at *Glassdrumman Lodge*, 85 Mill Rd (☎028/4376 8451; *www.visitcoastofdown.com/glassdrummanlodge*; ⑨), which has its own stylish restaurant. There's **camping** at the municipal *Marine Park* caravan site (☎028/4376 8736) by the harbour – a dreary place, landscaped in the shape of a shamrock. There's little in the way of places **to eat**, but right on the harbour, the *Harbour Inn* serves adequate lunches and evening meals, while the *Halfway House* north of town on the A2 offers bar meals and Sunday lunches.

Inland a mile or so from Annalong, signposts point to the **Silent Valley** (daily: Easter–Sept 10am–6.30pm; Oct–Easter 10am–4.30pm; car £3, pedestrians £1.50). Here you'll find Belfast and County Down's **reservoir**, a huge thirty-year engineering project that was completed in 1933. There's a car park by the lower reservoir, bound by the Mourne Wall, a sturdy 22-mile-long granite boundary to the catchment area that links the summits of fifteen mountains along its route. The views out to Slieve Binnian and Ben Crom, behind it to the west, are worth the effort of the three-mile circular **Viewpoint Walk** (starts at the car park). Less energetic, but still superb, is the half-mile Sally Lough stroll (or you can take the shuttle bus; £1.50) up to the dam at Ben Crom; again the views are spectacular.

Kilkeel and Ballymartin

Continuing south, **KILKEEL** – "the church of the narrows" – is a much grander version of Annalong, remarkable mainly for the even heftier stench of fish from the canneries on the harbour; the town is home to nearly a hundred trawlers. The biggest excitements here are the fish auctions that take place on the quayside when the fishing boats come home, and the annual summer **harbour festival**. Bang next to the harbour stands the **Nautilus Centre** which contains a small exhibition on the fishing industry, a fish shop (if you're subsequently tempted), a gift shop, café and conference centre.

The ruined "narrows" church, built in the fourteenth century, stands in the centre of Kilkeel in a ring fort. Kilkeel is a prosperous, predominantly Protestant place, but behind the village on the banks of its river memories of less happy days remain – small grave markers identify where the inmates of Kilkeel workhouse are buried. One of those buried here is the infamous **William Hare**, who murdered sixteen people in the space of a year in Edinburgh. Hare owned a lodging house and, when an old lodger died owing rent, he and his accomplice William Burke decided to sell the body to a medical school. The £7.10 they were paid spurred them on to greater efforts; however, their enthusiasm eventually raised the neighbours' suspicions and their profitable venture came to an end. Hare turned king's evidence and got his freedom, while Burke was hanged. Deciding to lie low, Hare came to Kilkeel and soon landed in the workhouse; his identity was only revealed to the locals when a Dr Reid, a former medical student from Edinburgh, recognized him.

There's a small **tourist office** in Kilkeel at 6 Newcastle St (Mon–Sat 9am–5.30pm; ☎028/4176 2525), which can help you to find **places to stay** in town and in **BALLYMARTIN**, a hamlet north on the Annalong road which has a good small beach. In Kilkeel the grandest hotel is the *Kilmorey Arms*, 41 Greencastle St (☎028/4176 2220; ⑥), whose **restaurant** has an *à la carte* menu, but the most atmospheric place to stay is *Morne Abbey Guest House*, 16 Greencastle Rd (☎028/4176 2426; *www.visitcoastofdown.com/morneabbeyguesthouse*; ③), set a couple of miles south of town on a mixed farm. Ballymartin has small **B&Bs** such as *Sharon Farm*, 6 Ballykeel Rd (☎028/4176 2521; ②), which has disabled access, and the award-winning *Wyncrest*, 30 Main Rd (☎028/4176 3012; ④), with delicious home cooking. If you're **camping**, take your pick of the seven campsites hereabouts – the best are along Cranfield Point, a flat piece of grassy land jutting out at the entrance to Carlingford Lough. Try *Sandilands Caravan Park* on Cranfield Rd (☎028/4176 3634) or *Chestnutt Caravan Park*, next to the beach on Grange Rd (☎028/4176 2653). **Restaurants** in Kilkeel are thin on the ground, but *The Fisherman*, 68 Greencastle St (☎028/4176 2130) has an extensive, though pricey, fish menu, while *Jacob Hall's*, 8 Greencastle St, at the other end of the price scale, does tasty grills and fish and chips.

Carlingford Lough

The eastern shore of **Carlingford Lough**, which borders the Mournes to the south, offers some wonderful views back to the mountains and across the lough itself. Driving round to **Warrenpoint**, though, the villages become increasingly politicized as you approach the border, IRA slogans alternating with Union Jacks.

Greencastle Fort

Guarding the mouth of the lough, **Greencastle Fort** (July & Aug Tues–Sat 10am–6pm, Sun 2–6pm; 75p) sits in brooding isolation about four miles southwest of Kilkeel, and its views alone are worth a diversion. The fort is a comparatively well-preserved Anglo-Norman edifice, with a unique rock ditch, built in the same year (1261) as Carlingford Castle on the southern side of the lough. After succumbing to several attacks from the local Magennis clan, and falling to Edward Bruce in 1316, it collapsed into complete ruin after the Cromwellian invasion and now only guards the farm across the road. It's hard to imagine the fort's great fireplaces providing a counterblast to the buffeting winds that sweep across from the lough – you can feel their full force by climbing up the corner turrets to the top storey, where you can look down on the sandy beach below and enjoy tremendous views of the lough.

Rostrevor

If you take the main road inland from Kilkeel (cutting behind Greencastle Fort), four or five miles out of Kilkeel a signpost points to the **Kilfeaghan dolmen**, a mile inland then a short walk through a couple of fields and kissing gates. Its capstone is enormous and could only have arrived here during the retreat of the glacial drift.

Further up the lough, the village of **ROSTREVOR** sits at the point where the bay waters dramatically begin to narrow towards Newry – and where the population and political climate turn more in favour of the Catholic communities of County Armagh and those across the ever-nearing border. Rostrevor is a charming and sleepy village of Victorian terraces and friendly pubs, meandering up the lower slopes of **Slieve Martin**. There are a couple of small **B&Bs**, including *An Tubar*, 2 Cherry Hill (☎028/4173 8712; ③) and *Fir Trees*, 16 Killowen Rd (☎028/4173 8602; ③). **Camping** is available at *Kilbroney Park*, Shore Rd (☎028/4173 8134), where you can hike up the hill to the thirty-ton **Cloughmore** ("big stone") for views across the lough to the Cooley Mountains over the border; geologists reckon the stone is a remnant of the Ice Age, but locals prefer a more spectacular story involving Fionn Mac Cumhaill. Opposite the church, *The Kilbroney Inn* is deservedly acclaimed for its wondrous **food**, including specialities such as roast monkfish. Other choices include the pubs *The Cloughmór Inn* and *The Corner House*, both on Bridge Street, and nearby *Goodfellows Cafe* for hearty lunches. The refurbished *Glenside Bar* is a grand place for a pint. The **Fiddler's Green Festival** in the last week of July is a big, enjoyable event, attracting folk and traditional musicians from across Europe.

Warrenpoint and around

WARRENPOINT is as picturesque as Rostrevor, with a colourful esplanade of seafront housing and a spacious central square. It's a much more traditional seaside resort than its neighbour and has been attracting visitors since the early 1800s, when an enterprising local man advertised warm baths for the "gentry, nobility and public". The **tourist office** (Mon–Fri 9am–5pm, plus weekends in summer; ☎028/4175 2256) is in the Town Hall on Church Street. There are handy **boat trips** across to Omeath on the opposite shore of Carlingford Lough in the Republic, which leave from just in front of the *Marine Tavern* (every 20min, tides permitting; June–Sept daily 1–6pm; £2 return). You can **rent bikes** at East Coast Adventure Centre (☎028/4173 9716), at Knockbarragh Lodge on the way to Rostrevor; they'll also set you up with jet-skis, wind-surfing boards, canoes and all the information on local sports you could want. For **horse riding** try Annett's Equestrian Centre, Rath Rd (☎028/4177 2976).

Less than a mile northwest of Warrenpoint along the Newry Road is the **Narrow Water Castle** (guided tours July & Aug Mon, Tues & Fri–Sun 11am–4.30pm; free). The original was built in 1212 by Hugh de Lacy to guard against access to Newry via the river, but this was burnt down during the 1641 Rebellion and the ruins here are of a building erected some twenty years later. In this serene setting, it's hard to grasp the fact that sixteen British soldiers were blown up here by the IRA, on the same day in 1979 that Lord Mountbatten was killed in Mullughmore Bay. There are very slight remains of the earlier castle nearby, and on the other side of the road an avenue leads up to **New Narrow Water Castle** (a private residence but can be viewed on request; 75p). A couple of miles to the north is the **Burren Heritage Centre** (June–Sept Mon–Fri 9am–1pm & 2–5pm; Oct–May Mon–Fri 9am–1pm; £1), a small interpretive museum which traces the locality's development through from prehistoric times.

PRACTICALITIES

You shouldn't have any trouble finding **accommodation** in Warrenpoint, except during the Maiden of the Mournes festival in August, a local version of the Rose of Tralee (see p.343). **B&Bs** include the seafront *Lough View*, 10 Osborne Promenade (☎028/4177 3067; ③), and nearby *The Mournes*, 16 Seaview (☎028/4177 2610; ③), as well as several in the hills above town, such as friendly *Fern Hill House*, 90 Clonallon Rd (☎028/4177 2677; ③) and *Mariann's*, 18 Upper Dromore Rd (☎028/4175 2085; ③), which has panoramic views.

For **food**, you can dine lavishly at *Aylesforte House* on the outskirts towards Newry; or for cheaper eating try *Diamond's* on the main square, which has a choice of low-priced specials. Wholesome food is also available at several pubs, including *Bennett's* on Church Street, and *Jack Ryan's* on the square. There's also cosy **drinking** at *Molly McCabe's* on Duke Street, uphill from the square, where the old boys gather – the bar can accommodate twelve people at the most. There's regular ceilidh **dancing** in St Peter's Gaelic Hall, and **traditional sessions** and discos in the *Forresters' Hall* on the seafront. Many of the pubs, including *The Victoria* on the square, and the *Duke Bar*, Duke Street, have music of the ballads and rock variety. The **disco** activity is at *Club Chéri* in the *Marine Tavern*, and *Shenanigans* in the nearby *Boathouse Inn*.

Newry

Although **NEWRY**, astride the border of Down and Armagh, is this area's most important commercial centre, bustling with urban vibrancy, it has little to sustain more than a short visit. Traditionally, it was the place for people from the Republic to come and shop and, despite the strength of sterling against the punt, the town still thrives economically, its already traffic-clogged streets suffering gridlock on **market day** (Thurs). Newry's **bus station** (☎028/3026 3051) is on Edward Street which runs west from the canal and Town Hall; services to and from other parts of County Down, County Armagh, Belfast and Dublin arrive and depart from here. Newry is the first stop in the North for trains from the Republic and its **train station** (☎028/3026 9271) is a mile west of town on Millvale Road and connected to the centre by local bus #341c (daily except Sun).

Newry was founded by Cistercian monks in 1144, but for most of its history has been a **garrison**, guarding the borders of Ulster at the narrow point between the mountains known as the Gap of the North. There's no trace at all of the bitterly contested early fortresses; rather what you see dates mostly from the eighteenth and nineteenth centuries, when a canal to Lough Neagh (cut in 1742, the first in the British Isles) brought the produce of the inland towns to the markets of Newry. This business has long gone, however, and Newry is probably better known from the news: the town and its immediate surroundings were repeatedly **bombed** by the IRA in the 1970s, and the area is still sometimes a hive of helicopter and police activity. Given its key position you're highly likely to pass through Newry, and it does make a possible base for exploring Slieve Gullion and the South Armagh district, but you're unlikely to be tempted to stay.

Perhaps the most interesting building in town is the **Catholic Cathedral** on Hill Street, in the pedestrian precinct. Despite an unpromising granite exterior, the rich mosaic pattern along its interior walls gives a Byzantine feel, and there's also a striking vaulted ceiling of decorative sweeping plaster arcs and vivid stained-glass windows. Nearby, there's a strange bronze totem pole by sculptor Paddy McElroy which depicts, in tortured relief, scenes from Newry's past. Not far away, the **Town Hall** is remarkable mainly because it's built on a bridge over the Clanrye river – it's half in Down, half in Armagh. Inside, the **Newry Museum** (Mon–Fri 10.30am–4.30pm; free) displays a variety of exhibits, including Nelson's table from *HMS Victory*, and local historical information. The **Newry and Mourne Arts Centre**, next door at 1a Bank Parade, hosts exhibitions of local artists' work, plays and all types of music in the auditorium.

Practicalities

Newry's **tourist office** is in the Town Hall (June–Sept Mon–Fri 9am–8pm, Sat 10am–4pm; Oct–May Mon–Fri 9am–1pm & 2–5pm; ☎028/3026 8877). If you want to **stay**, the *Mourne Country Hotel*, 52 Belfast Rd (☎028/3026 7922; ⑤), is luxurious but characterless; alternatively, there's the *Canal Court Hotel* on Merchants Quay (☎028/3025 1234; *www.canalcourthotel.com*; ⑦), equipped with a gym and sauna. There are a fair number of **B&Bs**, including the Georgian *Belmont Hall*, 18 Downshire Rd (☎028/3026 2163; *www.belmont-hall.co.uk*; ⑤), and the modern *Hillside Guesthouse*, 1 Rock Rd (☎028/3026 5484; *hillsideguesthouse@btinternet.com*; ③), off the main Belfast road. Newry's best **food** is at the *Brass Monkey* bar on Sandy Street, opposite the courthouse, with Kilkeel fish and local produce. There's little in the way of **nightlife**, but you could try Tuesdays at *The Cove*, Hilltown Road, or *Nan Rice's* on Frances Street, for **traditional sessions**. *Rosie O'Grady's Goodtime Emporium*, on the corner of Monaghan Street by the river, and the *Canal Court Hotel's* disco bar are the liveliest local nightspots.

Southwest of Belfast: central County Down

Heading west from Belfast, the M1 motorway offers very rapid access to Armagh and Tyrone, while the A1 road cuts southwest towards Newry. On the former route there's little to stop for until you're in County Armagh; on the latter there are contrasting attractions in picturesque Hillsborough and the bustling town of Banbridge, while the pleasant local countryside can be explored by following the Brontë Homeland Drive or taking a trip to the Legananny Dolmen.

Hillsborough

The historic village of **HILLSBOROUGH**, just a mile off the main A1 road and twelve miles southwest of Belfast, merits a quick detour. Its main street has a chintzy, Middle English ambience, reinforced by a sprinkling of tea rooms and antique shops. You get the best of Hillsborough by following a route that starts from the **war memorial** (where regular Ulsterbus services from Newry and Belfast stop) and heads up the magnificent approach to the rather spooky **parish church**. Bear right here for the main entrance to Hillsborough's elegant but ruined **fort** (April–Sept Tues–Sat 10am–7pm, Sun 2–7pm; Oct–March Tues–Sat 10am–4pm, Sun 2–4pm; free), constructed by Colonel Arthur Hill (after whom the village is named) in 1650 and remodelled in the eighteenth century as a fun palace. Beyond this, a deciduous **forest** opens up, curving around a **lake** stocked with brown and rainbow trout. Footpaths meander through the trees in all directions – a circuit of the lake takes around an hour.

Exiting via the car park, a driveway brings you out near the *White Gables Hotel* (☎028/9268 2755; ⑨), beyond which you'll notice a statue on a raised column, master of all it beholds – the third Marquis of Downshire, erstwhile owner of the estate. A right turn at the end of the drive brings you back into town, with **Hillsborough Castle** (April–Sept; call ☎028/9268 1300 for times; £5) on your left. Frankly, the ornate gates are the best part – and even these were transferred from Richhill in 1936. The mansion itself dates from 1797, and from 1925 to 1973 was the residence of the Governor of Northern Ireland. Since then it's been used mainly to house visiting diplomats, although it hit the headlines when the Anglo-Irish Agreement was signed here in 1985. More recently, Tony Blair stayed here during the April 1997 peace settlement talks, and the castle is now the official residence of the British Secretary of State for Northern Ireland.

Back on The Square, Hillsborough's **tourist office** (Mon–Sat 9am–5.30pm, July & Aug also Sun 2–6pm; ☎028/9268 9717) is housed in the elegant Georgian **courthouse**, which also now features a mildly interesting exhibition on the court system. By this time you'll be in need of **refreshment**, for which the *Plough Inn* across The Square is recommended. A little further down, the *Hillside Inn*, built in 1777, serves more substantial fare in a Victorian-style dining room. Best of all is the *Red Fox* tea shop (closed July) at the bottom of the hill, through an arch and behind a boutique of the same name. When you've finished here, you'll be back where you began, at the war memorial. However, if you want **to stay** there's **camping** three miles southeast at *Lakeside View*, 71 Magheraconluce Rd, Annahilt (Easter–Oct; ☎028/92682098) and a number of small **B&Bs** scattered around.

Banbridge and around

Follow the A1 south from Hillsborough and you'll pass through **BANBRIDGE** on the River Bann. A trim, mainly Protestant town, with a growing Catholic population, Banbridge was a major linen centre and also a stop on the old coach route to the Mourne Mountains. However, the steep hill – now the main street – to the south of the river presented problems to horse-drawn mail coaches. A threat to bypass the town was enough to initiate drastic action – and the result is the town's best-known feature. In 1834 the wide main street was divided into three with an **underpass**, known to locals as "the cut", carved out in the middle to lower the hill, and the **Downshire Bridge** was built over the gap. The town's most famous offspring is Captain Crozier, pioneer of the Northwest Passage (the sea route from the Atlantic to the Pacific via Arctic Canada), who was born in 1796 in a house on Church Square. The house now overlooks the Crozier Memorial, on which four polar bears gaze at the captain, who in turn gazes to the northwest.

The **tourist office**, known as Banbridge Gateway Tourist Information Centre, is a couple of miles south of town at 200 Newry Rd (July & Aug Mon–Sat 9am–7pm; rest of year Mon–Sat 10am–5pm; June–Sept also Sun 2–6pm; ☎028/4062 3322), and is the departure point for the six-hour **Linen Homelands Tour** (May–Sept Wed 10am; £10). This comprehensive and enjoyable tour explains the development of the manufacturing process by whizzing you around the district, with visits to a flax farmer's scutching mill, a local linen factory and the Irish Linen Centre and Museum in Lisburn (see p.594). The best **B&B** in the district is four miles northwest, just beyond Gilford at *Mount Pleasant*, 38 Banbridge Rd (☎028/3883 1522; ②). This vast castellated Georgian linen house sits on a grassy knoll with a fine view, and has bedrooms the size of tennis courts. There's little **nightlife** in Banbridge, although occasional club nights at the *Coach Inn*, Church Square draw the crowds and *Harry's Bar*, Dromore Street, serves great pub food and (a real rarity for Ireland) specializes in draught ales. Banbridge's proximity to the Bann offers numerous **angling** opportunities: advice, equipment and licences are available from James Coburn & Son, 32 Scarva St (☎028/4066 2207).

The area around Banbridge contains a number of sites of varied antiquity and importance. **Lisnagade Fort**, three miles west on the Scarva road, is an impressive circular earthwork, consisting of three massive ditch-separated banks. The diameter of the inner circle is a good thirty metres, but, though bronze artefacts have been recovered from the site, little is known about its occupants. A little more is understood about the **Loughbrickland Crannóg**, three miles southwest of Banbridge near the village of Loughbrickland (take the A1, then the B3 Milltown road). Constructed sometime around 500 AD this artificial island was inhabited in the seventeenth century by the Magennis family, who had vacated a castle that's thought to have been located on the lough shore. Lastly, and most notably, the **Legananny Dolmen** is worth a considerable detour. Its direction is signposted at the A50–B7 crossroads nine miles southeast of Banbridge, and also at the village of Leitrim, three miles north of Castlewellan.

THE BRONTË HOMELAND DRIVE

The start of the **Brontë Homeland Drive** is best approached by taking the A50 from Banbridge southeast to Moneyslane and thence to Ballyroney. If you've followed the signs correctly, you should end up at the Drumballyroney **interpretive centre** (March–Sept Tues–Fri 11am–5pm, Sat & Sun 2–6pm; £2), a minuscule place with a mock schoolroom. The drive itself is justified by a rather tenuous link – the Brontës in question are not the famous sisters or even Branwell, but father **Patrick Brontë** and his parents. Nor is there any evidence that the literary daughters ever visited Ireland, though there is a story that one of the uncles took his shillelagh and headed to England to sort out a reviewer critical of *Jane Eyre*. This is more the story of local boy made good: Patrick obviously dragged himself up by his bootlaces, working in the linen works by day and reading the classics by night. With help from a local rector, he got a place to read theology at Cambridge. In 1806 he came back to preach his first sermon at **Drumballyroney Church**, but eventually moved to Yorkshire where he married Maria Branwell and had his six children – all of whom he outlived. Little remains of Patrick's birthplace at **Emdale** but a few feet of stone wall. And several of the other sights are specious: **Knockiveagh**, a hilltop stopping point, seems to be on the signposted route mainly to give you a chance to get your bearings. But if the drive doesn't yield nuggets of literary history, it does offer a route – however difficult to follow – through lovely hillocky countryside that you might not otherwise explore.

Whichever your approach, you'll find yourself on narrow humped lanes, gradually ascending the southern edge of the Slieve range, and feeling increasingly distant from modern realities. You may also experience a sense of *déjà vu* when you arrive at the site, for the dolmen is a popular choice of guidebook and tourist board photographers. There's no doubting the impressiveness of the structure, looking for all the world like a giant stone tripod. Not too far away on the Castlewellan road to the east is a welcome oasis, the *Slieve Croob Inn* (☎028/4377 1412; *slievecroob@mcmail.com*; ⑤), a wonderfully situated **hotel** whose bistro and **restaurant** serve mouth-watering meals, and which also has self-catering accommodation (£190–£350 per week).

COUNTY ARMAGH

Recent history has hardly heightened **County Armagh**'s appeal for tourists. The villages of **South Armagh** – a predominantly Catholic area – were the heartland of violent Republicanism, so much so, in fact, that it has often been referred to as "Bandit Country" or "The Killing Fields", even by locals. On the other side of the sectarian divide, the name of **Portadown** has become synonymous with recalcitrant Unionism thanks to the stand-off at Drumcree church between the authorities and the Orange Order. Yet the county does warrant exploration, for it has some luscious landscapes and a history as rich as any county in Ireland: **Armagh city** has strong associations with St Patrick and early Christianity, while the sedately rural areas harbour some sites that are redolent of the island's legendary past, notably **Navan Fort** and **Slieve Gullion**.

North Armagh

Below **Lough Neagh**, the north of County Armagh is dominated by the developed industrial strip containing the almost connected towns of **Lurgan**, **Craigavon** and **Portadown**. There is little in this urban hinterland to attract you – and, indeed, Portadown's reputation as the most vehemently bigoted Loyalist town in the North is in itself deterrent enough. Outside the towns, however, there are a number of points of interest, and two stately homes, **Ardress** and the **Argory**, are features of some excellent cycling country north of **Loughgall**.

The far northeast

The **Lough Neagh Discovery Centre** (April–Sept daily 10am–7pm; Oct–March Wed–Sun 10am–5pm; £3) is to be found on **Oxford Island**, which is in fact a small peninsula jutting out into the lough – best approached from junction 10 of the M1. The woodlands and shoreline swamps draw a multitude of waterfowl and other birds, which can be viewed from various hides, while inside the centre you can learn more about the lough, its management and ornithology (and have some fun in the Ecolab games room). You can explore more a little to the east at **Kinnego Bay**, where there's a marina, boat trips, specialist powerboat and sailing courses, and a **campsite** and accommodation available in *Waterside House* **hostel** (for details of all activities call ☎028/3383 2573).

Further on to the west, the M1's junction 13 is the access point for **Peatlands Park** (daily 9am–dusk), where the visitor centre (Easter–July & Sept Sat & Sun 2–6pm; June–Aug daily 2–6pm) can tell you everything you ever wanted to know about peat. A narrow-gauge **railway** (£1) runs for a mile along part of the track once used by the previous owners, the Irish Peat Development Company, to transport extracted peat.

The roach-filled upper section of the River Bann, south of Portadown, is the place for coarse anglers to head, and another watery attraction is the **Newry Canal**, which flows into the river through a natural trough in the landscape, running through fourteen locks on the way. One of these features the restored **Moneypenny's Lockhouse** (Easter–Sept Sat & Sun 2–5pm; free), named after the family who kept the lock for 85 years – it's a two-mile stroll along the towpath from Shillingford Quay in Portadown.

Loughgall and around

LOUGHGALL, a small estate village about five miles west of Portadown (and the same distance north of Armagh along the B27) lies in the middle of apple orchard country, beautiful in the spring, and is worth visiting mainly for its historical connections. In 1988, the village was the scene of a British army ambush in which eight IRA men died, but both before and since has retained a genteel tranquillity. Like many of its neighbours in Armagh's rural north, Loughgall is strongly **Protestant**. It was three miles northeast of the village at Diamond Hill that the Battle of the Diamond took place in 1795, which led to the foundation of the first Protestant **Orange Order** (see box p.626) in the cottage of Dan Winter nearby. The cottage is now open to the public as the **Dan Winter Ancestral Home** (Mon–Sat 10.30am–8.30pm, Sun 2–8.30pm; voluntary donation) which, alongside seventeenth-century furniture, displays maps and relics from the battle, while the cottage roof still contains original lead-shot. Loughgall's tiny Orange Museum at **Sloane House** is part of a terrace at the northern end of the main street (key next door with Mrs Vallary), and includes such Orange paraphernalia as sashes, flags and the banner from the Dolly Brae victory, the first Orange Order warrant signed on a Catholic after the Battle of the Diamond, and a couple of UVF armbands. A new village amenity is **Loughgall Country Park** (entrance from Main Street; open daily until sunset; car £2.50) which offers waymarked trails and children's play areas. The main street has a couple of fine antique shops and, two miles east on Ballyhagan Road (off the B77 to Portadown) is the *Famous Grouse* (☎028/3889 1778), a lively **bar** with the best **restaurant** for miles around plus regular live music.

Five miles or so north of Loughgall are two National Trust stately homes a few miles apart that are worth visiting if you've more than a day in the area. **Ardress House** (April, May & Sept Sat & Sun 2–6pm; Easter week same times; June–Aug Mon &

THE ORANGE ORDER AND THE MARCHING TRADITION

Ireland's oldest political grouping, **The Grand Orange Lodge of Ireland**, was founded in September 1795 following the so-called **Battle of the Diamond**, which took place in Dan Winter's farm near **Loughgall**. The skirmish involved the Peep O'Day boys (Protestants) and the Defenders (Catholics) and was the culmination of a long-running dispute about control of the local linen trade. The Defenders attacked an inn, unaware that inside the Peep O'Day boys were armed and waiting. A dozen Defenders were killed, and in the glow of victory their opponents formed the Orange Order.

The first Orange Lodge march in celebration of the 1690 **Battle of the Boyne** (see p.669) took place in 1796, and they've been happening ever since. The Boyne is the Loyalist totem, even though the actual battle at Aughter which ended Jacobite rule did not take place until the following year. **William of Orange** is their icon, despite the fact that his campaign was supported by the Pope and most of the Catholic rulers of Europe, and that William himself had a noted reputation for religious tolerance. For Protestant Ulster, the Boyne came to represent a victory that enshrined Protestant supremacy and liberties, and the Orange Order became the bedrock of Protestant hegemony. Between 1921 and 1969, for example, 51 of the 54 ministers appointed to the Stormont government were members of the Orange Order; at its peak, so were two-thirds of the Protestant male population of the North.

The **Loyalist** "marching season" begins in March. Most of the Loyalist marches are uncontentious – small church parades, or commemorations of the Somme – but it can't be denied that some of them are something other than a vibrant expression of cultural identity. Marching can be a means by which one community asserts its dominance over the other – Loyalists selecting routes which deliberately pass through Nationalist areas, for instance, or their "Kick the Pope" fife and drum bands deliberately playing sectarian tunes and making provocative gestures such as the raising of five fingers on Belfast's **Lower Ormeau Road** (where five Catholics were shot dead in 1992) or the gratuitously offensive stamping dance performed by marchers in **Portadown** (where a young Catholic was kicked to death in 1998). The marching season culminates in celebration of the **Battle of the Boyne** on July 12, followed by the **Apprentice Boys'** traditional march around the walls of Derry on August 12.

Though Loyalist marches have tended to be the flashpoints for major disturbances in recent years, it shouldn't be forgotten that the marching tradition is common to both communities. Around three thousand marches take place throughout Northern Ireland each year and, although the vast majority are Loyalist parades, a significant number are **Nationalist**. The latter include the St Patrick's Day (March 17) marches of the Ancient Order of Hibernians and the Irish National Foresters, and commemorative parades and wreath-laying ceremonies by Sinn Féin and other Republican bodies on Easter Monday and various anniversaries.

Wed–Sun same times; £2.70) is a seventeenth-century manor house with ornate plasterwork by Michael Stapleton, a good collection of paintings, a sizeable working farmyard and wooded grounds. **The Argory** (same hours; £3) is a fine Neoclassical building dating back to 1824 which contains its original furniture and a fabulous cabinet barrel organ, and which is still lit by an original 1906 acetylene gas plant in the stable yard.

Armagh city and around

ARMAGH's small size disappoints some people, and certainly the city doesn't immediately present a greatly exciting prospect – but, rich in history at least, Armagh and its surroundings have plenty to keep you occupied for a day or two. The city offers **cathedrals**, **museums** and a **planetarium** set in handsome Georgian streets, and two miles west is the ancient site of once-grand **Navan Fort**. Armagh has been the site of the

THE DRUMCREE CHURCH PARADE

In the 1990s, it became clear that the Orangemen's march to the beat of the Lambeg drum was falling increasingly out of step with the political realities of Northern Ireland. What may well come to be seen as the turning point in the political fortunes of the Orange Order arrived during the summer of 1998.

For several years the **Drumcree church** parade in Portadown on the Sunday before the "Glorious Twelfth" (July 12 – the anniversary of the Battle of the Boyne) had been the focus for the Orange Order's assertion of their political identity, their march from the church down the Nationalist **Garvaghy Road** constituting a massive statement of the permanency of their power in Northern Ireland. Opposed to the peace settlement and the formation of the new Assembly, the Order made Drumcree its rallying cry, and was provoked to even greater stridency when the 1998 march was banned by the **Parades Commission**, a body formed specifically to limit the fractiousness (and cost) of marches by controlling or stopping them. The Order expected a massive security operation preventing their march, but failed to anticipate the subsequent Protestant violence which swept across the North, fuelled by Orange rhetoric and catalyzed by the hardline Loyalist Volunteer Force (LVF). Every day saw petrol bombings, vehicle hijacks, Catholic areas besieged and, hardest for the patriotic Orangemen to stomach, attacks on the RUC and troops. Early on the morning of Sunday July 12, 1998, a **petrol bomb** was thrown into a Catholic family's house on a largely Protestant estate in Ballymoney, County Antrim, killing three young brothers. The reaction of some Orange Lodge members, who seemed more concerned about maintaining their "traditional right to march" than with condemning the murder of innocent children, outraged people of both communities and exacerbated the divisions in the Order. Its chaplain called for Drumcree to be abandoned, and many Orangemen resigned. The RUC raided the protesters' camp and found weapons and explosives; the Protestant **Church of Ireland** then barred the protest from its grounds, forcing the abandonment of the Drumcree parade. The death of a policeman wounded by a blast bomb at Portadown further diminished the Orange Order's standing.

Subsequent years have again seen the Parades Commission refuse permission for the Garvaghy Road parade. While 1999 saw the Orange Order make only a symbolic protest, July 2000 witnessed a return to the demonstrators' more provocative stance, fuelled by the presence of **paramilitaries** from the LVF and the UDA (Ulster Defence Association). Drumcree remains a profoundly politicized gathering, and the events of 1998 will be recorded as a crucial episode in the modern political history of Ireland.

Catholic primacy of all Ireland since St Patrick established his church here, and has rather ambitiously adopted the title of the "Irish Rome" for itself – like Rome, it's positioned among seven small hills. Paradoxically, the city is also the seat of the **Protestant** Church of Ireland's Archbishop of Armagh.

The new **Ulsterbus** station (☎028/3752 2266) is on Lonsdale Road, just north of the centre. An excellent way to get around is with the free 1940s-style **bus** which operates throughout July and August, stopping outside all the city's attractions and the outlying Navan Centre (call ☎028/3752 9629 for times).

Some history

Armagh (*Ard Macha*, "Macha's height") was named after **Queen Macha**, wife of Nevry, who is said to have arrived in Ireland 608 years after the biblical flood. She built a fortress on the main hill where the Church of Ireland cathedral now stands and is sup-

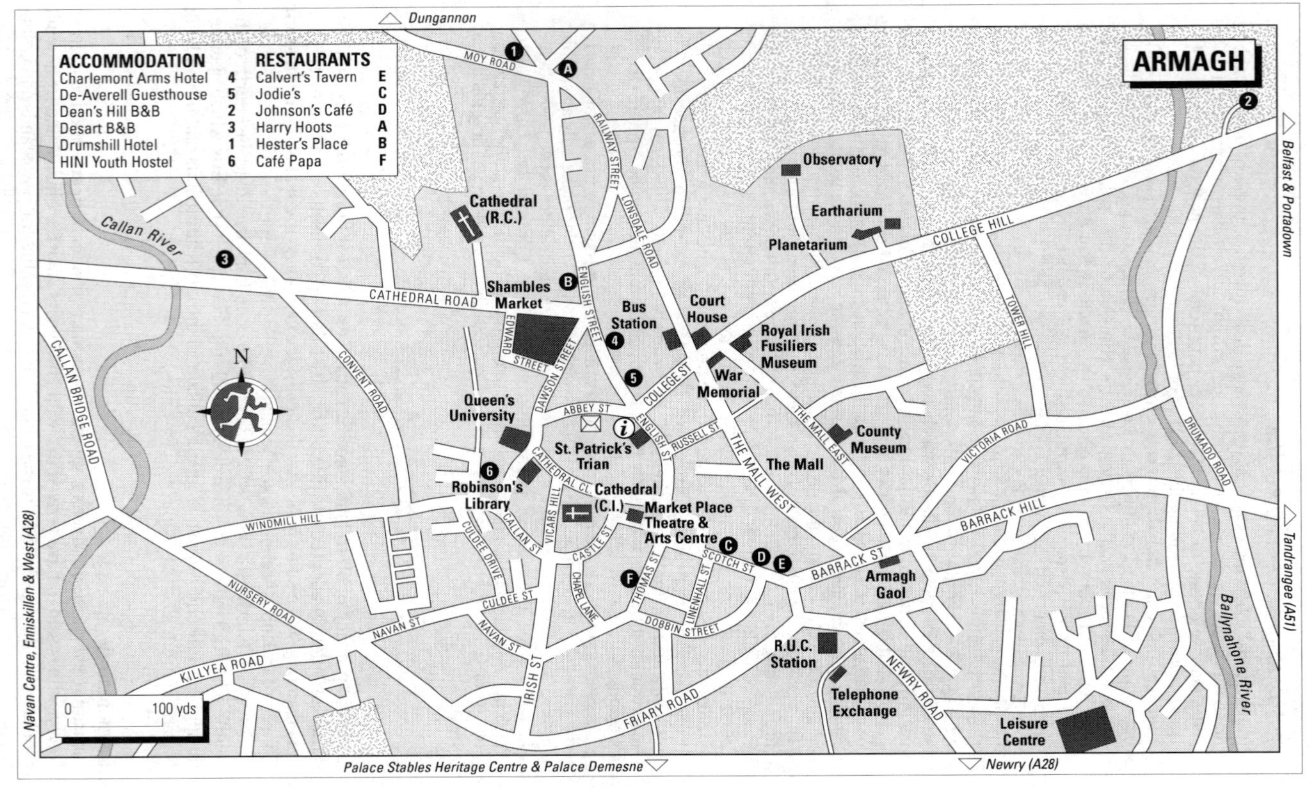
ARMAGH
ACCOMMODATION
Charlemont Arms Hotel 4
De-Averell Guesthouse 5
Dean's Hill B&B 2
Desart B&B 3
Drumshill Hotel 1
HINI Youth Hostel 6
RESTAURANTS
Calvert's Tavern E
Jodie's C
Johnson's Café D
Harry Hoots A
Hester's Place B
Café Papa F
Dungannon
Belfast & Portadown
Tandrangee (A51)
Newry (A28)
Palace Stables Heritage Centre & Palace Demesne
Navan Centre, Enniskillen & West (A28)
Callan River
Ballynahone River
MOY ROAD
RAILWAY STREET
LONSDALE ROAD
Cathedral (R.C.)
Observatory
Eartharium
Planetarium
COLLEGE HILL
CATHEDRAL ROAD
Shambles Market
ENGLISH STREET
Bus Station
Court House
Royal Irish Fusiliers Museum
EDWARD STREET
DAWSON STREET
COLLEGE ST
War Memorial
TOWER HILL
CALLAN BRIDGE ROAD
CONVENT ROAD
N
Queen's University
ABBEY ST
ENGLISH ST
RUSSELL ST
St. Patrick's Trian
THE MALL EAST
County Museum
VICTORIA ROAD
DRUMADO ROAD
THE MALL WEST
The Mall
CATHEDRAL CL.
Robinson's Library
Cathedral (C.I.)
Market Place Theatre & Arts Centre
WINDMILL HILL
VICARS HILL
CALLAN ST
CULDEE DRIVE
CASTLE ST
BARRACK HILL
BARRACK ST
SCOTCH ST
Armagh Gaol
THOMAS ST
LINENHALL ST
CHAPEL LANE
NURSERY ROAD
CULDEE ST
NAVAN ST
DOBBIN STREET
R.U.C. Station
KILLYEA ROAD
IRISH ST
NEWRY ROAD
Telephone Exchange
FRIARY ROAD
Leisure Centre
0
100 yds

posed to be buried somewhere in the hillside. The claim that Armagh is one of the oldest settlements in Ireland is supported by the city's position on one of the most ancient roads in the land, the Moyry Pass, which once stretched from the extreme south of Ireland, through Tara, to the north. In about 300 BC, the centre of power shifted westward across the River Callan to where another queen (of the same name, Macha) built the legendary **Navan Fort**.

After nearly seven hundred years, the ruling dynasty at Navan was defeated by the Collas brothers, and the new rulers re-established their main base back on the hill of Armagh. A hundred years later, in 445 AD, **St Patrick** declared the hill the site of his primacy and first bishopric and built his cathedral here (having first converted the local chieftain, Daire, a descendant of the Collas brothers). Other churches grew up around the cathedral, and Armagh became a pre-eminent centre of learning during the Dark Ages, the period when Ireland was known as the "Isle of Saints and Scholars". The settlement developed around three distinct districts *(Trians)*, their boundaries still reflected today by English, Irish and Scotch Streets. Armagh strongly challenges Downpatrick's claim to be the **burial place** of St Patrick; locals argue that since the relics of Patrick's book, bell and staff are here, his body must be too (though the burial site is not identified).

Between the ninth and the eleventh centuries, the city was repeatedly pillaged by the **Vikings**, mainly from the Norse settlements at Lough Neagh. The Irish king who claimed final victory over the Norsemen, **Brian Boru**, was killed at the Battle of Clontarf in 1014, and was buried in Armagh cathedral. The arrival of the **Normans** in the twelfth century saw the city become a constant battleground as the O'Neills sought to maintain their control. Despite this, Armagh's ecclesiastical power did not waver until the **Reformation**. Further local conflict ensued and it was not until the end of the Williamite wars that peace finally broke out. The arrival of Richard Robinson as Archbishop in 1765 saw a final flourish of building work, much of which survives today, despite the encroachment of recent supermarket developments. Modern Armagh is a predominantly Catholic city, strong on Gaelic sports, and, although physically it has borne up well to the Troubles (certainly in comparison to Newry and Derry), it has not avoided them.

The City

The best way to get your bearings is to walk up the steps of **St Patrick's Roman Catholic Cathedral** (Mon–Sat 10am–5pm), built on a hillside just northwest of the Shambles Market. The view of the town from here is impressive and you should be able to identify most of the key sites spread out below. The cathedral's foundation stone was laid in 1840, but completion was delayed by the Famine and a subsequent lack of funding. Whilst the Pope and local nobility chipped in, money was also raised by public collections and raffles – one prize of a grandfather clock has still not been claimed. On the outside the cathedral first appears little different to many of its nineteenth-century Gothic Revival contemporaries. But it is impressively large and airy; **inside**, as befits the seat of the Cardinal Archbishop, every inch of wall glistens with **mosaics**, in colours ranging from marine- and sky-blue to terracotta pinks and oranges. Other striking pieces include the white-granite "pincer-claw" **tabernacle holder**, reflected in a highly polished marble floor, and a **statue** of the Crucifixion which suggests (deliberately or otherwise) the old city's division into *Trians*. Armagh is known for its choral music, and the annual Charles Wood Summer School (check with the tourist office for dates) is worth catching.

Heading south along Dawson Street you'll soon reach Cathedral Close and **St Patrick's Church of Ireland Cathedral** (daily: April–Oct 10am–5pm; Nov–March 10am–4pm; tours June–Aug Mon–Sat 11.30am & 2.30pm). This lays claim to the summit of the principal hillock, Drum Saileach, where St Patrick founded his first church in 445 AD. It commands a distinctive Armagh view across to the other hills and down over the clutter of gable walls and pitched roofing on its own slopes. A series of churches occupied the site after 445 and, although the core of the present one is medieval, a nineteenth-century restoration coated the thirteenth-century outer walls in a sandstone plaster of which Thackeray remarked, "It is as neat and trim as a lady's dressing room." Many of the ancient decorations were removed, leaving the spartan interior you see today. Just as you enter from the highly distinctive timber porch, you'll see a few remnants of an eleventh-century **Celtic cross** and a startling **statue** of Thomas Molyneux. Inside, high up, you should be able to sight the medieval carved heads of men, women and monsters. One other unusual feature is the tilt of the chancel, a medieval building practice meant to represent the slumping head of the dying Christ. The **chapter house** has a small collection of stone statues (mostly gathered from elsewhere), the most noticeable of which are the Stone Age **Tandragee Idol** and a Sheila-na-Gig with an ass's ears.

Just down the hill from the cathedral, the **public library** (known locally as Robinson's; Mon–Fri 10am–1pm & 2–4pm; free but donations welcomed) has, among many rare tomes, a first edition of *Gulliver's Travels* annotated by Swift himself, and an early edition of Raleigh's *History of the World* (1614), as well as a collection of engravings, including some by Hogarth. The library was founded in 1771 by Archbishop Richard Robinson, who was described as converting Armagh "from mud to stone" and who is responsible for almost all the older buildings in Armagh – the nearby infirmary was one of his too, though it's now occupied by the university.

Cathedral Close leads downhill to the main shopping area, where an entry leads into the narrow winding lane of **McCrum's Court** where the rock-walled *Hole in the Wall* pub is well worth a visit. Walking back and a little way north up English Street you'll come to **St Patrick's Trian Centre**, an ambitious complex containing the **tourist office** and two separate exhibitions. The first of these, peopled with figures representing the Land of Lilliput and Jonathan Swift's connection with Armagh, occupies the former Presbyterian Meeting House, which was partly constructed from the ruined abbey of St Peter and St Paul – Swift is reputed to have commented that the masons were "chipping the popery out of the stones." The second installation, "The Armagh Story", is a multimedia account of both the town's growth and the nature of belief (opening times for both exhibitions: July & Aug Mon–Sat 10am–5.30pm, Sun 1–6pm; rest of year Mon–Sat 10am–5pm, Sun 2–5pm; joint ticket £3.75).

The Mall

Russell Street leads down to **The Mall**, an elegant tree-lined promenade fringed to the east by two terraces of handsome Georgian houses designed by the Armagh-born architect Francis Johnston, who worked primarily for Archbishop Robinson. Johnston was responsible for many of Dublin's best Georgian buildings and you'll encounter more examples of his work around town, including the classical **courthouse** at The Mall's northern end. Significantly, the former **jail** occupies the opposite position. In its late eighteenth-century heyday The Mall was a race course; nowadays there's nothing more athletic than the occasional jogger and Sunday cricket matches.

A former schoolhouse on the east side of The Mall houses the **County Museum** (Mon–Fri 10am–5pm, Sat 10am–1pm & 2–5pm; free), an old-style museum with all the usual local miscellany on display, including an alarmingly vivid collection of stuffed wildlife, plus a little **art gallery** tucked away on the upper floor. Here there are twenty or so mystical pastels, oils and cartoon sketches by the Irish turn-of-the-century poet **George Russell**, a much-neglected companion to Yeats, who acquired the alias AE as a result of a Dublin newspaper misprinting a letter that he had signed "Aeons". The prolific local artist J.B. Vallely is also represented with a superb oil showing five musicians enjoying a session; the theme of traditional music figures in more than three thousand of Vallely's canvases and, with his wife, Eithne, he currently runs the town's Armagh Pipers' Club. Elsewhere, a display devoted to railway history recounts the story of Ireland's worst railway disaster when two passenger trains collided outside Armagh in 1889, killing 89 people, many of whom are buried in the nearby St Mark's churchyard.

Further north along The Mall is the **Royal Irish Fusiliers Museum** (Mon–Fri 10am–12.30pm & 1.30–4pm; £2), built from the leftovers of the courthouse. It's pretty much as you'd expect: tons of weaponry, uniforms, medallions and regimental silverware from the regiment formed in 1793 in response to the Napoleonic crisis and subsequently known as the "Faughs" from their battle-cry *"Faugh a Ballagh!"* ("Clear the way!"). The Fusiliers subsequently fought in the Crimean and Boer Wars (where they relived the Siege of Ladysmith) and both world wars before amalgamating with the Inniskilling Fusiliers (see p.653) and Ulster Rifles in 1968.

The Observatory, Planetarium and Eartharium

College Hill, the road that heads east from The Mall alongside the Fusiliers museum, will take you to the **Observatory** (dome open April–Sept Mon–Fri 9.30am–4.30pm; free) – an ancient institution that celebrated its second centenary in 1990, but is still at the forefront of European astronomical research, with a ten-inch telescope. The nearby **Planetarium** (Mon–Fri 10am–4.45pm, Sat & Sun 1.15–4.45pm; £1; shows Mon–Fri 3pm, Sat & Sun 2pm, 3pm & 4pm; £3.75) is a more recent attraction, and its best feature are the **star theatre** shows where you whizz through the universe from the safety of a reclinable seat. It also has solar system galleries, various antique astronomical instruments from the earliest days of the Observatory, and high-tech equipment to show you the latest pictures from NASA's space telescope. Alongside is the **Eartharium** (same times and ticket) which – rather chillingly – allows you to zoom in on Belfast or Armagh using spy satellite pictures, or to predict the weather.

Armagh Friary

The ruins of **Armagh Friary**, founded by the Franciscans in 1263, lie within easy walking distance south of the city centre, just off Friary Road by the entrance to the grounds of the Archbishop's Palace (now the District Council offices). The ruins are those of the church alone, and the site is an unfortunate example of how atmosphere can be destroyed when a major road runs alongside. The focus now is the **Palace Stables Heritage Centre** (mid-May to Sept Mon–Sat 10am–5.30pm, Sun 1–6pm; rest of year Mon–Sat 10am–5pm, Sun 2–5pm; £3.50), where tableaux of life-sized figures depict July 23, 1776, the day on which Archbishop Robinson entertained agricultural entrepreneur Arthur Young – you're guided around by living history interpreters garbed in contemporary costumes. From here you move into the main part of the palace, which dates from around 1770, though the final storey was added in 1825, and was inhabited by subsequent archbishops until 1975 when the private Primate's Chapel next door was deconsecrated. In the grounds there's a well-preserved **ice house**, a curious **tunnel** by which servants accessed the basement kitchens, a stimulating **sensory garden** and, somewhat incongruously, the municipal dog pound.

Practicalities

The **tourist office** is in the Old Bank Building, 40 English St (June–Aug Mon–Sat 9am–5.30pm, Sun 1.30–5.30pm; rest of year closes 5pm; ☎028/3752 1800). Friendly *De-Averell Guest House*, 47 English St (☎028/3751 1213; ④), offers comfortable central **accommodation** and has an innovative basement restaurant, while the nearby *Charlemont Arms Hotel*, 63 English St (☎028/3752 2028; ⑤) is also noted for its menus.

Half a mile north of town on the Moy Road is *Drumsill Hotel* (☎028/3752 2009; ⑥). **B&Bs** are scarce, taking in *Desart*, 99 Cathedral Rd (☎028/3752 2387; ②), a fine detached house, and *Dean's Hill* on College Hill (☎028/3752 4923; ⑤), an eighteenth-century building in wooded grounds up past the Observatory. There's a fine, recently built and excellently equipped HINI **hostel** (☎028/3751 1800), superbly situated near the cathedral at 39 Abbey St. The nearest **camping** is *Gosford Forest Park*, seven miles southwest along the A28 near Markethill (☎028/3755 1277), with fine facilities set in wooded grounds around a castle.

Armagh has a number of **events** during the year, but the biggest concentration occurs during the May **Apple Blossom** festival when there are daily events, blues and dance festivals. As you'd expect, the local **St Patrick's Day Parade** (March 17) is one of the largest in the country. The County **Fleadh** (traditional music and dancing festival, usually with plenty of sessions around town) takes place in June, while November sees the **Bard of Armagh** poetry competition and one of Ireland's major *uilleann* piping events, the **William Kennedy Piping Festival**.

Eating, drinking and entertainment

Many of Armagh's pubs will serve bar **food** at lunchtime, but eating in the evening can be more problematic. Pick of the pubs with food is the lively *Calvert's Tavern*, 3 Scotch St. *Harry Hoots*, 143 Railway St, also has an excellent restaurant (with discos at the weekends); or you can always get a reasonably priced full meal at the *Drumsill Hotel*. *De-Averell House*'s basement restaurant and *The Market Place* (in the new theatre and arts complex; see opposite) are both highly recommended. Another excellent place with healthy food is *Jodies*, upstairs at 37 Scotch St. *Hester's Place* on Upper English Street and *Johnston's Cafe*, Scotch Street, both serve good-value lunches. The best coffee in the city is to be had at *Cafe Papa*, Thomas Street, with the *Pilgrim's Table* in the St Patrick's Trian Centre a close runner-up.

The most atmospheric **pub** for a pint is the *Hole in the Wall Bar* in McCrum's Court. The top end of English Street is a good area to pub-crawl in search of **music**; weekends are best but many places have sing-songs on Tuesdays and Thursdays. **Traditional music** is surprisingly scarce in the city and your best bet is to head for the villages of Mullaghbawn and Forkhill in the south of the county. The *Northern Bar*, 100 Railway

ROAD BOWLS

The sport of **road bowls** is popular in Holland and Germany and was once played throughout Ireland, but is now limited mainly to Cork and Armagh, where it's also known as "road bullets".

The game's principle is simple: a pair of rival contestants each propel a 28oz (800g) solid iron ball along a course of country roads (usually about two and a half miles long), the winner being the player who reaches the finishing line with the **fewest number of throws**. In practice, it's a complicated business. The Armagh roads twist and turn, up and down, and bowlers are assisted by a team of camp followers, including managers and road guides who advise on the most advantageous spots to aim and the force of the throw. Traditionally a male sport, it's become increasingly popular with women who've held their own championship since 1981.

Roads around Armagh where you're likely to catch sight of the game – usually on Sunday afternoons – include Cathedral Road, Napper Road, Blackwater Town Road, Rock Road, Tassa Road, Keady Road, Newtonhamilton Road and Madden Road. The most reliable information on forthcoming games is probably to be had in local pubs. One of the biggest competitions, **Ból Fada**, takes place in Keady, South Armagh, towards the end of April, with the **Ulster Championship** in Armagh city in June.

St, is the place for blues and rock. For **nightclubs**, your options are limited – locals head to nearby Keady, Moy or across the border to Castleblaney – but try *The Met* complex on Moy Road for weekend club nights.

Armagh's grandest new arrival is unquestionably **The Market Place Theatre and Arts Centre** (☎028/3752 1821) which features a 400-seat auditorium, a smaller studio theatre, gallery, bars, coffee house and bistro. The centre's reputation is growing, for its innovative programming and events and especially for bringing – for the first time in living memory – major names in Irish music (such as singer-songwriter Kieran Goss) to Armagh. Also on the Market Place is the **Armagh City Film House** (☎028/3751 1033), a four-screen cinema with a regular late show on Friday and Saturday nights.

Navan Fort

For nearly seven hundred years **Navan Fort** (open access; free) was the great seat of northern power, rivalling Tara in the south. It was here that the Kings of Ulster ruled and Queen Macha built her palace on the earthworks' summit. It's a site of deeply mystical significance, but one also of enormous archeological interest. The court of the **Knights of the Red Branch**, Ireland's most prestigious order of chivalry, was based here too. The knights, like those of the Round Table, are historical figures entirely subsumed into legend, their greatest champion being the legendary defender of Ulster, **Cúchulainn**. The stories of these warriors' deeds are recited and sung in what's now known as the *Ulster Cycle*. Their dynasty was finally vanquished in 332 AD, when three brothers (the Collas), in a conquest known as the Black Pig's Dyke, destroyed Navan Fort, razing it to the ground and leaving only the earthen mounds visible today. The defeated Red Branch Knights were driven eastwards into Down and Antrim, and were little heard of again.

The best approach to the fort (two miles west of Armagh on the A28; bus #73) is to visit the interpretive centre first. The **Navan Centre**, cut into the land near the site (April–Sept Mon–Fri 10am–6pm, Sat & Sun 11am–6pm; Oct–March Mon–Fri 10am–5pm, Sat 11am–5pm; last entry 1hr 15min before closing time; £3.95), is a circular grass-covered mound supported inside by columns, replicating the real fort as it's thought to have been structured. The seventy-minute **tour**, which deposits you at the doors leading to the fort proper, begins with an excellent talk on the history and archeology of the site, with some fascinating asides – the skull of a Barbary ape found at the fort, for example, implies trade links with North Africa. You then move onto an **audio-visual show** (with music supplied by Bill Whelan of *Riverdance* fame) that replays four key myths associated with this ancient fort, including that of Cúchulainn, the hound of Ulster, and the *Taín Bó Cuailngè* (Cattle Raid of Cooley).

The site area is defined by a massive bank with a defensive **ditch**. When you reach the fort, you find an **earthen mound** which gives a commanding view but no hint of its past. Excavation of the mound took place over a ten-year period (1961–71) and revealed a peculiar structure, apparently unique in the Celtic world. Archeologists reckon that around **100 BC** the buildings that had existed since the Neolithic period were cleared, and a huge structure 108ft in diameter was constructed. An outer wall of timber surrounded five concentric rings of large posts, 275 in all, with a massive post at the very centre. This was then filled with limestone boulders and **set on fire**, creating a mountain of ash that was then covered with sods of clay to make a high mound. It is anybody's guess what the purpose of the structure was – possibly a temple, or maybe a monumental funeral pyre.

Nearby you can visit for free other ancient archeological structures: a second fort, the earliest known artificial lake in Ireland, and a large natural lake which has yielded various archeological finds.

South Armagh

The **South Armagh** countryside is amongst the most attractive in the North, yet many visitors are deterred from coming here by the area's notoriety. Proximity to the border and a predominantly Catholic population have resulted in this being a nucleus of resistance to British rule, and evidence of military occupation is everywhere – from the hill-top surveillance posts to the constant whirring blades of helicopters monitoring the ground from above. Since the first ceasefire, however, many of the border controls and barriers have been removed, and South Armagh has remained a safe and remarkably welcoming place for tourists. Information on local sites and facilities is at *www.south-armagh.com* provided by the local tourism initiative.

The Ring of Gullion

Most of South Armagh's attractions are concentrated in and around the area known as the **Ring of Gullion**, a naturally formed ring-dyke of low-lying hills which encircles (and predates) the mountain at its core. People have lived here for more than six thousand years and there's a rich heritage of remains and monuments. On the ring's western fringe is **The Dorsey Enclosure**, two huge earthen banks and ditch ramparts dating from the Iron Age, running for a mile either side of the old route to Navan Fort. Elsewhere are numerous dolmens and cairns, Christian relics and monuments from the Plantation era.

Slieve Gullion (*sliabh gCuilinn*, "the mountain of Culainn"), which dominates the southeastern corner of County Armagh, is one of the most mysteriously beautiful mountains in the country. A store of romantic legends is attached to it, especially concerning **Cúchulainn**, who took his name here after slaying the hound (*Cú*) of the blacksmith Culainn. Due south at Glendhu is where Cúchulainn single-handedly halted the army of Queen Medb of Connaught, who was intent on capturing the great bull of Cooley. **Fionn Mac Cumhaill**, who founded the *Fianna*, a mythical national militia whose adventures are told in the *Fenian Cycle*, also appears in stories here.

A scenic way to approach the mountain is from the north, passing the turning to **BESSBROOK**, a nineteenth-century model village developed by a Quaker linen entrepreneur; the Cadbury family's Bourneville estate in Birmingham, England, followed a very similar layout. Just outside the village stands **Derrymore House** (May–Aug Thurs–Sat 2–5pm; £2), an eighteenth-century thatched manor house built for Isaac Corry, Chancellor of the Exchequer of the last Irish Parliament before the Act of Union, which was drafted in his drawing room here. After **CAMLOUGH** ("crooked lake"), where the Tricolour flutters, turn off the main road to go down by the eastern slopes of Camlough Mountain and you'll see the beautiful **lake**, set like a jewel within its green banks. A little further on, between Camlough Mountain and Slieve Gullion, are the **Killeavy churches** (*Cill Shléibhe* – "Church of the Mountain"). Two churches of different periods share the same gable wall: the west church is pre-Romanesque and one of the most important survivors of its kind in the country; the other, larger church dates from the thirteenth century. A granite slab marks the **grave of St Bline**, the founder of a fifth-century nunnery sited here – there's a holy well dedicated to her a little further up the slopes of Slieve Gullion, which pilgrims visit on her feast day (the Sunday nearest to July 6).

The official, tarmacked entrance up into Slieve Gullion is on the mountain's afforested southern face, after you've passed through the village of **KILLEAVY**. You'll find a small forest **park** (Easter–Sept daily 10am–dusk; car free), fronted by the **Courtyard Centre** (undergoing renovation at the time of writing), where there's a restaurant and self-catering **apartments** (☎028/3084 8084; £250–£350 per week; sleeps 6–8). From the centre it's an eight-mile winding drive up to the summit (or you can follow a walking trail), where there's a couple of megalithic **cairns**. Fionn Mac Cumhaill was bewitched here by Miluchra and local superstition holds that bathing in the small summit **lake** will turn your hair white; another tale states that under certain conditions a visitor to the site will be given the power to foresee everything that will happen that day. Various vertiginous viewpoints offer spectacular **views** over the Ring of Gullion and the surrounding countryside for miles around.

Jonesborough and around

JONESBOROUGH, east of the mountain, is the venue each Sunday for a vast open-air **market** (11am–5pm), drawing traders and customers from both sides of the border. The range of goods on offer is equally enormous and it's well worth experiencing. The excellent *Flurrybridge Inn* serves lunches Thursday to Sunday and holds occasional sessions.

Two miles south of Jonesborough is the **Pillar Stone of Kilnasaggart**, a beautifully inscribed monument, dating from 700 AD, which marks the site of an early Christian cemetery. Several small crosses are marked within circles on its back face, and the defaced markings on its edges are possibly *ogham* writing. It's surrounded by several other tiny stones with similar cross markings, all held within a pentagonal enclosure three fields away from the roadside, behind a farmhouse. Less than a mile west of here, on the other side of the train line, you should be able to see **Moyry Castle** on the hill. This is a timid affair and not really worth even this slight detour, but among its interesting features are several musket loopholes. It was built in 1601 by Lord Mountjoy, Queen Elizabeth I's deputy, as the defence for the Gap to the North.

Forkhill and Mullaghbawn

You might expect **FORKHILL** to lie in an elevated position, but this tiny village nestling in the southwestern foothills of Slieve Gullion derives its name from the Irish *foirceal* ("trough"). It's a simple, quiet and remote-looking place though dominated by the massive army encampment stacked upon the crown of an overlooking hill. The village is strong on traditional culture: O'Neill's *Welcome Inn* has a well-known **storyteller**, John Campbell, and **sessions** most Tuesday nights (and other music at the weekends); there's weekend music too at *The Forge*. Neighbouring **MULLAGHBAWN** (*an mullach bán* – "the white summit") to the north, has *O'Hanlons' Bridge House* which holds regular sessions on Fridays and Saturdays, and the innovative *Tí Chulainn* cultural activities centre (☎028/3088 8828; *www.tichulainn.ie*), dedicated to the promotion of the area's culture and literary heritage. South Armagh has a powerful **song tradition** and the centre hosts both the *Stray Leaf* singers' club (every second Saturday) and a number of annual events, including the Tommy Makem International Song School in the second week in June. The **Slieve Gullion Festival of Traditional Singing** takes place in both villages on the first weekend in October.

If you want to **stay**, there are a couple of B&Bs in Forkhill: *Lakeview*, 34 Church Rd (☎028/3088 8382; ③), with fine views of the mountain, and *Greenvale*, 141 Longfield Rd (☎028/3088 8314; ②), which also offers **pony trekking**. In Mullaghbawn there's *Lar Na Tuaithe*, 89 Maphoner Rd (☎028/3088 8897; ③), very close to the *Tí Chulainn* centre. Near here, the Ring of Gullion Centre on Lough Rd (☎028/3088 9311) also provides pony trekking and riding lessons.

Crossmaglen and around

In the far southwestern corner of Armagh just inside the border, **CROSSMAGLEN** has reputedly the largest market square in Ireland, the scene of a fortnightly Friday **market**. Face south and it's impossible to ignore the huge RUC/British army barracks here with its outcrops of aerials, cameras and sangars (small pillbox-like fortifications).

During the Troubles the town's reputation for armed struggle against the British was fearsome and, in truth, it has been a cauldron of activity ever since Partition. Indeed, had the 1924 Boundary Commission's proposals been fully implemented, the town and surrounding countryside would have been transferred to Dublin rule rather than staying inside the North. All this said, on arrival you'll find the pubs much friendlier than you might have expected and you're very unlikely to brush up against any trouble. Traditional-music sessions are abundant and the square comes vividly alive during the horse-trading fairs in September. There's **B&B** at *Murtagh's Bar*, 13 North St (☎028/3086 1378; ②) and at *Cnoc Mhuire*, 40 Annaghmare Rd (☎028/3086 1896; ①), the latter a hilltop farmhouse a mile or so north on the Newtownhamilton road. Lunches are available at *Murtagh's*, while several of the other bars, including *The Cartwheel* serve evening **meals**. *Keenan's* bar on The Square hosts a notable **traditional-music** session on Thursdays. The extremely helpful **tourist office** (Mon–Fri 9am–5pm, extended to 6pm and weekends in summer; ☎028/3086 8900) is in Ó Fiaich House on The Square.

A couple of miles east of Crossmaglen on the B30 Newry Road is **CREGGAN** and its **Poets' Graveyard**, so named because three eighteenth-century Gaelic poets are buried there: Art Mac Cooey, Patrick Mac Aliondain and Séamus Mór Mac Murphy (who was also an outlaw of some notoriety). The inscription on Mac Cooey's stone is taken from his most famous poem, *Úr-Chill an Chreagáin* – "That with the fragrant Gaels of Creggan I will be put in clay under the sod."

East of Creggan, a turning off the main road leads to **GLASSDRUMMOND** and *Hearty's Folk Cottage* (Sun 2–6pm), where you can admire the arts and crafts collections and enjoy excellent afternoon teas to the accompaniment of traditional music.

travel details

Trains

(services are far less frequent on Sundays)

Bangor to: Belfast (every 30min; 30min); Lisburn (every 30min; 1hr 10min); Lurgan (hourly; 1hr 30min); Portadown (hourly; 1hr 45min).

Newry to: Belfast (8 daily; 50min); Dublin (7 daily; 1hr 10min); Dundalk (7 daily; 15min).

Buses

The Mourne Rambler (☎028/4372 2296) is a circular service running in July and August from Newcastle to the Silent Valley and back. Buses depart Newcastle (Mon–Sat) at 10.10am, 11.35am, 2.05pm & 3.30pm; the return fare is £3.60.

The North Down Bus open-top service (☎028/9217 1143) runs from Bangor along the coastline to Ballywalter daily in July & August. Departures from Bangor are at 10.10am, 12.10pm, 2.15pm & 4.15pm; the return service departs Ballywalter approximately 45 minutes later; a day return is £2.90.

Armagh to: Belfast (11 Mon–Fri, 8 Sat, 4 Sun; 1hr–1hr 20min); Benburb (3 Mon–Fri, 2 Sat; 25min); Caledon via Navan Fort (10 Mon–Fri, 4 Sat; 20min); Castleblaney (5 Mon–Fri, 4 Sat, 1 Sun; 50min); Cavan (4 Mon–Sat, 1 Sun; 1hr 30min); Cork (1 daily; 9hr); Dublin (2 Mon–Sat, 1 Sun; 2hr 30min); Dungannon (7 Mon–Fri, 4 Sat; 40min); Enniskillen (1 daily, 1hr 45min); Galway (2 Mon–Sat, 1 Sun; 5hr 25min); Loughgall (7 Mon–Fri, 1 Sat; 15min); Markethill (9 Mon–Fri, 5 Sat; 20min); Monaghan (12 Mon–Fri, 10 Sat, 4 Sun; 30–45min); Newry (5 Mon–Sat; 1hr); Portadown (25 Mon–Fri, 15 Sat, 5 Sun; 30min); Portrush (1 Mon–Thurs, 2 Fri, 1 Sat & Sun; 2hr 20min).

Banbridge to: Belfast (30 Mon–Fri, 27 Sat, 11 Sun; 45min–1hr 15min); Dublin (5 Mon–Sat, 3 Sun; 2hr 20min); Newcastle (4 Mon–Fri, 3 Sat; 1hr); Newry (24 Mon–Fri, 21 Sat, 9 Sun; 30min).

Bangor to: Belfast (32 Mon–Fri, 27 Sat, 8 Sun; 45min); Donaghadee (18 Mon–Fri, 14 Sat, 5 Sun; 25min); Newtownards (31 Mon–Fri, 29 Sat, 7 Sun; 15min).

Donaghadee to: Bangor (17 Mon–Fri, 15 Sat, 5 Sun; 25min); Belfast (18 Mon–Fri, 15 Sat, 7 Sun; 55min).

Downpatrick to: Ardglass (11 Mon–Fri, 6 Sat, 2 Sun; 25 min); Ballyhornan (7 Mon–Fri, 5 Sat, 2 Sun; 35min); Belfast (26 Mon–Fri, 15 Sat, 5 Sun; 1hr); Kilkeel (13 Mon–Fri, 5 Sat, 1 Sun; 1hr 20min); Killyleagh (8 Mon–Wed, 10 Thurs & Fri, 4 Sat, 1 Sun; 20min); Killough (11 Mon–Fri, 6 Sat, 2 Sun; 15 min); Newcastle (15 Mon–Fri, 10 Sat, 3 Sun; 20–35 min); Newry (4 Mon–Sat, 2 Sun; 1hr); Raholp (6 Mon–Fri, 4 Sat; 15min); Strangford (8 Mon–Fri, 4 Sat; 25min).

Hillsborough to: Belfast (31 Mon–Fri, 29 Sat, 12 Sun; 45min).

Kilkeel to: Annalong (16 Mon–Fri, 11 Sat, 7 Sun; 15min); Greencastle (1 Mon, Tues, Wed, Thurs & Fri, 2 & Sat; 20 min); Newcastle (16 Mon–Fri, 11 Sat, 7 Sun; 30min); Newry (10 Mon–Sat, 4 Sun; 50min); Rostrevor (10 Mon–Sat, 4 Sun; 25min); Warrenpoint (10 Mon–Sat, 4 Sun; 35min).

Newcastle to: Annalong (16 Mon–Fri, 10 Sat, 6 Sun; 25min); Banbridge (2 Mon–Sat; 1hr); Belfast (19 Mon–Fri, 16 Sat, 10 Sun; 1hr 20min); Bryansford (5 Mon–Fri, 3 Sat, 2 Sun; 10min); Castlewellan (24 Mon–Fri, 17 Sat, 7 Sun; 10min); Downpatrick (15 Mon–Fri, 10 Sat, 5 Sun; 45min); Kilkeel (16 Mon–Fri, 10 Sat, 6 Sun; 40min); Newry (via Hilltown: 4 Mon–Sat, 2 Sun; 40min; via Kilkeel: 8 Mon–Fri, 9 Sat, 2 Sun; 1hr 50min).

Newry to: Armagh (7 Mon–Fri, 5 Sat; 1hr); Banbridge (24 Mon–Fri, 21 Sat, 9 Sun; 30min); Bessbrook (24 Mon–Fri, 16 Sat; 10min); Crossmaglen (6 Mon–Fri, 4 Sat; 55min); Downpatrick (4 Mon–Sat, 2 Sun; 1hr); Dublin (7 Mon–Sat, 3 Sun; 2hr); Forkhill (6 Mon–Fri, 4 Sat; 35min); Jonesborough (3 Mon–Wed & Fri, 5 Thurs & Sat; 15min); Mullaghbawn (6 Mon–Fri, 4 Sat; 30min); Newcastle (via Hilltown: 4 Mon–Sat, 2 Sun; 40min; via Kilkeel: 8 Mon–Fri, 4 Sat; 1hr 50min); Rostrevor (21 Mon–Fri, 14 Sat, 7 Sun; 25min); Warrenpoint (24 Mon–Fri, 15 Sat, 10 Sun; 15min).

Newtownards to: Bangor (33 Mon–Fri, 29 Sat, 7 Sun; 10min); Belfast (every 10–20min Mon–Sat, 12 Sun; 15min); Comber (16 Mon–Fri, 18 Sat, 7 Sun; 15min); Greyabbey (14 Mon–Fri, 8 Sat; 20min); Portaferry (14 Mon–Fri, 8 Sat & Sun; 50min–1hr 15min).

CHAPTER SEVENTEEN

TYRONE AND FERMANAGH

The bulk of inland Northern Ireland is formed by neighbouring **Tyrone** and **Fermanagh**, predominantly rural counties whose few sizeable towns lie at the eastern and western fringes of the region. The chief scenic attractions of County Tyrone are to be found in the wild and desolate **Sperrin Mountains** in the north, an area that's patchily covered by the local bus network, so you really need your own transport to explore it. Even in the southern lowlands, the scattered castles, archeological sites and heritage centres are sometimes difficult to reach without a car or bike, though an exception is the excellent **Ulster American Folk Park**, close to the county town, **Omagh**.

In contrast to Tyrone, County Fermanagh attracts plenty of visitors – chiefly for the water sports and fishing that are widely available. At its core is the great **Lough Erne**, a huge lake complex dotted with islands and surrounded by richly beautiful countryside. Its county town of **Enniskillen** evinces a strong sense of history, while the remnants of the medieval past – along with those of the seventeenth and eighteenth centuries – are found all over the region, on islands and mainland alike. As in Tyrone, sights of interest are dispersed, and buses mostly serve only the main routes; but the key to enjoying Fermanagh is to get out onto the water – and this is easy enough from Enniskillen and a number of the villages that rest on the lakes' shores.

COUNTY TYRONE

Stretching from the shores of the vast Lough Neagh in the east to the border of the Republic and Donegal in the west, County Tyrone lies bang in the middle of Northern Ireland. Its northeastern limits are high in the desolate and beautiful **Sperrin Mountains**, and in the south it reaches towards the lakes of County Fermanagh. This is first and foremost farming country, with little evidence of industrialization apart from the starchily neat planters' villages that grew up with the linen industry.

ACCOMMODATION PRICE CODES

Throughout this book, prices of hotels, guesthouses and B&Bs have been graded with the codes below, according to what you can expect to pay for a double room in high season. For more details on accommodation, see p.34.

① Under £26	④ £40–55	⑦ £90–110
② £26–33	⑤ £55–70	⑧ £110–130
③ £33–40	⑥ £70–90	⑨ Over £130

The Sperrin range offers major scenic attractions; it's rich in wildlife and is an excellent target for determined, lonesome walking. The place to head for is **Gortin**, a village on the **Ulster Way** footpath and the most easily accessible overnight stop in the area. Tyrone also has no shortage of archeological remains, the most remarkable being the **Beaghmore Stone Circles**, in the southeast of the Sperrins. The towns, though, are not much of a draw. **Omagh** is the county's largest town, agreeable enough but with little to warrant a stop. **Cookstown** and **Dungannon** in the east, and **Strabane** on the Donegal border, are similarly places to pass through, with minimal points of interest scattered around. The nearest the county's settlements get to being picturesque are the villages to the north and northwest of Omagh: **Castlederg**, **Newtownstewart**, **Sion Mills** and the tiny hamlets of the Sperrins. There's little else in the way of sights around the county beyond the **heritage centres** that celebrate the historic connections between Ulster and the US. Of these, the **Ulster American Folk Park** near Omagh is by far the best.

The only **local transport** in the region is Ulsterbus, which is reliable along main routes and not as infrequent as you might expect in such a rural area. Nonetheless, if this is your only way of getting around, it makes sense to pick up a timetable in a major bus station before you head off into the country. However, so scattered are Tyrone's attractions that you're likely to see little of the most interesting parts without a car or a bike. The one exception, of course, is in the Sperrins, where **hiking** is the best way to get around.

Some history

County Tyrone was the land of the **O'Neills**, who ruled Ulster from their seats in Omagh, Dungannon and Cookstown and claimed descent back to the legendary sons of "Niall of the Nine Hostages". Isolated geographically by bog, lake and mountain, Ulster was a key centre of Gaelic resistance to English rule. When Conn O'Neill received the English title Earl of Tyrone in the mid-sixteenth century, he followed the Gaelic Brehon Laws of inheritance and chose his youngest son, **Shane the Proud**, as successor, though the English favoured Matthew, his eldest son. After years of bitter feuding Matthew died in battle in 1558, and his son Hugh was taken to England to be educated. Meanwhile, Shane, elected The O'Neill and determined to extend his kingdom, attacked his neighbours and was promptly called to London to face Elizabeth I. The two cultures met in mutual incomprehension: the Queen sat surrounded by perfumed courtiers in silks and velvets, while O'Neill in saffron tunic and Irish mantle stood flanked by his wolfhounds and followers. He refused "to writhe his mouth in clattering English" or attend Protestant services. After six months he returned home and continued to pursue his aims. Finally he was murdered by the MacDonnells and his head sent to Dublin as a mark of their loyalty to the Crown.

It was Shane's nephew, **Hugh O'Neill**, who witnessed the final demise of Gaelic power in Ulster. In 1585, suitably anglicized, Hugh returned from England to Dungannon as the second Earl of Tyrone. Soon, however, he began to "go native". English spies carried tales to London and he was proclaimed a traitor. For five years he fought off English armies, but in 1601 Gaelic forces were defeated by Lord Mountjoy at the crucial battle of Kinsale. O'Neill signed the **Treaty of Mellifont** (1603), which compelled him to adopt English laws, language and dress and give up his clan title and his land. Ulster was divided into nine counties and English rule was enforced. In 1607, O'Neill led the **Flight of the Earls** out of Ireland with a retinue of Gaelic chiefs and their followers. It was the end of the old Gaelic chiefdoms and customs. Most of the *filí* (bards) – respected members of every noble family and clan historians – left with their patrons. The flight ended at the Church of St Pietro in **Rome**. Hugh O'Neill stayed on in Rome, where romantic legend has it that he died of sadness. He is buried in St Pietro before the high altar.

With the leaders of resistance gone, the subsequent "**plantation**" of Ulster under James I (1603–25) established the hegemony of the Crown, giving control of Tyrone to Protestant immigrants from England and Scotland. This was certainly not the end of Gaelic insurrection, and it was again from this part of Ulster that the next serious threat to English control came. The **Great Rebellion of 1641** began in Tyrone with Phelim O'Neill's capture of Dungannon and Charlemont. The rising spread throughout the country as Catholics all over Ireland joined together to claim their religious and civic rights. The rebellion was inevitably accompanied by considerable brutality, but horror stories grew to such an extent that settlers came to believe there was a concerted plan to butcher the entire Protestant population, and the alleged scale of the violence gave Cromwell his justification for the massacre at Drogheda ten years later. Ulster remained in the hands of the "planters", and it was they who introduced linen manufacture in the eighteenth century – Tyrone's only experience of industry until more recent times.

Omagh and around

On the afternoon of Saturday August 15, 1998, a 500-pound **car bomb**, planted by a dissident Republican group calling itself the Real IRA, exploded on Market Street in the centre of Tyrone's largest town, **OMAGH**. Twenty-six people were killed outright (a further three died later) and more than two hundred were injured. It was the worst single atrocity in the history of the Troubles and drew outrage and condemnation from every quarter. Indeed Sinn Féin's president, Gerry Adams, unprecedentedly denounced the bombing "without any equivocation whatsoever". Politicians moved frantically to save the peace process and prevent any Loyalist reprisals while the Irish and British governments announced their intentions to reinforce anti-terrorist legislation. Such efforts, however, offered scant consolation to the people of Omagh, a town more integrated and harmonious than most in Northern Ireland, and by then unified in its grief.

Much of the eastern part of Omagh's main street was devastated by the bombing and has since undergone major reconstruction. The area uphill to the west, originally thought to be the bombers' target on the basis of their misleading warning, remained unscathed and contains two adjacent buildings which would grace any town – the fine classical **courthouse** and the irregular twin spires of the Catholic **Sacred Heart Church**.

Practicalities

Omagh's **tourist office** is right in the centre of town at 1 Market St (Mon–Fri 9am–5pm; Easter–Sept also Sat 9am–5.30pm; ☎028/8224 7831). You'll need your own transport to see most of the region it promotes: you can rent **cars** from Johnson King Motors, 82 Derry Rd (☎028/8224 2788), and **bikes** from Conway Cycles (☎028/8224 6195) on Old Market Place. The **Ulsterbus** depot (☎028/8224 2711) is just across the river in Mountjoy Road (north off the High Street).

For **accommodation**, if you're hiking the Sperrins, a better bet might be to base yourself in Gortin (see p.645). Within Omagh, *Silverbirch Hotel*, 5 Gortin Rd (☎028/8224 2520; *www.silverbirchhotel.com*; ⑥), is relatively luxurious, while *Hawthorn House*, 72 Mountfield Rd, signposted to Killyclogher off the A505 (☎028/8225 2005; ④), is both friendly and comfortable. The nearest **B&B** is *Ardmore*, 12 Tamlaght Rd (☎028/8224 3381; ②), up the left fork in front of the Sacred Heart and along the second turning on your right. Also near the centre is *Bridie's*, 1 Georgian Villas, Hospital Rd (☎028/8224 5254; ②) – go down the main street away from the courthouse and, once across the river, turn to the right. The *Omagh Independent* **hostel** is two and a half miles north, at 9a Waterworks Rd (☎028/8224 1973; *mfyffe@netcomuk.co.uk*), signposted off the B48 and A505; the hostel managers will pick you up from Omagh bus station.

Omagh is a good place to stop for **food**, particularly during the daytime. The *Pink Elephant* in the High Street is a local favourite, serving breakfast and lunches in huge helpings. Almost as popular are the nearby *Carlton Coffee Lounge*, a little further down the hill, and the *Bridge Restaurant*, round the corner on Bridge Street. Plenty of pubs serve food, though the best is undoubtedly the *Coach Inn*, 1 Railway Terrace, offering tasty lunchtime specials and an extensive evening menu. *Hawthorn House* (see above) is extremely popular in the evenings, specializing in lobster and other seafood and steaks (allow £30 per head including wine). *Molly Sweeney's* on Gortin Road has an excellent fish menu and *Grant's* on George Street offers a bistro menu or snacks in the wine bar.

For **nightlife**, just outside town on the B4 Carrickmore Road is the Dún Uladh Cultural Heritage Centre of Ulster (☎028/8224 2777), the provincial branch of the national organization Comhaltas Ceoltóirí Éireann, which promotes Irish **traditional music and culture**. There's all manner of events running here, including a traditional session on Saturday nights. However, Omagh is showband country and most of the pubs and hotels have live **music** at weekends: you can usually find something happening at *McElroy's* on Castle Street or the *Silverbirch Hotel*, and traditionalists may be satisfied by occasional sessions at *Sally O'Brien's* on John Street or *Bogan's* near the tourist office.

The Ulster American Folk Park

The most successful of Northern Ireland's American heritage projects is the **Ulster American Folk Park** (Easter–Sept Mon–Sat 11am–6.30pm, Sun 11.30am–7pm; rest of year Mon–Fri 10.30am–5pm; *www.folkpark.com*; £4), only three miles north of Omagh in Camphill, a short hop on one of the regular Strabane-bound buses. The Folk Park makes a good afternoon out from Omagh and a fine day-trip if combined with the Ulster History Park near Gortin (see p.646).

The first significant **emigration** from Ireland to North America was that of Ulster men and women in the early eighteenth century, many of whom were of Scottish Protestant origin. Of all the immigrant communities in the United States, it was the Irish who most quickly – and profoundly – made their mark: the three first-generation **US presidents** were all of Ulster stock, and a further nine presidents could trace their roots to here. Throughout the eighteenth and nineteenth centuries thousands of people left to establish new lives in North America, a steady flow of emigrants which became a torrent during the Famine years.

You can find detailed information on the causes and patterns of migration in the Folk Park's indoor **gallery**, but the real attractions lie outside in the park itself, where **original buildings** have been transplanted or replicas constructed to provide a sense of Ulster life in the past. The disparity in living conditions is represented by a typical pre-Famine **single-room cabin** from the Sperrins which you'll pass on your way to the **Mellon Homestead**, a significantly more substantial dwelling from which the local Mellon family migrated in 1818. There's an austere **Presbyterian meeting house** and the squat **Tullyallen Mass House**, a Catholic chapel dating from 1768. A re-created Ulster street, including the impressively authentic Reilly's Spirit Grocers from Newtownbutler, leads to the *Union*, a full-size **brig** reconstructed to demonstrate the gruelling conditions endured during the voyage across the Atlantic. An American street leads to edifices constructed by the **Pennsylvanian settlers**, including a multipurpose log barn and massive six-roomed log farmhouse. There are plenty of other buildings and you'll meet costumed guides and craftworkers ready to explain their activities and answer questions, augmenting the Folk Park's attention to authenticity.

The complex also houses the **Centre for Emigration Studies** (Mon–Fri 9.30am–4.30pm), a major reference and research library that contains an enormous variety of material, such as emigrants' letters, passenger lists and contemporary newspaper articles.

Unfortunately, the onsite **restaurant** is basic – bring a picnic, or head across the road for more substantial fare at the *Mellon Country Inn*, which serves traditional Irish food in a cosmopolitan style; they can also provide you with walking routes and **maps** for the nearby Ulster Way, which enters the scenic Gortin area to the northeast.

Northwest Tyrone

The northwestern part of Tyrone is seldom visited by tourists yet has some of the county's most attractive towns and countryside. The fastest route through the area – and the only feasible one if you're hitching – is the A5 north to Derry or Letterkenny via **Newtownstewart**, **Sion Mills** and **Strabane**. A quieter alternative is the route via **Castlederg** along minor country roads and across the border to Castlefinn in County Donegal.

Castlederg

The friendly market village of **CASTLEDERG** sits around a spruced-up square beside the River Derg, across whose waters lie the ruins of a Plantation **castle**, built in 1619 and destroyed by Sir Phelim O'Neill during the 1641 Rebellion. Modern Castlederg retains something of its traditional flavour as a staging-post for travellers and a watering hole for pilgrims on their way to St Patrick's Purgatory on Lough Derg (see p.482). The town's bars and cafés make this a good place to stop for refuelling; and the **tourist office**, or Castlederg Visitor Centre, on the Lower Strabane Rd (April–Oct Tues–Fri 11am–4pm, Sat 11.30am–4pm, Sun 2–5pm; ☎028/8167 0794) will give you lots of information on local sites of interest. **Davy Crockett**'s family came from the Castlederg area and the visitor centre has a small display (£1.20) containing a model of the Alamo Fort where the celebrated frontiersman made his last stand. Close to each other one mile north of the village off the Lurganboy Road are two large **megalithic tombs** that stand as memorials to the area's pre-Christian past: Todd's Den is a cairn with a portal stone, but more impressive is the Druid's Altar, a chambered grave with two portal stones and capstones, one inscribed with *ogham* runes.

Accommodation in the town itself is limited to the *Derg Arms*, 43 Main St (☎028/8167 1644; ③). A few miles west off the Killeter road is *Ardmourne House and Stables*, 36 Corgary Rd (☎028/8167 0291; ②), with comfortable B&B and **riding** and **trekking** too. Surprisingly, the **nightlife** in Castlederg can often be quite lively, with various musical entertainments from sing-a-longs to discos, at bars such as the *Castle Inn* and *Gallen's*.

Newtownstewart and Sion Mills

The quicker route north from Omagh passes through rich farmland to **NEWTOWNSTEWART** which, surprisingly for its size, boasts remnants of two **castles**. In the main street a gable wall is all that remains of the Stewart castle burned down on the orders of James II; squatting in isolation on a hill to the southwest are the ruins of the fourteenth-century Harry Avery's castle, another O'Neill stronghold. But Newtownstewart's real draw is the gem of a **museum** that's housed in the tiny **tourist office** (May–Sept Tues–Fri 11am–4pm, Sat 11.30am–5pm, Sun 2–5pm; ☎028/8166 2414; £1.20) a couple of hundred yards down the Omagh road from the main street. Local historian Billy Dunbar, a walking encyclopedia, donated his collection of vintage packaging, man traps, stereoscopes and war memorabilia to the museum when he could no longer navigate from one end of his house to the other. Highlights include a Bordalous (a mini-chamberpot named after a French priest renowned for his over-long sermons), and a threepenny bit engraved with the Lord's Prayer.

Next door to Newtownstewart's museum is *Aunt Jane's* welcoming **café**, open seven days a week. There's **B&B** accommodation in the Baronscourt Forest area, three miles south on the B64 towards Drumquin, at *Hunting Lodge Hotel*, Letterbin (☎028/8166 1679; ④), a converted nineteenth-century schoolhouse. There's **camping** at the municipal *Harrigan Caravan Park* (☎028/8166 2414), just over the Mourne River on the north side of Newtownstewart, but you need to arrive before 5pm.

The linen industry of the eighteenth century made a big impact in Tyrone, as it did all over Ulster, but its traces are mostly faint ones – such as the disused mills along the Ballinderry River near Cookstown. **SION MILLS**, a planned linen village seven miles north of Newtownstewart, is the obvious exception. The quaint village, which belies the gruesome conditions of nineteenth-century factory work, is designated a conservation area, though the Herdman's linen works still operates, amidst security fences and cameras. You can skirt around it on foot and down to the Mourne River, where there's good **fishing**. For **B&B**, *Bide-a-Wee*, on the main Omagh–Strabane A5 at 181 Melmount Rd (☎028/8165 9571; ③), is friendly and has a swimming pool.

Strabane and around

Present-day **STRABANE**, north of Omagh, is pretty grim and often traffic-congested. As a small Catholic enclave surrounded by largely Protestant-owned farmland and sitting right on the border it has suffered more than most from the Troubles. Economic depression was a consequence and at one time the town had the highest unemployment rate in the country. In the eighteenth century, however, Strabane was an important printing and publishing centre. John Dunlap emigrated from here and went on to print the broadsheets of the American Declaration of Independence in 1776, as well as the *Pennsylvanian Packet*, America's first daily newspaper. All that is left in Strabane of these times is the cute, bow-windowed frontage of **Gray's Printing Shop**, 49 Main St, which is now owned by the National Trust. It has a small printing **museum** upstairs (Tues–Fri 11am–5pm, Sat 11.30am–5pm; £2) with a selection of old presses and an audiovisual show on print history, but sadly the shop's interior has been ripped out to provide maximum space for cards, completely destroying the scale and atmosphere the place must have once had.

One of Strabane's most famous sons was Brian O'Nolan, a multi-faceted writer better known as both the surreal and comic novelist **Flann O'Brien** and the brilliantly zany *Irish Times* columnist Myles na Gopaleen. Born in 1911 into an Irish-speaking household at 15 Bowling Green, he had a glittering academic career at University College Dublin and spent much of his working life as a civil servant. An irascible character with a fondness for drinking, he was unfortunate enough to produce his best work, *At Swim-Two-Birds*, just before the outbreak of World War II. Since his death in 1966 his absurdist novels have been republished and – much to his annoyance, no doubt – he has become a cult figure (for more on his work see p.722). Another, less entertaining individual to have his roots in the area is the American president **Woodrow Wilson**. Head east of Strabane two miles down the Plumbridge Road and you'll find the Wilson ancestral home in the village of **DERGALT** (July & Aug 2–5pm; £1) – the president's father, who was a printer in Strabane, lived in this small, traditional farmer's cottage. Stuffed with furniture and effects belonging to the family, it's now a target for American tourists, who dutifully meander through the hallowed rooms.

The **tourist office**, in a glass pagoda on Abercorn Square (April–Oct Mon–Thurs 9am–5.30pm, Fri & Sat 9am–4.30pm; ☎028/7138 2204), will help with finding **accommodation**. Top of the range is the *Fir Trees Hotel*, Melmount Rd (☎028/7138 2382; ⑤), which also has a fine **restaurant**, or try the central **B&B** *Bowling Green House*, 6 Bowling Green (☎028/7188 4787; ②). Wholesome daytime **meals** can be found at *Dempsey's*, Lower Main Street, while piscophiles should head for *Oysters Restaurant*, 37 Patrick St, for both lunch and evening fish specialities.

The Sperrins

The impressive, undulating **Sperrin Mountains** form the northeastern limits of County Tyrone. Wild, empty and beautiful, they reach 2240ft at their highest, yet the smooth and gradually curving slopes give them a deceptively low appearance. The covering of bog and heather adds to this effect, suggesting nothing more than high, open

WALKING THE SPERRINS

The forty-mile-wide range of the Sperrin Mountains offers good long-distance **walking**, without necessarily involving steep inclines. You can ramble wherever you like, but remember that – despite appearances – these are high mountains, and changeable weather makes them potentially dangerous. A map and compass are essential for serious walking.

For those not equipped for the high ground, the **Glenelly** and **Owenkillen** river valleys run through the heart of this stunning countryside from Plumbridge and Gortin respectively, and are particularly enjoyable for cyclists.

The official **Ulster Way** footpath takes an arduous 34-mile route – the steepish Glenelly Trail – from Dungiven up over Glenshane Mountain to Goles Forest. From Gortin a second stage of the Way leads to the Ulster American Folk Park, a ten-mile trek. Parts of both sections of the Way are on road, however, and along some stretches signposts have disappeared or, worse, point in the wrong direction. You can pick up a guidebook to the Ulster Way in tourist offices (see Basics, p.25) or from the Sports Council of Northern Ireland (☎028/9038 1222), but your best bet is to ask locals about the state of the path. For less strenuous walks, the Northern Ireland Tourist Board has produced route-plans for fourteen "mini-ways", the longest of which is thirteen miles; again, ask for them at local tourist offices.

moorland. For all this, views from the summits are panoramic, and the evenness of texture can make these mountains sumptuous when bathed in evening light. Once in the mountains, it's impossible not to catch sight of the **wildlife**. Sparrow hawks and kestrels hover above, and you might see buzzards or the far rarer hen harrier. They're attracted by rich prey in a landscape mostly undisturbed by development – the mountains teem with assorted rodents, rabbits, badgers and even the Irish hare. One threat to this delicately balanced ecosystem has been the rediscovery of **gold** in the mountains. Their future is in the balance, but for the moment at least, the Sperrins offer a wilderness to be enjoyed.

For local sheep-farming communities, however, the depopulation of the Sperrins is a real problem, and their traditional way of life is now slowly dying. The sparseness of the population and the lack of focal centres make it difficult for an outsider to key into this culture. For the same reason, hitching isn't easy, and walkers should bear in mind that there's a shortage of places to buy food, so **planning ahead** is essential. Rely only on large villages for provisions of any sort; hamlets often have nothing.

The **Sperrin Heritage Centre** (Easter–Oct Mon–Fri 11.30am–5.30pm, Sat 11.30am–6pm, Sun 2–6pm; £2) lies between Cranagh and Sperrin, nine miles east of Plumbridge (see below), and lets you explore the area's environmental and cultural issues without getting your feet wet. The video games and audiovisuals of this welcoming interpretive centre are quite a surprise – particularly the holographic storyteller and the quaint 3-D slide shows – and they also organize gold-panning expeditions or can rent you a pan. Its pleasant **tea room** serves homemade food and real coffee. The centre is tricky to reach without your own transport, although the weekday **Sperrin Link bus** passes by (see p.661).

Gortin and around

If you're tackling the Sperrins to the north of Omagh, there are really only two villages that can offer you any amenities at all – **Gortin** and its near-neighbour **Plumbridge**. And even these are comatose for much of the year.

GORTIN, ten miles north of Omagh and served by three buses daily, is a long one-street village with a surprising number of **pubs**, one of which, the *Badoney Tavern*, offers lunches and evening **meals**. Alternatively, there's an innovative menu at *The Pedlar's Restaurant*. The **Ulster Way** passes through Gortin, though the signposting which should connect it with Goles Forest is at the moment incomplete and stops at Craignaddy (984ft), two and a half miles north. However, the signposted Way does continue to the south of Gortin through the forest park, with its little loughs and wild deer, before swinging west to low farmland and the Ulster American Folk Park (see p.642). **Accommodation** is available at the *Gortin Outdoor Centre* **hostel** (July–Sept; ☎028/8264 8083), fifty yards south of the village crossroads, or the newly-opened **self-catering** *Gortin Village Accommodation* on Main St (☎028/8264 8346; £163-£325; sleeps 4–6). For **camping**, head to the *Gortin Glen Caravan Park* (☎028/8164 8108), three miles south on the Omagh road (3 buses daily); the site also has self-catering cottages. Smaller, but far more attractive, is the *Gortin Glen Forest Park* campsite opposite (☎028/8164 8217), a good place to stay if you're contemplating some hill-walking.

A little over three miles south of Gortin is the **Ulster History Park** (April–Sept daily 10am–5.30pm; July & Aug closes 6.30pm; Oct–March Mon–Fri 10am–5pm; last admission 1hr before closing; *www.omagh.gov.uk/uhpindex.htm*; £3.75), which features full-scale reconstructions of buildings in Ireland from 7000 BC up to the seventeenth century. Inside there are videos and displays that serve to distract in bad weather, but far more rewarding is the **interactive tour** on which a guide talks you round such authentic traditional dwellings as a stinking deerskin-covered teepee, shows you how to chip flint, explains ancient symbols and answers questions expertly, no matter how daft they are. The rath, *crannóg* and medieval castle are particularly interesting, and the latest addition is a seventeenth-century Plantation settlement.

PLUMBRIDGE, three and a half miles north of Gortin, sits clustered prettily on the banks of the Glenelly River. Apocryphally, it gets its name from the building of the village bridge: the engineer in charge didn't have a plumb line and so, from his scaffolding, spat in the water, using his spit to take the perpendicular. There's little here beyond a few bars and a couple of shops, and the liveliest times are during the annual Glenelly **sheepdog trials** in August. However, you might encounter the odd optimistic gold panner, convinced that the river's waters hold the key to their fortune.

Three and a half miles east of Gortin (on the B46 Creggan Road) is the tiny village of **ROUSKEY**, with the ruins of a "sweat lodge", an early form of sauna (after the steam treatment, the luckless invalid was plunged into the icy stream nearby). Widespread use of sweat lodges died out after the Famine years, possibly because the experience of typhoid that accompanied the Famine dealt a severe blow to people's confidence in traditional medicinal treatments, but some were still functioning up to the 1920s. Also in the village is *Teach Ceoil* (☎028/8167 1551), a restored stone barn worth investigating for its regular evenings of **traditional music** and dancing.

Prehistoric remains and the Beaghmore Stone Circles

County Tyrone is peppered with archeological remains: there are more than a thousand standing stones in the Sperrins alone and the county as a whole has numerous chambered graves. The **Lough Macrory** area, just east of Mountfield on the A505 Omagh–Cookstown road, is particularly rich in dolmens and megaliths, though many of these are hard to find and of specialist interest only.

The uninitiated will get most out of the Bronze Age **Beaghmore Stone Circles**, in the southeast of the Sperrins. From Gortin take the B46 east onto the A505, from where they're well signposted up a track three and a half miles north off the road. Although most of the stones on this lonely site are no more than three feet high, the complexity of the ritual they suggest is impressive: there are seven stone circles, ten stone rows and a dozen round cairns (burial mounds, some containing cremated human remains). All of the circles stand in pairs, except for one, which is filled with over eight hundred upright stones, known as Dragon's Teeth. The alignments correlate to movements of sun, moon and stars. Two of the rows point to sunrise at the summer solstice; another may point to moonrise at the same period.

An Creagán Visitor Centre

Just off the A505 roughly halfway between Omagh and Cookstown is **An Creagán Visitor Centre** (April–Sept daily 11am–6.30pm; Oct–March Mon–Fri 11am–4.30pm; £2), modelled on the many cairns that surround it – 44 of them in a five-mile radius. The centre is circular and built from local stone on the land of one of the last native speakers in the district, Peadar Joe Haughey, who died in the 1950s. Staff in the centre speak Irish, and the place is actually more of a cultural centre than a museum, with locals coming along to the **traditional-music** sessions, dancing, storytelling and singing events. But An Creagán also explores the rare raised bog terrain all around, with interpretive displays and signposted **rambling and cycling routes** over the countryside (they also rent bikes). The farmers driven to these bogs in the eighteenth century made huge efforts to reclaim the soil; there are limekilns from which they treated the reclaimed land, and you can still see the **potato ridges**: these grassed-over Copney spade ridges – a form of cultivation that maximized production – point back to the devastating Famine of 1845 to 1849 and the farmers' desperate attempts to survive. You can organize self-catering **accommodation** here (☎028/8076 1112; £110–£330 per week) in the traditional *clochán* settlement, with open turf fires supplemented, fortunately, by central heating.

Eastern Tyrone

The only places in the east of County Tyrone that could be described as anything more than villages are **Cookstown** and **Dungannon**. The dominant feature is the eastern shore of **Lough Neagh** and there are a number of relics of both the region's historical heritage, such as high crosses at **Ardboe** and **Donaghmore**, and its more recent industrial past at **Coalisland** and the **Welbrook Beetling Mill**. The village of **Benburb**, to the south, is one of the most attractively situated in the North.

Cookstown and the Lough Neagh shore

A planned planters' town, **COOKSTOWN** boasts the longest main street in Ireland, the site of an extensive Saturday market. The **tourist office** is at The Burnavon, Burns Rd (Mon–Fri 9am–5pm; Sat 10am–4pm; ☎028/8676 6727). The pick of the local **accommodation** is the very plush *Tullylagan Country House Hotel* (☎028/8676 5100; ⑥) set in thirty acres of grounds in Sandholes, four miles south of the town.

The **Wellbrook Beetling Mill**, three and a half miles west of Cookstown off the A505, is a National Trust-owned eighteenth-century water-powered linen mill (April–June & Sept Sat & Sun 2–6pm; July & Aug Mon & Wed–Sun 2–6pm; £2). "Beetling" was the final stage of production whereby linen was given a sheen and smoothness by hammering with heavy wooden "beetles". Though it ceased operation in 1961, the mill is excellently preserved, and all the engines still work.

For more monumental interest, two miles south of Cookstown on the B520 is **Tullaghoge Fort**, the erstwhile headquarters of the O'Hagans, chief justices of Ireland, who undertook the coronations of the O'Neill kings from the twelfth to the seventeenth century. From the road it appears to be simply a copse of beech and Scots pine on the top of a very gentle hill, but in fact these are very clear earthworks of the early Christian period – a circular outer bank with an inner oval enclosure. It was in Tullaghoge forest that O'Neill tribesmen hid after the Flight of the Earls.

It seems even the legendary Fionn Mac Cumhaill was unimpressed by east Tyrone's low-lying terrain. Legend has it that he took a massive lump of land from Ulster and hurled it across the Irish Sea. It landed and became the Isle of Man, and the hole it left behind became **Lough Neagh** (pronounced *nay*). The lough's shores form the county's eastern boundary and provide excellent **fishing** and plenty of bird life, but, beyond this, both land and lake are almost featureless. Small settlements house eel fishermen, whose catches go to the Toome Eel Fishery at **Toomebridge** (at the northern tip of the lake), the largest eel fishery in Europe.

Slight relief is to be found at **ARDBOE**, ten miles east of Cookstown, where there's a tenth-century **High Cross**. The elements have eroded the various biblical scenes carved onto the sandstone almost beyond recognition, but its exceptional size – 18ft high – is impressive. The cross stands in the grounds of an early monastery associated with **St Colman**, but the ruined church nearby dates from the seventeenth century and is of little interest. On a humid day, you'll also not fail to be impressed by the swarms of black Lough Neagh flies, a particularly pointless insect which, lacking a mouth, is born merely to copulate and die.

Ruined **Mountjoy Castle** lurks behind a farm eight miles south of here near Washing Bay. Built in 1602 as part of the English campaign against Hugh O'Neill, it was strategically important, but, sadly, the setting is disappointing. If you pass through the town of **COALISLAND** on the way to Dungannon, check out the **Cornmill Heritage Centre** on Lineside (Mon–Fri 10am–5pm; £1.50), a mélange of artefacts and exhibits from the area's industrial past, particularly coal-mining, and photographs of local luminaries (including **Dennis Taylor**, the former world snooker champion). The mill itself ground to a halt in 1978 after providing employment for more than seventy years. Coalisland is a sleepy place, but becomes more animated during its annual **international music festival** in July.

Dungannon and around

DUNGANNON, about ten miles south of Cookstown, is a dreary town with no trace of its illustrious past as the hilltop seat of the O'Neills, from which they ruled Ulster for over five centuries. Outside town, on the A45 Coalisland Road, is the **Tyrone Crystal factory** (tours Mon–Fri 9.30am, 11am, noon, 2pm & 3pm; £2) where you can see demonstrations of glass-blowing and hand-cutting. There's excellent **B&B** and home cooking in the Georgian *Grange Lodge*, 7 Grange Rd (☎028/8778 4212; ⑤) and surprisingly good lakeside **camping** in *Dungannon Park* on Moy Rd (☎028/8772 7327). At **DONAGHMORE**, three miles northwest, there's another **high cross** dating from the tenth century in front of the parish church, though whoever reassembled it in the nineteenth century clearly botched the job as there's an obvious join halfway down the shaft.

Between Dungannon and Armagh, the picturesque village of **BENBURB** merits a detour. The tiny cottages in Main Street were once apple-peeling sheds and the parish church, dating from 1618, is one of the oldest still in regular use in Ireland. This stands next to the gates of a **Servite Priory** – the monastic order of Servants of the Virgin, founded in Florence in 1233, but which did not establish itself in Ireland until 1948. The priory grounds offer a pleasant stroll, but far better are the walks along the Blackwater River in **Benburb Valley Park** (daily 10am–dusk), where, perched on a rock a hundred feet or so above the water are the substantial remains of a **castle** built by Viscount Powerscourt in 1615.

A mile south of Benburb village in the canalside hamlet of **MILLTOWN** is the **Benburb Valley Heritage Centre** (Easter–Sept daily 9am–6pm, £2), housed in a nineteenth-century weaving factory and containing a range of old linen-making machinery and a model of the 1646 Battle of Benburb, at which a Scottish army suffered catastrophic losses in an encounter with Owen Roe O'Neill. There's a tea shop and a **hostel** here too (April–Sept; ☎028/3754 9752).

The Clogher Valley

Ten miles or so west of Benburb, the Blackwater River forms the **Clogher Valley**, a twenty-mile stretch running from the market town of Aughnacloy (near the Monaghan border) through the villages of **Ballygawley**, **Augher** and **Clogher** to **Fivemiletown**. There's nothing here of special interest, but the pleasantly rolling countryside is sufficient in itself to justify a diversion.

Three miles east of **BALLYGAWLEY**, to the north of Aughnacloy, is the **Grant Ancestral Homestead**, signposted off the A4 Dungannon road (April–Sept Mon–Sat noon–5pm, Sun 2–6pm; £1.50). The land here was once a smallholding farmed by the maternal ancestors of the eighteenth US president, **Ulysses S. Grant** (1822–85), whose life and exploits during the American Civil War are depicted in the visitor centre. A tiny two-roomed cottage has been restored and refurnished in typical nineteenth-century style, while the surrounding working farm displays agricultural implements from the same period and is stocked with traditional breeds. Three miles west of Ballygawley, and signposted to the north, is a hill known as **Errigal Keerogue**, where there is an unfinished high cross and a ruined fifteenth-century church dedicated to St Ciaran.

At one time a railway connected the valley's villages and at **AUGHER** you can sample home baking in the old station, which now houses *Rosamund's Coffee Shop*. The village makes much of its connection with the writer **William Carleton** (1794–1869), whose most notable novel was *Black Prophet*, a sombre tale of the Famine years. A summer school celebrates his life and work each August. The cottage where the author was born is a mile south in **Springtown** (signposted from Augher) and is part of the longer of two Carleton Trails which start and finish at Clogher. A couple of miles northwest of Augher lies **Knockmany Forest**, where a cairn on the top of a steep wooded hill protects a Bronze Age passage tomb, said to be the resting place of Ainé, the mother-goddess with whom Fionn Mac Cumhaill was infatuated. The stones in the tomb are inscribed with complex swirling patterns, but you can merely peer at them from a distance through a locked grille. The only accommodation in Augher is **B&B** at *Beech Lodge*, 41 Glenhoy Rd (☎028/8554 8106; ③).

CLOGHER, further west, is a little more lively, its main street climbing gently upwards to its eighteenth-century Church of Ireland **cathedral**. The village lays claim to the oldest bishopric in Ireland – its first bishop was St MacCartan, a disciple of St Patrick – and there is also evidence of the place's earlier significance. In the park behind the cathedral is a recently excavated Iron Age **hill fort**, thought to be the seat of the old kings of Oriel. Inside the cathedral is "the golden stone", dating from the ninth century, and a gallery of portraits of former bishops bearing expressions of appropriate solemnity. On the main street, *The Rathmore* and *The Trident Inn* pubs provide **meals** and you can also dine in the evenings at *Corick House*, 20 Corick Rd (☎028/8554 8216; ④), which offers the best **B&B** in the area. Alternatively, there's *River Furey House*, 24 Monaghan Rd (☎028/8254 8843; ②), set on a working farm half a mile south on the B83, and **camping** at the *Clogher Valley Country Caravan Park* (April–Oct; ☎028/8554 8932) in Fardross Forest, a mile west on the A4.

The **Clogher Valley Scenic Drive** is ideally accessed from **FIVEMILETOWN**, seven miles west of Clogher, though the lack of signposts at certain crucial junctions means it's best tackled with an Ordnance Survey map. The complete circuit runs for about 25 miles in a loop either side of the A4, but the southerly section is easily the more enjoyable and takes you into the most isolated part of the county outside the Sperrins. Head south from the crossroads in Fivemiletown and, once you've picked up the first sign, you'll find yourself on narrow woodland lanes gradually ascending towards **Slieve Beagh**. It's more than likely that sheep will be your only company unless you encounter the odd hiker on the Ulster Way, which you'll traverse as the route enters moorland. The whole valley can be surveyed from the car park viewpoint before you descend into **Fardross Forest**. The only other site of note is a few miles onwards. Look out to your left for a bizarre, three-tiered hilltop tower known as **Brackenridge's Folly**, named after George Brackenridge, who had the tower constructed as his mausoleum – thus compelling the squirearchy who had looked down on him during his lifetime to look up to him once he was dead. Fivemiletown has a couple of **hotels** on the main street, the *Valley* (☎028/8952 1505; ④) and *Four Ways* (☎028/8952 1260; *fourwayshotel@lakelands.net*; ⑤). There's also **camping** at *Round Lake Caravan Park* (☎028/8776 7259), half a mile north off the Fintona road.

COUNTY FERMANAGH

Fermanagh is justly famous for the intense beauty of its **lakes**. Much of the landscape is dominated by their waters which, along with numerous rivers, constitute more than a third of the county's area. Though there are several attractive smaller loughs, it's the two interconnected parts of **Lough Erne** which draw the most visitors – Lower Lough Erne in the northwest and Upper Lough Erne in the southeast. Surrounding hills are wooded with oak, ash and beech, producing a scene of fresh, verdant greens in spring and rich and rusty colours in autumn. The water's rippling surface reflects whatever light there is, mirroring the palest of skies through to the ruddiest of magenta sunsets. It's a breathtaking landscape, where land and water complement each other in a resonant, stately harmony.

In winter **Lower Lough Erne** has the character of an inland sea, dangerous waves making even the locals wary of sailing. Fabulous vistas reach across to the shores of richly wooded, mostly uninhabited islands, on which are scattered early Christian ruins and evidence of earlier pagan cultures. The **Upper Lough** is quieter and less spectacular. The waterway here is a delightful muddle of little inlets and islands, where waters are shallower and shorelines reedy. Fields have shocks of bristly marsh-grasses; definitions between land and water are blurred. There are plenty of opportunities for **water sports**, and the less energetic can get out onto the lakes by renting a boat or taking one of the lough cruises. **Walkers** will find the countryside to be mostly gentle hills and woods, which rise to small mountains in the south and west of the county, made accessible by the Ulster Way. For **cyclists**, there are well-surfaced, empty roads (though routes around the Upper Lough are harder to negotiate, with little lanes often leading only to some empty reed-infested shore).

The county town of **Enniskillen** sits at the point where the Upper and Lower loughs meet. Long a strategic bridging point, it has more amenities than the rest of Fermanagh put together and, consequently, is a good base for exploring the region. With your own transport you can easily access Fermanagh's impressive series of planters' castles, while the county's two stately houses, **Florence Court** and **Castle Coole**, are both open to the public.

Public transport in the county is limited to Ulsterbus – although reliable enough, only the main routes from Enniskillen are served with any frequency. If you look like a foreign tourist, then **hitching** along main roads is possible during the summer months, though never easy: County Fermanagh is as friendly as anywhere in the North, but it is one of the few remaining areas still patrolled by the British Army.

Some history

The region's early history was dictated by the intricacies of the Lough Erne waterways, once even more confused and forested than today. Recorded history begins with the **early Christians**, who slowly permeated Celtic culture and established religious foun-

FISHING IN FERMANAGH

There are countless opportunities for **angling** in Fermanagh, with the two Lough Ernes, Upper and Lower Lough Macnean, Lough Melvin, thirty smaller lakes and numerous rivers. A good move is to get a copy of *Fishing in Fermanagh* from the tourist office in Enniskillen, which can also tell you of any temporary restrictions and allow you to secure particular waters in advance. Most of the waters of Lough Erne are suitable for **coarse fishing** and you can obtain a rod licence for this from tackle shops or the tourist office; if you're fishing for salmon or trout you'll need a **game licence** too. Note that a game licence must be held if you're fishing from a boat on Lower Lough Erne. There are signs at virtually all the designated fisheries providing information on the fish available and whether you'll need a permit from the water's owner.

As you'd expect, there are plenty of angling **boats for rent** and several **tackle shops** including, in Enniskillen, Home, Field and Stream on Church St (☎028/6632 2114), and Mullen's Pet and Shooting Supplies on Sligo Rd (☎028/6632 4975). Other outlets are the Carlton Fishing Centre, Main St, Belleek (☎028/6865 8181) and Erne Tackle, Main St, Lisnaskea (☎028/6772 1969).

dations. They appreciated the seclusion of the lakes, and ruins of **medieval monasteries** remain. Centres of ecclesiastical power and learning were dotted on islands in the lough, and it is likely they were visited by pilgrims on their way to St Patrick's Purgatory, the shrine on Lough Derg, across the border in Donegal. More brutal invaders found the lough complex difficult to infiltrate. Neither Vikings nor Normans ever managed to control the region, and throughout the medieval and Tudor periods, the **English** similarly failed to subdue it.

The land was unruly and hard to govern even for the Irish. The **Maguires**, who ruled the west of the kingdom of Oriel (Fermanagh, Monaghan, south Tyrone and Louth) from 1250 until 1600, were originally based at **Lisnaskea**, but the cattle raids of neighbouring chiefs forced them to move to **Enniskillen** in the early fifteenth century. The town was to become strategically crucial as the determination of the English to dominate Ireland increased during the sixteenth century. As the crossing point through the waterways it was one of only three land routes into Ulster available to the invaders, the others being over the river near Ballyshannon and the Moyry Pass between Dundalk and Newry. So Enniskillen and the Maguire castle became the focus of **Irish resistance** to the Tudors. It was taken in 1594, although shortly afterwards retaken by the Maguires. After its recapture in 1607, the planters arrived.

The usurpers were obliged to build a **ring of castles** around the lough in order to maintain control of their domain: Crom, Portora, Tully, Castle Archdale, Crevenish and Caldwell. Most importantly of all, the old Maguire castle at Enniskillen was enlarged and fortified. Given sizeable grants from the English Crown, the planters of Enniskillen built an Established church, a fort and a royal school, turning the place into a British colonial town. It became a **Loyalist** stronghold, which successfully defended itself against the Irish during the Great Rebellion of 1641 and against an attack by James's troops in 1689. The Loyalists of Enniskillen formed a regiment that William of Orange chose as his personal guard at the Boyne. In the late eighteenth century, Enniskillen proved to be of key military importance, with the threat of a **French invasion** through the northwest of Ireland. By now the town had two royal regiments – a unique phenomenon.

At **Partition**, Fermanagh became a part of the state of Northern Ireland, despite its predominantly Catholic population and their cultural affinities with Cavan in the Republic, with whom it shares the tail end of the Lough Erne complex. In 1921, the county returned a Nationalist majority in local government elections, an undesirable state of affairs for the British. The abolition of proportional representation in 1922, and the **gerrymandering** which followed, ensured the subsequent Loyalist majority. With a history of such blatant injustices, a large Catholic population and a lengthy border with the Republic, Fermanagh was a nucleus of **Republican** activity and today still has strong Sinn Féin sympathies. It was the constituency of Fermanagh and South Tyrone that in April 1981 returned **Bobby Sands** as MP to Westminster. At the time of the election Sands was serving a fourteen-year prison sentence at the Maze prison (see p.595) for possession of weapons and was leading a **hunger strike** for political status for IRA prisoners. His death from starvation after 66 days made him one of the most famous IRA heroes, and he appears iconically in Republican murals (see pp.538 & 539) while also being remembered as a songwriter of no little merit thanks to Christy Moore's recordings of his songs *Back Home in Derry* and *McIlhatton*.

Today Fermanagh remains largely sustained by agricultural subsidies and its **tourist industry** centred on Enniskillen and Lough Erne. It is the furthest of the Northern Irish counties from Belfast and many of its people feel a closer affinity to the five Southern counties it borders, with which it has much cultural interplay, not least through traditional music.

Enniskillen and around

A pleasant, conservative little town of around eleven thousand people, **ENNISKILLEN** sits on an island like an ornamental buckle, two narrow ribbons of water passing each side connecting the Lower and Upper lough complexes. The strategic strength of this position has long been recognized – indeed, the town takes its name from *Innis Ceithleann*, "the island of Kathleen", wife of Balor (see p.497), who sought refuge here after a defeat in battle. Later the island became a Maguire stronghold before William Cole, a planter from Cornwall, was appointed governor in 1607. The town played a major role in the 1641 Rebellion and the later Williamite wars, the latter leading to the formation of its two famous regiments, the **Inniskilling Dragoons** and the **Royal Inniskilling Fusiliers**, which played a significant role in the victory at the Battle of the Boyne.

With its historic **castle** and proximity to the elegant **Castle Coole**, plus a town centre relatively unspoilt by shopping developments, Enniskillen is worthy of a day's visit in its own right. It's also ideally situated as a base for exploring Lough Erne and touring the attractive local countryside. However, the name Enniskillen is still associated primarily with one of the most devastating atrocities of the Troubles. On Remembrance Day 1987, an IRA **bomb** killed eleven and injured 61 people as they gathered to commemorate the dead of the two world wars. The resulting widespread outrage was instrumental in directing parts of the Republican movement towards seeking a political solution to the Troubles.

Arrival, information and accommodation

Enniskillen's **bus station** (☎028/6632 2633), on Wellington Road a block south of the High Street, has services from Belfast, Derry, Dublin, Dungannon, Omagh and Sligo, as well as local buses. Next door is the **tourist office** (July & Aug Mon–Fri 9am–7pm, Sat 10am–6pm, Sun 11am–5pm; rest of year Mon–Fri closes 5.30pm; Oct–Easter closed Sat & Sun; ☎028/6632 3110). You can get **fishing licences and permits** here, and book a place on one of the summer guided **tours** of the town or Lough Erne. The Round "O" jetty for **lough cruises** is signposted off the Derrygonnelly Road northwest of town – see p.655 for more details of boat rental.

Enniskillen is on the 192-mile **Kingfisher Cycling Trail** which skirts around the loughs and runs through Cavan and Leitrim (☎028/6632 0121 for details); for **bike**

rental, try the Lakeland Canoe Centre on Castle Island (☎028/6632 4250; £10 per day) – the island is served by free ferries (8am–midnight) which leave from the Lakeland Forum leisure centre just behind the tourist office. Two **car rental** outlets are Lochside Garages, Tempo Rd (☎028/6632 4366), and Cyril Treacy, 115 Sligo Rd (☎028/6632 2727). Aside from the banks, the **post office** on East Bridge Street will change money.

Accommodation

The tourist office has comprehensive **accommodation** lists and will book a room for a small fee. You could try the conveniently central, family-run *Railway Hotel*, 34 Forthill St (☎028/6632 2408; ④), the grander *Fort Lodge Hotel*, 74 Forthill St (☎028/6632 3275; *www.advernet.ie/fortlodge/default.htm*; ⑤) or the spacious, modern *Ashberry Hotel*, 14–20 Tempo Rd (☎028/6632 0333; *reception@ashberry.freeserve.co.uk*; ⑤). Alternatively, *Killyhevlin Hotel* (☎028/6632 3481; *www.killyhevlin.com*; ⑦), a mile south of town on the Dublin road, offers luxurious rooms in a lakeside setting.

There's plenty of **B&B** options – pick of the bunch is *Mountview Guesthouse*, 61 Irvinestown Rd (☎028/6632 3147; *wendy@mauricem.flyer.co.uk*; ④), with TVs in all the rooms and a snooker room; or try *Lackaboy Farm Guesthouse*, Tempo Rd (☎028/6632 2488; ③). If you're driving, there are two country houses to sample: *Killyreagh* (☎028/6638 7221; ④), a couple of miles southeast of town on the A4 in Tamlaght; and *Tempo Manor* (☎028/6654 1450; ⑦), a Gothic fantasy in Tempo, about six miles northeast on the B80.

There's a handy **hostel** and a **campsite** at the *Lakeland Canoe Centre* (☎028/6632 4250) on Castle Island just offshore of Enniskillen (behind the bus station). Alternatively, the nearest HINI hostel is at Castle Archdale Country Park, eleven miles north of Enniskillen (see p.657) – though the HINI is planning to open a new hostel in Enniskillen town itself in the near future. All the other campsites are well out of town: *Blaney Caravan and Camping Park* (☎028/6864 1634), eight miles to the northwest off the A46, directly behind the Blaney service station, is a beautifully situated and well-equipped site.

The Town and around

Waterways loop their way around the core of Enniskillen, their glassy surface imbuing the town with a pervasive sense of calm and reflecting the mini-turrets of **Enniskillen Castle**. Rebuilt by William Cole, it stands on the site of the old Maguire castle damaged by siege in 1594, next to the island's westerly bridges. Cole's additions show obvious Scottish characteristics in the turrets corbelled out from the angles of the main wall. The castle houses the **Watergate History and Heritage Centre** (July & Aug Mon, Sat & Sun 2–5pm, Tues–Fri 10am–5pm; rest of year closed Sun; Oct–April closed Sat; £2), depicting life in the fifteenth to seventeenth centuries through models and audiovisual exhibits, archeological displays in the arcaded barracks and, in the keep, the **Regimental Museum of the Royal Inniskilling Fusiliers** (same ticket), a proud and polished display of the uniforms, flags and paraphernalia of the town's historic regiments.

The centre invites strolling: the main street undulates gently, lined with confident Victorian and Edwardian town houses, thriving shops and smart pub fronts. This street changes its name five times between the bridges at either end, running from Ann Street to East Bridge Street: lanes fall to either side down towards the water, and clustered together are three fine church buildings, Church of Ireland, Catholic and Methodist. Much of Enniskillen's character comes from wealth based on the care of a colonial presence. Evidence of British influence is widespread: on a hill to the west the stately **Portora Royal School** overlooks the town, discreetly reminding one of the continued elitism in the social order. It was founded by Charles I in 1626, though the present building dates from 1777; old boys include **Oscar Wilde** – the pride of the school, until his trial for homosexuality – and **Samuel Beckett**. Over on a hill to the east, **Cole's Monument**, a statue commemorating one of Wellington's generals, keeps an eye on the town from Forthill Park; catch the park-keeper and pay to ascend to the viewing gallery (May–Sept daily 2–6pm; 70p). Immediately below is the war memorial, scene of the 1987 bombing.

On Down Street, just off the High Street, the **Buttermarket** is a craft and design centre with a range of artisans working onsite all year round. These wonderfully renovated dairy market buildings date from 1835, and during the summer you'll find music and theatrical displays in the enclosed, yet airy courtyard. You can buy direct from the craft workers or from the shop attached to *Rebecca's* excellent coffee shop. For something less sedate, Thursday's general street **market** on Forthill Street is worth a trip.

Castle Coole, Tamlaght and Brookeborough

Evidence of how the richest of the colonists lived is found about a mile southeast of the town centre at **Castle Coole**, designed by James Wyatt and completed in 1798 as the lakeside home of the Earls of Belmore (April, May & Sept Sat & Sun 1–6pm; June–Aug Mon–Wed & Fri–Sun 1–6pm; last tour starts at 5.15pm; £3; grounds open all year; car £2, pedestrians free). It can be approached either from the Dublin Road (signposted just opposite the Ardhowen Theatre) or across the golf course from the Castlecoole Road. A perfect Palladian-fronted building of silver Portland stone, with elegant Regency furnishings and recently restored interior of exquisite plasterwork, the castle sits in a beautiful landscaped garden, exemplifying cultivated naturalness, part of a huge 700-acre estate.

A couple of miles further east on the A4 at **TAMLAGHT** is the **Carrothers Family Heritage Museum** (April–Oct Mon–Sat 11am–7pm; £1.50), an astonishing collection of old books, swords, bottles and various curios hoarded over two hundred and fifty years. Another specialist collection hereabouts is in the village of **BROOKEBOROUGH**, seven miles east of Tamlaght, where Robert Coalter's **Cycle Museum** (April–Sept Mon–Fri 5–9pm, Sat 2–8pm; £2) displays more than sixty vintage cycles, including post office and butcher's boys' bikes and a real old treasure from the 1870s with levers instead of pedals.

Eating, drinking and entertainment

Enniskillen has a handful of good cheap places to **eat**. The best of the bunch is unquestionably *Oscar's*, 29 Belmore St (Mon–Sat 5–10.30pm; ☎028/6632 7037) which serves a range of East Asian and European dishes in a 'child-friendly' setting. Alternatively, *Franco's* (Mon–Sat noon–11.30pm, Sun noon–10pm; ☎028/6632 4424) in Queen Elizabeth Road serves mouth-watering pizza, pasta and seafood. *Peppercorn*, on Townhall Street by the post office, serves large lunches and good coffee. A lot of the **bars** along the main street also do decent pub food, particularly *Mulligan's* on Darling Street, and, on Townhall Street, the *Vintage* and *Pat's Bar* – above which the *Melvin House* **restaurant** offers lunches, grills and dinners. The restaurant at the Ardhowen Theatre, a mile east of town on the Dublin Road (Mon–Sat 11am–3.30pm; ☎028/6632 5440), is worth visiting for its waterside setting (you can also enjoy the view from an excellent bar), should you be hungry after a traipse around Castle Coole.

Enniskillen is also well served for **cafés**, many of which do excellent inexpensive meals. Most imaginative is the *Barbizon* on East Bridge Street, specializing in home-baked produce. *Johnston's The Jolly Sandwich* further uphill is worth a try, too, for its fresh-baked pastries and breads. Nearby *Leslie's* on Church Street offers salads and good ice cream.

There's no shortage of cheerful **pubs**, and bar extensions until 1am are commonplace in summer. **Rock bands** play at *The Crow's Nest* in the main street every night and on Fridays and Saturdays at *Mulligan's* on Darling Street, while the *Fort Lodge Hotel*, Forthill Street, is a bastion of the local **country and Irish** scene at the weekends. For **traditional music** try the *Bush*, Townhall Street (Mon), the *Railway Hotel*, Forthill Street (Sun), or, on the main street, *Blakes of the Hollow* at the weekends, a traditional Victorian bar with original fittings, a fine pint and a chatty crowd. One of the best local traditional sessions is at *The Vintage*, Townhall Street (Fri), that is the rest of the time a disco bar with video jukebox and occasional rock bands. At the west end of town, the *Tippler's Brook* is the place for a quiet drink or to play cards with local farmers in town for the night. As ever, **discos** are in the pubs and hotels, in particular Forthill Street's *Willie Rumblers* (Wed, with other music Thurs-Sun) and the *Fort Lodge Hotel* on Saturday.

The hub of Enniskillen's **arts scene** is the Ardhowen Theatre (see above), which has a year-round programme of top-quality drama, film and ballet, and hosts a great range of music events – traditional Irish, jazz, opera, country, classical – as well as productions by local community groups and an annual **theatre festival** in March. Check with the tourist office for dates of the Fermanagh *feis* in March – lots of traditional music, dancing, drama and crafts – and the *Fleadh*, the competitive traditional music festival, in June. The new Enniskillen Complex, on Factory Road, is a seven-screen **cinema** showing the usual range of general release films.

Lough Erne

Lough Erne has had a profound effect on the history of Fermanagh. The earliest people to settle in the region lived on and around the two lakes; many of the islands here are in fact *crannógs* (early Celtic artificial islands). The lough's myriad connecting waterways were impenetrable to outsiders, protecting the settlers from invaders and creating an enduring cultural isolation. Evidence from stone carving suggests that

LOUGH ERNE CRUISES AND RENTALS

The *MV Kestrel*, operated by Erne Tours (☎028/6632 2882), sails from the **Round "O" jetty** northwest of Enniskillen (see p.652) around the Lower Lough, calling at Devenish Island (May & June Sun 2.30pm; July & Aug daily 10.30am, 2.15pm & 4.15pm; Sept Tues, Sat & Sun 2.30pm; morning cruises £5, afternoons £6). There are also additional evening cruises that include the Upper Lough (July & Aug Tues, Thurs & Sun 7.15pm; £6).

The *Inishcruiser* sails from the Inishclare restaurant complex at **Killadeas**, on the B82 Kesh road, on a two-hour trip around the Lower Lough (Wed–Sun: April–June & Sept 2.30pm & 5.30pm; July & Aug 11.30am, 2.30pm, 5.30pm & 7.30pm; ☎028/6862 1493; £7).

A "Viking longship" cruises the Upper Lough from the Share Holiday Village at **Smith's Strand**, signposted off the Lisnaskea–Derrylin road (April–June & Sept Sat & Sun 3pm; July & Aug Mon, Wed & Fri–Sun 3pm; ☎028/6772 2122; £4).

Renting your own boat is another possibility and there are a number of operators. Most offer open rowing boats, with or without outboard motor, though some have larger 20ft boats available. Prices range accordingly from £4 per hour to £75 for a full day, depending on the operator and boat size. The tourist office in Enniskillen has lists of rental companies and, if you fancy something grander, of cruisers available for rent (weekly prices in high season range from £565 for smaller boats to £1500 for 8-berth specials). Unless you're going out on a small lake you should always let the boat owner know where you're going and ask to borrow navigation charts – Lough Erne can be dangerous, especially outside the summer months.

Christianity was accepted far more slowly here than elsewhere: several pagan idols have been found on Christian sites, and the early Christian remains to be found on the islands show the strong influence of pagan culture. Here, Christian carving has something of the stark symmetry and vacancy of expression found in pagan statues. Particularly suggestive of earlier cults is the persistence of the human head motif in stone carving – in pagan times a symbol of divinity and the most important of religious symbols.

Devenish Island and **White Island**, the most popular of the Erne's ancient sites, are on the Lower Lough, as is **Boa Island** in the far north, which is linked to the mainland by a bridge at each end. The **Upper Lough** is less rewarding, but has interesting spots which repay a leisurely dawdle. Aside from **cruising** the waterways (see box on p.655) and visiting the islands, there are a number of minor attractions around the loughs that are worth dropping into during your stay. Perhaps the most impressive are the early seventeenth-century planters' **castles** scattered around the shoreline.

Devenish Island and around

If you don't have transport of your own, the easiest place to visit from Enniskillen is **Devenish Island**, in the south of the Lower Lough. There are **ferries** running continuously to the island from Trory Point, three miles north of Enniskillen off the A32 Irvinestown road (April–Sept Tues–Sat 10am–6pm, Sun 2–6pm; £2.25, includes admission to tower and museum). It's advisable to check times with the tourist office before setting out as poor weather can sometimes delay or cancel departures. To get to Trory Point from Enniskillen take one of the infrequent buses to Irvinestown or Pettigo.

A monastic settlement was founded on Devenish by St Molaise in the sixth century and became so important during the early Christian period that it had 1500 novices attached. Though plundered by Vikings in the ninth century and again in the twelfth, it continued to be an important religious centre up until the plantations. It's a delightful setting, not far from the lough shore, and the ruins are considerable, spanning the entire medieval period. Most impressive are the sturdy **oratory** and perfect **round tower**, both from the twelfth century; **St Molaise's Church**, a century older; and the ruined **Augustinian priory**, a fifteenth-century reconstruction of an earlier abbey. The priory has a fine Gothic sacristy door decorated with birds and vines. To the south is one of Ireland's finest **high crosses**, with highly complex, delicate carving. Other treasures found here – such as an early eleventh-century book shrine, the Soiscel Molaise – are now kept in the National Museum in Dublin, while the island's own small **museum** (joint ticket with ferry, or 75p if you've arrived in your own boat) includes other less notable relics and detailed information about Devenish itself.

Monea Castle (free open access), seven miles northwest of Enniskillen off the B81, is a particularly fine ruin of a planters' castle in a beautiful setting at the end of a beech-lined lane. Built around 1618, it bears the signs of Scottish influence in its design, with similar features to the reworked Maguire castle in Enniskillen. It was destroyed by fire in the Great Rebellion of 1641 and by Jacobite armies in 1689, and was eventually abandoned in 1750 after another fire. Five miles further north, beyond Derrygonnelly, the fortified house and bawn of restored **Tully Castle** (April–Sept Tues–Sat 10am–6pm, Sun 2–6pm; £1), itself burned by the Maguires in 1641, sits down by the lough shore. Further to the west, there are tremendous views of the lough and surrounds from **Lough Navar Forest** (daily 10am–dusk; car £2.50).

Castle Caldwell forest and Belleek

The **forest of Castle Caldwell**, on the A47 near the western extremity of Lower Lough Erne, is formed by two narrow promontories which make it a natural breeding site for waterfowl such as the common scoter (a species of duck) and a habitat of rarities such as the hen harrier, peregrine falcon and pine marten. However, its seventeenth-century **castle** has long since fallen into dilapidation and the surrounding estate is now a commercial, state-owned forest of spruce, pine and larch. At the castle's entrance look out for the giant stone fiddle in front of the gate lodge, the sobering memorial to Denis McCabe, a local musician who in 1770 tumbled from the Caldwells' barge while drunk, and drowned. Its inscription 'DDD' supposedly stands for "Denis died drunk"!

Lively **BELLEEK**, five miles further west, holds the **Fiddle Stone Festival** every June in McCabe's memory. Every Tuesday, the village streets are packed with the stalls of one of the area's liveliest and largest **markets**. Its other main attraction is the famous **Belleek Pottery** (tours every 20min; Mon–Fri 9.15am–12.15pm & 2.15pm–4.15pm; £2), which offers interesting tours of the works and a chance to buy the rather fussy products. On Main Street you'll find **Fermanagh Crystal** (Mon–Sat 10am–5pm), where you can watch the creation of glassware and even, funds permitting, commission your own piece. Across the river on the main A46 Enniskillen Road is the **Erne Gateway Centre**, which houses a **tourist office** (Easter–Sept daily 10.30am–6pm; ☎028/6865 8866) and the the **Explore Erne Exhibition** (same hours; £1), where a giant video wall screens an explanation of how the lake was formed and how it moulded the lives of lakeside dwellers over the centuries.

Belleek has grand **accommodation** at the recently restored *Hotel Carlton* (☎028/6665 8282; *www.lakelands.net/hotelcarlton*; ⑥) at the bottom of Main Street, and **B&B** further up the road in the *Fiddlestone* pub (☎028/6865 8008; ③). The village has a couple of cafés and *The Black Cat* provides excellent bar meals in an atmospheric setting. **Bikes** can be rented from Belleek Bicycle Hire on Main St (☎028/6865 8181).

Killadeas, Irvinestown and Castle Archdale

In **KILLADEAS** churchyard, seven miles north of Enniskillen on the eastern side of the lough (take the B82), stands the **Bishop's Stone**, carved some time between the ninth and eleventh centuries. It's one of the most striking examples of the appearance of pre-Christian images in early Christian culture, having a startled pagan-style face on one side and a bishop with bell and crozier on the other. There are other interesting carved stones in the graveyard, too, including two cross slabs and a rounded pillar, possibly a pagan phallic stone. If you want to get out onto the water from here, Manor House Marine (☎028/6634 8267) rents **motor boats** for £40 for a half-day, £60 for a full day.

The only site of any interest in **IRVINESTOWN**, a few miles northeast and inland, is Dr Patrick Delany's **church** built in 1734, though the clock tower and pinnacled battlements are all that remain. Jonathan Swift played an unlikely cupid to the rector, introducing him to court favourite and London society hostess, Mary Granville. They married, and Delany later became Dean of Down, while she left a revealing record of eighteenth-century Anglo-Irish society and gossip, gathered during their visits to the Big Houses. Irvinestown has a few **B&Bs**, including the central *Harlow's*, 60–62 Main St (☎028/6862 1241; ④) and the more rurally-set *Lettermoney House* on the Enniskillen–Omagh road (☎028/6638 8347; ②). Just outside town there's accommodation and **equestrian** activities in the splendid, woodland-situated *Necarne Castle* (☎028/6862 1919; ④); to get there take the road behind the town-centre clock and turn right at its end.

To immerse yourself thoroughly in the beauty of the lough scenery, you could hardly do better than stay in the HINI **hostel** set in the **Castle Archdale** forest park (March–Oct; ☎028/6862 8118), near Lisnarick, about five miles west of Irvinestown. If you're relying on public transport, the Pettigo **bus** (4 daily) will drop you a mile away at the park entrance; otherwise take one of the buses from Enniskillen to Kesh (4 daily) as far as Lisnarick and walk or hitch. The hostel is a perfect place for getting out to the lough and is a stone's throw from a large caravan park and **campsite** (☎028/6862 1333), which has a small supermarket and a fast-food outlet in high season. The **ferry** to White Island (see below) leaves from nearby, and you can also **rent boats** and **bikes** here in July and August. And, should you fancy exploring the area on **horseback**, Drumhoney Riding Stables (☎028/6862 1892), is handily adjacent too.

White Island

Mounted on the wall of a **ruined abbey**, the seven early Christian carvings of **White Island** look eerily pagan. Found early last century, they are thought to be caryatids – columns in human form – from a monastic church of the ninth to eleventh centuries. The most disconcerting statue is the lewd female figure known as a **Sheila-na-Gig**, with bulging cheeks, a big grin, open legs and arms pointing to her genitals. This could be a female fertility figure, a warning to monks of the sins of the flesh, or an expression of the demoniacal power of women, designed to ward off evil. (In the epic *Taín Bó Cuailngè*, Cúchulainn was stopped by an army of a hundred and fifty women led by their female chieftain Scannlach. Their only weapon was their display of nakedness, from which the boy Cúchulainn had to avert his face.)

Less equivocal figures continue left to right: a seated **Christ** figure holding the Gospels on his knees; a hooded figure with bell and crozier, possibly **St Anthony**; **David** carrying a shepherd's staff, his hand towards his mouth showing his role as author and singer; **Christ the Warrior** holding two griffins by the scruff of their necks; and another **Christ** figure with a fringe of curly hair wearing a brooch on his left shoulder and carrying a sword and shield – here he is the King of Glory at his Second Coming. There is an unfinished seventh stone and, on the far right, a carved head with a downturned mouth which is probably later than the other statues. The church of White Island also contains eleventh-century gravestones; the large earthworks round the outside date from an earlier monastery.

A **ferry** from Castle Archdale Country Park marina (☎028/6862 1333) runs to White Island on the hour (April–June Sat & Sun 11am–6pm; July & Aug daily 10am–6pm; £3).

Boa Island and around

One of the most evocative of the carvings of Lough Erne is the double-faced Janus figure of **Boa Island**, at the northern end of the Lower Lough – barely an island at all these days, as it's connected to the mainland by bridges. The landmark to look out for is **Caldragh cemetery**, signposted off the A47 about a mile west of Lusty Beg Island. Follow the signs down a lane and the graveyard is through a gate to your left.

This ancient Christian burial ground of broken moss-covered tombstones, shaded by low, encircling hazel trees, has an almost druidic setting. Here you'll find the **Janus figure**, an idol of yellow stone with very bold symmetrical features. It has the phallus on one side, and a belt and crossed limbs on the other. The figure was probably an invocation of fertility and a depiction of a god-hero, the belt being a reference to the bearing of weapons. Alongside it stands the smaller **"Lusty Man"**, so called since it was moved here from nearby Lustymore Island. This idol has only one eye fully carved, which may be to indicate blindness – Cúchulainn had a number of encounters with war goddesses, divine hags described as blind in the left eye.

Quiet **Lusty Beg Island** just off Boa Island is a popular weekend retreat for Enniskillen people: you'll find luxury **log cabins** with saunas (☎028/6863 2032; *lustybeg@dial.pipex.com*; £290–£490 a week; sleep 4–6), **B&B** in the guesthouse (⑤), **canoeing**, gentle **walks** and a **restaurant**. A free car-ferry will take you across; dial ☎0 from the telephone on the pier.

Kesh

KESH, four and a half miles east of Boa Island, is a possible overnight stop. **Accommodation** options in the village include the *Lough Erne Hotel*, Main St (☎028/6863 1275; *www.lakelands.net/loughernehotel*; ⑤), in a fine riverside setting with a restaurant and weekend entertainment, while **B&B** is available at *Roscolban House*, Enniskillen Rd (☎028/6863 1096; ②). If you've transport there's also the option of staying in the *Ardess Craft Centre* (☎028/6863 1267; ④), housed in a fine Georgian rectory, which offers day and residential courses in various crafts (from £25 per day); take the Enniskillen Road out of Kesh, turn left just before the police barracks, take a hard right, then follow the road for a mile and a half.

There are a few places to **eat** in Kesh, including the excellent *Riverside Restaurant*, 9 Main St (Tues–Sun 5–9.30pm & Sun lunch; ☎028/6863 2342), serving specialities such as duckling, and, further up the street, *Sarah Jane's Diner and Bakery* (Mon–Sat 9am–10.30pm), offering fine, inexpensive home cooking.

The chief recommendation of Kesh is its position on the lough. You can rent **motor boats** here from Mr R.A. Graham, Manville House (☎028/6863 1668; £25 a day, or £60 if he comes along and shows you the best trout spots), as well as from *Erinona Boats*, Boa Island Bridge (☎028/6863 2328; £40 a day). *Drumrush Watersports*, Boa Island Rd (☎028/6863 1578) offers everything from canoeing to jet-ski rental to banana boat rides; it also has its own guesthouse (③) and offers **camping** at its *Lakeland Caravan Park*. There's also camping available at *Loaneden Caravan Park* at Muckross Bay (☎028/6863 1603) and in *Clonelly Forest* (☎028/6863 1253), three miles north.

Upper Lough Erne and Lisnaskea

Upper Lough Erne holds nothing like the interest of the Lower lough, nor the scenic splendour, although it does have the best-preserved of the planters' castles nearby. The most you're really likely to do around the lough is disturb the anglers or get lost among its crazy causeways and waterways – fun on a boat, but frustrating on dry land.

Should you be tempted to venture further into the maze of reeds and water, a "Viking longship" runs **cruises** (see box on p.655) from the *Share Holiday Centre* (☎028/6722 2122; *www.village.com*) at Smith's Strand, signposted off the Lisnaskea–Derrylin road, where they also offer water-based activity holidays with facilities for disabled travellers, and B&B, self-catering chalets and a campsite.

The National Trust **Crom Estate** (April–Sept Mon–Sat 10am–6pm, Sun noon–6pm; car or boat £3), three miles southwest of Newtownbutler on the eastern shore of the lough, has the largest surviving area of **oak woodland** in Northern Ireland, home to rare species such as the purple hairstreak and wood white butterflies. There's a café and interpretive centre here, and you can rent **rowing boats** too. Unfortunately, the modern Crom Castle is privately occupied and not open to the public, though you can visit the ruins of the **old castle**. The estate has renovated courtyard **cottages** (☎028/4488 1204; £190–£480 per week for 2–6 people). The elegantly chiselled gravestones on **Galoon Island**, with their reliefs of skull and crossbones, hourglass and coffin, are worth a detour if you have transport. *Ports House*, right by the waterside at Ports, not far from Newtownbutler, offers **B&B** (☎028/6773 8528; ③).

Almost five miles north of Newtownbutler, **Castle Balfour** at **LISNASKEA** was built for Sir James Balfour, a Scottish planter, in the early seventeenth century and shows strong Scottish characteristics in the turrets and parapets, high-pitched gables and tall chimneys. Lisnaskea itself is one of Fermanagh's few towns – and a small one at that. Its tiny nineteenth-century Cornmarket yard has an early Christian **carved cross** depicting Adam and Eve beneath a tree, and the library up the road towards Enniskillen contains a diminutive but interesting **folk museum** (Mon, Tues & Fri 10am–5.30pm, Wed 10am–7.30pm, Sat 10am–1pm; free), with displays on local Gaelic traditions and festivals, including plenty of detail on the making of poteen. The town has several lively **bars** along Main Street, including the wonderfully named *Shoe the Donkey,* while the best place to **eat** is unquestionably the *Donn Carragh Hotel,* which specializes in seafood and provides the only local **accommodation** (☎028/6772 1206; ⑤), in a newly renovated setting. There's a **campsite** two miles north of Lisnaskea at Mullynascarthy (☎028/6772 1040).

Western Fermanagh

The stretch of countryside on the western edge of the county offers some good **walking** opportunities, particularly in the hills to the south. The **Ulster Way**, which runs northwest from the Upper Lough and east towards Tyrone, makes the riches of the terrain easily accessible.

This region also has two attractions that are well worth seeking out. The magnificent eighteenth-century **Florence Court** is the most assured achievement of the colonists, built a hundred and fifty years after the initial defensive planters' castles. If you have your own transport, a visit to the house can be combined with an hour or so at the **Marble Arch Caves**, the finest cave-system in Northern Ireland. Walkers can reach both along the Ulster Way, accessible from the A4 near Belcoo; the path runs four miles south past Lower Lough Macnean to the Marble Arch Caves and then a further five miles east to Florence Court.

Florence Court

The magnificent three-storey mansion of **Florence Court**, about eight miles southwest of Enniskillen (April & Sept Sat & Sun 1–6pm; May–Aug Mon & Wed–Sun 1–6pm; £3; grounds and forest park open all year 10am–dusk; £2 per car), was commissioned by John Cole, one of the Earls of Enniskillen, and named after his wife. The house, com-

THE ULSTER WAY IN WESTERN FERMANAGH

From Marble Arch Caves the **Ulster Way** heads past Lower and Upper Lough Macnean before taking you through the bog and granite heights of the Cuilcagh Mountains to **Ballintempo Forest**, where there are fabulous views over the loughs. The Way then continues north, through the **Lough Navar Forest**, a well-groomed conifer plantation with tarmacked roads and shorter trails. Although a great deal of fir plantation walking is dark and frustrating, this forest does, at points, provide some of the most spectacular **views** in Fermanagh, looking over Lower Lough Erne and the mountains of Tyrone, Donegal, Leitrim and Sligo. The Lough Navar Forest also sustains a small herd of red deer, as well as wild goats, foxes, badgers, hares and red squirrels.

Before setting out, it's well worth obtaining a copy of the *The Ulster Way: Southwest Section* from the tourist office in Enniskillen. This describes in detail the five connected trails constituting the Way's route through the county.

Accommodation along the Way is limited. There are a half a dozen B&Bs near **BELCOO**, two and a half miles west from the trail's ascent to the Ballintempo Forest: try *Bella Vista*, Cottage Drive (☎028/6638 6469; ③), or *Corralea Lodge*, Corralea (☎028/6638 6325; ③). There's a **campsite** and holiday cottages (£55 per cottage per night) in the *Tir Navar Holiday Village* (☎028/6864 1673) in **DERRYGONNELLY**, off the A46. A bit further away from the route of the Way, west near the border at **GARRISON** (take the minor road from Derrygonnelly), the *Lough Melvin Holiday Centre* (☎028/6865 8142; booking essential) offers caving, canoeing, wind-surfing and hill-walking – prices are from £5 per half-day, £55 per weekend. The centre has accommodation and camping, although you should ring ahead to check on space if you want to stop here.

pleted around 1775, is notable for its recently restored rococo plasterwork and rare Irish furnishings; the dining room is especially lavish, its ceiling hosting a cloud of cherubs with eagles flying out of a duck-egg blue sky. To get to the house from Enniskillen follow the A4 Sligo Road for three miles, branching off on the A32 Swanlinbar Road and taking the signposted right turn four miles further on. The Swanlinbar-bound **bus** passes this last junction, from where it's a mile's walk to the house.

You can **stay** in the pretty *Rose Cottage* in the Florence Court walled garden, well-equipped and with two double bedrooms (☎028/9571 0721; £190–£475 per week). There's award-winning accommodation nearby at *Arch Tullyhona House*, 59 Marble Arch Rd (☎028/6634 8452; *tullyguest60@hotmail.com*; ③), whose **restaurant** (Easter & June–Aug daily 10am–7pm) offers hearty home cooking; booking is essential.

The Marble Arch Caves

Fermanagh's caves are renowned, and while some are for experts only, the most spectacular system of all – the **Marble Arch Caves**, five miles west of Florence Court – is accessible to anyone. A tour of the system lasts around an hour and a quarter, beginning with a boat journey along a **subterranean river**, then on through brilliantly lit chambers, calcite-walled and dripping with stalactites and fragile mineral veils. **Tours** of the caves (daily: mid-March to June & Sept 10am–4.30pm; July & Aug 10am–5pm; ☎028/6634 8855; £6) are sometimes booked out by parties, so it makes sense to call ahead to check that your journey won't be wasted; in a steady Irish downpour the caves can be flooded, so check weather reports as well. You'll need to wear sturdy walking shoes and bring warm clothing as the temperature can drop significantly.

From whichever direction you approach the caves, you'll travel along the **Marlbank Scenic Loop**, with tremendous views of Lower Lough Macnean, and on either side you'll see limestone-flagged fields, much like those of the Burren in County Clare. It was fifty thousand years of gentle water seepage through the limestone that deposited the calcite for the amazing stalactite growths in the caves below.

Almost opposite the caves' entrance is the **Legnabrocky Trail** which runs through rugged limestone scenery and peatland to the shale covered slopes of **Cuilcagh Mountain**. This forms part of an environmental conservation area and offers a strenuous six- or seven-hour walk to the mountain's summit and back. A part of the Marble Arch centre is now devoted to exhibits and display describing the restoration of the mountain park's damaged peatland and bogland habitats.

travel details

Buses

The Sperrin Link runs from Omagh (Mon–Fri 2.15pm) through Gortin, Plumbridge and the Sperrins, and then across the County Derry border to Draperstown and Maghera (return service departs Maghera Mon–Fri 10.15am).

Cookstown to: Coalisland (9 Mon–Fri, 7 Sat, 2 Sun; 30min); Dungannon (9 Mon–Fri, 7 Sat, 2 Sun; 40min); Magherafelt (14 Mon–Fri, 11 Sat, 2 Sun; 30min); Moneymore (13 Mon–Fri, 10 Sat, 2 Sun; 15min).

Dungannon to: Armagh (7 Mon–Fri, 4 Sat; 45min); Coalisland (22 Mon–Fri; 12 Sat, 4 Sun; 20min); Cookstown (9 Mon–Fri, 7 Sat, 2 Sun; 40min); Omagh (8 Mon–Fri, 4 Sat; 1hr 20min).

Enniskillen to: Armagh (1 Mon–Sat; 1hr 50min); Ballyshannon (5 Mon–Sat, 3 Sun; 1hr); Belfast (8 Mon–Fri, 7 Sat, 6 Sun; 2hr 15min); Belleek (5 Mon–Sat, 3 Sun; 45min); Bundoran (5 Mon–Sat, 3

Sun; 1hr 10min); Clones (5 Mon–Sat, 3 Sun; 1hr 5min); Derry (7 Mon–Fri, 5 Sat, 4 Sun; 2hr 40min); Derrygonnelly (5 Mon–Sat; 25min); Dublin (3 daily; 3hr 45min); Fivemiletown (5 Mon–Fri, 4 Sat; 45min); Irvinestown (7 Mon–Fri, 4 Sat; 25 min); Kesh (5 Mon–Fri, 3 Sat; 45min); Lisnarick (6 Mon–Fri, 3 Sat; 35min); Lisnaskea (7 Mon–Fri, 5 Sat, 2 Sun; 30min); Monaghan (2 Mon–Sat; 1hr 20min); Omagh (7 Mon–Fri, 5 Sat, 4 Sun; 1hr 10min); Pettigo (4 Mon–Fri, 3 Sat; 1hr); Sligo (3 Mon–Sat, 1 Sun; 1hr 25min).

Omagh to: Athlone (1 Mon–Sat; 4hr); Belfast (7 Mon–Sat, 5 Sun; 1hr 50min); Cahir (1 daily; 7hr 30min); Castlederg (5 Mon–Fri, 1 Sat; 50min); Cookstown (1 daily; 1hr 10min); Cork (1 daily; 9hr); Cranagh (2 Tues & Fri; 55min); Derry (12 daily; 1hr 45min); Dublin (6 Mon–Sat, 5 Sun; 3hr); Dungannon (7 Mon–Fri, 5 Sat; 1hr 15min); Enniskillen (8 Mon–Fri, 5 Sat, 1 Sun; 1hr 10min); Gortin (5 Mon–Sat; 35min); Kesh (2 Mon & Thurs; 45min); Letterkenny (3 daily; 1hr); Strabane (13 Mon–Fri, 11 Sat, 6 Sun; 35min); the Ulster American Folk Park (13 Mon–Fri, 11 Sat, 6 Sun; 15min).

Strabane to: Belfast (7 Mon–Sat, 4 Sun; 2hr 30min); Castlederg (8 Mon–Fri, 5 Sat; 35min); Derry (18 Mon–Fri, 15 Sat, 9 Sun; 40min); Dublin (5 Mon–Sat, 3 Sun; 4hr); Enniskillen (1 daily; 3hr); Omagh (14 Mon–Fri, 10 Sat, 5 Sun; 35min).

PART THREE

THE CONTEXTS

THE HISTORICAL FRAMEWORK

An understanding of Ireland's history is essential in order to make sense of its troubled present. In these few pages, we cannot do more than provide a brief outline of that history, in the hope that it will serve as a starting point for further reading and discussion.

EARLIEST INHABITANTS

During the last Ice Age, when most of the country was covered by an icecap, low sea levels meant that Ireland was attached to Britain, and Britain to the European continent. As the climate warmed (from about 13,000 BC), and the ice gradually retreated, sea levels rose and the broad land connection between Ireland and Britain began to recede to one or more narrow land bridges. The first human inhabitants arrived over these routes, probably from Scotland, some time after 8000 BC. By about 7000 BC the land bridges were submerged and Ireland geographically isolated, while Britain remained connected to continental Europe for much longer.

The first inhabitants, **Mesolithic** (middle Stone Age) hunter-gatherers, found a densely forested land that could only be penetrated easily along its waterways, and, for the most part, they seem to have lived close to the sea, rivers and lakes (flint work from the period has been found in Antrim, Down, Louth and Dublin). Their way of life continued undisturbed until, from about 3500 BC, **Neolithic** (late Stone Age) farmers began arriving by sea, probably from Britain. With skills in animal and crop husbandry, weaving and pottery, the new arrivals used their stone axes to clear large tracts of forest for cultivation. The hunter-gatherer and agricultural economies were, however, complementary, and it is thought the two peoples co-existed for many centuries before the older way of life was gradually assimilated by the new.

The Neolithic people were the creators of Ireland's **megalithic remains**. There are more than 1200 such burial sites scattered throughout the country, with the greatest concentrations in the north and west. Such sites are also found all along the Atlantic seaboard of Europe, from Spain to Scandinavia – a sign of Ireland's ancestral and cultural links with the rest of Europe at this time and, in particular, with the peoples of Britain and Brittany.

The most dramatic and well-known megalithic remains in Ireland are the great **passage graves** at Knowth and Newgrange in County Meath, with their elaborate spiral engravings, cut into the stone entirely without the use of metal tools. It is thought that the function of these tombs was not purely religious or ceremonial; they were also territorial markers, which at times of population pressure staked a communal claim to the surrounding lands. Little is known of the people themselves, although their civilization was long-lasting, with thousands of years separating the earliest and the latest megalithic constructions. Only rarely have skeletons been found in the graves (in most cases only the cremated remains of bones are discovered), but what few there have been seem to indicate a short, dark, hairy people with a life expectancy of little more than 35 years.

Around 2000 BC the use of bronze spread to Ireland, though it is uncertain whether this was the result of the commercial contacts of the existing population or the migration of a new people. The next significant technological development, generally associated with the arrival of the Celts, was the introduction of iron around 700 BC.

THE CELTS

The **Celts** were an Indo-European group called Keltoi by the Greeks and Galli by the Romans, who spread south from central Europe into Italy and Spain and west through France and Britain. By 500 BC, Celtic language and culture were dominant in Ireland, but there is no evidence of any large-scale invasion or social upheaval. It is probably more accurate to think of their arrival as a gradual and relatively peaceful process that took place over hundreds of years.

Their settlements took the form of ring forts (or raths), and they divided the island into about one hundred small **kingdoms** or *Tuatha*, each with its own king. The *Tuatha* were grouped into the Five Fifths or provinces, which were Ulster (*Ulaid*), Meath (*Midhe*), Leinster (*Laigin*), Munster (*Muma*) and Connacht (which retains its Irish spelling). In theory, the High King (*Ard Rí*) ruled over all from his throne on the Hill of Tara – a place long associated with mysterious power – although only rarely did any one figure of sufficient strength emerge to lay undisputed claim to that title.

It is hard to separate the truth about the Celts from the stories they told of themselves. Theirs was an oral culture in which the immortality to be gained from being the hero of an epic tale was highly prized. With an enthusiasm for war little short of bloodthirsty, they celebrated battles decided by the single combat of great champions, guided and aided by the unpredictable whims of the gods. They also appropriated the religion and beliefs already current in Ireland and, although they had nothing to do with their building, megalithic sites continued to have great symbolic significance for them.

The two greatest heroes of the epics, **Cúchulainn** and **Fionn Mac Cumhaill** (Finn McCool), have been tentatively identified as warrior champions of the second and third centuries, transformed by legend into semi-divinities in much the same way as King Arthur was in England.

THE COMING OF CHRISTIANITY

The **christianization** of Ireland began as early as the fourth century AD, well before the arrival of St Patrick (whose existence is now the subject of some controversy). Vestiges did survive of the previous religion of the Celts, but after the collapse of the Roman Empire, Ireland assumed a position at the very forefront of European Christianity. (Also around this time the people of Ireland took the name Goidil – Gaels – for themselves from the Welsh Gwyddyl.)

In the sixth century, the early Christian leaders successfully adapted established church organization to suit the scattered and tribal nature of Gaelic society by setting up monastic foundations. The country became a haven for religious orders, the only sources of learning at this time. The sheer impassability of much of the landscape supported monastic development, and many of the great Irish monasteries, such as St Enda's on the Aran Islands, Clonmacnois in County Offaly and Clonard in County Meath, date from this period. **Ogham**, the Celtic line-based writing system seen on standing stones, was rapidly supplanted by the religious scholars, who introduced Latin. The first – and best-known – of their richly illuminated Latin manuscripts, the **Book of Kells**, can be seen in the Library of Trinity College, Dublin.

The traditional view of these times as "Dark Ages" of terror and chaos throughout Europe is not supported by events in Ireland. Although intertribal warfare was constant, the country enjoyed relative cultural and religious stability. Alongside this, well-established diplomatic and trading contact along the Atlantic seaboard encouraged the development of a strong missionary impulse in Irish Christianity. Between 500 and 800 the Irish church spread the gospel widely across the Continent. The most prominent of the many missionaries was St Columban, who founded monasteries in France, Switzerland, Germany and Austria, and at Bobbio in Italy – where he died in 615.

INVASION: VIKINGS AND NORMANS

From 795, Ireland was increasingly plagued by destructive **Viking raids**, in which many of the great monasteries were plundered and burned (though many more were destroyed as a result of indigenous intertribal warfare in the eighth and ninth centuries). The instability of the period led to the development of the **round towers**, which were used as lookout posts and places of sanctuary – and which characterize early Irish architecture. The Viking raids culminated in a full-scale invasion in 914 and the subsequent founding of walled cities, usually at the mouths of rivers, such as Dublin, Wexford, Waterford, Youghal, Cork, Bantry and Limerick. The decisive defeat of the Danes by the High King Brian Boru at the Battle of Clontarf in 1014 at least spared Ireland from becoming a Viking colony. However, the death of Brian Boru at the battle, and the subsequent divisions among his followers, meant that his victory was never consolidated by the formation of a strong unified kingdom. The Vikings that remained soon merged fully into the native Irish population.

From the time of the Norman conquest onwards, the kings of England coveted Ireland. The first of the **Anglo-Normans** to cross over to Ireland was a freelance adventurer, Richard FitzGilbert de Clare, more usually known as **Strongbow**. He came in 1169 at the invitation of Dermot MacMurrough, the exiled king of Leinster, who sought help to regain his throne. Henry II of England, however, was concerned that Strongbow might establish a threatening power base and therefore went personally to Ireland as overlord. He had earlier secured papal support and authorization over all powers – native, Norse and Norman – from, as chance would have it, the only English pope in history, Adrian IV.

In 1172, Pope Alexander III reaffirmed Henry II's lordship. This seemed to open the prospect of Anglo-Norman rule in which Gaelic tribal kingdoms would be reshaped into a feudal system on the English model, but the Irish resisted so effectively that royal authority outside the "English Pale" (an area surrounding Dublin) was little more than nominal (and gave rise to the pejorative English expression "beyond the pale", signifying a lack of civilization).

THE STATUTES OF KILKENNY

By the fourteenth century, the Anglo-Norman settlers had integrated with the native Irish population to such an extent that the Crown, eager to regain control, sought to drive a permanent wedge between the natives and the colonists with the introduction of The **Statutes of Kilkenny** (1366). This legislation prohibited intermarriage with the Irish, forbade the Irish from entering walled cities, and made the adoption of Irish names, dress, customs or speech illegal. The ineffectiveness of these measures allowed Gaelic influence to increase until, by the end of the fifteenth century, the "Pale" had been reduced to just a narrow strip of land around the capital.

THE TUDORS AND THE STUARTS

The continued isolation of Irish politics from English and Continental influence during the fifteenth century, and England's preoccupation with the Wars of the Roses, helped Ireland's most powerful Anglo-Norman family – the **FitzGeralds** of Kildare – to establish and consolidate control of the east and southeast of the country. For the most part, their growing authority was left unchallenged by the early Tudor monarchy, whose policy towards Ireland was based mainly on considerations of economy – it was cheaper to accept Kildare's rule than establish an English deputy who would need expensive military backing – and security – Irish discontent with English rule should not be allowed to take forms which might be exploited by England's foreign enemies.

THE REFORMATION

Henry VIII was able to retain his attitude of expedient caution until his break with Rome introduced several new factors. The clergy began to preach rebellion against the schismatical king, while Henry was able to reward his supporters with the spoils from the dissolution of religious houses. Convinced that his family's power was under threat, Kildare's son, Lord Offaly ("Silken Thomas"), staged an insurrection in the summer of 1534. Aid from the pope – who for the first time was seen as a potential supporter of opposition to England – was expected, but never came. Henry, inevitably, reacted forcibly and exchanged his policy of prudence for one of aggression. War dragged on until 1540, by which time Kildare and his supporters, their power all but crushed, were forced to submit to the Crown.

The Dublin parliament enacted legislation accepting Henry's **Act of Supremacy**, which made the king head of the Church. At least three distinct factions emerged in Ireland: the "Old English", who were loyal to the king but denied him spiritual primacy; the independent-minded and staunchly Catholic Gaelic Irish; and the new Protestants, many of whom had benefited materially by acquiring Church property. (At this stage, those "recusants" who refused to swear the oath acknowledging Henry as head of the Church were not yet subject to discrimination.) In an attempt to bind the chiefs and nobles of Ireland more closely to its authority, the Crown forced them to surrender their lands, only to return them again with the reduced status of landlords. Central to Henry's policy was the wish to rule Ireland cheaply, with least risk of foreign intervention, through Irish-born "deputies" whose loyalty was assured. But such loyalty could not be counted on, and after Henry's death the authority of the English Crown was again challenged.

ELIZABETH I AND JAMES I

During the reign of **Queen Elizabeth I** (1558–1603), a growing number of adventurers, mainly younger sons of the aristocracy, arrived from Protestant England to pillage Ireland. For the first time, the supposed moral imperative to turn the Gaelic Irish away from the papacy was used as an excuse to invade and dispossess. This justification for the suppression of Irish culture, religion and language was to be the trademark of English occupation of Ireland for many years to come.

Elizabeth's aim was to establish an English colony. This policy of **plantation** had been started, albeit unsuccessfully, some thirty years earlier during the reign of Mary I, when Laois – renamed "Queen's County" – and Offaly – "King's County" – were confiscated from their native Irish owners and given into the possession of loyal Old English. Elizabeth's first attempt, in the 1570s, to "plant" northeast Ulster, which was then the most Gaelic area of the country, failed miserably. However, the colonization process, when eventually completed, was the principal instrument in subjugating the entire country.

At least three major Irish **rebellions** were prompted by Elizabeth's policies. Two of these, led by the Desmonds of Munster, were easily put down; the Desmond lands were confiscated and given to English settlers. The third, last, and most serious was in Ulster, and was led by **Hugh O'Neill**. O'Neill, originally a protégé of the English court (see p.640), participated in crushing the revolt of the Desmonds, and had long been groomed to become chief of Ulster. He'd always imagined the role to be that of an autonomous Gaelic chieftain; he turned against his queen in 1595 when he began to appreciate the extent to which he would be the pawn of English Protestantism. His forces won a major victory over the English at the Battle of the Yellow Ford in 1598, but were defeated at **Kinsale** in December 1601 after failing to link up effectively with the Spanish reinforcements who had arrived there.

The Tudor conquest of Ireland was completed when O'Neill signed the **Treaty of Mellifont** in 1603, ignorant of the death of Elizabeth just a few days before. Half a million acres of land were confiscated from the native Irish, including all the estates of O'Neill and his fellow rebel Hugh O'Donnell, king of *Tír Chonaill* (Donegal). English plans to redistribute the land supposedly included generous endowments to the "natives". However, an abortive and unplanned insurrection was enough to frighten them into abandoning any such idea, and English and Scottish "planters" – many of whom were ex-soldiers – were brought over to be ensconced in fortified "bawns". Chiefs such as O'Neill were still nominally landlords but, unable to accept the loss of their ancient authority, and living under constant suspicion that they were plotting against the Crown, many chose instead to leave their country as exiles. Their mass departure to continental Europe in 1607 became known as the **Flight of the Earls**, an event which many identify as the beginning of the end for the old Gaelic order.

It was at this time that the character of Ulster began to change. James VI of Scotland had just become **James I** of England, and he encouraged many Scots to emigrate the short distance to Ulster where so much newly confiscated land awaited them. There was a great deal of bitterness on the part of the dispossessed native people, and little intermarriage with the planters, so that the whole country, and above all Ulster, became divided along Catholic and Protestant lines.

CHARLES I AND THE ENGLISH CIVIL WAR

The widespread belief in England and Ireland that James's successor, **Charles I**, harboured pro-Catholic sympathies was one of the spurs for the armed rebellion in Ulster in 1641. Terrifying stories circulated in England of the torture and murder of Protestant planters, and the rebels' (bogus) claim that they were acting with Charles's blessing did much to provoke the **English Civil War**. The origins of the current situation in the six northeast counties of Ulster can in many respects be traced to the policy and events of this period.

During the Civil War, the "Old English" in Ireland allied with the native Irish in the **Confederation of Kilkenny**, supporting the Royalist cause in the hope of bringing about the restoration of Catholicism. It was an uneasy alliance, characterized by inadequate leadership and personal rivalries, in which the Irish felt they had nothing to lose in pursuit of liberty, whereas the Old English lived in fear of a Protestant invasion should the forces of **Oliver Cromwell** achieve victory. The war did indeed end with the establishment of Cromwell's Protectorate and the execution of the king; and the conquest of Ireland became Cromwell's most immediate priority.

CROMWELL AND THE ACT OF SETTLEMENT

Cromwell's ruthless campaign in Ireland remains a source of great bitterness to this day. He arrived in Dublin with 12,000 men of the New Model Army in August 1649, and was soon joined by another force under General Ireton. **Drogheda** was stormed in September, and thousands, including civilians and children, were slaughtered. Cromwell continued south and quickly took Wexford and New Ross, whereupon the towns of Cork, Youghal and Kinsale in the southwest (all in the hands of Royalists) swiftly capitulated. Although Waterford held out for several months, it was not long before Cromwell's forces had overrun the entire country and broken the backbone of resistance.

By the time the struggle was over, almost two years on, one-quarter of the Catholic population was dead and those found wandering the country orphaned or dispossessed were sold into slavery in the West Indies. The **Act of Settlement** drawn up in 1652 confiscated land from the native Irish on a massive scale. All "transplantable persons" were ordered to move west of the River Shannon by May 1, 1654, on pain of death; in the famous phrase, it was a matter of indifference whether they went "to Hell or to Connacht". The mass exodus continued for months, with many of the old and sick dying on the journey. Cromwell's soldiers were paid off with gifts of appropriated land, and, remaining as settlers, constituted a permanent reminder of English injustice.

KING BILLY AND KING JAMES

Irish hopes were raised once more by the **Restoration** of Charles II in 1660. He had regained the English throne, however, only after lengthy negotiations with the Protestant parliamentarians of London and Dublin, and was in no position to give expression to any Catholic sympathies which he may have held.

Things changed only when Charles's brother James II succeeded him in 1685. He appointed a Catholic viceroy in Ireland and actually got as far as repealing the Act of Settlement. However, the Whigs and the Tories in England united to invite the Protestant William of Orange to take the throne. James fled and was soon raising an army in Ireland. He was successful until 1689, when he came to lay siege to the city of Derry in Ulster; young trade apprentices, known thereafter as the **Apprentice Boys**, shut the gates of the city in the face of James's troops – an event still celebrated today during the annual marching season.

However, arguably the most significant victory of Protestant over Catholic was on July 12, 1690, when William's army defeated that of James at the **Battle of the Boyne**. The repeal of the Act of Settlement was therefore never implemented – but the very idea that the Catholics still had claims to their old property which they might one day be able to reassert became established in the Protestant consciousness. As William's victory was consolidated, measures were taken to ensure irreversible Protestant control of the country.

THE PENAL LAWS TO THE ACT OF UNION

In 1641, 59 percent of the land in Ireland was owned by Catholics. In 1688, the figure was 22 percent, and by 1703 it was fourteen percent. The Protestant population, about one-tenth of the total, lived in fear of an uprising by the vast majority of dispossessed and embittered Catholics. In order to keep the native Catholics in a position of powerlessness, a number of Acts were passed, collectively known as the **penal laws**. Not only were Catholics forbidden to vote or join the army or navy, but it became illegal to educate a child in the Catholic faith; they could not teach, open their own schools or send their children to be educated abroad. Catholics could neither buy land nor inherit it, other than by the equal division of estates between all sons. There were vast rewards for turning Protestant; a male convert was entitled to all his brothers' inheritance, a female to her husband's property. Irish language, music and literature were banned, as was the saying of the Mass. The intention was to crush the identity of the Irish people through the suppression of their culture. However, clandestine "hedge schools" developed where outlawed Catholic teachers taught Irish language and music; Mass was said in secret, often at night in the open countryside, and although the erosion of the culture had begun, for the time being it remained strong (it wasn't until the devastating effects of the Famine that the culture went into serious decline).

GRATTAN'S PARLIAMENT

The next turning point in Irish history came in the late eighteenth century, when the increasingly prosperous merchant class ceased to identify its own interests exclusively with those of the British Crown. The British, in their turn, were forced to realize that the best guarantee of stability was the country's economic strength. This was an age of bourgeois revolution, and the events of the **American War of Independence** attracted much attention in Ireland. As early as 1771, Benjamin Franklin was in Dublin suggesting future transatlantic co-operation. Although the rebellion of the American colonies threatened Irish commercial interests, opposition to the war did not mean opposition to the American cause. Thus far, the bulk of Irish emigrants to the American colonies had been Ulster Presbyterians, Catholic emigration being subject to legal restrictions, and the Protestants of Ireland felt a deep sympathy with Washington's campaign. The demand for "no taxation without representation" struck an emotional chord with the parliamentarians of Henry Grattan's Patriot Party – although Ireland was not taxed directly by the British parliament, the Irish Protestants felt, increasingly, that their interests were not properly represented in the politics and policies of the British Isles as a whole.

Protestants and Catholics in Ireland made common cause to the extent that Grattan declared "the Irish Protestant could never be free till the Irish Catholic had ceased to be a slave". Its resources stretched to the limit by war, the British government was sufficiently intimidated by the thought of Irish rebellion to be in the mood for concessions. The land stipulations of the penal laws were repealed in 1778, and in 1782, **Grattan's Parliament** achieved what was felt at the time to be constitutional independence for Ireland, beyond the interference of the London parliament, although still subject to the veto of the king. In the **Renunciation Act** of 1783, the British parliament declared that the executive and judicial independence of Ireland should be "established and ascertained forever, and... at no time hereafter be questioned or questionable".

As it turned out, the independence of the Dublin parliament lasted for just eighteen years, and even those were long on dissent and short on achievement. Economic measures certainly benefited the merchants, but such issues as the extension of voting rights to Catholics – despite Grattan's personal support – were barely addressed. A major reason for its failure was the influence of the **French Revolution** in 1789.

WOLFE TONE AND THE UNITED IRISHMEN

In the 1770s, the threat of French invasion, coupled with the obvious inadequacy of the British force stationed in the country, had led to the formation throughout Ireland of bands of **Volunteers**. These were exclusively Protestant groups, at their strongest in Ulster and particularly Belfast, which rapidly acquired a political significance way beyond their role as a sort of Home Guard.

For Irish Nationalists of all persuasions the French Revolution transformed the thought of a French invasion from a menace to be feared to a prospective means of national liberation. **The Society of United Irishmen**, led by Wolfe Tone and built on the foundations of the Protestant Volunteers but attracting, if anything, more support from Catholics, rallied to the call of Liberty, Equality and Fraternity. Tone himself was a Protestant barrister, who saw equal rights for Protestants and Catholics in Ireland as the only route to independence from England. The United Irishmen were originally disposed towards non-violence, but for Tone the possibility of French aid was too appealing to resist. The British, and the majority of Ulster Protestants, were by contrast so alarmed by tales of the bloodshed in France that they also prepared for war; it was at this juncture that the Protestant Orange Society, later the Orange Order, was established (1795). Although influenced by revolutionary ideas from France, its main aim was to maintain Protestant power (for more on the Order, see p.745).

The uprising came in **1798** (see pp.225 & 421); disorganized fighting broke out in different parts of the island well before the French fleet – and Tone himself – arrived, and the scattered rebels were swiftly and bloodily suppressed. Tone was sentenced to be hanged, but committed suicide by cutting his own throat before his execution. The limited advances Henry Grattan had won for Catholics were withdrawn as a result of the rebellion.

THE ACT OF UNION

The destiny of Ireland during the period following the uprising was largely subject to the whim of political factions in England, ever ready to make an emotional *cause célèbre* of the latest developments. The rebellion of 1798 provoked Prime Minister William Pitt into support for the complete legislative union of Britain and Ireland and the dissolution of the Dublin parliament. Pitt argued that this offered the most hopeful road towards Catholic emancipation while also ensuring the perpetuation of the Protestant Ascendancy. In 1801, the **Act of Union** came into force, abolishing the 500-year-old Irish parliament and making Ireland part of the United Kingdom.

All hopes of independence seemed crushed. Ireland itself housed an utterly divided people, a minority Protestant ruling class and a politically powerless Catholic majority. Robert Emmet, a romantic figure in Irish history, inspired by Wolfe Tone, made one last stand for independence, and attempted a rising in 1803. His followers, however, were small in number and disorganized. The rising failed, and Emmet was executed.

DANIEL O'CONNELL

The quest for Catholic emancipation by peaceful constitutional means was the life's work of **Daniel O'Connell** (1775–1847), the lawyer who became known as "The Liberator" and whom Gladstone called "the greatest popular leader the world has ever seen". He founded the Catholic Association in 1823, which attracted a mass following in Ireland with its campaign for full political rights for Catholics. O'Connell himself was elected to the British House of Commons as the member for Ennis, County Clare in 1828. As a Catholic, he was forbidden to take his seat in Westminster; but the moral force of his victory was such that a change in the law had to be conceded. Royal assent was given to the **Catholic Emancipation Bill** on April 13, 1829, granting voting rights to some Catholics. Stringent property qualifications, however, ensured that the Catholic vote remained a small one.

At the height of his success, O'Connell's popularity was phenomenal. He was elected Lord Mayor of (Protestant) Dublin for the year of 1841, and two years later embarked on an ambitious campaign for the **repeal of the Union** with England. O'Connell addressed a series of vast "monster meetings" throughout Ireland; according to the conservative estimate of *The Times*, over a million people – one-eighth of the Irish population – attended the meeting symbolically held at the Hill of Tara.

The climax of O'Connell's campaign was to be a meeting at Clontarf (where Brian Boru had defeated the Danes in the eleventh century) on October 8, 1843. All Ireland was poised and waiting, conscious of the sympathy that O'Connell's profoundly peaceful movement had won from around the world. The pacifism which had led him to say that "no political change is worth the shedding of a single drop of human blood", and his determination always to act within the law, were, however, exploited by the British. One day before the Clontarf meeting it was declared to be an illegal gathering and O'Connell, remarkably, obliged by calling it off. The crowds which had already gathered, and the population at large, were baffled that O'Connell backed down from direct confrontation. His moment passed and the stage was left to those who, having seen pacifism fail to secure independence, believed that armed struggle would prove the only way forward. The **Young Ireland movement**, once aligned with O'Connell, attempted an armed uprising in 1848, but by then there was little chance of mass support. The country was already undergoing a national disaster.

THE FAMINE

The failure of the Irish potato crop from 1845 to 1849 plunged the island into appalling **famine**. Elsewhere in Europe, the blight was a resolvable problem but Irish subsistence farmers were utterly dependent on the crop. No disease affected grain, cattle, dairy produce or corn and throughout the disaster Irish produce that could have fed the hungry continued to be exported overseas. Millions were kept alive by charitable soup kitchens, and some individual landlords were supportive to their tenants; for millions more, the only choice lay between starvation and escape.

Between 1841 and 1851, census returns suggest that 1.4 million people died in Ireland and 1.4 million emigrated to the United States and elsewhere – though the exact numbers in each case were probably higher. Many emigrants were too ill to survive the journey on what became known as "coffin ships", some drowned when overcrowded ships sank, and still more died on arrival in the United States, Canada, Britain, Australia and New Zealand.

One consequence of **mass emigration** was the creation of large Irish communities abroad, which henceforth added an international dimension to the struggle for Irish independence. Financial support from the Irish overseas became crucial to such Nationalist organizations as the Irish Republican Brotherhood, also known as the **Fenians**. Their attempted uprising in 1867 was little short of a fiasco, but they nonetheless retained a loyal following both in the States and in England (where a number of bombings were carried out in their name).

The legacy of the Famine was such that the long-standing bitterness instilled by the English connection now deepened to a new level of emotional intensity. Resentment focused on the failure of the British government to intervene, and more specifically on the **absentee English landlords** who had continued to profit while remaining indifferent to the suffering of their tenants. Such landlords had little or no contact with the realities of life on their estates; rents were far higher than most tenants could pay, and evictions became widespread, most notoriously at Derryveagh in Donegal (see p.499).

PARNELL AND THE HOME RULE

The second half of the nineteenth century was characterized by a complex interplay of political and economic factors which contributed towards the exacerbation of religious differences. The most important of these was the struggle for land and for the rights of tenants. A coherent Nationalist movement with modest aims began to emerge, operating within British parliamentary democracy.

Charles Stewart Parnell (1846–91; see p.133), a Protestant who was elected to Westminster in 1875 and became leader of the **Home Rule Party** two years later, was the tenants' champion. He insisted that only the establishment of an Irish parliament in Dublin could be responsive to the needs of the people and, to that end, consistently disrupted the business of the British House of Commons.

Parnell also organized the Irish peasantry in defiance of particularly offensive landlords, adding a new word to the English language when the first such target was a Captain Boycott.

A breakthrough seemed to be approaching when Parnell won the support of the Prime Minister, Gladstone, but the **Phoenix Park** murders in Dublin in 1882 (see p.104) again hardened English opinion against the Irish. Three Home Rule Bills were defeated in the space of ten years; instead the Prevention of Crimes Act (temporarily) abolished trial by jury and increased police powers. The transparent honesty of Parnell's denials of complicity in the murders for a while served to boost his career, but public opinion finally swung against him in 1890, when he was cited in the divorce case of his colleague Captain O'Shea.

The attitude of many Irish Protestants to the agitation for Home Rule was summed up by the equation "Home Rule = Rome Rule"; such a threat was enough to unite the Anglican (broadly speaking, conservative gentry) and Presbyterian (liberal tradesmen) communities. These were certainly the people who were doing best from a modest boom in Ireland's economic fortunes, with Ulster, and specifically Belfast, having been the main beneficiary when the Industrial Revolution finally arrived in the country. Large-scale **industrialization**, in export industries such as shipbuilding, linen manufacture and engineering, gave the region an additional dependence on the British connection, while the fact that these industries were firmly under Protestant ownership increased social tensions.

The end of the nineteenth century saw a burst of activity aimed at the revival of interest in all aspects of Irish culture and identity. Ostensibly non-political organizations such as the **Gaelic League** and the Gaelic Athletic

Association were founded to promote Irish language, music and traditional sports, and these inevitably tended to attract the support of politically minded Nationalists. As well as those who sought to encourage the use of Irish, a body of writers, with W.B. Yeats in the forefront, embarked on an attempt to create a national literature in English.

In 1898, Arthur Griffith, a printer in Dublin, founded a newspaper called the *United Irishman*, in which he expounded the philosophy of **Sinn Féin**, meaning "We, Ourselves". His was a non-violent and essentially capitalist vision, arguing that the Irish MPs should simply abandon Westminster and set up their own parliament in Dublin, where, with or without the permission of the British, they would be able to govern Ireland by virtue of their unassailable moral authority. Such political freedom was a prerequisite for Ireland to achieve significant economic development. Sinn Féin incorporated itself into a political party in 1905. Meanwhile, socialist analyses of the situation in Ireland were appearing in the *Workers' Republic*, the newspaper of **James Connolly's** Irish Socialist Republican Party, pointing out that Ireland's frail prosperity rested on a basis of malnutrition, bad housing and social deprivation.

REACTION AND COUNTER-REACTION

In reaction to the declared intentions of Asquith's Liberal government in Britain in 1911 to see through the passage of yet another (exceptionally tame) Home Rule Bill, the Protestants of Ulster mobilized themselves under the leadership of **Sir Edward Carson**. A Dublin barrister who at first glance had little in common with the people of Ulster, a region he barely knew, his one great aim was to preserve the Union, in the face of the "nefarious conspiracy" hatched by the British government itself. To that end he declared that, in the event of the Home Rule Bill becoming law, the Unionists would defy it and set up their own parliament. In preparation for that eventuality, they organized their own militia, the **Ulster Volunteers**.

James Connolly, who had spent the years from 1903 to 1910 in disillusionment in the United States, found himself on less fertile ground when he tried to convert the workers of Belfast to socialism. He was impressed, however, by the example of the Ulster Volunteers, and the brutal police suppression of a protracted and bitter strike in Dublin, organized by James Larkin's Irish Transport Workers Union, gave him the opportunity to form the **Irish Citizen Army**. Other militant Republicans had also resolved to create an armed force in the south to parallel the Ulster Volunteers, and almost simultaneously, in November 1913, the **Irish Volunteers** came into being. The Gaelic League and Gaelic Athletic Association acted as prime recruiting places and provided such leaders as Pádraig Pearse. The movement should not, however, be seen in strictly sectarian terms; at least two of its most prominent leaders were Ulster Protestant.

REBELLION AND CIVIL WAR

The British parliament eventually passed the **Home Rule Bill** of 1912, and for a while the conditions appeared to exist for Ireland to erupt into civil war. Before this could happen, however, the outbreak of World War I dramatically altered the situation. An immediate consequence of war was that enactment of the Bill was indefinitely postponed.

For the majority of the Irish Volunteers, the primary aim of their movement was to safeguard the postwar introduction of Home Rule. Not simply to that end, but also out of loyalty to the British Crown, many of them joined the British Army. Some, however, led by Eoin MacNeill, in part supported the British war effort but were reluctant to commit too much of their strength towards defending Britain without a pledge of concrete rewards. These in turn fell under the domination of a small and secret militant faction, the revived **Irish Republican Brotherhood** (after 1916 they became the Irish Republican Army, or IRA), to whom "England's difficulty was Ireland's opportunity". They made tentative overtures for German support (and even contemplated installing a German prince as King of Ireland) but went ahead with preparations for armed insurrection regardless of whether or not they received foreign aid – indeed all but regardless of the virtual certainty of defeat.

THE EASTER RISING

The outbreak of fighting on the streets of Dublin on Easter Monday in 1916 was expected by neither the English nor the Irish Army, and was a source of bemusement to the Dubliners themselves. Republican forces swiftly took over a number of key buildings, although they missed an easy opportunity to capture the castle itself.

The leaders of the rising made their base in the General Post Office in O'Connell Street, and it was from there that Pádraig Pearse emerged to read the "Proclamation from The Provisional Government of the Irish Republic to the People of Ireland":

> *Ireland, through us, summons her children to the flag and strikes for her freedom... The Irish Republic is entitled to, and hereby claims, the allegiance of every Irishman and Irishwoman. The Republic guarantees religious and civil liberty, equal rights and equal opportunities to all its citizens... cherishing all the children of the nation equally, and oblivious of the differences carefully fostered by an alien Government, which have divided a minority from the majority in the past.*

To these fine democratic sentiments Pearse in particular added a quasi-mystical emphasis on the necessity for blood sacrifice; although potential allies such as Eoin MacNeill declined to join them with so little prospect of success, these were men prepared to give their lives as inspiration to others.

So weak was the rebel position that they only held out five days; at the time of their surrender they were even less popular with the mass of the nation than when they began, as a result of the terrible physical damage Dublin had suffered.

And yet, as the leaders of the rising were systematically and unceremoniously executed by the British – the wounded James Connolly was shot tied to a chair – sympathy did indeed grow for the Republicans and their cause. In the words of Yeats's *Easter 1916*:

> *... changed, changed utterly: A terrible beauty is born.*

WAR WITH BRITAIN

When the British government felt able once again to turn to Irish affairs, it found a dramatically altered situation. Sinn Féin won a resounding victory in the elections of 1918 and refused to take its seats at Westminster. Instead the newly elected MPs met in Dublin as the *Dáil Éireann* (Assembly of Ireland) and declared independence. Leadership passed to Eamonn de Valera, the sole surviving leader of the Easter Rising, whose sentence of death had been commuted. Michael Collins, the Minister of Finance in the new government and its most effective military organizer, began mobilizing the IRA for war. In January 1919, the killing of two members of the Royal Irish Constabulary (RIC), the main instrument of British power in Ireland, marked the beginning of the hostilities, which were to last for two and a half years.

The RIC experienced severe difficulties in recruiting sufficient new members (other than from Ulster). Newly demobilized British soldiers were therefore brought over from England, and by virtue of their distinctive uniforms became known as the **Black and Tans**. The Irish Republicans, fighting on home territory, were well able to hold their own in guerrilla fighting across the country, while the Black and Tans acquired an infamous and enduring reputation for brutality.

The **Government of Ireland Act** of 1920 created separate parliaments for "Northern Ireland" (Derry, Antrim, Fermanagh, Down, Tyrone and Armagh) and "Southern Ireland" (the 26 counties of the present-day Republic), to remain under the nominal authority of the British Crown. Elections were held for the two bodies in 1921, but the members elected to the Southern Parliament constituted themselves instead as the **Dáil Éireann**, with de Valera as their president. With the Protestants of Ulster still firmly pledged to the Union, and the fighting at a stalemate, a negotiated settlement seemed the only way out. A truce was called in July 1921 and de Valera sent emissaries to London, including Arthur Griffith and Michael Collins, to negotiate a treaty. Lloyd George persuaded them to agree to peace terms based on the partition of the island along the terms of the Government of Ireland Act. The 26 southern counties would become not a republic but an independent nation within the British Commonwealth – the Irish Free State. The northern border, Lloyd George suggested, would be so small as to preclude the North from being a viable entity, thus bringing about eventual unity. The alternative to the treaty was, he said, "immediate and terrible war".

CIVIL WAR

The **Anglo-Irish Treaty** was signed in London on December 6, 1921, and hailed by Lloyd

George as "one of the greatest days in the history of the British Empire". A provisional government was formed in Ireland in January 1922, pending elections. The link with Britain had been broken at last – but not completely or cleanly enough for a militant minority in Ireland. During the negotiations, Griffith and Collins in London and de Valera in Dublin had failed to agree a clear line on an acceptable outcome. On the negotiators' return, de Valera rejected the treaty as it veered too far from the Republican ideal. He resigned from office and left the Dáil; by July he and his military supporters had plunged Ireland into a squalid and economically devastating **civil war**.

Men who had been fighting alongside each other the year before were now pitched into a bitter conflict: the supporters of the treaty, the "Free Staters", against Republicans fighting for a united Ireland. In the North, the understandably alarmed Protestant community created the Ulster Special Constabulary, including the "**B Specials**" drawn from Carson's Ulster Volunteers, ostensibly to control the rioting which persistently broke out in response to events south of the border.

De Valera and his supporters were eventually forced to capitulate in May 1923; as he put it, "military victory must be allowed to rest for the moment with those who have destroyed the Republic".

THE IRISH FREE STATE

With the death of Michael Collins and Arthur Griffith during the civil war, the leadership of the Irish Free State fell to William T. Cosgrave, and finally in the summer of 1923 the new government began to reconstruct Ireland as an independent nation. A civil service was set up, along with a police force and the hydroelectric scheme on the River Shannon, which was to lead to the establishment of the ESB (Electricity Supply Board).

Meanwhile Eamonn de Valera, still an important political force, abandoned Sinn Féin's post-civil war policy of boycotting the Dáil to form his own political party in 1926. This took the explicitly mythological name of **Fianna Fáil** (Soldiers of Destiny) and was victorious in the 1932 general election. Under de Valera other state bodies were set up, including Coras Iompair Éireann (road and rail transport), Aer Lingus (air transport) and Bord na Mona (peat production). In 1933, the rival **Fine Gael** (Tribes of Gaels) party was founded.

The recession of the 1930s was made considerably worse for Ireland by the **Economic War**. De Valera had withheld repayments to England of loans made to tenants to buy their holdings; the British responded by imposing heavy duties on Irish goods.

In 1938, a new **constitution** came into effect, which finally declared Ireland's complete independence by renouncing British sovereignty. The Free State, under the new name of **Éire**, was to be governed by a two-chamber parliament (the Dáil and the Seanad), with a president (the Uachtarán), and a prime minister (the Taoiseach).

Ireland remained officially neutral during World War II, although considerable informal help was given to the Allies. De Valera, on the other hand, was the only government leader in the world to offer his commiserations – to a Nazi German minister in Dublin – on the suicide of Adolf Hitler.

THE REPUBLIC

It took the Republic (which finally came into being in 1949) twenty years to recover from the economic stagnation brought on by the war. Vast numbers of people, disproportionately drawn from among the young and talented, moved across to fill Britain's labour shortage. Not until a break was made with the past, with the accession to the premiership in 1959 of the vigorous and expansionist **Sean Lemass**, was a sufficient level of prosperity achieved to slow down the process of chronic emigration. Foreign enterprises began investing heavily in Ireland, unemployment fell by a third, and the way was paved for the country's successful application to join the European Economic Community in 1972. The immediate benefits were enjoyed by those employed in agriculture (twenty percent of the working population), although Irish fishing waters had now to be shared with other EEC members.

Ireland's and Britain's membership of the **EEC** did not, however, bring the Republic and Northern Ireland closer together. Their membership was made official on January 22, 1972; eight days later came Bloody Sunday (see p.678), and on February 2 the British Embassy in Dublin was destroyed by an angry mob.

The international recession hit Ireland very severely in the 1980s. Emigration rocketed once again and unemployment remained consistently high. Referenda on abortion in 1983 and divorce in 1986 (both remained illegal) reflected the Catholic Church's considerable influence.

CHARLES HAUGHEY

The 1987 general election, fought principally on the issues of taxation and unemployment, resulted in accession to power of the Fianna Fáil party, led by the resilient and wily **Charles Haughey**. In the summer of 1989, Mr Haughey called another election with the intention of increasing his majority. The result, however, was a Fianna Fáil/Progressive Democrat alliance, in which Haughey's hold on power always seemed tenuous.

The presidential election of 1991 yielded a surprise result when the feminist lawyer **Mary Robinson**, an independent candidate supported by Labour and The Workers' Party, was elected. Some in Haughey's party (and outside) accused the Taoiseach of sabotaging the campaign of his own party's candidate, Brian Lenihan (an old rival), but whatever the causes of her success, there can be no doubt that the president breathed new life into the office and into Irish politics in general: as a woman, and as a representative of causes outside the old two-party stalemate. In particular, her election gave hope to many that a new era of greater integrity and **liberalism** in politics, and perhaps some easing of positions on the intractable problems of the North, was about to dawn.

Early in 1992, Charles Haughey, whose government was weighed down by constant (and later to be proven) allegations of financial mismanagement and even corruption, resigned. The final straw came when Sean Doherty, speaker of the Seanad and a former minister under Haughey, claimed that he personally had delivered tapes of tapped phone calls, made by journalists unfriendly to Fianna Fáil, to Mr Haughey in 1982. Although Haughey denied any knowledge of such tapes, the threat of his coalition falling apart finally forced him to resign.

FROM ALBERT REYNOLDS TO BERTIE AHERN

The new prime minister, **Albert Reynolds**, took over the leadership of a seemingly exhausted Fianna Fáil party. His downfall, however, less than three years later, was due to a moral issue – as so often in Irish politics. Reynolds' years as prime minister were plagued by scandal and the powerful influence of the Church in public and political life. An early case was that of the fourteen-year-old rape victim whom the Irish High Court at first refused to allow to go to Britain to seek an abortion. In May 1992 came the dramatic confessions of an American woman, former lover of Dr Eamonn Casey, the Bishop of Galway, who had apparently been using church funds to bring up his teenage son. Then, in 1993, it emerged that warrants from Belfast for the extradition of the paedophile priest Father Brendan Smyth had been ignored for several months. The government – under pressure from the Church – continued to cover up the scandal, but in November 1994, after questions in the Dáil, the prime minister's part in the affair came to light and he was forced to resign. It didn't help that at the same time a 68-year-old priest, Liam Cosgrave, died in a Dublin gay sauna club; this spate of clerical scandals caused disarray among Irish Catholics and would appear to have irrevocably undermined the Church's authority on moral issues.

Since 1994, there has been a series of coalition governments. The current one is Fianna Fáil-led, under their new leader **Bertie Ahern**. Ahern's term in office has been dogged with damaging **financial scandals**, involving leading figures in his party, notably Charles Haughey and foreign minister, Ray Burke. Haughey was found guilty in 1997 of taking a "gift" of £1.3 million from top Irish businessman, Ben Dunne. Shortly afterwards, Burke resigned when it was revealed he had received £30,000 from a company wanting to develop land in his constituency. The **Flood Commission's** subequent investigations pulled further skeletons from their closets, but one positive outcome of these scandals has been the passing of an Ethics in Public Office Act – evidence that Ireland is developing into something approaching a mature democracy.

The presidential election in October 1997 saw another woman, **Mary McAleese**, elected to the post. Her politics, however, differ fundamentally from her predecessor's. Born in Belfast, President McAleese's politics are Nationalist and influenced by her strongly-held Catholic beliefs (she is ardently pro-life). However, it was the greenness of her Nationalism not her social conservatism that caused concern for some southerners during her election campaign. There were fears that she might alienate Ulster Unionists at a delicate time in the peace process (she had once described Northern Ireland as "the archetypal police state"). Other critics worried that her campaigning zeal, most in evidence in her role as Vice-Chancellor of Queen's University, Belfast, would be inappropriate for the apolitical position of president. These fears, however, have not been realized.

One of the most significant developments in Irish society in the last decade has been the staggering growth of the country's GDP, earning it the epithet "**Celtic Tiger**". The reasons for this impressive performance are manifold, but are chiefly due to the granting of generous tax concessions to multinationals, economic support from Europe and a young, highly educated workforce. However, there are doubts over the sustainability of this growth. The main criticism of the economy is that growth is concentrated in five high-tech sectors, owned by multinationals, attracted to Ireland by generous tax concessions. Indigenous industries, on the other hand, are showing no real growth in comparison. This has resulted in a high-growth multinational and a sluggish indigenous sector sitting uncomfortably side by side. There are also concerns that only certain sectors of society are benefiting from the recent wealth-creation and that social inequalities are growing.

NORTHERN IRELAND FROM 1921

On June 22, 1921, the new political entity of Northern Ireland came into existence with the opening of the **Northern Irish Parliament** in Belfast's City Hall. In order to understand the present situation in the North it is necessary to grasp the political background to this development. Since the settlements of the seventeenth century, the Protestant descendants of the settlers had been concentrated in the northern part of the island; they rarely intermarried with the local people or assimilated into the native culture, feeling both superior to and threatened by the Catholics, who formed the vast majority of the population of Ireland as a whole. The economically dominant group in the northern counties was essentially Protestant, and when an industrial base developed in this part of the island, the prosperity of the region was inextricably tied to the trading power of Britain. In negotiating for their exclusion from the new Irish state, Carson and the Unionist Council decided to accept just six counties of Ulster out of a possible nine, because only in this way could a safe Protestant majority be guaranteed. Thus Westminster gave political power into the hands of those whose pro-British sympathies were certain.

The Unionists were not slow to exploit their supremacy: a Protestant police force and military were set up, and "gerrymandering" (the redrawing of boundary lines in order to control the outcome of elections) was commonplace, so securing Protestant control even in areas with Catholic majorities. Thus Derry city, with a two-thirds Catholic majority, returned a two-thirds Protestant council. Nothing was done to rectify the situation for several decades. The Catholic community was to benefit from the British welfare state, but they were discriminated against in innumerable ways, most notoriously in jobs and also in housing, an area controlled by Protestant local authorities.

CIVIL RIGHTS

In 1967, inspired by the civil rights movement in America, the Northern Irish **Civil Rights Movement** was born, a non-sectarian organization demanding equality of rights for all. Massively supported by the Catholic community, the campaign led to huge protest marches, some of which were viciously attacked by Loyalist mobs. The **RUC** (Royal Ulster Constabulary) rarely intervened, and when they did take action, it was generally not to protect the Catholics. The Apprentice Boys' march of 1969 proved to be the flashpoint. This triumphal procession, commemorating the city's siege in 1689 (see p.669), annually passed through Derry's Catholic areas (though in recent times it has been truncated first by the Parades Commission and subsequently by mutual agreement with the city council). The 1969 march provoked rioting that ended in the Catholic community barricading themselves in and Jack Lynch, the Irish prime minister, mobilizing Irish troops and setting up field hospitals on the border.

On August 14, British troops were sent to Derry to protect the besieged minority, and at first they were welcomed by the Catholics, who were relieved to see the troops pushing back the RUC and B Specials. Belief in the neutrality of the British army did not last long, as escalating violence between the two communities across the North forced the army into a more interventionist role, but confusion arose as to whether **Stormont** (the Northern parliament) or Westminster was giving the orders. Before long the army was acting not as a protective force but as a retaliatory one, and it was clear that retaliation against the Catholics was far harsher than measures taken against the Protestants. With the Catholics again vulnerable, the resurgent IRA quickly assumed the role of defenders of the ghetto areas of Derry and Belfast. Within a few months the **Provisional IRA**, now stronger than the less militant Official wing of the organization, had launched an intensive bombing and shooting campaign across the North.

At the request of Northern Ireland's Prime Minister, Brian Faulkner, **internment without trial** was introduced in 1971, a measure which was used as an indiscriminate weapon against the minority population. Then, on Sunday, January 30, 1972, thirteen unarmed civil rights demonstrators were shot dead by British paratroopers in Derry, an event that shocked the world and was to become known as **Bloody Sunday**. The Irish government declared February 2 a national day of mourning; on the same day an angry crowd in Dublin burned down the British Embassy. Stormont was suspended and direct rule from Westminster imposed.

POWER SHARING AND ITS AFTERMATH

In 1973 a conference was held at **Sunningdale** between representatives of the British and Irish governments and both sections of the community in Northern Ireland, a meeting that led to the creation of a power-sharing executive representing both Unionists and Nationalists, as well as proposals for a Council of Ireland, a non-executive body bringing together politicians from both North and South. An elected executive took office in January 1974, but Ulster Unionist opposition to the Council of Ireland forced Faulkner's resignation. More significantly, inspired by the Reverend Ian Paisley and his Democratic Unionist Party's vehement opposition to the end of majority rule, the Ulster Workers' Council responded by organizing a massive strike in May 1974 which, enforced by the roadblocks of the UDA (Ulster Defence Association), crippled the power stations and other essential services run by a strongly Unionist workforce. In the same week as the strike, three car bombs planted by the UDA exploded during rush hour in Dublin without warning – 33 people were killed, the highest death toll since 1969. By the end of the month, the Sunningdale executive – the first ever to have Catholic representation – was disbanded, and direct rule from Westminster continued until the implementation of the Good Friday peace agreement in 1999 (see p.681).

Throughout 1973 and 1974 the IRA had been conducting a **bombing campaign** in Britain, aimed at destabilizing the government by provoking public revulsion. Twenty-one people were killed in a pub bombing in Birmingham in 1974, and in the same month seven people died in simultaneous pub bombings in Woolwich and **Guildford**. However, a ceasefire was declared in late December, at a time, it subsequently emerged, when the IRA leadership was involved in secret negotiations with the British government. Though some concessions were made, the British refusal to consider the question of Irish unity saw a resumption of the bombing campaign early in 1975. The British responded by introducing the **Prevention of Terrorism Act**, permitting lengthy detention without charge. Four people were arrested for the Guildford bombings and convicted on the basis of confessions and forensic evidence which even at the time were thought by many people to be unreliable. After fifteen years in jail, the prisoners were released when the judiciary finally conceded, with no hint of regret for the injustice, that they were indeed innocent. Six Irish people were given life sentences for the Birmingham attack, and their convictions, too, were finally overthrown in 1991.

In 1976 Special Category Status was abolished for future prisoners in Northern Ireland (previously those arrested for offences connected with what had become known as the Troubles enjoyed the status of political prisoners, involving free association). When Republican prisoners refused to wear prison uniforms in accordance with their change in status they were locked naked in their cells in Long Kesh (also known as The Maze) – the beginning of the famous "**blanket protest**" (see p.595), which soon developed into the "dirty protest" where prisoners smeared excrement on their cell walls rather than slopping out. In 1978 Britain was found guilty by the European Court of Human Rights of "inhuman and degrading treatment" of Republican prisoners. In late 1980 a **hunger strike** for the same demands was called off after six weeks when one of the strikers was close to death. The following March, a hunger strike was begun by **Bobby Sands**, the commander of the Republican prisoners in The Maze, who on April 11 was elected as MP for Fermanagh and South Tyrone as part of a campaign to highlight the protest. By the time of this election, nine other Republicans had joined the hunger strike. All ten died, an outcome that brought widespread condemnation of British intransigence.

THE ANGLO-IRISH AGREEMENT AND THE DOWNING STREET DECLARATION

The year 1982 saw the British government make a timid attempt to break the impasse, introducing the **Northern Ireland Assembly**, a power-sharing body with some legislative but no executive powers. It was boycotted by the Nationalists, and survived only until 1985, by which time the final stages had been reached in the negotiations over the **Anglo-Irish Agreement**. Largely drafted by John Hume, the leader of the moderate Nationalist SDLP, and signed in 1986, it instituted official co-operation between Dublin and Westminster on security and other issues, and strengthened the consultative part played by Dublin in Northern affairs. Unfortunately, the Agreement was weakened by the non-participation of the Ulster Unionists, who had not been involved in its preparation, in the processes it inaugurated.

Throughout the early 1980s Republicans had increasingly become involved in the democratic process. **Gerry Adams** was elected MP for West Belfast in June 1983 and became Sinn Féin's president in November that year. Three years later, the party ended its policy of refusing to take up seats in the Dáil following election gains in the South, though significantly Adams and fellow-MP **Martin McGuinness** have always abstained from attending at Westminster. For many this combination of armed and political Republican activity was encapsulated in ex-internee and Sinn Féin member Danny Morrison's famous question to his party conference, "Would anyone here object if, with the ballot paper in this hand and an Armalite in this hand, we take power in Ireland?" However, by the early 1990s the IRA had increased the pressure through a series of bombing campaigns in both Northern Ireland and England (the latter including an audacious attempt to mortar-bomb the British Prime Minister, John Major, and his Cabinet while meeting in 10 Downing Street). Loyalist reprisals in Northern Ireland, featuring their old speciality, the random attack, were so widespread that, for the first time since 1975, deaths from their activities were more numerous than those resulting from the actions of Republican paramilitaries.

The next major step in addressing the stalemate in the North came with the **Downing Street Declaration** of December 1993. Brokered courageously, once again, by John Hume, and issued jointly by the Irish and British premiers, Albert Reynolds and John Major, it signalled a new readiness for dialogue with all sides involved in the Troubles – including Sinn Féin and the IRA. Previously, the Republican movement had been "psychopaths, godfathers, crypto-fascists", and worse; now, in a remarkable volte-face, they were people who could be reasoned with. They were repeatedly assured of their place at a negotiating table if they embraced the Downing Street Declaration and if the violence stopped.

The Irish government's ban on broadcast of interviews with, or direct statements by, representatives of Sinn Féin, the IRA and other organizations associated with militant Republicanism or militant Loyalism fell due for renewal just a month after the Downing Street Declaration. This ban, which provided the inspiration for a similar, though less restrictive, prohibition in Britain, had been consistently opposed by civil liberties organizations and media professionals, and the government had it under review for months before the Downing Street Declaration. In a rare example of liberal leadership to Britain, the Irish government decided not to renew the ban, and was subsequently followed by the British government.

THE CEASEFIRE, THE PEACE PROCESS AND THE GOOD FRIDAY AGREEMENT

In July 1994, a Sinn Féin conference rejected the Downing Street Declaration, but continued political bargaining by Albert Reynolds and lobbying by Irish-American groups eventually persuaded the party of the virtues of participation in a Nationalist coalition. On August 31, 1994, the IRA declared a "complete cessation" of military activities. Loyalist paramilitaries announced their own **ceasefire** two months later.

After further negotiation, in February 1995, the London and Dublin governments produced a framework document which attempted to satisfy some of the Republicans' constitutional demands, including provision for an all-Ireland authority with far-reaching executive powers.

Major's precondition that the IRA should commence decommissioning its weaponry before Sinn Féin be allowed to participate in the all-party talks proved a huge stumbling block. Seen by Republicans as a demand for the IRA's unconditional surrender, the deadlock was not broken until the establishment of an international commission in November 1995 to advise on the decommissioning process. Chaired by the US senator George Mitchell, it recommended that talks should go ahead in tandem with the handing over of weapons. Crucially, the report detailed six conditions for participation in such talks. Known as the **Mitchell Principles**, these included an overriding commitment to peaceful and democratic principles and all-party consensus and acceptance of the outcome of the political process. However, in the absence of any weaponry being yielded, and bowing to Unionist pressure, the British Government unilaterally announced its intention to hold elections in May 1997 for participation in the all-party talks which would commence in June if the IRA maintained its ceasefire.

The patience of Republicans, however, was being severely tested by what they saw as British intransigence. Sinn Féin's insistence on the whole of the Irish people's right to national self-determination meant that it could not accept the principle of majority consent in Northern Ireland. The IRA's ceasefire was itself essentially fragile and its threats of a return to violence if the political process did not achieve its desired ends became reality with the explosion on February 9, 1996 of a massive **bomb** near London's **Canary Wharf**, killing two people, injuring many more and causing several hundred million pounds of damage to buildings.

Many feared this was the end of the process, but support for political change in Northern Ireland remained powerful and vociferous. The key players remained active, not least the SDLP leader, John Hume, who saw negotiation in the absence of Sinn Féin as redundant and resumed contact with Gerry Adams, seeking a restoration of the IRA's ceasefire. This call was reiterated by **Bill Clinton** whose support for the peace process had become much greater than a simple desire to target the Irish-American vote. Adams was permitted entry to the United States and the White House became a vital intermediary, risking the displeasure of its traditional ally. Signs that the political stalemate might be over came with the election of new parties and leaders in both Britain and the Republic. Elected by an enormous majority, the first Labour Prime Minister for eighteen years, **Tony Blair**, made clear his commitment to the Northern Ireland peace process in his visit to Belfast less than two weeks after his election in May 1997. **Mo Mowlam** was his inspired choice as Northern Ireland Secretary. As the first woman to hold the post, her bluff no-nonsense "matey" approach was to undermine significantly the suspicions of many involved in the peace process. The following month, Bertie Ahern's Fianna Fáil won the Republic's General Election. **Ahern**, along with Foreign Secretary **Dick Spring**, was to play a major role in subsequent events, not least in becoming the first Taoiseach to meet the leader of the Ulster Unionists. It was his securing of the trust of David Trimble which was to have huge significance in later events.

The elections for the **all-party talks** took place at the end of May 1997. Sinn Féin had obtained a large enough vote to participate, but could not do so because of the IRA's refusal to return to a state of ceasefire. However, intense lobbying within Republican circles resulted in the IRA's announcement of "an unequivocal restoration of the ceasefire of August 1994" on July 19, 1997. Though Sinn Féin was now actively engaged and **Gerry Adams** was to make a historic visit to **Downing Street**, at Blair's invitation, on December 9, 1997, little demonstrable progress was made until the following year. Violation of the principles set out by George Mitchell, who had been appointed chair of the talks, led to representatives of the Loyalist paramilitaries and, later, Sinn Féin being suspended. Moreover, the INLA's assassination of the LVF's leader, **Billy Wright**, in the Maze prison just before Christmas 1997 threatened a full-scale return to the violence of the past. The IRA's and Loyalist groups' ceasefires seemed increasingly precarious, especially once dissident Loyalists embarked on a spree of random sectarian attacks. In March 1998, two close friends were shot dead in the Railway Bar in **Poyntzpass**, County Armagh, a village regarded as one of the friendliest and most integrated in Northern Ireland. That one of the pair was Catholic and the other Protestant enhanced the general outrage at the killings and the increasing pointlessness of violence as a solution to the Troubles. Blair seized the impetus by declaring that the all-party talks had to reach a compromise by April 9, 1998 or the process was finished for the foreseeable future.

As the deadline loomed nearer, the chances of a successful conclusion seemed to recede and the day and night of April 9 saw a frenzy of activity and frantic negotiation. Finally, a settlement was somehow negotiated and the accord, known as the **Good Friday Agreement**, was signed on April 10, 1998. It was, without doubt, the most important development in the political history of Northern Ireland. The agreement committed its signatories "to partnership, equality and mutual respect as the basis of relationships within Northern Ireland" and reaffirmed the participants' dedication "to exclusively democratic and peaceful means of resolving differences on political issues". The principle of "consent" lay at the agreement's core. Hugely significant in securing Unionist and Loyalist support, this categorically stated that both governments would respect the legitimacy of the wishes of the majority of the people of Northern Ireland, whether that be to remain part of the United Kingdom or, at some later date, to become part of a united Ireland. In reinforcement, the two governments also agreed to make legal changes – the British Government to repeal the Government of Ireland Act 1920 asserting the sovereignty of the United Kingdom's Parliament over Ireland, and the Irish to hold a referendum on Articles Two and Three of its constitution, claiming territorial sovereignty over the North.

Further provisions included the establishment of a 108-member **Assembly**, elected by proportional representation to ensure the rights of Nationalists, and with a twelve-strong executive committee of ministers appointed on a cross-community basis. The Assembly would have legislative and executive authority over six departments previously run by the British government's Northern Ireland Ministers. An inter-governmental Council of the Isles was also to be established, with membership from the Assembly, Dáil, Commons and the new devolved Welsh and Scottish assemblies. The signatories also committed themselves to the incorporation of the European Convention of Human Rights into Northern Ireland law and the establishment of a new Northern Ireland Human Rights Commission. Apart from the consent principle, the most controversial aspects of the agreement dealt with the accelerated release of political prisoners (an issue that divided the Ulster Unionist Party) and the establishment of an independent commission to review the RUC and the future of policing in the North. In addition, the agreement's signatories "reaffirmed their commitment to the total disarmament of all paramilitary organization". However, the issue of the decommissioning of terrorist weaponry remained the most thorny part of the agreement, until the IRA's surprise announcement early in 2000 (see p.683).

On May 22, 1998, the people of Northern Ireland took part in a **referendum** on the agreement while, simultaneously, the people of the Republic voted on the proposal to amend the Irish constitution. There were strong divisions within the Unionist camp with both Ian Paisley's DUP and Bob McCartney's UKU urging opposition to any potential loosening of the bonds with the United Kingdom. The turnout in the North was an unprecedented 81 percent, of whom 71.12 percent supported the settlement, enough to suggest that Trimble had been backed by a majority of Unionist voters. Though the Republic's turn-out was lower, a massive 94.4 percent ratified the deal. In the consequent Assembly elections in June, enough pro-agreement Ulster Unionists and Progressive Unionists were returned to guarantee Trimble a working majority over dissident Unionist parties, while the SDLP and Sinn Féin both received handsome support. For the first time since 1972, Northern Ireland had its own form of government and, for the first time ever, one that largely represented the composition of the electorate. **David Trimble** was elected its **First Minister** and the SDLP's **Seamus Mallon** his **deputy**.

DRUMCREE AND OMAGH

The first test for the new political order in Northern Ireland came in July 1998, the traditional climax of the Orange Order's marching season. Since 1995, the Orangemen's march on the Sunday before the "Glorious 12th" from **Drumcree church** to its lodge in Portadown, County Armagh, via the predominantly Nationalist Garvaghy Road, had become a focus for the assertion of traditional Unionist rights and identity. The **July 1998 parade** took on extra significance in the light of the peace agreement and the asserted intention of many dissident Unionists to embody the spirit of their opposition in the march. However, when the march was banned by the Parades Commission, Orangemen reacted by employing a strategy of brinkmanship, calling Unionists and Loyalists from all over Northern Ireland to assemble at Portadown, knowing full well that the RUC and army had already set up blockades to prevent them marching down the Garvaghy Road. Mass demonstrations at the barricades inspired an astonishing wave of violence throughout Northern Ireland. There were numerous attacks on Catholics and their property and, much to the horror of more conservative Unionists, on members of the RUC itself. A tragic event in County Antrim led to many Orangemen abandoning their protest. Early in the morning of July 12, the home of Chrissie Quinn, a Catholic woman living on the mainly Protestant Carmany estate in Ballymoney, County Antrim, was fire-bombed. In the resulting conflagration, three of her four young sons were burned to death. Condemnation of this outrage brought to the boil divisions within the Orange Order which had already been simmering over the tactics employed at Drumcree. Rev William Bingham, the Order's County Chaplain for Armagh, called for the demonstrations to be abandoned, asserting that "a fifteen-minute walk down Garvaghy Road would be ... in the shadow of the coffins of three little boys who wouldn't even know what the Orange Order is about". David Trimble, who had played an important role in previous Drumcree confrontations, stated simply that "no road is worth these lives". The Church of Ireland refused the Order permission to camp on its land and the demonstration gradually fizzled out, leaving residual questions about the continued relevance of the Orange Order to the new Northern Ireland.

Many hoped that the tragic deaths of the Quinn children in Ballymoney would be the last politically motivated killings in Northern Ireland, but this illusion was shattered by events on Saturday, August 15, 1998 in the County Tyrone town of **Omagh**. A dissident Republican group calling itself the **Real IRA** had embarked upon a campaign of town centre bombings to express its opposition to the Accord and jeopardize continued Republican involvement in the peace process. Misleading telephone warnings led the RUC to evacuate people to the very area where a bomb had been planted and 29 people were killed and hundreds injured when the device exploded. It was the worst single atrocity in the entire thirty years of conflict in Northern Ireland. Politicians acted frantically to deter a Loyalist backlash, but were aided by an unprecedented statement by Gerry Adams who, visiting Omagh, declared his unequivocal condemnation of the bombing. Both Irish and British governments announced their intention to strengthen existing legislation against terrorism and, two weeks later, the Real IRA declared a ceasefire.

The Real IRA's announcement helped to ease the tension surrounding the historic first **face-to-face meeting** between David Trimble and Gerry Adams at the beginning of September 1998. They may have stopped short of shaking hands, but their very contact demonstrated just how much progress had been made towards a lasting settlement. The international community's recognition of this came in October 1998 with the award of the **Nobel peace prize** to Trimble and John Hume.

THE ASSEMBLY AND THE IRA STATEMENT

Most of 1999 passed quietly in the wake of the Omagh bombing, as politicians prepared for the opening of the Assembly while paramilitaries maintained their ceasefires (with the exception of the small breakaway Continuity IRA which had never declared one). However, while general optimism remained in place, the implementation of parts of the Good Friday Agreement began to make their ramifications apparent. Army numbers were reduced and many of their security installations, including some notable Belfast landmarks, were demolished or removed. However, the two key issues, interrelated in the eyes of many Unionists, were the release of political prisoners and the decommissioning of weaponry. Firmly opposed to the Agreement, Paisley's DUP called for Sinn Féin members to be barred from taking up their allotted ministerial positions, if the IRA had made no move towards decommissioning. Increasing numbers of Ulster Unionists too began to question what they saw as a precipitous release of prisoners while the IRA remained apparently committed to its armed struggle.

Around the turn of the year, David Trimble found himself conducting two acts of political brinkmanship, first persuading his party to vote narrowly in favour of participation in the Assembly (but only until the end of February 2000, if the IRA had not announced its decommissioning plans) and, secondly, just winning a leadership challenge from the Rev Martin Smyth, an anti-Agreement Unionist. The UUP's concerns were further exacerbated by the report of the **Patten Commission** into the future of the **Royal Ulster Constabulary**. Chaired by the former Tory minister, Chris Patten, who, in his role as Governor of Hong Kong, had overseen the protectorate's return to China, the report astonished Unionists by proposing the RUC's abolition and replacement by a body called the Police Service of Northern Ireland which would recruit its members equally from both Catholic and Loyalist communities. The loss of the words "Royal" and "Ulster" from the new organization's title were impossible for Unionists to accept and the new Secretary of State, **Peter Mandelson** (who had replaced Mo Mowlam) bowed to pressure by rejecting many of the Commission's findings, despite strong Nationalist and Republican protest.

The Assembly got up and running on December 1, 1999 and Sinn Féin's two ministers took up their executive positions, most notably, Martin McGuinness as the new Education Minister, an appointment which alarmed Unionists. Their concern did not persist for long, however, as the row over decommissioning boiled over in early 2000 and Mandelson suspended the Assembly after a mere few months in operation. Sinn Féin's leadership was aghast at this new development, arguing that, as a political party, it had met all the conditions of the Good Friday Agreement and had no powers over decommissioning. Many now feared for the future of devolution, fearing that this apparent dead end in the political process would see many IRA members defecting to the increasingly active Real IRA based on the belief that the Adams-McGuinness strategy for political progress had been a mistake. If Gerry Adams could not persuade the IRA to decommission, they reasoned, then nobody could, while the absence from the political arena of John Hume, who had fallen seriously ill the previous Christmas, represented another significant vacuum.

As Mandelson resumed the mantle of power in Northern Ireland, the next two months saw last-ditch attempts to save the Agreement. While the process saw Adams and McGuinness invited by Tony Blair for talks at Chequers, attention focussed increasingly on the key figure of John Taylor, deputy leader of the Ulster Unionists, whose continued support for Trimble was essential if devolution were to remain a reality. Yet, suddenly, on May 6, 2000 came an event which even the most hardened participants in Northern Ireland's political roller-coaster ride would have found hard to predict. It came in the unexpected form of **a statement from the leadership of the IRA** which, while not renouncing its avowed aim of securing a united Ireland, declared its continued commitment to the peace process. While this itself was of extreme significance, another part of the statement immediately changed the whole context of political debate in Northern Ireland by declaring that "the IRA leadership will initiate a process that will completely and verifiably put IRA arms beyond use". A number of its arms dumps were to be sealed and inspected by agreed third parties, and the IRA had already identified its two favoured inspectors, Cyril Ramaphosa (former secretary-general of the African National Congress) and the ex-president of Finland, Martti Ahtisaari. The IRA's statement had not so much moved the decommissioning goal posts, but marked out an entirely new pitch.

Unionism's troubled waters had still to be calmed, however, and efforts now concentrated on securing backing for the acceptance of the IRA's proposals. The DUP had no intention of doing so, but David Trimble was successful in persuading the Ulster Unionist's ruling council to do so, despite last minute doubts over whether or not John Taylor's support had been secured. Subsequently, Trimble announced his intention to reform membership of the council, many of whose 860 delegates were in attendance as representatives of the Orange Order. Devolution was now back in business and the Assembly was reinstated, despite the renewed efforts of the Real IRA to undermine Republican faith in the process. Their campaign, allegedly co-ordinated from Dundalk in the Republic by the Provisional IRA's ex-quartermaster, set out to prove that the armed struggle was not over, and their most notable success was the bombing of Hammersmith Bridge in London – a target selected simply because the IRA's own bomb, a few years previously, had failed to detonate. Later that year, in September, in a grim reminder of its prowess, the Real IRA mortared an RUC station in Armagh and bombed an Army training camp at Magilligan, County Derry, at the very time that the inquest into the Omagh bombing was in session. Indeed, Omagh has continued to receive coded bomb warnings each week since the original outrage.

Loyalist marching remained a contentious issue. While the 1999 Drumcree parade had been relatively peaceful (its leaders delivering a simple message of protest at the barricade), the 2000 affair saw opponents of the Agreement determined to make a stand, both within the Orange Order and beyond. Yet again, permission to march down the Garvaghy Road was refused by the Parades Commission and once more barricades were mounted by the RUC, bolstered by a huge British Army presence. Observers were concerned to see many Loyalist paramilitaries present at the protest, most notably the recently-released leader of the UDA, **Johnny Adair**. However, while order was largely maintained, subsequent months in Northern Ireland were characterized by a formidable **feud between Loyalist paramilitary groups**. The UDA, joined by the closely linked UFF, embarked on a campaign against its rival, the UVF, which included murder, arson, reprisals and the wounding of an eleven-year-old girl in Coleraine. Some suggested that the dispute was little more than a turf war between rival groups of gangsters over the control of the North's drugs trade, while others regarded the feud as an introspective blood-letting, signifying the hardline Loyalist community's opposition to the Agreement. Whatever the case, the battle precipitated an increased Army presence in areas such as the Falls Road and the return to incarceration of Johnny Adair, the first released political prisoner to be sent back to his cell.

ENVIRONMENT AND WILDLIFE

Ireland conjures up images of a romantic wild territory unscarred by human activity – a somewhat rosy picture, but with more than a little truth to it. Genuine wilderness may be scarce, but centuries of economic deprivation have ensured that most of Ireland is a rural landscape in which the only intervention has come from generations of farmers.

The topography of Ireland is fairly homogenous: there are few high mountain ranges and most of the centre of the country is covered by a flat boggy plain. And with only four degrees of latitude from north to south, it lacks extremes of weather, the enveloping Atlantic Ocean producing a mild, damp climate. Summers are rarely hot, winters rarely cold, and in parts of the west it rains on two days out of every three.

In these conditions you'd expect to find broad-leaved woodland, but intensive pressure on the landscape during the centuries leading up to the famine of 1845 to 1849 denuded the country of its original tree cover. It has been replaced mostly by a patchwork of small grass fields divided by wild untidy hedgerows – long lines of trees acting as refuges for the former woodland community of plants and animals. The small population in Ireland today means that over much of the country the intensity of land use is lower than in many other European countries. Mixed farms are still more common than specialized intensive units.

Natural habitats such as peat bogs, dunes and wetlands still survive here, having all but disappeared elsewhere under the relentless pace of modern development. However, the pressures are growing. The great midland bogs are being rapidly stripped for fuel; mountainsides are disappearing under blankets of exotic conifers; shoals of dead fish are becoming all too frequent a sight in Irish waterways; and rapid housing developments threaten some of Ireland's most valuable habitats, most notably in coastal regions.

FLORA

The flowers of the Irish countryside are impressive perhaps more in their profusion than in their variety. Certainly for anyone travelling from Britain only a few of the common species are going to be unfamiliar, and on the whole it is in the sheer abundance of habitats that the interest lies, rather than any particularly unusual plants.

WOODLANDS

At one time Ireland was covered in oakwoods. This great forest canopy also included elm and alder, and holly grew beneath the tall trees. The first major clearances of woodlands were in the late Stone Age (5000 years ago), but vast areas of forest survived well into the medieval period. By the eighteenth century felling for housing, shipping and smelting had been so extensive that wood actually started to be imported. Today only six percent of Ireland is woodland (the lowest percentage of any European country), and afforestation in recent decades has tended to be coniferous, doing immense damage to natural habitats. As a result, **indigenous oak forests** are extremely rare, though good examples can still be seen at Glengarriff and in the National Parks at Killarney and Glenveagh.

Throughout the country strong westerly winds keep the treeline low (about 150m in the west to 350m in the east) and small trees growing diagonally towards the east as if swept by one almighty blast are a common sight in exposed areas, particularly in the west. The lim-

BOGS

Bogs – or peatland – cover around one sixth of Ireland's total landmass, a proportion in Europe topped only by Finland. Now recognized internationally as providing habitats of great ecological value, considerable progress has been made in the conservation of blanket bogs, but there's no room for complacency. Taking the three main categories as a whole – raised bog, blanket bog and fen – the Irish government has only conserved 61 percent of its proposed target area.

Bogs have formed over the last 10,000 years: at the end of the last Ice Age retreating glaciers and ice sheets left central Ireland covered by shallow lakes that filled with vegetation, which then dried and partly decomposed. Today they form a remarkable legacy, not only in terms of biodiversity, but also as a living repository of cultural history. The bog is a great natural preservative, and as well as providing botanists with a calendar of plant history over the past nine thousand years, it has bequeathed a great deal to archeologists – dug-out canoes, gold and silver artefacts, shoes, amber beads and, of course, bodies in extraordinarily good condition. Bog pools were revered during the Bronze Age, and votive offerings such as weapons and ornaments placed there. The Iron Age saw the construction of *tochair*, or wooden pathways, to cross the bog, and these too have been discovered.

The **exploitation of boglands** has been going on for centuries. Dried peat sods have always been used for fuel; the top layer of matted vegetation was once used to insulate thatched roofs; preserved timbers dug from the bog – some of them 5000 years old – provided stout beams for lintels; and the lime-rich marl below the peat was used to fertilize the land. Bogs have a unique place in folk history too and the annual ritual of "saving the turf" is well represented in stories, poetry and song, carrying with it traditions as strong as any other form of harvest.

Blanket bogs are characterized by a layer of peat between two and six metres thick spreading over large areas of land, and are found in both low-lying and mountainous areas. Connemara, Mayo and Donegal provide particularly dramatic landscapes, with huge expanses of open countryside, wild, treeless and exposed, and blanket bogs are also found in Cork, Kerry and the Wicklow Mountains. But it's the Slieve Bloom Mountains, straddling counties Laois and Offaly, which offer the finest examples of relatively undamaged blanket bog, and the two mountain roads that divide the range rise to 1300ft, with wonderful views in every direction.

Somewhat smaller, and favoured by commercial operators, **raised bogs** are found in the central lowlands, domed in shape, with an average peat layer of seven metres, though they can develop to nearly twice that. To see a raised bog of international importance, go to Mongan Bog in County Offaly.

Fens are found in water-logged areas and lakesides and are different to blanket and raised bogs in that the layer of peat is only about two metres deep and plants are fed by mineral-rich water as opposed to just rainwater. Pollardstown Fen, two miles northeast of Newbridge, is a fine expanse of fen. **Peatland World**, nearby in Lullymore, County Kildare, provides an excellent introduction to Irish bogs (see p.143).

ited range of flowers found in forests includes **foxgloves**, **violets** and **primroses** – this last growing in abundance, and flowering from March to May.

THE WEST

County Kerry and the peninsulas of west Cork benefit from a damp climate which, because of the Gulf Stream, is far warmer than elsewhere in the country. Consequently it's here that you'll find Ireland's limited number of fairly exotic plant species, including palm trees, the Mediterranean **strawberry tree** (or arbutus) and very rare Lusitanian plants including Irish spurge and **St Patrick's Cabbage**, the latter found nowhere else in Europe. In the valleys of Killarney National Park you can also see **holly** and **rowan trees**, and common on the mountainsides are various heathers, forming a beautiful purple cloak when in bloom in September. Hedgerows throughout the southwest are commonly full of the brilliant purple-red bulbs of **fuschia**, and musky-scented **honeysuckle** clambers over walls and hedges. A shock of bright orange **mont bretia** is a common sight along many quiet laneways in the west, as are the dramatic pink spears of foxgloves that grow throughout the country. Other species which you may come across include the Kerry butterwort, the Kerry lily and occasionally Cornish moneywort.

The mountains of Connemara have a somewhat colder climate and here the plantlife is more spartan, but you will find **St Dabeoc's heath** and, in the west of the region, wild **London pride**.

In some counties, notably Donegal, Mayo and Kerry there are extensive **sand dunes**. In summer these are clothed in a profusion of wild flowers such as the yellow **bird's-foot trefoil** and pink sea bindweed. Prickly-leafed sea-holly, sea-pansy and kidney vetch are common, and the exotic-looking **bee orchid** is one of the rarities sometimes found in the dunes. Sea pinks thrive on cliffs and in sandy places, and on coastal cliffs in Donegal you will find wild lovage and dwarf willow. The shoreline is always worth exploring for the splendid varieties of **seaweed** that flourish, including kelp, bladder wrack and thong weed.

The limestone karst region of **the Burren** in County Clare is an extraordinary landscape (see also "Wetlands" below). From a distance its virtually treeless slopes appear completely barren, but the long cracks and grooves in the limestone support and shelter an astonishing array of both **alpine and arctic plants**: hart's tongue and maidenhair ferns grow well, and the profusion of wild flowers include the blue spring gentian and mountain avens, saxifrages and a number of orchid species; the best times to visit are spring and early summer.

WETLANDS

Much of Ireland is low-lying, and coupled with high rainfall this means there's an abundance of wetland environments. Irish **bogs** support a range of plantlife: black bog rush, purple moor grass, **sphagnum mosses** and milkwort are all commonly found on blanket bogs. On raised bogs you are likely to find **bog cotton**, sphagnum moss, sundew, ling heather, cranberry and cladonia lichen. The plantlife in fens, where the water source is mineral-rich, is quite different, and you can expect to find fen rush, bog bean, saw sedge and pond weed. Fens also support various **orchids**, particularly marsh helleborine and the marsh orchid, and the **marsh marigold** and **flag iris** are both fairly common.

Alongside many rivers are callows – areas of meadow which are flooded during periods of high rainfall, producing nutrient-rich soil where **herbs** such as **meadowsweet**, **loosestrife** and **marsh pea** thrive.

Turloughs, found most readily in the Burren of County Clare, are hollows which appear as meadows for most of the year, but become lakes after flooding. Generally found in areas of limestone, they support a range of grasses, but you may also find cinquefoil, creeping buttercup and various sedges.

MAMMALS

Ireland, like many islands, has a relatively small number of mammal species; besides its famous lack of snakes, there are no moles, for example. However, the largely undeveloped landscapes mean that there are plenty of opportunities for observing mammals in the wild, particularly in remote areas.

THE COASTS

Ireland's **marine life** is particularly impressive. The remoteness of islands off the west coast make them havens for wildlife: **grey seals** breed on island beaches and in caves during autumn months. Due to lack of disturbance, nocturnal animals like **otters** can be seen during daylight, hunting for food among rocks and pools. Herds of **common seals** can be seen basking on sand banks in numerous locations all around the coast, especially in the west and at Strangford Lough in the northeast, where there are literally hundreds of them in late June when the new pups are born.

Patient sea-watching from a western headland may also be rewarded with a school of **dolphins** or porpoises, or the occasional **whale** feeding in the rich inshore waters. Whales might also be seen off the east coast of the Ards Peninsula, and if you're lucky you may see basking sharks.

INLAND

Inland there's far less of interest. Small mammals include both grey and red squirrels in Ireland's diminished woodlands; stoats, rabbits and foxes are common, as is the pygmy shrew, and the **Irish hare** is a wonderful sight spotted from time to time running across huge areas of bog. You may well see **badgers** late at night scuttling along a country lane away from car headlamps, though the location of a sett is often kept secret for fear of baiting. The rare **pine marten** is occasionally sighted darting amongst the rocks of the Burren, County Clare, near low hazel scrub, a furry brown weasel-like creature with cream markings on its throat and ears.

Around a quarter of all land mammals in Ireland are **bats**, which tend to roost in undisturbed buildings, old trees and the cracks of old stone bridges, certain species moving to underground sites such as caves and cellars during the winter months. Bats can be spotted at night as they flit through the air hunting for insects, and are especially easy to see when flying low over water.

The only mammals of any size that you are likely to encounter are wild **goats**, which generally keep to remote hillsides – though on occasion they have been known to explore Mayo villages – and herds of **red deer**, which roam in the remote valleys of the Glenveagh National Park.

BIRDS

What Ireland may lack in mammals it more than makes up for in bird life. The spectacular coastline provides superb opportunities for spotting seabirds and, in season, flocks of migrating species. There's interest inland too, with wetlands providing largely undisturbed habitats for a great range of waterbirds and mountainous areas harbouring birds of prey.

THE COASTS

Ireland has over two thousand miles of **coast**, most of it undeveloped, and hundreds of **islands**, providing a wealth of opportunities for observing the country's rich bird life. It's the wild coasts of the west and the north that have the most dramatic scenic appeal and it's here you'll find some of the best opportunities for observing **seabirds**.

Kerry has Ireland's largest concentration of seabirds: the Blasket Islands, the Skelligs and Puffin Island are home to impressive colonies of puffins, and Little Skellig is also home to around twenty thousand pairs of gannets, a fabulous sight as they dive for food from heights of 120ft. Kerry's islands also have a great number of Manx shearwaters and the world's largest colonies of stormy petrels.

Clear Island, off the west Cork coast, has an important observatory recording the patterns of **migratory birds**, and here you can see huge numbers of Manx shearwaters, particularly during July and August. Other species here in abundance include stormy petrels, gannets, cormorants, fulmars and kittiwakes.

In the southeast the Wexford Sloblands are the wintering ground for around ten thousand Greenland white-fronted geese – over a third of the world population – and along with these there are mute and Bewick swans, godwits, oystercatchers and coots. At Tacumshane Lake south of here wintering wildfowl include brent geese and scaups.

A trip to the bird sanctuary on the Saltees Islands off the Wexford coast, especially in late spring or early summer, is rewarded with the sight of puffins, razorbills, cormorants, auks and kittiwakes. The nearby Hook Head Peninsula also makes an exhilarating spot from which to observe migrating seabirds in spring and autumn.

In the northeast, Strangford Lough has all the characteristics of a marine environment, despite the fact that its opening to the sea is exteremely narrow. It's most famous as a wintering ground for migrating birds: the annual arrival of the pale-bellied brent geese from Arctic Canada is expected in late August and by the end of October their population can reach twelve thousand. The sheer variety of bird life on the lough is stupendous: Icelandic whooper swans, wigeon, pintail and shoveler are all common here, and overwintering waders include golden plovers and oystercatchers. In the summer huge numbers of terns arrive from their winter residences in Africa.

The spectacular cliffs of Horn Head, County Donegal, has Ireland's largest colony of razorbill, and the magnificent Antrim coast offers excellent opportunities for observing **cliff-breeding birds**, especially at Rathlin Island with its colonies of fulmar, guillemot, puffin, kittiwake and Manx shearwater.

Ireland's low coasts, especially on the east and south, are punctuated by estuaries, some with vast, lonely mudflats. Despite their bare appearance, below the surface they harbour countless shellfish and other burrowing animals, attracting feeding **waders** and **wildfowl**. From October to April the estuaries are alive with the calls of curlews, redshanks, godwits, widgeon, teal and shoveler.

Ireland's absence of tree cover means few breeding birds, but cuckoos are a special feature of Irish sand dunes, as they exploit the nests of the ubiquitous meadow pipits. The chough, a comparatively rare crow, breeds extensively on the south and west coasts and can be seen in large flocks feeding in sand dune systems.

WETLANDS

Travellers in the Midlands and west of Ireland will encounter numerous small **lakes** and reed-fringed **marshes**. High rainfall and poor drainage ensure plentiful surface water, especially in winter, and breeding **water birds** are extremely common as a result. Every waterway has its resident pair of swans, moorhens and herons. Wetlands of international importance include Lough Neagh, which supports a dozen species of duck, large numbers of Bewick and whooper swans, terns and grebes, and the **Shannon Callows** near Clonmacnois, where in late summer you can listen for corncrakes as they search for mates. For Ireland's biggest corncrake population, however, you will need to travel to Inishowen – and most particularly Malin Head.

MOUNTAINS

Mountainous regions provide rocky crags and cliffs for **birds of prey**: the little-visited Sperrins Mountains are noted for buzzards, hen harriers and sparrowhawks, and both here and in the Mourne Mountains you can see peregrine falcons and kestrels. In the uplands of the Wicklow Mountains hen harriers are easily sighted, and other species include ouzel and red grouse, typical of heather-clad moorland. The wild mountains of Cork were Ireland's last habitat for golden eagles, but today you can still see merlins and sparrowhawks.

USEFUL CONTACTS

ENFO, 17 St. Andrew Street, Dublin 2 (☎01/6793144).
Invaluable resource centre for information on environmental issues and campaign groups in the Republic; personal visits welcome, and a wealth of literature available.

Northern Irish Tourist Board, 59 North Street, Belfast, BT1 1NB (☎028/9024 6609).
Detailed information on birdwatching in Northern Ireland.

ARCHITECTURE

BEGINNINGS

The most tangible legacy left by the inhabitants of prehistoric Ireland are the numerous stone tombs, found throughout the country. The earliest of these date from the Neolithic period (3700–2000 BC) and the simplest form is the **dolmen**. Resembling a tripod, this is usually formed by several standing stones supporting one or two capstones, the largest of which can be as much as 20ft long. While these simply marked a grave, the **court-cairn** was more complex, consisting of a rectangular burial chamber, again built with large stones, and covered by a mound of earth. Conceptually similar, though most advanced of all, however, are the **passage tombs**, of which the best-known examples are clustered near Drogheda, in the valley of the River Boyne, at Newgrange, Howth and Dowth. As the name suggests, a passage from the edge of the mound provides access to one or two burial chambers. The **Newgrange** grave is positioned inside a circle of standing stones; its 280ft diameter mound is almost 35ft high and the passage is 60ft long. The burial chamber's roof shows its builders' grasp of the technique of corbelling where layers of flat stones are placed on top of each other, each layer projecting gradually outwards below the next. Most striking here, however, is that an opening in the stonework was created to allow sunlight to penetrate the tomb on the winter solstice, December 21, the shortest day of the year, evidence of a society sophisticated in its understanding of the calendar.

The **Bronze Age** (2000–500 BC) saw further tomb-building, though the constructions were generally smaller. Most tombs surviving from this period were plain compartments of stone, though some more elaborate chambers were covered by a wedge-shaped mound. Domestic structures are thought to have been constructed of wood and daub and the most significant development, circular fortified enclosures built on hilltops, came towards the end of the period. However, the finest examples of these **hill forts** date from the **Iron Age**. The huge fortress of **Dún Aengus** on the Aran Island of Inishmore sits spectacularly on the cliff-top, while, the partially restored **Grianán of Aileach**, near Derry, affords staggering views down to Inishowen and for miles around in all directions. There is evidence of many other smaller ring forts, built of stone or earth, which were probably fortified dwellings. The Iron Age also saw the building of **crannógs**, artificial islands, set in defensive isolation in the middle of lakes.

EARLY CHRISTIAN AND MEDIEVAL PERIOD

Christianity arrived in Ireland in the fifth century and, consequently, most of the architectural remains from this period until medieval times are **ecclesiastical**. Ireland was divided into bishoprics which resulted in a system of scattered monasteries. Most buildings were constructed of wood and daub and none, whether religious or domestic, has survived. The stone churches you now see when visiting early monastic sites were constructed during a later era. However, among the ruins of **St Fionan's Abbey** on the rocky crag of Skellig Michael off the Kerry coast is a group of six dry-stone beehive huts, built according to the corbel technique. **Stone churches** began to be built in the ninth century, and an exceptional example dating from this time is **Gallarus Oratory** on the Dingle Peninsula, which represents a transition from the round beehive shape to the later rectangular church. The remains of **round towers** are often found on early monastic sites. These slender, stone, tapering structures, sometimes more than 100ft high, are a specifically Irish phenomenon. The entrance is usually several feet above ground level and it was once believed that this signified a defensive purpose.

However, it now seems that they were used as bell-towers and the doorway's elevation was purely for structural purposes. One of the best-preserved towers is part of the St Molaise monastic complex on **Devenish Island** in Lower Lough Erne, near Enniskillen, Co. Fermanagh.

Increasing contact with England and continental Europe saw the introduction of the highly decorative **Romanesque** style to Irish ecclesiastical architecture from the twelfth century onwards. Built between 1127 and 1134, the beautiful, twin-towered **Cormac's Chapel** in Cashel, Co. Tipperary, is the earliest and best surviving example, though much smaller in scale than its European counterparts. Gradually, the simple box style of church architecture began to be superseded by the **basilica** style, characterized by a nave, side aisles and a round apse at the eastern end. Often, church doorways and chancel arches were decorated with intricate sculpture using traditional Celtic motifs, such as interlacing and animal patterns, seen to tremendous effect in the wonderful six-arched doorway of **Clonfert Cathedral**, Co. Galway.

Further changes resulted from the arrival of monastic orders, such as the Cistercians, Dominicans and Benedictines. They favoured large cruciform churches and their settlements, typified by the Cistercian **Boyle Abbey**, Co. Roscommon, were very European in their layout of a cloister surrounded by church, chapter house and domestic buildings.

Much of Ireland was under **Norman** subjugation by the end of the twelfth century and the invaders constructed fortifications to protect their new domains. The earliest of these were earthworks surmounted by wooden forts. However, soon more substantial **stone castles**, distinguished by a massive keep, began to be constructed, such as those at **Carrickfergus**, Co. Antrim, and **Trim**, Co. Meath. The fifteenth-century castle at **Cahir** in Co. Tipperary, surrounded by high enclosing walls and defended by eight towers, is the most impressive of the surviving feudal strongholds.

Simultaneously, the Anglo-Normans, as they came to be known, introduced **Gothic** architecture to Ireland. The huge new **cathedrals**, constructed in the main towns, were characterized by the use of high-pointed arches and clustered columns. Dublin's two thirteenth-century cathedrals, **St Patrick's** and **Christchurch**, are among the finest examples of this innovation.

Later Anglo-Norman fortifications tended to be smaller in size, typified by the **tower houses** which began to be constructed during the fifteenth century and continued to be built over the next two hundred years. There are the remains of hundreds of these rectangular, fortified multistorey residences across the island, several in relatively close proximity and varying states of ruin around **Strangford Lough**, Co. Down. In the west, two such houses have been restored and are open to the public – elaborate **Bunratty Castle**, Co. Clare, and the sixteenth-century **Dunguaire Castle**, Co. Galway.

THE SEVENTEENTH AND EIGHTEENTH CENTURIES

Few purely domestic residences constructed before the **seventeenth century** have survived. One such, **Rothe House** in Kilkenny, built in 1594, is a unique example of an Irish merchant's home from the prosperous Tudor period and is now open as a museum. Most domestic buildings from this period show some evidence of fortification, reflecting a turbulent time in Irish history. The first **unfortified mansion** is claimed to be **Beaulieu House**, Co. Louth, built in the 1660s following Cromwell's departure. A red-brick, hipped-roof dwelling, it closely follows the **Dutch style** popular in contemporary England. This century also saw the first **thatched cottages**, constructed of clay, whitewashed both inside and out, and consisting of merely one or two rooms poorly illuminated by small windows. Though these may have suited the damp Irish climate, the humble conditions reflected the continuation of a repressively feudal social system in which the rights of the landlord held sway.

Classical buildings began to appear in Ireland in the late-seventeenth century, the finest example of this period being the **Royal Hospital at Kilmainham**, Dublin, built between 1680 and 1687. It was designed by Sir William Robinson who used as his model Les Invalides in Paris, the home for retired soldiers. The building's core is an arcaded courtyard around which are ranged a great hall and chapel on one side and living quarters on the other three. During the 1980s, the now derelict building was fully restored at a cost of £20 million and reopened in 1991 as the Irish Museum of Modern Art.

The following century witnessed massive developments in public and private building. The Irish ruling class, known sometimes as the Protestant Ascendancy, drew its prosperity in part from lands granted or acquired during the 1600s and consolidated its position on them through the construction of mansions. The presence of an Irish Parliament in Dublin, though still subject to Westminster, gave the city a new confidence, and evidence of its consequent wealth is present in the many fine public buildings and elegant squares that still exist today. The Ascendancy's dominance was reinforced through the enactment of the repressive penal laws which prevented Catholics from holding public office, owning property or practising their religion. As a result, hardly a Catholic church was constructed during this period, though a notable survivor is the South Parish Church in Cork, built in 1766.

The architectural style favoured by the Ascendancy was influenced by the work and publications of the sixteenth-century Italian architect, Andrea Palladio. Equally popular in England, **Palladian** designs first appeared in Ireland in the 1720s and the largest and most palatial Palladian country house is **Castletown** in Co. Kildare, completed in 1732 and designed by Alessandro Galilei and Sir Edward Lovett Pearce. Elsewhere, the Palladian style was utilized in the construction of simpler houses built as much for utility as for ostentation, such as **Hazelwood**, Co. Sligo, and **Ledwithstown**, Co. Longford. Pearce was also responsible for the design of the great **Parliament House** (now the Bank of Ireland) in Dublin's College Green, constructed between 1729 and 1739. It is the earliest large-scale Palladian public building in all Ireland or England, and the model, a century later, for the British Museum in London. Another notable architect of the period was the German, Richard Castle, responsible for **Leinster House** (1745), commissioned as a town house for the dukes of Leinster, and now the seat of the Dáil.

Towards the end of the eighteenth century, **Neoclassicism** became the prevailing architectural style, taking ancient Greece and Rome as even more direct influences than its predecessor. A refined Neoclassical creation is the **Casino at Marino**, just northeast of Dublin, designed during the 1760s by Sir William Chambers as a country house for Lord Charlemont. **Castle Coole**, near Enniskillen, Co. Fermanagh, was designed by James Wyatt and is unarguably the best Neoclassical house in Ireland. The house is now owned by the British National Trust and has been lavishly, if controversially, restored – the new colour scheme involves a shade that the previous owner, who still lives there, calls "Germolene pink".

The great architect of this period was undoubtedly **James Gandon** (1743–1823) who designed some of the most important public buildings in Dublin, including the **Custom House** and the **Four Courts**, both dating from the 1780s. Each building has an impressive columned riverside facade, topped by a magnificent dome.

Sadly, however, much of Ireland's Georgian architecture has vanished. As late as the 1950s, Dublin was still one of the most perfectly intact eighteenth-century cities in Europe, but much has since been lost (for more on this see opposite). Irish independence and the subsequent civil war led to a decline in the fortunes of the **Anglo-Irish Ascendancy**, resulting in the sale of many estates and **Big Houses**. Many of the houses themselves still lie in ruins following their destruction by a people who had long been repressed by a political system completely identified with their erstwhile owners. In recent years, however, there has been something approaching a *rapprochement* and the Anglo-Irish heritage is beginning to be seen as something inherently Irish. A good example of this change is **Strokestown Park House**, Co. Roscommon, an outstanding Palladian dwelling which has been meticulously restored by a local garage business and is now open to the public.

THE NINETEENTH CENTURY

Although the Act of Union (1801) dissolved Ireland's independent government and diminished localized power and prosperity, architecture continued to flourish throughout the nineteenth century. Indeed the expansion in numbers of Irish-born members of the profession led to the establishment of the **Royal Institute of the Architects of Ireland** in 1839. At the same time, many English architects continued to be commissioned.

Perhaps feeling further isolated from their English contemporaries after Dublin ceased to be a centre of power, the Anglo-Irish Ascendancy embarked on a spate of building during the first few decades. Neoclassicism remained the predominant style, exemplified by such buildings as the **General Post Office** in Dublin's O'Connell Street, designed by Francis Johnston and completed in 1818, and William Morrison's **Carlow Courthouse**, dating from 1828.

The nineteenth century was also notable for the revival of the Gothic style, the catalyst for which was Catholic emancipation in 1829, leading to the construction of numerous **new churches**, influenced by the French style of slender towers and pointed spires surrounded by smaller pinnacles. Examples include **St Finbarr's Cathedral** in Cork and **St Colman's Cathedral**, Cobh, both begun in the 1860s. The similarly aged **Ashford Castle**, Co. Mayo, demonstrates the adaptation of the Gothic style to domestic architecture. Elsewhere, there are many examples of the architectural eclecticism which characterized the nineteenth century. **St Mary's Pro-Cathedral** in Dublin, started in 1814, shows a marked **Greek Revival** influence, a style more often associated with large-scale public building. **Tudor** and **Oriental** styles were also popular and it was almost as though architects saw the rapid development of the **railway system** as an opportunity to test the limits of their imagination in the design of station buildings.

Towards the end of the century, the **Celtic revival**, associated with the Gaelic literary movement, had a limited impact on architectural design, most noticeably in church-building. The favoured style was Hiberno-Romanesque and examples of its influence are visible in the design of the **Honan Chapel**, University College Cork, and **Spiddal Church**, Co. Galway.

TO THE PRESENT

A history of Ireland's twentieth-century architecture is as much about what has been lost as about what was built. Any post-colonial country necessarily inherits a complicated relation to its past, and buildings are one of the most tangible reminders of past eras. After Independence in 1922, the country entered a state of dormancy, from which it has only begun to emerge in the last three decades. The great public buildings of the colonizer continued to function as intended under the new order. Country house architecture fared badly with only a few hundred period houses left intact (see p.692), and Dublin's elaborate Georgian squares and domestic architecture have been vandalized as much by central government as by the property developers. The eminent English architectural historian Sir John Summerson was employed by the Electricity Supply Board in the 1960s to justify the demolition of a range of Georgian houses on Fitzwilliam Square, Dublin. Sir John said he believed that the interjection of some modern buildings would greatly relieve the monotony of red brick!

This is not to say that nothing notable was built between 1922 and 1960. The dominant influence during this period was **Art Deco**. While a restrained use of the style was invoked to good effect in the construction of institutions such as hospitals, it barely disguised their sombre debt to the workhouses of the mid-nineteenth century. As in the development of the visual arts, **modernism** reached Ireland relatively late in the twentieth century. Indeed, the first significant modern construction was the **Dublin Airport terminal**, designed by Desmond Fitzgerald, in 1940. One of the first postwar constructions to express this modernity with comfort was the **Busáras** station in Store Street, Dublin, which was designed in 1953 by Michael Scott, later to become one of the leading exponents of modern architecture in Ireland. The bus station contains a theatre, a sign of a bygone era's benevolence.

The economic boom of the 1960s and 1970s saw considerable expansion in architecture, though the demands of industry paid little heed to the heritage of the past. Systematic and effective legislation preserving buildings and monuments presupposes a buoyant economy and a sort of uncomplicated approach to the past which had not developed. Innately conservative Irish society had yet to discover any meaningful understanding of the importance of preservation and the rapid changes to the urban landscapes of Dublin and other cities took place without hindrance of debate or planning. For instance, it was only in the 1970s that **factory builders** began to consider the impact of such construction on the aesthetic nature of the local environment. Carroll's cigarette factory in Dundalk, designed by Ronald Tallon, is a worthy example of attractive development.

Similar modernist trends became visible in **school building**, such as Birr School by Peter and Mary Doyle, 1980, which applied new designs to accommodate contemporary educational theory. The most significant work in **ecclesiastical architecture** has been undertaken by Liam McCormick from Derry, whose style is marked by a consideration of the natural landmarks which overshadow his projects. Fine examples of his church designs are to be found in the Donegal villages of Burt, Creeslough and Glenties.

The recession of the 1980s reduced building activity and increasing worldwide awareness of environmental issues stimulated debate among architects about the cultivation of a new Irish architecture. Greater concerns for context and progressive town planning came to dominate new architectural theory. Postwar barbarism gradually became subsumed by desires to maintain the remnants of the country's built heritage and considerable state funding was provided for the restoration of buildings such as the **Custom House**, **Dublin Castle**, the **Casino at Marino** and the **Royal Hospital**, Kilmainham which was converted into the Irish Museum of Modern Art.

The grim public housing style of the 1960s, deck-access low- and high-rise blocks, was abandoned in favour of schemes such as **City Quay**, Dublin, and **Share Housing** in Cork. These 1980s developments paid far greater attention to street pattern and context and set the template for future designs. Similarly, private housing has undergone radical changes, though the virtual absence of planning regulations has resulted in a blight of **bungalow construction** which mars the landscape all the way from Kerry to Donegal. Conversely, many rural areas are equally sullied by dilapidated properties which have been deliberately allowed to fall into ruin.

Sadly, Dublin's cityscape is also marred by far too many examples of retarded modernist building. One of the worst examples of this trend is the Civic Offices at Wood Quay. Commonly known as the "bunkers", these offensive structures are doubly horrible in that they were constructed on the most important early Viking archeological site in Europe before it was fully excavated. In contrast, an especially fine example of the juxtaposition of old and modern buildings can be seen at New Square in Trinity College, Dublin.

Over the last decade, Ireland has been the beneficiary of considerable funding, resulting from its membership of the European Union. At the same time, tax incentives have encouraged private investment in the redevelopment of run-down areas in the major urban centres and towns. As a direct consequence, the country has witnessed a building boom of a magnitude similar to the accelerated urban expansion of the eighteenth century. The most significant changes have again taken place in the city centres, most notably in the construction of massive new shopping centres and in adaptations of Ireland's industrial and commercial past. Redevelopment of the semi-derelict **Temple Bar** area of Dublin was the subject of a competition. Revitalized as Dublin's answer to Paris's Left Bank or London's Covent Garden, the streets have been cobbled and pedestrianized, public sculptures installed, and a host of cultural institutions and fashionable bars and shops occupy the restored or newly constructed premises. The gains are there for all to see, but the downside is that Dublin's appearance is edging nearer and nearer to that of any other European city.

Much state funding has also been directed towards tourism. Virtually every town now seems to have its own heritage or interpretive centre, no matter the level of justification. While existing buildings are, for the most part, converted to accommodate these attractions, several new buildings have been constructed. The Office of Public Works is at the forefront of this trend. Several large-scale interpretive centres have already been completed by them, including **Dunquin**, County Kerry, and **Ceíde Fields**, County Mayo and others have been developed through Heritage funding, such as **Ardara**, County Donegal. The marketing of the past in the service of economic recovery has touched every country town. Fake timber shopfronts abound, creating an illusory but gentler version of the past, which has more to do with cultural stereotypes than with the grim historical realities of the subsistence of the majority of Irish people.

Finally, in complete contrast, Ireland is currently in the grip of a **property pricing boom** comparable to the worst excesses of London in the 1980s. The cost of housing in Dublin and the most popular tourist and holiday home areas has risen to levels that prohibit all but the wealthiest from purchase. Though prices in the North remain relatively low, certain areas there too have seen a dramatic escalation. While homelessness has become a way of life for some in the Republic, there have been significant changes in the landscape, especially resulting from an apparently ever-broadening commuting range. Ugly new housing developments have sprung up around towns even as far as eighty or ninety miles from Dublin, and, if you drive around, the whole country can sometimes seem like one constant road-widening or resurfacing scheme. Coming to terms with these changes will be a major challenge for Ireland as the twenty-first century progresses.

THE ART OF IRELAND

Irish art has long been overshadowed by the island's literature and, to some extent, its music. For the lay majority, Irish art is generally associated with the products of a Celtic culture in the centuries preceding and following the arrival of Christianity, and few, if pressed, are able to name a single Irish artist of the modern period. There is, however, a significant body of modern Irish work that deserves broader recognition.

THE STONE, BRONZE AND IRON AGES

The oldest art works in Ireland available to us can be found in the Stone Age tombs of the Boyne Valley, especially the passage grave at **Newgrange** (see "Architecture", p.690). The stones and slabs of this 5000-year-old burial chamber are adorned with basic, but impressive whorls, zigzags and geometric forms whose purpose has long since been lost to us. The site has also yielded stone balls and beads as well as the remains of some rudimentary pottery.

Other decorative work on stone has survived from the **Bronze Age** (2000–500 BC), an epoch more notable for some startling work in goldsmithery. The National Museum of Ireland in Dublin houses a stunning collection of artefacts and jewellery, including a variety of lunulae (crescent-shaped collars of beaten gold), earrings and torques (twisted gold necklaces and armbands). One of the finest examples is the **Gleninsheen Gorget**, an elaborate gold neck ornament with roundel fastenings, dating from around 800 BC.

The subsequent **Iron Age** witnessed continuing developments. There are a number of fine examples of figurative stone carving scattered around the country. Among the most notable are the **Janus statue**, two conjoined and grotesque figures carved back to back, in Calgach Cemetery on Boa Island, Co. Fermanagh, and the **Tandragee Idol**, now in the Church of Ireland Cathedral, Armagh city. Linear designs of flowing tendrils, typical of the La Tène style of Celtic art found in continental Europe, are visible on a number of surviving works, including the well-known **Turoe stone** in Co. Galway (see p.388). The National Museum holds several good examples of this style, including the **Somerset box lid** (also from Galway) and the so-called **Petrie Crown** gold collar, part of a hoard unearthed in 1896 in Broighter, Co. Derry, which also included a wonderful miniature sailing boat complete with oars.

EARLY CHRISTIAN ART

In Ireland, the early Christian era (432–1170 AD) is often described as the **Golden Age**. Irish society remained unscathed by the turmoil in the centuries following the fall of the Roman Empire and its society based on small tribal units was not disturbed radically by the advent of Christianity. Indeed, artists and craftworkers retained a privileged status, continuing to develop skills in metalwork and other areas. The period attained its zenith with the production of justifiably famous illuminated manuscripts such as the **Book of Kells**, but other wonderful artefacts have also survived from this era and a visit to the magnificent **high crosses** will take you to some of the most beautiful parts of the country.

ILLUMINATED MANUSCRIPTS

The first of the surviving manuscripts is an early seventh-century book of psalms known as **the Cathach** (pronounced Kohok), now housed in the library of the Royal Irish Academy in Dublin. Only the initial letter of each paragraph of Latin text is decorated and such illustration consists of scrolls and animals in a limited range of colours. These motifs set the style for the greater books that followed.

The first of the truly magnificent illuminated texts is the **Book of Durrow**, dating from around 675 AD, and displayed alongside the *Book of Kells* in the Old Library in Trinity College, Dublin. The *Book of Durrow* was produced by the monastery of the same name in Co. Offaly and consists of a copy of the four gospels. Though the artist's palette was limited to red, yellow and green, the three major stylistic components of spirals, animals and interlacing bands, typical of the great books, are plainly evident. These bands, like the dots which surround some of the initial letters in the *Cathach*, suggest a stylistic link with Coptic or other Middle Eastern sources. The *Book* is also notable for its full-page illustrations (called carpet pages) devoted entirely to ornamentation or a depiction of the saint whose gospel follows.

Other books were produced during the next hundred and fifty years. Two others displayed in Trinity College are the **Book of Armagh**, commissioned in 807 by Torbach, Bishop of Armagh, and the **Book of Dimma**, typical of a smaller pocket format designed to be carried around. Similar illuminated manuscripts, such as the *Lindisfarne Gospels*, can be found in museums and libraries abroad, reflecting the travels of many of the monks of the period. St Columba, for example, spread the Gospels and founded monasteries around Britain and Europe.

However, it was in the **Book of Kells** that this art form found its highest expression in Ireland. Again a copy of the Gospels in Latin, this glorious manuscript is a perfect synthesis of all the motifs and styles – both imported or developed locally – used in earlier books. Its origins are obscure and some suggest that it was produced by monks from Iona, St Columba's first Scottish base. Created around 800 AD, it takes its name from the Columban monastery at Kells, Co. Meath, where it was kept for centuries until it was transferred to Trinity in 1654 for protection during the Cromwellian wars. Mere words cannot convey the beauty of the book's illustrations, from the vividly ornamental geometric and floral patterns to the human and animal forms gracing the page margins. It is no wonder at all that the *Book of Kells* is easily Ireland's most popular visitor attraction and queueing for a view is an essential part of a trip to the island.

METALWORK AND JEWELLERY

The decorative style of the illuminated manuscripts is reflected in the best of the period's metalwork, including two impressive chalices. The first is part of the eighth- or ninth-century **Derrynaflan Hoard**, discovered in Co. Tipperary in 1980, while the second, a century older, was found at **Ardagh**. Both chalices are roughly eight inches high and similar in shape, with a rounded cup and a conical base, though the elaborately engraved Ardagh chalice is technically more refined than its plainer predecessor. However, for evidence that secular art also flourished during this period, look no further than the eighth-century bronze **Tara Brooch**, found on the seashore near Bettystown, Co. Louth, in 1850. Covered with gold and decorated with amber, glass and fine metalwork, intricate designs on both its sides bear close similarities to patterns in the *Book of Kells*. Both chalices and the brooch are on view in the National Museum.

The development of metalwork over the following centuries showed the increasing influence of Romanesque and Viking styles. While the latter is apparent in numerous examples of brooches and other jewellery, the former is best exemplified by the magnificent **Cross of Cong**. The Cross was made around 1123 in order to contain and protect a chip from the True Cross, presented by Pope Calixtus II to the King of Connacht, Turlough O'Connor. It is made of oak, encased in gilt bronze, copper and silver, and the arms are decorated with fine gold filigree. There is a central bronze boss into which is set a polished crystal.

HIGH CROSSES AND SHEILA-NA-GIGS

The Cross of Cong predated by several centuries another great, but also relatively short-lived, genre of Irish art, the **high crosses**. An early simple, but gloriously executed example is the seventh-century **Donagh Cross**, near Carndonagh, Co. Donegal. The interlaced design of the head of the cross is typical of many and, while each face is decorated, the east face depicts a number of biblical scenes, including the crucifixion. A pair of more elaborate crosses is to be found at **Ahenny**, Co. Tipperary. Here the arms of each cross are joined by a circle, a form which served as a prototype for subsequent sculptures.

The best of the later scriptural crosses can be ranked amongst Ireland's finest artistic achievements. One such is the **Cross of Moone**, Co. Kildare. Although its setting is less picturesque than others, there is an instant appeal about this long, narrowly proportioned cross with its almost naive flat figures depicting biblical scenes.

Other more striking examples are to be found at the beautiful locations of **Clonmacnois**, Co. Offaly, and at **Monasterboice**, Co. Louth. The former's Great Cross unusually includes a secular scene, while, at Monasterboice, the graphic biblical scenes of Muiredach's cross have survived a thousand years of Ireland's inclement climate. Elsewhere, various examples can be seen in **Kells**, Co. Meath, and at **Donaghmore** and **Ardboe** in Co. Tyrone. Sadly, many crosses were carved from local sandstone and their carvings have not withstood the elements, but the granite **Castledermot Crosses**, in Co. Kildare, have fared better than many.

Crosses continued to be carved in stone right up to the twelfth century, although there were significant changes in style. For instance, the White Cross of Tola at **Dysert O'Dea**, Co. Clare, where large figures in relief of Christ and a bishop have replaced flatter charactered biblical panels. The arms of this cross are not joined by a circle.

Evidence that Irish Christianity retained some idiosyncrasies is provided by the stone sculptured **Sheila-na-Gigs** found on some early church decorations and in castle walls (see p.208). A pair of these pagan fertility symbols are exhibited in the National Museum, but to see one in situ, a visit to **White Island** in Lower Lough Erne, Co. Fermanagh, is essential (see p.658). The figures are undeniably female, but what is also indisputable is the sheer provocative lewdness of their representation. The White Island figure grins lasciviously, her cheeks bulging, legs wide open and arms pointing towards her genitalia.

NORMAN AND MEDIEVAL ART

Until the dissolution of the monasteries in the sixteenth century, virtually all Irish art was religious in context and content and the church was the principal patron. Following the Norman invasion in the twelfth century, the earliest stone figure carvings were of bishops, such as those still visible in the Norman cathedrals of **St Patrick** and **Christ Church** in Dublin. Not to be outdone, some Norman knights also had effigies carved of themselves: that of Strongbow in Christ Church was reckoned to be one of the best until it was destroyed by the collapse of a wall and replaced by an anonymous earl.

The most notable achievement of this period was probably the refinement of stone-carving techniques and there are numerous surviving examples. The fifteenth-century cloister carvings at the important Cistercian monastery of **Jerpoint,** near Thomastown, Co. Kilkenny, were the work of the nearby Callan carvers, who were also responsible for the tomb of Piers Fitz Oge Butler in **Kilcooly Abbey**, Co. Tipperary. New stones were used by the craftworkers and a startling example from the sixteenth century is the beautiful black marble effigies of Piers Butler and Lady Margaret Fitzgerald, his countess, in **St Canice's Cathedral**, Kilkenny.

Fortunately, examples of the woodcarver's art have survived too. The earliest is thought to be the thirteenth-century **Kilcorban Madonna and Child**, displayed in the Loughrea Museum, Co. Galway, while, in Dublin, the National Museum has the **St Molaise of Inishmurray** and **God the Father** from Fethard, Co. Tipperary. St Mary's Cathedral in Limerick has the only set of misericords in the country – black oak choir seats, carved with various animals, both fabulous and real, in bold relief. Limerick's Catholic cathedral, **St John's**, is worth visiting for its fifteenth-century mitre and carved crosier and mitre, thought to be the finest religious artefacts of the Middle Ages in Ireland.

Protective shrines or casings in metalwork have survived from the first millennium, and some of these were reworked in medieval style. **The Cathach Shrine**, for example, has work dating from about 1050, but the most impressive panels are possibly fifteenth century. This, the **Breac Maodhóg** and the **Domhnach Airgid** shrines can all be seen in the National Museum. Each is lavishly decorated with bronze or silver gilt illustrations of the Crucifixion, the saints or other religious themes.

SEVENTEENTH- TO NINETEENTH-CENTURY ART

Following the models of England and continental Europe, guilds of urban craftworkers began to form during the later medieval period. A new "professionalism" produced significant technical advances in the decorative arts of goldsmithery, plasterwork, silver, glass and furniture, and some guilds, such as the Goldsmiths' Company, had acquired power in their own right. The visual arts were stimulated by the desire of the new Anglo-Irish ruling class to display images of itself and many such works were commissioned from painters and sculptors. Easel-based portrait painting thus became the dominant mode and a "painters' guild" was formed in 1670. Later prominent members included **Garrett Morphey**, noted for his portraits of the martyred Oliver Plunkett, and **James Latham**, probably the first Irish artist of major ability. Latham had studied at Antwerp, and the depth of perception displayed in his work, especially his portrait of the philosopher Bishop George Berkeley, influenced Irish art for decades.

Drawing Schools were founded in Dublin around 1740 and many artists, such as **Robert Healy**, were trained in charcoal and chalk techniques. Both his and the pastelist **Hugh Hamilton's** work can be seen in the National Gallery, while the latter was to become a distinguished painter in the Neoclassical style, which became popular later in the century. The greatest stimulus to the visual arts, however, came from **Edmund Burke's** theory of aesthetics, described in *A Philosophical Enquiry into the Origins of our Ideas of The Sublime and Beautiful*, published in 1756. Two major painters of the period, **George Barret** and **James Barry** were protégés of Burke and attempted to embody his aesthetic principles in their work. Influenced by such ideas as the excitement of pain or danger (the sublime) or love (the beautiful), the subject-matter of Irish painting broadened to include historical and some landscape work, often with classical or mythological allusions. Barry later became Professor of Painting at the Royal Academy, London, a position he held from 1782 until he was sacked in 1795 following an altercation with colleagues. Two paintings in the National Gallery, his *Self Portrait* and *Adam and Eve*, are typical of his style.

Another influential artist of the period was **Nathaniel Hone**, the first painter of note in a family which would much later produce other major artists. He was noted for his portraits of children and miniatures, but his most famous work, *The Conjurer*, now in the National Gallery, Dublin, was a satire on Sir Joshua Reynolds' attempts to emulate the Old Masters. Unsurprisingly, it was rejected for exhibition by the Royal Academy in London in 1775 and Hone defiantly held his own one-man show instead.

George Barret adopted Burke's principles to his landscapes and these paintings, together with **Robert Carver's**, were often characteristically romantic. However, a later Classical school developed, deriving much from the Frenchman Claude Lorraine, and including landscapists such as **Thomas Roberts** and **William Ashford**. Paintings of this genre typically featured a green and brown foreground, green middle-distance and often, further back, a Gothic-style ruin set against a lighter, blue background. Topography, too, gradually became an important concern and its finest proponent was **James Malton**, a former draughtsman in the architect James Gandon's practice. His series of line drawings, *Views of Dublin*, drawn in 1790 to 1791, include some marvellous aspects of contemporary Irish architecture.

Classical and rococo styles were also seen in the applied arts in the eighteenth century, particularly in stucco work. Dublin's **Powerscourt Town House**, recently restored as an imaginatively designed shopping centre, has a magnificent ceiling by **Michael Stapleton** (also responsible for the plasterwork at Trinity) and a staircase by **James McCullagh** and **Michael Reynolds**, which have been decorated with motifs of urns, scrolls and heads. The rich Baroque ceiling of the **chapel** in the Rotunda Maternity Hospital by **Bartholomew Cramillion** is unlike anything else in the country. Life-size figures by the Swiss-Italian **Francini brothers**, the foremost contemporary stuccoists, and detailed birds and musical instruments by Robert West decorate **Newman House** at 85/86 St Stephen's Green. The extraordinary beauty of these make it all the more poignant that heartless town "planners" and "developers" have allowed the wanton destruction or neglect of many equally fine interiors in Ireland's principal city.

The eighteenth century was also noted for heavy, deep-cut glasswork and for high-quality silverware, some of which, such as three-legged sugar bowls, were made in characteristically Irish shapes. Sculpture in classical and Neoclassical styles can be seen on a number of buildings such as the **Custom House**, the **City Hall** and the **Casino in Marino**, Dublin.

During the early years of the nineteenth century, following the 1801 Act of Union, many artists emigrated to London. Those who remained formed new organizations aimed at consolidating art in Ireland. The leading body was the Royal Hibernian Academy, established in 1823, and directly modelled on its London equivalent, holding annual exhibitions and seeking to stimulate debate on the direction and concerns of painting.

Nineteenth-century Irish art is dominated by the landscapists, led by **James Arthur O'Connor**. Though he was partially influenced by seventeenth-century Dutch works, the persistence of classical and romantic styles is visible in his *Homeward Bound* and **Edwin Hayes'** seascape *The Emigrant Ship*. The landscape tradition was further developed by **George Chinnery**, **William Sadler**, **Cecilia Campbell** and **Henry O'Neill** working in a variety of media – watercolour, gouache and oil. **George Petrie**, a distinguished archeologist who was for some time attached to the Irish Ordnance Survey, also produced many topographical illustrations for travel books, a popular publishing genre of the time.

Portrait painting continued, though occasionally it followed the Victorian English trend for cloying sentimentality, as in **Richard Rothwell's** *The Young Mother's Pastime*. Beginning as a pencil portraitist, Cork-born **Daniel Maclise** went on to produce historical frescoes, such as *The Meeting of Wellington and Blücher* and *The Death of Nelson*, both of which are displayed in the House of Lords' Royal Gallery; he also illustrated works by Dickens and Tennyson. His contemporary, **William Mulready** from Ennis, also studied at the Royal Academy and had an equally significant impact on English art through his studies *Barber's Shop* and *Boys Fishing*. **Francis Danby** was also notable for his large historical and biblical paintings, characterized by the romanticism still popular among Irish painters.

John Henry Foley, **John Lawlor** and **Samuel Ferris Lynn** collaborated with British sculptors to produce the Albert Memorial in London. Foley was also noted for his classical-style busts, but his major works were the commissions he received for **public monuments**; several examples of his work still stand in Dublin, such as the memorials to Oliver Goldsmith and Edmund Burke in College Green, and to Daniel O'Connell in O'Connell Street. There is some fine stucco work from this time, too, such as that in the hall of Ballyfin House, Co. Laois, by **Richard Morrison**.

FROM IMPRESSIONISM TO THE PRESENT DAY

Developments in European art markedly influenced Irish painting from the late nineteenth century onwards. The landscapes of **Nathaniel Hone**, the great-grandnephew of his namesake, and early paintings of **Walter Osborne** were inspired by the rustic realism of Jules Bastien-Lepage, though Osborne became one of many native artists stimulated by Impressionism, its influence visible in such works as *Tea in the Garden*. His *St Patrick's Close* depicted the griminess of working-class Dublin. Post-Impressionism had a powerful impact on the work of **Roderic O'Conor**, and his *Field of Corn* in the Ulster Museum, Belfast, is reminiscent of Cezanne and perhaps Van Gogh.

Other notable artists of the period include **William Orpen**, a precociously talented draughtsman who began training at the Dublin Metropolitan School of Art at the age of eleven. Later, as a young instructor at the school, he painted some marvellous coastal scenes with figures near Howth, but he is better-known for his sketches and paintings at the front during World War I and at the subsequent Paris Peace Conference, where he was official painter. His portraits are worth seeing simply for their vitality and feeling for character. Similarly adept was **John Lavery**, many of whose works are displayed in the Ulster Museum in his home-town, Belfast. In his early career, he too was influenced by Bastien-Lepage. Lavery studied in Glasgow, London and Paris and became a significant portraitist, especially during the 1920s when he painted many of the leading contemporary Irish political figures, including Carson and Collins.

Most prominent among artists of this period were **Jack Butler Yeats** and **Paul Henry**. Son of a successful portraitist and brother of the poet W.B. Yeats, Jack Yeats is probably the best-known Irish twentieth-century painter, though he worked originally as an illustrator, sketching horses for *Paddock Life* magazine and drawing the first cartoon strip version of Sherlock Holmes, *Chubblock Homes*, for *Comic Cuts*. Like his father, he was a fine portraitist although he later developed a highly personal Expressionist style, marked by extremely vivid colour and loose brush technique. Yeats' subjects were Celtic mythology and everyday Irish life, yet though he undoubtedly contributed to the upsurge of nationalist sentiment in the arts, following Irish independence, his influence on Irish art was largely osmotic, for he took no pupils and was never seen at work. Paul Henry studied first at his native Belfast School of Art before continuing his education in Paris. Like Yeats, he was originally an illustrator, working with high competence through the medium of charcoal. His early paintings were heavily influenced by Millet and, while living on Achill Island, County Mayo, he produced a number of works on Irish country life in which Millet's characteristic "peasant" poses were apparent. Later, Henry fell under the spell of Whistler and studied at his new Paris studio. Returning to Dublin he became active in the local arts world and, along with his wife, Grace Mitchell Henry, and a number of other painters, including Yeats, formed the **Society of Dublin Painters** in 1920. He had already developed his own characteristic style which remained hardly altered for the rest of his life and it is for his Connemara landscapes that he is most remembered. Using a palette of matt blues and greys, his paintings commonly consist of a few elements, natural or man-made, set in bold composition against a cloud-filled sky. *Lakeside Cottages* (circa. 1930) is a typical example. In the 1920s, some of Henry's works were reproduced as posters and were also used in tourist literature and government publications. Such was the demand for similar pictures, that Henry's subsequent work almost sank to the level of romantic caricature.

In contrast to Post-Impressionism, abstract art was relatively late in arriving in Ireland. Some artists, such as **Seán Keating**, **Maurice MacGonigal** and **Sean O'Sullivan**, continued to work in the landscape tradition. Other young Irish artists travelled abroad to absorb the advances of Cubism and Futurism; the most influential on their return were **Mainie Jellett** and **Evie Hone** who had both trained under André Lhote and Albert Gleizes in Paris. Interestingly, early modernism's masculinist avant garde was given little credence in Ireland, leaving space for women like Jellett and Hone to be the main proponents of Irish modernism. Evie Hone was best known as a distinguished member of An Túr Gloine, a school for stained glass, founded by the painter Sarah Purser, and her best works include windows in the chapel at Eton College in England and the CIE headquarters in O'Connell Street, Dublin. In 1943, along with fellow abstract artists Louis Le Brocquy and Norah McGuinness, Hone and Jellett, founded the **Irish Exhibition of Living Art** as an alternative showcase for modernist work rejected by the compilers of the Royal Hibernian Academy's annual exhibitions.

Postwar Ireland saw major advances in sculpture. **Clíona Cussen**, **Hilary Heron** and **Oisín Kelly** pioneered the use of new casting techniques and developed the concept of an Irish vernacular sculpture. Kelly's *Children of Lir*, inspired by the Celtic legend, stands in Parnell Square, one of a number of public monuments placed around the capital by the Dublin Corporation. Sculptors of achievement have included **Michael Bulfin**, **John Behan**, **Edward Delaney**, **Conor Fallon** and **John Burke**. More recently, sculptors such as **Christopher Keaney** and **Jill Crowley** have produced remarkable figures, the latter wittily caricaturing Irish men.

One expressionist painter using a uniquely Irish context for his work is the prolific Armagh artist and *uilleann* piper, **J.B. (Brian) Vallely**, who has produced more than four thousand canvases. Many of these centre on his love of traditional music, often showing musicians in action, and demonstrate an extraordinary dynamism and vitality.

The influence of the Exhibition of Living Art developed during the 1950s, serving as a focus for the works of artists like **Barrie Cooke**, **Cecil King**, **Nano Reid** and **Camille Souter**, while the landscape tradition was maintained by **Patrick Collins** and **Tony O'Malley**. Le Brocquy's contorted human shapes dominated abstract art and an idiosyncratic school of primitive artists developed on **Tory Island** (see p.496) off the coast of Donegal. Partly as a result of government funding, the visual arts have flourished in Ireland since the 1970s, and, in more recent years, in the North. In the 1980s, Living Art opened its doors to video and performance artists, exhibiting the works of **Aileen**

MacKeough, **Nigel Rolfe**, **Eilis O'Connell** and a host of others. A strong new expressionist movement has emerged from the Independent Artists group, represented by **Michael Kane**, **Patrick Hall**, **Brian Maguire**, **Patrick Graham**, **Eithne Jordan**, **Michael Mulcahy** and **Michael Cullen**.

Along with increased support, there has been a steady expansion in the number of exhibition spaces. In Dublin, the Irish Museum of Modern Art, opened in 1991, and the Douglas Hyde Gallery, in Trinity College, both offer opportunities for new experimentalism. There's a host of commercial galleries here too, such as the Kerlin and Green on Red, ensuring that a steady stream of contemporary Irish art is always on show, and around the country there are numerous local art centres and galleries such as the Triskel, Cork, and the Model Art Centre, Sligo. In Northern Ireland, the Orchard Gallery in Derry has a long history of top-quality exhibitions, and the Ormeau Baths Gallery in Belfast regularly presents an equally strong contemporary Northern Irish programme. Names to watch out for include John Carson, Brian Connolly, Rita Duffy, Philip Napler and Louise Walsh. Animated debates in the pages of *Circa* (published in both Dublin and Belfast) testify to the continued revitalization of the Irish arts.

Additionally, recent years have seen major developments in contemporary applied arts and design, especially in such fields as jewellery, glass, furniture and ceramics. In the Republic, such work has been supported by a government agency, the Craft Council of Ireland. The two capitals are the best locations for viewing, though there are plenty of others dotted around the island. In Dublin, there is the **Crafts Council gallery** in the Powerscourt Town House and several outlets in **Temple Bar**, including DESIGNyard, while in Belfast, work can be viewed in the **Craftworks gallery** in Bedford Street.

THE IRISH IN FILM

The international profile of filmmaking in Ireland has reached new heights over tha last decade as a result of financial incentives for foreign filmmakers. Increased government funding for indigenous filmmakers has spawned a thriving film community, catapulted onto the world stage thanks largely to the activities and successes of directors Neil Jordan and Jim Sheridan.

The Irish have always been conscious of the stereotypical images of Irishness in foreign, particularly American, pictures: the country a pastoral idyll, its people a good-humoured mix of priests and nuns, fiery redheads and hard-drinking and -fighting men. More recently, however, films made in and about Ireland have started to explore broader themes, reflecting the changing state of Irish society and giving the world a very different image of Irishness: urban, diverse and outward-looking.

The films below are listed in chronological order, each title followed by the director and year of release.

Knocknagow (Fred O'Donovan, 1917).
Set in the post-Famine years of the 1840s, this sprawling landlord/tenant silent drama, produced by the largely Nationalist Film Company of Ireland is effectively a call to arms and was considered propagandist by the British authorities.

Willie Reilly and his Colleen Bawn (John McDonagh, 1920).
Political drama set in the 1740s in which the rights of the landowning classes are upheld regardless of religion. Protestant squire's daughter Helen and Catholic gentleman Willie Reilly fall in love; rival suitor and anti-Catholic bigot Sir Whitecroft attempts to use the Penal Laws to dispossess Reilly, burning down his house in the process. Sympathetic Protestants come to the beleaguered Willie's assistance and ultimately justice prevails.

Irish Destiny (George Dewhurst,1926).
The first fictionalized film about the War of Independence and the civil war, with plenty of horrific detail including footage of the burning of Cork city and the Custom House, and the brutality of the Black and Tans. The film was banned by the British Board of Censors in 1926, but was received enthusiastically in Ireland and America.

Mother Machree (John Ford, 1928).
Silent movie made for the Irish-American market in which an impoverished Irish immigrant is forced to surrender her son for adoption and devote her energies to raising the child of her own employer, only to find both son and daughter fall in love in adult life.

Man of Aran (Robert O'Flaherty, 1934).
Landmark documentary about life on the Aran Islands. Long criticized as portraying the islanders' primitive struggle against the elements in an overly romanticized, epic form that runs contrary to its documentary status, it nonetheless remains a thrilling film.

The Quiet Man (John Ford, 1952)
US film included here because it represents the pinnacle of Hollywood "Oirishness". This romantic comedy stars John Wayne as the prize fighter who has hung up his gloves and returned to the auld sod from the States, and focuses on his courtship of the feisty Maureen O'Hara and the hostility he encounters from her pugilist brother.

Shake Hands With The Devil
(Michael Anderson, 1959).
The first international production to be made at Ardmore Studios in Bray, Co. Wicklow. Melodrama starring James Cagney in which an IRA man develops a taste for violence as an end in itself.

Saoirse? ("Freedom?" George Morrison, 1961).
Documentary account of the emergence of the

modern Irish state, focusing on events from 1918 to the civil war.

Ryan's Daughter (David Lean, 1970).
Set amid the gorgeous scenery of the Dingle Peninsula, the adulterous affair between a British officer (Christopher Jones) and the local schoolteacher's wife (Sarah Miles) is common knowledge by the time a boatload of IRA guns arrive to be intercepted by British forces; the year is 1916. The locals set upon Miles, believing her to be responsible for the treachery. For all this, a rather lacklustre film.

Down the Corner (Joe Comerford, 1974).
The first urban working-class film shot in Ireland by an Irish director, the action centres around the escapades of five adolescent boys. Their surrounding adult world is characterized by alcoholism, unemployment and memories of the 1916 Rising.

Withdrawal (Joe Comerford, 1974).
Film dealing with mental illness and drug addiction in an uncharacteristically raw manner.

On a Paving Stone Mounted
(Thaddeus O'Sullivan, 1978).
A tale of the lives of Irish emigrants in London, significant not just for its subject matter, but also for the improvisational scope given to its actors. The film deploys a mix of drama and documentary styles and presents a dislocated collage of memory and experience.

Our Boys (Cathal Black, 1981).
Iconoclastic milestone in Irish film history which combined documentary and drama to highlight the inequities of Irish Christian Brothers' schools. "The Brothers" were notorious for their insensitivity and the outbursts of savage brutishness which they inflicted on pupils. It was deemed so subversive that RTE, one of the film's backers, refused to broadcast it for the best part of a decade after its release.

Angel
(Neil Jordan, 1982/ US title "Danny Boy").
Fine revenge thriller set in Northern Ireland, in which a saxophonist pursues the murderer of a mute girl and is thus drawn into a world of violence.

Cal (Pat O'Connor, 1984).
Fatalistic love story set in the context of the Troubles in Northern Ireland. Cal, an IRA volunteer, seeks redemption for his part in the murder of a policeman from the dead man's widow. Love blooms all too briefly and their relationship is destroyed when the past catches up with them.

Eat the Peach (Peter Ormrod, 1986).
Droll and quirky movie in which protagonists Arthur and Vinnie set out to build a motorcycle wall-of-death to relieve the unrelenting tedium of their bleak and desolate bogland home.

Reefer and the Model (Joe Comerford, 1987).
Highly enjoyable thriller in which an ex-prostitute heroin user, now pregnant, and an ex-IRA man meet up and rampage through Connemara, rob a mobile bank and effect a getaway of sorts.

My Left Foot (Jim Sheridan, 1989).
A fine and touching film based on Christy Brown's best-selling autobiography. Brown, almost entirely paralyzed by cerebral palsy, except for his left foot, retells the story of his courageous battle with disability.

December Bride (Thaddeus O'Sullivan, 1990).
Family drama set at the turn of the century, beautifully shot on location at Strangford Lough. Central to the film is one pregnant woman's refusal to marry at the behest of the local minister, and her growing understanding of the sacrifices that must be made for the sake of future generations. The film was commended at the 1990 European Film Awards for its rich and varied portrayal of Northern Protestants.

The Field (Jim Sheridan, 1990).
Sentimentalized story about one man's fight to keep the field he's created and tended over the years. A crude allegory of land ownership and the dignity of toil.

The Commitments (Alan Parker, 1991).
One of the most popular film treatments of working class Dublin. Adapted from Roddy Doyle's novel, the film follows the rise of the eponymous soul band and is chiefly enjoyable for its rather obvious comedy and R&B/soul classics.

Hear My Song (Peter Chelsom, 1991).
Engaging light comedy in which Liverpool nightclub manager Micky O'Neill hopes to revive his fortunes by luring legendary tenor Josef Locke to perform in his ailing club. However, O'Neill has underrated the complexities of Locke's past and things do not run smoothly.

The Crying Game (Neil Jordan, 1992).
Excellent thriller in which an IRA man becomes haunted by his part in the death of a British

hostage and subsequently develops an intimate relationship with the dead man's lover. However, things are not that simple, and this gripping film comes to an unexpected ironic conclusion.

Into the West (Mike Newell, 1992).
Clichéd but nonetheless charming contemporary working of the Tír na nÓg myth – the quest for the Land of Eternal Youth. The film focuses on the horseback adventures of two young boys and their father's struggle to accept the death of their mother. The film fuses gritty Dublin realism with the magical landscape of the west.

In The Name of The Father
(Jim Sheridan, 1993).
Based on the true story of the Guildford Four who were wrongfully imprisoned for the 1974 IRA Guildford pub bombing in which five people died. The film focuses on the imprisonment of Gerry Conlon and his father Guiseppe, and the attempt to clear the family name. Although marred by historical inaccuracies and a ludicrous final courtroom scene, this remains a powerful drama, thanks chiefly to the towering performance of Daniel Day Lewis as Gerry.

Korea (Cathal Black, 1994).
Set in the border country of the 1950s. An adolescent boy's romance forces his father to confront a changing world and put local enmities dating back to the civil war behind him.

A Man of No Importance
(Suri Krishnamma, 1995).
Light movie in which gay bus conductor Alfie Byrne, played by a delightful Albert Finney, attempts to loosen up the travelling public in a repressive Dublin of the 1960s. Action revolves around his efforts to stage a production of Wilde's *Salome* in a church hall.

Circle of Friends (Pat O'Connor, 1995).
Light, chocolate-box tale of young romance and betrayal in 50s Ireland. This adaptation of a Maeve Binchy novel remains cosy and warm-hearted throughout.

Guiltrip (Gerard Stembridge, 1995).
Adultery, impotence and frustration drive squaddie Liam, an army corporal, to extremes in this tense small town drama.

Nothing Personal
(Thaddeus O'Sullivan, 1995).
Action-packed Troubles movie in which innocent individuals are caught up in the terrorists' war. Criticized as having pro-Republican sympathies, the film can be credited with some honest scrutiny of the motivations and inner tensions of Loyalist organizations. As the film comes to its awful conclusion, the inevitability that violence begets violence is made horribly clear, and so too is the message that this is a war in which everyone loses.

The Run of the Country (Peter Yates, 1995).
The quiet, forgotten border country is the setting for this adolescent rite of passage, the drama centring around a cross-border romance and an unwanted pregnancy. Fine scenery and pale shadows of IRA activity provide a modicum of local colour.

The Boy From Mercury (Martin Duffy, 1996).
Slight, amusing film about a boy's obsession with science fiction, in particular Flash Gordon movies. The young James Cronin pulls through the trials of boyhood with the help of his wide-eyed imagination and the outer-space fantasies of the local cinema.

Michael Collins (Neil Jordan, 1996).
Hugely important biopic in which Republican leader Collins, played by Liam Neeson, is portrayed as an heroic figure in the struggle against imperial Britain. The film includes a powerful dramatization of the 1916 Easter Rising and, although it skirts over the details of the Treaty negotiations of 1921, follows Collins through the founding of the Free State to the civil war and his assassination.

Some Mother's Son (Terry George, 1996).
Enthralling and moving film about the 1981 Irish hunger strikers in the Maze prison, focusing on the effect of their endeavour on two mothers of differing political beliefs. Despite occasional lapses into sentimentality, this is a convincing evocation of those times and includes superb performances by Fionnula Flanagan and Helen Mirren.

The Van (Stephen Frears, 1996).
Based on Roddy Doyle's novel, this Dublin working-class comedy revolves around protagonist Bimbo's attempt to launch a chip van business in time for Ireland's World Cup games.

The Boxer
(Jim Sheridan, 1997/ US title "Hell's Kitchen").
Circles of violence explored as ex-con boxer returns to his Republican community to discover the continuing demands of sectarianism are as

restricting as life inside. A very convincing portrayal of the men of violence's stranglehold on a community.

The General (John Boorman, 1998).
Based on the true-life story of a notorious Dublin art thief. The "general" becomes fatally caught up in the complexities of the political underworld when the UVF prove the only organization capable of buying his haul. A magnificent performance by Brendan Gleeson in the central role.

The Butcher Boy (Neil Jordan, 1998).
Powerful dark comedy set in small-town Ireland in which a young boy's failure to cope with the dysfunctional society in which he finds himself leads to violence. From the Patrick McCabe novel of the same name.

Angela's Ashes (Alan Parker, 1999).
Moving and faithful adaptation of Frank McCourt's international bestseller based on his Limerick childhood. Despite the child deaths, the father's drinking and above all the unrelenting poverty, this is a tale suffused with humour.

Nora (Pat Murphy, 1999).
Biopic following the courtship and early married life of Nora Barnacle and James Joyce. The title suggests Murphy's feminist agenda: we find Nora portrayed here as a robust and down-to-earth character, with tensions between the couple generated by Joyce's sexual jealousies and insecurities. An especially powerful performance by Susan Lynch in the leading role.

The Last September (Deborah Warner, 1999).
Set in 1920, the film explores some of the contradictory impulses of the Anglo-Irish Ascendancy at this critical period in their history. Upper-class Lois is drawn to stereotypical IRA rebel Peter – brooding, attractive and misogynous – despite the advances of an eligible English captain with whom, arguably, she has more in common. An atmospheric portrait of a fading world.

When the Sky Falls (John MacKenzie, 1999).
Fictionalized account of the investigations into Dublin's drug world by journalist Veronica Guerin and her subsequent murder. Guerin actually assisted Jim Sheridan in the development of an early screenplay. Criticized for its sympathetic portrayal of the IRA.

MUSIC

Ireland and music are as inseparable as fish and chips. Traditional music may form the well-known cultural backbone, but there is also an important, though often ignored, body of classical composition. Artistes such as Van Morrison, Thin Lizzy, U2, The Corrs and Sinéad O'Connor have ensured Ireland's prominence in the world gazetteer of rock while also carving out a niche in the pop world through a succession of successful boy bands such as Boyzone and Westlife and their girl counterparts B*witched.

TRADITIONAL MUSIC

Kept alive by a combination of historical, political and cultural forces, Irish traditional music remains one of the richest musical cultures in the Western world. In Ireland itself, the growing interest in traditional music is further evidence of a national maturity that allows Irish people to be more relaxed about aspects of their traditional culture. Consequently, traditional music is neither seen as backward, rural and something shameful, nor is it a stick of cultural purity for fending off the twenty-first century. Long after much traditional music in the industrialized West has ceased to exist in any meaningful way, Irish music continues to refashion itself, not as introverted, stagnant, and nationalistic, but as an evolving and progressive part of a common, universal oral folk tradition.

Most of the instrumental music the visitor will hear in Ireland is **dance music** (such as reels, jigs and hornpipes), originally played in kitchens, barns and at crossroads, usually to mark an occasion, such as a wedding or a wake. The melody of any dance tune is but bare bones to a traditional musician; it's dependent on performance for flesh, blood and soul. Through ornamentation, decoration and embellishments the performer breathes life into the music and this controlled extemporization allows the player to re-create a tune with each rendition.

SEAN NÓS AND THE VOCAL TRADITION

Songs in the Irish language are at the heart of Irish music and the most important belong to a tradition known as **sean nós** (literally "in the old style"). An unaccompanied singing style of great beauty and complexity, it is thought to derive in part from the bardic tradition which died out in the seventeenth century with the demise of the old Gaelic order, though other recent research has suggested links to North Africa. Hugely demanding for both singer and listener, it requires the skill of the former to vary the interpretation of each verse by means of subtle changes in tempo, ornamentation, timbre and stress, while the latter needs to possess the knowledge and discrimination to appreciate fully the singer's efforts. To the untutored ear it can easily "sound all the same", with its slightly nasal tone and unemotional manner of performance, but perseverance will lead to great rewards. Sean nós remains strongest in the *Gaeltacht* areas, especially Connemara, while the marvellous **Iarla O'Lionáird** (from west Cork) has taken the art form to international audiences, especially through his work with the roots-dance fusion outfit Afro Celt Sound System.

THE SESSION: MUSIC AND CRACK

Travellers to Ireland will most likely come across traditional music in a pub setting and these quasi-impromptu musical get-togethers are known as "**sessions**". These are the life-blood of traditional music, accompanied by the associated notion of **craic** (or crack) whereby music, conversation and drink combine to produce an evening of fun. A session is not strictly a performance, but more of a dynamic of entertainer and listener – a group of people enjoying the *craic* together. While sessions take place all year round in the major cities, summer is the optimal time for sessions in traditional music's heartland, the west of Ireland, and a few enquiries locally will point you to the best.

The instrumental repertoire mainly consists of dance tunes, but there are also pieces known as **Fonn Mall** – "slow airs" – played without accompaniment and usually to hushed attention. Most are laments or the melodies of songs, some so old that the words have been lost. The *uilleann* pipes (see box p.708) are particularly well suited to the performance of airs, as their plaintive tone and ability to produce complex ornamentation cleanly allows them to approach the style of sean nós singers (see p.708).

Playing in groups or with accompaniment is a prominent feature of traditional music performance today. One of the most exciting exponents of this style is the band **De Dannan**, which in its heyday featured three women singers who went on to have solo careers in commercial rock: **Mary Black**, **Dolores Keane**, and **Maura O'Connell**. Ireland's best-known traditional band, **The Chieftains**, carry on the virtuoso tradition, too. This group was the spearhead of the 1960s' revival of Irish traditional music, which itself was largely due to the efforts of the group's founder, composer and arranger, **Seán Ó Riada**. Living in the *Gaeltacht* (Irish-speaking area) of Cuil Aodha, renowned for its singers and passionate devotion to music, Ó Riada hit on the idea of ensemble music-making using traditional instruments like the pipes, fiddle and whistle. It was a brilliantly obvious innovation and, over the past

INSTRUMENTS AND PLAYERS

We've included mention of some of the best instrumentalists on the Irish music scene in this round-up of traditional instruments. If you get the chance to see any of them at the festivals, don't miss it.

The harp

There are references to harp playing in Ireland from as early as the eighth century. Indeed, in Irish legend the harp is credited with magical powers and it was adopted as the island's symbol in the seventeenth century (and somewhat later by Guinness). As court musicians to the Gaelic aristocracy, the old Irish harpists were a musical elite and had a close acquaintance with the court music of Baroque Europe. The couple of hundred surviving tunes by the greatest of eighteenth-century harpists, Turlough Carolan, clearly reflect his regard for the Italian composer Corelli.

Their harp was metal-stringed and played with the fingernails. Today's harpists play (with their fingerpads) a chromatic, gut- or nylon-string version, which one of its best exponents, **Máire Ni Chathaisaigh**, describes as "neo-Irish". Máire has been notably successful in adapting dance music for the instrument, drawing on her knowledge and love of the piping tradition as inspiration. The younger generation of harpists following in Máire's wake include the vivacious **Laoise Kelly** who has demonstrated the harp's potential in ensemble playing in the band **Bumblebees**.

Be warned that there is also a bland, anodyne type of twee Irish music played on a gut-strung instrument, often as accompaniment to ersatz medieval banquets held at tourist locations around the country. About as traditional as green beer, it should be given a wide berth.

Uilleann pipes

"Seven years learning, seven years practising, and seven years playing" is reputedly what it takes to master the *uilleann* (pronounced *illun* or *illyun*, depending on local dialect) pipes. Perhaps the world's most technically sophisticated bagpipe, it is highly temperamental and difficult to master. The melody is played on a nine-holed chanter with a two-octave range blown by the air from a bag squeezed under the left arm, itself fed by a bellows squeezed under the right elbow. As well as the usual set of drones, the *uilleann* pipes are marked by their possession of a set of regulators, which can be switched on and off to provide chords. In the hands of a master, such as the late **Leo Rowsome**, they can provide a sensitive backing for slow airs and an excitingly rhythmic springboard for dance music.

The pipes arrived in Ireland in the early eighteenth century and reached their present form in the 1890s. Taken up by members of the gentry, who became known as "gentlemen pipers", they were also beloved of the Irish tinkers or travellers, and two different styles evolved: the restrained and delicate parlour style exemplified by the late **Séamus Ennis**, and the traveller style (known as "open" or "legato") which, designed as it was to coax money from the pockets of visitors to country fairs, is highly ornamented and often showy.

Some of the most acclaimed musicians of recent years have been pipers: Séamus Ennis, **Willie Clancy**, and travellers **Johnny** and **Felix Doran**, all alas now dead. Today **Liam O'Flynn** is regarded as one of the country's foremost practitioners and has pushed forward the possibilities for piping through his association with classical composer **Shaun Davey** and with the band Planxty. Other contemporary exponents include **Paddy Keenan**, one-time star of the Bothy Band, and **Davy Spillane**, who learned much of his technique from travelling pipers.

four decades, The Chieftains, led by whistler and piper **Paddy Moloney**, have developed the concept of ensemble playing to the point where it has become universally accepted and adopted. In addition, Ó Riada brought his genius for interpretation to bear on choral, liturgical and orchestral music.

A widely known musician exploring the ensemble format is **Sharon Shannon**. Playing furiously energetic dance music, Shannon is a mesmerizing button accordion player who can also turn her hand to the fiddle and spent some time with The Waterboys before forming her own band. Her first solo album mixed well-known and much-played tunes like *The Silver Spire* and *O'Keefes* with cajun, Swedish, and new material in traditional style. Her profile was further enhanced by her involvement with the *Woman's Heart* album combining with Maura O'Connell, Frances and Mary Black,

The bodhrán

The *bodhrán* (pronounced *bore-run*) is an instrument much in evidence at traditional sessions and a relatively recent addition to the dance music line-up. It is not universally welcome, partly because it looks like an easy way into playing – and it isn't. The great piper Séamus Ennis, when asked how a *bodhrán* should be played, replied "with a penknife". The *bodhrán* is a frame drum usually made of goatskin and originally associated with "wren boys" or mummers who went out revelling and playing music on Wrens Day (Dec 26). It looks like a large tambourine without jingles and can be played with a small wooden stick or with the back of the hand.

When played well by the likes of famed Galway musician **Johnny "Ringo" MacDonagh**, or **Colm Murphy**, **Mel Mercier** and **Tommy Hayes**, the *bodhrán* sounds wonderful, a sympathetic support to the running rhythms of traditional music. Since it was introduced into mainstream traditional music in the 1960s by the great innovator Seán Ó Riada, it has come on by leaps and bounds, and new techniques are constantly being invented. Many traditional ensembles now regard it as *de rigueur*.

Flutes and whistles

It's the wooden flute of a simple type that is used in Irish music, played mostly in a fairly low register with a quiet and confidential tone which means that it's not heard at its best in pub sessions. Played solo by such musicians as **Matt Molloy** or **Desi Wilkinson**, its clear flow of notes displays a gentler side to the rushing melodies of jigs and reels.

While anyone can get a note, though not necessarily the right one, out of its little cousin the tin whistle, it can take a long time to develop an embouchure capable of producing a beautiful flute tone, and so piper Finbar Furey has introduced the low whistle, which takes the place of the flute when there is no proper flute player around. In the right hands, those of **Paddy Moloney**, **Seán Ryan** or **Mary Bergin**, for example, the tin whistle itself is no mean instrument, but it's also suitable for the beginner. If you're interested, make sure you get a D-whistle, as most Irish music is in this key.

Fiddles

The fiddle is popular all over Ireland, and each area has its own particular characteristics: Donegal breeds fiddlers with a smooth melodic approach but lively, attacking bowing techniques, whereas the Sligo style, exemplified in the playing of the great **Michael Coleman**, is more elaborate and flamboyant. Alongside his Sligo contemporary, **James Morrison**, Coleman's 1920s recordings in America still wield an incredible influence on contemporary fiddling. Currently worth catching are the US-based Clare fiddler **Martin Hayes**, who works as a duo with guitarist Dennis Cahill, the semi-legendary Donegal fiddler **Tommy Peoples** and, of the younger breed, **Dezi Donnelly**.

The bouzouki

At first sight it might seem odd to include the bouzouki on a list of traditional Irish instruments. Nevertheless, its light but piercing tone makes it eminently suitable both for melodies and providing a restrained chordal backing within an ensemble, and since its introduction to the island by Johnny Moynihan, in the late 1960s, and subsequent popularization by Dónal Lunny, it has taken firm root. In the process it has lost much of its original Greek form, and with its flat back the Irish bouzouki is really closer to a member of the mandolin family. Along with other string instruments like the guitar and banjo, which provide supporting harmonies in a "folky" idiom, bouzoukis crop up at sessions all over the country, and some of the best accompanists are bouzouki players.

Dolores Keane and Eleanor McEvoy to produce one of the most successful traditional albums of all time, while her more recent albums, *Each Little Thing* and *The Diamond Mountain Sessions,* are less traditional but exude the ebullience that has become her trademark. Donegal-based **Altan** derive their energy from a twin fiddle attack led by **Mairéad Ní Mhaonaigh** and **Ciaran Tourish** coupled with the phenomenal accordion work of **Dermot Byrne**, while their earlier recordings feature the exquisite flute playing of the late **Frankie Kennedy** – all can be appreciated on their stunning album *Island Angel.* **Dervish**, based in neighbouring Sligo, are another effervescent grouping and feature the extraordinary range of singer Cathy Jordan, a dab hand on bones and *bodhrán* too. Other bands to look out for include **Danú**, from County Waterford, who create a mighty musical confection, enhanced by another remarkable sean nós singer, **Ciarán Ó Geabháin**, and the Cork-based **Nomos**, featuring the remarkable concertina player, **Niall Vallely**. **Coolfin**, led by traditional alumnus, **Dónal Lunny**, brings together some staggering talent, including singer **Maighread Ní Dhomhnaill** and piper **John McSherry**, who himself was a one-time member of **Lúnasa**, a band which harnesses the instrumental prowess of fiddler **Seán Smyth** and flute-player **Kevin Crawford**. The American band **Solas** represent a marvellous dynamic between aggression and tenderness, drawing on the skills of multi-instrumentalist **Seamus Egan**, fiddler **Winifred Horan** and singer **Deirdre Scanlan**.

FOLK MEETS TRADITIONAL

Singing **folk songs** to instrumental accompaniment became enormously popular in Ireland in the 1960s with the triumphal return from America of **The Clancy Brothers and Tommy Makem** (three brothers from Tipperary joined by a member of a well-known Armagh musical family). The Clancys had taken New York's Carnegie Hall and the networked *Ed Sullivan Show* by storm, and they were welcomed home to Ireland as conquering heroes. Their heady blend of rousing ballads accompanied by guitar, harmonica, and five-string banjo revitalized a genre of folk song that had all but vanished. Hundreds of sound-alike ballad groups sprang up, decked out in a motley selection of ganseys – The Clancys' and Makem's hallmark was the Aran sweater. Before the ballad group fashion petered out, it had laid the foundations for a revival of interest in popular folk singing that endures to this day. Still going strong is another great group of this era, **The Dubliners**. With an uncompromisingly urban image, in contrast to the rather twee Oirishness of The Clancys, their work was often bawdy and their ribald spirit was captured in the most popular song of this era, *Seven Drunken Nights* (although the Dubliners only recorded five of them, it still managed to be banned from Irish radio). Earthiness may have been part of the reason why their true musical accomplishment was never fully appreciated for, as well as fielding two unique singers, **Luke Kelly** (who died in 1984) and **Ronnie Drew**, they boasted two fine instrumentalists, banjoist **Barney McKenna** and fiddler **John Sheahan**. In many ways they helped lay the groundwork for the fusion of the traditional/ballad genre explored by bands such as **Sweeney's Men**, **The Johnstons**, **The Bothy Band** and, most influential of all, **Planxty**.

Planxty was formed from the musicians recording Christy Moore's *Prosperous* album and the evolution of traditional music can be traced through the band members' post-Planxty recordings. The band consisted of **Liam O'Flynn**, **Dónal Lunny**, **Andy Irvine** and **Christy Moore** and their self-titled first album (known as "The Black Album") mixed traditional, modern folk and ballad singing through harmonies backed by O'Flynn's superlative pipe playing. They recorded three albums before their split and a selection from each is available on the 1976 album *The Planxty Collection.* The band reformed again in 1978, adding the former Bothy Band and currently Chieftains' flute-player, **Matt Molloy**, to their ranks. Their best work in this period is *The Woman I Loved So Well* but the band split finally when Lunny and Moore moved on to stretch the traditional genre even further with the formation of Moving Hearts.

Moving Hearts radically attempted to fuse traditional and rock music and almost succeeded. Consisting of two pipers, saxophone, bass and lead guitars, electric bouzouki, drums and percussion, their gigs were memorable feasts of exciting music, seeming simultaneously familiar and new. Too large to survive financially, the band sadly folded in 1984. Since then there have been a few reunions which have played to crowds of fans old and new. Released after their break-up, their 1985 album *The Storm* is a landmark in its pioneering use of rock and jazz idioms to redefine the harmonic and rhythmic foundations of Irish music.

Moore has since moved on to become possibly Ireland's best loved singer recording a number of highly successful and acclaimed albums. In his first recordings, such as the album *Prosperous*, he was overtly political in the style of Woody Guthrie or the early Bob Dylan. This commitment is also evident in his recordings with Moving Hearts, such as his protest against state repression *No Time for Love* and, in the mid-1980s album *The Time has Come*, his song *Section 31* which criticizes the Republic's media censorship of Sinn Féin. Though Moore has become less politically engaged, his popularity has been maintained through stunning live performances, including regular mainstays such as the comic *Lisdoonvarna* and the ballad, *Ride On*. Finally, in 1996, after years of singing others' songs, he released a self-penned album *Graffiti Tongue*. In 1998 he announced his retirement on the grounds of ill-health, but returned at the end of the following year with a grand new album and a barn-storming series of gigs.

Moore's brother Barry records under the name **Luka Bloom** (a combination of Suzanne Vega's song and the protagonist of *Ulysses*). Early on he backed his brother who recorded some of Bloom's work, most notably *The City of Chicago*. With a reputation himself for magnificent live performances he has also made some fine albums including *Turf* and *Salty Heaven*.

Of the other musicians recording crossover traditional music and folk in the Sixties, **Paul Brady** continues to produce music of an exceptional standard. From Strabane in County Tyrone, Brady became involved in the Dublin folk renaissance while studying there in the 1960s. His first recordings were made with the Johnstons with whom he made seven albums before leaving for London and New York, returning in 1974 to join Planxty for a short time. In 1976 he teamed up with Planxty member Andy Irvine and the album they produced, with its unique and sensitive interpretations of songs such as *Arthur McBride*, make it one of the finest albums in the traditional canon. His work in the late Seventies was of an equally high standard culminating in arguably his best solo album, *Welcome Here Kind Stranger*, in 1978, featuring his benchmark rendition of *The Lakes of Pontchartrain*. The 1980s saw Brady move away from his traditional roots through *Hard Station* (1981) which included the passionate exposé of anti-Irish racism, *Nothing but the Same Old Story*. Subsequent albums have further highlighted his tremendous songwriting talents – he's been recorded by Tina Turner and Eric Clapton among many others and the best way of sampling these is his remastered compilation *Nobody Knows*.

Contemporary bands striving for new ways to express the tradition are the excellent **Kíla**, whose latest album *Lemonade & Buns* mixes traditional singing with African rhythms, the superb **Afro-Celt Sound System**, **Anam**, who draw on a rich variety of musical influences from jazz and blues, and **Anúna**, a vocal group spanning classical, folk, traditional and contemporary. Other experimental outfits include **Flook**, featuring the astonishing young *bodhrán* player **John Joe Kelly** and a twin flute attack, and **Cran** whose blend of flute, *uilleann* pipes and bouzouki is married to song arrangements of both exceptional candour and beauty. Originally a jazz-influenced folk band, **Clannad**'s mix of atmospherics (sometimes known as "Celtic hush" music) has brought the group huge international success.

Any examination of Irish traditional music must include a reference to **The Pogues**. Originally known as Pogue Mahone ("kiss my arse" in Irish), this London Irish band emerged in the early 1980s playing a chaotic set of "Oirish" standards and rebel songs. Iconoclasts to the core, they brought a punk energy to the Irish ballad. They were also blessed with one of the finest Irish songwriters of recent years, **Shane McGowan**. His songs captured the casualties and condition of Irish exile in London and, said fan and producer Elvis Costello, "saved folk from the folkies". Certainly they helped bring a new audience, and a new generation of musicians, back to look at its roots. McGowan subsequently formed his own band The Popes and released three albums, though none matched the glorious exuberance of The Pogues' *Red Roses for Me* or *Rum, Sodomy and the Lash*.

ROCK, POP AND WHATEVER YOU WILL

Naturally, Ireland's rock scene has always borne close similarities to Britain's. Physical proximity, the permeation of British mass-media, especially radio and the influential rock press, and British stars' use of Dublin as a tax haven have all facilitated a musical currency between the two. What happens in London, Liverpool or Manchester tends to be mirrored in Belfast and Dublin and, occasionally, vice versa. However, there are two significant exceptions. First, apart from mavericks like Richard Thompson, British rock and pop bear little indication of any traditional folk origins, whereas Irish rock culture is steeped in it – a hardly surprising conclusion considering the number of Irish musicians who learn a traditional instrument and its associated tunes at an early age. Secondly, the overwhelmingly mono-cultural nature of Irish society means that important components of the British scene – reggae, ragga, bhangra, black dance and soul music in its many variations – are rarely experienced first-hand or develop from cultural traditions. Two Tone, for instance, could never have happened in Dublin, just as a host of Clannad clones is never likely to appear in Coventry. Nevertheless, the country's rock heritage is a rich one and, for every dozen bands trying to be the new Radiohead, there's always something happening in the pubs and clubs of Dublin, Belfast and Derry.

SHOWBANDS AND BEAT

For most of the 1960s and the following decade, live music was dominated by that peculiarly Irish phenomenon, the **showband**. These groups of neatly-coiffed, shiny-suited cover-version merchants toured the country, playing their selections in vast ballrooms (barely a few of which survive today). Enthusiasm tended to supersede talent, but their regimentation did provide a training ground for future stars such as Rory Gallagher and Eric Bell (Thin Lizzy's first guitarist).

The showbands' dominance was undermined by the arrival of **beat music**, conveyed by radio and, like Liverpool, by sailors bringing American R&B records to the ports of Dublin and Belfast. By the mid-1960s Dublin was awash with beat groups, the majority of whom are long- (and perhaps best-) forgotten, though you can hear examples of the recordings of The Greenbeats, The Movement, Purple Pussycat and a horde of others on the Sequel collection *Ireland's Beat Groups: 1964–69*. The most successful group was **Bluesville**, led by Ian Whitcomb, an American studying at Trinity College, which had a US top ten hit with *You Turn Me On*. Meanwhile, in Belfast, George Ivan Morrison had got together with guitarist Billy Harrison to

TWENTY ESSENTIAL IRISH ROCK ALBUMS

A House *I Am the Greatest* (1991;Setanta UK).

Paul Brady *Hard Station* (1981; Mercury UK).

Mary Coughlan *Under the Influence* (1987; WEA UK).

The Divine Comedy *Casanova* (1996; Setanta UK; Red Ink US).

The Fat Lady Sings *John Son* (1993; East West UK).

The Frames[dc] *Fitzcarraldo* (1996; ZTT UK; WEA/Elektra US).

Gavin Friday *Shag Tobacco* (1995; Island UK).

Hothouse Flowers *People* (1988; London UK; Polygram US).

Microdisney *The Clock Comes Down the Stairs* (1985; Rev-Ola UK).

Van Morrison *It's Too Late to Stop Now* (1974; Warner UK; A&M US).

Moving Hearts *Moving Hearts* (1981; WEA UK).

The Pogues *Rum, Sodomy and the Lash* (1984; Stiff UK).

Sinéad O'Connor *I Do Not Want What I Haven't Got* (1991; Ensign UK; Chrysalis US).

The Stars of Heaven *Sacred Heart Hotel* (1986; Rough Trade UK).

Taste *On the Boards* (1970; Polydor UK).

Them *Angry Young Them* (1965; Decca UK).

Thin Lizzy *Jailbreak* (1976; Vertigo UK; Polygram US).

Pierce Turner *The Compilation* (1998; Beggars Banquet UK).

The Undertones *The Undertones* (1979; Sire UK; Ryko US).

U2 *The Joshua Tree* (1987; Island UK; Polygram US).

form **Them**. **Van Morrison** had toured with another Belfast band, The Monarchs, since 1959, when he was only 14, but Them's successes with *Baby, Please Don't Go* (the B-side was the wonderful *Gloria*) and *Here Comes the Night* established musical credentials which he has never relinquished. Dissatisfied with his management, constant personnel changes and the quality of the band's first two albums, Morrison left and moved to the US. After disastrous experiences with the Bang label, he signed with Warner Brothers; his first two albums with them achieved astonishing critical, if not entirely commercial, success and established the hallmarks of his style. The marvellously atmospheric *Astral Weeks* was recorded in only two days, consisting of apparent improvisation by an adept band adroitly working around Van's range of vocal stylings and poetic lyrics. *Moondance* followed two years later, in 1970, revealing his ability to construct compact songs characterized by a sense of relaxation, though driven by extremely tight instrumentation. Since then Morrison has released numerous albums, of late almost annually, but while none has attained the excellence of the early pair, he remains the consummate professional and a tremendous experience live.

Morrison's love of the blues was shared by the Donegal-born guitarist **Rory Gallagher**. Extracting himself from the showband scene, Gallagher was first successful as leader of the progressive blues band **Taste** where he developed a reputation for his powerful rolling guitar licks. Taste split acrimoniously in 1970, citing the then popular "musical differences" and Gallagher launched a creditable solo career, using a variety of bassists and drummers, notable for his range of checked shirts and the intensity of his live performances (captured semi-successfully on *Irish Tour* and *Live! in Europe*). His later career was bedevilled by health problems and, sadly, he died in 1995. For a flavour of Gallagher's music try the recently released compilation album *Etched in Blue* (1999).

THE SEVENTIES

Ireland dabbled with psychedelia and for a time the music scene was dominated by bands such as Granny's Intentions, Dr Strangely Strange and Eire Apparent. However, it was **Skid Row**'s more straight-out-the-barrel rock which was to have a lasting impact. The original band featured the bassist **Brush Shiels** (still playing regularly in Dublin), an astonishingly young Belfast lad, **Gary Moore**, on guitar and, for a while, **Phil Lynott** as singer. Skid Row released two progressive albums in the early 1970s, after which Moore left – he later played with a variety of other bands running the gamut of rock to heavy metal before establishing himself as a major solo performer.

Phil Lynott, however, formed **Thin Lizzy**, the first Irish band to crack the world market which led to Lynott becoming the first black Irish superstar. Initial success came with a reworking of the traditional *Whiskey in the Jar* in 1973. Then followed a series of albums, dominated by Lynott's romantic lyrics and a characteristic twin lead guitar sound. The 1976 album *Jailbreak* retains its initial impact, even if the macho posturing of its biggest hit, *The Boys are Back in Town*, jangles raucously in an era of more considered sensibilities. Lynott later produced a couple of fine, though sadly overlooked, solo albums (*Solo in Soho* is the better), before dying from kidney and liver failure in 1986.

Elsewhere, two more folk-oriented bands enjoyed a modicum of popularity in the early 1970s. The acoustic duo **Tír na nÓg** supported virtually everybody and made a couple of whimsical albums for Chrysalis. Meanwhile, **Horslips** were almost single-handedly responsible for Celtic Rock. Retrospectively, their Irish legend-based concept albums such as *The Tain* (1973) and *The Book of Invasions* (1976) seem clumsily contrived in context and obscure in content – as many such albums were – but their use of traditional instruments in a rock setting was of durable influence and they blazed a trail for later bands to follow, such as **Moving Hearts** (see p.710), **In Tua Nua** and **Lick the Tins**.

There may have been fewer Irish dinosaurs to be declared extinct, but the advent of punk and new wave in the second half of the 1970s reinvigorated the home scene. However, the initial success of **The Boomtown Rats**, led by **Bob Geldof**, relied on their ability to produce powerful three-minute pop songs such as *Rat Trap* (1978) and *I Don't Like Mondays* (1979). For a while the Dublin scene thrived through bands such as **The Radiators from Space** (featuring later Pogues guitarist Philip Chevron), **The Virgin Prunes**, **The Blades** and a very young bunch of hopefuls called **The Hype**. Perhaps the greater successes, however, were in the North. **Stiff Little Fingers** first came to notice in 1978 with their astonishingly powerful debut single *Suspect Device*, a song whose driving beat struggled to contain an equally powerful lyric of political discontent. Meanwhile, **The Undertones** had been formed in Derry in 1974, but failed to achieve any success until the BBC Radio One disc jockey John Peel adopted their *Teenage Kicks* as a virtual personal anthem. Four albums of finely-crafted perceptive songs followed, mixing in perfect harmony the **O'Neill Brothers** songs of adolescent yearning, **Feargal Sharkey's** idiosyncratic tremolo voice and a pumping beat. After their split in 1983 Sharkey had a couple of hit singles while Damien and John O'Neill formed **That Petrol Emotion** whose initial releases were marked by powerful political sentiments questioning the continued British presence in Ireland.

U2 TO THE CORRS

The Hype, having changed their name to **U2**, went on to become the biggest rock band in the world. Listening to their first album *Boy* (1980), it's just about possible to understand the reason. Then, as now, U2's ability to try their hand at a range of styles is very much apparent, even if the original efforts lacked their subsequent polish and grasp of studio technique. Nevertheless, the key elements have remained the same: a tight rhythm bedrock of **Adam Clayton** (bass) and **Larry Mullen** (drums) setting the framework for **Dave Evans**'s innovative chordal guitar stylings and **Bono**'s soaring voice. Their anthems proved ideal American stadium fodder and the video of *Under a Blood Red Sky* (1983) brought them an even wider audience. 1987's *The Joshua Tree*, however, was their major breakthrough, despite the bleakness of songs such as *Where the Streets Have No Name* and *I Still Haven't Found What I'm Looking For*. The album even spawned a notable group of Dublin parodists, **The Joshua Trio**, featuring one of the future author's of *Father Ted*. The release of subsequent U2 albums and their associated tours have become major international events and Bono has become Ireland's greatest living love-hate figure, derided for his occasional pomposity (such as his on-stage telephone calls to political leaders), but revered for his undeniable care for his country (such as his appearance at Ash's 1998 peace settlement gig with the politicians David Trimble and John Hume). The year 2000 saw the band return to their musical roots with an album, *All You Can't Leave Behind*, which exudes the style, confidence and distinctive rock melodies that won them such acclaim in the 1980s.

Following U2's ascent to glory, Dublin's bars and clubs were awash with agents and talent scouts trying to sign "the next big thing". Most of the recordings of these bands have sunk without trace and few now recall Aslan, Cactus World News, Cry Before Dawn or Light a Big Fire. A couple are worth noting – the country-tinged **Stars of Heaven**, who sadly split before the talent displayed in their debut *Sacred Heart Hotel* could evolve further, and the continued efforts of **Gavin Friday** (first with the Virgin Prunes and later solo) to gain the audience he deserves for his original confection of the baroque and bizarre. A significantly successful signing, however, was the then shaven-headed young singer, **Sinéad O'Connor**, first with her Prince-written single *Nothing Compares 2 U* and later with the album *I Do Not Want What I Haven't Got* (1990). Yet it was her outspoken public pronouncements on Ireland, abortion and papal power which brought her even greater attention. Oppressed by her fame, she left Ireland and moved to London to rear her children, only to return after undergoing a much-publicized religious conversion, which she claims to be the inspiration behind her disappointing latest album *Faith and Courage* (2000).

Every musical genre seems to be represented in the Ireland of the 1990s. There are plenty of solo singers ploughing their lonely furrows. Apart from Paul Brady and Christy Moore (see p.710), the currently popular include **Sinéad Lohan**, **Kieran Goss**, **Nick Kelly** (formerly leader of the excellent The Fat Lady Sings), **Paddy Casey** and three from the North, **Brian Houston**, **Andy White** and **Brian Kennedy** who also works regularly with Van Morrison. Also worth seeking out are the sporadically released albums by **Pierce Turner** (quirky avant-garde meets Irish sensibility), the blues and jazz of the smoky-voiced **Mary Coughlan**, while *Metropolis Blue* (2000) has seen the sublime **Jack Lukeman** receive the recognition he has long deserved. **The Cranberries**, after enjoying brief global success in the mid-1990s, have re-established themselves with *Bury the*

Hatchet (1999). At one time it seemed as though the film *The Commitments* would sire a host of spin-off bands – only one, Glenn Hansard's **The Frames** has had any lasting impact with their 2000 album *Dance the Devil* hugely popular in the alternative music scene. Other bands to enjoy success have included **Hothouse Flowers** (led by Liam O'Maonlai), **The Frank and Walters**, **A House**, **An Emotional Fish**, **Something Happens**, **the Sultans of Ping FC** and two notable results from the break-up of the wonderfully angry 1980s band **Microdisney** – the raw psychopathy of Cathal Coughlan's **Fatima Mansions** and the Beach Boys-inspired work of **The High Llamas**, led by Sean O'Hagan. **Coughlan** has since released a highly impressive solo album *Black River Falls* (2000). Mention must also be made of the traditional-inspired soft rock of Donegal's **Clannad** and the more ambient, but exceedingly popular, doodles of their fellow family member **Enya**. The Enniskillen band **Celtus** is currently exploring a similar vein. There's a thriving dance scene in Ireland, too, with the most innovative and universally acclaimed work being produced by **David Holmes** from Belfast. 1999 saw Holmes release a box set of 12-inch remixes, *Stop Arresting Artists*, followed in 2000 by arguably the finest Irish album of the year, *Bow Down to the Exit Sign*, which succeeds in capturing the seedy underside of New York City where the album was recorded. Ethereal electronica can be found in *My Fault* (2000) the debut album of **Metisse** fronted by sensual French vocalist Aida.

At the forefront of the resurgence of Northern Ireland as a hotbed for young talent are **Ash** from Downpatrick who, having showed precocious polish on their debut album *1977*, have come of musical age with their edgy follow-up *Nu-clear Sounds* (1999). One-man band, **Neil Hannon**, better-known as **The Divine Comedy**, has gained a loyal following with quirky recordings such as *Casanova* (1995) which evoke the sharp-suited romance of a James Bond movie. Recently written off by many critics, Larne's **Therapy?** have bounced back with a vengeance with the exhilarating and frenetic *Semi-detached* (1999). Other bands worth looking out for are **Watercress**, who hit the mark with their infectiously poppy *Bummer* album (1999), **Snow Patrol** (originally from Belfast though now based in Glasgow), **Booley** and Derry's **Cuckoo** who released the frantic *Breathing Lesson* in 1999. In the Republic, bands with significant potential include **Ten Speed Racer**, **The Hitchers** (fronted by former Cranberries vocalist Niall Quinn), the punky **Joan of Arse**, the country-inspired **Great Western Squares**, and the former darling of the music press, **Junkster**. Ireland's only rock paper, the superb *Hot Press*, is the place to look for information.

However, apart from the old reliables (Moore, Morrison and so on), the favourite Irish artistes of the moment, naturally, come from the more mainstream areas. The teen market is catered for by bands fathered by Ireland's pop impresario Louis Walsh, the man responsible for boy-bands **Boyzone** and **Westlife**, though the lads are being outshone of late by his latest teen sensation **Samantha Mumba**. The girl-band **B*witched** released the album *Awake and Breathe* (1999) and claim to be the youngest girl-band to have recorded a number one hit in the UK pop charts. The middle-aged, of course, are not left out and their darling is **Daniel O'Donnell**, the homely Donegal singer of standards, country and western and gospel. Lastly, tapping the sensitivities of *Rumours*-period Fleetwood Mac, albeit with a strong Irish traditional influence, are the family foursome, **The Corrs** (three sisters, one brother), whose bright good looks and anodyne, but catchy, songs have been recorded on two hugely popular albums *Forgiven not Forgotten* (1997) and *Talk on Corners* (1998) which have guaranteed them global popularity and healthy bank accounts for years to come.

CLASSICAL MUSIC

As in the visual arts, Ireland has a strong classical music tradition, though it's little-known outside the island. The dominant instrument of early music was the **harp**, though we know little of how it was played since no written record has survived. However, more than two hundred works by the poet, harpist and composer **Turlough O'Carolan** (1670–1738) have survived. His work, together with the performances of the participants at the 1792 **Belfast Harp Festival**, transcribed and published by **Edward Bunting**, were the prime sources of the airs which have formed a major component of Irish music since that time.

During the eighteenth century, Dublin became an important musical centre and attracted many European composers, including **Handel**, who staged the premiere of the *Messiah* in the capital in 1742. The first native classical composer of note was **John Field** (1782–1837), who, as a child prodigy, was apprenticed to Clementi to demonstrate pianos. He taught in Europe for several years and produced a significant body of keyboard work, especially his *19 Nocturnes* which considerably influenced Chopin and other Romantics.

Another precocious child was **Michael Balfe** (1808–70), who made his debut as a violinist at the age of nine, though he had already begun composing two years earlier. During the 1820s, he studied under Rossini and became converted to the opera form. Numerous compositions followed and his *The Bohemian Girl* was a success of the time. From 1846, he was conductor of the London Italian Opera. Similarly popular were the operas of Waterford man **Vincent Wallace** (1813–65), particularly *Maritana* and *Lurina*. This Irish operatic tradition was continued by **Victor Herbert** (1859–1924), a cellist who played in the orchestras of Joseph Strauss before emigrating to the US to join the New York Metropolitan Opera Company. His forte was the comic opera and he became popular for songs such as *Sweet Mystery of Life* before settling down to pen more serious work. Most prolific in this period, however, was **Charles Villiers Stanford** (1852–1924), who was organist at Trinity College, Cambridge. After a stint teaching at the Royal College of Music he became Professor of Music at Cambridge and taught numerous young British composers of the era. In his own right he adapted Tennyson's poetry to choral settings, wrote a number of operas and religious pieces. His origins are reflected by his *Irish Symphony* and *Six Irish Rhapsodies*.

In the first half of the twentieth century, **Hamilton Harty** (1880–1941), from Hillsborough, Co. Down, attained a degree of fame through his conducting of the Hallé Orchestra from 1920 to 1933 and revived Handel's popularity through his arrangements of the *Fireworks* and *Water Music* suites. However, his own work, including an *Irish Symphony* utilizing the strains and melodies of traditional songs, is less well known. **A.J. Potter** (1918–80), the son of a blind Belfast piano-tuner, was Professor of Composition at the Royal Irish Academy of Music for almost twenty years and his own eclectic style influenced many of his students. Other notable figures have included the popular conductor **Brian Boydell** (b.1917) whose works for orchestra and string quartet are influenced by Bartok and Hindesmith, and **Gerard Victory** (1921–1995), who became well-known via his work with the RTE Symphony Orchestra from 1967 onwards. Head of Music at the RTE for some of the same time was **John Kinsella** (b.1932) until he resigned in 1988 to devote himself to full-time composition, subsequently producing a number of influential works. **Seóirse Bodley** (b.1933) has written five full symphonies and numerous other works revealing influences ranging from the European avant-garde to traditional song. **Gerald Barry** (b.1952) studied composition under Stockhausen and has had many works commissioned by the BBC, additionally penning operas for the ICA and Channel 4. The flautist **John Buckley** (b.1951) has produced a range of works for solo instruments and various ensembles. Intriguingly, the latest generation of composers producing influential work includes a significant number of **young women**, including Elaine Agnew, Rhona Clarke, Siobhan Cleary and Deirdre Gribbin – a trend which bodes well for the future.

Finally, the more popular end of the home market has come to be dominated recently by composers experimenting with adaptations and reformulations of Irish traditional music. Notable exponents include **Patrick Cassidy**, **Michael Alcorn** and **Shaun Davey**. While **Michael Ó Súilleabháin**'s recordings in this genre, such as *The Dolphin's Way* and *Flowing*, have attained considerable success. However, without any doubt, the most famous (or notorious, depending on your viewpoint) is **Bill Whelan**, responsible for the *Riverdance* phenomenon and a huge increase in the sale of dancing shoes.

LITERATURE

Oscar Wilde once sighed to Yeats that "we Irish have done nothing, but we are the greatest talkers since the Greeks"; Samuel Beckett claimed that Irish writers had been "buggered into existence by the English army and the Roman pope". Irish writing has always flouted and challenged, experimented and fantasized, from the great anti-novel, Joyce's *Ulysses*, to what some see as the great anti-play, Beckett's *Waiting for Godot*. Much Irish writing concerns the dysfunction of real life, but this is usually laced with wild, fantastical and spiritual imaginings; one of the country's great contemporary novelists, Patrick McCabe, claims, in a typical Irish inversion, this should be deemed "social fantastic" not "poetic realism". Authors from Swift to Roddy Doyle present us with the conflict between high ideals and sordid reality, a conflict captured by Beckett when he claimed he wanted to "sit around, scratch my arse and think of Dante." Tension has also come from writing in a language that belongs, essentially, to another tradition. This is most clearly articulated by Nobel laureate Seamus Heaney who sees the conflict between his folk background, what he deems "hearth culture", and expressing himself in poetry, the most formal genre in Engish, as the central dynamic in his work. Thus any study of Irish literature must begin with an examination of the folk culture and tradition to which Irish writers belong.

THE GAELS

Irish writing first appeared in the fifth century AD when monastic settlers brought Classical culture into contact with a Gaelic civilization that had a long and sophisticated oral tradition. Faced with the resistance of the pagan bards, the newcomers set about incorporating the Celtic sagas into the comparatively young system of Christian belief. These ancient tales told of war and famine, madness and love, death and magical rebirth – story sequences from deep in the folk memory. One of the earliest of these, the *Taín Bó Cuailnge* (Cattle Raid of Cooley), deals with a rumpus between **Cúchulainn**, a prototypical Celtic superman, and the mighty Queen Medb, over the theft of a prize bull. The best translation of the epic is, without doubt, Thomas Kinsella's *The Taín* (1969), which has an excellent introduction and a map of areas relating to the tale. The series of tales concerning Cúchulainn, known as the **Ulster Cycle**, were, from the eighth century, superseded by those concerning the exploits of **Fionn Mac Cumhaill** and his posse, the Fianna, known as the **Ossianic Cycle**. Fionn was a more disturbing and sophisticated figure, not only a warrior but a poet, sage and mystic; in the most prominent tale in the cycle, *Tóraigheacht Dhiarmada agus Ghráinne* (Pursuit of Diarmaid and Gráinne), Fionn is represented as a jealous, ageing warrior, irate at being cuckolded by the young Diarmaid and chasing him and his former lover Gráinne around Ireland.

Later Irish artists made much of the early tales, sometimes with less than proper reverence; in Beckett's novel *Murphy* (1938), for instance, a character attempts suicide by banging his head repeatedly against the bronze buttocks of the statue of Cúchulainn, which adorns the lobby of Dublin's GPO. Another tale which has proved an inspiration to many writers is *Buile Shuibne* (Frenzy of Sweeney), a twelfth-century text detailing the adventures of the king **Sweeney** who, driven mad by the noise of incessant warfare, seeks refuge in the tree tops of Ireland, where he writes lyrical nature poetry. This tale was one of the inspirations behind Flann O'Brien's novel *At Swim-Two-Birds* (see p.722), while Seamus Heaney's *Sweeney Astray* (1983) is a lyrical translation of the mythical wanderings of the mad king.

Fairy tales from this Celtic era reveal a world of witches, imps and banshees, all jollying around in a Manichaean struggle with the forces of love, wisdom and goodness – which, refreshingly, do not always triumph. Check out Kevin Danaher's *In Ireland Long Ago* (1962) for full-blooded retellings.

A LITERATURE OF RESISTANCE

The first of many incursions from England took place in the twelfth century, when gangs of Norman adventurers invaded at the invitation of an Irish king. But it wasn't until four centuries later that the English presence found its way into the literature, when the excesses of English rule began finally to provoke an early literature of resistance.

The high point of this Irish-language tradition is the long poem from 1773 by **Eibhlín Dhubh Ní Chonaill** (1748–1800), *Caoineadh Airt Uí Laoghaire* (A Lament for Art O'Leary). A traditional *caoineadh* or lament infused with a new political awareness, it deals with the execution of the poet's lover, who had refused to sell his prized white horse to the Sheriff of Cork and was therefore hunted down and killed; even in translation this has a sparse and chilling beauty.

Other marvellous laments include the anonymous *Donal Óg*, Lady Gregory's translation of which was included with cheeky but effective licence in the 1985 John Huston film of Joyce's short story, *The Dead*. But the early written tradition wasn't all tears, and some pieces harked back to a pre-Christian earthiness. One such text from the later Irish-language era is **Brian Merriman**'s satirical *aisling* (vision poem), *Cúirt an Mheán Oíche* (The Midnight Court), a trenchant attack on the sexual inadequacy of the Irish male. One translation which preserves the earthiness of the original is by **Frank O'Connor**, in *Kings, Lords and Commons* (1959).

Despite persecution, the Irish language persisted as a majority tongue well into the last century, and **Séan Ó Tuama** and **Thomas Kinsella's** book of translations, *An Duanaire: Poems of the Dispossessed*, records the voices of those marginalized by foreign rule and famine. However, defying both economic realities and the ineptitude of successive Irish governments, the Irish language has survived, and in recent years has produced an impressive canon of its own, far removed from the rural preoccupations it is often associated with. Such preoccupations were exemplified by storyteller **Peig Sayers** (1873–1958) – still perhaps the most famous Irish-language author in the country – whose recounting of the misery of life on one of Ireland's westerly outposts was the set text in Irish schools and which, not surprisingly, turned bored urban schoolchildren against the language for life. Far preferable is **Pádraig Ó Conaire** (1883–1928), whose statue stands in Eyre Square, Galway. His *Scothscéalta* reads like Maupassant, capturing the stark cruelty of the Irish landscape and the petty malices of rural life.

The first step towards modernity in Irish writing was, in many ways, the wickedly satirical and hilariously funny, *An Béal Bocht* (The Poor Mouth) by **Myles na Gopaleen**, aka Flann O'Brien (1941 – see p.722), which satirized such classic Gaelic works on the difficulty of life on Ireland's western seaboard. **Seán Ó Ríordáin** (1916–77) from West Cork drew heavily on both the Gaelic and modernist traditions in his poems, while the poetry of **Máirtín Ó Díreáin** (1910–88) from the Aran Islands explores the themes of deracination and the anonymity of urban life. This modernist tradition greatly influenced a group of poets working out of University College Cork, the **Innti** group, whose writing embraced all manner of urban and popular cultural references. The most prominent of this group is **Nuala Ní Dhomhnaill** (b.1952), whose work marks an engagement between the feminist and Gaelic traditions and is well received both in Irish and English translation; for a flavour of her work try either *The Astrakhan Cloak* (1991), with translations by Paul Muldoon, or *The Water Horse* (1999), a selection from her earlier works *Feis* and *Cead Aighnis* with translations by Medbh McGuckian. **Gabriel Rosenstock** (b.1949) and **Cathal Ósearcaigh** (b.1956) are prolific writers and translators, working closely with Seamus Heaney, the latter's latest work *Out in the Open* (1997) causing a stir because of its sexual candidness. Other contemporary poets writing in Irish are **Michael O'Siadhail** (b.1947) whose collected poems were published in 1999 and **Michael Davitt** (b.1950) whose work, heavily influenced by American Beat poetry, can be read in *Freacnairc Mhearcair* (The Oomph of Quicksilver).

THE START OF THE LITERARY TRADITION

Between the 1690s and the 1720s the hated penal laws were passed, denying Catholics rights to property, education, political activity and religious practice. British misrule created widespread poverty which devastated the countryside and ravaged the population. It's in this period that **Anglo-Irish literature** began.

One of the most prominent of the early pamphleteers and agitators was **John Toland** (1670–1722), whom the authorities gave the dubious distinction of being the first Irish writer to have his work publicly burned. But the first big-league player arrived in the angry little shape of **Jonathan Swift** (1667–1745), Dean of St Patrick's Cathedral, Dublin. Swift was a cantankerous but basically compassionate man who used his pen to expose viciousness, hypocrisy and corruption whenever he saw it, which in eighteenth-century Dublin was pretty often. Swift was a master of satire; in one of his 75 pamphlets, *A Modest Proposal*, he proposed that the children of the poor should be cooked to feed the rich, thereby getting rid of poverty and increasing affluence, and his masterpiece, *Gulliver's Travels* (1726), is as terrifying now as it ever was. He died a bitter man, leaving in his will an endowment to build Dublin's first lunatic asylum, adding in a pithy codicil that if he'd had enough money he would have arranged for a 20ft-high wall to be built around the entire island. He is buried in the vault of St Patrick's, where, as his epitaph says, "Savage indignation can rend his heart no more".

The other great satirist of the eighteenth century was **Laurence Sterne** (1713–1768). A tremendous wit with more mad whimsy than venom, his greatest work *Tristram Shandy* was once memorably described as "the greatest shaggy dog story in the language".

The elegant prose of **Edmund Burke** (1729–97) – graduate of Trinity College, philosopher, journalist and MP – argued for order in all things, decrying the French Revolution for its destruction of humanity's basic need for faith. He is a complex and difficult figure, and his ideas are claimed in Ireland both by the civil-liberties-trampling Right and by elements of the progressive Left.

1780–1880: THE CELTIC REVIVAL

Towards the end of the eighteenth century, a Europe-wide vogue for all things Celtic prompted a renaissance in Irish music and literature. This period also saw the birth of that misty, ineffable Celtic spirit, which was to influence Yeats a century later. A couple of important books appeared, including **Joseph Cooper Walker**'s *Historical Memoirs of the Irish Bards* (1786) and **Edward Bunting**'s *General Collection of Irish Music* (1796).

Dublin at the time of the Act of Union with Britain (1801) had long been a truly European city, frequently visited by French, German and Italian composers. Indeed, Handel's *Messiah* was first performed in Dublin's Fishamble Street. One Irish composer and writer who thrived under the European influence was the harpist **Turlough O'Carolan** (1670–1738), who met and traded riffs with the Italian composer Geminiani.

At the turn of the century a series of Irish harp festivals began, their purpose being to recover the rapidly disappearing ancient music. With their evocation of the bardic tradition they became a focus not just for nifty fingerwork but for political agitation. The harpists continued into the nineteenth century until **Thomas Moore** (1779–1852) finally stole many of their traditional airs, wrote words for them, published them as *Moore's Irish Melodies* (1808) and made a lot of money.

The concomitant literary revival entailed a resurrection of the Irish language too, and although few went so far as to learn it, it became a vague symbol of an heroic literary past that implied a fundamentally nationalist world view. John Mitchell's Fenian movement, provoked by Britain's callous response to the Famine, was at least as influenced by the Celtic Revival as it was by the new revolutionary ideas being imported all the time from Europe. The Fenians were to provide a bridge between the heroic past and the demands of modernism and had a huge impact on the thinking of Yeats and other leaders of the Celtic revival. One of their supporters, **James Clarence Mangan** (1803–49), inaugurated in *My Dark Rosaleen* (1846) the image of suffering Ireland as a brutalized woman, awaiting defence by an heroic man. In a country where visual and literary imagery of the Virgin Mary is ubiquitous, the symbolism escaped nobody.

THE NINETEENTH-CENTURY NOVEL

The unease generated among the aristocracy by the growth of Irish Nationalism and the Fenian Rebellion of 1848 found expression in novels showing the peasantry plotting away in their cottages against their masters up in the mansion – the "Big House" sub-genre of Anglo-Irish writing, represented by such writers as **Lady Morgan** (1775–1859). Typically, such a book would involve an evil-smelling Irish hoodlum inheriting the mansion and either turning it into a barn or burning it to the ground. *Castle Rackrent* (1800) by **Maria Edgeworth**

(1776–1849) is one of the few good Big House novels, its craftily resourceful narrator telling the story of the great family's demise with a subtle glee.

The Irish fought back, appropriating the well-made novel for themselves. **Gerald Griffin** (1803–40), **John Banim** (1798–1842), **William Carleton** (1794–1869) and **Charles Lever** (1806–72) emerged as the voice of the new middle class, protesting at the stereotyping of the Irish as savages, and demanding political and economic rights.

This period also saw the entry of the Anglo-Irish into the crisis that would haunt them until their complete demise in the 1920s, as they struggled between the specifically "Anglo" and "Irish" sides of their identity. This kind of angst can be found running throughout the work of **Sir Samuel Ferguson** (1810–86), **Standish O'Grady** (1846–1928), and **Douglas Hyde** (1860–1949), the founder of the Gaelic League (1893) who went on to become Ireland's first president in 1937.

The writing of **E.O. Sommerville** (1858–1949) and **(Violet) Martin Ross** (1861–1915) – cousins and increasingly impoverished daughters of the Ascendancy – is typical of nineteenth-century Anglo-Irish confusion. Their work, such as *Some Recollections and Further Experiences of an Irish RM* (1899) and the powerful novel *The Real Charlotte* (1894), is imbued with a genuine love of Ireland and the ways of the Irish peasantry, yet occasionally there's a chilling sense that the status quo is in danger. The peasants, previously marginalized in the tradition, now seem to keep intruding in unwelcome ways, sneaking into the upstairs rooms, interrupting their betters or conspiring behind the bushes in the estate's well-kept gardens.

Meanwhile **Bram Stoker** (1847–1912) was busily writing his way into the history books with a novel that would enter modern popular culture in all its forms, from the movies to the comic book. *Dracula* is a wonderful novel, more of a psychological Gothic thriller than a schlock horror bloodbath, and its concerns – the nature of the soul versus the bestial allure of the body, for instance – are curiously Irish. But even this had its political implications. With its pseudo-folkloric style and its pitting of the noble peasants against the aristocratic monster debauching away in his castle, its symbolism is inescapably revolutionary and romantic.

THE STORY OF THE STAGE IRISHMAN

It's one of the delicious twists of fate which seem to beset Irish literary history that the country's most important early dramatist only took up writing by mistake. One evening a young Derry actor named **George Farquhar** was playing a bit part in the duel scene of Dryden's *Indian Emperor* at the Dublin *Smock Alley* theatre when, in a moment of tragic enthusiasm, he accidentally stabbed a fellow actor, almost killing him. Understandably shaken, Farquhar gave up the stage for good and went off to London to write plays instead.

Farquhar (1677–1707) is often credited with the invention of the stage Irishman, the descendants of whom can still be seen in many soap operas and situation comedies on British television to this day. Effusive in his own way, but basically sly, stupid and violent, this stock character stumbled through the dramas of **Steele** (1672–1729), **Chaigneau** (1709–81), **Goldsmith** (1728–74) and **Sheridan** (1751–1816), tugging his forelock, bumping into the furniture and going "bejayzus" at every available moment. In fact Irish stereotypes had existed in the British tradition for many centuries before these dramatists had at least the good sense to make some money out of them. The stage Irishman was brought to his ultimate idiocy by **Dion Boucicault** (1820–90), whose leprechaunic characters seemed to have staggered straight out of the Big House novel and onto the London stage. Boucicault, however, has undergone something of a revival in recent years, with a few critics arguing that his unstable and unpredictable dramas were subversive attacks against the version of colonial reality imposed upon Ireland in the nineteenth century.

Boucicault's chum, **George Bernard Shaw** (1856–1950), turned out to be the kind of stage Irishman the English couldn't patronize out of existence. A radical socialist and feminist, he championed all kinds of cranky causes and some very admirable ones, and lived long enough to be a founder member of CND. His cerebral and often polemical plays – of which *Saint Joan* is perhaps the best – have remained a mainstay of theatre repertoire.

Yet even Shaw paled in comparison to the ultimate king of the one-line put-down, **Oscar Wilde** (1856–1900). After a brilliant career at

Oxford – during which he lost both his virginity and his Irish accent – Wilde went on to set literary London alight, creating the smiling resentment that would finally destroy him. In *The Picture of Dorian Gray* he expanded on the Gothic tradition of Stoker and Sheridan Le Fanu (1814–73) to explore the fundamental duality of the romantic hero. But it was in his satirical plays, particularly *The Importance of Being Earnest*, that he was at his most acerbic. A brilliant and gentle man, he poured scorn on his critics, openly espoused home rule for Ireland and lived with consummate style until the debacle of his affair with Lord Alfred Douglas. This self-obsessed bimbo persuaded Wilde into a foolish libel action against his thuggish father, the Marquess of Queensbury, which Wilde lost. Immediately afterwards he was arrested for homosexuality, publicly disgraced and privately condemned by his many fair-weather friends. He served two years in prison where he wrote his finest works, *The Ballad of Reading Gaol* and *De Profundis* (published after his death in 1905). In early 1900 one of Ireland's greatest, and most tragic, writers, died alone and distraught in Paris. "I will never live into the new century", he declared. "The English would just not allow it."

IRISH MODERNISM: POETRY AND DRAMA

Shortly before Wilde's death, the myth of the fallen hero had entered the vocabulary of Irish literature with the demise of Charles Stuart Parnell, Protestant hero of the Irish Nationalist community. Savaged from the pulpit and the editorial page for his adulterous involvement with Kitty O'Shea, Parnell had resigned in disgrace, defended by only a few lonely voices in the literary world. He died shortly afterwards, and Irish constitutional politics died with him.

The changed atmosphere of Irish life is caught in the work of **J.M. Synge** (1871–1909) and **George Moore** (1852–1933), who wrestled to accommodate a tradition they now saw rapidly slipping into the hands of the priests. Synge's *The Playboy of the Western World* (1907), with its parricidal hero, is the last and perhaps the most brilliant attempt at a fundamentally English view of Irish peasant life, and was greeted by riots when it opened at The Abbey. His friend George Moore identified Catholicism as a life-denying and authoritarian creed, and his extraordinary volume *The Untilled Field* (1903) in many ways anticipates much later writers.

Meanwhile the separatist Sinn Féin party made great advances, and in 1916, led by the poet **Pádraig Pearse** (1879–1916) and **James Connolly** (1868–1916), an important socialist figure and powerful writer, there was an armed insurrection in Dublin. It was crushed savagely. Connolly and all the other leaders were court-martialled and shot, thereby becoming heroes overnight, and leading Yeats to observe that everything had been "changed utterly" and that "a terrible beauty" had been born.

William Butler Yeats (1865–1939) is one of the most written-about but most elusive characters in Irish literature. A Protestant aristocrat who argued for Irish independence, he helped found the world's first national theatre, The Abbey, before the nation even existed. He wrote early lyrical ballads about gossamer fairies and stunning sunsets until, stricken with desire for the beautiful Maude Gonne, he began reaming out some of the century's greatest works of unrequited love. Much of the work of his middle period lambasts the Dublin middle class for its money-grabbing complacency – *September 1913* is well worth a read if white-lipped rage is your thing. In 1923 Yeats was awarded the Nobel Prize for Literature, though he had become somewhat disillusioned with the world, expressed in his bleak poem *The Second Coming*, part of the collection *Michael Robartes and the Dancer* (1921). Yeats' later period is more problematic, however, producing a series of spare, lucid but complex meditations on the artist's task. The influence of Yeats, in many ways the father of modern Irish literature and one of the most important English language poets of all time, cannot be underestimated.

Until the 1920s Yeats kept up a friendship with **Sean O'Casey** (1884–1964), who was that rarest of things, a working-class Irish writer. The Dublin slums in which he was born were later immortalized in his trilogy, *Shadow of a Gunman* (1923), *Juno and the Paycock* (1924) and *The Plough and the Stars* (1926). As with Synge, O'Casey's first nights were occasions for rioting and were usually attended by more policemen than punters – *The Plough and the Stars'* overt criticism of Irish nationalism particularly enraged the Dublin audience. It was actually Yeats who had to lead the coppers' charge into the stalls to break up the fracas and he later harangued the audience, screeching that the very fact they had broken up his play meant that O'Casey was a genius, and that "this was his apotheosis"; O'Casey's journal records that while he smiled nervously and twiddled his thumbs backstage he couldn't wait to get home so that he could look up the word "apotheosis" in the dictionary. In 1928, after the rejection of his play *The Silver Tassie*, dealing with World War I, O'Casey moved to England, eventually settling in Devon, where he wrote several plays on the subject of workers' struggles and injustice.

IRISH MODERNISM: FICTION

As the tide of history turned towards Nationalism and Republicanism, and Yeats wondered glumly whether the tradition would die with the aristocracy, one of the seminal figures of literary modernism was emerging in Dublin. While still a student at the new University College – established in 1908 as a college for Catholic middle-class youth along lines suggested by Cardinal John Henry Newman – **James Joyce** (1882–1941) set himself against the world of politics and religion, and announced that he would become, in his own phrase, "a high priest of art". His subsequent career was to be the epitome of obsessive dedication.

Dubliners (1914), his first book, continued where George Moore had left off, evoking the city as a deathly place, its citizens quietly atrophying in a state of emotional paralysis. *A Portrait of the Artist as a Young Man* is largely autobiographical and deals with Stephen Dedalus's decision to leave Ireland, criticizing the country as a priest-ridden and superstitious dump. After ten years of trying to get it published, Joyce finally had the bad luck to get it printed in 1916, the year of the Easter Rising. Perhaps understandably, lack of patriotism was not fashionable. Joyce was condemned by just about everyone who mattered and quite a few people who didn't.

His next novel, *Ulysses*, came out in 1922, another flashpoint in Irish history, as the new Irish government went to war with its former comrades. Modelled on Homer's *Odyssey*, the book follows Stephen Dedalus and Leopold Bloom through one day and one night of Dublin life, recording their experiences with a relish and precision that repulsed the critics, including Virginia Woolf and D.H. Lawrence. The book was widely banned and its self-exiled author was condemned as a pornographer. *Ulysses* is a kaleidoscope of narrative techniques; Joyce's last work, the vast *Finnegans Wake* (1939), is the only true polyglot novel, a bewitching – and often impenetrable – stew of languages, representing the history of the world as dreamed by its hero, Humphrey Chimpden Earwicker (alias "Here Comes Everybody", "Haveth Childers Everywhere" etc). Critics of different persuasions see it as either the pinnacle of literary modernism or the greatest folly in the history of the novel.

The other great Irish modernist, **Samuel Beckett** (1906–89), emigrated to Paris and became Joyce's secretary in 1932. One writer has remarked that while Joyce tried to include everything in his work Beckett tried to leave everything out, and that's a pretty good summary. Beckett is bleak, pared down, exploring the fundamental paradox of the futility of speech and yet its absolute necessity. A modernist in his devotion to verbal precision, Beckett is on the other hand a dominant figure in what has been termed the postmodern "literature of exhaustion". As he said shortly before his death – "I have never been on my way anywhere, but simply on my way." Despite his reputation for terseness, Beckett was a prolific writer – the best places to start are the trilogy of novels, *Molloy*, *Malone Dies* (both 1952) and *The Unnamable* (1953), and the play *Waiting for Godot* (1949).

The absurd prose and hilarious satire of **Flann O'Brien** (1912–66) has earned him the reputation of being Ireland's greatest comic writer. His comic vision of Purgatory, *The Third Policeman* (1967), includes the famous molecular theory, which proposes that excessive riding of a bicycle can lead to the mixing of the molecules of rider and machine – hence a character who is half-man, half-bike. O'Brien's other great book, *At Swim-Two-Birds* (1939), is a weird mélange of mythology and pastiche that plays around with the notion that fictional characters might have a life independent of their creators. Under one of his several pseudonyms, Myles Na Gopaleen (Myles of the Little Horses), he wrote a daily column for the *Irish Times* for many years, and his hilarious journalism is collected in *The Best of Myles* and *Myles Away from Dublin*.

Traditional fiction continued, of course – for instance, **Brinsley MacNamara** (1890–1963) devastatingly portrayed small-town life in *The Valley of the Squinting Windows* (1918). But many writers had moved away from social observation and into a kind of modernist fantasy that had its roots way back in the Celtic twilight. **James Stephens** (1882–1950), a writer with an unjustly insignificant international reputation, used absurdity as a route to high lyricism. His *The Crock of Gold* (1912), is a profoundly moving fantasy on the Irish mythological tradition, part fairy story and part post-Joycean satire – in a sense, a precursor of "Magic Realism".

POSTWAR LITERATURE

Ireland in the late 1940s and 1950s suffered severe economic recession and another wave of emigration began. Added to this, the people had in 1937 passed a constitution – still operational today – which enshrined the Catholic Church's teachings in the laws of the land. Intolerance and xenophobia were bolstered by an economic war against Britain and a campaign of state censorship which was truly Stalinist in its vigour. Books which had never been read were snipped, shredded and scorched by committees of pious civil servants.

No history of postwar Irish literature would be complete without at least a mention of *The Bell*, a highly influential but now defunct literary magazine. In its two runs, between 1940 and 1948 and 1950 and 1954, it was a forum for writers like **Frank O'Connor** (1903–66), **Seán Ó Faolain** (1900–91) and **Liam O'Flaherty** (1897–1984), all of whom were veterans of the independence war, and all of whom became outstanding short-story writers. They chronicled the raging betrayal they felt at state censorship and social intolerance – O'Connor's *Guests of the Nation* (1931) is perhaps the most eloquent epitaph for Ireland's revolutionary generation, a terrifying tale of the execution of two British soldiers by the IRA that influenced Brendan Behan's *The Hostage* (1958) enormously. *The Bell* also opened its pages to writers like **Peadar O'Donnell** (1893–1985), a radical socialist who, only six months before he died, publicly burned his honorary degree from the National University of Ireland on the occasion of a similar honour being conferred on Ronald Reagan.

In an infamous speech President Eamonn de Valera envisaged a new rural Ireland full of "comely maidens dancing at the crossroads and the laughter of athletic youths". But writers such as **Denis Devlin** (1908–59), **Francis Stuart** (1902–90), **Mary Lavin** (1912–96) and **Brian Moore** (1921–99) took up the fight for truth against propaganda. Their youths and maidens didn't dance. They were too busy packing their bags, or wandering in bewilderment across the desolate pages of an Ireland that had failed to live up to its possibilities. In their poetry **Austin Clarke** (1896–1974) and **Thomas Kinsella** (b.1928) mourned the passing of hope into despair and fragmentation.

Patrick Kavanagh (1906–67) was an exception to all the rules. His poetry is almost entirely parochial, celebrating what he called "the spirit-shocking wonder of a black slanting Ulster hill", and his contemplative celebrations of the ordinary made him perhaps Ireland's best-loved poet. But as time went on, the harshness of reality began to press in on his work. His long poem *The Great Hunger* (1942) portrays rural Ireland – the same Ireland he had formerly extolled – as physically barren, with the blasted landscape an incisive metaphor for sexual repression. Its publication was widely condemned and the writer was even questioned by the police, an event he discussed with customary venom in his own short-lived journal, *Kavanagh's Weekly*.

The forces of reaction were again about to wage war on Irish literature. O'Casey's anti-clerical play *The Drums of Father Ned* was produced in Dublin in 1955 and received aggressive reviews. Three years later there was a proposal to revive it for the new Dublin Theatre Festival. The Catholic Archbishop of Dublin, John Charles McQuaid, insisted that the plans be dropped, and when the trade unions stepped into the fray on his behalf, he succeeded. The year before, the young director Alan Simpson had been arrested and his entire cast threatened with imprisonment for indecency following the first night in Dublin of Tennessee Williams's play *The Rose Tattoo*. The important novelist **John McGahern** (b.1935) lost his teaching job in a Catholic school in 1966 following the publication of his second book, *The Dark* (1965), which was immediately banned. It's a marvellous novel, dealing tenderly with adolescence and clerical celibacy.

A more celebrated literary victim – in this case a self-destructive one – was **Brendan Behan**, who died in 1964, only six years after the publication of his first book, *Borstal Boy*. He spent the last years of his life as a minor celebrity, reciting his books into tape recorders in Dublin pubs, drunk and surrounded by equally drunk admirers, some of whom sobered up for long enough to try and save him from becoming the victim of his own myth.

CONTEMPORARY WRITING

It was only in the 1970s that the post-revolutionary climate of repression began to lift, and a sophisticated and largely progressive generation began having their works published. **Seamus Heaney** (b.1939) is the leading light of an unofficial group of Northern Irish poets who combine a sophistication of technique with a self-conscious political commitment. Heaney's first work, *Death of a Naturalist* (1966), is easily accessible and is firmly rooted in his childhood experiences in south Derry. *Door into the Dark* (1969) and *Wintering Out* (1972) see Heaney trying to find a voice to deal with the increasing sectarian violence in the North. *North* (1975) was Heaney's most controversial work, with many commentators criticizing the lack of condmenation when dealing with the violence of the Troubles. In 1995 Heaney's poetic world changed: not only did he become Ireland's fourth Nobel literary laureate (after Yeats, Shaw and Beckett), but, with the emergence of the peace process in the North, he found a refreshed poetic voice. His most recent works have been *Beowulf* (1999), a a widely acclaimed translation of the Anglo-Saxon epic into his native south Derry vernacular, and *Open Ground* (2000), a selection of his poetry from 1966 to 1996.

John Banville (b.1945) is another writer who prefers to remain at a tangent to the national identity, taking Ireland (when he writes of it at all) as the means rather than the end of his artistic vision. His first book, *Long Lankin*, appeared in 1970, a precocious debut that has been followed by a string of extraordinarily inventive novels, the most recent being *The Untouchable* (1997), a fictional treatment of the life of Anthony Blunt, and a superb exploration of treachery and deception.

The Irish Writers' Co-op produced novelists such as **Desmond Hogan** (b.1951), **Ronan Sheehan** (b.1953) and **Neil Jordan** (b.1951), the last of whom has gone on to major international success as a film director (see "The Irish in Film", p.703). Jordan's work (much like Banville's), is located firmly within the counter-tradition of the novel coming out of Joyce, which in its turn owed something to the fantastic narratives of the sagas and to the rejection of the traditional novel form – what Joyce saw as its built-in British view of the world. The 1970s also saw the establishment of courageous publishing companies founded by writers, including Peter Fallon's Gallery, Dermot Bolger's Raven Arts Press, and Steve McDonogh's Brandon.

At the end of the decade **Paul Durcan** (b.1944) emerged as the inheritor of Kavanagh's mantle. He is a quirkily witty and profoundly religious poet, whose work encompasses social issues such as IRA bombings and Ireland's prohibition, until recently, of divorce and continuing ban on abortion, but always addresses them in personal terms. His most recent collection *Greetings to Our Friends in Brazil* (1999) is somewhat mellower, with Durcan feeling that some of his poetic visions have been met; indeed many of the poems centre on a priest who, far from being repressive and hypocritical as in his earlier works, is in fact honourable and truly spiritual.

Other important poets include **Padraic Fiacc** (b.1924), **Richard Murphy** (b.1927), **Michael Hartnett** (b.1934), **Brendan Kennelly** (b.1936), and **Derek Mahon** (b.1941). **Michael Longley** (b.1939) seems doomed always to be cited as the husband of the major revisionist critic Edna Longley, but his poetry is innovative and striking, and the last decade has seen him publish three exceptional volumes, *Gorse Fires* (1991), *The Ghost Orchid* (1995) and *The Weather in Japan* (2000), which show Longley as a highly skilled poet with a strong moral voice. Two poets having close relations with the US, **Paul Muldoon** (b.1951), born in Mayo but now living in New York, and **John Montague** (b.1929), born in Brooklyn of Irish parents but brought up in Tyrone, explore the relations between different poetic traditions on the island. **Christopher Nolan** (b.1965), a severely disabled writer, has proved to be an amazing talent, employing a rich language reminiscent of Dylan Thomas. His first book of poetry, *Damburst of Dreams* (1988), received great acclaim, and he later won the Whitbread Prize for his autobiographical novel *Under the Eye of the Clock* (1988), while Nolan has recently completed his second novel, *The Banyan Tree* (2000).

Perhaps the most exciting contemporary verse in Ireland is being written by women writers who, in the absence of civic or political opportunities, have turned to poetry to express their experiences of the modern state. Up and down the country poetry groups and workshops turn out collections that deal with the realities of being an Irish daughter, wife or mother. In this they receive support from established poets such as **Eiléan Ní Chuilleanáin** (b.1942), **Eavan Boland** (b.1944), and **Medbh McGuckian** (b.1950). Boland, especially, has explored the complexities of modern Irish female experience in particularly enabling ways. McGuckian's poetry is tremendously imaginative, and in *Selected Poems* (1997) she creates ephemeral worlds where language is fluid, meaning forever shifting.

Without doubt, the most successful theatre company and cultural initiative on the island in recent times has been **Field Day**, a Northern-based team founded by **Seamus Deane** (b.1940), **Tom Paulin** (b.1949), **Brian Friel** (b.1929), **Seamus Heaney** and actor **Stephen Rea**. As well as being established poets, Deane and Paulin are also insightful critics who from their locations in England and the US continue to do battle with all comers over the rights to Irish literary history. Friel, who turned from short-story writing to the theatre in the 1960s, wrote some of Ireland's best loved plays in the 1960's including *Philadelphia Here I Come!* (1964), *The Loves of Cass Maguire* (1966) and *Lovers* (1967). The outbreak of violence in the North drew a response from Friel in two plays, *The Freedom of the City* (1973), loosely based on the events in Derry on Bloody Sunday (see p.678) and *Volunteers* (1975) which treated Irish history in a more symbolic manner. It was Friel's play *Translations* (1980) which broached the subject of rewriting history which provided Field Day with their greatest success, a subject he came back to with his last play for the company *History* (1988). However, after giving his hugely popular work, *Dancing at Lughnasa* (1990), to Dublin's Abbey Theatre, he left the group and has since written three highly acclaimed works *In Wonderful Tennessee* (1993), *Molly Sweeney* (1994) and *Give Me Your Answer, Do!* (1997).

Any list of Ireland's innovative theatre writers must include **Tom Murphy** (b.1936) who is celebrated in many corners as Ireland's greatest living playwright. Murphy's plays are hugely critical of contemporary Ireland; his 1998 production, *The Wake*, about an Irish whore returning home to her native village for a funeral, was met with universal acclaim. **Thomas Kilroy** (b.1934) was another playwright closely associated with the Field Day Project whose most recent work *The Secret Fall of Constance Wilde* (1997) deals with the tragic relationship between Oscar Wilde and his wife.

While many cite Murphy as Ireland's leading dramatist others point to Ulsterman, **Frank McGuinness** (b.1953). His play *Observe the Sons of Ulster Marching Towards the Somme* (1995), staged in Dublin as talks began on the Anglo-Irish agreement, focuses on the participation of a group of Northern Loyalists in the battle of the Somme. Its imagery exploits the symbolism of the whole Irish tradition, permitting a range of readings, in which the Somme represents the current situation in the North, or the battlefield of the Boyne, or the slaughters of the early sagas. It was his 1987 piece, *Carthaginians*, a play set in Derry city, which thrust him into the major league of Irish writers. The play found a vocabulary in which to explore ancient Irish themes – the nature of political allegiance, death and resurrection, the relationship between Britain, Ireland and the North, sexuality, religion – in a way that seems to sum up the whole tradition while simultaneously threatening to demolish it. Never afraid to articulate the unfashionable, he asks questions of nationalism in a manner that demands attention: his *Someone To Watch Over Me* (1992) starts out appealing to our readiness to accept crude national stereotypes, but ultimately becomes, among other things, a homage to the English literary tradition. McGuiness's work provides, if not some hope of unifying the various strands of Ireland's long cultural histories, at least the imperative to understand what divides them; in this act of enquiry lies great humanity.

The Irish stage has produced numerous, exciting new dramatists in recent years: **Sebastian Barry** (b.1955) takes figures from his recent ancestry and weaves plays from their unique junction with history – the finest example of which is *The Steward of Christendom*

(1995), a piece of staggering poetic intensity. The plays of **Alex Johnston** and **Conor McPherson** (b.1971) are set in contemporary Ireland; McPherson's work in particular has met with considerable critical acclaim: in *This Lime Tree Bower* (1996) he brings pace and pathos – at times with acute hilarity – to stories of provincial life; his most recent play, *The Weir* (1998), confirms his reputation as a compelling dramatist. Belfast writer **Gary Mitchell** has produced some fine work, most notably *In a Little World of Our Own* (1997) and *As the Beast Sleeps* (1998), plays which centre around a Loyalist housing estate, the latter dealing with militants trying to come to terms with the encroaching ceasefire while *Tearing the Loom* (1999) explores the political complexities of the 1798 United Irish rebellion.

One of the freshest voice in Irish drama at the moment is **Marina Carr** (b.1969) whose plays, *Patricia Coughlan* (1996), *Bog of Cats* (1998) and *On Raftery's Hill* (2000), deal with the dark side of human poverty and feature powerfully-written, energetic dialogue, often in the voice of her native midlands. Arguably the most successful dramatist to be writing plays in an Irish context right now is in fact English: **Martin McDonagh**, the Jack Charlton of contemporary Irish theatre, sets his work in an Irish west coast of the imagination, managing to both exploit and explode its associated myths. Heavily reminiscent of Synge, he deploys the traditional themes of murder, ignorance, familial hatred and isolation with swift, dark humour. McDonagh is a gifted storyteller, and *The Beauty Queen of Leenane*, *The Cripple of Inishmaan*, and *The Lonesome West* have all proved immensely popular. Other exciting dramatists to emerge in recent years are **Mark O'Rowe,** whose *Howie the Rookie* took the Edinburgh Festival by storm in 1999 and Corkman **Enda Walsh** whose powerful one act plays *Disco Pigs* (1997) and *Misterman* (1999) have been hugely popular with audiences more familiar with clubbing than theatre-going.

It is perhaps in the novel and in autobiography that the richest seam of contemporary Irish literature is to be discovered. Over the past decade or so, writers like Colin Bateman, Hugo Hamilton (b.1953), Anne Enright (b1962), Eoin McNamee, Ferdia McAnna (1955), Ronan Bennett (1956), Michael O'Loughlin(b.1958), Glen Patterson (b.1961) and Robert MacLiam Wilson (b.1964**)** have begun to turn the accepted version of Irish literary tradition on its head. **Dermot Bolger** (b.1959), as well as being a gifted poet and playwright, has produced hard-hitting yet lyrical novels of contemporary Dublin. **Colm Toibín** (b.1955) has written two deceptively understated novels of Irish experience at home and abroad in *The South* (1990) and *The Heather Blazing* (1992); in *The Story of the Night* (1996), set in Argentina at the time of the Generals, he achieves a novel of breathtaking poise while his latest work *The Blackwater Lightship* (1999) tells the story of an AIDS victim. *The Butcher Boy* (1992) by **Patrick McCabe** (b.1955) won numerous awards as well as being shortlisted for the prestigious Booker Prize, and the grisly comedy of that novel reappeared in even grimmer form in *The Dead School* (1995). In the novel, *Breakfast on Pluto* (1998), McCabe's mordant humour shifts its focus to a violent, seedy London underworld while *Mondo Desperado!*(2000) is an hilarious and at times absurd ride into small town Irish life.

Younger writers such as **Joseph O'Connor** (b.1963) and **Emma Donoghue** (b.1969) are typical inasmuch as they work in a number of genres besides the novel. Their writing responds to the new Ireland of sex and drugs and rock 'n' roll in which they grew up, with Donoghue producing in her first two novels *Stir-fry* (1994) and *Hood* (1995), perhaps the first happy lesbian love stories in Irish fiction. Other new female writers worth reading are **Mary Morrissey** whose acclaimed first novel *Mother of Pearl* (1998) has been followed by the equally enjoyable *The Pretender* (2000) about a Polish factory worker who thinks she is the daughter of Anastasia. **Antonia Logue** from Derry has written the most exciting first novel in recent years, *Shadow Box* (2000), which deals with the relationship between black heavyweight boxer Jack Johnston, a white modernist poet and one of the foremost figures in the Dadaist movement in the States.

Without doubt, the most successful of the new generation of novelists has been **Roddy Doyle** (b.1958), a writer who, along with Bolger and others, disdains the critical title of "Northside realist" (referring to the north side of the River Liffey where most of their work is set). All three novels of *The Barrytown Trilogy*, *The Commitments* (1987), *The Snapper* (1990) and *The Van* (1991), have been made into successful films, and Doyle snapped up the Booker Prize in 1993 for *Paddy Clarke Ha Ha Ha* which was followed in 1996 by *The Woman Who Walked Into Doors*, which tackles the darker theme of domestic violence. Doyle's fiction makes deceptively easy reading, while the enormous sales figures for his books must compensate somewhat for the criticism that he merely reproduces modern urban variations on the stage Irishman. Perhaps with this in mind Doyle spent three years researching and writing latest work *A Star Called Henry* (1999) an historical novel, set around the struggle for Irish independence from 1916 to 1921. This novel, like all of Doyle's work is highly accessible but, unlike some of his previous works, is of huge literary significance in its powerful critique of the accepted ideologies that underpin the Irish state.

This young generation of novelists of the 1980s and 1990s gave short shrift to the hackneyed themes of the traditional canon: the Catholic Church, the lure of the land, the repression of sexuality. Irish novels and short stories began to anatomize social change rather than conservatism, revealing an Ireland populated by women as well as men, Protestants as well as Catholics, fervent atheists as well as true believers, gays as well as straights, people who feel British as well as people who feel Irish, and writers for whom Ireland is no longer a necessary subject. It is interesting then that after such a great loosening of the soil, there emerged in the 1990s a couple of writers who returned to explore these themes via personal memoir, and in so doing found that their experiences of repression, denial and acute poverty struck a deep resonance in the consciousness of an older generation. **Nuala O'Faolain**'s *Are You Somebody?* (1996), an autobiography which deftly portrays the desolate marginalization of women, and **Frank McCourt**'s (b.1930) *Angela's Ashes* (1996), an extraordinary book showing the degradation and poverty of an entire class of Irish people, were both enormously popular, and perhaps cathartic, in an Ireland moving to publicly come to terms with huge areas of deprivation in its immediate past. His follow-up to this *'Tis* (1999) has none of the warmth or humour of *Angela's Ashes* and was a great disappointment.

Less emotively, but no less successfully, in the North, too, childhood has proved fertile ground for novelists. **Seamus Deane's** (b.1940) semi-autobiographical *Reading in the Dark* (1996) stands as a powerful, myth-spectred work, a child's world full of half-gleaned tales of superstition, political reprisals and fear, and **Ciaran Carson's** (b.1948) *The Star Factory* (1997) delivers a Belfast ringing bright with poetic imagery, fresh and full of life. Childhood Belfast is also the subject of **Eugene McEldowney's** endearing novel The *Faloorie Man* (2000), an intimate portrait of childhood life from an author more generally associated with the thriller genre. King of the Irish thriller at the moment is **John Connolly** whose *Every Dead Thing* (1999) is a pulsating read. The nineties have seen some novels of great inventiveness too: Ciaran Carson's *Last Night's Fun* (1996) is an astonishing book conjuring up the spontaneous magic of the world of traditional music; **Philip Casey's** (b.1950) first novel *The Fabulists* is a fine love story, skilfully understated, while his second *The Water Star* (1999), set in postwar Britain and Ireland, realized a lot of the promise shown in *The Fabulists*. **Ann Haverty**'s (b.1959) *One Day As a Tiger* (1997) is a delightfully mischievous tale drawing us in to consider the emotional and romantic possibilities of life in an age of genetic engineering, while *The Beauty of the Moon* (1999) is a collection of delicately crafted poems. The best selling novels in Ireland remain romance, most of them published by **Poolbeg**; if romantic escapism is your thing then look out for Cathy Kelly or Colette Caddle amongst others.

BOOKS

Most of the books listed below are in print and in paperback – those that are out of print (o/p) should be easy to track down in secondhand bookshops. Publishers follow each title; first the UK or Irish publisher, then the US. Only one publisher is listed if the UK/Irish and US publishers are the same. Where books are published in only one of these countries, UK, IRE or US follows the publisher's name.

HISTORY AND POLITICS

John Ardagh, *Ireland and the Irish: Portrait of a Changing Society* (Penguin). Comprehensive and lively, this is an excellent anatomy of Irish society and its efforts to come to terms with the modern world.

Jonathan Bardon, *A History of Ulster* (Blackstaff; Dufour). A comprehensive account from early settlements to the current Troubles.

Brian Barton, *A Pocket History of Ulster* (O'Brien; Irish American Book Co.). Accessible account of Northern Irish politics from the years prior to Partition to the present day.

J.C. Beckett, *The Making of Modern Ireland 1603–1923* (Faber; Trafalgar o/p). Concise and elegant, this is probably the best introduction to the complexities of Irish history.

David Beresford, *Ten Men Dead* (HarperCollins; Atlantic Monthly). Revelatory account of the 1981 hunger strike, using the prison correspondence as its basic material; a powerful refutation of the demonologies of the British press.

Angela Bourke, *The Burning of Bridget Cleary* (Pimlico UK). Impeccably researched account of nefarious goings-on in Tipperary in the 1890s, describing the sensational case of a young woman supposedly taken by the fairies, tortured and murdered, and the subsequent trial of her husband, father, aunt and four cousins.

Terence Brown, *Ireland: A Social and Cultural History 1922 to the Present* (HarperCollins; Cornell University Press). Brilliantly perceptive survey of writers' responses to the dog's breakfast made of postrevolutionary Ireland by its leaders.

Max Caulfield, *The Easter Rebellion* (Gill & Macmillan; Roberts Rinehart o/p). Recently revised account of the events of 1916, originally published in 1963, brought to life with interviews with those involved.

Michael Collins, *In His Own Words* (Gill & Macmillan IRE). A collection of extracts from the revolutionary's writings and speeches.

S.J. Connolly (ed), *The Oxford Companion to Irish History* (OUP). A massive introduction to almost every aspect of Irish history.

Tim Pat Coogan, *The Troubles: Ireland's Ordeal 1969–1995 and the Search for Peace* (Arrow; Museum of Denver). The former *Irish Press* editor's popular-history writing has many followers and his *The IRA* (Fontana; Roberts Rinehart) is a contemporary classic. His earlier books on two icons of modern Ireland, *Michael Collins* (Arrow; Roberts Rinehart o/p) and *De Valera: Long Fellow, Long Shadow* (Arrow; Harper o/p), are essential reading.

Sean Duffy, *The Atlas of Irish History* (Gill & Macmillan IRE). A good introduction to Irish history, rich with maps, diagrams and drawings.

Peter Berresford Ellis, *Hell or Connaught* (Blackstaff; Dufour) and *The Boyne Water* (o/p). Vivid popular histories of Cromwell's rampage and the pivotal Battle of the Boyne.

Michael Farrell, *Arming the Protestants: The Formation of the Ulster Special Constabulary and the Royal Ulster Constabulary, 1920–1927* (Pluto o/p; Longwood o/p). Farrell is a fine journalist and veteran of Northern Ireland's civil rights campaigns. In *Northern Ireland: The Orange State* (Pluto UK) he argues, as the title implies, from a Republican standpoint; it's an occasionally tendentious but extremely persuasive political account of the development of Northern Ireland.

Garret FitzGerald, *All in a Life* (Gill & Macmillan UK o/p). The first former Taoiseach to write his memoirs has produced an extraordinary book, characteristically frank, and full of detail on the working of government.

David Fitzpatrick, *Oceans of Consolation: Personal Accounts of Migration to Australia.* (Cork University Press; Cornell University Press). Using over a hundred unedited letters largely written around the 1850s and 1860s, this book brings to life the experiences of loss and longing of Irish emigrants to Australia.

R.F. Foster, *Modern Ireland 1600–1972* (Penguin). Superb and provocative new book, generally reckoned to be unrivalled in its scholarship and acuity, although it has been criticized for what some feel to be an excessive sympathy towards the Anglo-Irish. Not recommended for beginners.

Kathleen Hughes and Ann Hamlin, *The Modern Traveller to the Early Irish Church* (Four Courts Press IRE). The remains of monastic settlements are found all over Ireland and this revised edition enhances the visitor's appreciation by reconstructing the daily religious and secular life of Ireland in the Early Christian Period; also includes a detailed list of recommended sites.

Gemma Hussey, *Ireland Today: Anatomy of a Changing State* (Penguin o/p). A well-regarded and invaluable source of information on Ireland's changing identity by this ex-government minister.

Robert Kee, *The Green Flag* (Penguin; 3 vols). Scrupulous history of Irish Nationalism from the first plantations to the creation of the Free State. Masterful as narrative and as analysis.

Dáire Keogh and Nicholas Furlong (eds), *The Women of 1798* (Four Courts Press IRE). Women are often "hidden" in Irish history and this collection of essays reasserts the vital role many played in the 1798 Rebellion, from Matilda Tone (wife of Wolfe) who redefined the role of woman as patriot, to the Belfast revolutionary Mary Anne McCracken.

Christine Kinealy, *This Great Calamity: The Irish Famine* (Gill & MacMillan; Roberts Rinehart o/p). Unravels fact from fiction through systematic analysis of primary source material related to the Great Famine.

F.S.L. Lyons, *Ireland Since the Famine* (HarperCollins UK). The most complete overview of recent Irish history; either iconoclastic or revisionist, depending on your point of view.

T.W. Moody and F.X. Martin (eds), *The Course of Irish History* (Mercier; Madison Books). Highly readable collection of essays on many aspects of Irish history.

R.J. Scally, *The End of the Hidden Ireland: Rebellion, Famine and Emigration* (OUP UK). History revealing the strategies deployed by one particular Roscommon peasant community in their struggle to avoid eviction and emigration; this book also details their exploitation by Irish Catholic middlemen.

David Sharrock & Mark Prendergast, *Man of War, Man of Peace? The Unauthorised Biography of Gerry Adams* (MacMillan UK). Lengthy, detailed account of the Sinn Féin leader's rise to prominence.

Cecil Woodham Smith, *The Great Hunger: Ireland 1845–1849* (Penguin). The classic history of the Famine, superseded by recent research, but still a superb and harrowing narrative.

A.T.Q. Stewart, *The Narrow Ground* (Blackstaff Press IRE). A Unionist overview of the history of the North from 1609 to the 1960s, providing an essential background to the current situation.

Ruth Taillon, *Women of 1916* (Beyond the Pale IRE). Key documentation of the part played by women in the struggle for independence.

Peter Taylor, *Provos: The IRA and Sinn Féin* (Bloomsbury), published in USA as *Behind the Mask* (TV Books). Study of the historical development of the Provisional IRA, including fascinating interviews with IRA members.

Kevin Toolis, *Rebel Hearts: Journeys within the IRA's Soul* (Picador; St Martin's Press). Highly acclaimed and topical account of what makes the IRA tick by this journalist and screenwriter.

GAELIC TALES

Kevin Danaher, *Folk Tales of the Irish Countryside* (Mercier IRE). The best volume on fairy and folk tales, recorded with a civil servant's meticulousness and a novelist's literary style.

Myles Dillon (ed), *Irish Sagas* (Mercier IRE). An excellent examination of Cúchulainn, Fionn Mac Cumhaill, etc in literary and socio-psychological terms.

Seamus Heaney, *Buile Suibhne*; in English, *Sweeney Astray* (Faber; Noonday). A modern reworking of the ancient Irish saga of the mad king Sweeney.

Pádraig Ó Conaire, *Finest Stories* (Poolbeg o/p; Dufour o/p). Ó Conaire's dispassionate eye roams over the cruelties of peasant life.

Tomás Ó Criomhtháin, (sometimes Thomas O'Crohan), *An tOileánach*; in English, *The Islandman* (OUP UK). Similar to Ó Conaire but non-fiction and, if possible, even more raw.

Seán Ó Tuama and Thomas Kinsella, *An Duanaire: Poems of the Dispossessed* (Dolmen o/p; University of Pennsylvania, o/p). Excellent translations of stark Irish-language poems on famine and death. See also Kinsella's translation of one of the earliest sagas, the *Táin Bó Cúailnge* (OUP UK o/p).

Peig Sayers, *An Old Woman's Reflections* (OUP UK). Unfortunately, Sayers' complacent acceptance of her own powerlessness is still held up as an example to Irish schoolchildren. Still, in spite of itself, a frightening insight into the eradication of the Irish language through emigration, poverty and political failure. A funny deconstruction of the Sayers style is Flann O'Brien's *An Beál Bocht*; in English, *The Poor Mouth* (HarperCollins; Dalkey Archive).

Alan Titley, *A Pocket History of Gaelic Culture* (O'Brien Press IRE). Concise, witty and sometimes irreverent analysis of the nature of Gaelic culture, its survival in Ireland and lasting impact.

William Butler Yeats (ed), *Irish Fairy and Folk Tales* (Hippocrene Press; Simon & Schuster). Yeats gets all misty-eyed about an Ireland that never existed.

FICTION

Peter Ackroyd, *The Last Testament of Oscar Wilde* (Penguin UK). Witty re-creation of the life of the tragic, abused artist in exile; a superb parody and an absolute must for anyone so familiar with Wilde's epigrams, they wish he'd written more.

John Banville, *The Newton Letter* (Minerva; David R. Godine); *The Book of Evidence* (Picador; Warner); *Ghosts* (Picador; Vintage); *Athena* (Picador; Vintage); *The Untouchable* (Picador; Vintage). Five novels from first-rate Irish novelist, including his 1989, Booker Prize nomination, *The Book of Evidence*, a sleazy tale of a weird Dublin murder. *The Untouchable* is a superb fiction based on the life of Anthony Blunt, full of deception and treachery. Banville's talents show no sign of waning in his most recent novel *Eclipse* (Picador), in which an actor plays out his own psychological crisis by a return to his childhood home.

Leland Bardwell, *The House* (Brandon Books o/p; Longwood o/p); *There We Have Been* (Attic; InBook o/p). Quirky, bleak prose, often dealing with domestic violence, male cruelty, drink and poverty; but funny too, in a black way.

Sebastian Barry, *The Whereabouts of Eneas McNulty* (Picador; Penguin). Tremendously moving, tragic account of one of Barry's ancestors who fought for the British in both world wars, and the life he then had to lead as a consequence.

Colin Bateman, *Cycle of Violence*; *Divorcing Jack*; *Of Wee Sweetie Mice and Men* (all HarperCollins; Arcade); and *Empire State* (HarperCollins; Acacia). Sparkling and increasingly fast-paced tales of violence and men in crisis by one of the North's most successful novelists.

Samuel Beckett, *More Pricks Than Kicks* (Calder; Grove); *Beckett Trilogy*, including *Molloy*, *Malone Dies* and *The Unnamable* (Calder; Grove). Beckett's early short stories, grotesque tales set around the eccentric character of Belacqua Shuah, were followed by his wonderful and increasingly bleak trilogy of breakdown and glum humour.

Brendan Behan, *Borstal Boy* (Arrow; David R. Godine). Behan's gutsy *roman à clef* about his early life in the IRA and in jail.

Dermot Bolger, *The Journey Home* (Penguin UK). Dublin unforgettably imagined as both heaven and hell. *A Second Life* (Penguin UK) is an assured novel about a man who, miraculously given a second chance at life, sets out to find out the truth about his adoption. *Father's Music* (Flamingo; HarperCollins). Dublin's criminal underworld is the setting for this psychological thriller.

Elizabeth Bowen, *The Death of the Heart* (Penguin; Anchor) and *The Last September* (Vintage). The former is a finely tuned tale of the anguish of unrequited love, generally rated as the masterpiece of this obliquely stylish writer. In the latter, the immense political change of 1920s Cork forms the setting for a tale of an upper class woman's coming of age; now a film by Neil Jordan.

Clare Boylan, *Home Rule* (Abacus UK); *Room For a Single Lady* (Abacus UK); *Holy Pictures* (Abacus UK) and *Nail on the Head* (Penguin o/p; Viking o/p). A rising star of contemporary Irish fiction, her *Room for a Single Lady* features 1950s Dublin and a cast of eccentric lodgers.

Philip Casey, *The Fabulists* (Lilliput; Serif). Deftly woven tale of love and storytelling; a fine first novel. *The Water Star* (Picador UK) is a similarly compassionate novel about a group of people rebuilding their lives in postwar London.

Seamus Deane *Reading in the Dark* (Vintage). A turbulent semi-autobiographical tale set in Derry in the 1950s and 1960s, full of ghosts, fear and political enmities.

J.P. Donleavy, *The Ginger Man* (Abacus; Atlantic Monthly). Outlandish exploits of a consummate bounder; semi-autobiographical; banned in Ireland for some time.

Emma Donoghue, *Stir-fry* (Penguin; Harper o/p). Well-wrought love story from young Irish lesbian writer. *Hood* (Penguin; Alyson). Painful and at times funny story about overcoming bereavement.

Roddy Doyle, *Paddy Clarke Ha Ha Ha* (Minerva; Penguin). Hilarious and deeply moving novel of Dublin family strife that won the Booker Prize in 1993. The earlier *Barrytown Trilogy*, including *The Commitments*, *The Snapper* and *The Van* (Vintage; Penguin), is lighter and funnier and made Doyle's reputation. In *The Woman Who Walked Into Doors* (Minerva; Penguin), Doyle shifts to the darker theme of domestic violence, while *A Star called Henry* (Jonathan Cape; Penguin) is an irreverent romp through early twentieth-century Irish history.

Maria Edgeworth, *Castle Rackrent* (OUP). Best of the "Big House" books, in which Edgeworth displays a subversively subtle sympathy with her peasant narrator. Would have shocked her fellow aristos if they'd been able to figure it out.

Anne Enright, *The Portable Virgin* (Vintage; Butterworth-Heinemann o/p). Highly original stories of life on the outside. *The Wig My Father Wore* (Minerva UK). A tale of sex, death and reproduction.

Oliver Goldsmith, *The Vicar of Wakefield* (Penguin; OUP). An affecting celebration of simple virtue.

Hugo Hamilton, *The Love Test* (Faber UK o/p). Irish-German novelist's thriller set on both sides of the Berlin Wall, before and after its fall, combines excitement with a tender portrait of a disintegrating marriage. *Dublin Where the Palm Trees Grow* (Faber UK o/p) is a fine collection of stories set with equal assurance in Berlin and middle-class Dublin.

Anne Haverty, *One Day as a Tiger* (Vintage; Ecco). Delightful, arcadian tale of love and genetic engineering twists as the betrayals set in. A sentimental journey for our times.

Dermot Healy, *A Goat's Song* (Harvill Press; Harcourt Brace). Dark and deep novel which convincingly weaves a study of obsessive love into a fresh view of the Northern conflict. *The Bend for Home* (Harvill Press; Harcourt Brace) is a touching memoir of the author's family life.

Aidan Higgins, *Flotsam & Jetsam* (Minerva UK); *Langrishe, Go Down* (Minerva; Riverrun); *Lions of the Grunewald* (Minerva UK). The most European of Irish writers, whose later works play with language in a mordantly humorous and deeply personal way.

Desmond Hogan, *The Ikon Maker* (Faber UK). Impressive, impressionistic first novel from one of Ireland's most lyrical prose writers, about angst-ridden adolescence in the 1970s, before Ireland was hip. *A Farewell to Prague* (Faber UK) is an intense, episodic, autobiographical novel that wanders lonely through late-twentieth-century Europe.

Neil Jordan, *Night in Tunisia* (Vintage; Random House o/p). Film director Jordan first made his name with this impressive collection, which prefigures treatments and themes of his films. His most recent novel, *Sunrise with Sea Monster* (Vintage UK), is a delicate, powerful study in love and betrayal. *The Past* (Vintage UK) deals with the troubled early years of the Irish Free State.

James Joyce, *Dubliners*; *Portrait of the Artist as a Young Man*; *Ulysses* (all Penguin; Vintage); *Finnegans Wake* (Penguin). No novel written in English this century can match the linguistic verve of *Ulysses*, Joyce's monumental evocation of 24 hours in the life of Dublin. From the time of its completion until shortly before his death – a period of sixteen years – he laboured at *Finnegans Wake*, a dream-language recapitulation of the cycles of world history. Though indigestible as a whole, it contains passages of incomparable lyricism and wit – try the "Anna Livia Plurabelle" section, and you could be hooked.

Molly Keane, *Good Behaviour* (Abacus; Knopf o/p). Highly successful comic reworking of the "Big House" novel.

Benedict Kiely, *God's Own Country: Selected Stories 1963–1993* (Mandarin UK). A good introduction to the quirky fiction of a veteran novelist and travel writer.

Mary Lavin, *In a Café: Selected Stories* (Town House; Penguin). New collection of previously published stories by one of the great short-story writers, in the Chekhov tradition. Earlier books include *The House on Clewe Street* (Virago o/p; Viking o/p) and *Stories* (Constable; Viking o/p).

Hugh Leonard, *Parnell and the Englishwoman* (Deutsch UK). Fictional biography focusing on Parnell's affair with Kitty O'Shea.

Antonia Logue, *Shadow-Box* (Bloomsbury; Grove). This extraordinary first novel is an exhilarating mix of surrealism and boxing inspired by the life of Dadaist poet Mina Loy.

Bernard MacLaverty, *Cal* (Vintage; Norton); *Lamb* (Penguin; Norton). Both novels of love beset by crisis; the first deals with an unwilling IRA man and the widow of one of his victims. *Lamb* is the disturbing tale of a Christian Brother who absconds from a borstal with a young boy. *Grace Notes* (Vintage; Norton). Finely crafted novel about grief, love and creativity.

Deirdre Madden, *Hidden Symptoms* (Faber o/p); *The Birds of the Innocent Wood* (Faber UK); *Remembering Light and Stone* (Faber UK); and *Nothing is Black* (Faber UK). Evocatively grim novels of life in the North.

Aidan Mathews, *Lipstick on the Host* (Minerva; Harcourt Brace o/p). Delicate stories of breathtaking skill.

Eugene McCabe, *Death and Nightingales* (Vintage UK). Powerfully relevant novel of love, land and violence, set in late-nineteenth-century Ireland.

Patrick McCabe, *The Butcher Boy* (Picador; Dell); *The Dead School* (Picador; Delta). Scary, disturbing, but funny tales of Irish small-town life. *Breakfast on Pluto* (Picador; Harperperennial) is a camp and macabre satire in which McCabe's protagonist takes his cross-dressing from his sleepy parochial home to a sleazy London underworld, and there's now a fresh crop of absurd short stories in *Mondo Desperado* (Picador; HarperCollins).

Eugene McEldowney, *The Faloorie Man* (New Island Books IRE). Pleasantly understated autobiographical novel set in pre-Troubles Belfast, enjoyable chiefly for the affectionate nature of the reminiscences.

John McGahern, *The Dark* (Faber; Viking o/p); *The Barracks* (Faber UK); *Amongst Women* (Faber; Penguin); *Collected Stories* (Faber; Vintage). *The Barracks* is classic McGahern; stark, murderous and not a spare adjective in sight. *Amongst Women* is an excellent tale of an old Republican and the oppression of rural and family life.

Eoin McNamee, *Resurrection Man* (Picador). A darkly poetic and gripping tale of sectarian killings and the minds of the perpetrators, loosely based upon the Shankill Butchers.

Frances Molloy, *No Mate For The Magpie* (Virago o/p; Persea). Written wholly in dialect, this is the moving tale of a working class northern woman who finds herself demonstrating outside the American Embassy in Dublin.

Brian Moore, *The Lonely Passion of Judith Hearne* (Flamingo; McClelland & Stewart). Moore's early novels are rooted in the landscape of his native Belfast; this was his first, a poignant tale of emotional blight and the possibilities of late redemption by love. The somewhat Cartlandesque *The Magician's Wife* (Bloomsbury; Penguin) is a tale of pernickety sexual repression at the court of Napoleon III, while *Black Robe* (Flamingo; Plume) re-creates an extraordinary culture clash between seventeenth-century missionary Jesuits and native North American Indians.

Mary Morrissey, *A Lazy Eye* (Vintage; Simon & Schuster o/p); *Mother of Pearl* (Vintage UK).

impressive stories and a novel by a rising star in the new generation of writers. Her *The Pretender* (Jonathan Cape UK) tells the story of the Polish factory worker who claimed to be Anastasia, daughter of the last tsar of Russia.

Christopher Nolan, *Under the Eye of the Clock* (Phoenix; Arcade). Extraordinary and explosive fiction debut: the largely autobiographical story of a handicapped boy's celebration of the power of language. *The Banyan Tree* (Phoenix; Arcade) is an evocative tale, chock full of poetry, about an elderly woman's love for her family and the land.

Edna O'Brien, *The Country Girls* (Penguin); *Down by the River* (Phoenix; Plume o/p). *The Country Girls* is a sensitively wrought novel from a top-class writer sometimes accused, unjustly, of wavering too much towards Mills and Boon. In *Down by the River*, incest and bigotry in parochial Ireland is dealt with head-on and delivered with brutal poetry.

Flann O'Brien, *The Third Policeman* (HarperCollins; Dalkey Archive). O'Brien's masterpiece of the ominously absurd and fiendishly humorous. *At Swim-Two-Birds* (Penguin; Dalkey Archive) is a complicated and hilarious blend of Gaelic fable and surrealism; essential reading. Also see "Memoirs and Journalism", p.737, under Myles na Gopaleen.

Frank O'Connor, *Guests of the Nation* (Poolbeg; Irish Books & Media o/p). Arguably the best Irish political fiction of the twentieth century. *My Oedipus Complex & Other Stories* (Penguin UK). Witty short stories from a master of the genre, especially enjoyable for Catholics.

Joseph O'Connor, *True Believers* (HarperCollins; Trafalgar o/p); *Cowboys and Indians* (HarperCollins; Trafalgar o/p). *Desperadoes* (Flamingo UK); *The Salesman* (Secker; Picador); *Inishowen* (Secker & Warburg). The first two titles deal with life on the peripheries in London and Dublin: love and loss, madness and redemption. *Desperadoes* is a love story ranging from 1950s' Dublin to modern Nicaragua, while *The Salesman* is a pacy revenge thriller in which a man hunts the thief who has left his daughter in a coma. *Inishowen* is a comic novel set in small-town Donegal.

Peadar O'Donnell, *Islanders* (Mercier o/p; Dufour o/p). Evocative, mesmerizing prose from important Republican figure.

Julia O'Faolain, *No Country for Young Men* (Penguin o/p; Carroll & Graf o/p). Spanning four generations, this ambitious novel traces the personal repercussions of the civil war.

Seán Ó Faoláin, *Midsummer Night Madness* (Penguin). A master of the short-story form and the juiciness of rural dialect.

Liam O'Flaherty, *Short Stories* (Wolfhound IRE); *The Collected Stories* (St Martin's Press US). Best of the postwar generation of former IRA men turned writers.

Kate O'Riordan, *Involved* (HarperCollins UK). A young Dublin woman's struggle to understand the passions at the root of Northern Irish republicanism.

Glenn Patterson, *Burning Your Own* (Minerva UK). Distinctive young Northern writer gives Protestant child's-eye view of late 1960s' Northern Ireland just about to explode. *Fat Lad* (Minerva UK). A man gives up a promising career to return to Belfast; an uncompromising yet positive portrayal of the city. *The International* (Anchor UK). A fine novel set in pre-Troubles Belfast based around the lives of staff and guests of what was then just an ordinary provincial hotel.

E.O. Somerville and (Violet) Martin Ross, *The Irish RM* (Abacus; Little, Brown o/p). Hilarious tales in which the locals always outwit the resident magistrate. *Some Experiences of an Irish RM* (Dent UK). The needle pushes the begorra factor a little too heavily here and there, but Somerville and Ross write with witty flair and their tales are very significant for what they unwittingly reveal about a dying class.

James Stephens, *The Crock of Gold* (Gill & MacMillan; Dover); *The Charwoman's Daughter* (Gill & Macmillan o/p; North Books); *The Demi-Gods* (Butler o/p). Three fabulous masterpieces from the country's most underrated genius.

Laurence Sterne, *The Life and Opinion of Tristram Shandy* (Penguin) and *A Sentimental Journey Through France and Italy* (Penguin; Oxford World's Classics). Essential reading from an eighteenth-century comic genius.

Bram Stoker, *Dracula* (Penguin; Signet). Stoker woke up after a nightmare brought on by a hefty lobster supper, and proceeded to write his way into the nightmares of the twentieth century.

Francis Stuart, *Black List Section H* (Lilliput; Penguin). Once a protégé of Yeats, Stuart has consistently maintained a stance of opposition, in his life and his art. *Black List Section H*, his masterpiece, depicts the life of an Irishman in wartime Germany.

Eamon Sweeney, *Waiting for the Healer* (Picador). A single father's bleak descent into drink handled with wry humour. *There's Only One Red Army* (New Island Books IRE). A fictional memoir of a life led through alcoholism and an obsession with a third-rate football team.

Jonathan Swift, *Gulliver's Travels* (Penguin; Oxford World's Classics); *The Tale of a Tub and Other Stories* (Oxford University Press UK). Acerbic satire from the only writer in the English language with as sharp a pen as Voltaire.

Colm Tóibín, *The South* (Picador; Penguin); *The Heather Blazing* (Picador; Penguin); *The Story of the Night* (Picador; Henry Holt); *The Blackwater Lightship* (Picador; Scribner). In *The South* a woman turns her back on Ireland for Spain and returns thirty years later to resolve her life, and to die. A powerfully understated novel, *The Heather Blazing* explores themes of personal and political loss, while his *Story of the Night* is a haunting love story set in Argentina at the time of the Generals. *The Blackwater Lightship* follows the grim journey of an ordinary family confronting AIDS.

William Trevor, *Collected Stories* (Penguin). Five of Trevor's short-story collections in one volume, revealing more about Ireland than many a turgid sociological thesis. Often desperately moving, these stories confirm Trevor as one of the true giants of Irish fiction. *Two Lives* (Penguin), including *Reading Turgenev*, a sensitive account of an unhappy marriage, was shortlisted for the 1991 Booker Prize.

Oscar Wilde, *The Picture of Dorian Gray* (Penguin; Dover). Wilde's exploration of moral schizophrenia. A debauched socialite maintains his youthful good looks, while his portrait in the attic slowly disintegrates into a vision of evil.

Robert McLiam Wilson, *Ripley Bogle* (Minerva; Ballantine). Very funny first novel in which the irrepressible and precocious down and out Bogle tells his tale in wonderfully extravagant tones. *Eureka Street* (Minerva; Ballantine). Acerbic, irreverent humour in both pre- and post-ceasefire Belfast.

POETRY AND DRAMA

Sebastian Barry, *The Steward of Chistendom* (Methuen UK), *Boss Grady's Boys* and *Prayers of Sherkin* (Methuen UK), and *Our Lady of Sligo*. Characters from Barry's family history are central to these plays, all characterized by his richly poetic use of language.

Samuel Beckett, *Collected Shorter Plays* and *Waiting for Godot* (Faber; Grove). Bleak hilarity from the laureate of the void. All essential for swanning around Dublin coffee shops.

Brendan Behan, *The Complete Plays* (Methuen; Grove). Flashes of brilliance from a writer destroyed by alcoholism. His *The Quare Fellow* takes up where Wilde's *Ballad of Reading Gaol* leaves off.

Eavan Boland, *The Journey* (Carcanet UK o/p); *Selected Poems* (Carcanet UK) and *Outside History* (Carcanet; Norton). Thoughtful, spare and elegant verse from one of Ireland's most significant poets.

Pat Boran, *The Unwound Clock* (Dedalus UK o/p). Wry, insightful poems of contemporary Irish life.

Marina Carr, *Portia Coughlan* (Faber UK), *The Mai* (Gallery IRE) and *On Raftery's Hill* (Faber UK). Three plays by one of Ireland's most promising playwrights.

Ciaran Carson, *The Twelfth of Never* (Gallery IRE). Richly allusive poetry that will baffle those not steeped in Irish history and politics; Carson's novels offer a more accessible taste of one of Ireland's most musical literary voices.

Austin Clarke, *Selected Poems* (Colin Smythe; Penguin). Clarke's tender work evokes the same stark grandeur as the paintings of Jack Yeats.

Patrick Crotty (ed), *Modern Irish Poetry: An Anthology* (Blackstaff; Dufour). This anthology covers a broad range of poetry from 1922 onwards, includes Irish and English translations of a number of poems, and provides highly accessible introductions to both the period and the individual poets represented.

Denis Devlin, *Collected Poems* (Wake-Forest US). Pre-eminent Irish poet of the 1930s, owing allegiance to a European modern tradition rather than the prevailing Yeatsian.

Paul Durcan, *A Snail in My Prime* (Harvill; Penguin); *O Westport in the Light of Asia Minor* (Harvill UK); *The Berlin Wall Café* (Harvill UK); *Greetings to our Friends in Brazil* (Harvill). Ireland's most popular and readable poet. *Berlin Wall* is a lament for a broken marriage, recounted with agonizing honesty, dignity and, ultimately, forgiveness.

Peter Fallon, *News of the World* (Gallery; Wake-Forest). Reflections on a reassuring landscape, the present consciously linked to the past, punctuated by the petty rivalries and discrete madnesses of country life.

George Farquhar, *The Recruiting Officer* (OUP). The usual helping of cross-dressing and mistaken identity, yet this goes beyond the implications of most Restoration comedy, even flirting with feminism before finally marrying everyone off in the last scene.

Padraic Fiacc, *Missa Terribilis* (Blackstaff UK o/p). Fiacc's work is informed by the political and social tribalisms of Northern Ireland, and explores personal relationships in these contexts.

Brian Friel, *Dancing at Lughnasa* (Faber). Family drama by Derry playwright examining the coexistence of Catholicism and paganism in Irish society, and the tensions between them. *Plays 1* (Faber) contains six of his greatest works, including *Translations* and *Faith Healer*.

Oliver Goldsmith, *She Stoops to Conquer* (A&C Black; W.W. Norton). Sparky dialogue, with a more English sheen than Farquhar.

Augusta, Lady Gregory, *Collected Plays* (Colin Smythe; Dufour). The Anglo-Irish writer who understood most about the cadences of the Irish language. This gives not only her translations, but also her original drama an authenticity lacking in the work of others.

Seamus Heaney, *Death of a Naturalist* (Faber); *Station Island, Seeing Things* and *Opened Ground: Poems 1966–96* (Faber; Farrar Straus & Giroux). The most important Irish poet since Yeats. His poems are immediate and passionate, even when dealing with intellectual problems and radical social divisions. *The Redress of Poetry* (Faber o/p; Farrar Straus & Giroux) is an example of his energetic prose, consisting of the lectures he gave while Professor of Poetry at Oxford from 1989 to 1994. The title of *The Spirit Level* (Faber), winner of the 1997 Whitbread Prize, alludes to the delicate balances of private and political life following the ceasefire; cool, reassuring poetry with its own quiet music. *Opened Ground* is a massive new collection selected from all his previous published work.

Patrick Kavanagh, *Selected Poems* (Penguin UK). Joyfully mystic exploration of the rural countryside and the lives of its inhabitants by one of Ireland's most popular poets. See also his autobiographical novel, *Tarry Flynn* (Penguin UK).

Brendan Kennelly, *Cromwell* (Bloodaxe; Dufour). Speculative meditation on the role of the conqueror in Irish history. *Poetry My Arse* (Bloodaxe; Dufour) is an epic poem which "sinks its teeth into the pants of poetry itself", while *Begin* (Bloodaxe UK) presents an accessible and highly enjoyable selection of Kennelly's "echopoems".

Thomas Kinsella, *Collected Poems: 1956–1994* (OUP), and his first-rate anthology *The New Oxford Book of Irish Verse* (OUP).

Shane MacGowan, *Poguetry* (Faber UK o/p). Powerful and pungent lyrics by the former Pogues' bardperson. Not for Yeats fans.

Louis MacNeice, *Collected Poems* (Faber UK) or *Selected Poems* (Faber; Wake-Forest). Good chum of Auden, Spender and the rest of the "1930s' generation", Carrickfergus-born MacNeice achieves a fruitier texture and an even more detached tone.

Derek Mahon, *Selected Poems* (Penguin UK); *Collected Poems* (Dufour US); *The Hudson Letter* (Gallery UK); *The Yellow Book* (Gallery; Wake-Forest). One of the finest contemporary Northern Irish poets. See also his *Penguin Book of Contemporary Irish Poetry* (ed with Peter Fallon).

Martin McDonagh, *The Beauty Queen of Linnane, The Skull of Connemara* and *The Lonesome West* (all Methuen UK).Festering familial hatred, murder and isolation on the west coast of Ireland dished up with aplomb.

Medbh McGuckian, *Venus in the Rain* (Gallery; Dufour); *Selected Poems* (Gallery; Wake Forest). Trawling the subconscious for their imagery, McGuckian's sensuous and elusive poems are highly demanding and equally rewarding.

Frank McGuinness, *Observe the Sons of Ulster Marching Towards the Somme* (Faber). An exploration of the Ulster Protestant experience of World War I by one of Ireland's most important playwrights. *Someone to Watch Over Me* (Faber) reveals the resources of cultural history and personality that sustain three hostages – one Irish, one American and one British.

Conor McPherson, *McPherson: Four Plays* (Nick Hern Books). A collection including *This Lime Tree Bower*, a very funny play in which the lives of three men change in the course of a weekend, and *The Weir*, an eerie, compelling drama set in an isolated village in the west of Ireland. *A Dublin Carol* (Nick Hern Books) is a moving piece set around the seasonal reflections of a Dublin undertaker.

Paula Meehan, *The Man who was Marked by Winter* (Gallery; Eastern Washington University); *Pillow Talk* (Gallery UK); *Dharmakaya* (Carcanet). Memorable work, often concerned with women's lives, issues of family, gender and sexuality and rooted in the inner-city experience.

Gary Mitchell, *Tearing the Loom & In a Little World of our Own*, *Trust* and *The Force of Change* (all Nick Hern Books UK). Fine plays from one of Belfast's leading playwrights, chiefly focusing on the changing lives of the Loyalist community.

John Montague, *Collected Poems* (Gallery; Wake-Forest). Terse poetry concerned with history, community and social decay. See also his anthology, *The Book of Irish Verse* (Faber; Budget Book Service).

Paul Muldoon, *New Selected Poems* (Faber UK). Muldoon's own selection of his more accessible, witty and inventive poetry taken from work spanning thirty years.

Tom Murphy, *Famine*, *The Patriot Game*, *The Blue Macushla* and *The Gigli Concert* (Methuen/Heinemand). Along with Friel and McGuinness, Murphy is one of the three outstanding contemporary playwrights.

Eileán Ní Chuilleanáin, *The Rose Geranium* (Gallery IRE); *The Brazen Serpent* (Gallery; Wake-Forest). Manages to carve something new, purposeful and whole from the iconography and language of religion; quietly impressive.

Nuala Ní Dhomhnaill, *Selected Poems* (Raven Arts Press; New Island o/p) is in Irish and English. Haunting translations of her modern erotic verse by the fine poet Michael Hartnett are included in *Raven Introductions 3* (Colin Smythe UK) and in Frank Ormsby's anthology (see below).

Sean O'Casey, *Three Dublin Plays* (Faber). Contains his powerful Dublin trilogy, *Juno and the Paycock*, *Shadow of a Gunman* and *The Plough and the Stars*, set against the backdrop of the civil war.

Frank Ormsby (ed), *The Long Embrace: Twentieth Century Irish Love Poems* (Blackstaff UK o/p). Excellent anthology with major chunks from the work of almost every important twentieth-century Irish poet from Yeats to the present day. *A Rage To Order* (ed) (Blackstaff IRE o/p); impressive anthology of poetry born of the Troubles. Horror, pain, anger and pity somehow all wrestled into some sense of form; an absorbing book. See also his *Poets from the North of Ireland* anthology (Blackstaff; Dufour).

Tom Paulin, *Fivemiletown*; *The Strange Museum*; *Walking a Line*; *Selected Poems 1972–90* (all Faber). Often called "dry" both in praise and accusation, Paulin's work reverberates with thoughtful political commitment and a sophisticated irony.

John Millington Synge, *The Complete Plays* (Methuen; Vintage). Lots of begorras and mavourneens and other dialogue kindly invented for the Irish peasantry by Synge; but *The Playboy of the Western World* (Penguin) is a brilliant and unique work, greeted in Dublin by riots, threats and moral outrage.

Oscar Wilde, *Complete Plays* (Methuen). His drama is characterized by bittersweet satire, subversive one-liners and profound existentialist philosophy all masquerading as well-made, drawing-room farce. In his poem, *The Ballad of Reading Gaol*, the great comedian achieves his greatest success, in tragedy.

William Butler Yeats, *The Poems* (Everyman UK) and *The Collected Poems* (Scribner US). They're all here, poems of rhapsody, love, revolution and eventual rage at a disconnected and failed Ireland "fumbling in the greasy till".

BIOGRAPHY AND CRITICISM

A.M. Brady and Brian Cleeve (eds), *Biographical Dictionary of Irish Writers* (Lilliput o/p; St Martin's Press o/p). Succinct entries on all the greats, better used as a magical mystery tour through the lost byways of Irish literature.

Anthony Cronin, *Samuel Beckett: The Last Modernist* (Flamingo; Da Capo). Accessible, anecdotal biography, good on the Irish background. *No Laughing Matter: The Life and Times of Flann O'Brien* (Fromm US). Witty and insightful biography, and particularly interesting on 1950s Dublin.

Seamus Deane, *Short History of Irish Literature* (Hutchinson o/p; University of Notre Dame Press). Deane brings a poet's sensitivity to a massive and sometimes unwieldy tradition, with skill and a profound sense of sociopolitical context. See also his shorter analysis of modern writing in *Irish Writers* (Eason UK).

Richard Ellmann, *James Joyce* (OUP US); *Oscar Wilde* (Penguin o/p). Ellman's *Joyce* is a major literary work in itself, a massive and brilliant book. His *Oscar Wilde* is at least its equal, an eloquent corrective to the image of Wilde as an intellectual mayfly.

Roy Foster, *W.B. Yeats – A Life – The Apprentice Mage,* Volume One of two volumes (OUP). This is a superb biography – dispassionate, scholarly, and bound to augment your understanding of, though not necessarily your feelings for, the great man.

Michael Holroyd, *Bernard Shaw: A Biography* (Chatto & Windus; Random House). Unfairly slammed by the critics, this is actually a pretty successful stab at understanding one of the most difficult and complex authors of the whole Anglo-Irish canon.

Robert Kee, *The Laurel & the Ivy: The Story of Charles Stewart Parnell* (Penguin). Illuminating account of the life and times of the great statesman by one of Ireland's most respected historians.

Declan Kiberd, *Inventing Ireland* (Vintage; Harvard University Press). A massively scrupulous assessment of modern Irish literature from Yeats to Friel, set against a background of flux and turmoil.

James Knowlson, *Damned to Fame: The Life of Samuel Beckett* (Bloomsbury o/p; Simon & Schuster). Stunning biography: thorough, balanced and scholarly.

Brenda Maddox, *Nora: A Biography of Nora Joyce* (Minerva; Houghton Mifflin). Eminently readable story of the funny, irreverent and formidable Nora Barnacle and her life with James Joyce – an interesting complement to Ellmann's Joyce biography.

Ulick O'Connor, *Brendan Behan* (Abacus UK). Moving account of the dramatist's life.

Margaret Ward, *Hannah Sheehy Skeffington: A Life* (Cork University Press IRE). Fascinating, scholarly biography of a militant suffragist; co-founder of the Irish Women's Franchise League in 1908, Skeffington was one of the most important political activists of her day.

Robert Welch (ed), *Oxford Companion to Irish Literature* (OUP). This encyclopedic tour through who's who and what they've written fills a long-standing need.

MEMOIRS AND JOURNALISM

Dr Noel Browne, *Against the Tide* (Blackstaff IRE). Tremendously important autobiography and account of Irish political life by one of Ireland's key twentieth-century radicals. Dr Browne pulls no punches and leaves you feeling both appalled and inspired.

Ciaran Carson, *The Star Factory* (Granta; Arcade). Magical account of growing up in 1950s and 1960s Belfast; Carson has a poetic ingenuity reminiscent of Dylan Thomas.

Liam Fay, *Beyond Belief* (Hot Press UK o/p). Hilarious, irreverent look at the state of religion in Ireland.

Myles na Gopaleen, (aka Flann O'Brien), *The Best of Myles* (HarperCollins UK). Priceless extracts from a daily humorous newspaper column by O'Brien's alter ego.

Frank McCourt, *Angela's Ashes* (Flamingo; Touchstone). Stunning memoir of a Limerick childhood; a tale of bleak, desperate poverty, laced with astonishing moments of humour and a deep respect for the lives led. In the sequel, *'Tis* (Flamingo; Simon & Schuster), McCourt finds both escape and a sense of purpose through education in New York.

Nuala O'Faolain, *Are You Somebody?* (New Island Books; Owl Books). Despite a life rich in ideas and experience, this memoir reveals an Ireland that until recently treated women with, at best, indifference. Neat sketches of literary Dublin in the 1950s, puncturing one or two cosy myths along the way.

Colm Tóibín, *The Sign of the Cross: Travels in Catholic Europe* (Vintage; Pantheon). Novelist Tóibín uses his journalistic skills to find the old-time religion in Ireland and elsewhere. *Bad Blood* (Vintage UK) is a perceptive account of a journey along the line that divides Northern Ireland from the rest of the island.

John Waters, *Jiving at the Crossroads* (Blackstaff; Dufour o/p). Curiously engaging autobiography which traces a fascination with Fianna Fáil politics through the formative years of a western youth in the 1970s and 1980s.

ART AND MUSIC

Bruce Arnold, *Irish Art: A Concise History* (Thames & Hudson UK). Updated edition provides a fuller account of Irish modernism.

Breandán Breathnach, *Folk Music and Dances of Ireland* (Ossian). Breathnach's classic developmental account and analysis of the structure of Irish music is essential reading. A companion CD features all the songs and tunes from the book's closing section.

Ciaran Carson *The Pocket Guide to Irish Traditional Music* (Appletree Press; Irish Books & Media). Useful introduction to the world or traditional music, while *Last Night's Fun* (Pimlico; North Point Press) is a wonderful evocation of the elusive pleasures of traditional music sessions.

Tony Clayton-Lea & Richard Taylor, *Irish Rock* (Gill & MacMillan UK). Popular account of the growth of the Irish music scene, particularly good on the punk and new wave years.

P.J. Curtis, *Notes form the Heart* (Poolbeg IRE). Criminally ignored on first publication, P.J.'s opening chapters provide an admirable overview of the music's twentieth-century developments, while the remainder focuses on major figures in County Clare's music.

Brian Fallon, *Irish Art 1830–1990* (Appletree Press UK). The development of art in Ireland and its reflection of questions of national identity and culture.

Caoimhín ó hAllmhuráin, *Between the Jigs and Reels: The Donegal Fiddle Tradition* (Drumlin Publications IRE). A marvellous book which truly captures the richness of the county's musical heritage through a detailed analysis of its history, informative biographies of many musicians and valuable descriptions of their various techniques.

Christy Moore, *One Voice* (Hodder & Stoughton). Not just a scintillating account of Moore's own life through song, but a hard-hitting analysis of Ireland over the last thirty years.

Thomas Moore, *Moore's Irish Melodies;* (Ossian; Dover). Various editions of the prettied-up tunes Moore stole from the harpists, along with lyrics of mind-numbingly perfect rhythm. Moore is an important historical figure, who expressed the Nationalism of the emerging middle class and brought revolution into the parlour.

Nuala O'Connor, *Bringing It All Back Home* (BBC UK). Detailed account of the history of traditional Irish music written to accompany a 1991 BBC TV series.

George Petrie, *The Complete Collection of Irish Music* (Llanerch UK). One of the most important cultural documents in Irish history.

Mark J. Prendergast, *Irish Rock: Roots, Personalities and Directions* (O'Brien Press IRE). Dated, but still the best in-depth account of the development of Irish rock music.

Fintan Vallely (ed), *The Companion to Irish Traditional Music* (Cork University Press IRE). Provides constant delight in its copious accounts of the music's form, style and qualities, and brief biographies of many key participants; required reading.

Geoff Wallis and Sue Wilson, *The Rough Guide to Irish Music* (Rough Guides). A quintessential account of the roots and current state of traditional music in Ireland, containing a comprehensive directory of more than four hundred singers, musicians and groups and details of the best places to see them in action.

LANDSCAPE AND TOPOGRAPHY

Aalen, Whelan and Stout, (eds), *Atlas of the Irish Rural Landscape* (Cork University Press; University of Toronto). Wholly absorbing collection of essays, maps and illustrations revealing and analysing the changing landscape of

Ireland; a must for all concerned with its history and future.

Deirdre Flanagan & Lawrence Flanagan, *Irish Place Names* (Gill & MacMillan; Irish Books & Media). Expertly researched account of the origins of virtually everywhere on the island – a dipper's delight.

Breandán & Ruarí ó hEithir, *An Aran Reader* (Lilliput IRE). A fascinating anthology of writings about the Aran Islands, including the works of early travellers, anthropologists, poets and islanders.

Tim Robinson, *The Stones of Aran: Pilgrimage* (Penguin UK). Treats the largest of the Aran Islands to a scrutiny of Proustian detail. *The Stones of Aran: Labyrinth* (Penguin UK) completes the project, to form a uniquely challenging travel book.

GUIDES

Kevin Corcoran, *West Cork Walks* (O'Brien; Irish American). A good, accessible guide to ten walks, including a wealth of interesting material on the history and natural history of the county.

Paddy Dillon, *Twelve Walks in Glendalough* (Drimbane IRE). A lightweight, easy-to-use guide to walks around Glendalough, ranging from short and easy to long and very strenuous. Colour photographs and clear maps are included.

David Herman, *Hill Walkers' Donegal* (Shanksmore Publications UK). Over thirty walks in the county described in excellent detail.

Joss Lynam (ed), *Best Irish Walks* (Gill & MacMillan; Passport). Seventy-six walks through some of the most beautiful and remote parts of the country. *Easy Walks near Dublin* (Gill & Macmillan IRE). An excellent guide to forty walks, many in the Wicklow Mountains, and several with details about access by public transport from Dublin.

Sally and John McKenna, *Bridgestone Irish Food Guide* (Estragon UK). The best in an almost non-existent field of Irish food writing. The same authors' smaller guides, to restaurants and places to stay, are also popular.

Seán Ó Súilleabháin, *Walk Guide: South West of Ireland – Third Edition* (Gill & MacMillan UK). Forty-seven well-written and clearly illustrated walks; indispensable for anyone planning walking in Kerry and on the Beara Peninsula.

Patrick Simms and Tony Whilde, *West of Ireland Walk Guide* (Gill & MacMillan UK). Detailed descriptions of west and northwest walks from counties Clare to Derry.

Brendan Walsh, *Irish Cycling Guide* (Moorland; Irish Books & Media). This is a grand tour of the country, in 36 stages, taking the roads with least traffic.

Alan Warner, *Walking the Ulster Way* (Appletree Press; Irish Books & Media). The first man to walk the entire five hundred miles describes his journey in detailed and sometimes whimsical diaries.

LANGUAGE

A visitor to Ireland will probably have little or no contact with the Irish language, unless they seek to do so in the *Gaeltacht* (Irish-speaking areas mostly in the west of the country). However, the legacy of the language still pervades many aspects of Irish life, be it in the rhythms of speech patterns in English, the town and townland names throughout the country or in traditional poetry or song. It has been said for decades that Irish is a dying language and although there is little chance of it becoming the first tongue of more than a small minority of the people of Ireland, the recent rebirth of interest has ensured that it will not follow in the linguistic footsteps of its deceased Celtic cousins.

The Celtic settlement of Ireland probably began in the seventh century BC; the later migration of Irish tribes to the Isle of Man and to Scotland established Irish-speaking kingdoms in those areas. With the rise of Rome the Celtic languages survived only in the peripheral western areas – today, Celtic languages are limited to parts of Scotland, Wales and Brittany in addition to Ireland. Cornish, another Celtic derivative, died out in the eighteenth century and, in the twentieth century, Manx ceased to be a community language.

The earliest form of script in Celtic Ireland, known as **ogham**, is found on standing stones dating from the fourth to seventh centuries. Employing a twenty-character alphabet derived from Latin, the letters were represented by varying strokes and notches, and read from the bottom upwards. Following the establishment of monasteries, a written form of the language, more closely resembling its modern-day form, evolved, with monks recording significant events in the areas in which they were based. The best known non-religious text of this period is the *Táin Bó Cúailgne* ("The cattle raid of Cooley"), which dates back to the seventh century. With the first Viking raid of 795, the world of the monastery was thrown into chaos and the thread of the language, now known as **Old Irish**, was cut, giving way to a less scholastic and more vernacular-based written language referred to as **Middle Irish**. It was in the later part of this era that the **Fenian Cycle** emerged, charting the exploits of Fionn Mac Cumhaill and his Fianna (band), tales which were very popular with the peasantry.

The period from 1200 to 1600 is considered the **Classical Period** in the development of the language, when the grammatical chaos of Middle Irish was brought under control. A succession of invaders speaking Norse, French and English were assimilated into the population, with a resulting cross-fertilization of languages. There were, however, concerted attempts to stamp out the use of the language, one example being in 1367 when the Statutes of Kilkenny declared that, among other things, "the English may not entertain or make gifts to Irish minstrels, rhymers or storytellers". Despite these attempts to preserve an English-speaking culture, the first Anglo-Norman aristocracy became thoroughly Gaelicized, and even as late as 1578 the Lord Chancellor could report that "all English, and most part with delight, even in Dublin, speak Irish and greatly are spotted in manners, habit and conditions with Irish stains".

However, after the Battle of Kinsale in 1601, the Gaelic aristocracy disappeared, as did the king's court, the Brehon system of law and the bardic schools. Poets soon became a class of wandering minstrel, known as "rakarees" (from the Irish *recaire* – "one who recites") and were persecuted since they represented "the old way".

Although the use of Irish was still widespread in the nineteenth century, the language was further weakened by the establishment of the **National School System** in 1831, which decreed that all children should be educated through the medium of English, despite the fact that many of their parents only spoke Irish. A further blow to the language was the **Great**

Famine which hit hardest in many Irish-speaking areas and in many places left a psychological legacy that survival itself depended on the mastery of the English language. Even mass movement politics of a vaguely nationalistic nature eschewed the use of Irish, and Daniel O'Connell, despite being a fluent speaker, preferred to use English both at his rallies and in his propaganda.

Despite the language's decline in the nineteenth century, some organizations sprang up to preserve its use: ironically, considering today's political climate, it was northern Protestants who spearheaded this campaign, the most prominent being the Rev William Nelson. In the late nineteenth century, a catalyst for the revival of Irish was the poet **Thomas Davis** who promoted the use of Irish as a living language. His efforts were followed by the formation of the **Gaelic League** that works to this day in the field of language promotion.

Immediately after Independence in 1921, Irish was installed as the first national language and steps were taken to revive it as a community tongue. Apart from an intensive education programme, the government attempted in other ways to "Gaelicize" Ireland, the most obvious example being the planting of Gaelic-speaking communities in the heart of English-speaking areas (one such community still remains in Raith Cairn, County Meath). This enthusiasm has, however, in postwar years, given way to apathy and governments' efforts at promoting the language have been tokenistic at best; Article 8 Section 1 of the Constitution states that Irish is the first language, though this is viewed in most political circles as anachronistic and irrelevant.

Despite these factors militating against the survival of the language, it is still estimated that in the designated Irish-speaking (*Gaeltacht*) areas – in counties Donegal, Galway and north Mayo, and in counties Kerry, Cork and Waterford – there are around seventy thousand speakers of the language, which is 77 percent of the *Gaeltacht* population. In parallel to this, there is growing **grassroots interest** in the promotion and use of Irish. It is in many ways evidence of an increasing national confidence that instead of seeing Irish as backward, it is nowadays embraced by some of the most progressive elements in society. 1967 saw the establishment of the **Irish-language radio station**, Radio na Gaeltachta, and the latter half of the twentieth century has seen many fine writers writing in Irish about subjects that are far removed from the rural preoccupations some associate with Irish-language literature: the first staging-post towards modernity in Irish writing was *An Béal Bocht* by Myles na Gopaleen, followed by the poetry of Seán Ó Ríordáin and Máirtín Ó Díreáin, and latterly by the contemporary poetry of Nuala Ní Dhomhnaill, Gabriel Rosentock and Cathal Ó Searcaigh. In the North, the rise in the use of Irish has been both cultural and political: in the 1970s, Republican prisoners began to learn Irish, though owing to the insular nature of its usage and the lack of professional teaching, it mutated into a kind of pidgin that was known as "jailic". Perhaps the most conspicuous evidence of this revived interest came in the form of the new national **television station**, Teilifís na Gaeilge, which, through its progressive and inventive programming and its energetic youth-oriented presentation, presents the contemporary face of the Irish language.

LANGUAGE BOOKS AND RESOURCES

Buntus Cainte (Gael Linn). A series of easy to follow books and cassettes aimed at the complete beginner.

Irish for Beginners, Angela Wilkes (Usborne). Humorous illustrations and puzzles help make learning more fun.

Lazy Way to Irish, O Riain, Flann (Y Lolfa; New South Wales University Press). A good introduction to some useful words and phrases.

Learn Irish – CD ROM Words and Phrases for Beginners. Not the greatest CD ROM ever but is as good a place to start as any.

Learning Irish, Mícheál Ó Siadháil (Yale University Press). Modern guide to language through speaking. Cassettes available. Strong on grammar; Connacht dialect preferred.

Now You're Talking (Gael Media). Based on the RTE BBC N.Ireland television programme of the same name, this is a good resource for both the beginner and those wishing to brush up on their language.

Teach Yourself Irish, Miles Dillon/Donncha Ó Cróinín (Hodder o/p; NTC o/p). Archaic teaching methods; student needs to be a saint; southern dialects favoured.

IRISH WORDS COMMONLY FOUND IN PLACE NAMES

Irish	English
abha	river
achadh	field
árd	height
áth	ford
baile	town
bán	white
barr	top
beag	small
béal	small
bó	cow
bóthar	road
buí	yellow
bun	base
caisleán	castle
caoin	pleasant
caol	narrow
carraig	rock
ceann	head
cill	church
cloch	stone
cluain	meadow
cnoc	hill
coill	wood
cos	foot, mouth of a river
currach	marsh
dearg	red
doire	oak tree
droichead	bridge
dubh	black
eaglais	church
eas	waterfall
eó	yew tree
fál	hedge
fiodh	wood
fionn	white, fair
fraoch	heather
gall	foreigner
garbh	rough
garraí	garden
geal	bright
glas	green or grey
gleann	valley
gort	field
grian	sun
inis	island
iúr	yew tree
lag	hollow
lann	church
leaba	bed
leath	half
léim	leap
leitir	hillside
loch	lake
machaire	plain
mainstir	abbey
maol	smooth
móin	peat bog
muc	pig
mullach	summit
nead	nest
nua	new
ráth	ring fort
reilig	ring fort
rua	red
sagart	priest
sean	old
sí	fairy
sliabh	mountain
sráid	street
suí	seat
teach, tí	house, monastery
teampall	church
tír	country, territory
tobar	well
trá	beach
tulach	small hill
uisce	water
uaimhe	cave

PRONUNCIATION OF IRISH

A few basic pointers on pronouncing Irish are given below. Bear in mind, however, that the language has three distinct dialects which differ in pronunciation and grammar. These dialects are commonly referred to as Connaught Irish, spoken in the *Gaeltacht* areas of Galway and Mayo, Munster Irish, found mostly in Cork, Kerry and, to a lesser extent, Waterford, and Ulster Irish spoken in the western areas of Donegal.

Vowels

Irish uses an accent known as a *fada* to lengthen vowel sounds.

a as in "mat"
á as in "saw"
e as in "met"
é as in "hey"
i as in "sit"
í as in "fine"
o as in "son"
ó as in "cow"
u as in "but"
ú as in "put"

Consonants

c–hard as in "cat"
ch – the glottal sound found in English words with Gaelic origins such as "loch"
d – hard as in the English "do" when followed by "o" or "u", or soft like the "j" in "jelly" when followed by "e" or "i"
dh – like the "y" in young when followed by "e" or "i", or as a soft "g" sound as in "huge" when followed by an "o" or "u"
t – soft resembling the "ch" in "church" when followed by an "e" or an "i", or hard as in the "t" in "toe" when followed by an "o" or "u"
th – the same sound as "h" in "hop"
s – pronounced as the "sh" in "shirt" or as in "sugar"

CLASSES AND COURSES

For information about Irish language classes, contact Conrad na Gaeilge, 6 Harcourt St, Dublin 2. For books relating to the language, Siopa Leabhair (Book Shop) at the same address is the best place in Dublin.

If you want to combine language learning and cultural activities such as walking, *bodhrán* playing or dancing then contact the excellent Oideas Gael (☎073/30248), which runs courses in Glencolmcille in Donegal.

AN IRISH GLOSSARY

ALLIANCE PARTY A moderate, centrist, non-sectarian Northern Ireland party led by Lord (John) Alderdice, now speaker of the Assembly.

BAWN A castle enclosure or castlefold.

BODHRÁN (pronounced *bore-run*) A hand-held, shallow, goatskin drum.

B SPECIALS Auxiliary police force of the Stormont government; disbanded in 1971.

CASHEL A kind of rath (see overleaf), distinguished by a circular outer stone wall instead of earthen ramparts.

CLOCHÁN A beehive-shaped, weatherproof hut built of tightly fitted stone without mortar. Clocháns date from the early Christian period.

THE CONTINUITY IRA Small breakaway organization maintaining the armed struggle against British rule and now thought to have amalagamated with The Real IRA.

"THE CRACK" Good conversation, a good time, often accompanying drinking. "What's the crack?" means "what's the gossip?" or "what's going on?"

CRANNÓG An artificial island in the middle of a lake, dating from the Bronze Age.

CURRACH/CURRAGH Small fishing vessel used off the west coast; traditionally made of leather stretched over a light wood frame, modern currachs are of tar-coated canvas.

THE DÁIL Lower house of the Irish parliament.

DOLMEN (or "portal tomb") A chamber formed by standing stones that support a massive capstone. The capstone often slopes to form the entrance of the chamber. Dates from the Copper Age (2000–1750 BC).

DRUMLIN Small, oval, hummocky hill formed from the detritus of a retreating glacier.

DUP The Democratic Unionist Party. A traditionalist, anti-Republican right-wing party founded by Ian Paisley and Desmond Boal in 1971. Paisley has remained leader since then and is the only European political leader this century to have founded his own church. The DUP is fundamentally opposed to the Good Friday Agreement and any loosening of the bonds with the United Kingdom.

ÉIRE Irish name for Ireland, but officially indicates the 26 counties.

FIANNA FÁIL The largest and most successful of Ireland's two main political parties since Independence. Essentially a conservative party, it has its origins in the Republican faction of Sinn Féin, and fought against pro-Treaty forces in the civil war. During the 1930s, the party did much to assert Ireland's separateness from Britain.

FINE GAEL Ireland's second largest political party, Fine Gael sprang from the pro-Treaty faction of Sinn Féin which formed the first Free State government in 1921. Since that time it has not been able to gain a strong majority, and periods in office have been in coalitions. It advocates more liberal policies than Fianna Fáil in terms of social welfare, but in fact there is very little to distinguish the two main parties.

FIR Men (sign on men's public toilets).

GAELTACHT Any region in Ireland in which Irish Gaelic is the vernacular speech; these are chiefly in the west.

GALLERY GRAVE A simple burial chamber of squared stones, generally found under a long mound.

GARDAÍ The police force of the Republic of Ireland.

INLA Irish National Liberation Army. Extreme splinter group of the IRA. Its aim is the creation through physical force of a united socialist 32-county republic.

IRA Irish Republican Army. The upholders of the Irish Fenian tradition, ultimately dedicated to the establishment of a united 32-county republic by whatever means possible and notorious both for its bombing campaigns and the extreme sophistication of its organizational structure.

IRSP Irish Republican Socialist Party. The most revolutionary, if small, party in Northern Ireland and the political wing of the INLA.

LVF Loyalist Volunteer Force. Banned paramilitary organization based in and around Portadown, led by Billy Wright until his assassination by the INLA in the Maze prison, December 1997.

LOYALIST A person loyal to the British Crown, usually a Northern Irish Protestant.

MARTELLO TOWER Circular coastal tower once used for defence.

MNÁ Women (sign on women's public toilets).

MOTTE A circular mound, flat on top, which the Normans used as a fortification.

NATIONALISTS Those who wish to see a united Ireland.

THE NORTH Term referring to Northern Ireland used by many people.

OGHAM (rhyming with poem) The earliest form of writing used by the Irish (fourth to seventh centuries), and found on the edge of standing stones. Employing a twenty-character alphabet derived from Latin, the letters were represented by varying strokes and notches, and read from the bottom upwards.

ORANGE ORDER A Loyalist Protestant organization, found throughout Northern Ireland, which promotes the Union with Britain. The name comes from William of Orange ("King Billy"), the Protestant king who defeated the Catholic James II at the Battle of the Boyne (1690) and at the Battle of Aughrim (1691). Most Unionist MPs are Orangemen, and outside of Northern Ireland, Orange Lodges (branches) are found amongst Loyalist expats. Also see p.670.

PASSAGE GRAVE A megalithic tomb from the Neolithic period. A simple corridor of large, square, vertical stones lead to a burial chamber, and the whole tomb is covered with earth. The stones are decorated with simple patterns: double spirals, triangles, zigzag lines, and the sun symbol.

POTEEN/POITÍN (pronounced potcheen) Highly alcoholic (and often toxic) and illegal spirit, usually distilled from potatoes.

PUP Progressive Unionist Party. Seen as the political wing of the UVF. Many of its leading lights are former Loyalist paramilitaries, including David Ervine, a major player in ensuring Loyalist support for the Good Friday Agreement.

RATH or RINGFORT A farmstead dating from the first millennium AD. A circular timber enclosure banked by earth and surrounded by a ditch formed the outer walls, within which roofed dwellings were built and, in times of danger, cattle were herded. Today raths are visible as circular earthworks.

THE REAL IRA Breakaway faction led by the IRA's former quartermaster which rejects the political process and maintains the armed struggle; responsible for the Omagh bombing, The Real IRA has attacked RUC and Army installations and exploded bombs in England, most notably at Hammersmith Bridge.

REPUBLICANS Supporters of the ideals incorporated in the 1916 Proclamation of the Republic, the overthrow of British rule in Ireland and the promotion of Irish language and culture.

ROUND TOWER Narrow, tall (65–110ft) and circular tower, tapering to a conical roof. Built from the ninth century onwards, they are unique to Ireland. They are found on the sites of early monasteries, and served to call the monks to prayer. The entrance is usually a doorway 10–15ft above the ground, which was reached by a wooden or rope ladder that could be pulled up for safety.

RUC Royal Ulster Constabulary. Northern Ireland's regular, but armed, police force.

SDLP Social Democratic and Labour Party. The largest Nationalist party, centrist left, founded in 1970 and led by John Hume since 1979.

SINN FÉIN ("Ourselves Alone") Sinn Féin's history has been colourful, eventful and characterized by splits. Re-emerging in the 1970s, it subsequently became a major political force in Northern Ireland, aiming to achieve national self-determination and the formation of a 32-county socialist republic, based on the principles of the Proclamation of 1916 and the beliefs of Tone, Pearse and Connolly. It has been labelled by some as the political wing of the IRA. Its leader since 1983 has been Gerry Adams who has gradually steered Republicanism towards democratic resolution of its goals.

THE SIX COUNTIES Nationalist/Republican name for Northern Ireland.

SOUTERRAIN Underground passage that served as a hiding place in times of danger; also used to store food and valuables.

TAOISEACH Irish prime minister.

TD Teachta Dála. Member of the Irish parliament.

32-COUNTY SOVEREIGNTY COMMITTEE The alleged political wing of The Real IRA.

TRICOLOUR The green, white and orange flag of the Republic.

THE TWENTY-SIX COUNTIES The Republic of Ireland (Éire).

UDA Ulster Defence Association. A Loyalist paramilitary organization, the largest in Northern Ireland.

UDP Ulster Democratic Party. Political wing of the UDA, led by Gary McMichael.

UDR Ulster Defence Regiment. A regular regiment of the British army recruited in Northern Ireland.

UFF Ulster Freedom Fighters. Another illegal Protestant paramilitary faction; linked to the UDA.

UKU United Kingdom Unionists. Virtually a one-person Unionist Party, sharing similar views to the DUP and led by Robert McCartney, MP for North Down.

ULSTER One of Ireland's four provinces, often erroneously used by Unionists and journalists as a synonym for Northern Ireland, thus ignoring the counties of Cavan, Donegal and Monaghan which Ulster also comprises.

UNIONISTS Those (predominantly Protestant) who wish to keep Northern Ireland in union with the rest of the United Kingdom.

UUP Ulster Unionist Party. Founded in 1905 by Edward Carson, the UUP was in power in Northern Ireland from 1921 until the dissolution of Stormont in 1972. Known as the Official Unionists, the largest party in the North is led by David Trimble, a key player in the peace process and now First Minister in the Assembly.

UVF Ulster Volunteer Force. Yet another illegal Protestant paramilitary organization, originally formed in 1912 to oppose any British plans to impose a united Ireland on Northern Irish Protestants; banned in 1966 following its random sectarian murders of Catholics.

INDEX

A

B

D

G

H

I